VOLUME 001-003

# Amazing_Agent Luna
OMNIBUS I

art by Shiei

story by Nunzio DeFilippis
and Christina Weir

[CONFIDENTIAL]

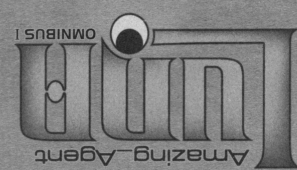

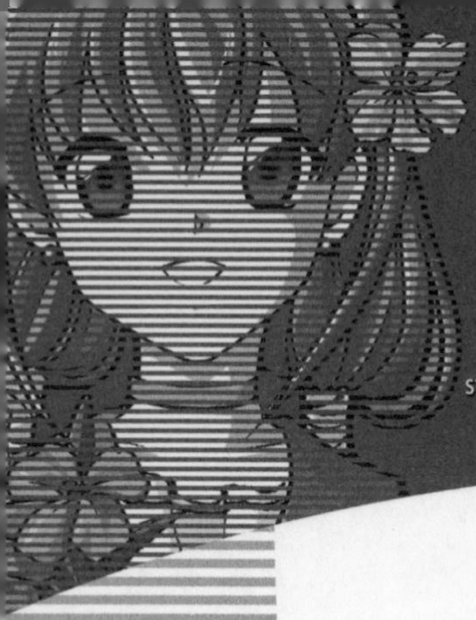

# Amazing Agent Luna

OMNIBUS I

story by Nunzio DeFilippis & Christina Weir

art by Shiei

## STAFF CREDITS

| | |
|---|---|
| toning | **Jay Jimenez, Roland Amago** |
| background assists | **Roland Amago** |
| lettering | **Nicky Lim, Cheese** |
| graphic design | **Culture Crash, Nicky Lim, Adam Arnold** |
| cover design | **Nicky Lim** |
| assistant editor | **Adam Arnold** |
| editor | **Jason DeAngelis** |



Visit us online at www.gomanga.com

Seven Seas

ISBN: 978-1-933164-74-8

Printed in Canada

First printing: April 2008

10 9 8 7 6 5 4 3 2 1

# AMAZING AGENT LUNA - CONTENTS

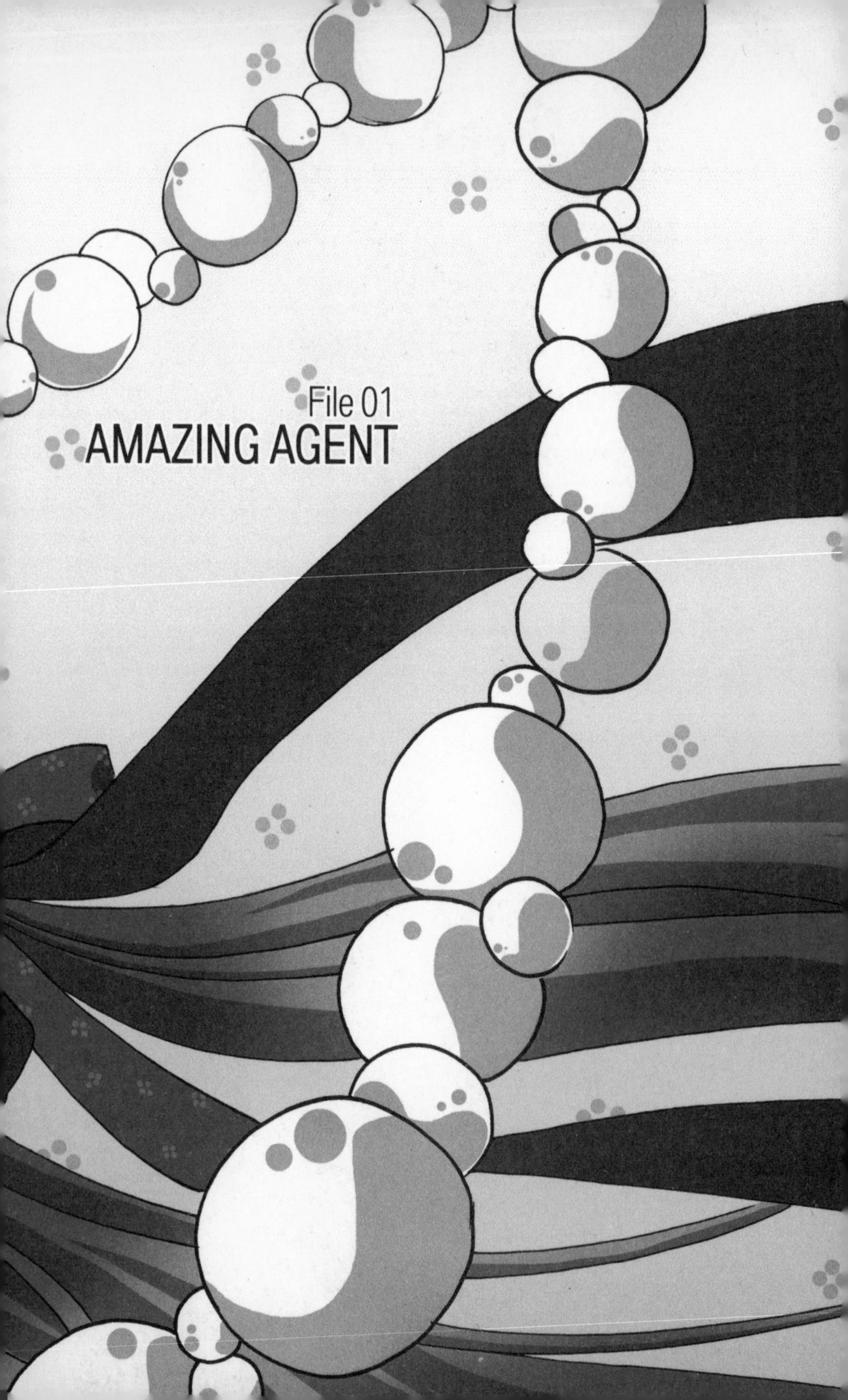
File 01
AMAZING AGENT

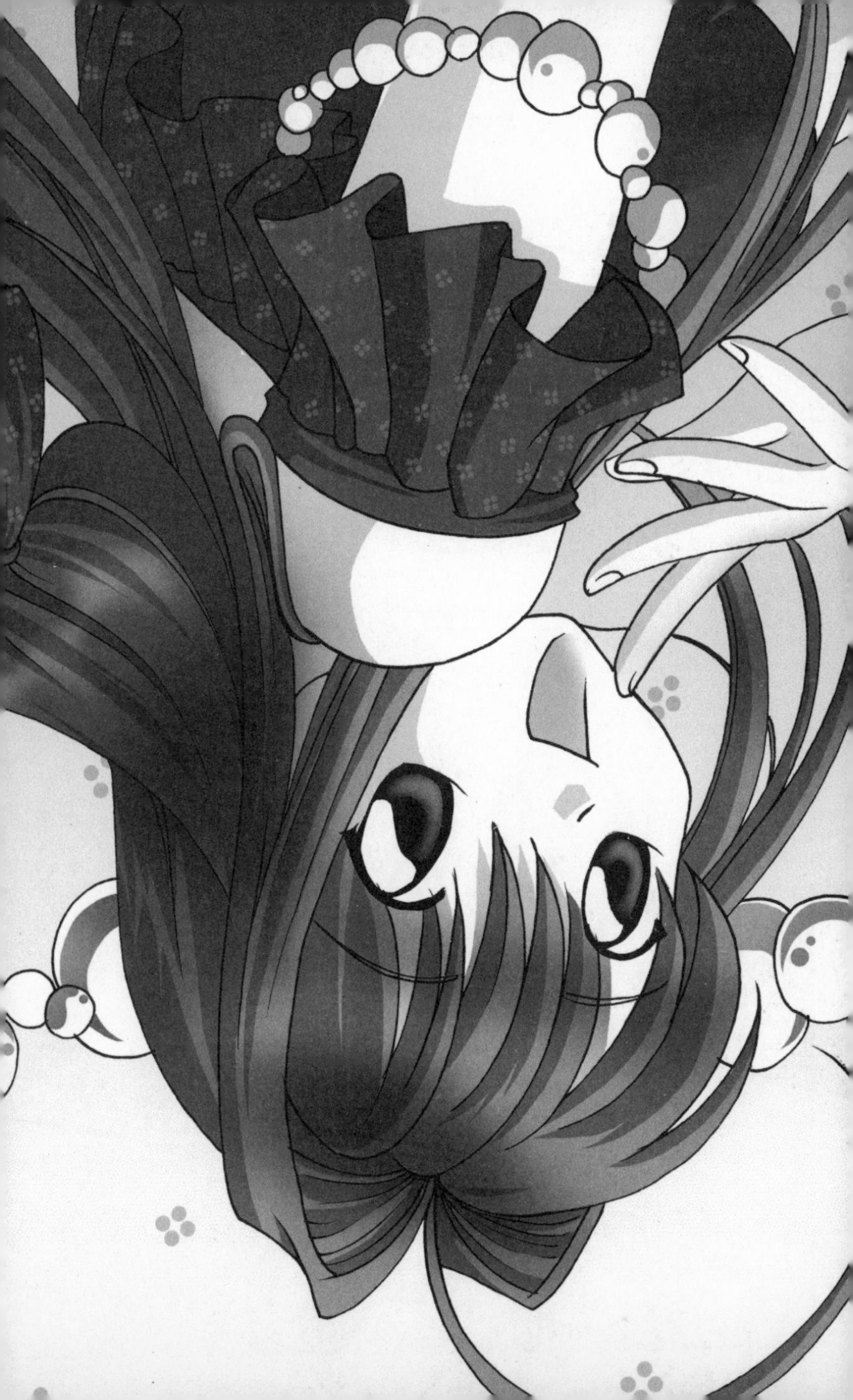

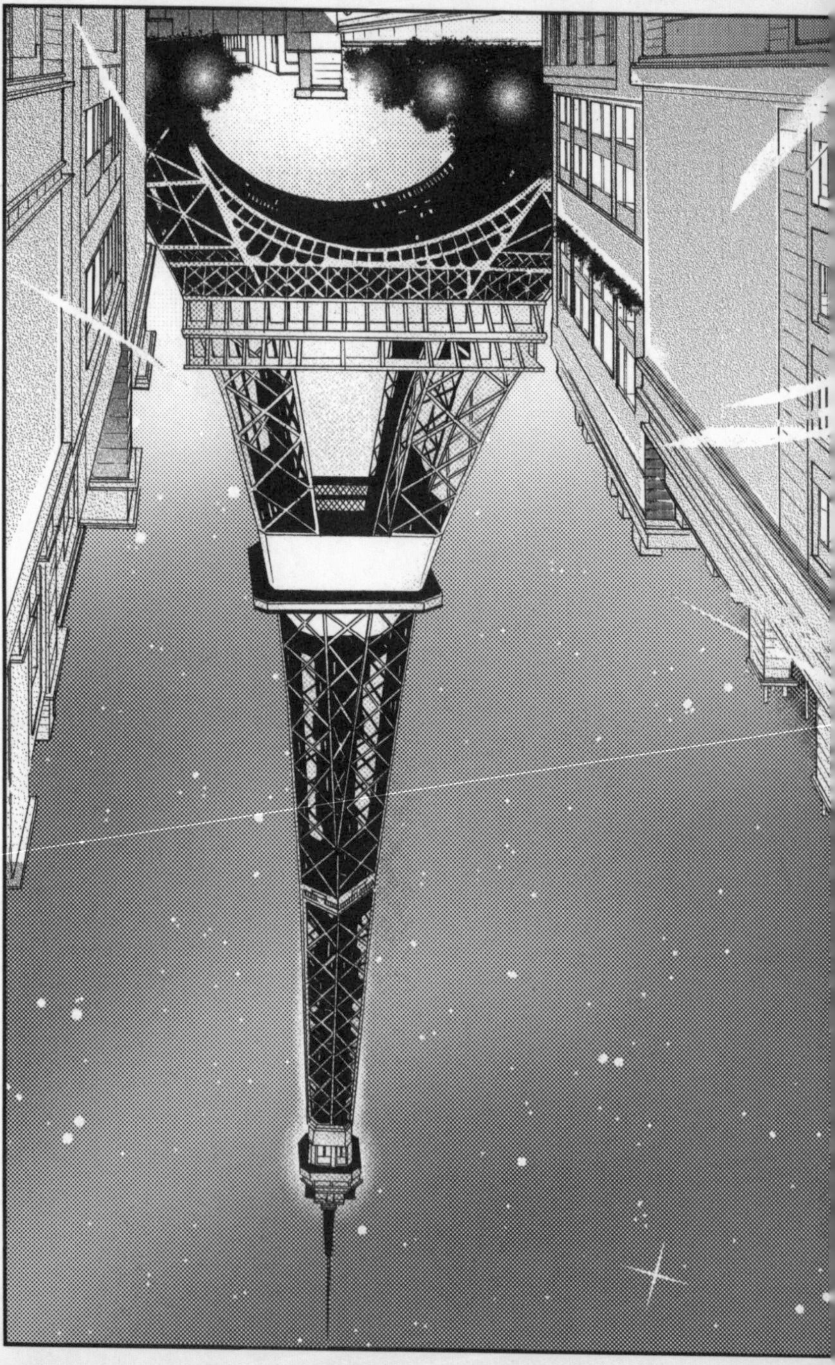

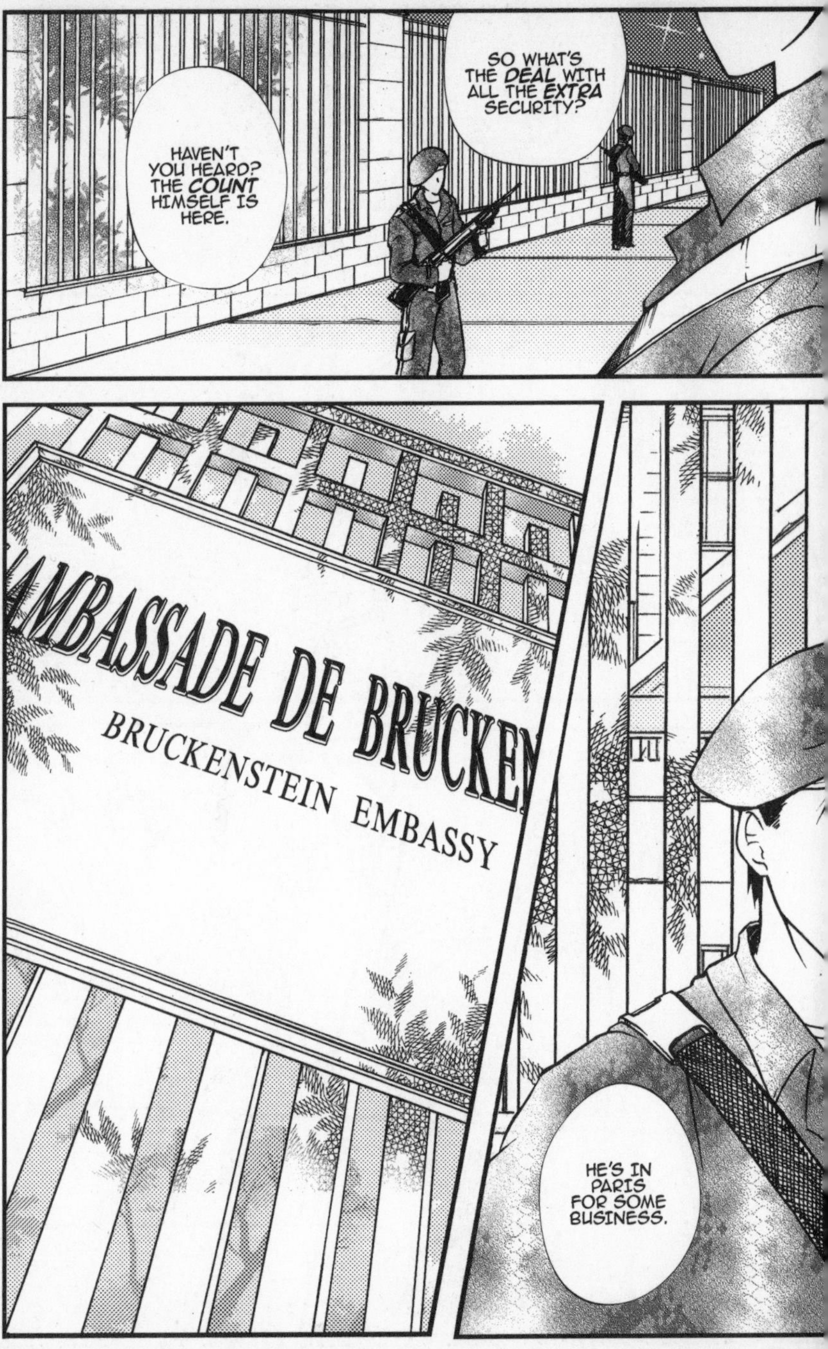
SO WHAT'S THE DEAL WITH ALL THE EXTRA SECURITY?
HAVEN'T YOU HEARD? THE COUNT HIMSELF IS HERE.
HE'S IN PARIS FOR SOME BUSINESS.
AMBASSADE DE BRUCKEN
BRUCKENSTEIN EMBASSY

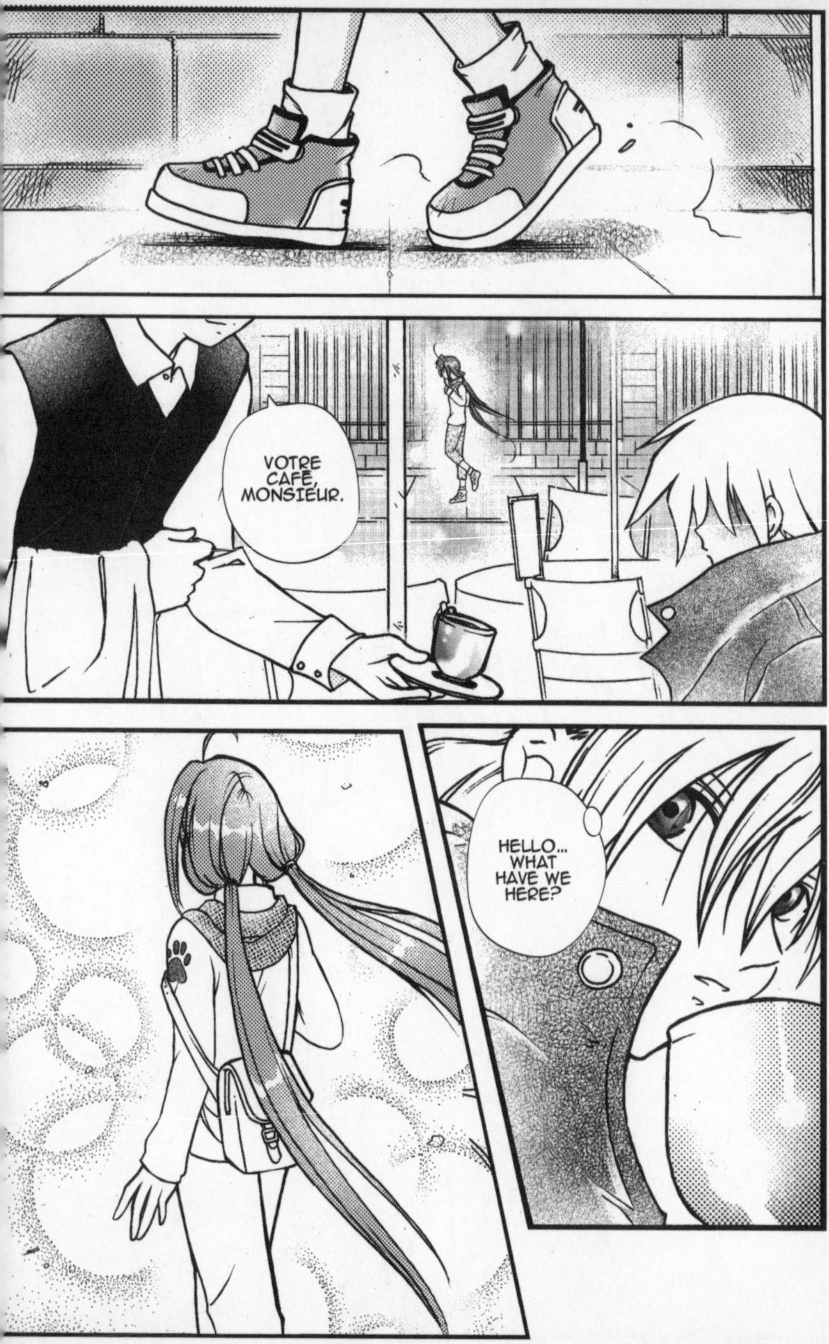
VOTRE CAFÉ, MONSIEUR.
HELLO... WHAT HAVE WE HERE?

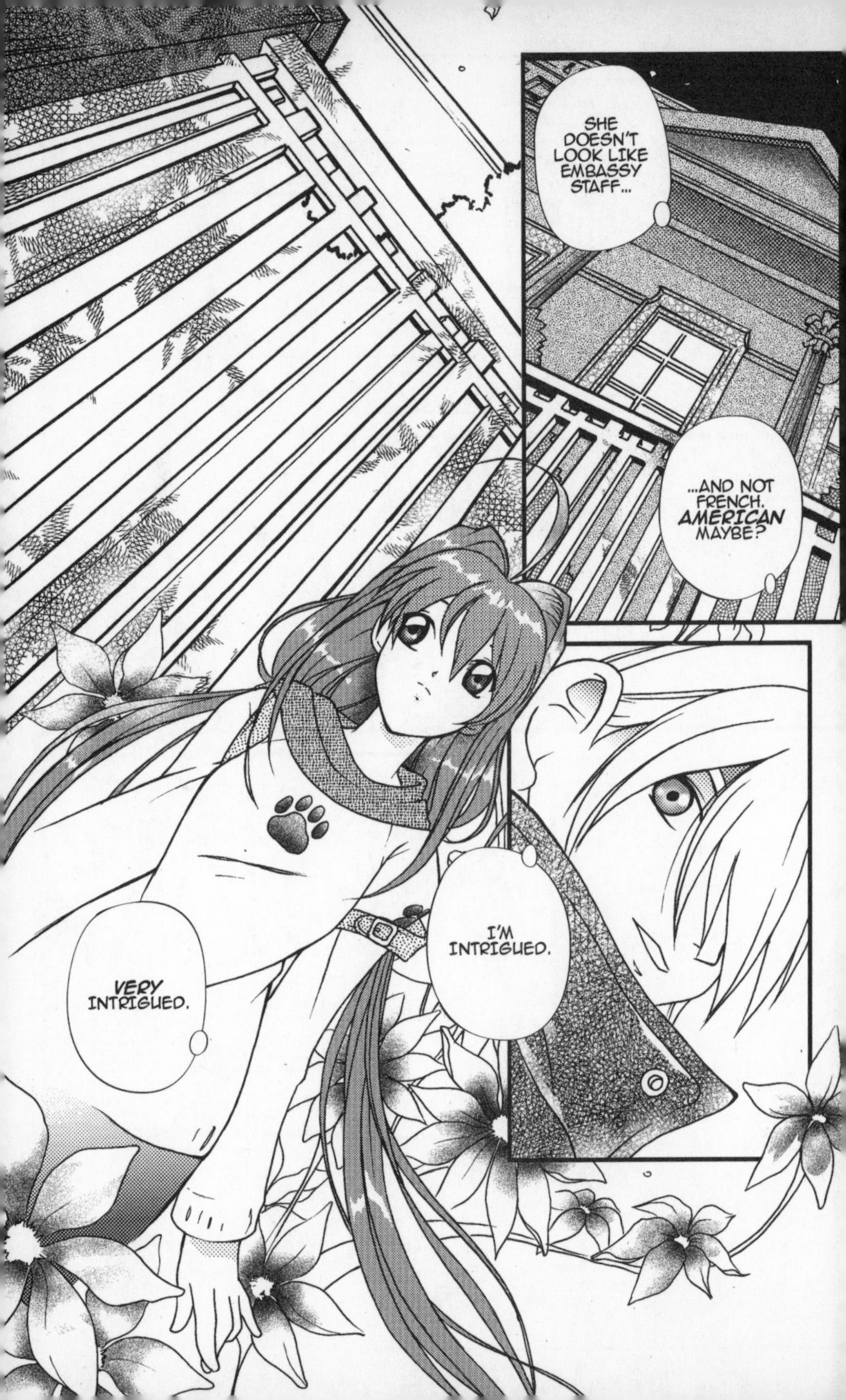
SHE DOESN'T LOOK LIKE EMBASSY STAFF...
...AND NOT FRENCH. **AMERICAN** MAYBE?
I'M INTRIGUED.
**VERY** INTRIGUED.

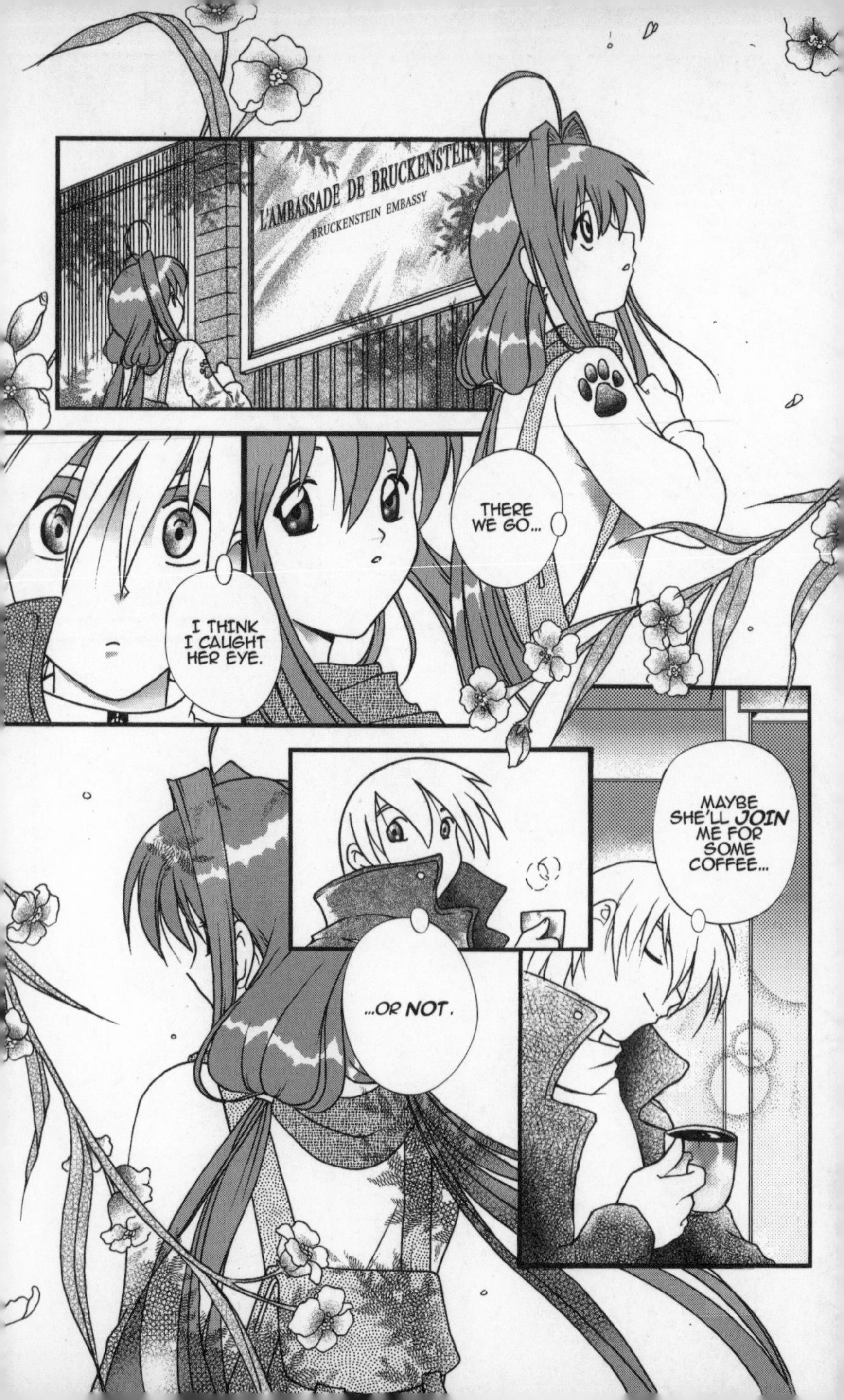
L'AMBASSADE DE BRUCKENSTEIN
BRUCKENSTEIN EMBASSY
THERE WE GO...
I THINK I CAUGHT HER EYE.
MAYBE SHE'LL JOIN ME FOR SOME COFFEE...
...OR NOT.

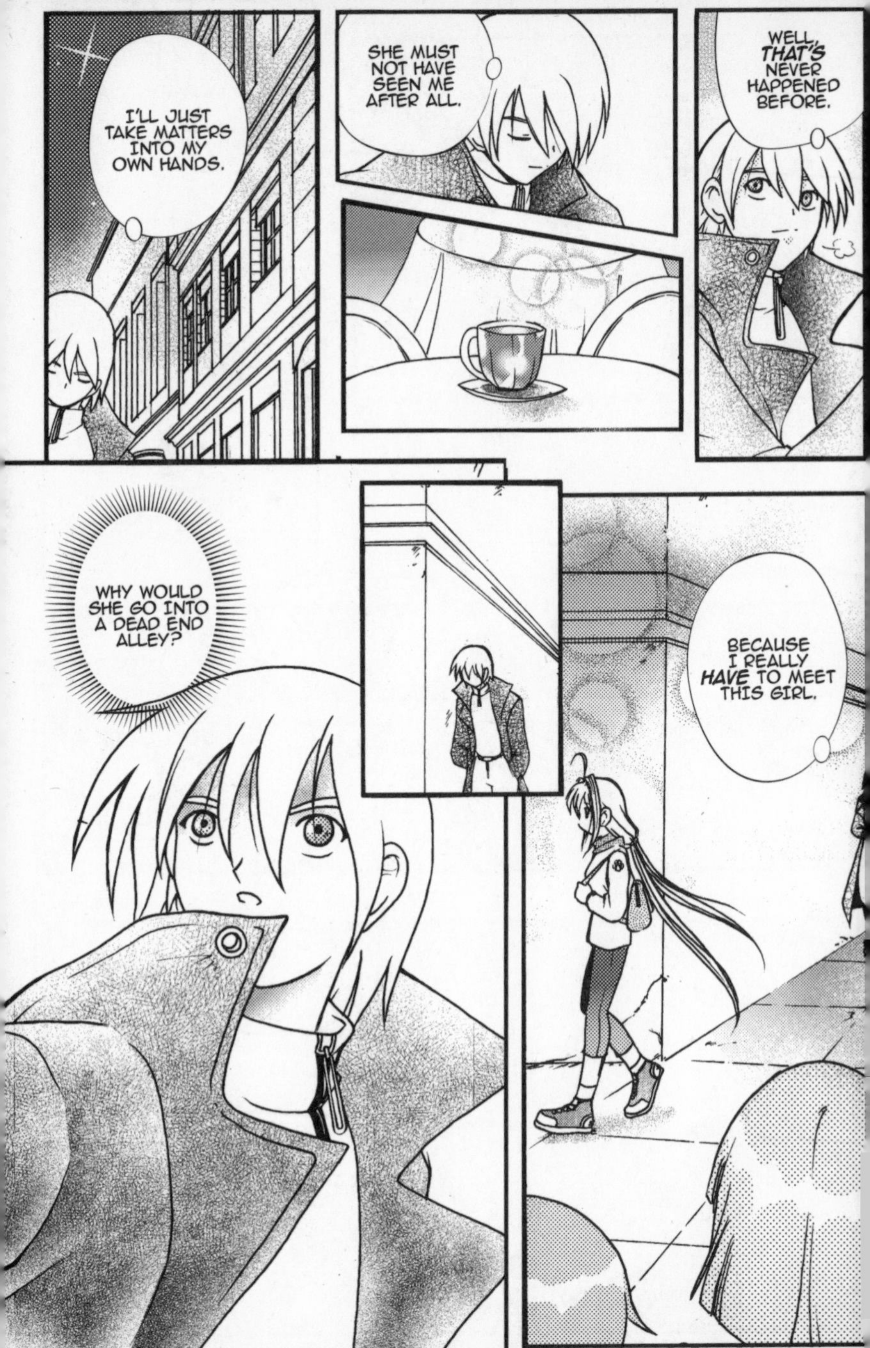
WELL, ***THAT'S*** NEVER HAPPENED BEFORE.
SHE MUST NOT HAVE SEEN ME AFTER ALL.
I'LL JUST TAKE MATTERS INTO MY OWN HANDS.
BECAUSE I REALLY ***HAVE*** TO MEET THIS GIRL.
WHY WOULD SHE GO INTO A DEAD END ALLEY?

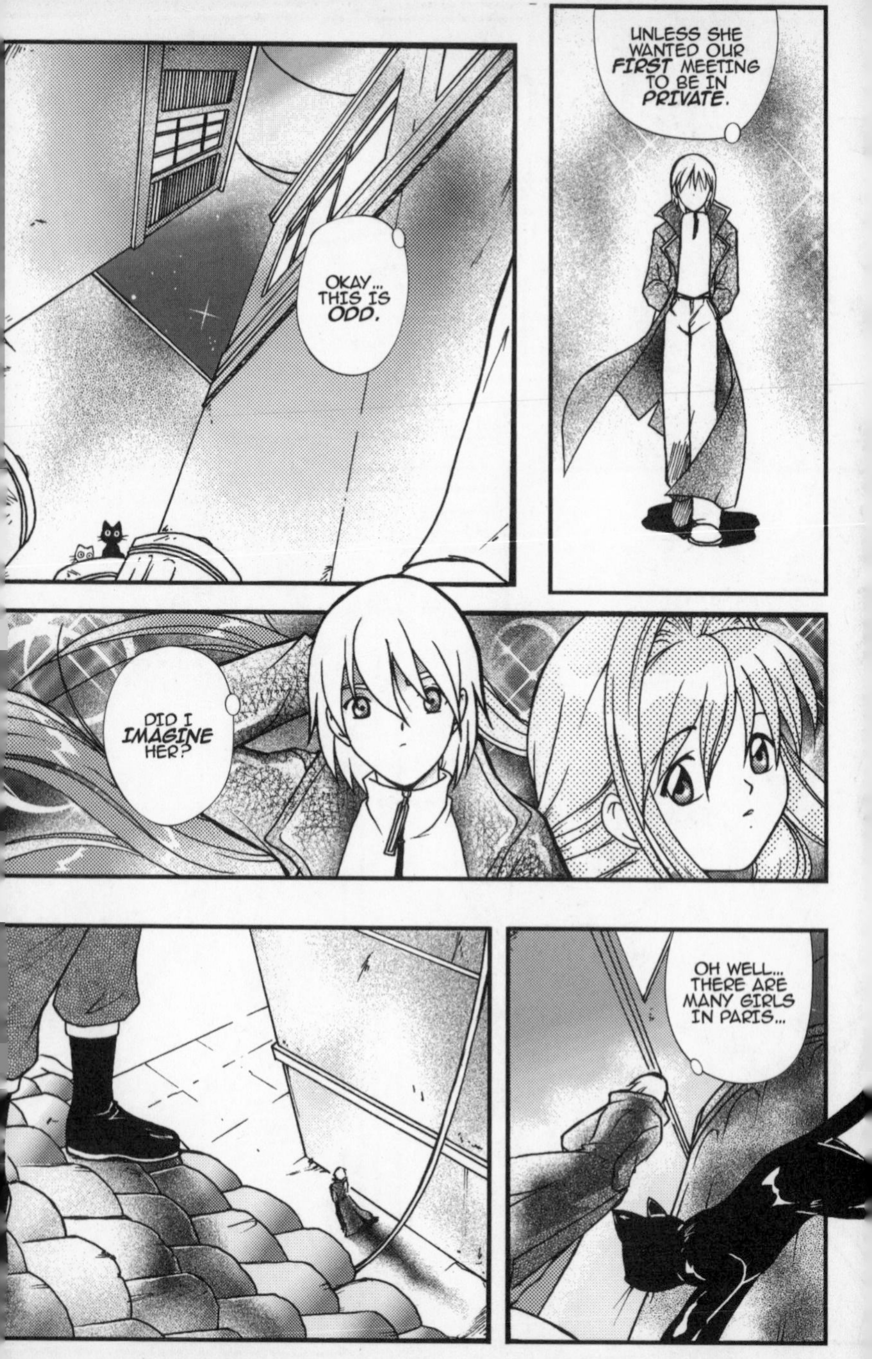
UNLESS SHE WANTED OUR FIRST MEETING TO BE IN PRIVATE.
OKAY... THIS IS ODD.
DID I IMAGINE HER?
OH WELL... THERE ARE MANY GIRLS IN PARIS...

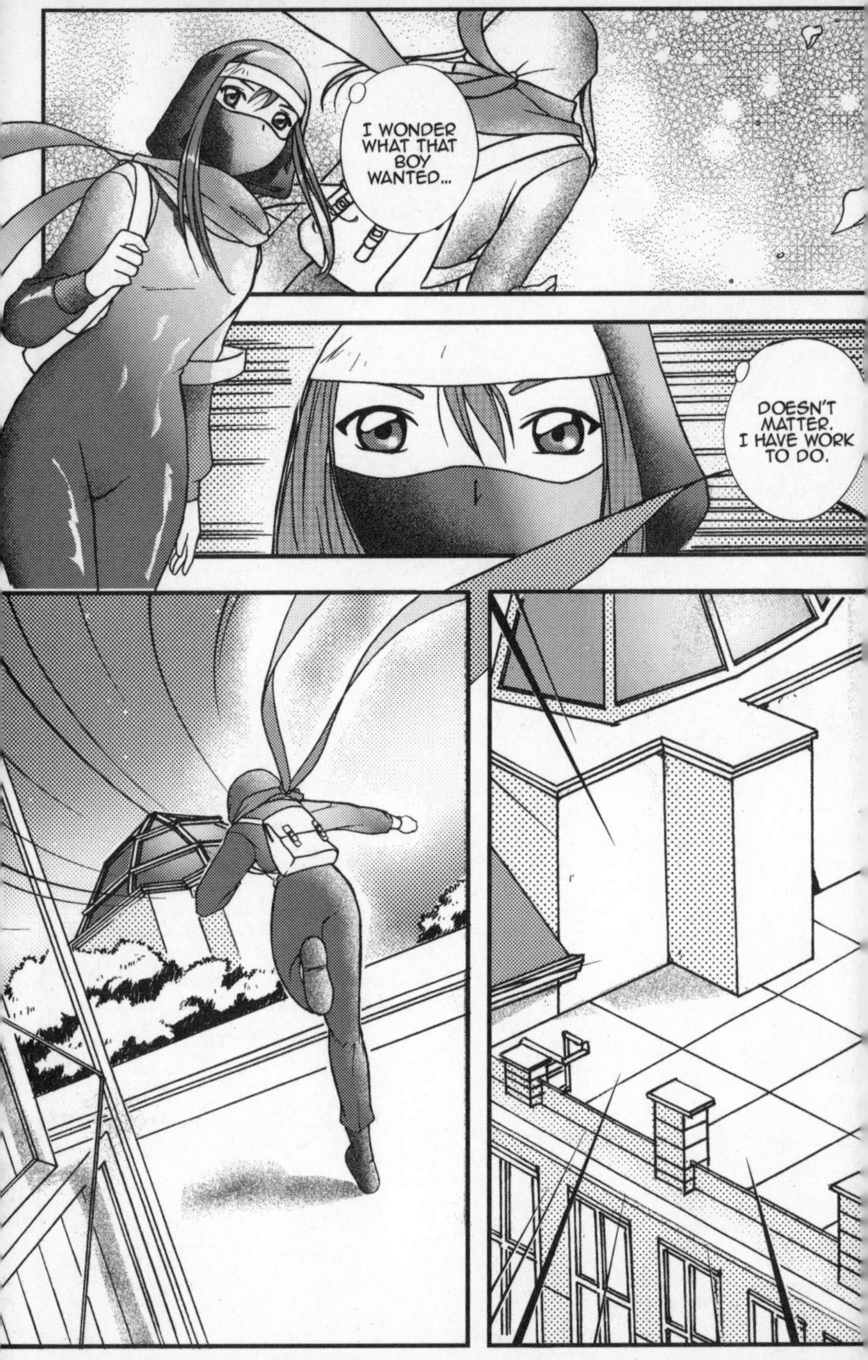
I WONDER WHAT THAT BOY WANTED...
DOESN'T MATTER. I HAVE WORK TO DO.

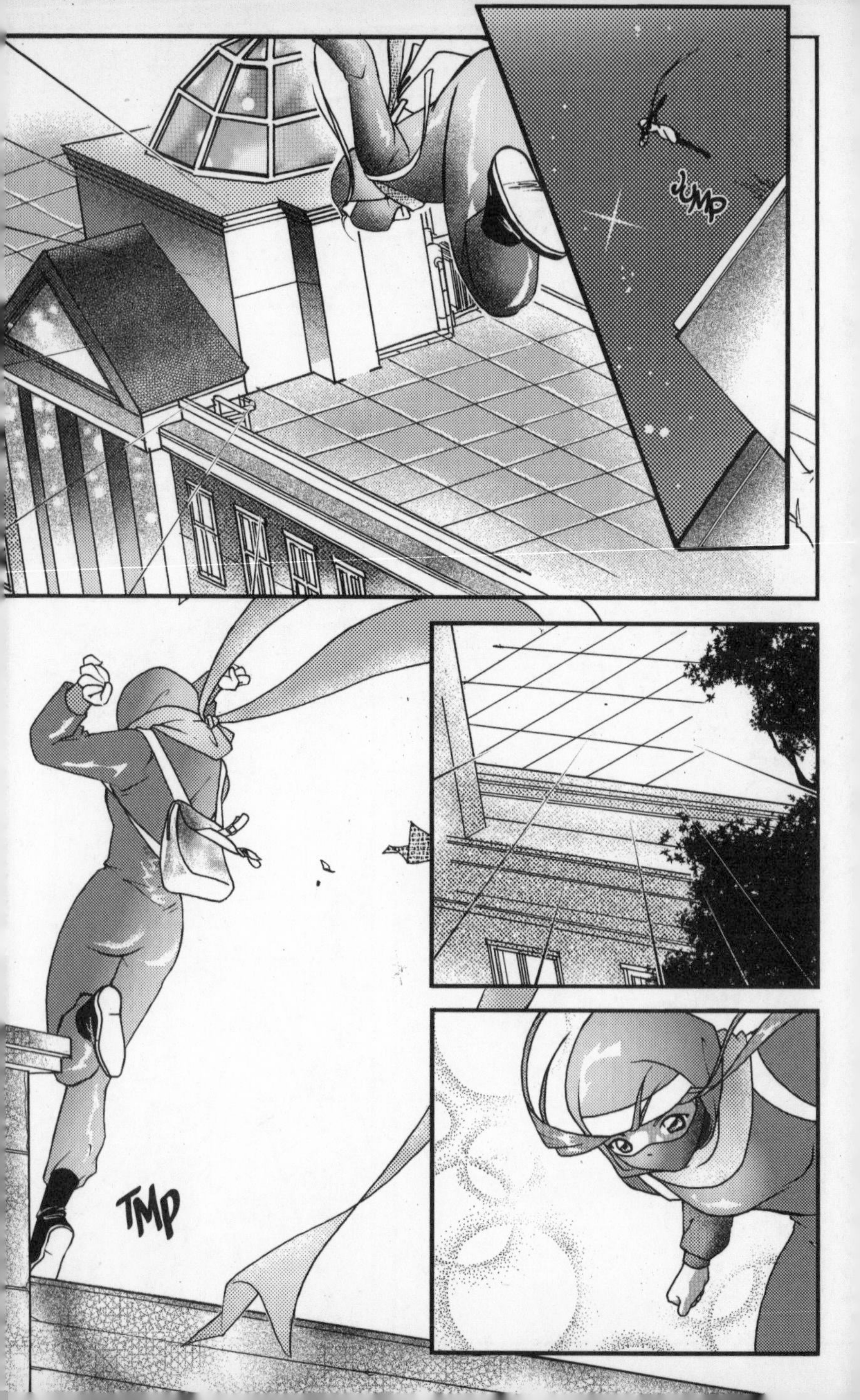
JUMP
TMP

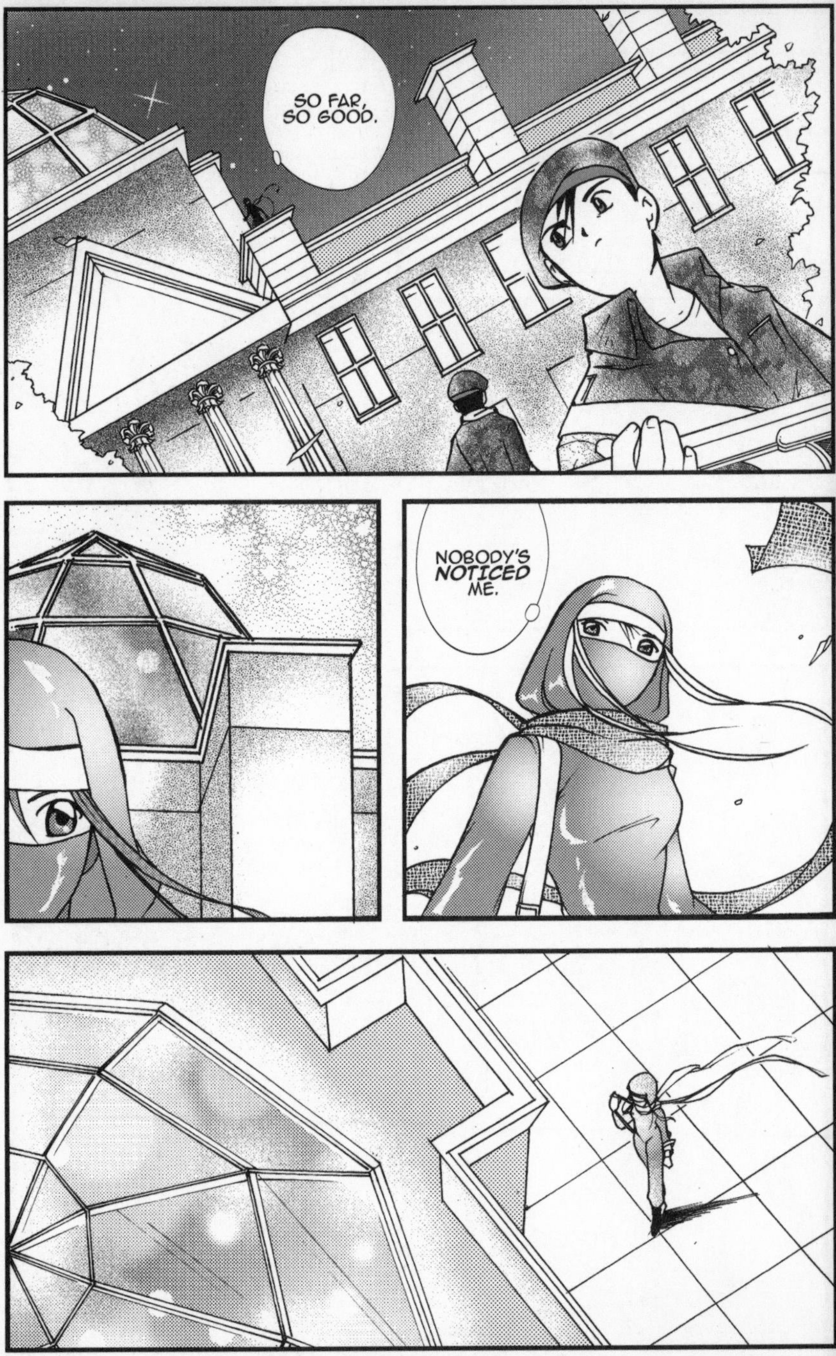
SO FAR, SO GOOD.
NOBODY'S *NOTICED* ME.

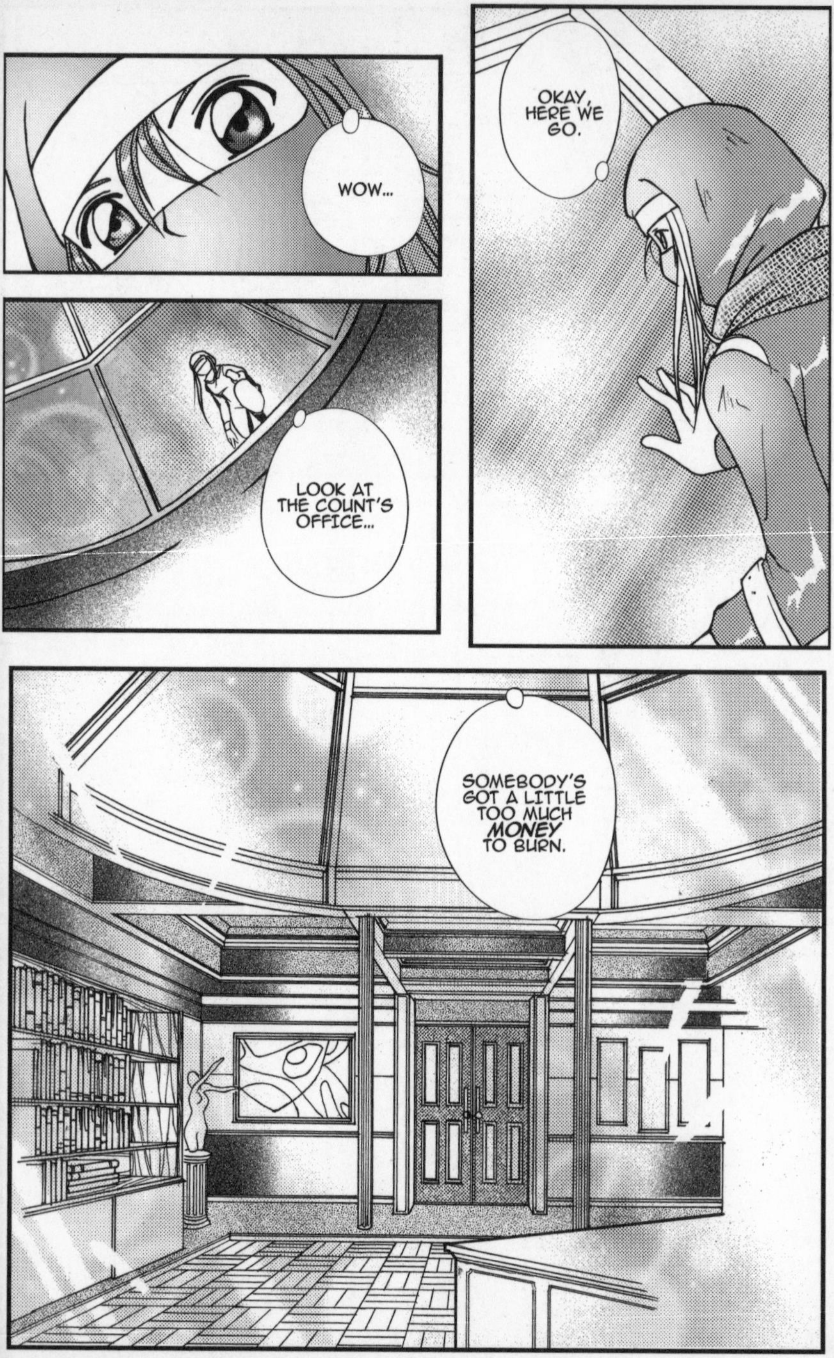
OKAY, HERE WE GO.
WOW...
LOOK AT THE COUNT'S OFFICE...
SOMEBODY'S GOT A LITTLE TOO MUCH ***MONEY*** TO BURN.

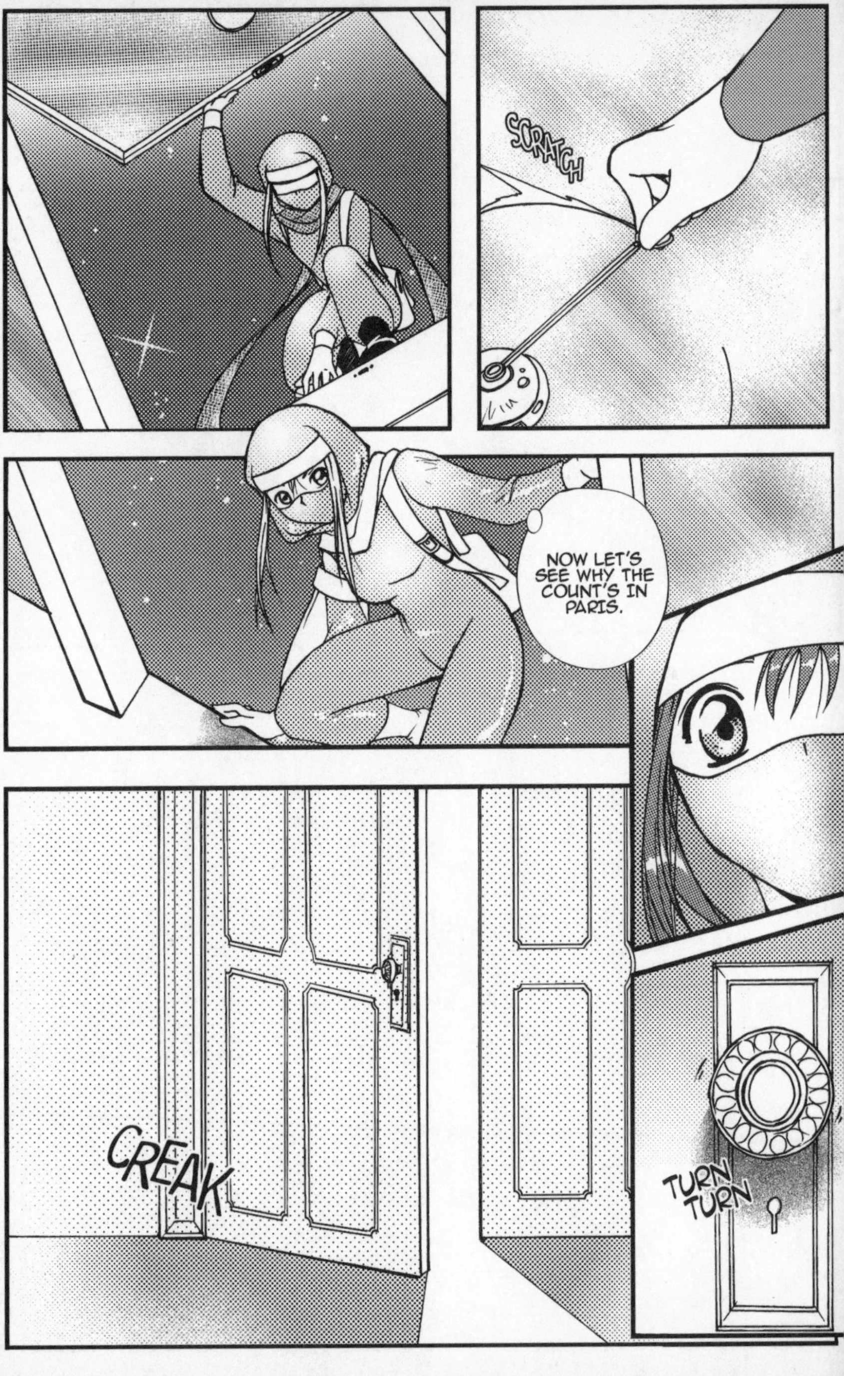
SCRATCH
NOW LET'S SEE WHY THE COUNT'S IN PARIS.
TURN TURN
CREAK

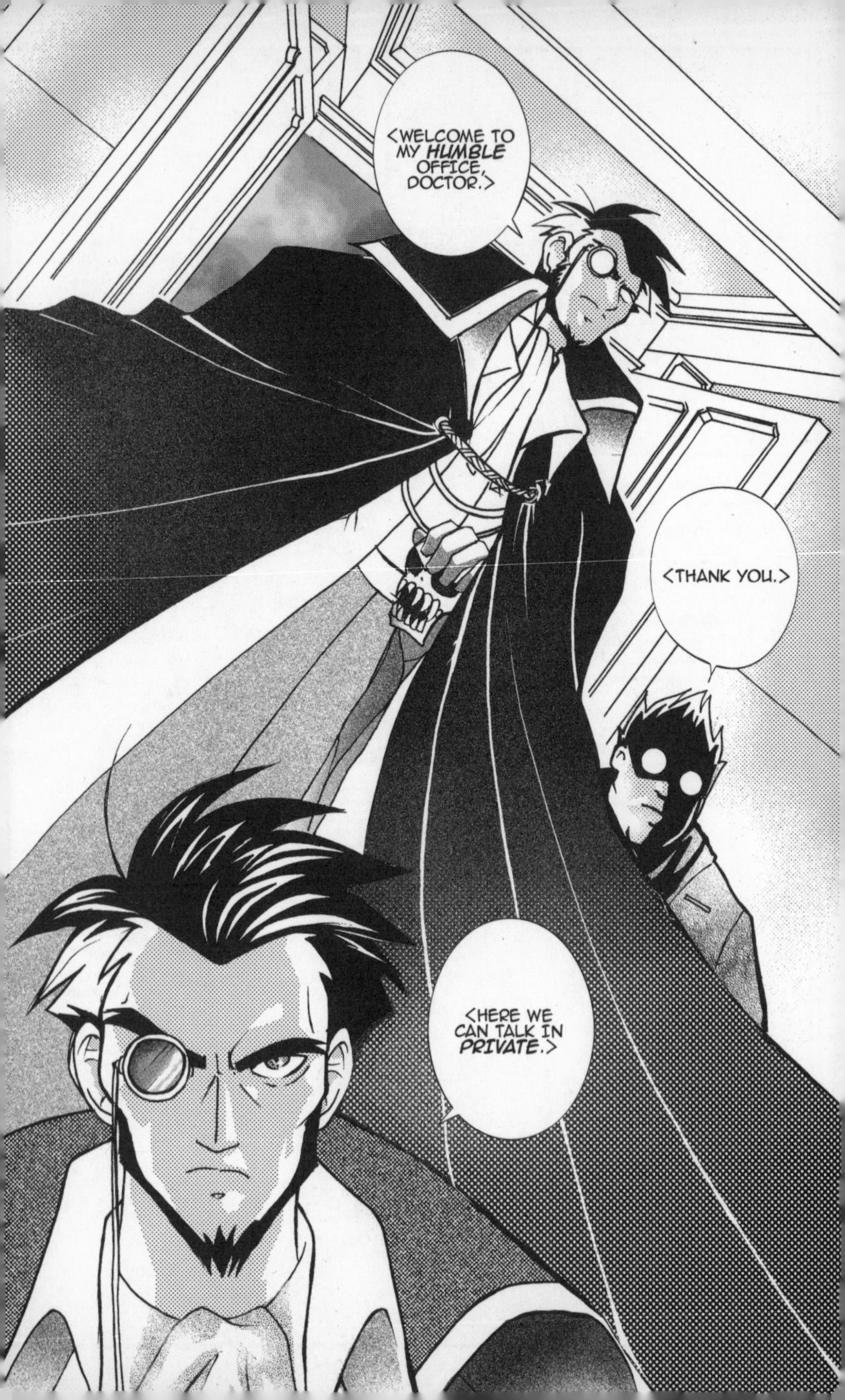
<WELCOME TO MY *HUMBLE* OFFICE, DOCTOR.>
<THANK YOU.>
<HERE WE CAN TALK IN *PRIVATE*.>

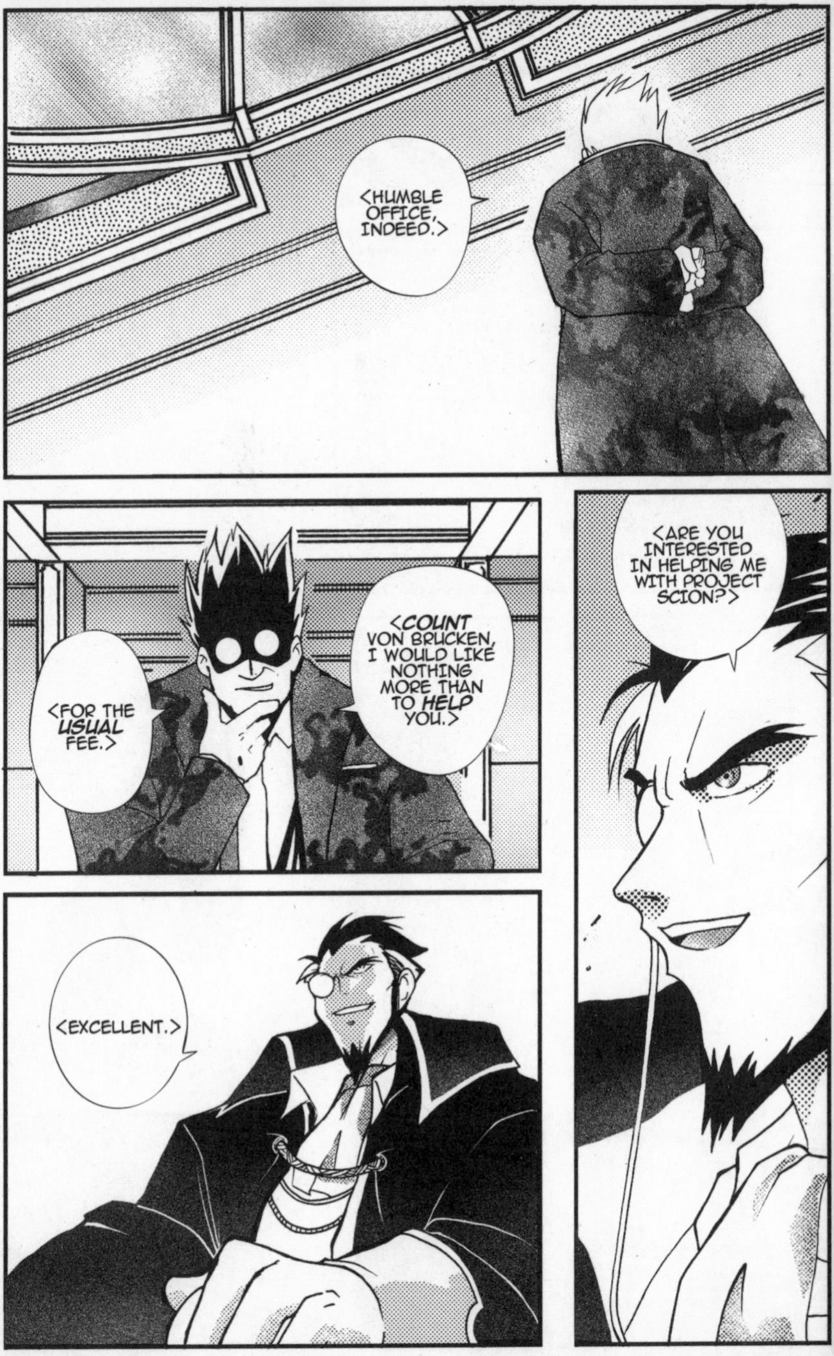
<HUMBLE OFFICE, INDEED.>
<ARE YOU INTERESTED IN HELPING ME WITH PROJECT SCION?>
<**COUNT** VON BRUCKEN, I WOULD LIKE NOTHING MORE THAN TO **HELP** YOU.>
<FOR THE **USUAL** FEE.>
<EXCELLENT.>

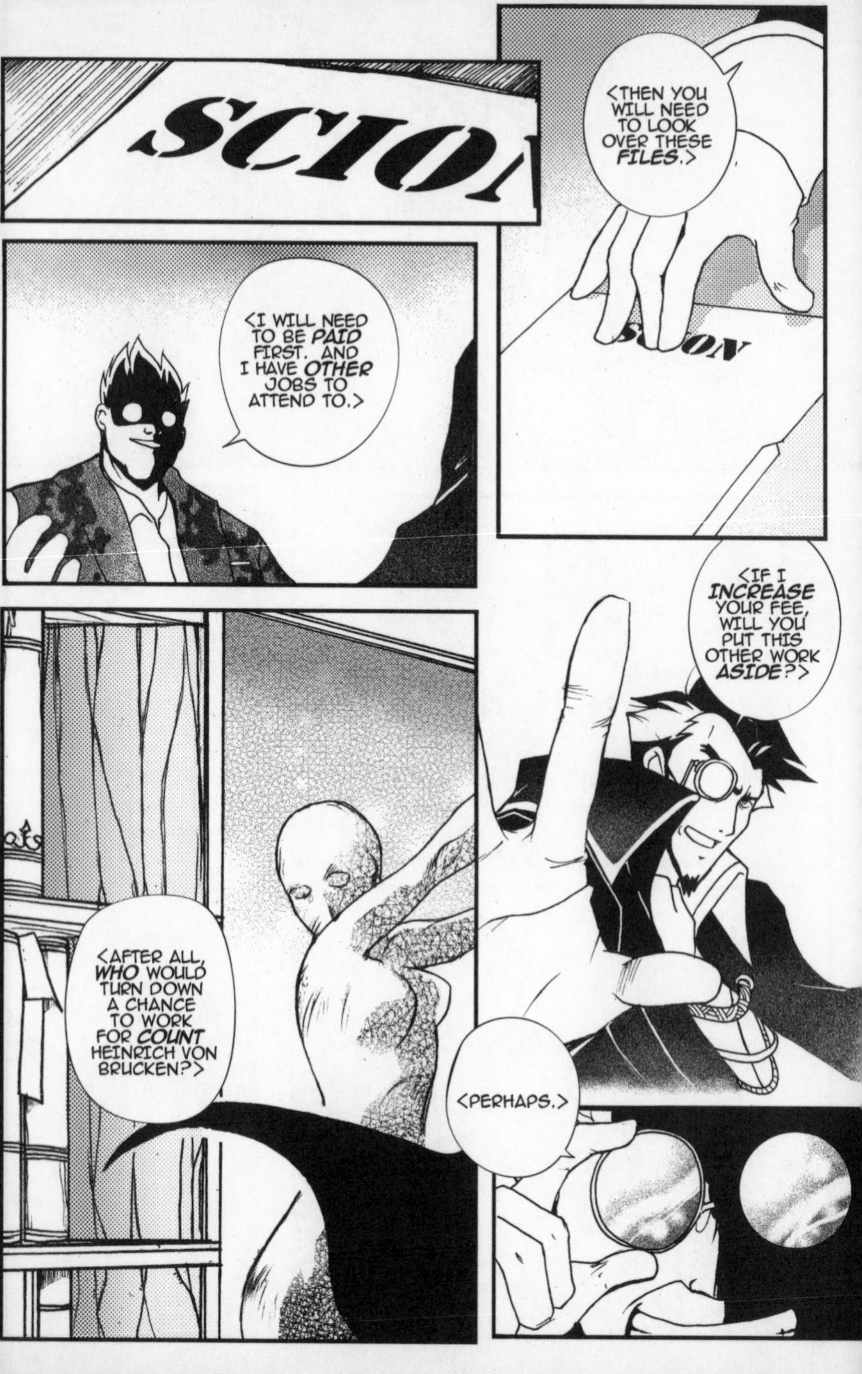
<THEN YOU WILL NEED TO LOOK OVER THESE *FILES*.>
SCIO
S ON
<I WILL NEED TO BE *PAID* FIRST. AND I HAVE *OTHER* JOBS TO ATTEND TO.>
<IF I *INCREASE* YOUR FEE, WILL YOU PUT THIS OTHER WORK *ASIDE*?>
<PERHAPS.>
<AFTER ALL, *WHO* WOULD TURN DOWN A CHANCE TO WORK FOR *COUNT* HEINRICH VON BRUCKEN?>

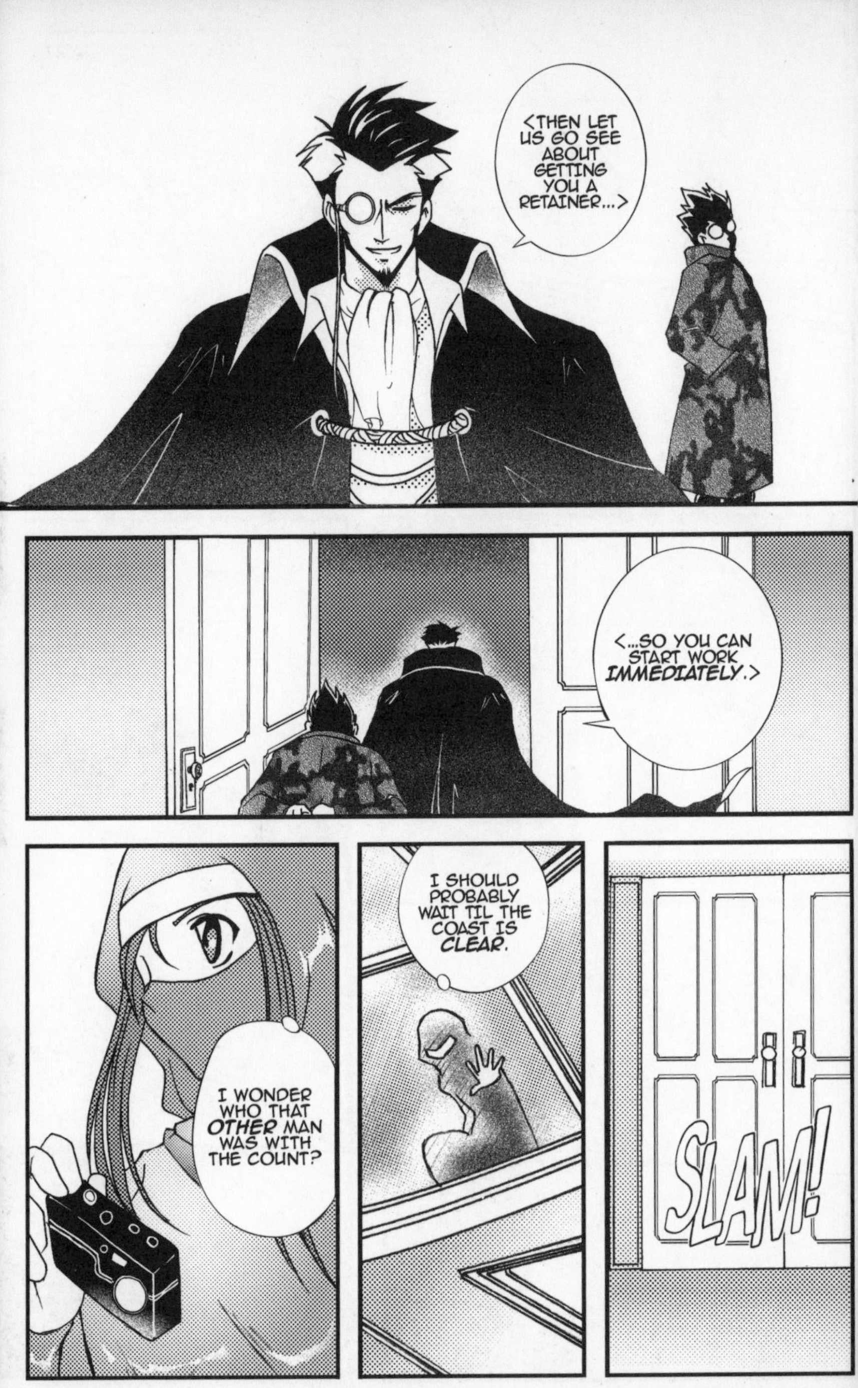
<THEN LET US GO SEE ABOUT GETTING YOU A RETAINER...>
<...SO YOU CAN START WORK *IMMEDIATELY*.>
SLAM!
I SHOULD PROBABLY WAIT TIL THE COAST IS *CLEAR*.
I WONDER WHO THAT *OTHER* MAN WAS WITH THE COUNT?

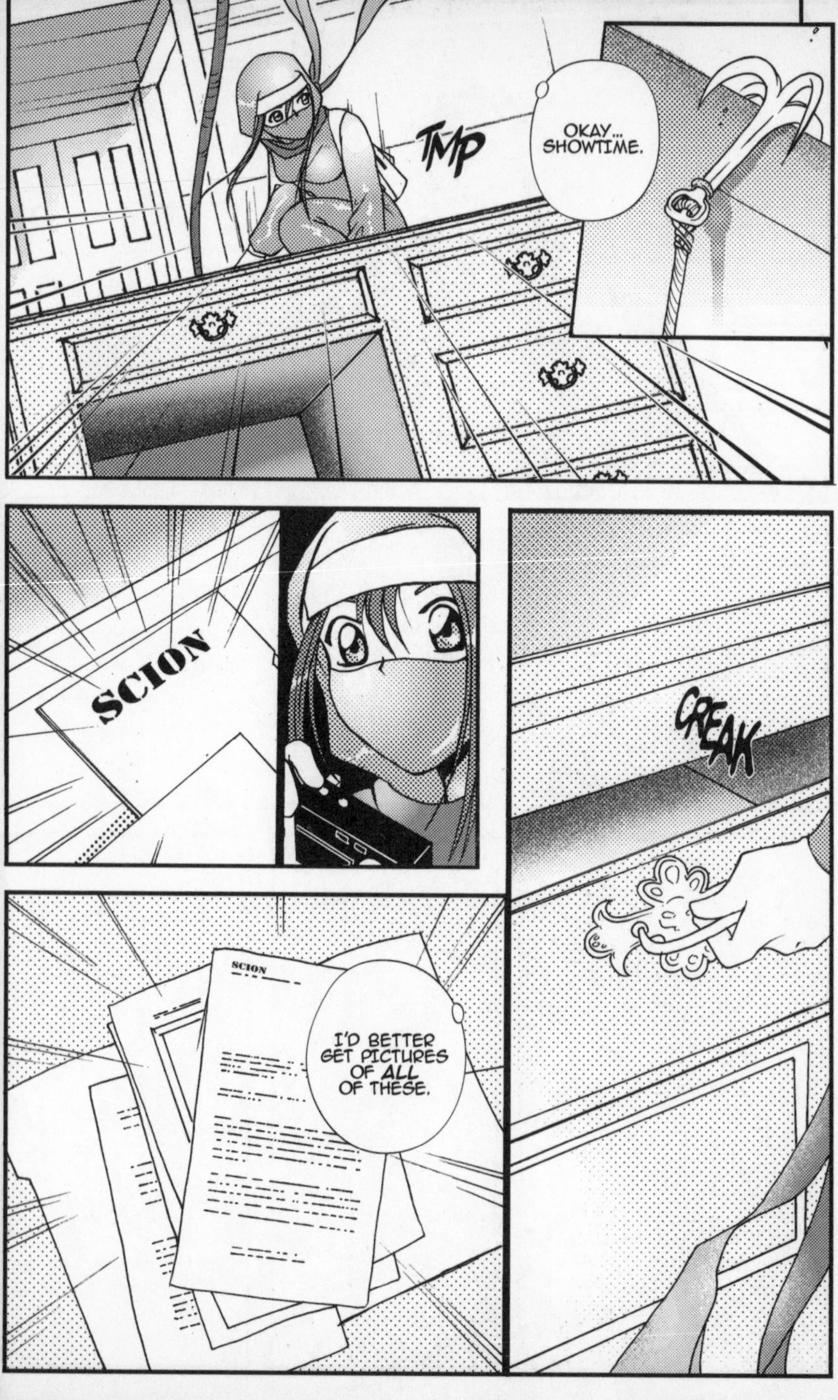
OKAY... SHOWTIME.
TMP
CREAK
SCION
SCION
I'D BETTER GET PICTURES OF ALL OF THESE.

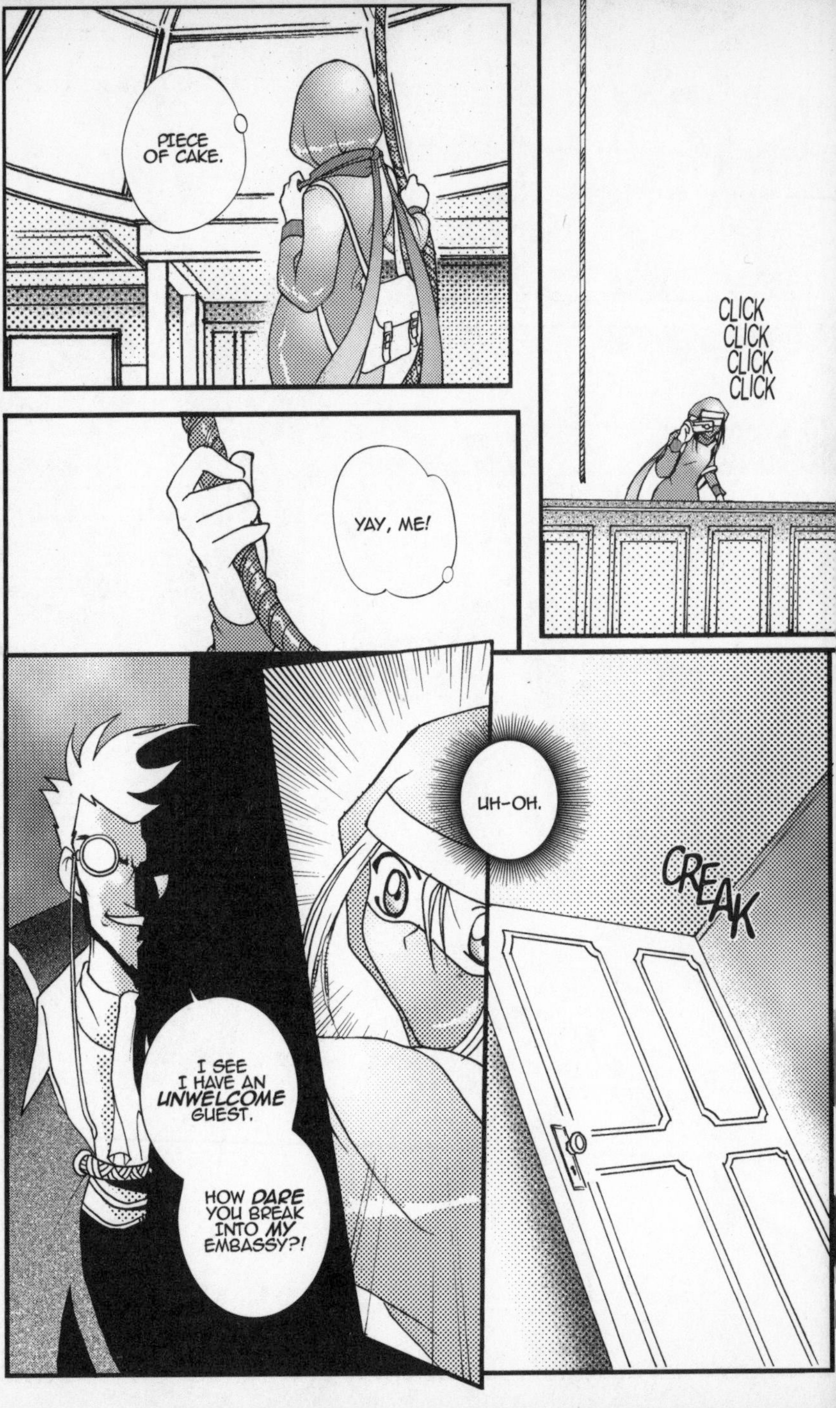
CLICK CLICK CLICK CLICK
PIECE OF CAKE.
YAY, ME!
UH-OH.
CREAK
I SEE I HAVE AN *UNWELCOME* GUEST.
HOW *DARE* YOU BREAK INTO *MY* EMBASSY?!

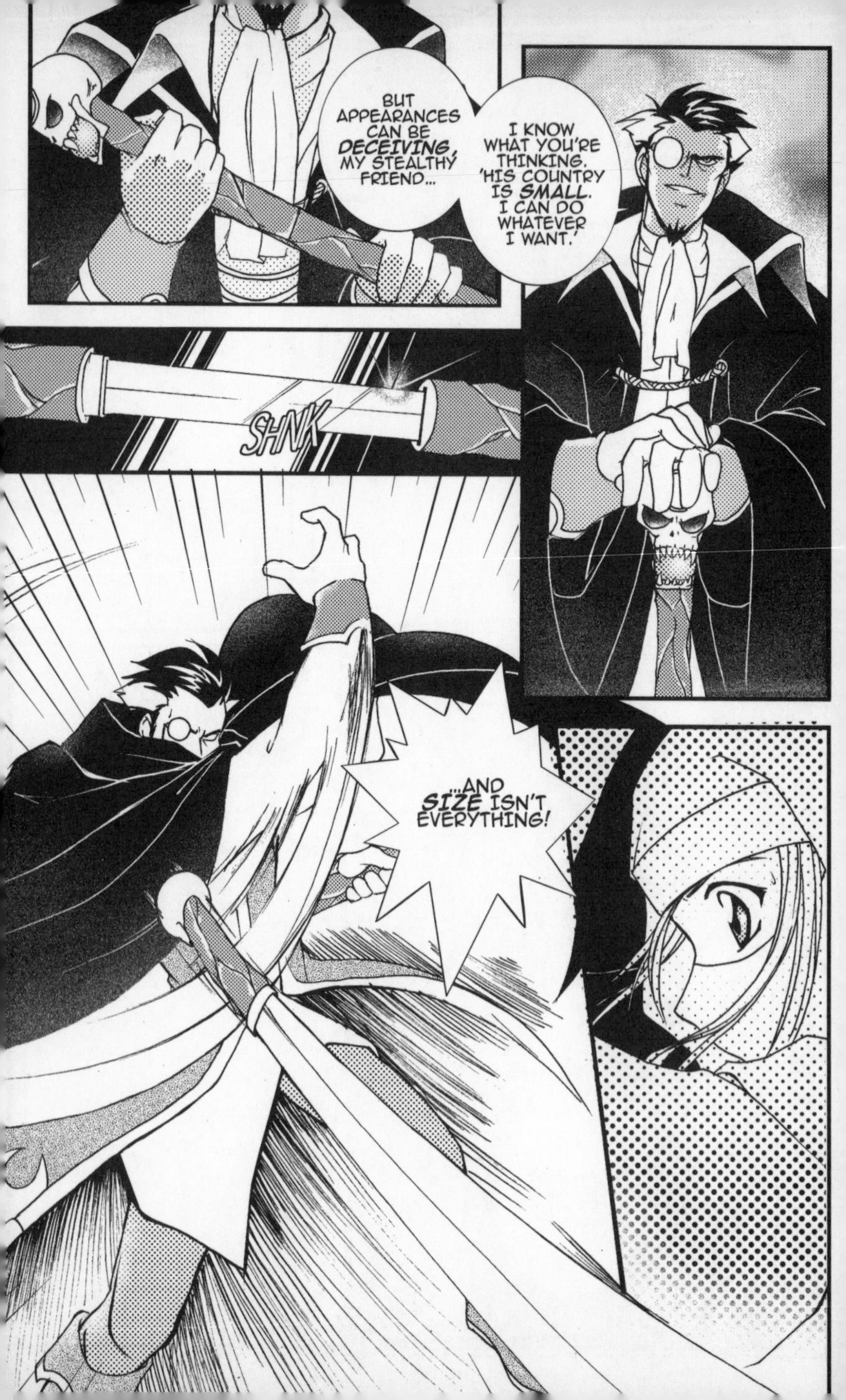
I KNOW WHAT YOU'RE THINKING. 'HIS COUNTRY IS SMALL. I CAN DO WHATEVER I WANT.'
BUT APPEARANCES CAN BE DECEIVING, MY STEALTHY FRIEND...
SHNK
...AND SIZE ISN'T EVERYTHING!

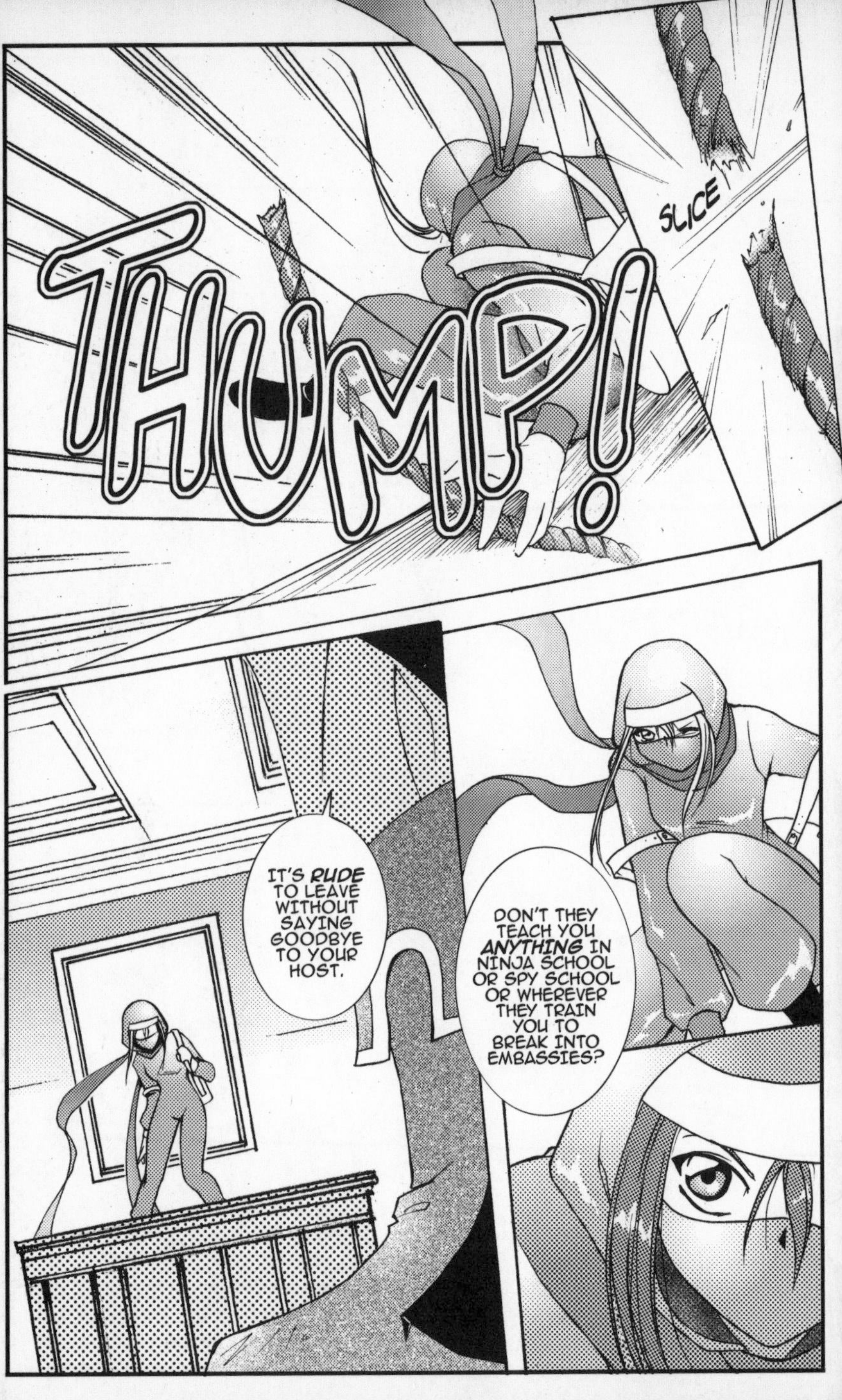
SLICE
THUMP!
IT'S ***RUDE*** TO LEAVE WITHOUT SAYING GOODBYE TO YOUR HOST.
DON'T THEY TEACH YOU ***ANYTHING*** IN NINJA SCHOOL OR SPY SCHOOL OR WHEREVER THEY TRAIN YOU TO BREAK INTO EMBASSIES?

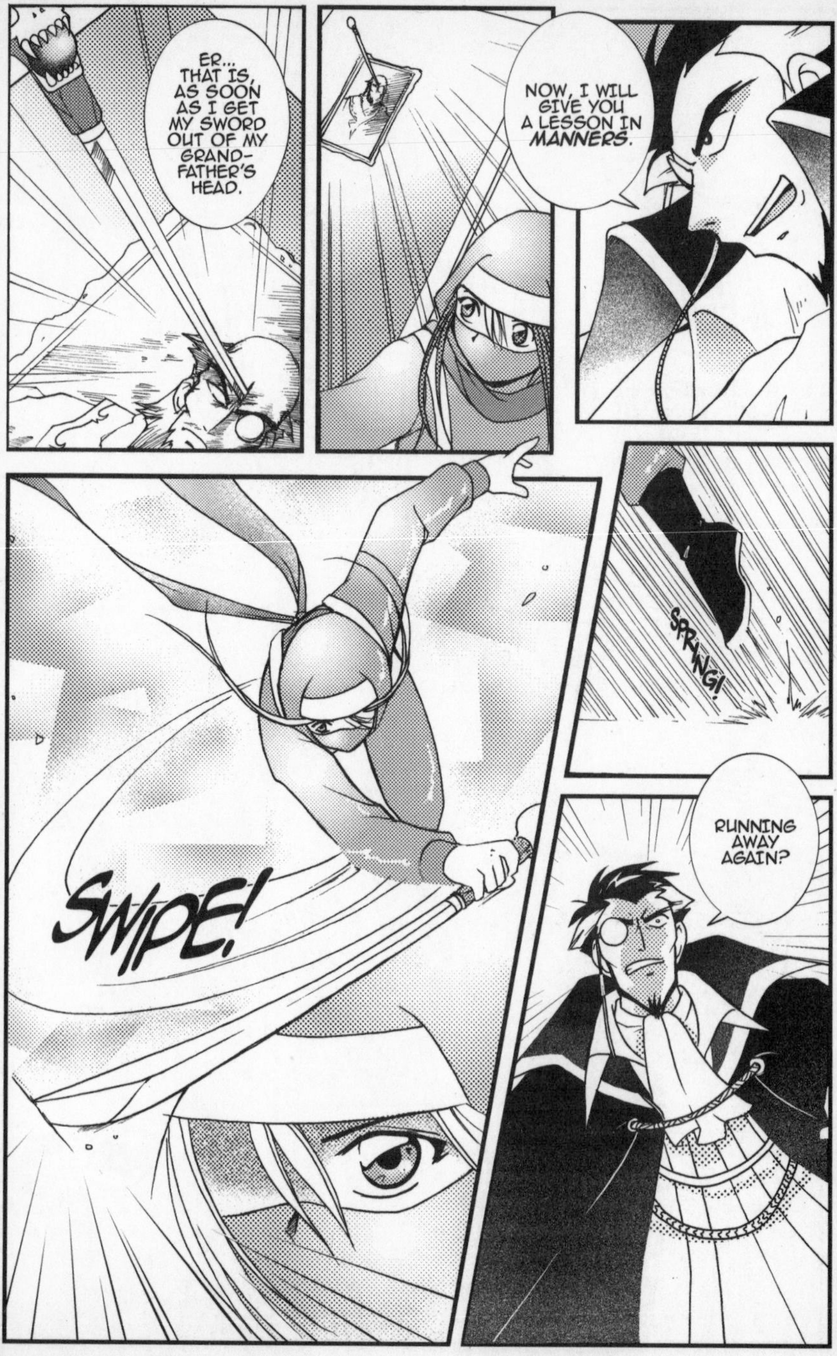
NOW, I WILL GIVE YOU A LESSON IN MANNERS.
ER... THAT IS, AS SOON AS I GET MY SWORD OUT OF MY GRAND-FATHER'S HEAD.
SPRING!
RUNNING AWAY AGAIN?
SWIPE!

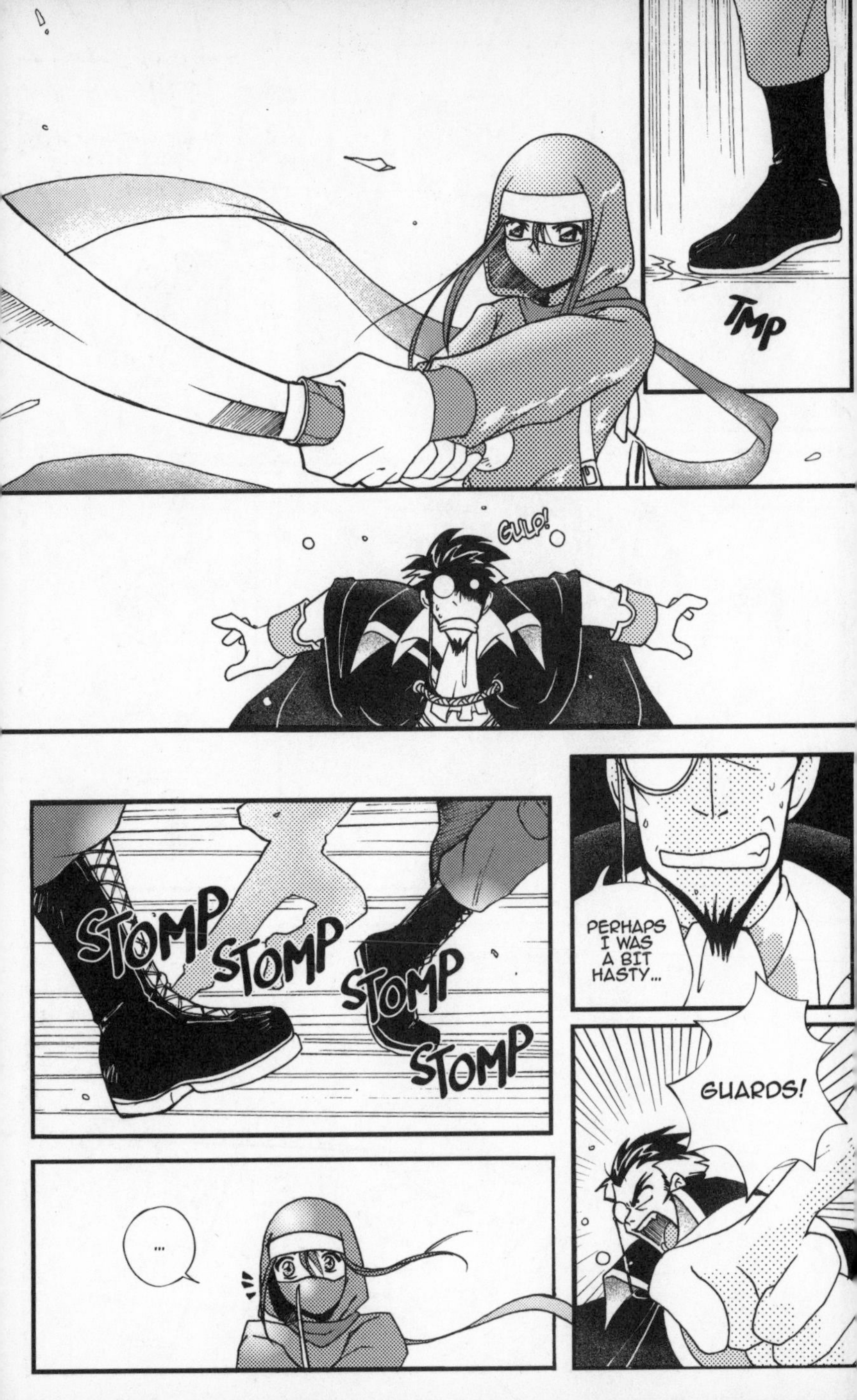
TMP
GULP!
PERHAPS I WAS A BIT HASTY...
STOMP
STOMP
STOMP
STOMP
GUARDS!
...

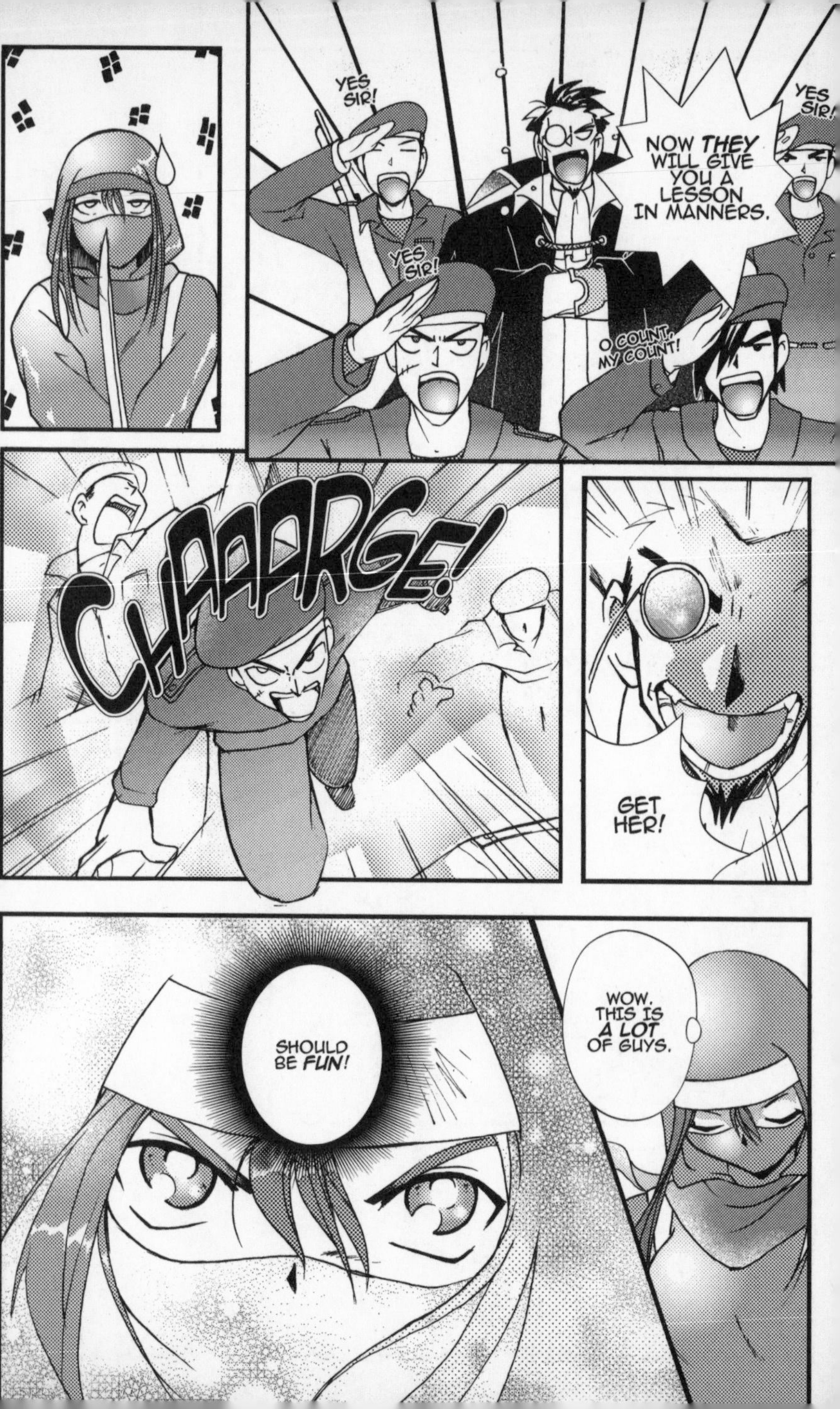
NOW THEY WILL GIVE YOU A LESSON IN MANNERS.
YES SIR!
O COUNT, MY COUNT!
YES SIR!
YES SIR!
GET HER!
CHAAARGE!
WOW. THIS IS A LOT OF GUYS.
SHOULD BE FUN!

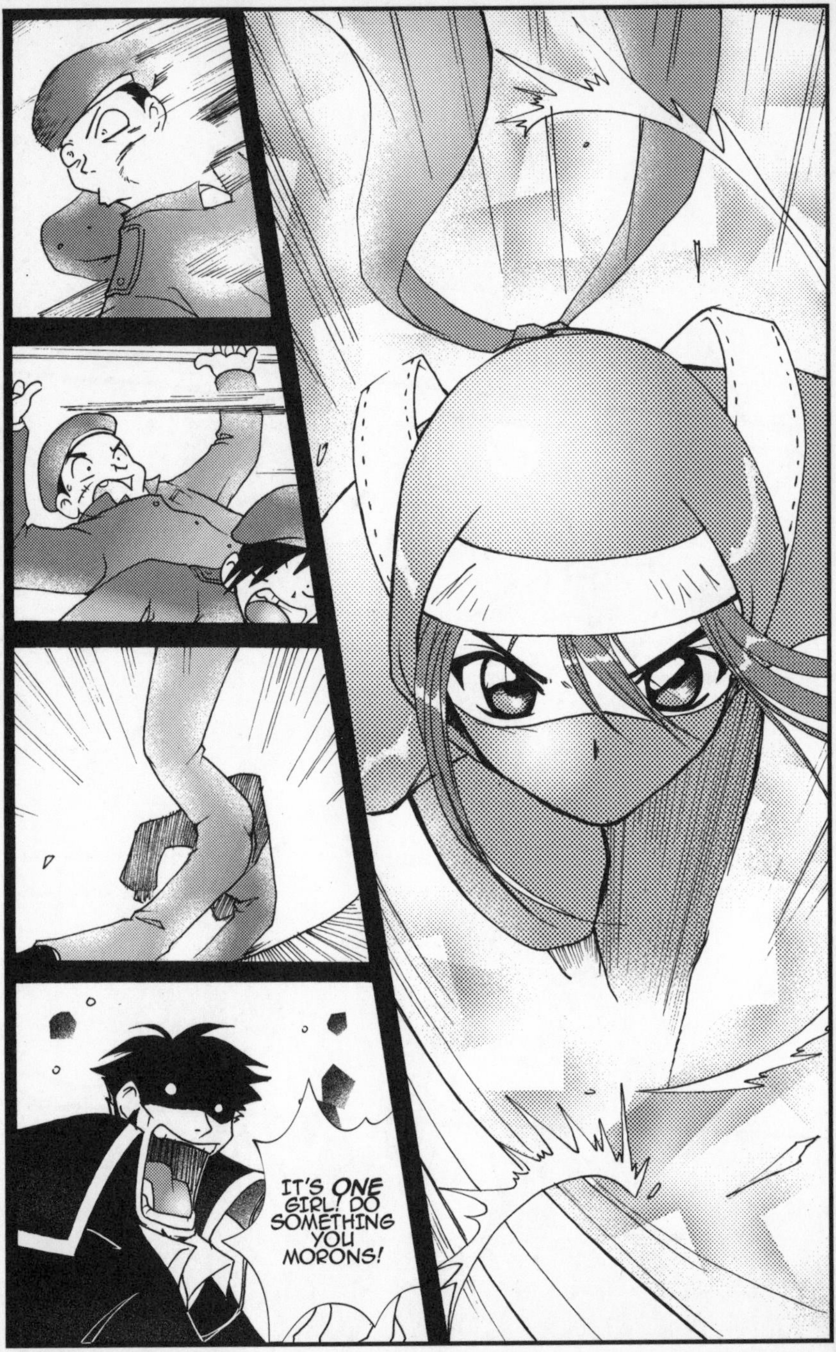
IT'S ONE GIRL! DO SOMETHING YOU MORONS!

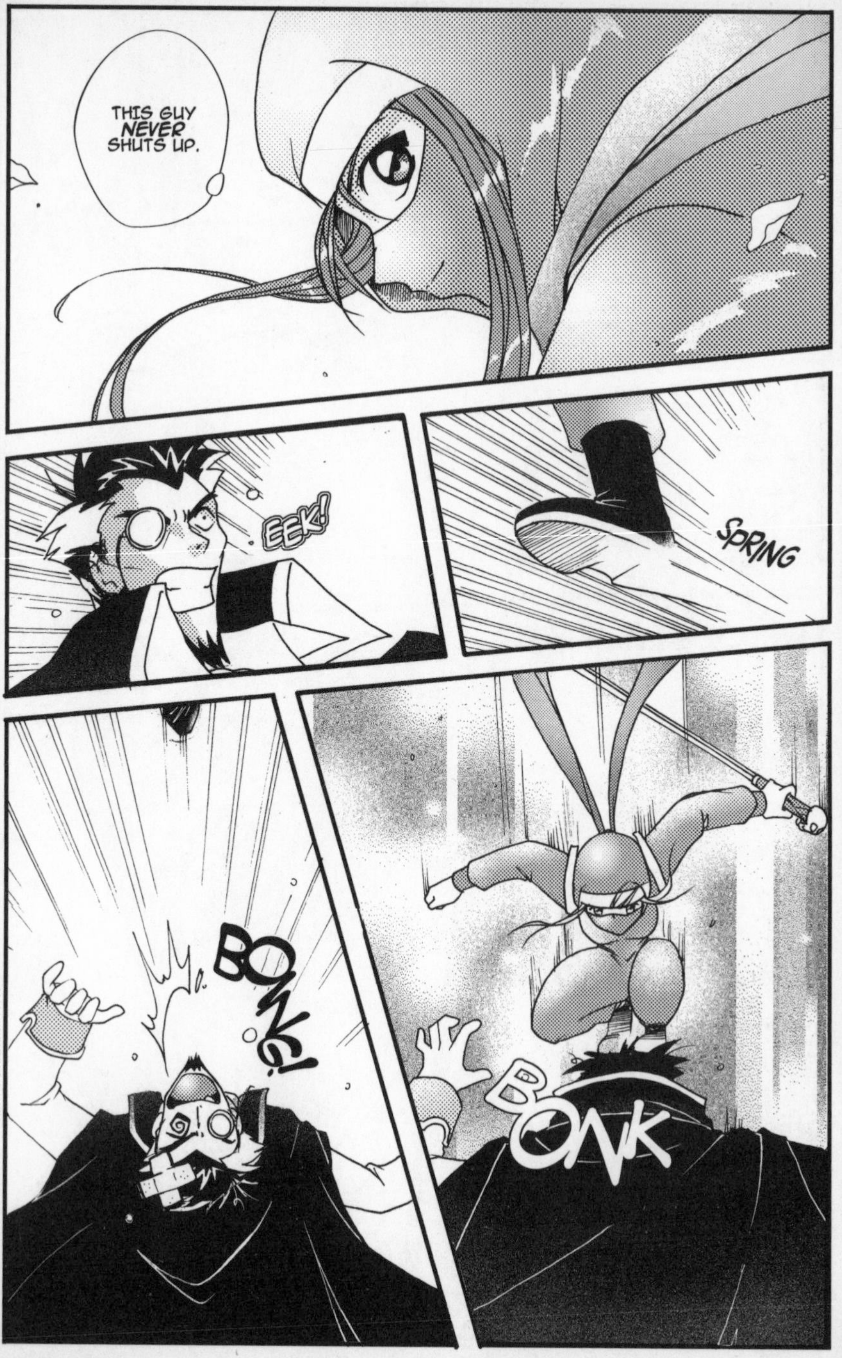
THIS GUY NEVER SHUTS UP.
SPRING
EEK!
BONK
BONG!

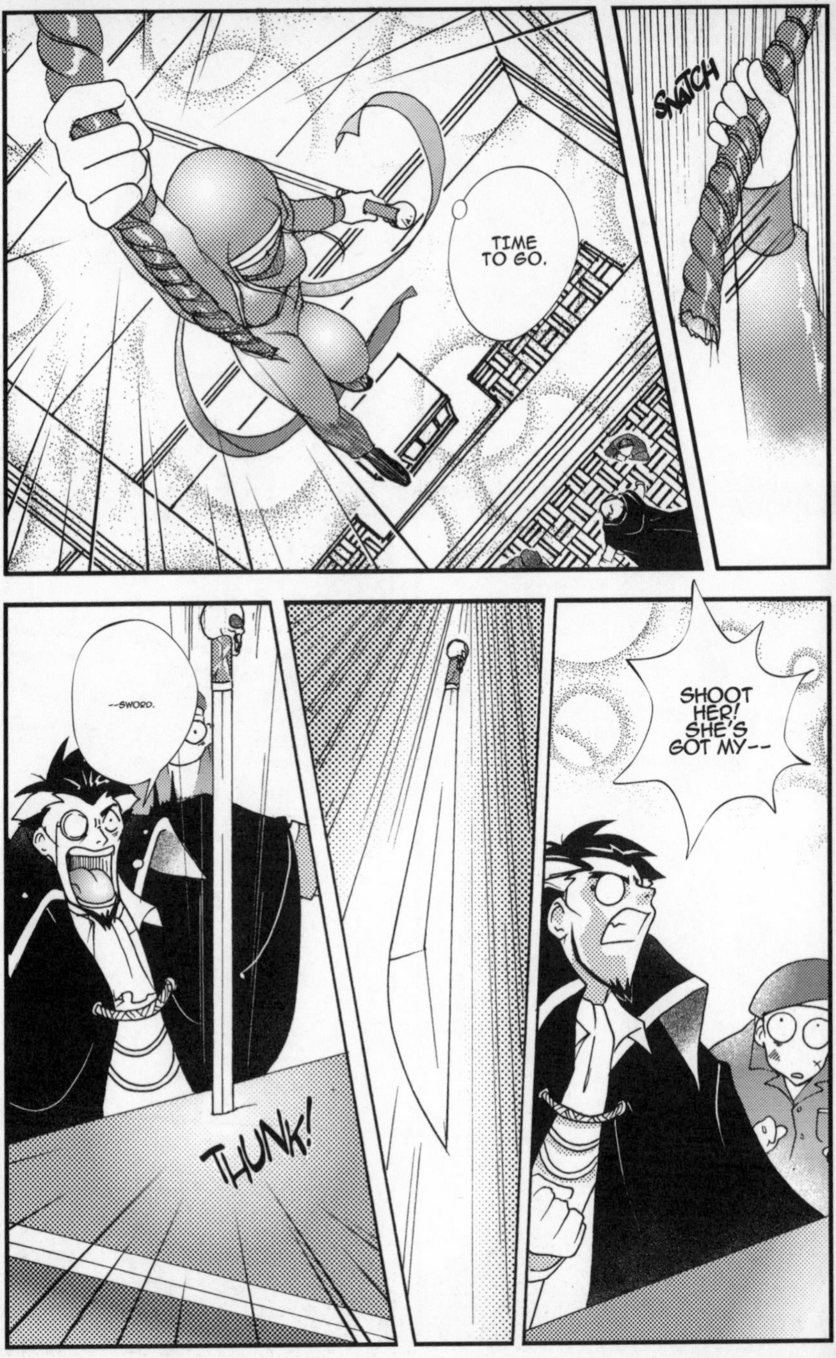
SNATCH
TIME TO GO.
SHOOT HER! SHE'S GOT MY--
--SWORD.
THUNK!

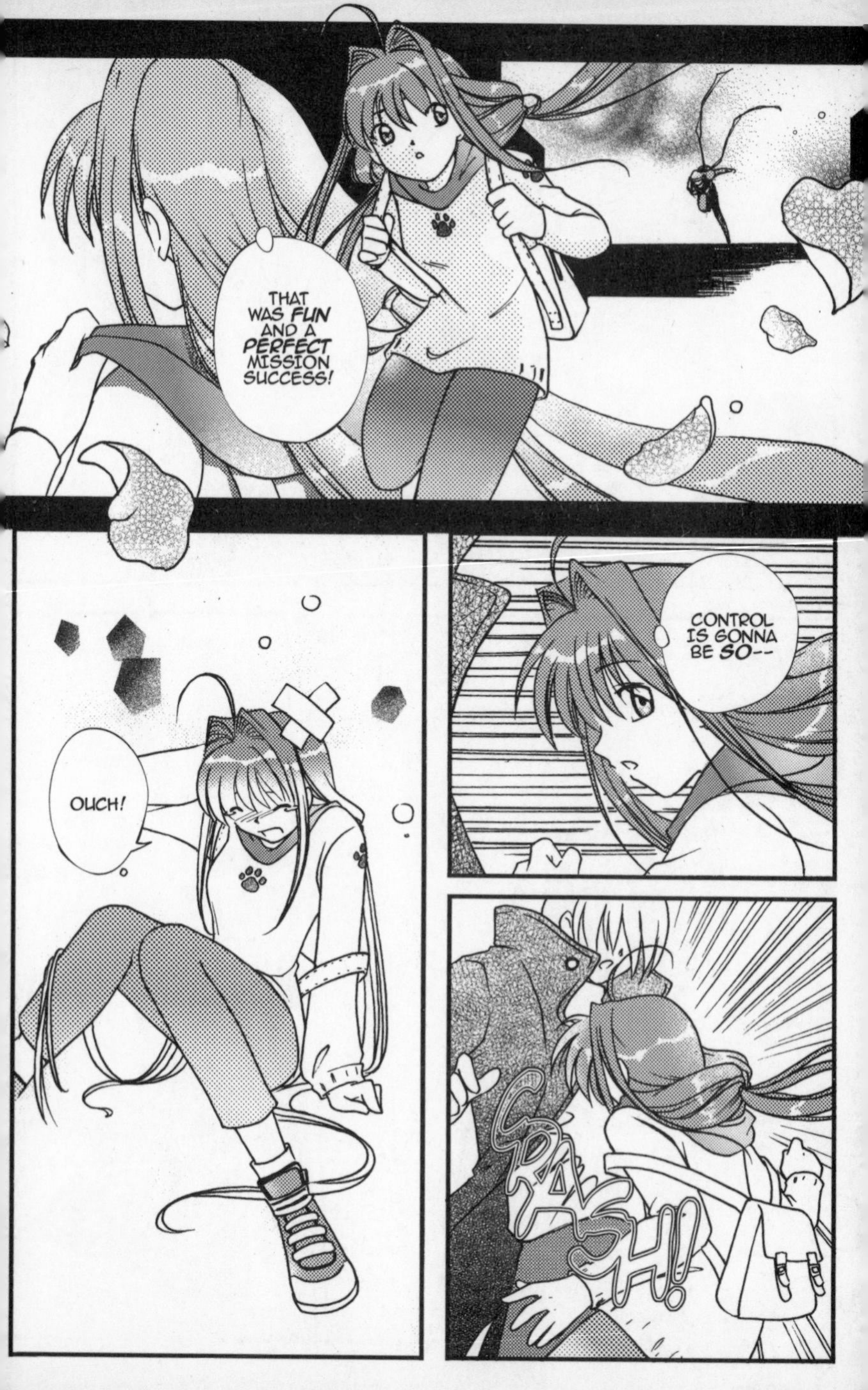
THAT WAS FUN AND A PERFECT MISSION SUCCESS!
CONTROL IS GONNA BE SO--
SPLASH!
OUCH!

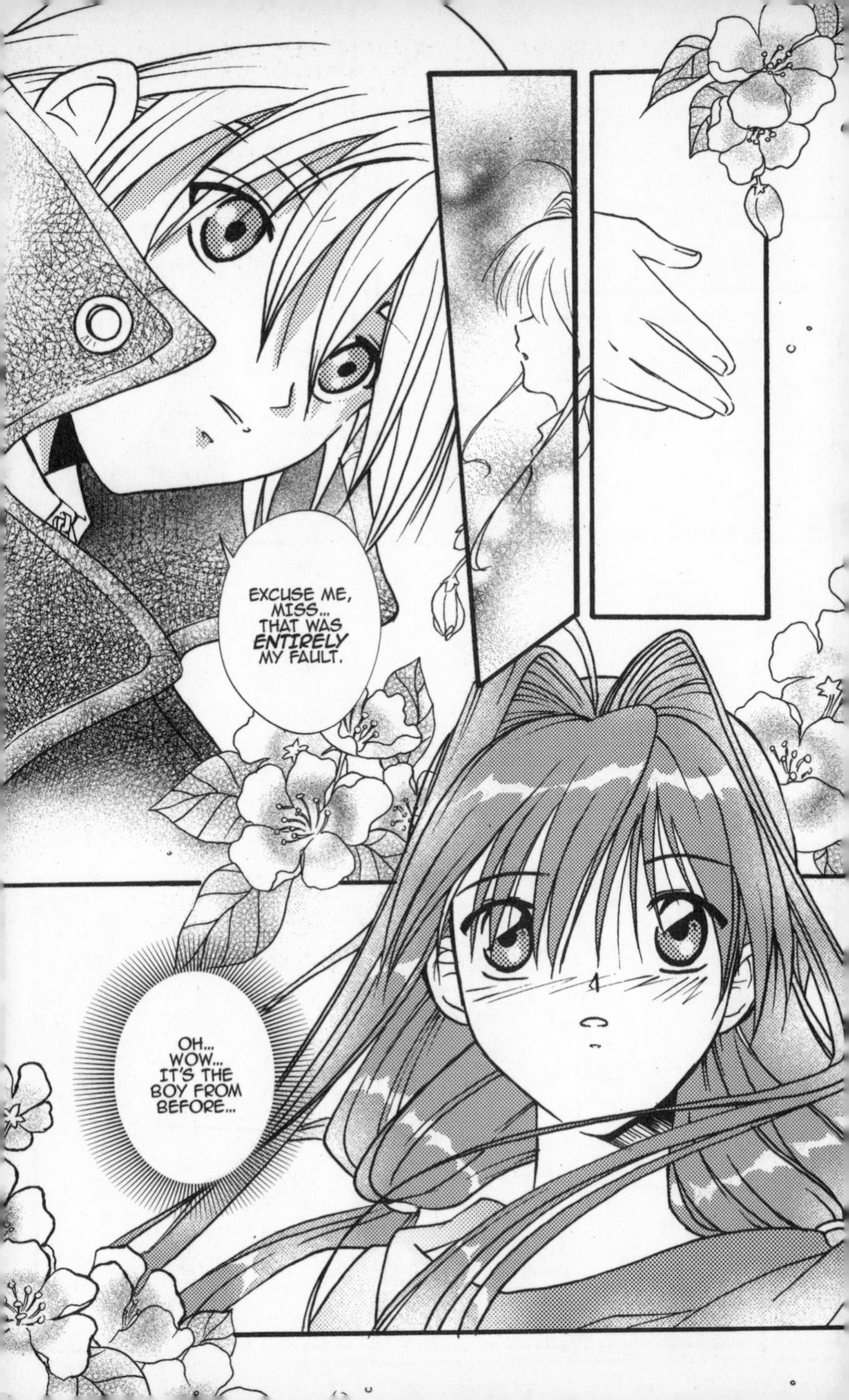
EXCUSE ME, MISS... THAT WAS ***ENTIRELY*** MY FAULT.
OH... WOW... IT'S THE BOY FROM BEFORE...

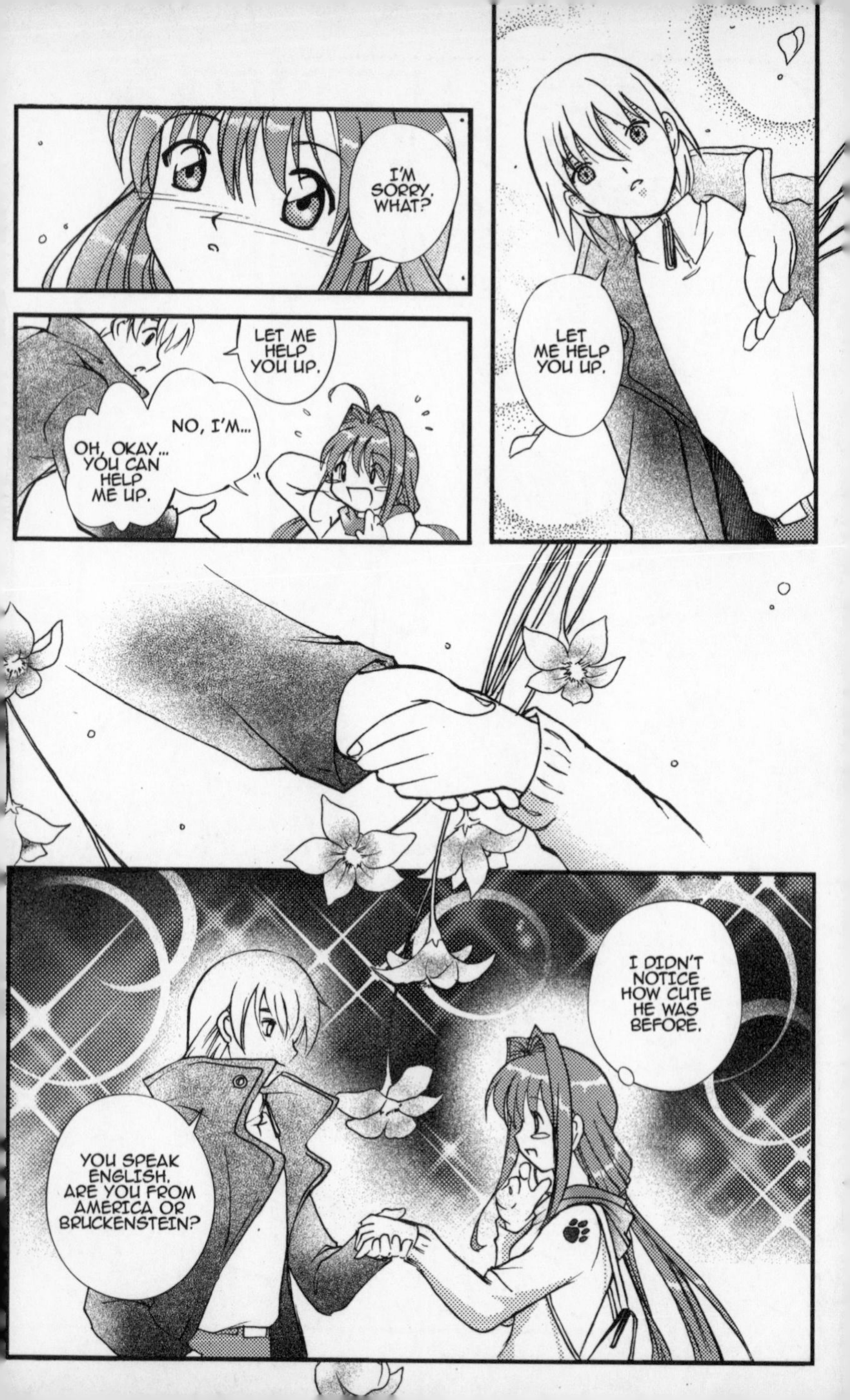
LET ME HELP YOU UP.
I'M SORRY. WHAT?
LET ME HELP YOU UP.
NO, I'M...
OH, OKAY... YOU CAN HELP ME UP.
I DIDN'T NOTICE HOW CUTE HE WAS BEFORE.
YOU SPEAK ENGLISH. ARE YOU FROM AMERICA OR BRUCKENSTEIN?

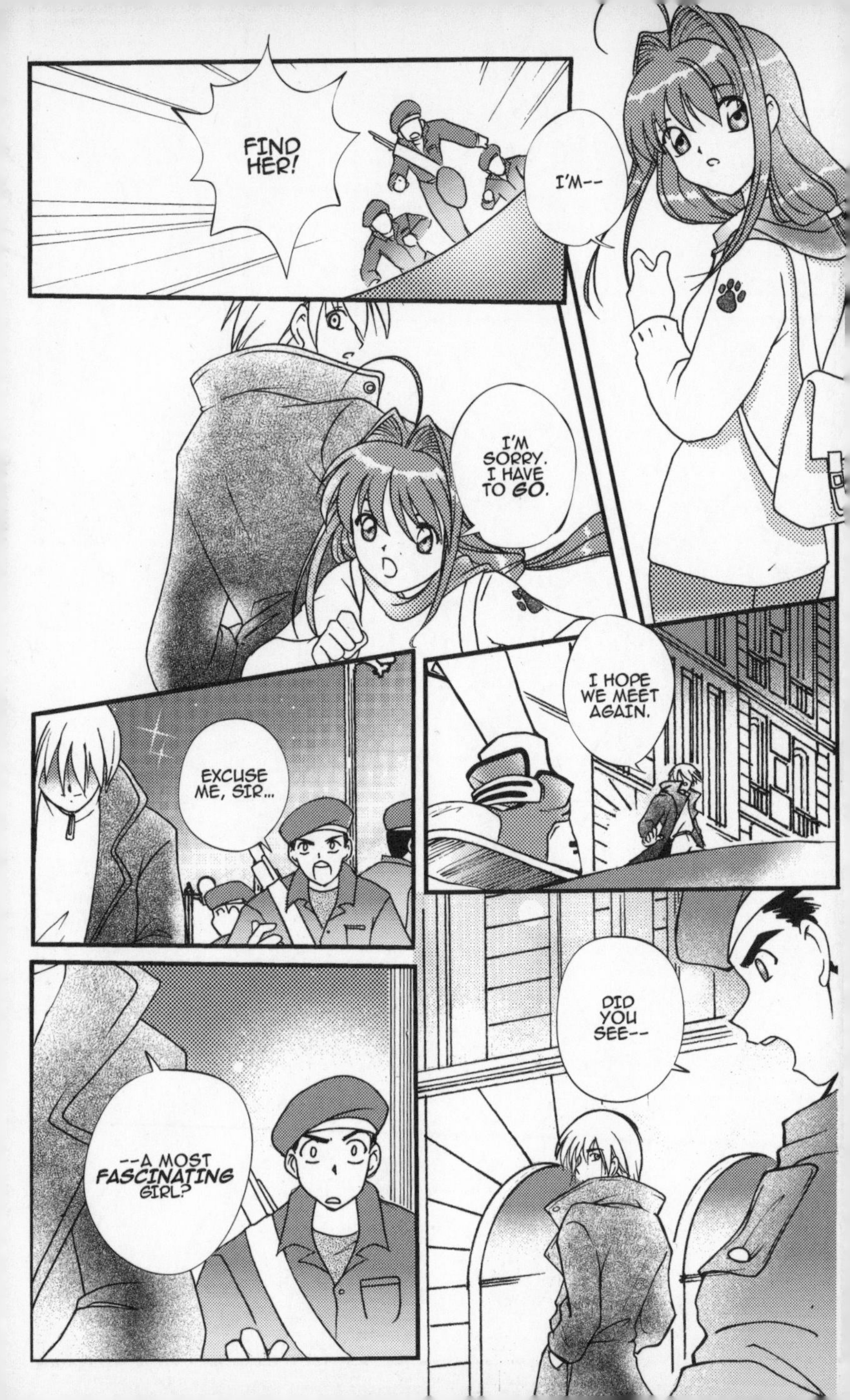
I'M--
FIND HER!
I'M SORRY. I HAVE TO GO.
I HOPE WE MEET AGAIN.
EXCUSE ME, SIR...
DID YOU SEE--
--A MOST FASCINATING GIRL?

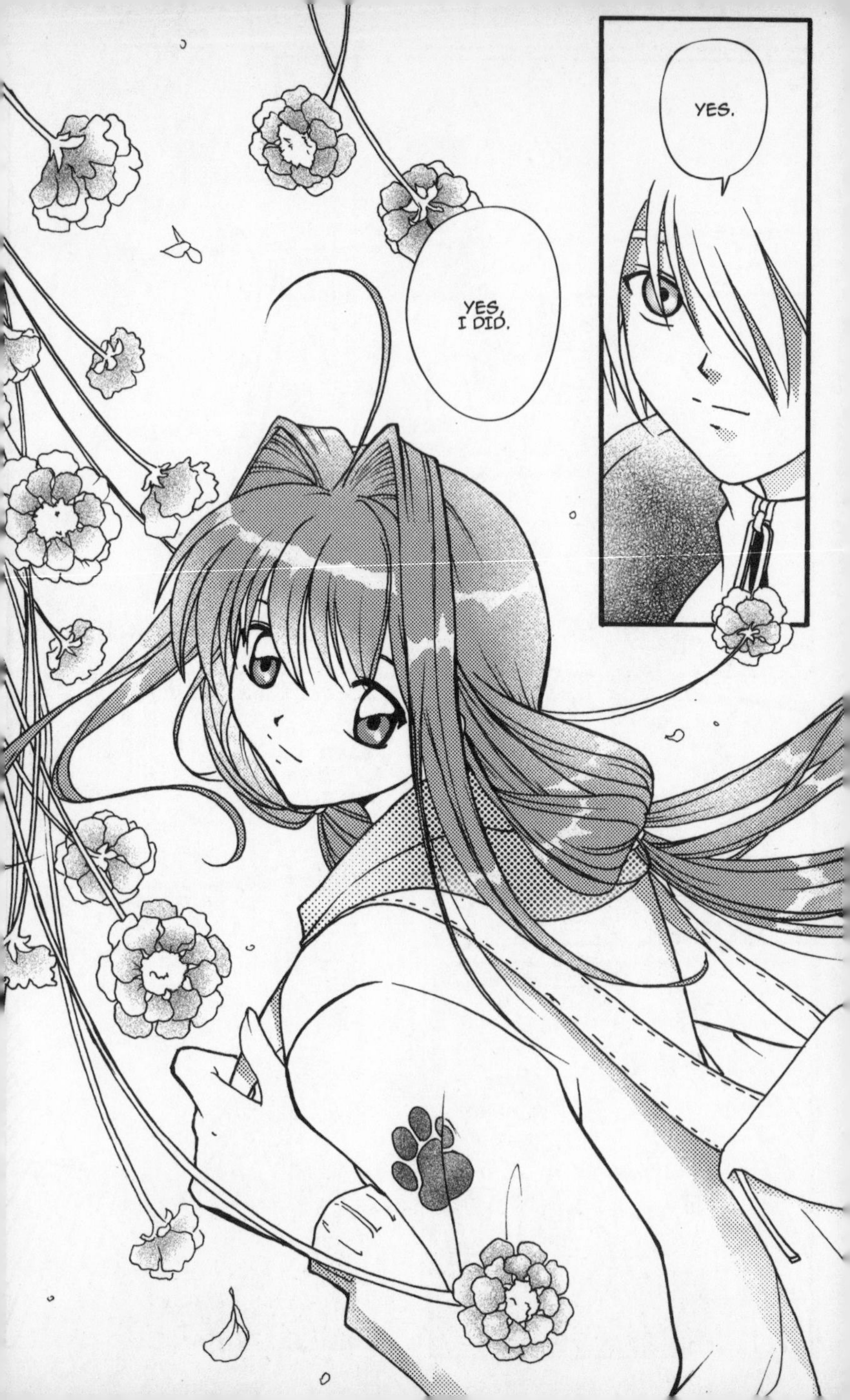
YES.
YES, I DID.

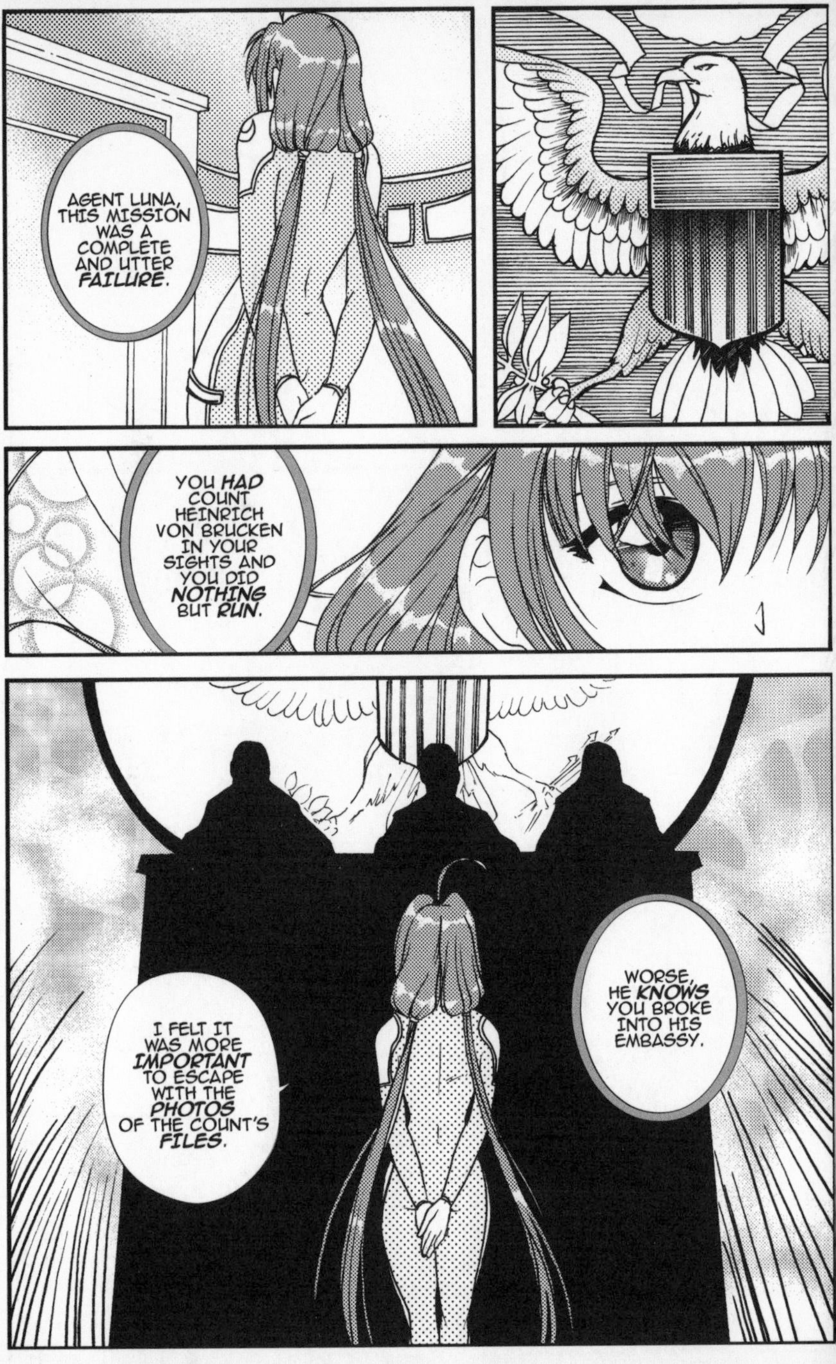
AGENT LUNA, THIS MISSION WAS A COMPLETE AND UTTER FAILURE.
YOU HAD COUNT HEINRICH VON BRUCKEN IN YOUR SIGHTS AND YOU DID NOTHING BUT RUN.
WORSE, HE KNOWS YOU BROKE INTO HIS EMBASSY.
I FELT IT WAS MORE IMPORTANT TO ESCAPE WITH THE PHOTOS OF THE COUNT'S FILES.

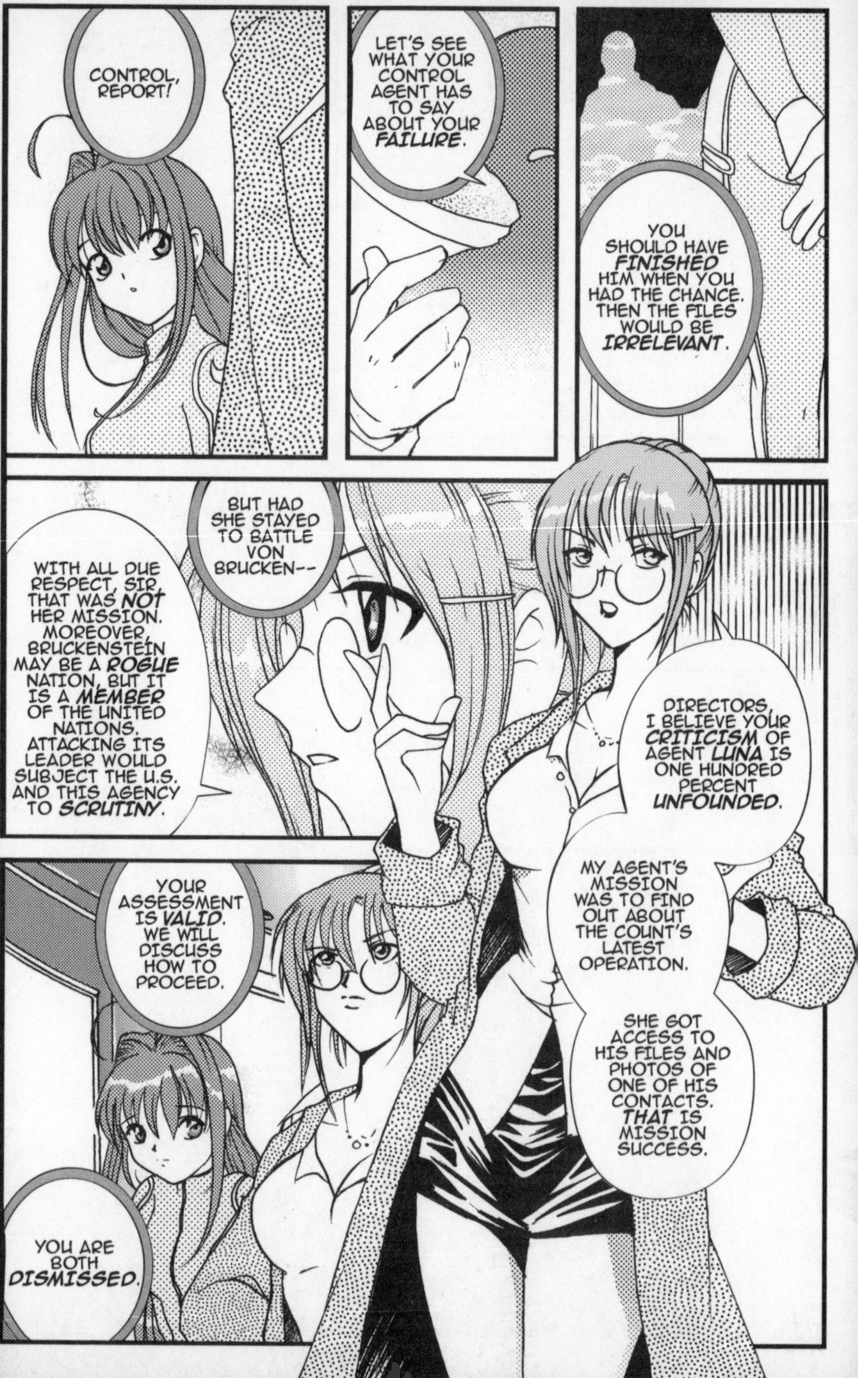
YOU SHOULD HAVE FINISHED HIM WHEN YOU HAD THE CHANCE. THEN THE FILES WOULD BE IRRELEVANT.
LET'S SEE WHAT YOUR CONTROL AGENT HAS TO SAY ABOUT YOUR FAILURE.
CONTROL, REPORT!
DIRECTORS, I BELIEVE YOUR CRITICISM OF AGENT LUNA IS ONE HUNDRED PERCENT UNFOUNDED.
BUT HAD SHE STAYED TO BATTLE VON BRUCKEN--
WITH ALL DUE RESPECT, SIR, THAT WAS NOT HER MISSION. MOREOVER, BRUCKENSTEIN MAY BE A ROGUE NATION, BUT IT IS A MEMBER OF THE UNITED NATIONS. ATTACKING ITS LEADER WOULD SUBJECT THE U.S. AND THIS AGENCY TO SCRUTINY.
MY AGENT'S MISSION WAS TO FIND OUT ABOUT THE COUNT'S LATEST OPERATION.
SHE GOT ACCESS TO HIS FILES AND PHOTOS OF ONE OF HIS CONTACTS. THAT IS MISSION SUCCESS.
YOUR ASSESSMENT IS VALID. WE WILL DISCUSS HOW TO PROCEED.
YOU ARE BOTH DISMISSED.

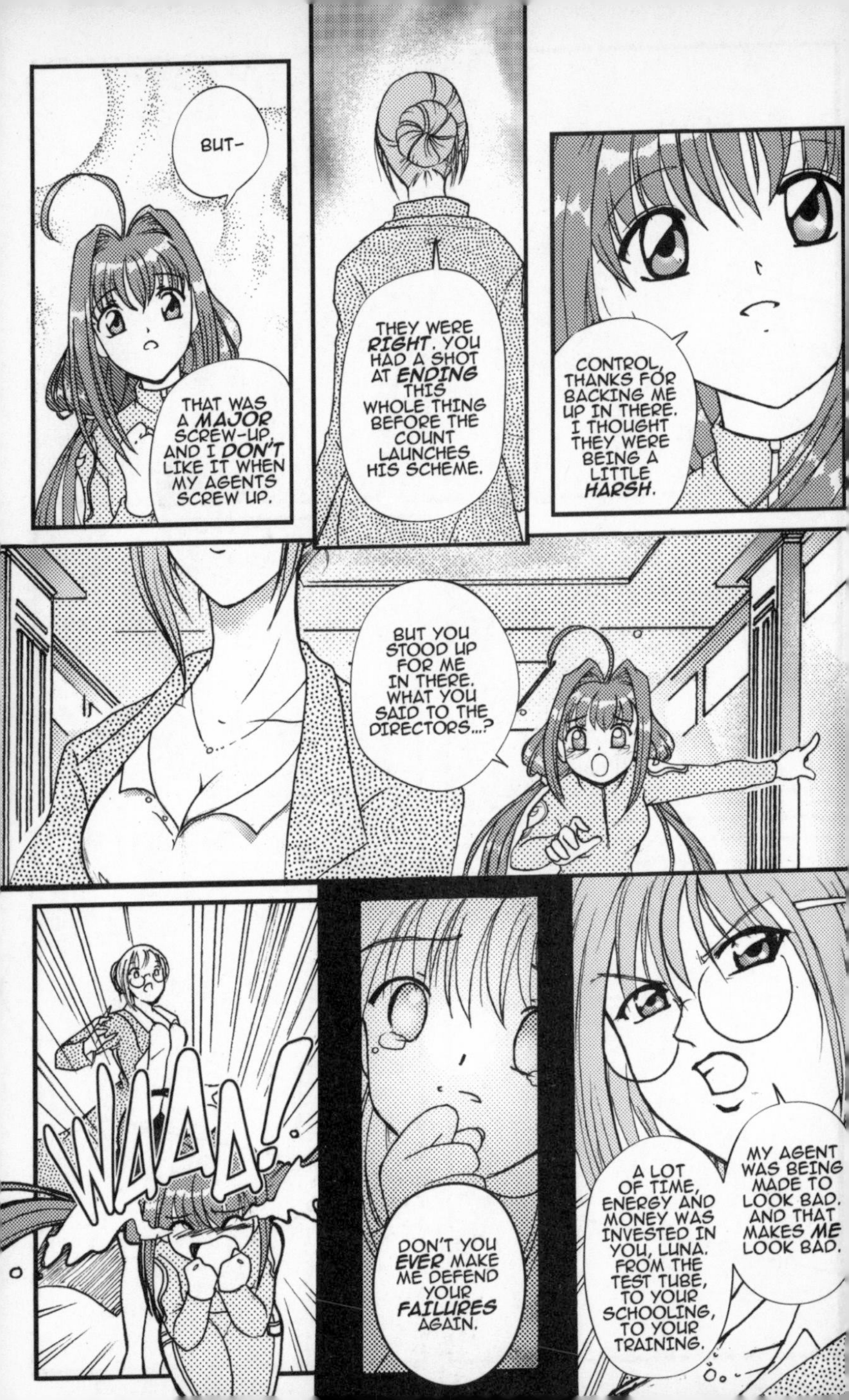
CONTROL, THANKS FOR BACKING ME UP IN THERE. I THOUGHT THEY WERE BEING A LITTLE **HARSH**.
THEY WERE **RIGHT**. YOU HAD A SHOT AT **ENDING** THIS WHOLE THING BEFORE THE COUNT LAUNCHES HIS SCHEME.
THAT WAS A **MAJOR** SCREW-UP, AND I **DON'T** LIKE IT WHEN MY AGENTS SCREW UP.
BUT-
BUT YOU STOOD UP FOR ME IN THERE. WHAT YOU SAID TO THE DIRECTORS...?
MY AGENT WAS BEING MADE TO LOOK BAD. AND THAT MAKES **ME** LOOK BAD.
A LOT OF TIME, ENERGY AND MONEY WAS INVESTED IN YOU, LUNA. FROM THE TEST TUBE, TO YOUR SCHOOLING, TO YOUR TRAINING.
DON'T YOU **EVER** MAKE ME DEFEND YOUR **FAILURES** AGAIN.
WAAA!

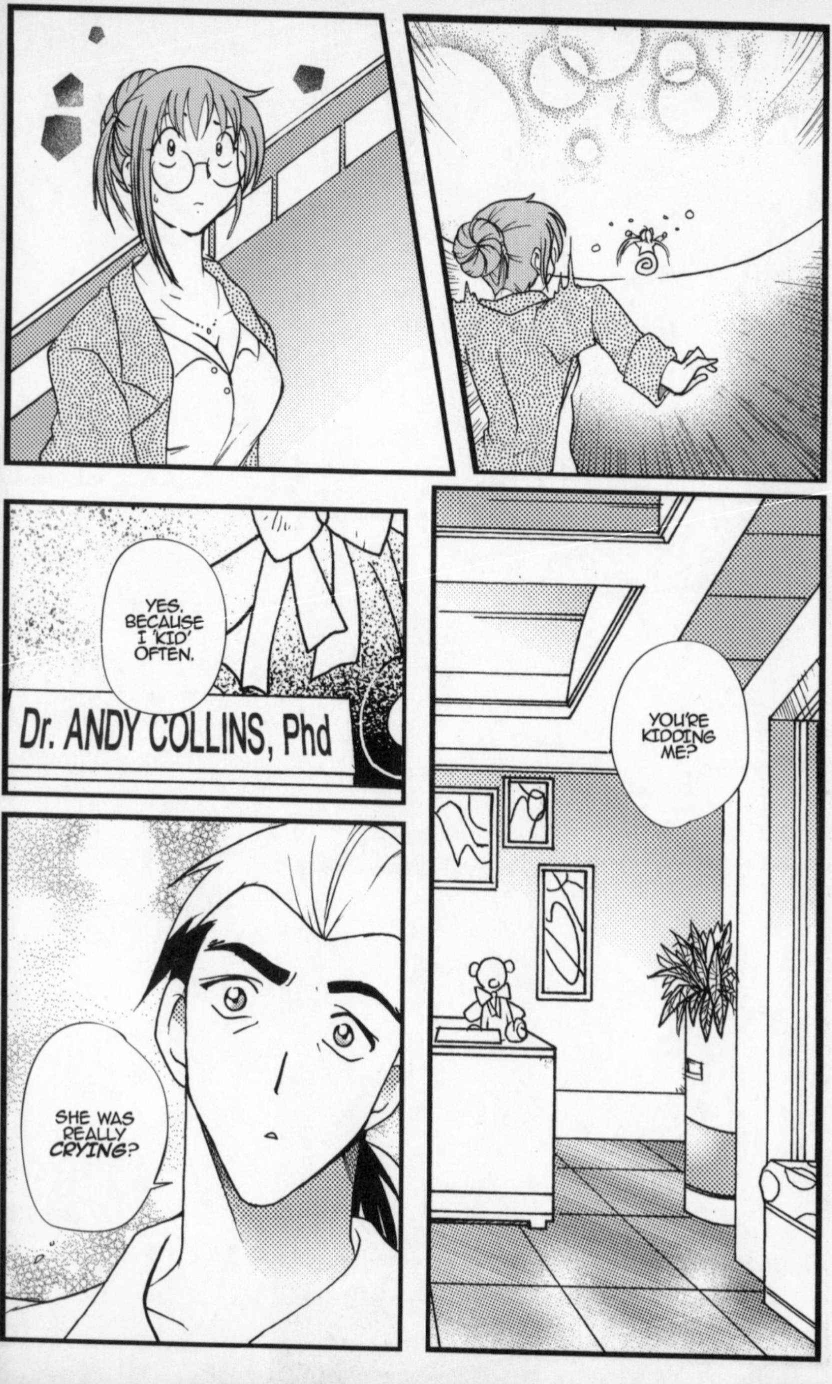
YOU'RE KIDDING ME?
YES. BECAUSE I 'KID' OFTEN.
Dr. ANDY COLLINS, Phd
SHE WAS REALLY CRYING?

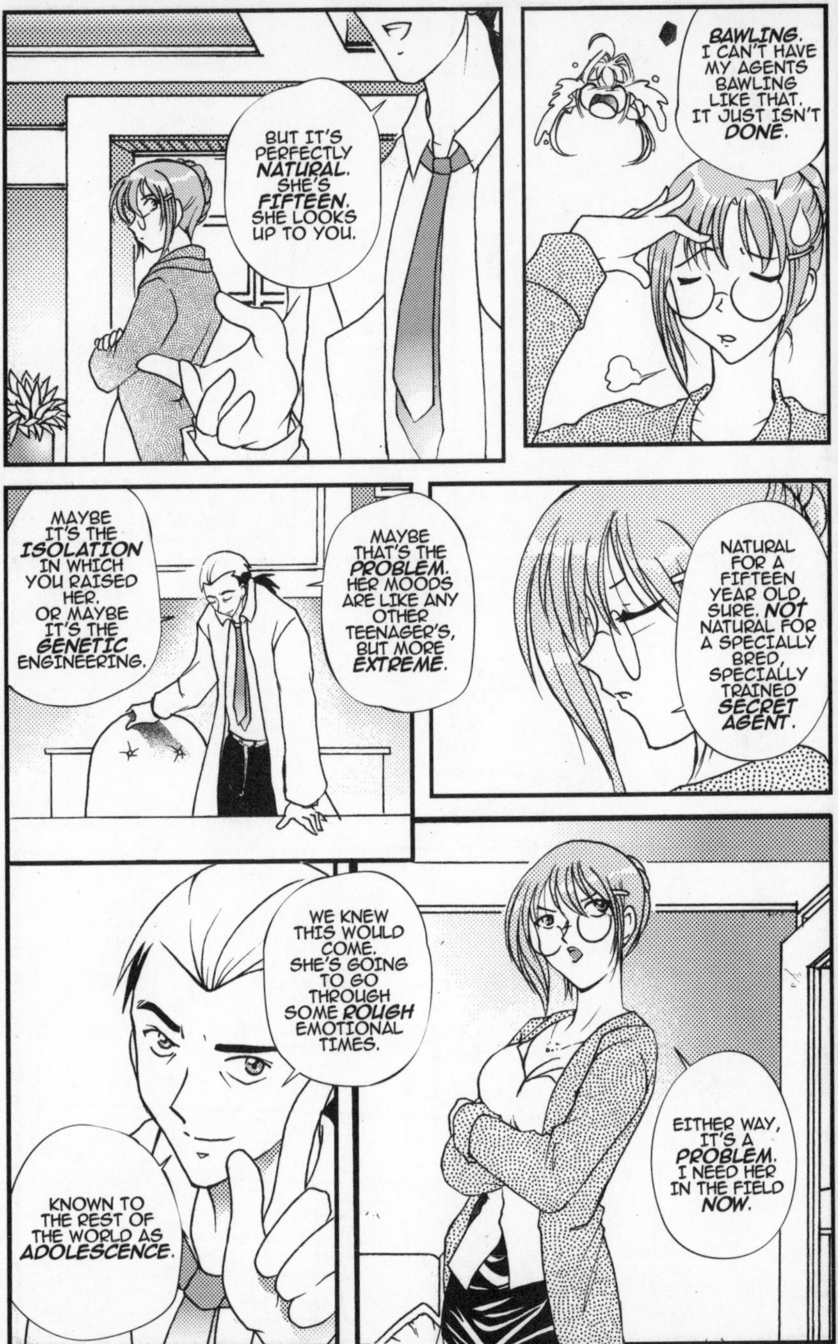
BAWLING. I CAN'T HAVE MY AGENTS BAWLING LIKE THAT. IT JUST ISN'T DONE.
BUT IT'S PERFECTLY NATURAL. SHE'S FIFTEEN. SHE LOOKS UP TO YOU.
NATURAL FOR A FIFTEEN YEAR OLD, SURE. NOT NATURAL FOR A SPECIALLY BRED, SPECIALLY TRAINED SECRET AGENT.
MAYBE THAT'S THE PROBLEM. HER MOODS ARE LIKE ANY OTHER TEENAGER'S, BUT MORE EXTREME.
MAYBE IT'S THE ISOLATION IN WHICH YOU RAISED HER. OR MAYBE IT'S THE GENETIC ENGINEERING.
EITHER WAY, IT'S A PROBLEM. I NEED HER IN THE FIELD NOW.
WE KNEW THIS WOULD COME. SHE'S GOING TO GO THROUGH SOME ROUGH EMOTIONAL TIMES.
KNOWN TO THE REST OF THE WORLD AS ADOLESCENCE.

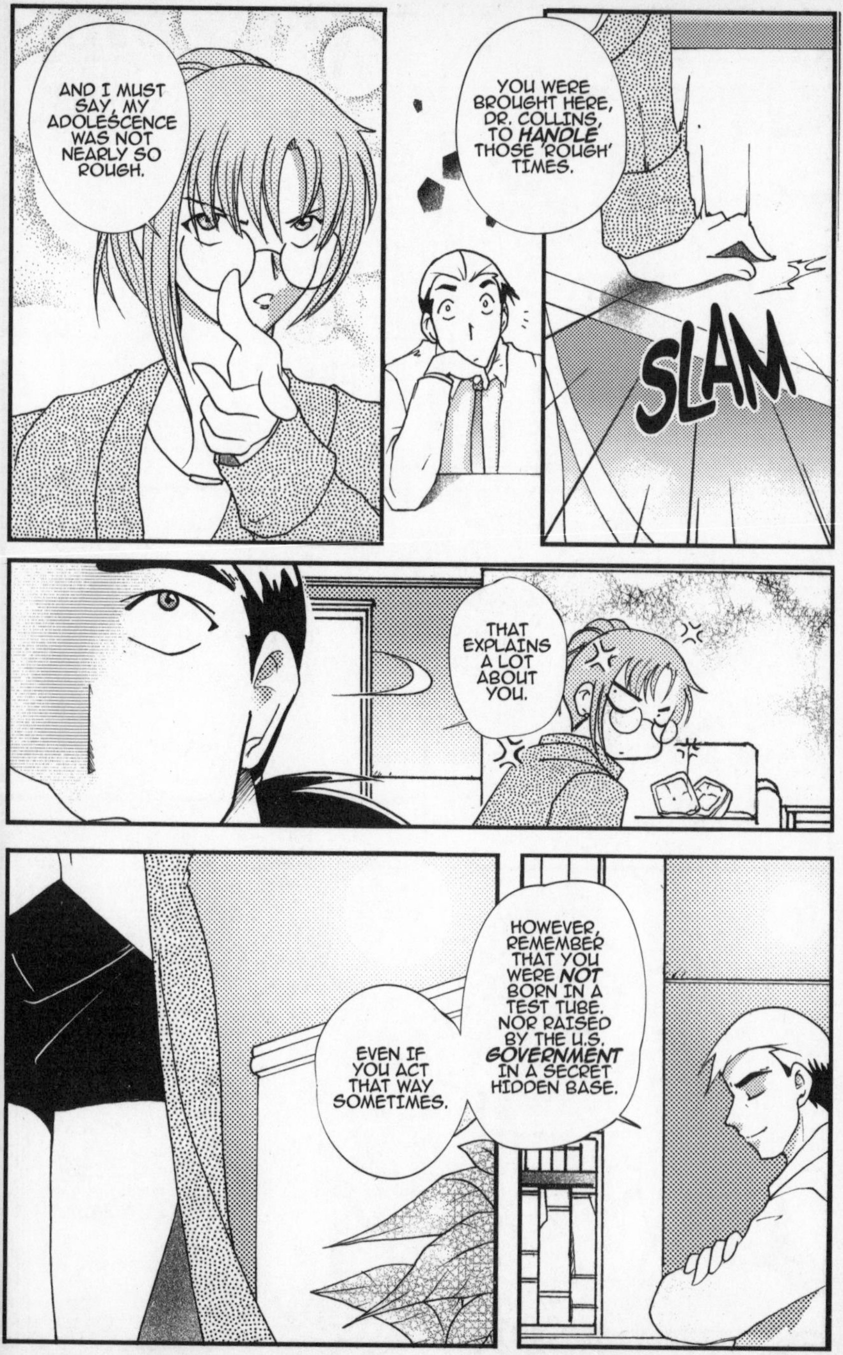
SLAM
YOU WERE BROUGHT HERE, DR. COLLINS, TO HANDLE THOSE 'ROUGH' TIMES.
AND I MUST SAY, MY ADOLESCENCE WAS NOT NEARLY SO ROUGH.
THAT EXPLAINS A LOT ABOUT YOU.
HOWEVER, REMEMBER THAT YOU WERE NOT BORN IN A TEST TUBE, NOR RAISED BY THE U.S. GOVERNMENT IN A SECRET HIDDEN BASE.
EVEN IF YOU ACT THAT WAY SOMETIMES.

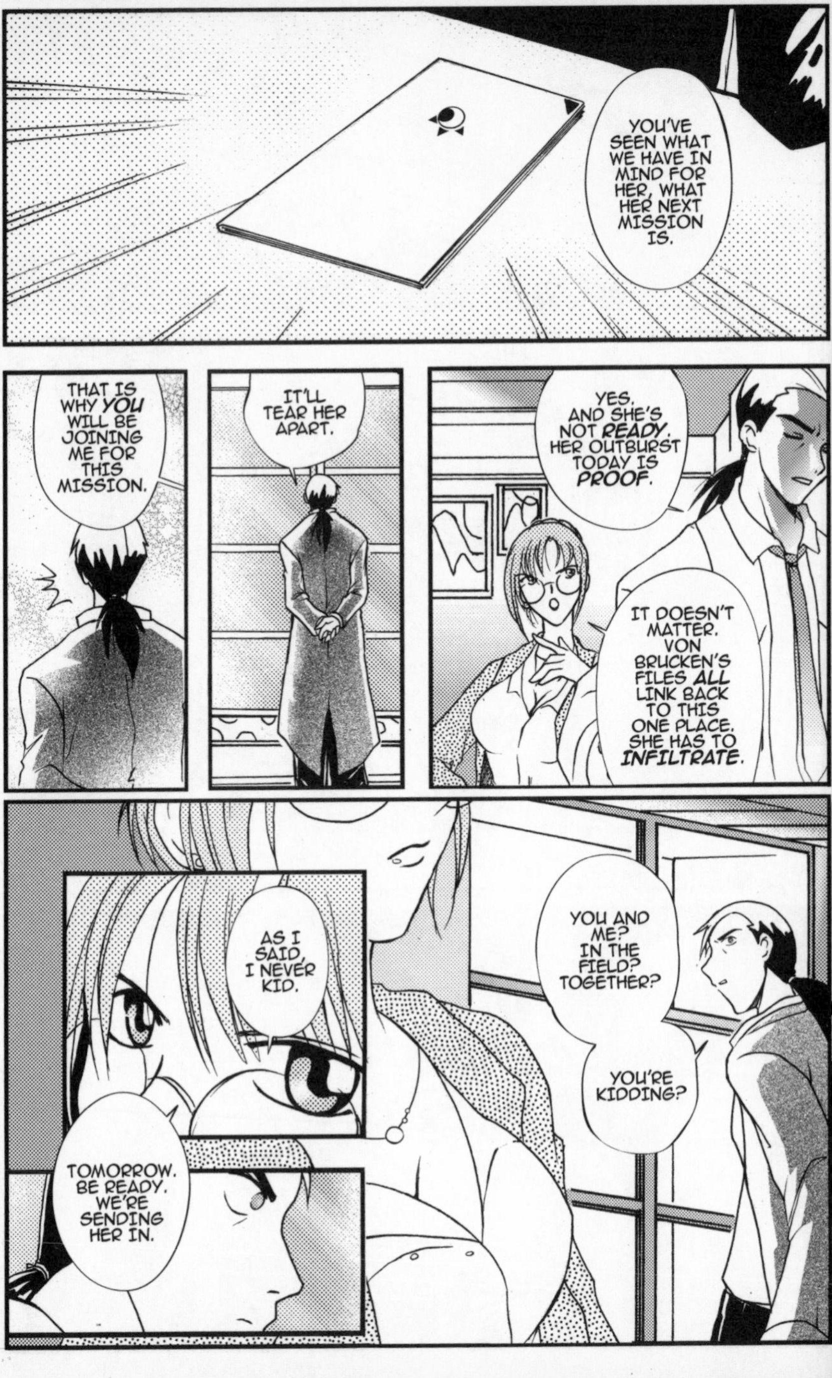
YOU'VE SEEN WHAT WE HAVE IN MIND FOR HER, WHAT HER NEXT MISSION IS.
YES. AND SHE'S NOT *READY*. HER OUTBURST TODAY IS *PROOF*.
IT DOESN'T MATTER. VON BRUCKEN'S FILES *ALL* LINK BACK TO THIS ONE PLACE. SHE HAS TO *INFILTRATE*.
IT'LL TEAR HER APART.
THAT IS WHY *YOU* WILL BE JOINING ME FOR THIS MISSION.
YOU AND ME? IN THE FIELD? TOGETHER?
YOU'RE KIDDING?
AS I SAID, I NEVER KID.
TOMORROW. BE READY. WE'RE SENDING HER IN.

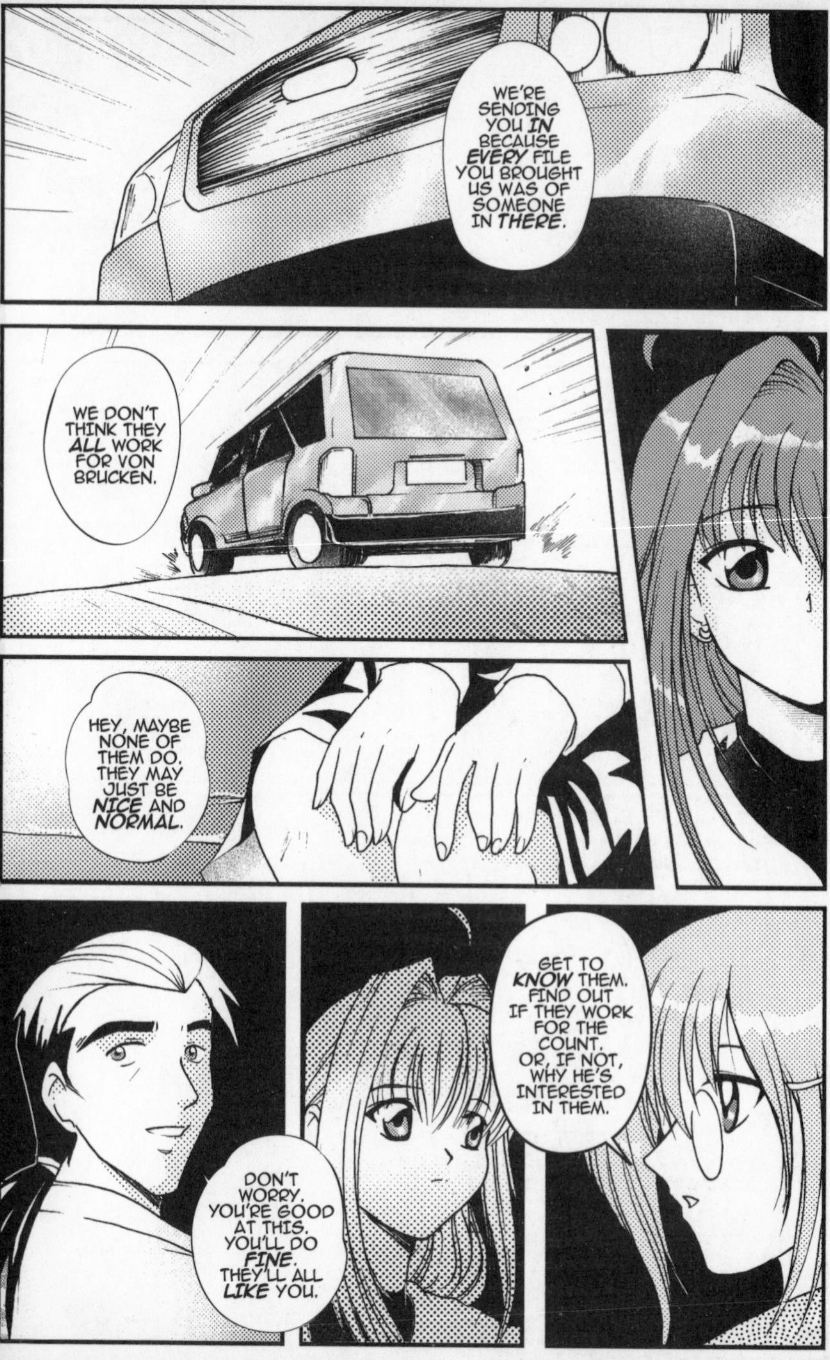
WE'RE SENDING YOU IN BECAUSE EVERY FILE YOU BROUGHT US WAS OF SOMEONE IN THERE.
WE DON'T THINK THEY ALL WORK FOR VON BRUCKEN.
HEY, MAYBE NONE OF THEM DO. THEY MAY JUST BE NICE AND NORMAL.
GET TO KNOW THEM. FIND OUT IF THEY WORK FOR THE COUNT. OR, IF NOT, WHY HE'S INTERESTED IN THEM.
DON'T WORRY. YOU'RE GOOD AT THIS. YOU'LL DO FINE. THEY'LL ALL LIKE YOU.

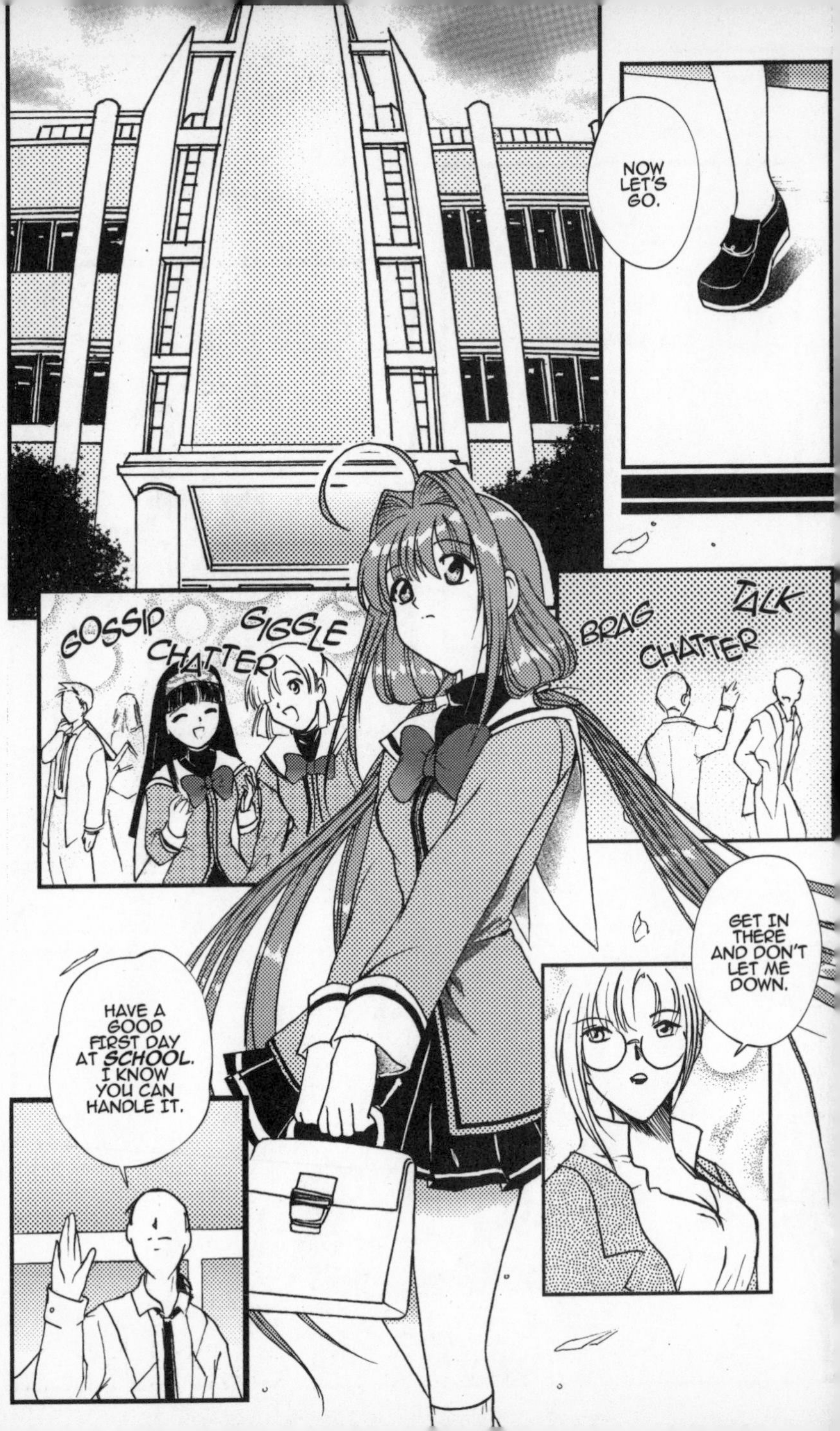
NOW LET'S GO.
TALK
BRAG
CHATTER
GOSSIP
GIGGLE
CHATTER
GET IN THERE AND DON'T LET ME DOWN.
HAVE A GOOD FIRST DAY AT SCHOOL. I KNOW YOU CAN HANDLE IT.

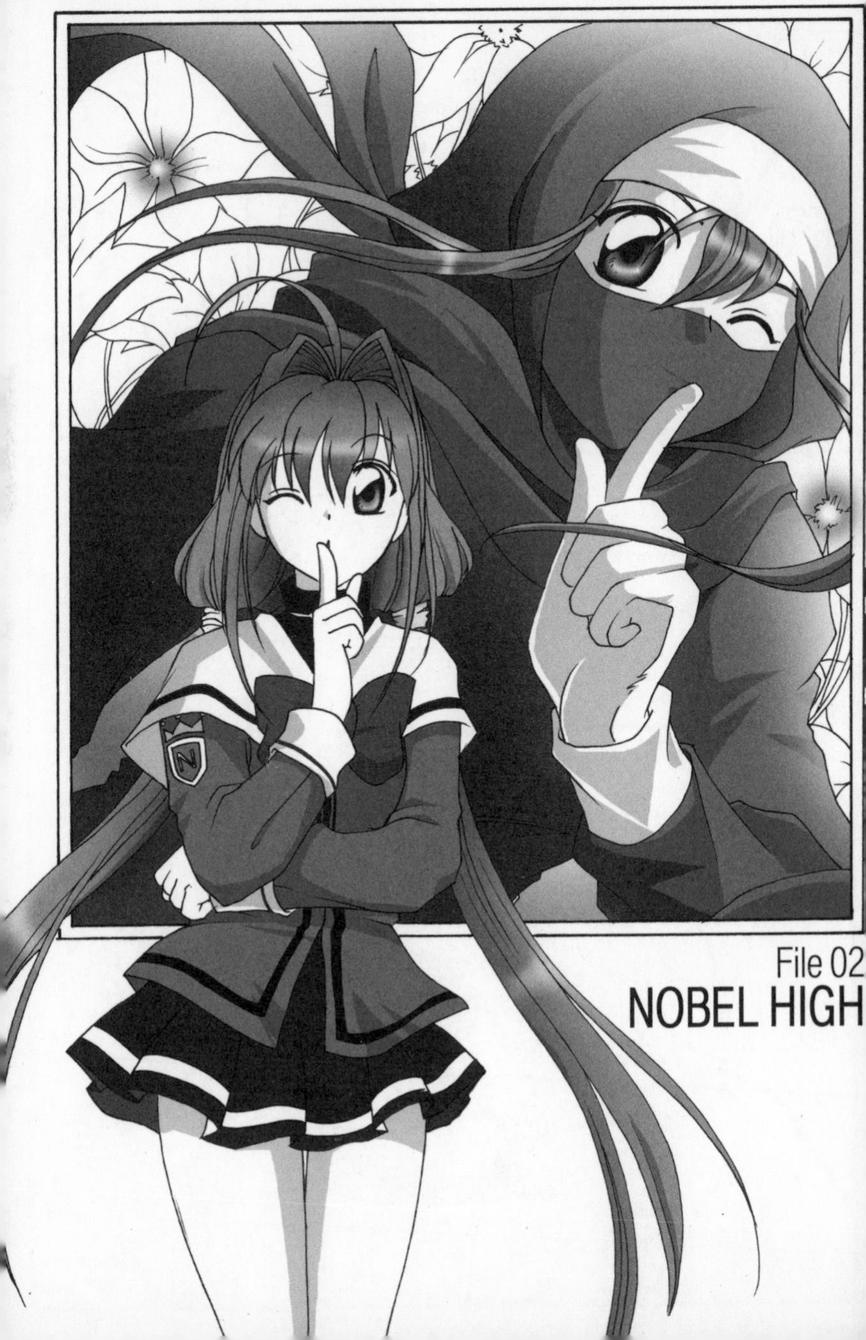

# File 02
# NOBEL HIGH

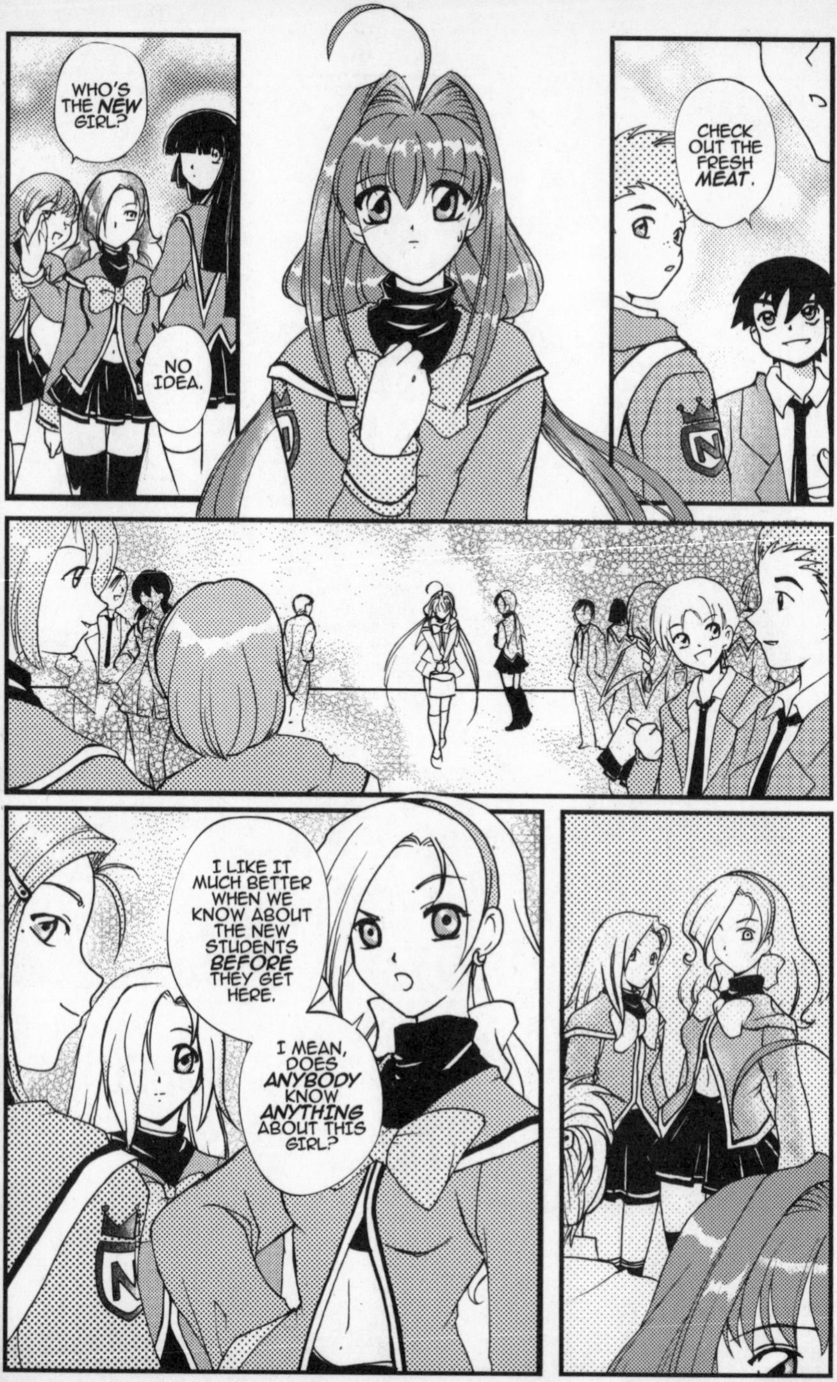
CHECK OUT THE FRESH MEAT.
WHO'S THE NEW GIRL?
NO IDEA.
I LIKE IT MUCH BETTER WHEN WE KNOW ABOUT THE NEW STUDENTS BEFORE THEY GET HERE.
I MEAN, DOES ANYBODY KNOW ANYTHING ABOUT THIS GIRL?

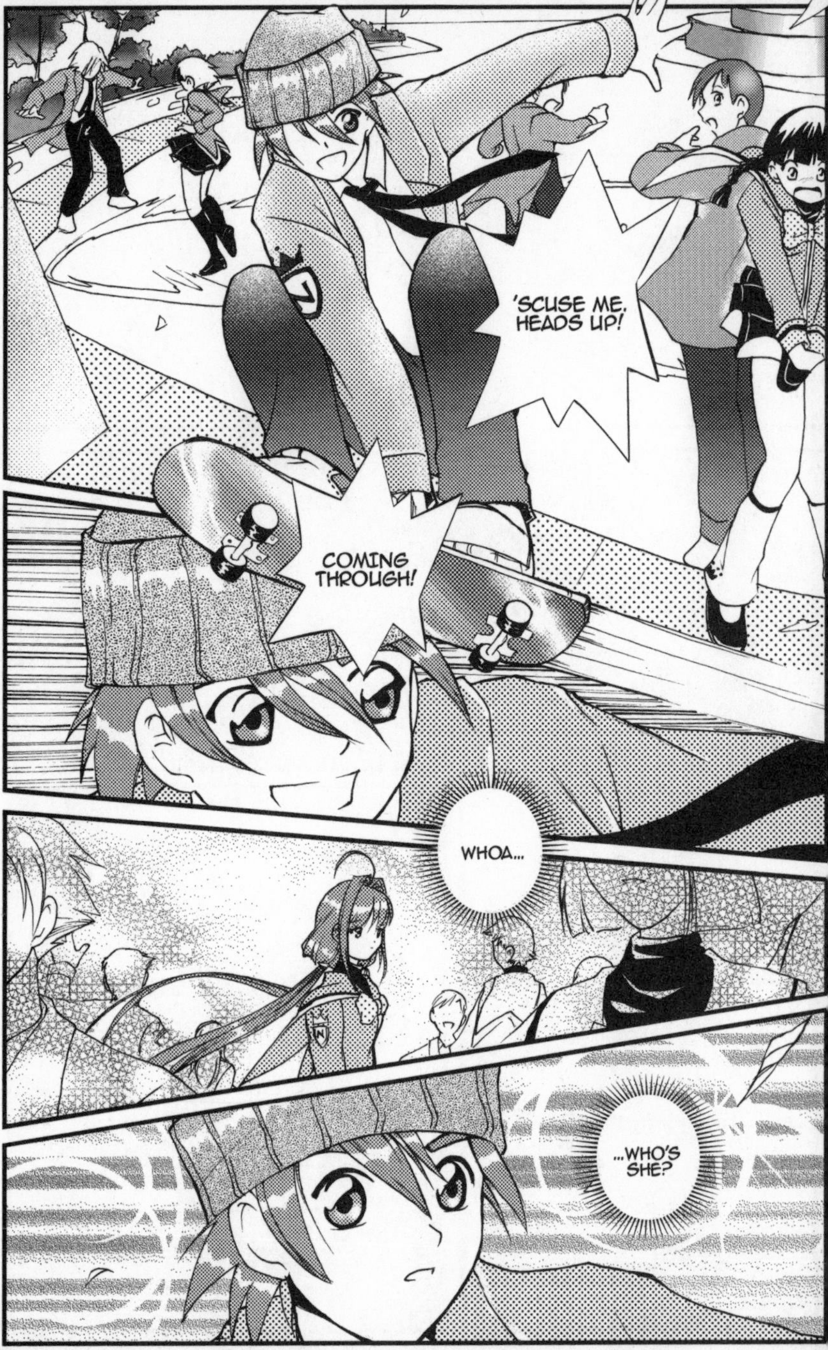
'SCUSE ME. HEADS UP!
COMING THROUGH!
WHOA...
...WHO'S SHE?

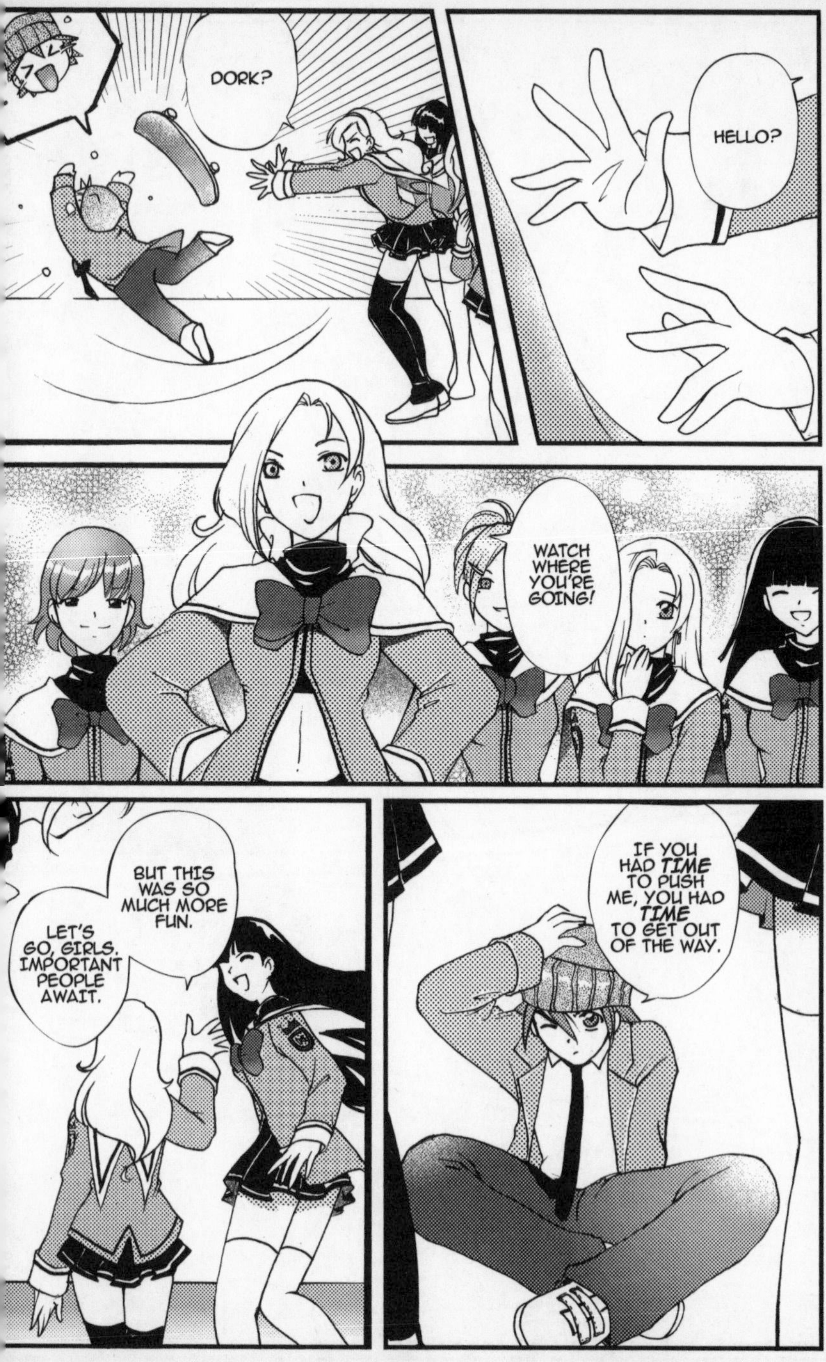
HELLO?
DORK?
WATCH WHERE YOU'RE GOING!
IF YOU HAD *TIME* TO PUSH ME, YOU HAD *TIME* TO GET OUT OF THE WAY.
BUT THIS WAS SO MUCH MORE FUN.
LET'S GO, GIRLS. IMPORTANT PEOPLE AWAIT.

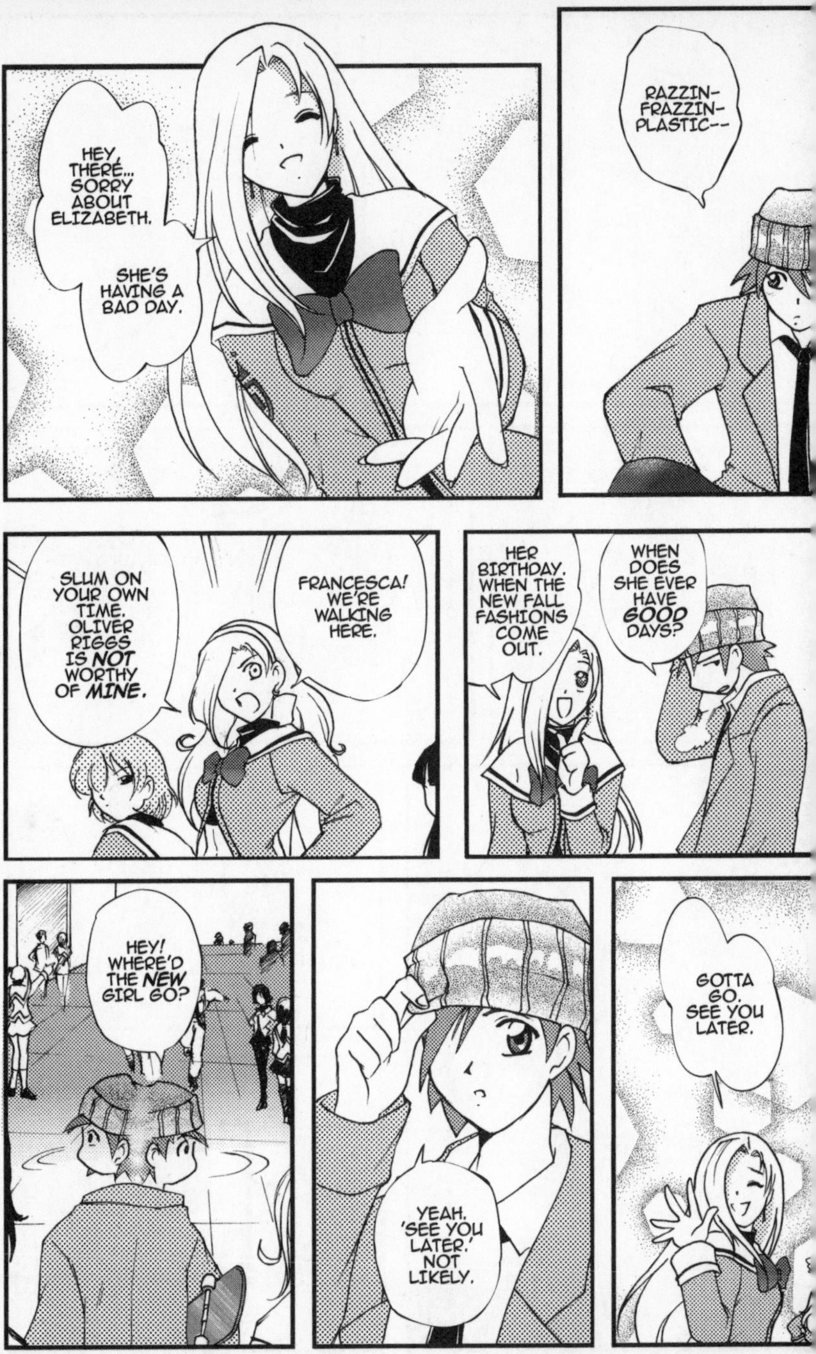
RAZZIN-FRAZZIN-PLASTIC--
HEY, THERE... SORRY ABOUT ELIZABETH.
SHE'S HAVING A BAD DAY.
WHEN DOES SHE EVER HAVE *GOOD* DAYS?
HER BIRTHDAY. WHEN THE NEW FALL FASHIONS COME OUT.
FRANCESCA! WE'RE WALKING HERE.
SLUM ON YOUR OWN TIME. OLIVER RIGGS IS *NOT* WORTHY OF *MINE*.
GOTTA GO. SEE YOU LATER.
YEAH. 'SEE YOU LATER.' NOT LIKELY.
HEY! WHERE'D THE *NEW* GIRL GO?

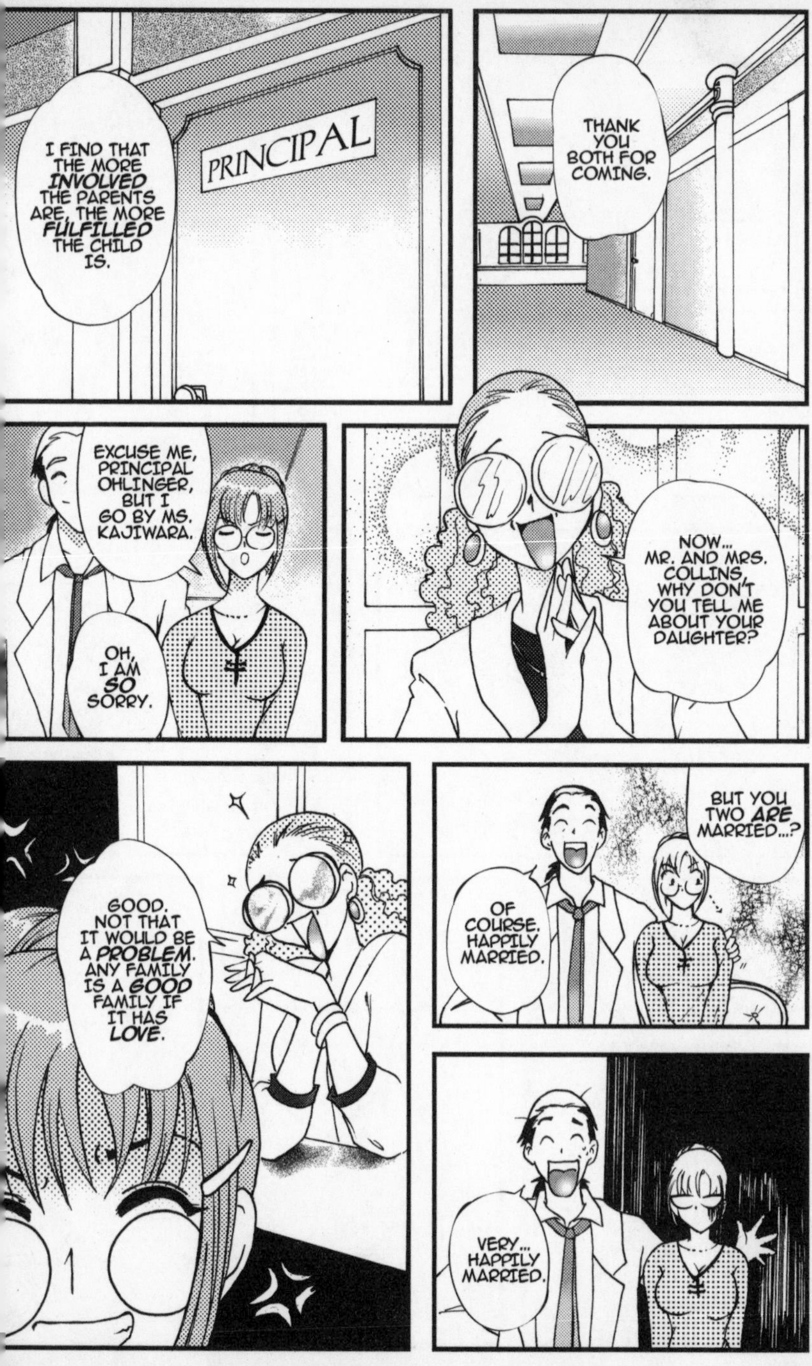
THANK YOU BOTH FOR COMING.
PRINCIPAL
I FIND THAT THE MORE INVOLVED THE PARENTS ARE, THE MORE FULFILLED THE CHILD IS.
NOW... MR. AND MRS. COLLINS, WHY DON'T YOU TELL ME ABOUT YOUR DAUGHTER?
EXCUSE ME, PRINCIPAL OHLINGER, BUT I GO BY MS. KAJIWARA.
OH, I AM SO SORRY.
BUT YOU TWO ARE MARRIED...?
OF COURSE. HAPPILY MARRIED.
VERY... HAPPILY MARRIED.
GOOD. NOT THAT IT WOULD BE A PROBLEM. ANY FAMILY IS A GOOD FAMILY IF IT HAS LOVE.

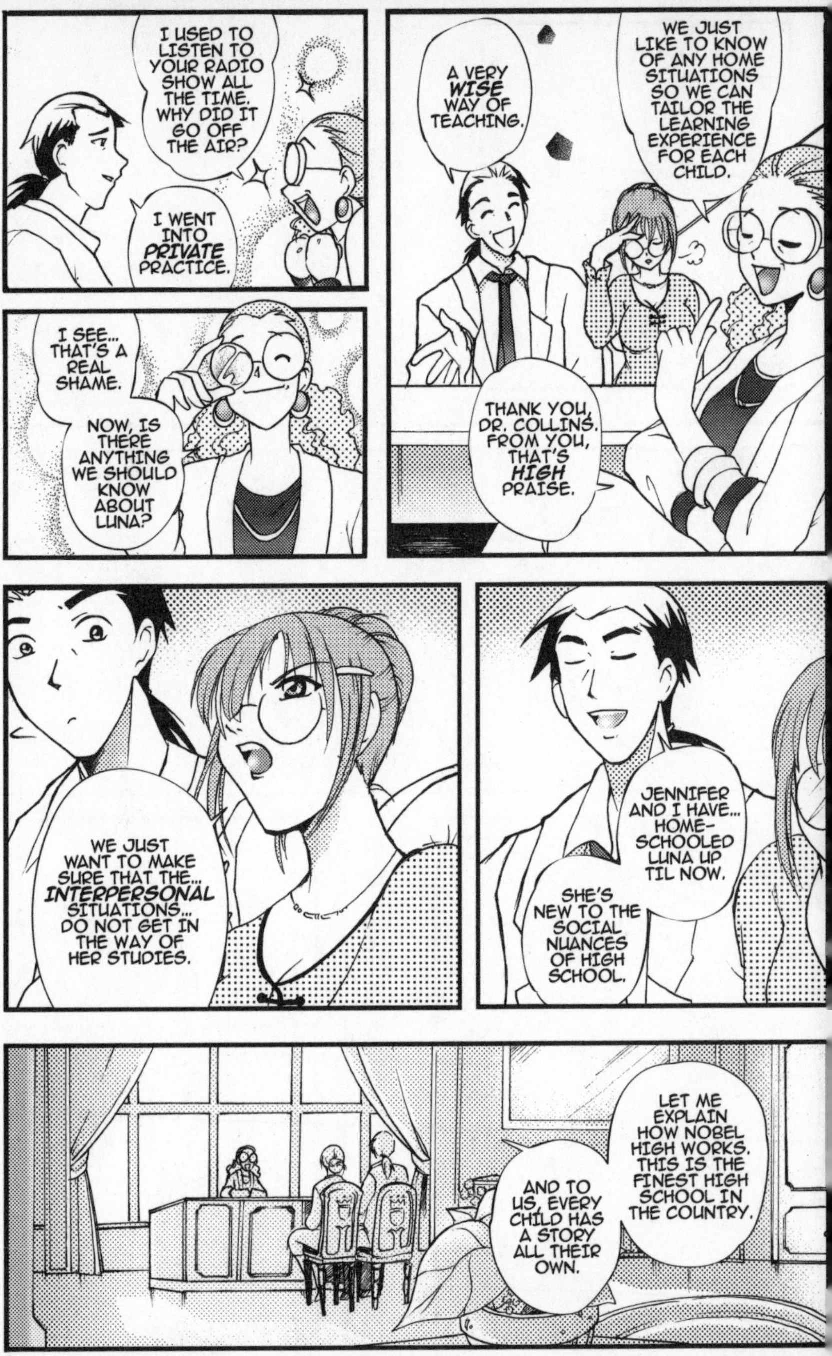
WE JUST LIKE TO KNOW OF ANY HOME SITUATIONS SO WE CAN TAILOR THE LEARNING EXPERIENCE FOR EACH CHILD.
A VERY **WISE** WAY OF TEACHING.
THANK YOU, DR. COLLINS. FROM YOU, THAT'S **HIGH** PRAISE.
I USED TO LISTEN TO YOUR RADIO SHOW ALL THE TIME. WHY DID IT GO OFF THE AIR?
I WENT INTO **PRIVATE** PRACTICE.
I SEE... THAT'S A REAL SHAME.
NOW, IS THERE ANYTHING WE SHOULD KNOW ABOUT LUNA?
JENNIFER AND I HAVE... HOME-SCHOOLED LUNA UP TIL NOW.
SHE'S NEW TO THE SOCIAL NUANCES OF HIGH SCHOOL.
WE JUST WANT TO MAKE SURE THAT THE... **INTERPERSONAL** SITUATIONS... DO NOT GET IN THE WAY OF HER STUDIES.
LET ME EXPLAIN HOW NOBEL HIGH WORKS. THIS IS THE FINEST HIGH SCHOOL IN THE COUNTRY.
AND TO US, EVERY CHILD HAS A STORY ALL THEIR OWN.

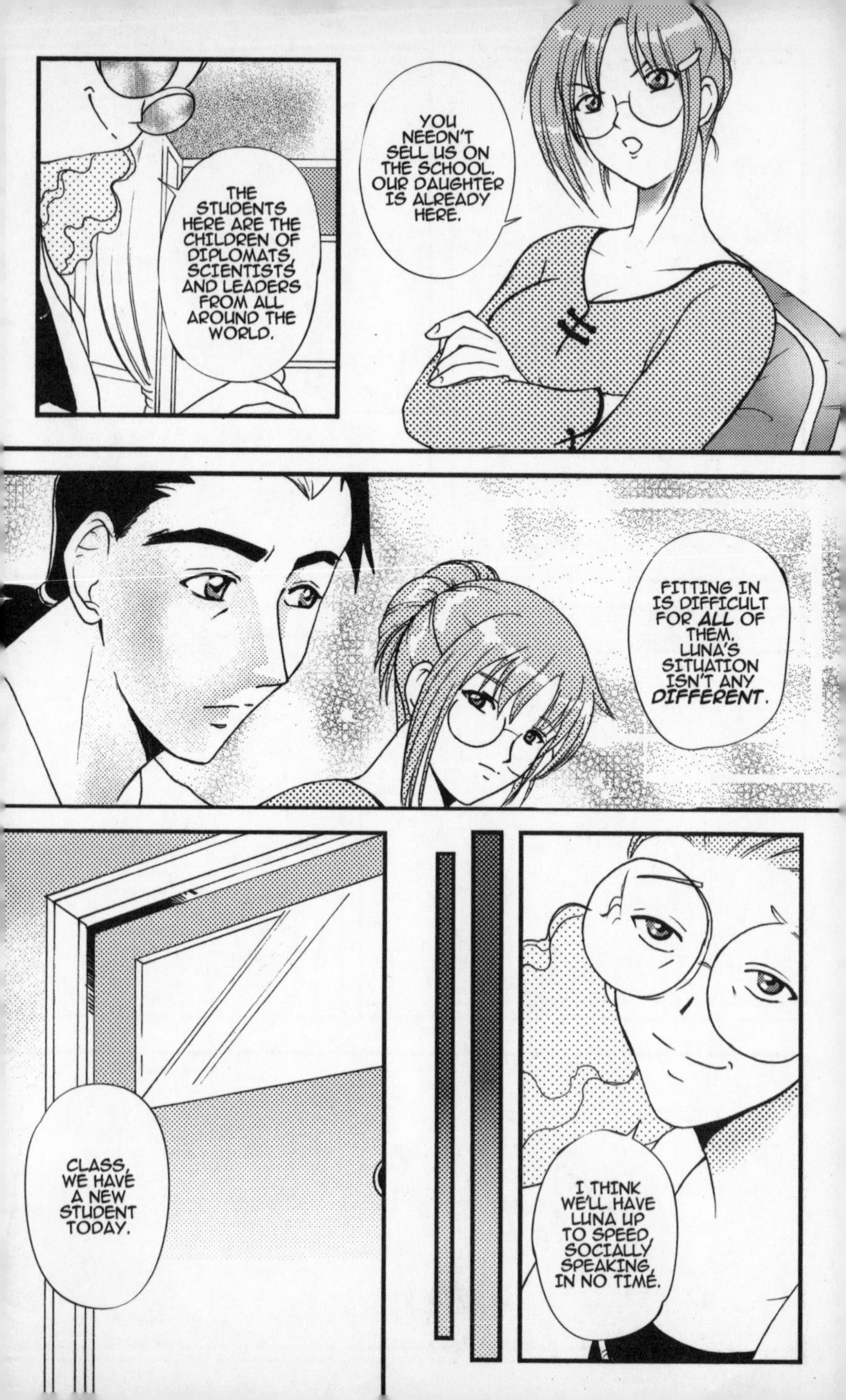
YOU NEEDN'T SELL US ON THE SCHOOL. OUR DAUGHTER IS ALREADY HERE.
THE STUDENTS HERE ARE THE CHILDREN OF DIPLOMATS, SCIENTISTS AND LEADERS FROM ALL AROUND THE WORLD.
FITTING IN IS DIFFICULT FOR *ALL* OF THEM. LUNA'S SITUATION ISN'T ANY *DIFFERENT*.
I THINK WE'LL HAVE LUNA UP TO SPEED, SOCIALLY SPEAKING, IN NO TIME.
CLASS, WE HAVE A NEW STUDENT TODAY.

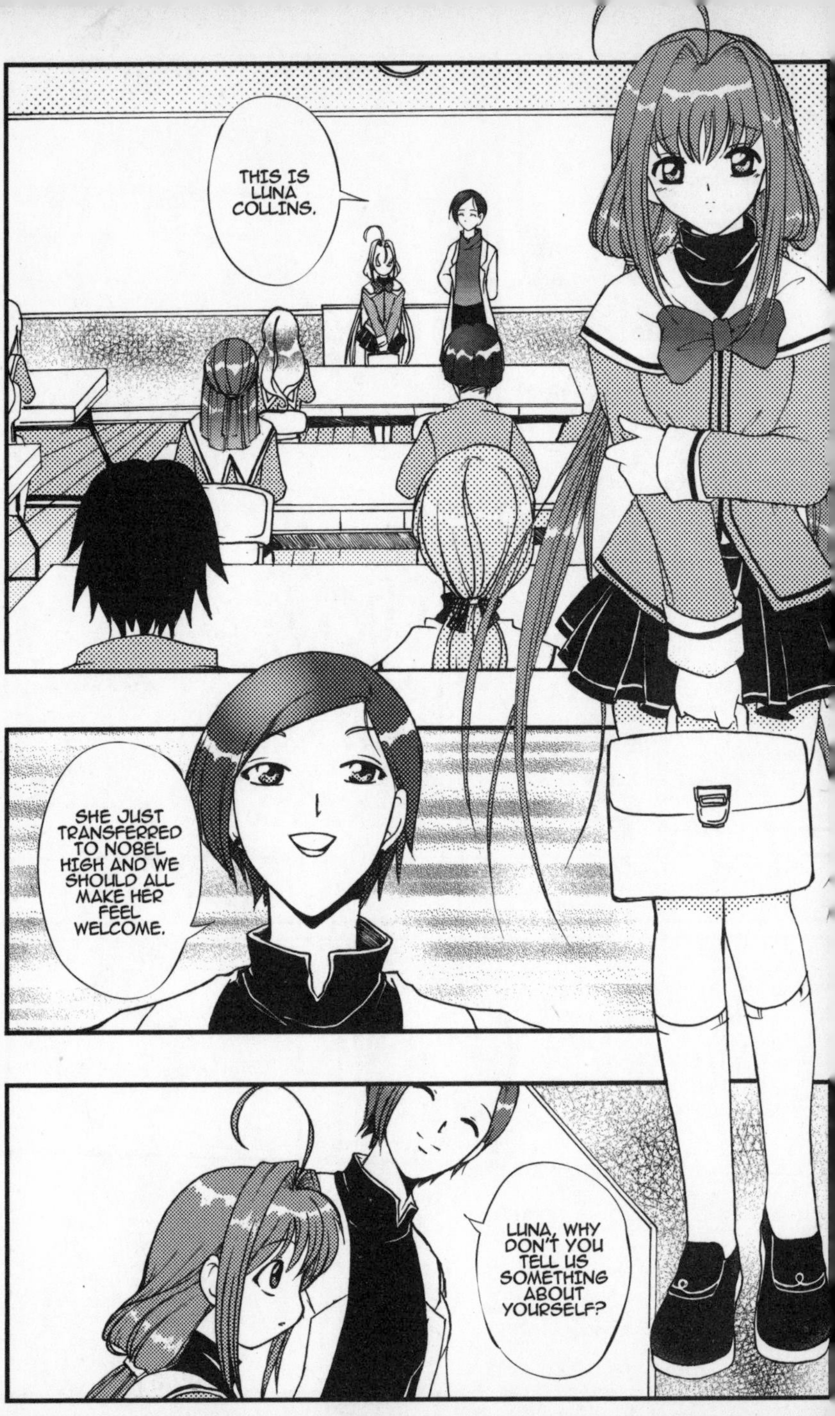
THIS IS LUNA COLLINS.
SHE JUST TRANSFERRED TO NOBEL HIGH AND WE SHOULD ALL MAKE HER FEEL WELCOME.
LUNA, WHY DON'T YOU TELL US SOMETHING ABOUT YOURSELF?

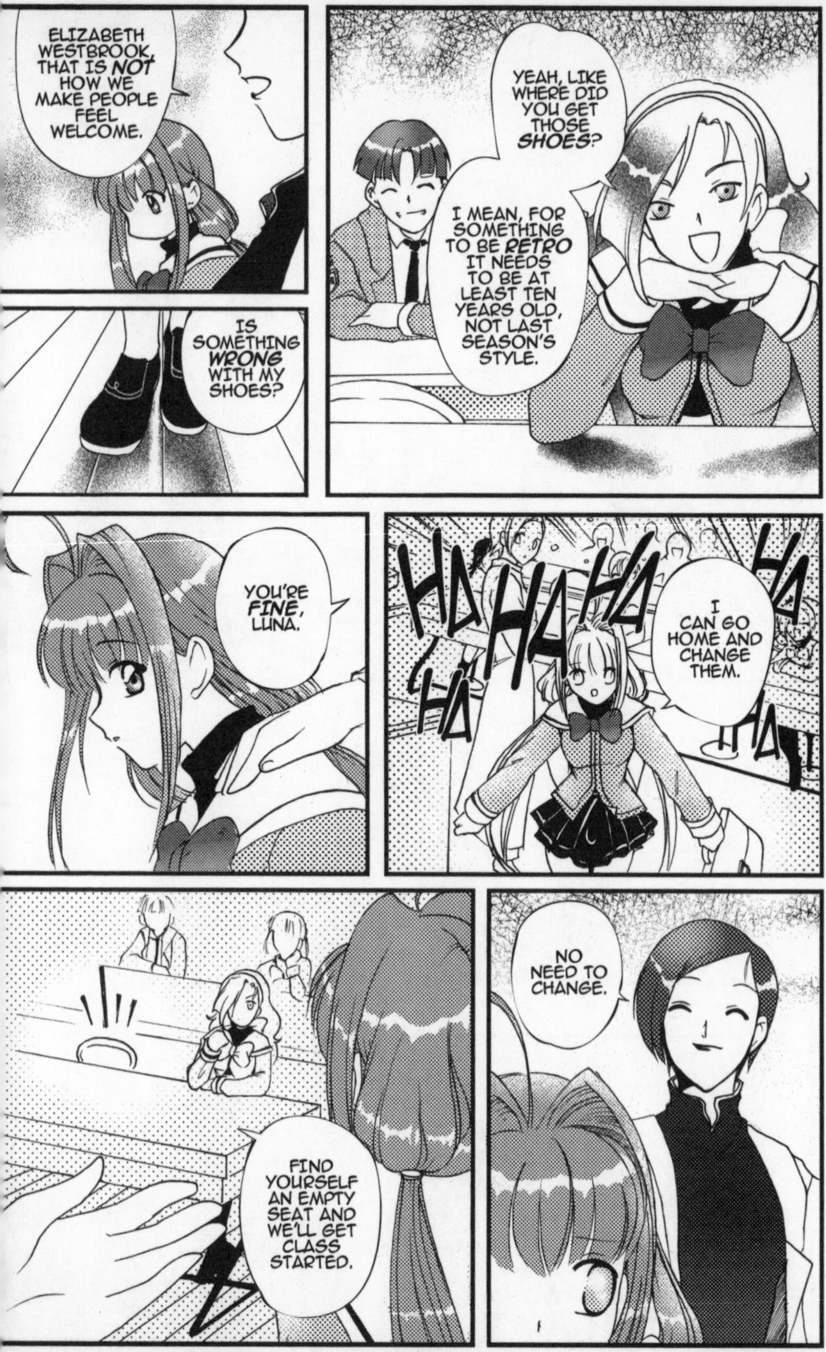
YEAH, LIKE WHERE DID YOU GET THOSE *SHOES*?
I MEAN, FOR SOMETHING TO BE *RETRO* IT NEEDS TO BE AT LEAST TEN YEARS OLD, NOT LAST SEASON'S STYLE.
ELIZABETH WESTBROOK, THAT IS *NOT* HOW WE MAKE PEOPLE FEEL WELCOME.
IS SOMETHING *WRONG* WITH MY SHOES?
HA HA HA HA HA HA HA HA!
I CAN GO HOME AND CHANGE THEM.
YOU'RE *FINE*, LUNA.
NO NEED TO CHANGE.
FIND YOURSELF AN EMPTY SEAT AND WE'LL GET CLASS STARTED.

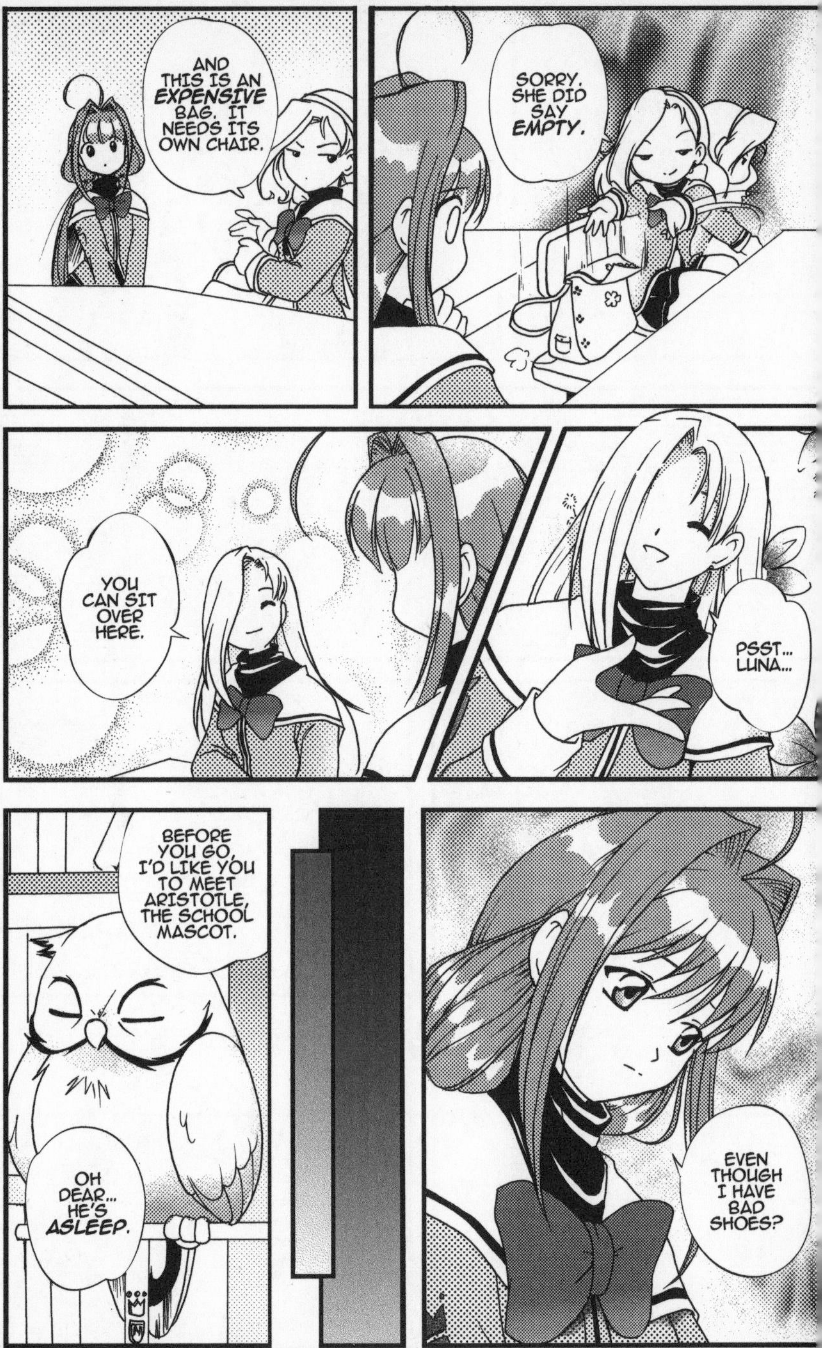
SORRY. SHE DID SAY EMPTY.
AND THIS IS AN EXPENSIVE BAG. IT NEEDS ITS OWN CHAIR.
PSST... LUNA...
YOU CAN SIT OVER HERE.
EVEN THOUGH I HAVE BAD SHOES?
BEFORE YOU GO, I'D LIKE YOU TO MEET ARISTOTLE, THE SCHOOL MASCOT.
OH DEAR... HE'S ASLEEP.

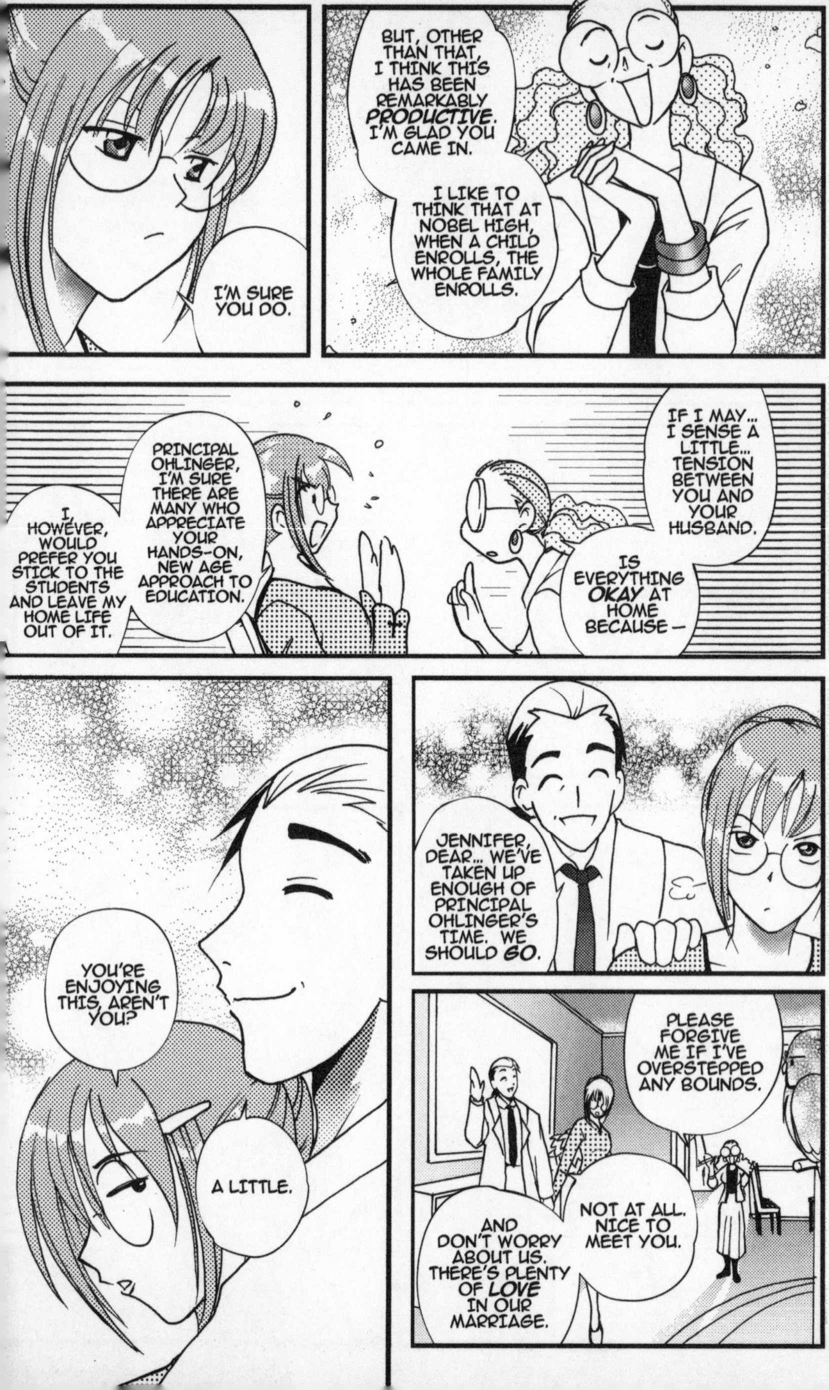
BUT, OTHER THAN THAT, I THINK THIS HAS BEEN REMARKABLY **PRODUCTIVE**. I'M GLAD YOU CAME IN.
I LIKE TO THINK THAT AT NOBEL HIGH, WHEN A CHILD ENROLLS, THE WHOLE FAMILY ENROLLS.
I'M SURE YOU DO.
IF I MAY... I SENSE A LITTLE... TENSION BETWEEN YOU AND YOUR HUSBAND.
IS EVERYTHING **OKAY** AT HOME BECAUSE —
PRINCIPAL OHLINGER, I'M SURE THERE ARE MANY WHO APPRECIATE YOUR HANDS-ON, NEW AGE APPROACH TO EDUCATION.
I, HOWEVER, WOULD PREFER YOU STICK TO THE STUDENTS AND LEAVE MY HOME LIFE OUT OF IT.
JENNIFER, DEAR... WE'VE TAKEN UP ENOUGH OF PRINCIPAL OHLINGER'S TIME. WE SHOULD **GO**.
PLEASE FORGIVE ME IF I'VE OVERSTEPPED ANY BOUNDS.
NOT AT ALL. NICE TO MEET YOU.
AND DON'T WORRY ABOUT US. THERE'S PLENTY OF **LOVE** IN OUR MARRIAGE.
YOU'RE ENJOYING THIS, AREN'T YOU?
A LITTLE.

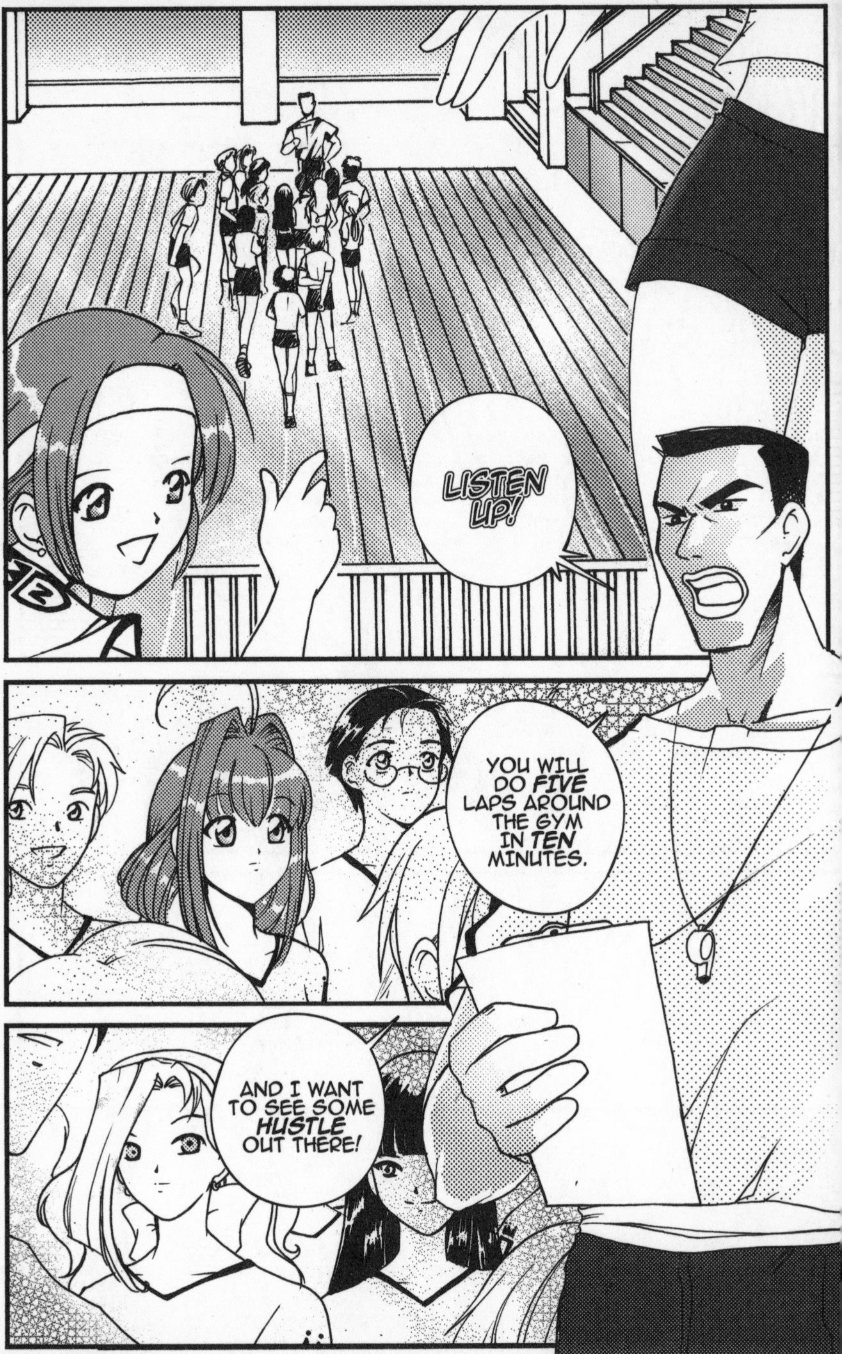
LISTEN UP!
YOU WILL DO *FIVE* LAPS AROUND THE GYM IN *TEN* MINUTES.
AND I WANT TO SEE SOME *HUSTLE* OUT THERE!

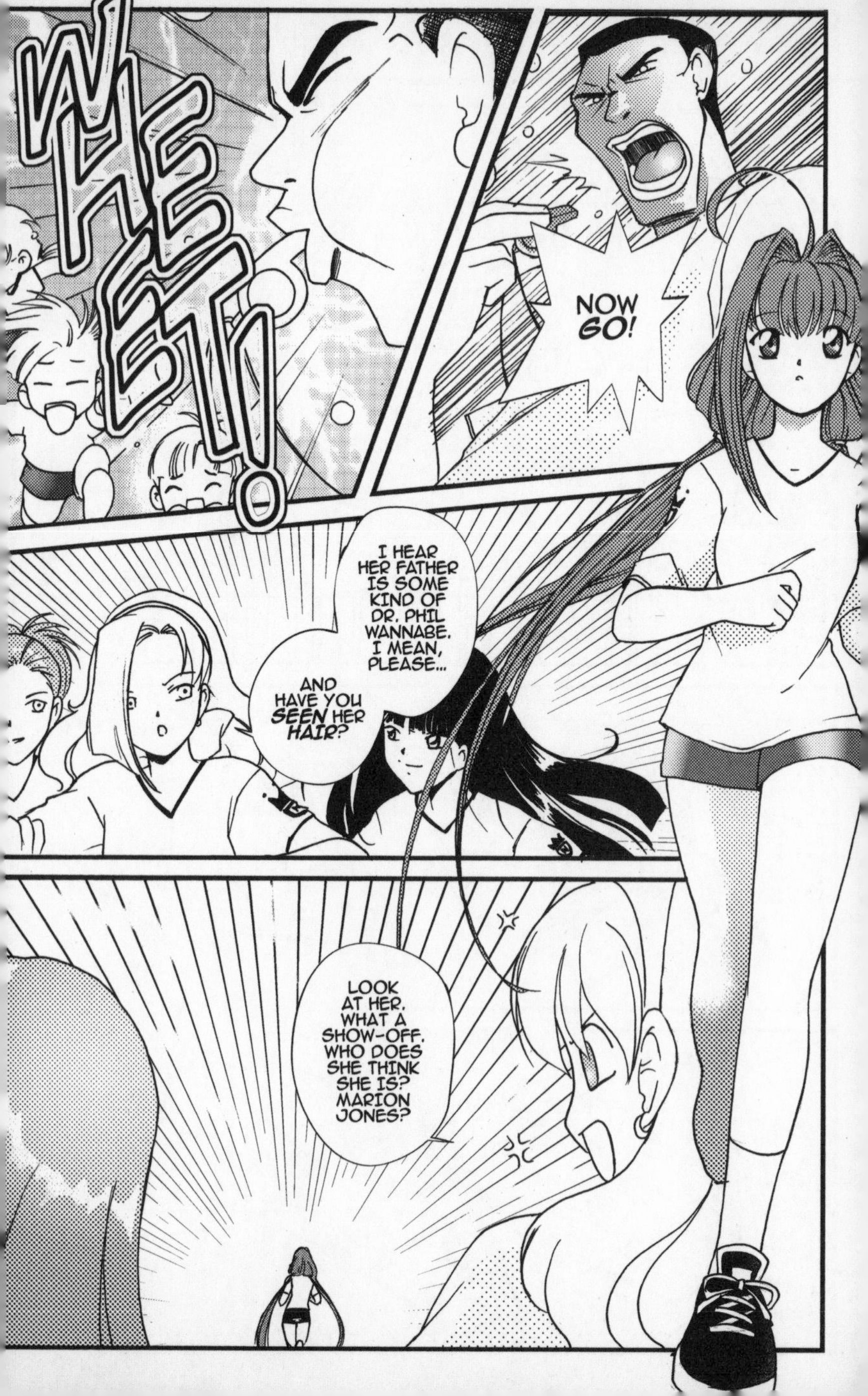
NOW GO!
WHEEET!
I HEAR HER FATHER IS SOME KIND OF DR. PHIL WANNABE. I MEAN, PLEASE...
AND HAVE YOU SEEN HER HAIR?
LOOK AT HER. WHAT A SHOW-OFF. WHO DOES SHE THINK SHE IS? MARION JONES?

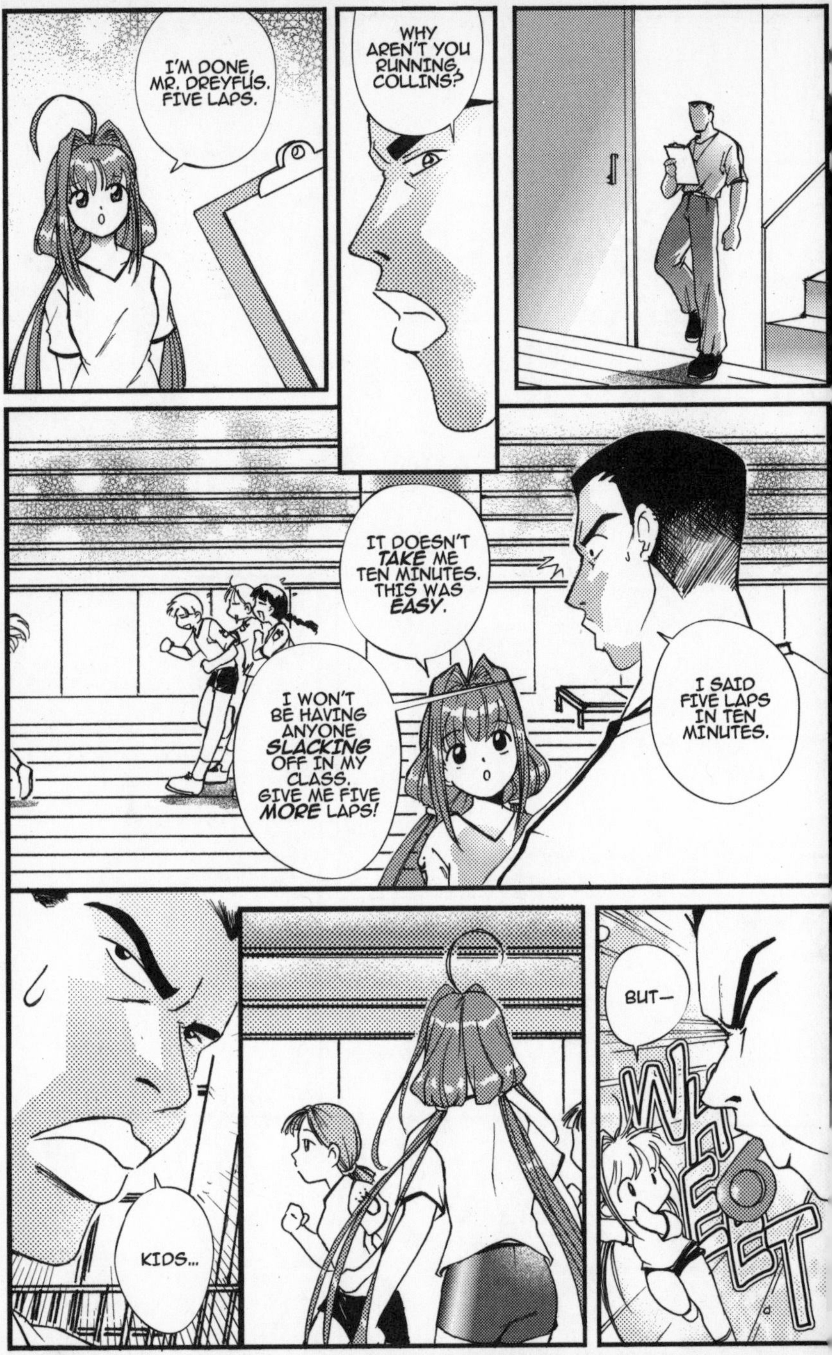
WHY AREN'T YOU RUNNING, COLLINS?
I'M DONE, MR. DREYFUS. FIVE LAPS.
I SAID FIVE LAPS IN TEN MINUTES.
IT DOESN'T *TAKE* ME TEN MINUTES. THIS WAS *EASY*.
I WON'T BE HAVING ANYONE *SLACKING* OFF IN MY CLASS. GIVE ME FIVE *MORE* LAPS!
BUT—
WHAT THE FFT
KIDS...

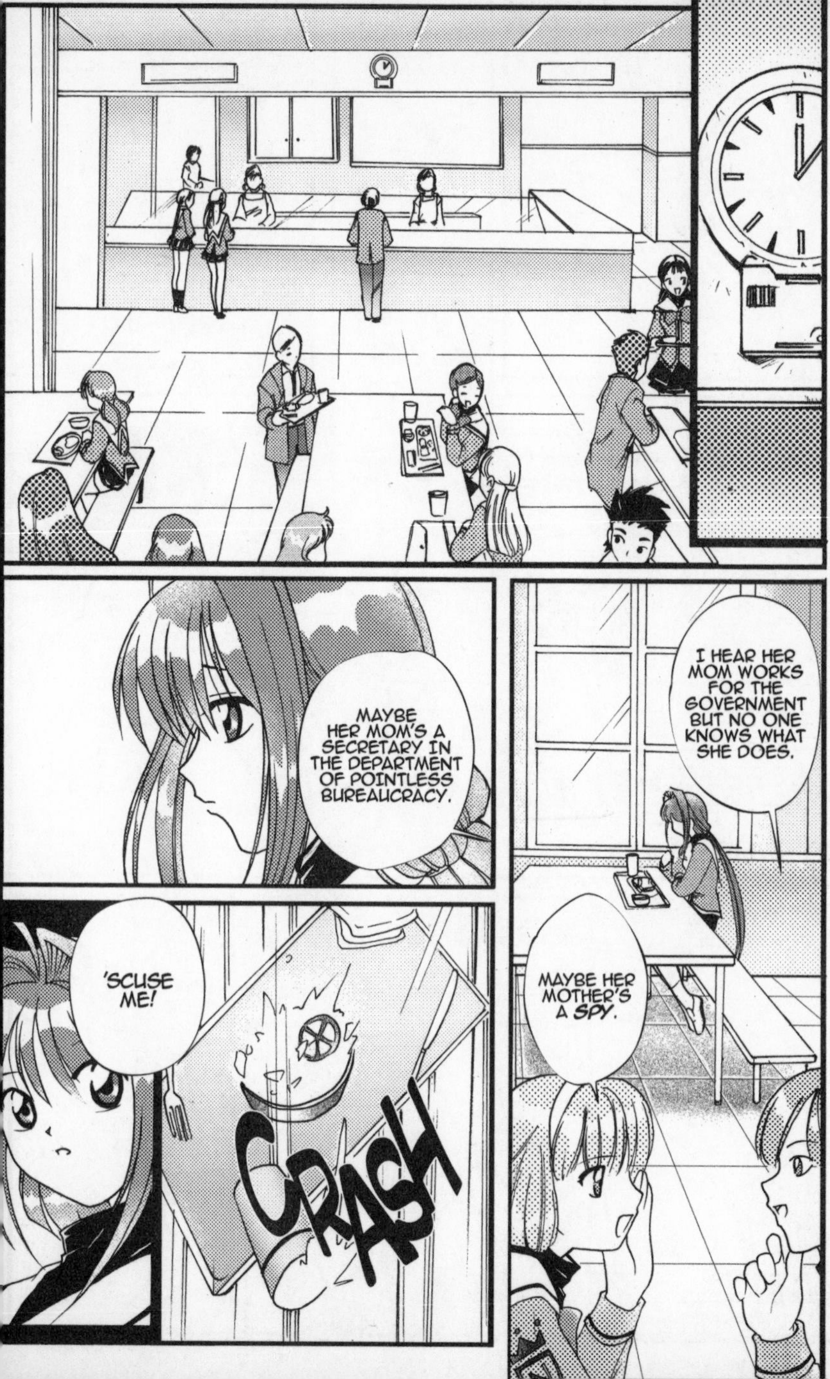
I HEAR HER MOM WORKS FOR THE GOVERNMENT BUT NO ONE KNOWS WHAT SHE DOES.
MAYBE HER MOTHER'S A *SPY*.
MAYBE HER MOM'S A SECRETARY IN THE DEPARTMENT OF POINTLESS BUREAUCRACY.
CRASH
'SCUSE ME!

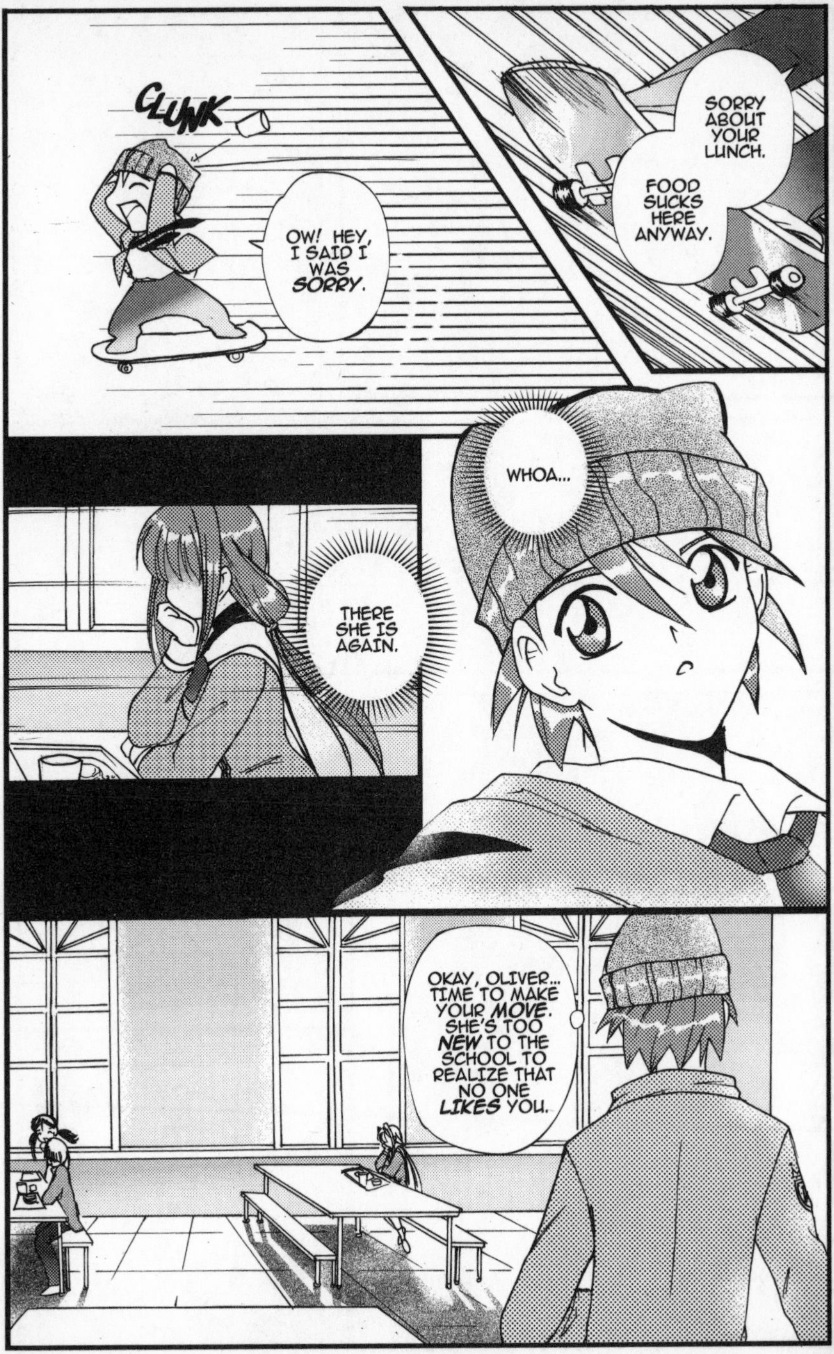
SORRY ABOUT YOUR LUNCH.
FOOD SUCKS HERE ANYWAY.
CLUNK
OW! HEY, I SAID I WAS *SORRY*.
WHOA...
THERE SHE IS AGAIN.
OKAY, OLIVER... TIME TO MAKE YOUR *MOVE*. SHE'S TOO *NEW* TO THE SCHOOL TO REALIZE THAT NO ONE *LIKES* YOU.

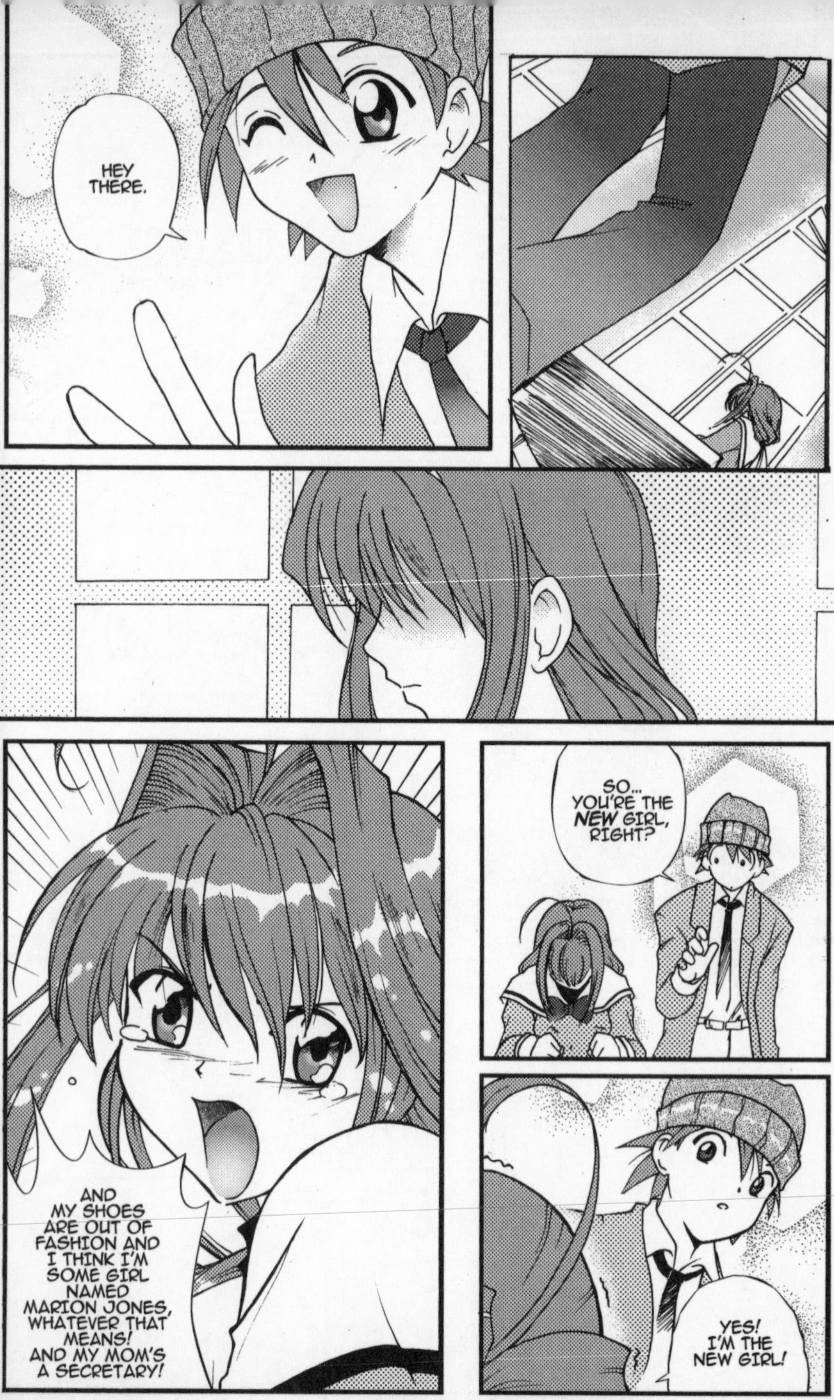
HEY THERE.
SO... YOU'RE THE NEW GIRL, RIGHT?
YES! I'M THE NEW GIRL!
AND MY SHOES ARE OUT OF FASHION AND I THINK I'M SOME GIRL NAMED MARION JONES, WHATEVER THAT MEANS! AND MY MOM'S A SECRETARY!

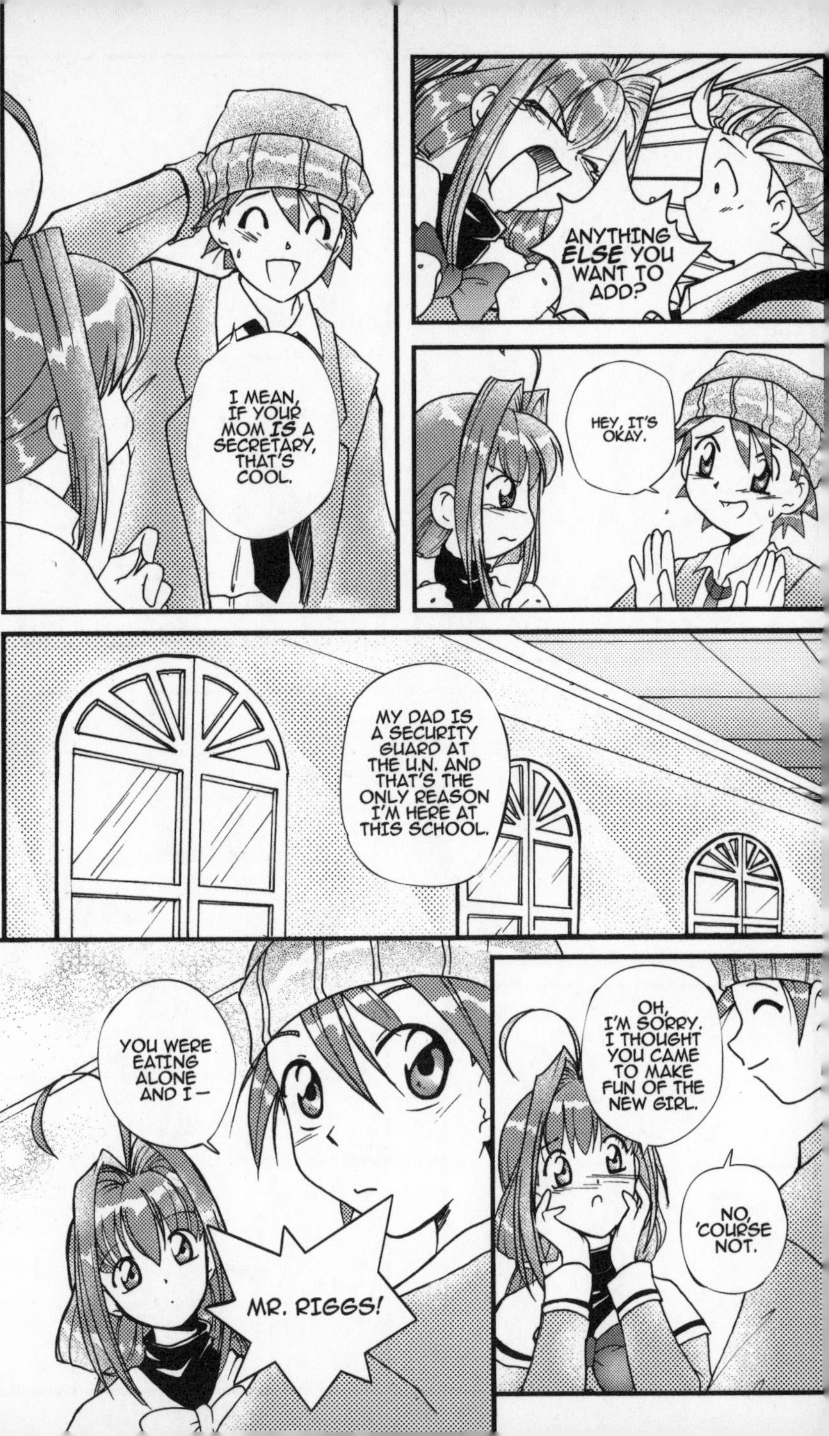
ANYTHING ELSE YOU WANT TO ADD?
HEY, IT'S OKAY.
I MEAN, IF YOUR MOM IS A SECRETARY, THAT'S COOL.
MY DAD IS A SECURITY GUARD AT THE U.N. AND THAT'S THE ONLY REASON I'M HERE AT THIS SCHOOL.
OH, I'M SORRY. I THOUGHT YOU CAME TO MAKE FUN OF THE NEW GIRL.
NO, 'COURSE NOT.
YOU WERE EATING ALONE AND I—
MR. RIGGS!

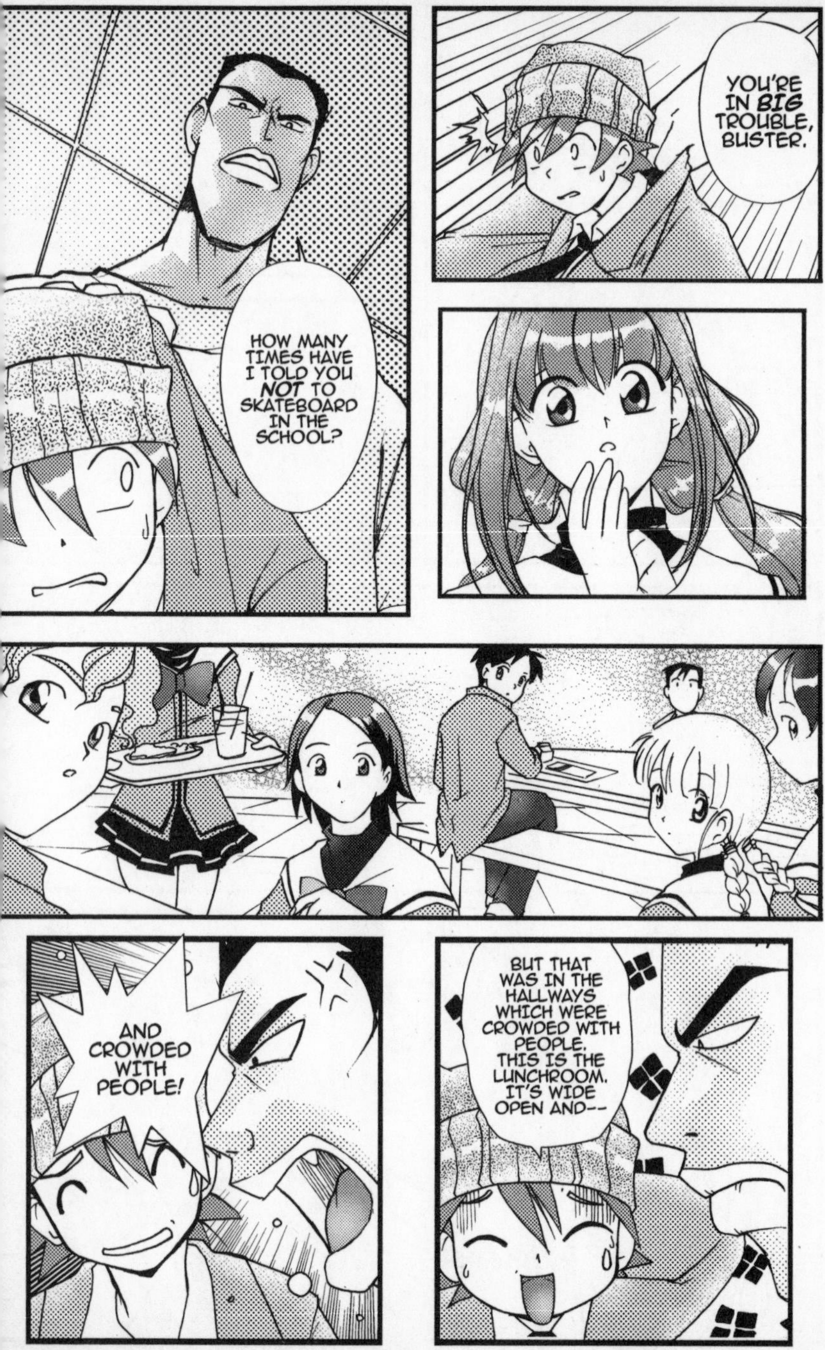
YOU'RE IN **BIG** TROUBLE, BUSTER.
HOW MANY TIMES HAVE I TOLD YOU **NOT** TO SKATEBOARD IN THE SCHOOL?
BUT THAT WAS IN THE HALLWAYS WHICH WERE CROWDED WITH PEOPLE. THIS IS THE LUNCHROOM. IT'S WIDE OPEN AND--
AND CROWDED WITH PEOPLE!

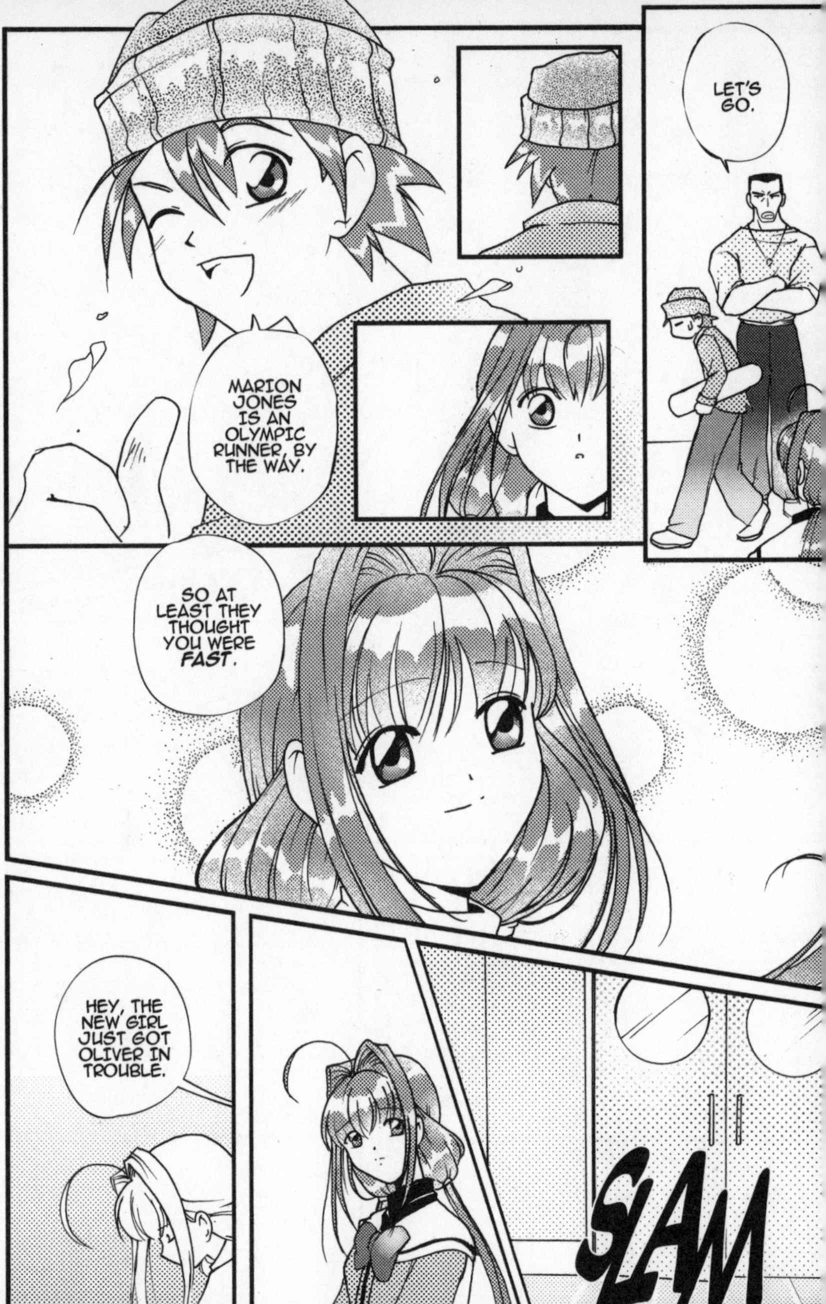
LET'S GO.
MARION JONES IS AN OLYMPIC RUNNER, BY THE WAY.
SO AT LEAST THEY THOUGHT YOU WERE *FAST*.
SLAM
HEY, THE NEW GIRL JUST GOT OLIVER IN TROUBLE.

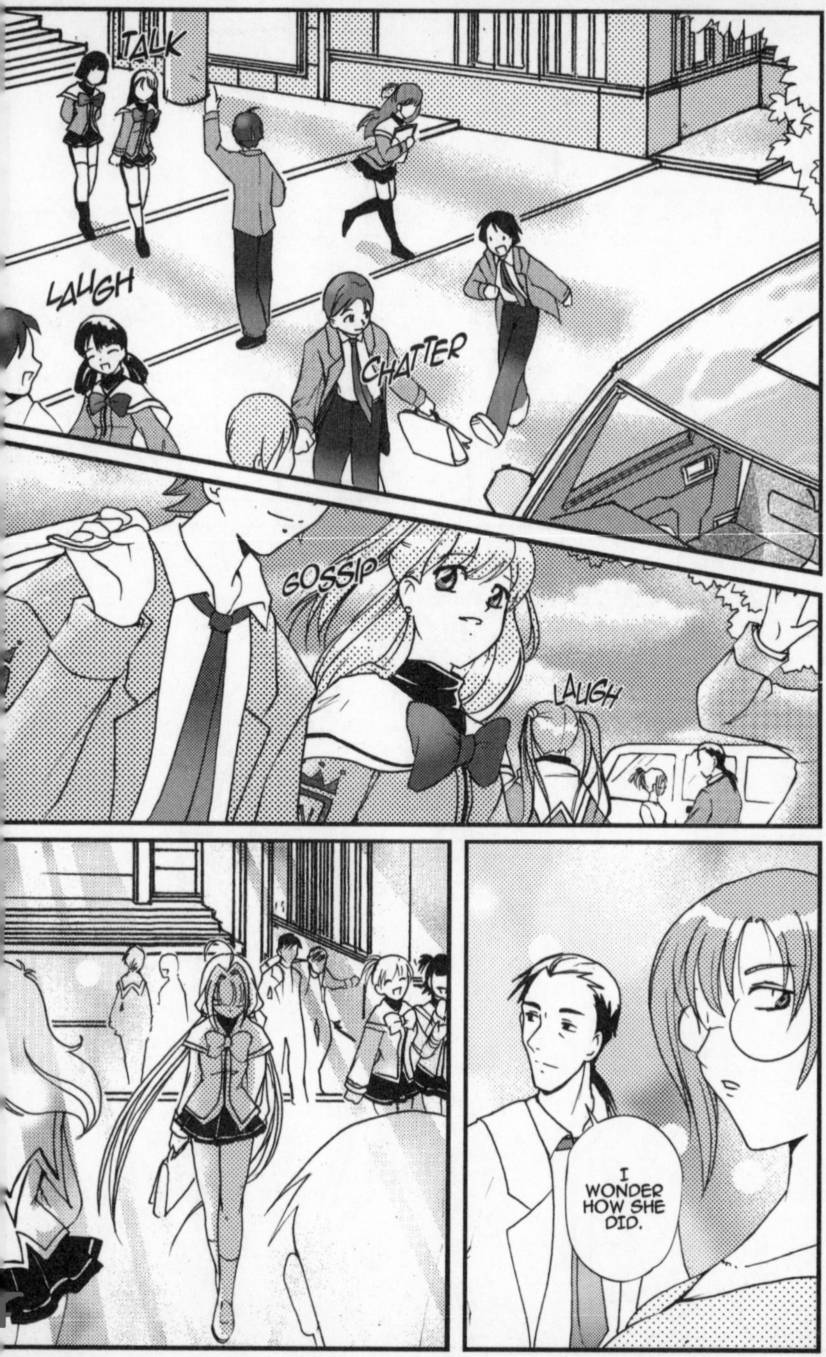
TALK
LAUGH
CHATTER
GOSSIP
LAUGH
I WONDER HOW SHE DID.

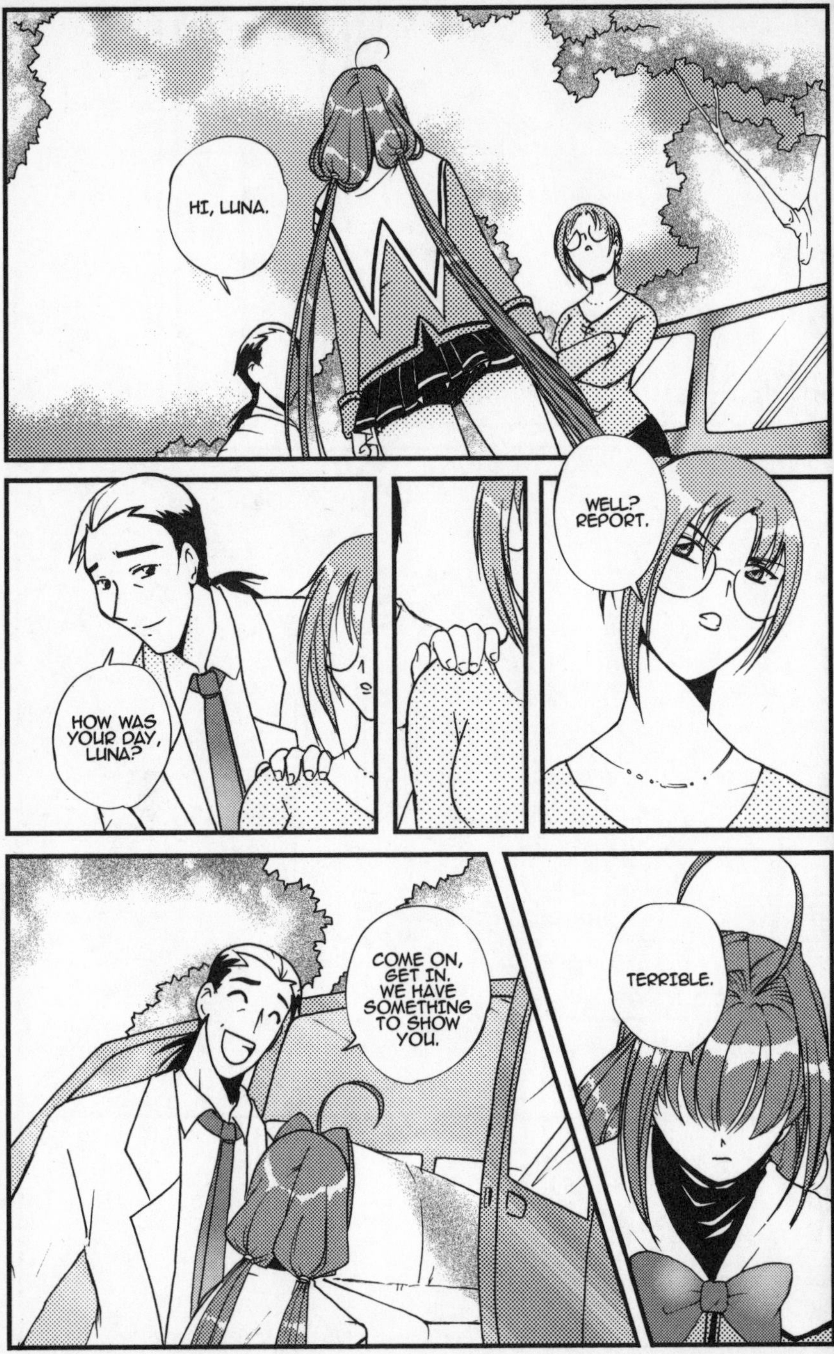
HI, LUNA.
WELL? REPORT.
HOW WAS YOUR DAY, LUNA?
TERRIBLE.
COME ON, GET IN. WE HAVE SOMETHING TO SHOW YOU.

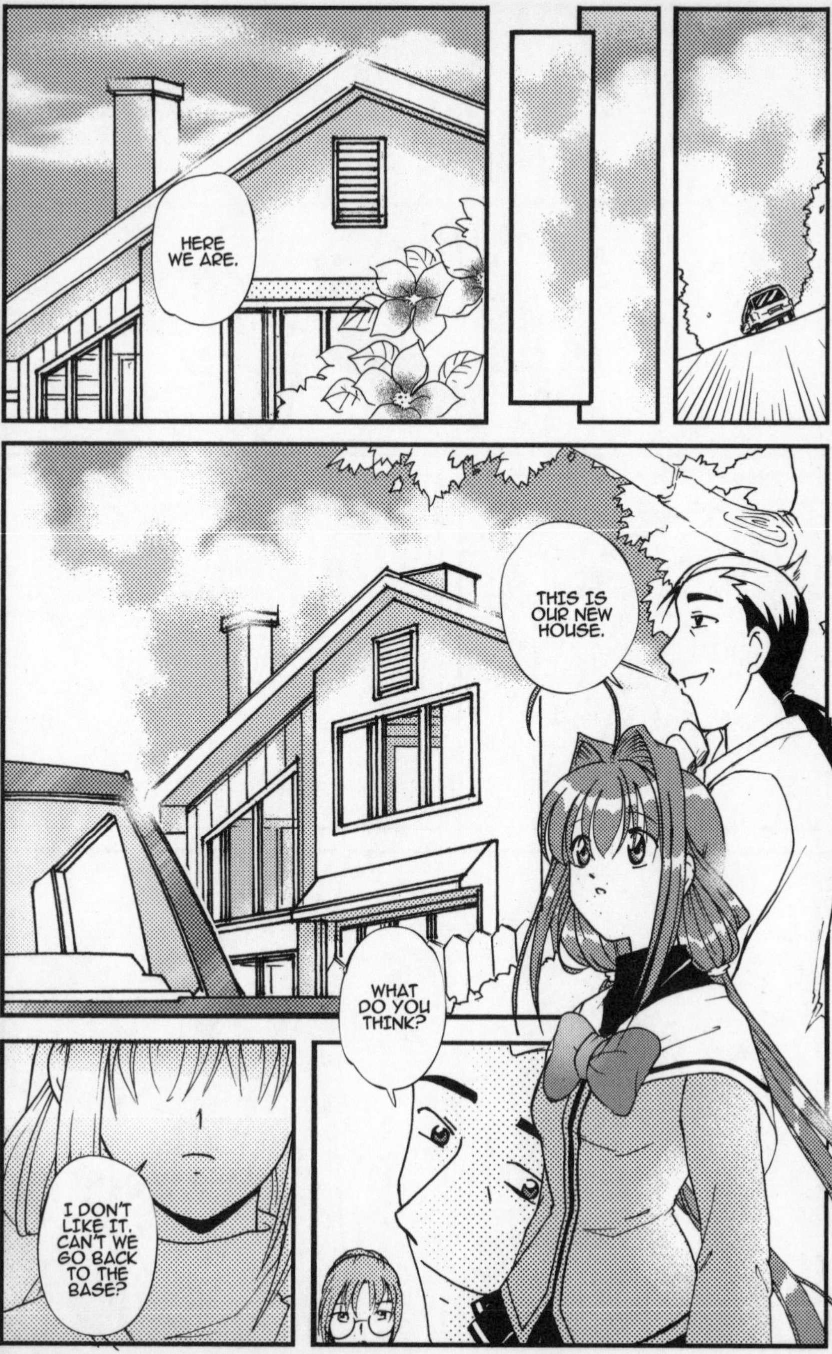
HERE WE ARE.
THIS IS OUR NEW HOUSE.
WHAT DO YOU THINK?
I DON'T LIKE IT. CAN'T WE GO BACK TO THE BASE?

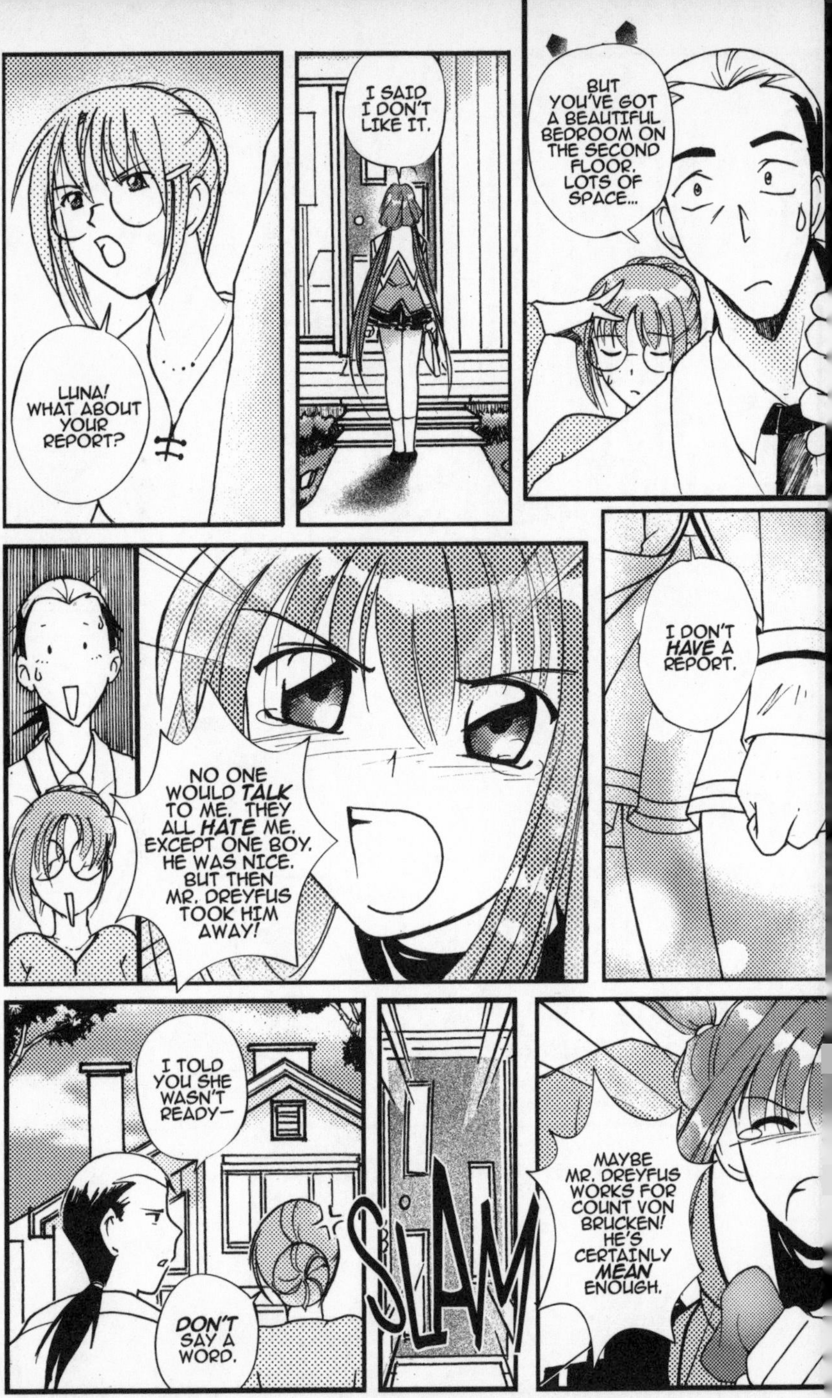
BUT YOU'VE GOT A BEAUTIFUL BEDROOM ON THE SECOND FLOOR. LOTS OF SPACE...
I SAID I DON'T LIKE IT.
LUNA! WHAT ABOUT YOUR REPORT?
I DON'T *HAVE* A REPORT.
NO ONE WOULD *TALK* TO ME. THEY ALL *HATE* ME. EXCEPT ONE BOY. HE WAS NICE. BUT THEN MR. DREYFUS TOOK HIM AWAY!
MAYBE MR. DREYFUS WORKS FOR COUNT VON BRUCKEN! HE'S CERTAINLY *MEAN* ENOUGH.
SLAM
I TOLD YOU SHE WASN'T READY—
*DON'T* SAY A WORD.

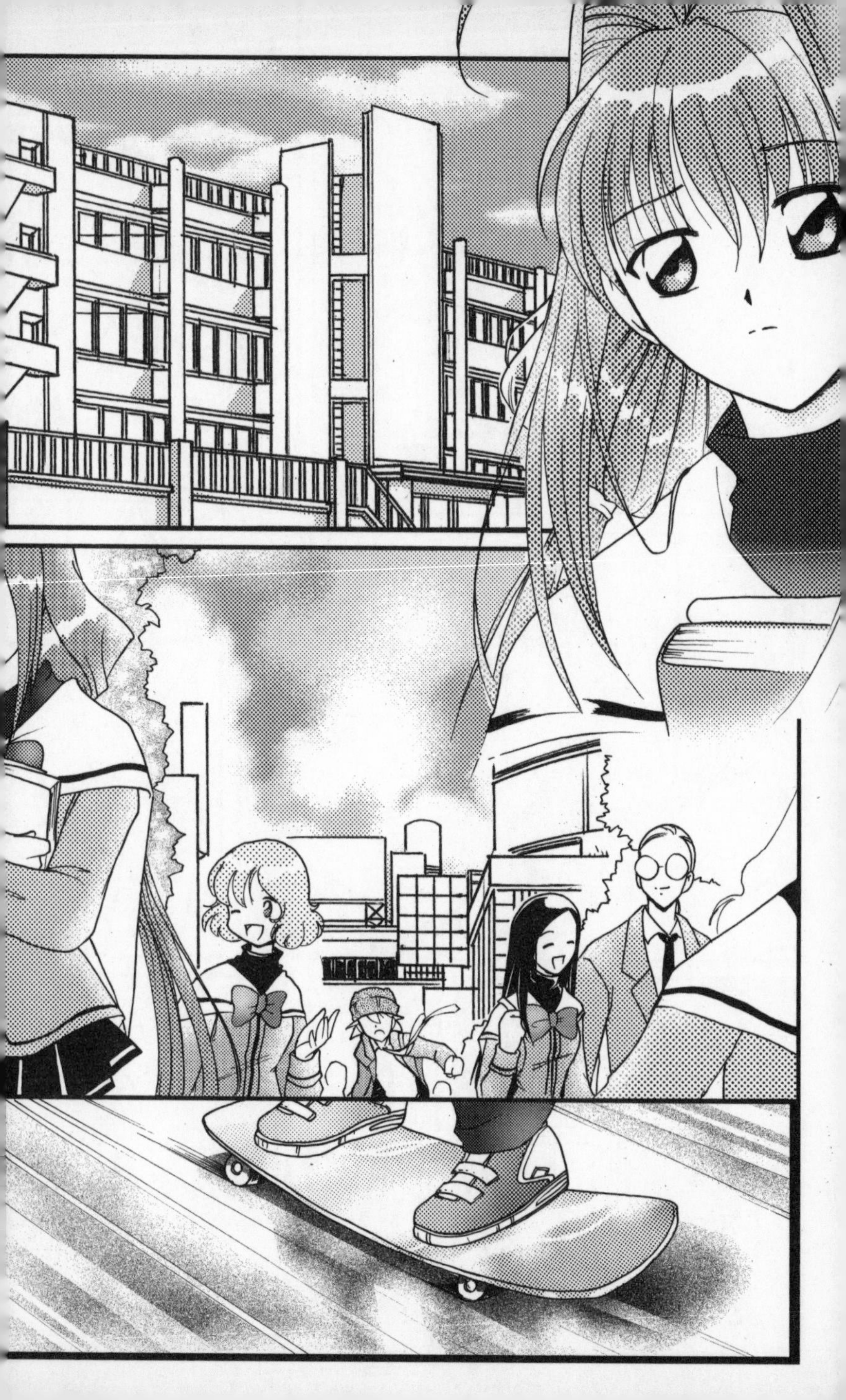

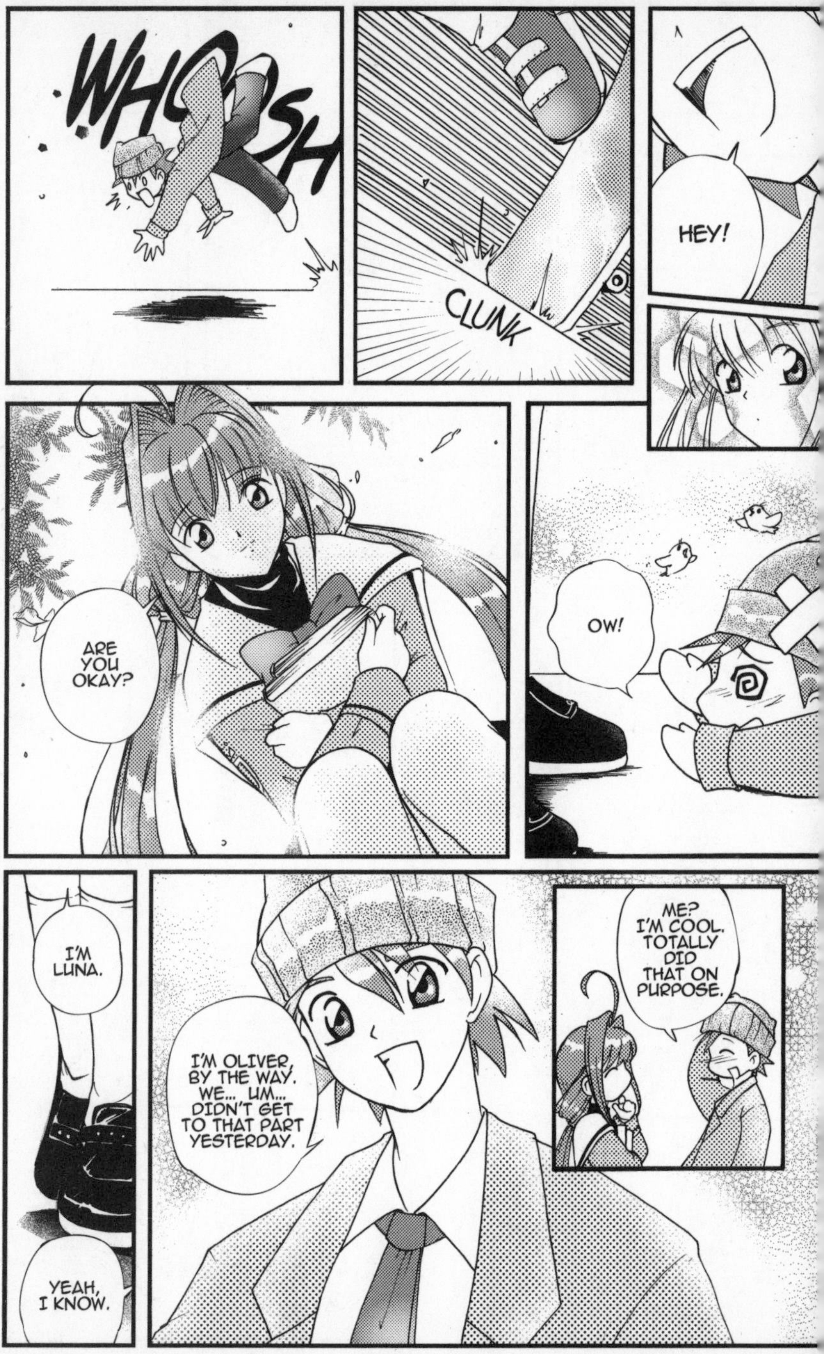
HEY!
CLUNK
WHOOSH
OW!
ARE YOU OKAY?
ME? I'M COOL. TOTALLY DID THAT ON PURPOSE.
I'M OLIVER, BY THE WAY. WE... UM... DIDN'T GET TO THAT PART YESTERDAY.
I'M LUNA.
YEAH, I KNOW.

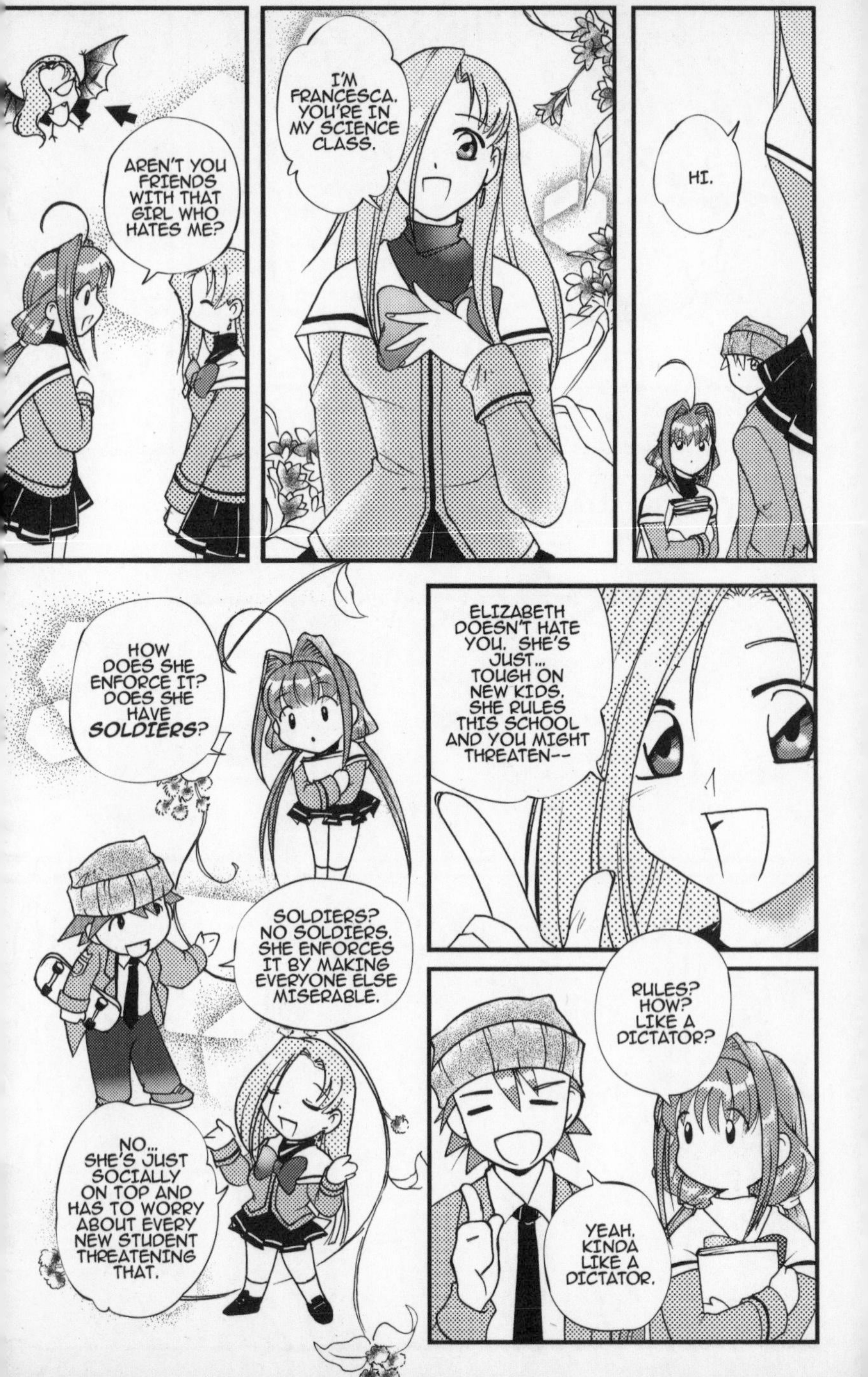
HI.
I'M FRANCESCA. YOU'RE IN MY SCIENCE CLASS.
AREN'T YOU FRIENDS WITH THAT GIRL WHO HATES ME?
ELIZABETH DOESN'T HATE YOU. SHE'S JUST... TOUGH ON NEW KIDS. SHE RULES THIS SCHOOL AND YOU MIGHT THREATEN--
RULES? HOW? LIKE A DICTATOR?
YEAH. KINDA LIKE A DICTATOR.
HOW DOES SHE ENFORCE IT? DOES SHE HAVE SOLDIERS?
SOLDIERS? NO SOLDIERS. SHE ENFORCES IT BY MAKING EVERYONE ELSE MISERABLE.
NO... SHE'S JUST SOCIALLY ON TOP AND HAS TO WORRY ABOUT EVERY NEW STUDENT THREATENING THAT.

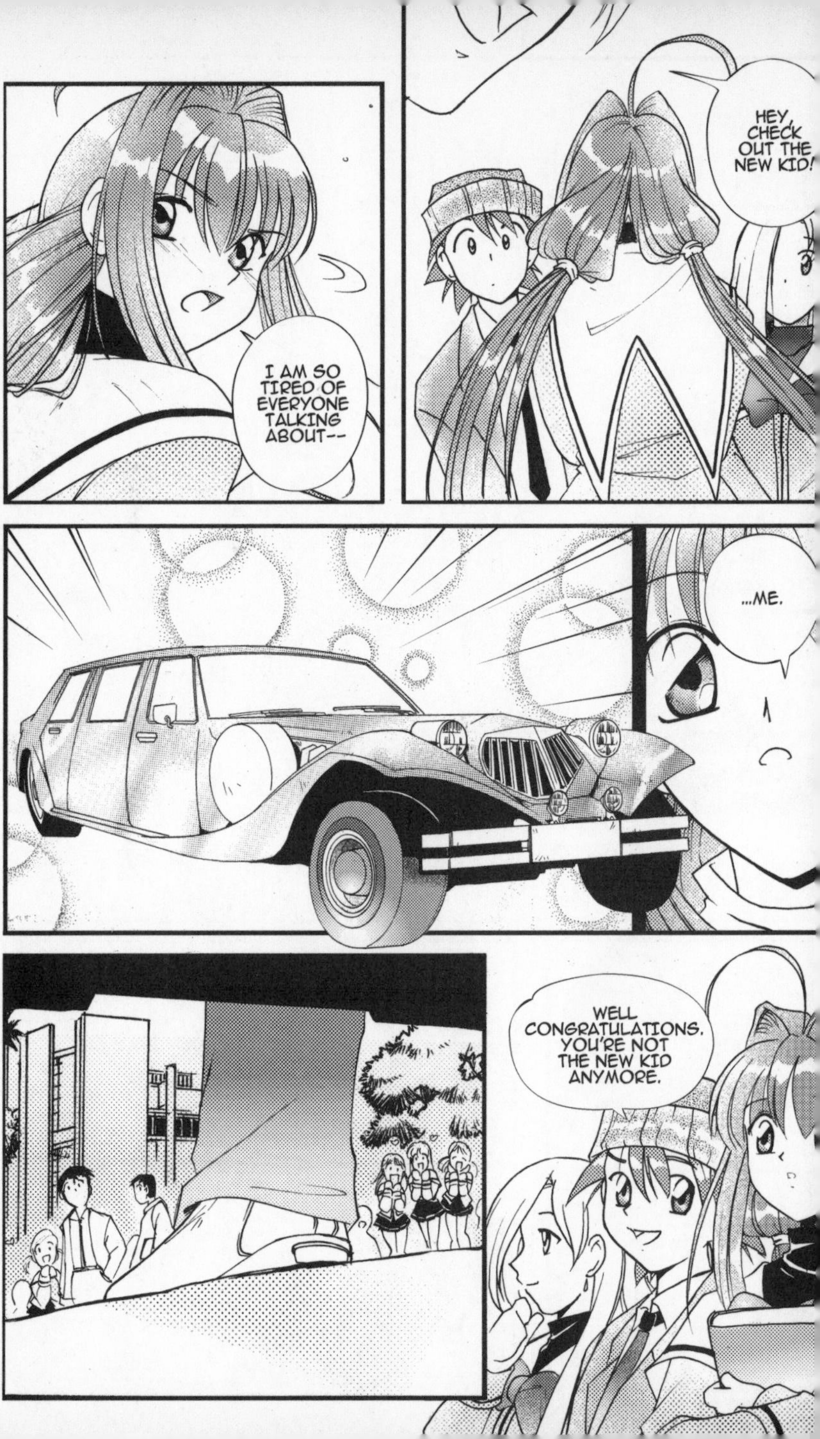
HEY, CHECK OUT THE NEW KID!
I AM SO TIRED OF EVERYONE TALKING ABOUT--
...ME.
WELL CONGRATULATIONS. YOU'RE NOT THE NEW KID ANYMORE.

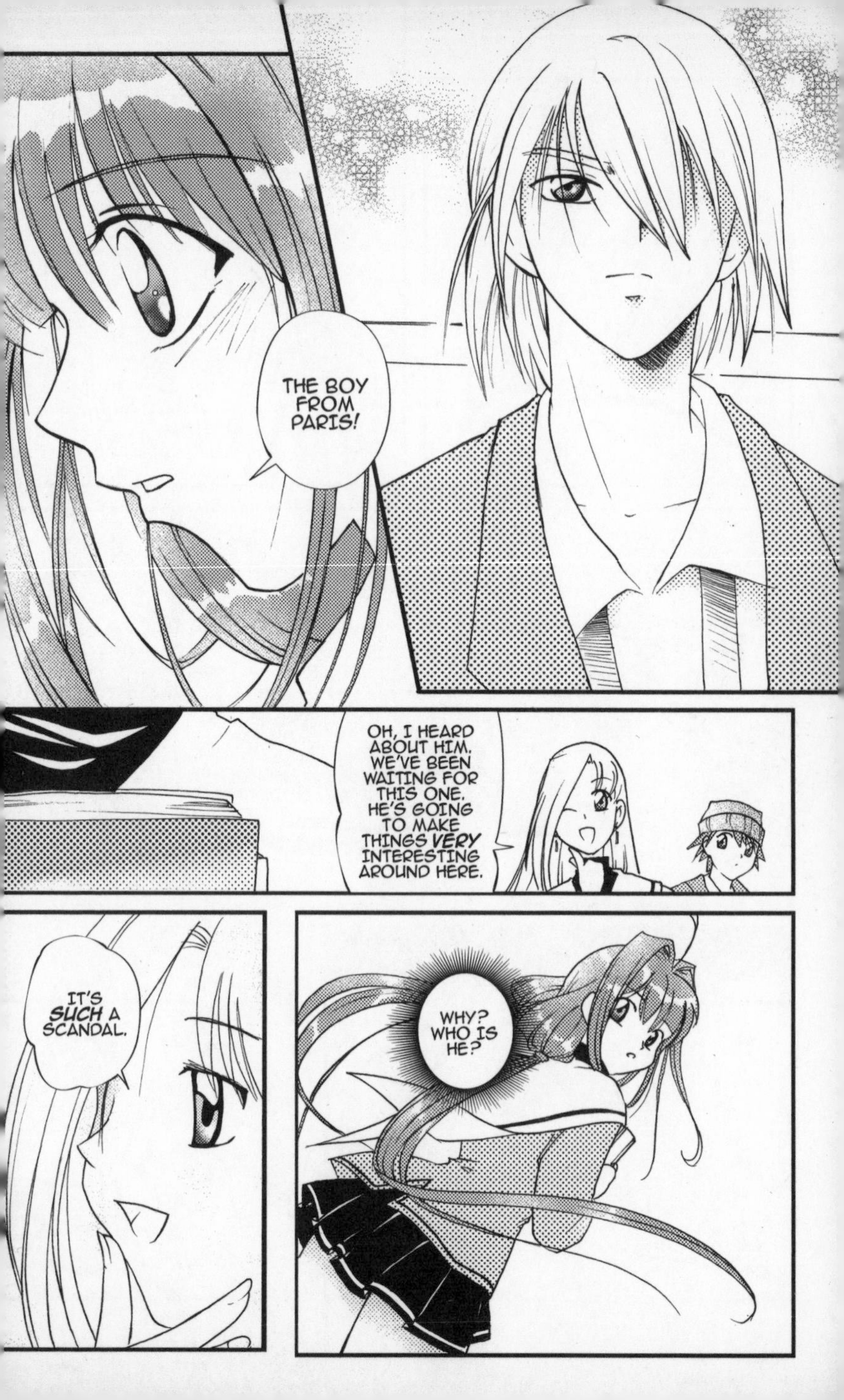
THE BOY FROM PARIS!
OH, I HEARD ABOUT HIM. WE'VE BEEN WAITING FOR THIS ONE. HE'S GOING TO MAKE THINGS ***VERY*** INTERESTING AROUND HERE.
WHY? WHO IS HE?
IT'S ***SUCH*** A SCANDAL.

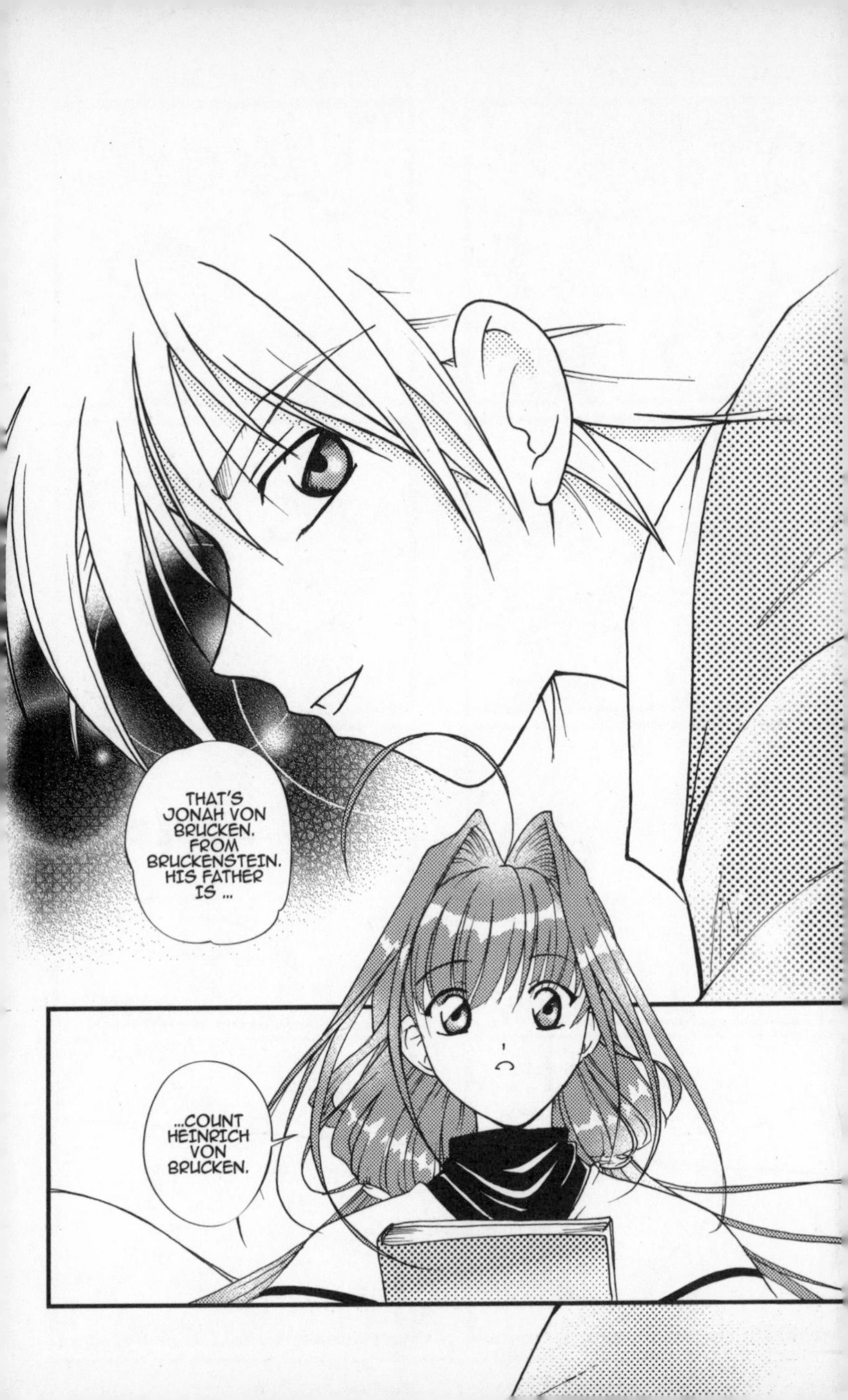
THAT'S JONAH VON BRUCKEN. FROM BRUCKENSTEIN. HIS FATHER IS ...
...COUNT HEINRICH VON BRUCKEN.

## WRITING PROCESS

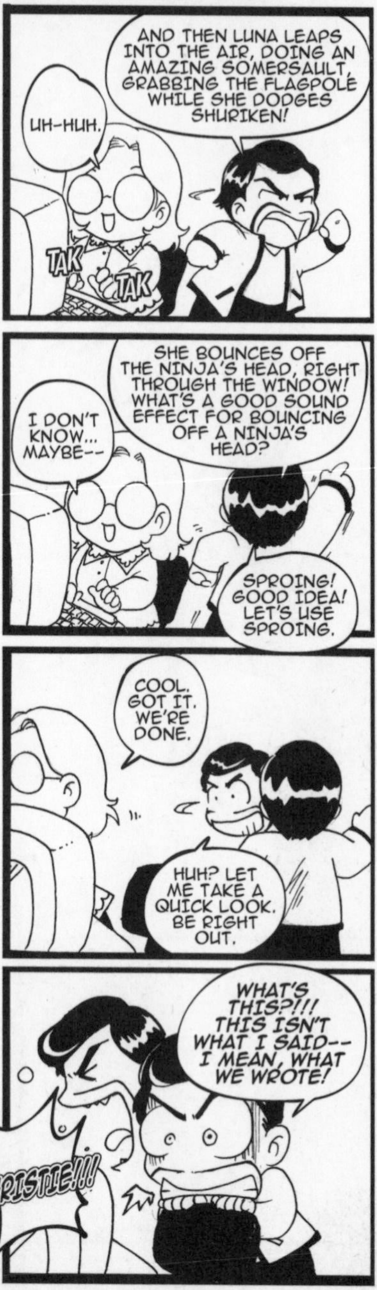
AND THEN LUNA LEAPS INTO THE AIR, DOING AN AMAZING SOMERSAULT, GRABBING THE FLAGPOLE WHILE SHE DODGES SHURIKEN!
UH-HUH.
TAK
TAK
SHE BOUNCES OFF THE NINJA'S HEAD, RIGHT THROUGH THE WINDOW! WHAT'S A GOOD SOUND EFFECT FOR BOUNCING OFF A NINJA'S HEAD?
I DON'T KNOW... MAYBE--
SPROING! GOOD IDEA! LET'S USE SPROING.
COOL. GOT IT. WE'RE DONE.
HUH? LET ME TAKE A QUICK LOOK. BE RIGHT OUT.
WHAT'S THIS?!!! THIS ISN'T WHAT I SAID-- I MEAN, WHAT WE WROTE!
CHRISTIE!!!

## IN YOUR DREAMS

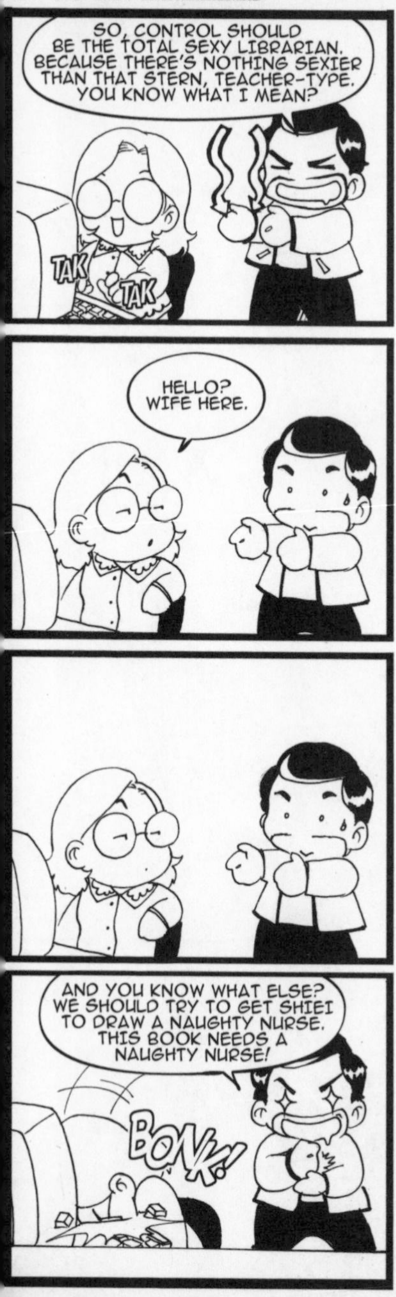
SO, CONTROL SHOULD BE THE TOTAL SEXY LIBRARIAN. BECAUSE THERE'S NOTHING SEXIER THAN THAT STERN, TEACHER-TYPE. YOU KNOW WHAT I MEAN?
TAK
TAK
HELLO? WIFE HERE.
AND YOU KNOW WHAT ELSE? WE SHOULD TRY TO GET SHIEI TO DRAW A NAUGHTY NURSE. THIS BOOK NEEDS A NAUGHTY NURSE!
BONK!

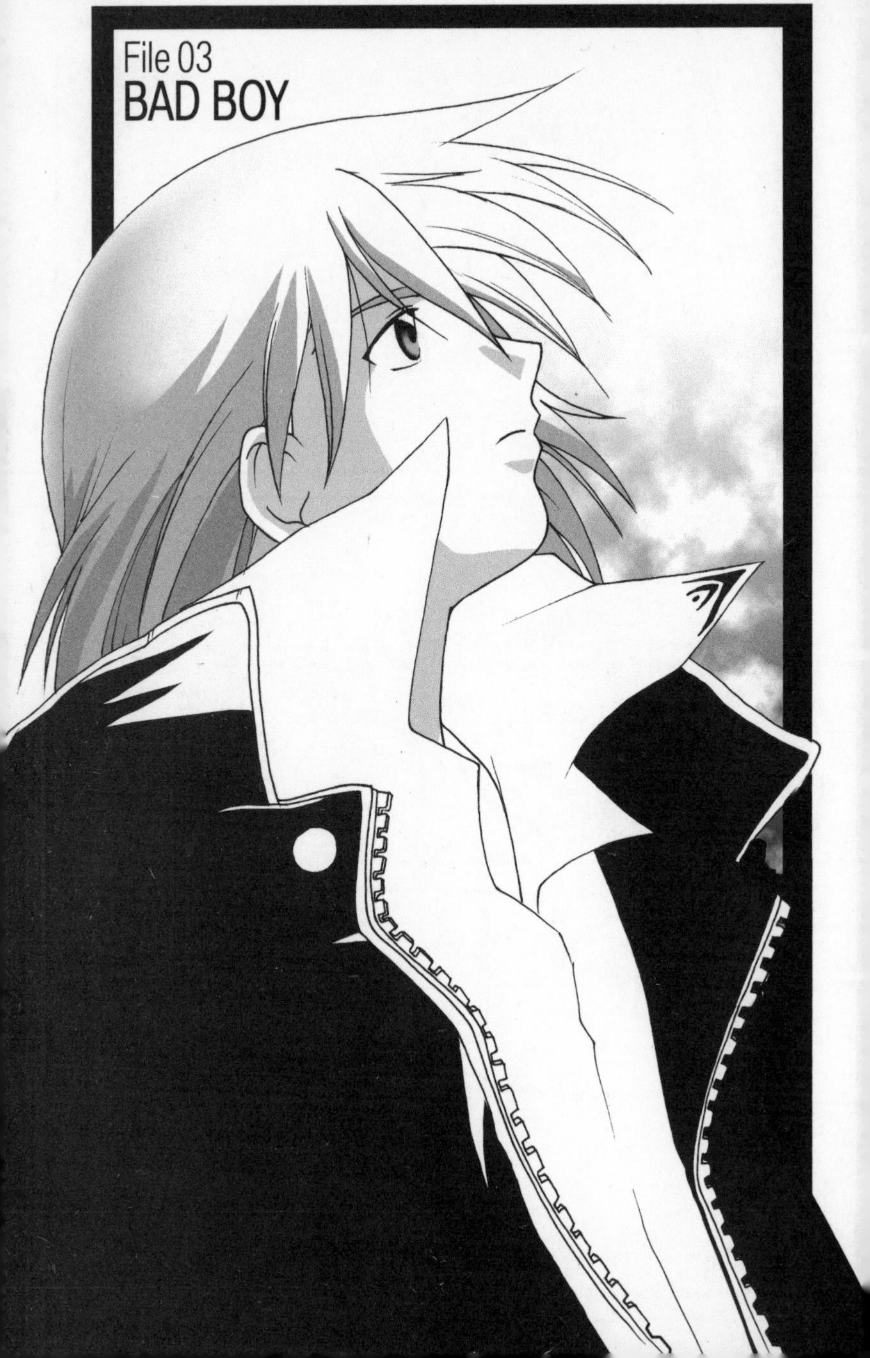
File 03
BAD BOY

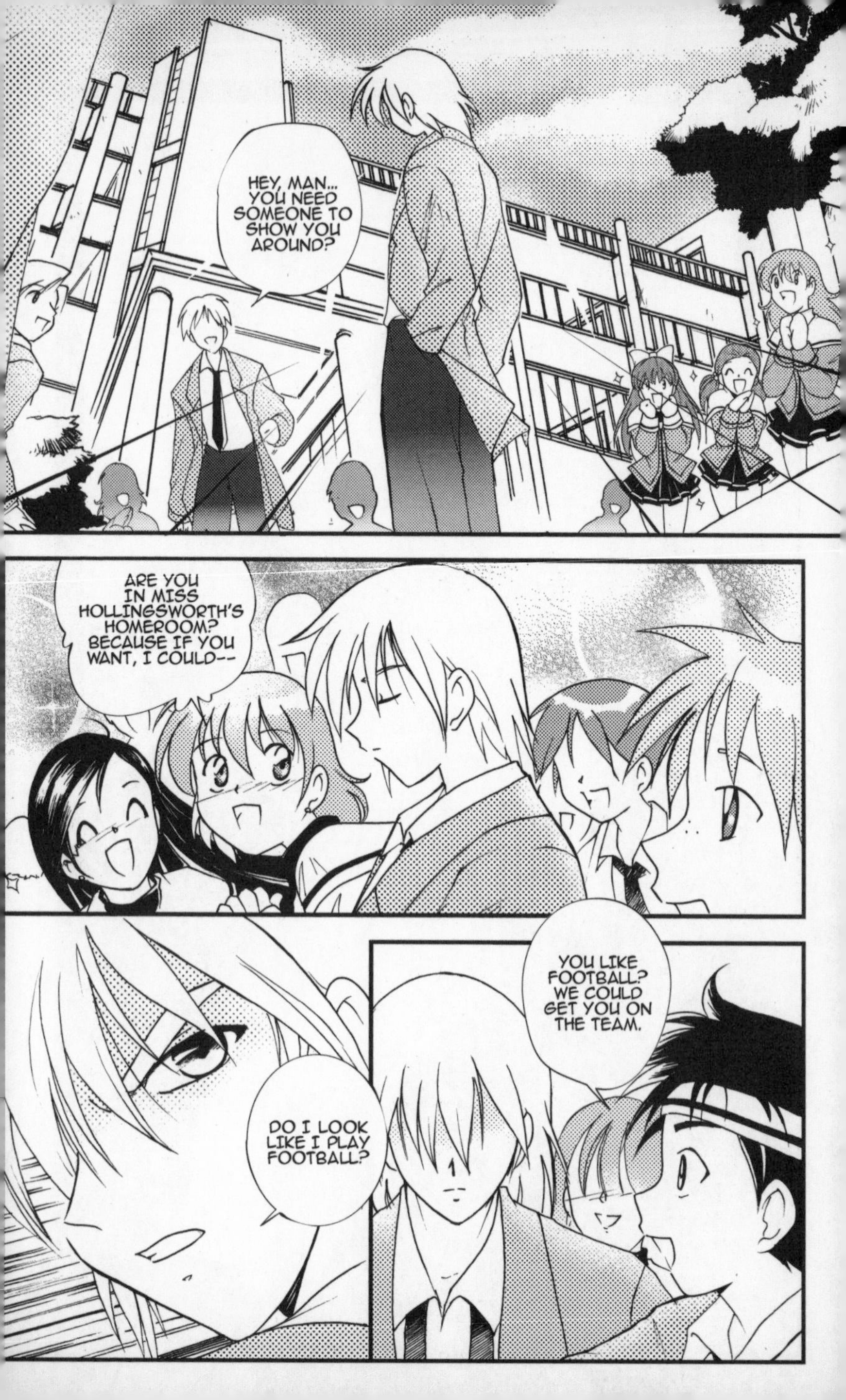
HEY, MAN... YOU NEED SOMEONE TO SHOW YOU AROUND?
ARE YOU IN MISS HOLLINGSWORTH'S HOMEROOM? BECAUSE IF YOU WANT, I COULD--
YOU LIKE FOOTBALL? WE COULD GET YOU ON THE TEAM.
DO I LOOK LIKE I PLAY FOOTBALL?

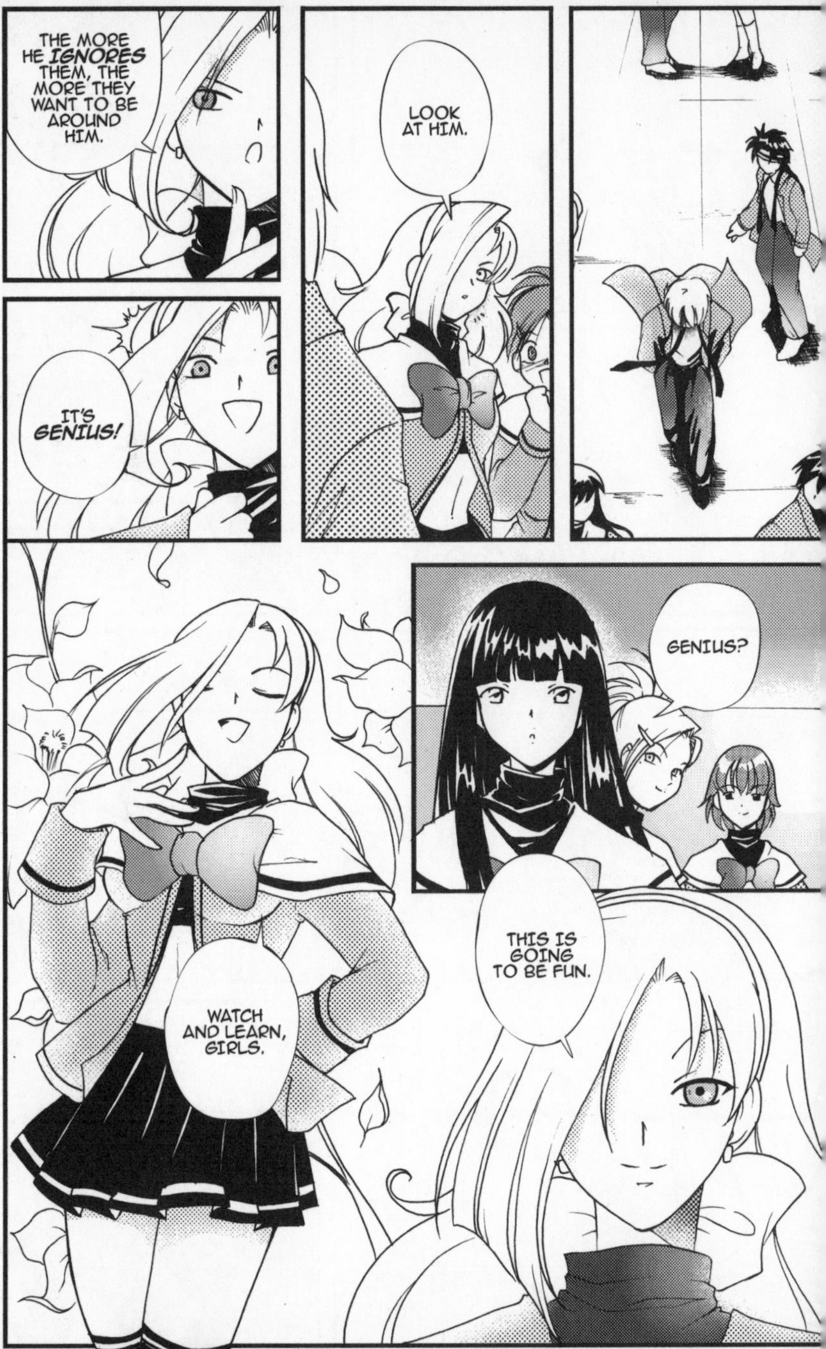
LOOK AT HIM.
THE MORE HE ***IGNORES*** THEM, THE MORE THEY WANT TO BE AROUND HIM.
IT'S ***GENIUS!***
GENIUS?
THIS IS GOING TO BE FUN.
WATCH AND LEARN, GIRLS.

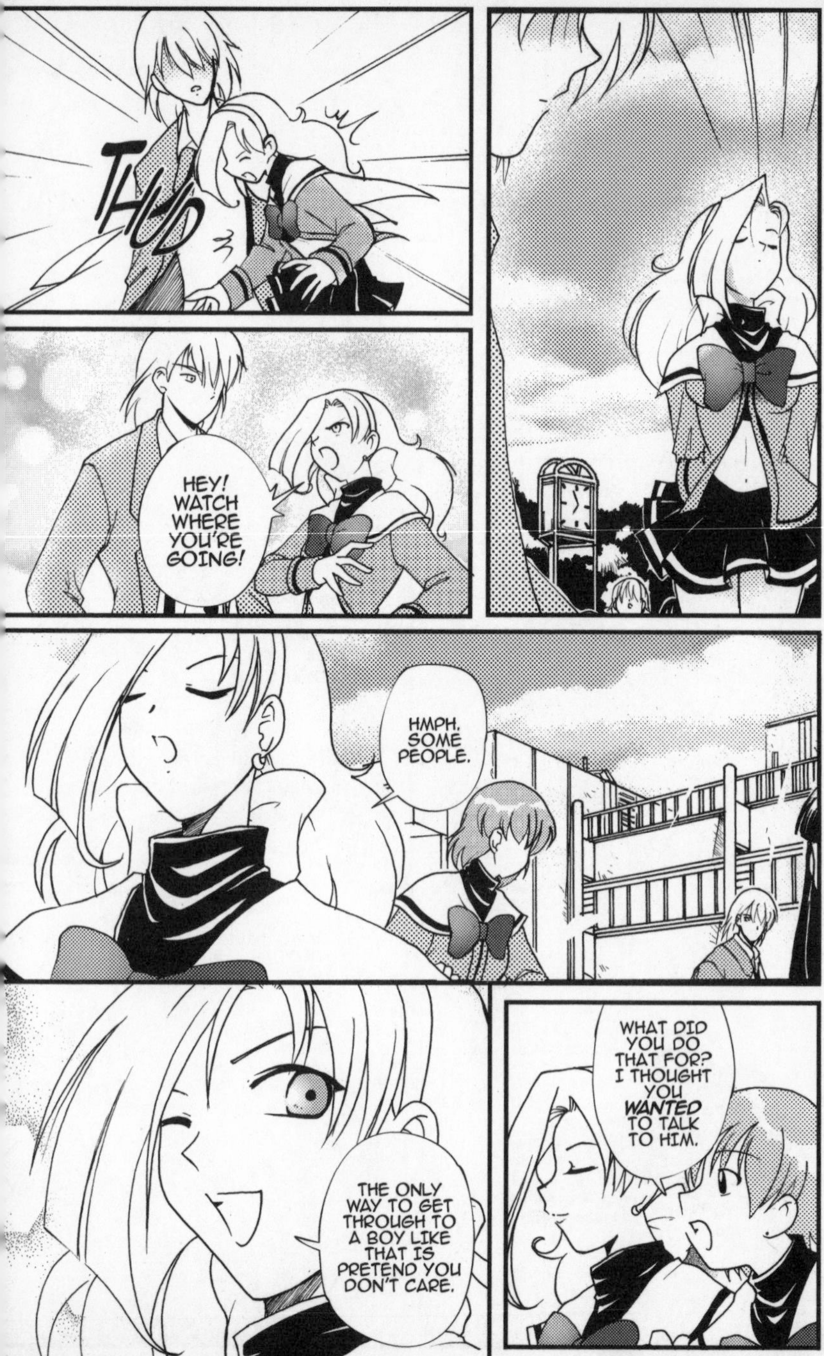
THUD
HEY! WATCH WHERE YOU'RE GOING!
HMPH, SOME PEOPLE.
WHAT DID YOU DO THAT FOR? I THOUGHT YOU *WANTED* TO TALK TO HIM.
THE ONLY WAY TO GET THROUGH TO A BOY LIKE THAT IS PRETEND YOU DON'T CARE.

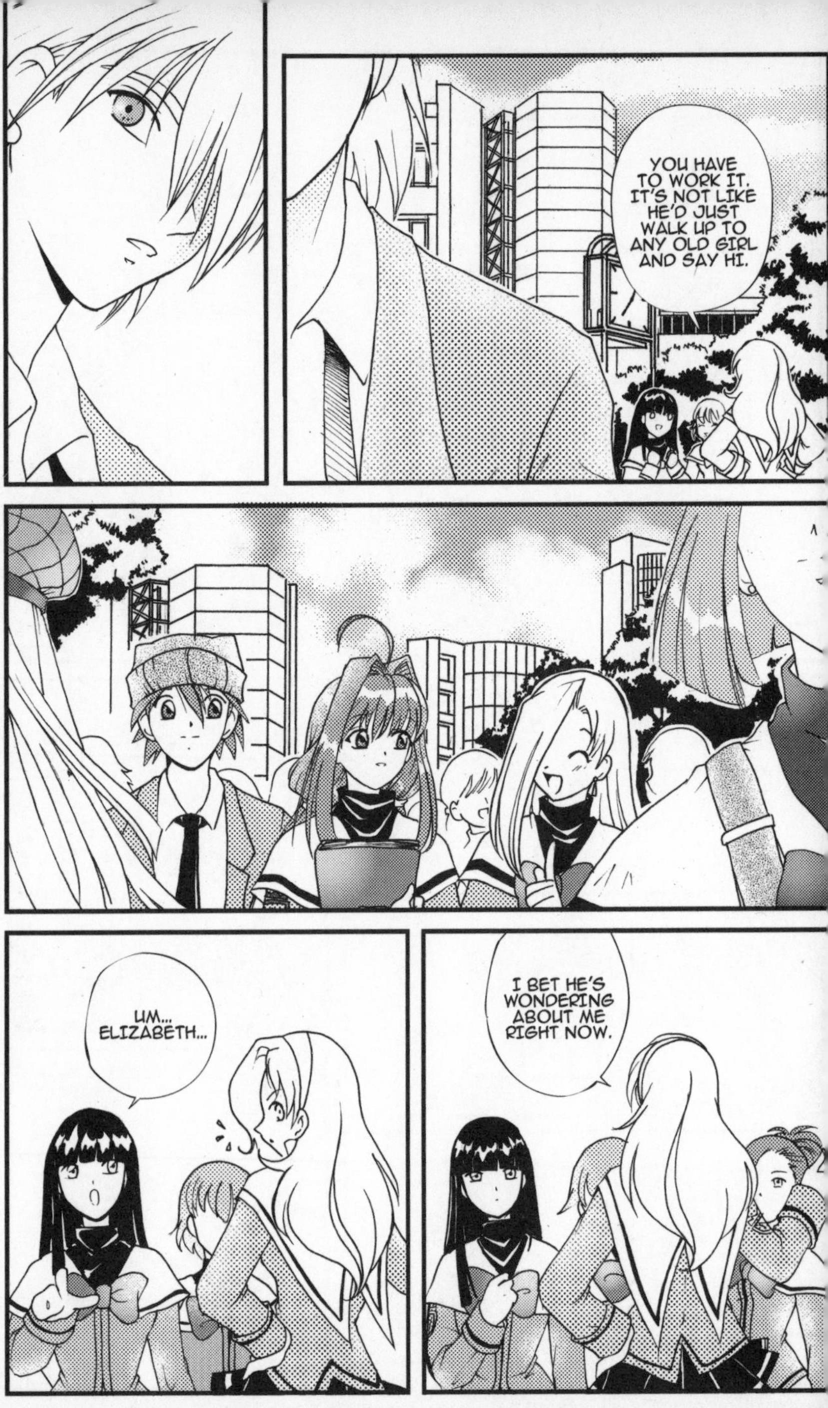
YOU HAVE TO WORK IT. IT'S NOT LIKE HE'D JUST WALK UP TO ANY OLD GIRL AND SAY HI.
I BET HE'S WONDERING ABOUT ME RIGHT NOW.
UM... ELIZABETH...

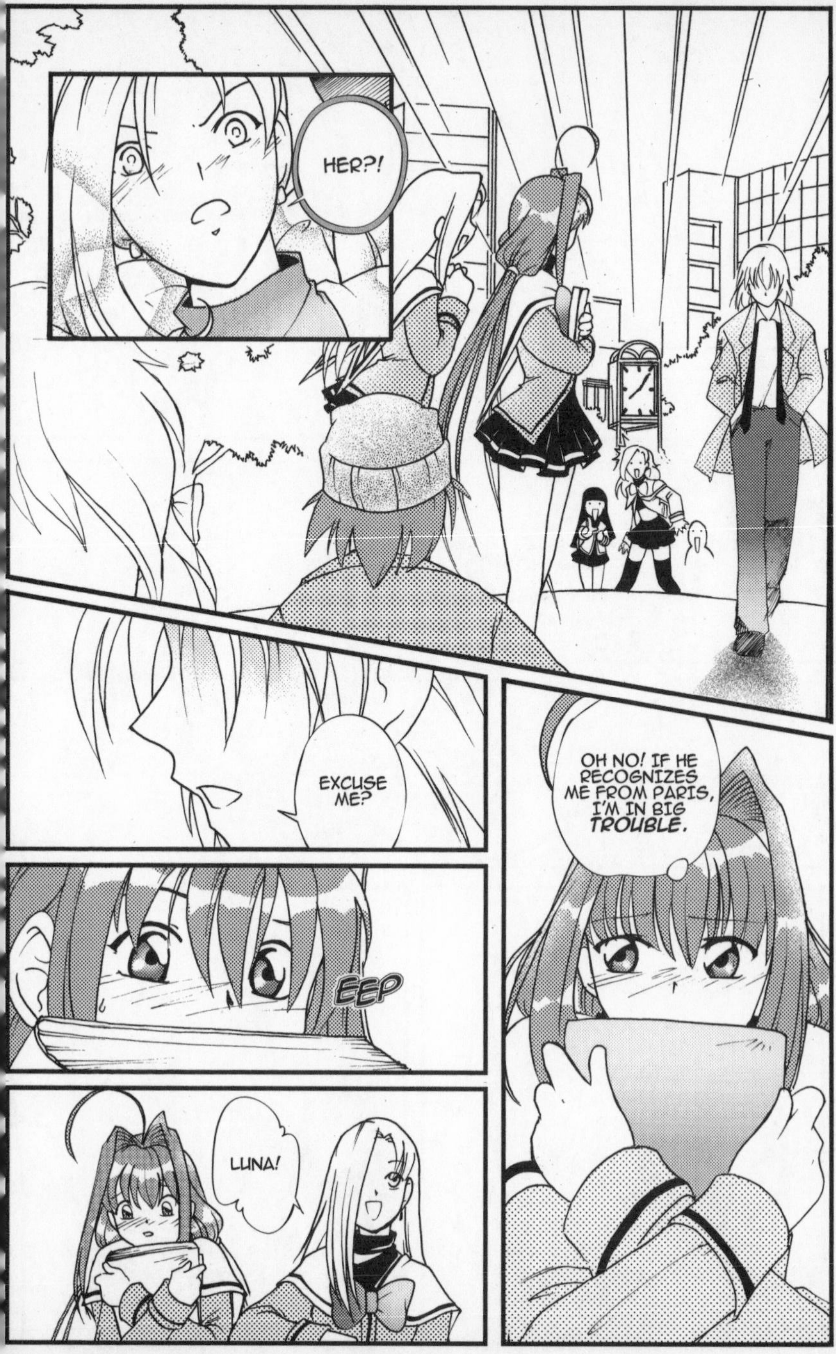
HER?!
OH NO! IF HE RECOGNIZES ME FROM PARIS, I'M IN BIG TROUBLE.
EXCUSE ME?
EEP
LUNA!

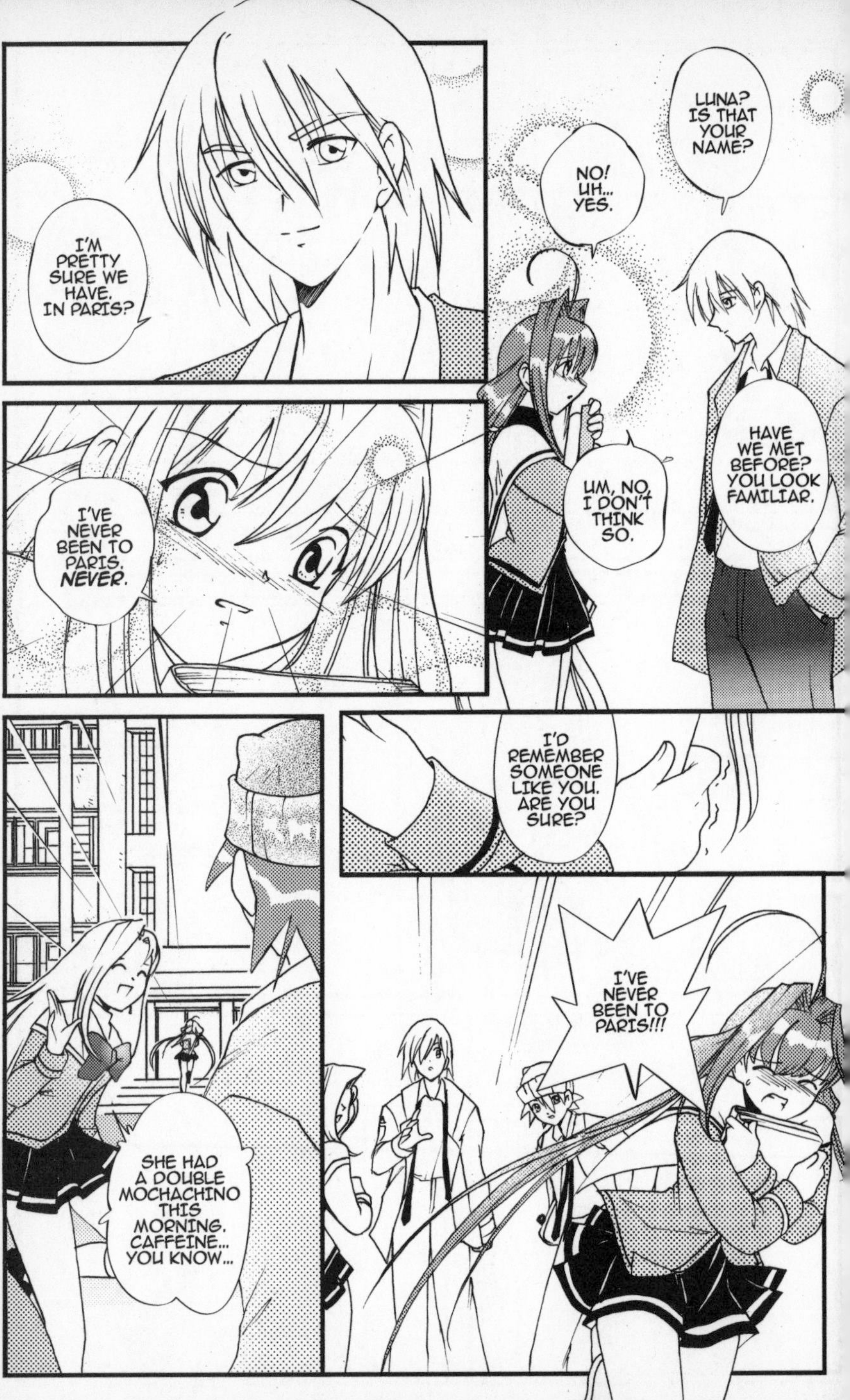
LUNA? IS THAT YOUR NAME?
NO! UH... YES.
HAVE WE MET BEFORE? YOU LOOK FAMILIAR.
UM, NO, I DON'T THINK SO.
I'M PRETTY SURE WE HAVE. IN PARIS?
I'VE NEVER BEEN TO PARIS. NEVER.
I'D REMEMBER SOMEONE LIKE YOU. ARE YOU SURE?
I'VE NEVER BEEN TO PARIS!!!
SHE HAD A DOUBLE MOCHACHINO THIS MORNING. CAFFEINE... YOU KNOW...

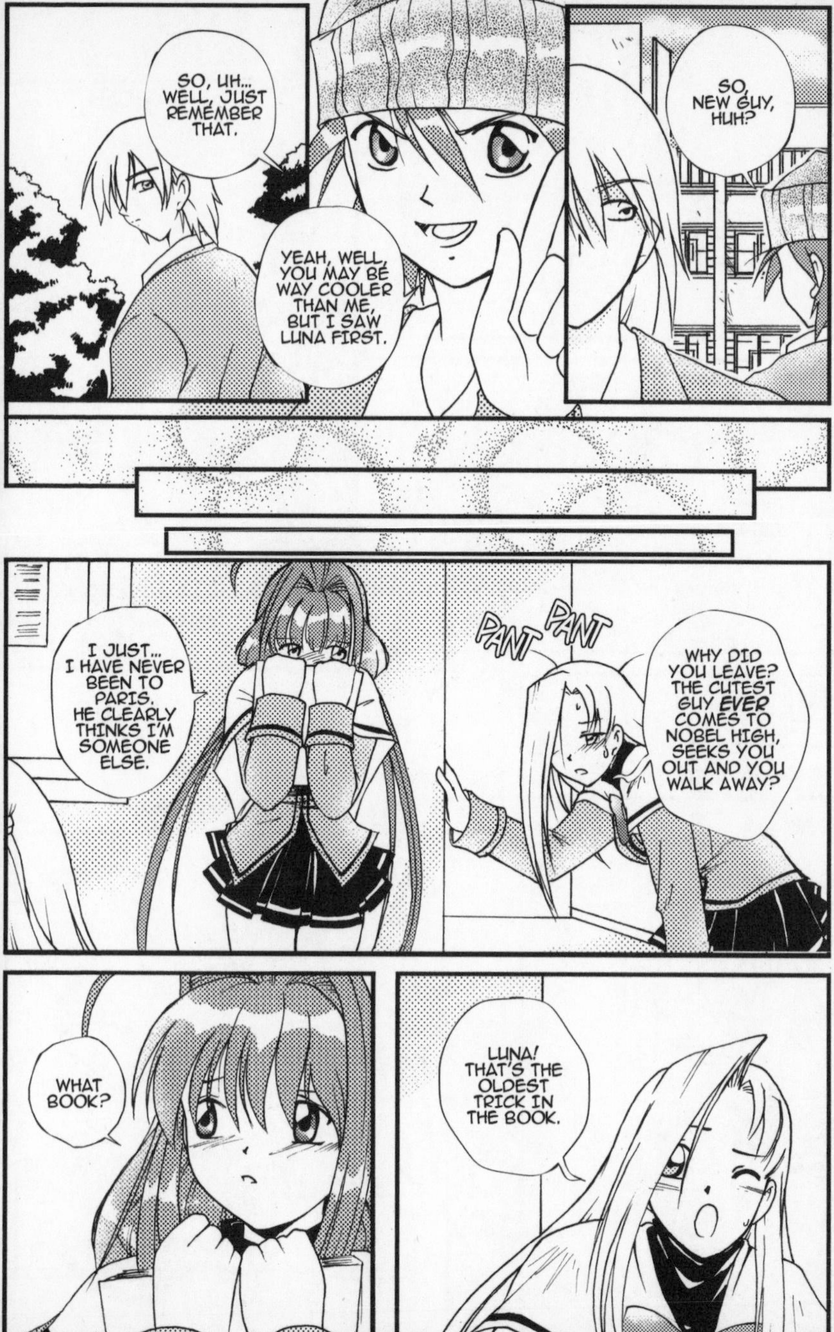
SO, NEW GUY, HUH?
YEAH, WELL, YOU MAY BE WAY COOLER THAN ME, BUT I SAW LUNA FIRST.
SO, UH... WELL, JUST REMEMBER THAT.
PANT PANT
WHY DID YOU LEAVE? THE CUTEST GUY ***EVER*** COMES TO NOBEL HIGH, SEEKS YOU OUT AND YOU WALK AWAY?
I JUST... I HAVE NEVER BEEN TO PARIS. HE CLEARLY THINKS I'M SOMEONE ELSE.
LUNA! THAT'S THE OLDEST TRICK IN THE BOOK.
WHAT BOOK?

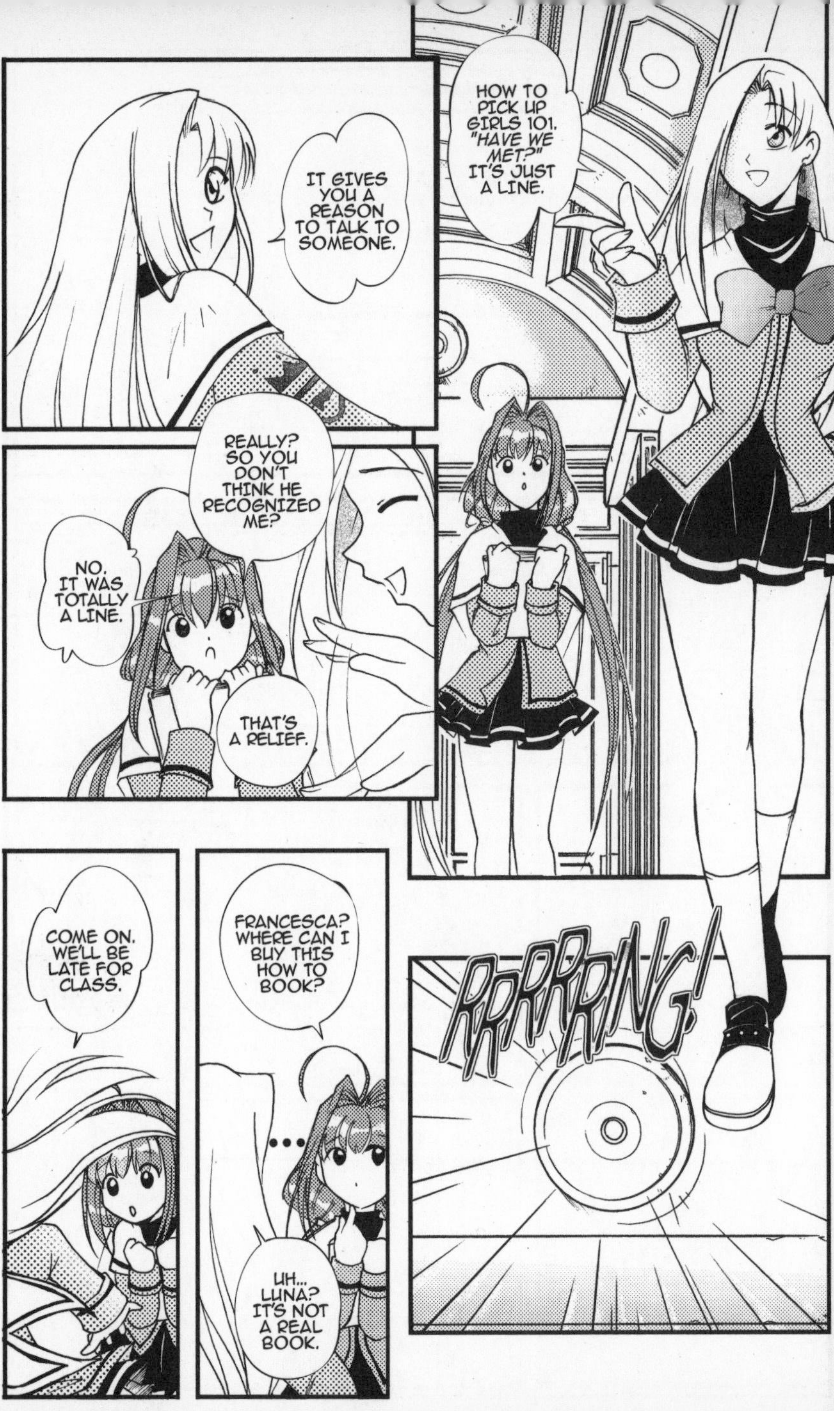
HOW TO PICK UP GIRLS 101. "HAVE WE MET?" IT'S JUST A LINE.
IT GIVES YOU A REASON TO TALK TO SOMEONE.
REALLY? SO YOU DON'T THINK HE RECOGNIZED ME?
NO. IT WAS TOTALLY A LINE.
THAT'S A RELIEF.
RRRRRRING!
FRANCESCA? WHERE CAN I BUY THIS HOW TO BOOK?
...
UH... LUNA? IT'S NOT A REAL BOOK.
COME ON. WE'LL BE LATE FOR CLASS.

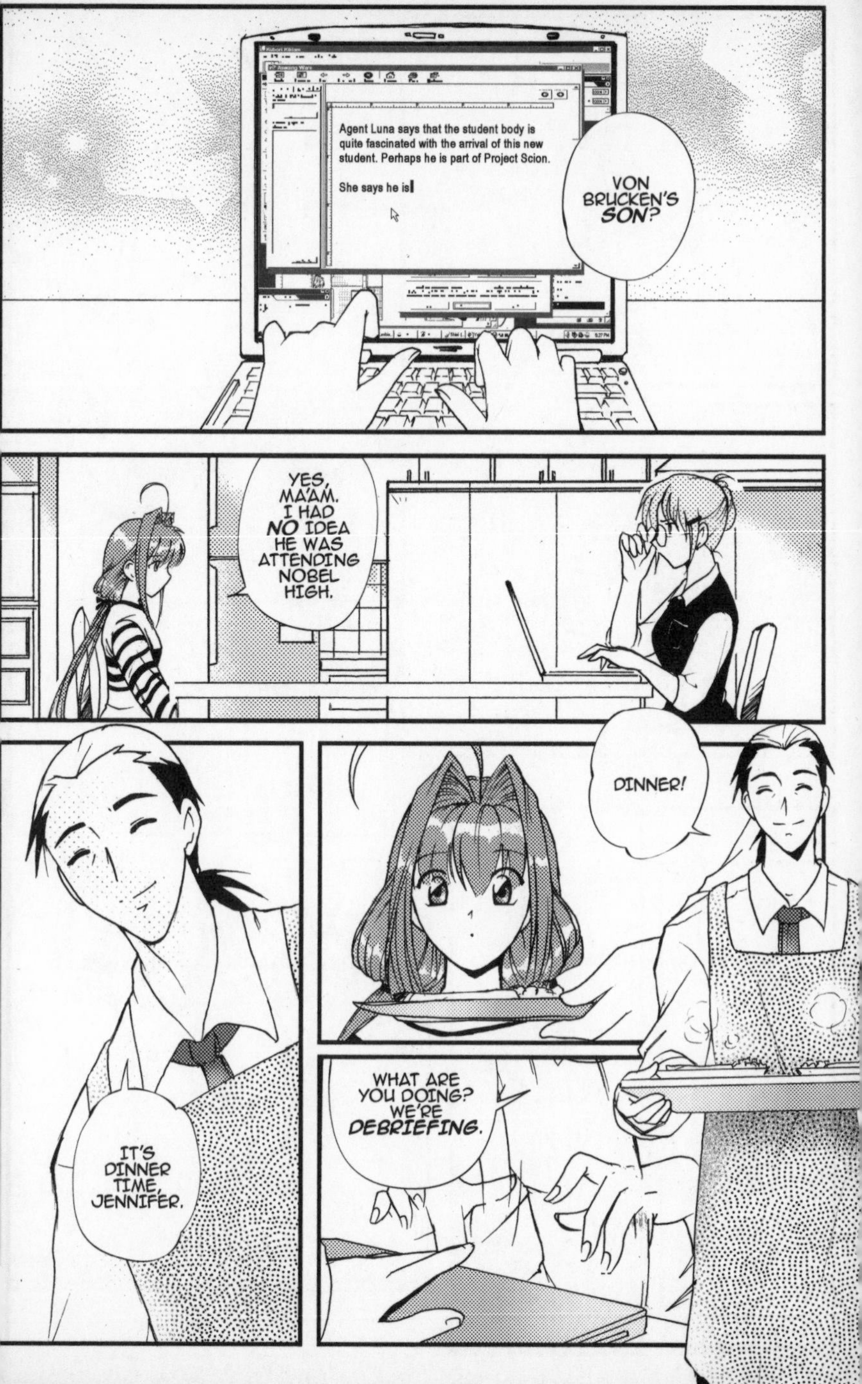
Agent Luna says that the student body is quite fascinated with the arrival of this new student. Perhaps he is part of Project Scion.
She says he is
VON BRUCKEN'S SON?
YES, MA'AM. I HAD NO IDEA HE WAS ATTENDING NOBEL HIGH.
DINNER!
WHAT ARE YOU DOING? WE'RE DEBRIEFING.
IT'S DINNER TIME, JENNIFER.

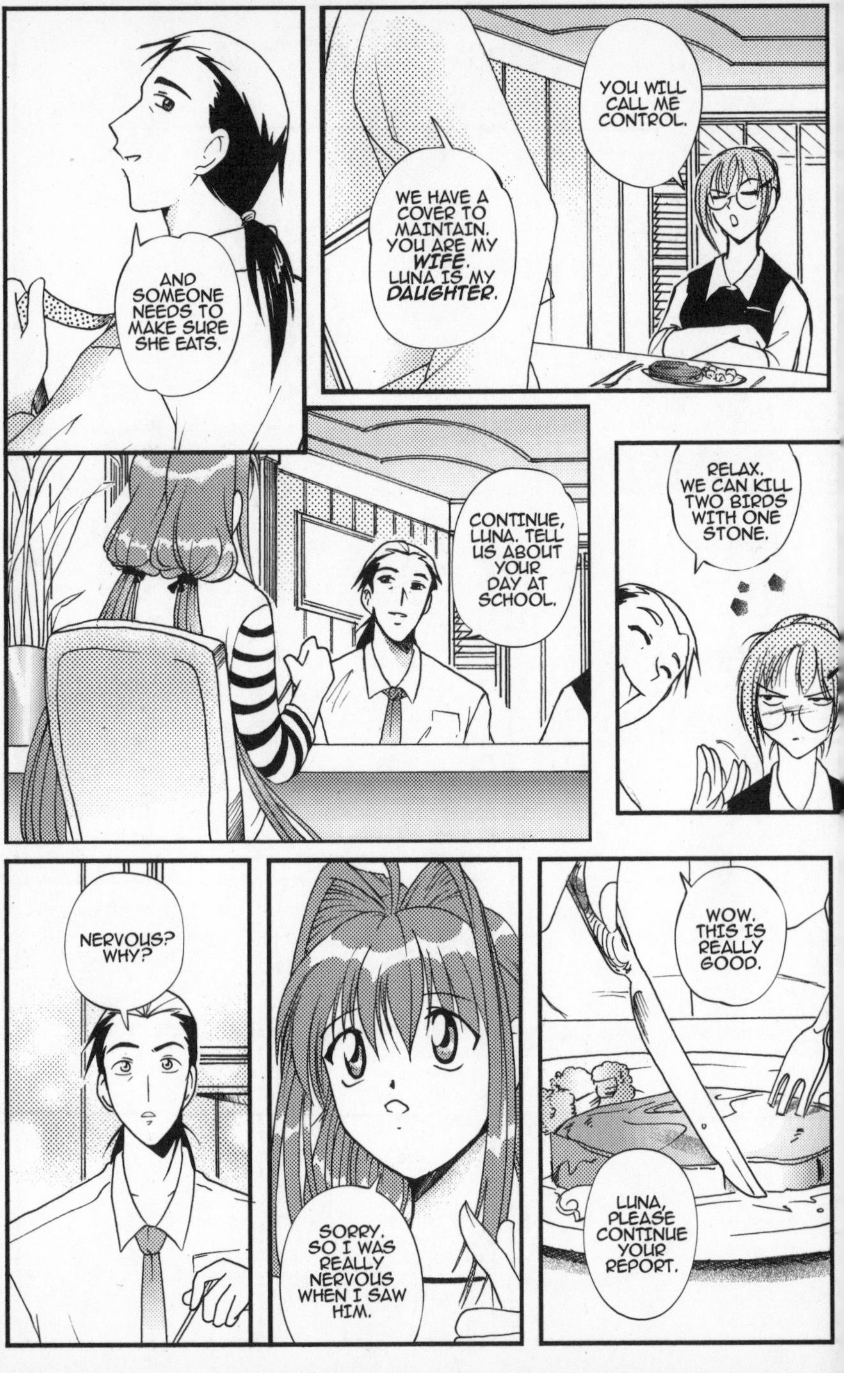
YOU WILL CALL ME CONTROL.
WE HAVE A COVER TO MAINTAIN. YOU ARE MY ***WIFE***. LUNA IS MY ***DAUGHTER***.
AND SOMEONE NEEDS TO MAKE SURE SHE EATS.
RELAX. WE CAN KILL TWO BIRDS WITH ONE STONE.
CONTINUE, LUNA. TELL US ABOUT YOUR DAY AT SCHOOL.
WOW. THIS IS REALLY GOOD.
LUNA, PLEASE CONTINUE YOUR REPORT.
SORRY. SO I WAS REALLY NERVOUS WHEN I SAW HIM.
NERVOUS? WHY?

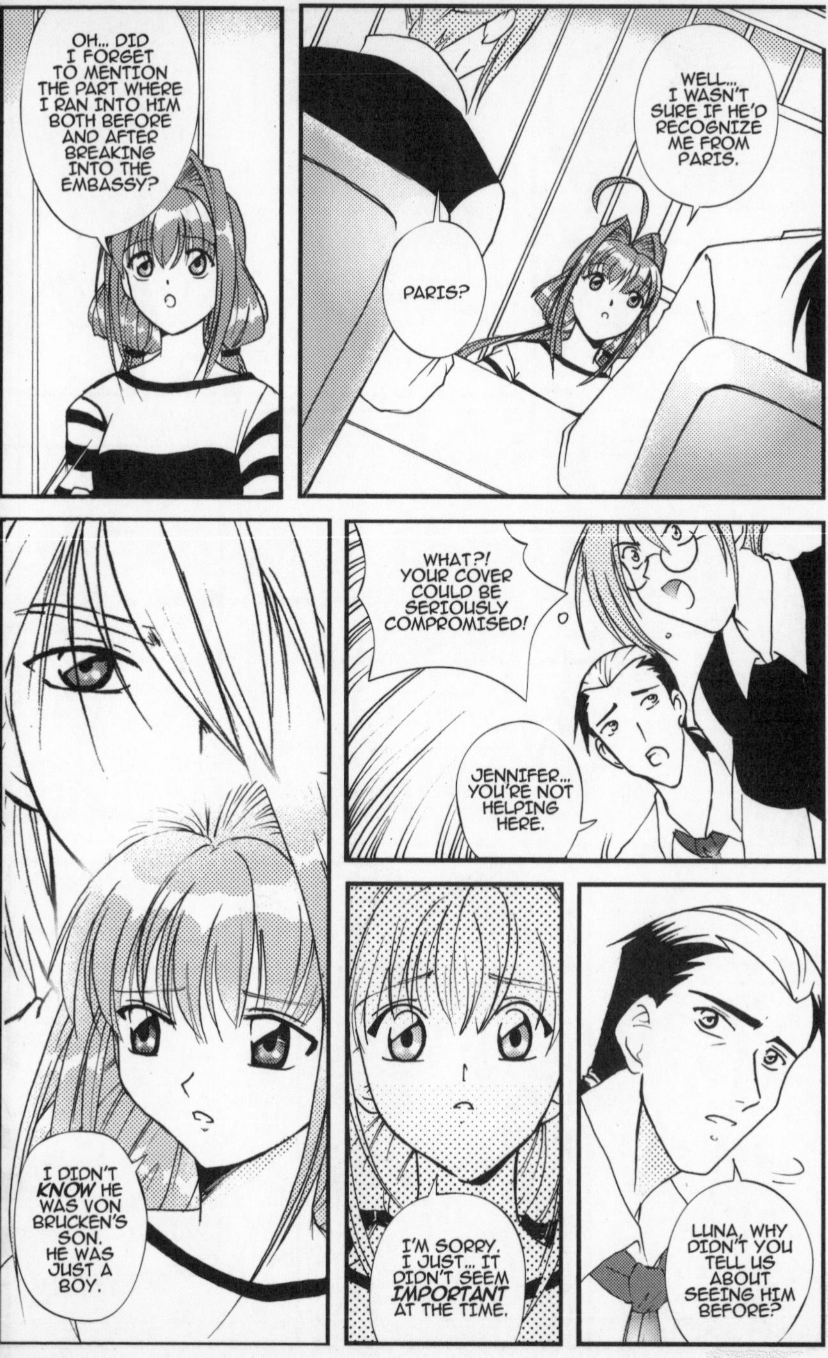
WELL... I WASN'T SURE IF HE'D RECOGNIZE ME FROM PARIS.
PARIS?
OH... DID I FORGET TO MENTION THE PART WHERE I RAN INTO HIM BOTH BEFORE AND AFTER BREAKING INTO THE EMBASSY?
WHAT?! YOUR COVER COULD BE SERIOUSLY COMPROMISED!
JENNIFER... YOU'RE NOT HELPING HERE.
LUNA, WHY DIDN'T YOU TELL US ABOUT SEEING HIM BEFORE?
I'M SORRY. I JUST... IT DIDN'T SEEM IMPORTANT AT THE TIME.
I DIDN'T KNOW HE WAS VON BRUCKEN'S SON. HE WAS JUST A BOY.

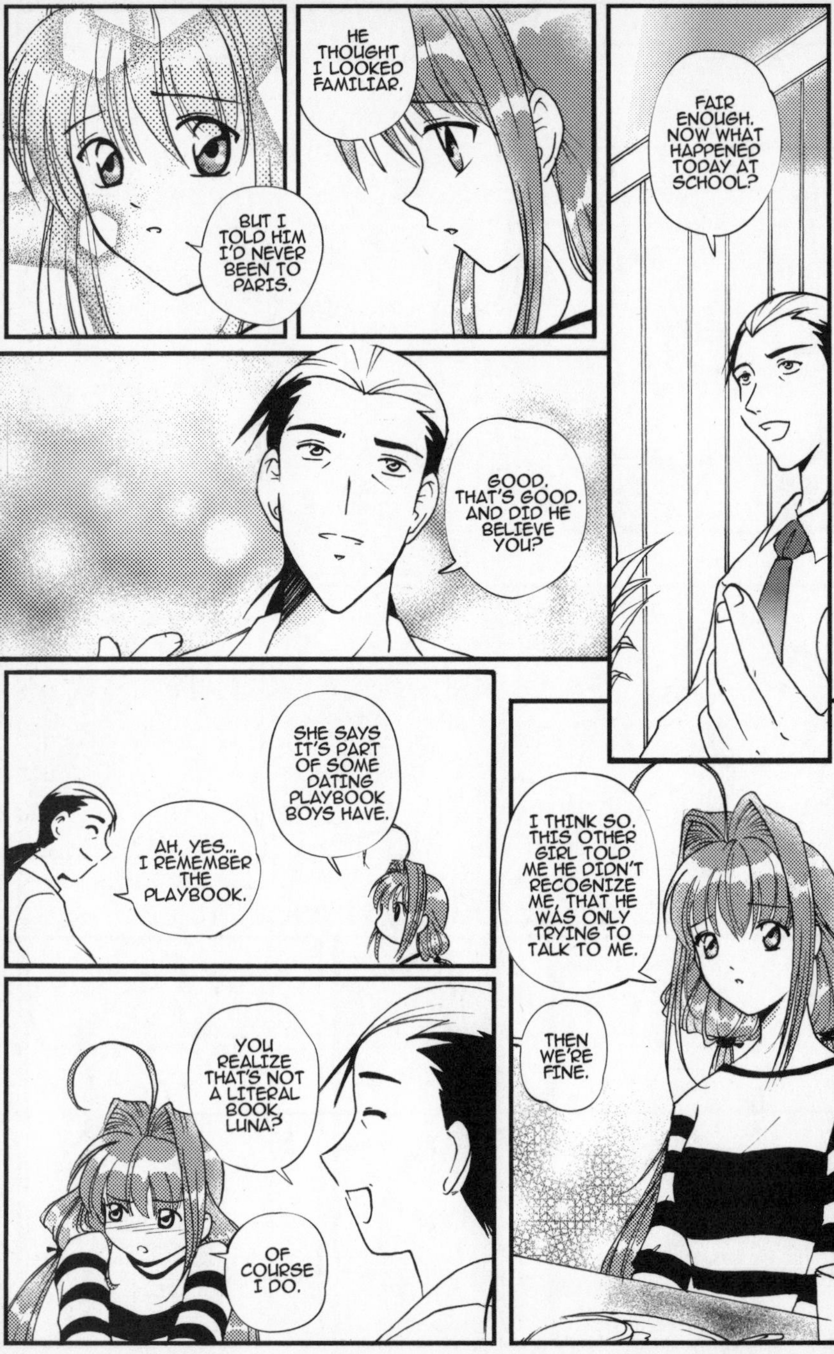
FAIR ENOUGH. NOW WHAT HAPPENED TODAY AT SCHOOL?
HE THOUGHT I LOOKED FAMILIAR.
BUT I TOLD HIM I'D NEVER BEEN TO PARIS.
GOOD. THAT'S GOOD. AND DID HE BELIEVE YOU?
I THINK SO. THIS OTHER GIRL TOLD ME HE DIDN'T RECOGNIZE ME, THAT HE WAS ONLY TRYING TO TALK TO ME.
THEN WE'RE FINE.
SHE SAYS IT'S PART OF SOME DATING PLAYBOOK BOYS HAVE.
AH, YES... I REMEMBER THE PLAYBOOK.
YOU REALIZE THAT'S NOT A LITERAL BOOK, LUNA?
OF COURSE I DO.

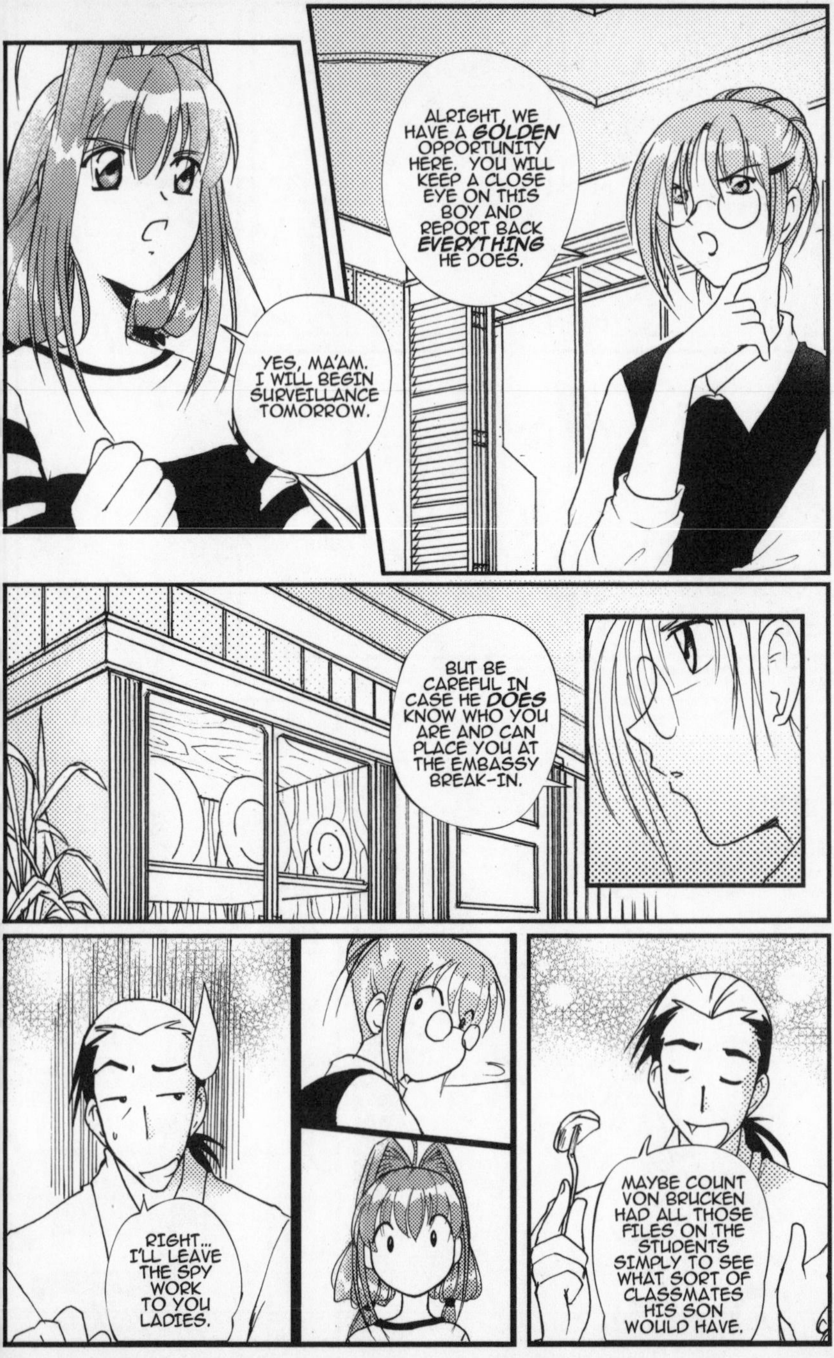
ALRIGHT, WE HAVE A GOLDEN OPPORTUNITY HERE. YOU WILL KEEP A CLOSE EYE ON THIS BOY AND REPORT BACK EVERYTHING HE DOES.
YES, MA'AM. I WILL BEGIN SURVEILLANCE TOMORROW.
BUT BE CAREFUL IN CASE HE DOES KNOW WHO YOU ARE AND CAN PLACE YOU AT THE EMBASSY BREAK-IN.
MAYBE COUNT VON BRUCKEN HAD ALL THOSE FILES ON THE STUDENTS SIMPLY TO SEE WHAT SORT OF CLASSMATES HIS SON WOULD HAVE.
RIGHT... I'LL LEAVE THE SPY WORK TO YOU LADIES.

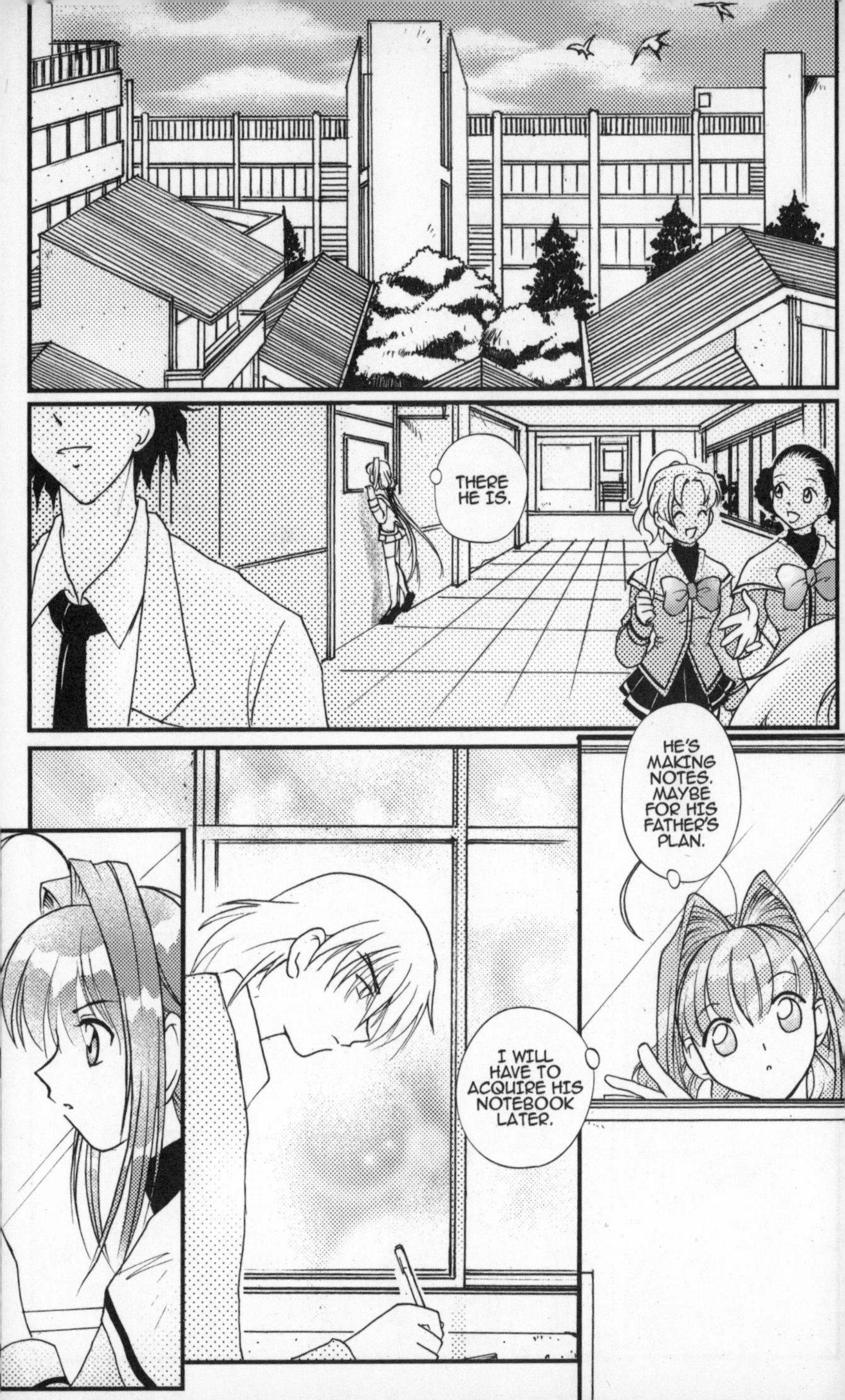
THERE HE IS.
HE'S MAKING NOTES. MAYBE FOR HIS FATHER'S PLAN.
I WILL HAVE TO ACQUIRE HIS NOTEBOOK LATER.

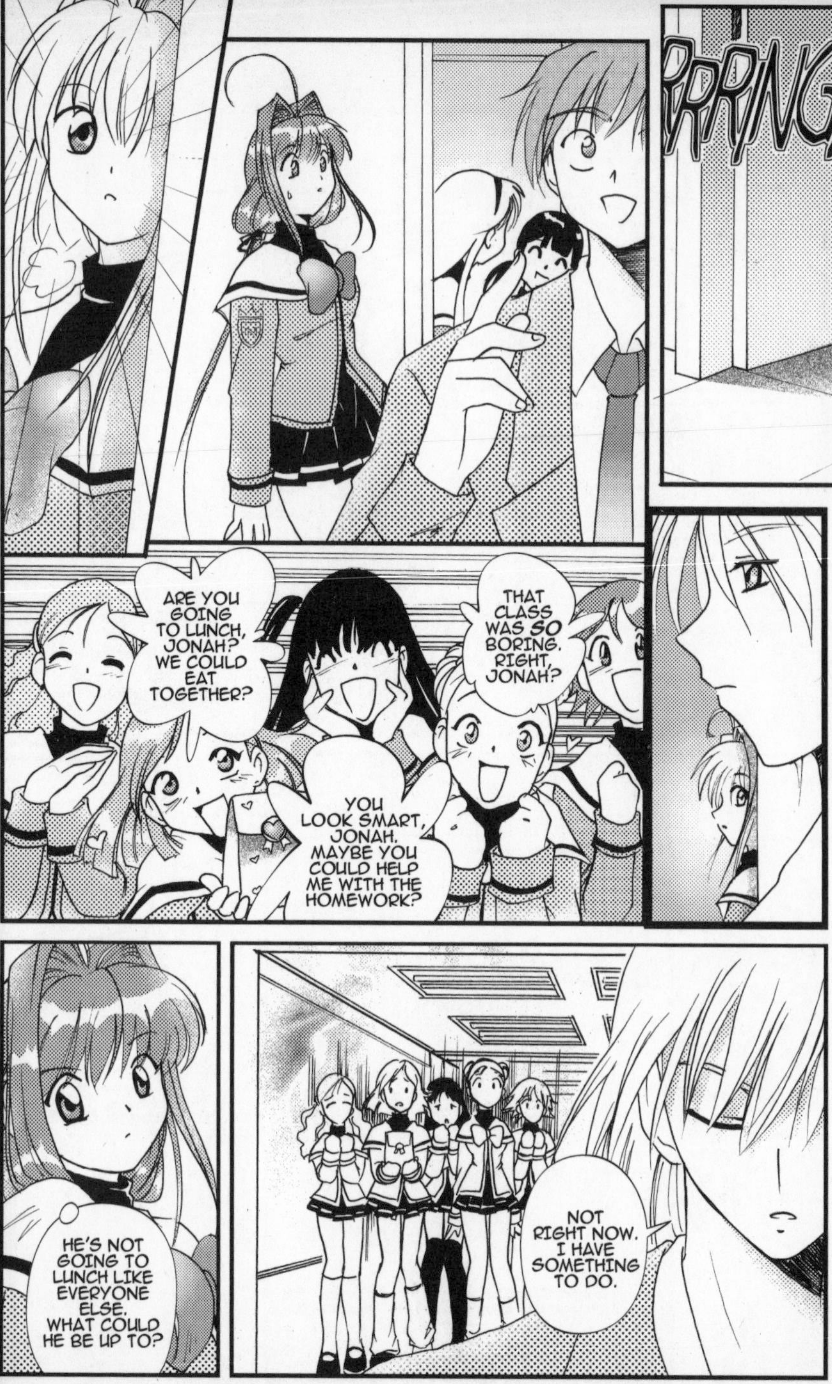
RRRING!
THAT CLASS WAS SO BORING, RIGHT, JONAH?
YOU LOOK SMART, JONAH. MAYBE YOU COULD HELP ME WITH THE HOMEWORK?
ARE YOU GOING TO LUNCH, JONAH? WE COULD EAT TOGETHER?
NOT RIGHT NOW. I HAVE SOMETHING TO DO.
HE'S NOT GOING TO LUNCH LIKE EVERYONE ELSE. WHAT COULD HE BE UP TO?

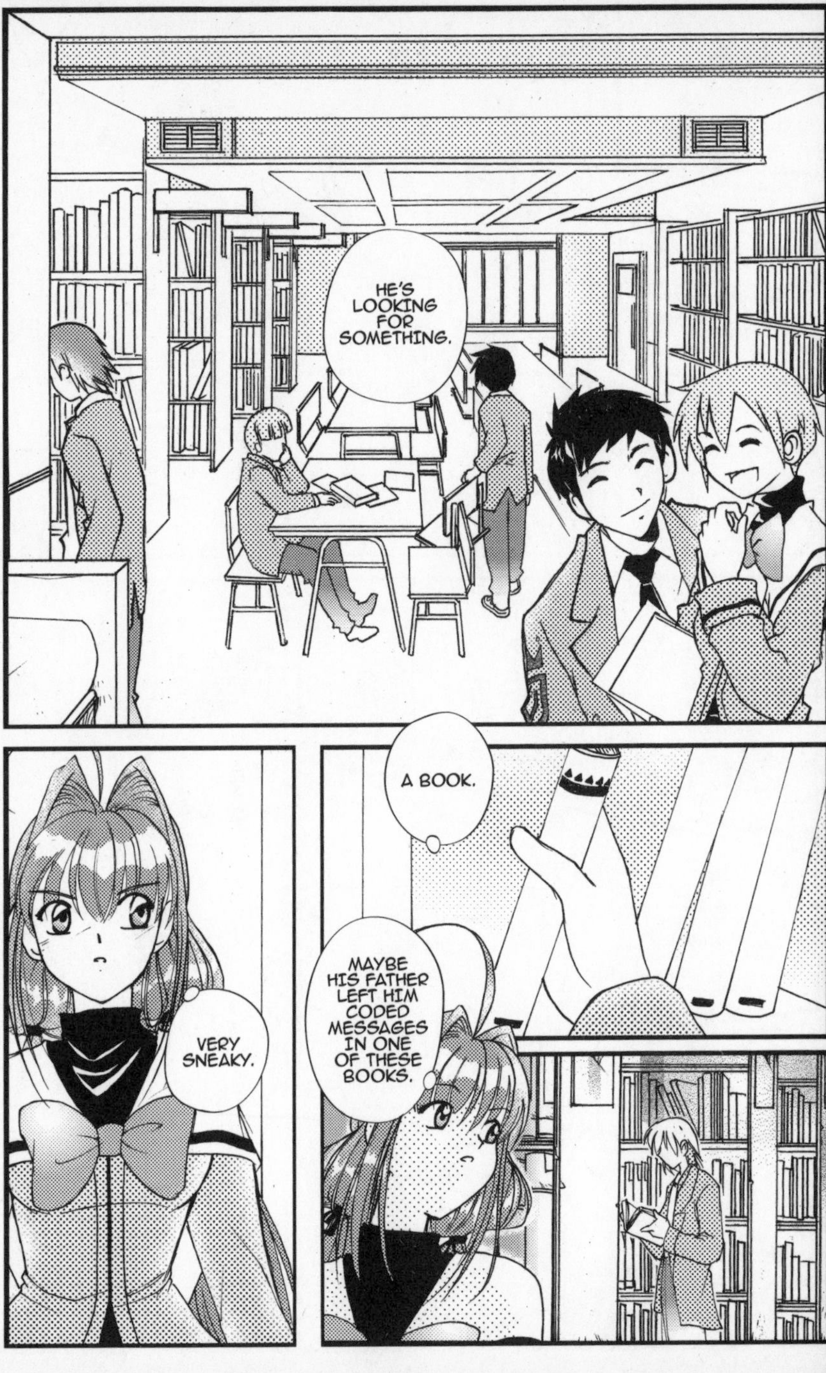
HE'S LOOKING FOR SOMETHING.
A BOOK.
MAYBE HIS FATHER LEFT HIM CODED MESSAGES IN ONE OF THESE BOOKS.
VERY SNEAKY.

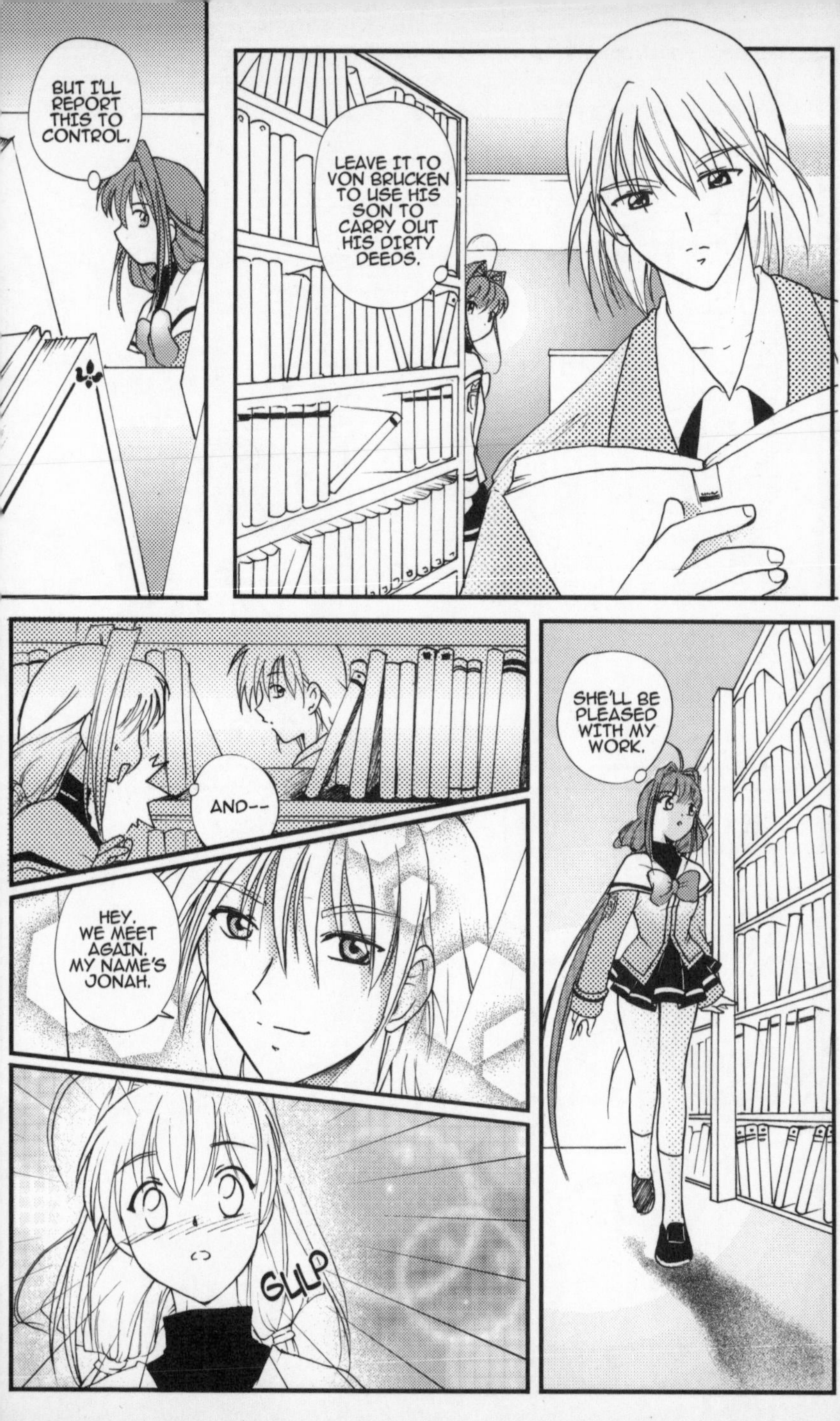
LEAVE IT TO VON BRUCKEN TO USE HIS SON TO CARRY OUT HIS DIRTY DEEDS.
BUT I'LL REPORT THIS TO CONTROL.
SHE'LL BE PLEASED WITH MY WORK.
AND--
HEY. WE MEET AGAIN. MY NAME'S JONAH.
GULP

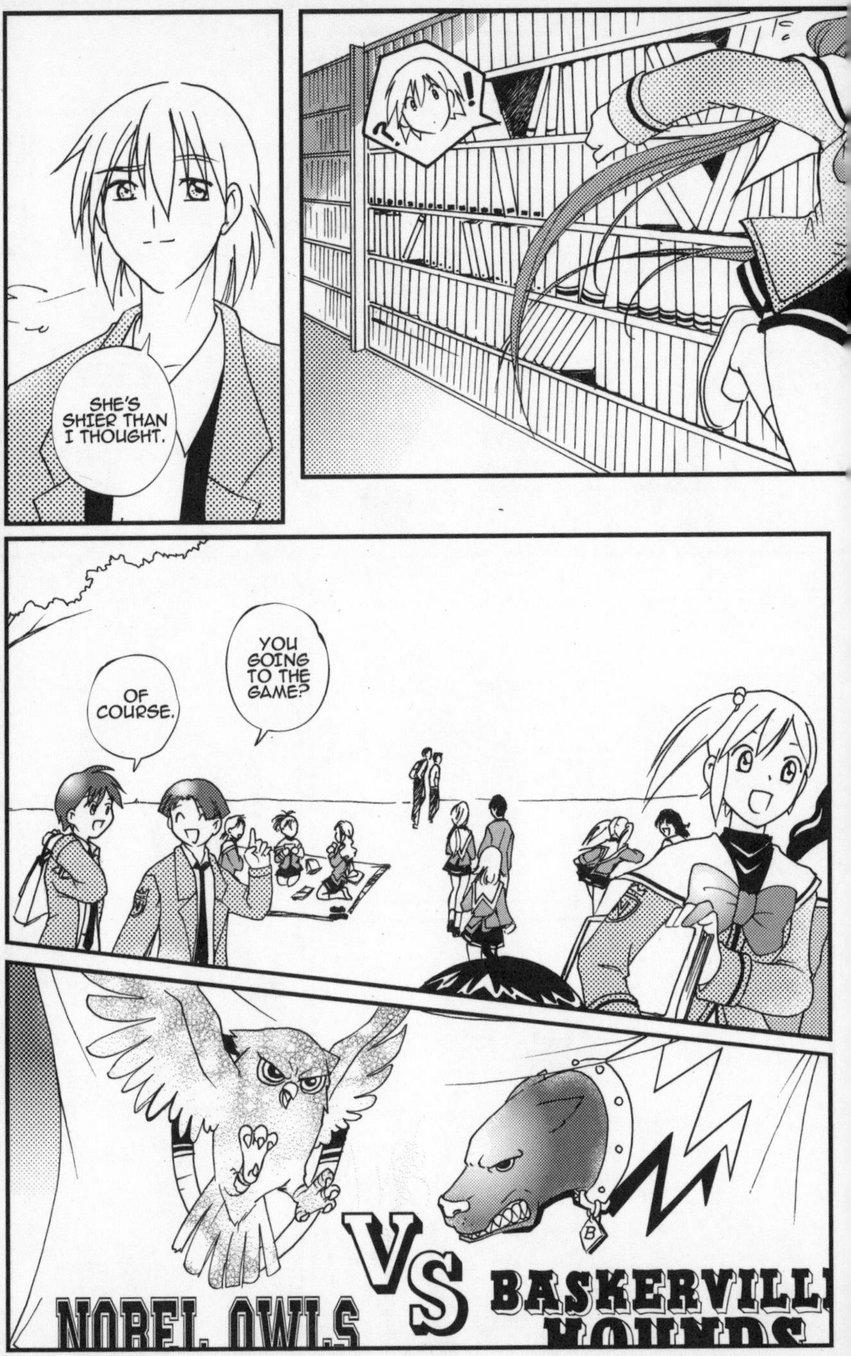
?!
SHE'S SHIER THAN I THOUGHT.
YOU GOING TO THE GAME?
OF COURSE.
NOBEL OWLS
VS
BASKERVILL
HOUNDS

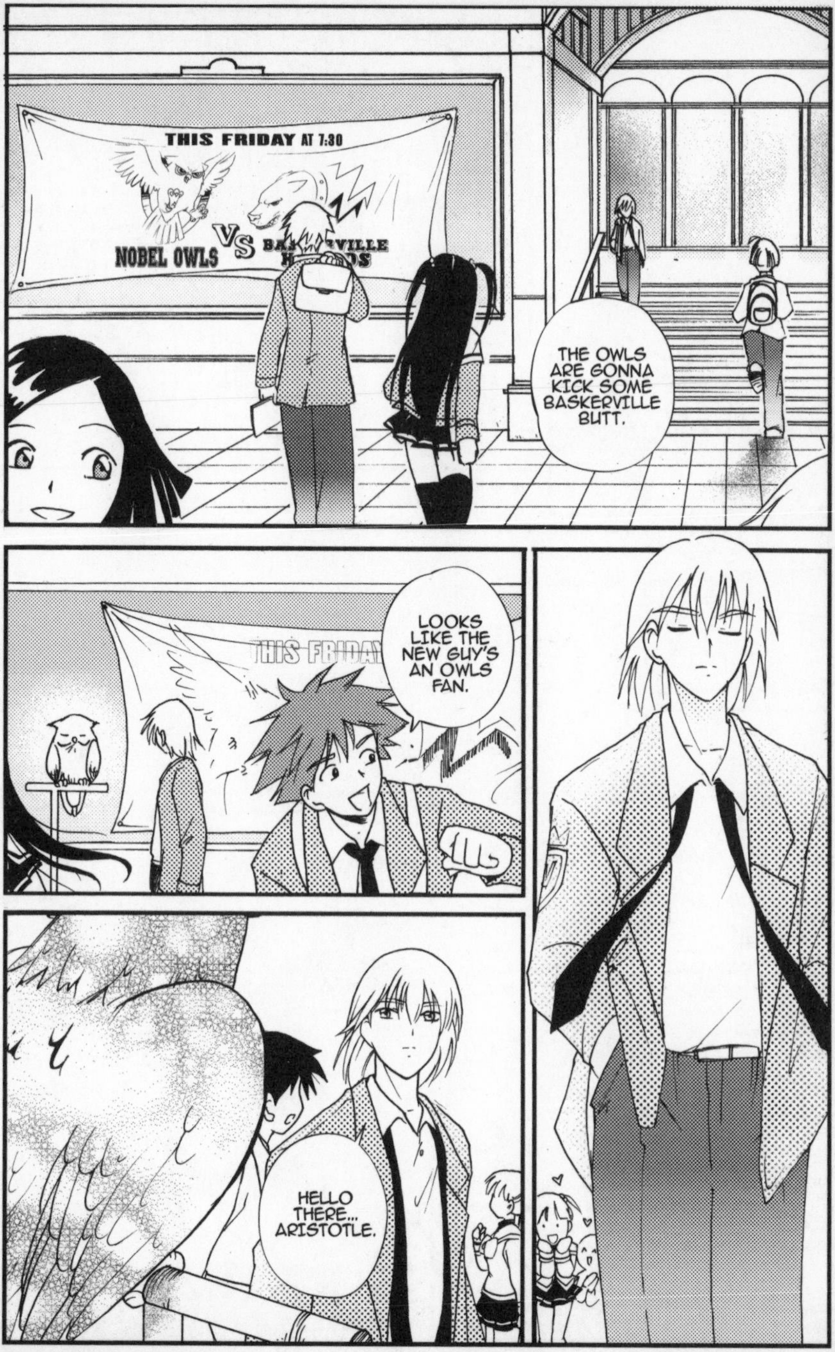
THIS FRIDAY AT 7:30
NOBEL OWLS
VS
THE OWLS ARE GONNA KICK SOME BASKERVILLE BUTT.
LOOKS LIKE THE NEW GUY'S AN OWLS FAN.
HELLO THERE... ARISTOTLE.

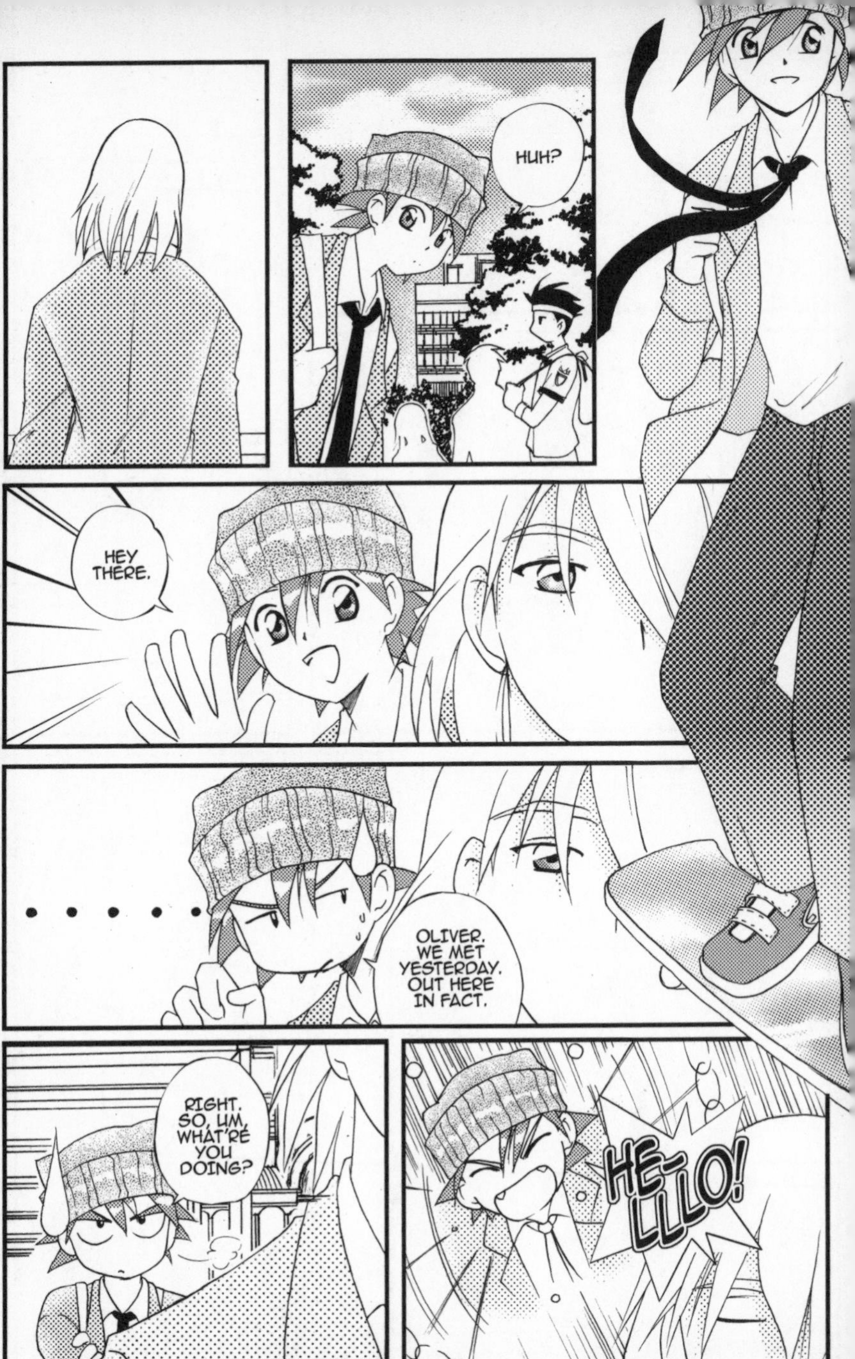
HUH?
HEY THERE.
. . . . .
OLIVER. WE MET YESTERDAY. OUT HERE IN FACT.
HE-LLLO!
RIGHT. SO, UM, WHAT'RE YOU DOING?

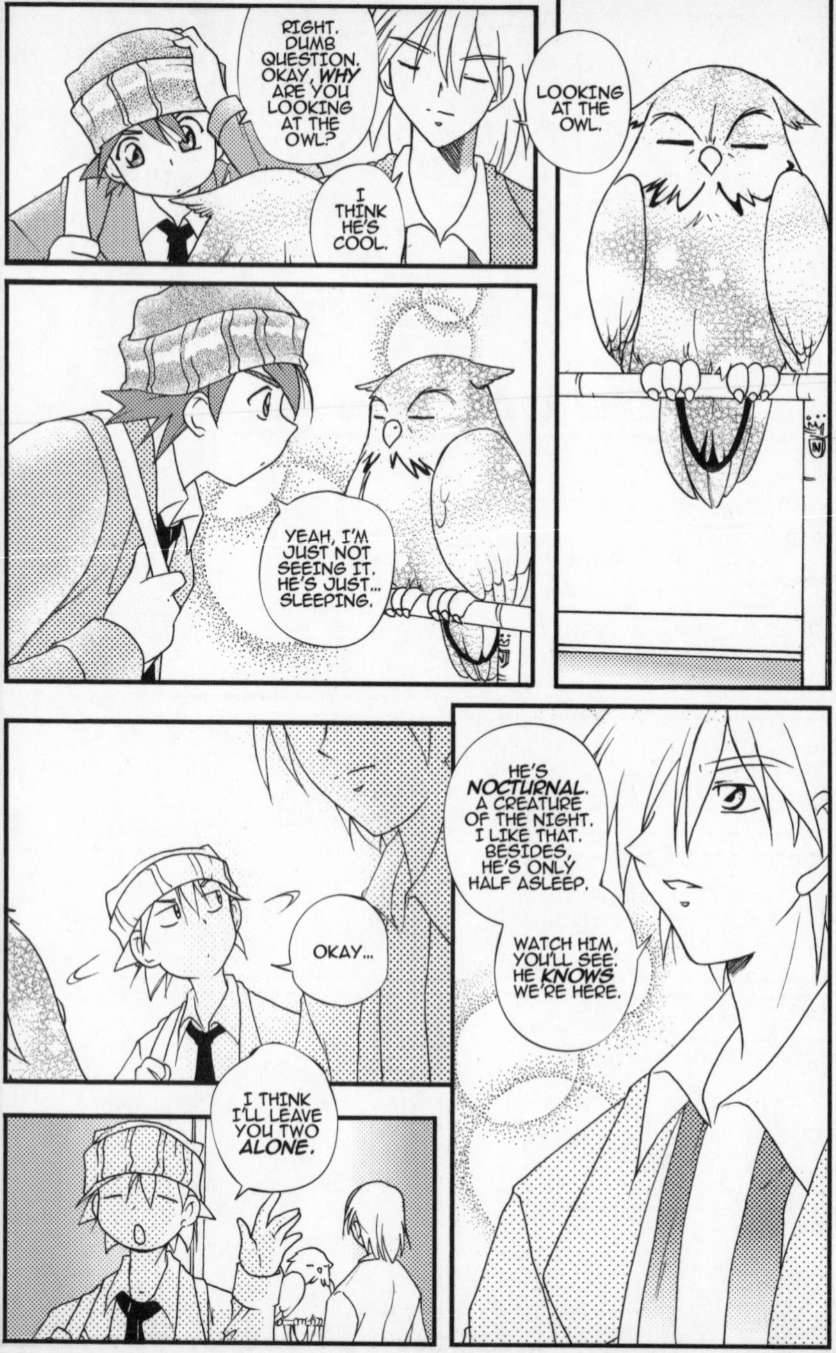
LOOKING AT THE OWL.
RIGHT. DUMB QUESTION. OKAY, *WHY* ARE YOU LOOKING AT THE OWL?
I THINK HE'S COOL.
YEAH, I'M JUST NOT SEEING IT. HE'S JUST... SLEEPING.
HE'S *NOCTURNAL*. A CREATURE OF THE NIGHT. I LIKE THAT. BESIDES, HE'S ONLY HALF ASLEEP.
WATCH HIM, YOU'LL SEE. HE *KNOWS* WE'RE HERE.
OKAY...
I THINK I'LL LEAVE YOU TWO *ALONE*.

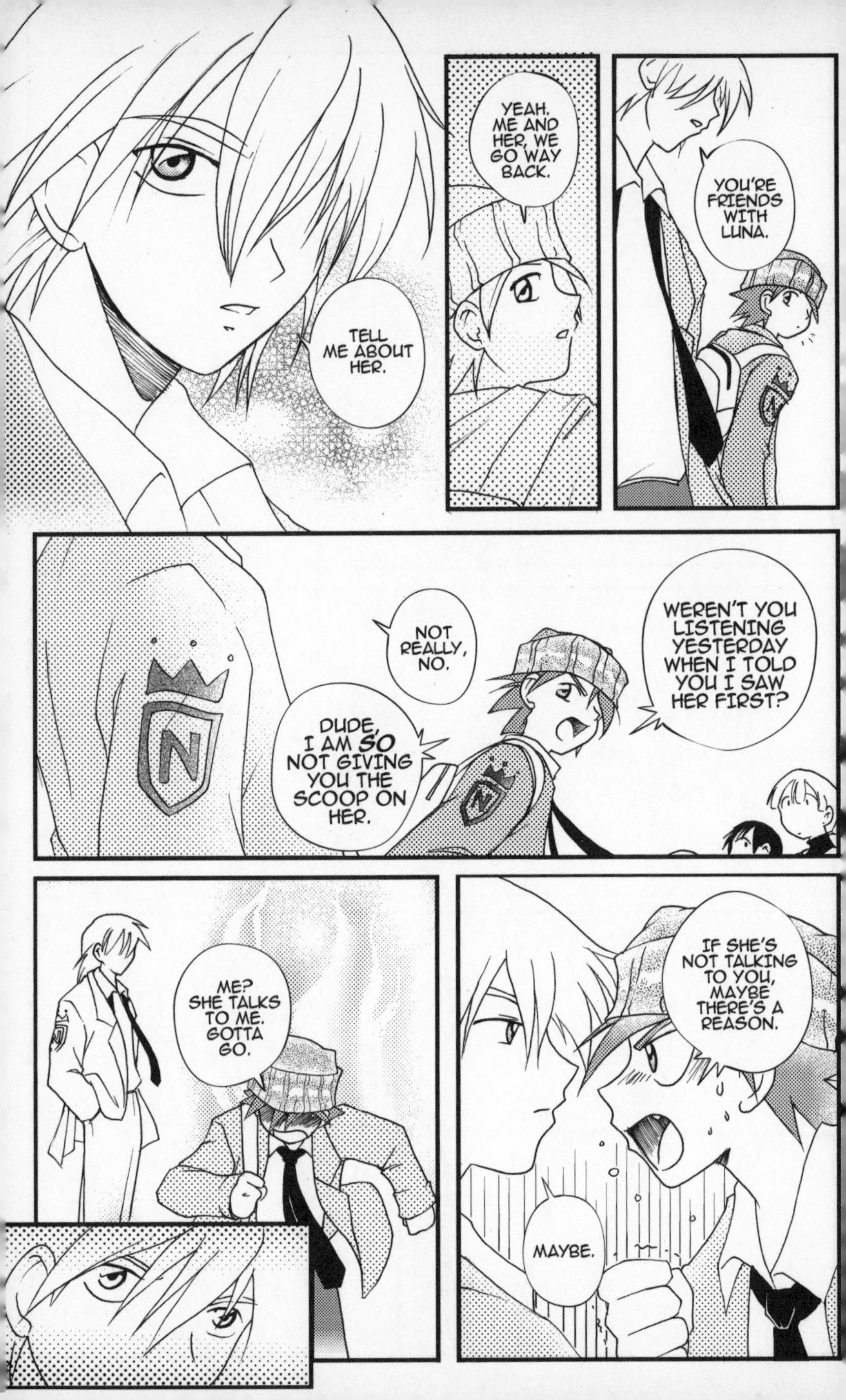
YOU'RE FRIENDS WITH LUNA.
YEAH, ME AND HER, WE GO WAY BACK.
TELL ME ABOUT HER.
WEREN'T YOU LISTENING YESTERDAY WHEN I TOLD YOU I SAW HER FIRST?
NOT REALLY, NO.
DUDE, I AM *SO* NOT GIVING YOU THE SCOOP ON HER.
IF SHE'S NOT TALKING TO YOU, MAYBE THERE'S A REASON.
MAYBE.
ME? SHE TALKS TO ME. GOTTA GO.

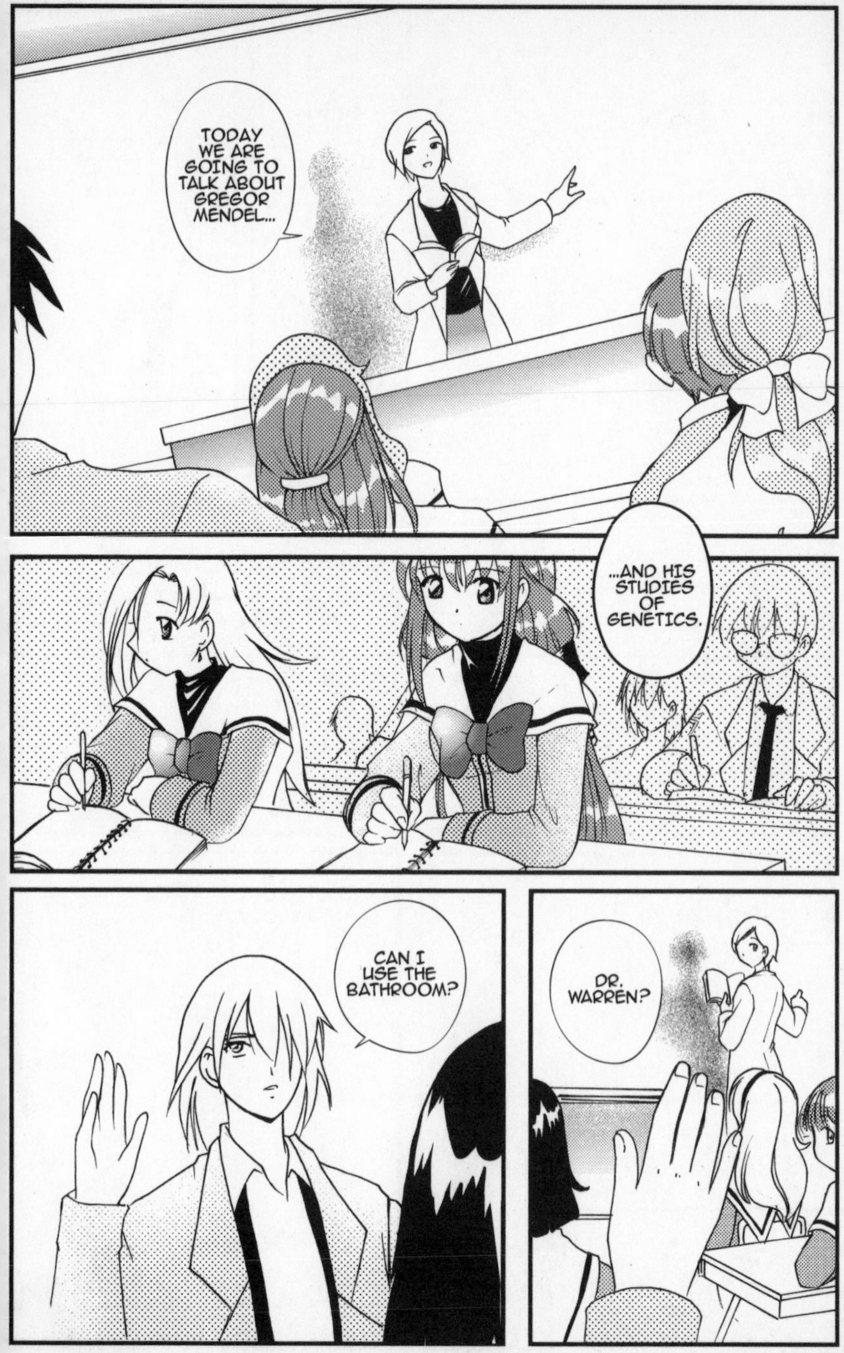
TODAY WE ARE GOING TO TALK ABOUT GREGOR MENDEL...
...AND HIS STUDIES OF GENETICS.
DR. WARREN?
CAN I USE THE BATHROOM?

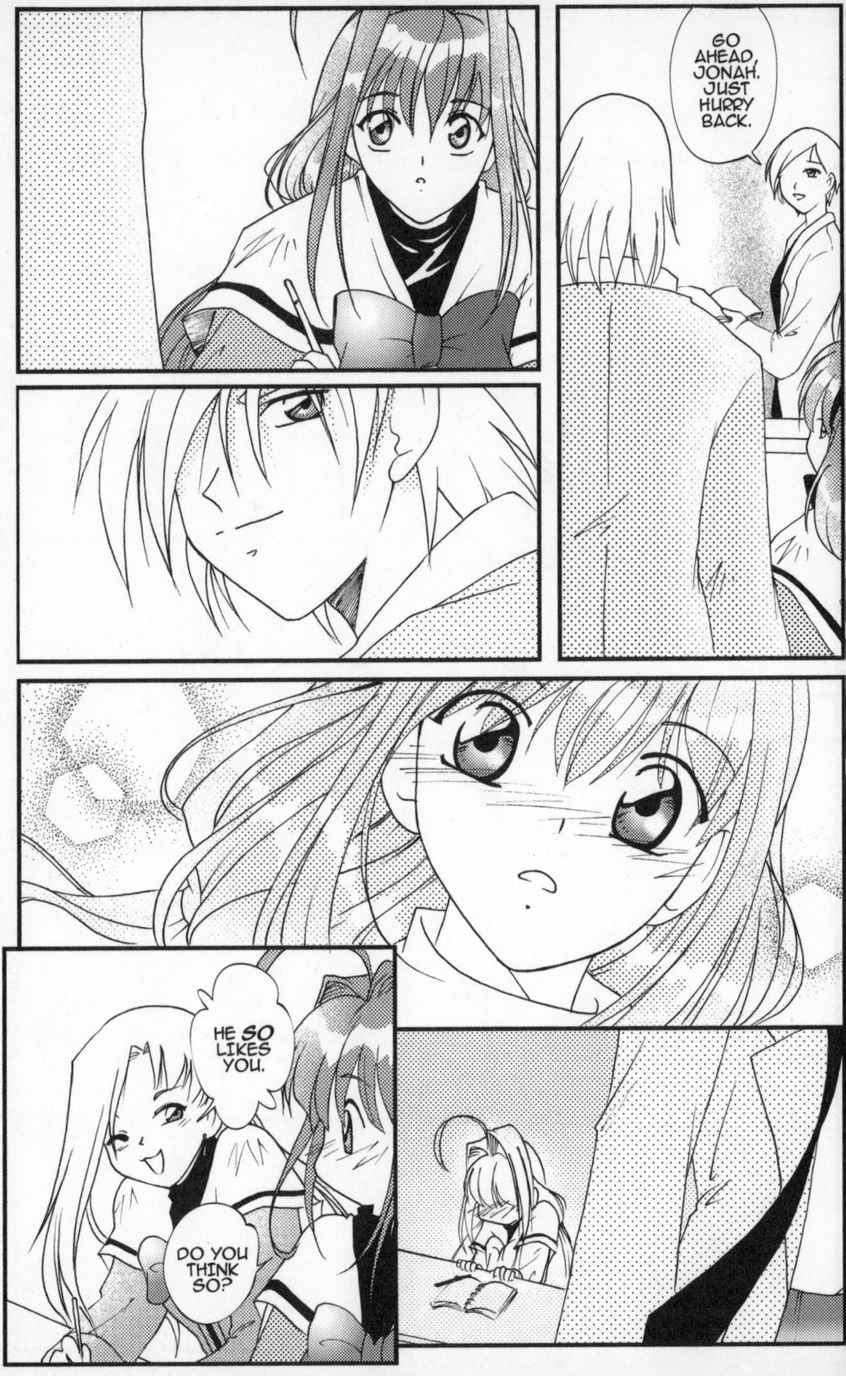
GO AHEAD, JONAH. JUST HURRY BACK.
HE SO LIKES YOU.
DO YOU THINK SO?

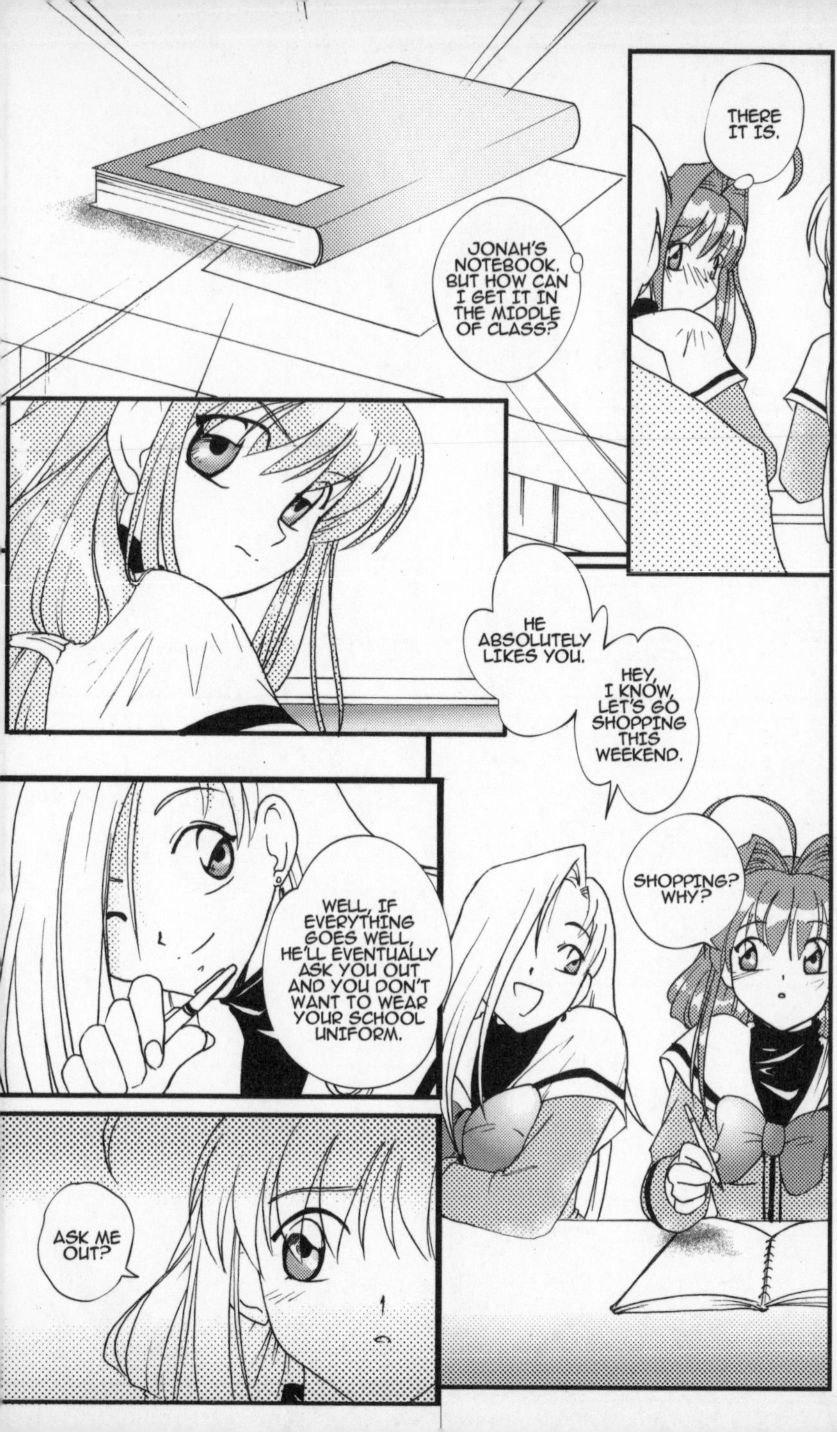
THERE IT IS.
JONAH'S NOTEBOOK. BUT HOW CAN I GET IT IN THE MIDDLE OF CLASS?
HE ABSOLUTELY LIKES YOU.
HEY, I KNOW, LET'S GO SHOPPING THIS WEEKEND.
SHOPPING? WHY?
WELL, IF EVERYTHING GOES WELL, HE'LL EVENTUALLY ASK YOU OUT AND YOU DON'T WANT TO WEAR YOUR SCHOOL UNIFORM.
ASK ME OUT?

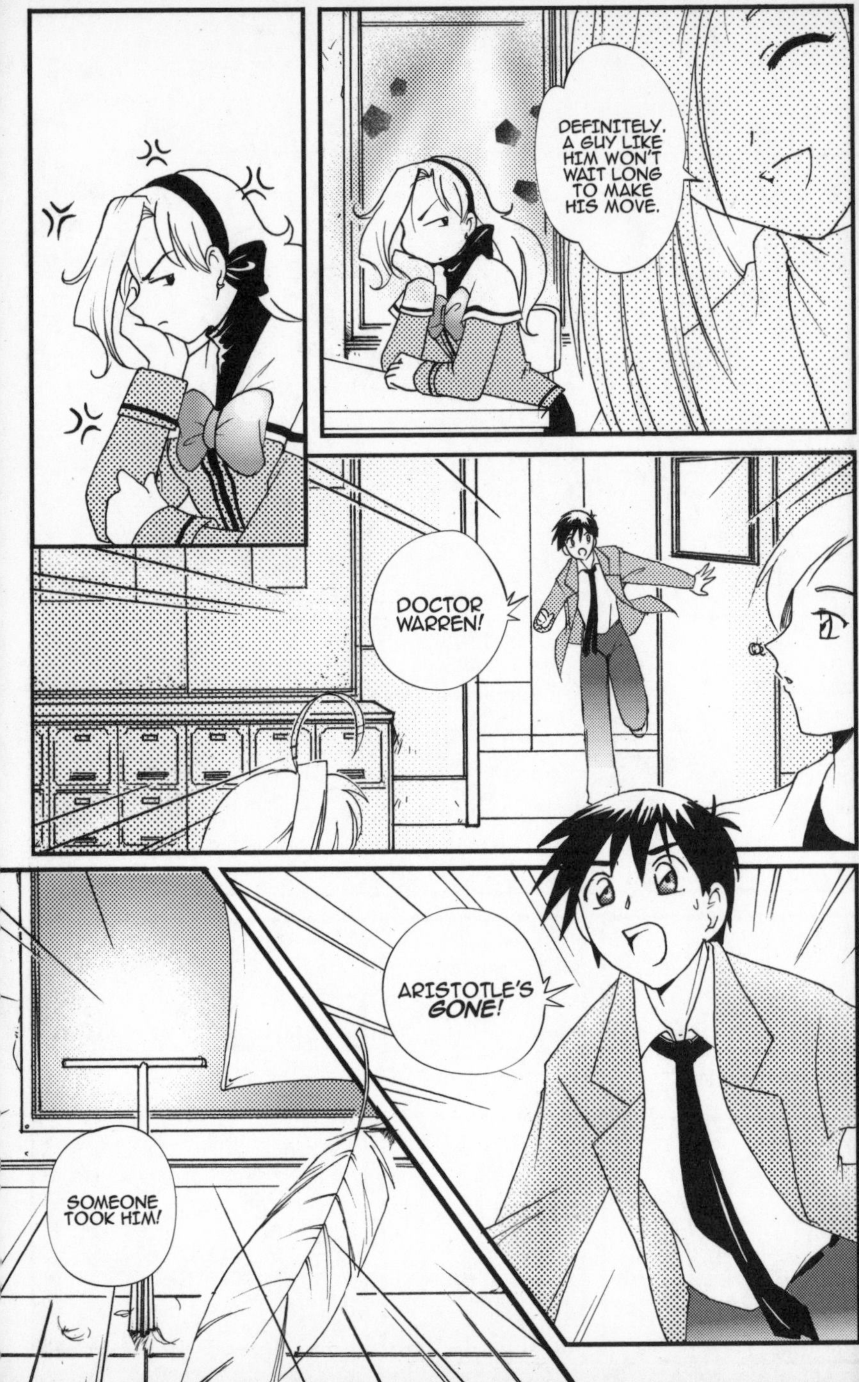
DEFINITELY. A GUY LIKE HIM WON'T WAIT LONG TO MAKE HIS MOVE.
DOCTOR WARREN!
ARISTOTLE'S GONE!
SOMEONE TOOK HIM!

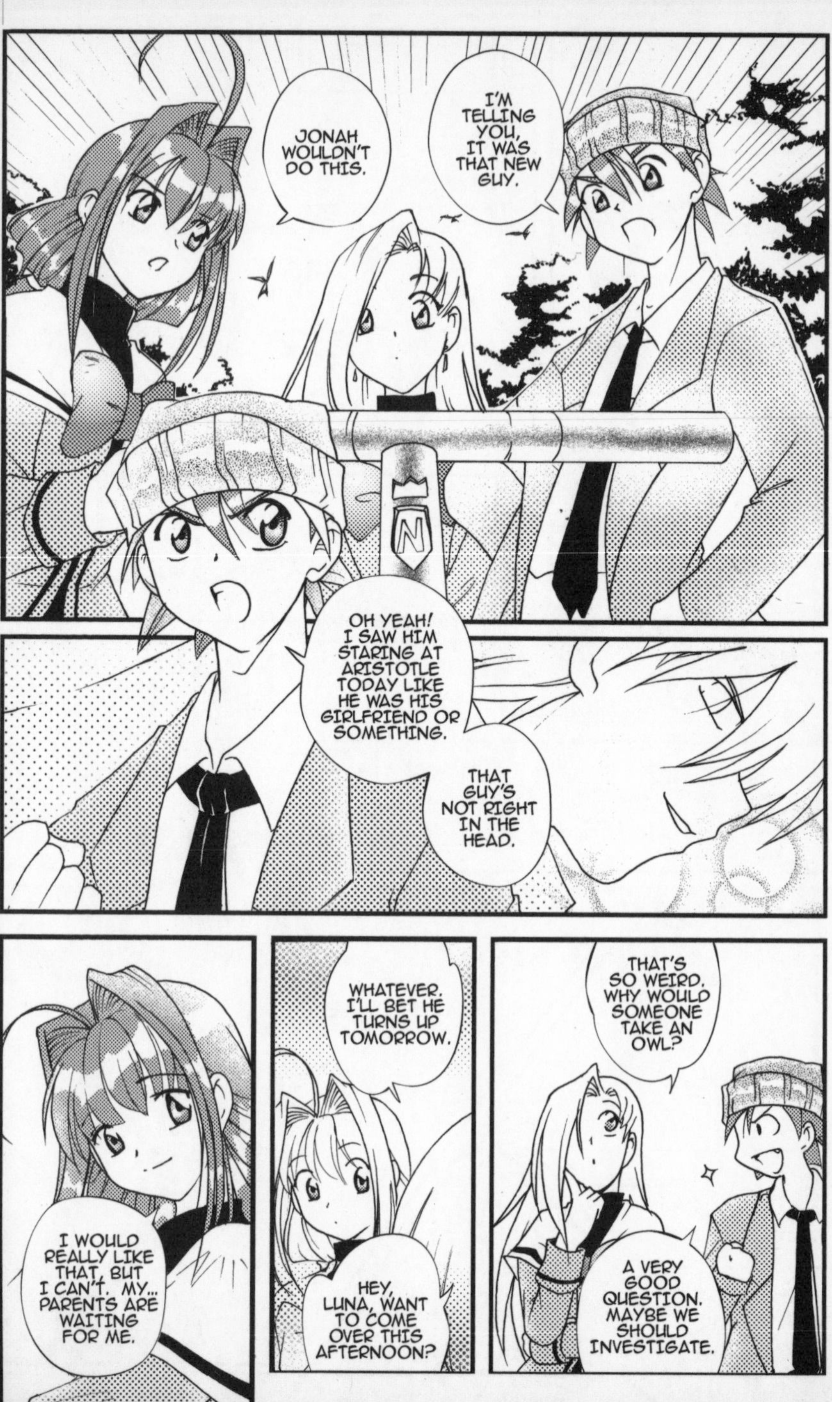
I'M TELLING YOU, IT WAS THAT NEW GUY.
JONAH WOULDN'T DO THIS.
OH YEAH! I SAW HIM STARING AT ARISTOTLE TODAY LIKE HE WAS HIS GIRLFRIEND OR SOMETHING.
THAT GUY'S NOT RIGHT IN THE HEAD.
THAT'S SO WEIRD. WHY WOULD SOMEONE TAKE AN OWL?
A VERY GOOD QUESTION. MAYBE WE SHOULD INVESTIGATE.
WHATEVER. I'LL BET HE TURNS UP TOMORROW.
HEY, LUNA, WANT TO COME OVER THIS AFTERNOON?
I WOULD REALLY LIKE THAT, BUT I CAN'T. MY... PARENTS ARE WAITING FOR ME.

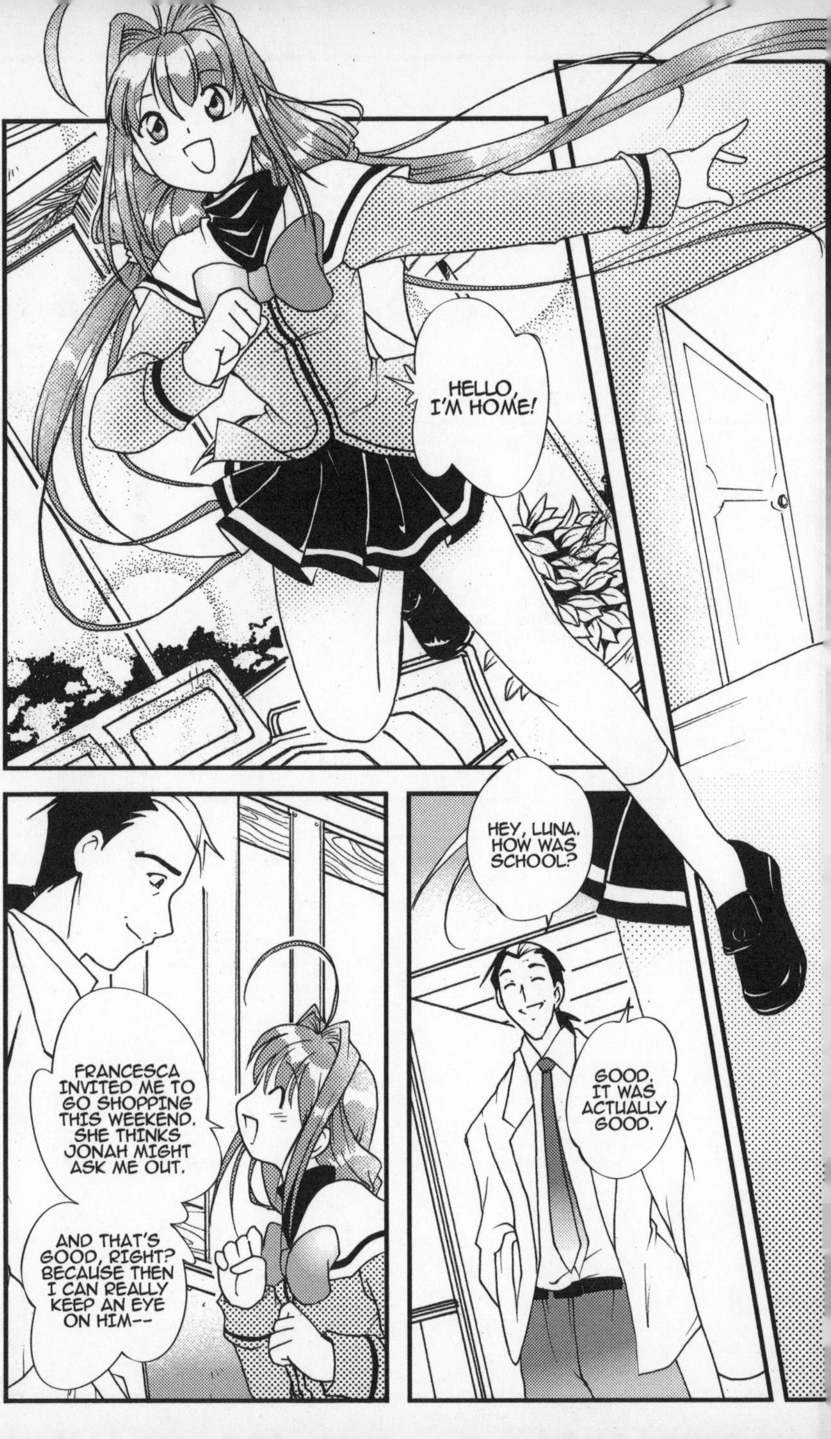
HELLO, I'M HOME!
HEY, LUNA. HOW WAS SCHOOL?
GOOD, IT WAS ACTUALLY GOOD.
FRANCESCA INVITED ME TO GO SHOPPING THIS WEEKEND. SHE THINKS JONAH MIGHT ASK ME OUT.
AND THAT'S GOOD, RIGHT? BECAUSE THEN I CAN REALLY KEEP AN EYE ON HIM--

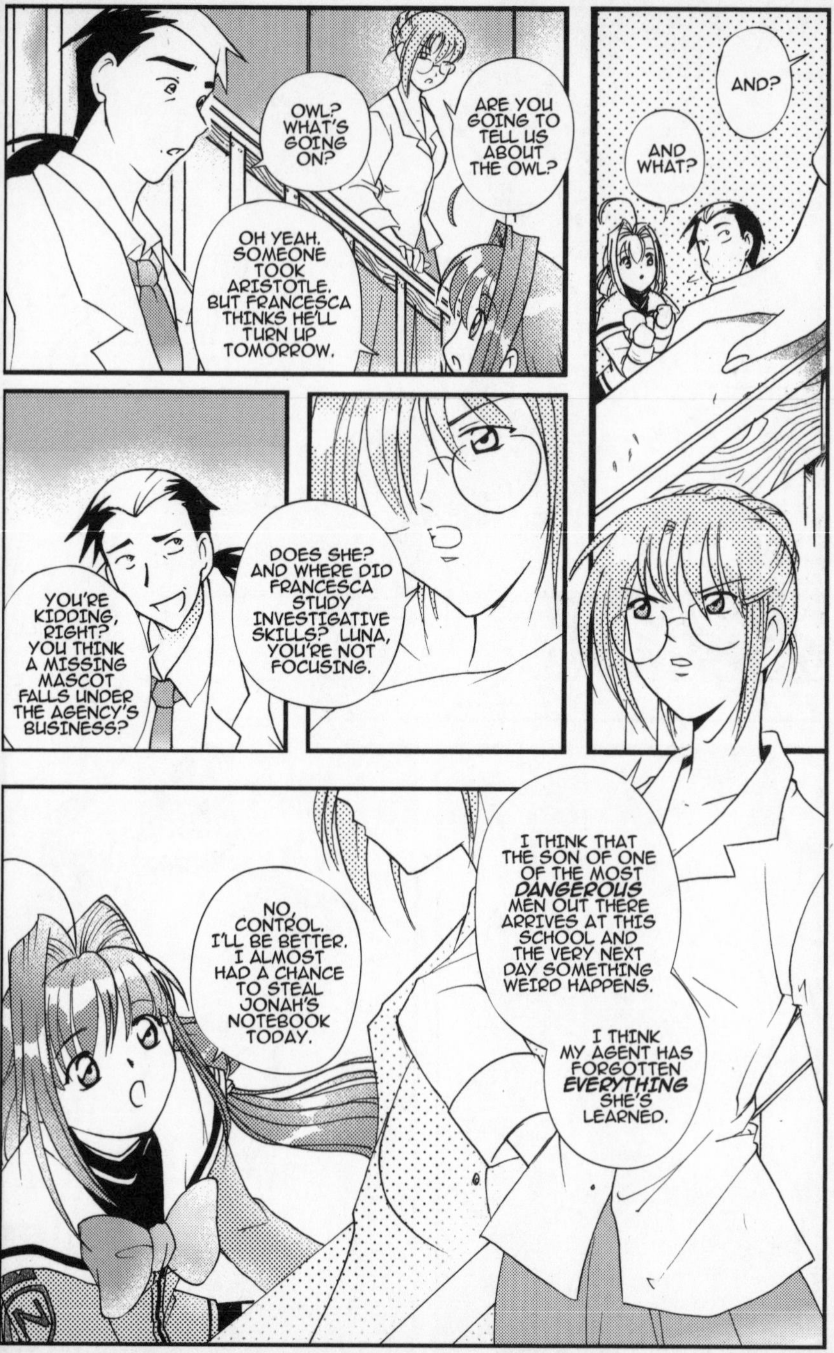
AND?
AND WHAT?
ARE YOU GOING TO TELL US ABOUT THE OWL?
OWL? WHAT'S GOING ON?
OH YEAH. SOMEONE TOOK ARISTOTLE. BUT FRANCESCA THINKS HE'LL TURN UP TOMORROW.
DOES SHE? AND WHERE DID FRANCESCA STUDY INVESTIGATIVE SKILLS? LUNA, YOU'RE NOT FOCUSING.
YOU'RE KIDDING, RIGHT? YOU THINK A MISSING MASCOT FALLS UNDER THE AGENCY'S BUSINESS?
I THINK THAT THE SON OF ONE OF THE MOST DANGEROUS MEN OUT THERE ARRIVES AT THIS SCHOOL AND THE VERY NEXT DAY SOMETHING WEIRD HAPPENS.
I THINK MY AGENT HAS FORGOTTEN EVERYTHING SHE'S LEARNED.
NO, CONTROL. I'LL BE BETTER. I ALMOST HAD A CHANCE TO STEAL JONAH'S NOTEBOOK TODAY.

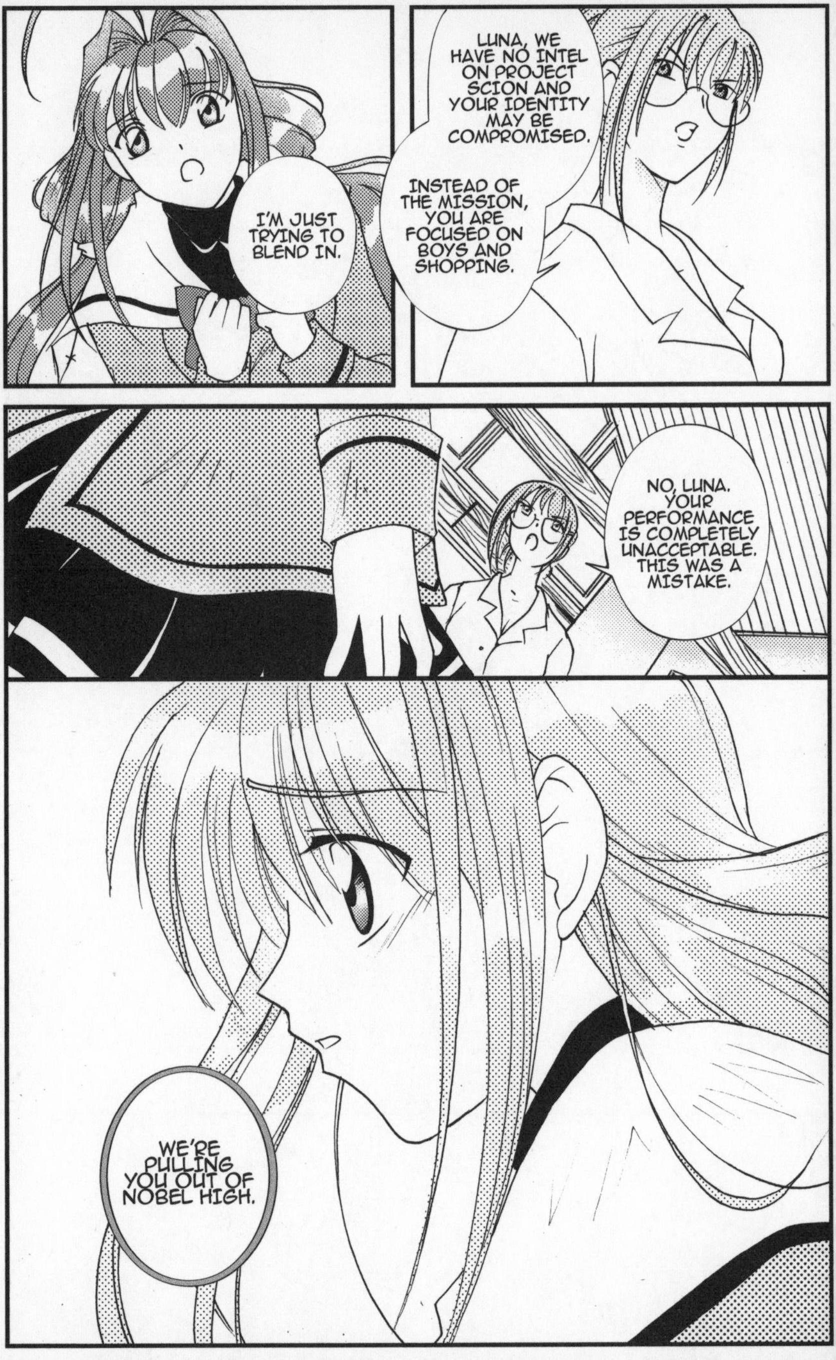
LUNA, WE HAVE NO INTEL ON PROJECT SCION AND YOUR IDENTITY MAY BE COMPROMISED.
INSTEAD OF THE MISSION, YOU ARE FOCUSED ON BOYS AND SHOPPING.
I'M JUST TRYING TO BLEND IN.
NO, LUNA. YOUR PERFORMANCE IS COMPLETELY UNACCEPTABLE. THIS WAS A MISTAKE.
WE'RE PULLING YOU OUT OF NOBEL HIGH.

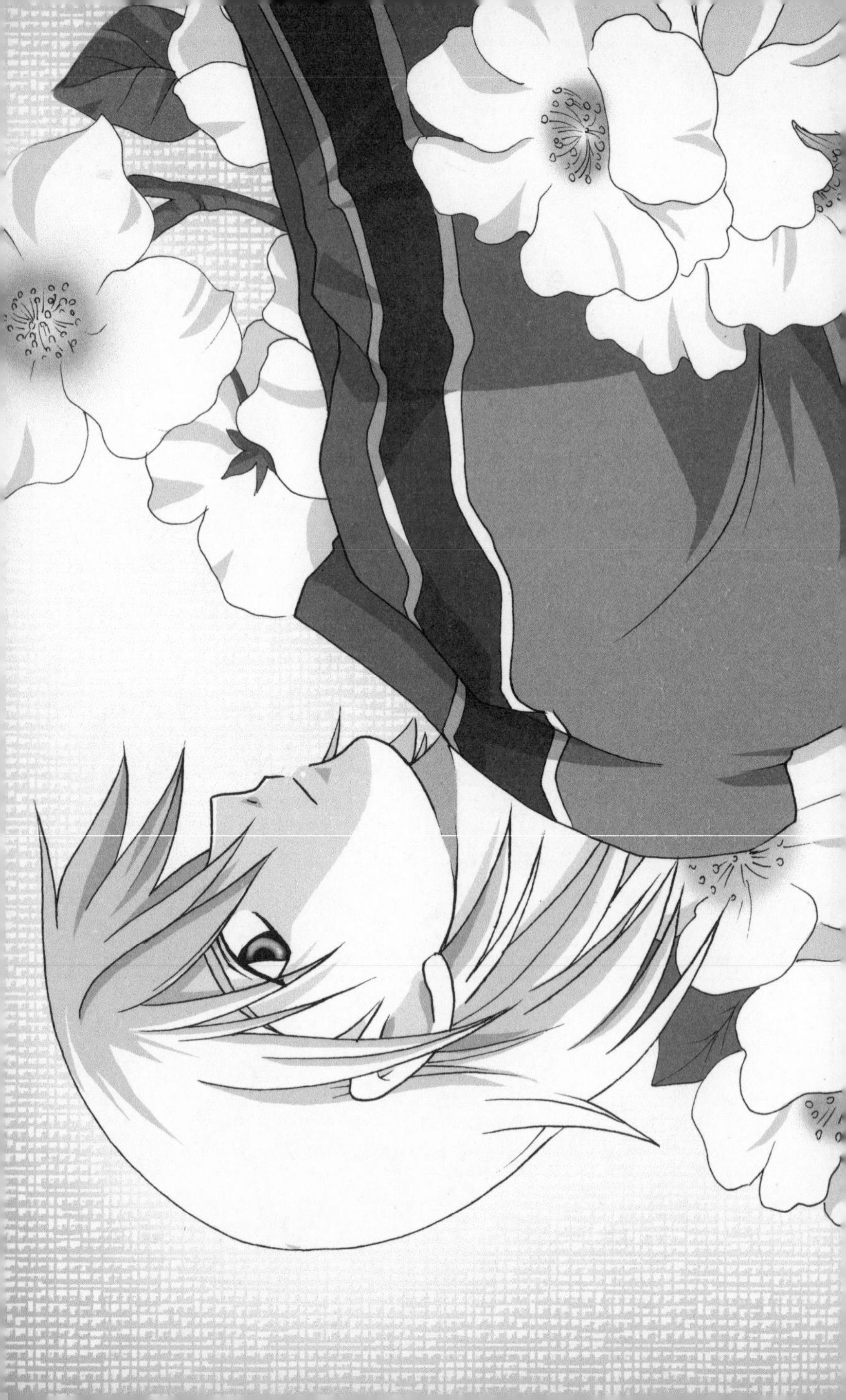

## File 04
# FIRST CRUSH

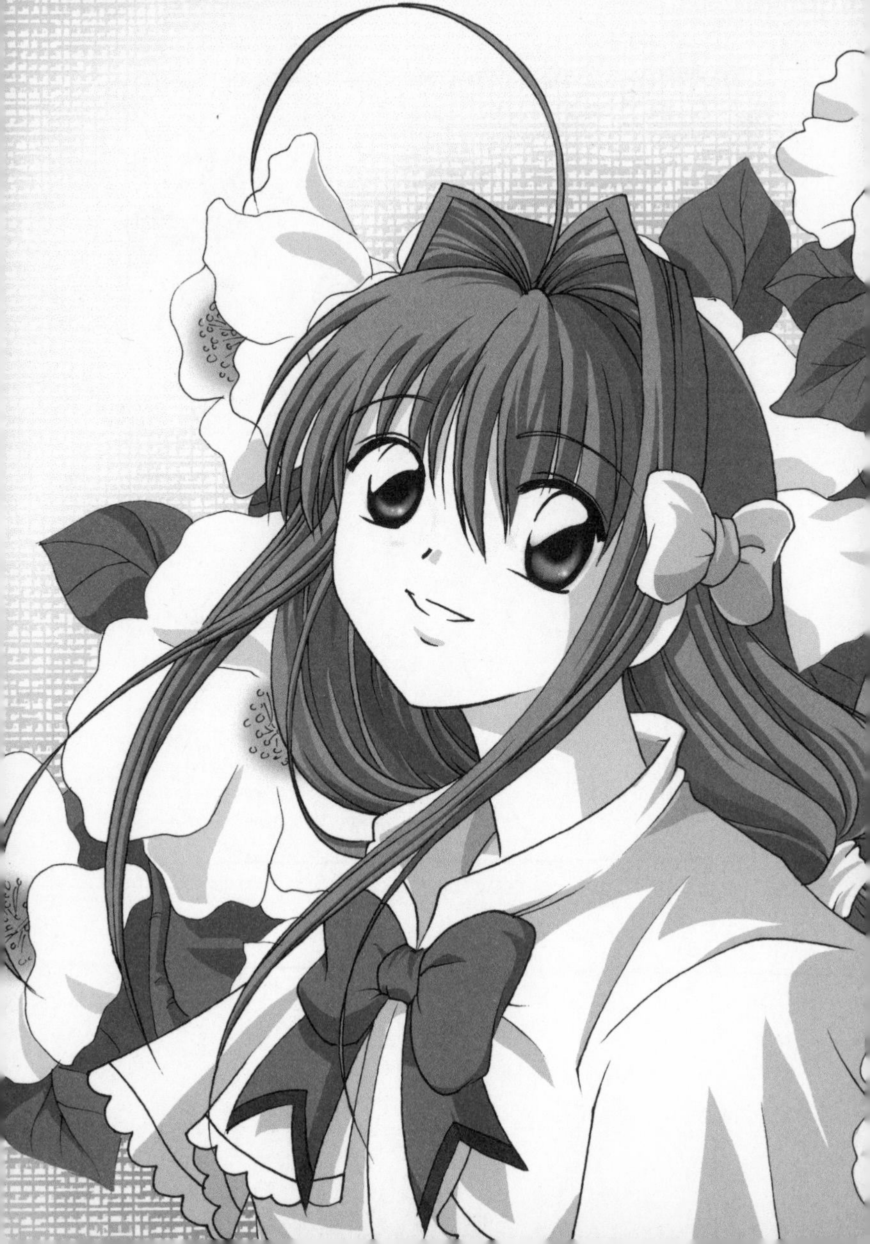

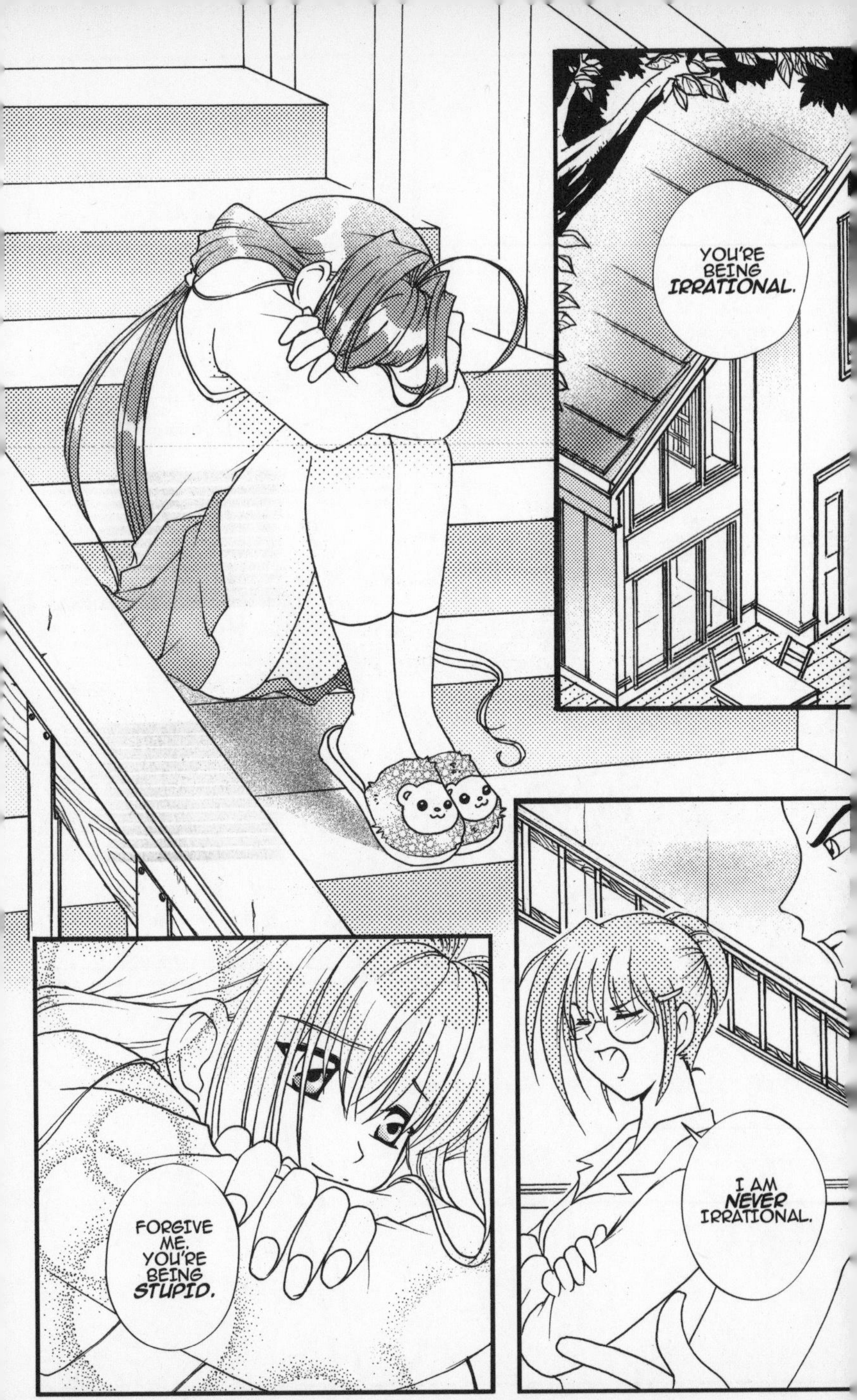
YOU'RE BEING IRRATIONAL.
I AM NEVER IRRATIONAL.
FORGIVE ME. YOU'RE BEING STUPID.

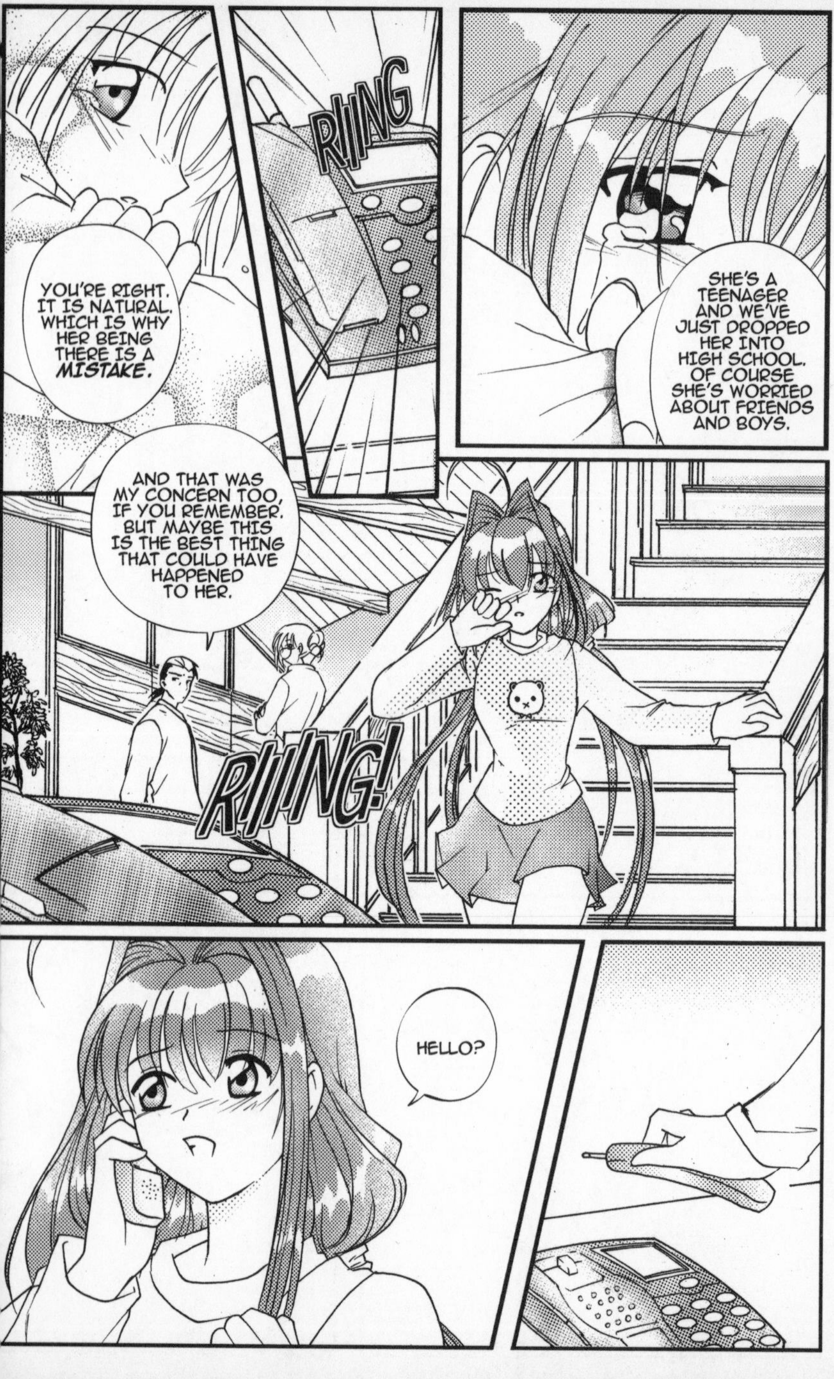
SHE'S A TEENAGER AND WE'VE JUST DROPPED HER INTO HIGH SCHOOL. OF COURSE SHE'S WORRIED ABOUT FRIENDS AND BOYS.
RIIING
YOU'RE RIGHT. IT IS NATURAL. WHICH IS WHY HER BEING THERE IS A *MISTAKE*.
AND THAT WAS MY CONCERN TOO, IF YOU REMEMBER. BUT MAYBE THIS IS THE BEST THING THAT COULD HAVE HAPPENED TO HER.
RIIING!
HELLO?

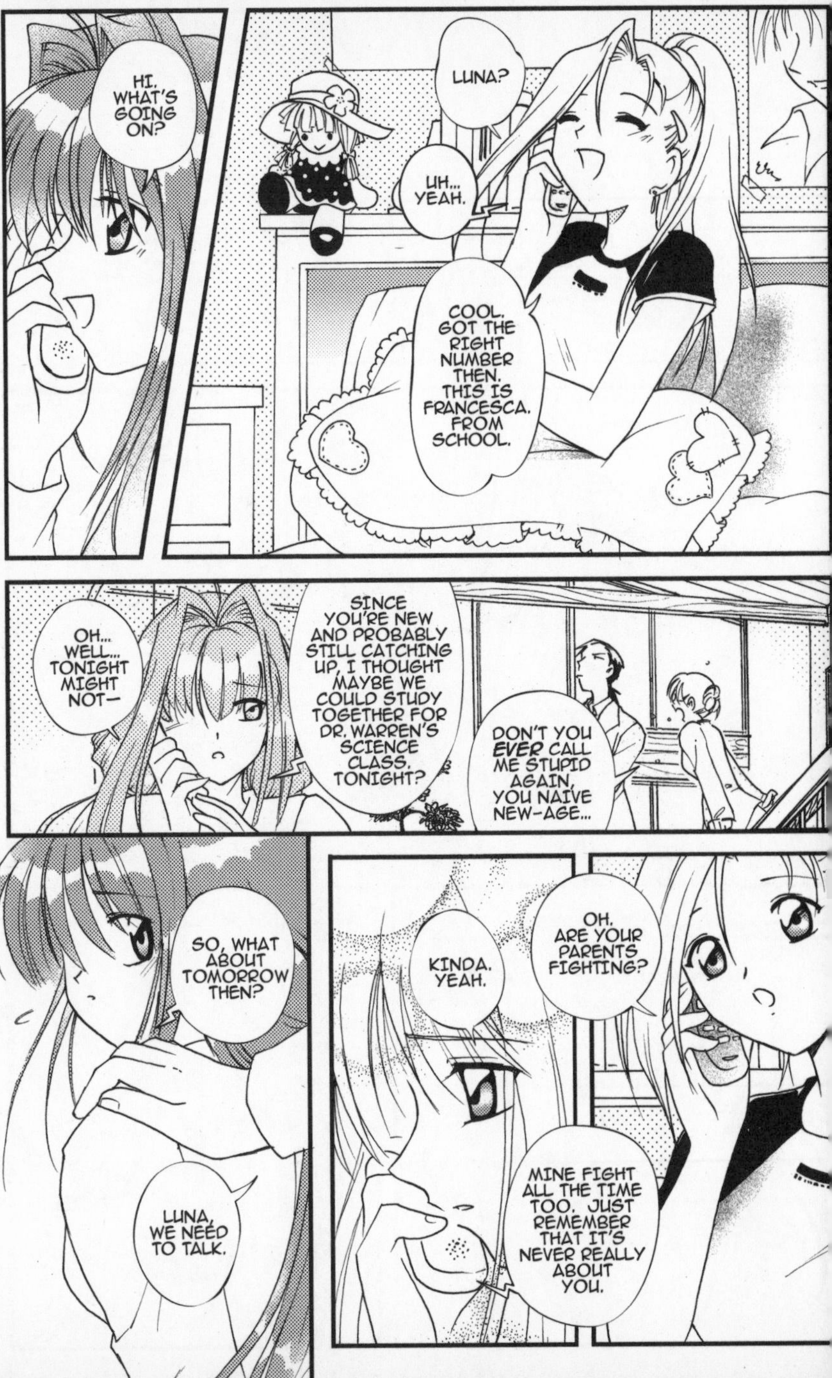
LUNA?
UH... YEAH.
COOL. GOT THE RIGHT NUMBER THEN. THIS IS FRANCESCA. FROM SCHOOL.
HI. WHAT'S GOING ON?
DON'T YOU *EVER* CALL ME STUPID AGAIN, YOU NAIVE NEW-AGE...
SINCE YOU'RE NEW AND PROBABLY STILL CATCHING UP, I THOUGHT MAYBE WE COULD STUDY TOGETHER FOR DR. WARREN'S SCIENCE CLASS. TONIGHT?
OH... WELL... TONIGHT MIGHT NOT—
OH. ARE YOUR PARENTS FIGHTING?
KINDA. YEAH.
MINE FIGHT ALL THE TIME TOO. JUST REMEMBER THAT IT'S NEVER REALLY ABOUT YOU.
SO, WHAT ABOUT TOMORROW THEN?
LUNA, WE NEED TO TALK.

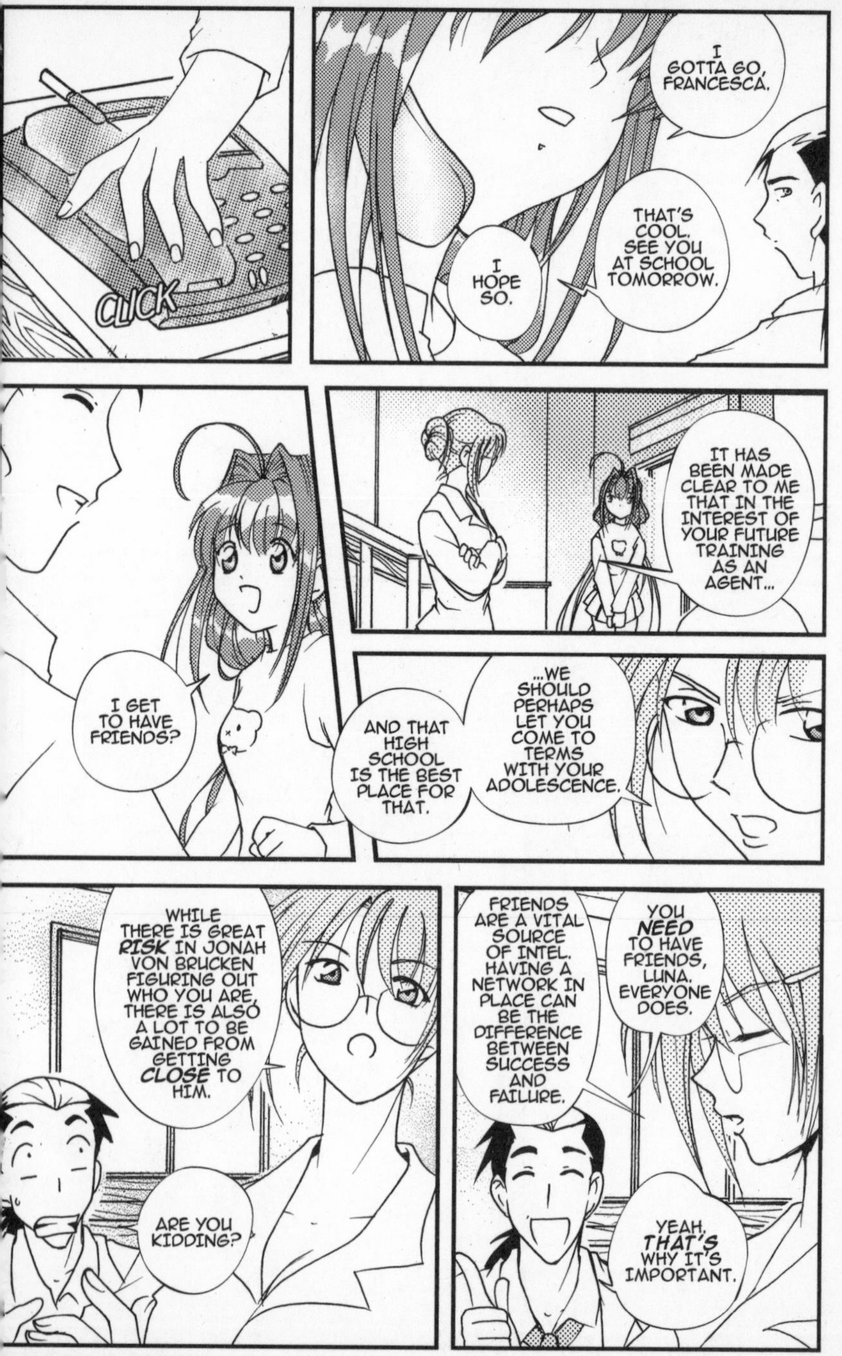

I GOTTA GO, FRANCESCA.
THAT'S COOL. SEE YOU AT SCHOOL TOMORROW.
I HOPE SO.
CLICK
IT HAS BEEN MADE CLEAR TO ME THAT IN THE INTEREST OF YOUR FUTURE TRAINING AS AN AGENT...
...WE SHOULD PERHAPS LET YOU COME TO TERMS WITH YOUR ADOLESCENCE.
AND THAT HIGH SCHOOL IS THE BEST PLACE FOR THAT.
I GET TO HAVE FRIENDS?
YOU *NEED* TO HAVE FRIENDS, LUNA. EVERYONE DOES.
FRIENDS ARE A VITAL SOURCE OF INTEL. HAVING A NETWORK IN PLACE CAN BE THE DIFFERENCE BETWEEN SUCCESS AND FAILURE.
YEAH, *THAT'S* WHY IT'S IMPORTANT.
WHILE THERE IS GREAT *RISK* IN JONAH VON BRUCKEN FIGURING OUT WHO YOU ARE, THERE IS ALSO A LOT TO BE GAINED FROM GETTING *CLOSE* TO HIM.
ARE YOU KIDDING?

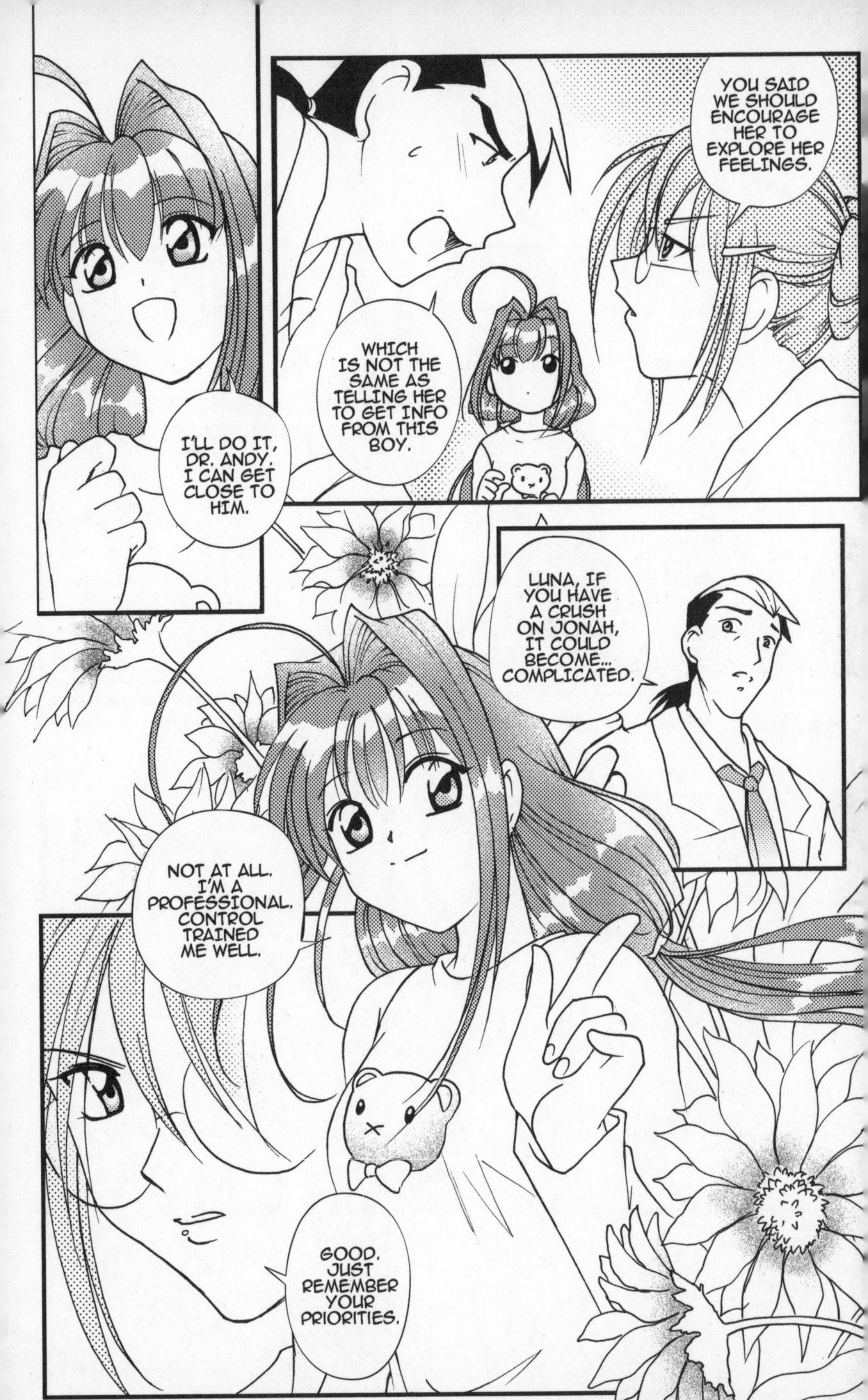
YOU SAID WE SHOULD ENCOURAGE HER TO EXPLORE HER FEELINGS.
WHICH IS NOT THE SAME AS TELLING HER TO GET INFO FROM THIS BOY.
I'LL DO IT, DR. ANDY. I CAN GET CLOSE TO HIM.
LUNA, IF YOU HAVE A CRUSH ON JONAH, IT COULD BECOME... COMPLICATED.
NOT AT ALL. I'M A PROFESSIONAL. CONTROL TRAINED ME WELL.
GOOD. JUST REMEMBER YOUR PRIORITIES.

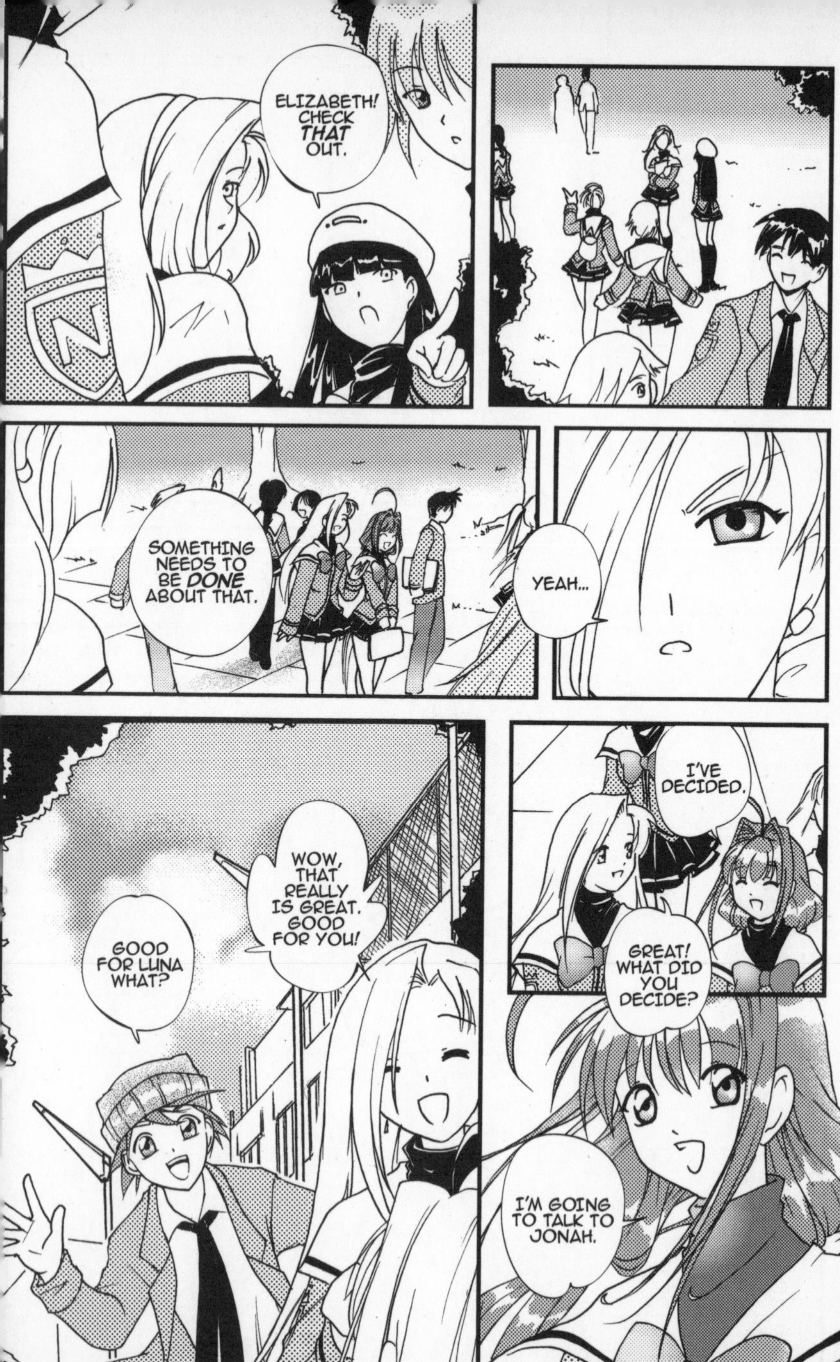
ELIZABETH! CHECK *THAT* OUT.
YEAH...
SOMETHING NEEDS TO BE *DONE* ABOUT THAT.
I'VE DECIDED.
GREAT! WHAT DID YOU DECIDE?
I'M GOING TO TALK TO JONAH.
WOW, THAT REALLY IS GREAT. GOOD FOR YOU!
GOOD FOR LUNA WHAT?

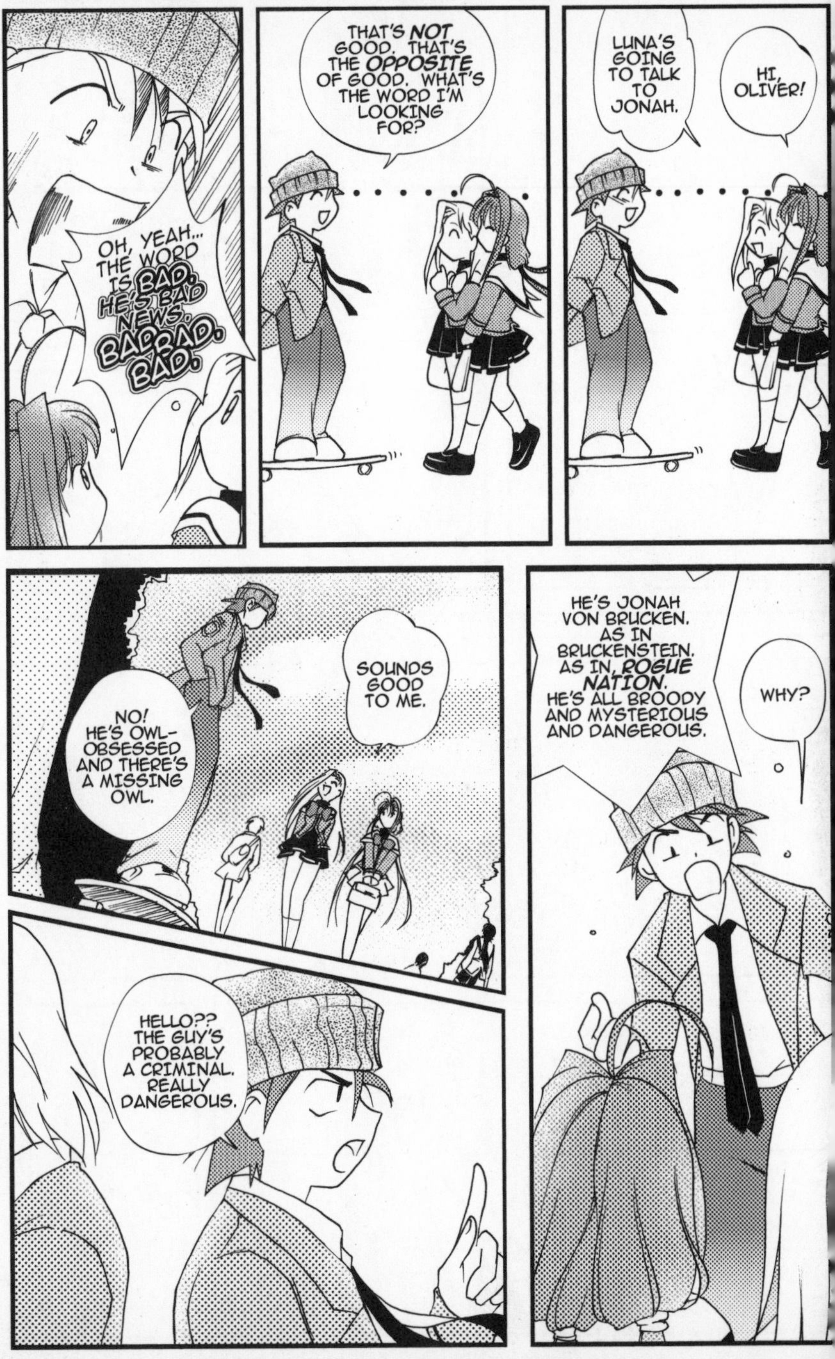
HI, OLIVER!
LUNA'S GOING TO TALK TO JONAH.
THAT'S **NOT** GOOD. THAT'S THE **OPPOSITE** OF GOOD. WHAT'S THE WORD I'M LOOKING FOR?
OH, YEAH... THE WORD IS BAD. HE'S BAD NEWS. BAD BAD. BAD.
WHY?
HE'S JONAH VON BRUCKEN. AS IN BRUCKENSTEIN. AS IN, ***ROGUE NATION***. HE'S ALL BROODY AND MYSTERIOUS AND DANGEROUS.
SOUNDS GOOD TO ME.
NO! HE'S OWL-OBSESSED AND THERE'S A MISSING OWL.
HELLO?? THE GUY'S PROBABLY A CRIMINAL. REALLY DANGEROUS.

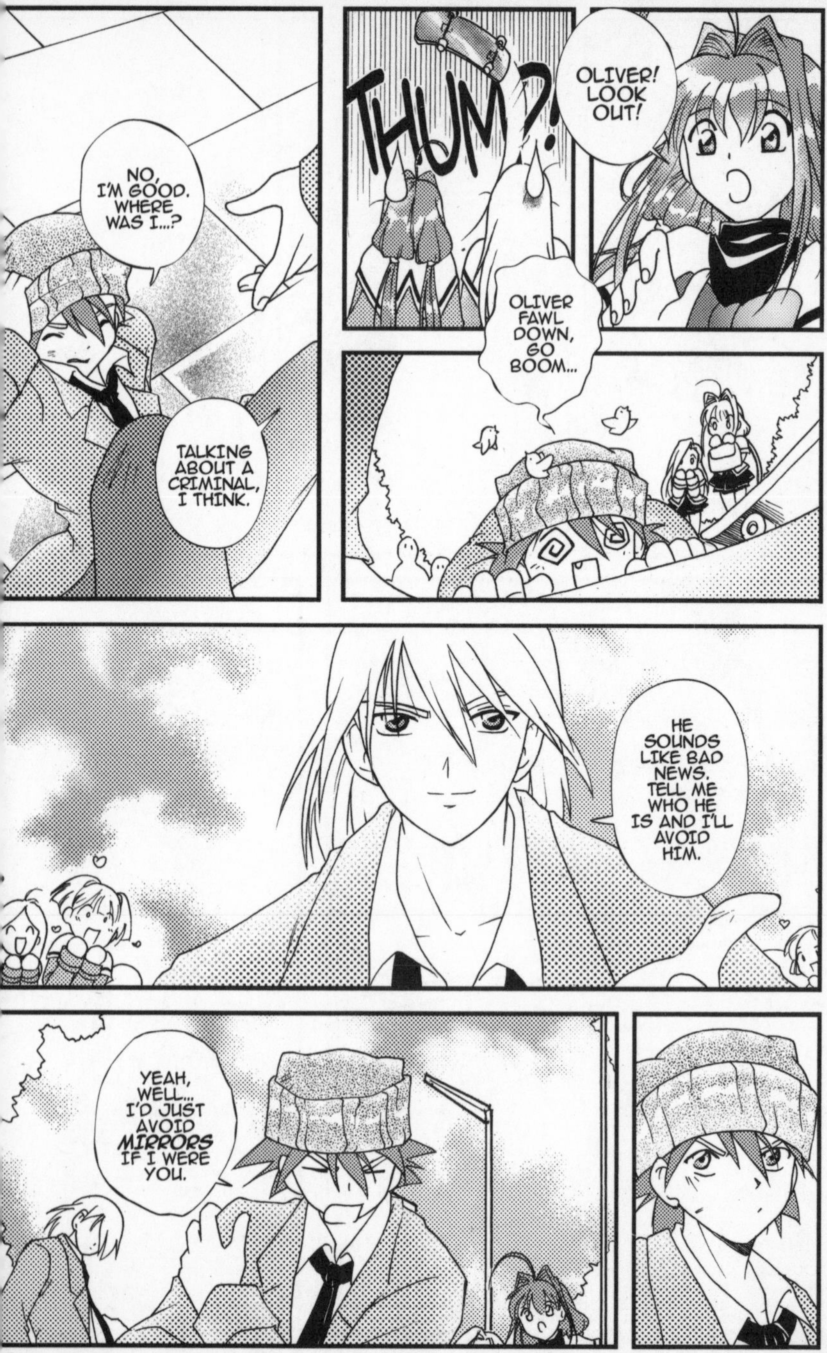
OLIVER! LOOK OUT!
THUM
?!
OLIVER FAWL DOWN, GO BOOM...
NO, I'M GOOD. WHERE WAS I...?
TALKING ABOUT A CRIMINAL, I THINK.
HE SOUNDS LIKE BAD NEWS. TELL ME WHO HE IS AND I'LL AVOID HIM.
YEAH, WELL... I'D JUST AVOID **MIRRORS** IF I WERE YOU.

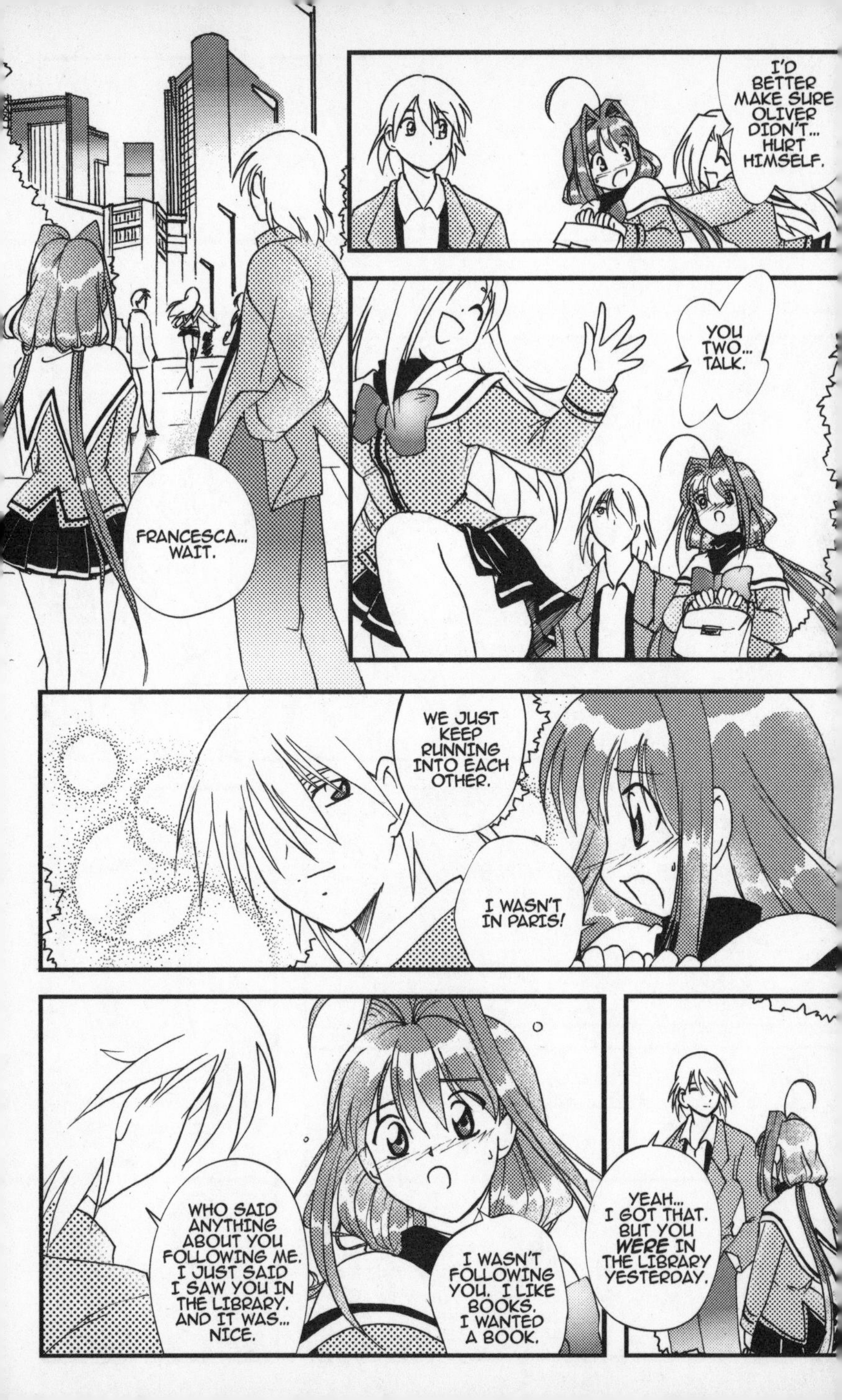
I'D BETTER MAKE SURE OLIVER DIDN'T... HURT HIMSELF.
YOU TWO... TALK.
FRANCESCA... WAIT.
WE JUST KEEP RUNNING INTO EACH OTHER.
I WASN'T IN PARIS!
YEAH... I GOT THAT. BUT YOU *WERE* IN THE LIBRARY YESTERDAY.
I WASN'T FOLLOWING YOU. I LIKE BOOKS. I WANTED A BOOK.
WHO SAID ANYTHING ABOUT YOU FOLLOWING ME. I JUST SAID I SAW YOU IN THE LIBRARY. AND IT WAS... NICE.

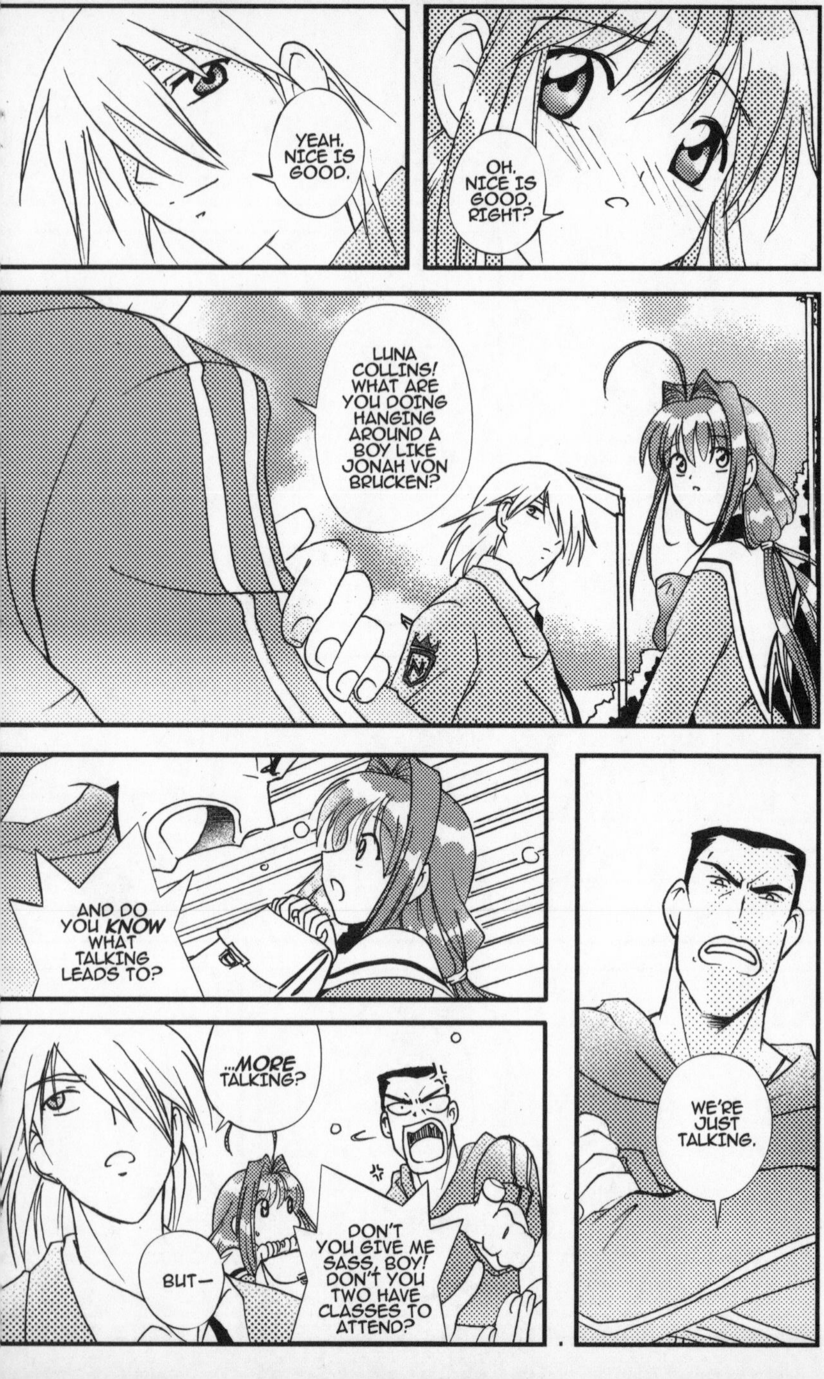
OH. NICE IS GOOD, RIGHT?
YEAH. NICE IS GOOD.
LUNA COLLINS! WHAT ARE YOU DOING HANGING AROUND A BOY LIKE JONAH VON BRUCKEN?
WE'RE JUST TALKING.
AND DO YOU ***KNOW*** WHAT TALKING LEADS TO?
...***MORE*** TALKING?
DON'T YOU GIVE ME SASS, BOY! DON'T YOU TWO HAVE CLASSES TO ATTEND?
BUT—

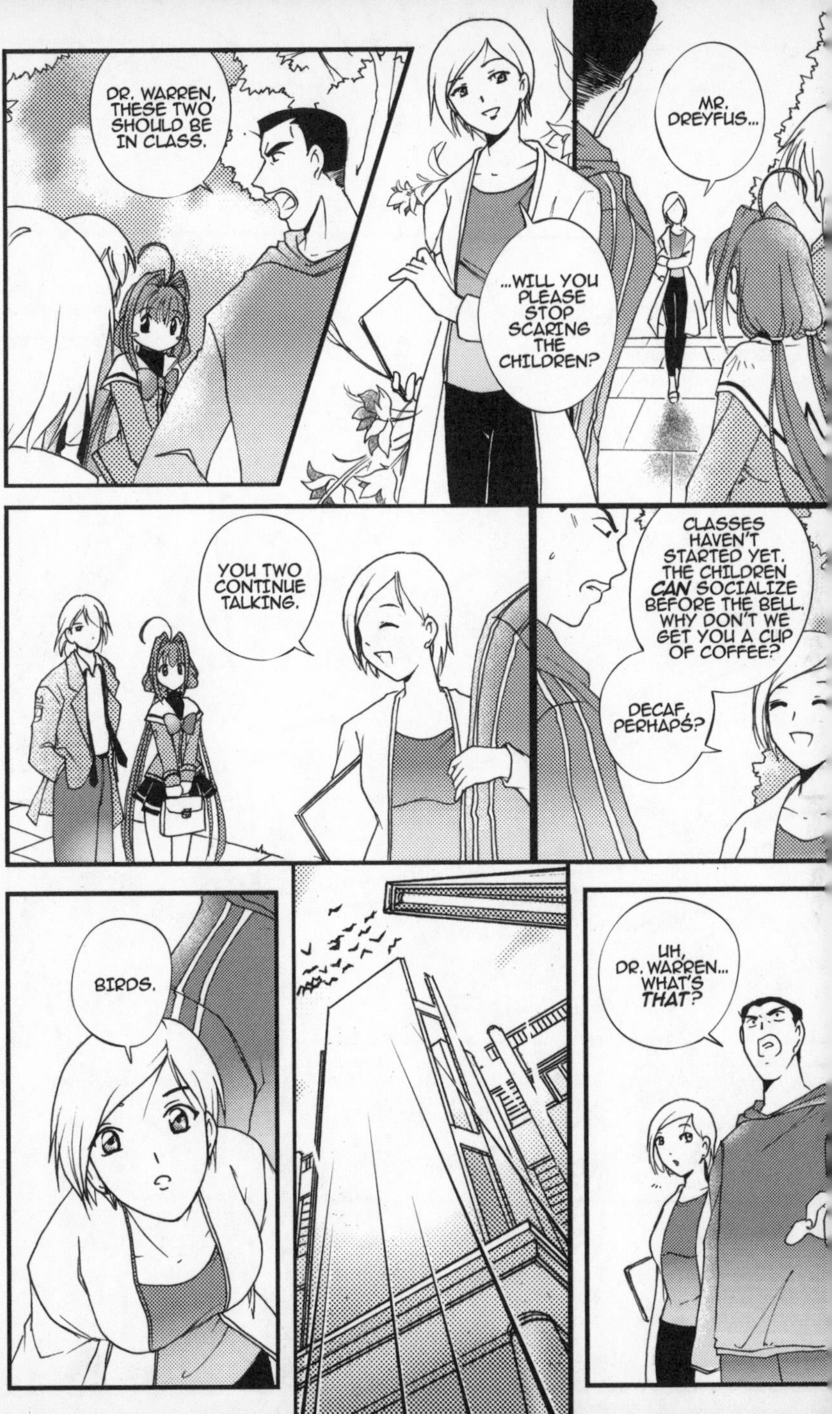
MR. DREYFUS...
...WILL YOU PLEASE STOP SCARING THE CHILDREN?
DR. WARREN, THESE TWO SHOULD BE IN CLASS.
CLASSES HAVEN'T STARTED YET. THE CHILDREN CAN SOCIALIZE BEFORE THE BELL. WHY DON'T WE GET YOU A CUP OF COFFEE?
DECAF, PERHAPS?
YOU TWO CONTINUE TALKING.
UH, DR. WARREN... WHAT'S THAT?
BIRDS.

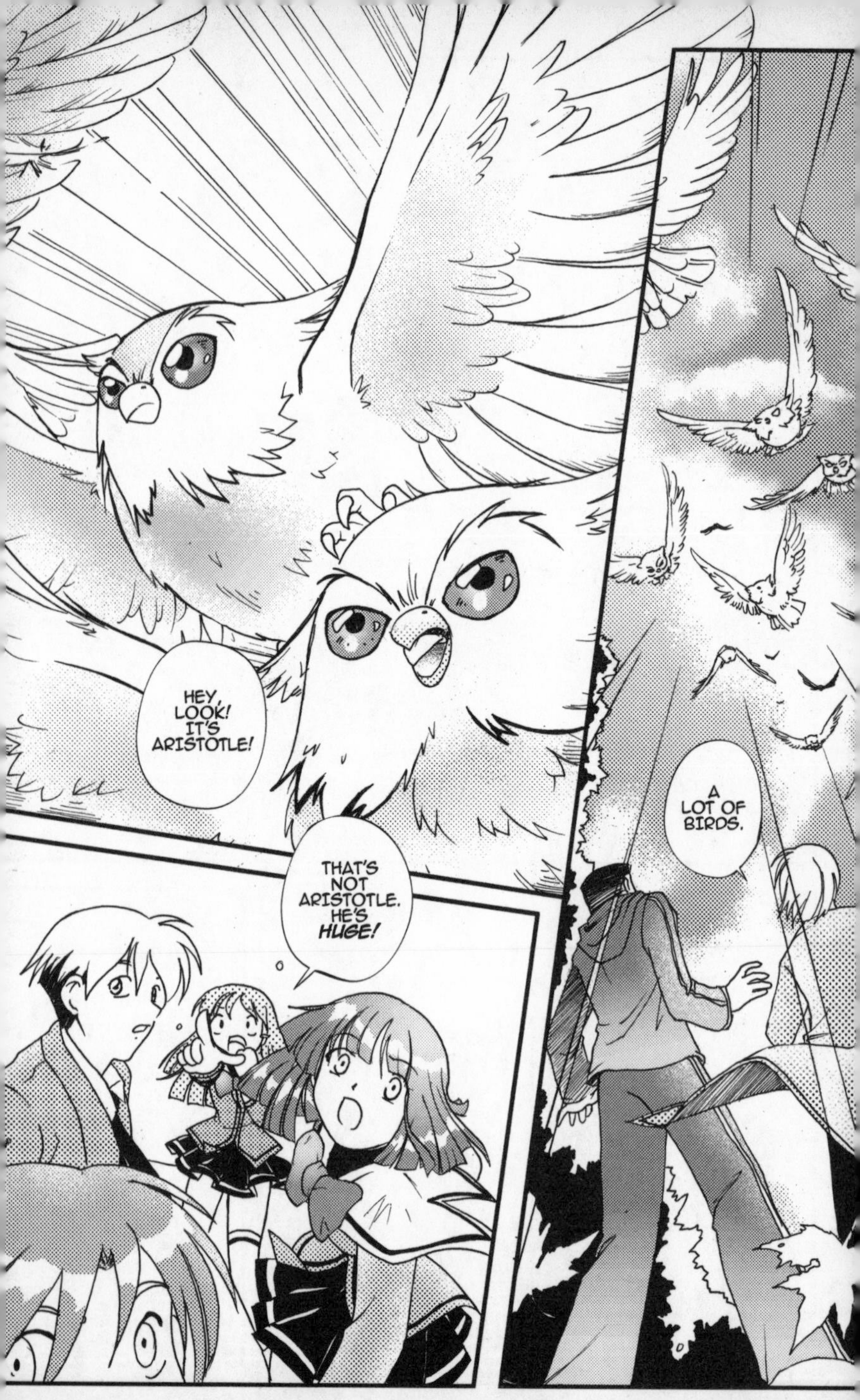
A LOT OF BIRDS.
HEY, LOOK! IT'S ARISTOTLE!
THAT'S NOT ARISTOTLE. HE'S *HUGE!*

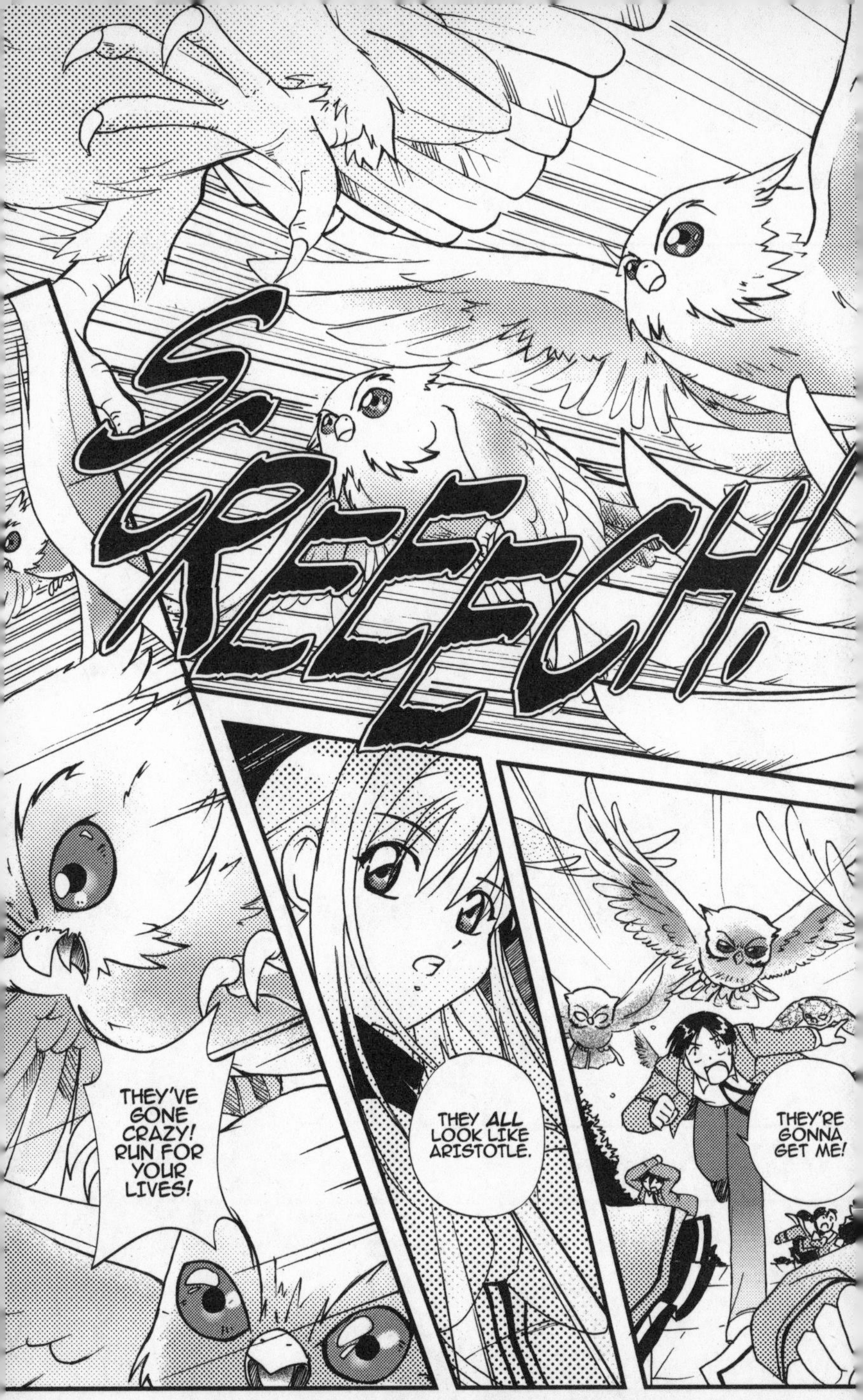
SKREEECH!
THEY'RE GONNA GET ME!
THEY *ALL* LOOK LIKE ARISTOTLE.
THEY'VE GONE CRAZY! RUN FOR YOUR LIVES!

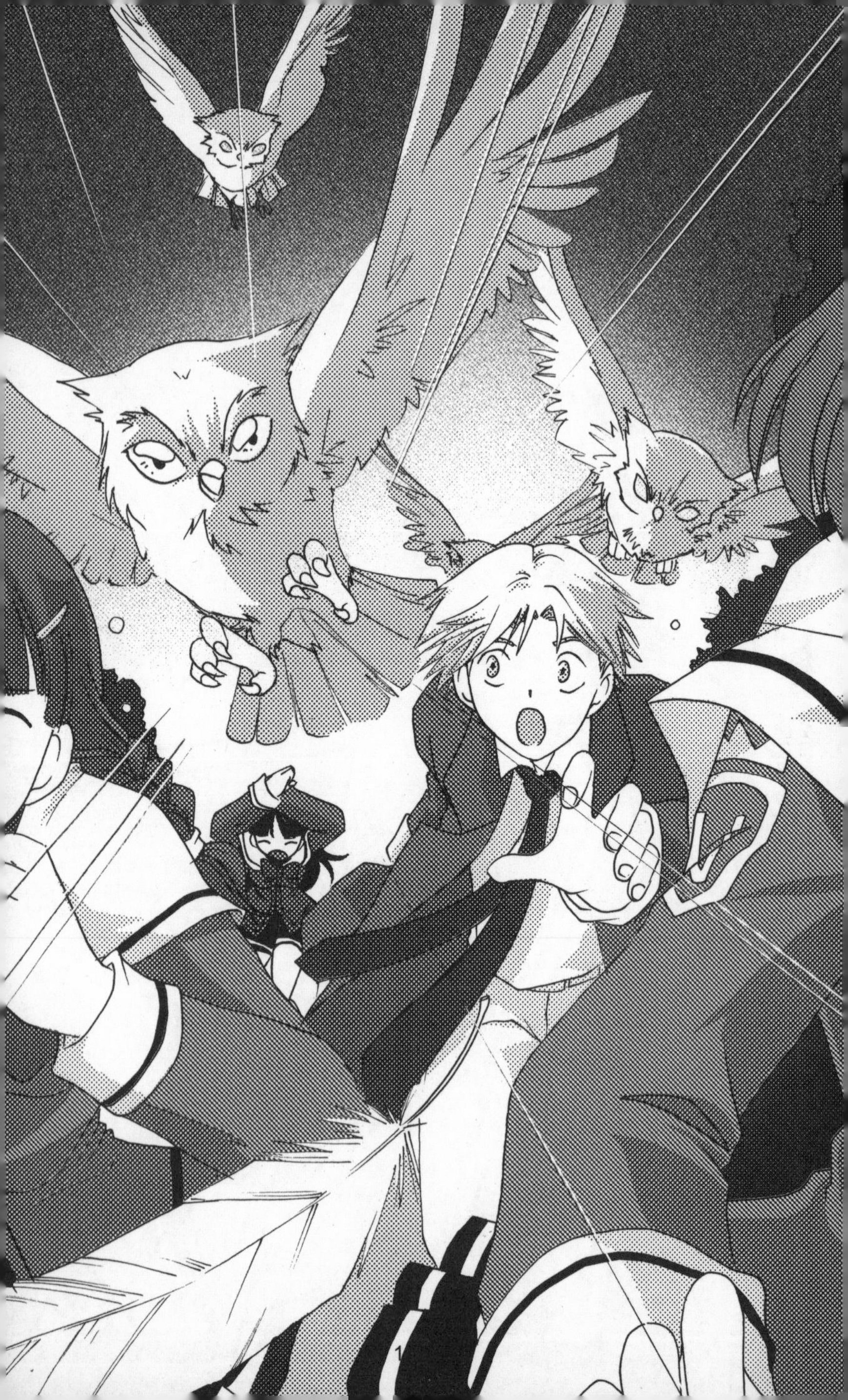

# File 05
# MYSTERIOUS BIRDS

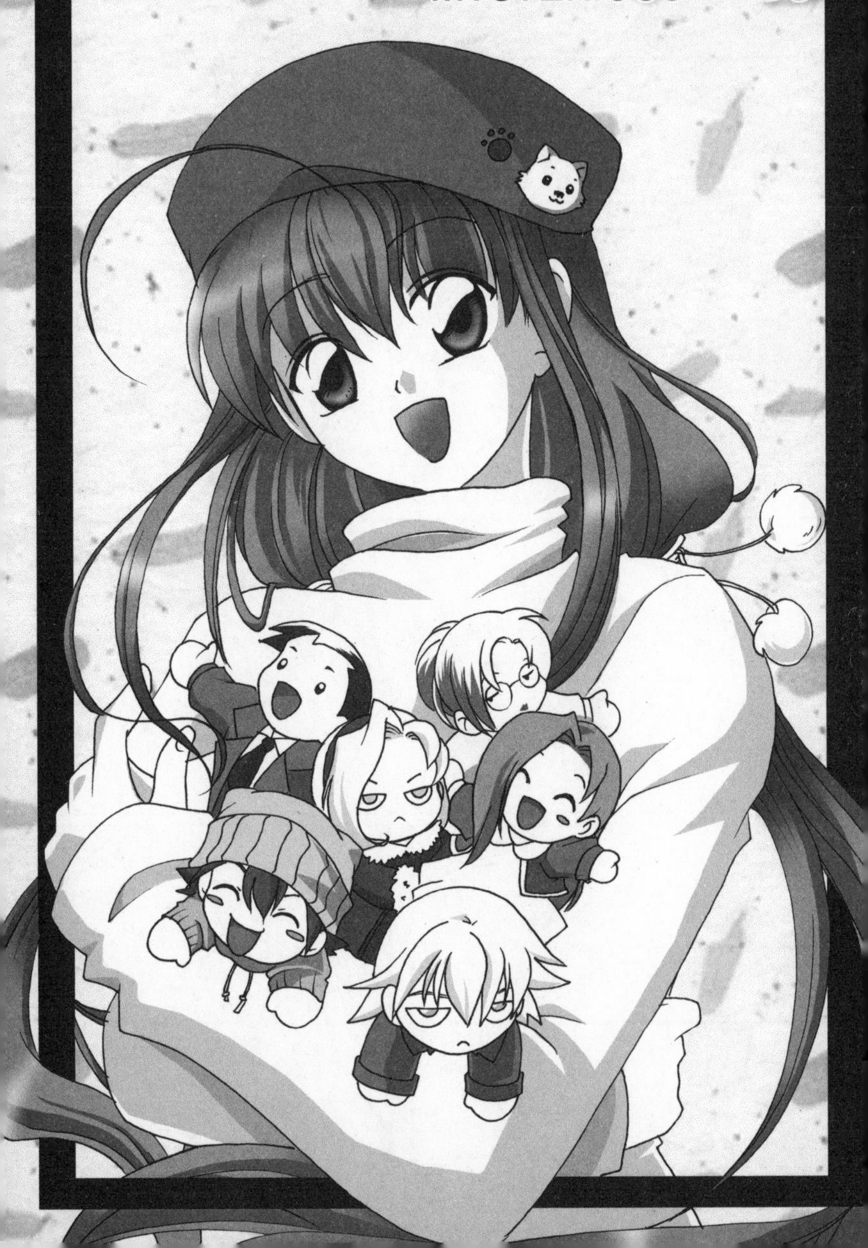

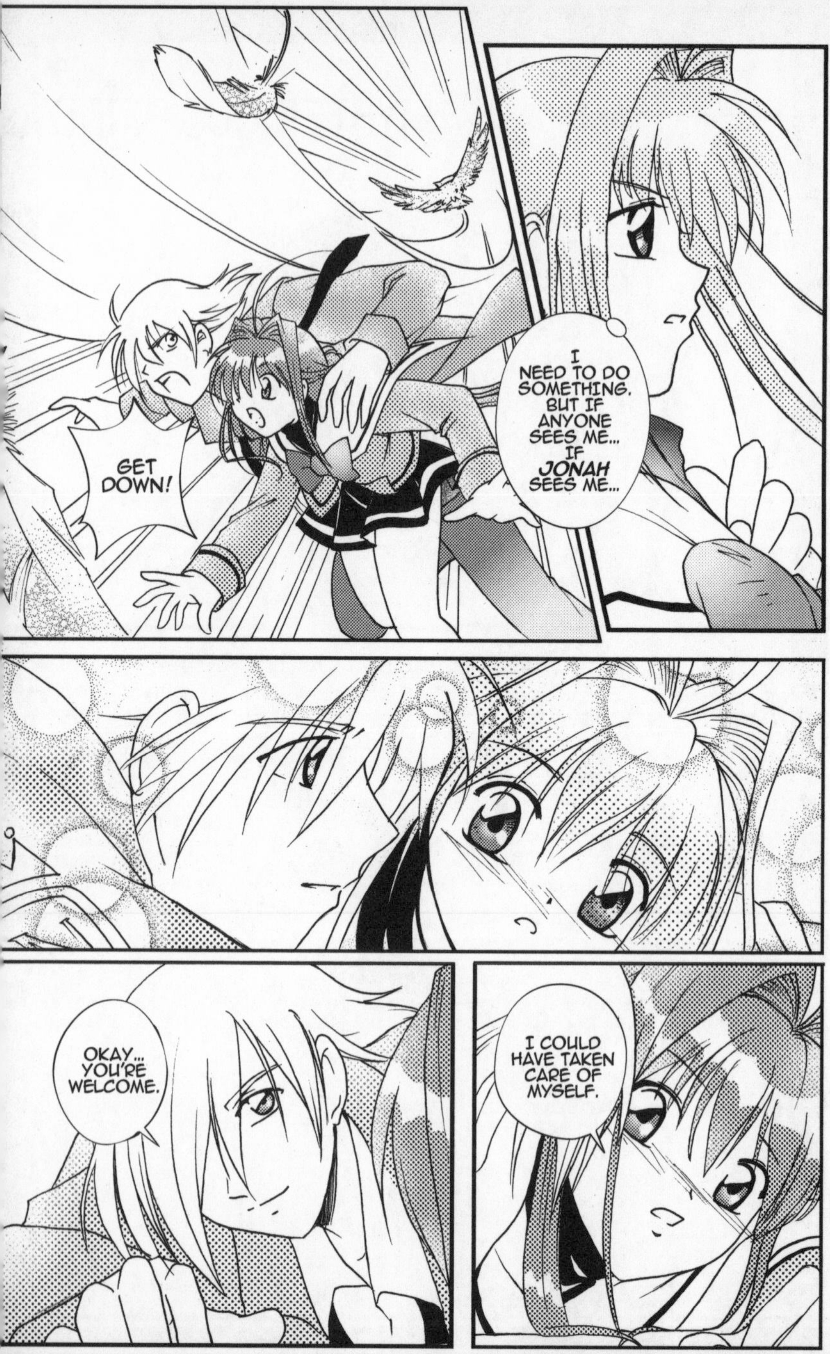
I NEED TO DO SOMETHING. BUT IF ANYONE SEES ME... IF *JONAH* SEES ME...
GET DOWN!
I COULD HAVE TAKEN CARE OF MYSELF.
OKAY... YOU'RE WELCOME.

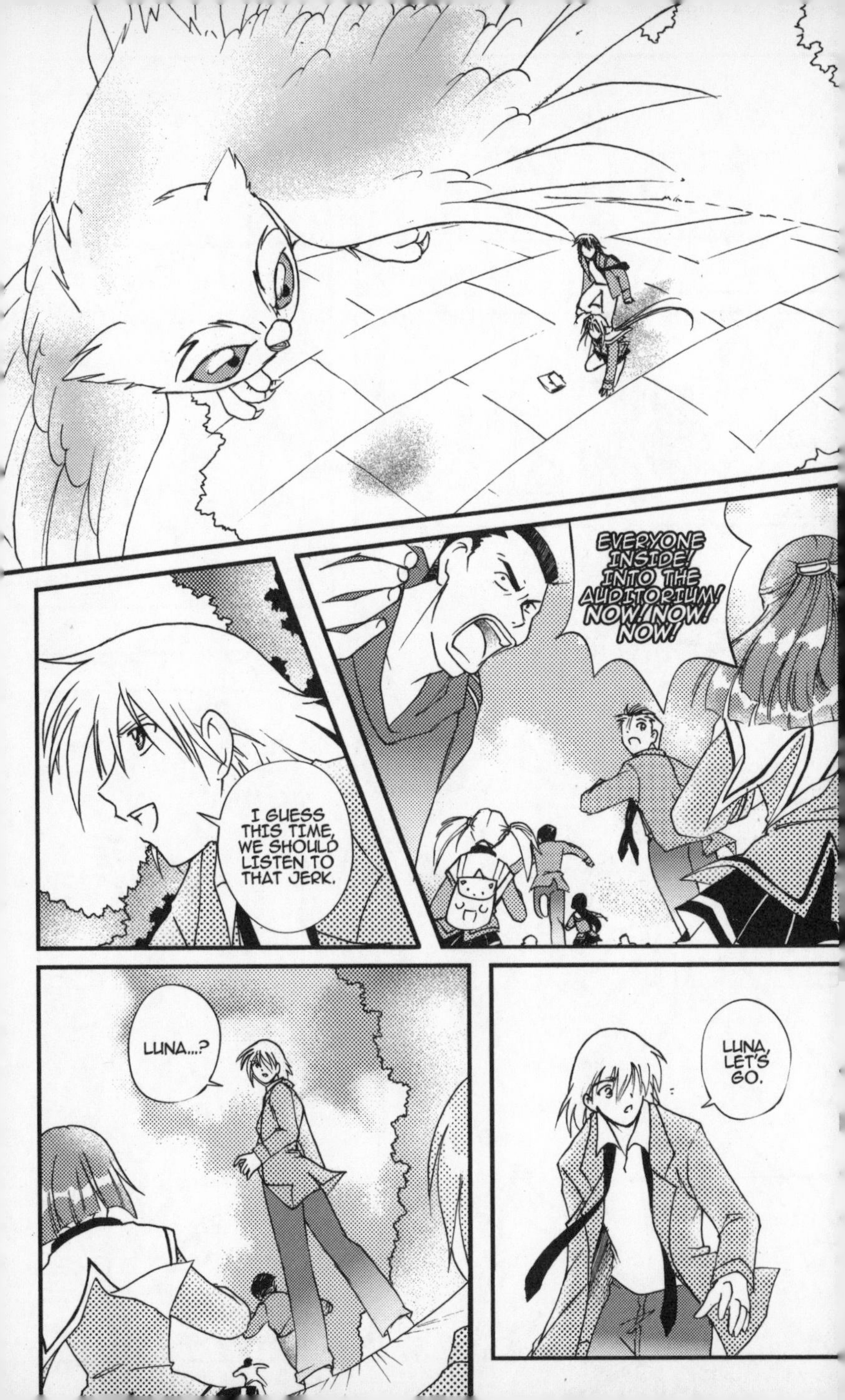
EVERYONE INSIDE! INTO THE AUDITORIUM! NOW! NOW! NOW!
I GUESS THIS TIME, WE SHOULD LISTEN TO THAT JERK.
LUNA, LET'S GO.
LUNA...?

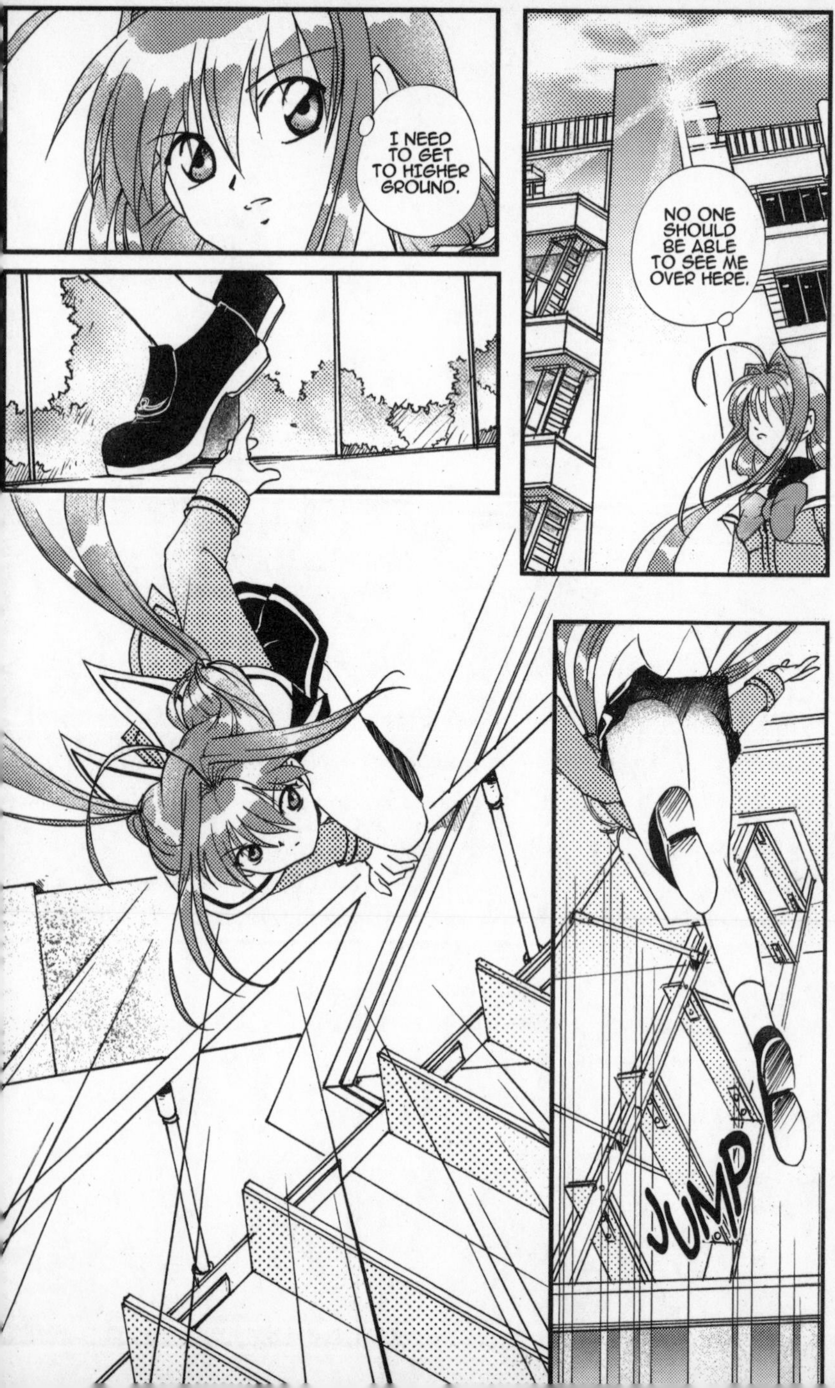
NO ONE SHOULD BE ABLE TO SEE ME OVER HERE.
I NEED TO GET TO HIGHER GROUND.
JUMP

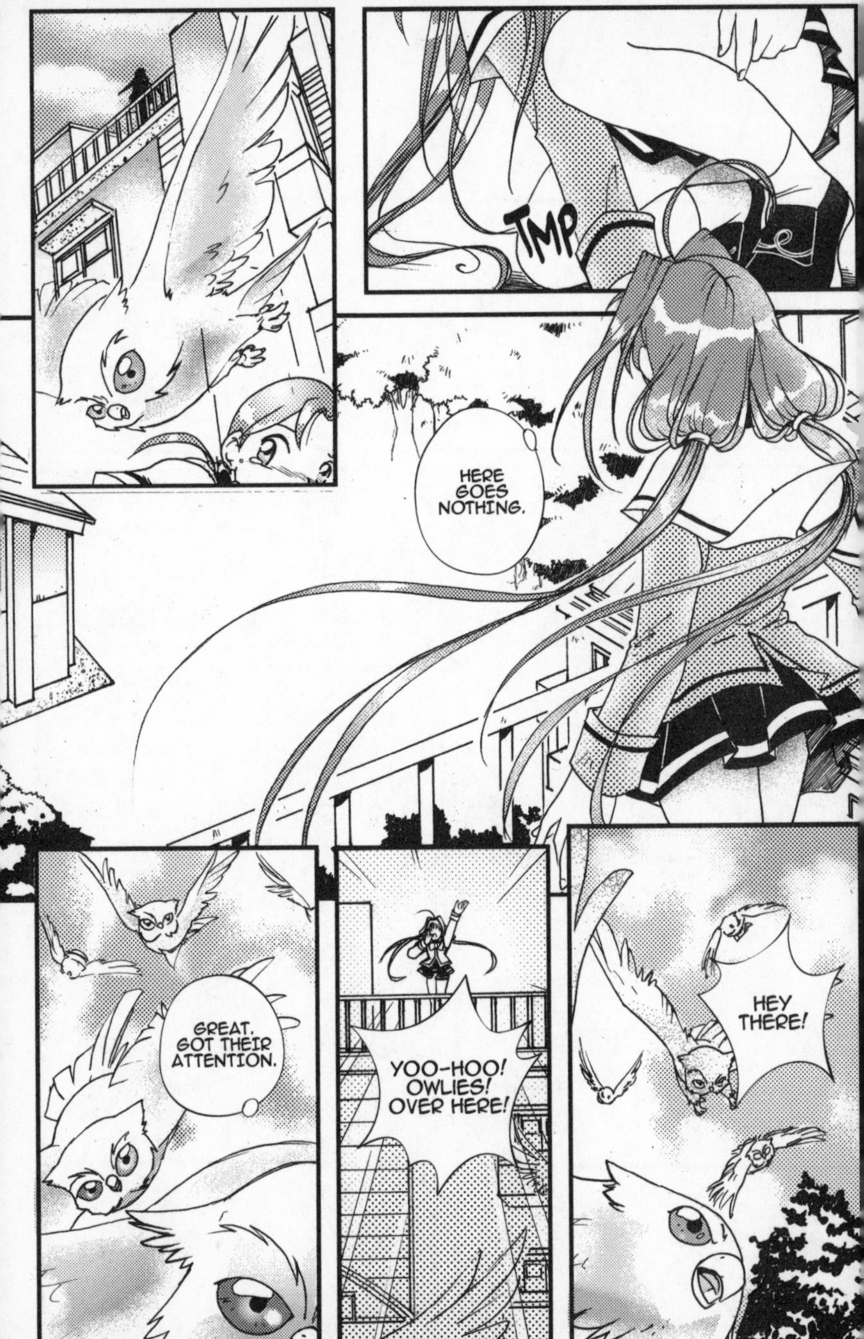
TMP
HERE GOES NOTHING.
HEY THERE!
YOO-HOO! OWLIES! OVER HERE!
GREAT. GOT THEIR ATTENTION.

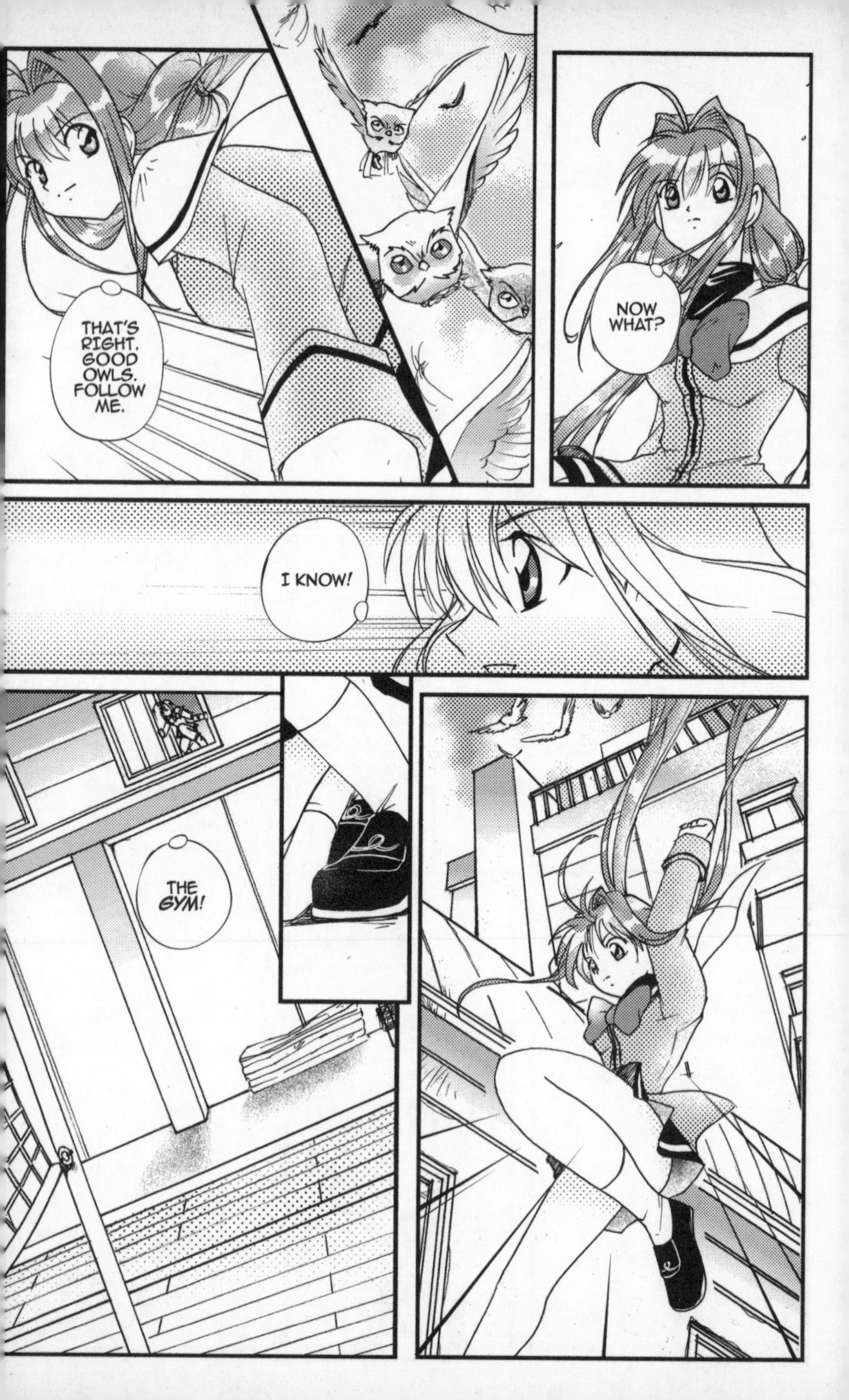
NOW WHAT?
THAT'S RIGHT. GOOD OWLS. FOLLOW ME.
I KNOW!
THE GYM!

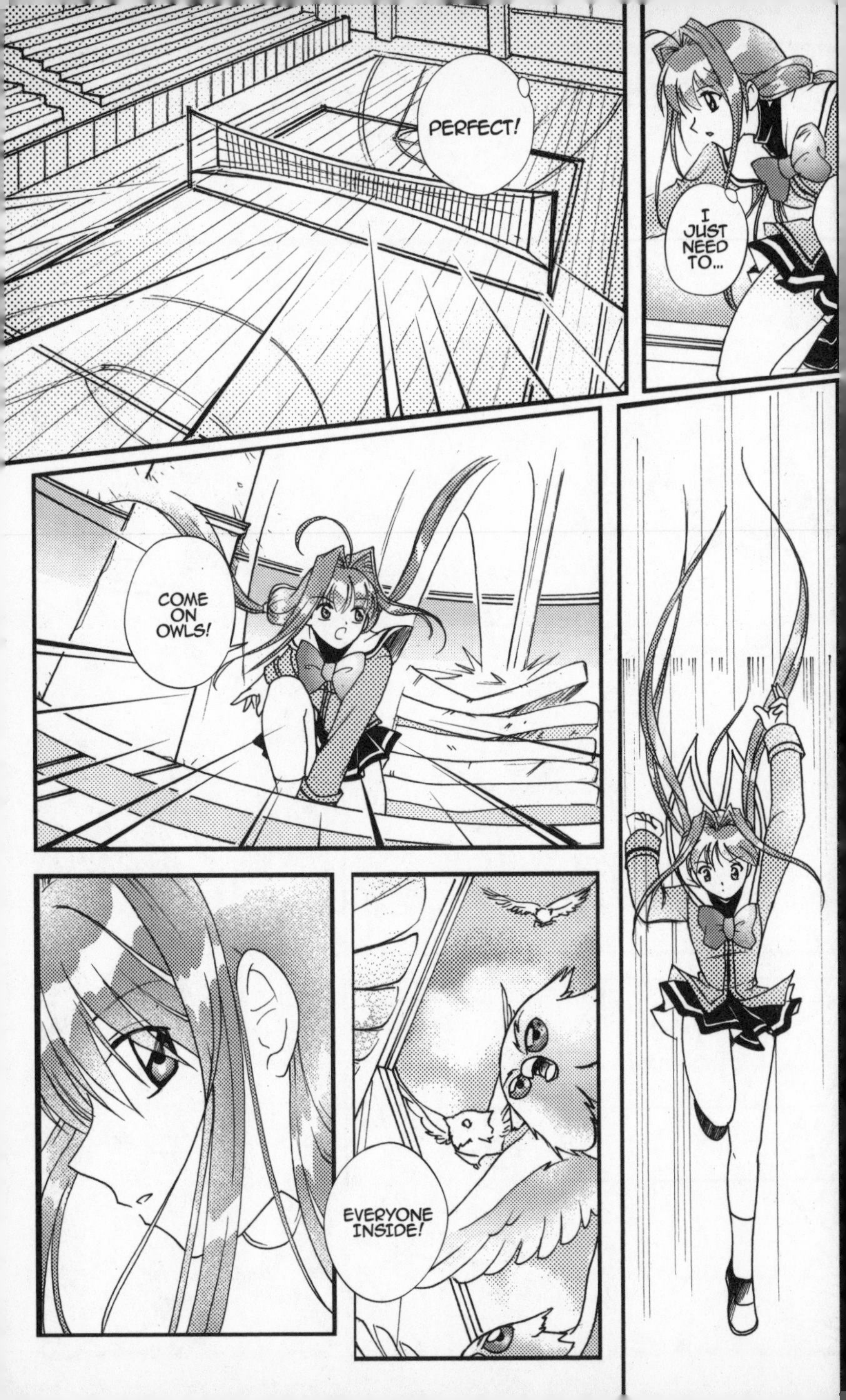
I JUST NEED TO...
PERFECT!
COME ON OWLS!
EVERYONE INSIDE!

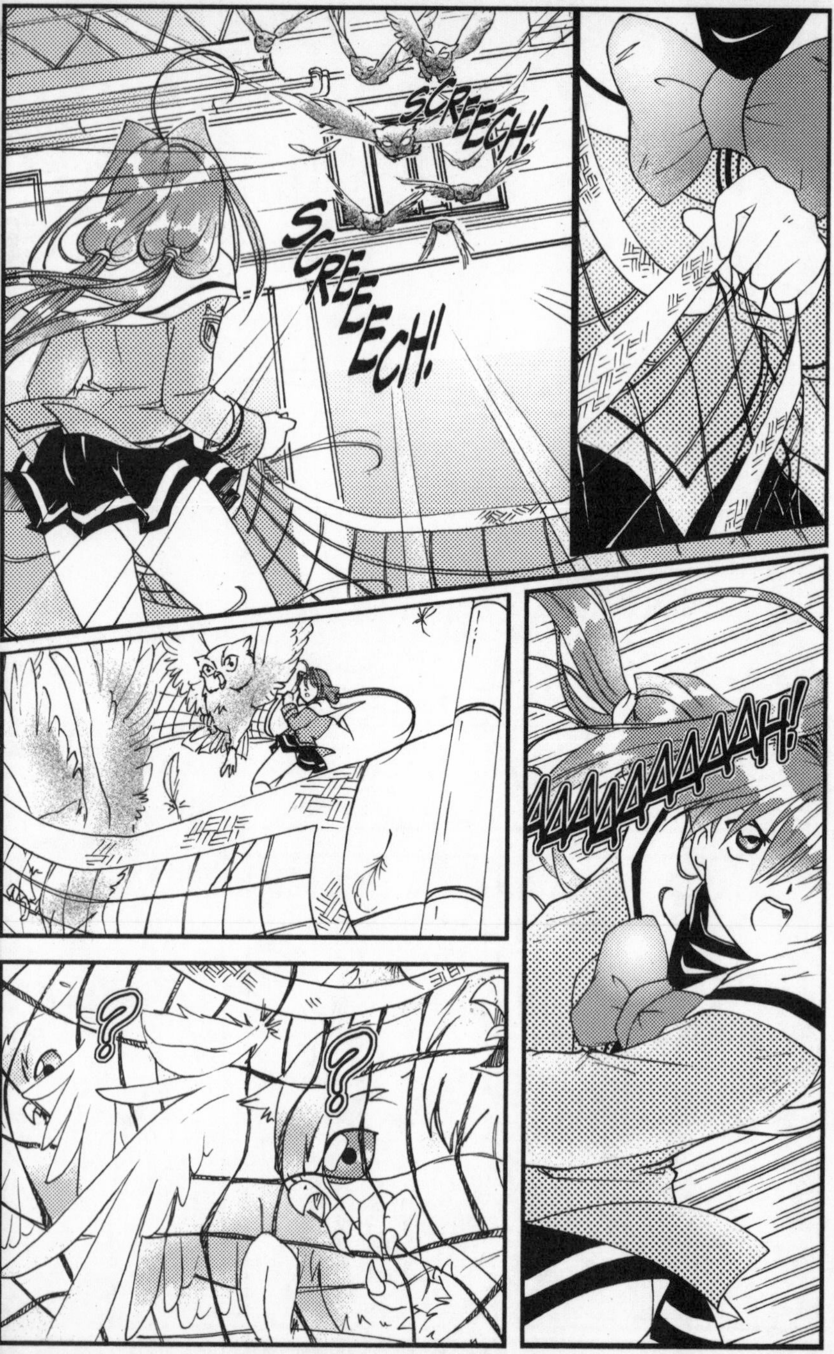
SCREEECH!
SCREEECH!
AAAAAAAAAAAAH!

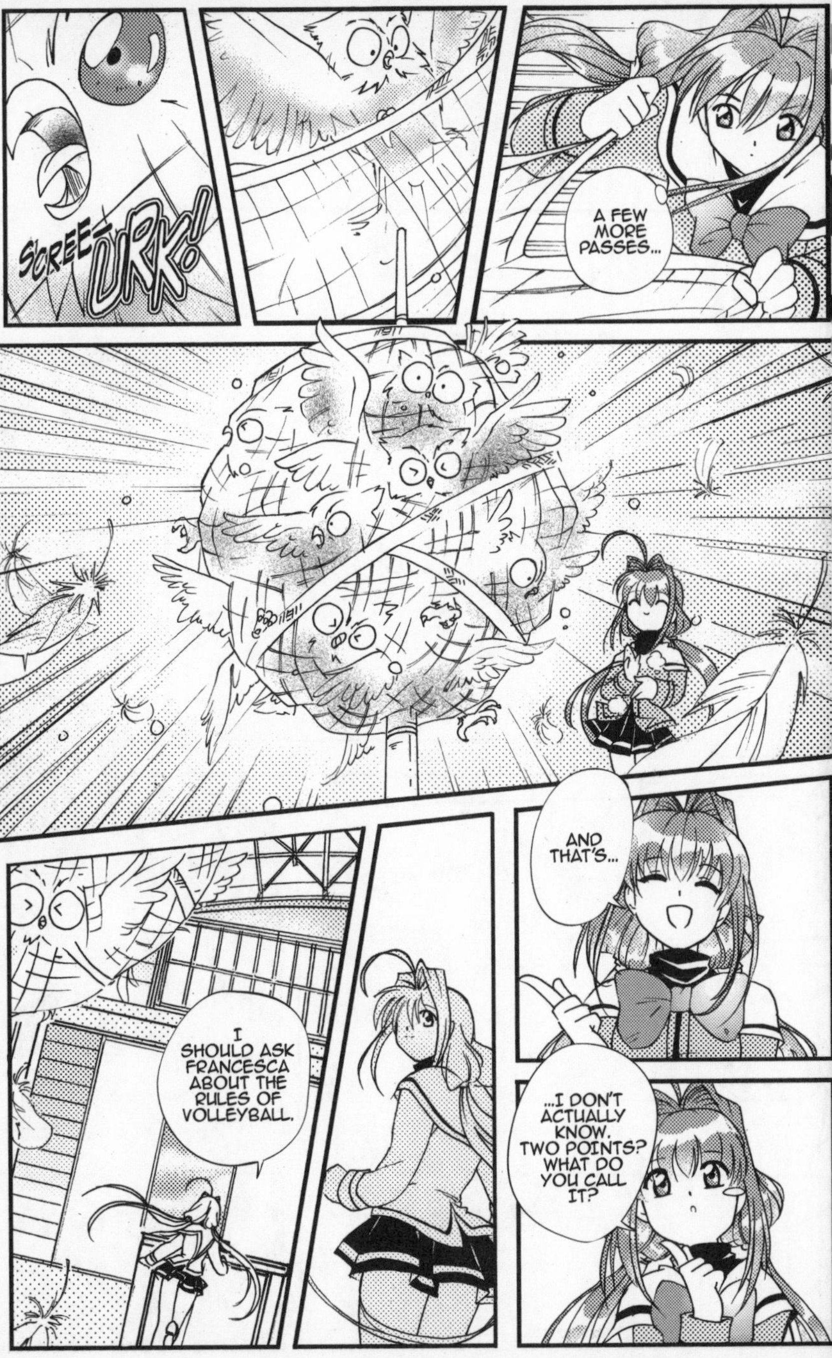
A FEW MORE PASSES...
SCREE-URK!
AND THAT'S...
...I DON'T ACTUALLY KNOW. TWO POINTS? WHAT DO YOU CALL IT?
I SHOULD ASK FRANCESCA ABOUT THE RULES OF VOLLEYBALL.

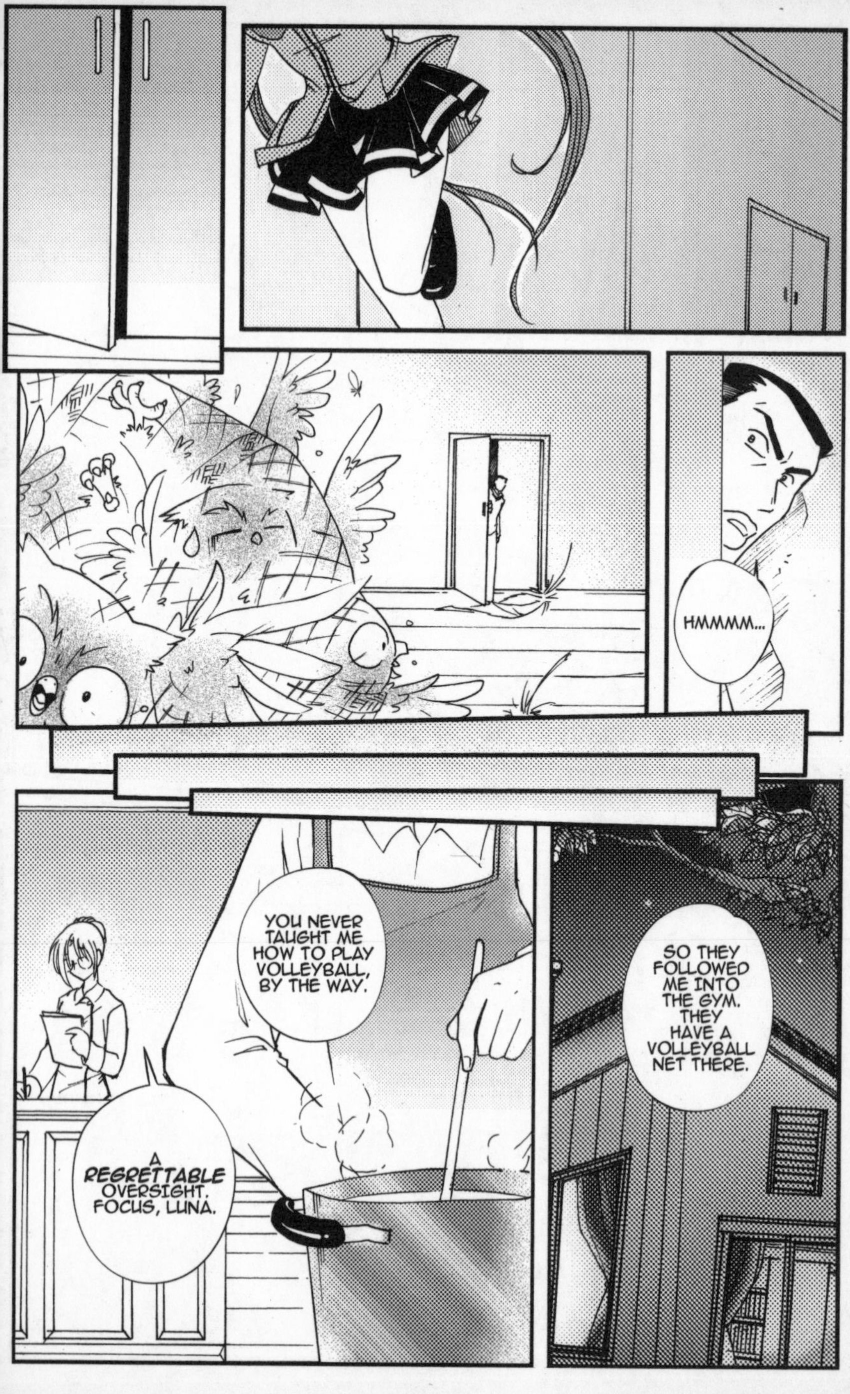
HMMMM...
SO THEY FOLLOWED ME INTO THE GYM. THEY HAVE A VOLLEYBALL NET THERE.
YOU NEVER TAUGHT ME HOW TO PLAY VOLLEYBALL, BY THE WAY.
A REGRETTABLE OVERSIGHT. FOCUS, LUNA.

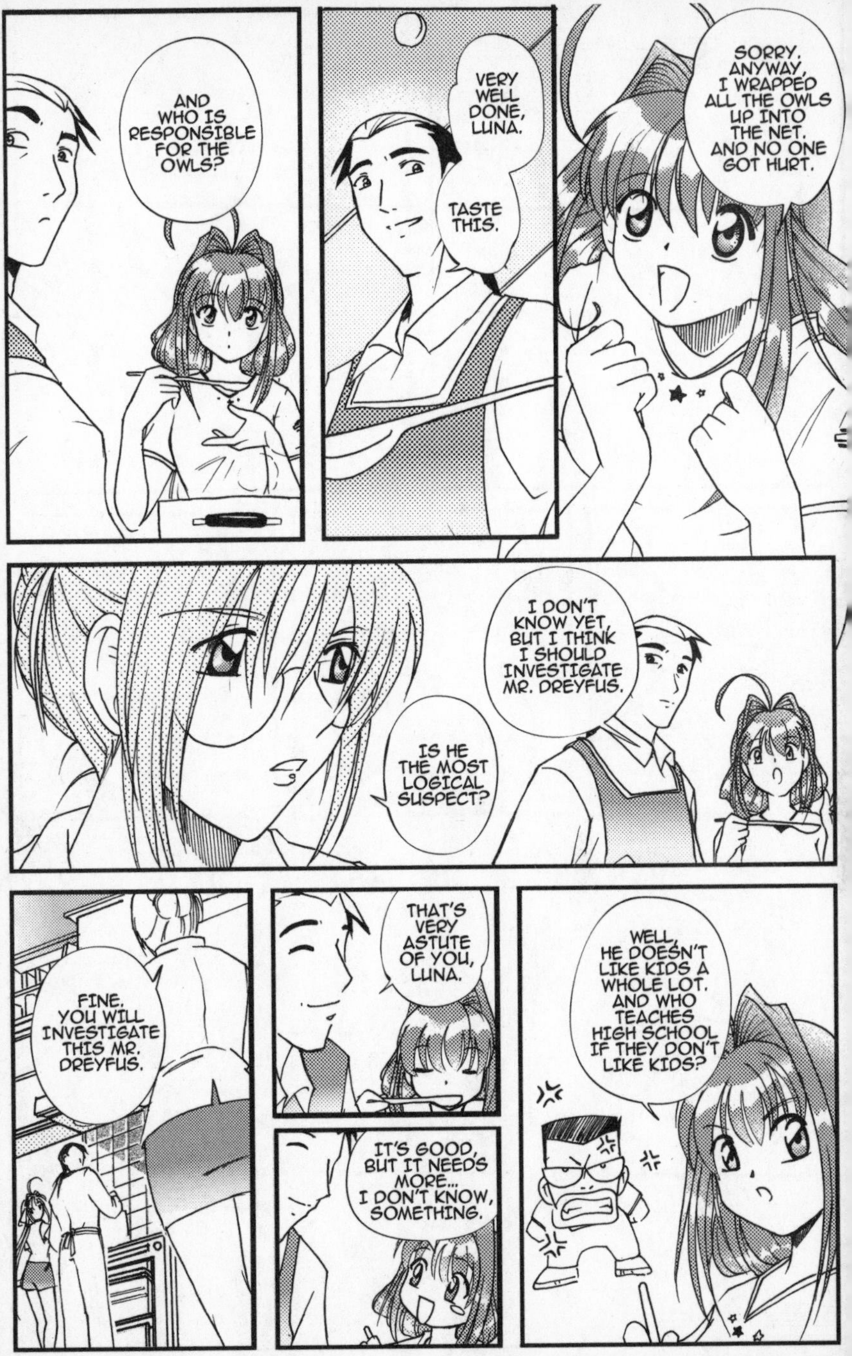
SORRY, ANYWAY, I WRAPPED ALL THE OWLS UP INTO THE NET. AND NO ONE GOT HURT.
VERY WELL DONE, LUNA.
TASTE THIS.
AND WHO IS RESPONSIBLE FOR THE OWLS?
I DON'T KNOW YET, BUT I THINK I SHOULD INVESTIGATE MR. DREYFUS.
IS HE THE MOST LOGICAL SUSPECT?
WELL, HE DOESN'T LIKE KIDS A WHOLE LOT. AND WHO TEACHES HIGH SCHOOL IF THEY DON'T LIKE KIDS?
THAT'S VERY ASTUTE OF YOU, LUNA.
IT'S GOOD, BUT IT NEEDS MORE... I DON'T KNOW, SOMETHING.
FINE. YOU WILL INVESTIGATE THIS MR. DREYFUS.

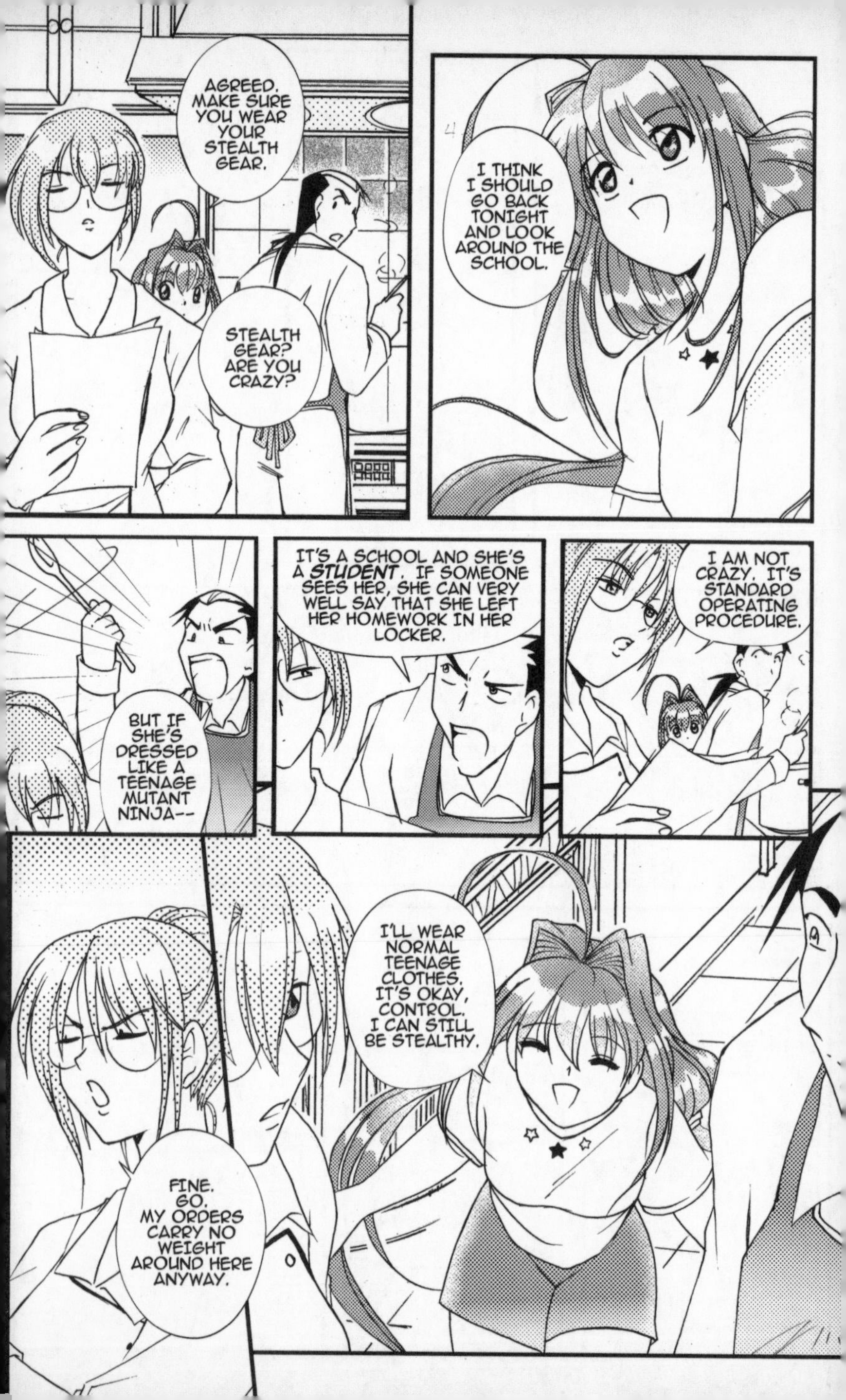
I THINK I SHOULD GO BACK TONIGHT AND LOOK AROUND THE SCHOOL.
AGREED. MAKE SURE YOU WEAR YOUR STEALTH GEAR.
STEALTH GEAR? ARE YOU CRAZY?
I AM NOT CRAZY. IT'S STANDARD OPERATING PROCEDURE.
IT'S A SCHOOL AND SHE'S A *STUDENT*. IF SOMEONE SEES HER, SHE CAN VERY WELL SAY THAT SHE LEFT HER HOMEWORK IN HER LOCKER.
BUT IF SHE'S DRESSED LIKE A TEENAGE MUTANT NINJA--
I'LL WEAR NORMAL TEENAGE CLOTHES. IT'S OKAY, CONTROL. I CAN STILL BE STEALTHY.
FINE. GO. MY ORDERS CARRY NO WEIGHT AROUND HERE ANYWAY.

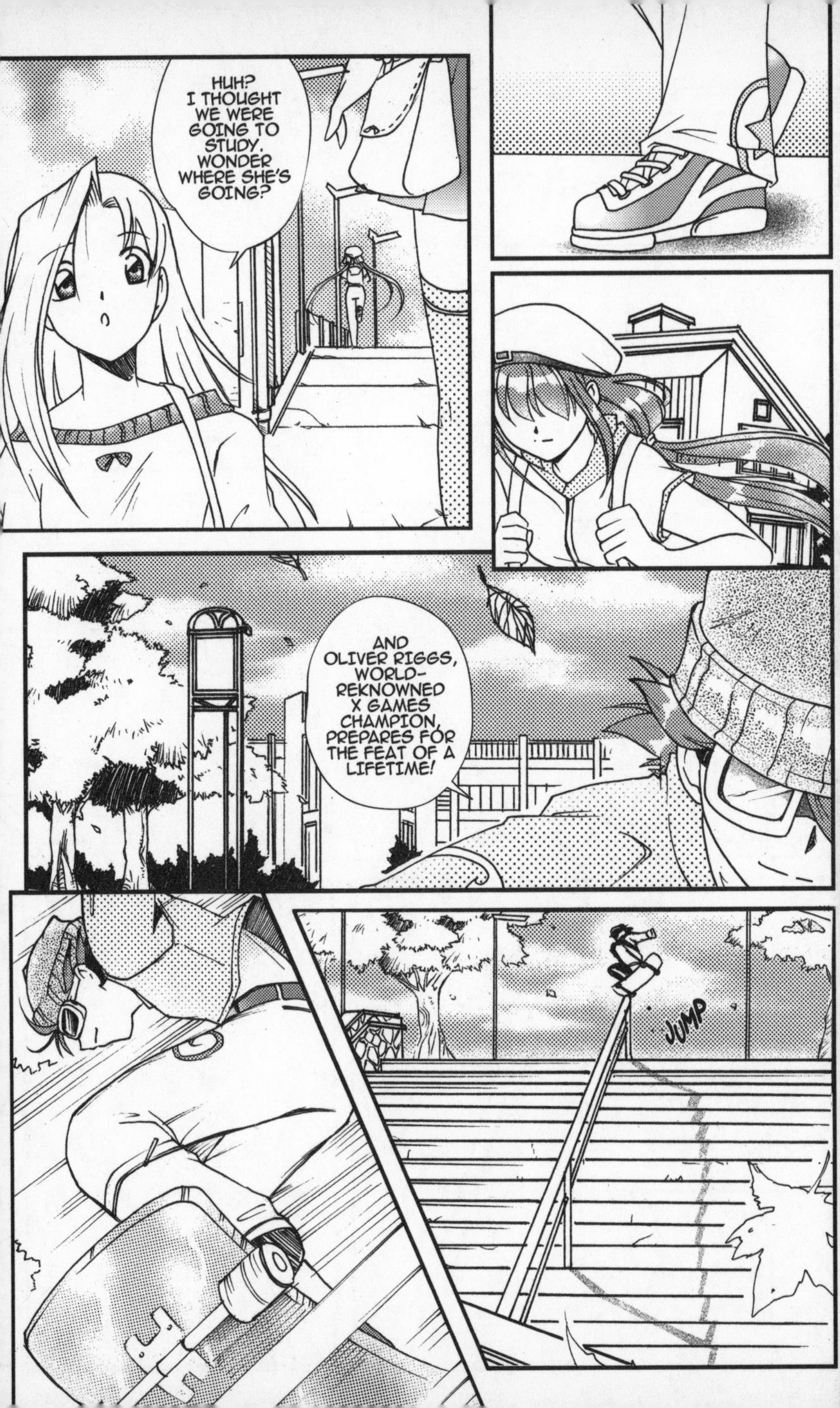
HUH? I THOUGHT WE WERE GOING TO STUDY. WONDER WHERE SHE'S GOING?
AND OLIVER RIGGS, WORLD-REKNOWNED X GAMES CHAMPION, PREPARES FOR THE FEAT OF A LIFETIME!
JUMP

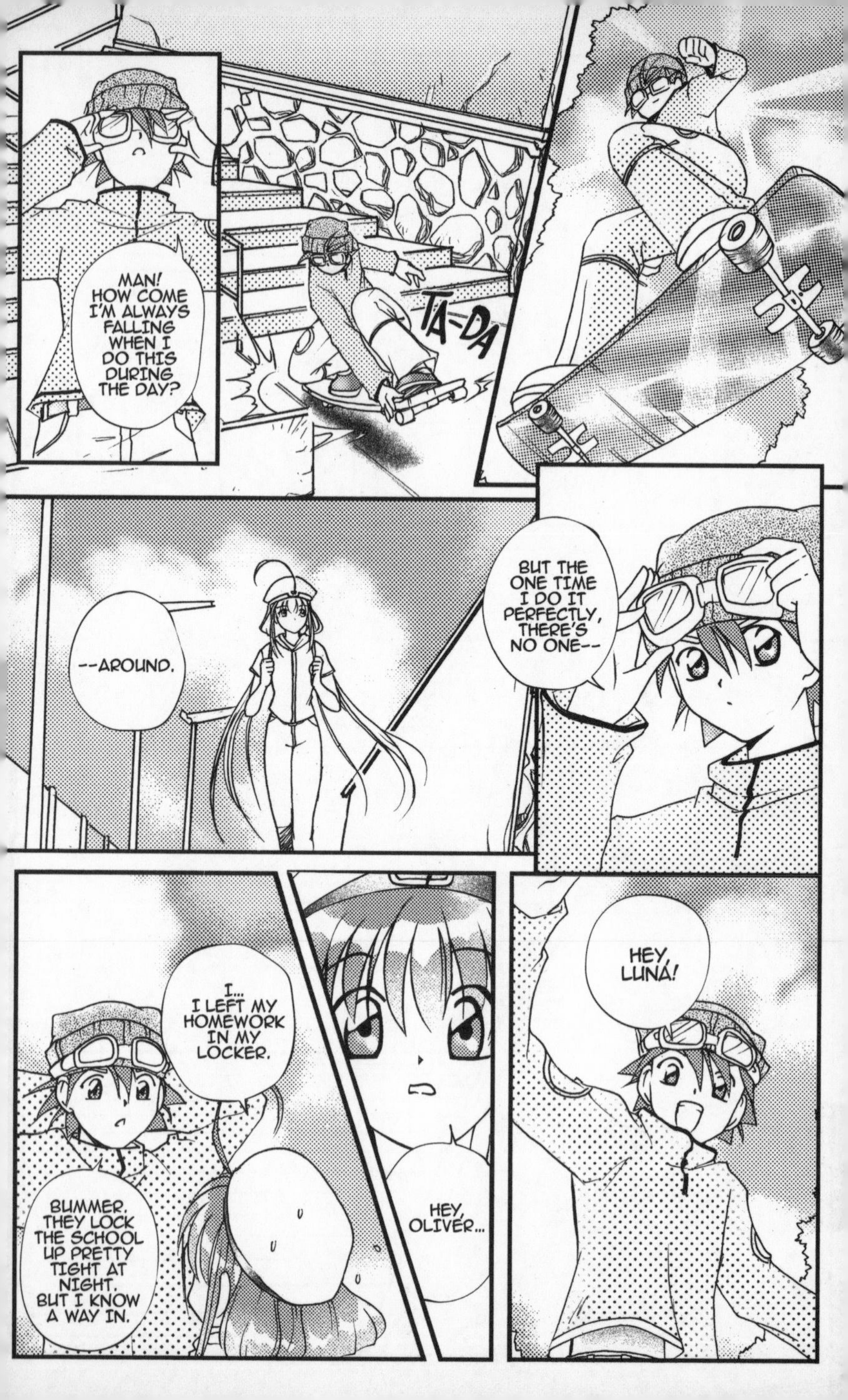
TA-DA
MAN! HOW COME I'M ALWAYS FALLING WHEN I DO THIS DURING THE DAY?
BUT THE ONE TIME I DO IT PERFECTLY, THERE'S NO ONE--
--AROUND.
HEY, LUNA!
HEY, OLIVER...
I... I LEFT MY HOMEWORK IN MY LOCKER.
BUMMER. THEY LOCK THE SCHOOL UP PRETTY TIGHT AT NIGHT. BUT I KNOW A WAY IN.

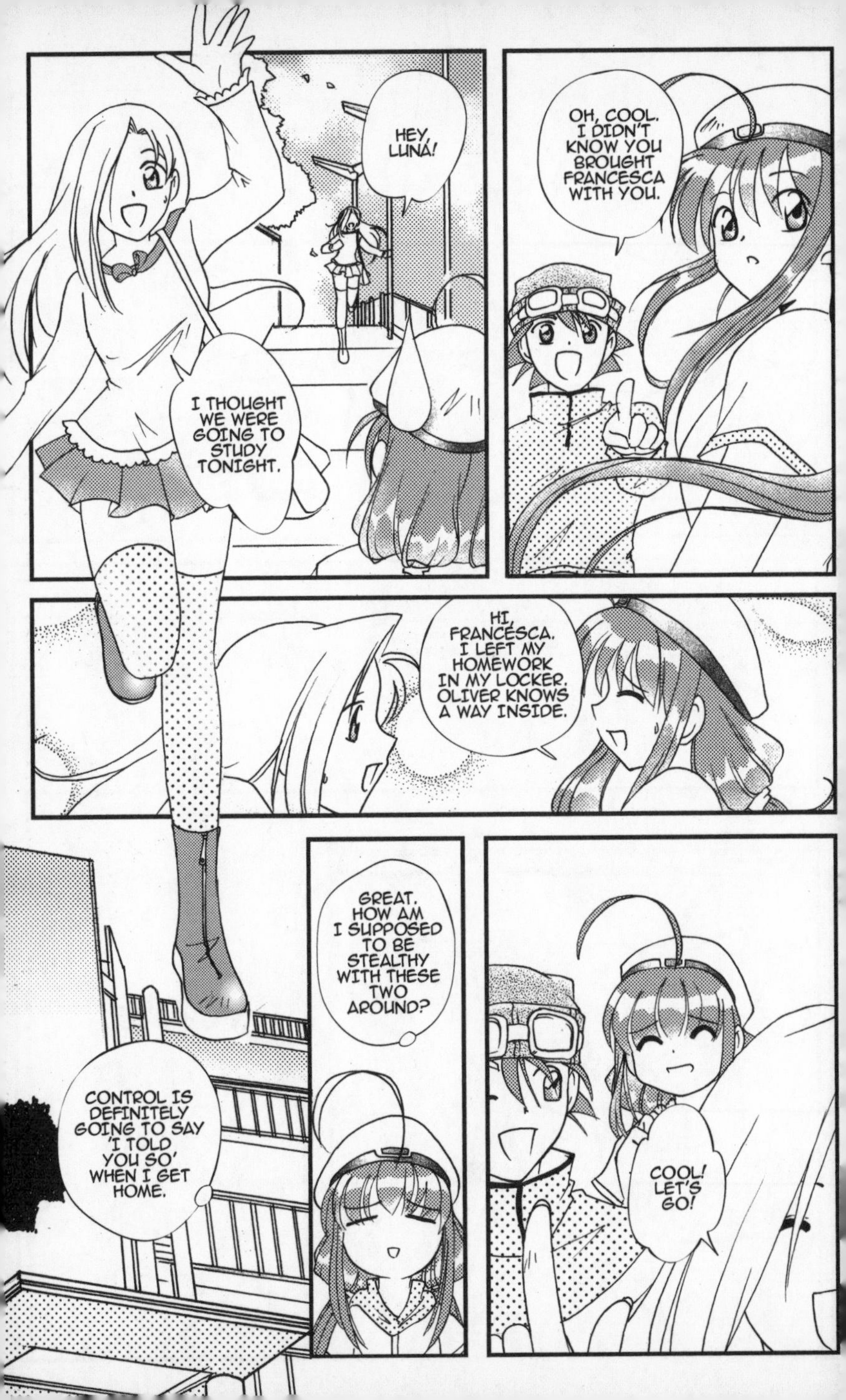
OH, COOL. I DIDN'T KNOW YOU BROUGHT FRANCESCA WITH YOU.
HEY, LUNA!
I THOUGHT WE WERE GOING TO STUDY TONIGHT.
HI, FRANCESCA. I LEFT MY HOMEWORK IN MY LOCKER. OLIVER KNOWS A WAY INSIDE.
COOL! LET'S GO!
GREAT. HOW AM I SUPPOSED TO BE STEALTHY WITH THESE TWO AROUND?
CONTROL IS DEFINITELY GOING TO SAY 'I TOLD YOU SO' WHEN I GET HOME.

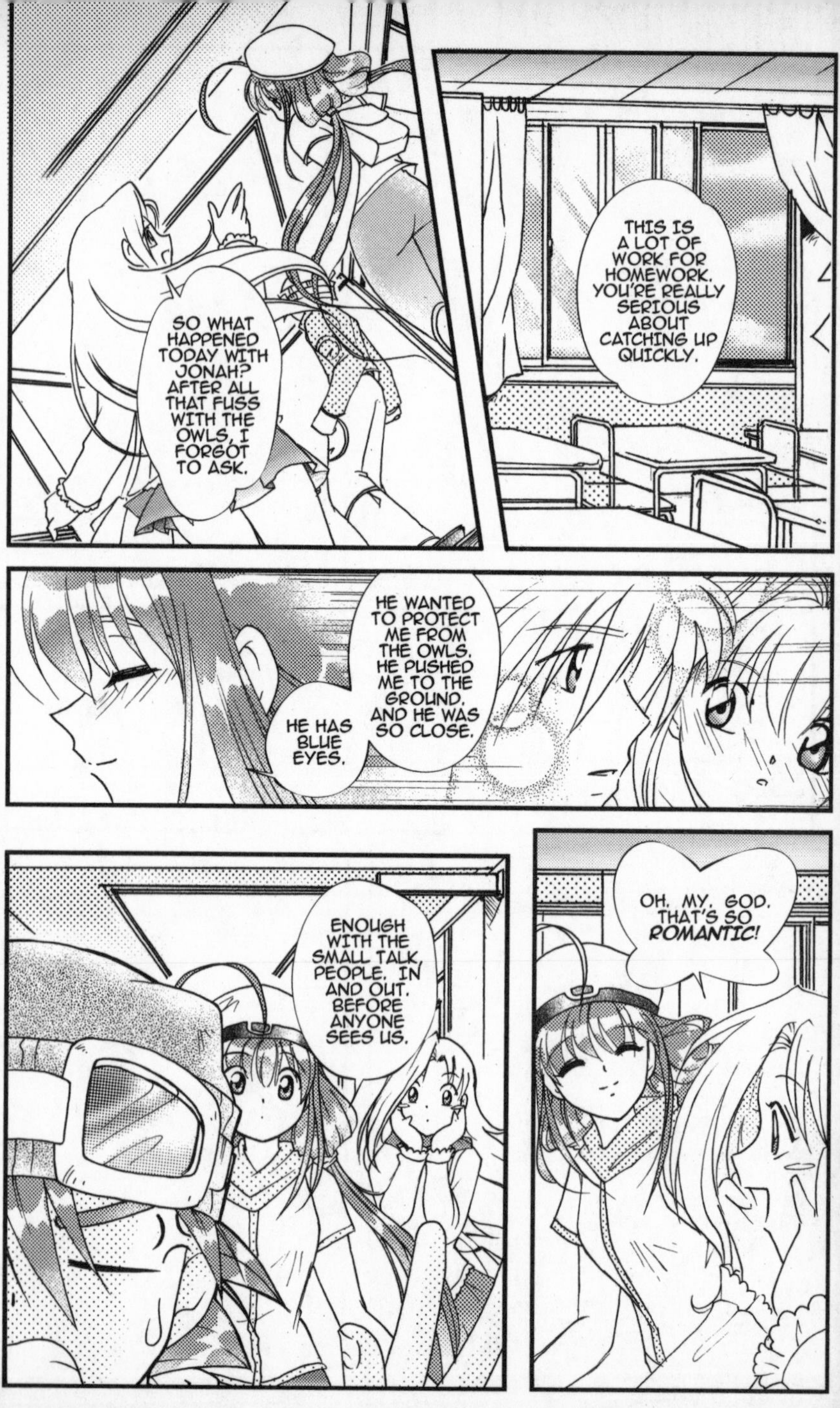
THIS IS A LOT OF WORK FOR HOMEWORK. YOU'RE REALLY SERIOUS ABOUT CATCHING UP QUICKLY.
SO WHAT HAPPENED TODAY WITH JONAH? AFTER ALL THAT FUSS WITH THE OWLS, I FORGOT TO ASK.
HE WANTED TO PROTECT ME FROM THE OWLS. HE PUSHED ME TO THE GROUND, AND HE WAS SO CLOSE.
HE HAS BLUE EYES.
OH. MY. GOD. THAT'S SO *ROMANTIC!*
ENOUGH WITH THE SMALL TALK, PEOPLE. IN AND OUT. BEFORE ANYONE SEES US.

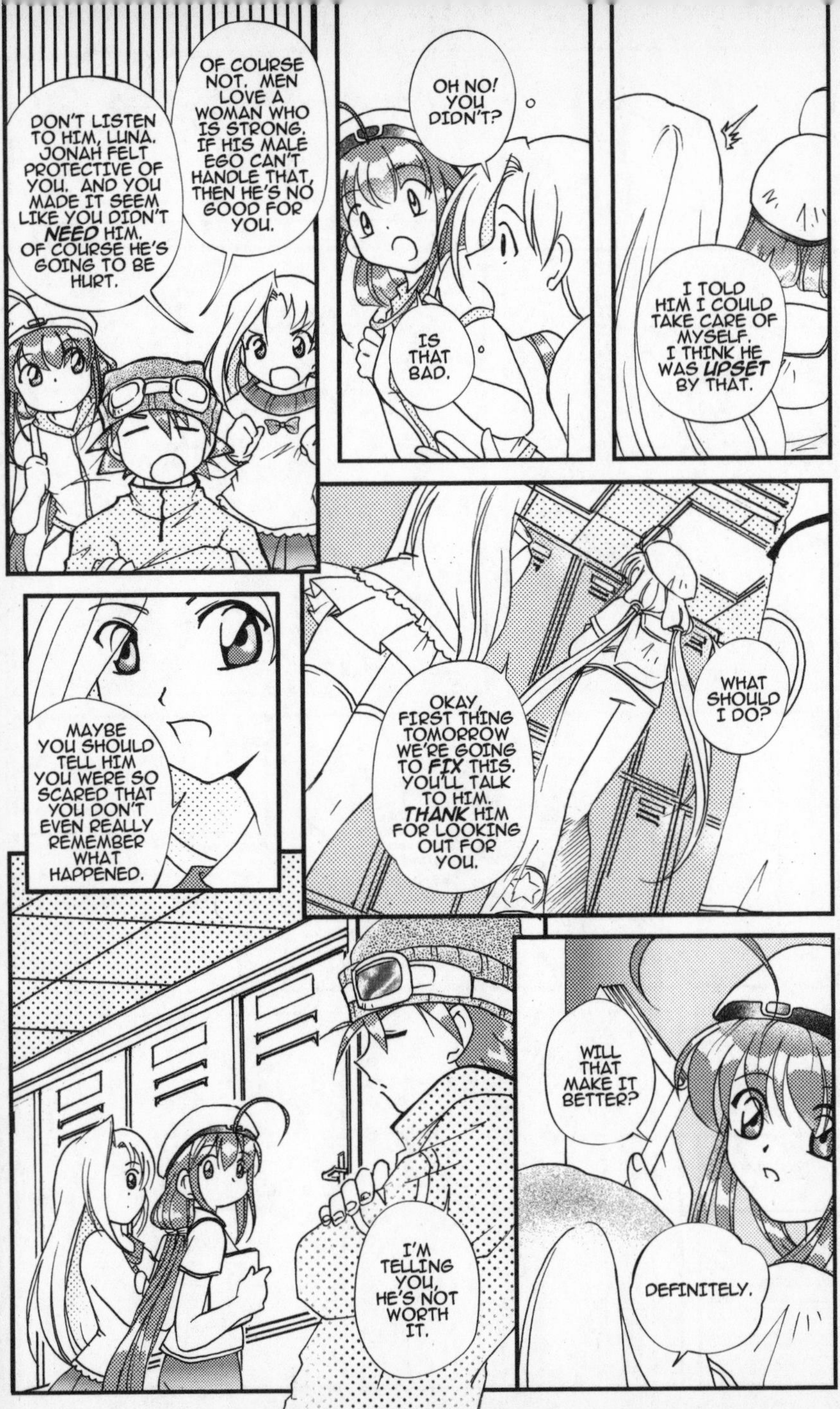
I TOLD HIM I COULD TAKE CARE OF MYSELF. I THINK HE WAS *UPSET* BY THAT.
OH NO! YOU DIDN'T?
IS THAT BAD.
OF COURSE NOT. MEN LOVE A WOMAN WHO IS STRONG. IF HIS MALE EGO CAN'T HANDLE THAT, THEN HE'S NO GOOD FOR YOU.
DON'T LISTEN TO HIM, LUNA. JONAH FELT PROTECTIVE OF YOU. AND YOU MADE IT SEEM LIKE YOU DIDN'T *NEED* HIM. OF COURSE HE'S GOING TO BE HURT.
WHAT SHOULD I DO?
OKAY, FIRST THING TOMORROW WE'RE GOING TO *FIX* THIS. YOU'LL TALK TO HIM. *THANK* HIM FOR LOOKING OUT FOR YOU.
MAYBE YOU SHOULD TELL HIM YOU WERE SO SCARED THAT YOU DON'T EVEN REALLY REMEMBER WHAT HAPPENED.
WILL THAT MAKE IT BETTER?
DEFINITELY.
I'M TELLING YOU, HE'S NOT WORTH IT.

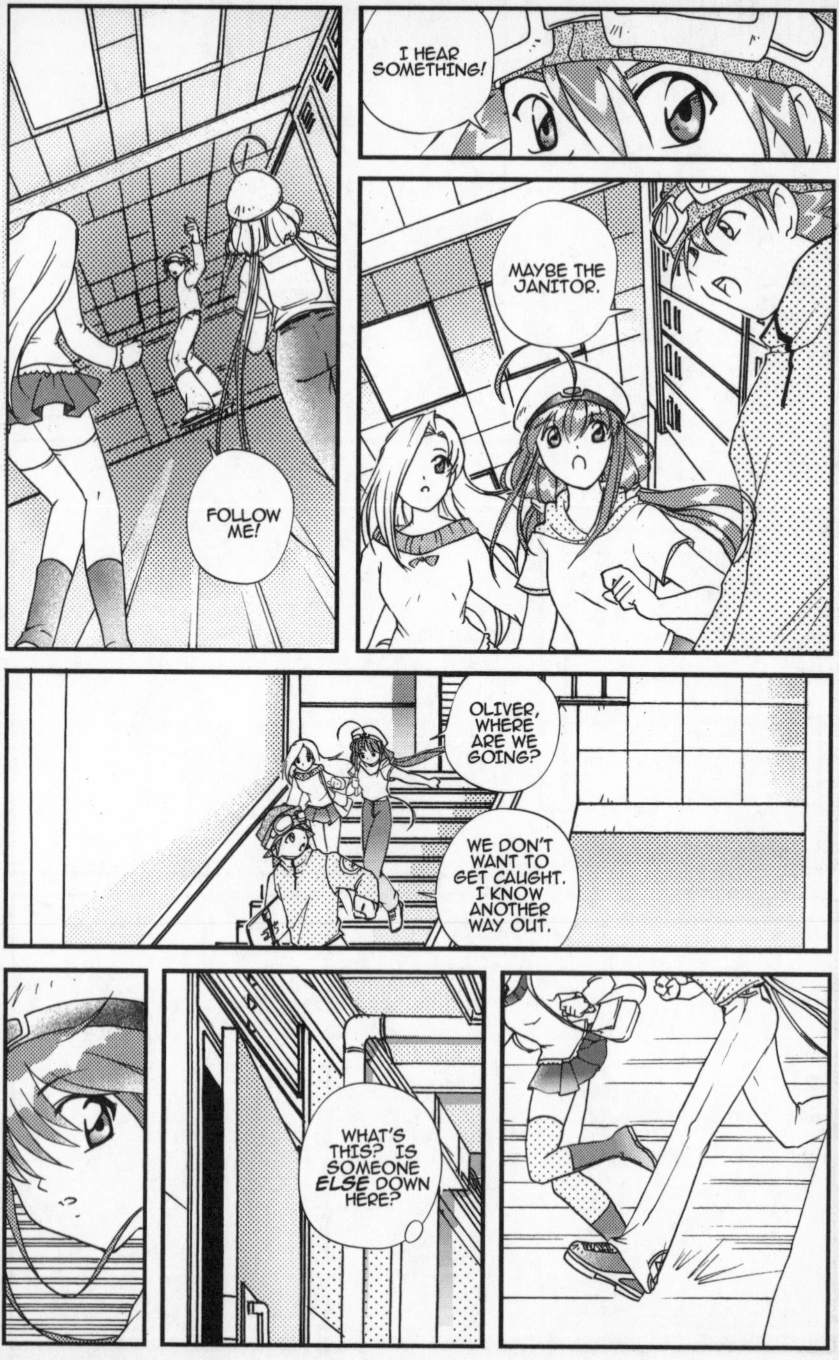
I HEAR SOMETHING!
MAYBE THE JANITOR.
FOLLOW ME!
OLIVER, WHERE ARE WE GOING?
WE DON'T WANT TO GET CAUGHT. I KNOW ANOTHER WAY OUT.
WHAT'S THIS? IS SOMEONE *ELSE* DOWN HERE?

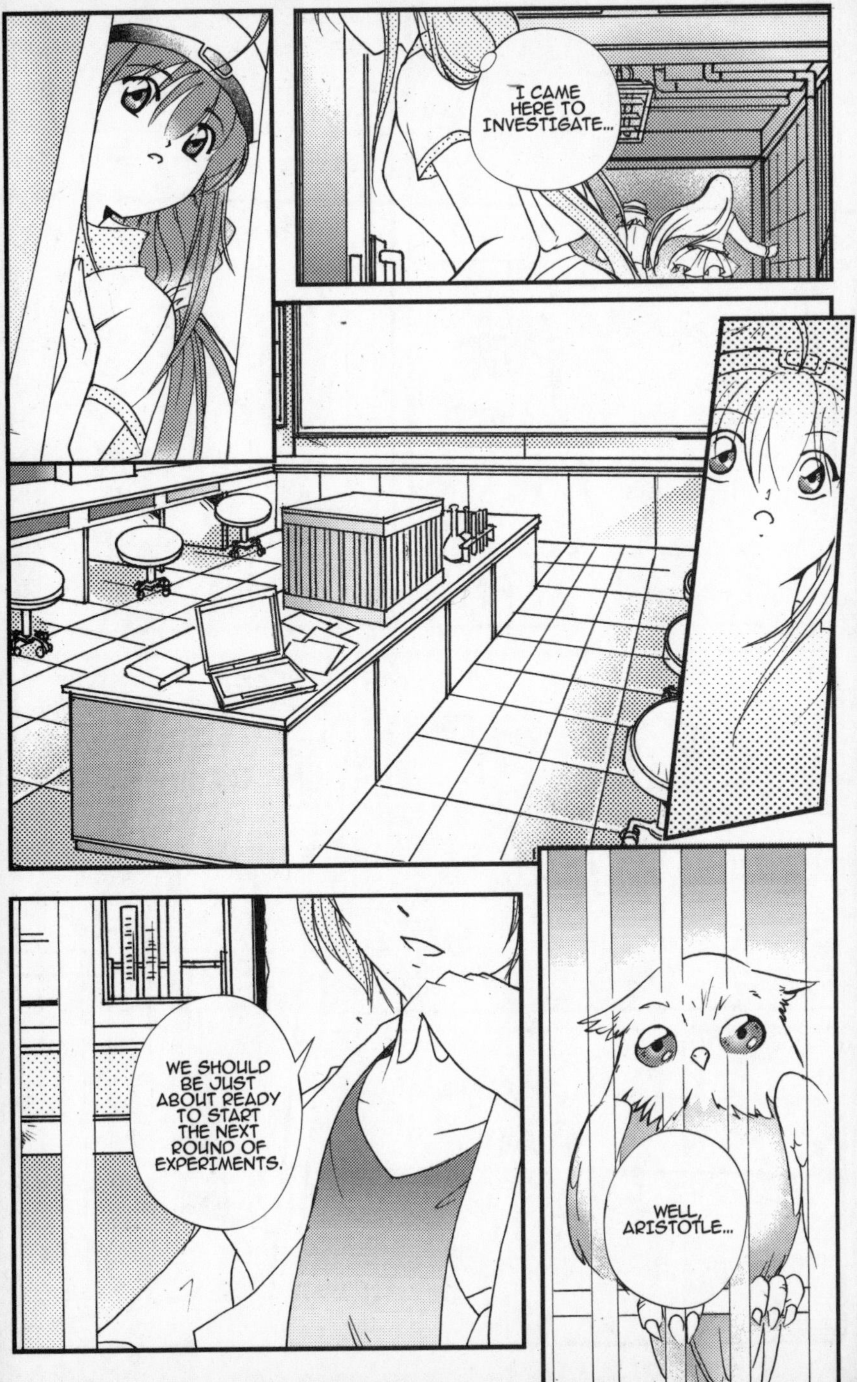
I CAME HERE TO INVESTIGATE...
WELL, ARISTOTLE...
WE SHOULD BE JUST ABOUT READY TO START THE NEXT ROUND OF EXPERIMENTS.

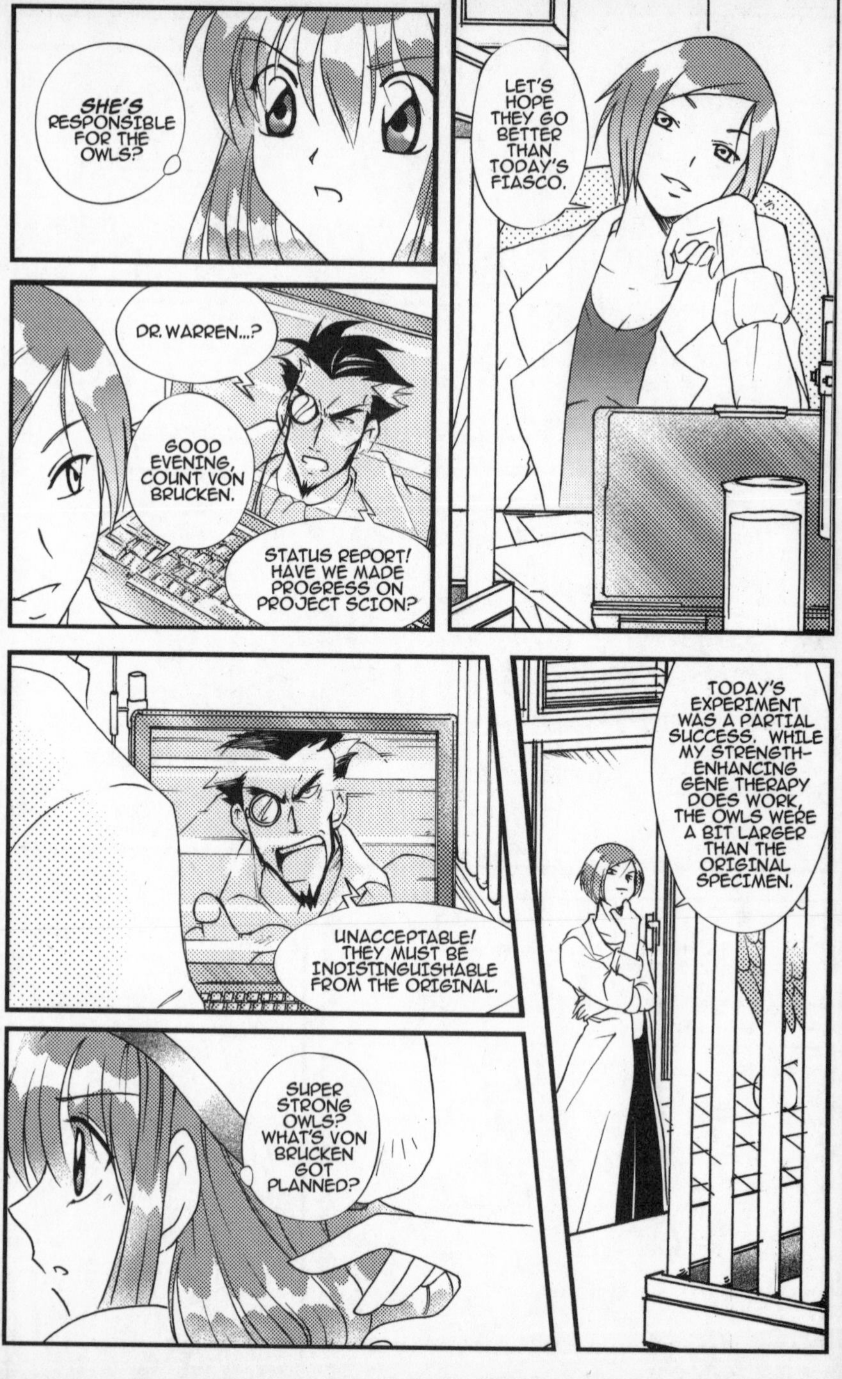
LET'S HOPE THEY GO BETTER THAN TODAY'S FIASCO.
SHE'S RESPONSIBLE FOR THE OWLS?
DR. WARREN...?
GOOD EVENING, COUNT VON BRUCKEN.
STATUS REPORT! HAVE WE MADE PROGRESS ON PROJECT SCION?
TODAY'S EXPERIMENT WAS A PARTIAL SUCCESS. WHILE MY STRENGTH-ENHANCING GENE THERAPY DOES WORK, THE OWLS WERE A BIT LARGER THAN THE ORIGINAL SPECIMEN.
UNACCEPTABLE! THEY MUST BE INDISTINGUISHABLE FROM THE ORIGINAL.
SUPER STRONG OWLS? WHAT'S VON BRUCKEN GOT PLANNED?

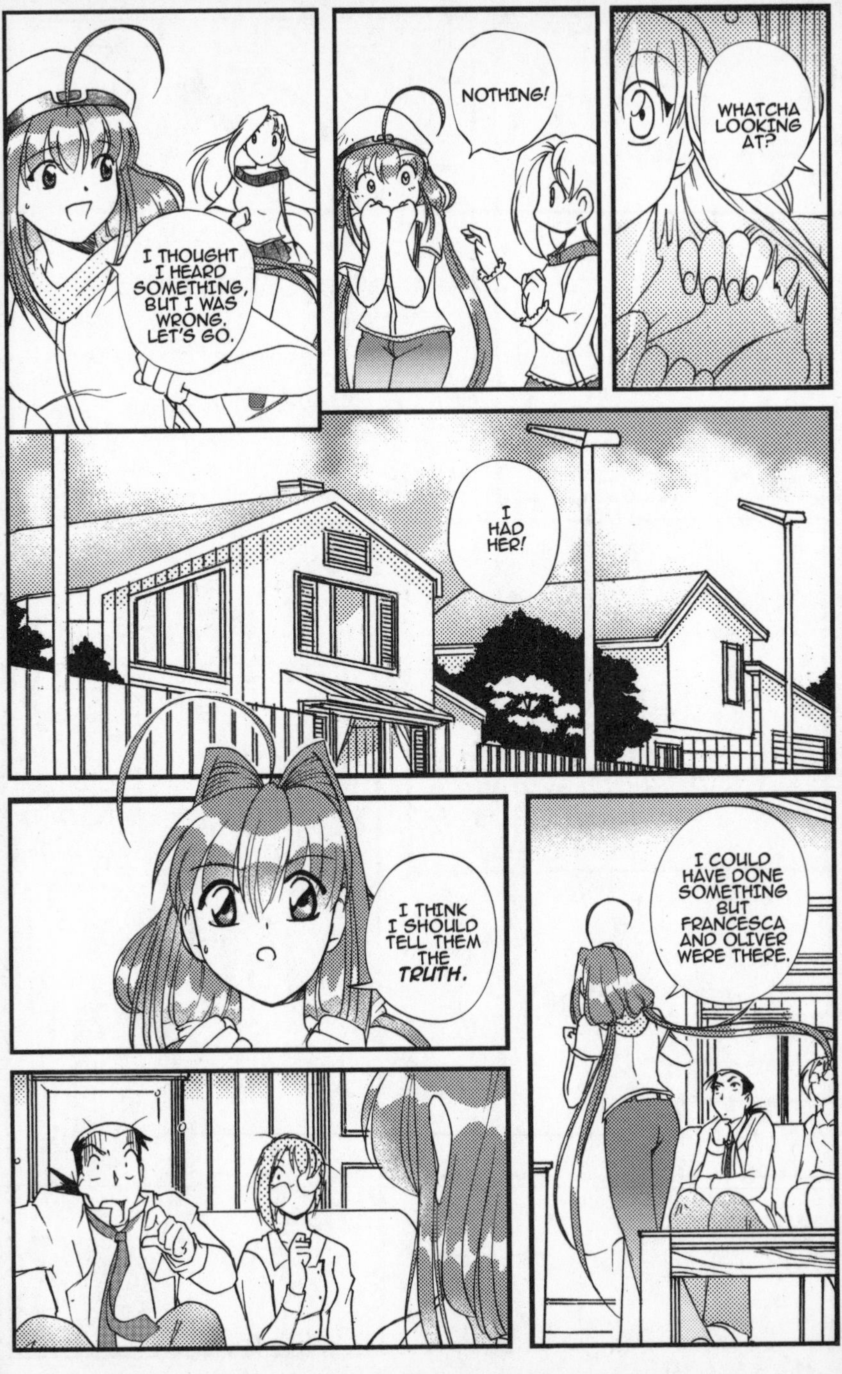
WHATCHA LOOKING AT?
NOTHING!
I THOUGHT I HEARD SOMETHING, BUT I WAS WRONG. LET'S GO.
I HAD HER!
I COULD HAVE DONE SOMETHING BUT FRANCESCA AND OLIVER WERE THERE.
I THINK I SHOULD TELL THEM THE *TRUTH*.

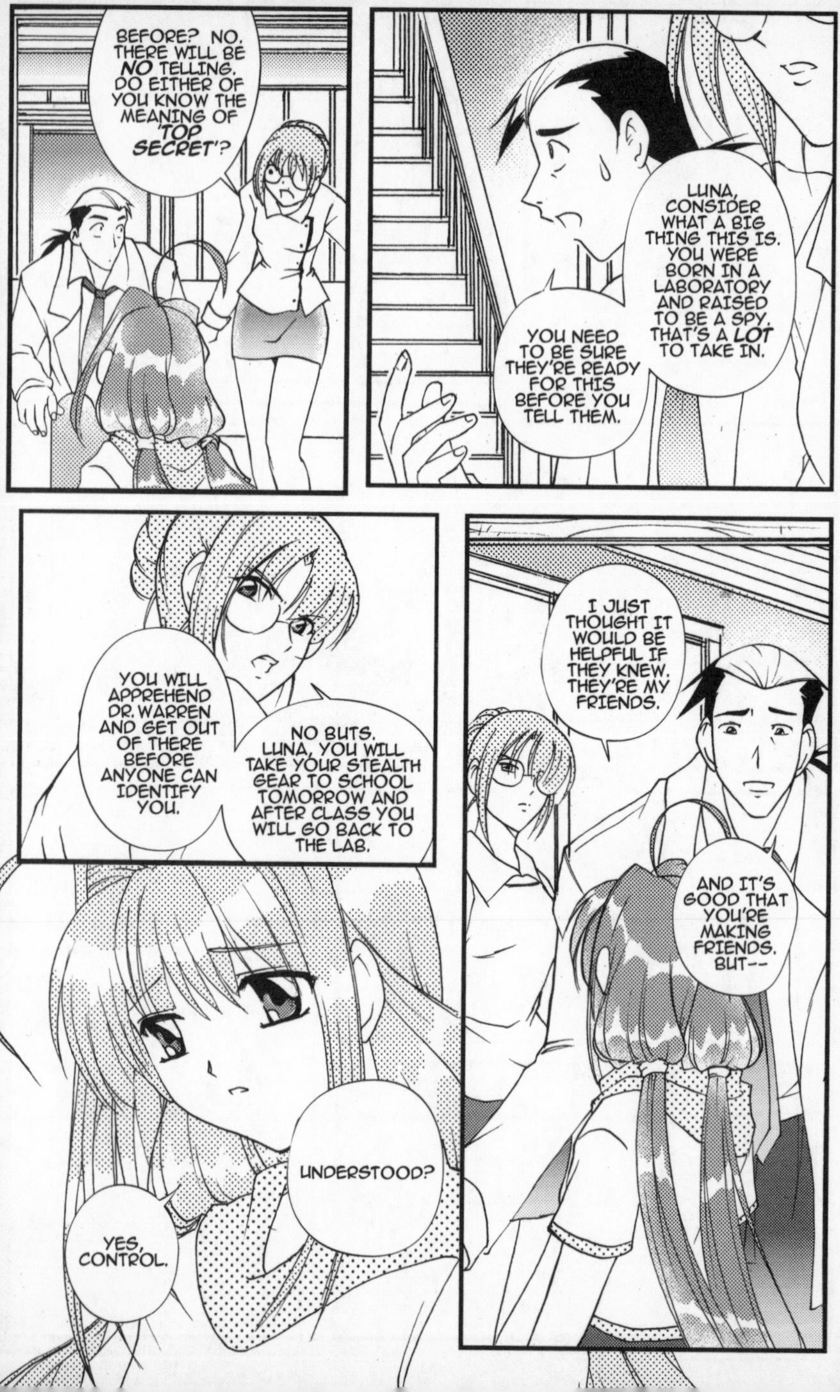
LUNA, CONSIDER WHAT A BIG THING THIS IS. YOU WERE BORN IN A LABORATORY AND RAISED TO BE A SPY. THAT'S A **LOT** TO TAKE IN.
YOU NEED TO BE SURE THEY'RE READY FOR THIS BEFORE YOU TELL THEM.
BEFORE? NO. THERE WILL BE **NO** TELLING. DO EITHER OF YOU KNOW THE MEANING OF '**TOP SECRET**'?
I JUST THOUGHT IT WOULD BE HELPFUL IF THEY KNEW. THEY'RE MY FRIENDS.
AND IT'S GOOD THAT YOU'RE MAKING FRIENDS. BUT--
NO BUTS. LUNA, YOU WILL TAKE YOUR STEALTH GEAR TO SCHOOL TOMORROW AND AFTER CLASS YOU WILL GO BACK TO THE LAB.
YOU WILL APPREHEND DR. WARREN AND GET OUT OF THERE BEFORE ANYONE CAN IDENTIFY YOU.
UNDERSTOOD?
YES, CONTROL.

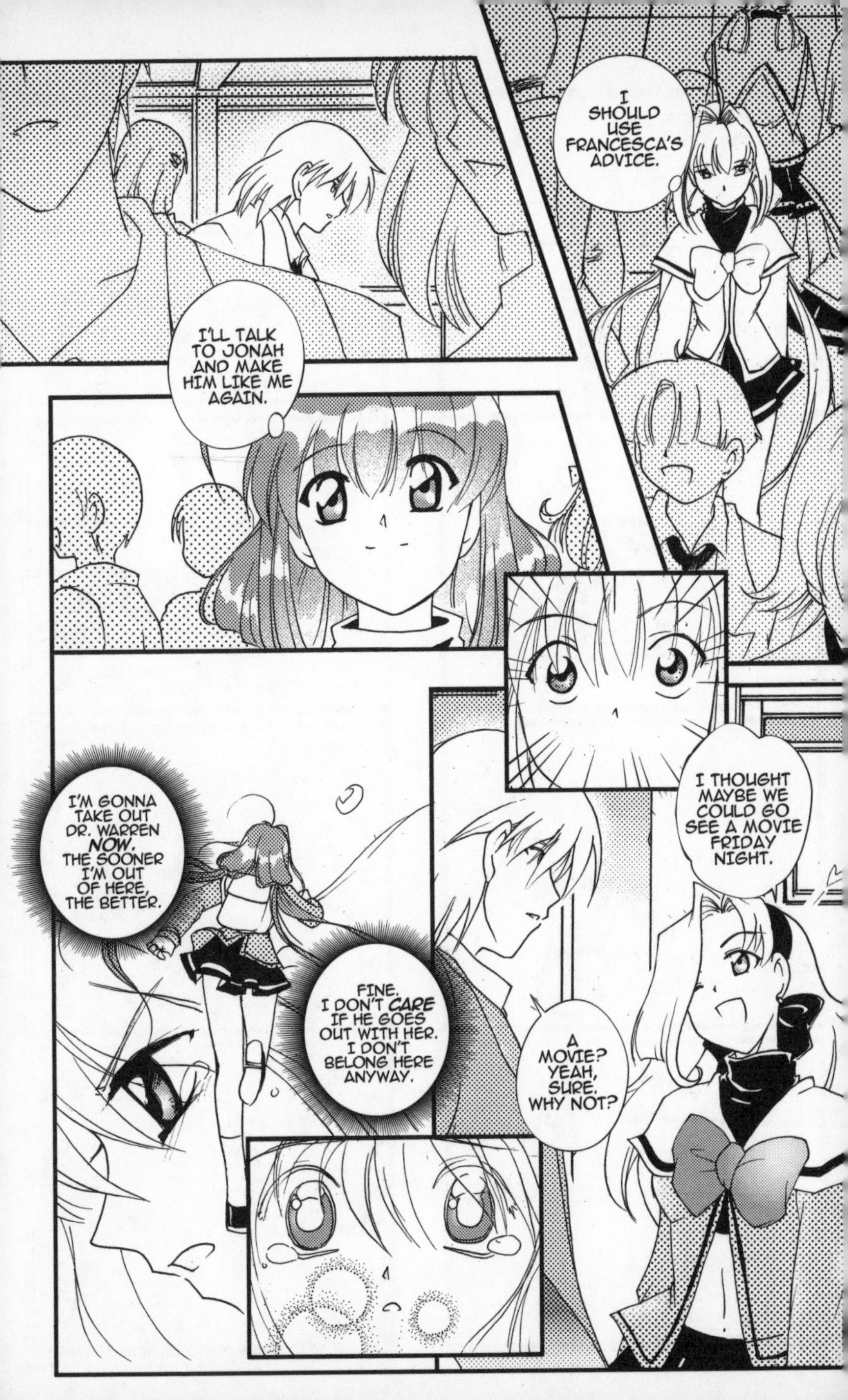
I SHOULD USE FRANCESCA'S ADVICE.
I'LL TALK TO JONAH AND MAKE HIM LIKE ME AGAIN.
I THOUGHT MAYBE WE COULD GO SEE A MOVIE FRIDAY NIGHT.
A MOVIE? YEAH, SURE. WHY NOT?
FINE. I DON'T *CARE* IF HE GOES OUT WITH HER. I DON'T BELONG HERE ANYWAY.
I'M GONNA TAKE OUT DR. WARREN ***NOW***. THE SOONER I'M OUT OF HERE, THE BETTER.

AMAZING ARTIST SHIEI

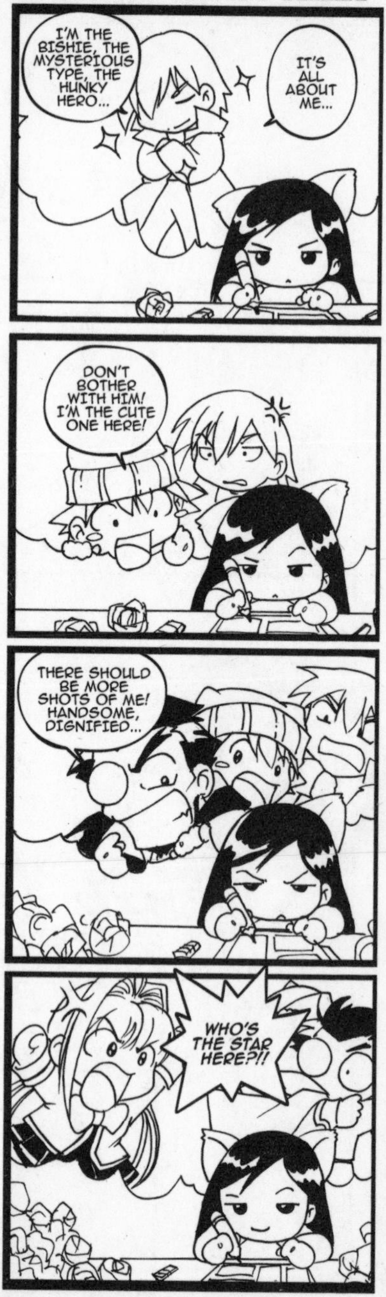
IT'S ALL ABOUT ME...
I'M THE BISHIE, THE MYSTERIOUS TYPE, THE HUNKY HERO...
DON'T BOTHER WITH HIM! I'M THE CUTE ONE HERE!
THERE SHOULD BE MORE SHOTS OF ME! HANDSOME, DIGNIFIED...
WHO'S THE STAR HERE?!!

FINISHED

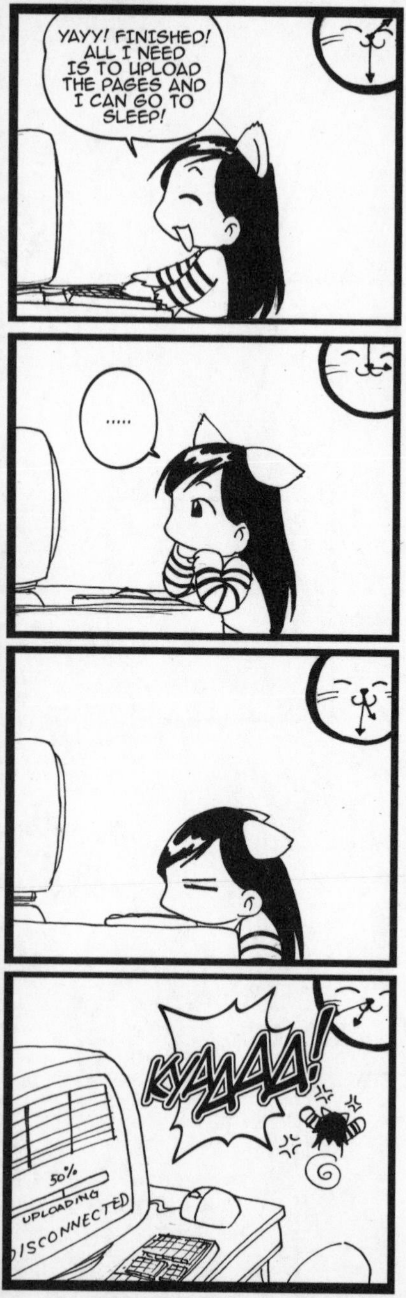
YAYY! FINISHED! ALL I NEED IS TO UPLOAD THE PAGES AND I CAN GO TO SLEEP!
.....
KYAAAA!
50%
UPLOADING
DISCONNECTED

## File 06
# MISSION ACCOMPLISHED?

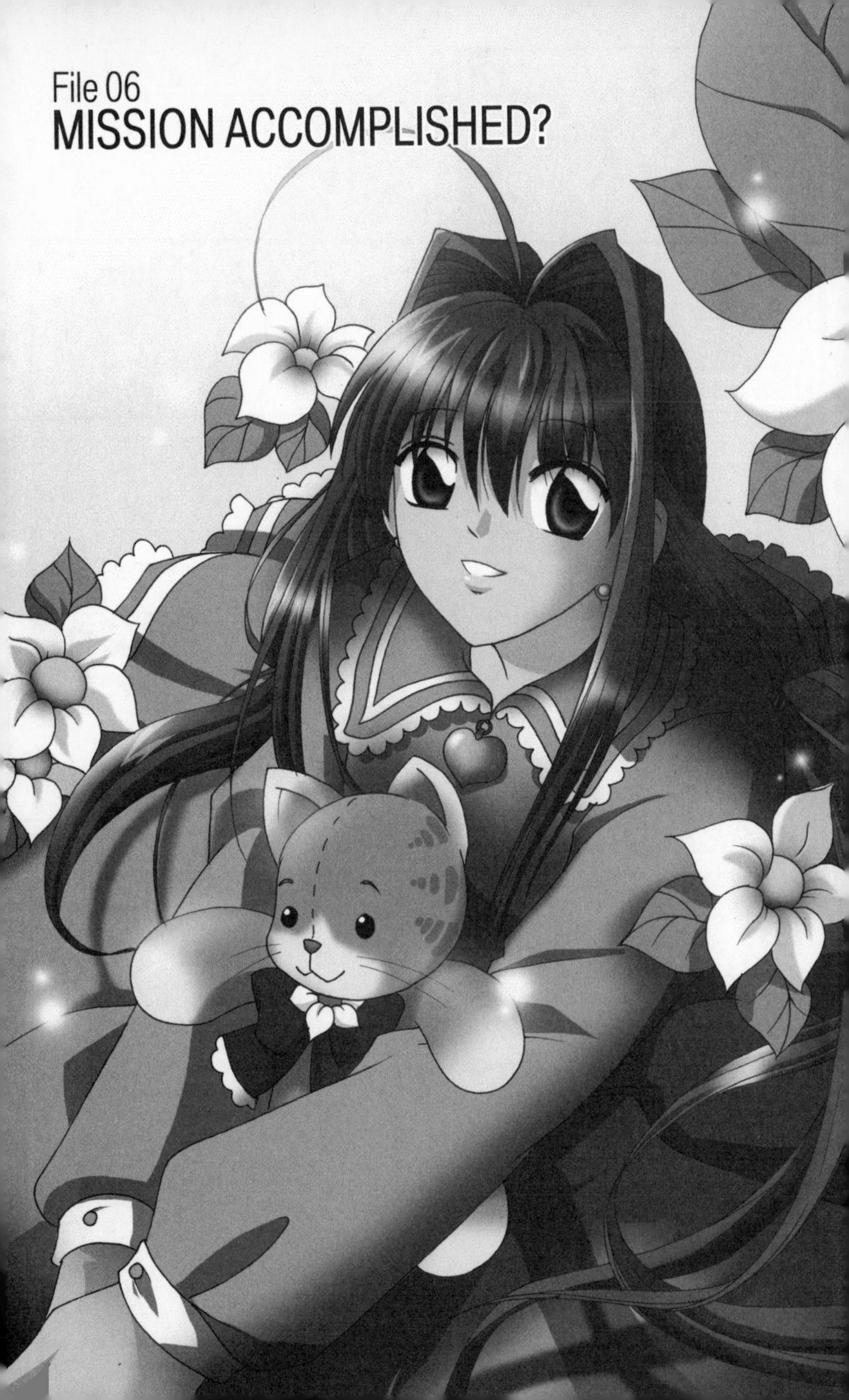

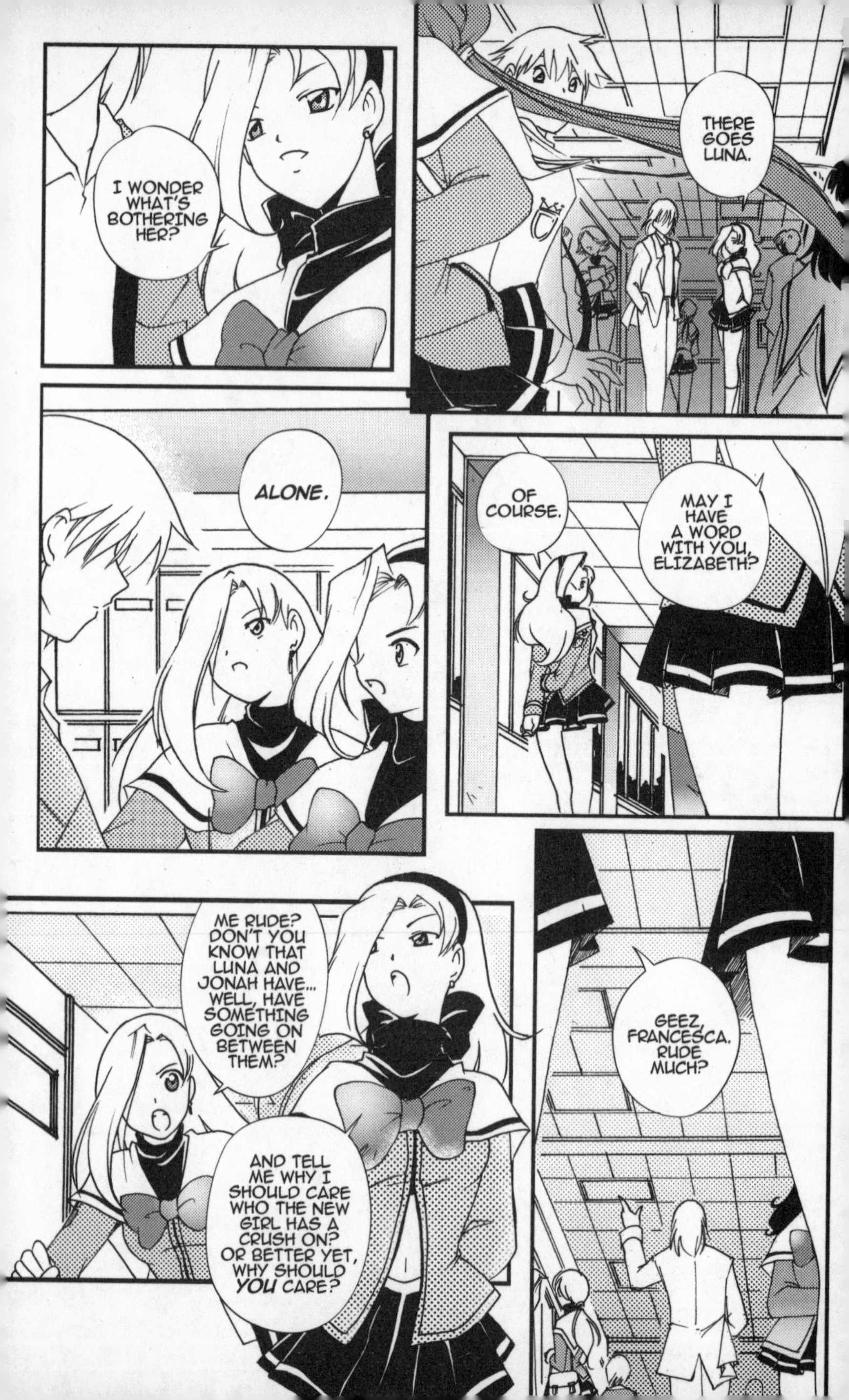
THERE GOES LUNA.
I WONDER WHAT'S BOTHERING HER?
MAY I HAVE A WORD WITH YOU, ELIZABETH?
OF COURSE.
ALONE.
GEEZ, FRANCESCA, RUDE MUCH?
ME RUDE? DON'T YOU KNOW THAT LUNA AND JONAH HAVE... WELL, HAVE SOMETHING GOING ON BETWEEN THEM?
AND TELL ME WHY I SHOULD CARE WHO THE NEW GIRL HAS A CRUSH ON? OR BETTER YET, WHY SHOULD YOU CARE?

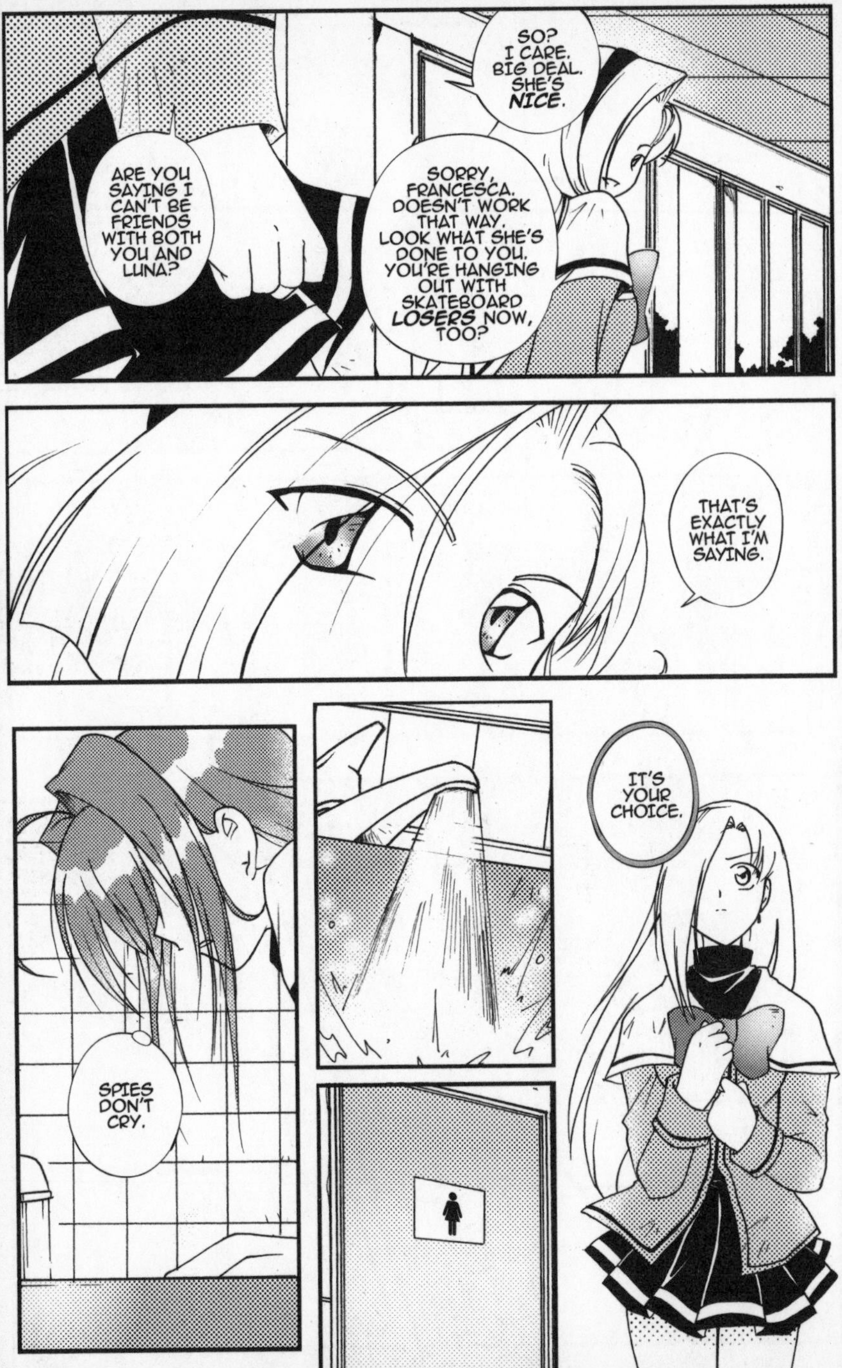
SO? I CARE. BIG DEAL. SHE'S *NICE*.
SORRY, FRANCESCA. DOESN'T WORK THAT WAY. LOOK WHAT SHE'S DONE TO YOU. YOU'RE HANGING OUT WITH SKATEBOARD **LOSERS** NOW, TOO?
ARE YOU SAYING I CAN'T BE FRIENDS WITH BOTH YOU AND LUNA?
THAT'S EXACTLY WHAT I'M SAYING.
IT'S YOUR CHOICE.
SPIES DON'T CRY.

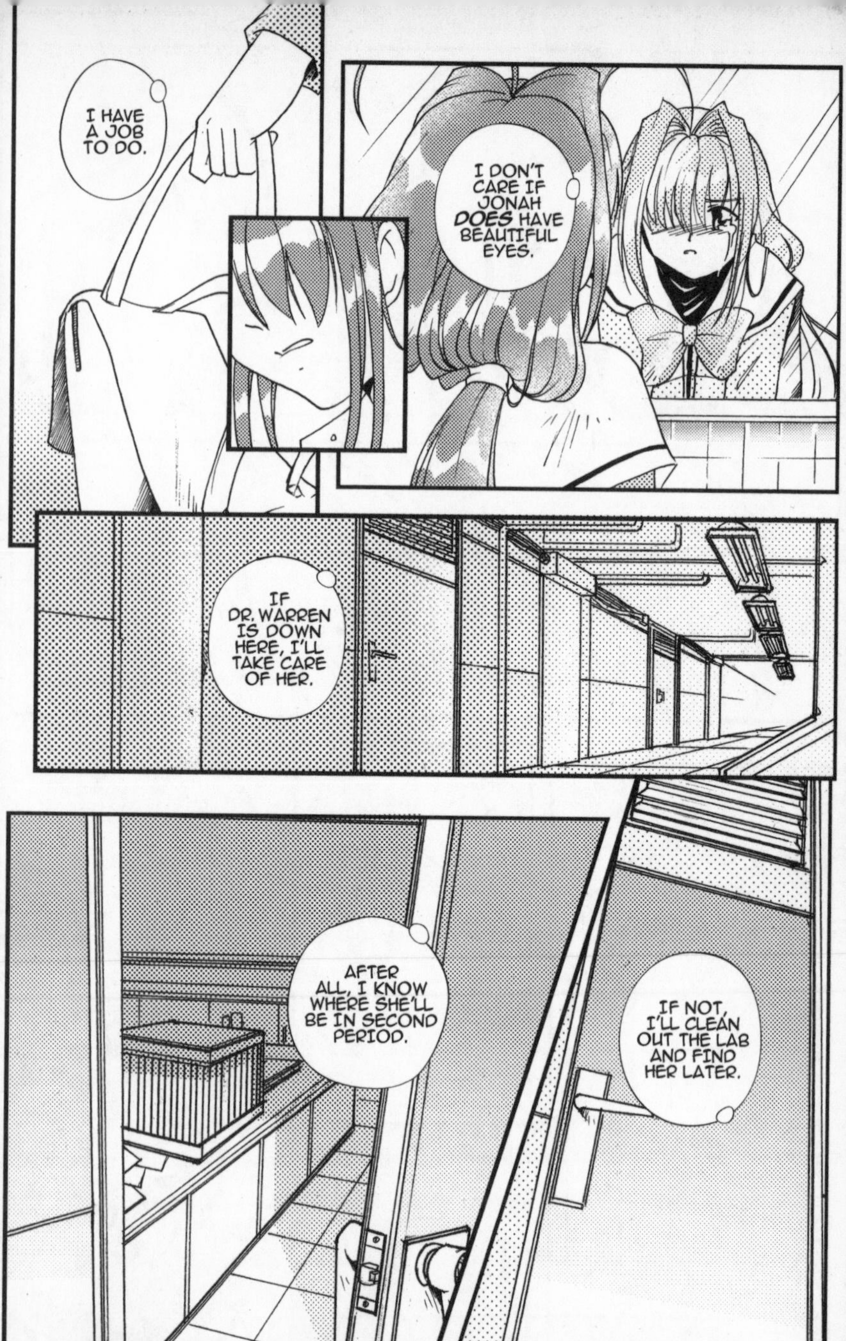
I DON'T CARE IF JONAH DOES HAVE BEAUTIFUL EYES.
I HAVE A JOB TO DO.
IF DR. WARREN IS DOWN HERE, I'LL TAKE CARE OF HER.
IF NOT, I'LL CLEAN OUT THE LAB AND FIND HER LATER.
AFTER ALL, I KNOW WHERE SHE'LL BE IN SECOND PERIOD.

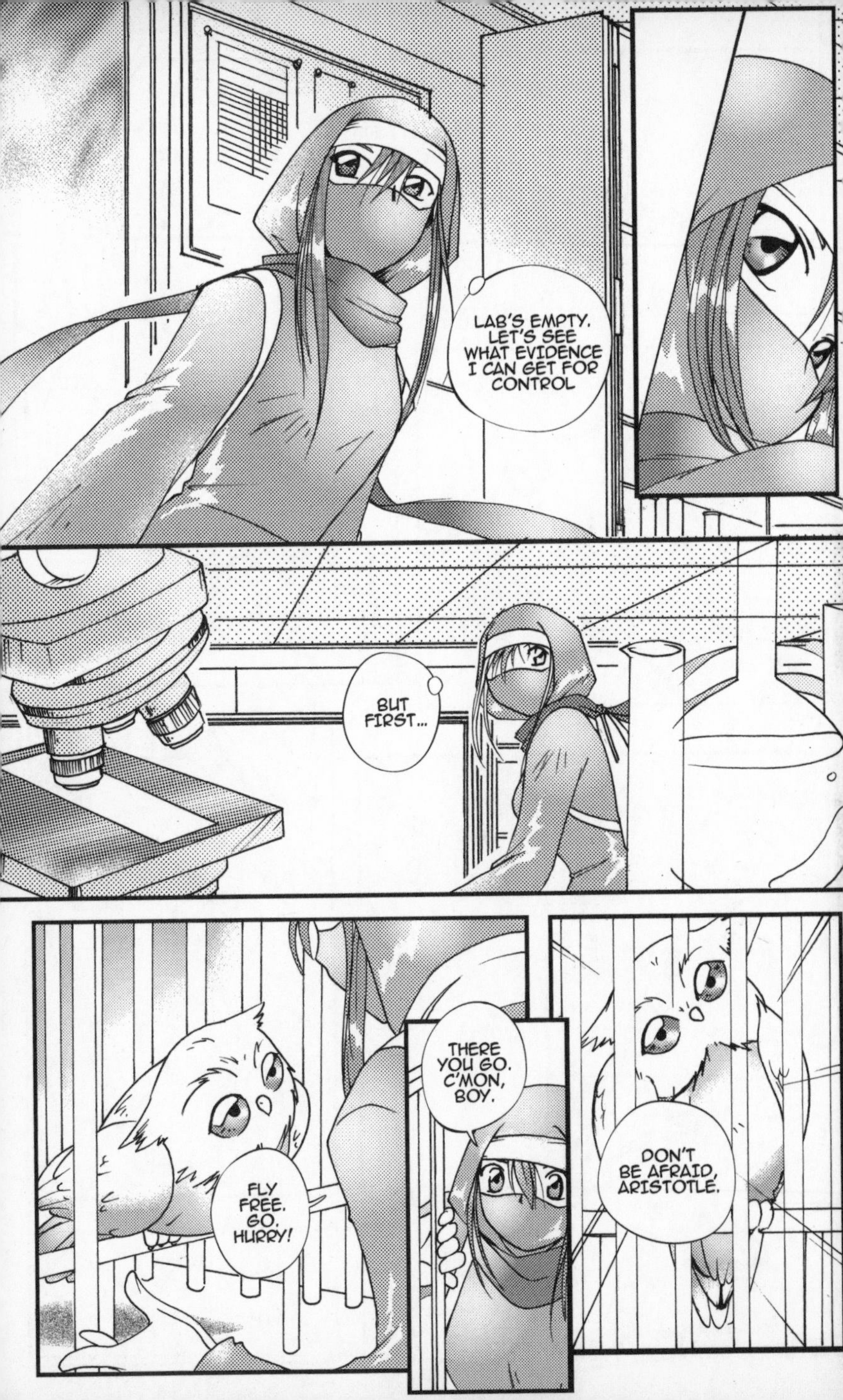
LAB'S EMPTY. LET'S SEE WHAT EVIDENCE I CAN GET FOR CONTROL
BUT FIRST...
DON'T BE AFRAID, ARISTOTLE.
THERE YOU GO. C'MON, BOY.
FLY FREE. GO. HURRY!

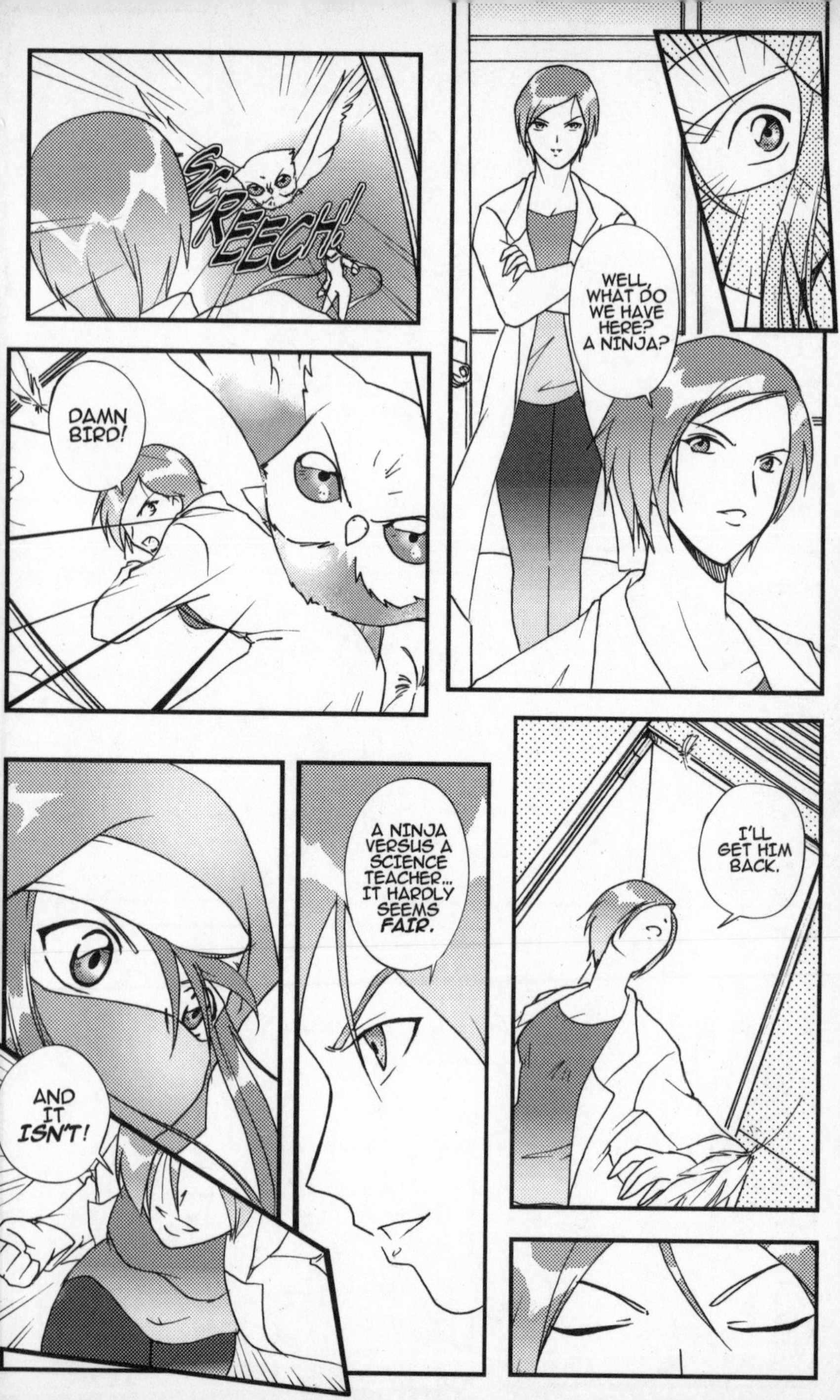
WELL, WHAT DO WE HAVE HERE? A NINJA?
SCREEEECH!
DAMN BIRD!
I'LL GET HIM BACK.
A NINJA VERSUS A SCIENCE TEACHER... IT HARDLY SEEMS *FAIR*.
AND IT *ISN'T*!

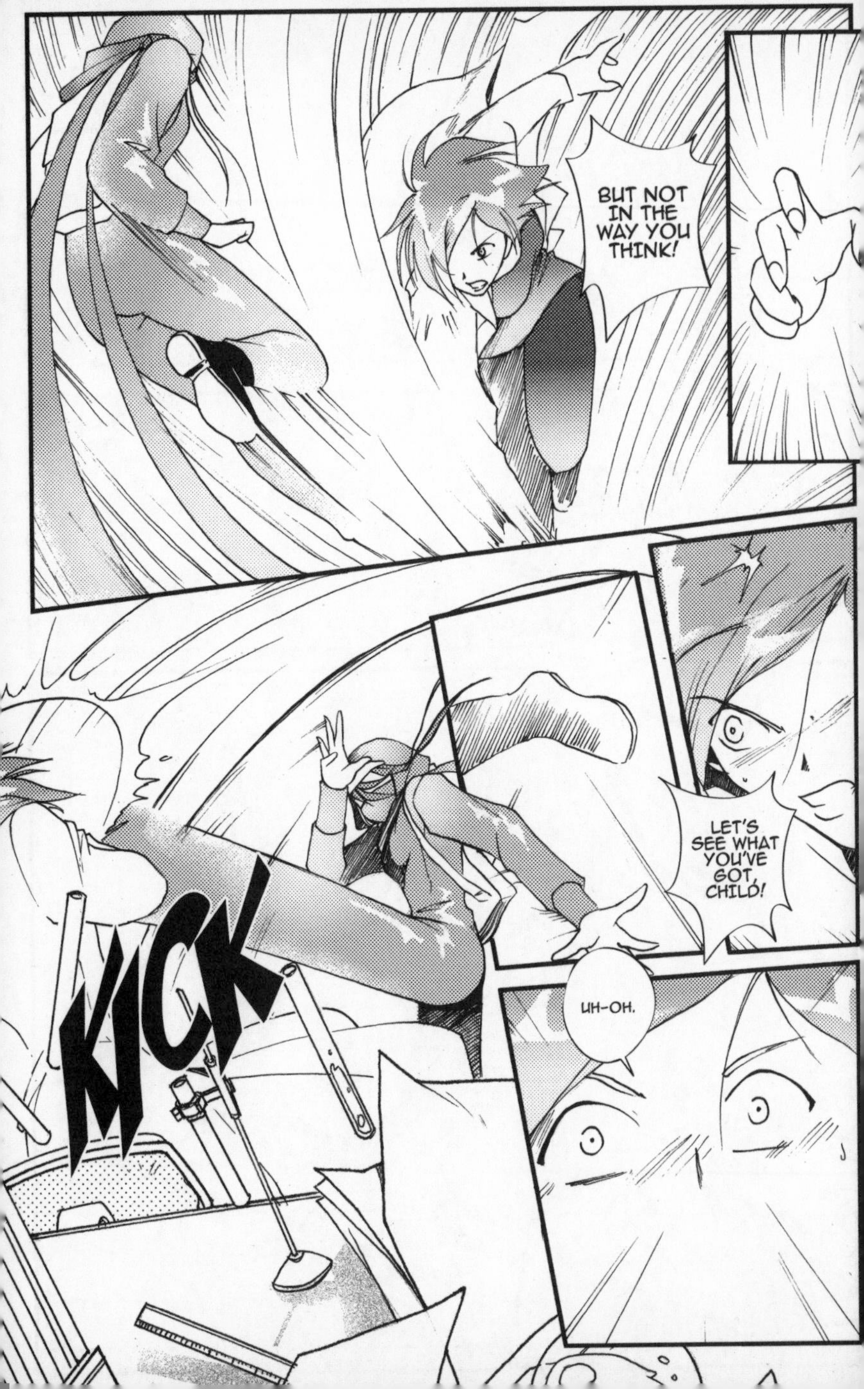
BUT NOT IN THE WAY YOU THINK!
LET'S SEE WHAT YOU'VE GOT, CHILD!
KICK
UH-OH.

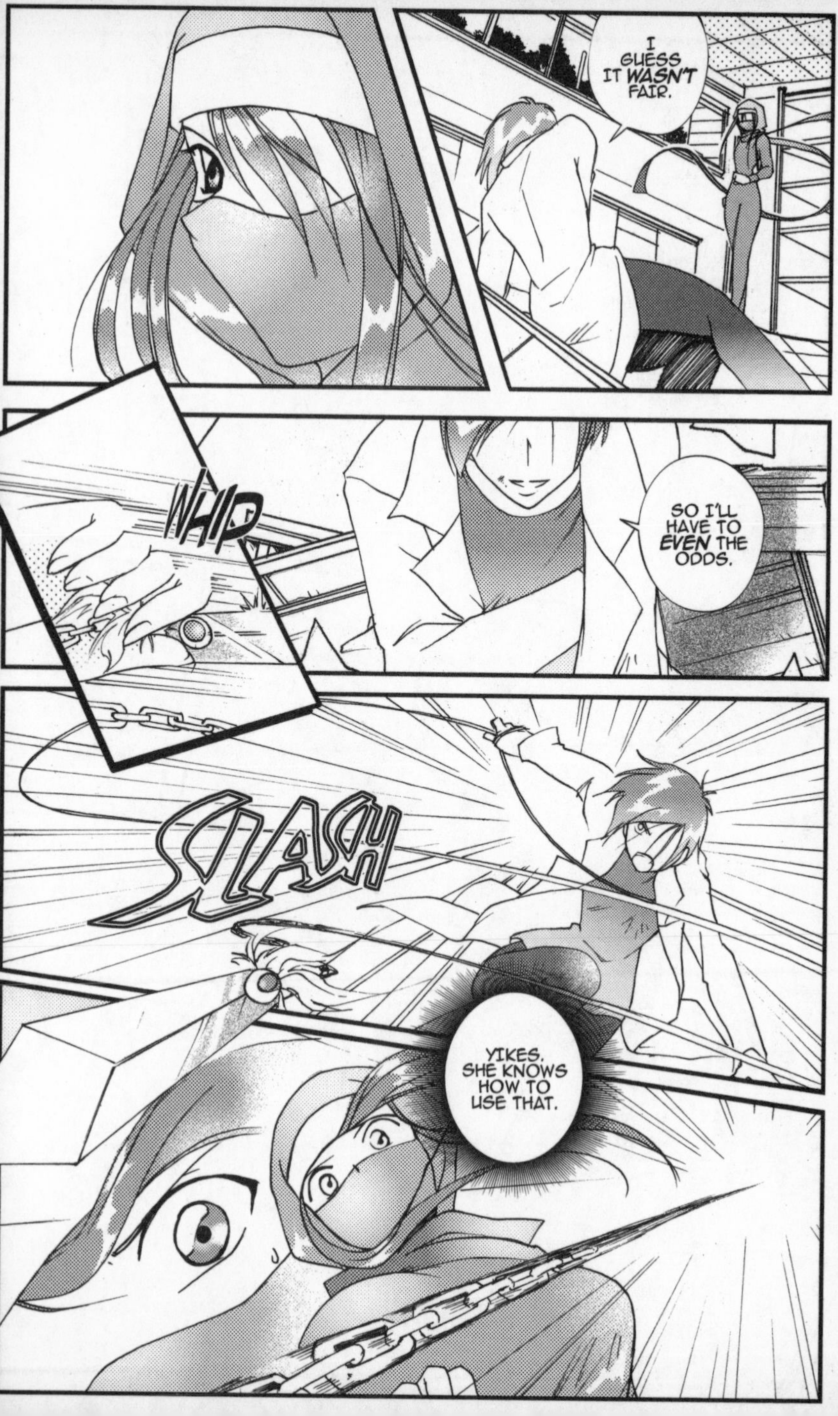
I GUESS IT WASN'T FAIR.
SO I'LL HAVE TO EVEN THE ODDS.
WHIP
SLASH
YIKES. SHE KNOWS HOW TO USE THAT.

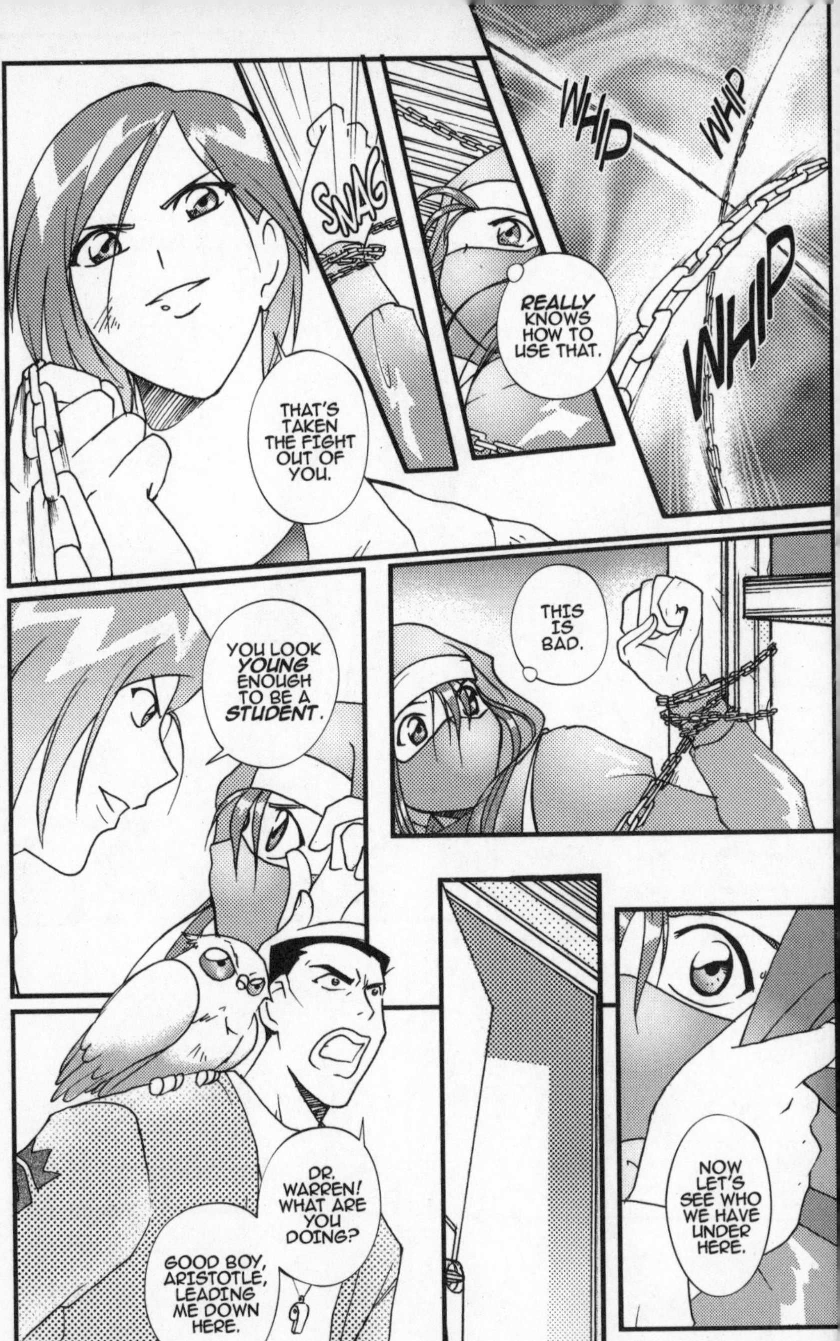
WHIP
WHIP
WHIP
WHIP
REALLY KNOWS HOW TO USE THAT.
SNAG
THAT'S TAKEN THE FIGHT OUT OF YOU.
THIS IS BAD.
YOU LOOK YOUNG ENOUGH TO BE A STUDENT.
NOW LET'S SEE WHO WE HAVE UNDER HERE.
DR. WARREN! WHAT ARE YOU DOING?
GOOD BOY, ARISTOTLE, LEADING ME DOWN HERE.

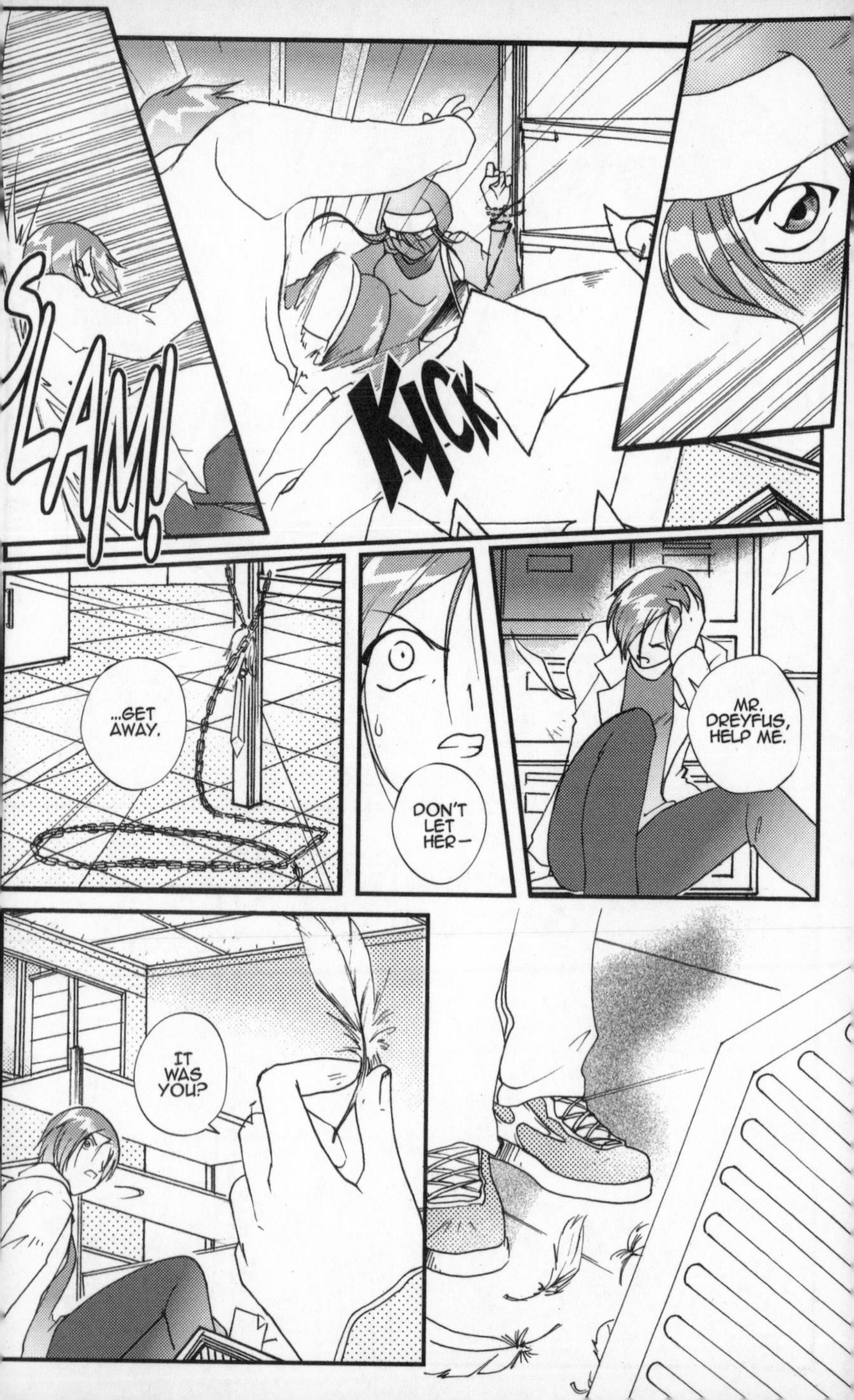
KICK
SLAM!
MR. DREYFUS, HELP ME.
DON'T LET HER—
...GET AWAY.
IT WAS YOU?

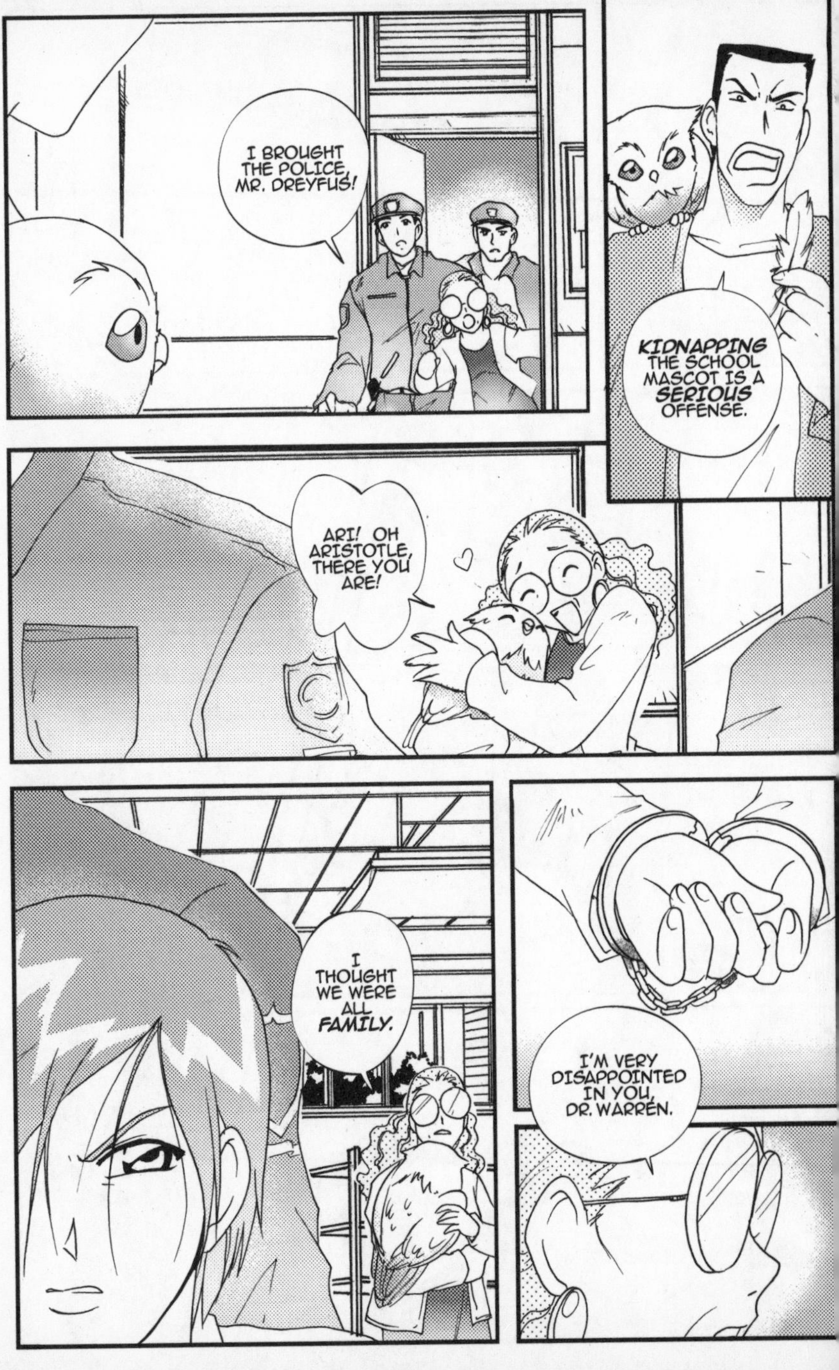
KIDNAPPING THE SCHOOL MASCOT IS A SERIOUS OFFENSE.
I BROUGHT THE POLICE, MR. DREYFUS!
ARI! OH ARISTOTLE, THERE YOU ARE!
I'M VERY DISAPPOINTED IN YOU, DR. WARREN.
I THOUGHT WE WERE ALL FAMILY.

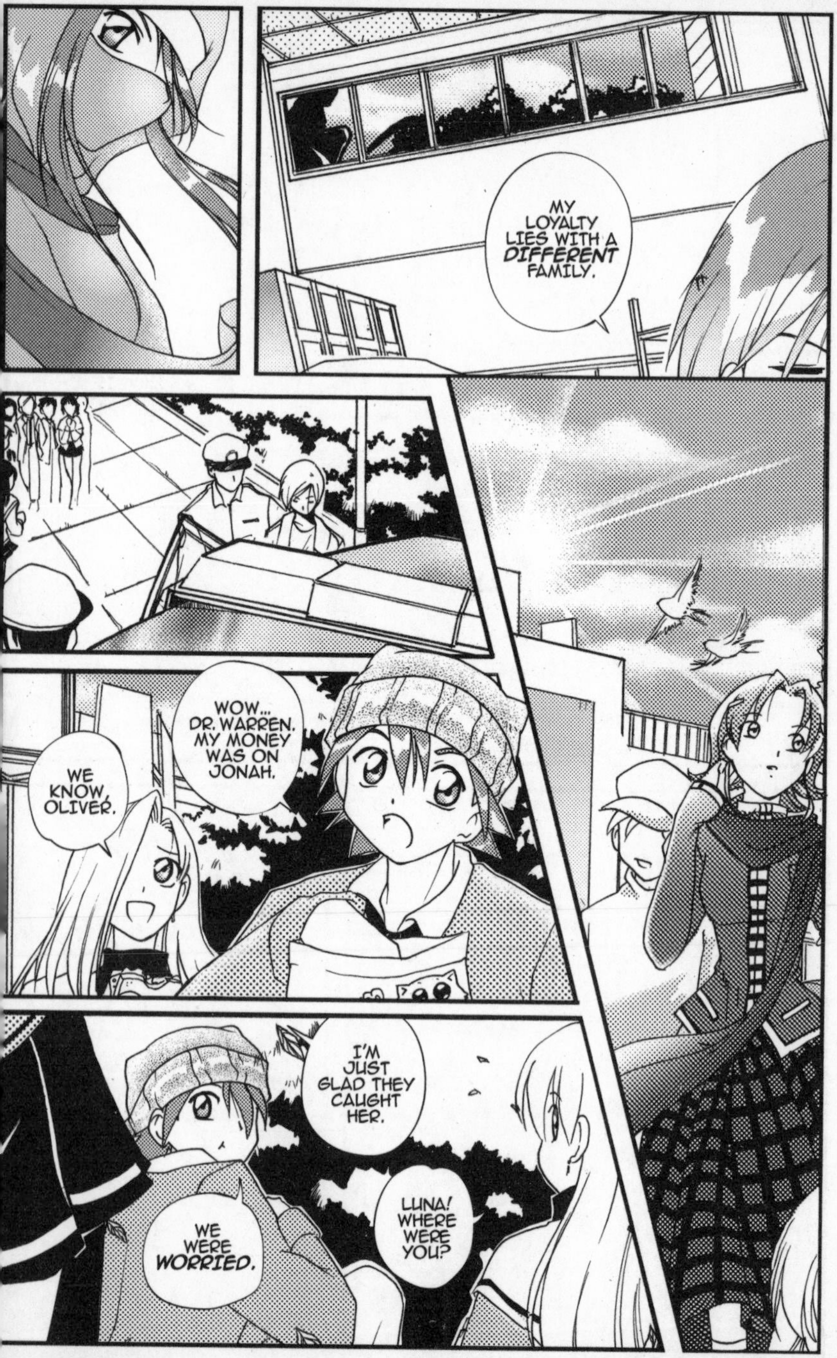
MY LOYALTY LIES WITH A DIFFERENT FAMILY.
WOW... DR. WARREN. MY MONEY WAS ON JONAH.
WE KNOW, OLIVER.
I'M JUST GLAD THEY CAUGHT HER.
LUNA! WHERE WERE YOU?
WE WERE WORRIED.

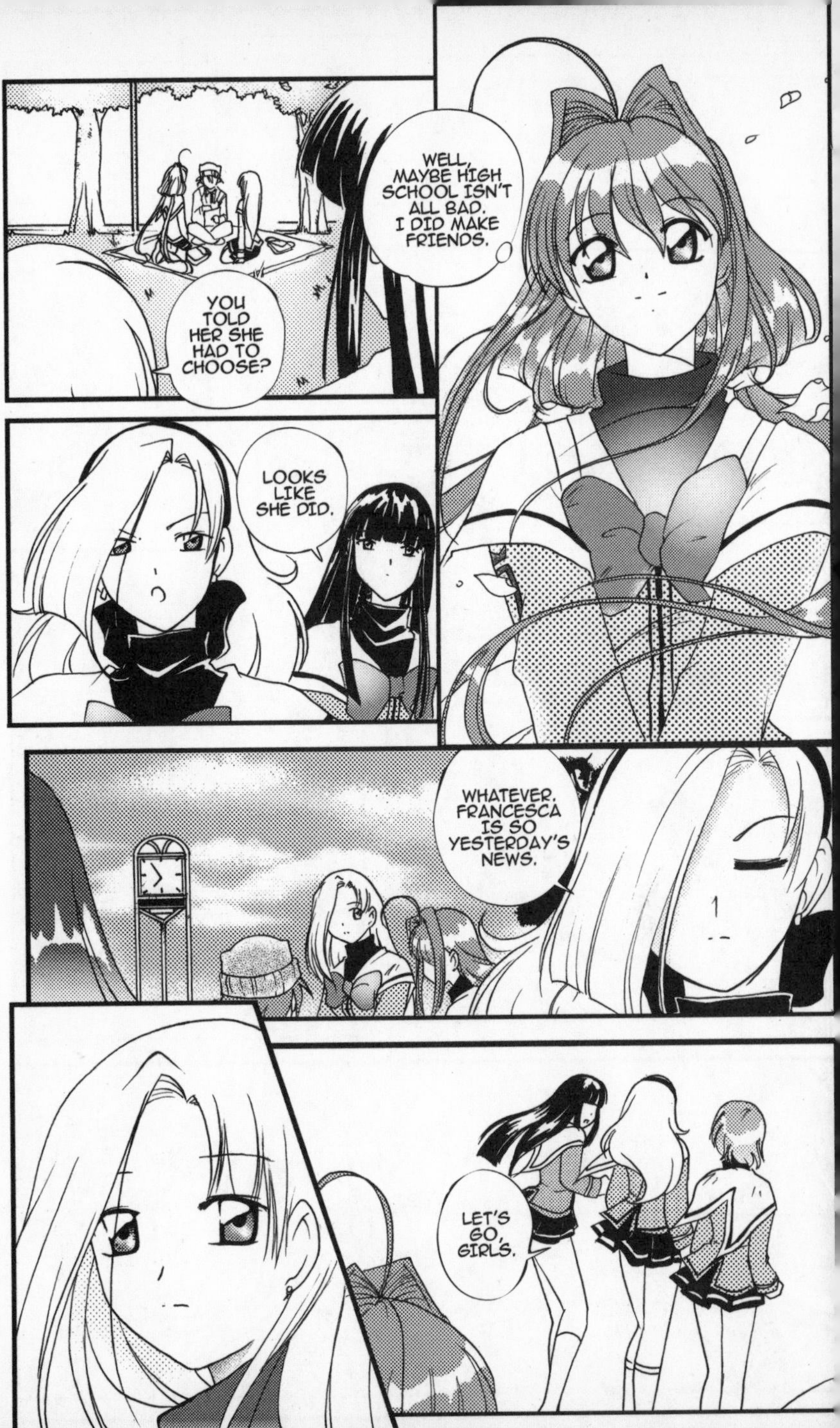
WELL, MAYBE HIGH SCHOOL ISN'T ALL BAD. I DID MAKE FRIENDS.
YOU TOLD HER SHE HAD TO CHOOSE?
LOOKS LIKE SHE DID.
WHATEVER. FRANCESCA IS SO YESTERDAY'S NEWS.
LET'S GO, GIRLS.

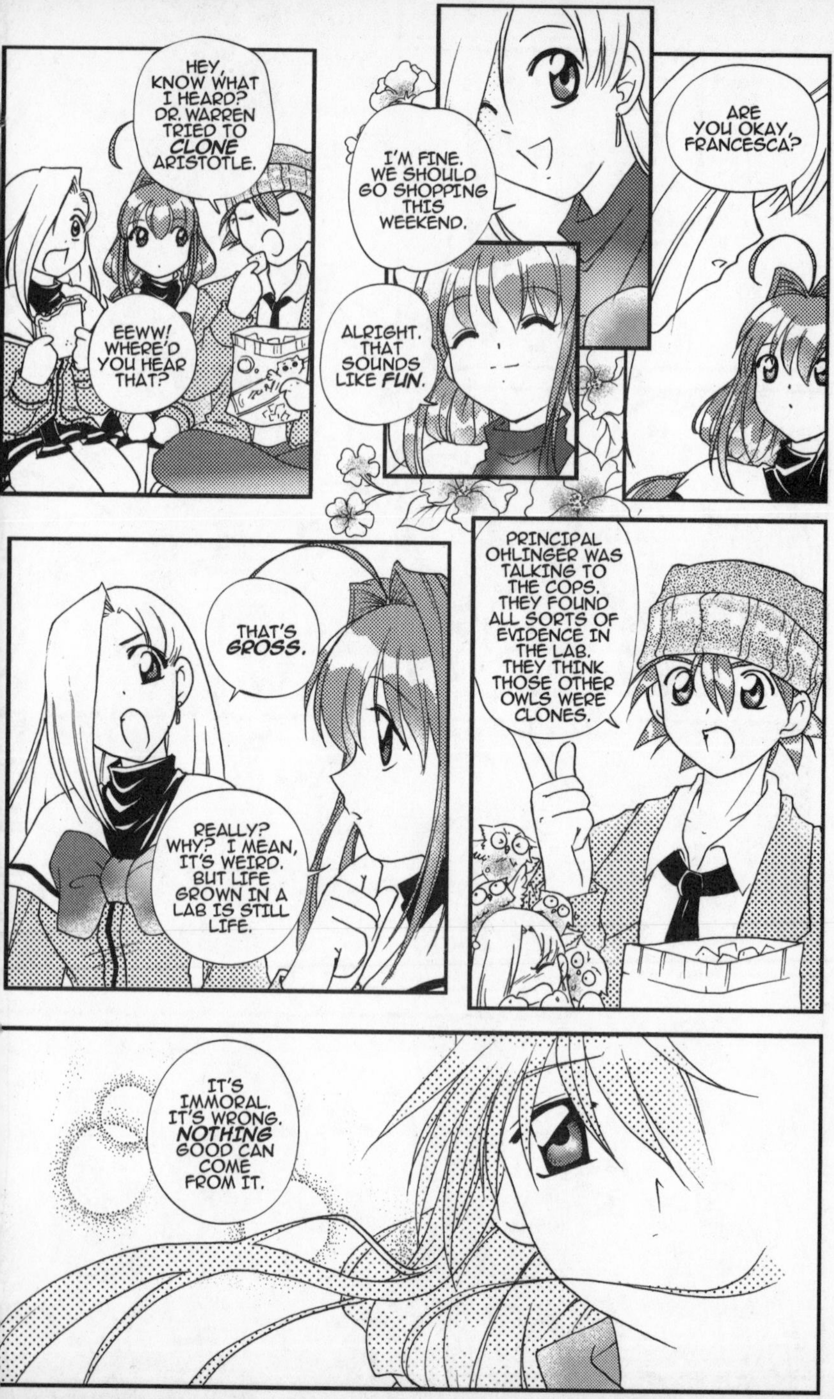
ARE YOU OKAY, FRANCESCA?
I'M FINE. WE SHOULD GO SHOPPING THIS WEEKEND.
ALRIGHT. THAT SOUNDS LIKE *FUN*.
HEY, KNOW WHAT I HEARD? DR. WARREN TRIED TO *CLONE* ARISTOTLE.
EEWW! WHERE'D YOU HEAR THAT?
PRINCIPAL OHLINGER WAS TALKING TO THE COPS. THEY FOUND ALL SORTS OF EVIDENCE IN THE LAB. THEY THINK THOSE OTHER OWLS WERE CLONES.
THAT'S *GROSS*.
REALLY? WHY? I MEAN, IT'S WEIRD. BUT LIFE GROWN IN A LAB IS STILL LIFE.
IT'S IMMORAL. IT'S WRONG. *NOTHING* GOOD CAN COME FROM IT.

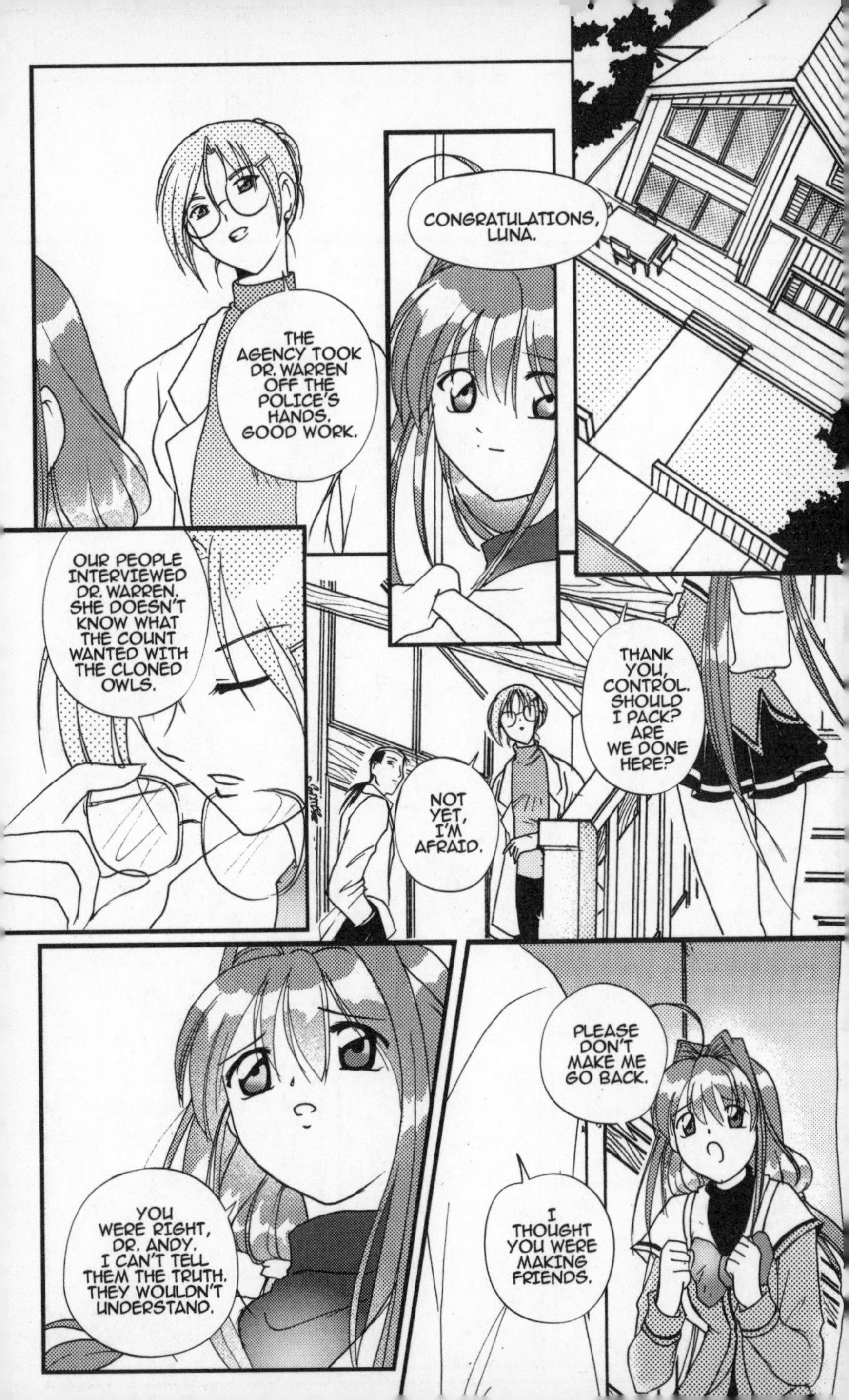
CONGRATULATIONS, LUNA.
THE AGENCY TOOK DR. WARREN OFF THE POLICE'S HANDS. GOOD WORK.
THANK YOU, CONTROL. SHOULD I PACK? ARE WE DONE HERE?
NOT YET, I'M AFRAID.
OUR PEOPLE INTERVIEWED DR. WARREN. SHE DOESN'T KNOW WHAT THE COUNT WANTED WITH THE CLONED OWLS.
PLEASE DON'T MAKE ME GO BACK.
I THOUGHT YOU WERE MAKING FRIENDS.
YOU WERE RIGHT, DR. ANDY. I CAN'T TELL THEM THE TRUTH. THEY WOULDN'T UNDERSTAND.

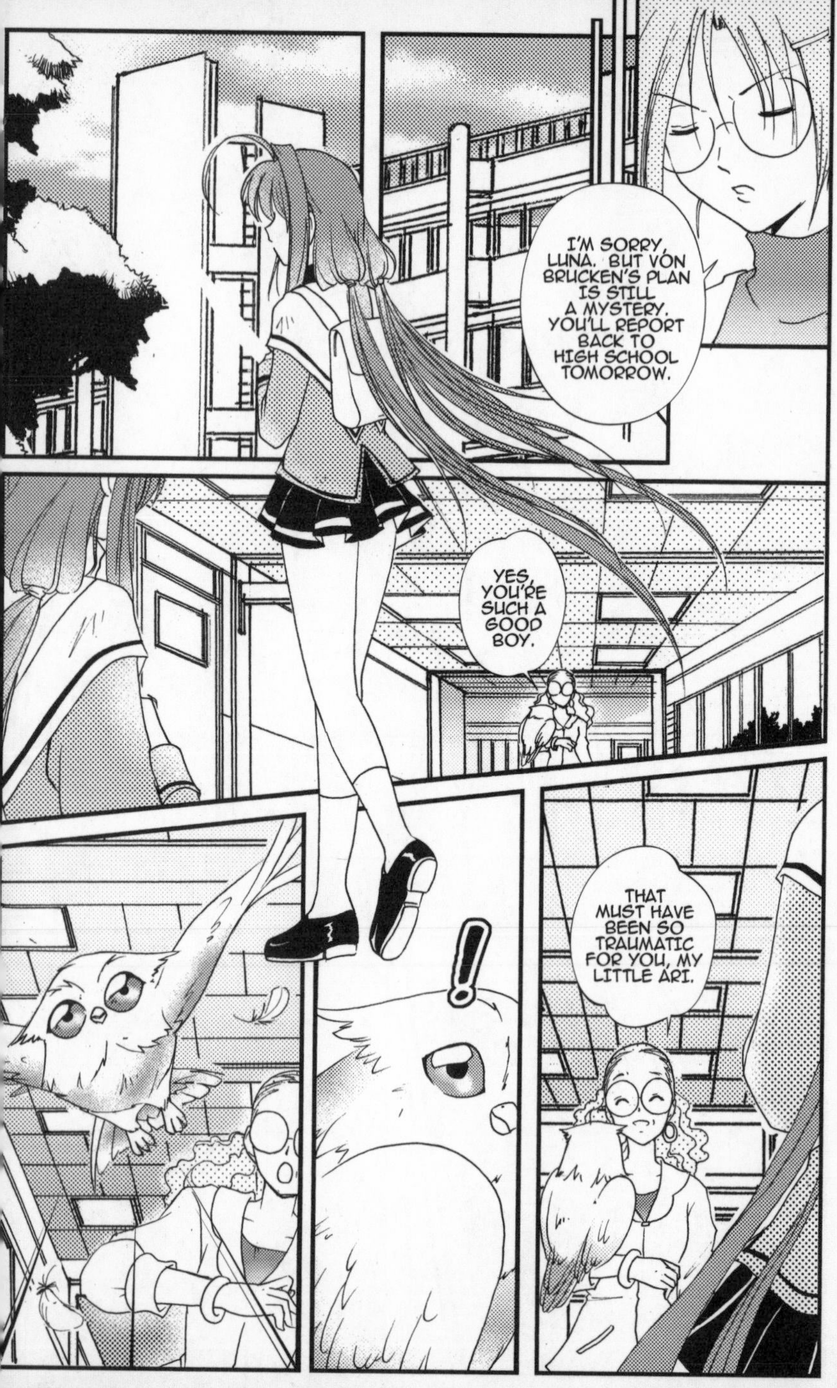
I'M SORRY, LUNA. BUT VON BRUCKEN'S PLAN IS STILL A MYSTERY. YOU'LL REPORT BACK TO HIGH SCHOOL TOMORROW.
YES, YOU'RE SUCH A GOOD BOY.
THAT MUST HAVE BEEN SO TRAUMATIC FOR YOU, MY LITTLE ARI.

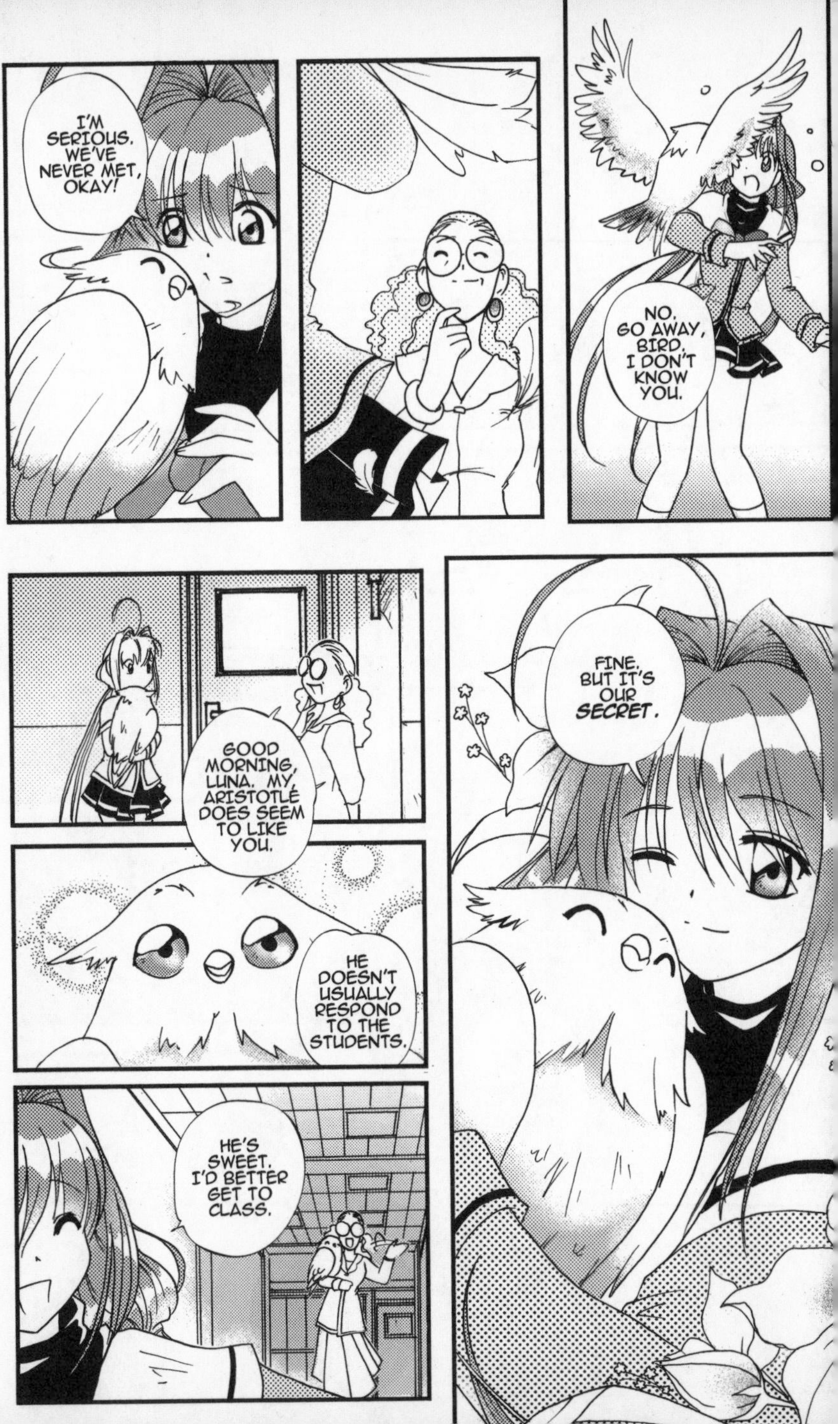
NO. GO AWAY, BIRD, I DON'T KNOW YOU.
I'M SERIOUS. WE'VE NEVER MET, OKAY!
FINE. BUT IT'S OUR SECRET.
GOOD MORNING, LUNA. MY, ARISTOTLE DOES SEEM TO LIKE YOU.
HE DOESN'T USUALLY RESPOND TO THE STUDENTS.
HE'S SWEET. I'D BETTER GET TO CLASS.

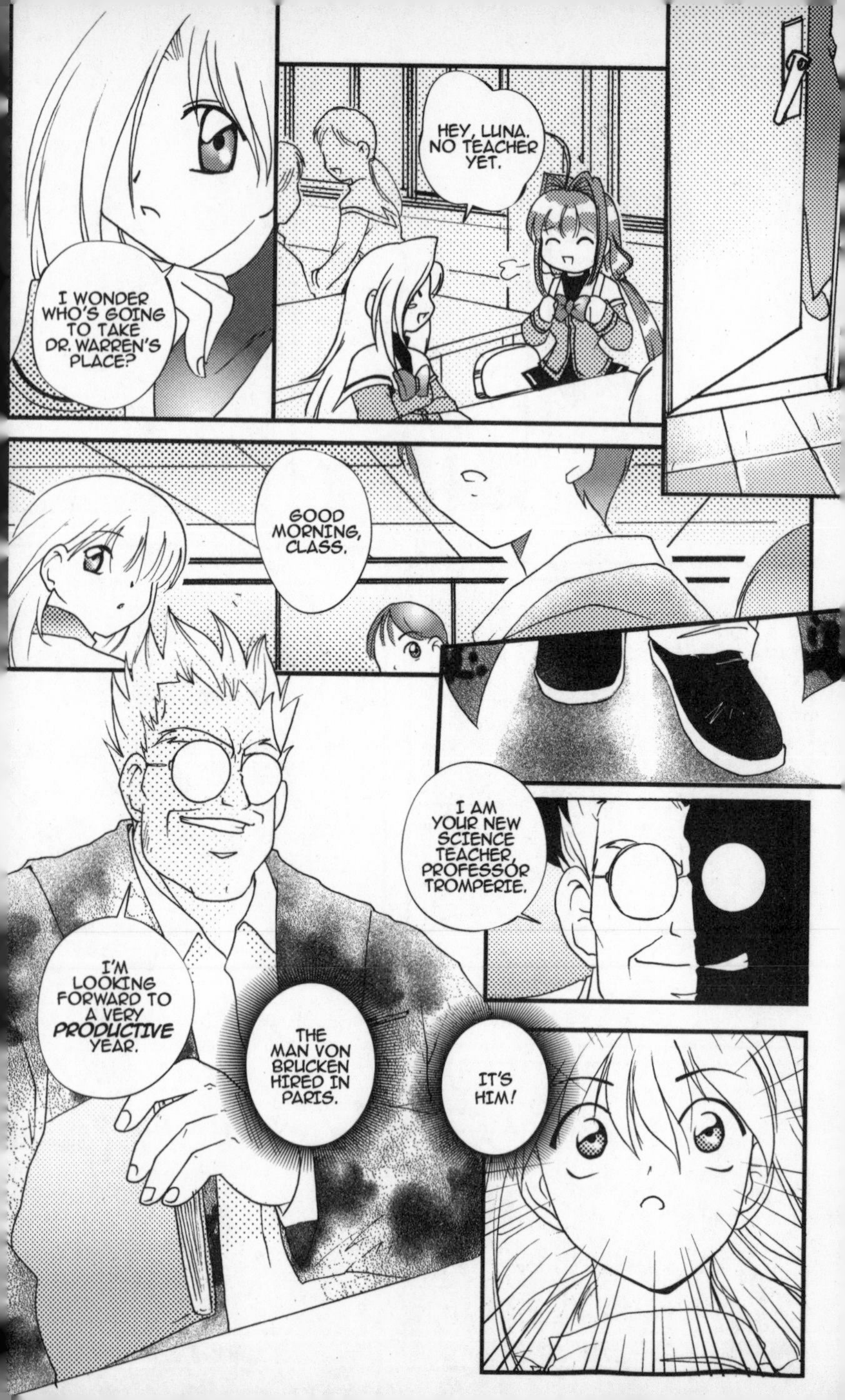
HEY, LUNA. NO TEACHER YET.
I WONDER WHO'S GOING TO TAKE DR. WARREN'S PLACE?
GOOD MORNING, CLASS.
I AM YOUR NEW SCIENCE TEACHER, PROFESSOR TROMPERIE.
I'M LOOKING FORWARD TO A VERY *PRODUCTIVE* YEAR.
THE MAN VON BRUCKEN HIRED IN PARIS.
IT'S HIM!

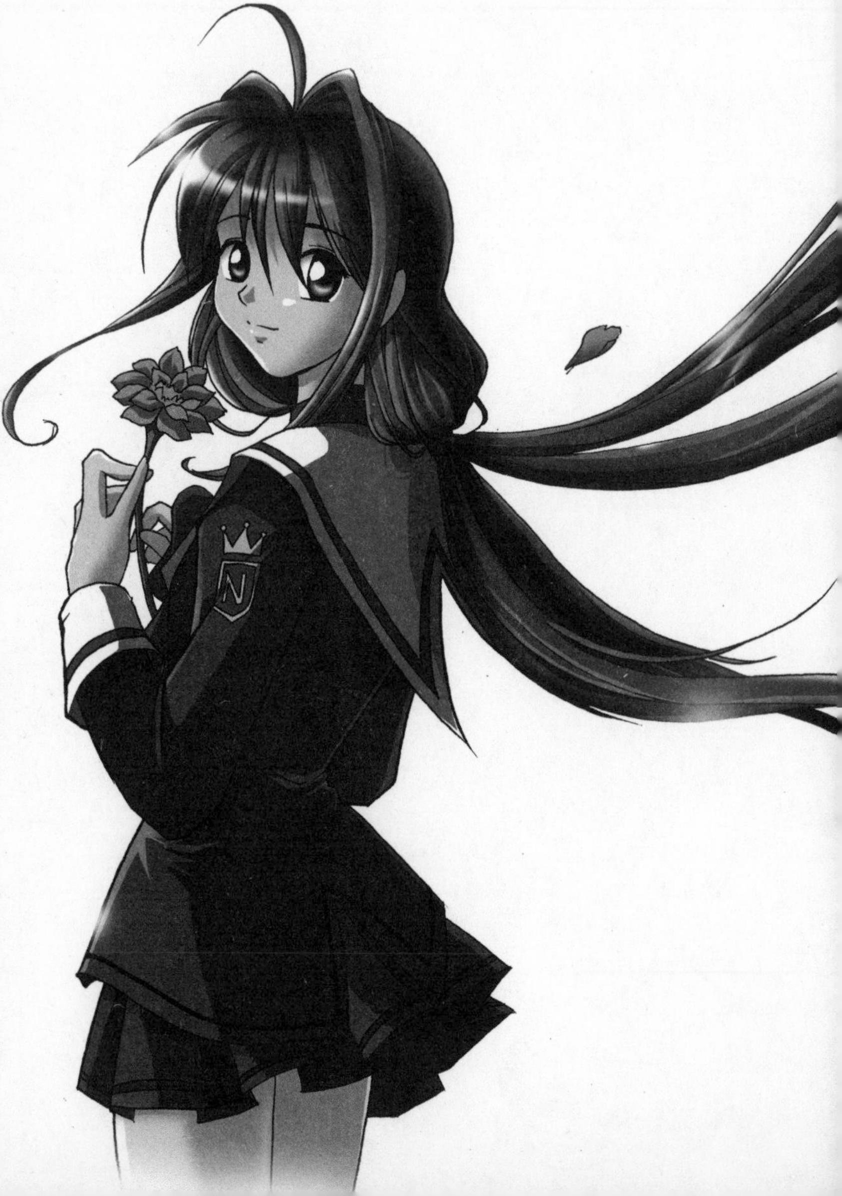

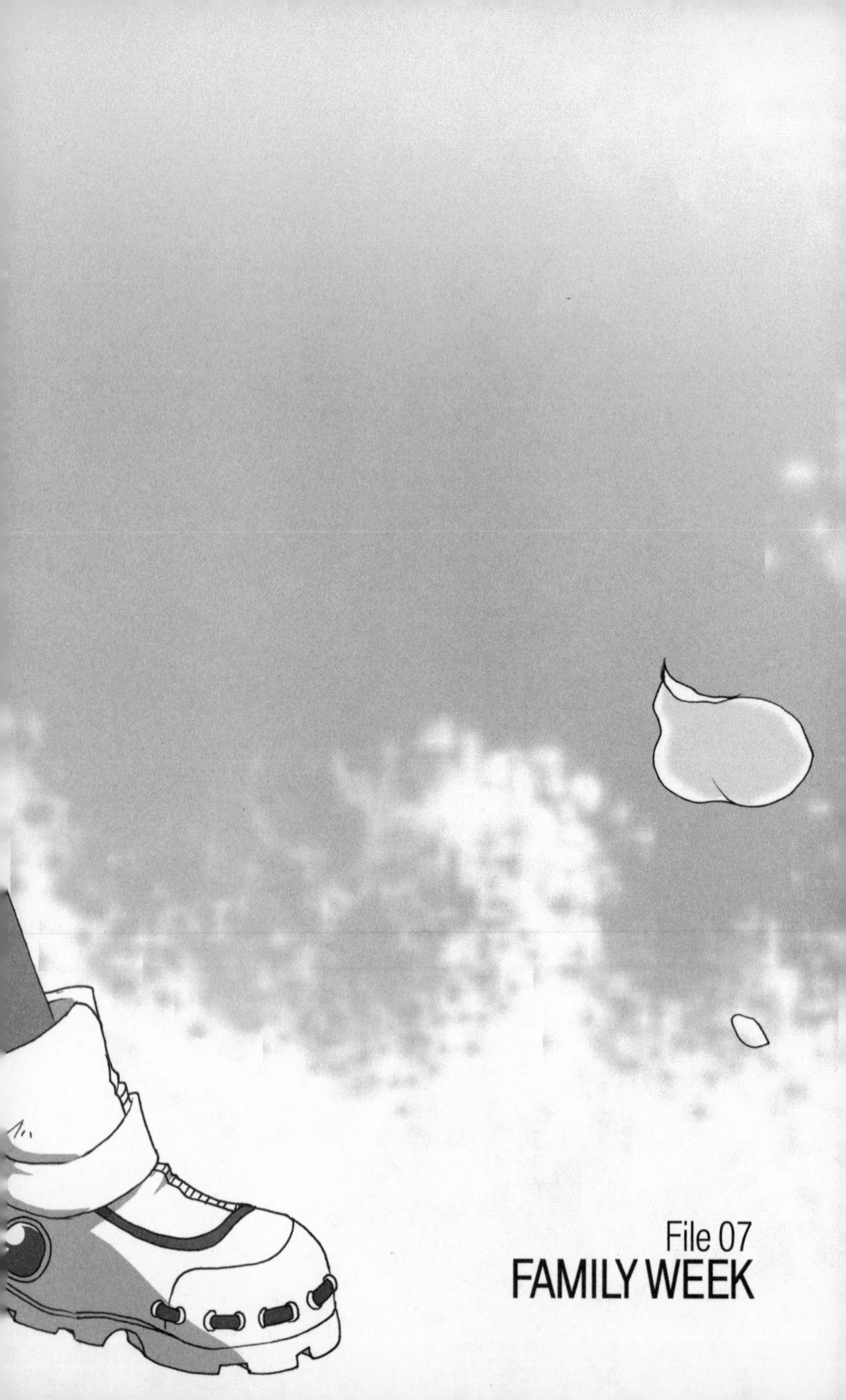

# File 07
# FAMILY WEEK

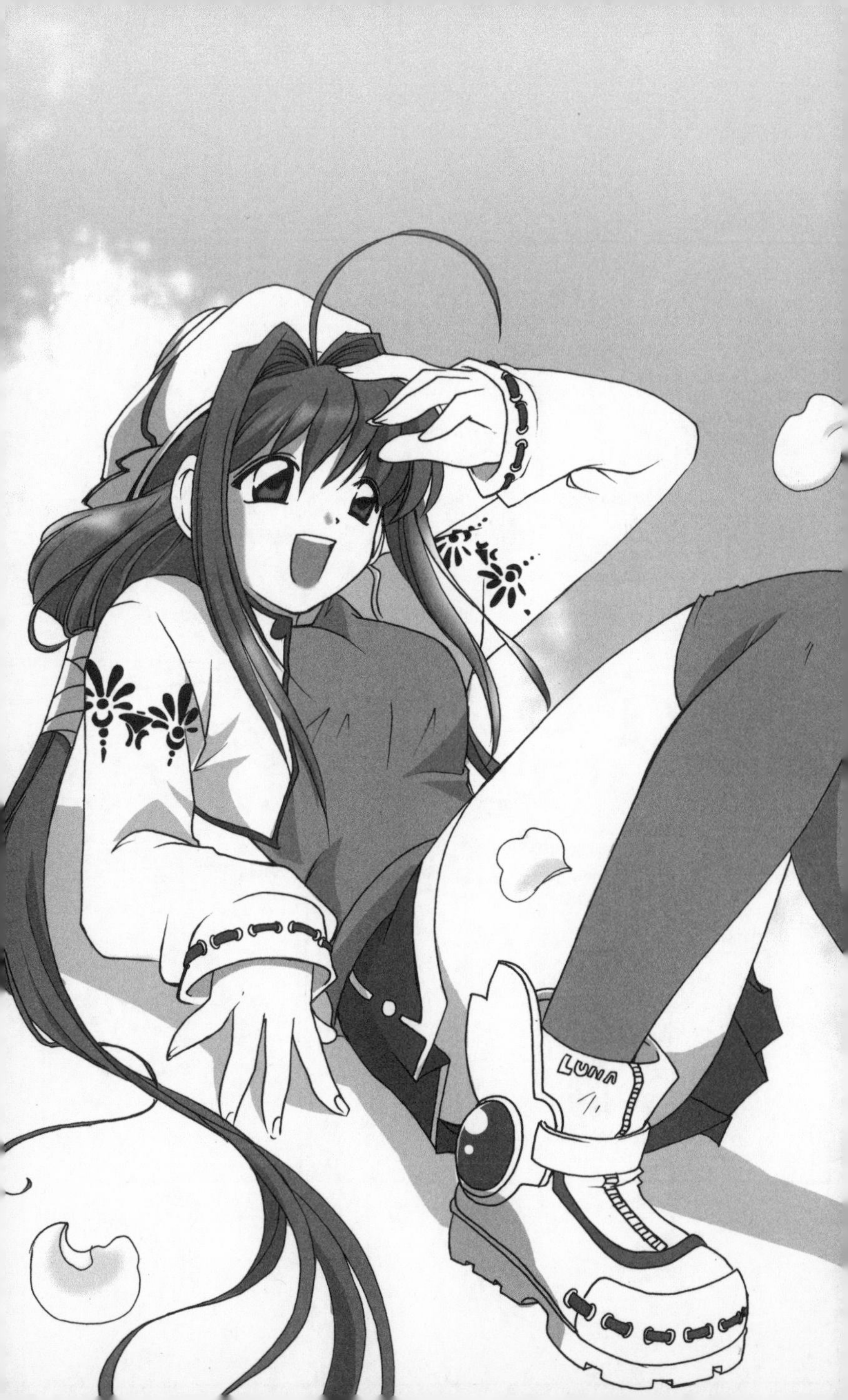
LUNA

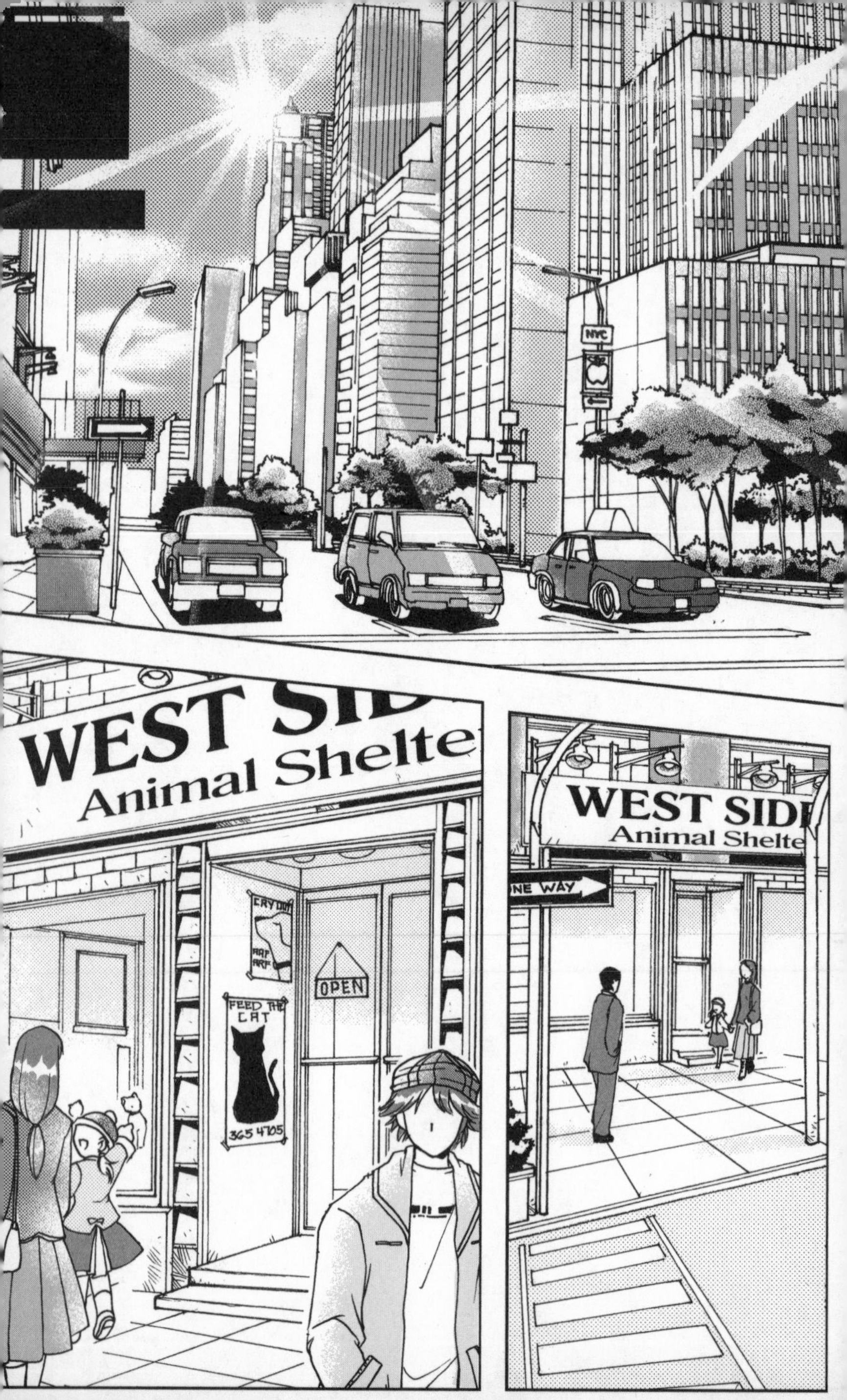
NYC
WEST SIDI
Animal Shelte
ONE WAY
WEST SID
Animal Shelte
OPEN
FEED THE CAT
365 4705

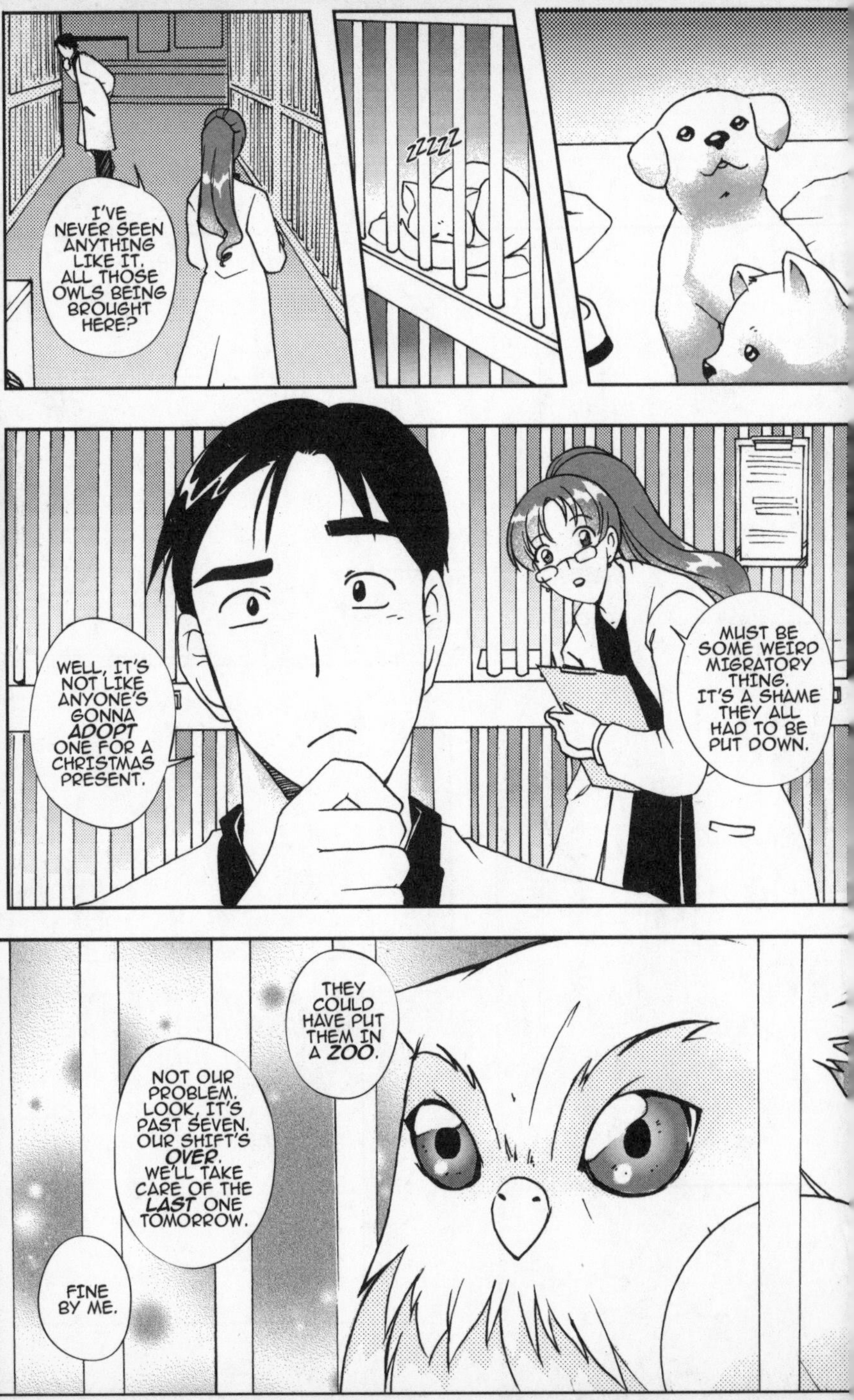
ZZZZZ
I'VE NEVER SEEN ANYTHING LIKE IT. ALL THOSE OWLS BEING BROUGHT HERE?
MUST BE SOME WEIRD MIGRATORY THING. IT'S A SHAME THEY ALL HAD TO BE PUT DOWN.
WELL, IT'S NOT LIKE ANYONE'S GONNA ADOPT ONE FOR A CHRISTMAS PRESENT.
THEY COULD HAVE PUT THEM IN A ZOO.
NOT OUR PROBLEM. LOOK, IT'S PAST SEVEN. OUR SHIFT'S OVER. WE'LL TAKE CARE OF THE LAST ONE TOMORROW.
FINE BY ME.

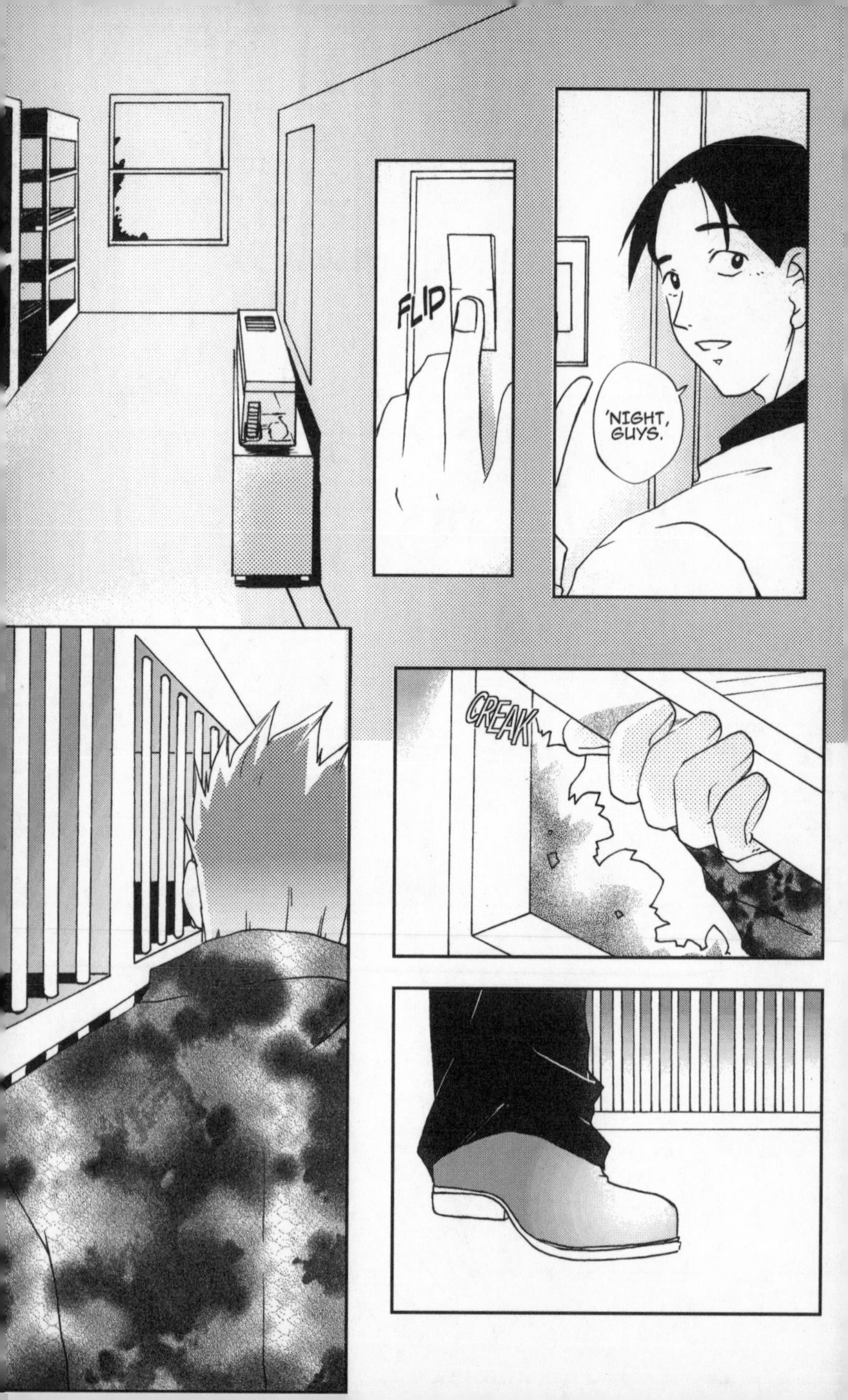
'NIGHT, GUYS.
FLIP
CREAK

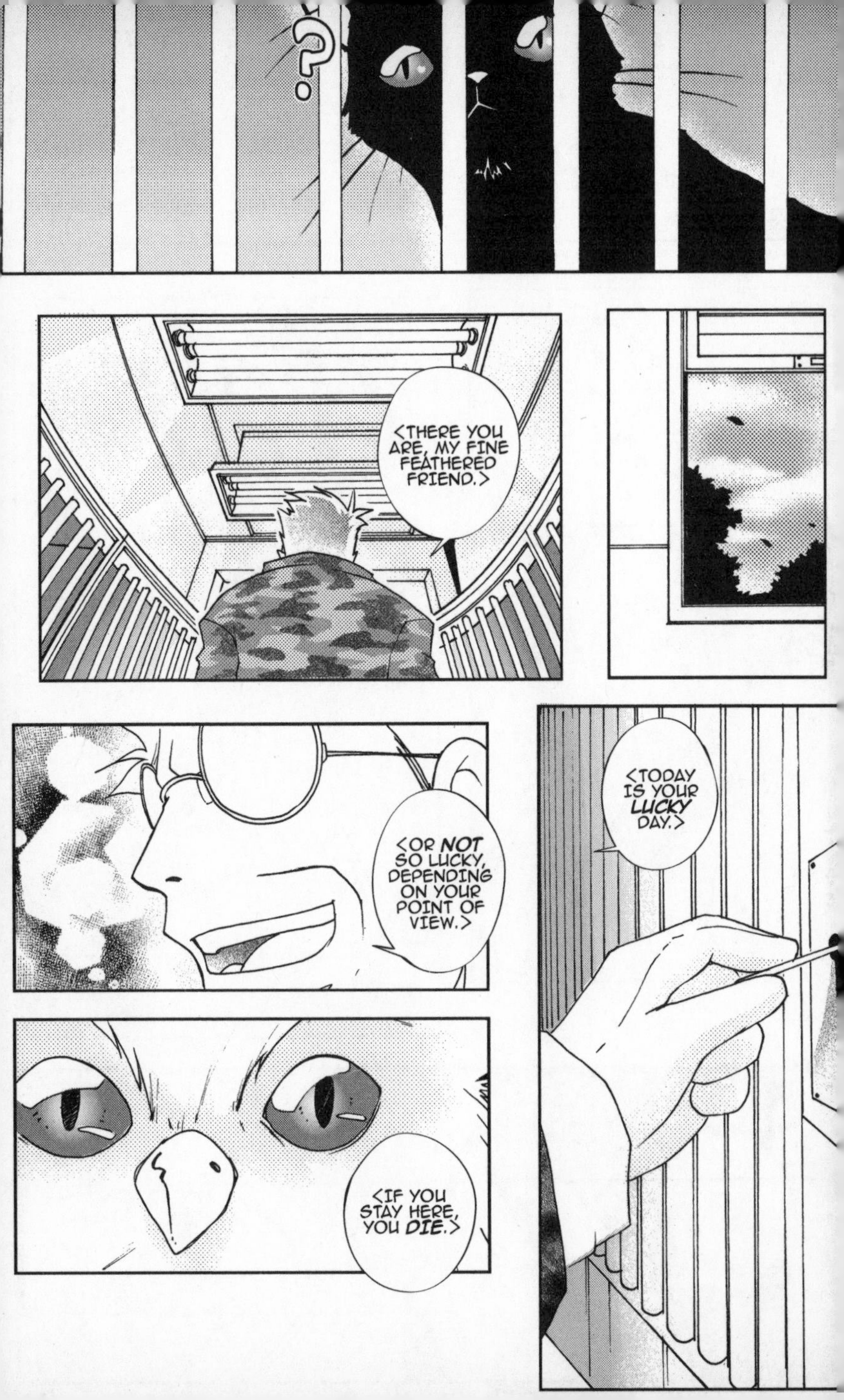
?
<THERE YOU ARE, MY FINE FEATHERED FRIEND.>
<TODAY IS YOUR ***LUCKY*** DAY.>
<OR ***NOT*** SO LUCKY, DEPENDING ON YOUR POINT OF VIEW.>
<IF YOU STAY HERE, YOU ***DIE***.>

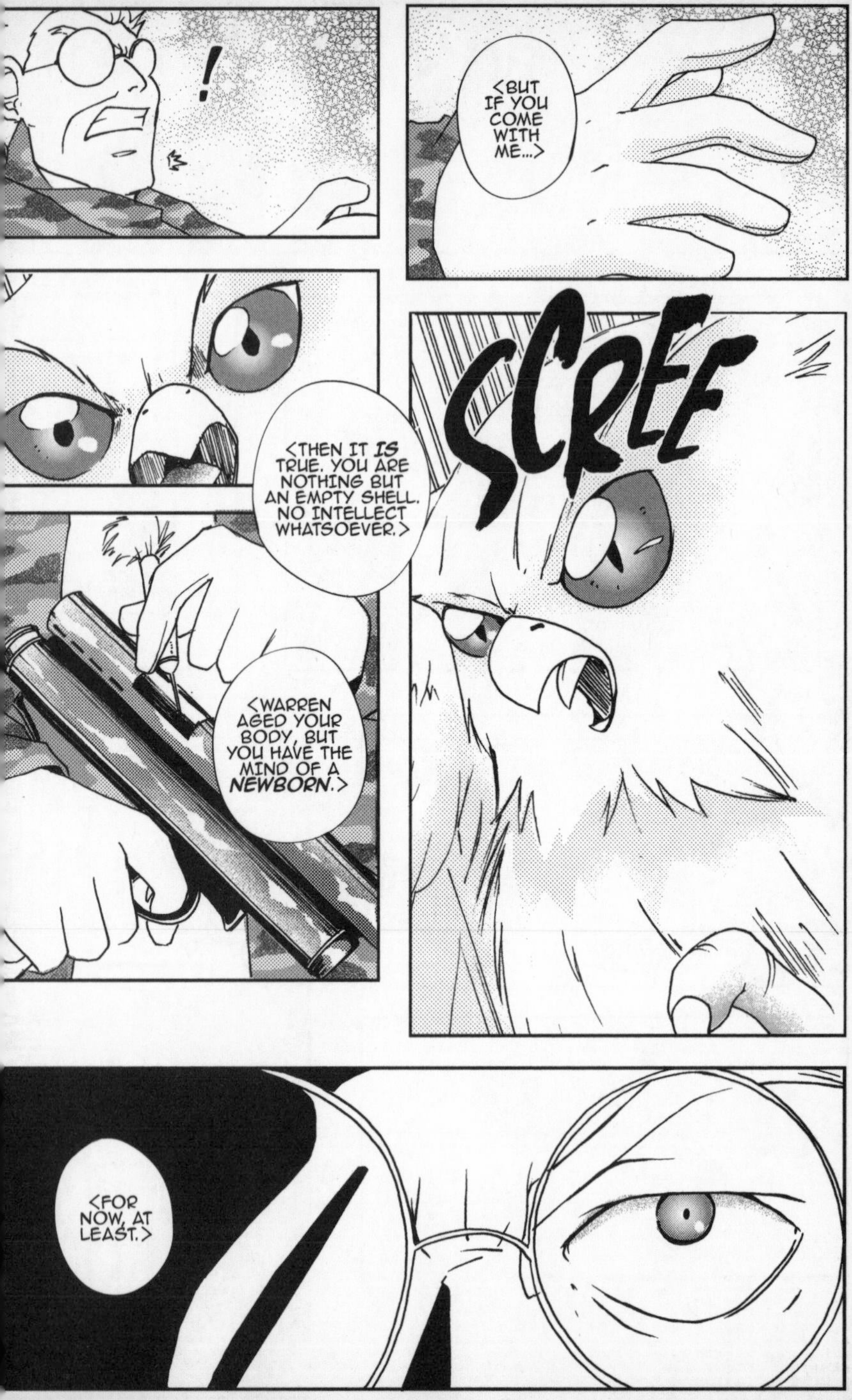
<BUT IF YOU COME WITH ME...>
!
SCREE
<THEN IT IS TRUE. YOU ARE NOTHING BUT AN EMPTY SHELL. NO INTELLECT WHATSOEVER.>
<WARREN AGED YOUR BODY, BUT YOU HAVE THE MIND OF A NEWBORN.>
<FOR NOW, AT LEAST.>

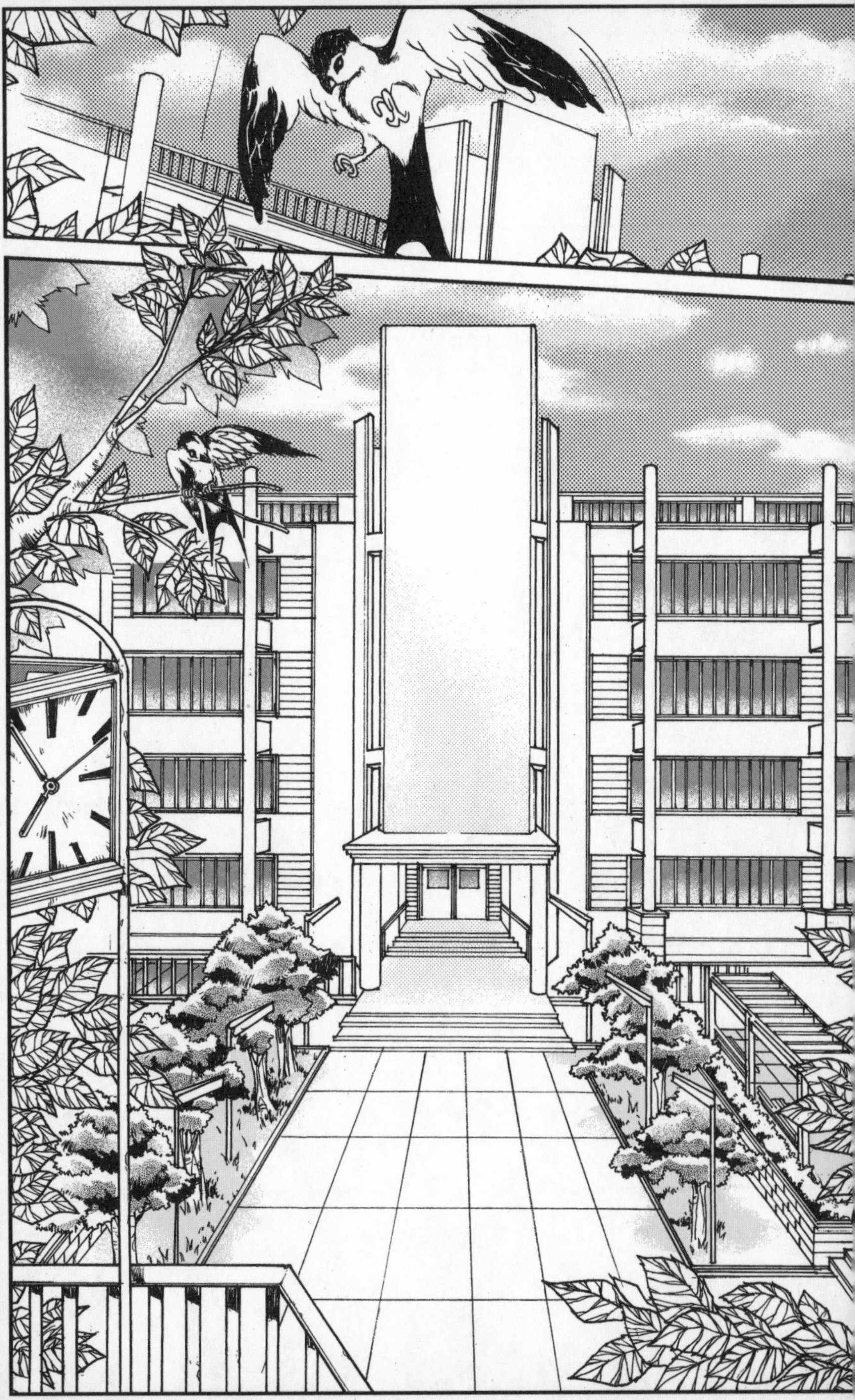

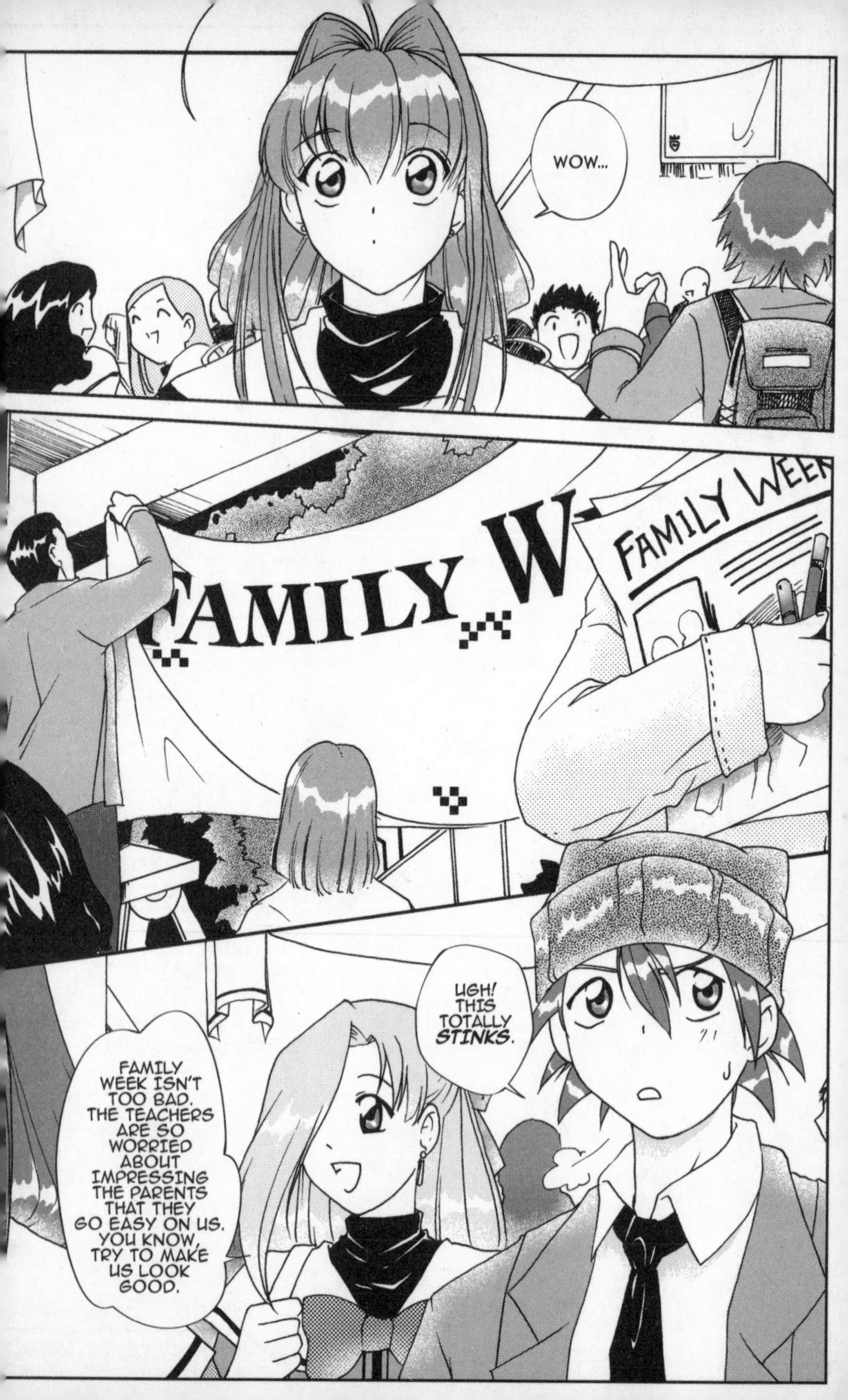
WOW...
FAMILY W
FAMILY WEEK
FAMILY WEE
UGH! THIS TOTALLY STINKS.
FAMILY WEEK ISN'T TOO BAD. THE TEACHERS ARE SO WORRIED ABOUT IMPRESSING THE PARENTS THAT THEY GO EASY ON US. YOU KNOW, TRY TO MAKE US LOOK GOOD.

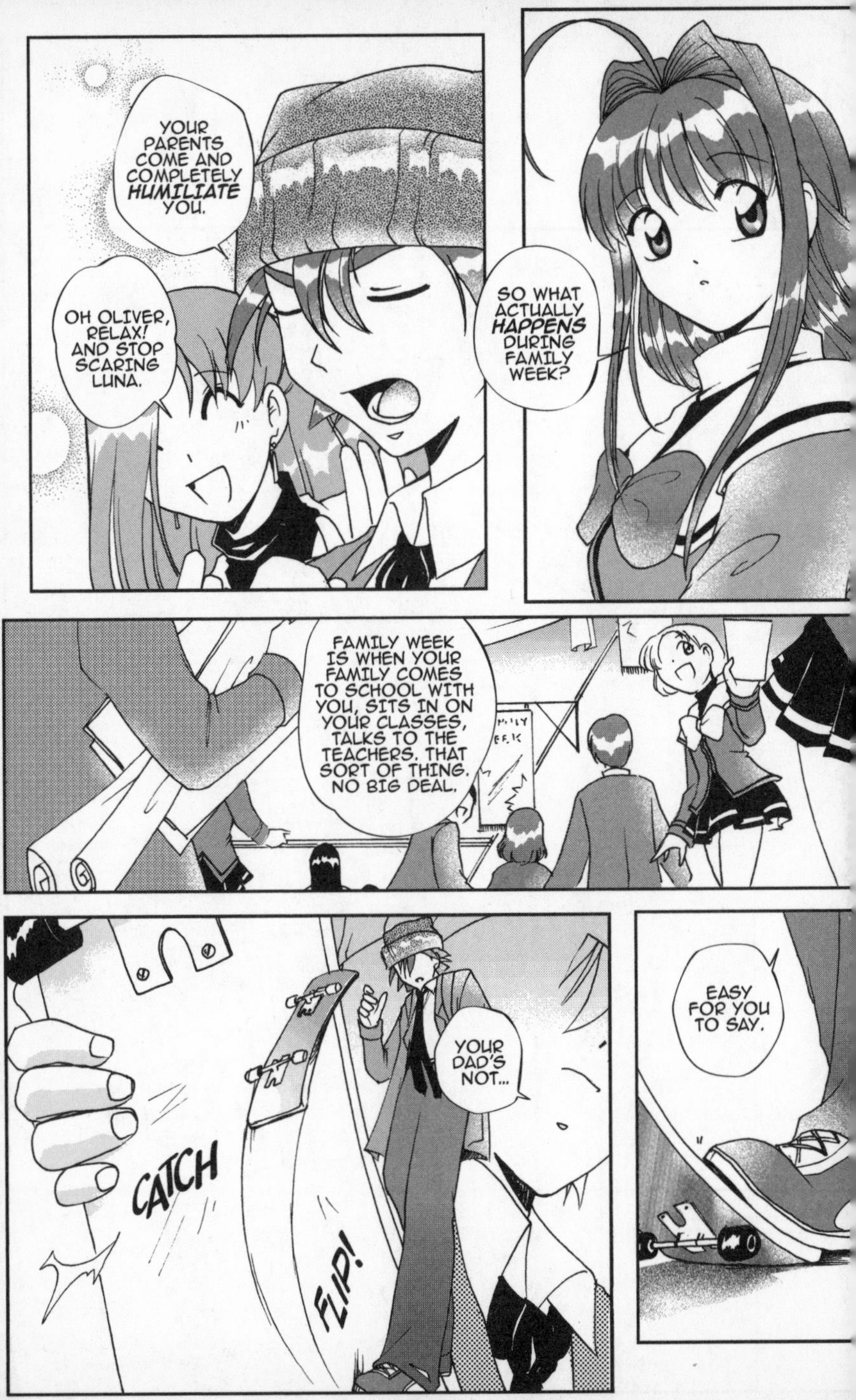
SO WHAT ACTUALLY HAPPENS DURING FAMILY WEEK?
YOUR PARENTS COME AND COMPLETELY HUMILIATE YOU.
OH OLIVER, RELAX! AND STOP SCARING LUNA.
FAMILY WEEK IS WHEN YOUR FAMILY COMES TO SCHOOL WITH YOU, SITS IN ON YOUR CLASSES, TALKS TO THE TEACHERS. THAT SORT OF THING. NO BIG DEAL.
EASY FOR YOU TO SAY.
YOUR DAD'S NOT...
CATCH
FLIP!

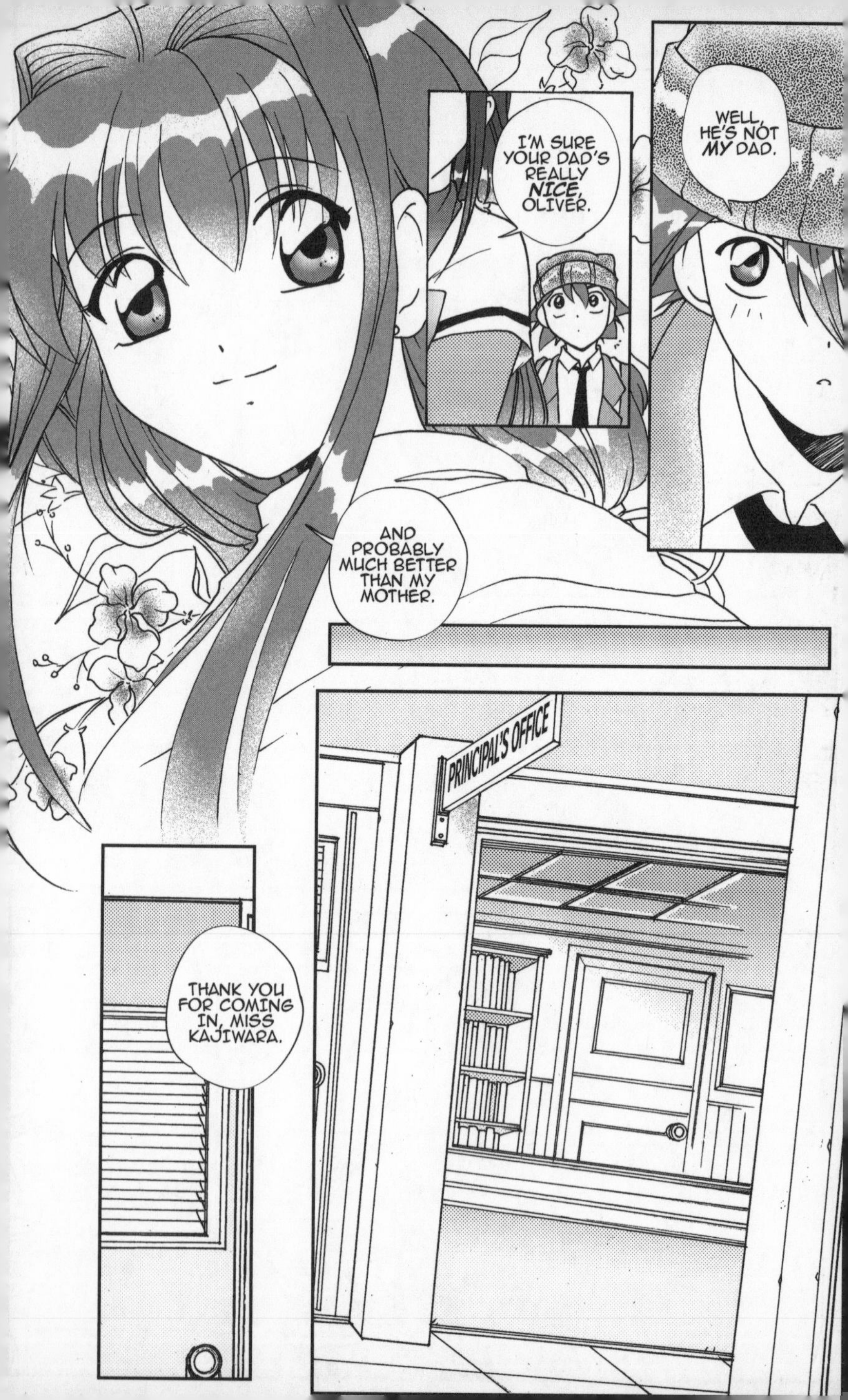
WELL, HE'S NOT MY DAD.
I'M SURE YOUR DAD'S REALLY NICE, OLIVER.
AND PROBABLY MUCH BETTER THAN MY MOTHER.
PRINCIPAL'S OFFICE
THANK YOU FOR COMING IN, MISS KAJIWARA.

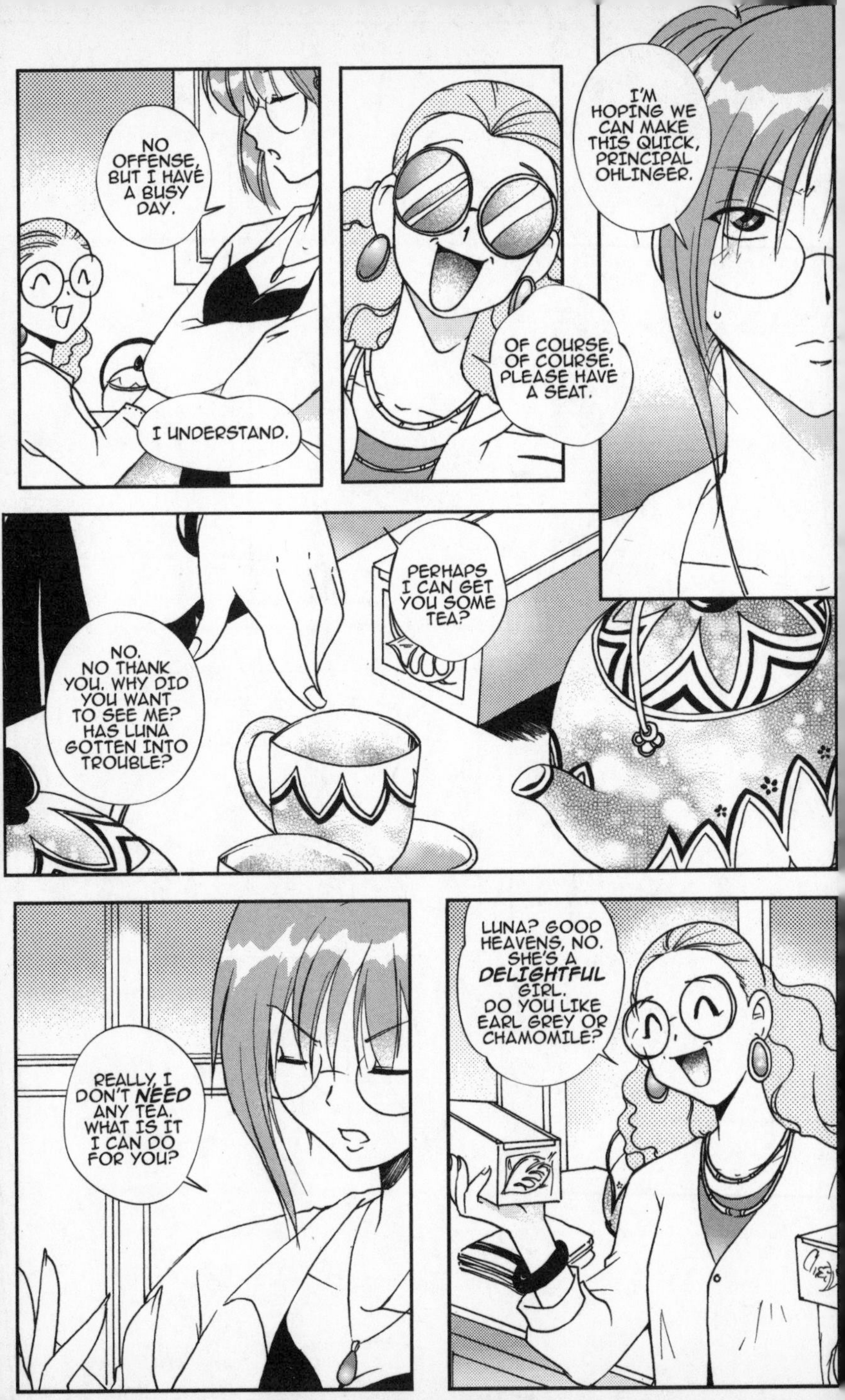
I'M HOPING WE CAN MAKE THIS QUICK, PRINCIPAL OHLINGER.
OF COURSE, OF COURSE. PLEASE HAVE A SEAT.
NO OFFENSE, BUT I HAVE A BUSY DAY.
I UNDERSTAND.
PERHAPS I CAN GET YOU SOME TEA?
NO. NO THANK YOU. WHY DID YOU WANT TO SEE ME? HAS LUNA GOTTEN INTO TROUBLE?
LUNA? GOOD HEAVENS, NO. SHE'S A **DELIGHTFUL** GIRL. DO YOU LIKE EARL GREY OR CHAMOMILE?
REALLY, I DON'T **NEED** ANY TEA. WHAT IS IT I CAN DO FOR YOU?

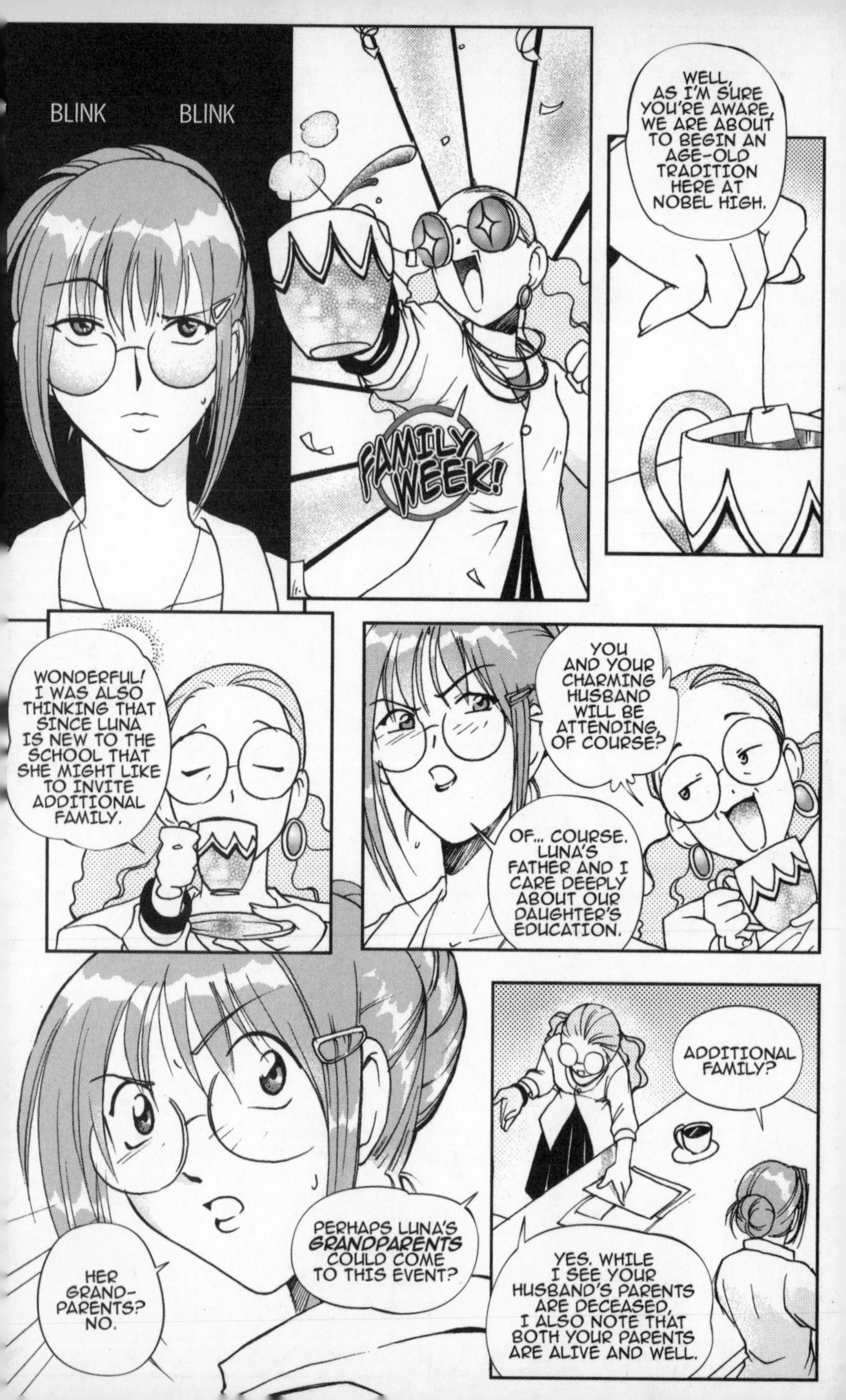
WELL, AS I'M SURE YOU'RE AWARE, WE ARE ABOUT TO BEGIN AN AGE-OLD TRADITION HERE AT NOBEL HIGH.
FAMILY WEEK!
BLINK
BLINK
YOU AND YOUR CHARMING HUSBAND WILL BE ATTENDING, OF COURSE?
OF... COURSE. LUNA'S FATHER AND I CARE DEEPLY ABOUT OUR DAUGHTER'S EDUCATION.
WONDERFUL! I WAS ALSO THINKING THAT SINCE LUNA IS NEW TO THE SCHOOL THAT SHE MIGHT LIKE TO INVITE ADDITIONAL FAMILY.
ADDITIONAL FAMILY?
YES. WHILE I SEE YOUR HUSBAND'S PARENTS ARE DECEASED, I ALSO NOTE THAT BOTH YOUR PARENTS ARE ALIVE AND WELL.
PERHAPS LUNA'S **GRANDPARENTS** COULD COME TO THIS EVENT?
HER GRAND-PARENTS? NO.

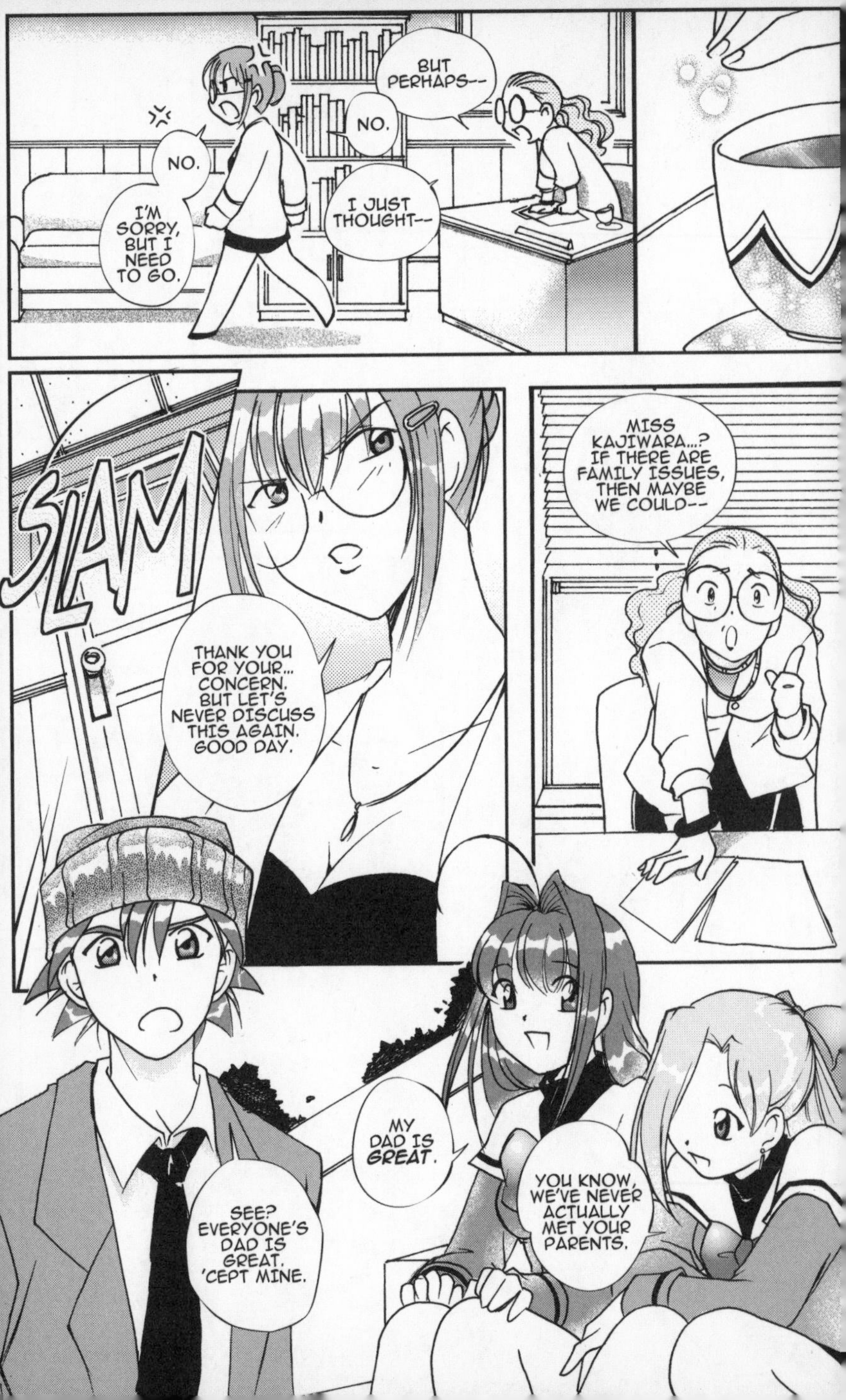

BUT PERHAPS--
NO.
I JUST THOUGHT--
NO.
I'M SORRY, BUT I NEED TO GO.
MISS KAJIWARA...? IF THERE ARE FAMILY ISSUES, THEN MAYBE WE COULD--
SLAM
THANK YOU FOR YOUR... CONCERN. BUT LET'S NEVER DISCUSS THIS AGAIN. GOOD DAY.
YOU KNOW, WE'VE NEVER ACTUALLY MET YOUR PARENTS.
MY DAD IS GREAT.
SEE? EVERYONE'S DAD IS GREAT, 'CEPT MINE.

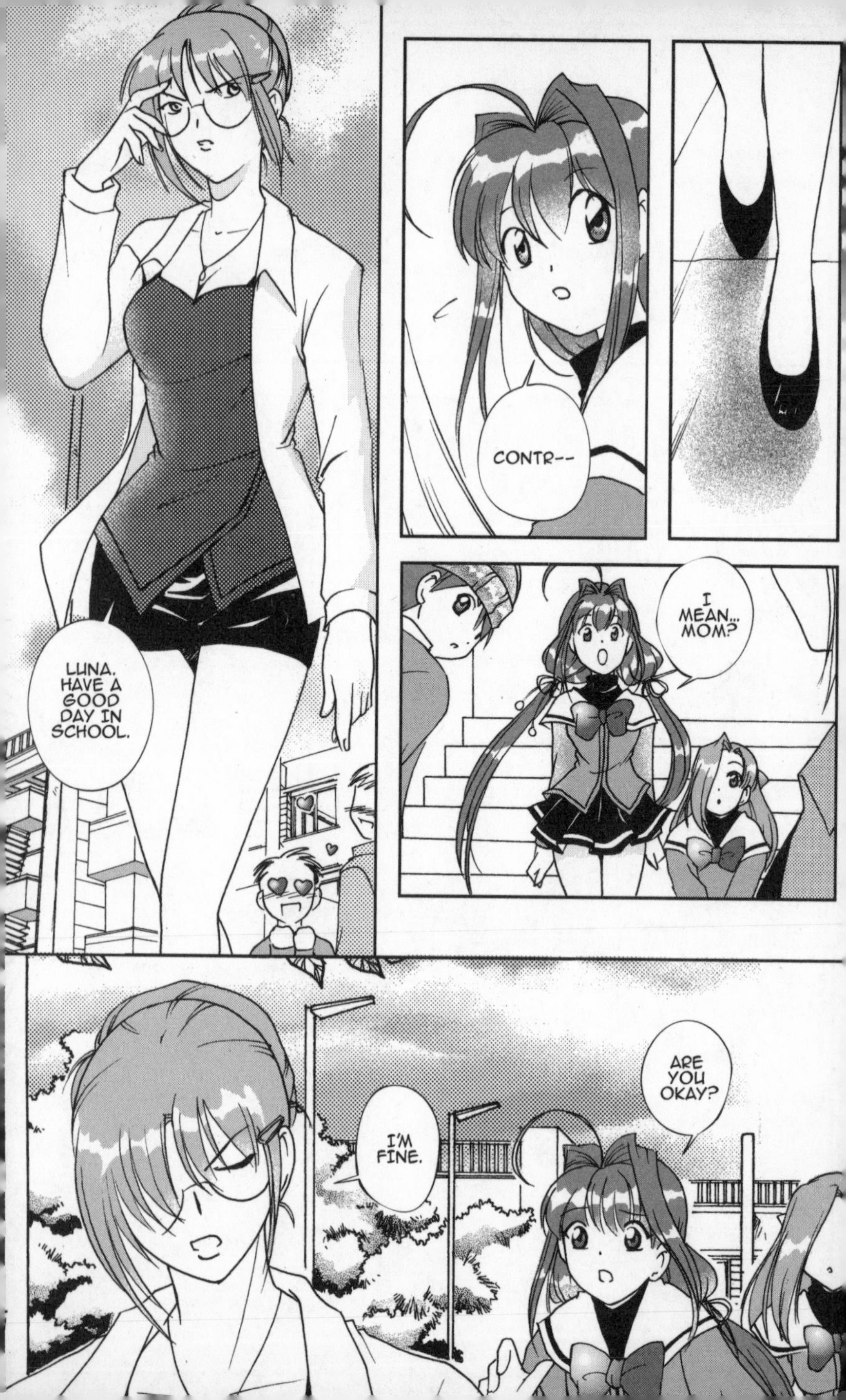
CONTR--
I MEAN... MOM?
LUNA. HAVE A GOOD DAY IN SCHOOL.
ARE YOU OKAY?
I'M FINE.

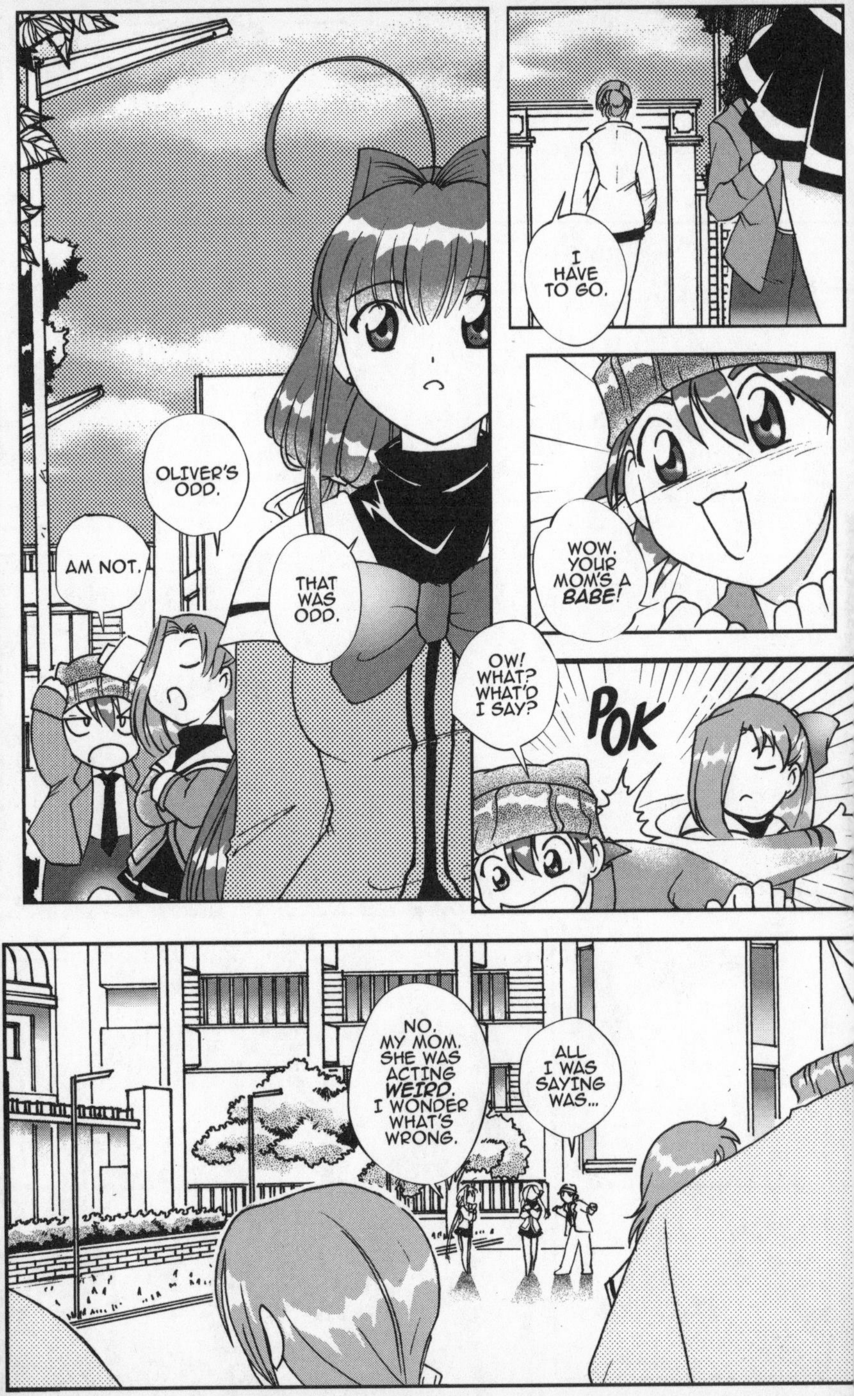
I HAVE TO GO.
WOW. YOUR MOM'S A *BABE*!
POK
OW! WHAT? WHAT'D I SAY?
THAT WAS ODD.
OLIVER'S ODD.
AM NOT.
ALL I WAS SAYING WAS...
NO. MY MOM. SHE WAS ACTING *WEIRD*. I WONDER WHAT'S WRONG.

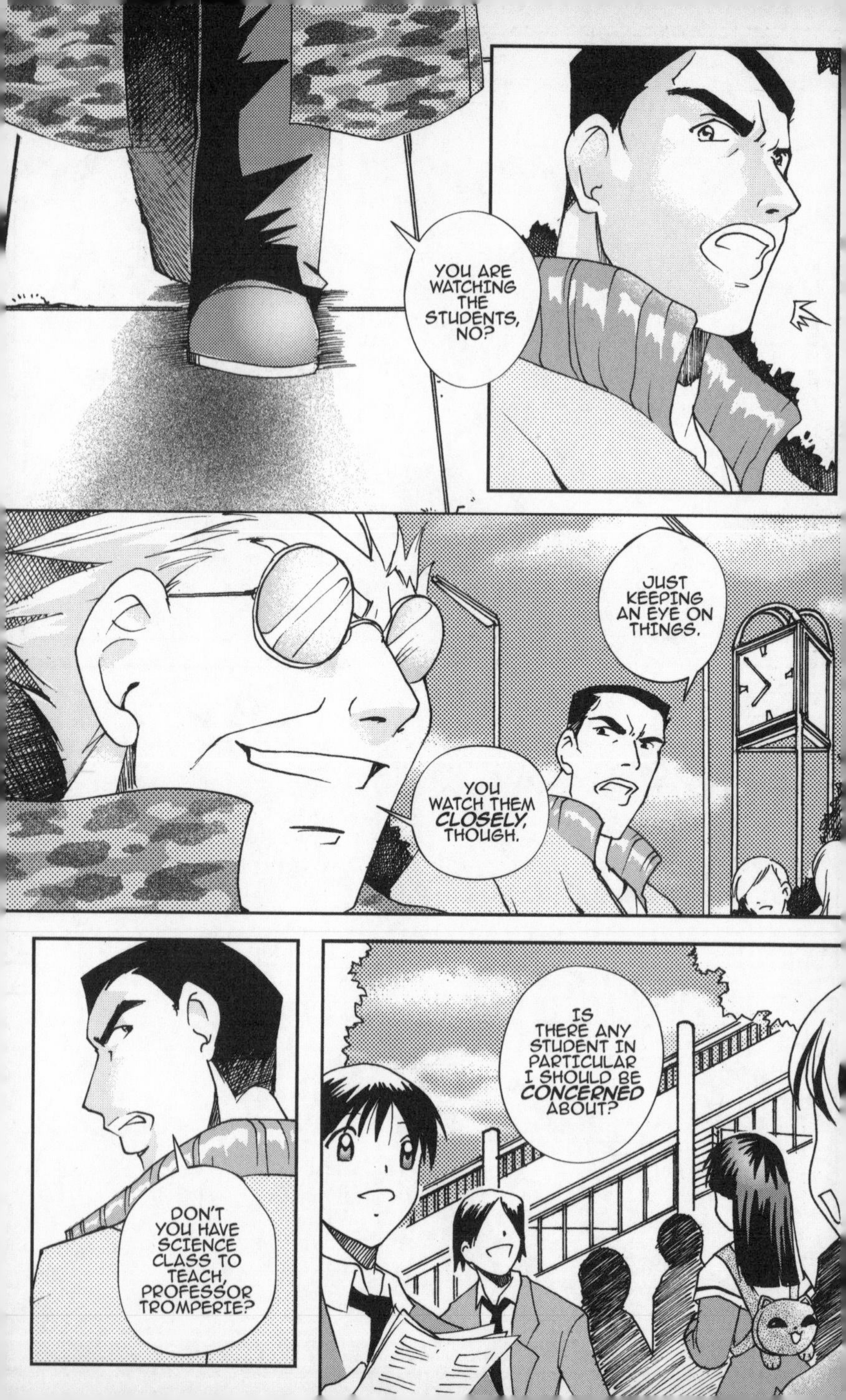
YOU ARE WATCHING THE STUDENTS, NO?
JUST KEEPING AN EYE ON THINGS.
YOU WATCH THEM **CLOSELY**, THOUGH.
IS THERE ANY STUDENT IN PARTICULAR I SHOULD BE **CONCERNED** ABOUT?
DON'T YOU HAVE SCIENCE CLASS TO TEACH, PROFESSOR TROMPERIE?

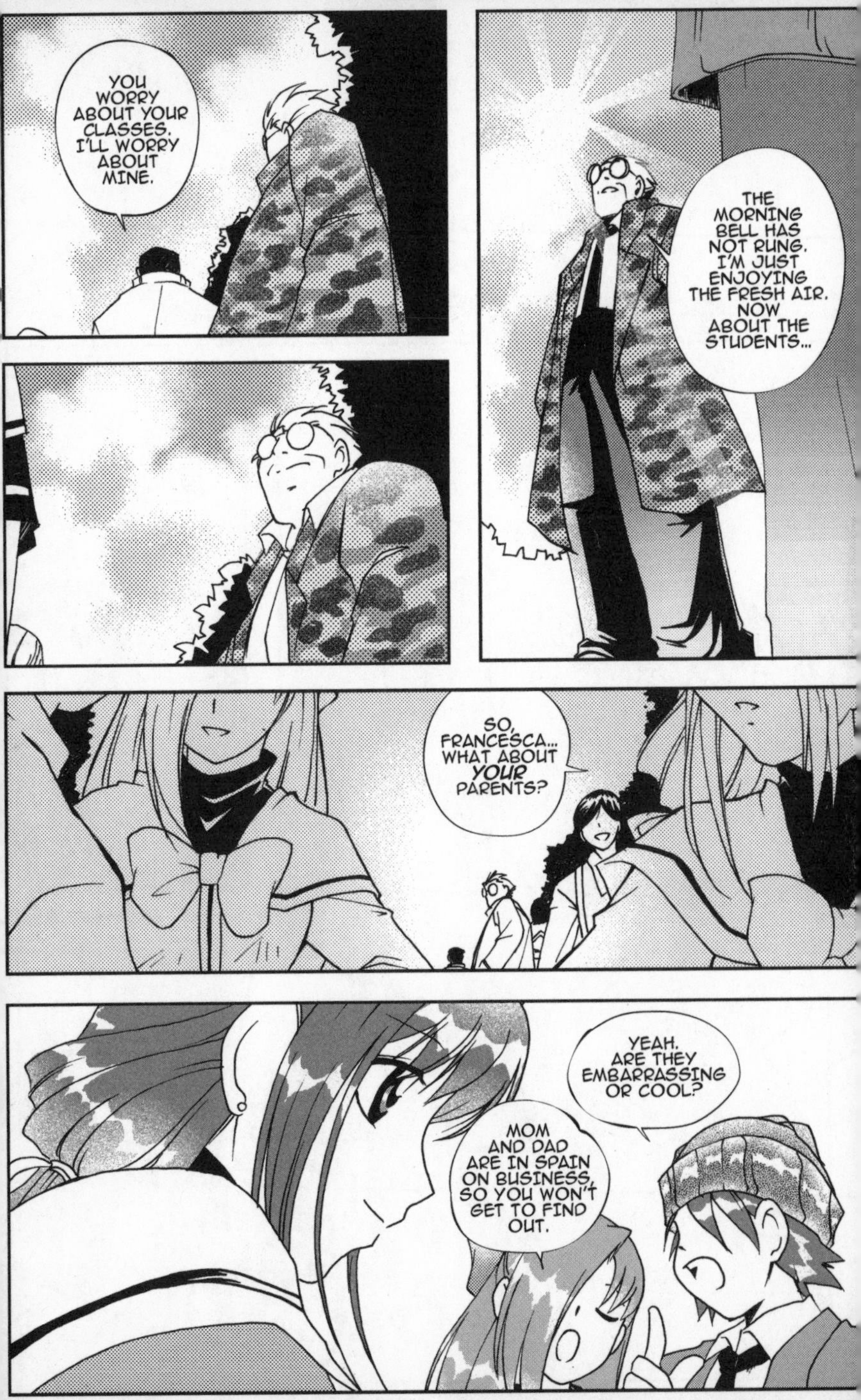
THE MORNING BELL HAS NOT RUNG. I'M JUST ENJOYING THE FRESH AIR. NOW ABOUT THE STUDENTS...
YOU WORRY ABOUT YOUR CLASSES. I'LL WORRY ABOUT MINE.
SO, FRANCESCA... WHAT ABOUT YOUR PARENTS?
YEAH. ARE THEY EMBARRASSING OR COOL?
MOM AND DAD ARE IN SPAIN ON BUSINESS, SO YOU WON'T GET TO FIND OUT.

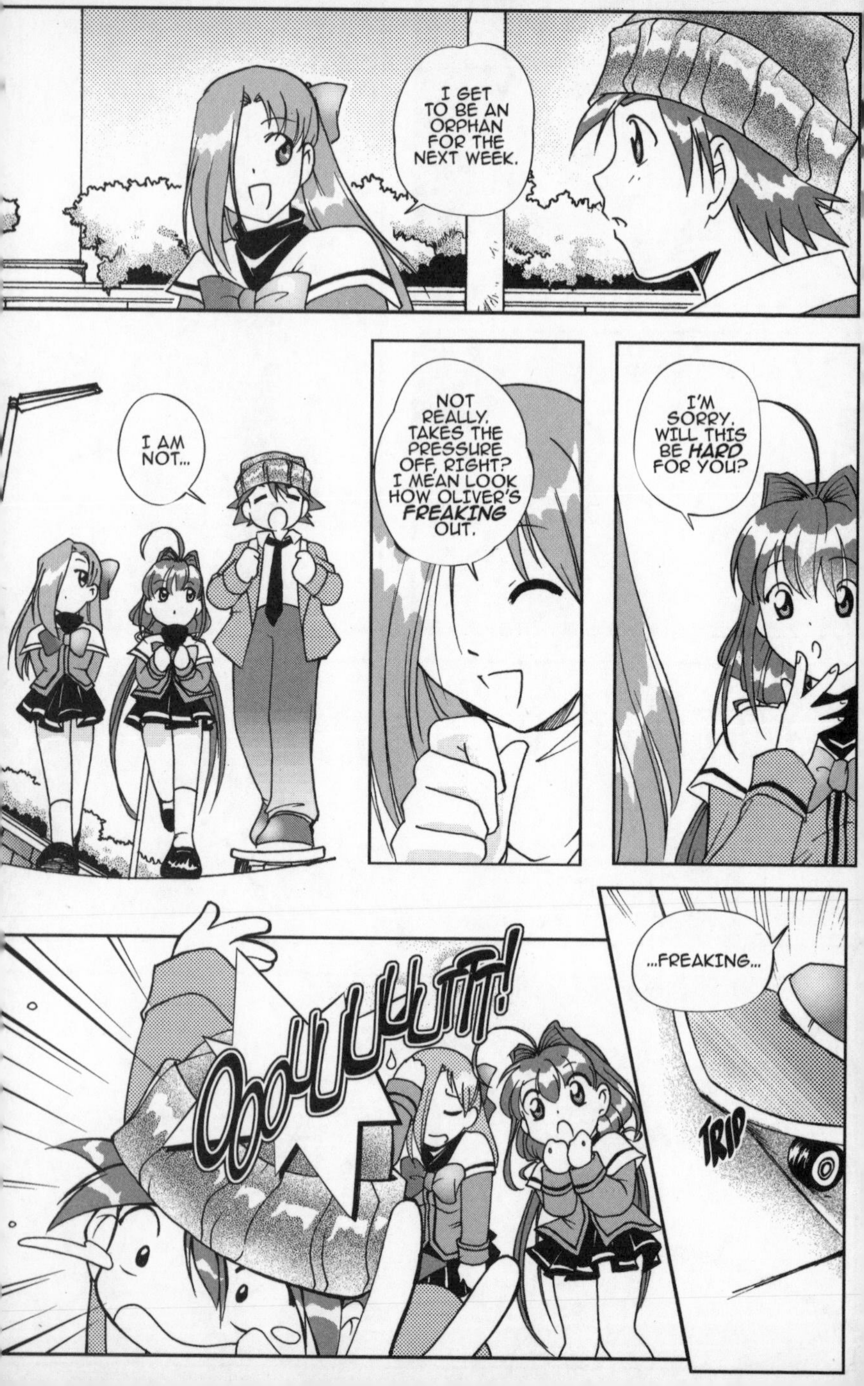
I GET TO BE AN ORPHAN FOR THE NEXT WEEK.
I'M SORRY. WILL THIS BE *HARD* FOR YOU?
NOT REALLY. TAKES THE PRESSURE OFF, RIGHT? I MEAN LOOK HOW OLIVER'S *FREAKING* OUT.
I AM NOT...
...FREAKING...
TRIP
OOOUUUUUTT!

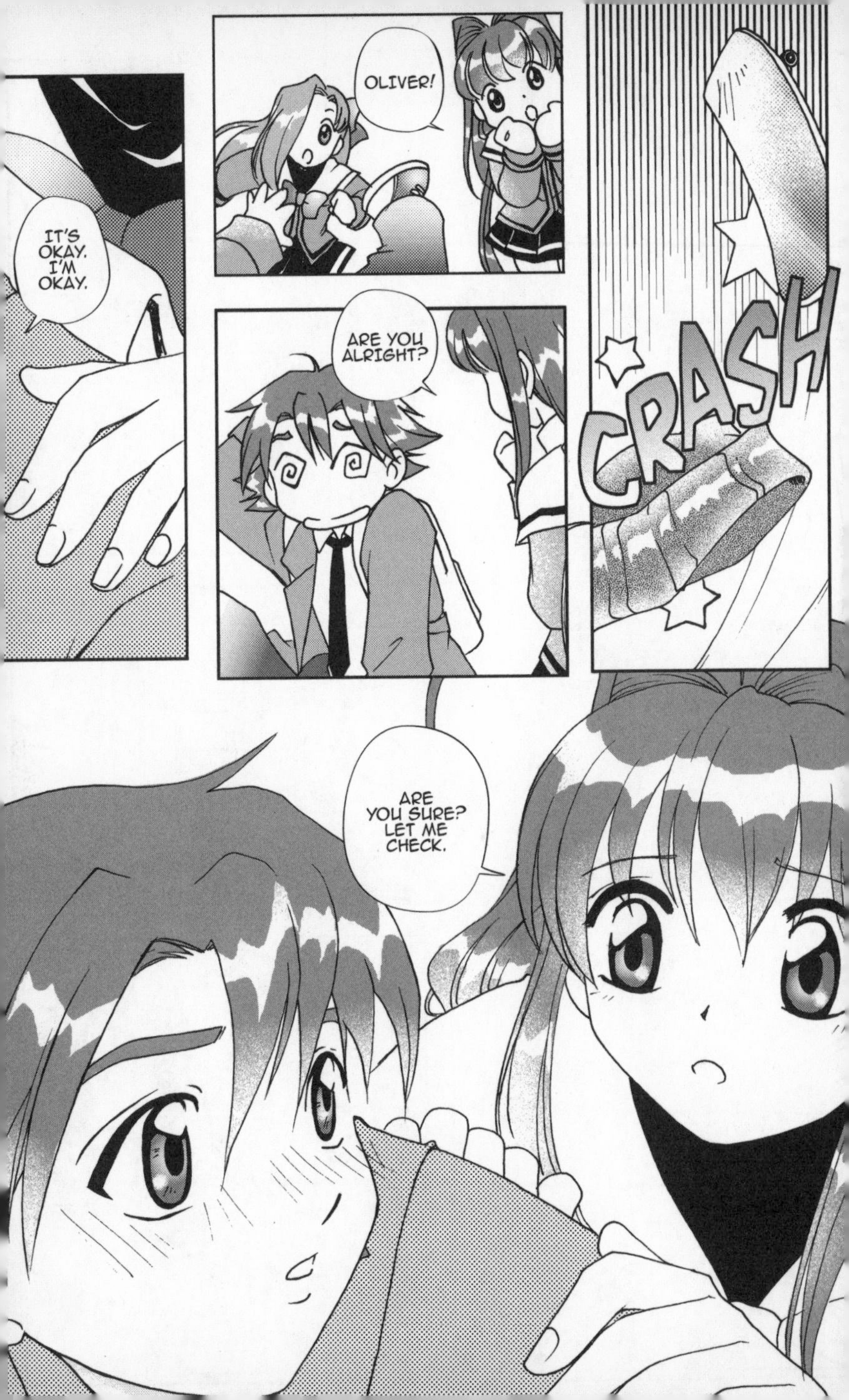
CRASH
OLIVER!
ARE YOU ALRIGHT?
IT'S OKAY. I'M OKAY.
ARE YOU SURE? LET ME CHECK.

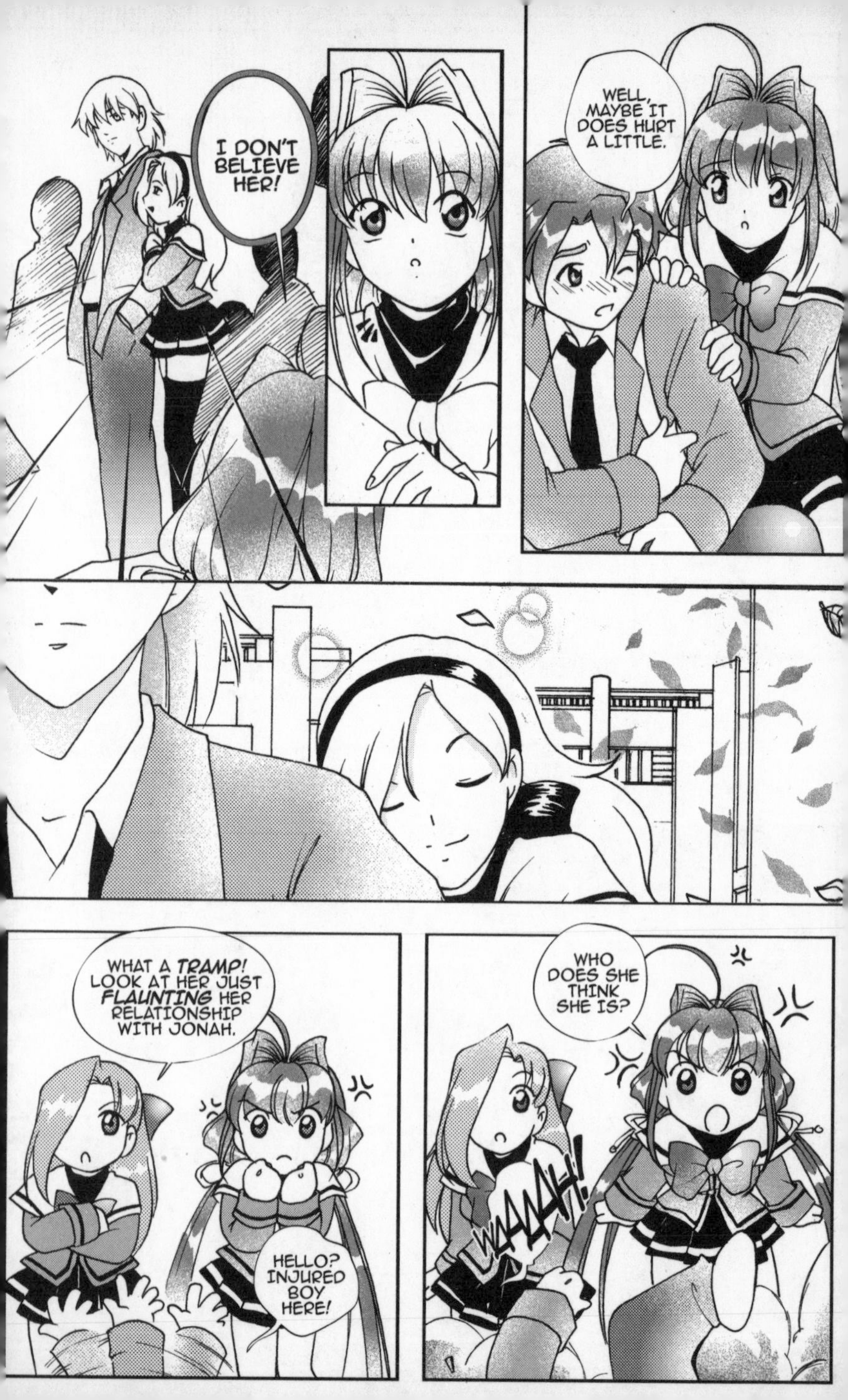

WELL, MAYBE IT DOES HURT A LITTLE.
I DON'T BELIEVE HER!
WHO DOES SHE THINK SHE IS?
WAAAH!
WHAT A TRAMP! LOOK AT HER JUST FLAUNTING HER RELATIONSHIP WITH JONAH.
HELLO? INJURED BOY HERE!

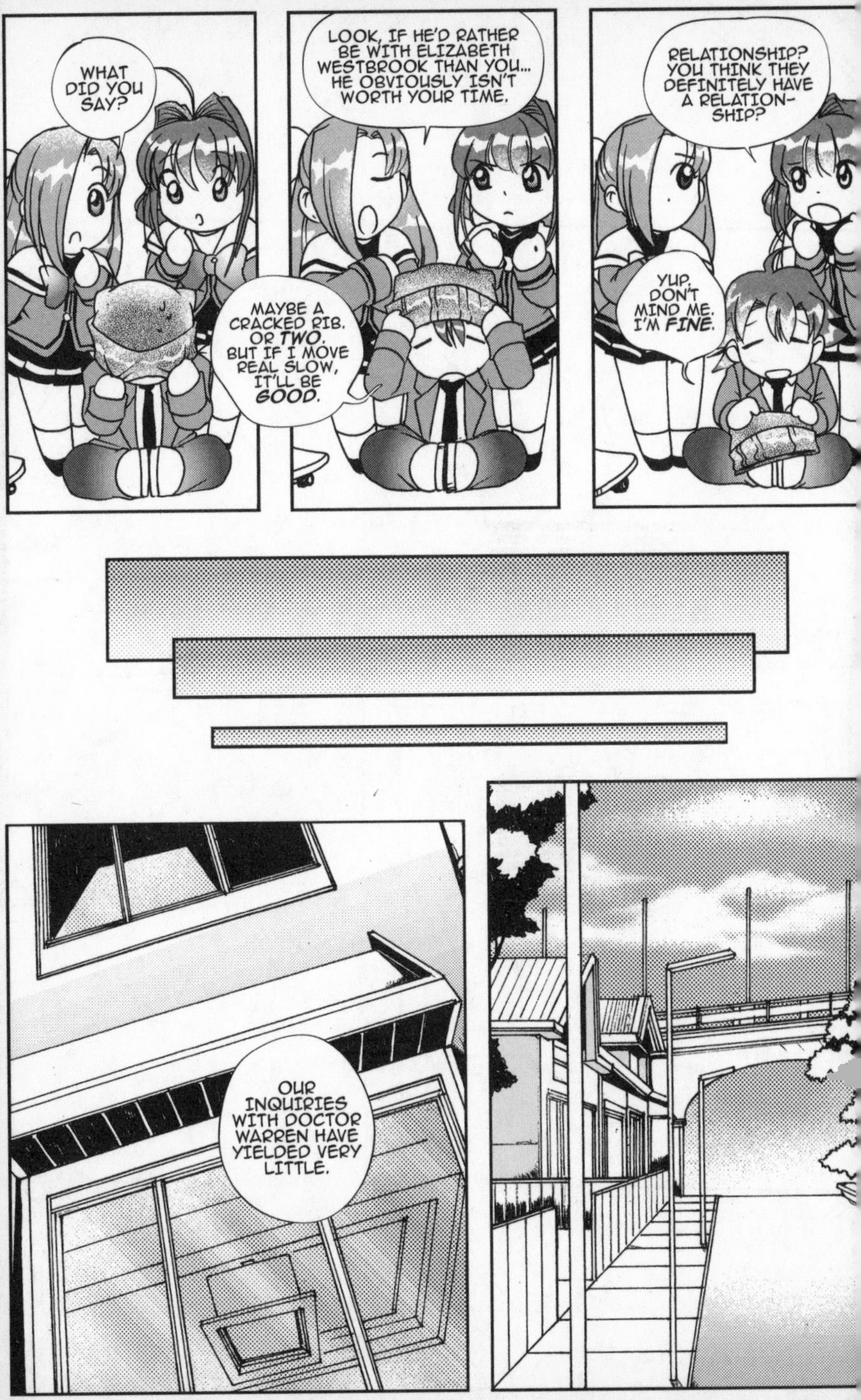
WHAT DID YOU SAY?
LOOK, IF HE'D RATHER BE WITH ELIZABETH WESTBROOK THAN YOU... HE OBVIOUSLY ISN'T WORTH YOUR TIME.
MAYBE A CRACKED RIB. OR **TWO**. BUT IF I MOVE REAL SLOW, IT'LL BE **GOOD**.
RELATIONSHIP? YOU THINK THEY DEFINITELY HAVE A RELATION-SHIP?
YUP, DON'T MIND ME. I'M **FINE**.
OUR INQUIRIES WITH DOCTOR WARREN HAVE YIELDED VERY LITTLE.

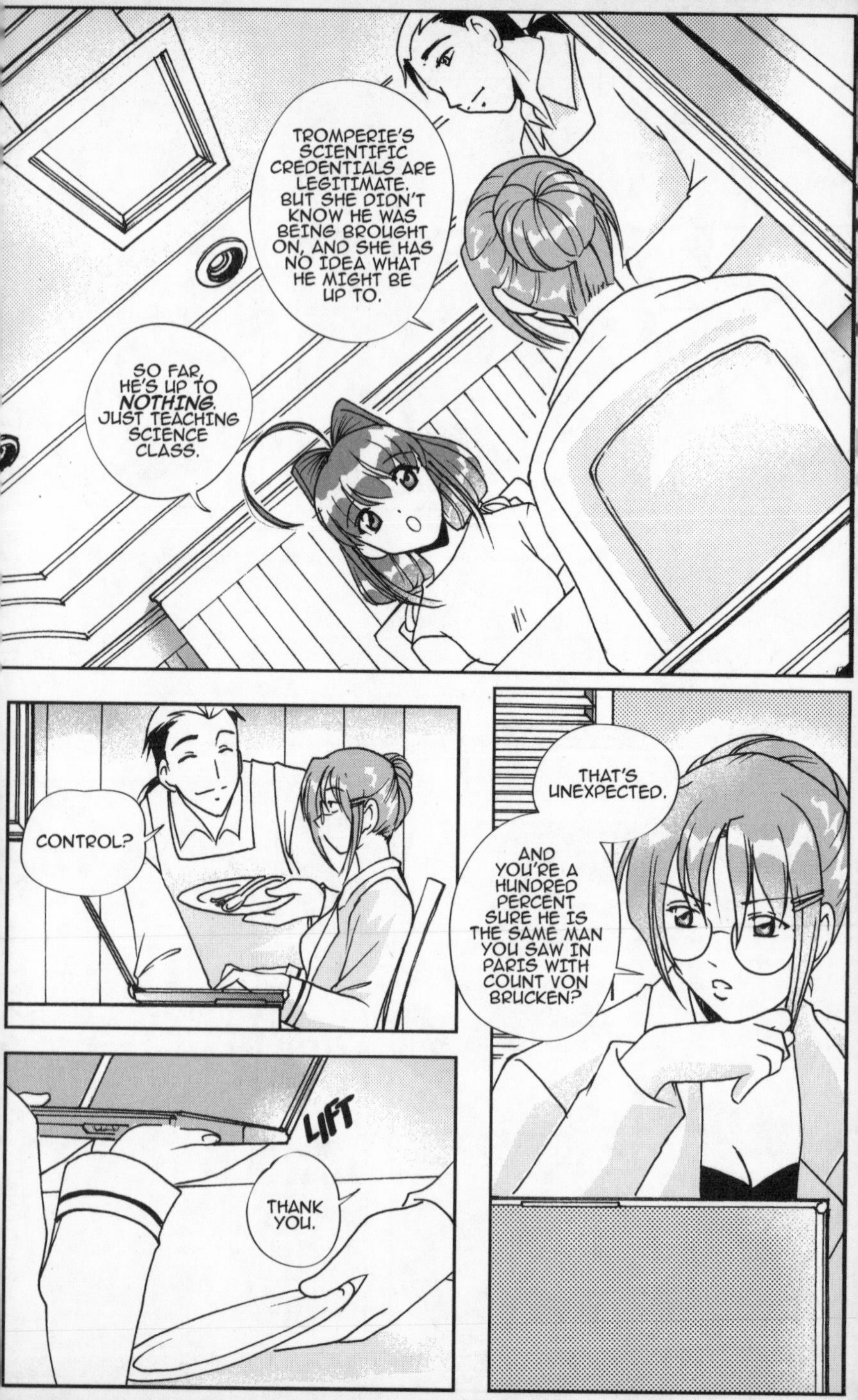
TROMPERIE'S SCIENTIFIC CREDENTIALS ARE LEGITIMATE. BUT SHE DIDN'T KNOW HE WAS BEING BROUGHT ON, AND SHE HAS NO IDEA WHAT HE MIGHT BE UP TO.
SO FAR, HE'S UP TO *NOTHING*. JUST TEACHING SCIENCE CLASS.
THAT'S UNEXPECTED.
AND YOU'RE A HUNDRED PERCENT SURE HE IS THE SAME MAN YOU SAW IN PARIS WITH COUNT VON BRUCKEN?
CONTROL?
LIFT
THANK YOU.

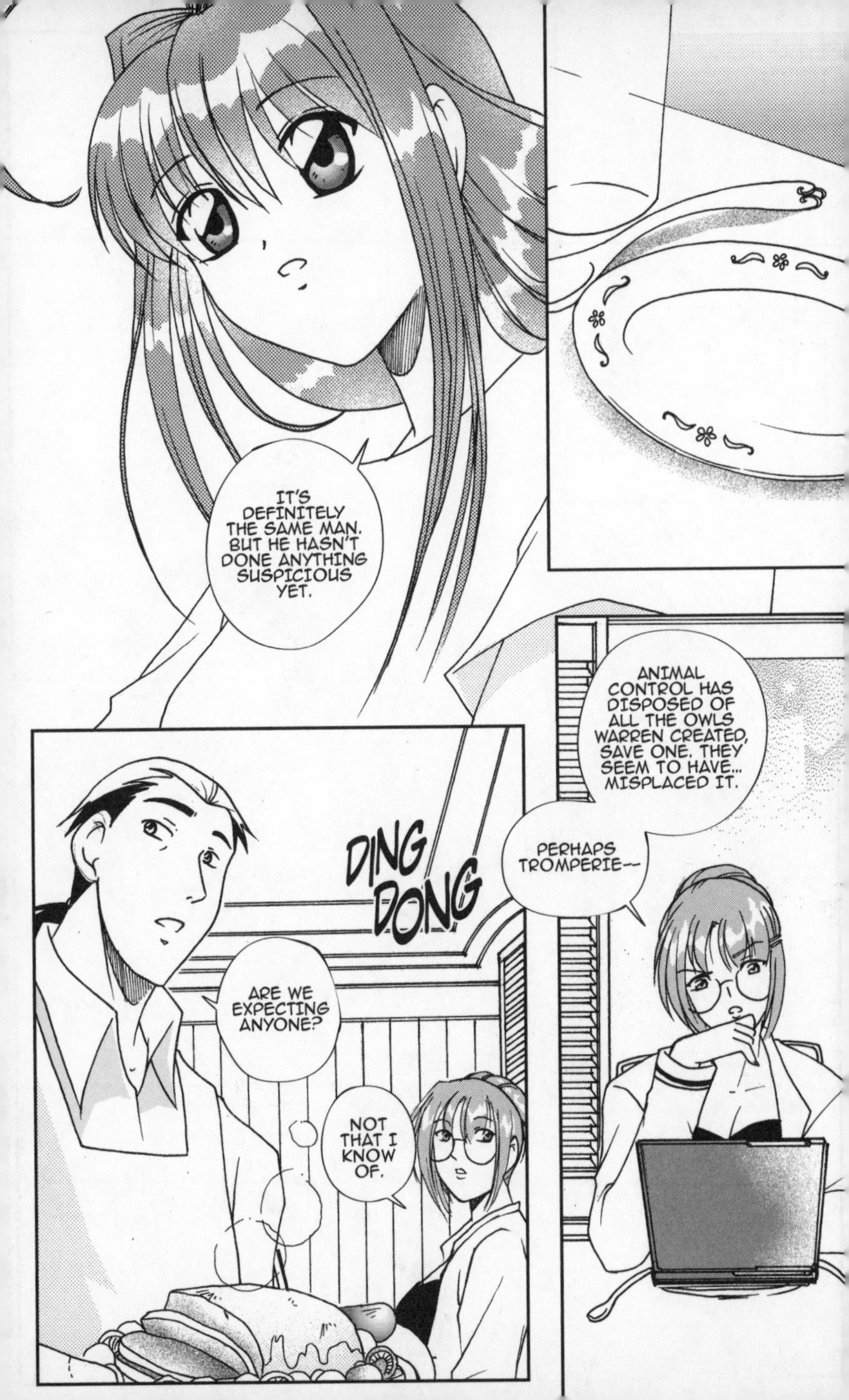
IT'S DEFINITELY THE SAME MAN. BUT HE HASN'T DONE ANYTHING SUSPICIOUS YET.
ANIMAL CONTROL HAS DISPOSED OF ALL THE OWLS WARREN CREATED, SAVE ONE. THEY SEEM TO HAVE... MISPLACED IT.
PERHAPS TROMPERIE--
DING DONG
ARE WE EXPECTING ANYONE?
NOT THAT I KNOW OF.

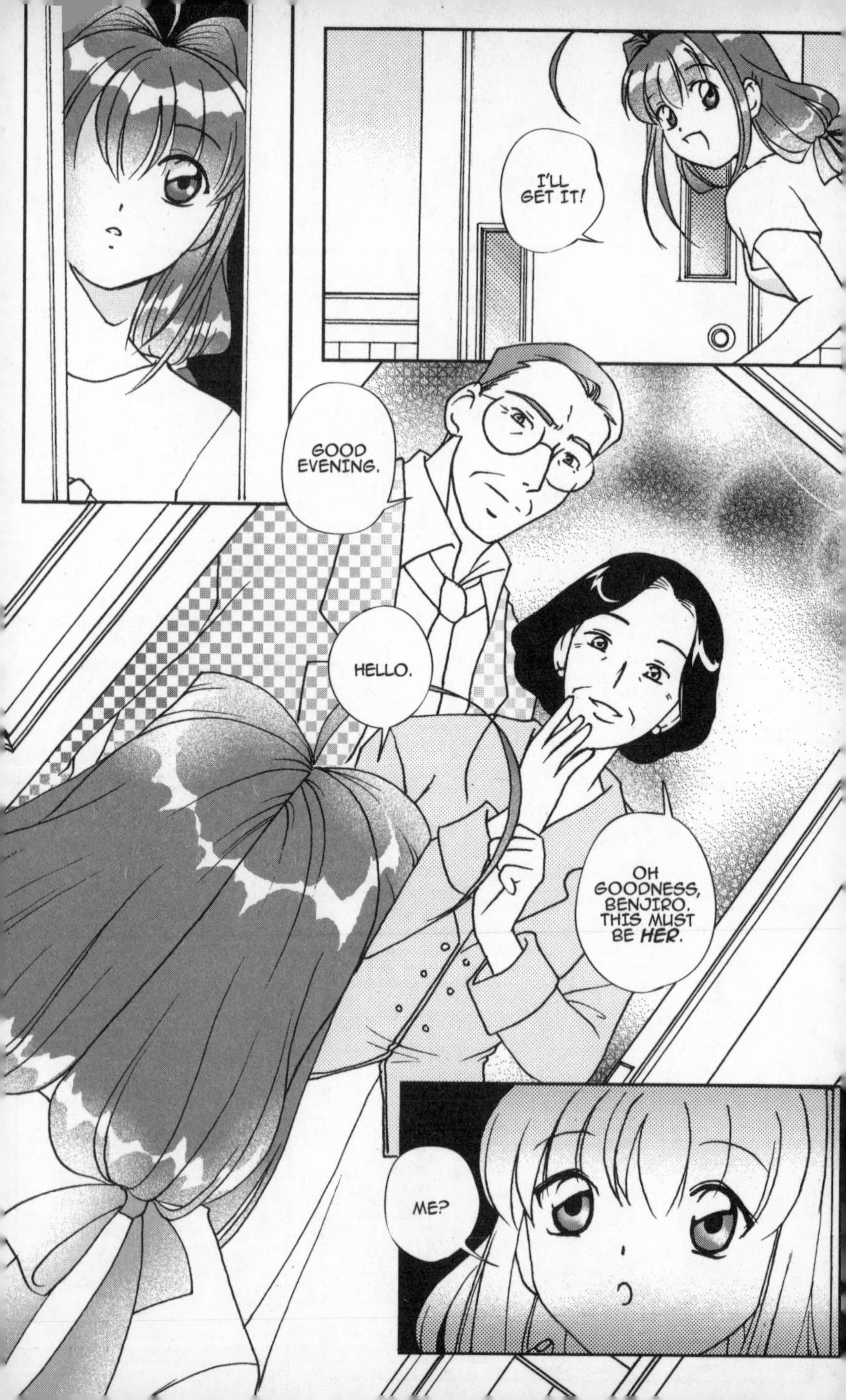
I'LL GET IT!
GOOD EVENING.
HELLO.
OH GOODNESS, BENJIRO. THIS MUST BE ***HER***.
ME?

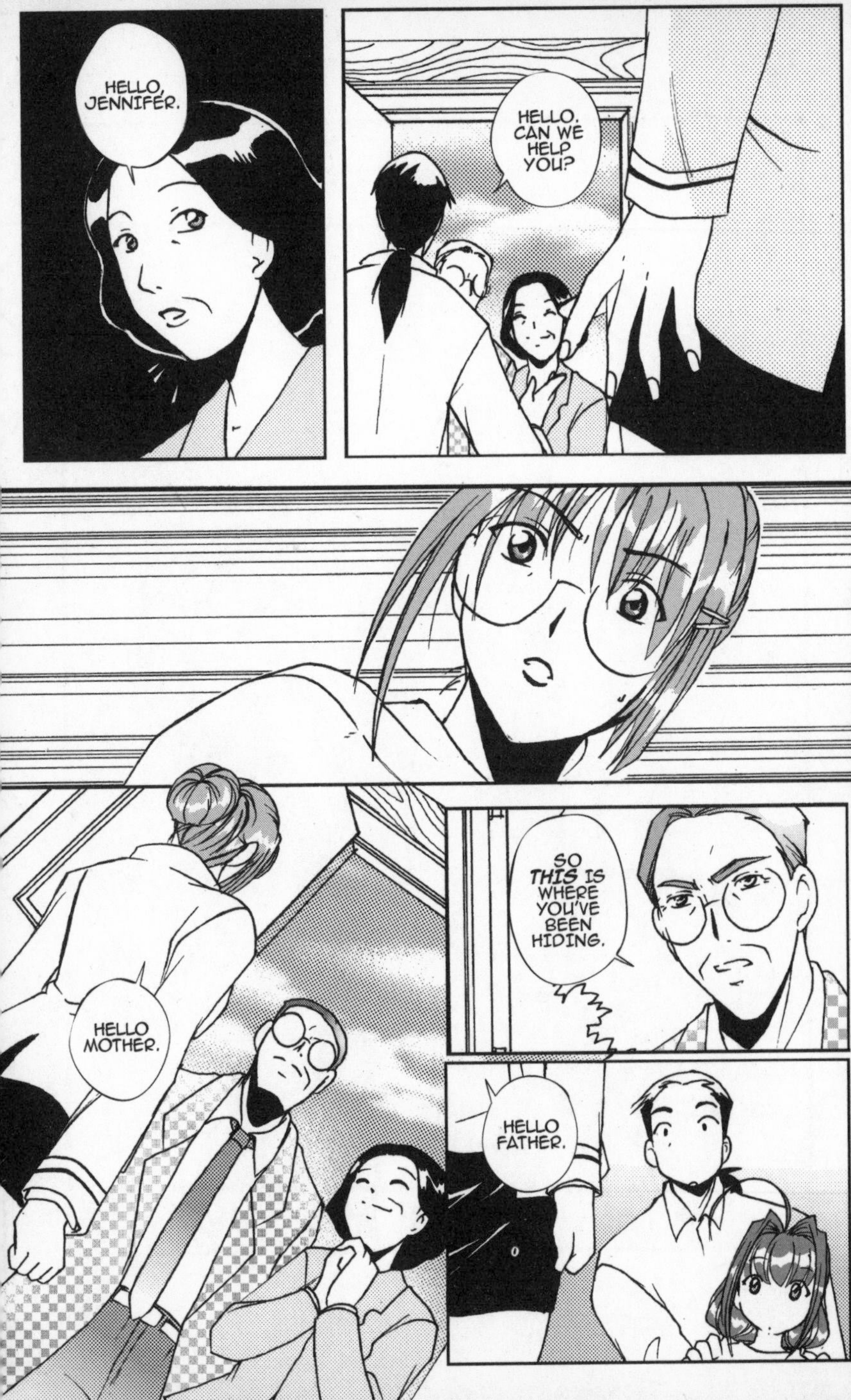
HELLO. CAN WE HELP YOU?
HELLO, JENNIFER.
SO *THIS* IS WHERE YOU'VE BEEN HIDING.
HELLO FATHER.
HELLO MOTHER.

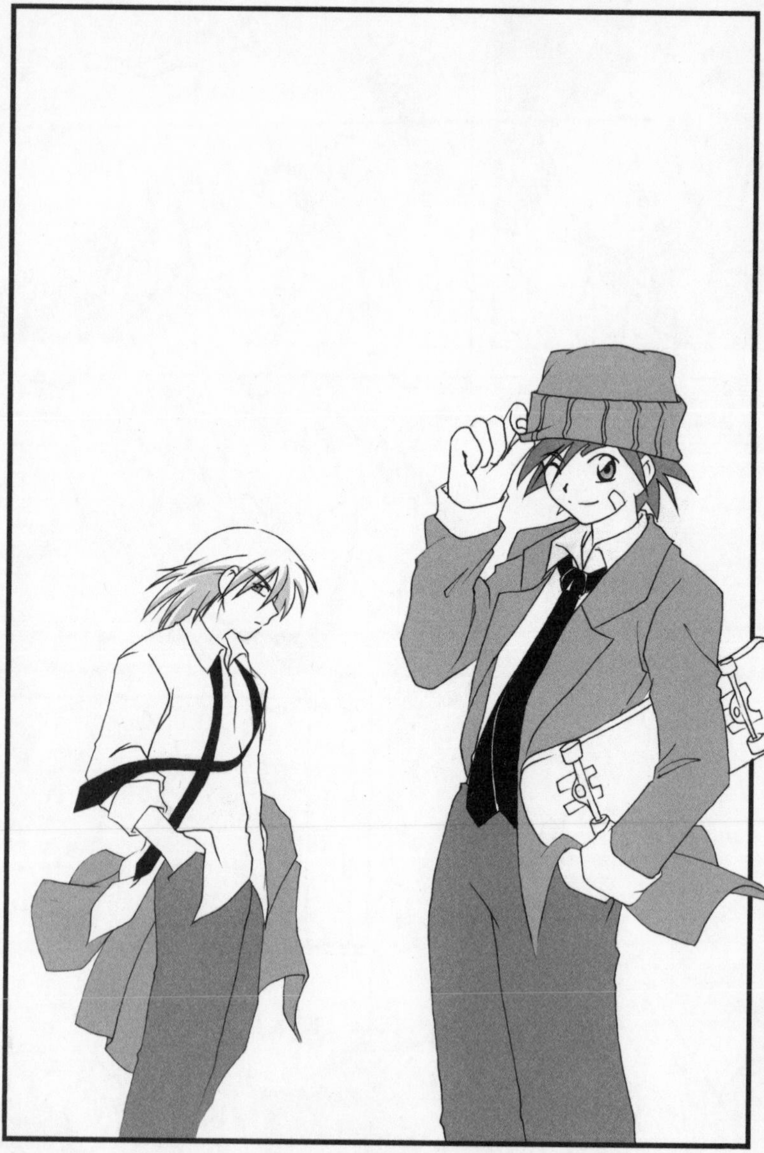

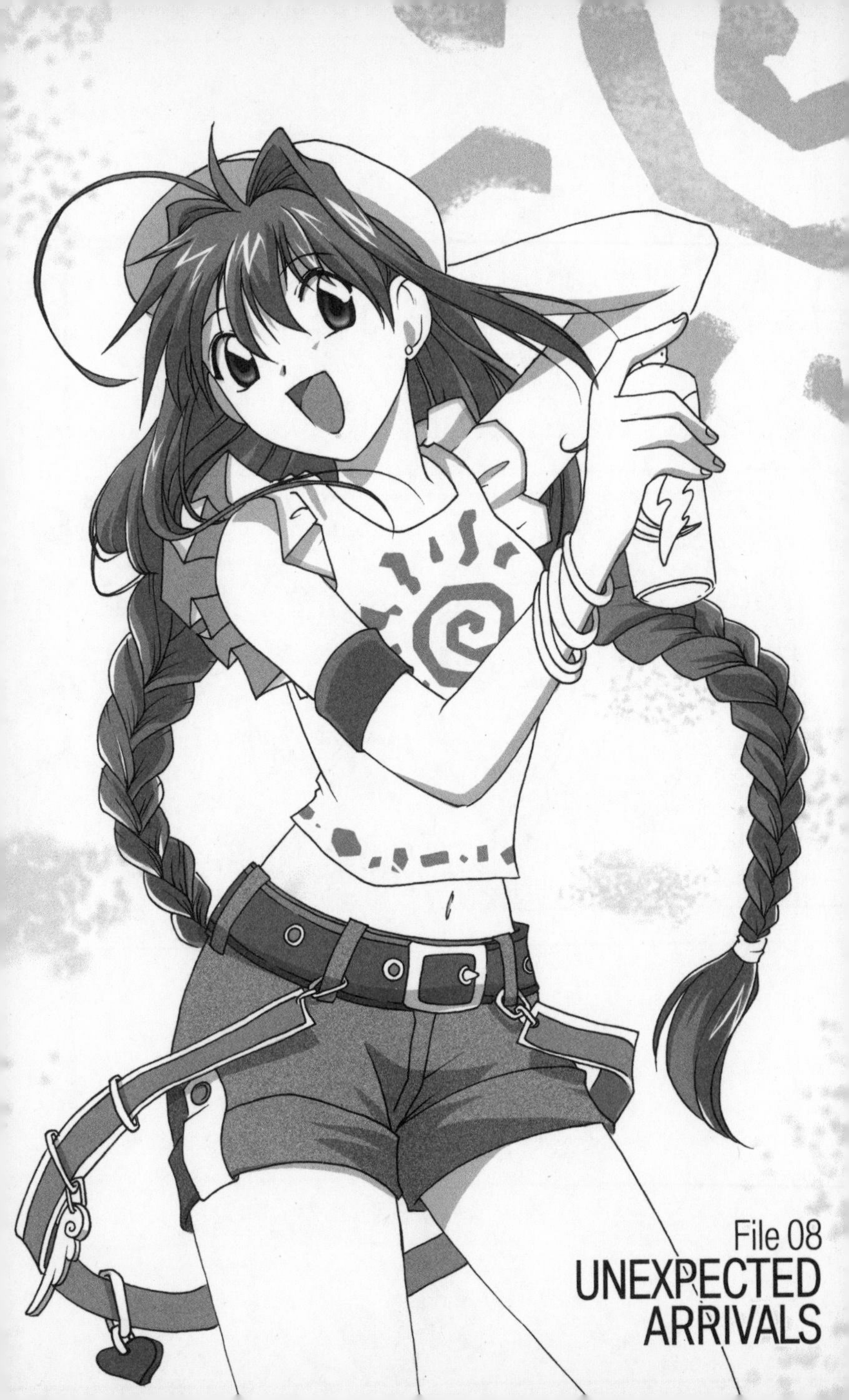

File 08
# UNEXPECTED ARRIVALS

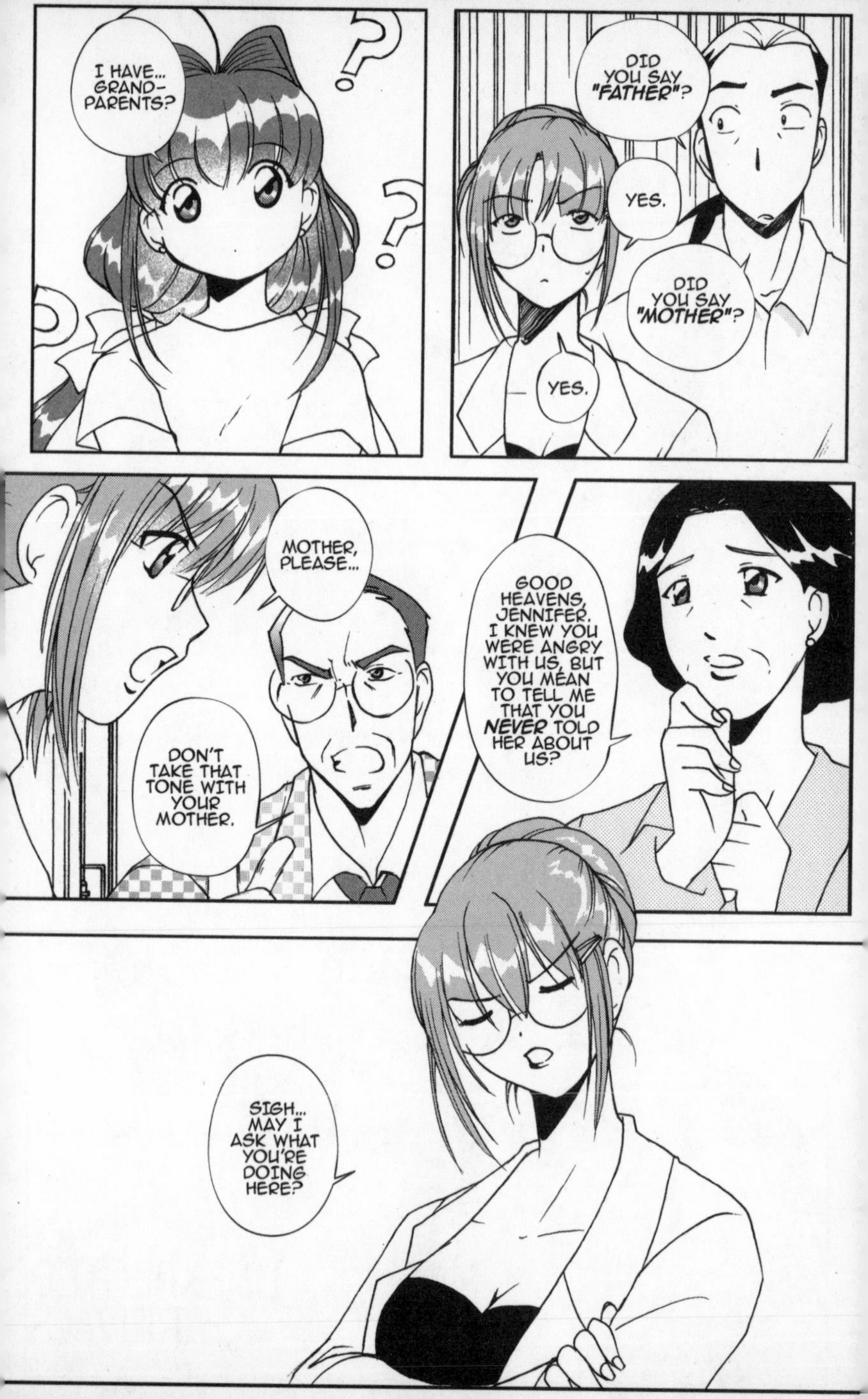
DID YOU SAY "*FATHER*"?
YES.
DID YOU SAY "*MOTHER*"?
YES.
I HAVE... GRAND-PARENTS?
GOOD HEAVENS, JENNIFER. I KNEW YOU WERE ANGRY WITH US, BUT YOU MEAN TO TELL ME THAT YOU ***NEVER*** TOLD HER ABOUT US?
MOTHER, PLEASE...
DON'T TAKE THAT TONE WITH YOUR MOTHER.
SIGH... MAY I ASK WHAT YOU'RE DOING HERE?

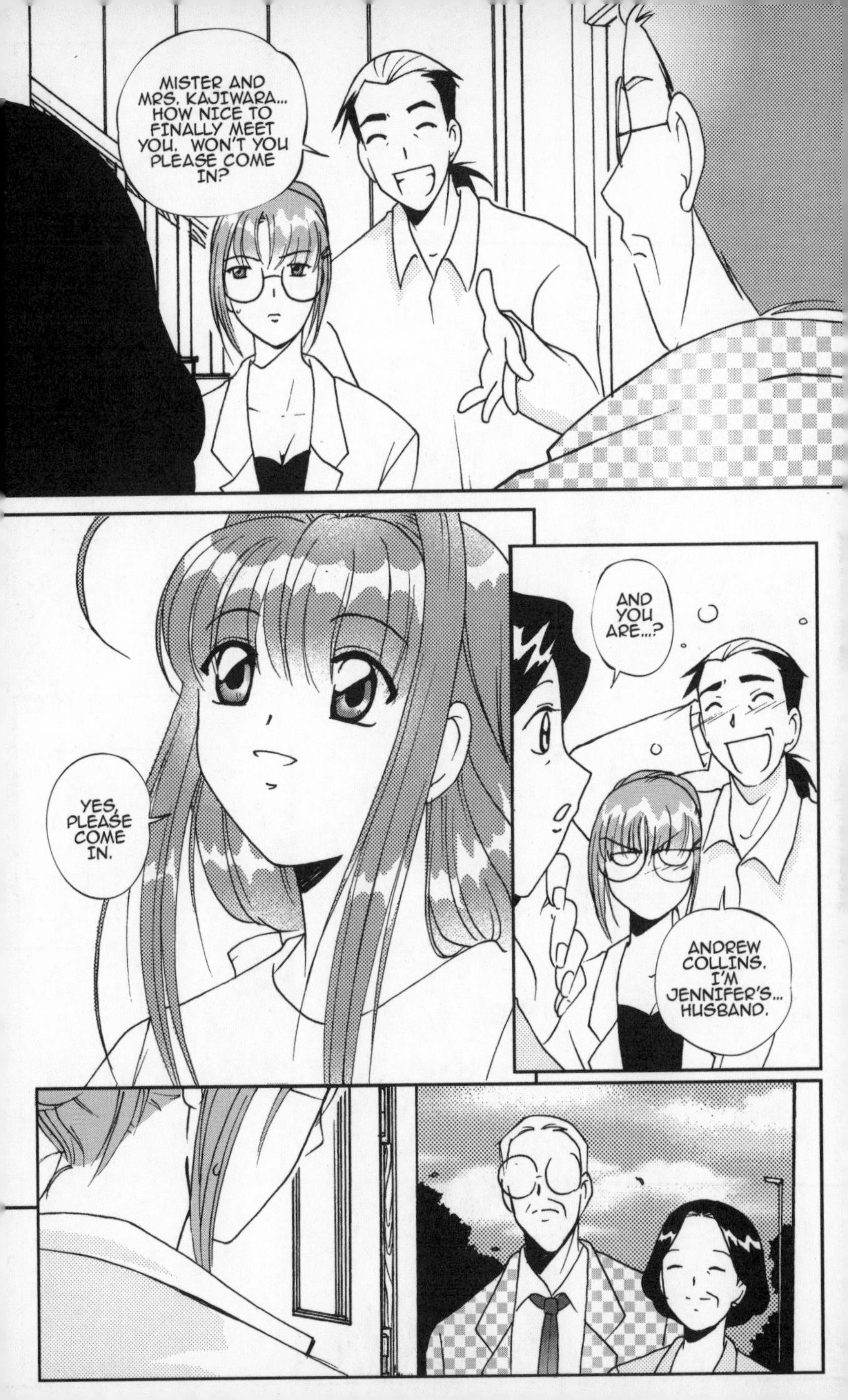
MISTER AND MRS. KAJIWARA... HOW NICE TO FINALLY MEET YOU. WON'T YOU PLEASE COME IN?
AND YOU ARE...?
ANDREW COLLINS. I'M JENNIFER'S... HUSBAND.
YES, PLEASE COME IN.

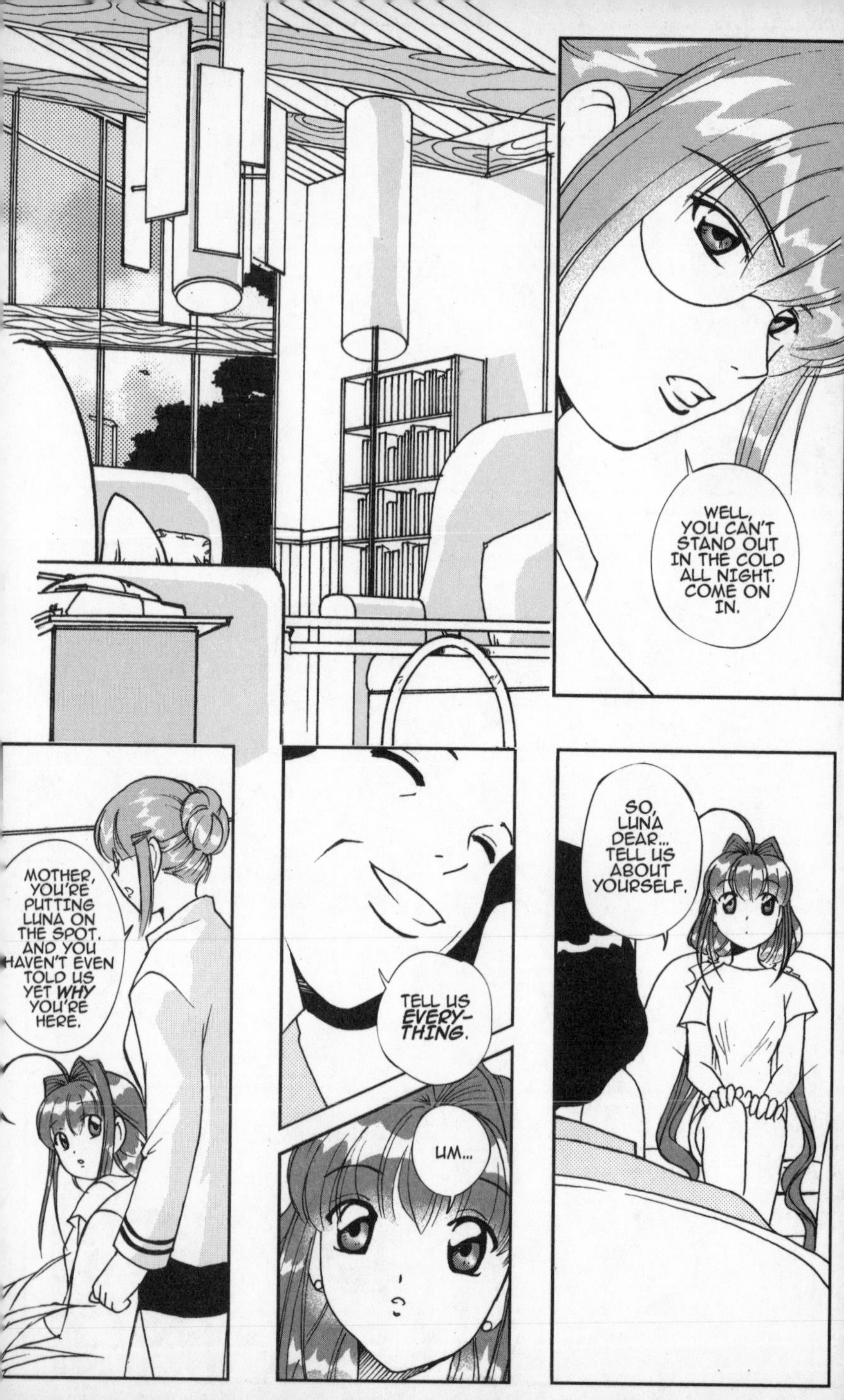
WELL, YOU CAN'T STAND OUT IN THE COLD ALL NIGHT. COME ON IN.
SO, LUNA DEAR... TELL US ABOUT YOURSELF.
TELL US *EVERYTHING*.
UM...
MOTHER, YOU'RE PUTTING LUNA ON THE SPOT, AND YOU HAVEN'T EVEN TOLD US YET *WHY* YOU'RE HERE.

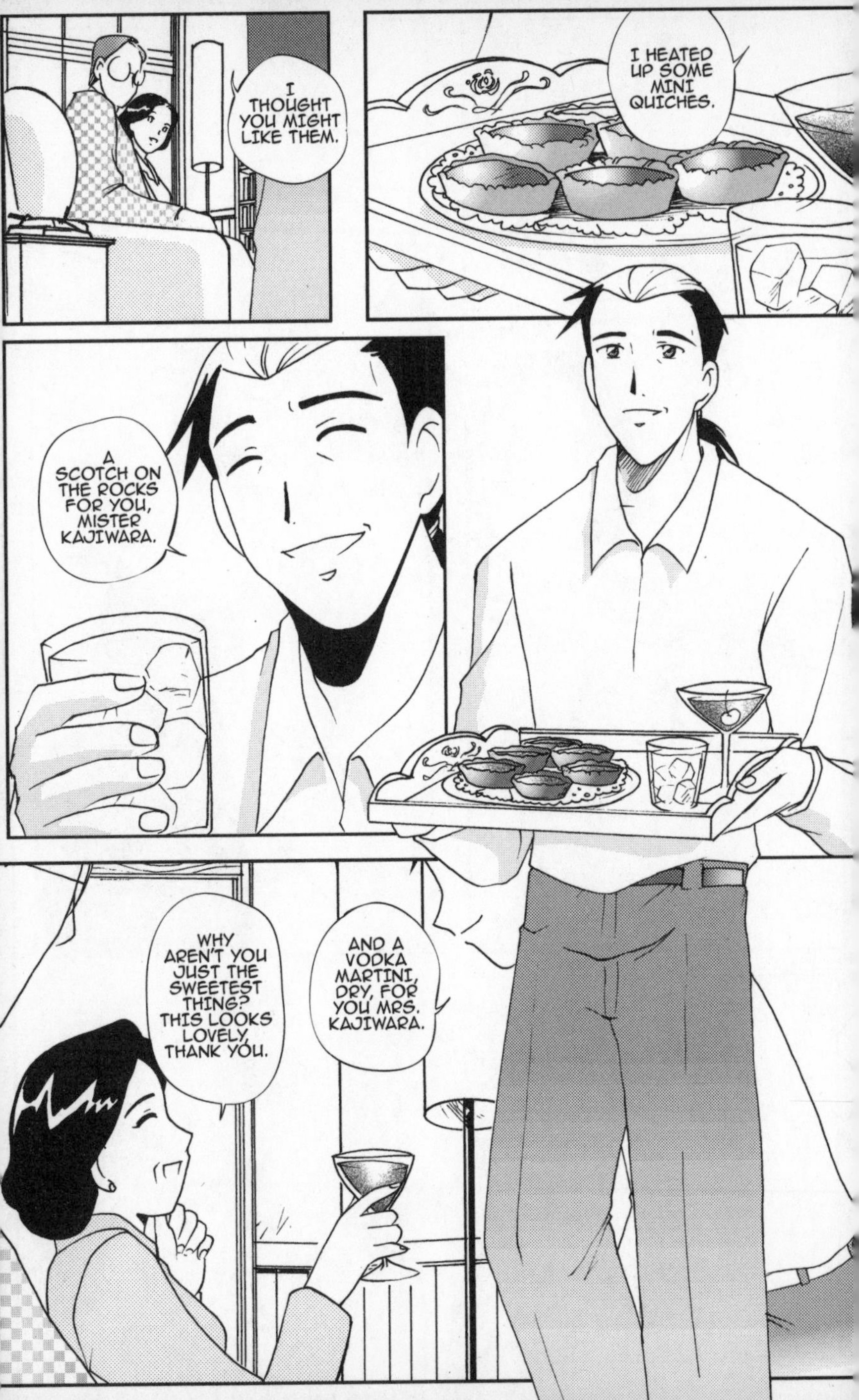
I HEATED UP SOME MINI QUICHES.
I THOUGHT YOU MIGHT LIKE THEM.
A SCOTCH ON THE ROCKS FOR YOU, MISTER KAJIWARA.
AND A VODKA MARTINI, DRY, FOR YOU MRS. KAJIWARA.
WHY AREN'T YOU JUST THE SWEETEST THING? THIS LOOKS LOVELY, THANK YOU.

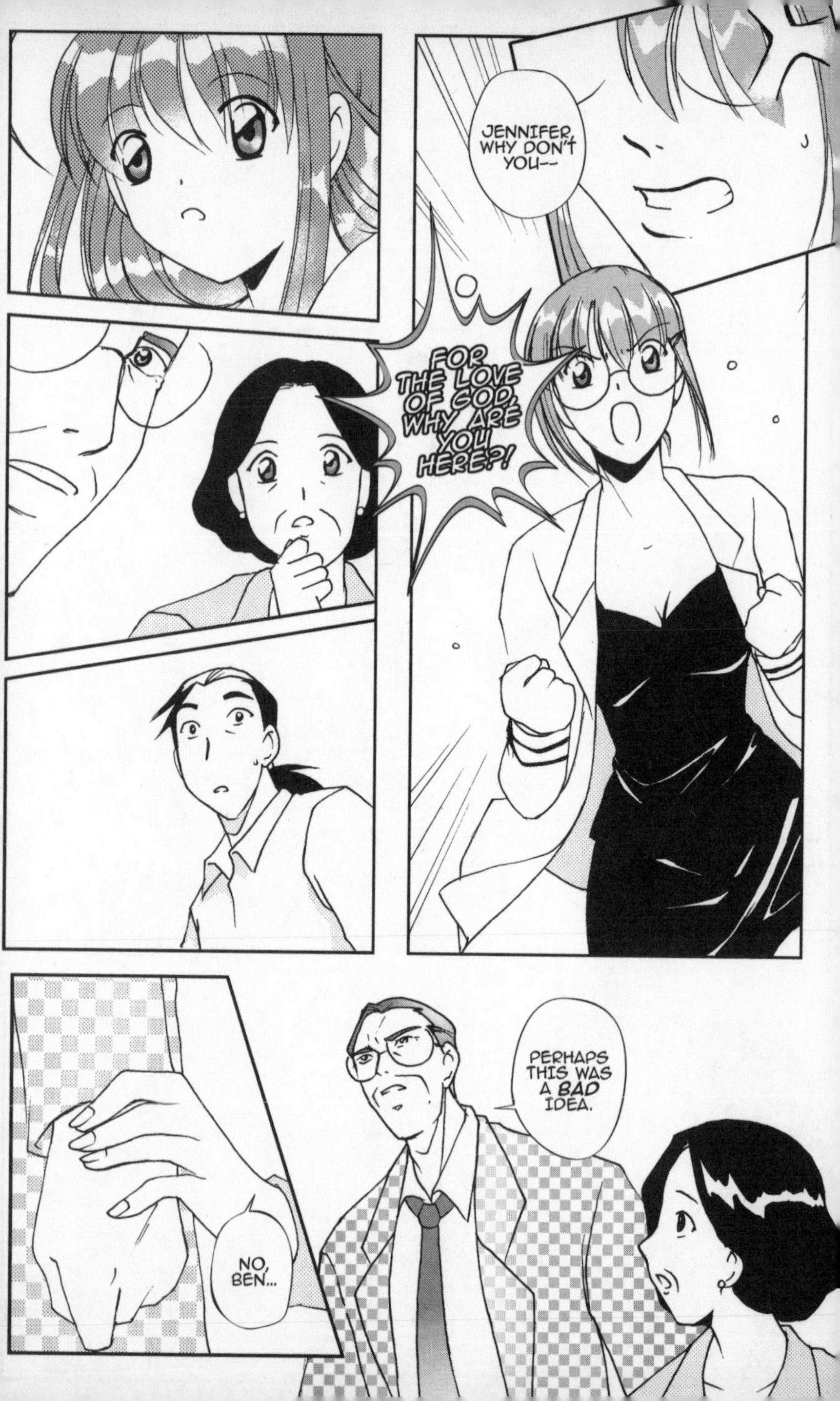
JENNIFER, WHY DON'T YOU--
FOR THE LOVE OF GOD, WHY ARE YOU HERE?!
PERHAPS THIS WAS A *BAD* IDEA.
NO, BEN...

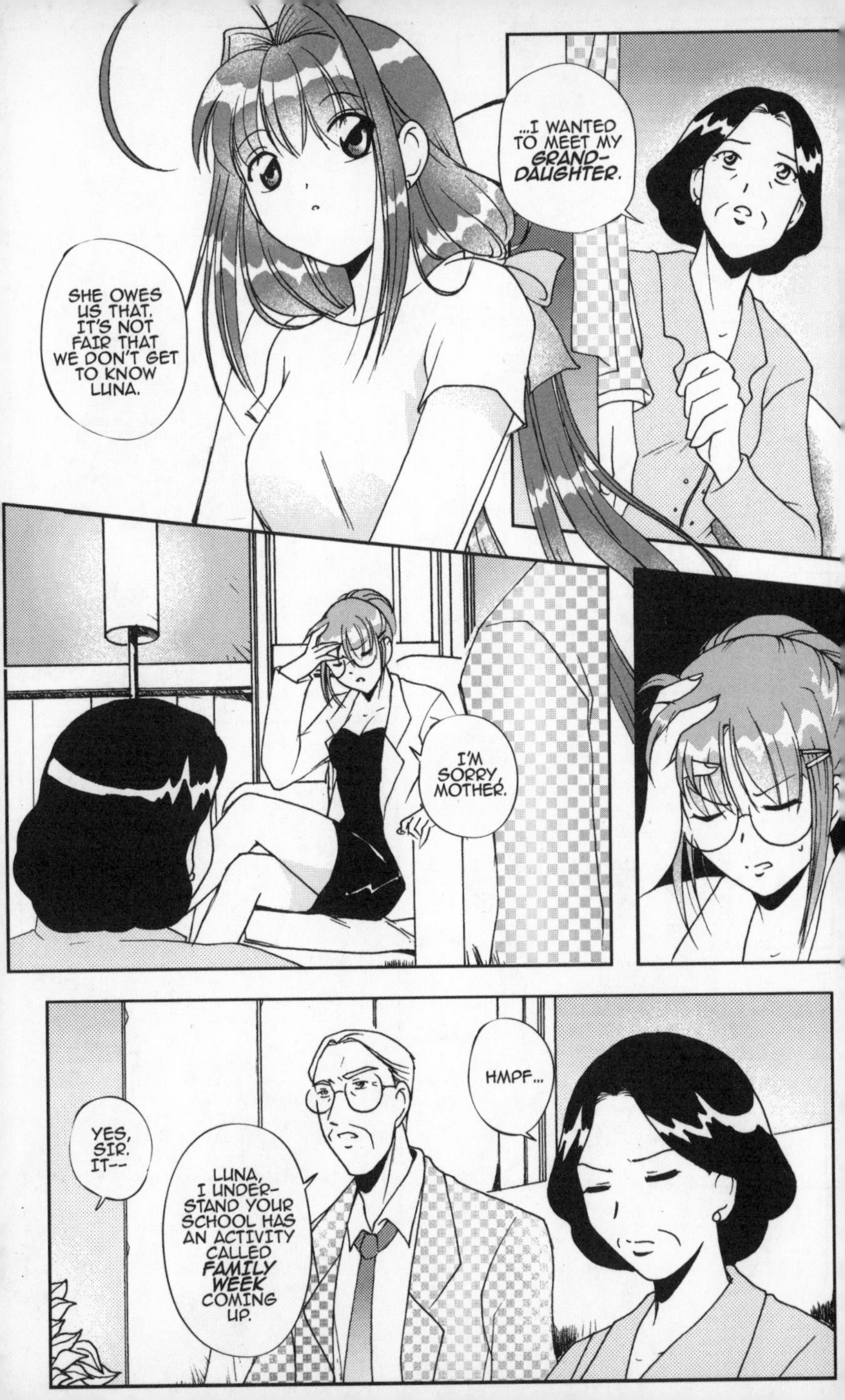
...I WANTED TO MEET MY GRAND-DAUGHTER.
SHE OWES US THAT. IT'S NOT FAIR THAT WE DON'T GET TO KNOW LUNA.
I'M SORRY, MOTHER.
HMPF...
LUNA, I UNDER-STAND YOUR SCHOOL HAS AN ACTIVITY CALLED FAMILY WEEK COMING UP.
YES, SIR. IT--

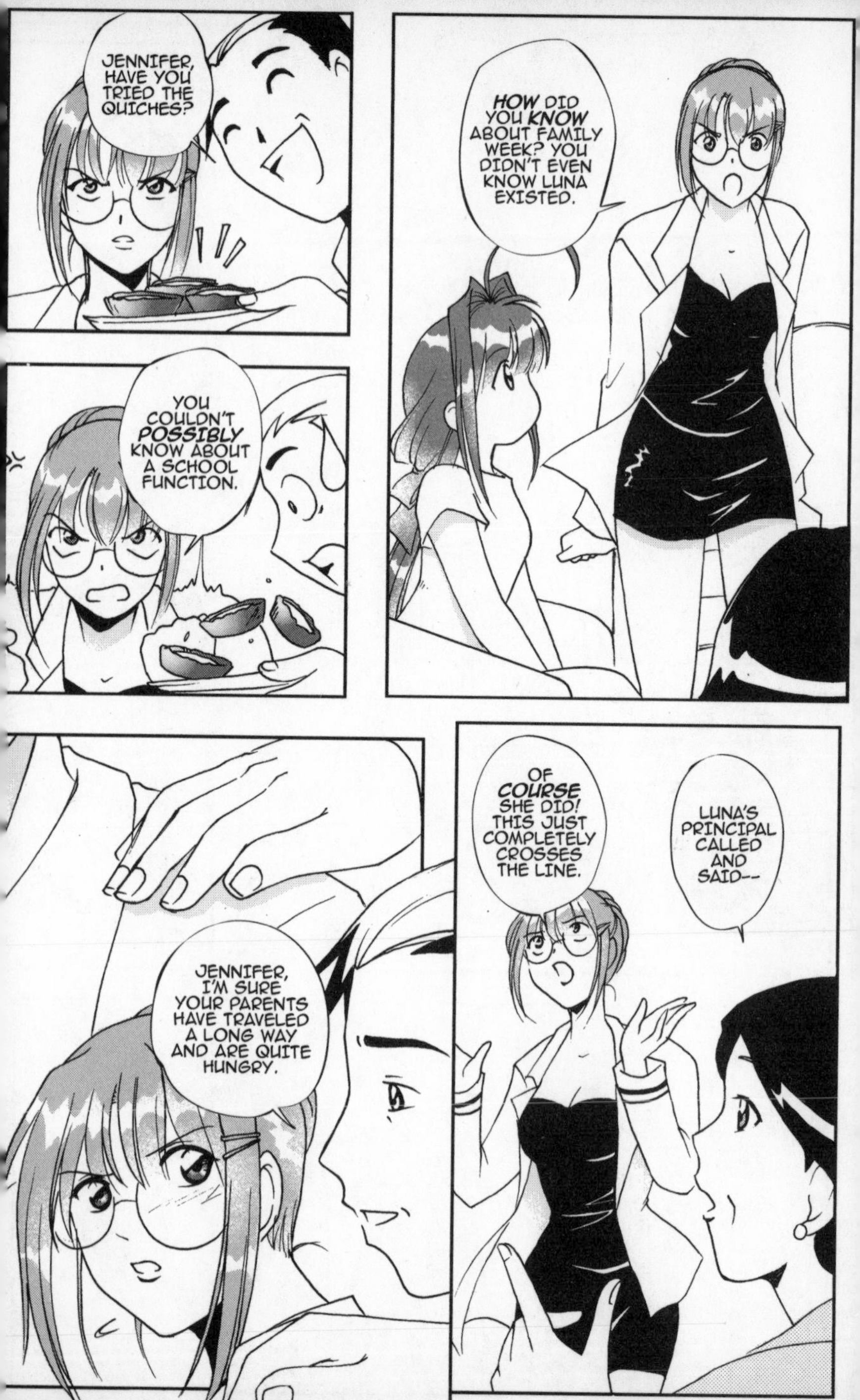
HOW DID YOU KNOW ABOUT FAMILY WEEK? YOU DIDN'T EVEN KNOW LUNA EXISTED.
JENNIFER, HAVE YOU TRIED THE QUICHES?
YOU COULDN'T POSSIBLY KNOW ABOUT A SCHOOL FUNCTION.
LUNA'S PRINCIPAL CALLED AND SAID--
OF COURSE SHE DID! THIS JUST COMPLETELY CROSSES THE LINE.
JENNIFER, I'M SURE YOUR PARENTS HAVE TRAVELED A LONG WAY AND ARE QUITE HUNGRY.

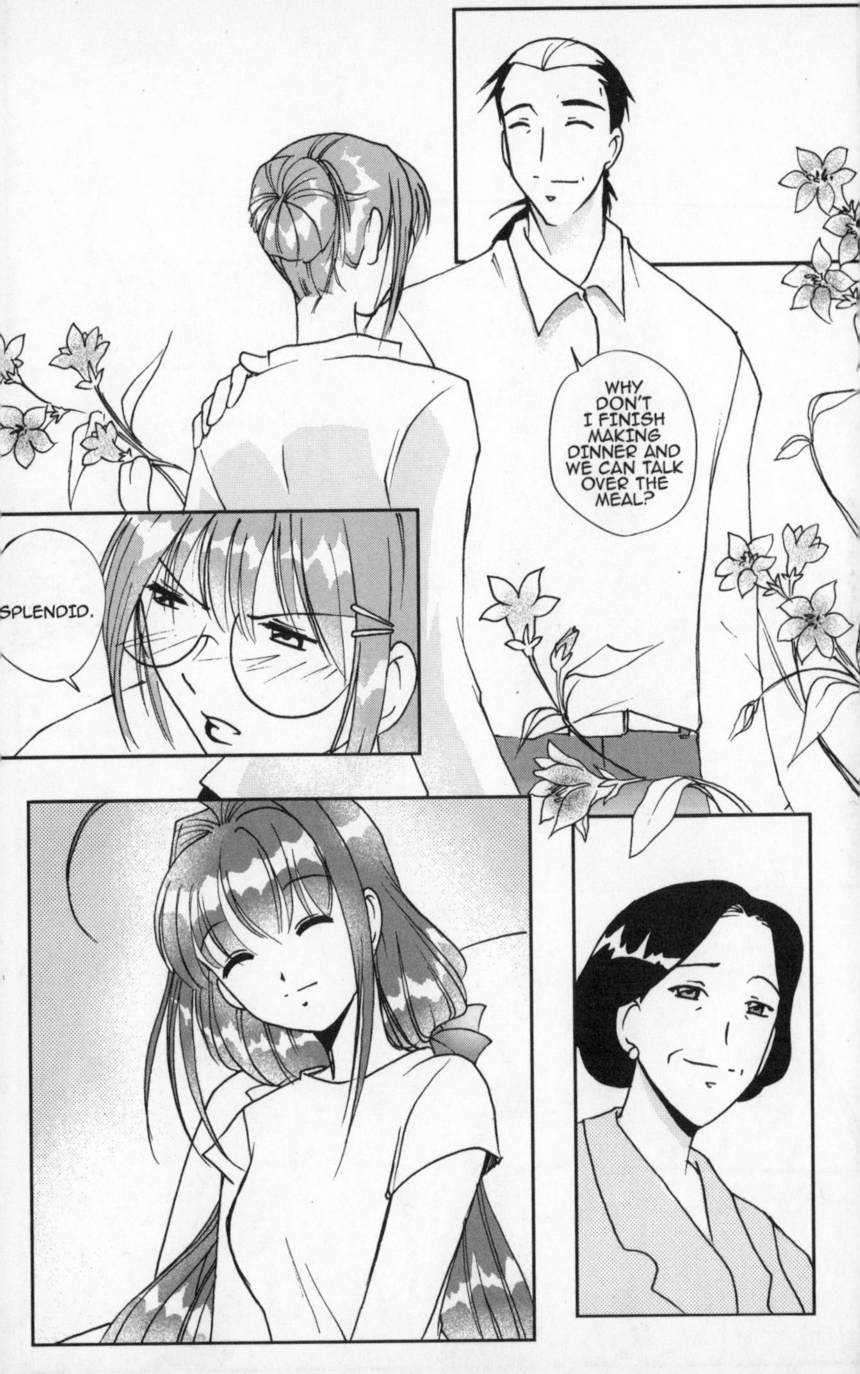
WHY DON'T I FINISH MAKING DINNER AND WE CAN TALK OVER THE MEAL?
SPLENDID.

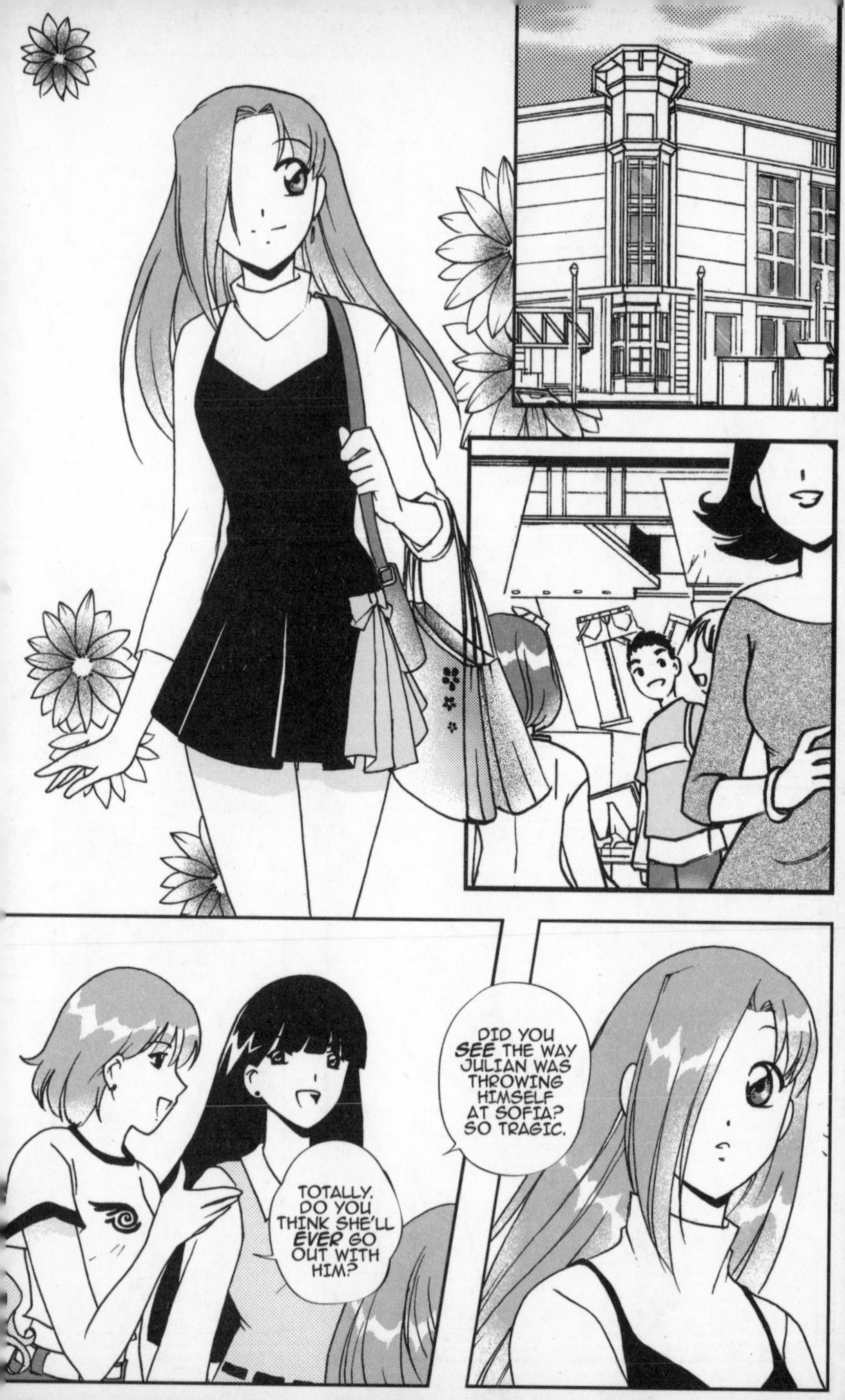
DID YOU SEE THE WAY JULIAN WAS THROWING HIMSELF AT SOFIA? SO TRAGIC.
TOTALLY. DO YOU THINK SHE'LL EVER GO OUT WITH HIM?

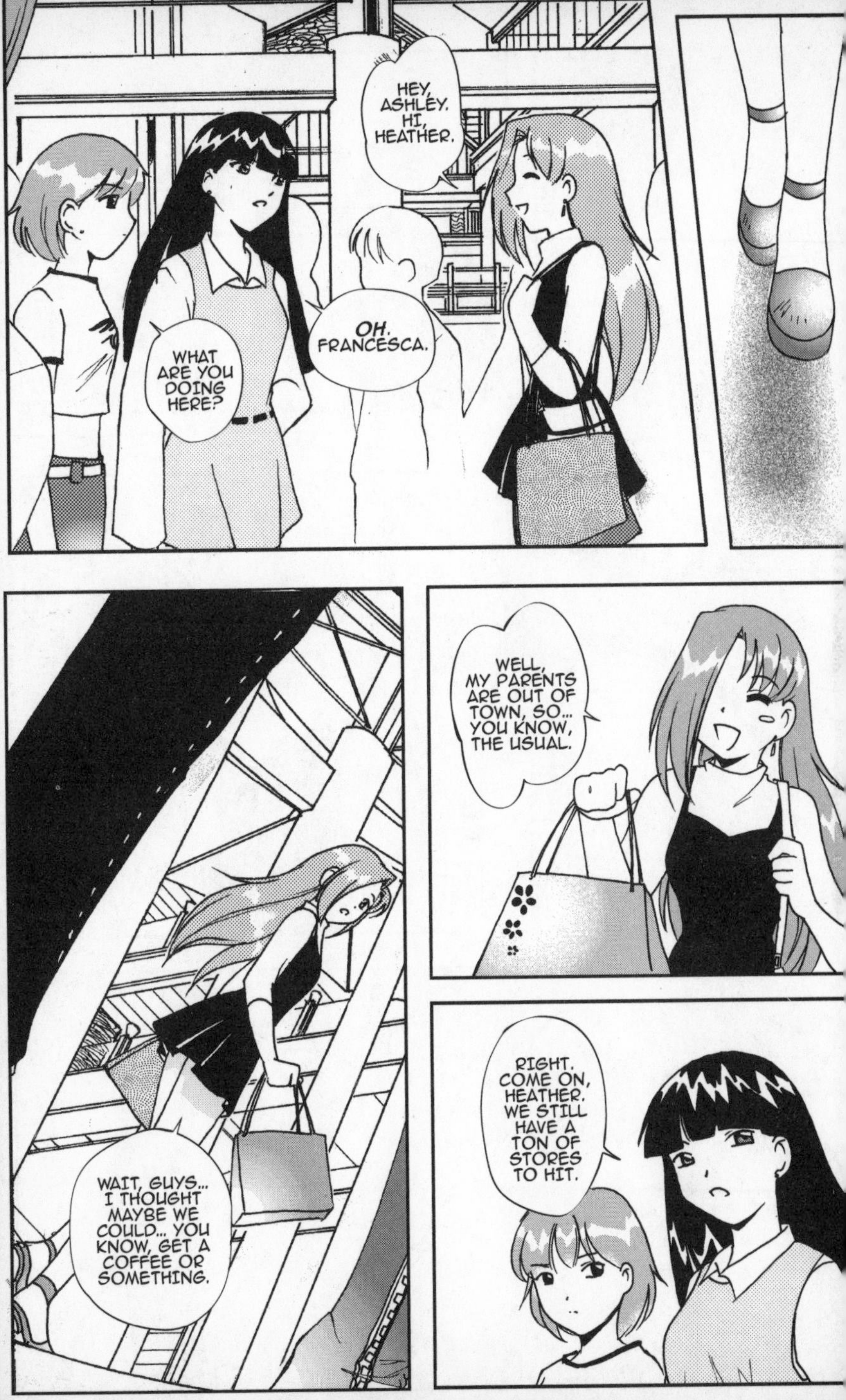
HEY, ASHLEY. HI, HEATHER.
OH. FRANCESCA.
WHAT ARE YOU DOING HERE?
WELL, MY PARENTS ARE OUT OF TOWN, SO... YOU KNOW, THE USUAL.
RIGHT. COME ON, HEATHER. WE STILL HAVE A TON OF STORES TO HIT.
WAIT, GUYS... I THOUGHT MAYBE WE COULD... YOU KNOW, GET A COFFEE OR SOMETHING.

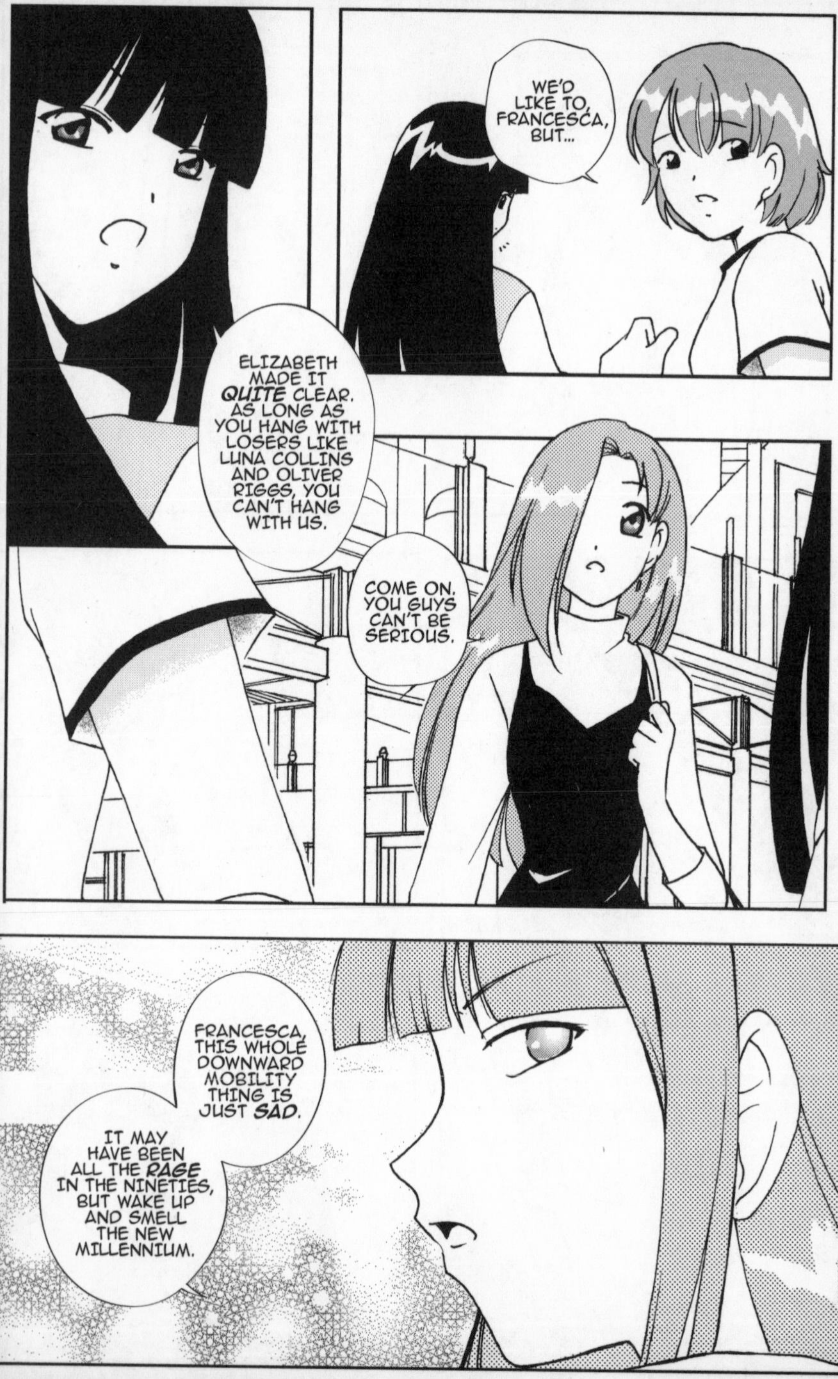
WE'D LIKE TO, FRANCESCA, BUT...
ELIZABETH MADE IT QUITE CLEAR. AS LONG AS YOU HANG WITH LOSERS LIKE LUNA COLLINS AND OLIVER RIGGS, YOU CAN'T HANG WITH US.
COME ON. YOU GUYS CAN'T BE SERIOUS.
FRANCESCA, THIS WHOLE DOWNWARD MOBILITY THING IS JUST SAD.
IT MAY HAVE BEEN ALL THE RAGE IN THE NINETIES, BUT WAKE UP AND SMELL THE NEW MILLENNIUM.

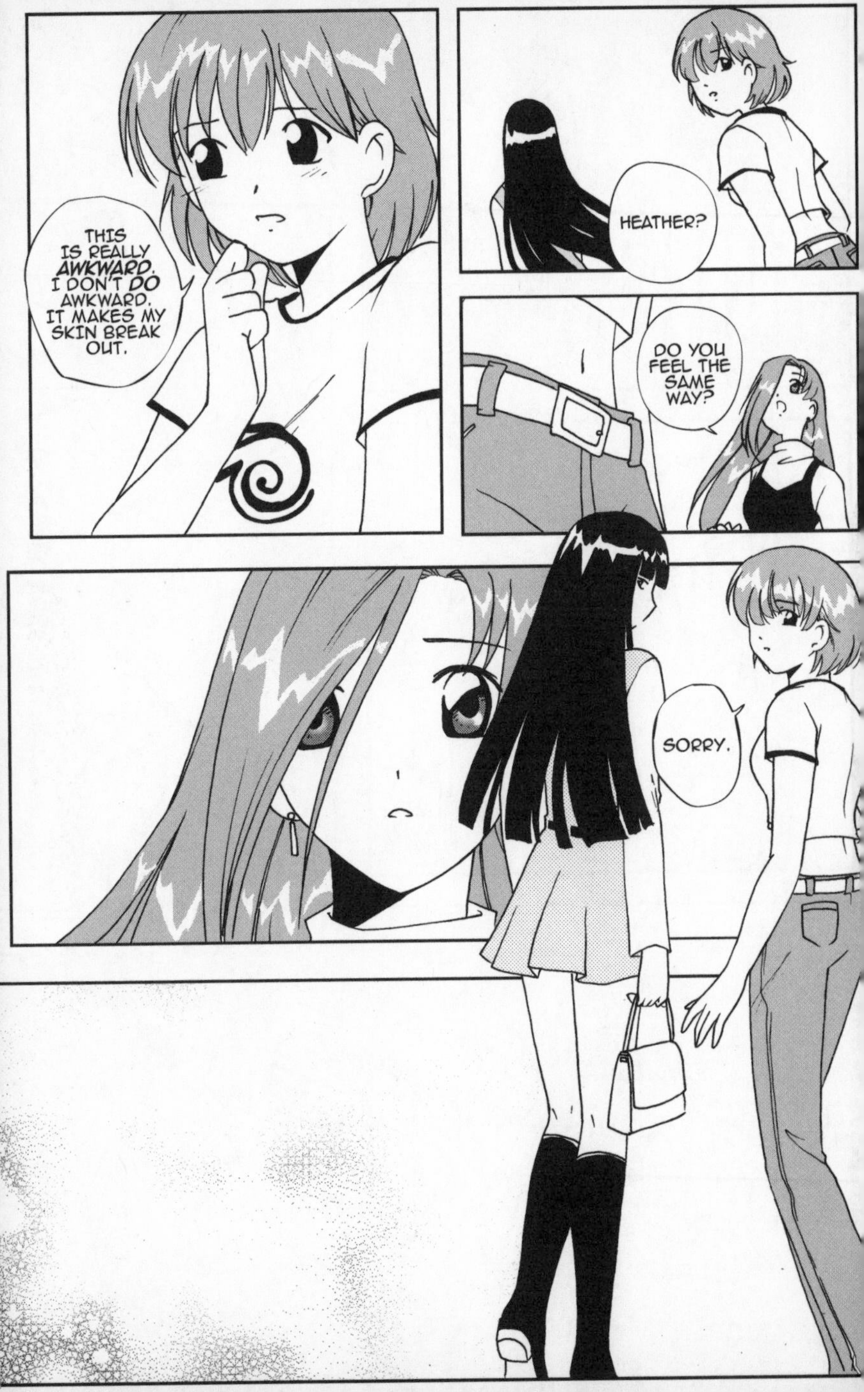
HEATHER?
DO YOU FEEL THE SAME WAY?
THIS IS REALLY AWKWARD. I DON'T DO AWKWARD. IT MAKES MY SKIN BREAK OUT.
SORRY.

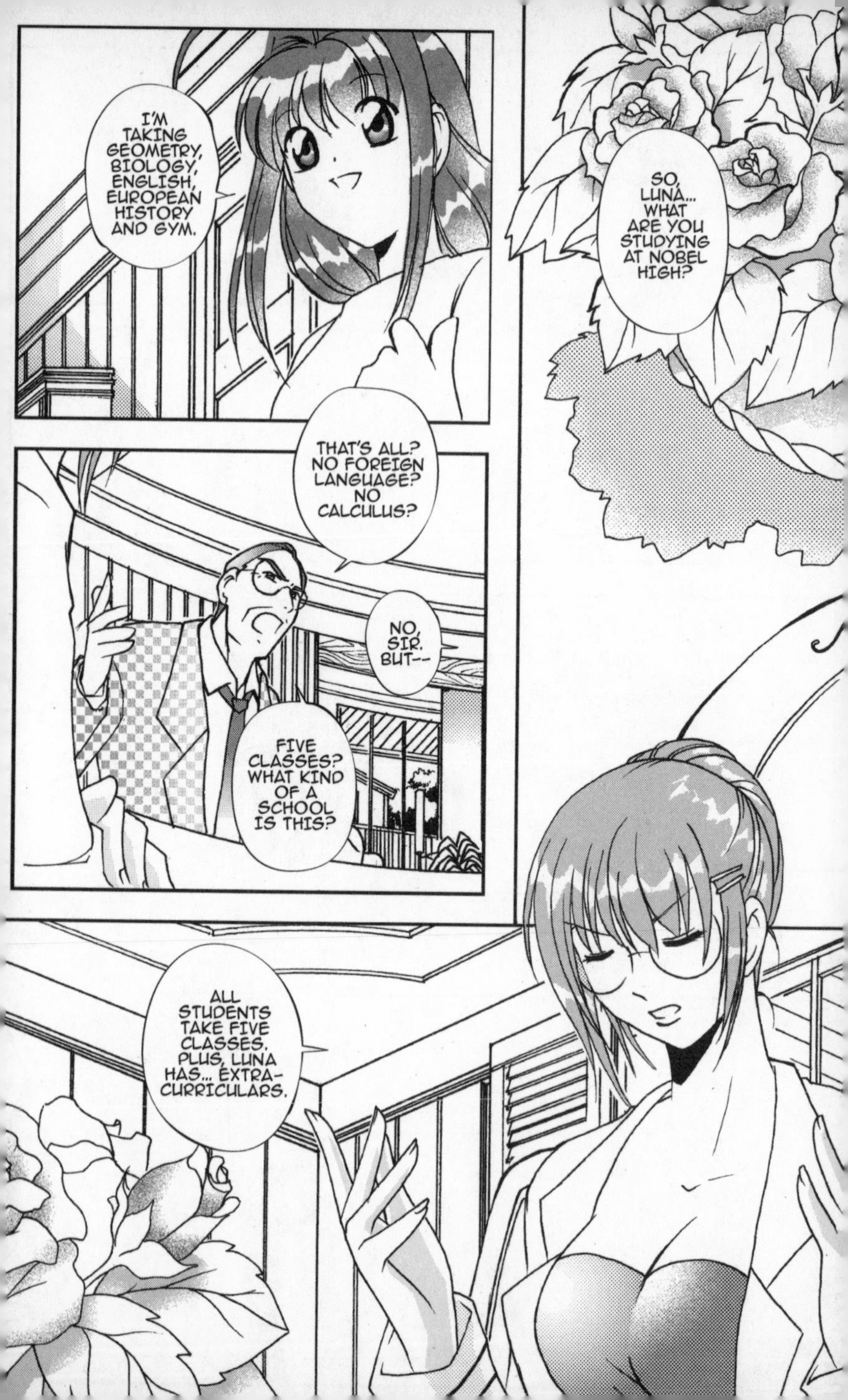
SO, LUNA... WHAT ARE YOU STUDYING AT NOBEL HIGH?
I'M TAKING GEOMETRY, BIOLOGY, ENGLISH, EUROPEAN HISTORY AND GYM.
THAT'S ALL? NO FOREIGN LANGUAGE? NO CALCULUS?
NO, SIR. BUT--
FIVE CLASSES? WHAT KIND OF A SCHOOL IS THIS?
ALL STUDENTS TAKE FIVE CLASSES. PLUS, LUNA HAS... EXTRA-CURRICULARS.

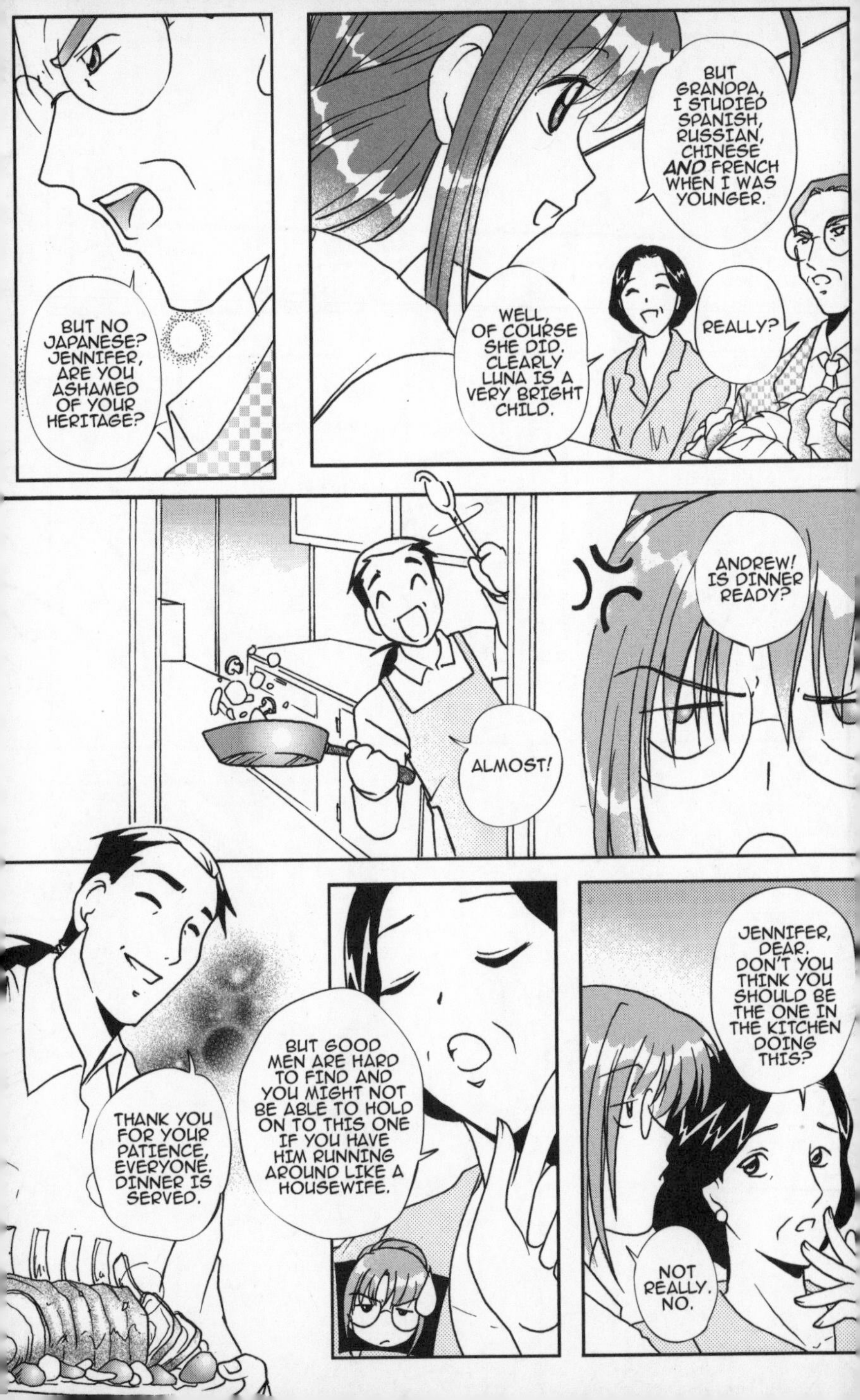
BUT GRANDPA, I STUDIED SPANISH, RUSSIAN, CHINESE *AND* FRENCH WHEN I WAS YOUNGER.
REALLY?
WELL, OF COURSE SHE DID. CLEARLY LUNA IS A VERY BRIGHT CHILD.
BUT NO JAPANESE? JENNIFER, ARE YOU ASHAMED OF YOUR HERITAGE?
ANDREW! IS DINNER READY?
ALMOST!
JENNIFER, DEAR. DON'T YOU THINK YOU SHOULD BE THE ONE IN THE KITCHEN DOING THIS?
NOT REALLY. NO.
BUT GOOD MEN ARE HARD TO FIND AND YOU MIGHT NOT BE ABLE TO HOLD ON TO THIS ONE IF YOU HAVE HIM RUNNING AROUND LIKE A HOUSEWIFE.
THANK YOU FOR YOUR PATIENCE, EVERYONE. DINNER IS SERVED.

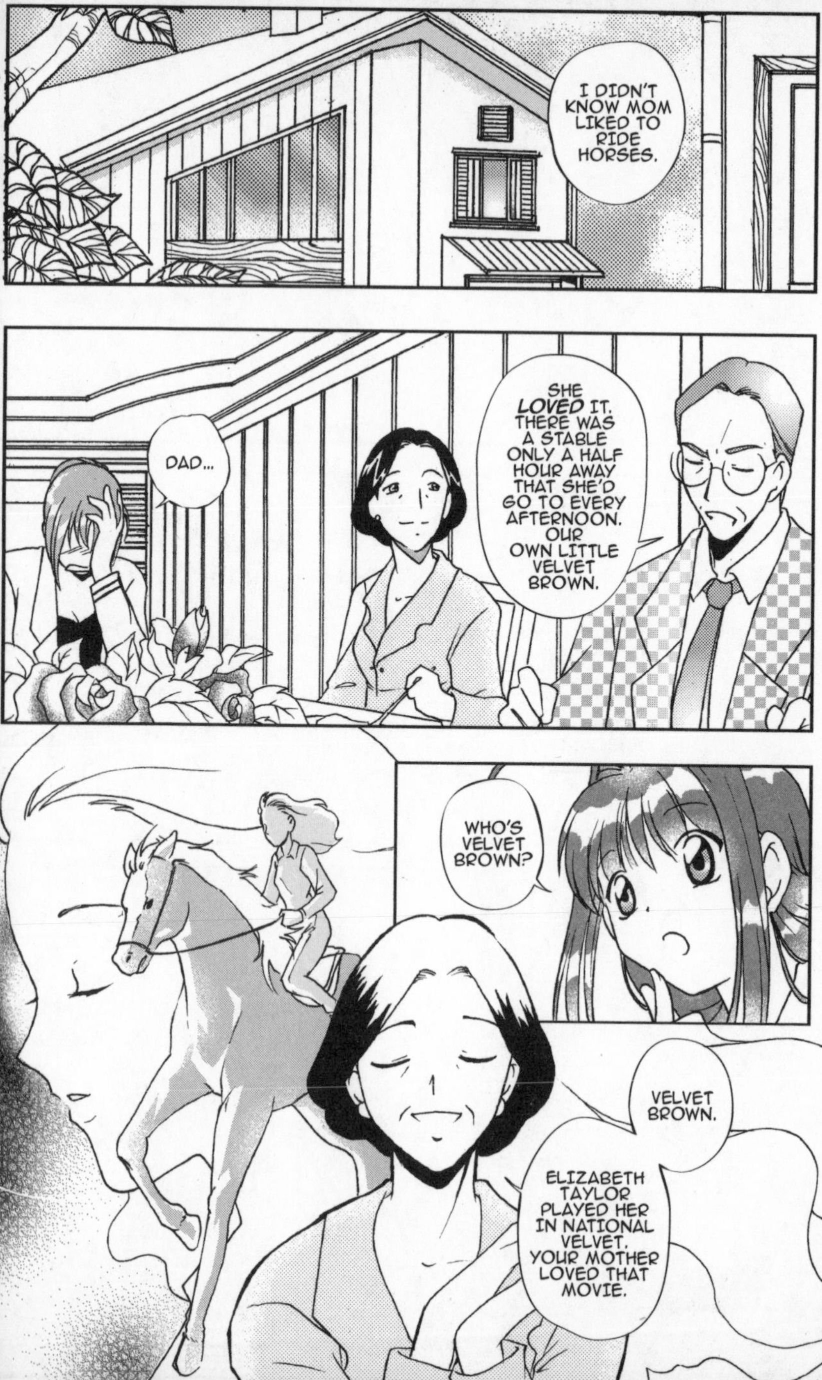
I DIDN'T KNOW MOM LIKED TO RIDE HORSES.
SHE *LOVED* IT. THERE WAS A STABLE ONLY A HALF HOUR AWAY THAT SHE'D GO TO EVERY AFTERNOON. OUR OWN LITTLE VELVET BROWN.
DAD...
WHO'S VELVET BROWN?
VELVET BROWN.
ELIZABETH TAYLOR PLAYED HER IN NATIONAL VELVET. YOUR MOTHER LOVED THAT MOVIE.

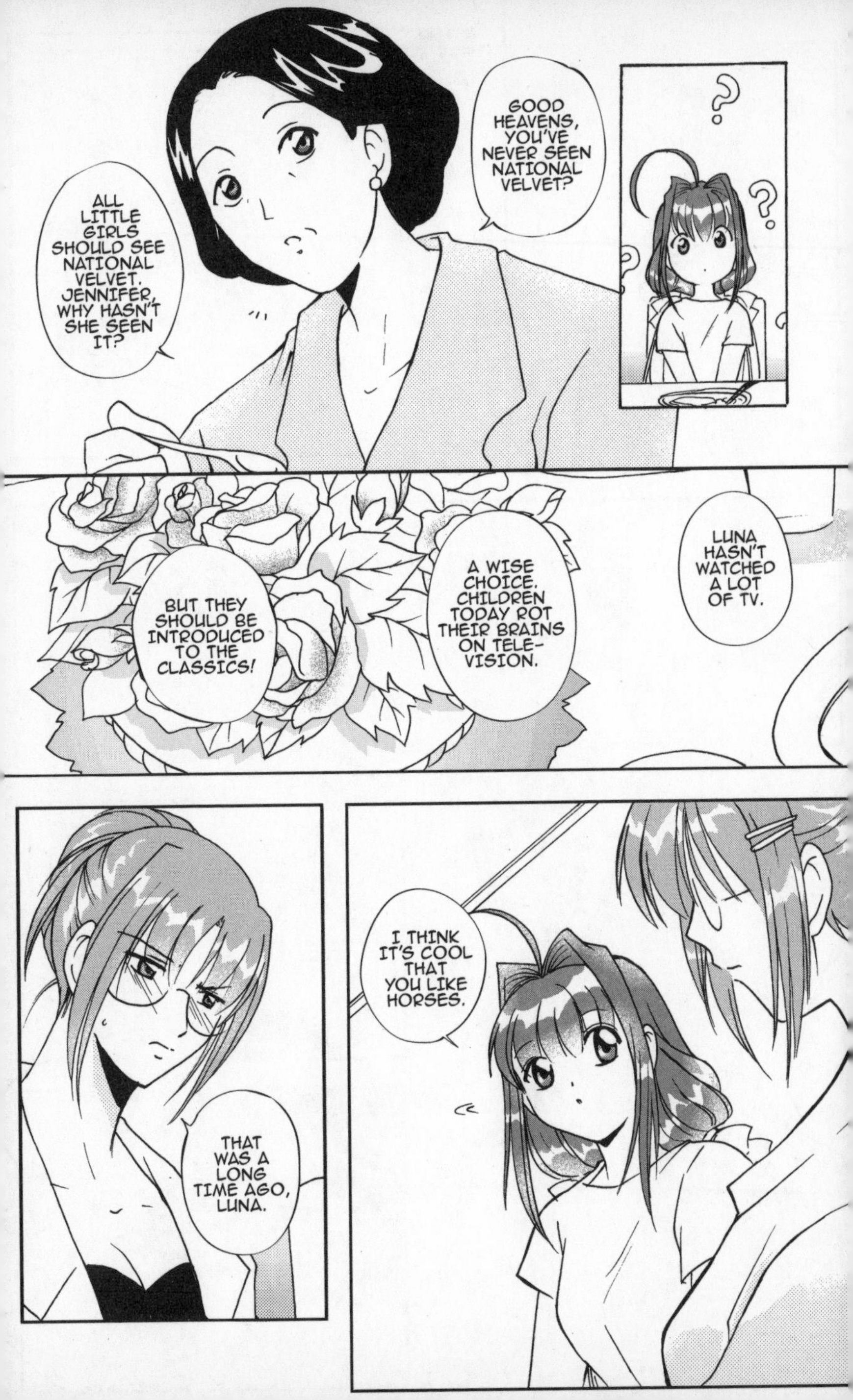
GOOD HEAVENS, YOU'VE NEVER SEEN NATIONAL VELVET?
ALL LITTLE GIRLS SHOULD SEE NATIONAL VELVET. JENNIFER, WHY HASN'T SHE SEEN IT?
LUNA HASN'T WATCHED A LOT OF TV.
A WISE CHOICE. CHILDREN TODAY ROT THEIR BRAINS ON TELE-VISION.
BUT THEY SHOULD BE INTRODUCED TO THE CLASSICS!
I THINK IT'S COOL THAT YOU LIKE HORSES.
THAT WAS A LONG TIME AGO, LUNA.

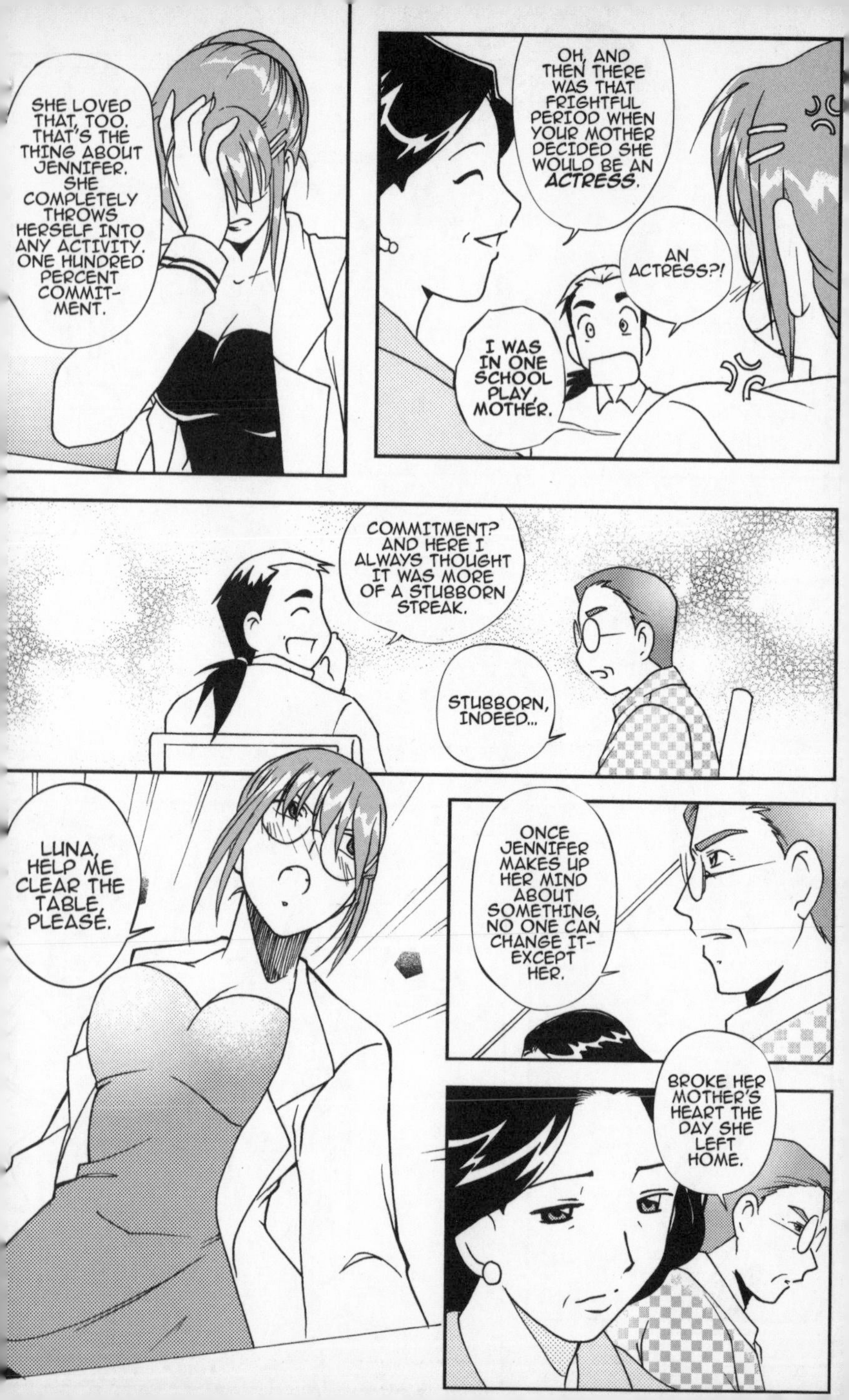

OH, AND THEN THERE WAS THAT FRIGHTFUL PERIOD WHEN YOUR MOTHER DECIDED SHE WOULD BE AN *ACTRESS*.
AN ACTRESS?!
I WAS IN ONE SCHOOL PLAY, MOTHER.
SHE LOVED THAT, TOO. THAT'S THE THING ABOUT JENNIFER. SHE COMPLETELY THROWS HERSELF INTO ANY ACTIVITY. ONE HUNDRED PERCENT COMMIT-MENT.
COMMITMENT? AND HERE I ALWAYS THOUGHT IT WAS MORE OF A STUBBORN STREAK.
STUBBORN, INDEED...
ONCE JENNIFER MAKES UP HER MIND ABOUT SOMETHING, NO ONE CAN CHANGE IT-EXCEPT HER.
BROKE HER MOTHER'S HEART THE DAY SHE LEFT HOME.
LUNA, HELP ME CLEAR THE TABLE, PLEASE.

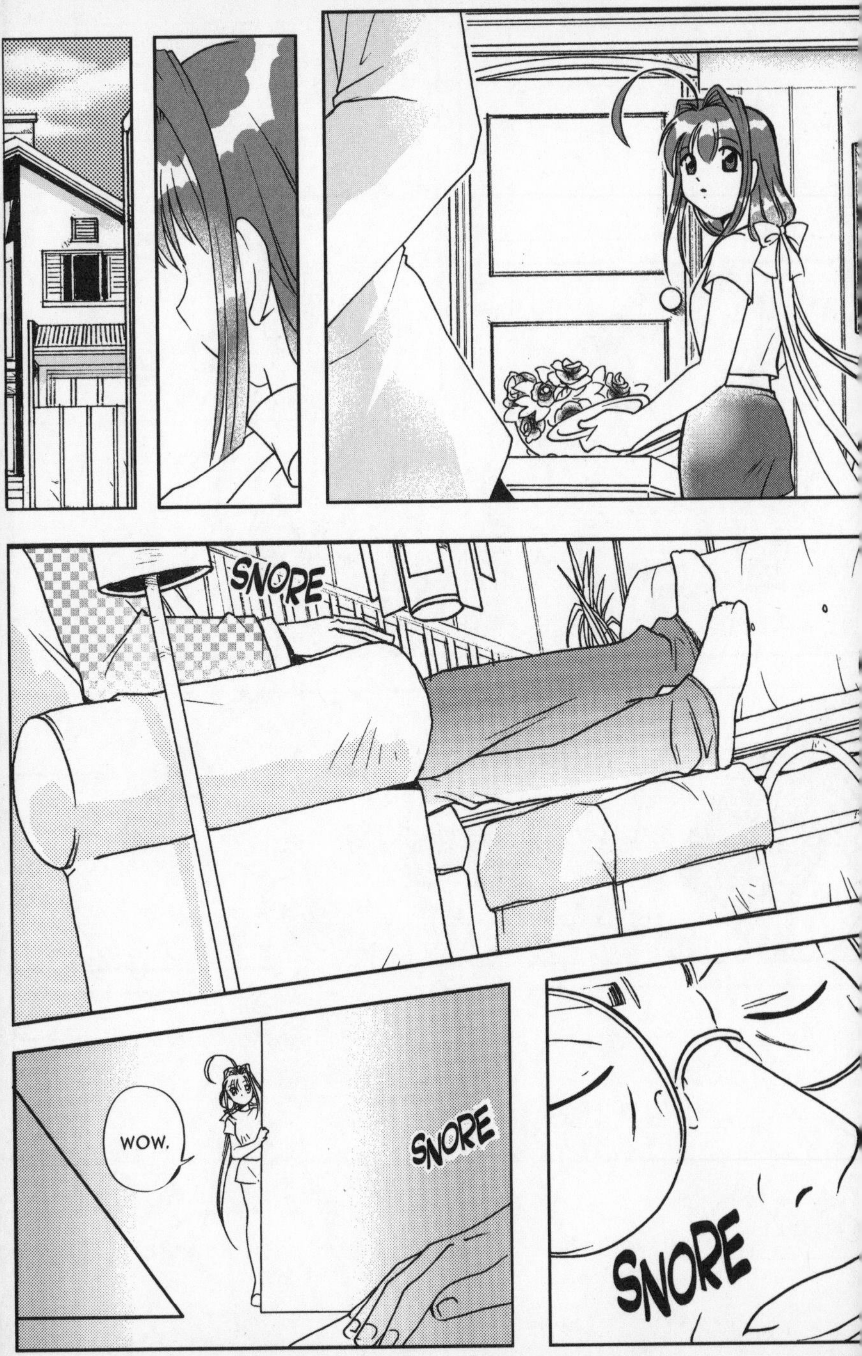
SNORE
SNORE
SNORE
WOW.

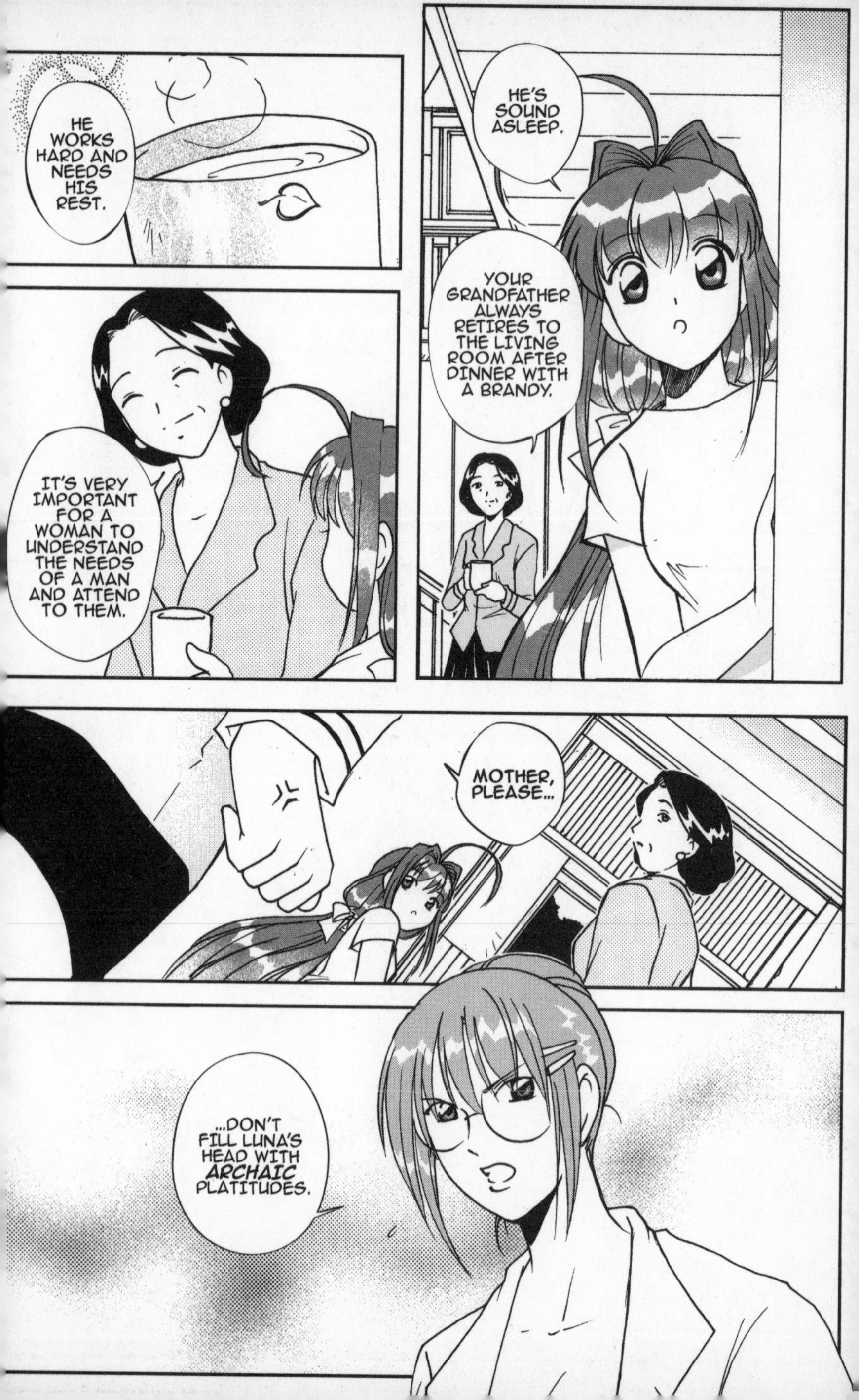
HE'S SOUND ASLEEP.
YOUR GRANDFATHER ALWAYS RETIRES TO THE LIVING ROOM AFTER DINNER WITH A BRANDY.
HE WORKS HARD AND NEEDS HIS REST.
IT'S VERY IMPORTANT FOR A WOMAN TO UNDERSTAND THE NEEDS OF A MAN AND ATTEND TO THEM.
MOTHER, PLEASE...
...DON'T FILL LUNA'S HEAD WITH *ARCHAIC* PLATITUDES.

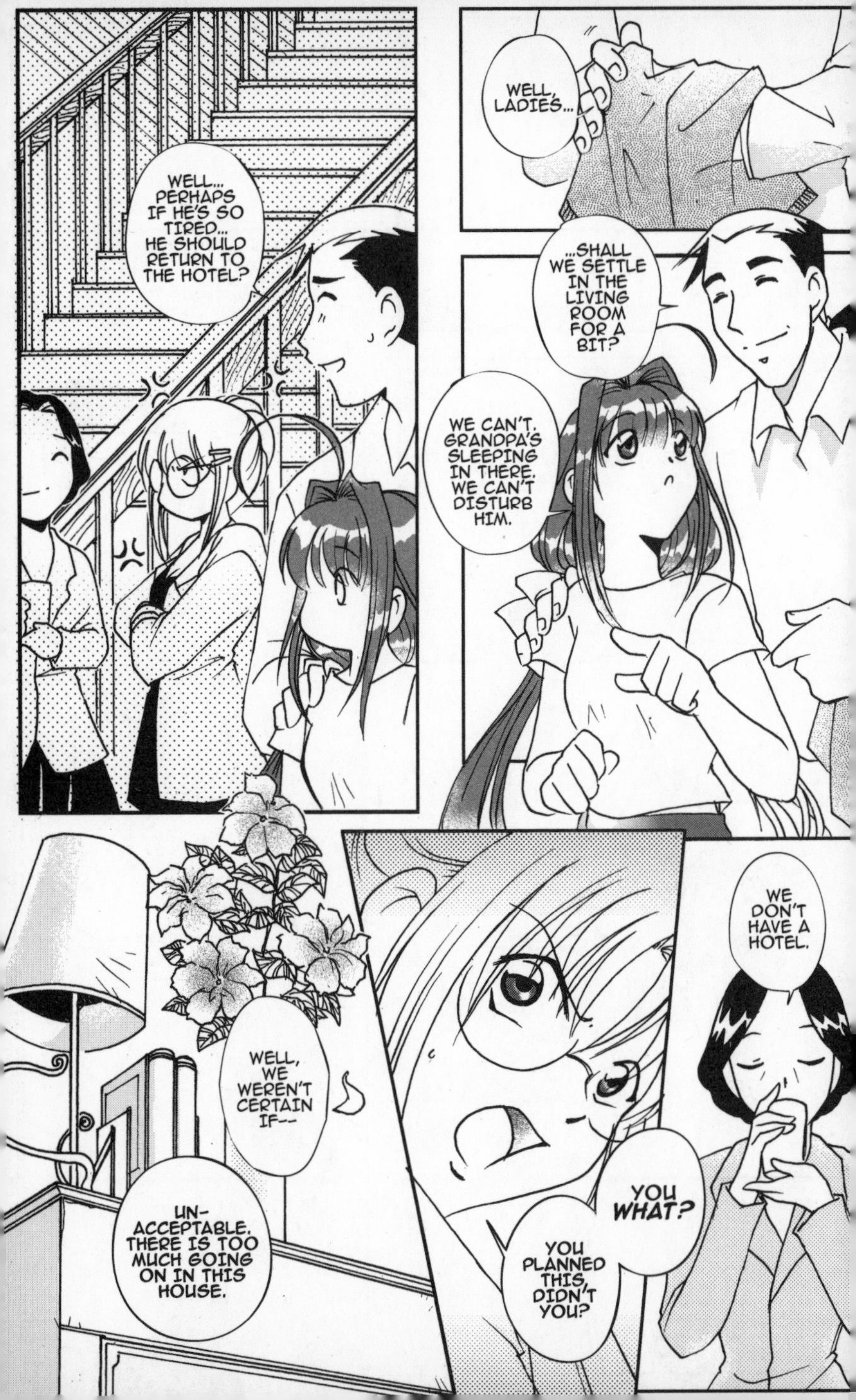
WELL, LADIES...
...SHALL WE SETTLE IN THE LIVING ROOM FOR A BIT?
WE CAN'T. GRANDPA'S SLEEPING IN THERE. WE CAN'T DISTURB HIM.
WELL... PERHAPS IF HE'S SO TIRED... HE SHOULD RETURN TO THE HOTEL?
WE DON'T HAVE A HOTEL.
YOU *WHAT?*
YOU PLANNED THIS, DIDN'T YOU?
WELL, WE WEREN'T CERTAIN IF--
UN-ACCEPTABLE. THERE IS TOO MUCH GOING ON IN THIS HOUSE.

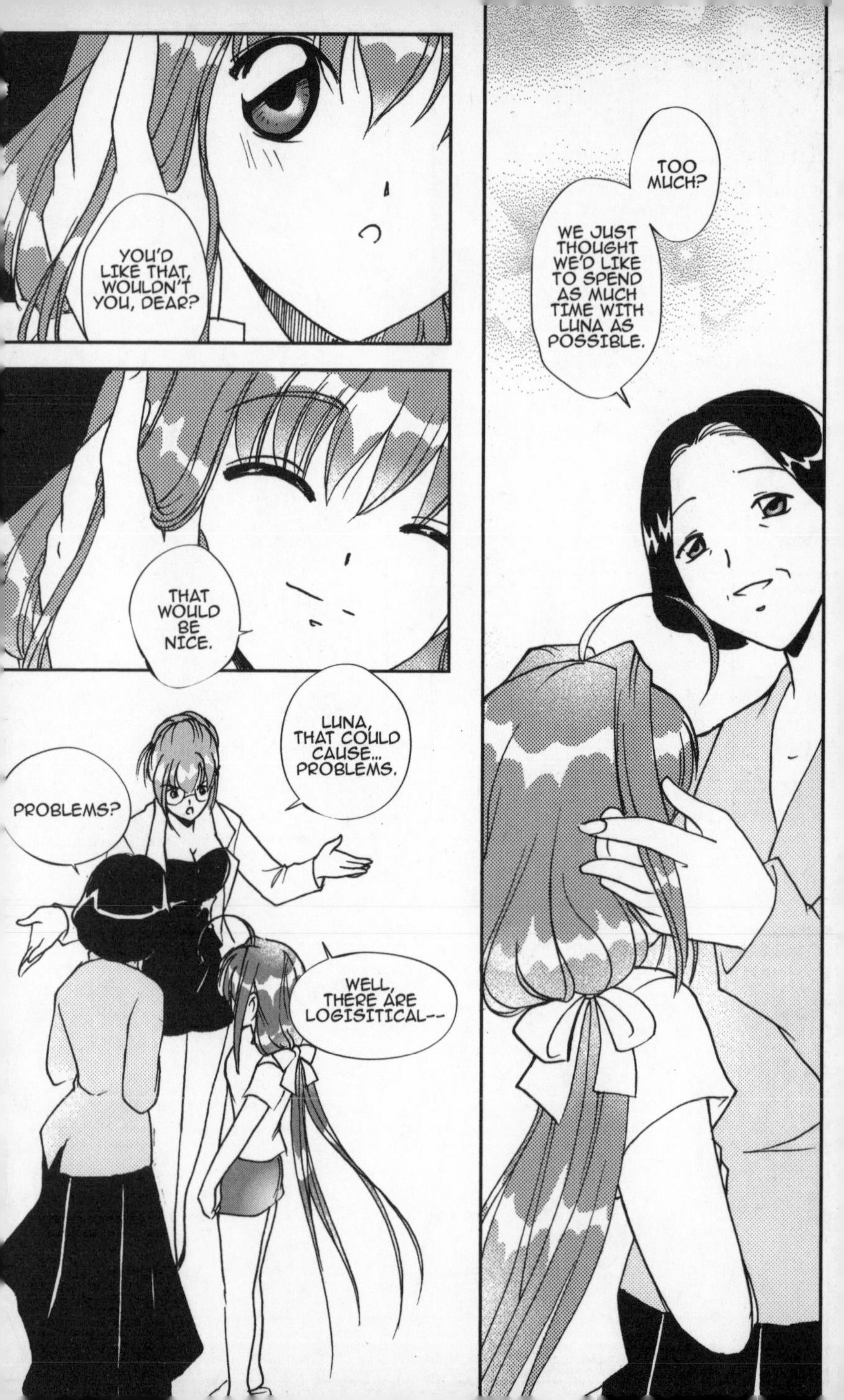
TOO MUCH?
WE JUST THOUGHT WE'D LIKE TO SPEND AS MUCH TIME WITH LUNA AS POSSIBLE.
YOU'D LIKE THAT, WOULDN'T YOU, DEAR?
THAT WOULD BE NICE.
LUNA, THAT COULD CAUSE... PROBLEMS.
PROBLEMS?
WELL, THERE ARE LOGISITICAL--

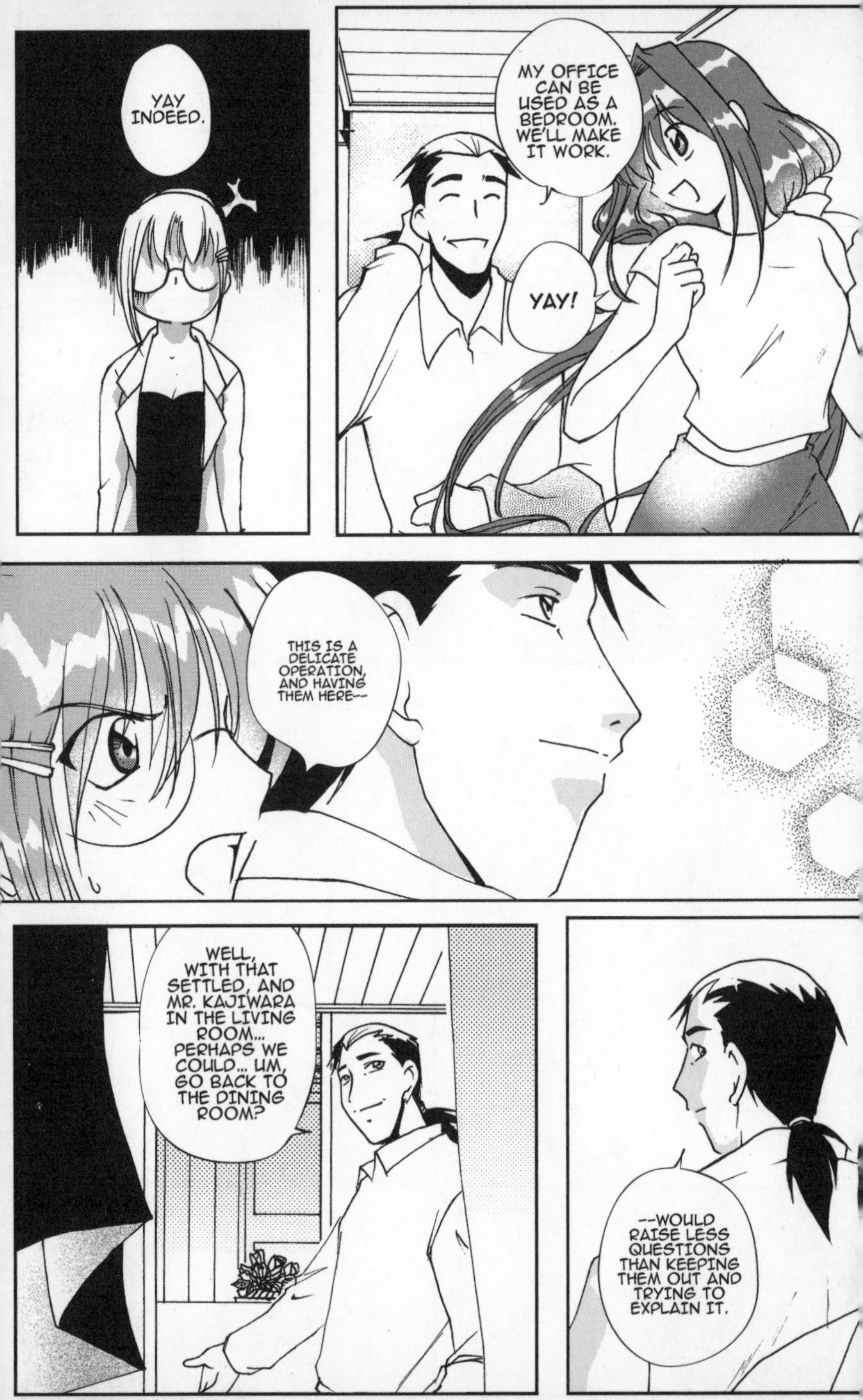
MY OFFICE CAN BE USED AS A BEDROOM. WE'LL MAKE IT WORK.
YAY!
YAY INDEED.
THIS IS A DELICATE OPERATION, AND HAVING THEM HERE--
--WOULD RAISE LESS QUESTIONS THAN KEEPING THEM OUT AND TRYING TO EXPLAIN IT.
WELL, WITH THAT SETTLED, AND MR. KAJIWARA IN THE LIVING ROOM... PERHAPS WE COULD... UM, GO BACK TO THE DINING ROOM?

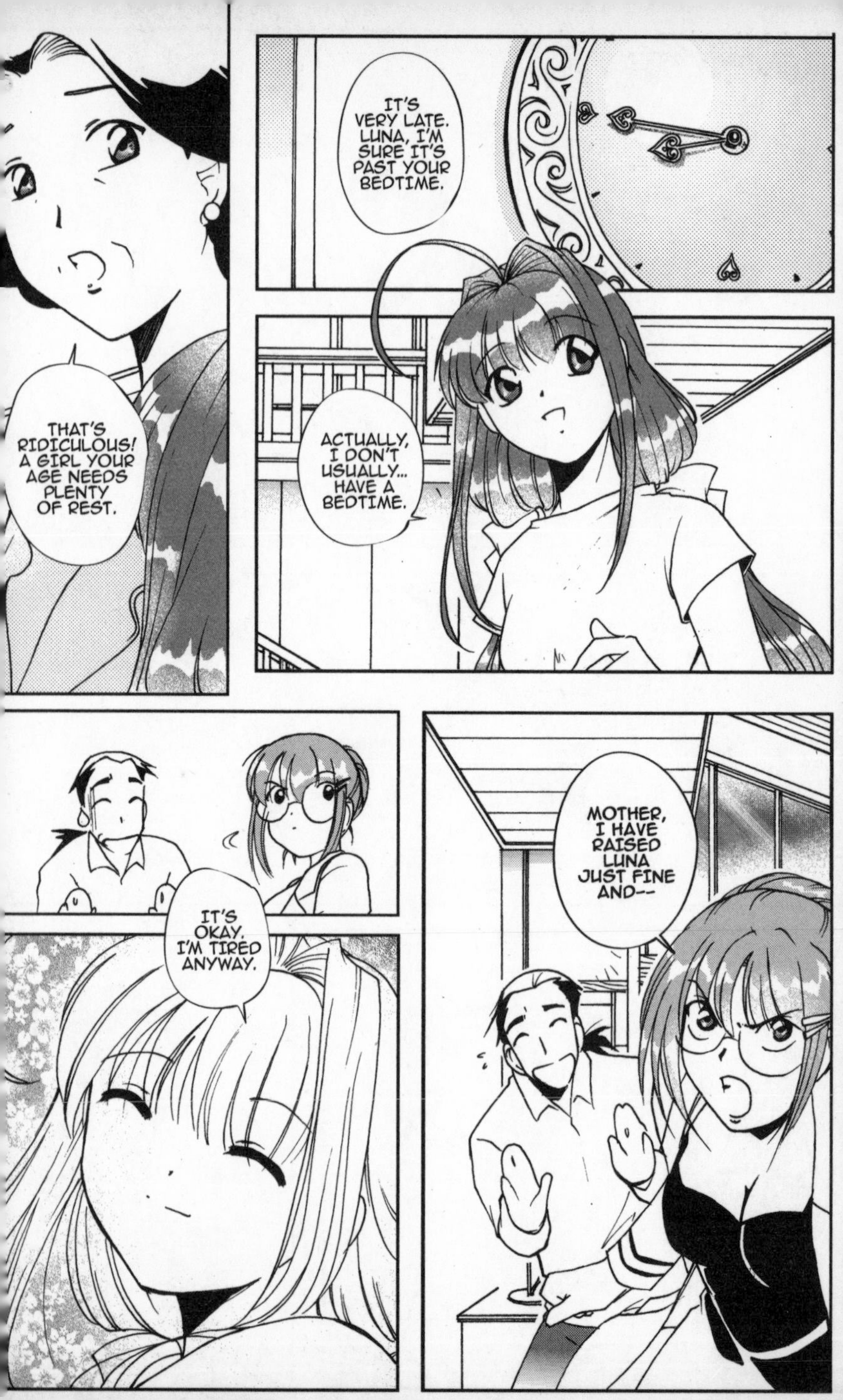
IT'S VERY LATE. LUNA, I'M SURE IT'S PAST YOUR BEDTIME.
ACTUALLY, I DON'T USUALLY... HAVE A BEDTIME.
THAT'S RIDICULOUS! A GIRL YOUR AGE NEEDS PLENTY OF REST.
MOTHER, I HAVE RAISED LUNA JUST FINE AND--
IT'S OKAY. I'M TIRED ANYWAY.

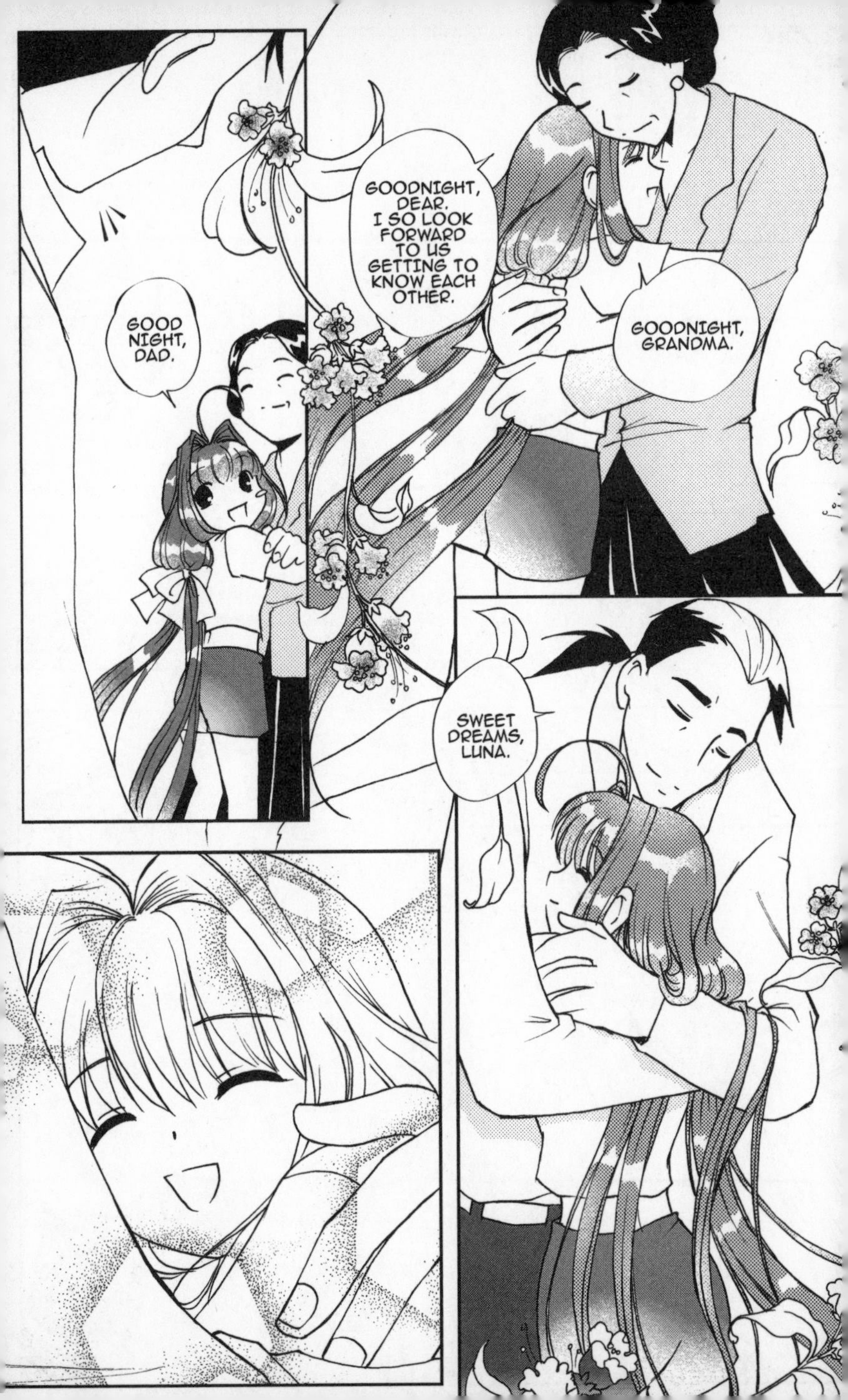
GOODNIGHT, DEAR. I SO LOOK FORWARD TO US GETTING TO KNOW EACH OTHER.
GOODNIGHT, GRANDMA.
GOOD NIGHT, DAD.
SWEET DREAMS, LUNA.

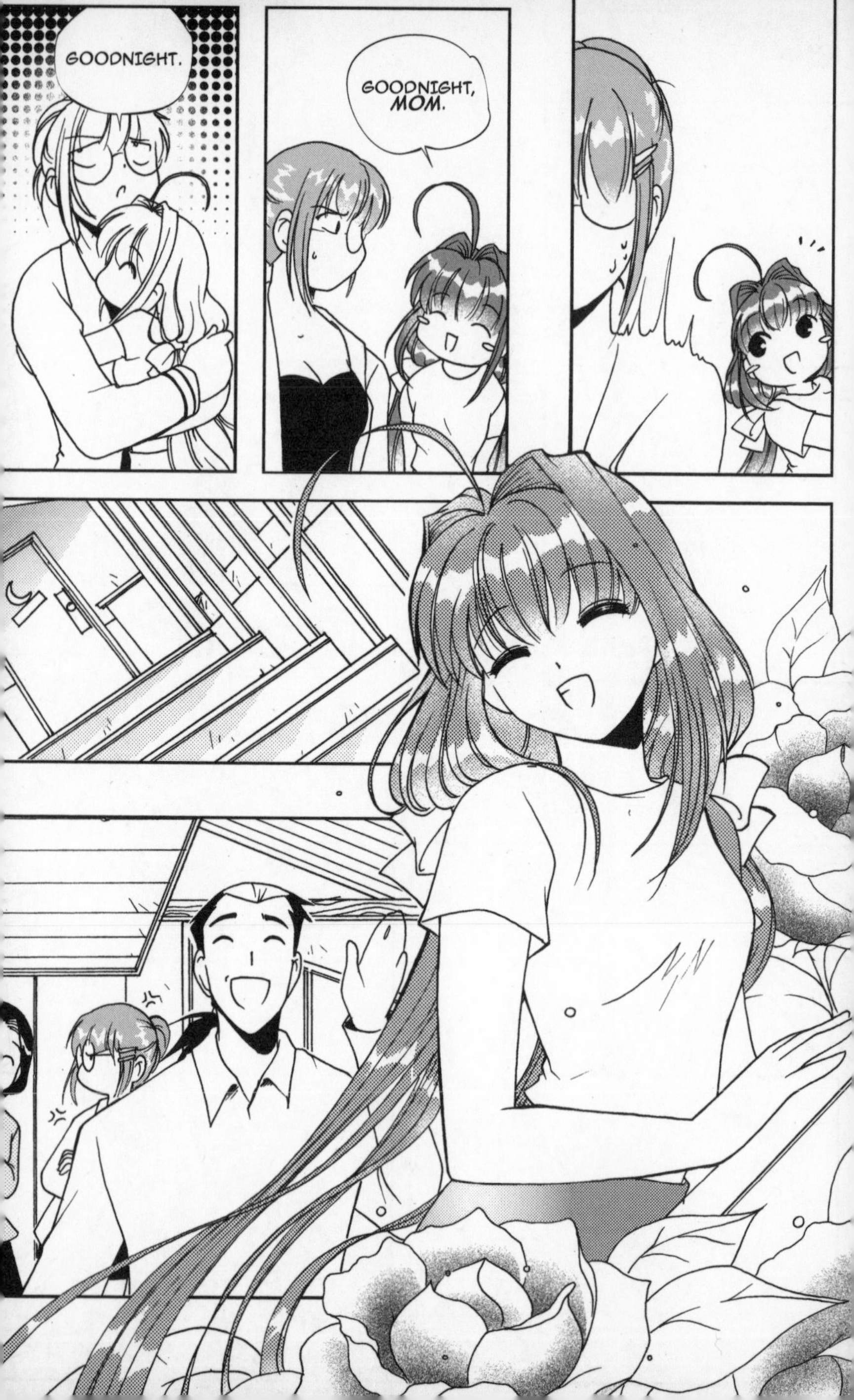
GOODNIGHT, MOM.
GOODNIGHT.

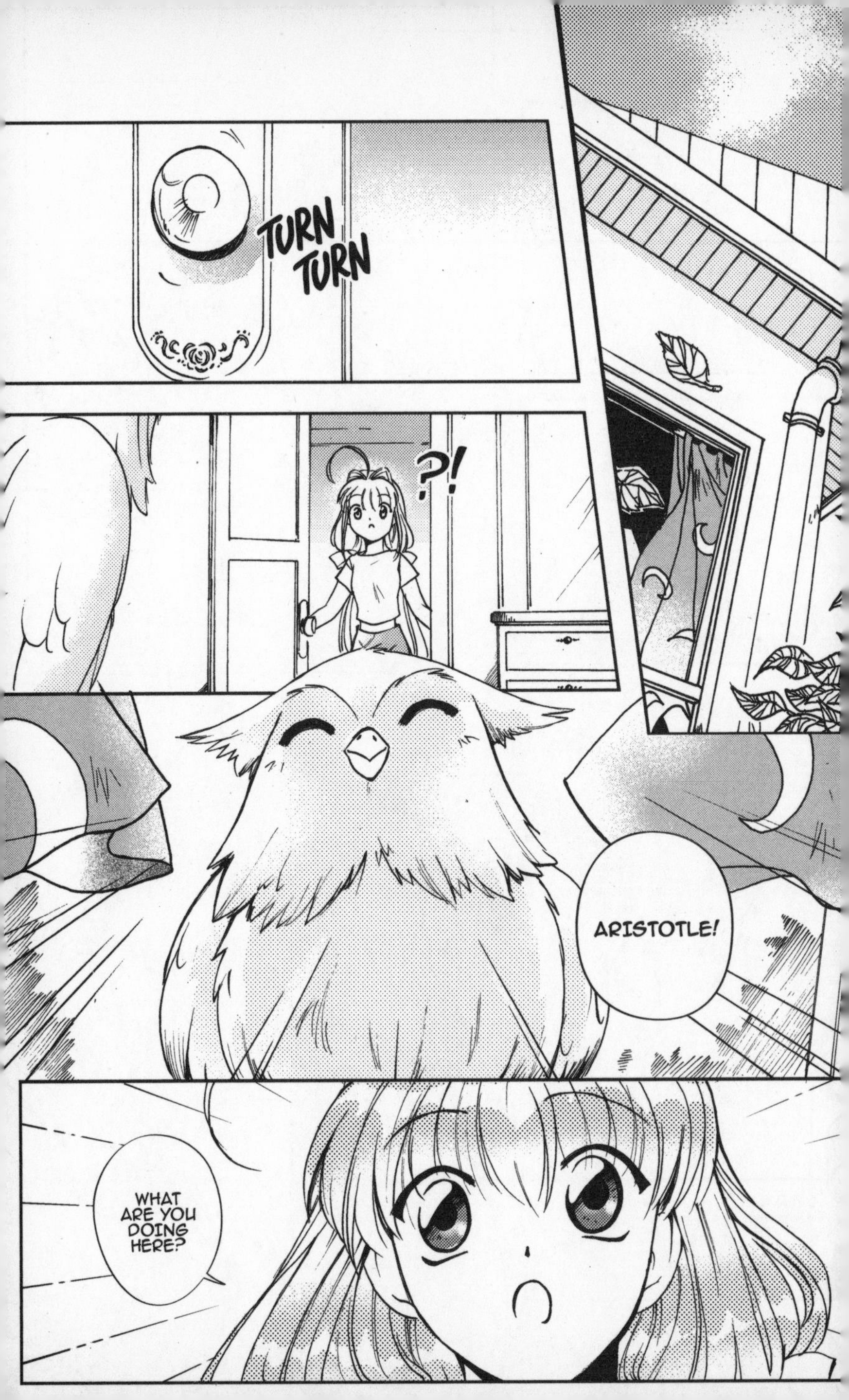

TURN TURN
?!
ARISTOTLE!
WHAT ARE YOU DOING HERE?

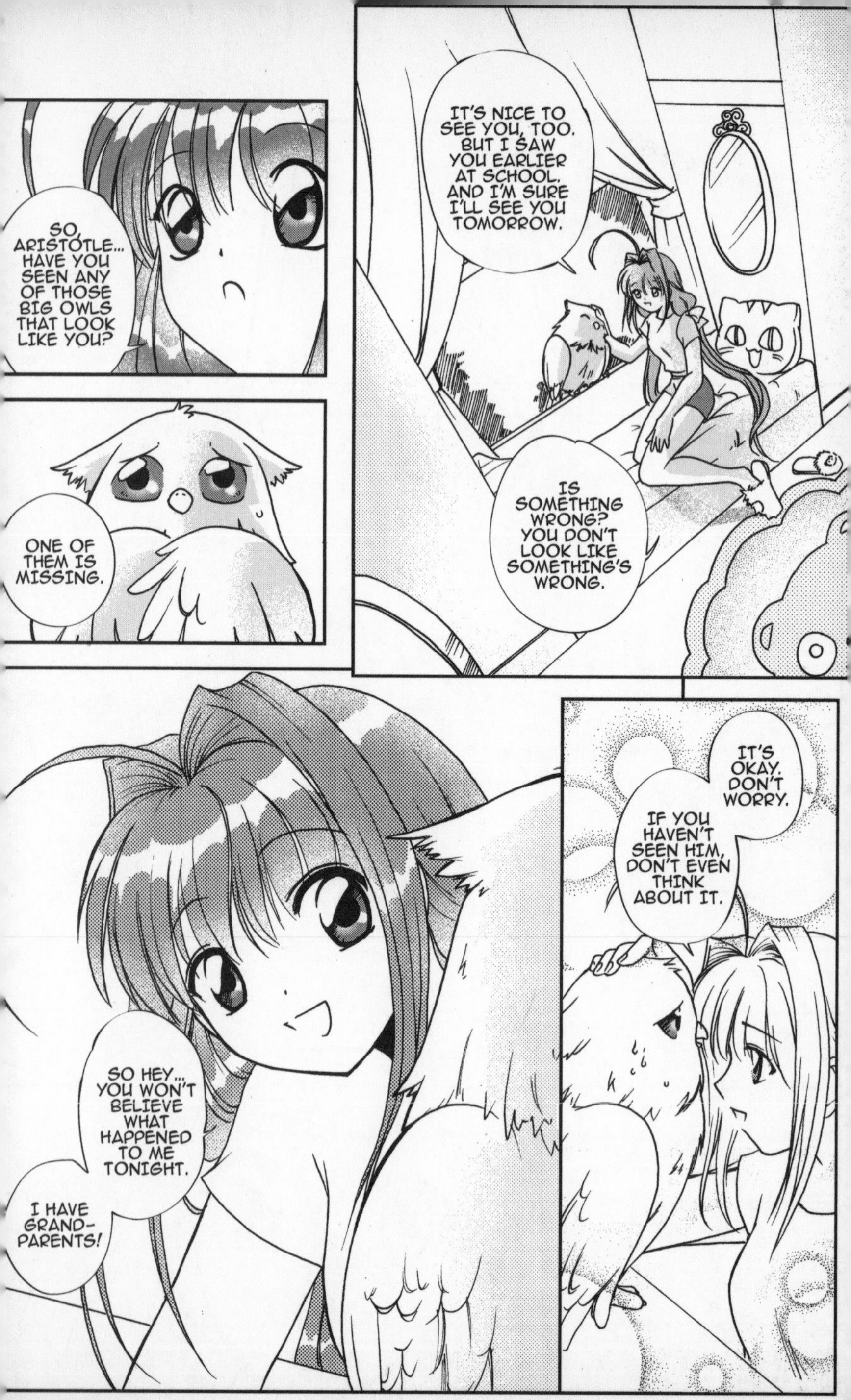
IT'S NICE TO SEE YOU, TOO. BUT I SAW YOU EARLIER AT SCHOOL. AND I'M SURE I'LL SEE YOU TOMORROW.
IS SOMETHING WRONG? YOU DON'T LOOK LIKE SOMETHING'S WRONG.
SO, ARISTOTLE... HAVE YOU SEEN ANY OF THOSE BIG OWLS THAT LOOK LIKE YOU?
ONE OF THEM IS MISSING.
IT'S OKAY. DON'T WORRY.
IF YOU HAVEN'T SEEN HIM, DON'T EVEN THINK ABOUT IT.
SO HEY... YOU WON'T BELIEVE WHAT HAPPENED TO ME TONIGHT.
I HAVE GRAND-PARENTS!

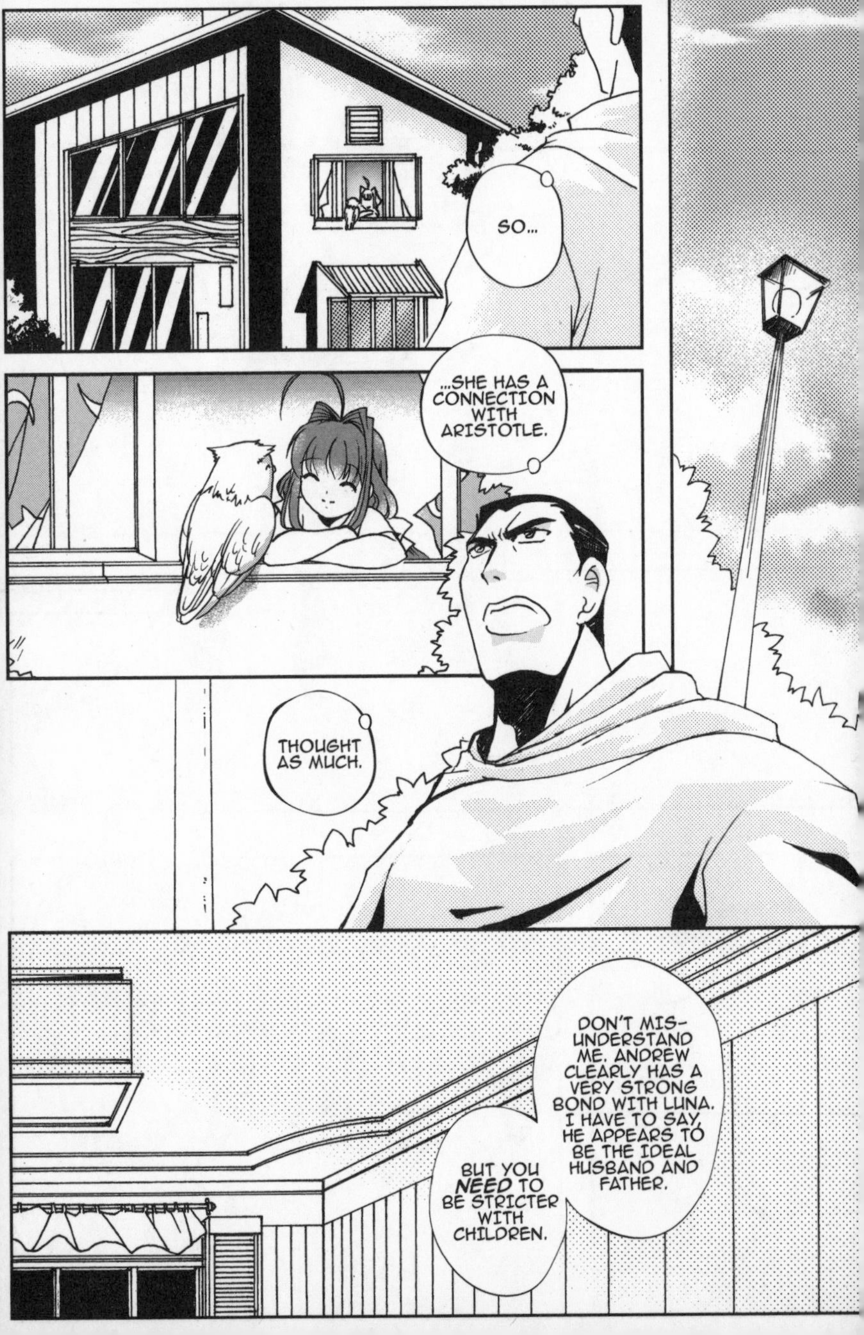
SO...
...SHE HAS A CONNECTION WITH ARISTOTLE.
THOUGHT AS MUCH.
DON'T MIS-UNDERSTAND ME. ANDREW CLEARLY HAS A VERY STRONG BOND WITH LUNA. I HAVE TO SAY, HE APPEARS TO BE THE IDEAL HUSBAND AND FATHER.
BUT YOU *NEED* TO BE STRICTER WITH CHILDREN.

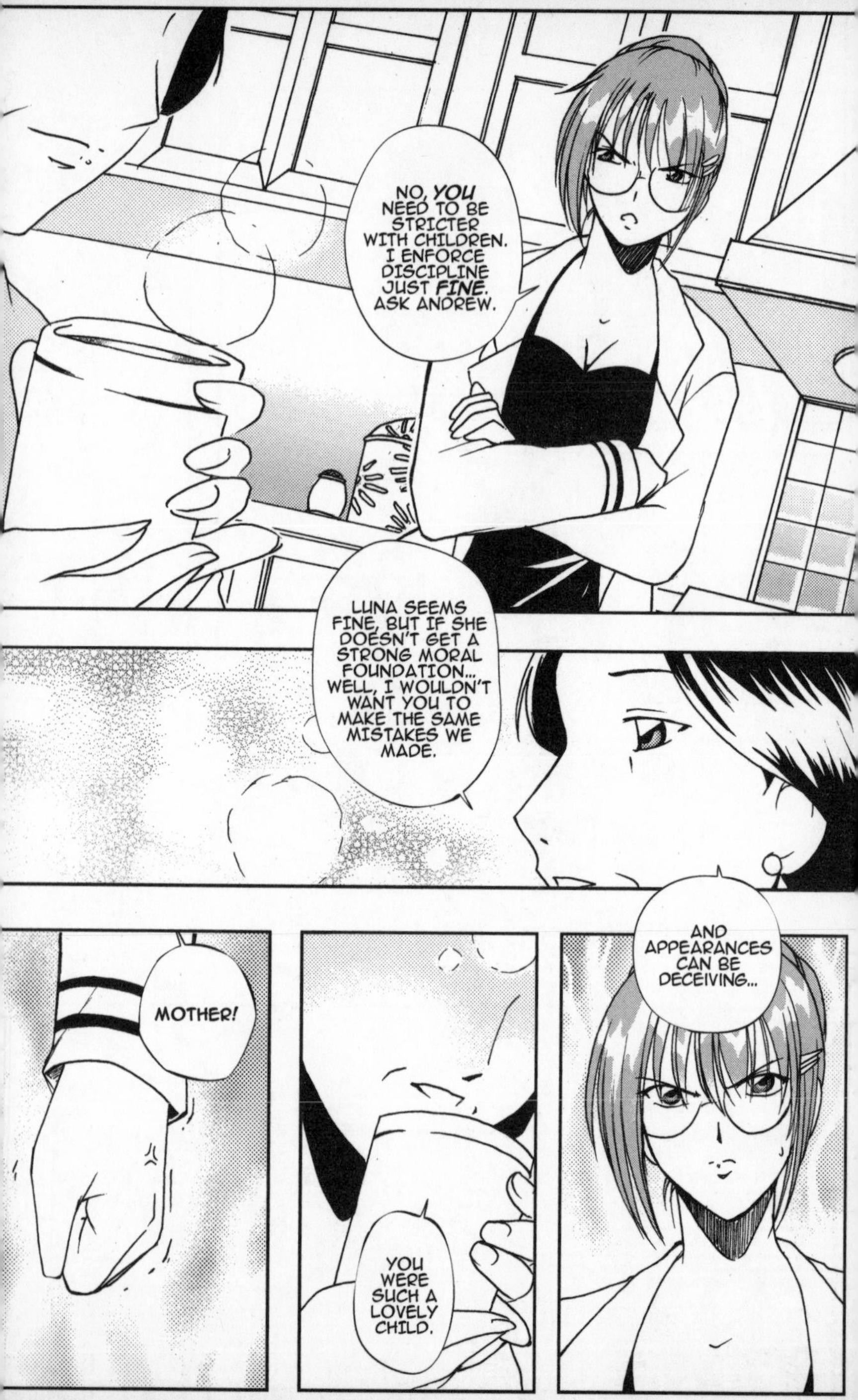
NO, *YOU* NEED TO BE STRICTER WITH CHILDREN. I ENFORCE DISCIPLINE JUST *FINE*. ASK ANDREW.
LUNA SEEMS FINE, BUT IF SHE DOESN'T GET A STRONG MORAL FOUNDATION... WELL, I WOULDN'T WANT YOU TO MAKE THE SAME MISTAKES WE MADE.
AND APPEARANCES CAN BE DECEIVING...
YOU WERE SUCH A LOVELY CHILD.
MOTHER!

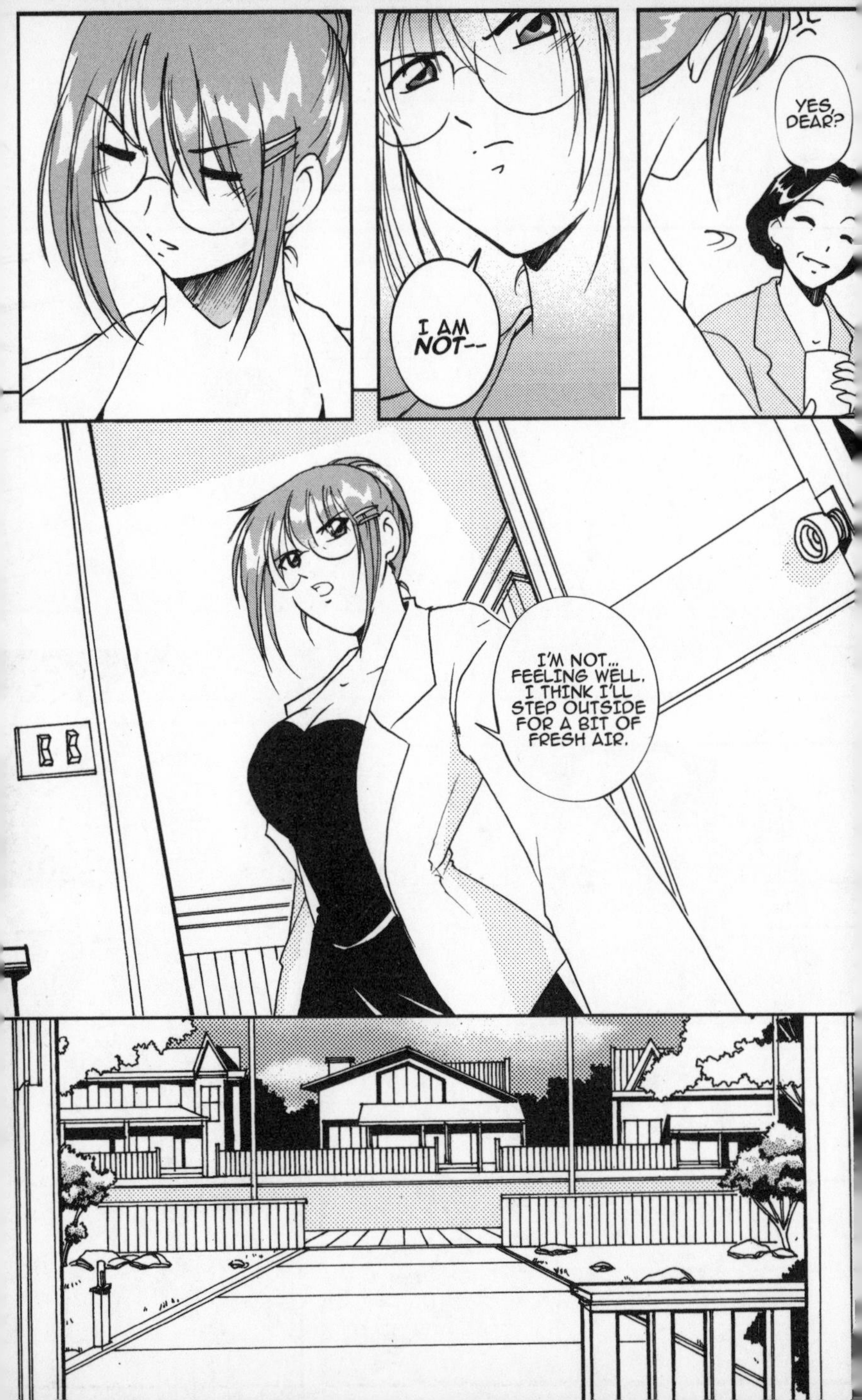
YES, DEAR?
I AM NOT--
I'M NOT... FEELING WELL. I THINK I'LL STEP OUTSIDE FOR A BIT OF FRESH AIR.

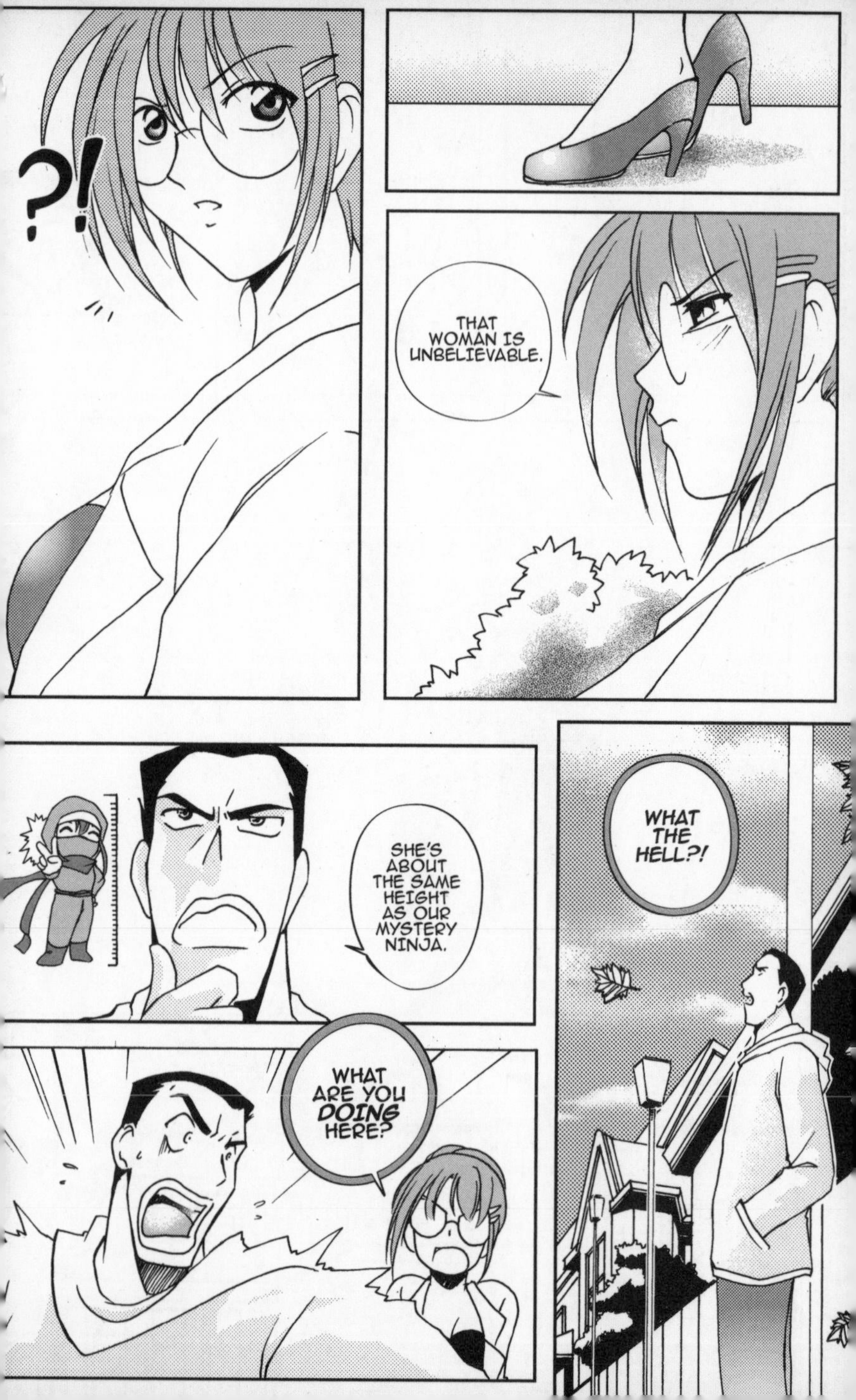
THAT WOMAN IS UNBELIEVABLE.
?!
WHAT THE HELL?!
SHE'S ABOUT THE SAME HEIGHT AS OUR MYSTERY NINJA.
WHAT ARE YOU *DOING* HERE?

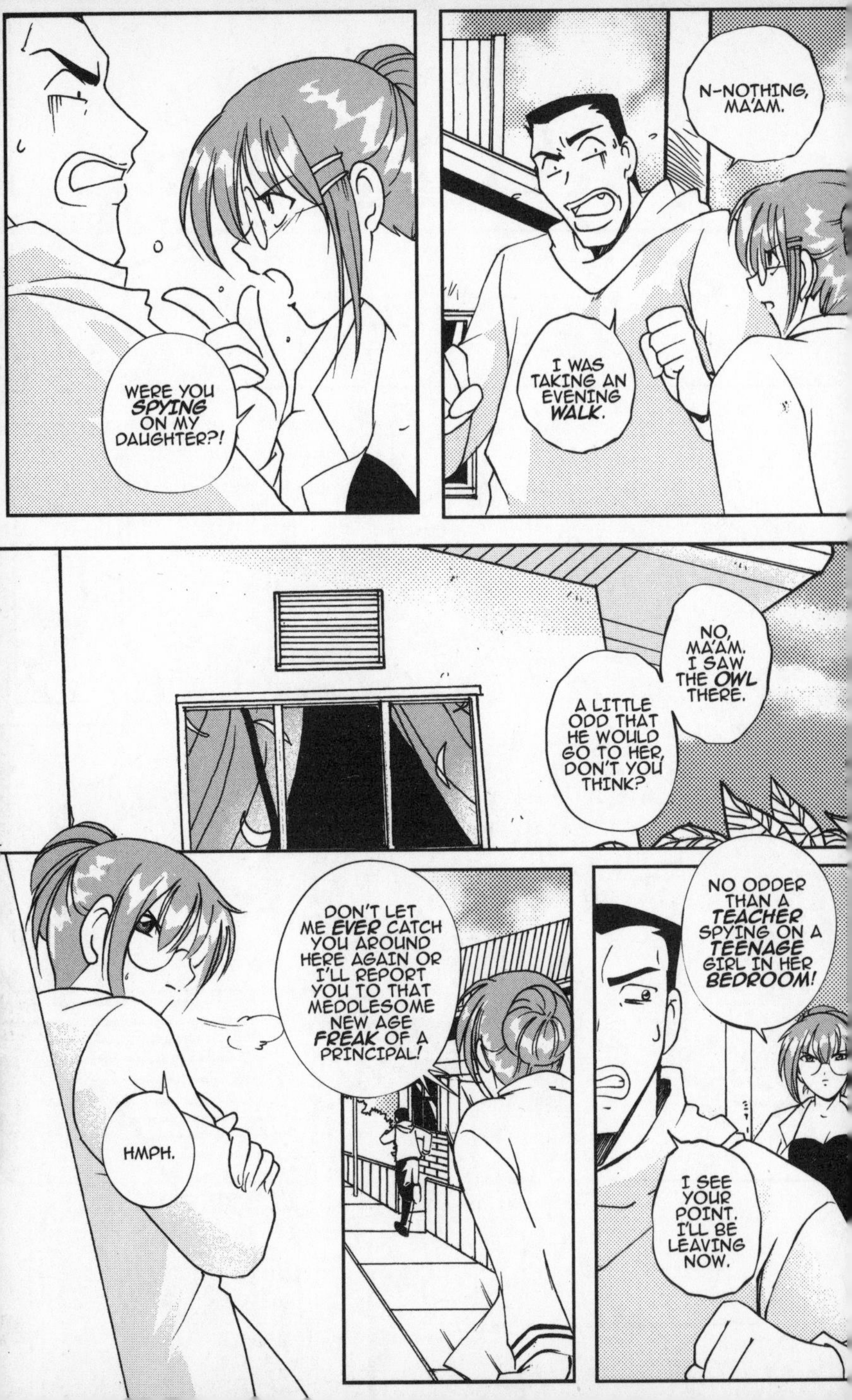

N-NOTHING, MA'AM.
I WAS TAKING AN EVENING **WALK**.
WERE YOU **SPYING** ON MY DAUGHTER?!
NO, MA'AM. I SAW THE **OWL** THERE.
A LITTLE ODD THAT HE WOULD GO TO HER, DON'T YOU THINK?
NO ODDER THAN A **TEACHER** SPYING ON A **TEENAGE** GIRL IN HER **BEDROOM**!
I SEE YOUR POINT. I'LL BE LEAVING NOW.
DON'T LET ME **EVER** CATCH YOU AROUND HERE AGAIN OR I'LL REPORT YOU TO THAT MEDDLESOME NEW AGE **FREAK** OF A PRINCIPAL!
HMPH.

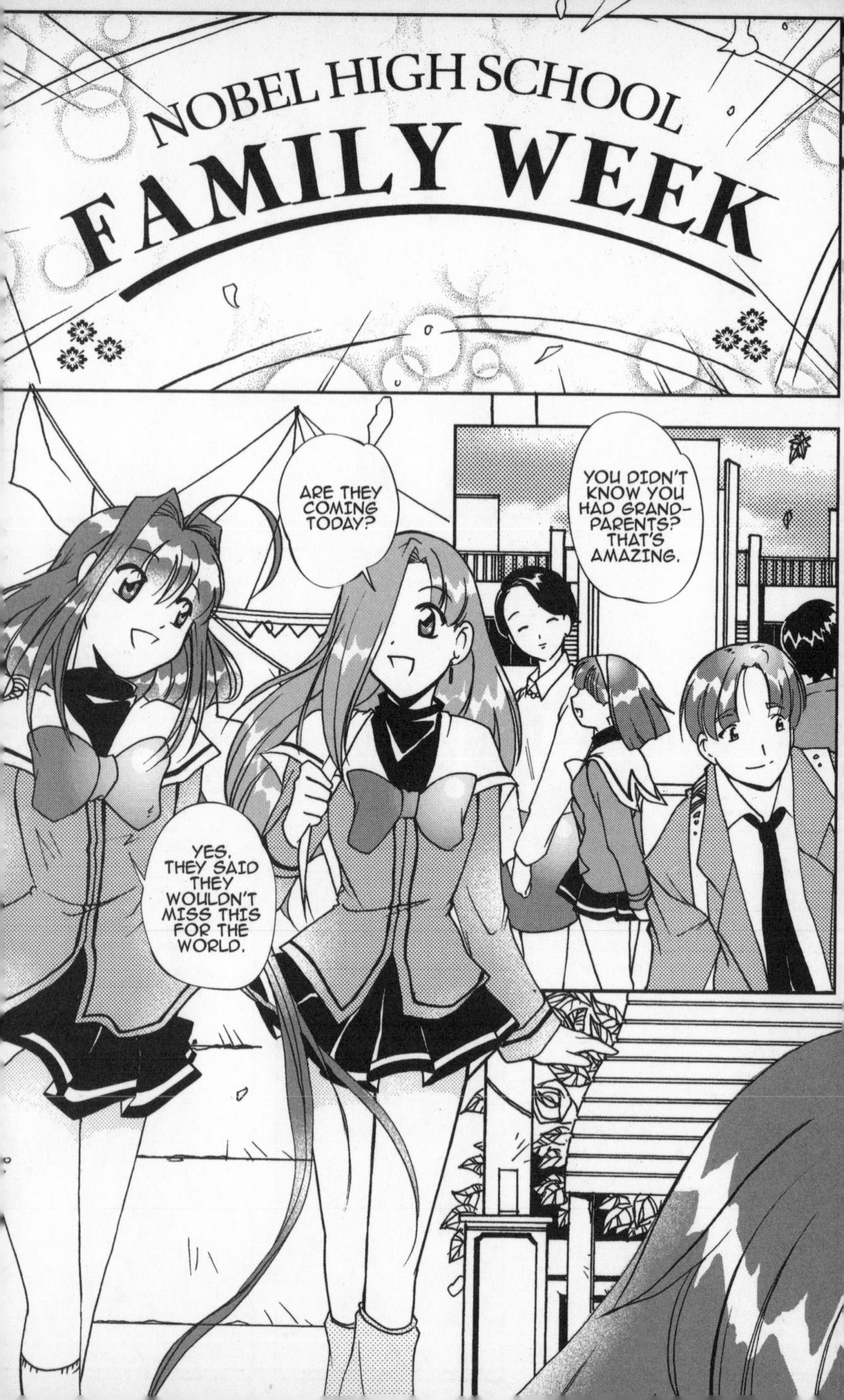
NOBEL HIGH SCHOOL
FAMILY WEEK
YOU DIDN'T KNOW YOU HAD GRAND-PARENTS? THAT'S AMAZING.
ARE THEY COMING TODAY?
YES. THEY SAID THEY WOULDN'T MISS THIS FOR THE WORLD.

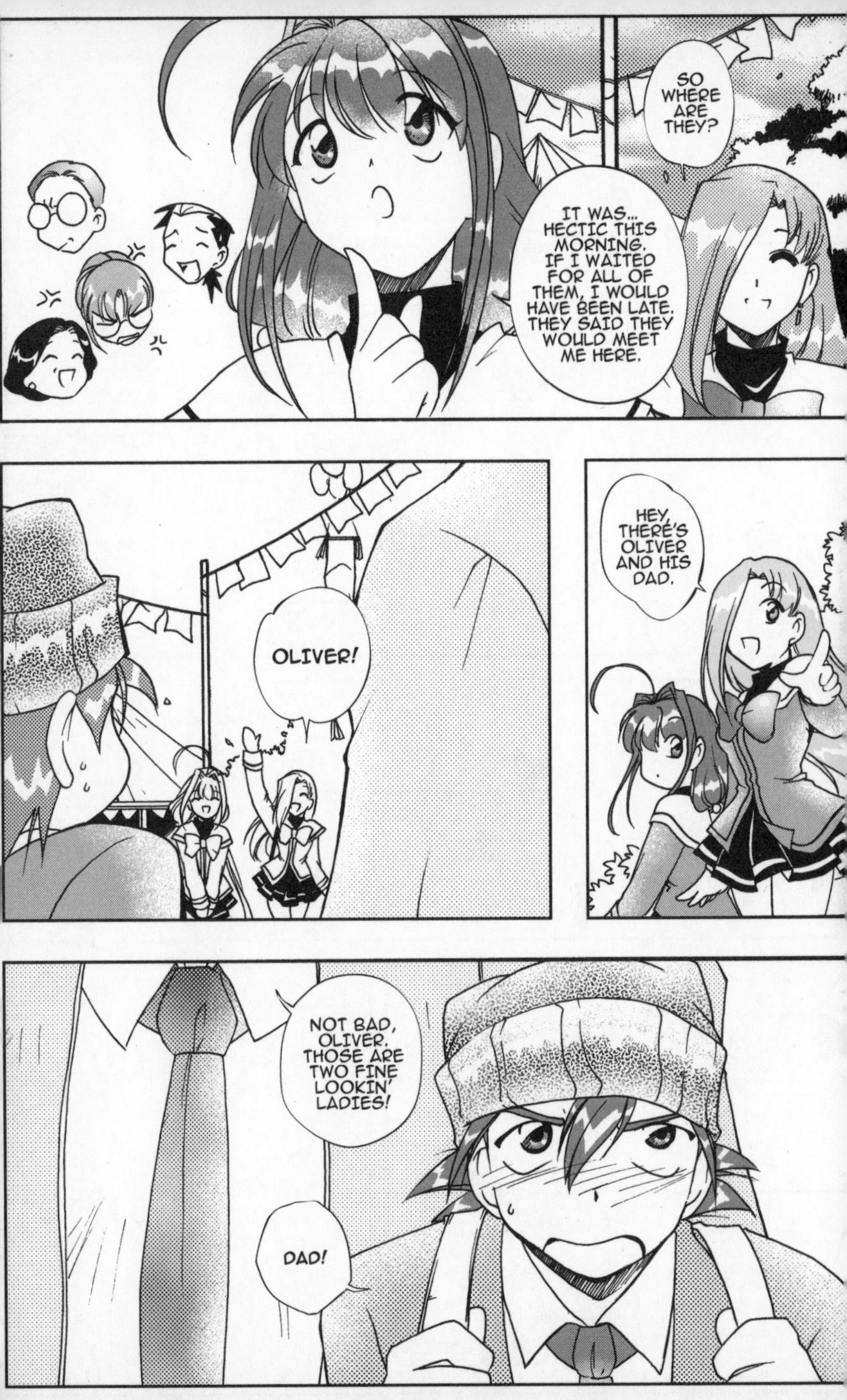
SO WHERE ARE THEY?
IT WAS... HECTIC THIS MORNING. IF I WAITED FOR ALL OF THEM, I WOULD HAVE BEEN LATE. THEY SAID THEY WOULD MEET ME HERE.
HEY, THERE'S OLIVER AND HIS DAD.
OLIVER!
NOT BAD, OLIVER. THOSE ARE TWO FINE LOOKIN' LADIES!
DAD!

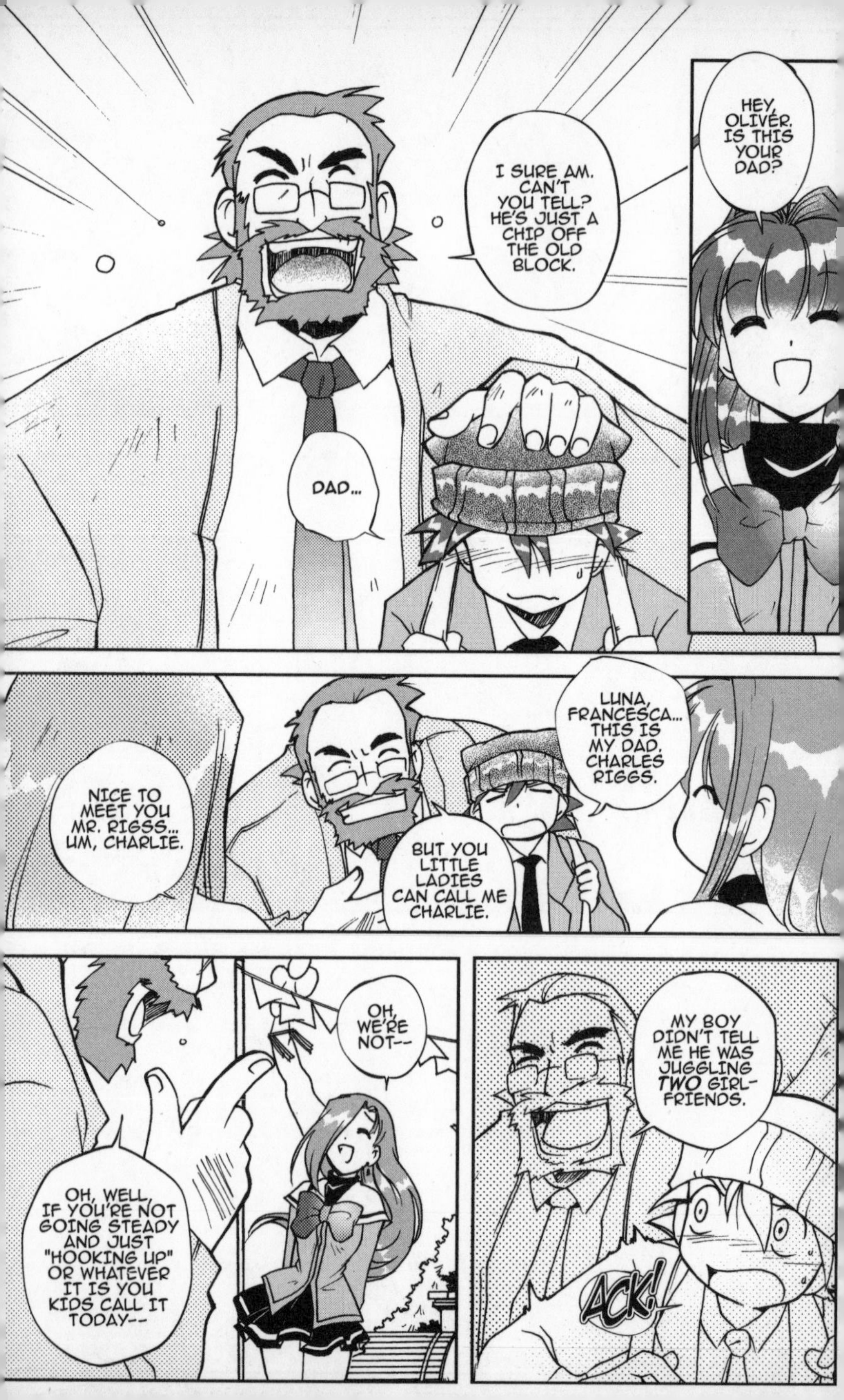
HEY, OLIVER. IS THIS YOUR DAD?
I SURE AM. CAN'T YOU TELL? HE'S JUST A CHIP OFF THE OLD BLOCK.
DAD...
LUNA, FRANCESCA... THIS IS MY DAD. CHARLES RIGGS.
NICE TO MEET YOU MR. RIGSS... UM, CHARLIE.
BUT YOU LITTLE LADIES CAN CALL ME CHARLIE.
MY BOY DIDN'T TELL ME HE WAS JUGGLING *TWO* GIRL-FRIENDS.
ACK!
OH, WE'RE NOT--
OH, WELL, IF YOU'RE NOT GOING STEADY AND JUST "HOOKING UP" OR WHATEVER IT IS YOU KIDS CALL IT TODAY--

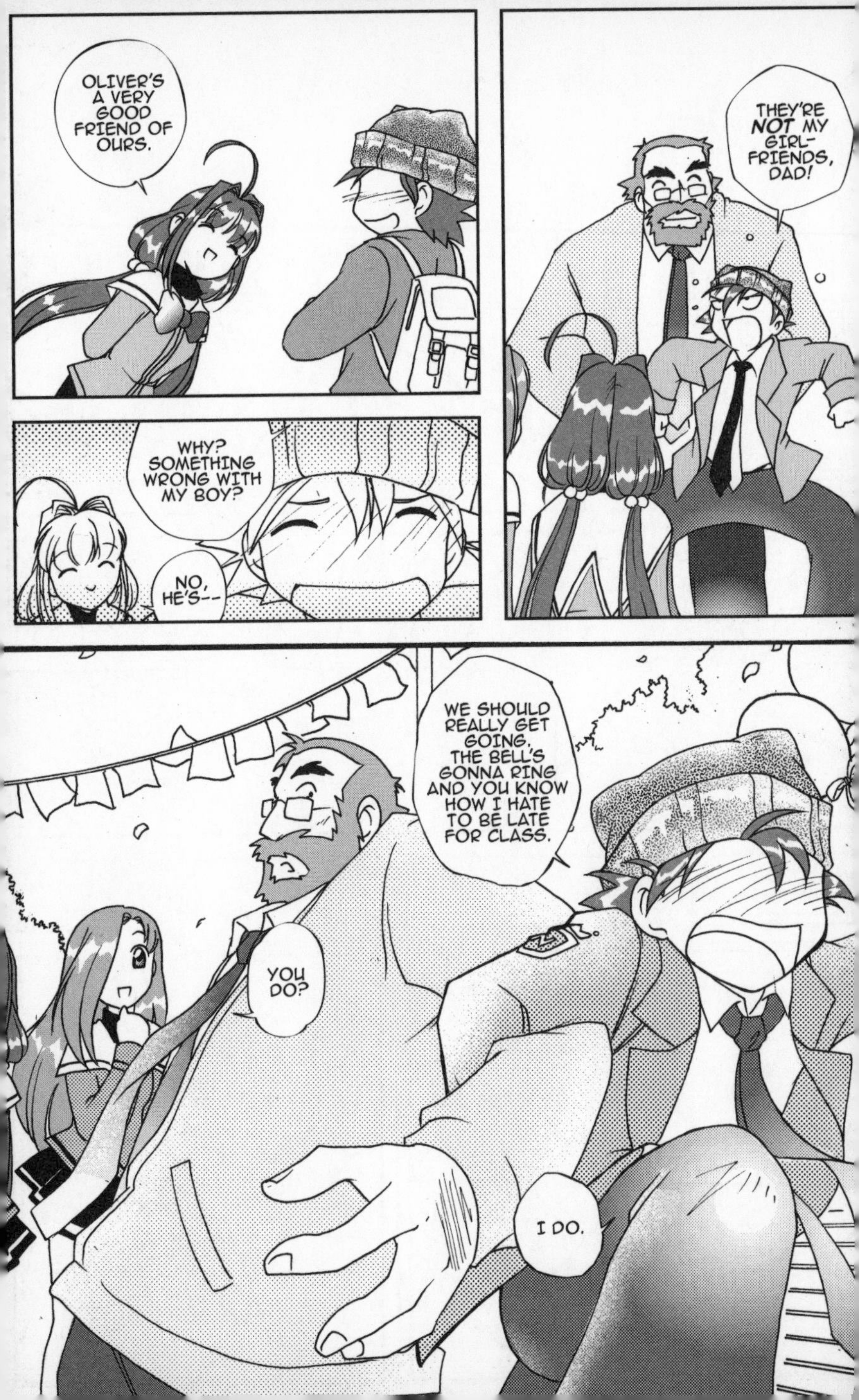
THEY'RE **NOT** MY GIRL-FRIENDS, DAD!
OLIVER'S A VERY GOOD FRIEND OF OURS.
WHY? SOMETHING WRONG WITH MY BOY?
NO, HE'S--
WE SHOULD REALLY GET GOING. THE BELL'S GONNA RING AND YOU KNOW HOW I HATE TO BE LATE FOR CLASS.
YOU DO?
I DO.

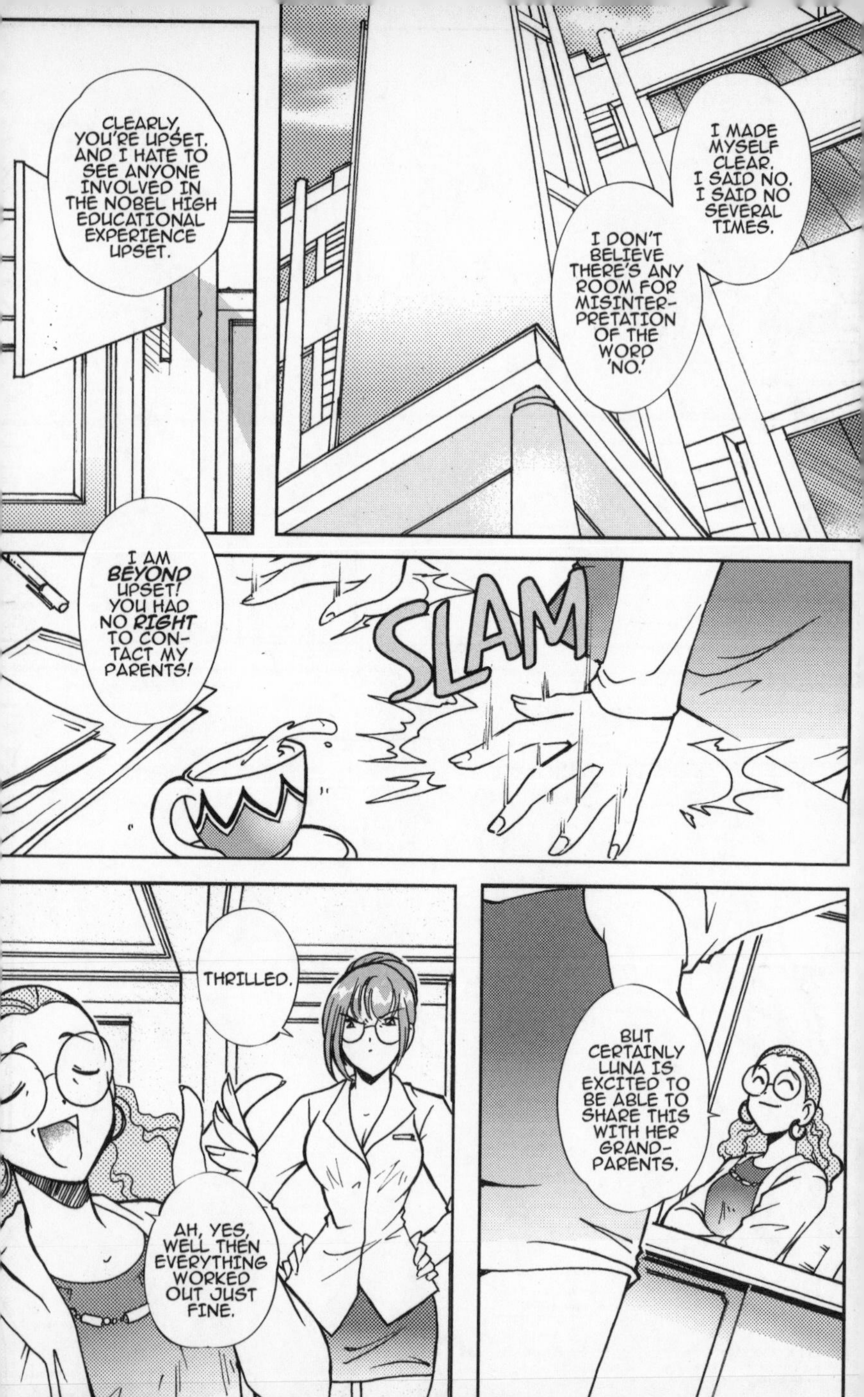
I MADE MYSELF CLEAR. I SAID NO. I SAID NO SEVERAL TIMES.
I DON'T BELIEVE THERE'S ANY ROOM FOR MISINTERPRETATION OF THE WORD 'NO.'
CLEARLY, YOU'RE UPSET. AND I HATE TO SEE ANYONE INVOLVED IN THE NOBEL HIGH EDUCATIONAL EXPERIENCE UPSET.
I AM *BEYOND* UPSET! YOU HAD NO *RIGHT* TO CONTACT MY PARENTS!
SLAM
BUT CERTAINLY LUNA IS EXCITED TO BE ABLE TO SHARE THIS WITH HER GRANDPARENTS.
THRILLED.
AH, YES, WELL THEN EVERYTHING WORKED OUT JUST FINE.

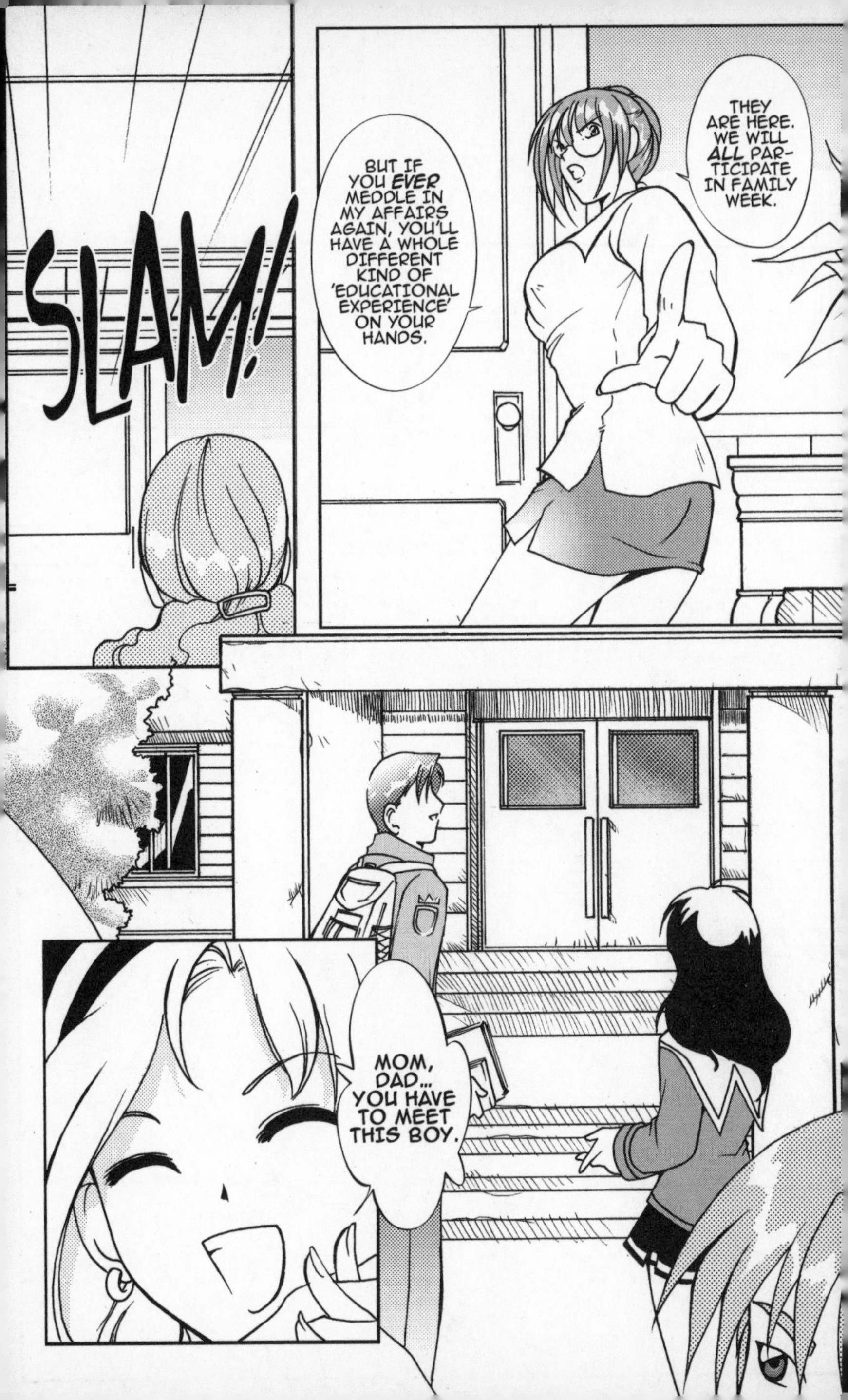
THEY ARE HERE. WE WILL ALL PARTICIPATE IN FAMILY WEEK.
BUT IF YOU EVER MEDDLE IN MY AFFAIRS AGAIN, YOU'LL HAVE A WHOLE DIFFERENT KIND OF 'EDUCATIONAL EXPERIENCE' ON YOUR HANDS.
SLAM!
MOM, DAD... YOU HAVE TO MEET THIS BOY.

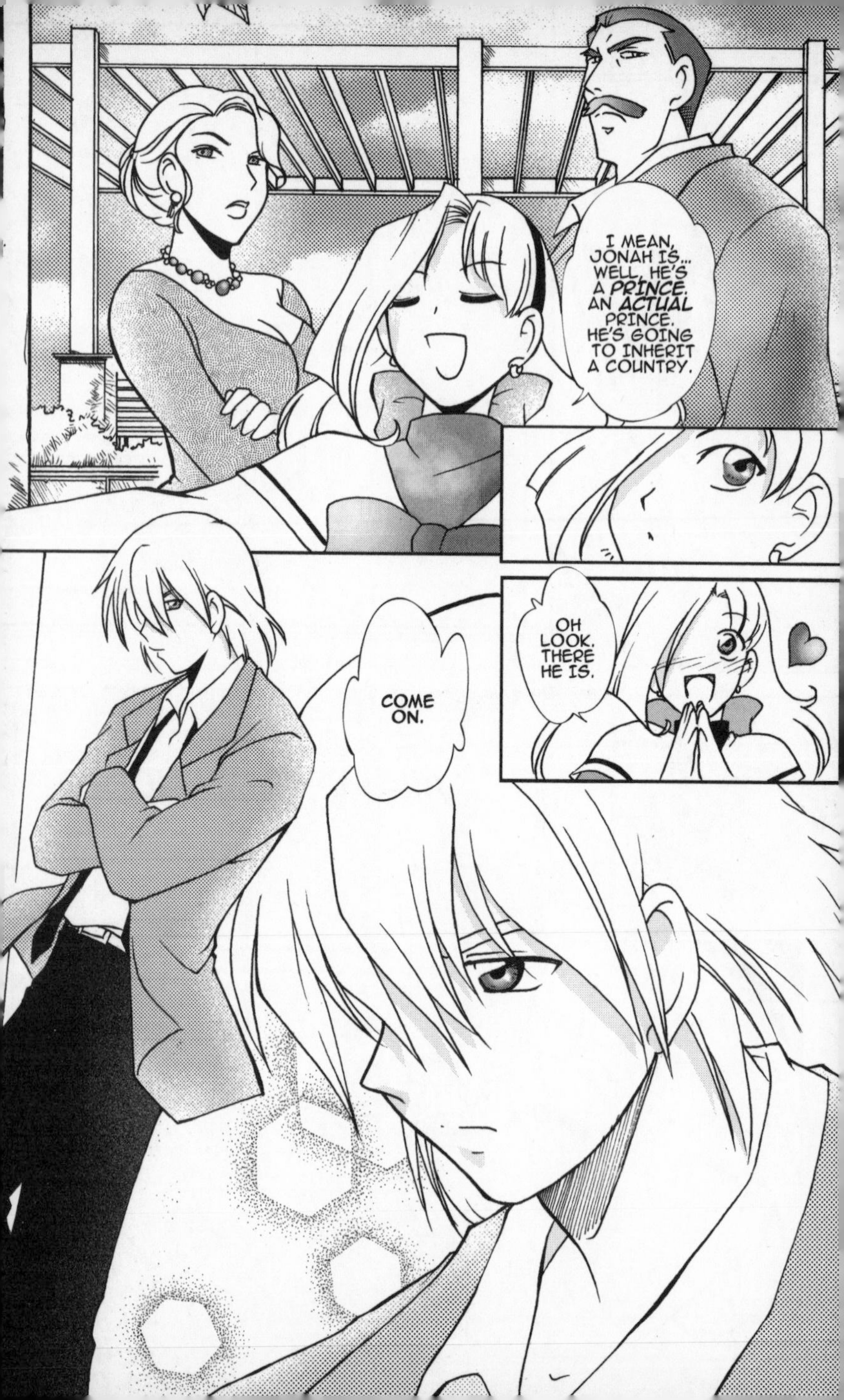
I MEAN, JONAH IS... WELL, HE'S A *PRINCE*. AN *ACTUAL* PRINCE. HE'S GOING TO INHERIT A COUNTRY.
OH LOOK. THERE HE IS.
COME ON.

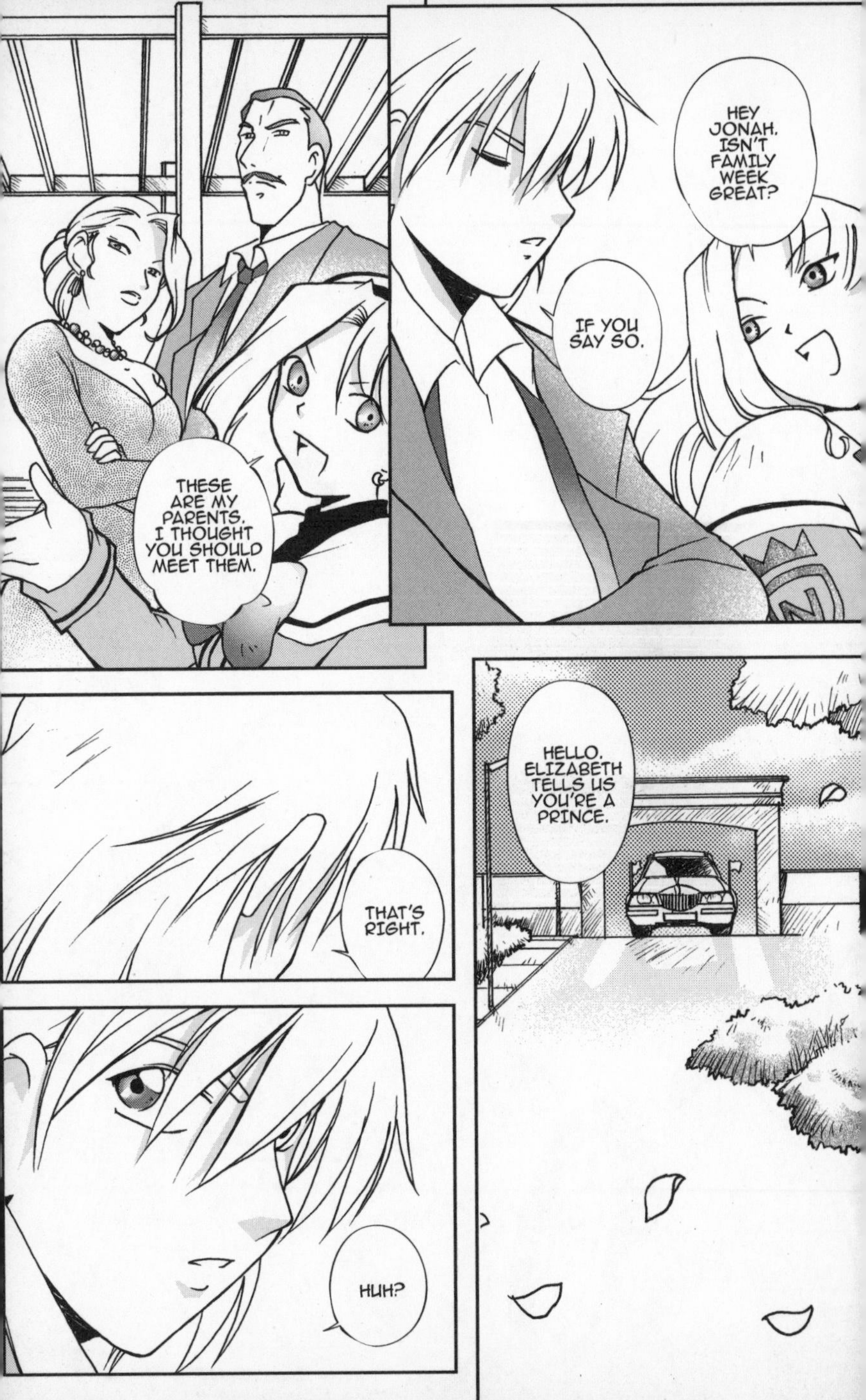
HEY JONAH. ISN'T FAMILY WEEK GREAT?
IF YOU SAY SO.
THESE ARE MY PARENTS. I THOUGHT YOU SHOULD MEET THEM.
HELLO. ELIZABETH TELLS US YOU'RE A PRINCE.
THAT'S RIGHT.
HUH?

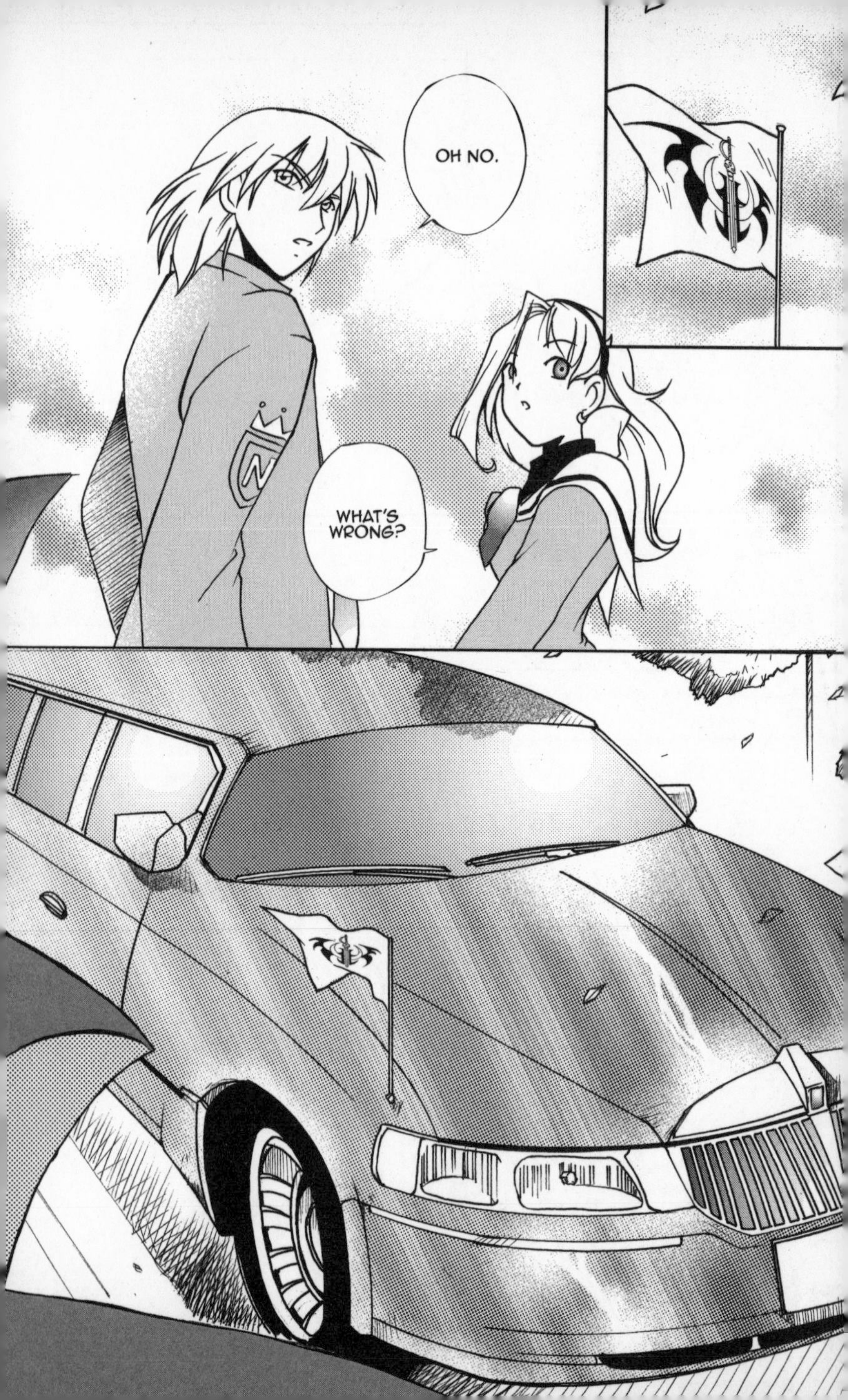
OH NO.
WHAT'S WRONG?

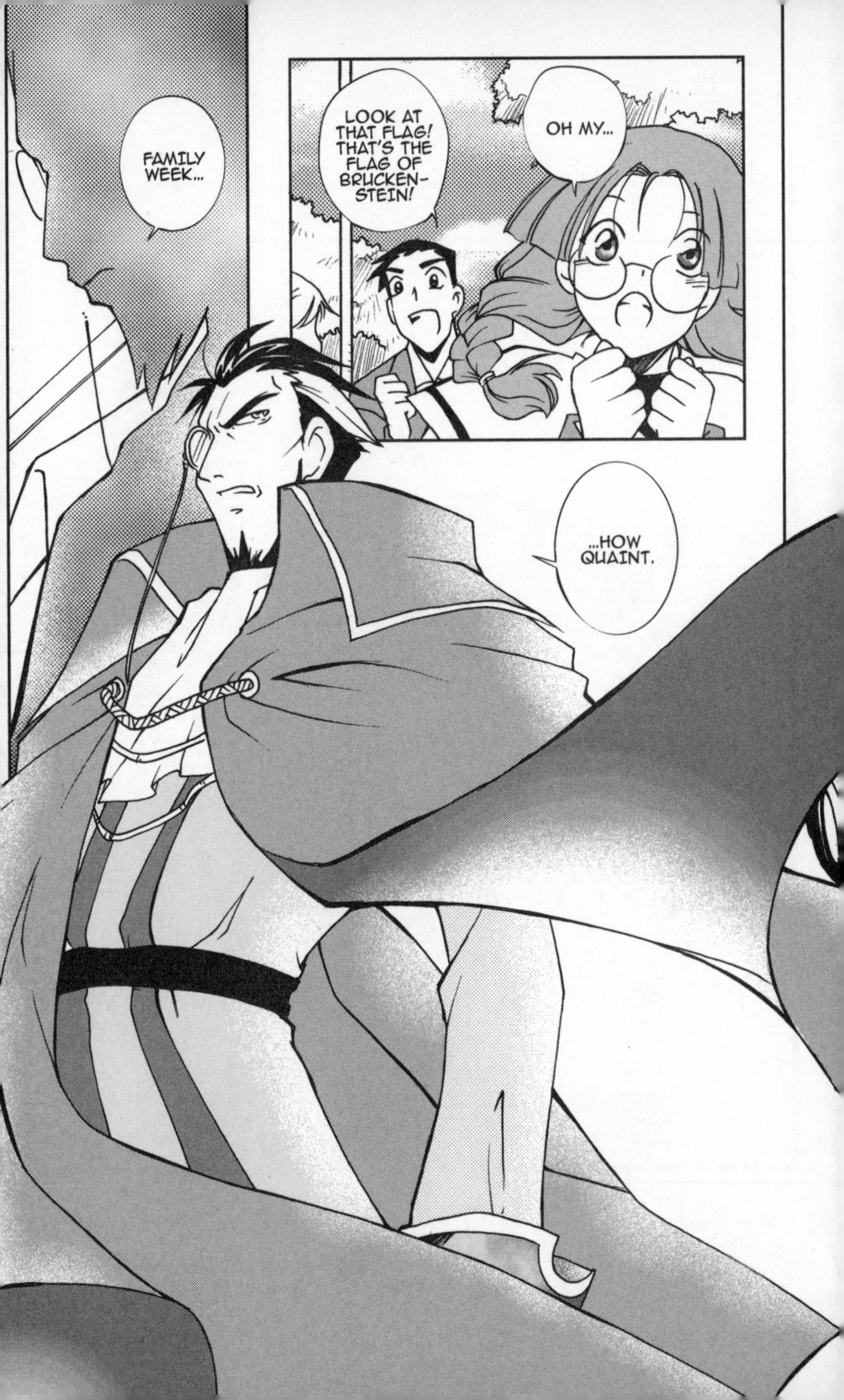
OH MY...
LOOK AT THAT FLAG! THAT'S THE FLAG OF BRUCKEN-STEIN!
FAMILY WEEK...
...HOW QUAINT.

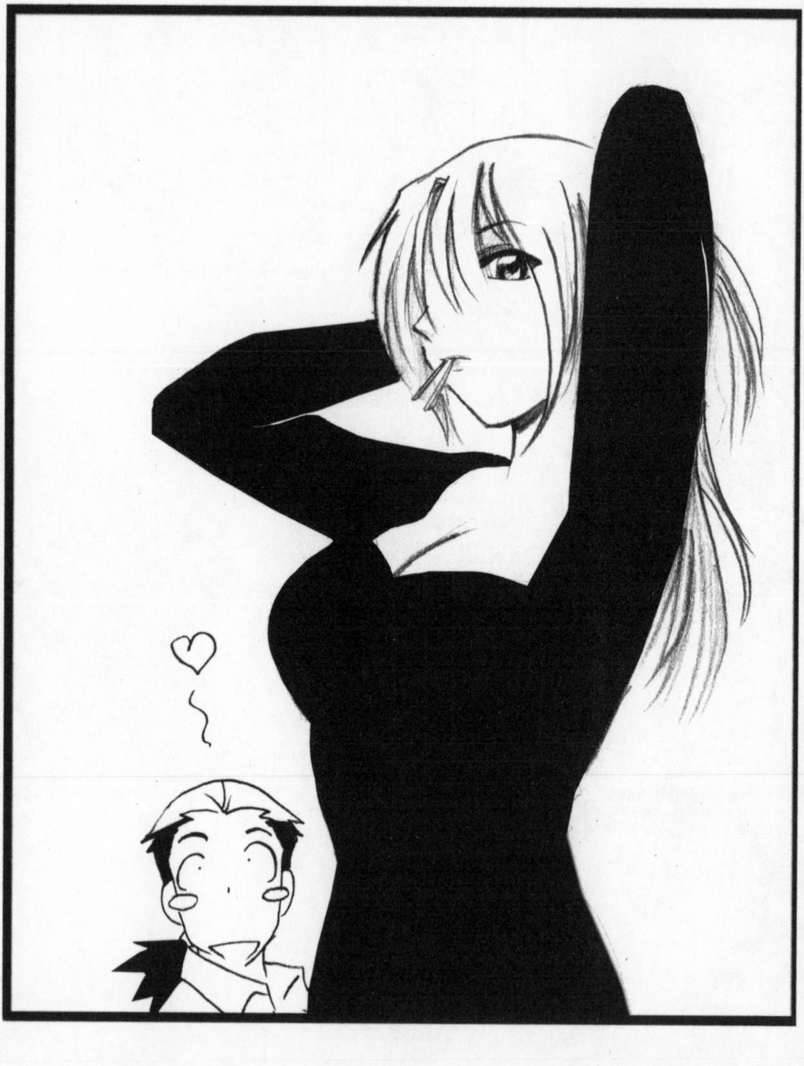

# File 09
# BONDING

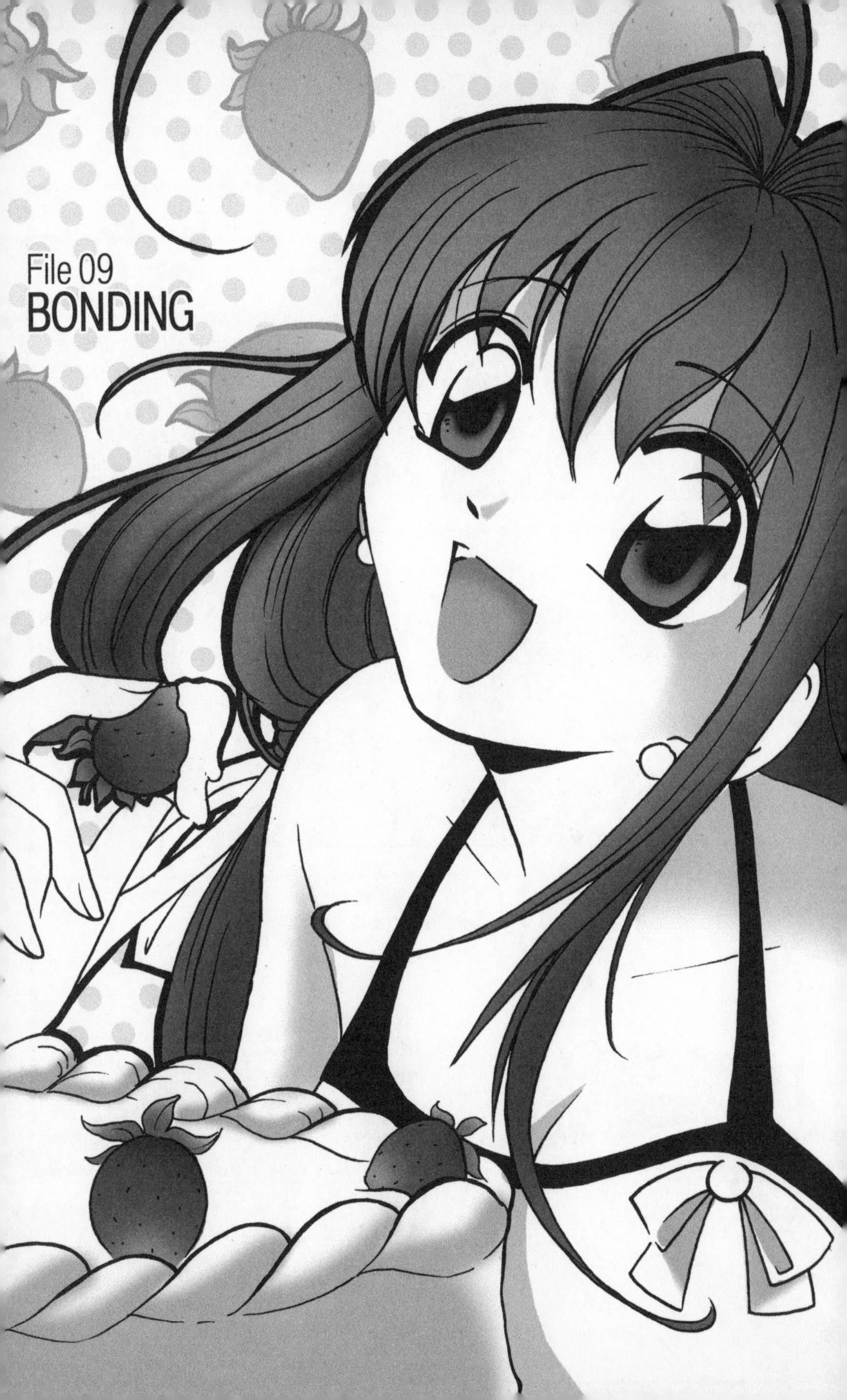

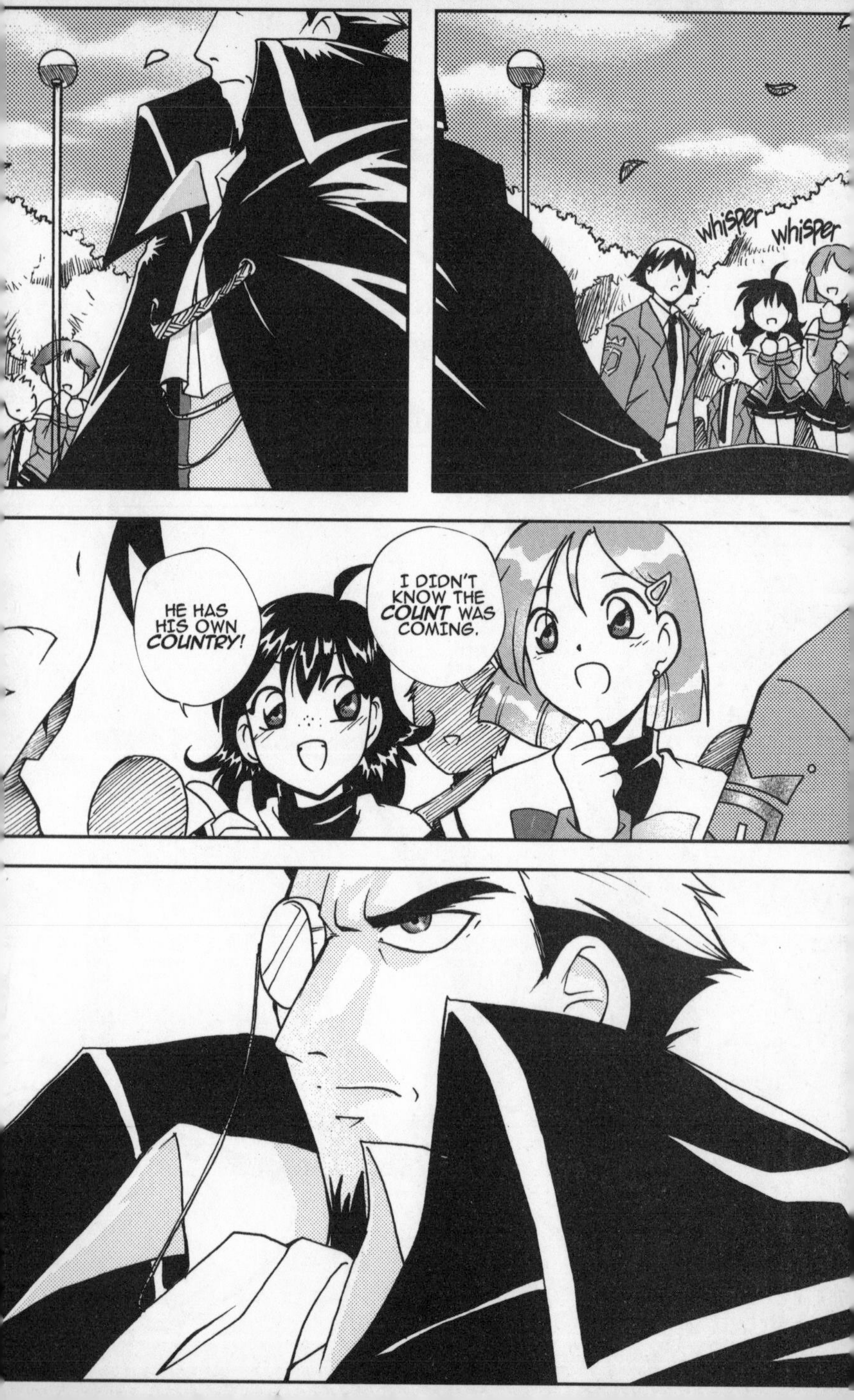
whisper
whisper
I DIDN'T KNOW THE COUNT WAS COMING.
HE HAS HIS OWN COUNTRY!

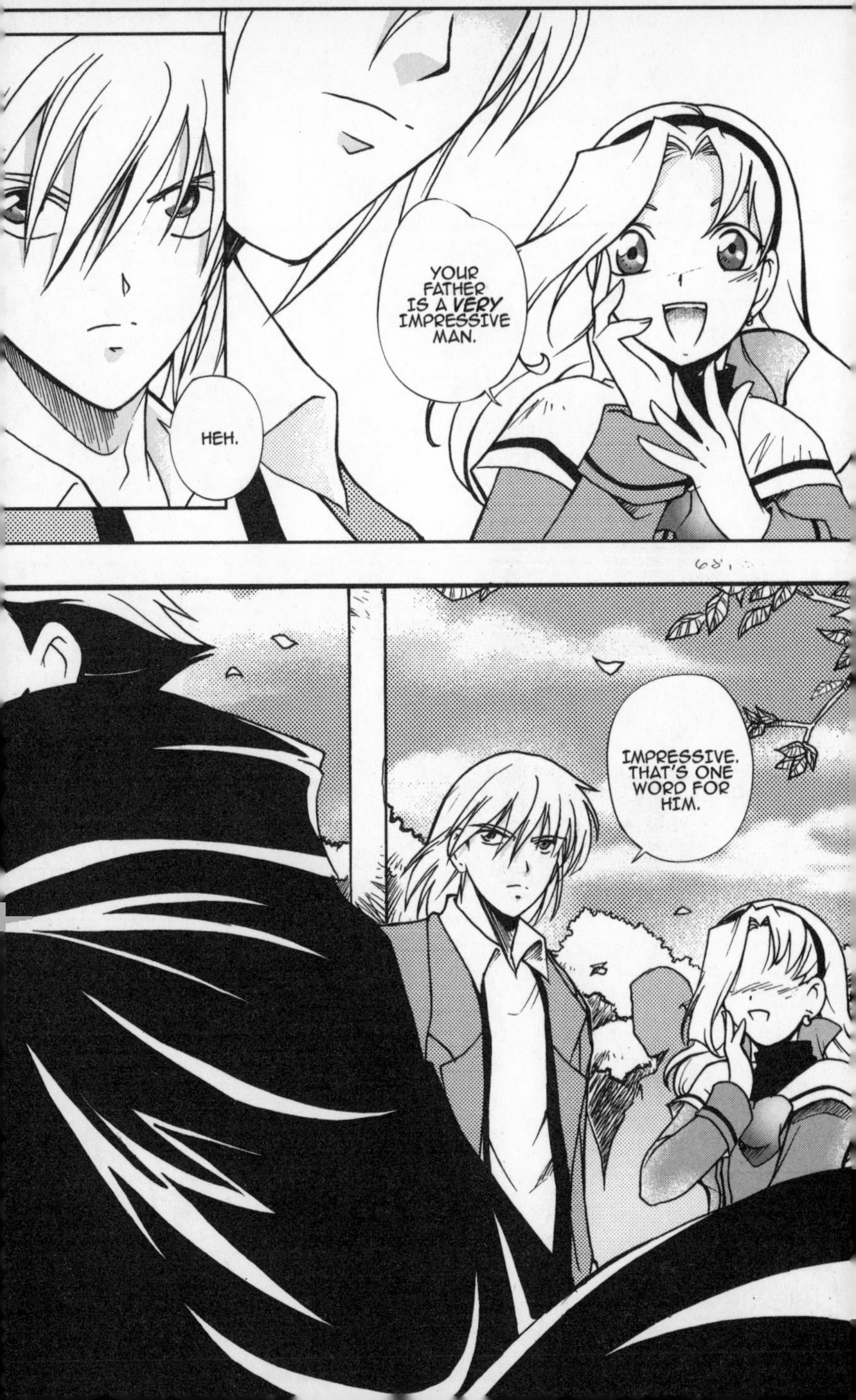
YOUR FATHER IS A VERY IMPRESSIVE MAN.
HEH.
IMPRESSIVE. THAT'S ONE WORD FOR HIM.

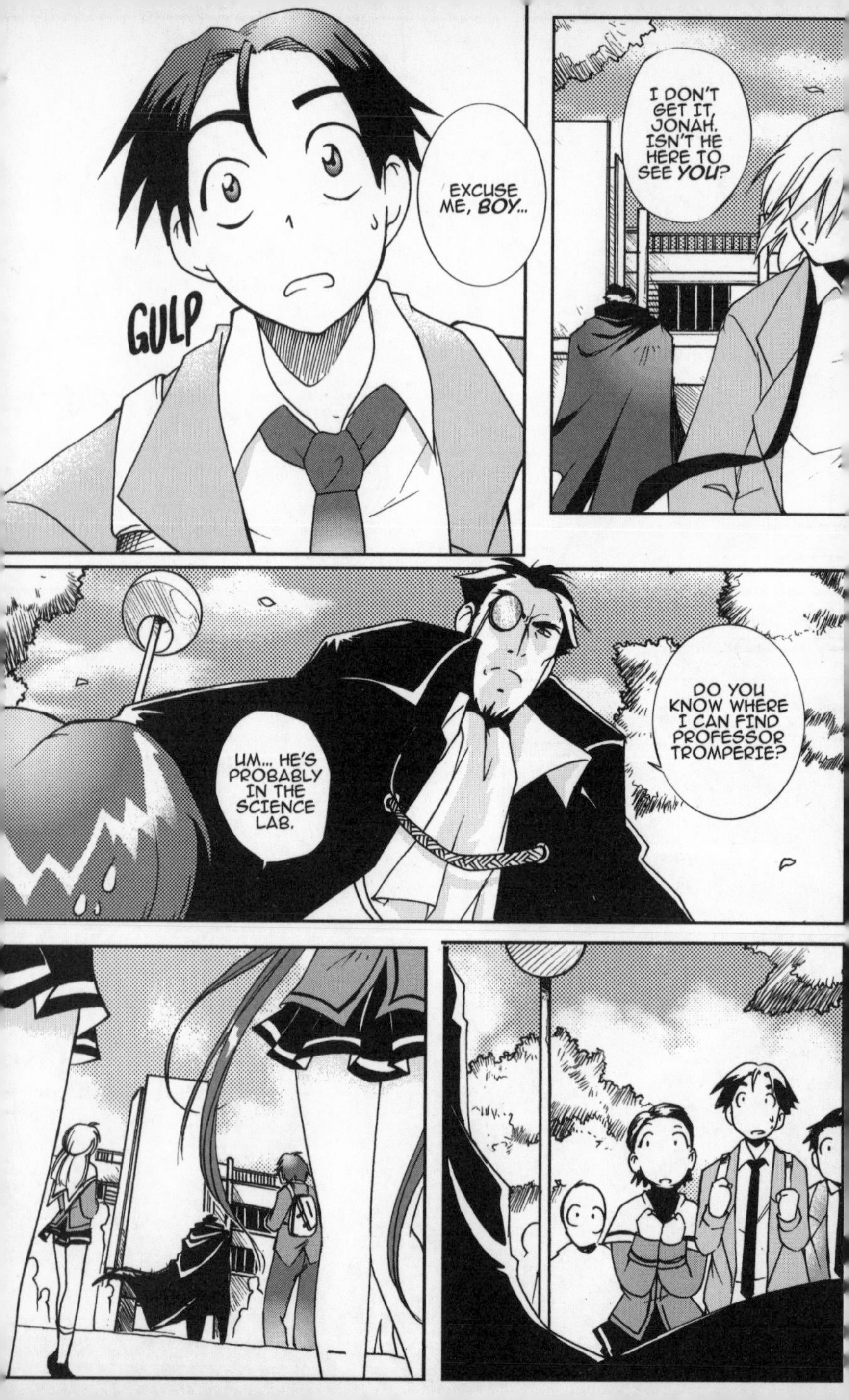
I DON'T GET IT, JONAH. ISN'T HE HERE TO SEE *YOU*?
EXCUSE ME, *BOY*...
GULP
DO YOU KNOW WHERE I CAN FIND PROFESSOR TROMPERIE?
UM... HE'S PROBABLY IN THE SCIENCE LAB.

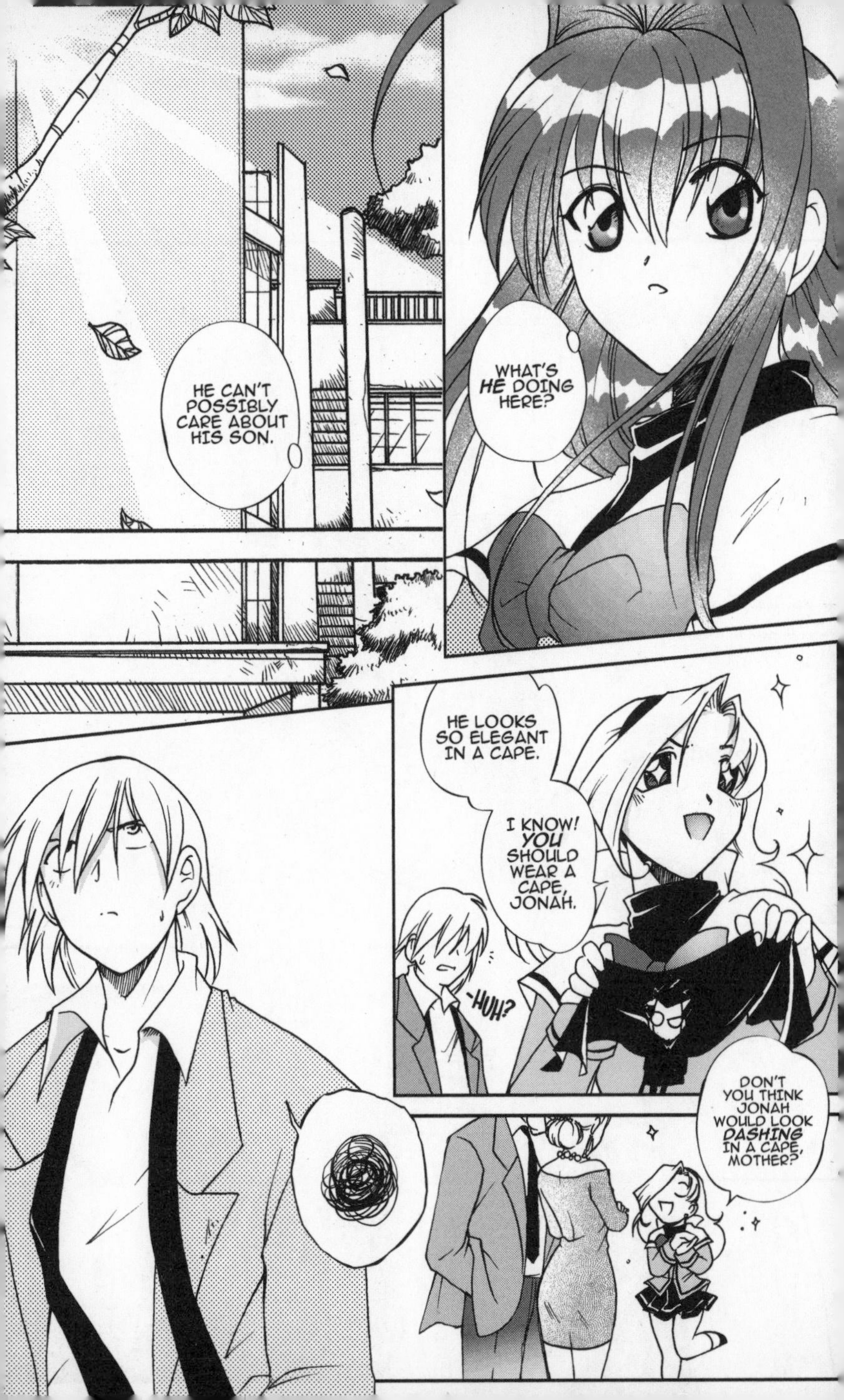
WHAT'S HE DOING HERE?
HE CAN'T POSSIBLY CARE ABOUT HIS SON.
HE LOOKS SO ELEGANT IN A CAPE.
I KNOW! YOU SHOULD WEAR A CAPE, JONAH.
-HUH?
DON'T YOU THINK JONAH WOULD LOOK DASHING IN A CAPE, MOTHER?

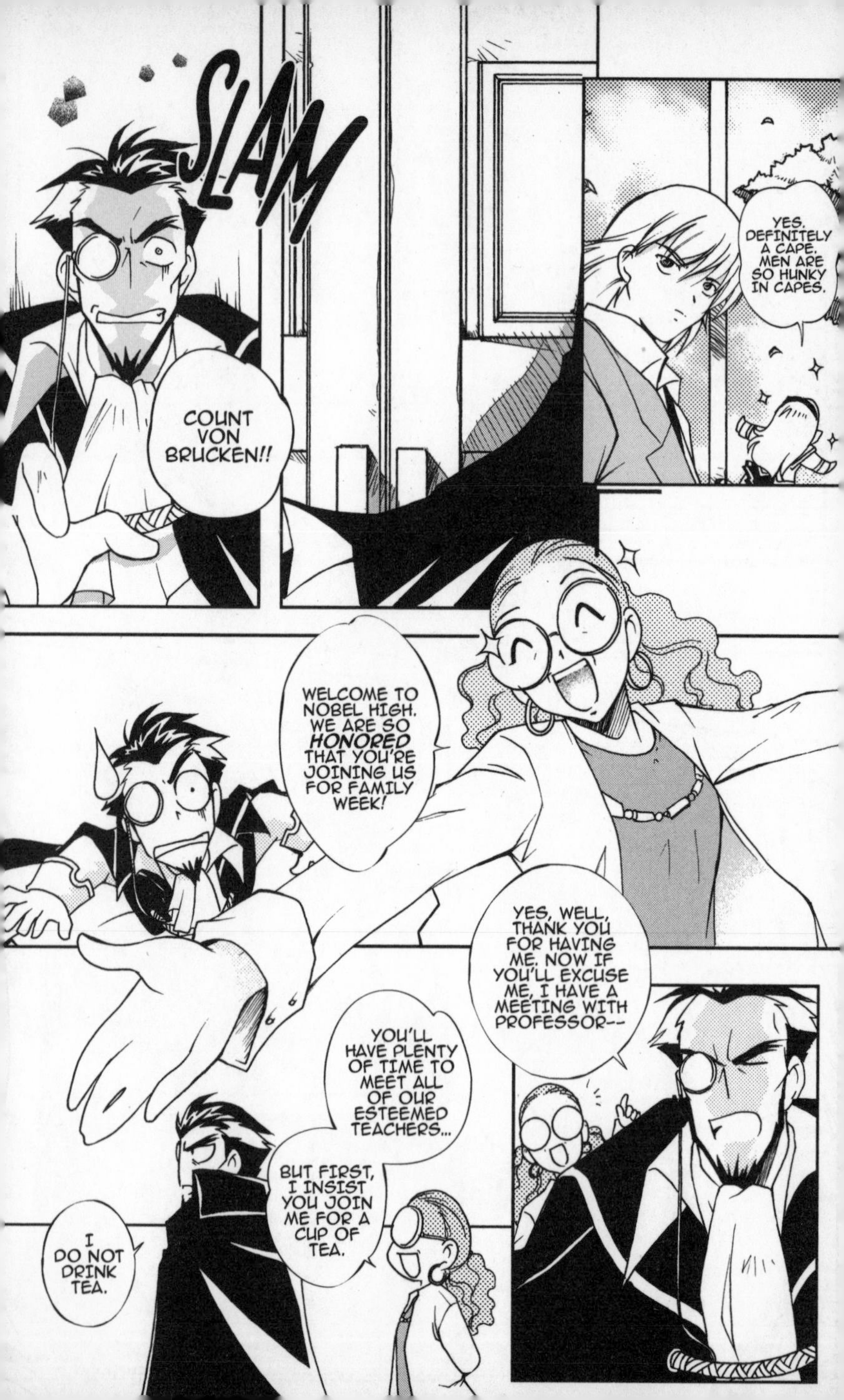
YES. DEFINITELY A CAPE. MEN ARE SO HUNKY IN CAPES.
SLAM
COUNT VON BRUCKEN!!
WELCOME TO NOBEL HIGH. WE ARE SO HONORED THAT YOU'RE JOINING US FOR FAMILY WEEK!
YES, WELL, THANK YOU FOR HAVING ME. NOW IF YOU'LL EXCUSE ME, I HAVE A MEETING WITH PROFESSOR--
YOU'LL HAVE PLENTY OF TIME TO MEET ALL OF OUR ESTEEMED TEACHERS...
BUT FIRST, I INSIST YOU JOIN ME FOR A CUP OF TEA.
I DO NOT DRINK TEA.

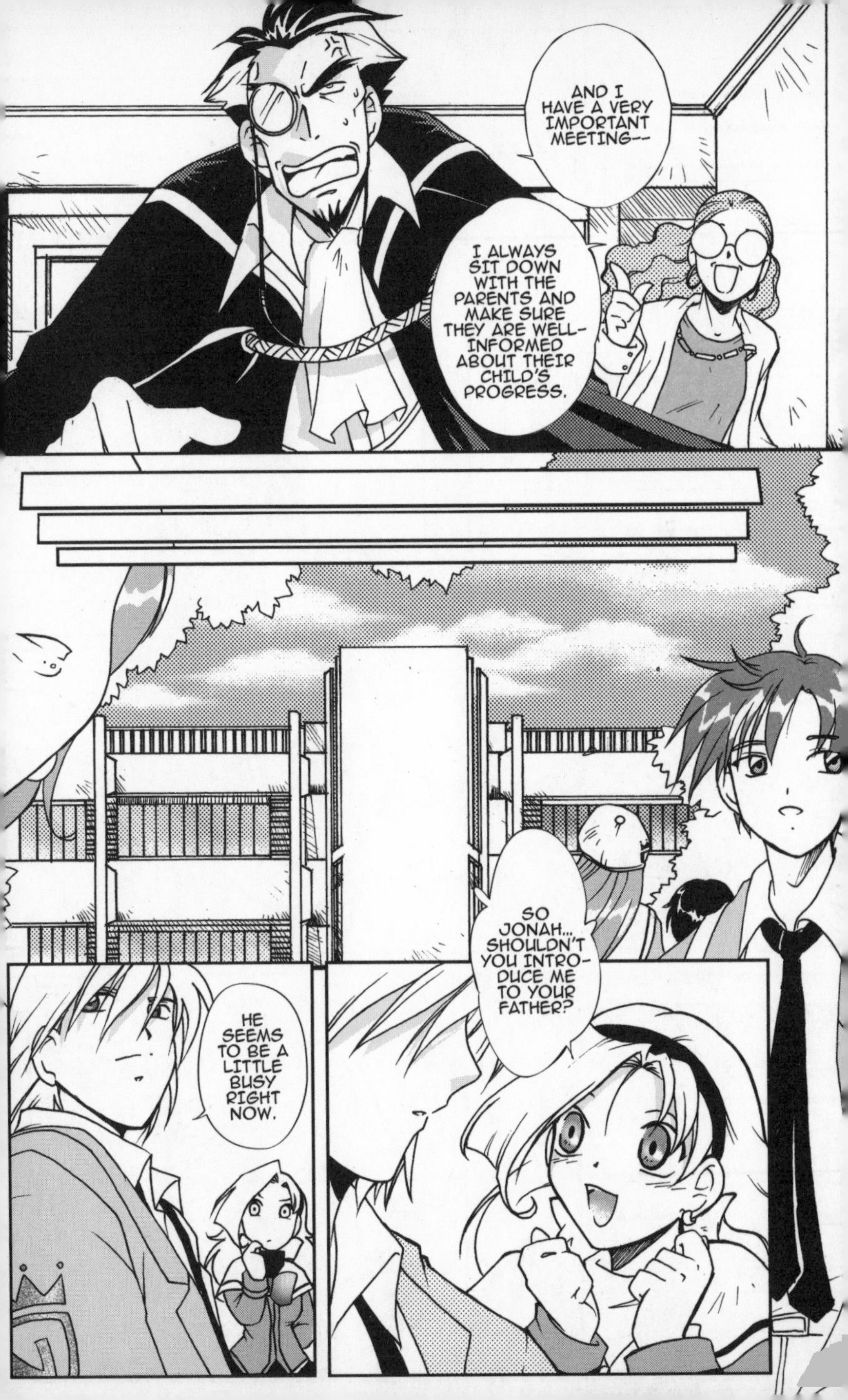
AND I HAVE A VERY IMPORTANT MEETING--
I ALWAYS SIT DOWN WITH THE PARENTS AND MAKE SURE THEY ARE WELL-INFORMED ABOUT THEIR CHILD'S PROGRESS.
SO JONAH... SHOULDN'T YOU INTRODUCE ME TO YOUR FATHER?
HE SEEMS TO BE A LITTLE BUSY RIGHT NOW.

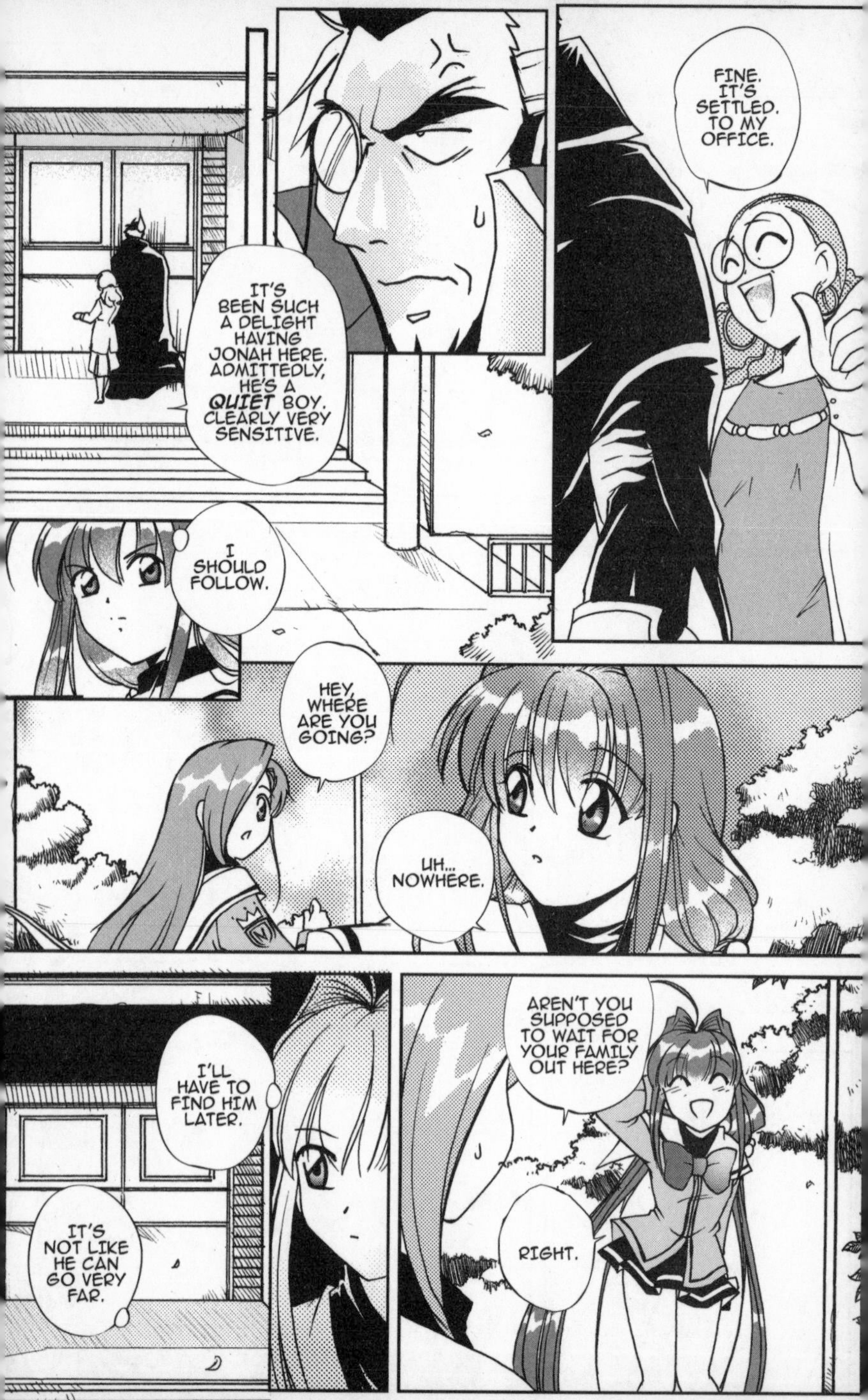
FINE. IT'S SETTLED. TO MY OFFICE.
IT'S BEEN SUCH A DELIGHT HAVING JONAH HERE. ADMITTEDLY, HE'S A *QUIET* BOY. CLEARLY VERY SENSITIVE.
I SHOULD FOLLOW.
HEY, WHERE ARE YOU GOING?
UH... NOWHERE.
AREN'T YOU SUPPOSED TO WAIT FOR YOUR FAMILY OUT HERE?
RIGHT.
I'LL HAVE TO FIND HIM LATER.
IT'S NOT LIKE HE CAN GO VERY FAR.

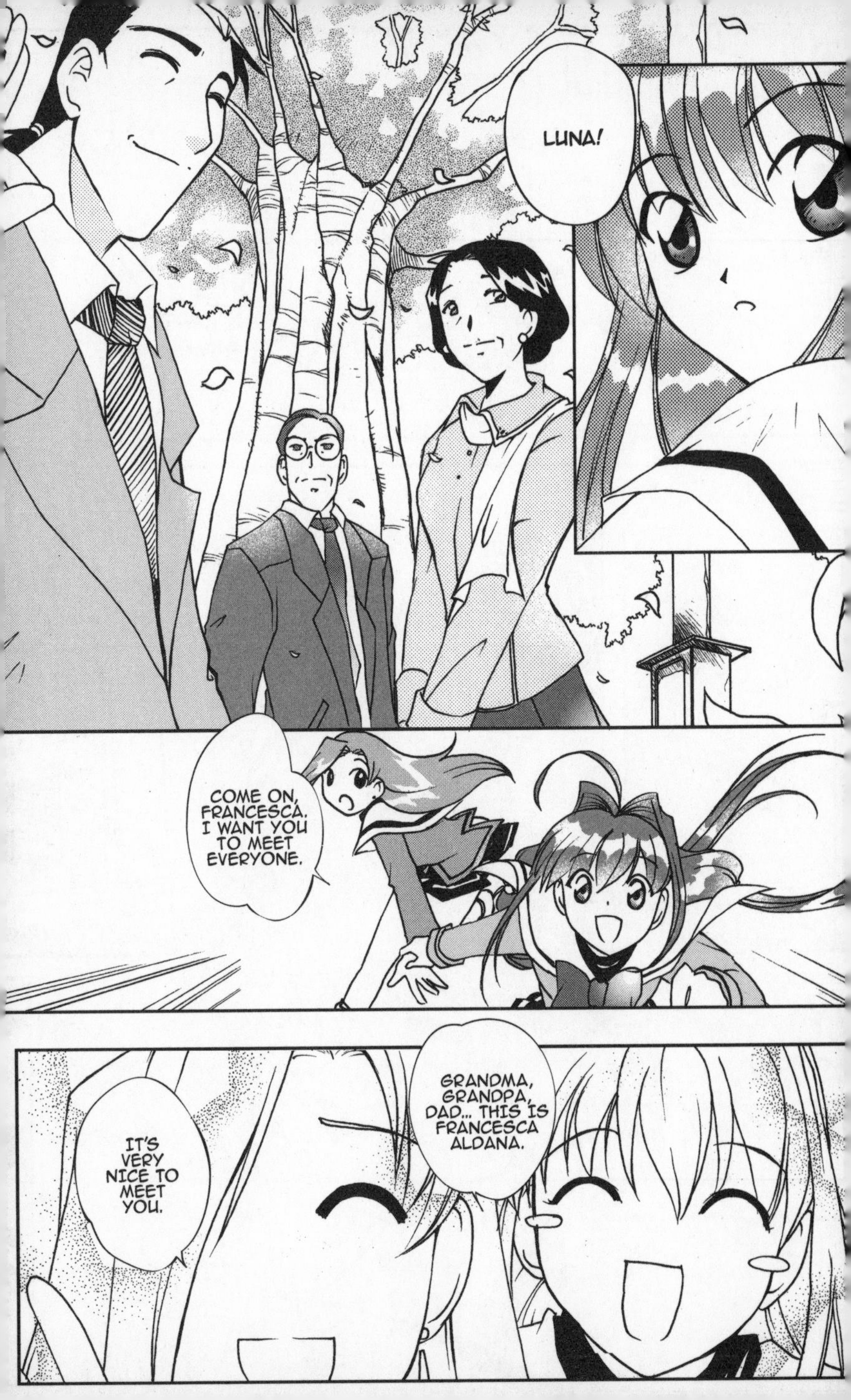
LUNA!
COME ON, FRANCESCA. I WANT YOU TO MEET EVERYONE.
GRANDMA, GRANDPA, DAD... THIS IS FRANCESCA ALDANA.
IT'S VERY NICE TO MEET YOU.

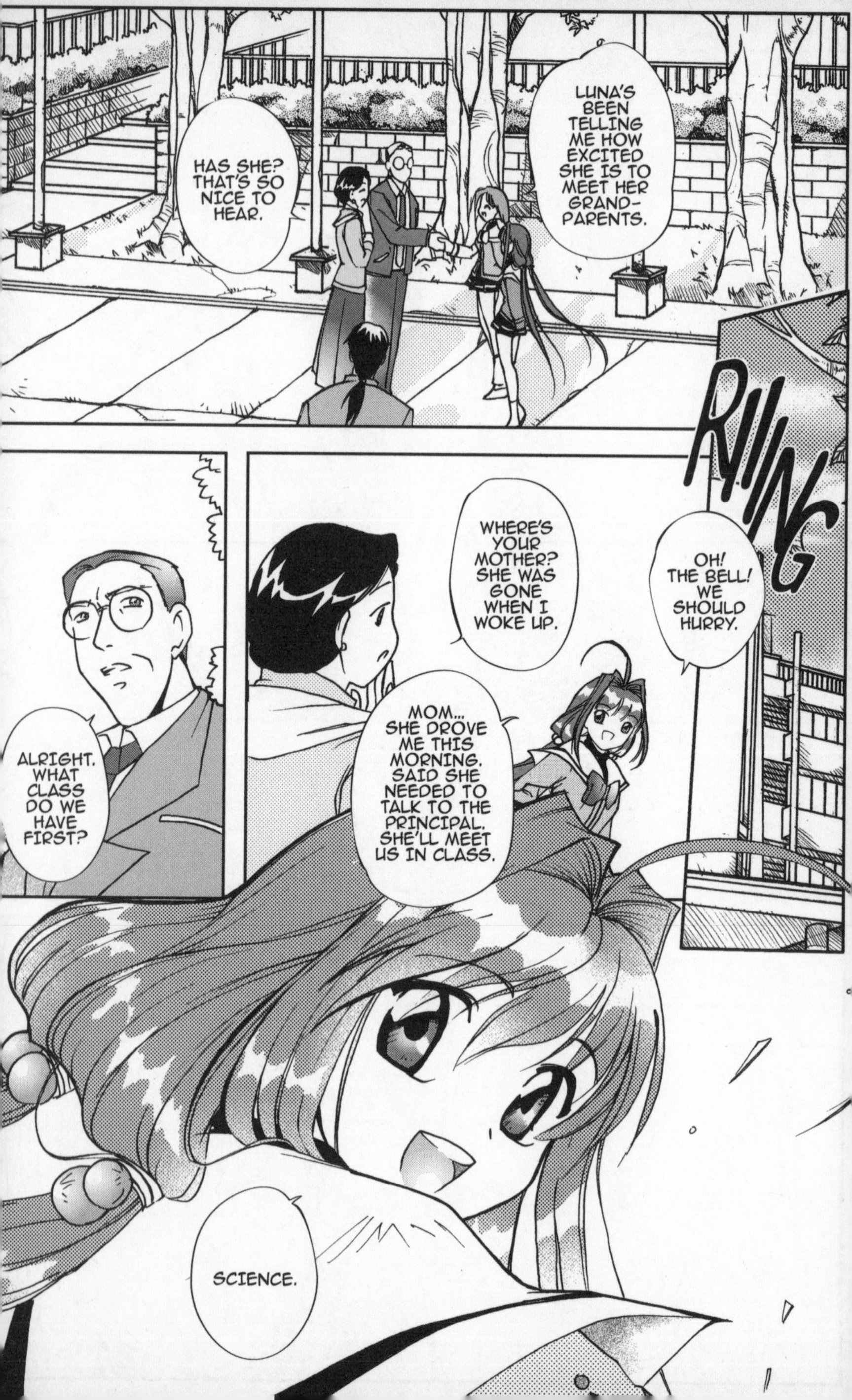
LUNA'S BEEN TELLING ME HOW EXCITED SHE IS TO MEET HER GRAND-PARENTS.
HAS SHE? THAT'S SO NICE TO HEAR.
RIING
OH! THE BELL! WE SHOULD HURRY.
WHERE'S YOUR MOTHER? SHE WAS GONE WHEN I WOKE UP.
MOM... SHE DROVE ME THIS MORNING. SAID SHE NEEDED TO TALK TO THE PRINCIPAL. SHE'LL MEET US IN CLASS.
ALRIGHT. WHAT CLASS DO WE HAVE FIRST?
SCIENCE.

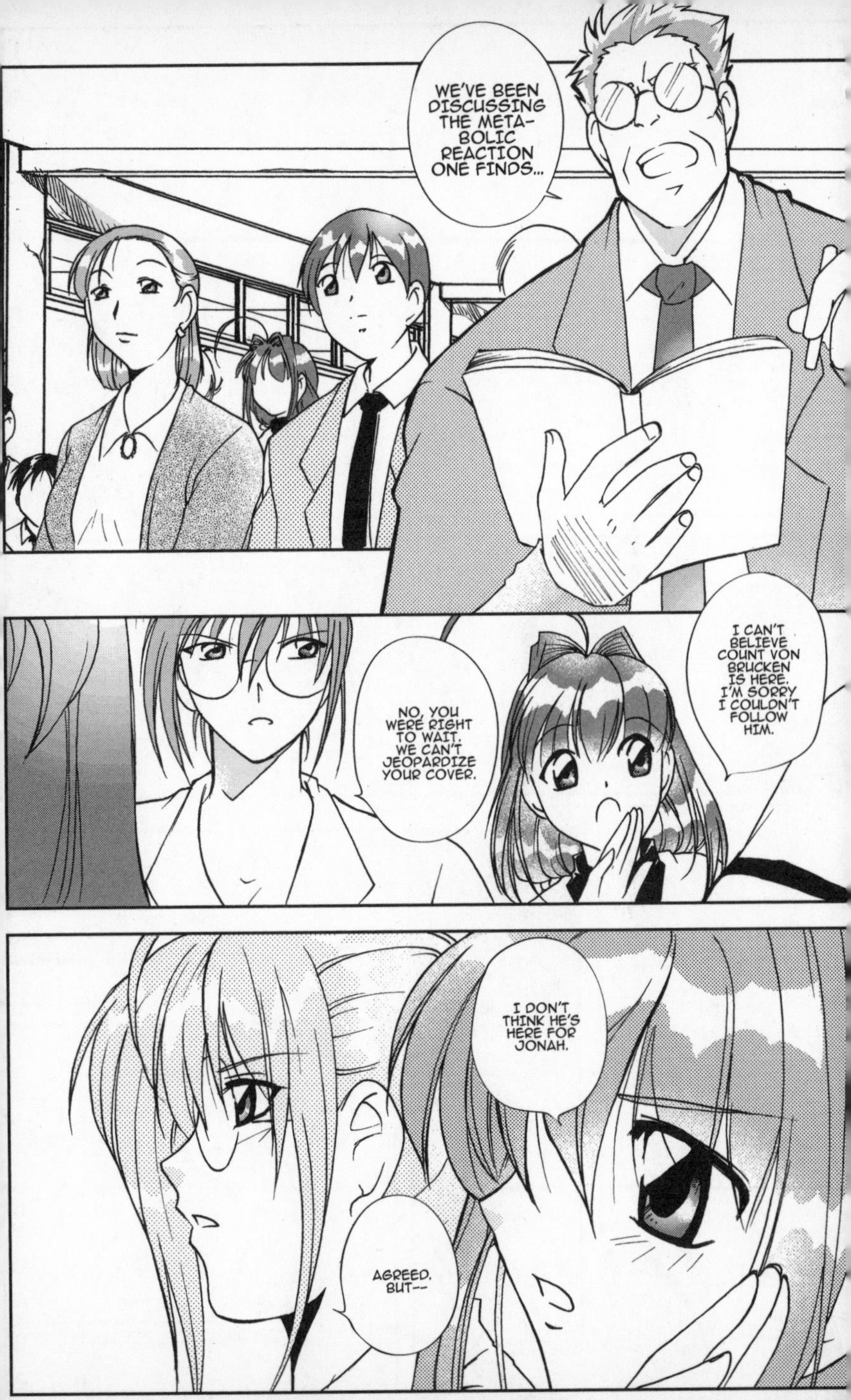
WE'VE BEEN DISCUSSING THE META-BOLIC REACTION ONE FINDS...
I CAN'T BELIEVE COUNT VON BRUCKEN IS HERE. I'M SORRY I COULDN'T FOLLOW HIM.
NO, YOU WERE RIGHT TO WAIT. WE CAN'T JEOPARDIZE YOUR COVER.
I DON'T THINK HE'S HERE FOR JONAH.
AGREED. BUT--

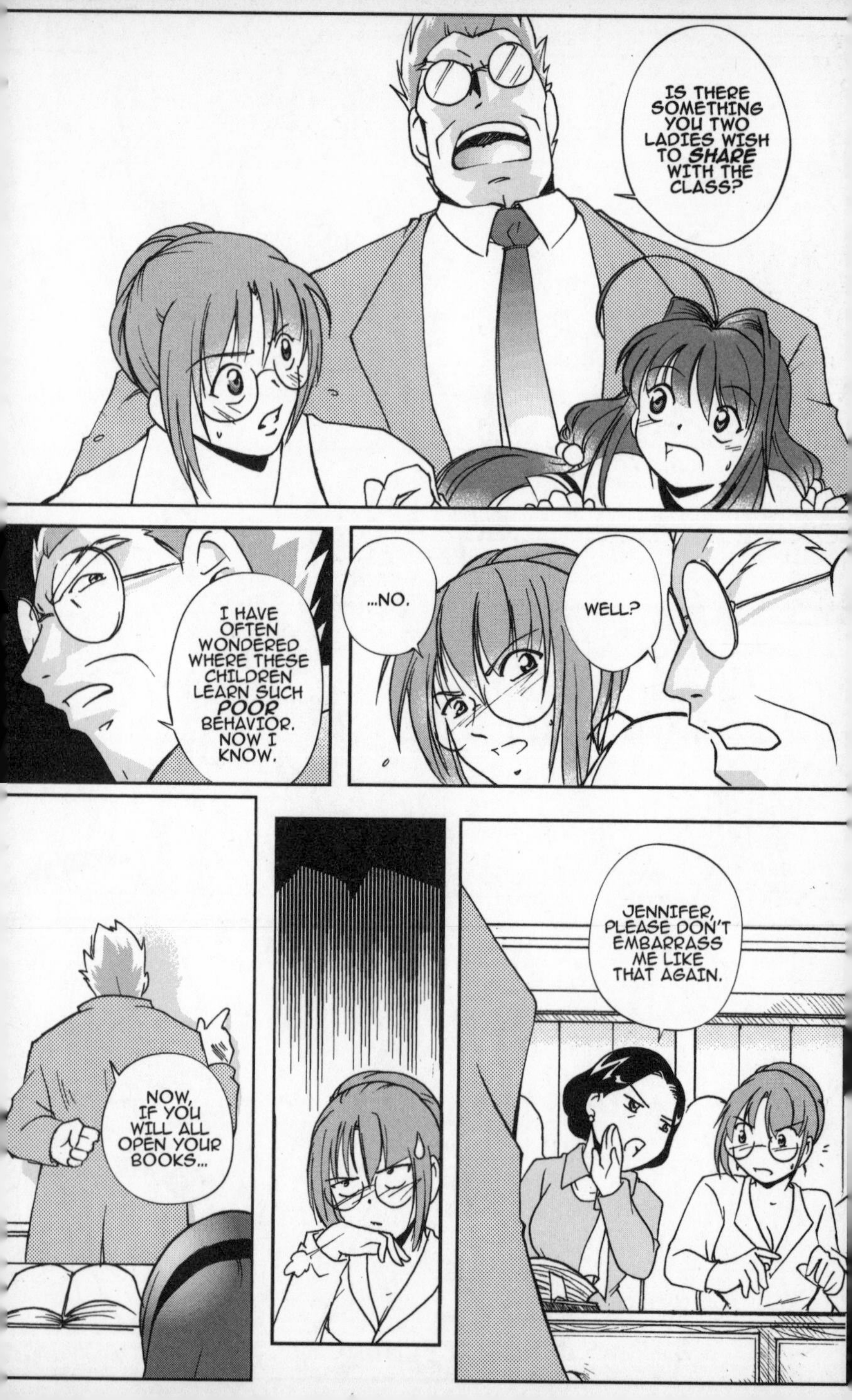
IS THERE SOMETHING YOU TWO LADIES WISH TO SHARE WITH THE CLASS?
WELL?
...NO.
I HAVE OFTEN WONDERED WHERE THESE CHILDREN LEARN SUCH POOR BEHAVIOR. NOW I KNOW.
JENNIFER, PLEASE DON'T EMBARRASS ME LIKE THAT AGAIN.
NOW, IF YOU WILL ALL OPEN YOUR BOOKS...

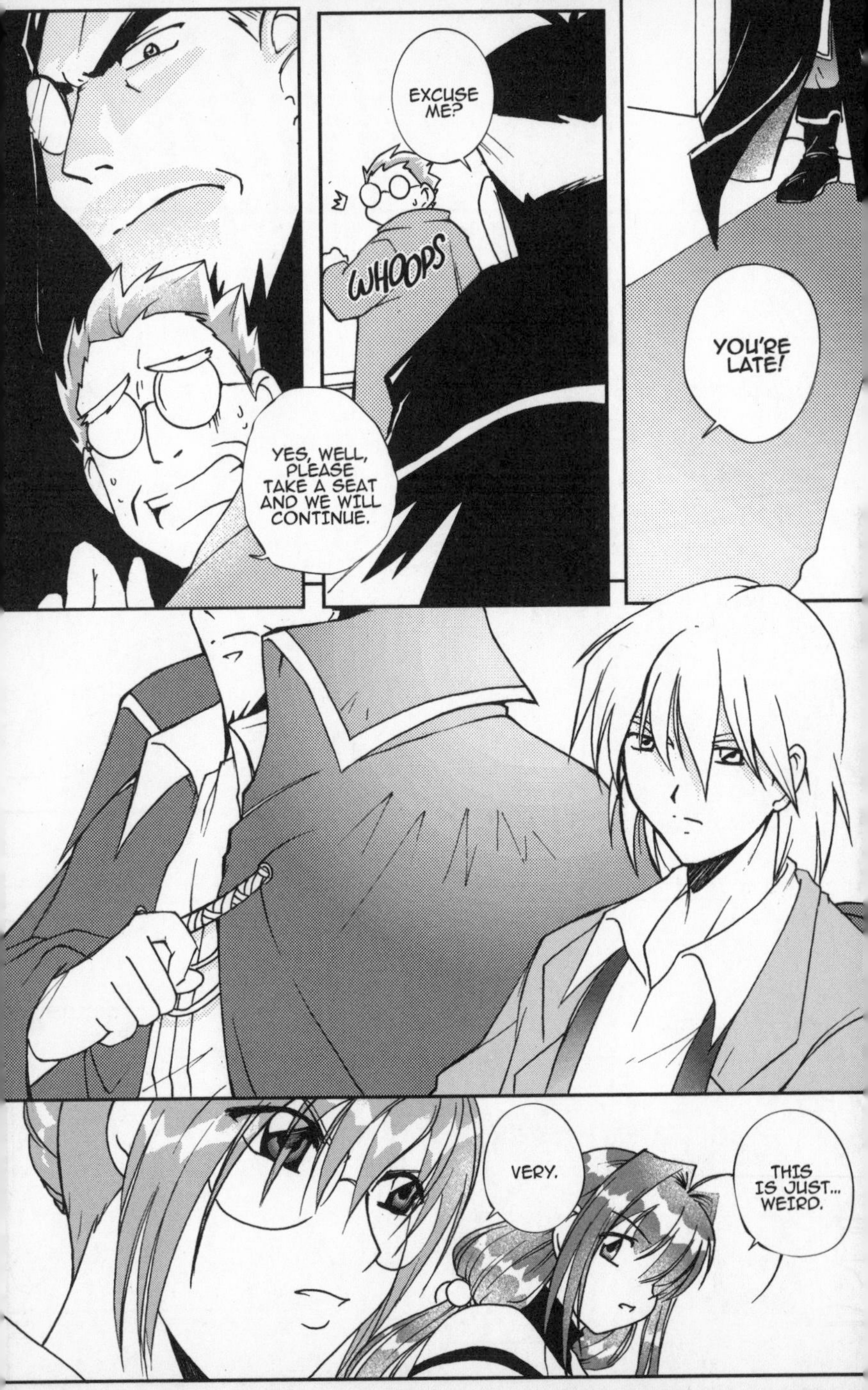
YOU'RE LATE!
EXCUSE ME?
WHOOPS
YES, WELL, PLEASE TAKE A SEAT AND WE WILL CONTINUE.
THIS IS JUST... WEIRD.
VERY.

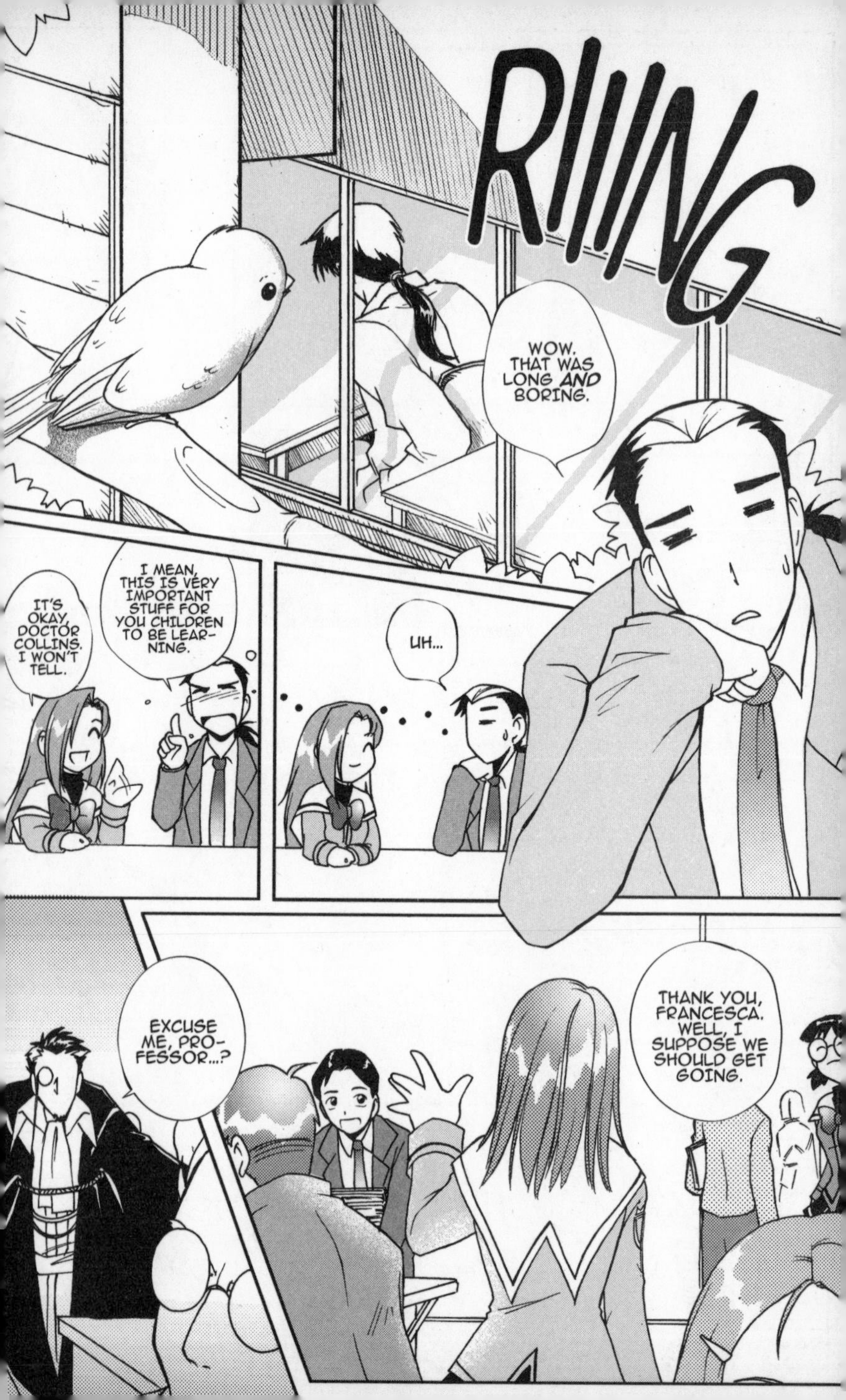
RIIING
WOW. THAT WAS LONG AND BORING.
UH...
I MEAN, THIS IS VERY IMPORTANT STUFF FOR YOU CHILDREN TO BE LEARNING.
IT'S OKAY, DOCTOR COLLINS. I WON'T TELL.
THANK YOU, FRANCESCA. WELL, I SUPPOSE WE SHOULD GET GOING.
EXCUSE ME, PRO-FESSOR...?

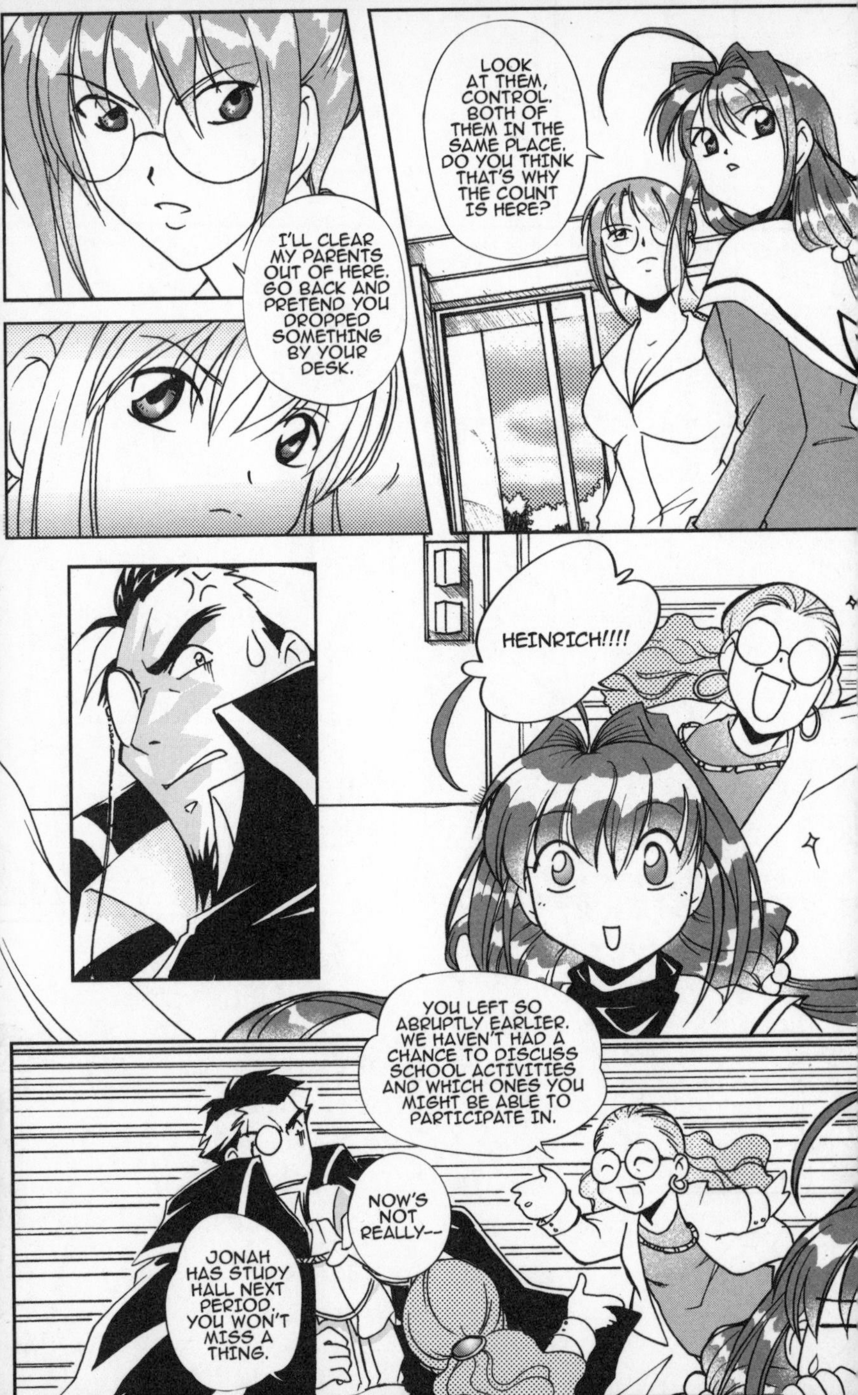
LOOK AT THEM, CONTROL. BOTH OF THEM IN THE SAME PLACE. DO YOU THINK THAT'S WHY THE COUNT IS HERE?
I'LL CLEAR MY PARENTS OUT OF HERE. GO BACK AND PRETEND YOU DROPPED SOMETHING BY YOUR DESK.
HEINRICH!!!!
YOU LEFT SO ABRUPTLY EARLIER. WE HAVEN'T HAD A CHANCE TO DISCUSS SCHOOL ACTIVITIES AND WHICH ONES YOU MIGHT BE ABLE TO PARTICIPATE IN.
NOW'S NOT REALLY--
JONAH HAS STUDY HALL NEXT PERIOD. YOU WON'T MISS A THING.

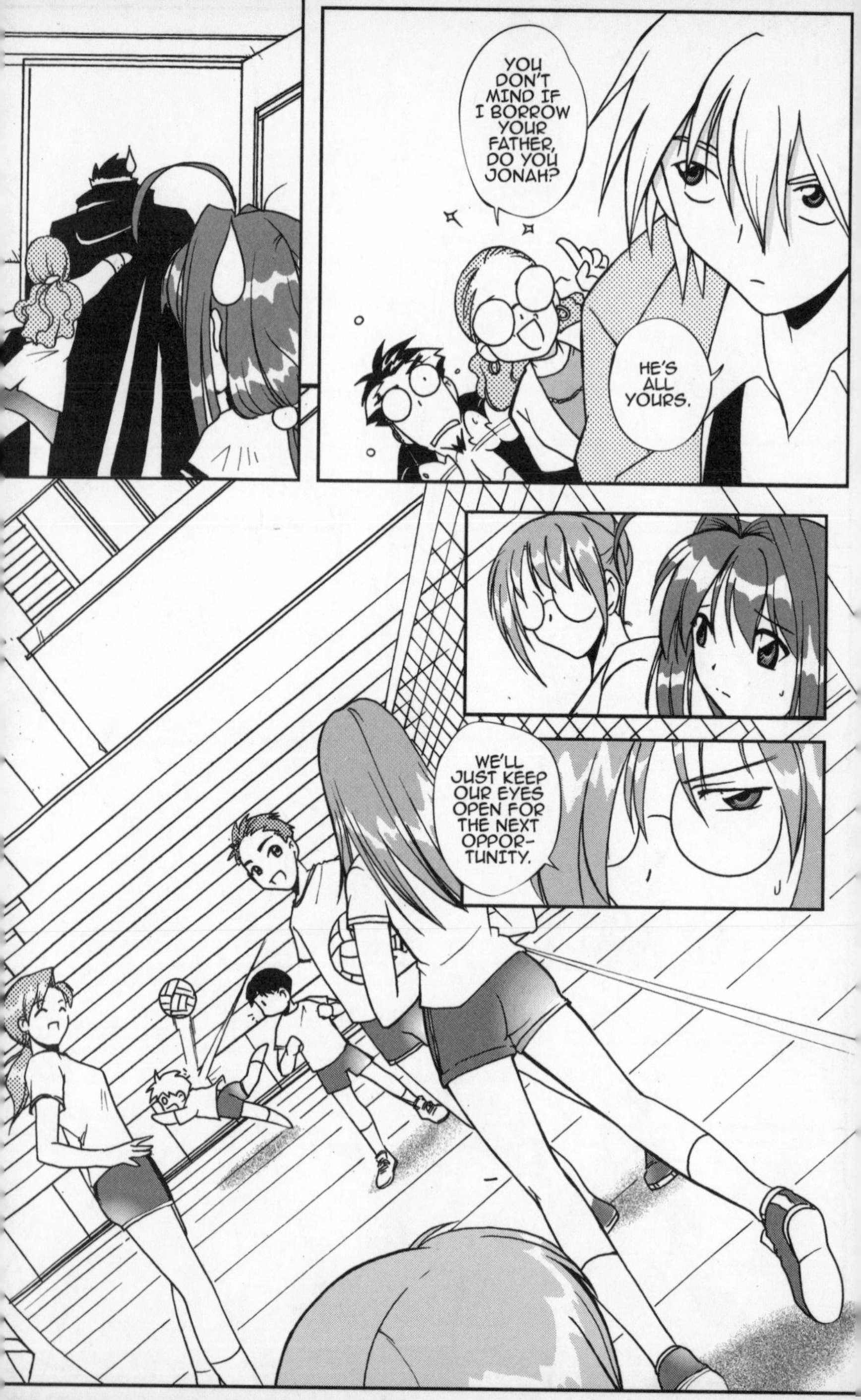
YOU DON'T MIND IF I BORROW YOUR FATHER, DO YOU JONAH?
HE'S ALL YOURS.
WE'LL JUST KEEP OUR EYES OPEN FOR THE NEXT OPPOR-TUNITY.

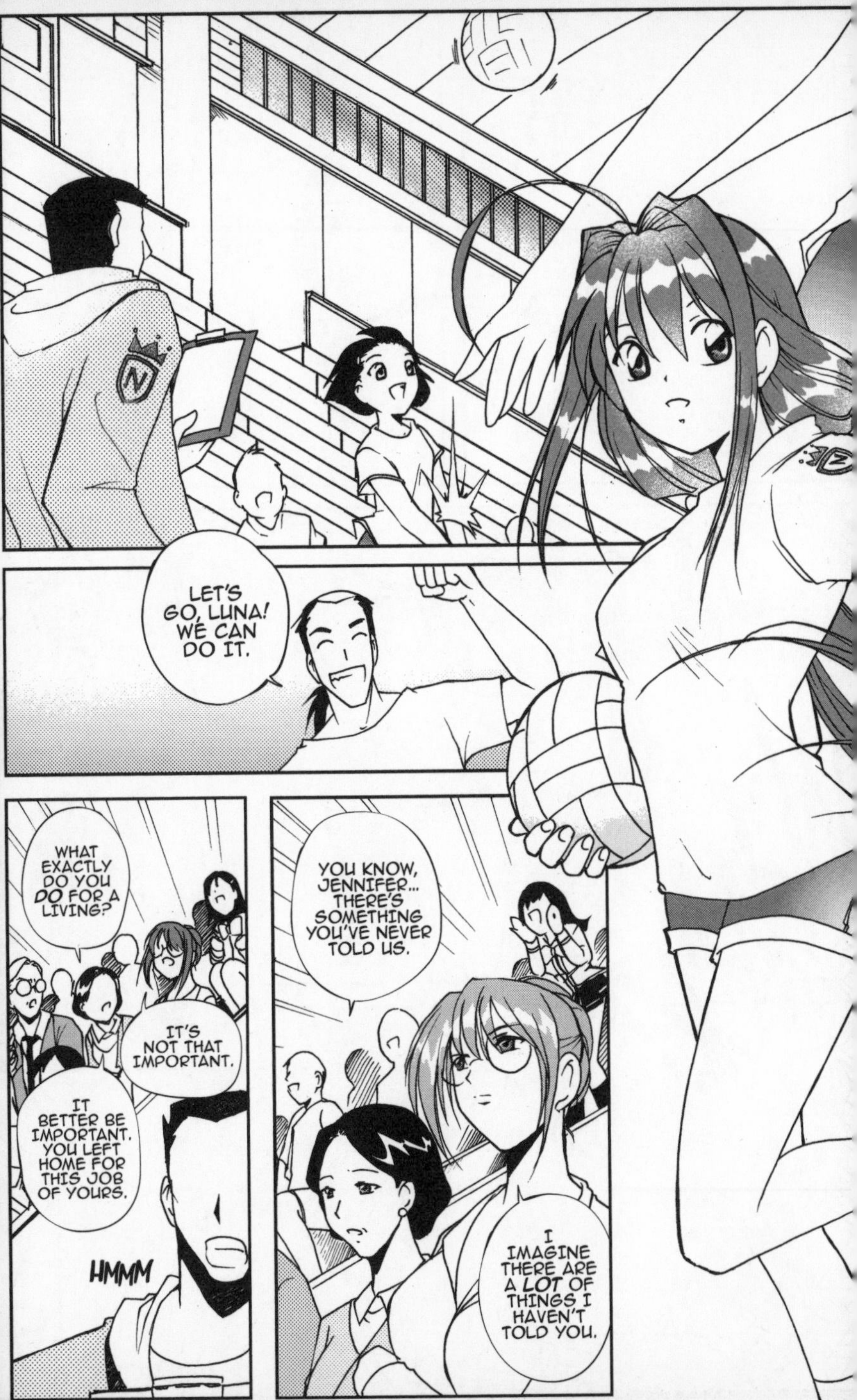
LET'S GO, LUNA! WE CAN DO IT.
YOU KNOW, JENNIFER... THERE'S SOMETHING YOU'VE NEVER TOLD US.
I IMAGINE THERE ARE A *LOT* OF THINGS I HAVEN'T TOLD YOU.
WHAT EXACTLY DO YOU *DO* FOR A LIVING?
IT'S NOT THAT IMPORTANT.
IT BETTER BE IMPORTANT. YOU LEFT HOME FOR THIS JOB OF YOURS.
HMMM

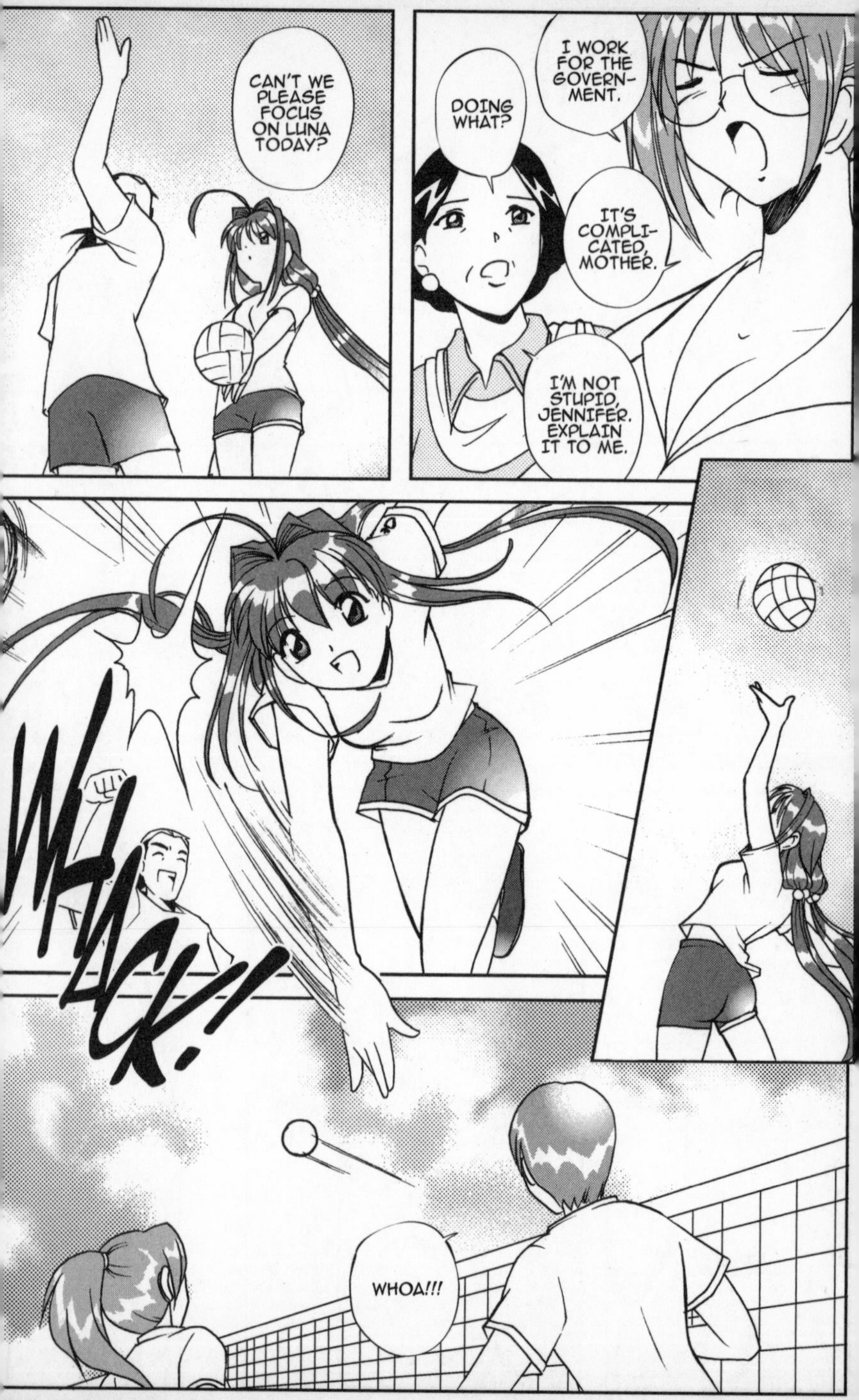
I WORK FOR THE GOVERNMENT.
DOING WHAT?
IT'S COMPLICATED, MOTHER.
I'M NOT STUPID, JENNIFER. EXPLAIN IT TO ME.
CAN'T WE PLEASE FOCUS ON LUNA TODAY?
WHACK!!
WHOA!!!

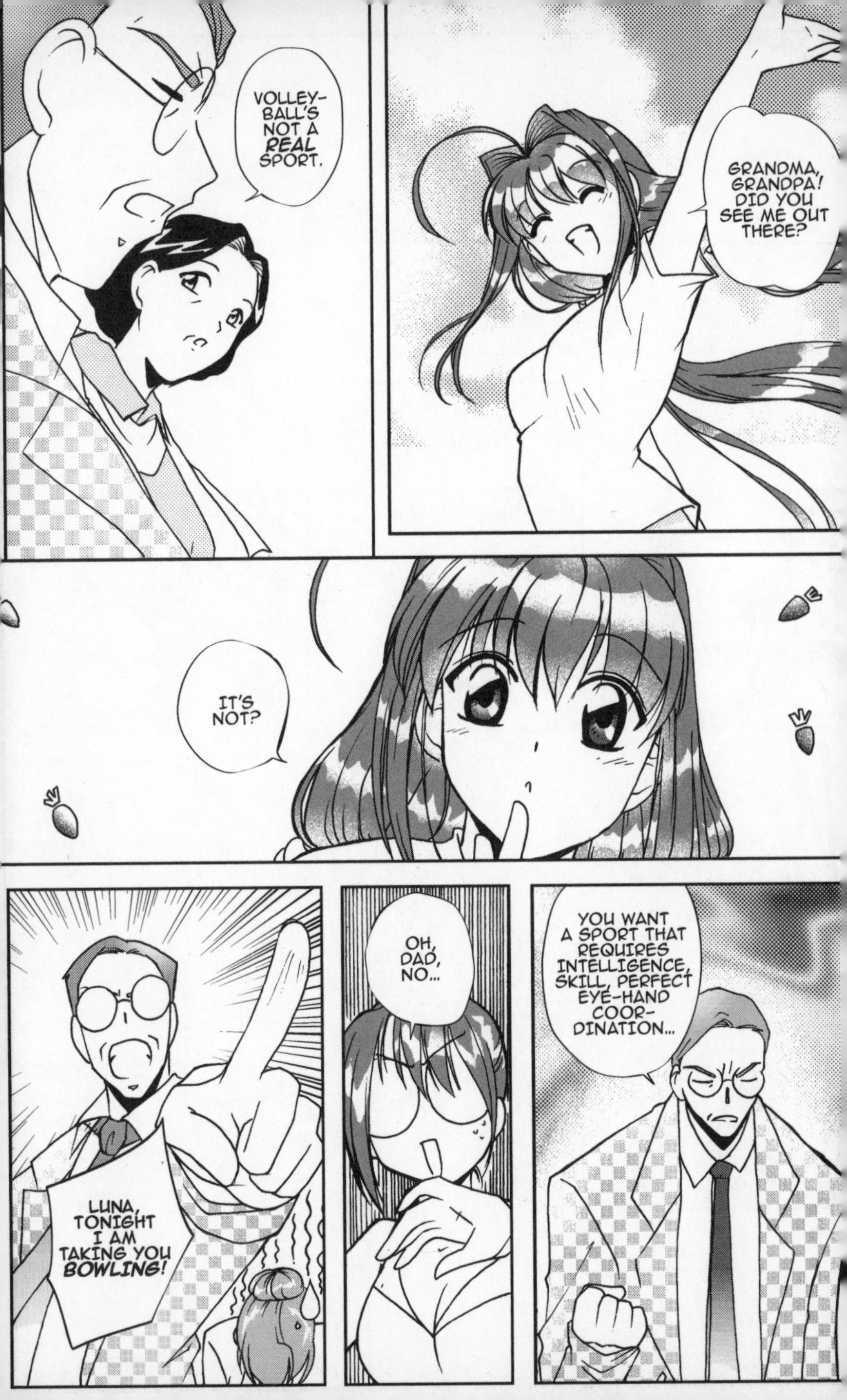
GRANDMA, GRANDPA! DID YOU SEE ME OUT THERE?
VOLLEY-BALL'S NOT A *REAL* SPORT.
IT'S NOT?
YOU WANT A SPORT THAT REQUIRES INTELLIGENCE, SKILL, PERFECT EYE-HAND COOR-DINATION...
OH, DAD, NO...
LUNA, TONIGHT I AM TAKING YOU *BOWLING*!

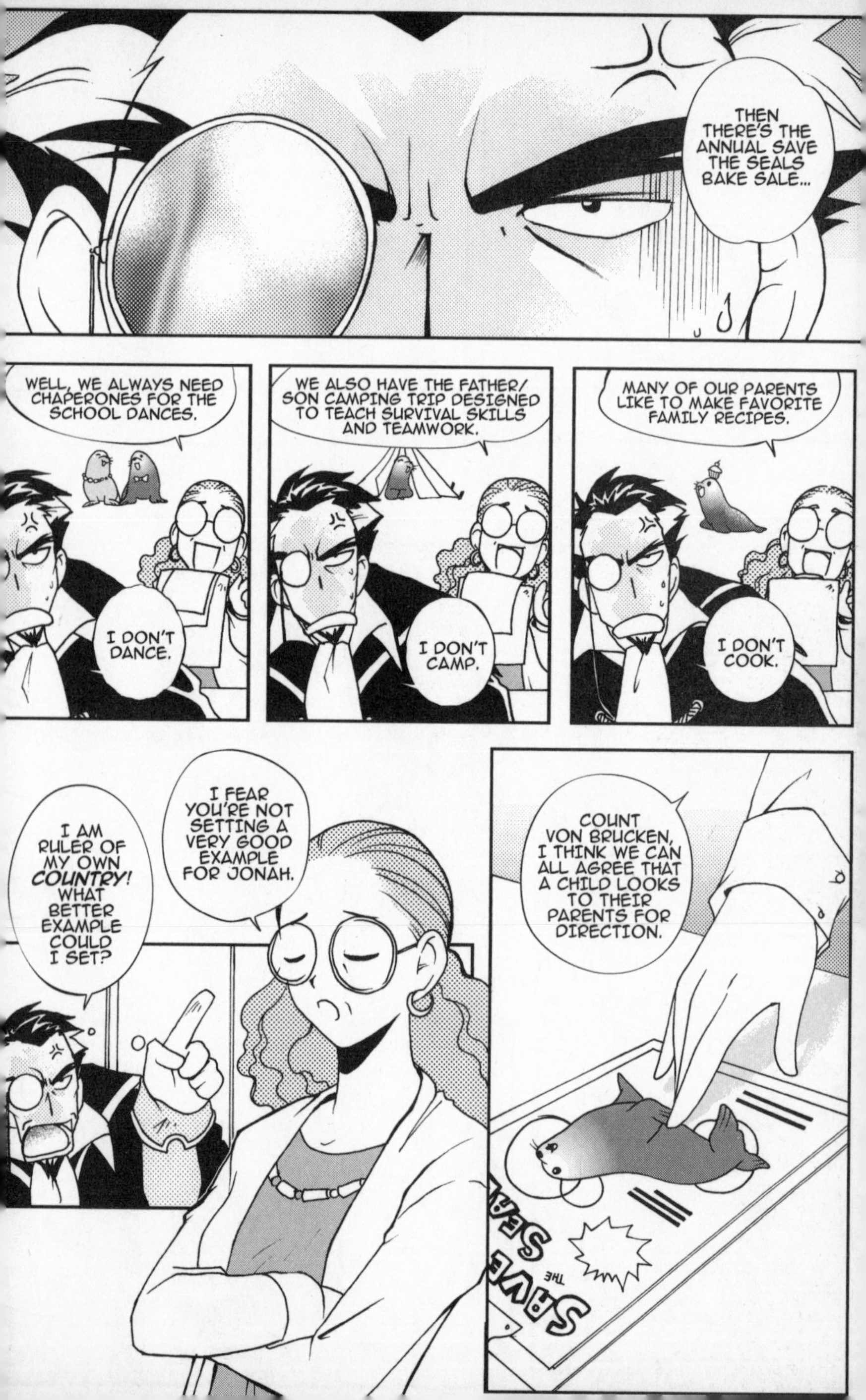
THEN THERE'S THE ANNUAL SAVE THE SEALS BAKE SALE...
MANY OF OUR PARENTS LIKE TO MAKE FAVORITE FAMILY RECIPES.
I DON'T COOK.
WE ALSO HAVE THE FATHER/SON CAMPING TRIP DESIGNED TO TEACH SURVIVAL SKILLS AND TEAMWORK.
I DON'T CAMP.
WELL, WE ALWAYS NEED CHAPERONES FOR THE SCHOOL DANCES.
I DON'T DANCE.
COUNT VON BRUCKEN, I THINK WE CAN ALL AGREE THAT A CHILD LOOKS TO THEIR PARENTS FOR DIRECTION.
SAVE THE
I FEAR YOU'RE NOT SETTING A VERY GOOD EXAMPLE FOR JONAH.
I AM RULER OF MY OWN ***COUNTRY***! WHAT BETTER EXAMPLE COULD I SET?

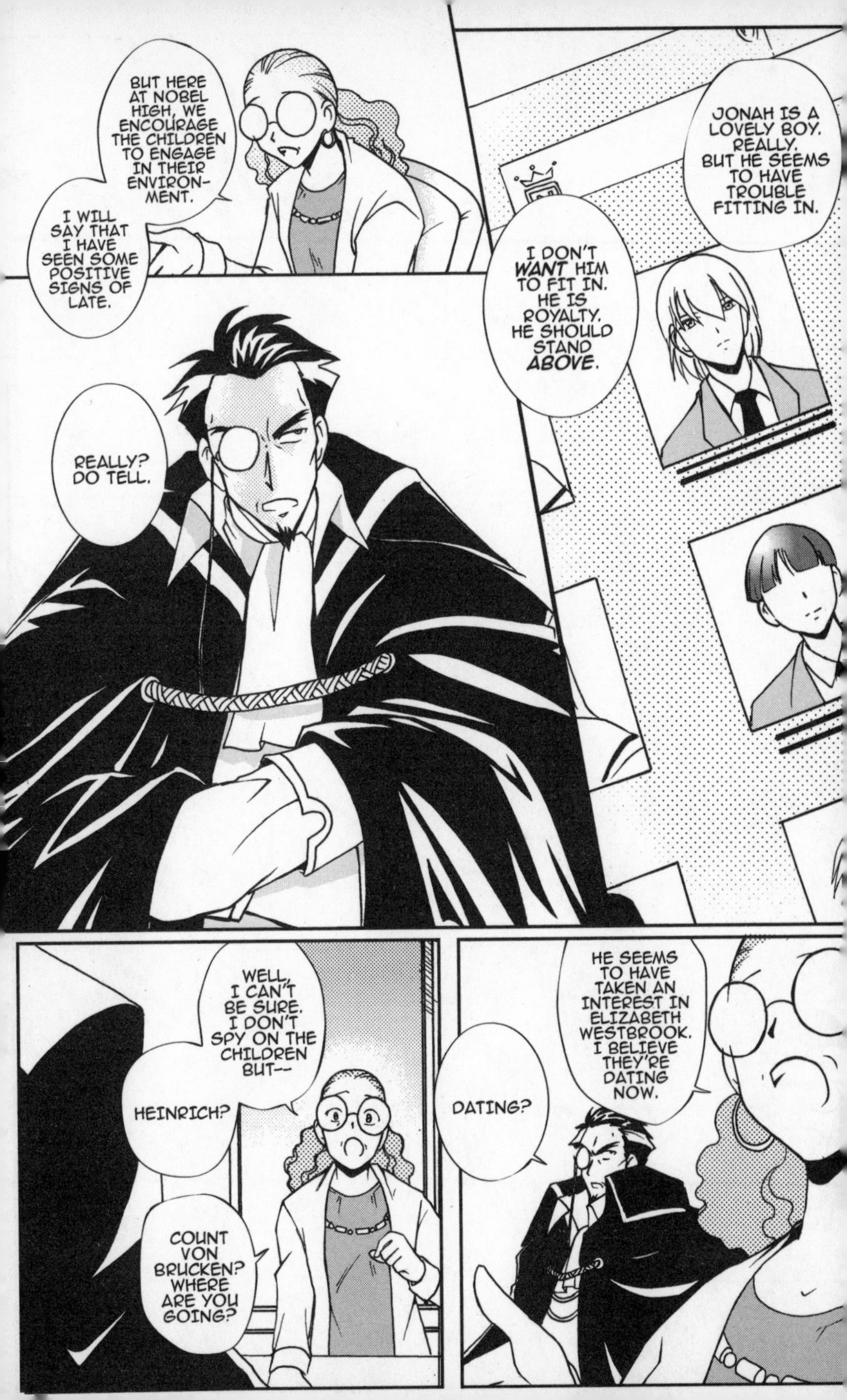
JONAH IS A LOVELY BOY. REALLY. BUT HE SEEMS TO HAVE TROUBLE FITTING IN.
I DON'T *WANT* HIM TO FIT IN. HE IS ROYALTY. HE SHOULD STAND *ABOVE*.
BUT HERE AT NOBEL HIGH, WE ENCOURAGE THE CHILDREN TO ENGAGE IN THEIR ENVIRONMENT.
I WILL SAY THAT I HAVE SEEN SOME POSITIVE SIGNS OF LATE.
REALLY? DO TELL.
HE SEEMS TO HAVE TAKEN AN INTEREST IN ELIZABETH WESTBROOK. I BELIEVE THEY'RE DATING NOW.
DATING?
WELL, I CAN'T BE SURE. I DON'T SPY ON THE CHILDREN BUT--
HEINRICH?
COUNT VON BRUCKEN? WHERE ARE YOU GOING?

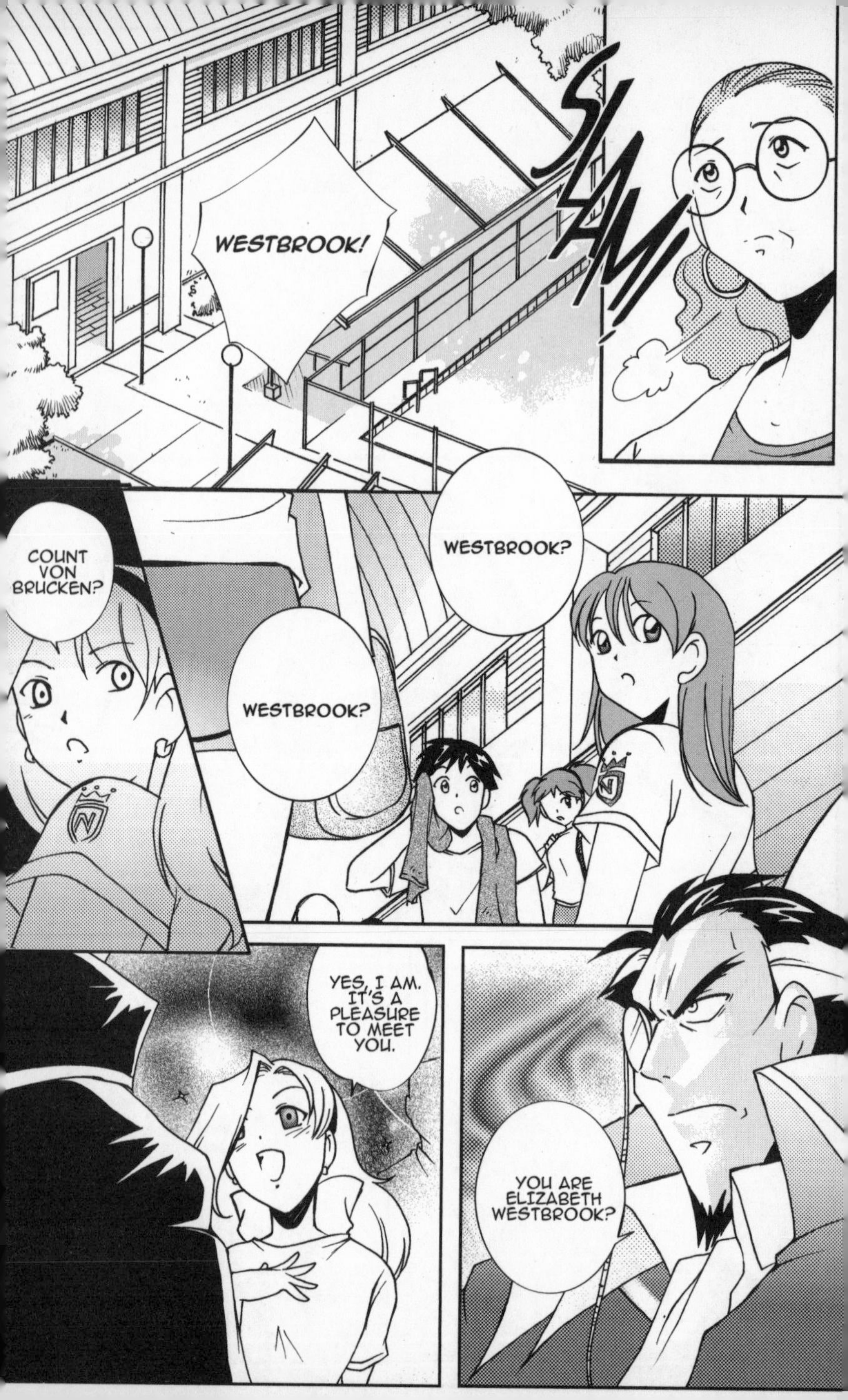
SLAM!
WESTBROOK!
WESTBROOK?
WESTBROOK?
COUNT VON BRUCKEN?
YOU ARE ELIZABETH WESTBROOK?
YES, I AM. IT'S A PLEASURE TO MEET YOU.

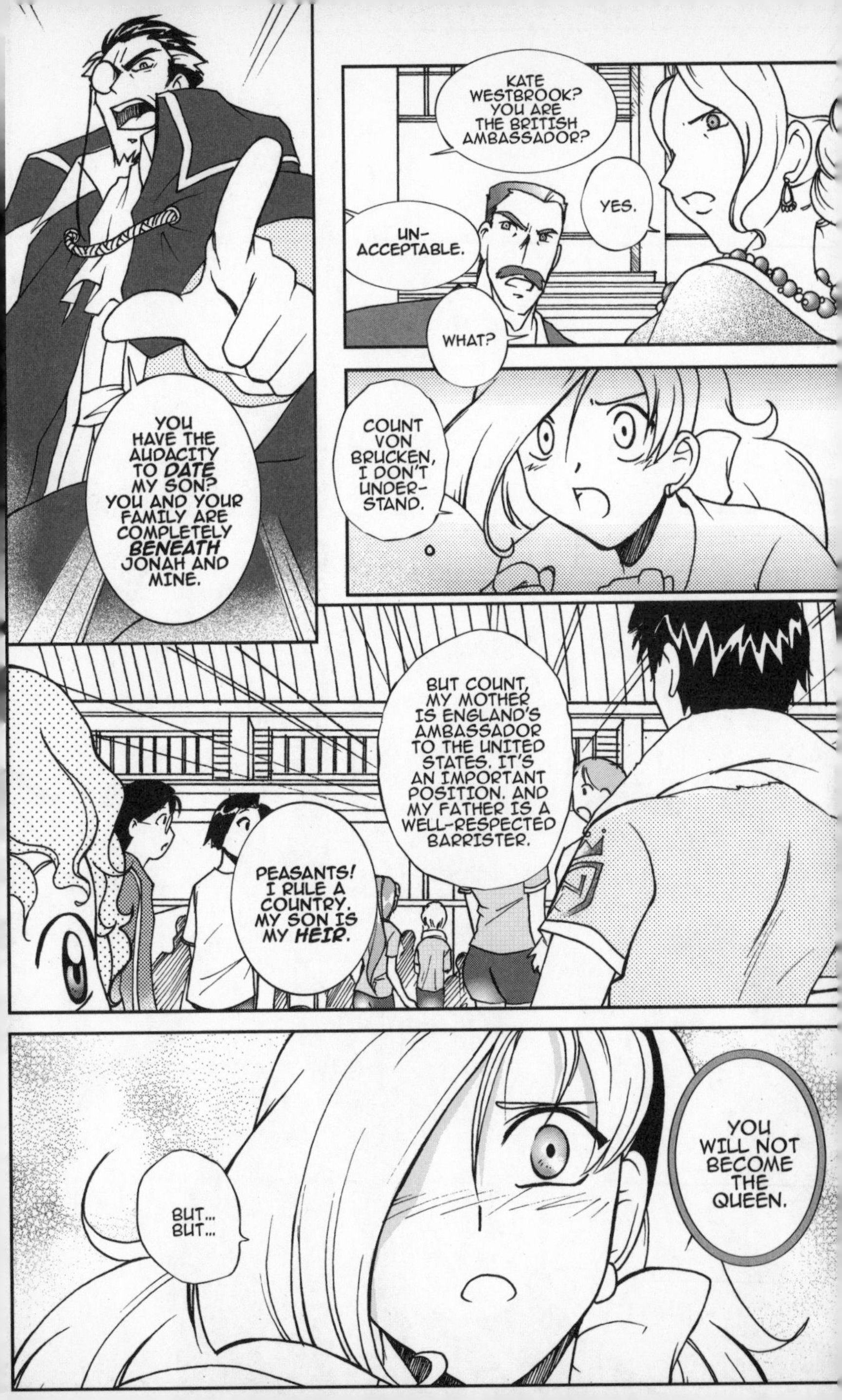
KATE WESTBROOK? YOU ARE THE BRITISH AMBASSADOR?
YES.
UN-ACCEPTABLE.
WHAT?
COUNT VON BRUCKEN, I DON'T UNDER-STAND.
YOU HAVE THE AUDACITY TO *DATE* MY SON? YOU AND YOUR FAMILY ARE COMPLETELY ***BENEATH*** JONAH AND MINE.
BUT COUNT, MY MOTHER IS ENGLAND'S AMBASSADOR TO THE UNITED STATES. IT'S AN IMPORTANT POSITION. AND MY FATHER IS A WELL-RESPECTED BARRISTER.
PEASANTS! I RULE A COUNTRY. MY SON IS MY ***HEIR***.
YOU WILL NOT BECOME THE QUEEN.
BUT... BUT...

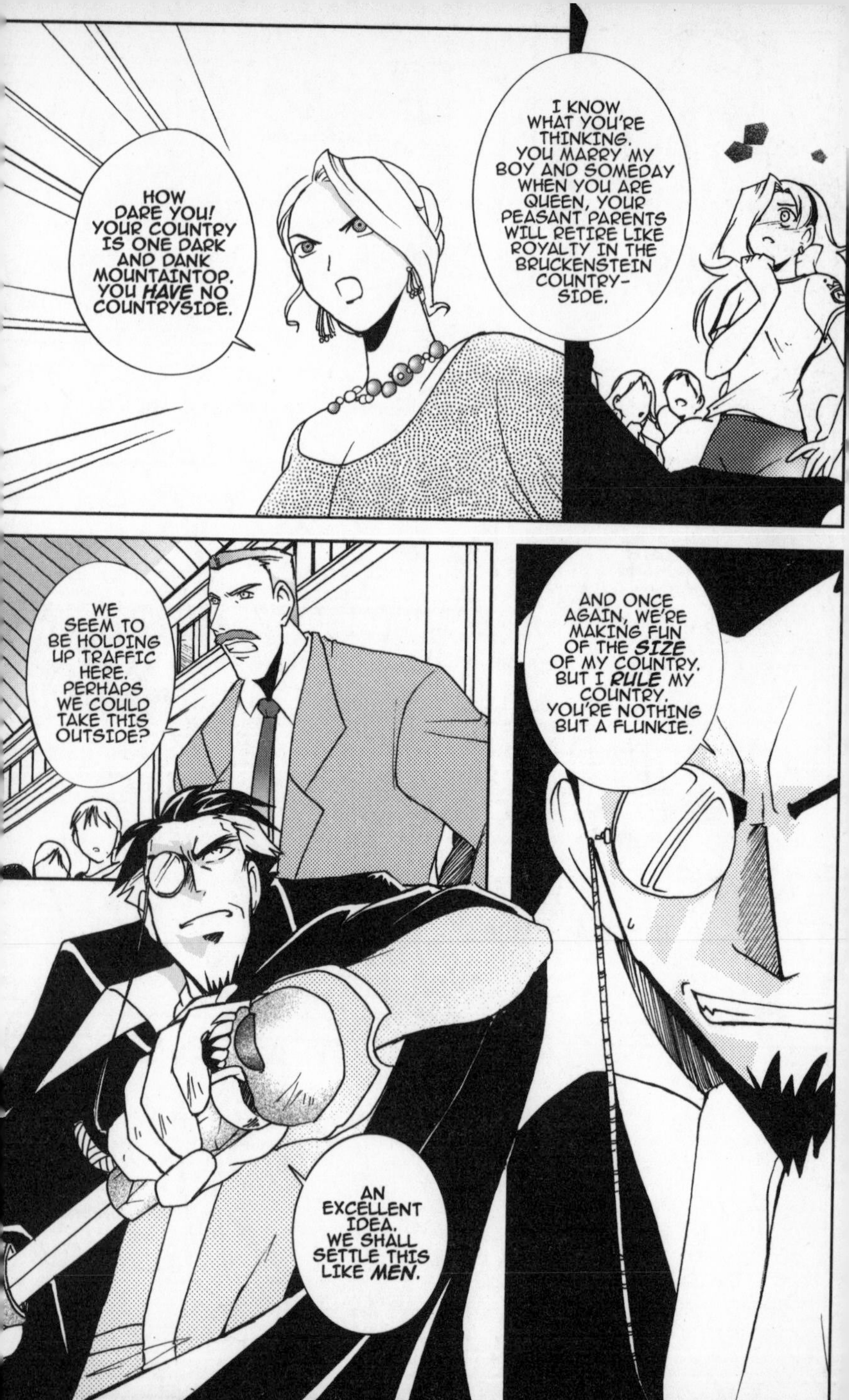
I KNOW WHAT YOU'RE THINKING. YOU MARRY MY BOY AND SOMEDAY WHEN YOU ARE QUEEN, YOUR PEASANT PARENTS WILL RETIRE LIKE ROYALTY IN THE BRUCKENSTEIN COUNTRY-SIDE.
HOW DARE YOU! YOUR COUNTRY IS ONE DARK AND DANK MOUNTAINTOP. YOU *HAVE* NO COUNTRYSIDE.
AND ONCE AGAIN, WE'RE MAKING FUN OF THE *SIZE* OF MY COUNTRY. BUT I *RULE* MY COUNTRY. YOU'RE NOTHING BUT A FLUNKIE.
WE SEEM TO BE HOLDING UP TRAFFIC HERE. PERHAPS WE COULD TAKE THIS OUTSIDE?
AN EXCELLENT IDEA. WE SHALL SETTLE THIS LIKE *MEN*.

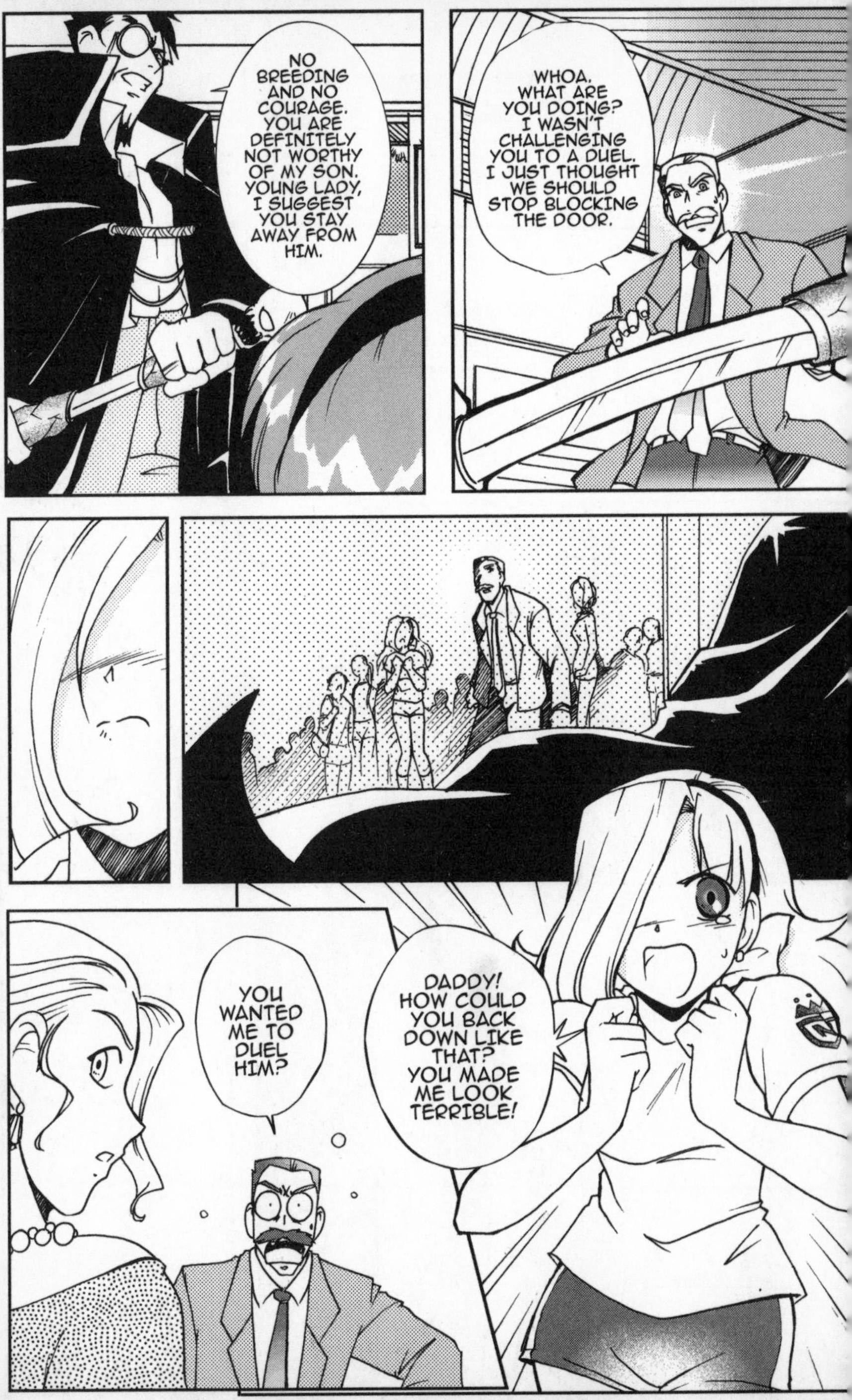
WHOA. WHAT ARE YOU DOING? I WASN'T CHALLENGING YOU TO A DUEL. I JUST THOUGHT WE SHOULD STOP BLOCKING THE DOOR.
NO BREEDING AND NO COURAGE. YOU ARE DEFINITELY NOT WORTHY OF MY SON. YOUNG LADY, I SUGGEST YOU STAY AWAY FROM HIM.
DADDY! HOW COULD YOU BACK DOWN LIKE THAT? YOU MADE ME LOOK TERRIBLE!
YOU WANTED ME TO DUEL HIM?

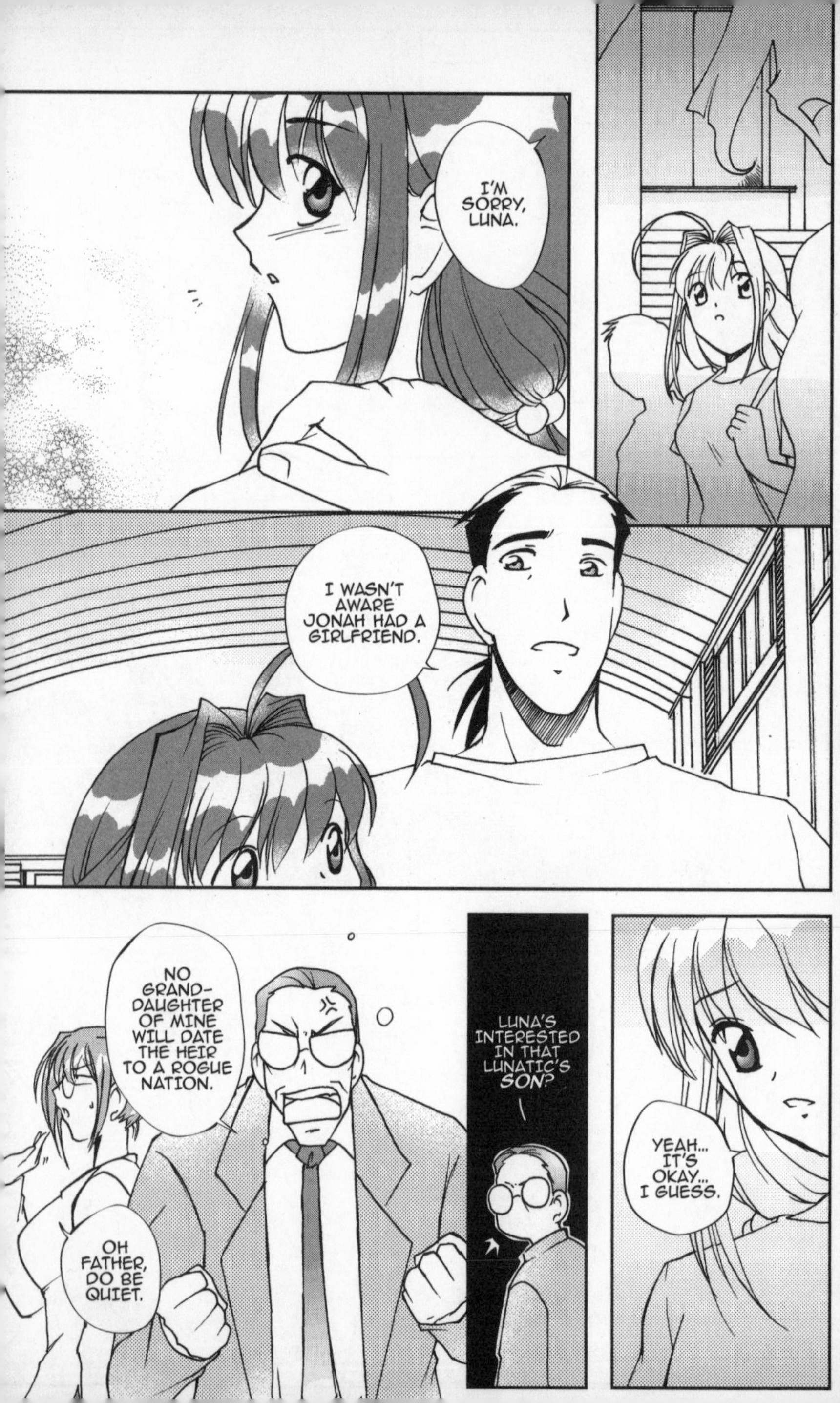
I'M SORRY, LUNA.
I WASN'T AWARE JONAH HAD A GIRLFRIEND.
YEAH... IT'S OKAY... I GUESS.
LUNA'S INTERESTED IN THAT LUNATIC'S *SON*?
NO GRAND-DAUGHTER OF MINE WILL DATE THE HEIR TO A ROGUE NATION.
OH FATHER, DO BE QUIET.

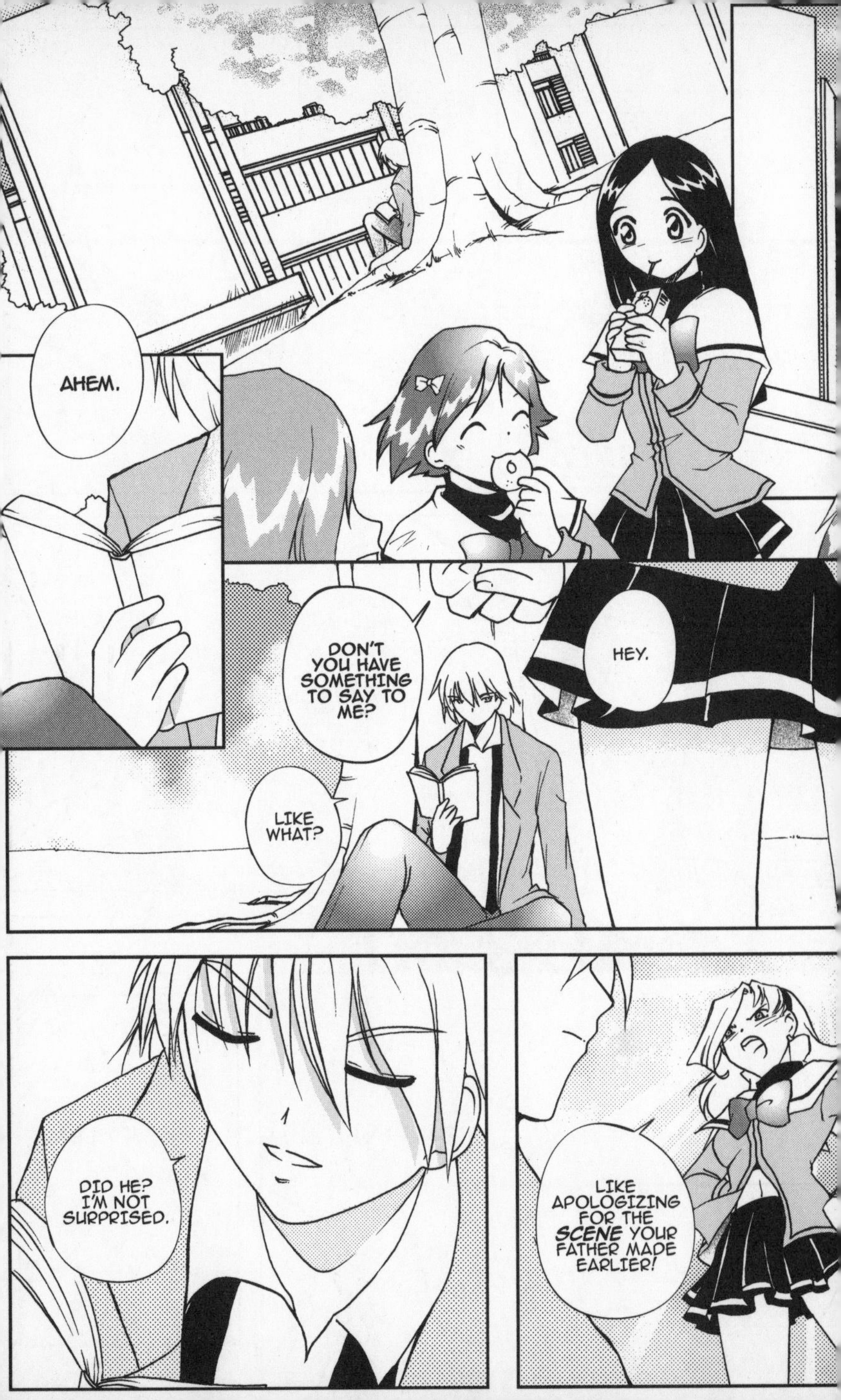
AHEM.
HEY.
DON'T YOU HAVE SOMETHING TO SAY TO ME?
LIKE WHAT?
LIKE APOLOGIZING FOR THE SCENE YOUR FATHER MADE EARLIER!
DID HE? I'M NOT SURPRISED.

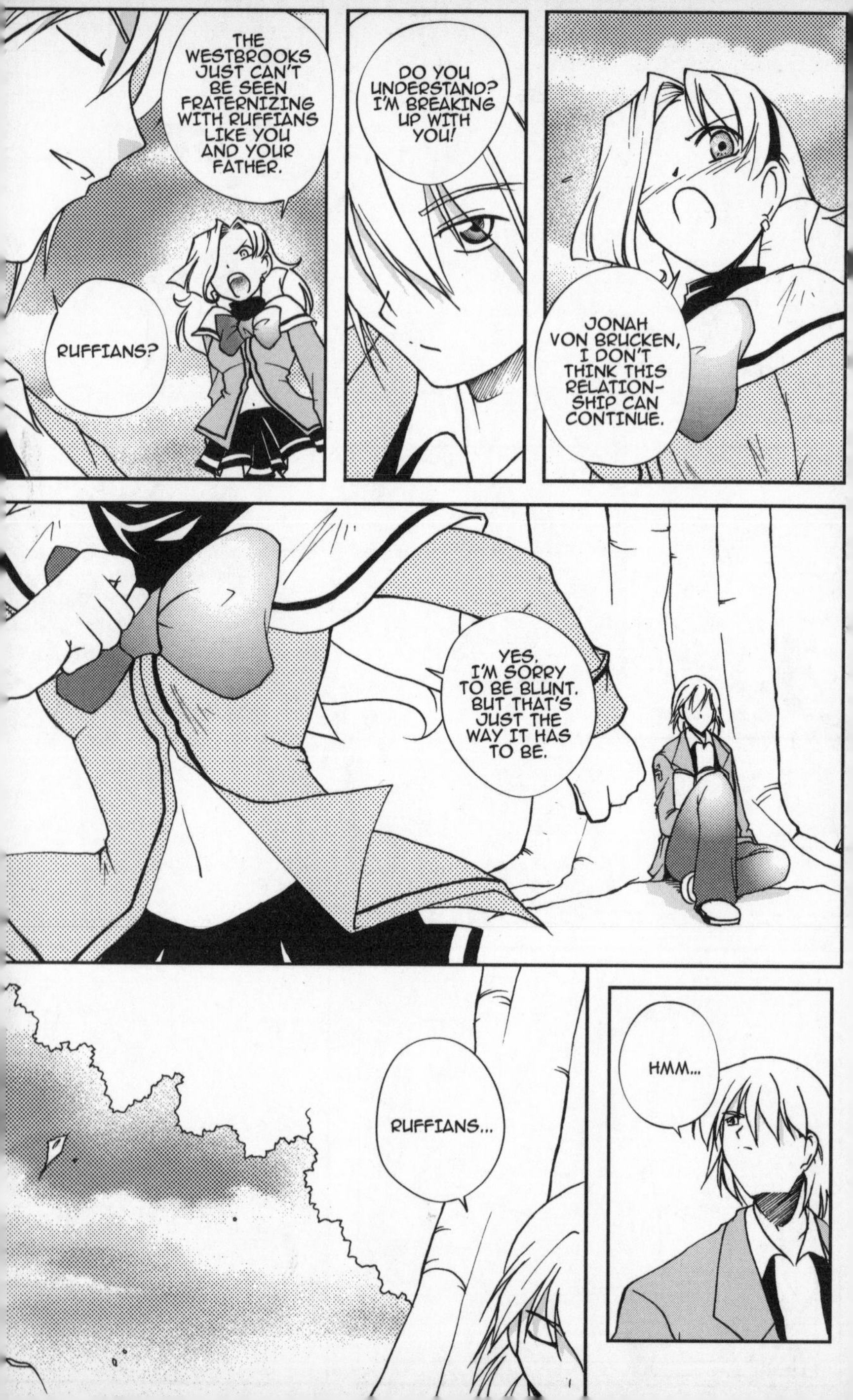
JONAH VON BRUCKEN, I DON'T THINK THIS RELATION-SHIP CAN CONTINUE.
DO YOU UNDERSTAND? I'M BREAKING UP WITH YOU!
THE WESTBROOKS JUST CAN'T BE SEEN FRATERNIZING WITH RUFFIANS LIKE YOU AND YOUR FATHER.
RUFFIANS?
YES. I'M SORRY TO BE BLUNT. BUT THAT'S JUST THE WAY IT HAS TO BE.
HMM...
RUFFIANS...

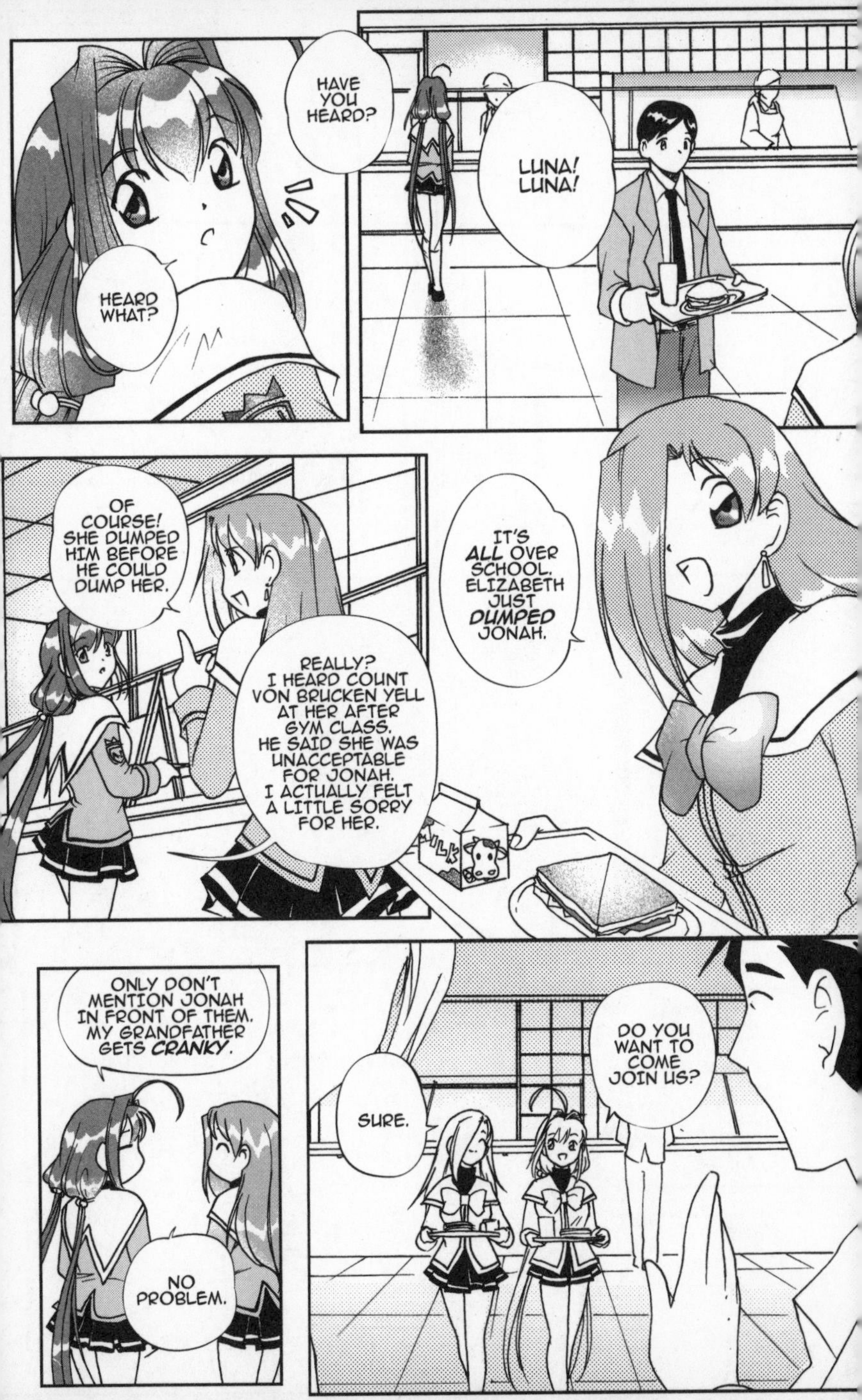
LUNA! LUNA!
HAVE YOU HEARD?
HEARD WHAT?
IT'S *ALL* OVER SCHOOL. ELIZABETH JUST *DUMPED* JONAH.
OF COURSE! SHE DUMPED HIM BEFORE HE COULD DUMP HER.
REALLY? I HEARD COUNT VON BRUCKEN YELL AT HER AFTER GYM CLASS. HE SAID SHE WAS UNACCEPTABLE FOR JONAH. I ACTUALLY FELT A LITTLE SORRY FOR HER.
MILK
DO YOU WANT TO COME JOIN US?
SURE.
ONLY DON'T MENTION JONAH IN FRONT OF THEM. MY GRANDFATHER GETS *CRANKY*.
NO PROBLEM.

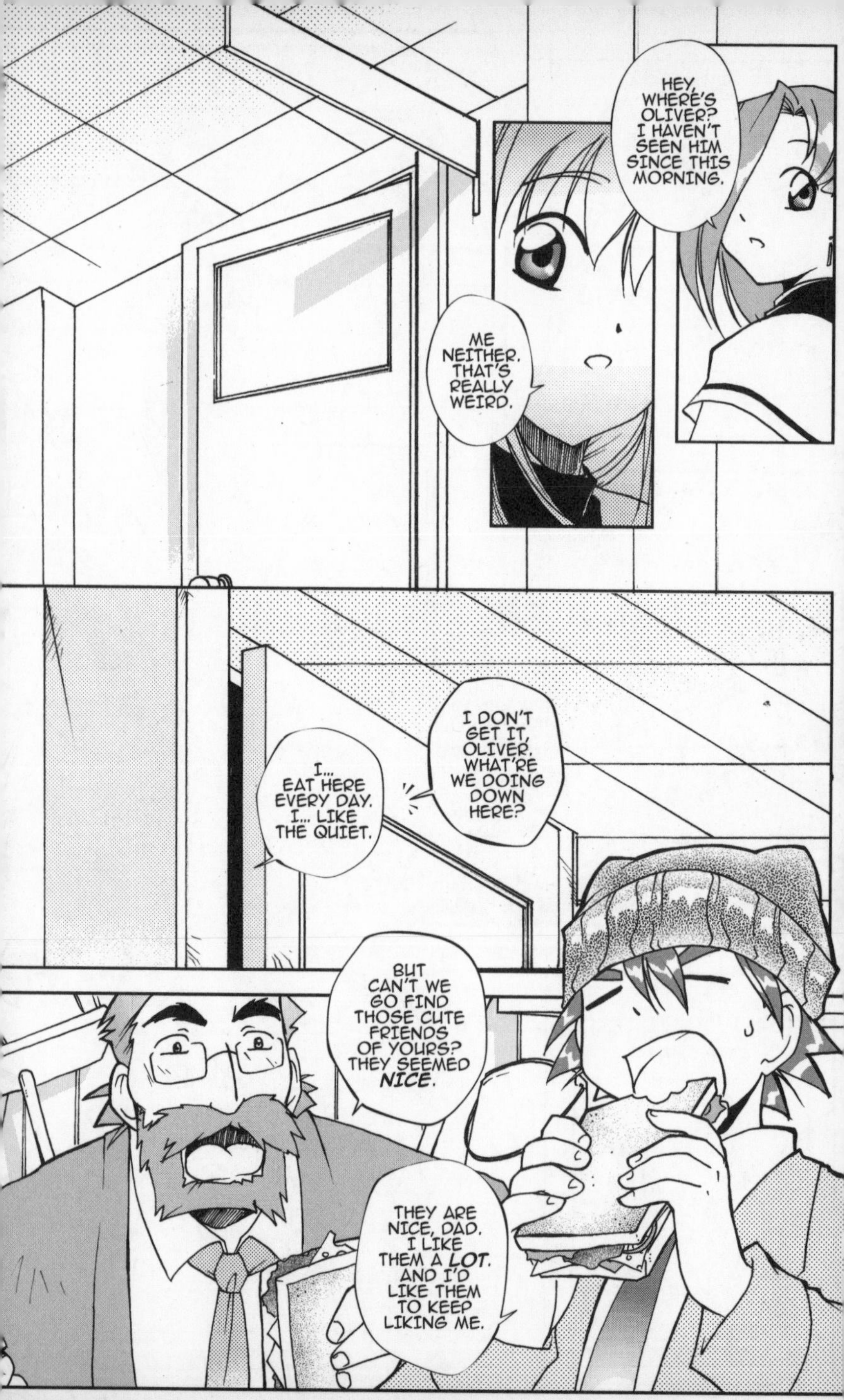
HEY, WHERE'S OLIVER? I HAVEN'T SEEN HIM SINCE THIS MORNING.
ME NEITHER. THAT'S REALLY WEIRD.
I DON'T GET IT, OLIVER. WHAT'RE WE DOING DOWN HERE?
I... EAT HERE EVERY DAY. I... LIKE THE QUIET.
BUT CAN'T WE GO FIND THOSE CUTE FRIENDS OF YOURS? THEY SEEMED *NICE*.
THEY ARE NICE, DAD. I LIKE THEM A *LOT*. AND I'D LIKE THEM TO KEEP LIKING ME.

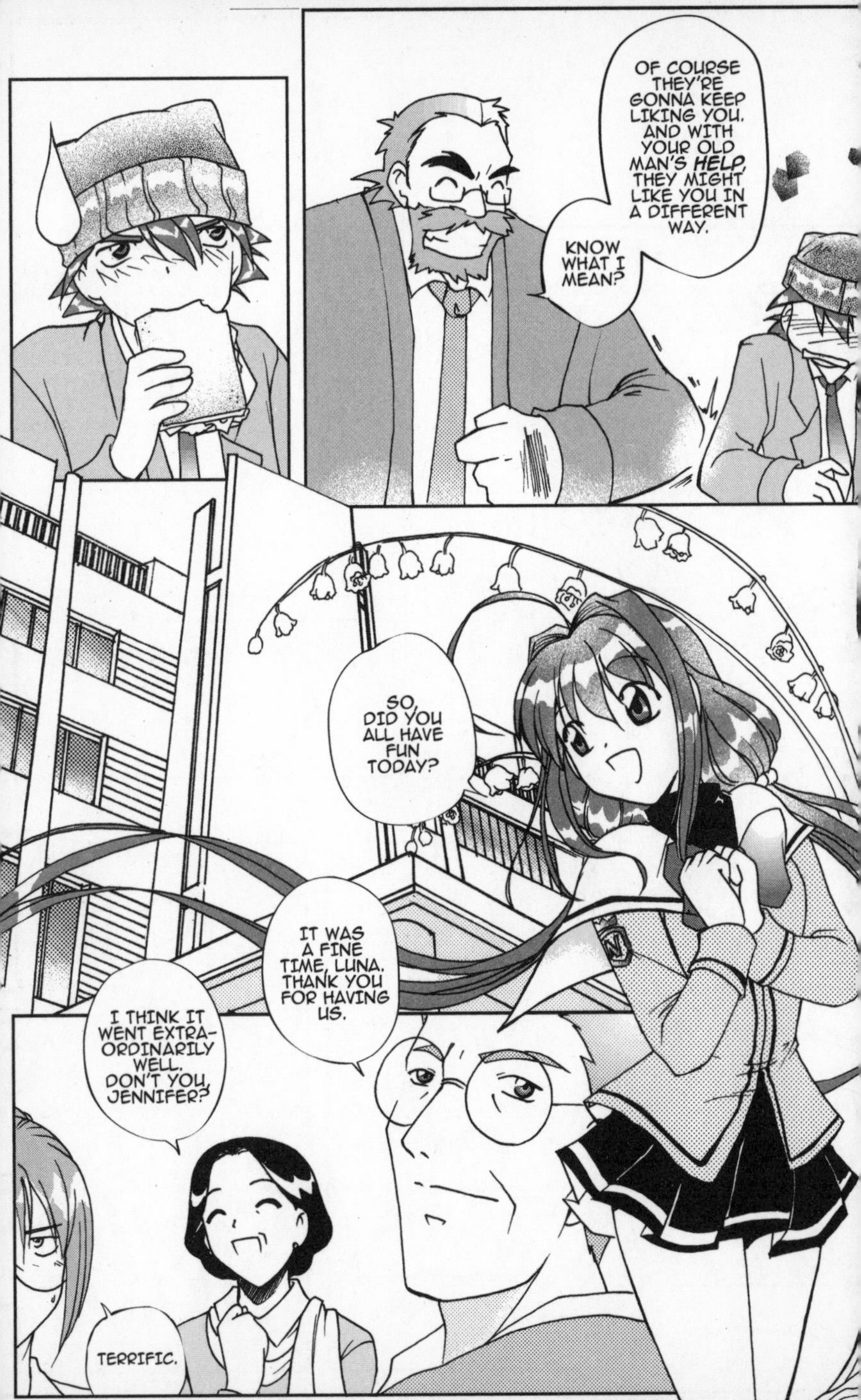
OF COURSE THEY'RE GONNA KEEP LIKING YOU. AND WITH YOUR OLD MAN'S **HELP**, THEY MIGHT LIKE YOU IN A DIFFERENT WAY.
KNOW WHAT I MEAN?
SO, DID YOU ALL HAVE FUN TODAY?
IT WAS A FINE TIME, LUNA. THANK YOU FOR HAVING US.
I THINK IT WENT EXTRA-ORDINARILY WELL. DON'T YOU, JENNIFER?
TERRIFIC.

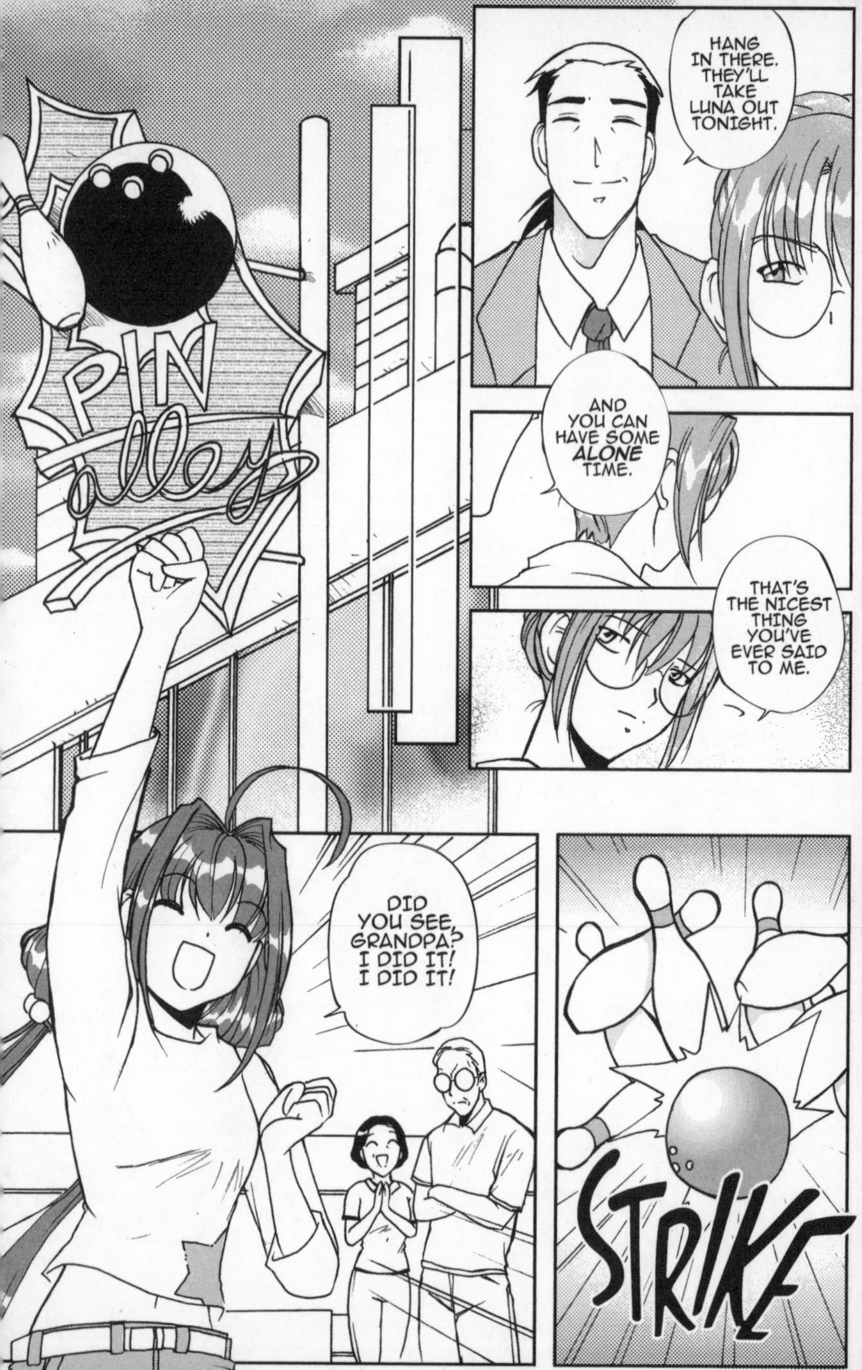
HANG IN THERE. THEY'LL TAKE LUNA OUT TONIGHT.
AND YOU CAN HAVE SOME ***ALONE*** TIME.
THAT'S THE NICEST THING YOU'VE EVER SAID TO ME.
PIN alley
STRIKE
DID YOU SEE, GRANDPA? I DID IT! I DID IT!

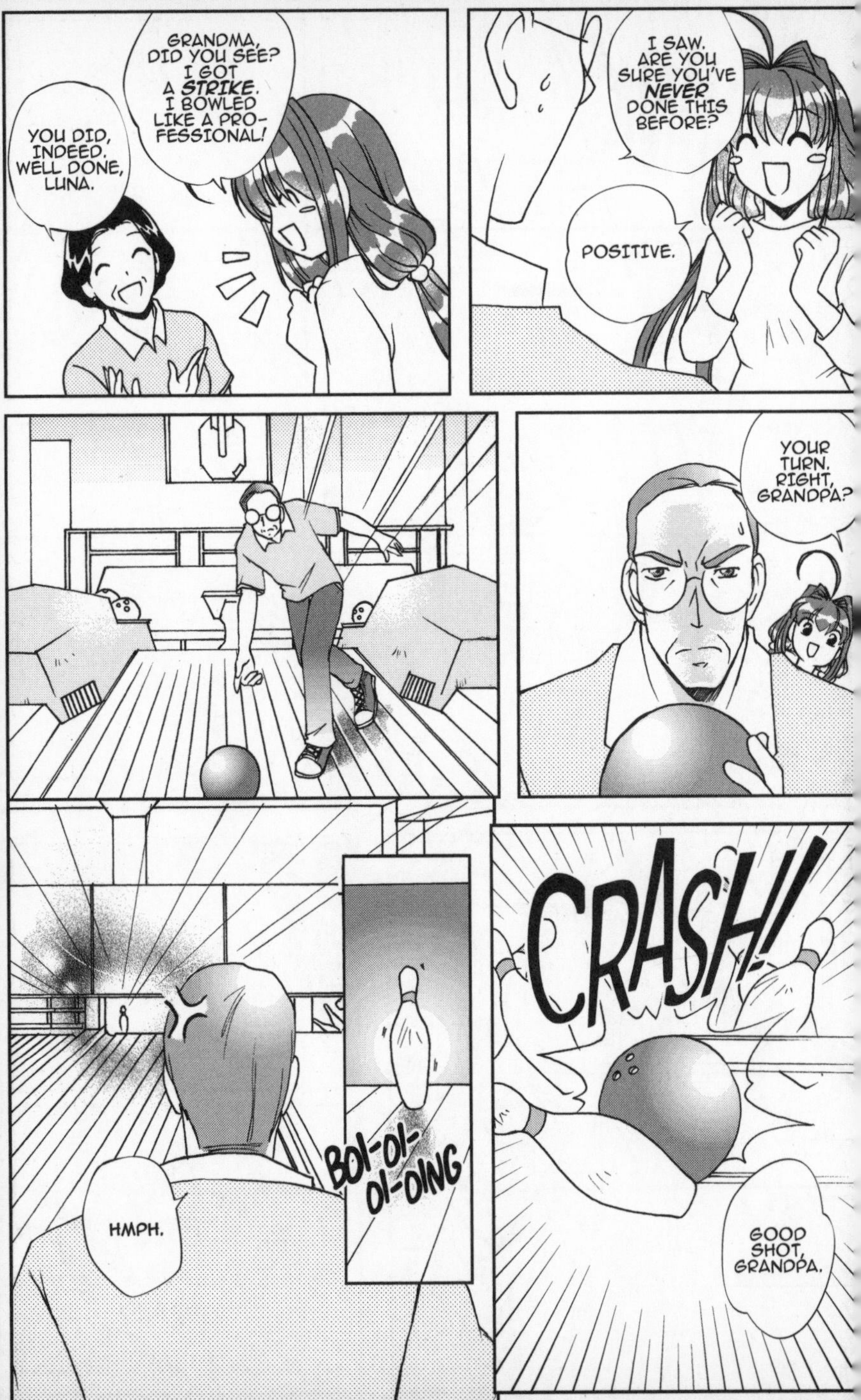
I SAW. ARE YOU SURE YOU'VE **NEVER** DONE THIS BEFORE?
POSITIVE.
GRANDMA, DID YOU SEE? I GOT A **STRIKE**. I BOWLED LIKE A PRO-FESSIONAL!
YOU DID, INDEED. WELL DONE, LUNA.
YOUR TURN. RIGHT, GRANDPA?
CRASH!!
GOOD SHOT, GRANDPA.
BOI-OI-OI-OING
HMPH.

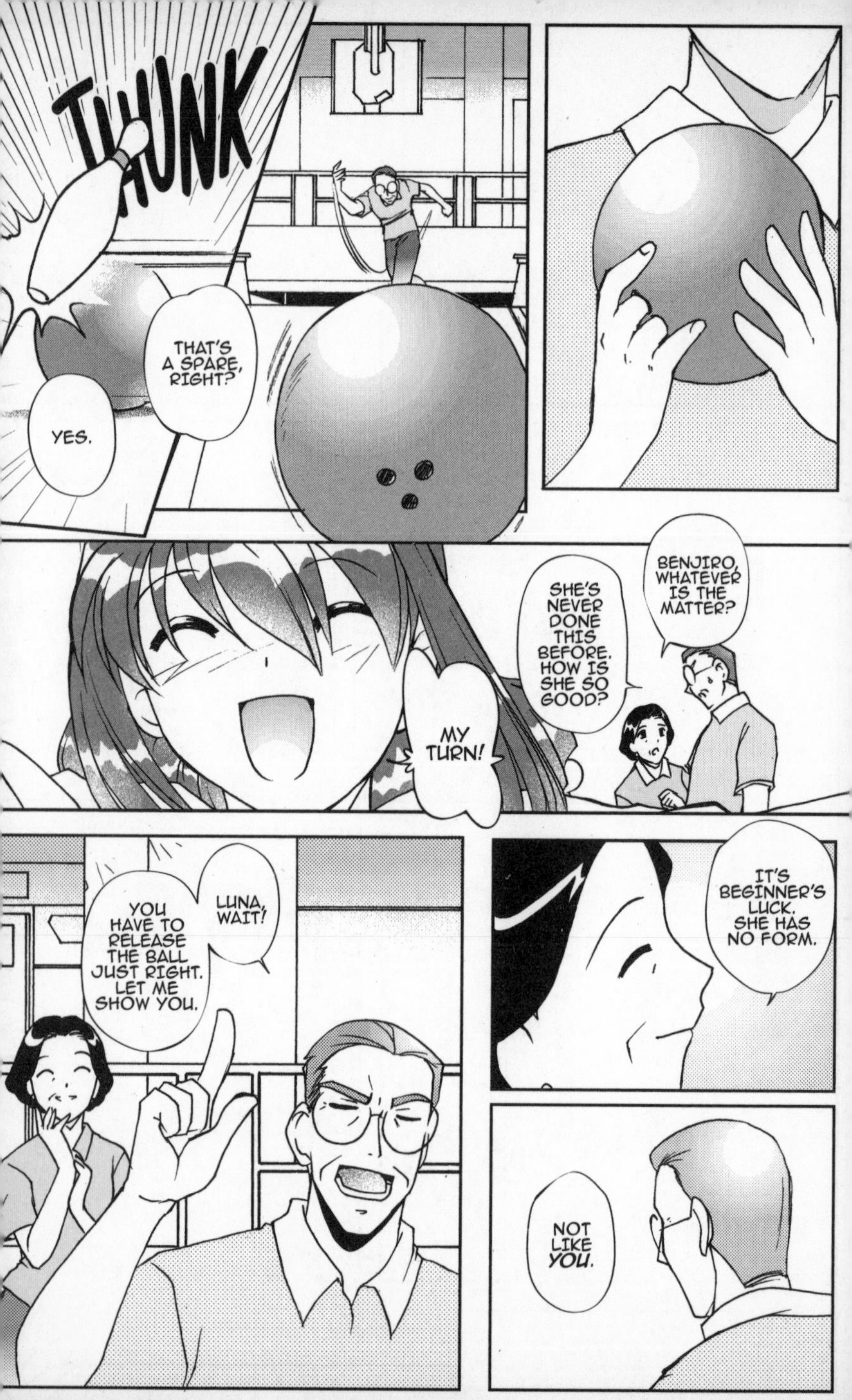
THUNK
THAT'S A SPARE, RIGHT?
YES.
BENJIRO, WHATEVER IS THE MATTER?
SHE'S NEVER DONE THIS BEFORE. HOW IS SHE SO GOOD?
MY TURN!
IT'S BEGINNER'S LUCK. SHE HAS NO FORM.
NOT LIKE *YOU*.
LUNA, WAIT!
YOU HAVE TO RELEASE THE BALL JUST RIGHT. LET ME SHOW YOU.

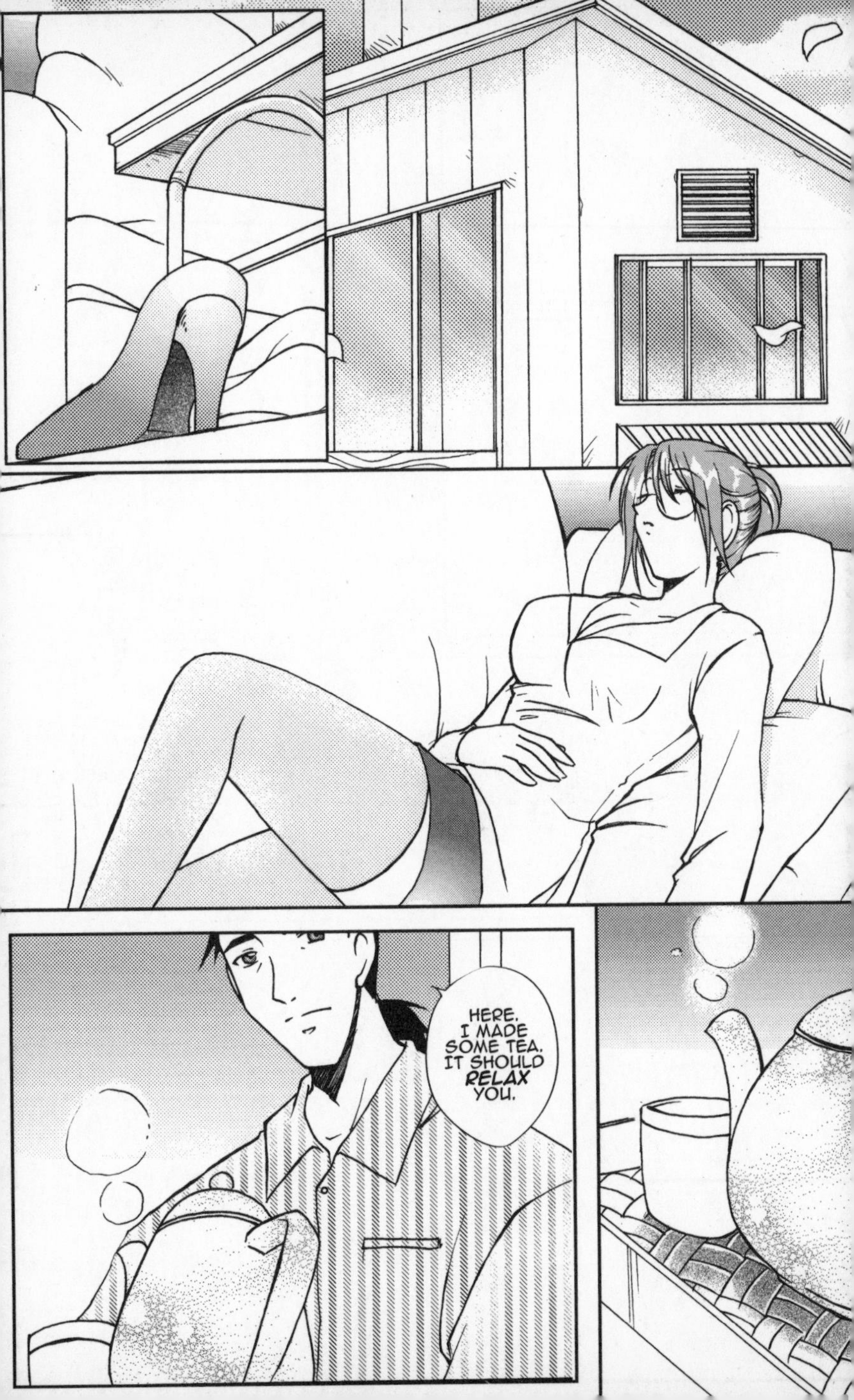
HERE. I MADE SOME TEA. IT SHOULD RELAX YOU.

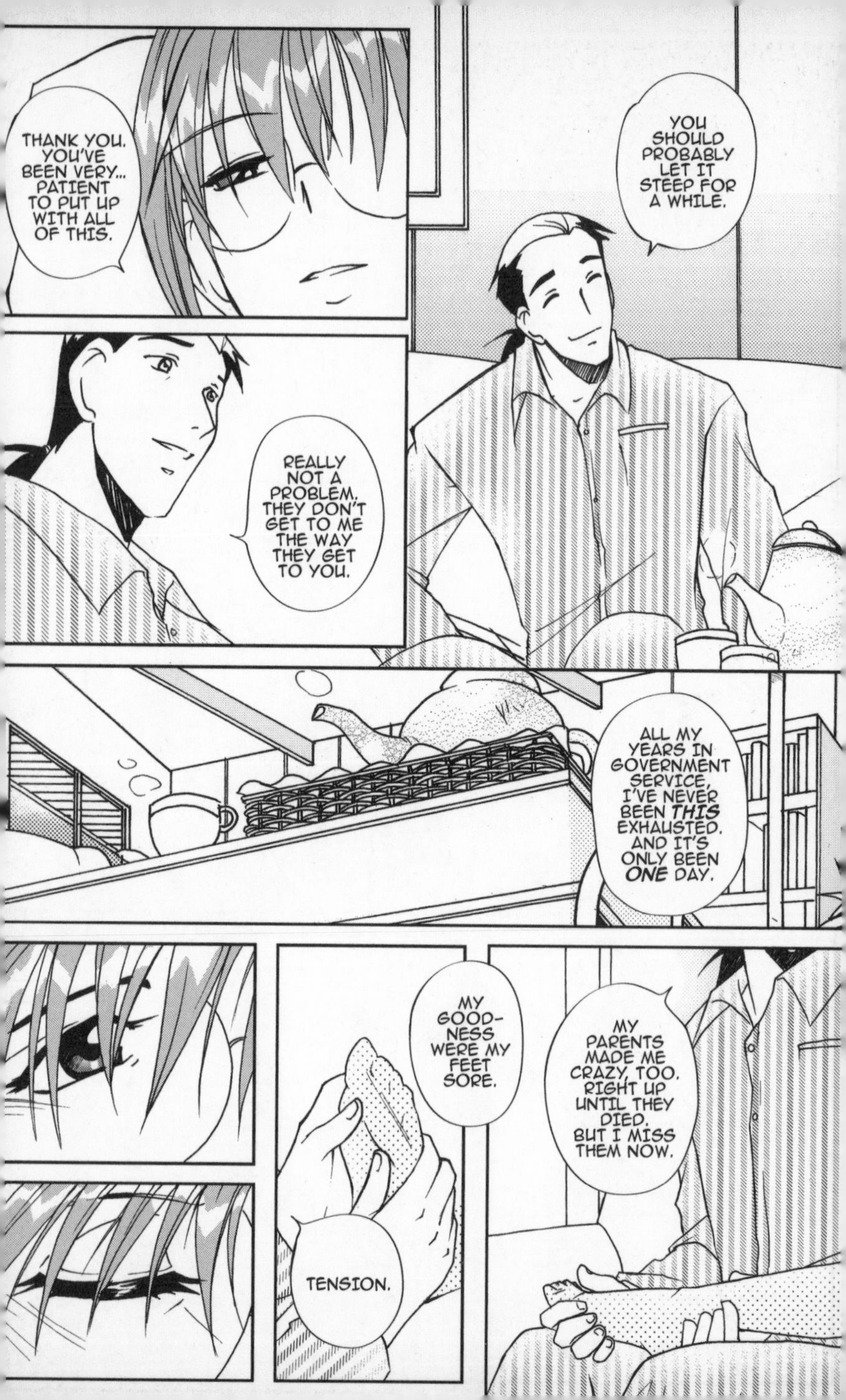
YOU SHOULD PROBABLY LET IT STEEP FOR A WHILE.
THANK YOU. YOU'VE BEEN VERY... PATIENT TO PUT UP WITH ALL OF THIS.
REALLY NOT A PROBLEM. THEY DON'T GET TO ME THE WAY THEY GET TO YOU.
ALL MY YEARS IN GOVERNMENT SERVICE, I'VE NEVER BEEN *THIS* EXHAUSTED. AND IT'S ONLY BEEN *ONE* DAY.
MY PARENTS MADE ME CRAZY, TOO. RIGHT UP UNTIL THEY DIED. BUT I MISS THEM NOW.
MY GOODNESS WERE MY FEET SORE.
TENSION.

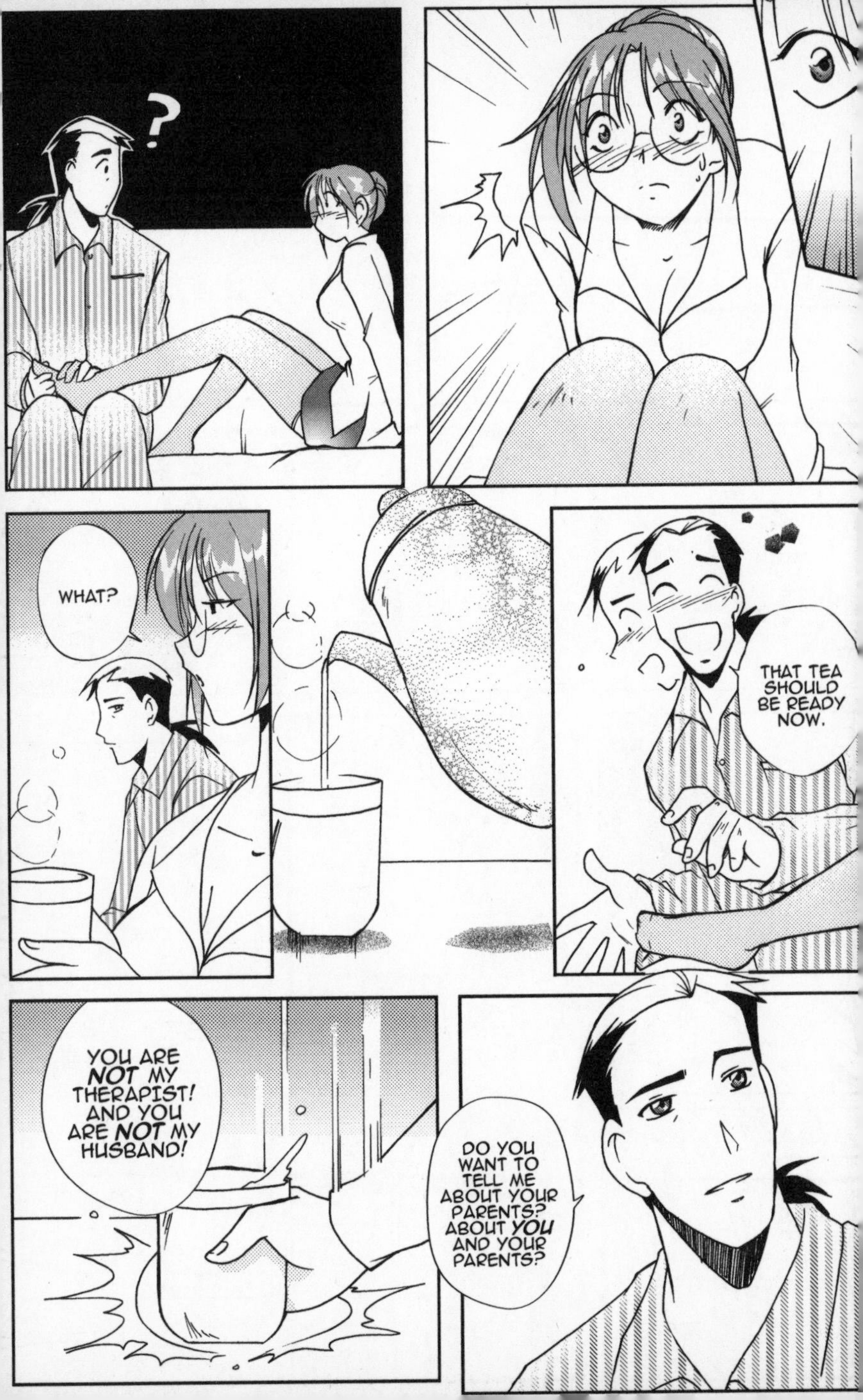
?
THAT TEA SHOULD BE READY NOW.
WHAT?
DO YOU WANT TO TELL ME ABOUT YOUR PARENTS? ABOUT *YOU* AND YOUR PARENTS?
YOU ARE ***NOT*** MY THERAPIST! AND YOU ARE ***NOT*** MY HUSBAND!

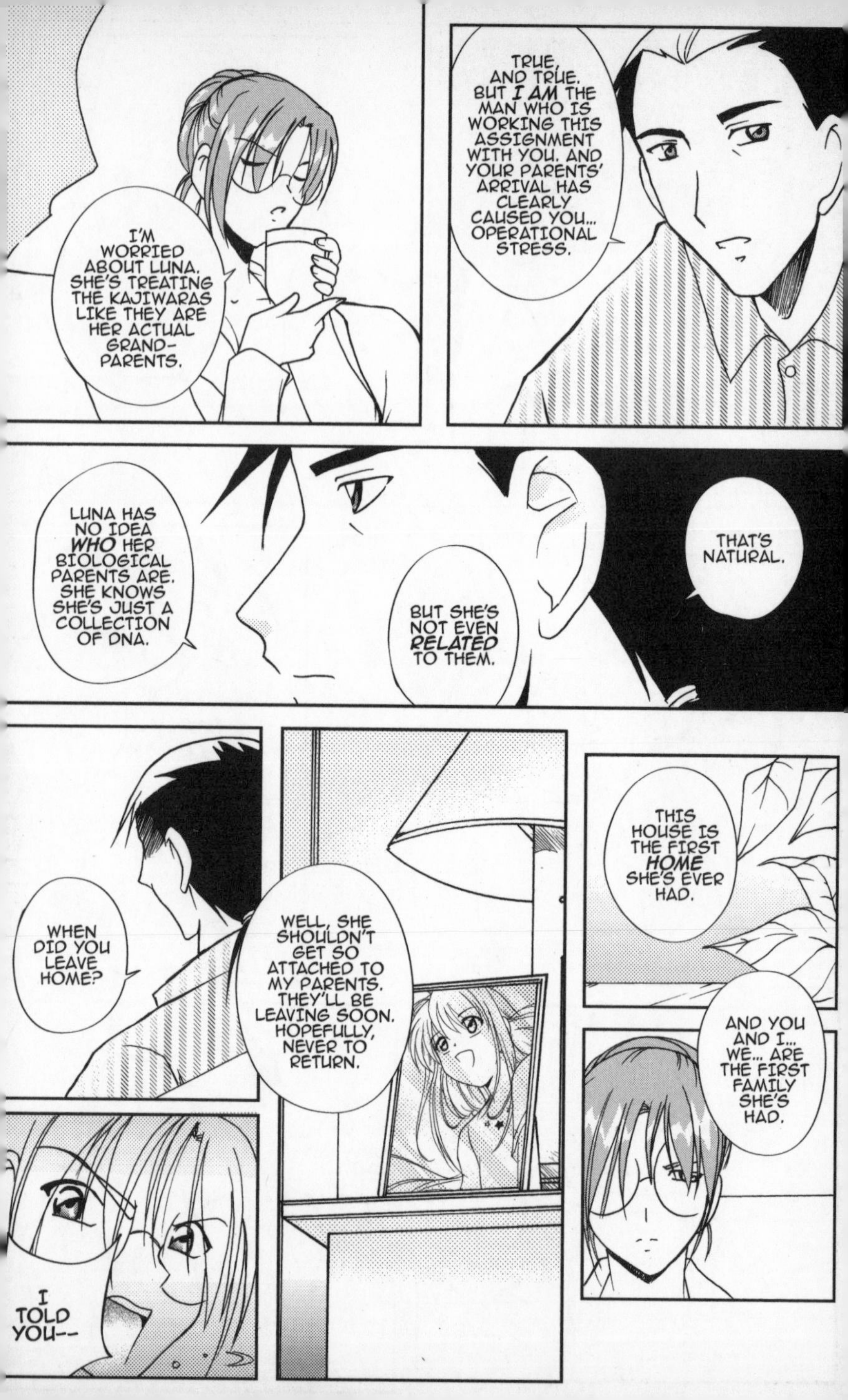
TRUE, AND TRUE. BUT I AM THE MAN WHO IS WORKING THIS ASSIGNMENT WITH YOU. AND YOUR PARENTS' ARRIVAL HAS CLEARLY CAUSED YOU... OPERATIONAL STRESS.
I'M WORRIED ABOUT LUNA. SHE'S TREATING THE KAJIWARAS LIKE THEY ARE HER ACTUAL GRAND-PARENTS.
THAT'S NATURAL.
BUT SHE'S NOT EVEN RELATED TO THEM.
LUNA HAS NO IDEA WHO HER BIOLOGICAL PARENTS ARE. SHE KNOWS SHE'S JUST A COLLECTION OF DNA.
THIS HOUSE IS THE FIRST HOME SHE'S EVER HAD.
AND YOU AND I... WE... ARE THE FIRST FAMILY SHE'S HAD.
WELL, SHE SHOULDN'T GET SO ATTACHED TO MY PARENTS. THEY'LL BE LEAVING SOON. HOPEFULLY, NEVER TO RETURN.
WHEN DID YOU LEAVE HOME?
I TOLD YOU--

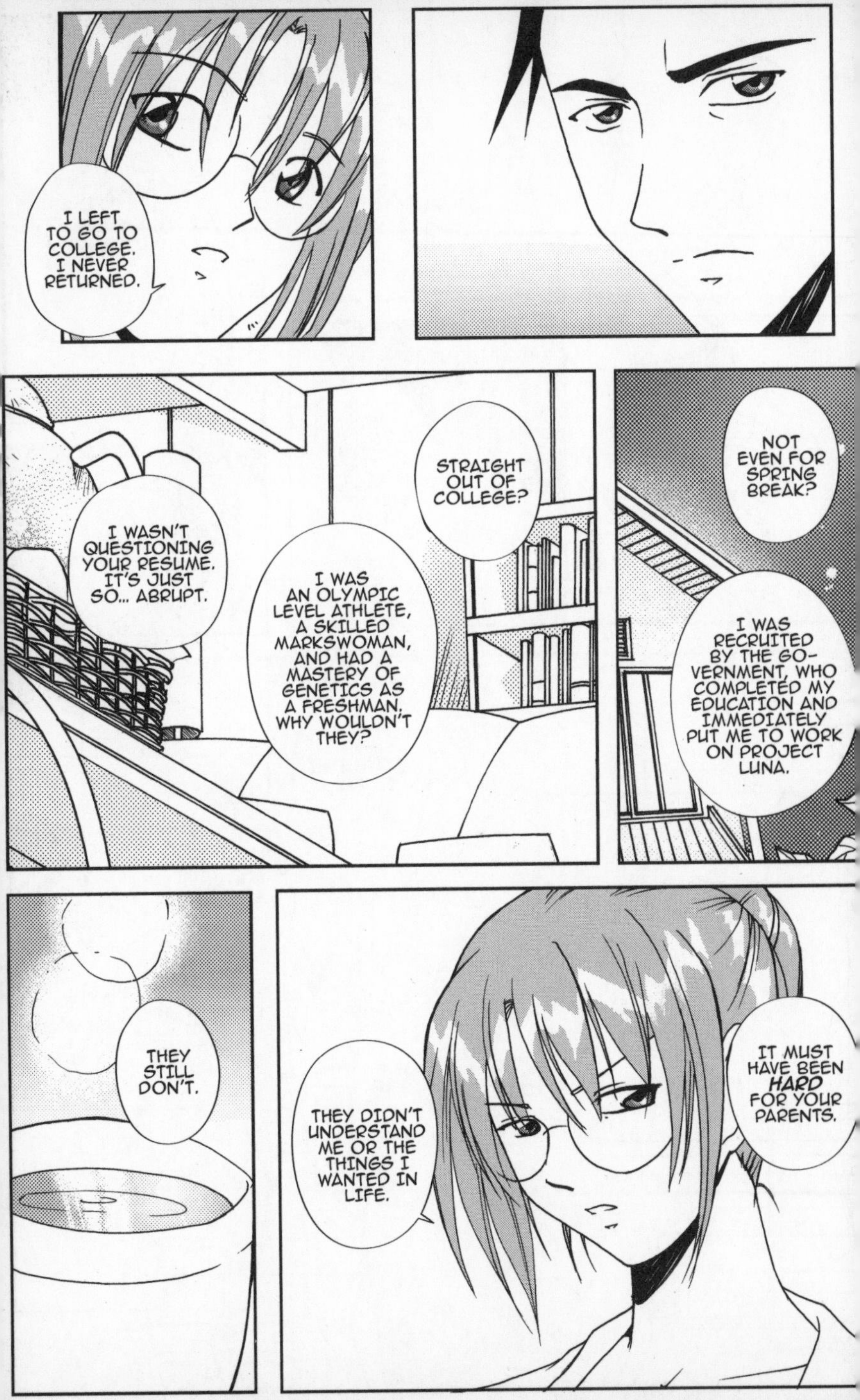
I LEFT TO GO TO COLLEGE. I NEVER RETURNED.
NOT EVEN FOR SPRING BREAK?
I WAS RECRUITED BY THE GO-VERNMENT, WHO COMPLETED MY EDUCATION AND IMMEDIATELY PUT ME TO WORK ON PROJECT LUNA.
STRAIGHT OUT OF COLLEGE?
I WAS AN OLYMPIC LEVEL ATHLETE, A SKILLED MARKSWOMAN, AND HAD A MASTERY OF GENETICS AS A FRESHMAN. WHY WOULDN'T THEY?
I WASN'T QUESTIONING YOUR RESUME. IT'S JUST SO... ABRUPT.
IT MUST HAVE BEEN *HARD* FOR YOUR PARENTS.
THEY DIDN'T UNDERSTAND ME OR THE THINGS I WANTED IN LIFE.
THEY STILL DON'T.

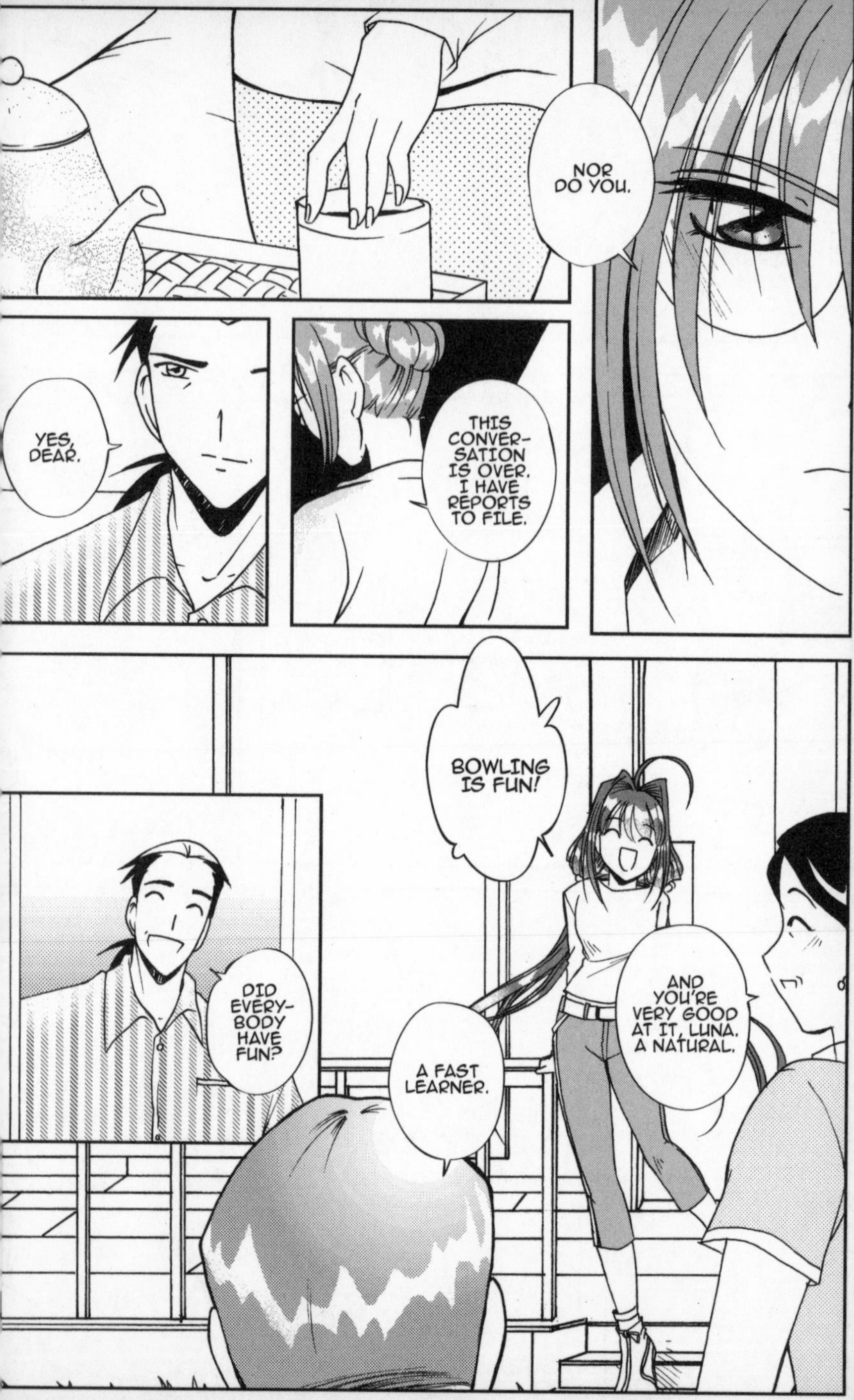
NOR DO YOU.
THIS CONVERSATION IS OVER. I HAVE REPORTS TO FILE.
YES, DEAR.
BOWLING IS FUN!
AND YOU'RE VERY GOOD AT IT, LUNA. A NATURAL.
DID EVERYBODY HAVE FUN?
A FAST LEARNER.

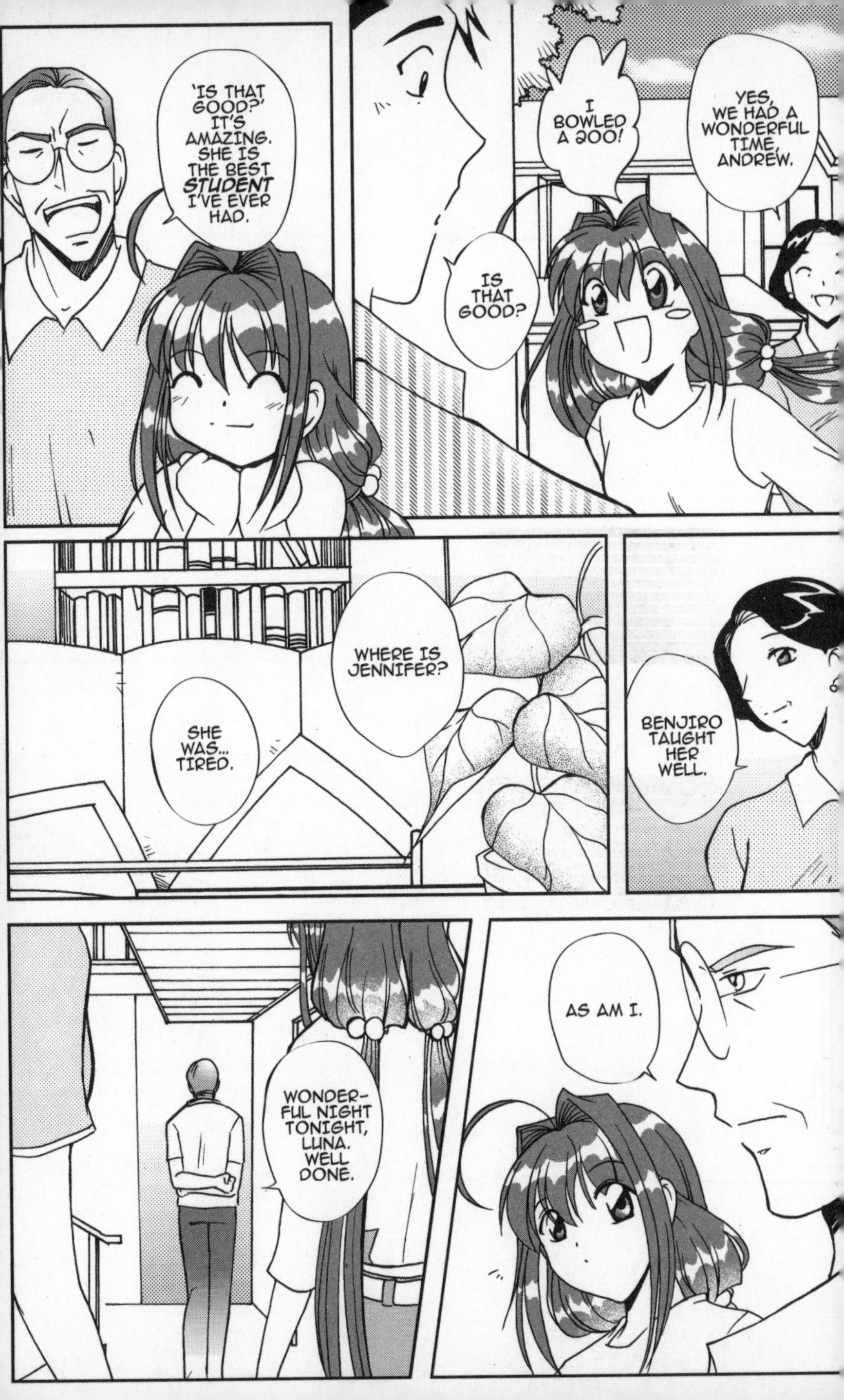
YES, WE HAD A WONDERFUL TIME, ANDREW.
I BOWLED A 200!
IS THAT GOOD?
'IS THAT GOOD?' IT'S AMAZING. SHE IS THE BEST **STUDENT** I'VE EVER HAD.
BENJIRO TAUGHT HER WELL.
WHERE IS JENNIFER?
SHE WAS... TIRED.
AS AM I.
WONDER-FUL NIGHT TONIGHT, LUNA. WELL DONE.

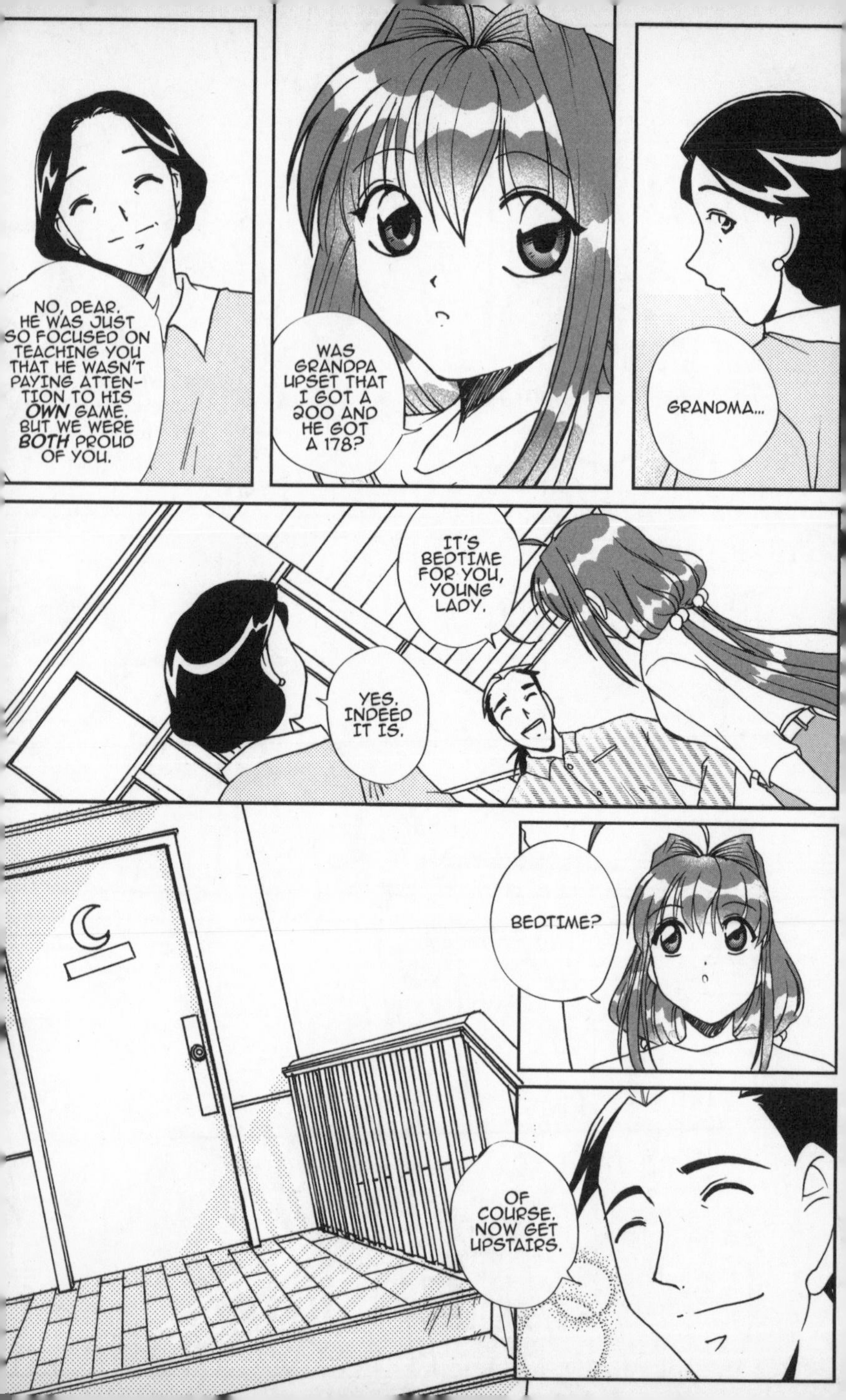
GRANDMA...
WAS GRANDPA UPSET THAT I GOT A 200 AND HE GOT A 178?
NO, DEAR. HE WAS JUST SO FOCUSED ON TEACHING YOU THAT HE WASN'T PAYING ATTENTION TO HIS OWN GAME. BUT WE WERE BOTH PROUD OF YOU.
IT'S BEDTIME FOR YOU, YOUNG LADY.
YES. INDEED IT IS.
BEDTIME?
OF COURSE. NOW GET UPSTAIRS.

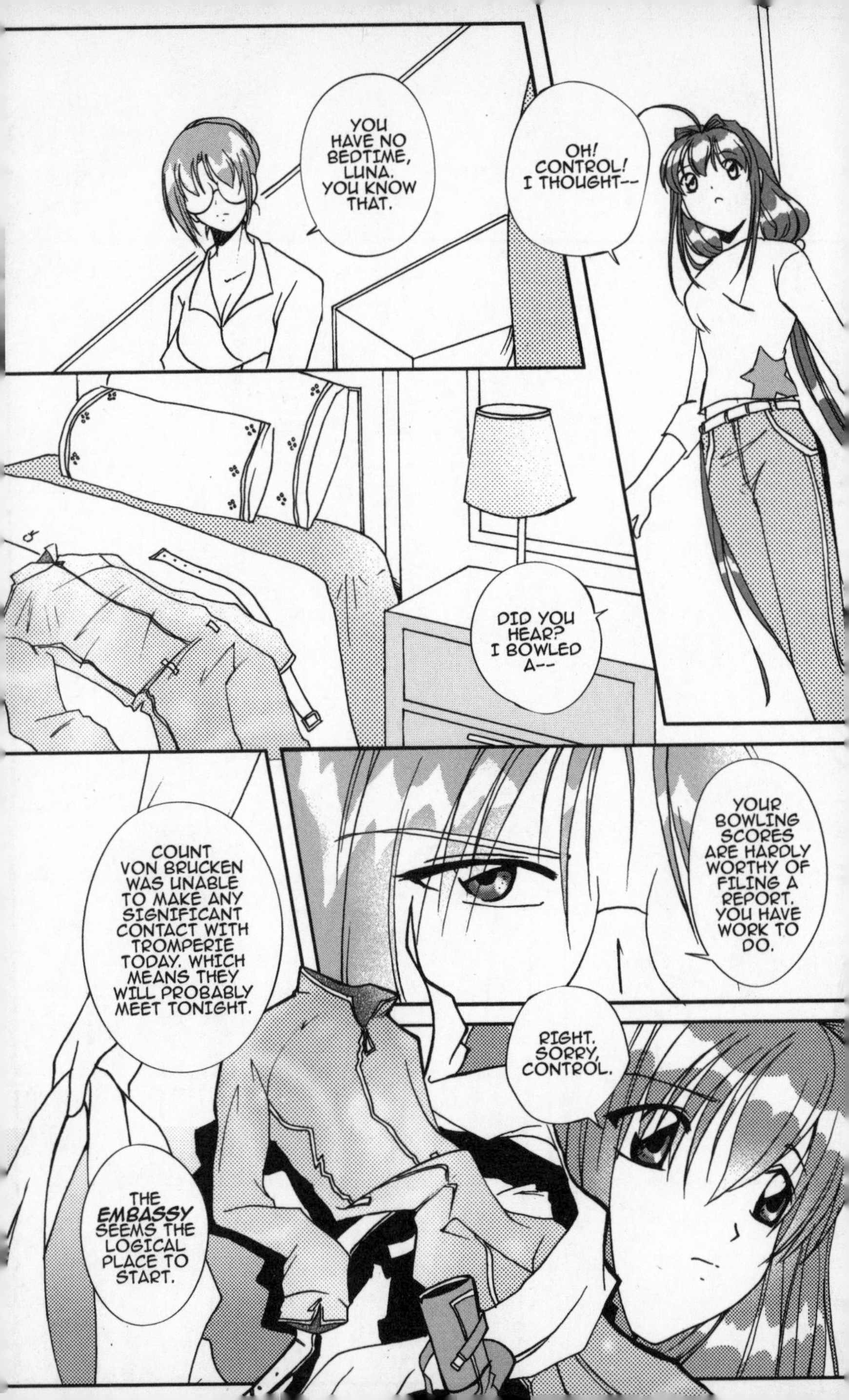
OH! CONTROL! I THOUGHT--
YOU HAVE NO BEDTIME, LUNA. YOU KNOW THAT.
DID YOU HEAR? I BOWLED A--
YOUR BOWLING SCORES ARE HARDLY WORTHY OF FILING A REPORT. YOU HAVE WORK TO DO.
COUNT VON BRUCKEN WAS UNABLE TO MAKE ANY SIGNIFICANT CONTACT WITH TROMPERIE TODAY. WHICH MEANS THEY WILL PROBABLY MEET TONIGHT.
RIGHT. SORRY, CONTROL.
THE *EMBASSY* SEEMS THE LOGICAL PLACE TO START.

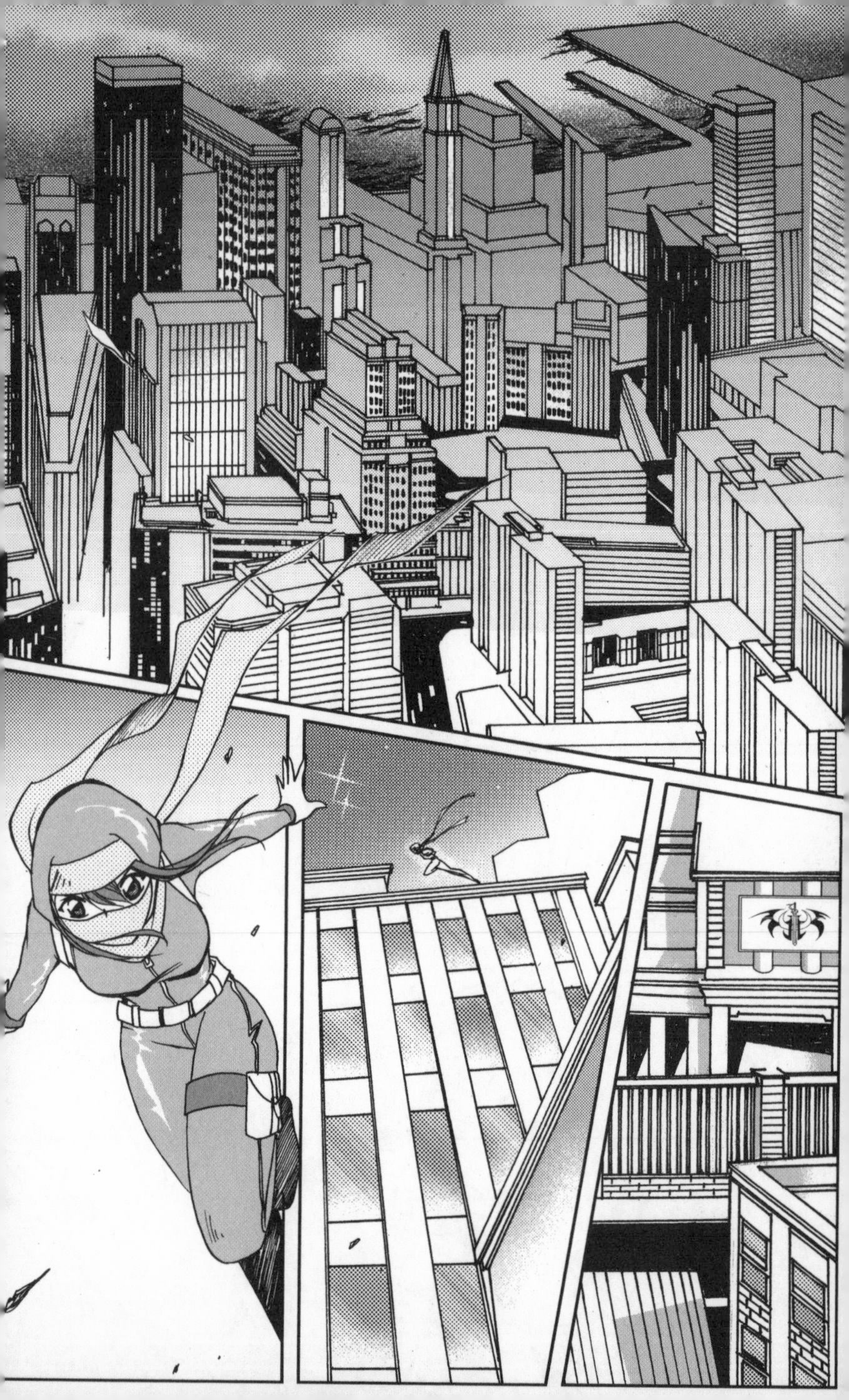

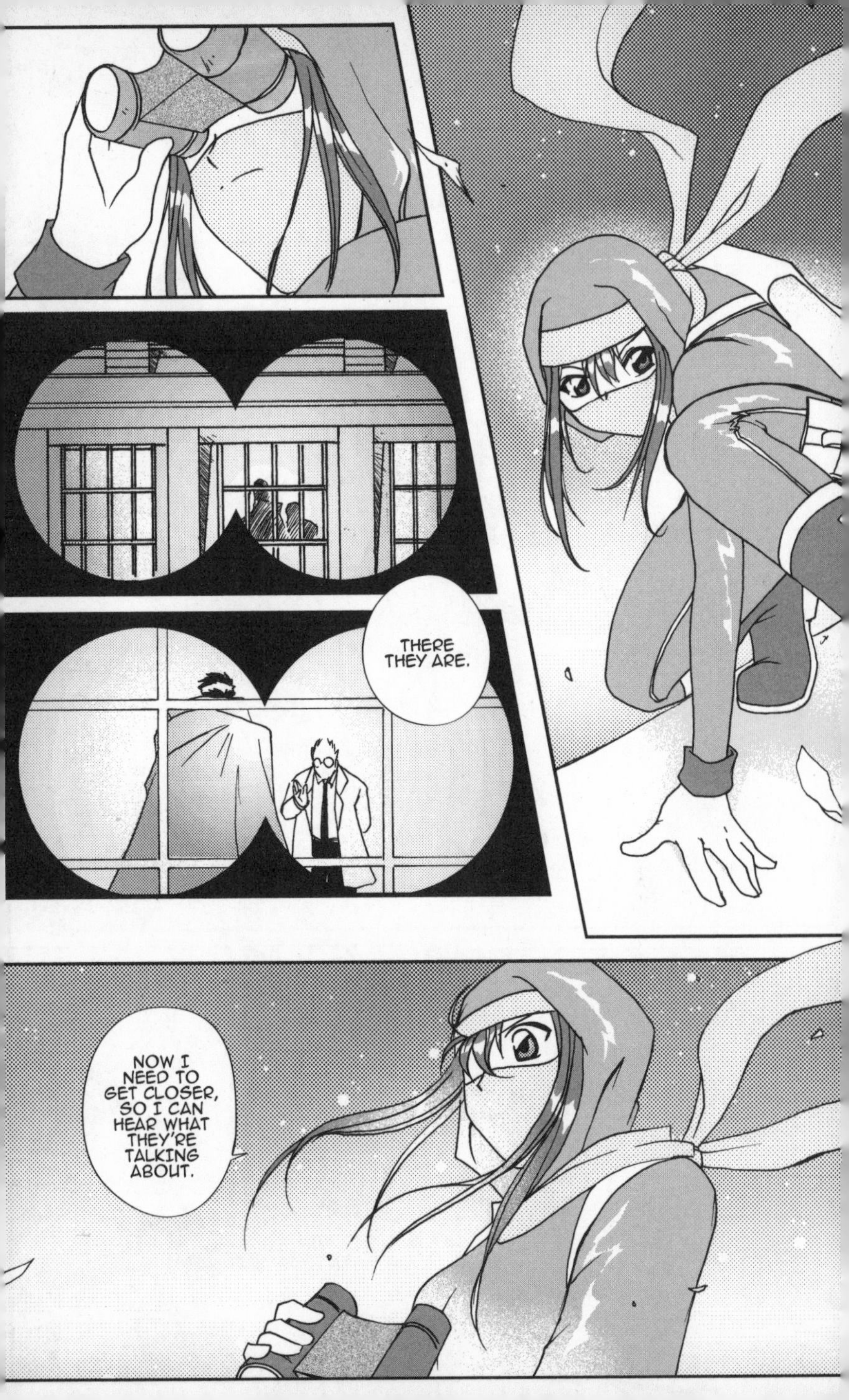
THERE THEY ARE.
NOW I NEED TO GET CLOSER, SO I CAN HEAR WHAT THEY'RE TALKING ABOUT.

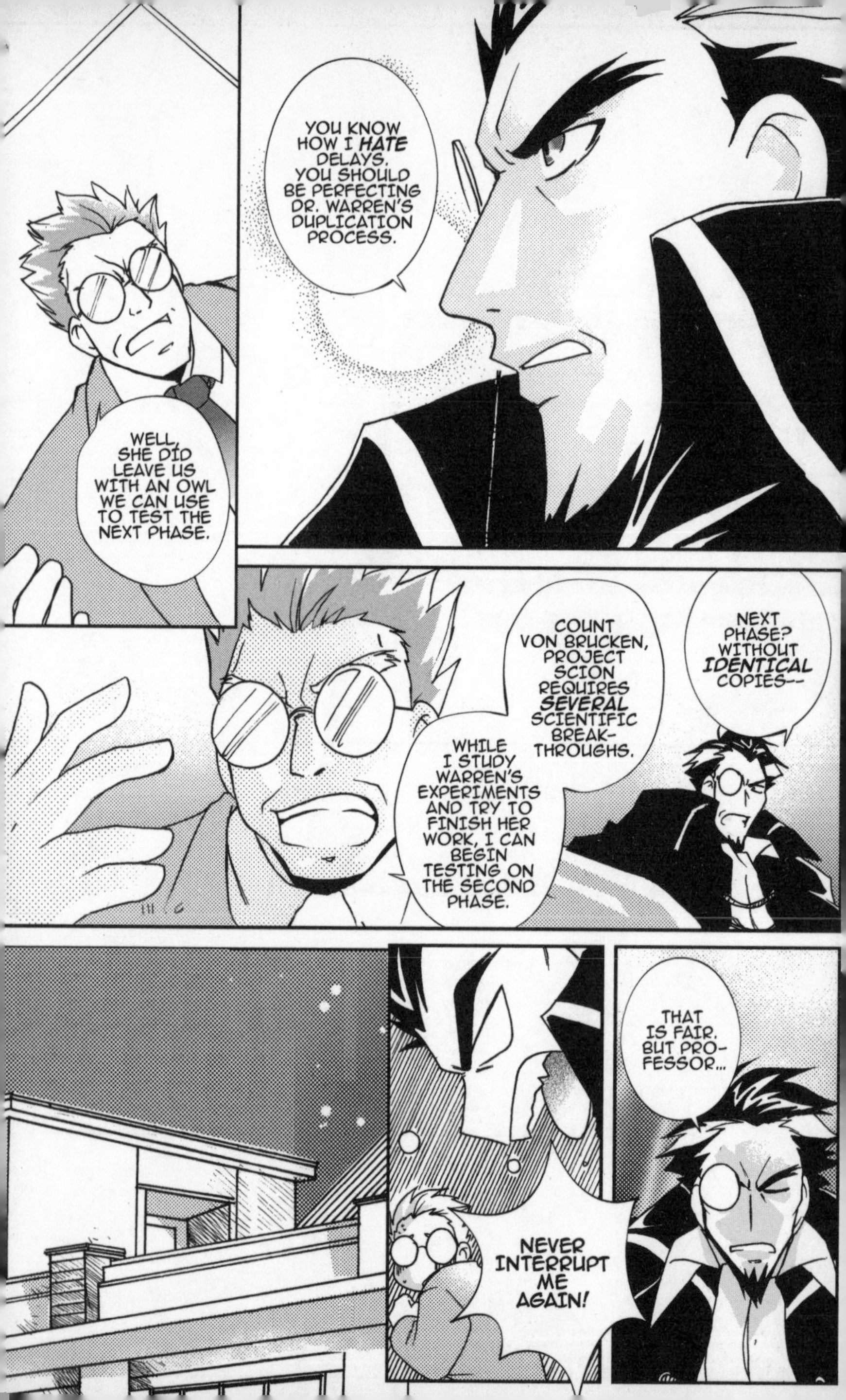
YOU KNOW HOW I **HATE** DELAYS. YOU SHOULD BE PERFECTING DR. WARREN'S DUPLICATION PROCESS.
WELL, SHE DID LEAVE US WITH AN OWL WE CAN USE TO TEST THE NEXT PHASE.
NEXT PHASE? WITHOUT ***IDENTICAL*** COPIES--
COUNT VON BRUCKEN, PROJECT SCION REQUIRES ***SEVERAL*** SCIENTIFIC BREAK-THROUGHS.
WHILE I STUDY WARREN'S EXPERIMENTS AND TRY TO FINISH HER WORK, I CAN BEGIN TESTING ON THE SECOND PHASE.
THAT IS FAIR. BUT PRO-FESSOR...
NEVER INTERRUPT ME AGAIN!

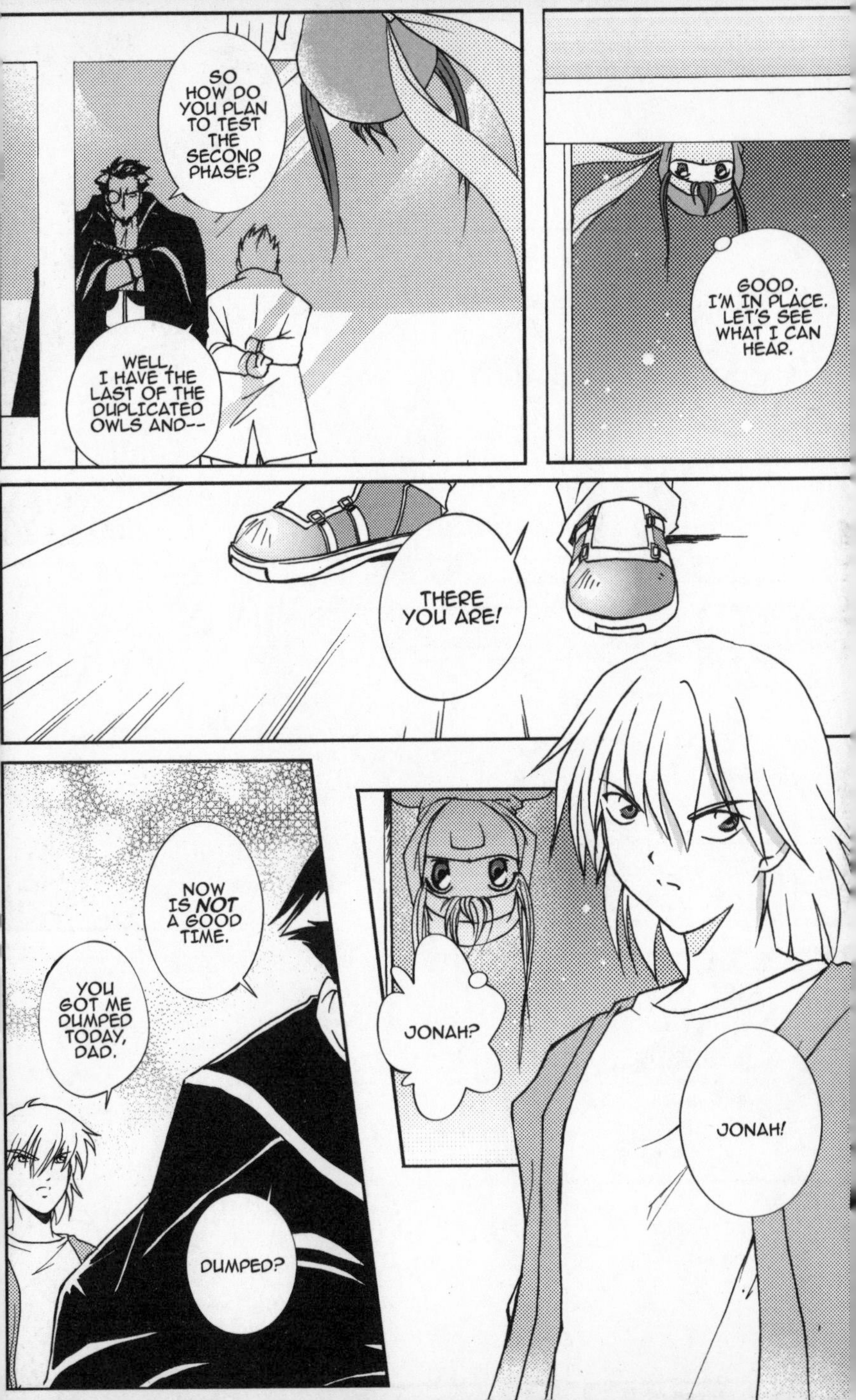
GOOD. I'M IN PLACE. LET'S SEE WHAT I CAN HEAR.
SO HOW DO YOU PLAN TO TEST THE SECOND PHASE?
WELL, I HAVE THE LAST OF THE DUPLICATED OWLS AND--
THERE YOU ARE!
JONAH!
JONAH?
NOW IS *NOT* A GOOD TIME.
YOU GOT ME DUMPED TODAY, DAD.
DUMPED?

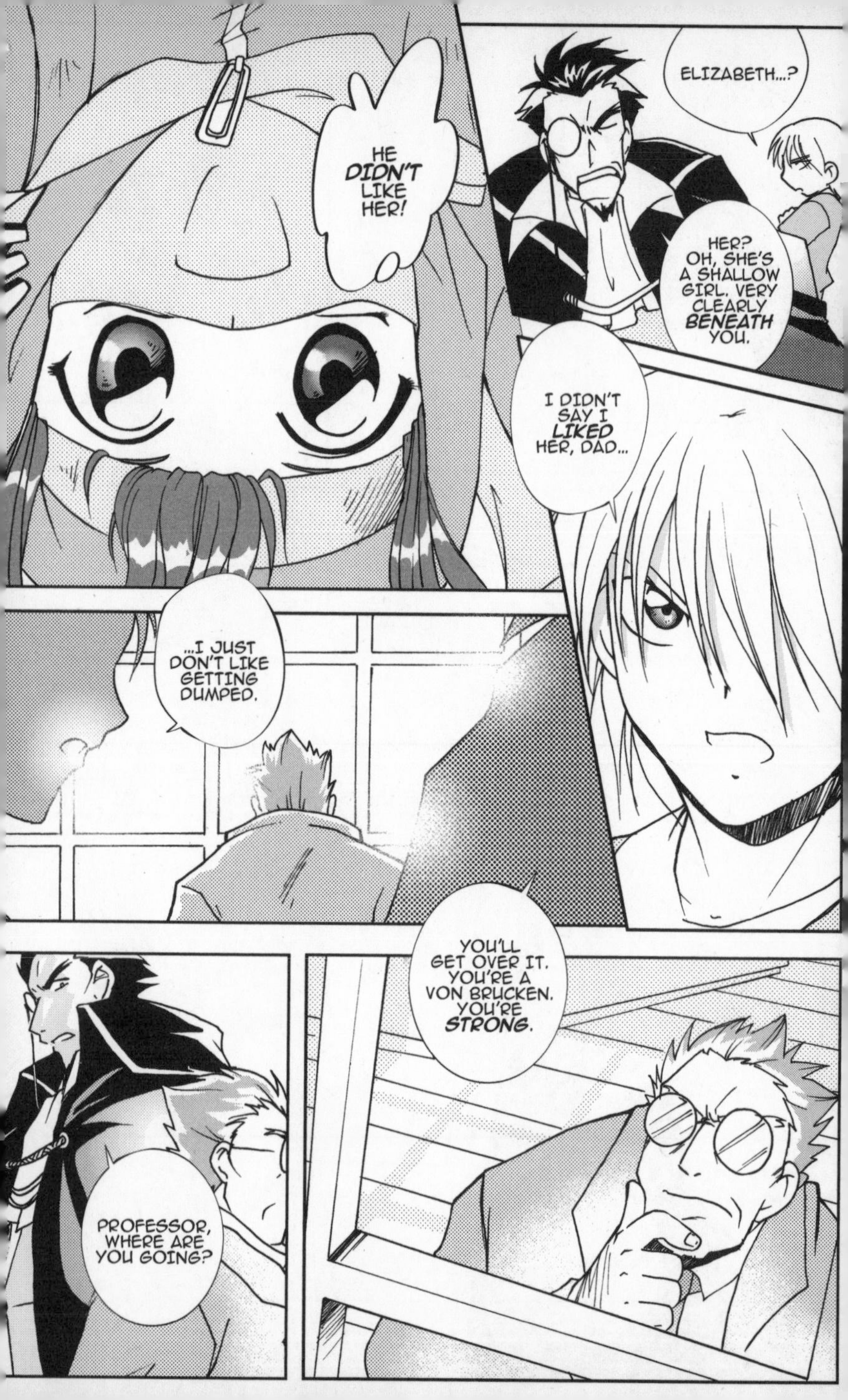
ELIZABETH...?
HER? OH, SHE'S A SHALLOW GIRL. VERY CLEARLY BENEATH YOU.
HE DIDN'T LIKE HER!
I DIDN'T SAY I LIKED HER, DAD...
...I JUST DON'T LIKE GETTING DUMPED.
YOU'LL GET OVER IT. YOU'RE A VON BRUCKEN. YOU'RE STRONG.
PROFESSOR, WHERE ARE YOU GOING?

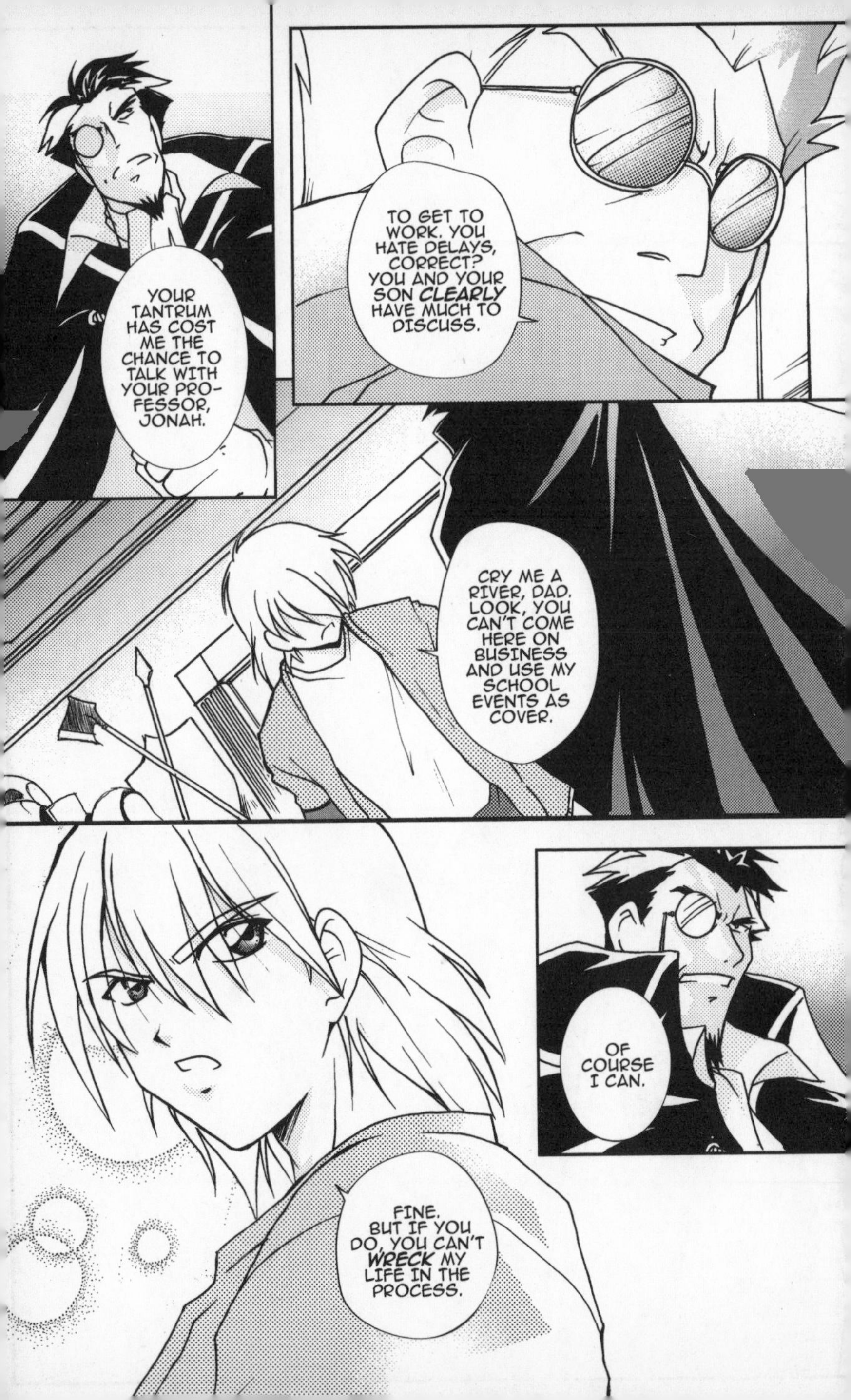
TO GET TO WORK. YOU HATE DELAYS, CORRECT? YOU AND YOUR SON *CLEARLY* HAVE MUCH TO DISCUSS.
YOUR TANTRUM HAS COST ME THE CHANCE TO TALK WITH YOUR PRO-FESSOR, JONAH.
CRY ME A RIVER, DAD. LOOK, YOU CAN'T COME HERE ON BUSINESS AND USE MY SCHOOL EVENTS AS COVER.
OF COURSE I CAN.
FINE. BUT IF YOU DO, YOU CAN'T *WRECK* MY LIFE IN THE PROCESS.

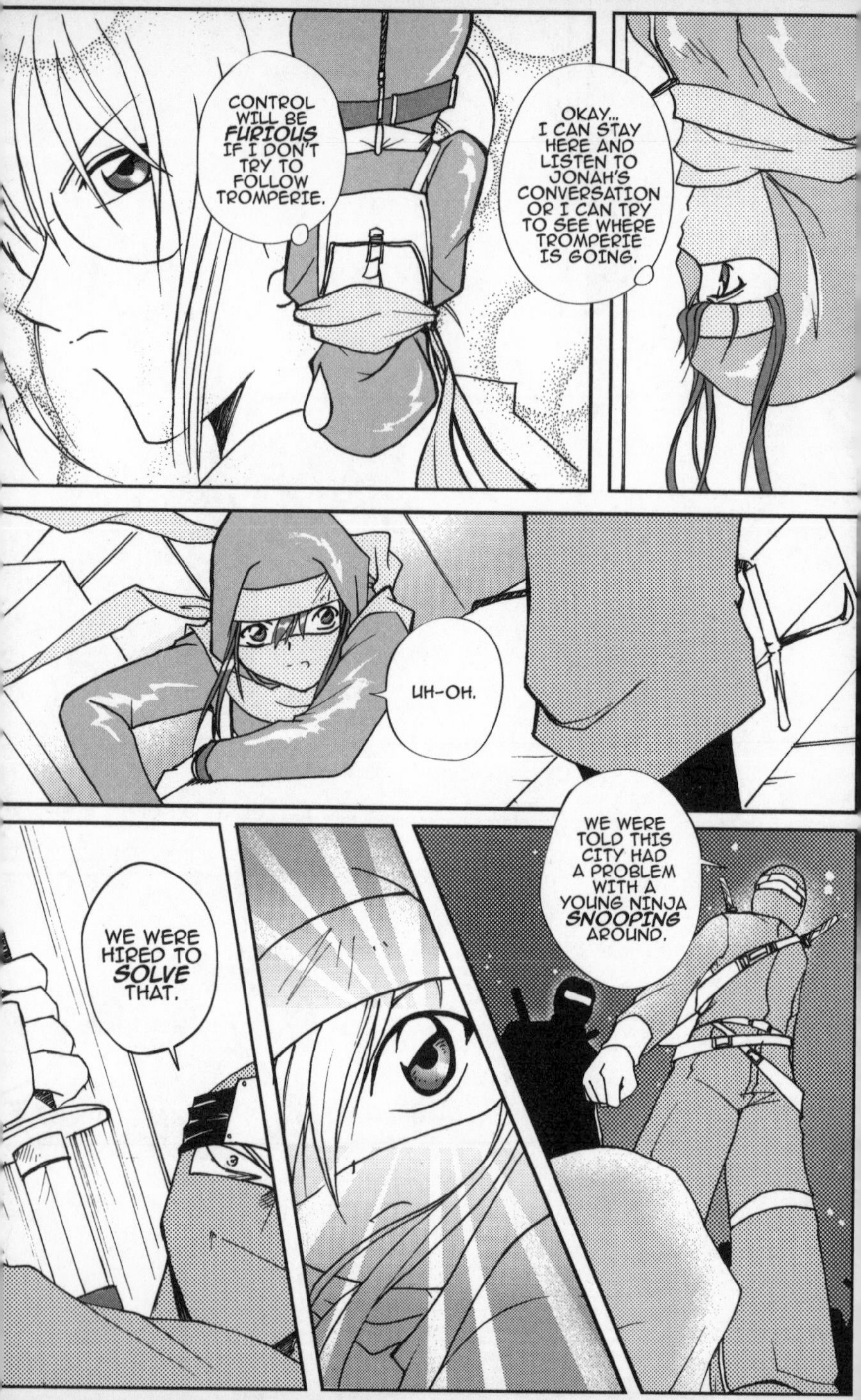
OKAY... I CAN STAY HERE AND LISTEN TO JONAH'S CONVERSATION OR I CAN TRY TO SEE WHERE TROMPERIE IS GOING.
CONTROL WILL BE ***FURIOUS*** IF I DON'T TRY TO FOLLOW TROMPERIE.
UH-OH.
WE WERE TOLD THIS CITY HAD A PROBLEM WITH A YOUNG NINJA ***SNOOPING*** AROUND.
WE WERE HIRED TO ***SOLVE*** THAT.

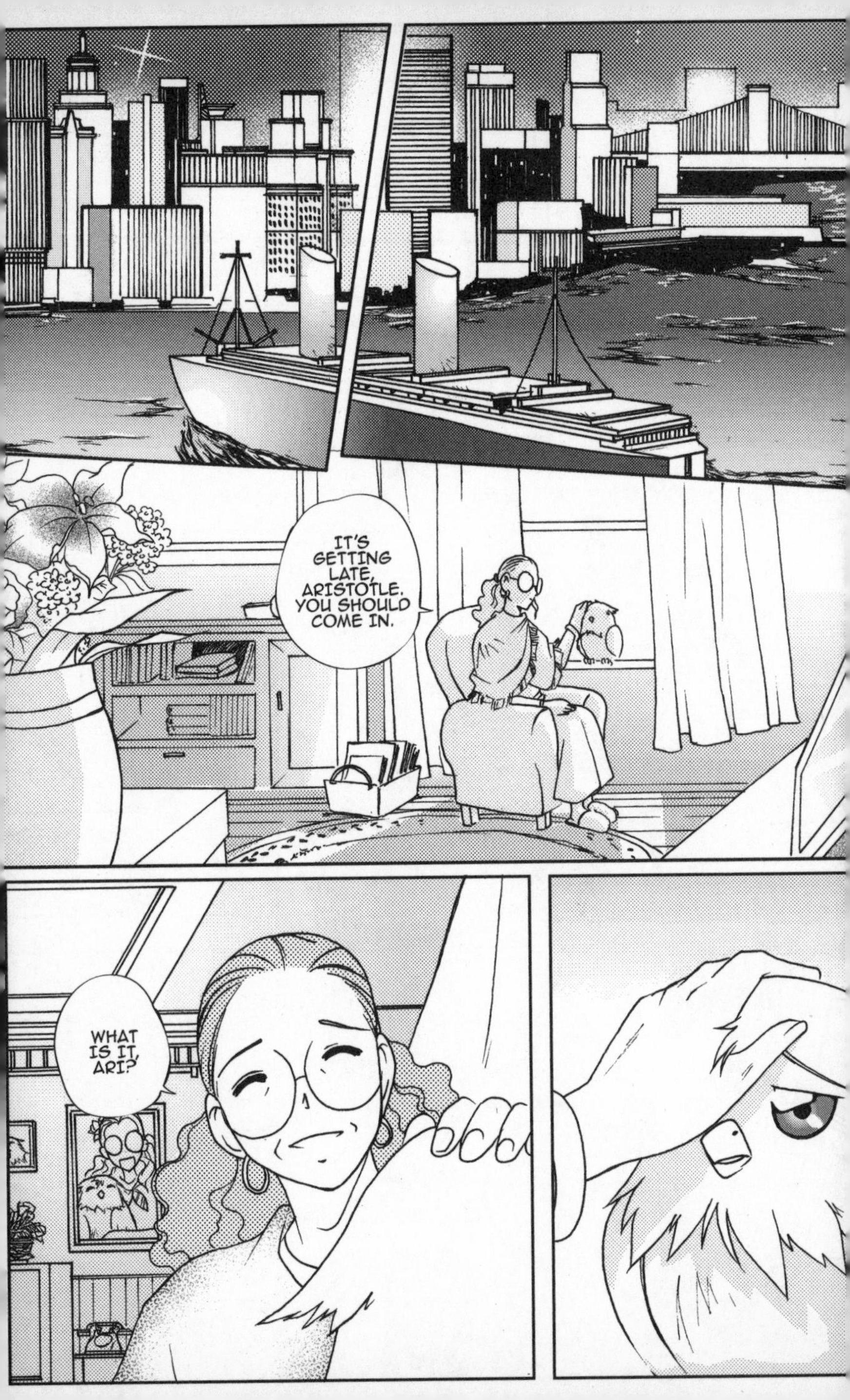
IT'S GETTING LATE, ARISTOTLE. YOU SHOULD COME IN.
WHAT IS IT, ARI?

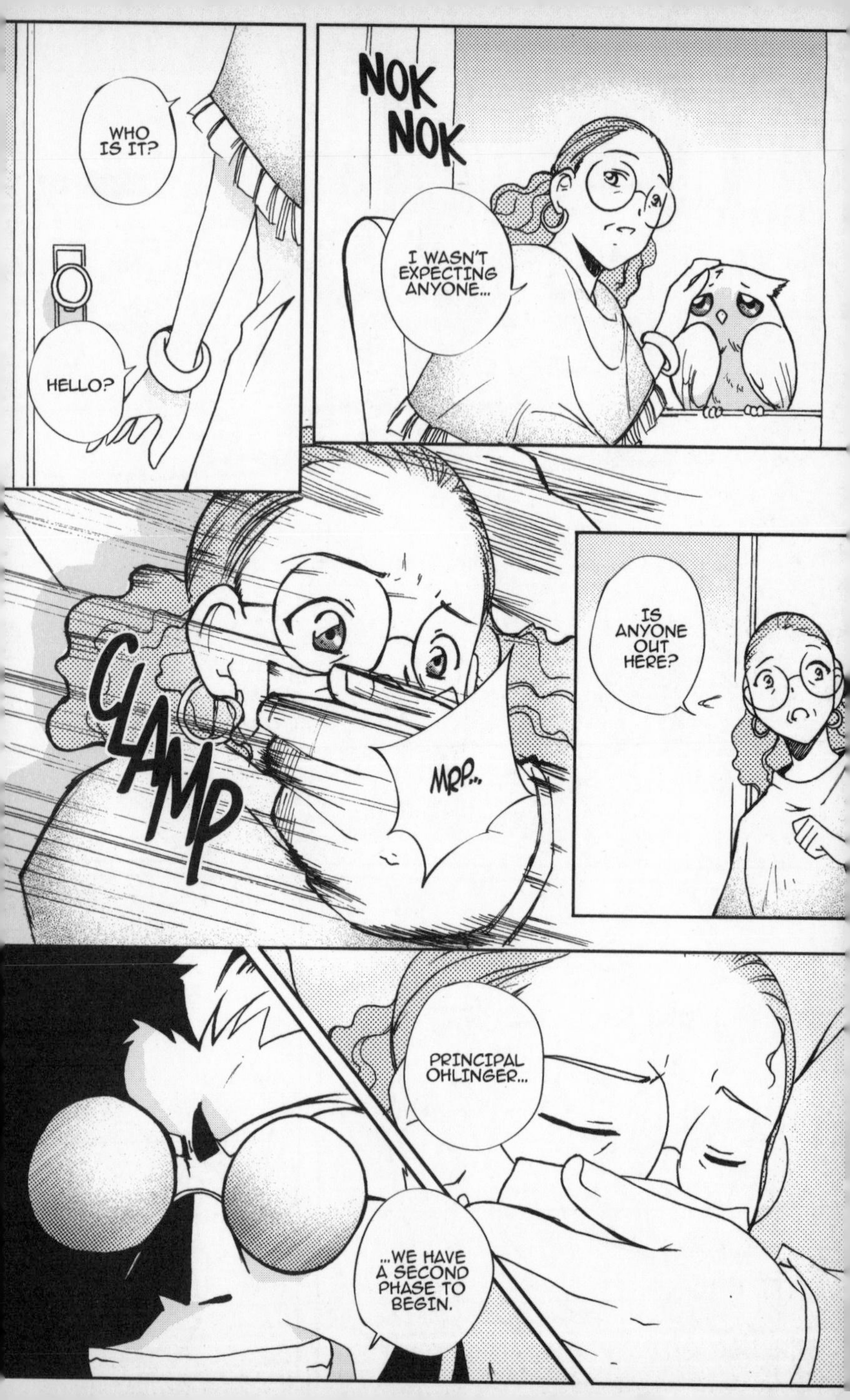
NOK NOK
I WASN'T EXPECTING ANYONE...
WHO IS IT?
HELLO?
IS ANYONE OUT HERE?
CLAMP
MRP...
PRINCIPAL OHLINGER...
...WE HAVE A SECOND PHASE TO BEGIN.

# File 10
# MEMORIES

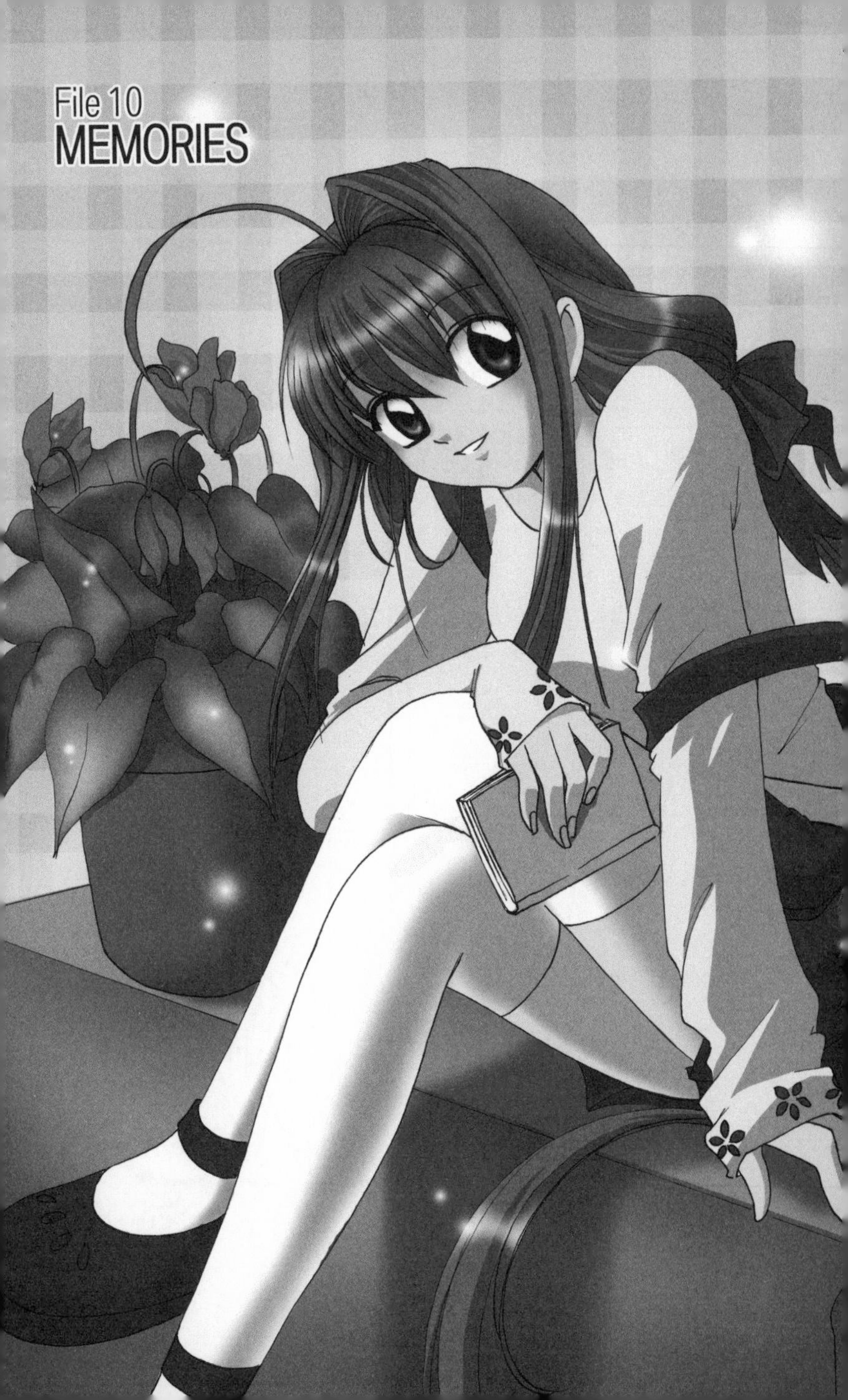

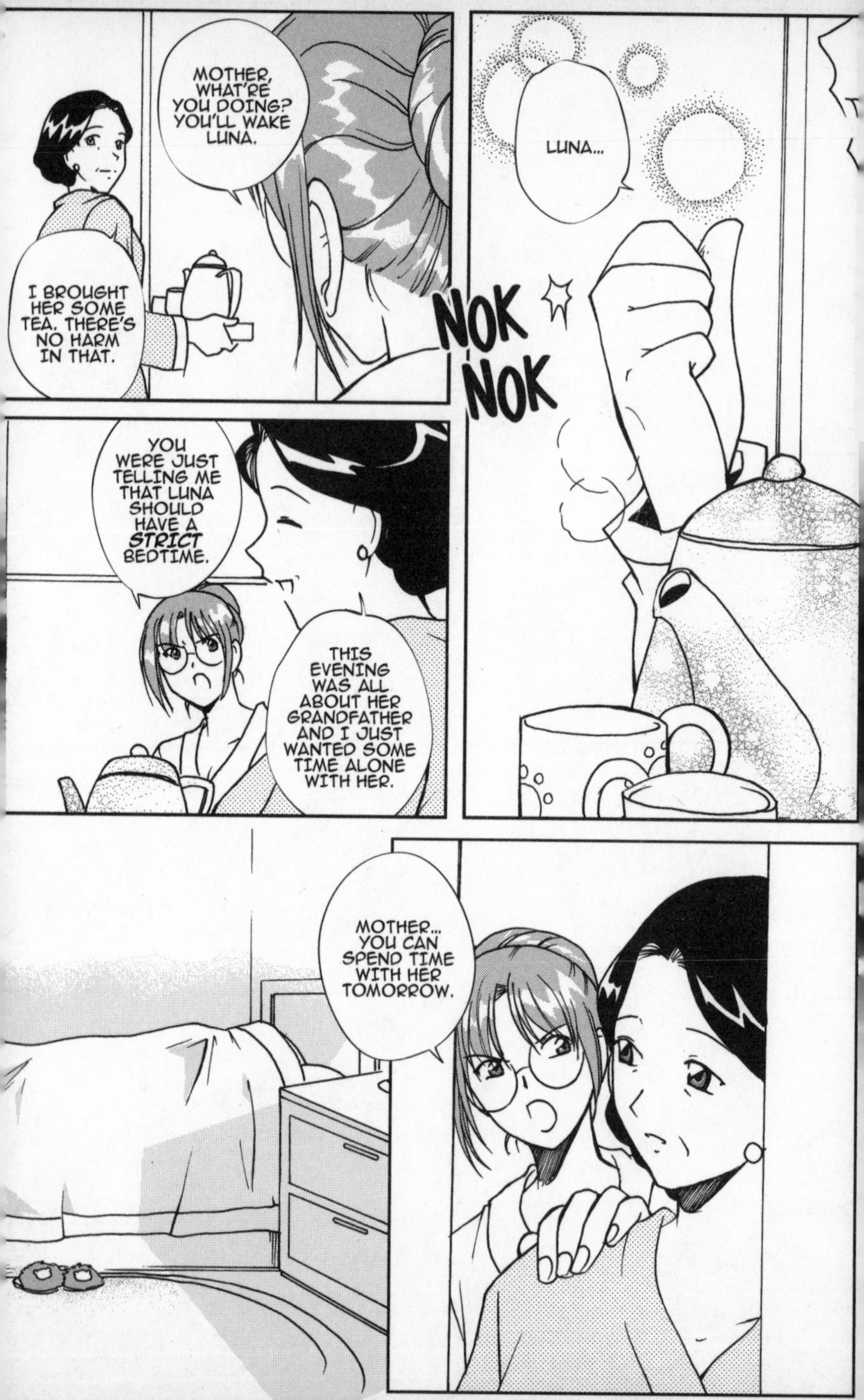
LUNA...
NOK NOK
MOTHER, WHAT'RE YOU DOING? YOU'LL WAKE LUNA.
I BROUGHT HER SOME TEA. THERE'S NO HARM IN THAT.
YOU WERE JUST TELLING ME THAT LUNA SHOULD HAVE A *STRICT* BEDTIME.
THIS EVENING WAS ALL ABOUT HER GRANDFATHER AND I JUST WANTED SOME TIME ALONE WITH HER.
MOTHER... YOU CAN SPEND TIME WITH HER TOMORROW.

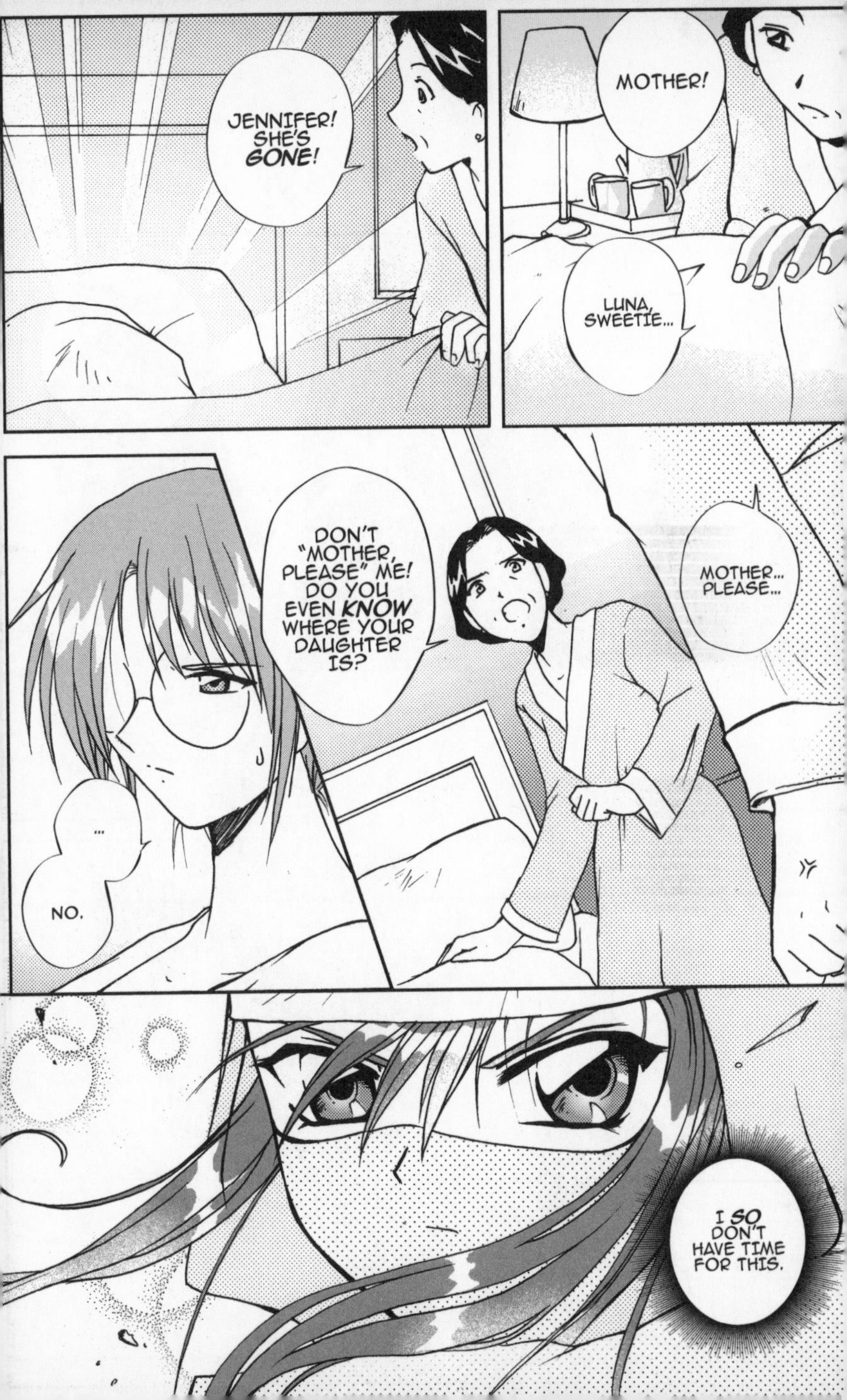
MOTHER!
LUNA, SWEETIE...
JENNIFER! SHE'S GONE!
MOTHER... PLEASE...
DON'T "MOTHER, PLEASE" ME! DO YOU EVEN KNOW WHERE YOUR DAUGHTER IS?
...
NO.
I SO DON'T HAVE TIME FOR THIS.

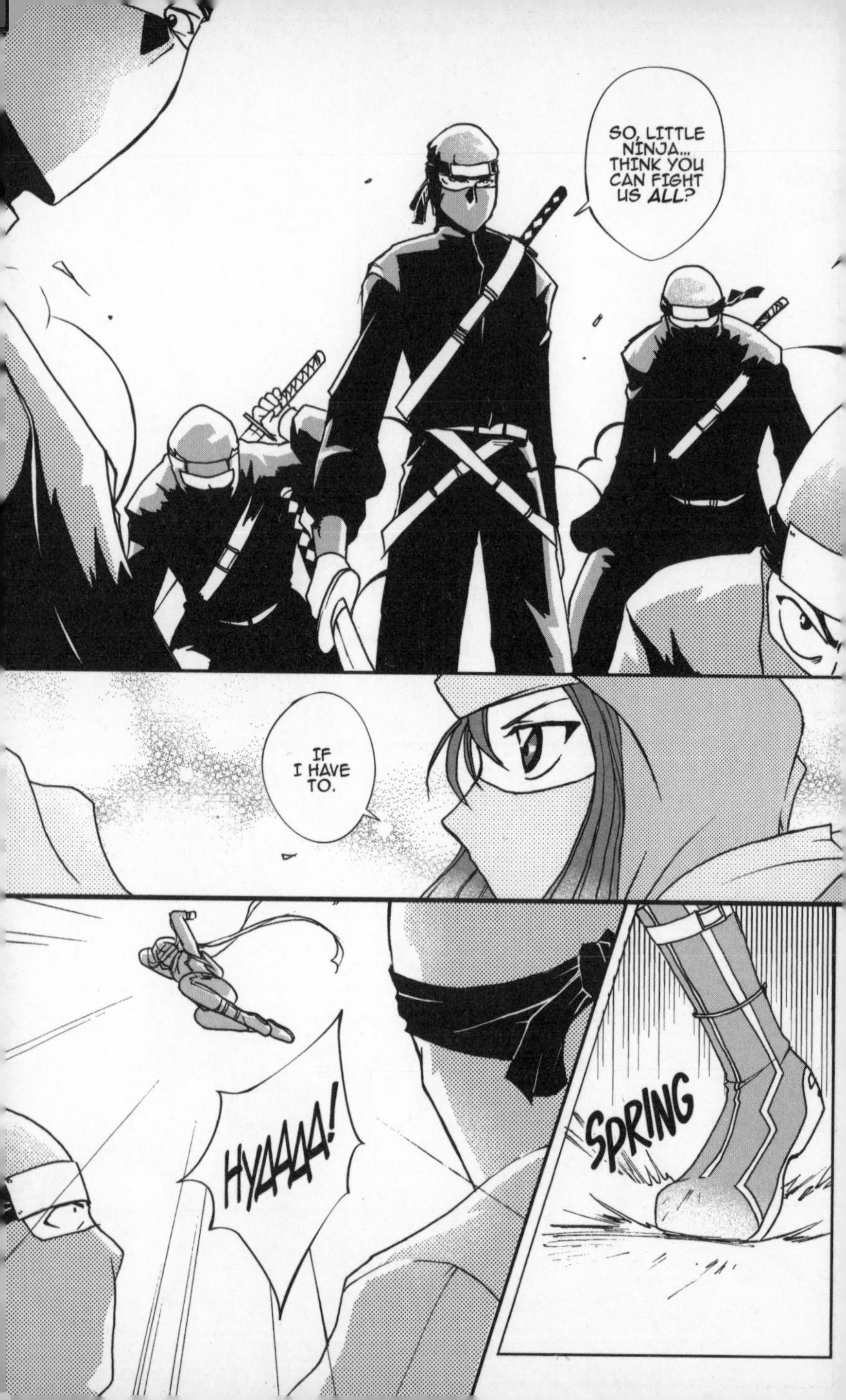
SO, LITTLE NINJA... THINK YOU CAN FIGHT US ALL?
IF I HAVE TO.
SPRING
HYAAAA!

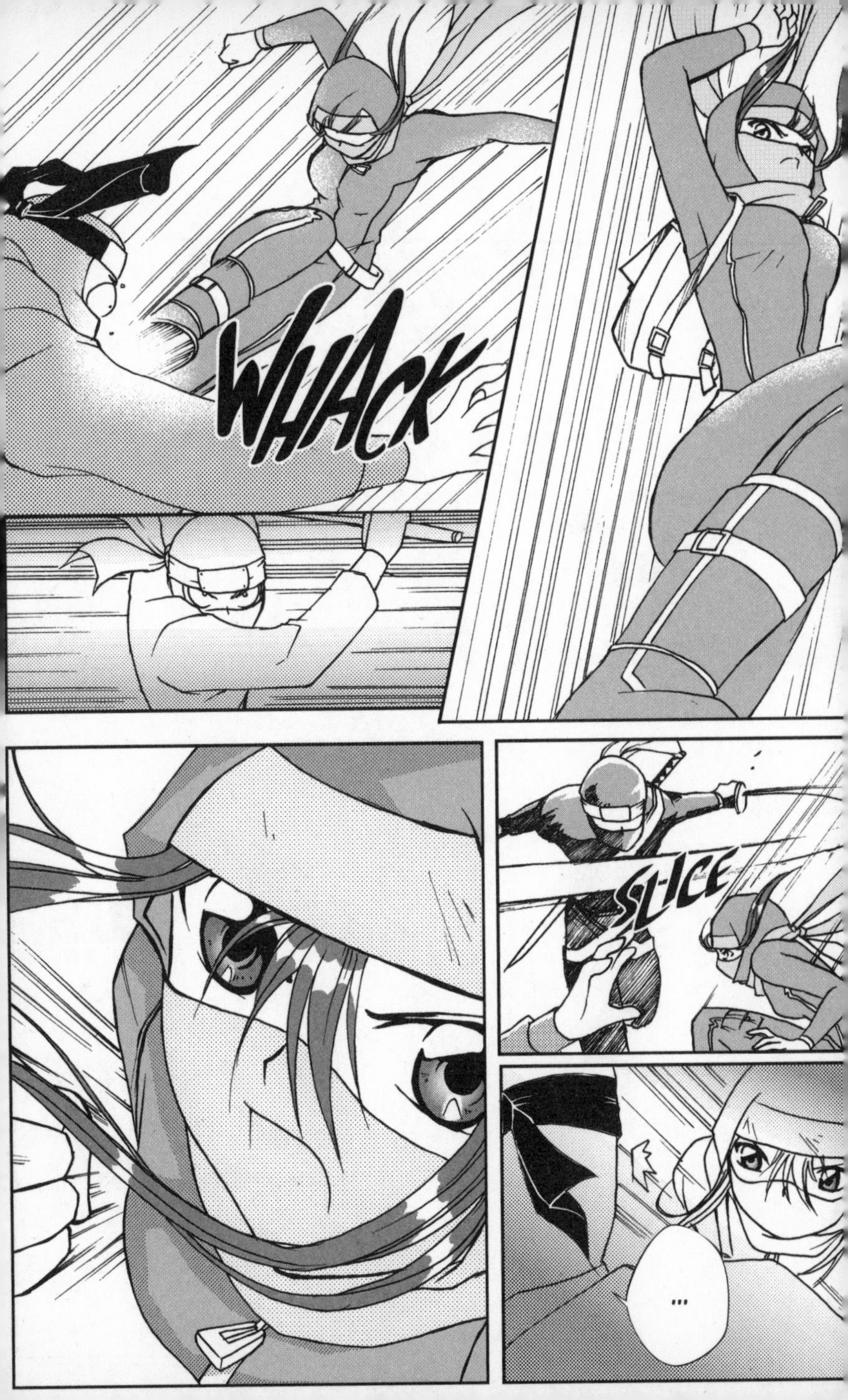
WHACK
SLICE
...

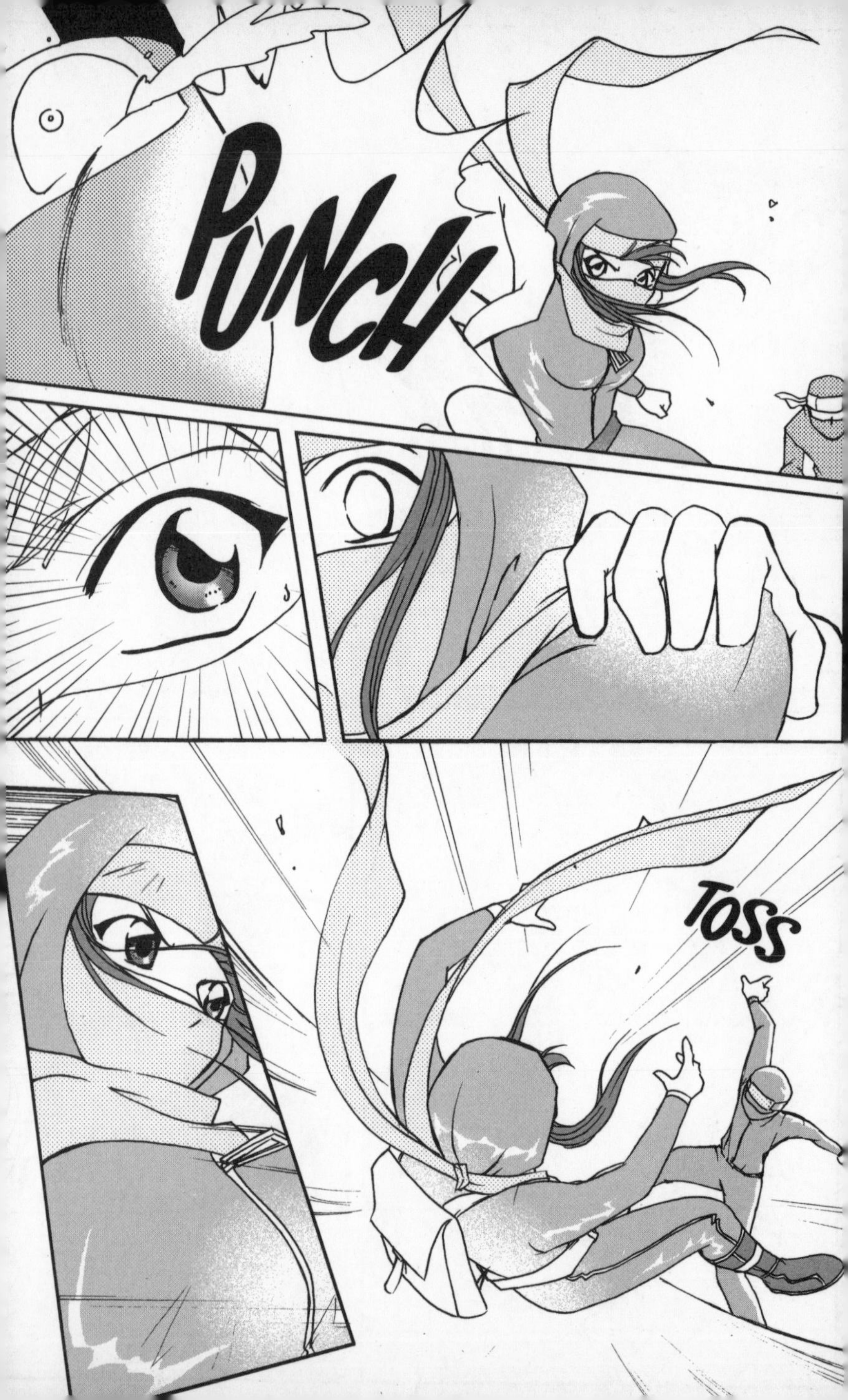
PUNCH
TOSS

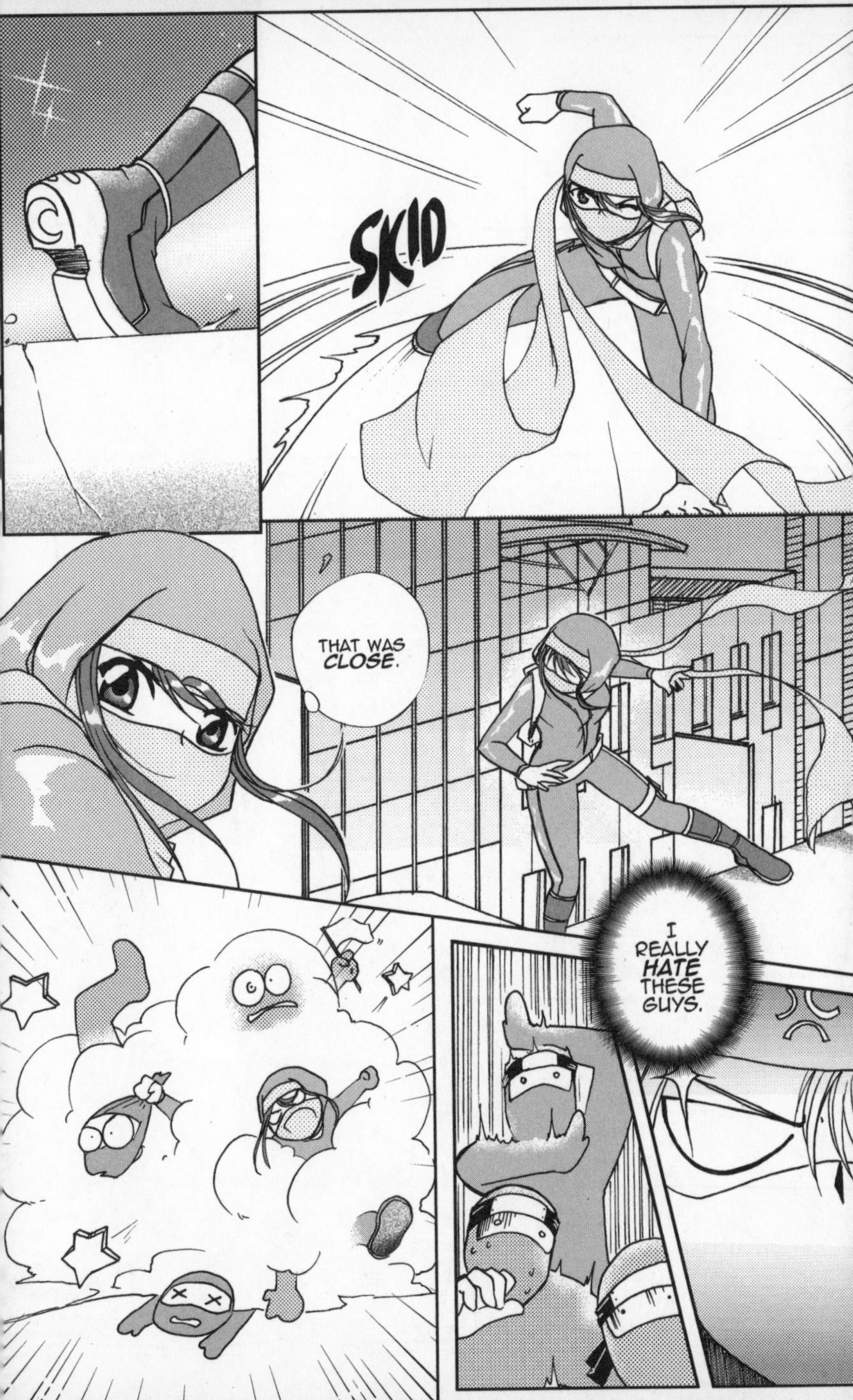
SKID
THAT WAS CLOSE.
I REALLY HATE THESE GUYS.

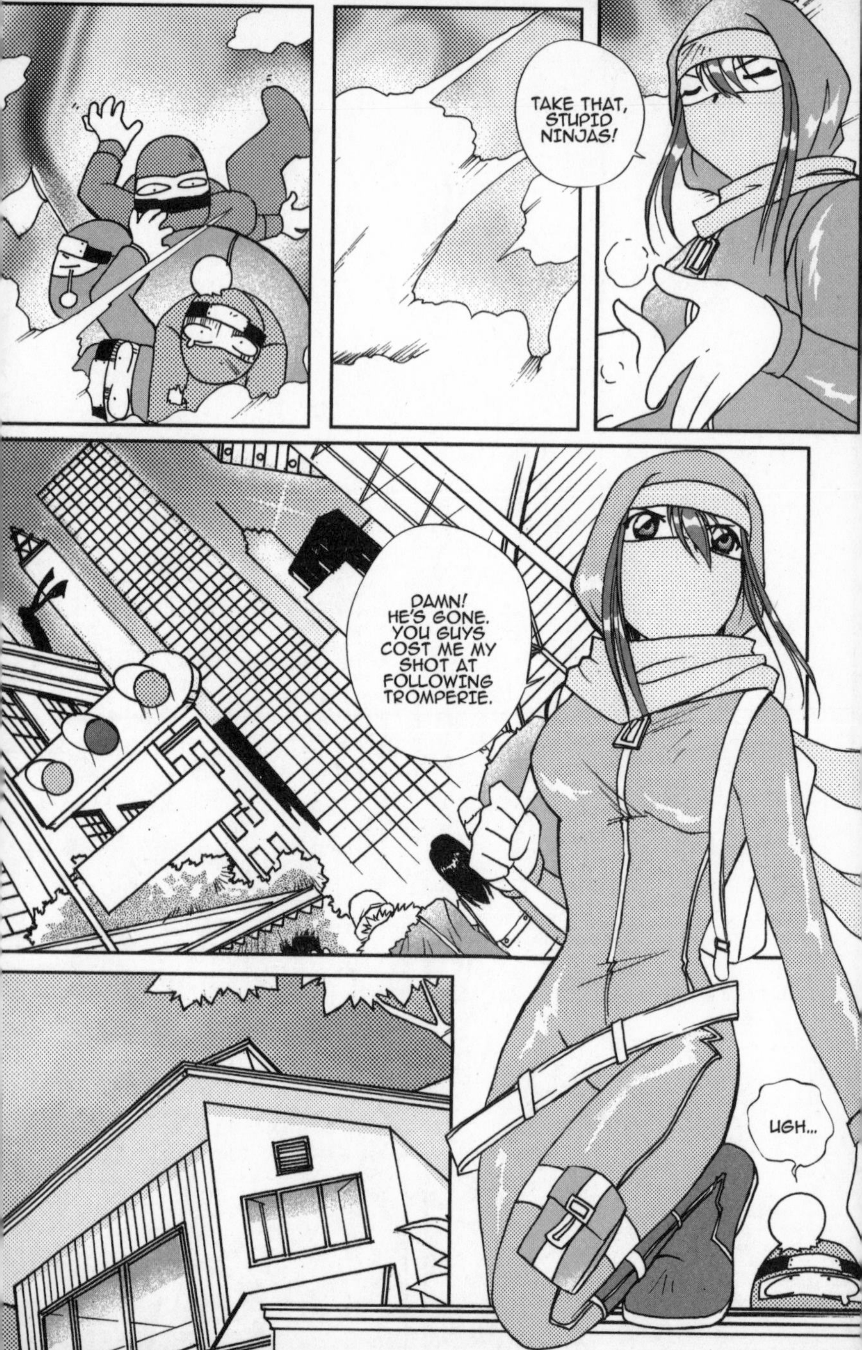
TAKE THAT, STUPID NINJAS!
DAMN! HE'S GONE. YOU GUYS COST ME MY SHOT AT FOLLOWING TROMPERIE.
UGH...

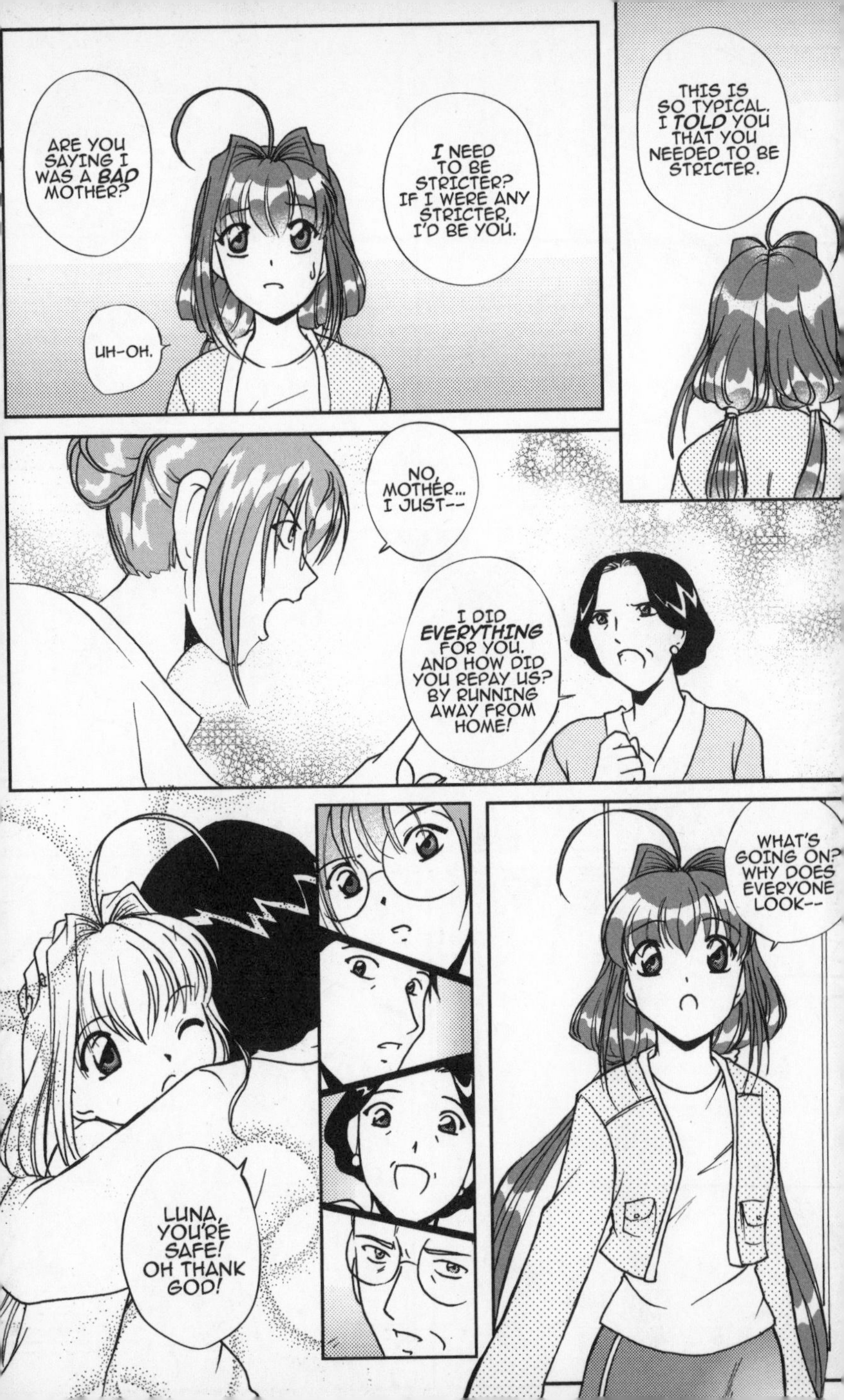
THIS IS SO TYPICAL. I TOLD YOU THAT YOU NEEDED TO BE STRICTER.
I NEED TO BE STRICTER? IF I WERE ANY STRICTER, I'D BE YOU.
ARE YOU SAYING I WAS A BAD MOTHER?
UH-OH.
NO, MOTHER... I JUST--
I DID EVERYTHING FOR YOU. AND HOW DID YOU REPAY US? BY RUNNING AWAY FROM HOME!
WHAT'S GOING ON? WHY DOES EVERYONE LOOK--
LUNA, YOU'RE SAFE! OH THANK GOD!

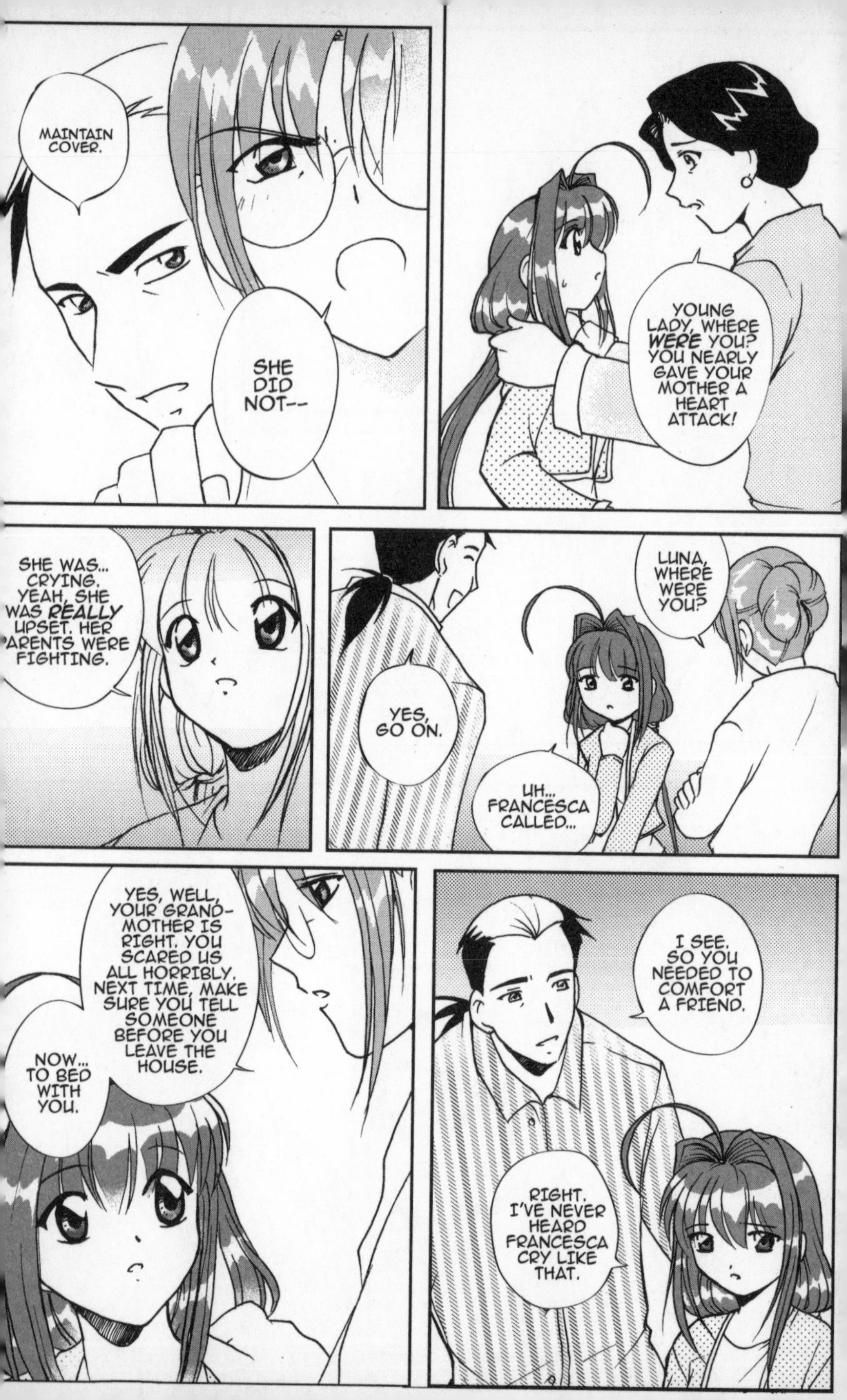
YOUNG LADY, WHERE *WERE* YOU? YOU NEARLY GAVE YOUR MOTHER A HEART ATTACK!
SHE DID NOT--
MAINTAIN COVER.
LUNA, WHERE WERE YOU?
UH... FRANCESCA CALLED...
YES, GO ON.
SHE WAS... CRYING. YEAH, SHE WAS *REALLY* UPSET. HER PARENTS WERE FIGHTING.
I SEE. SO YOU NEEDED TO COMFORT A FRIEND.
RIGHT. I'VE NEVER HEARD FRANCESCA CRY LIKE THAT.
YES, WELL, YOUR GRAND-MOTHER IS RIGHT. YOU SCARED US ALL HORRIBLY. NEXT TIME, MAKE SURE YOU TELL SOMEONE BEFORE YOU LEAVE THE HOUSE.
NOW... TO BED WITH YOU.

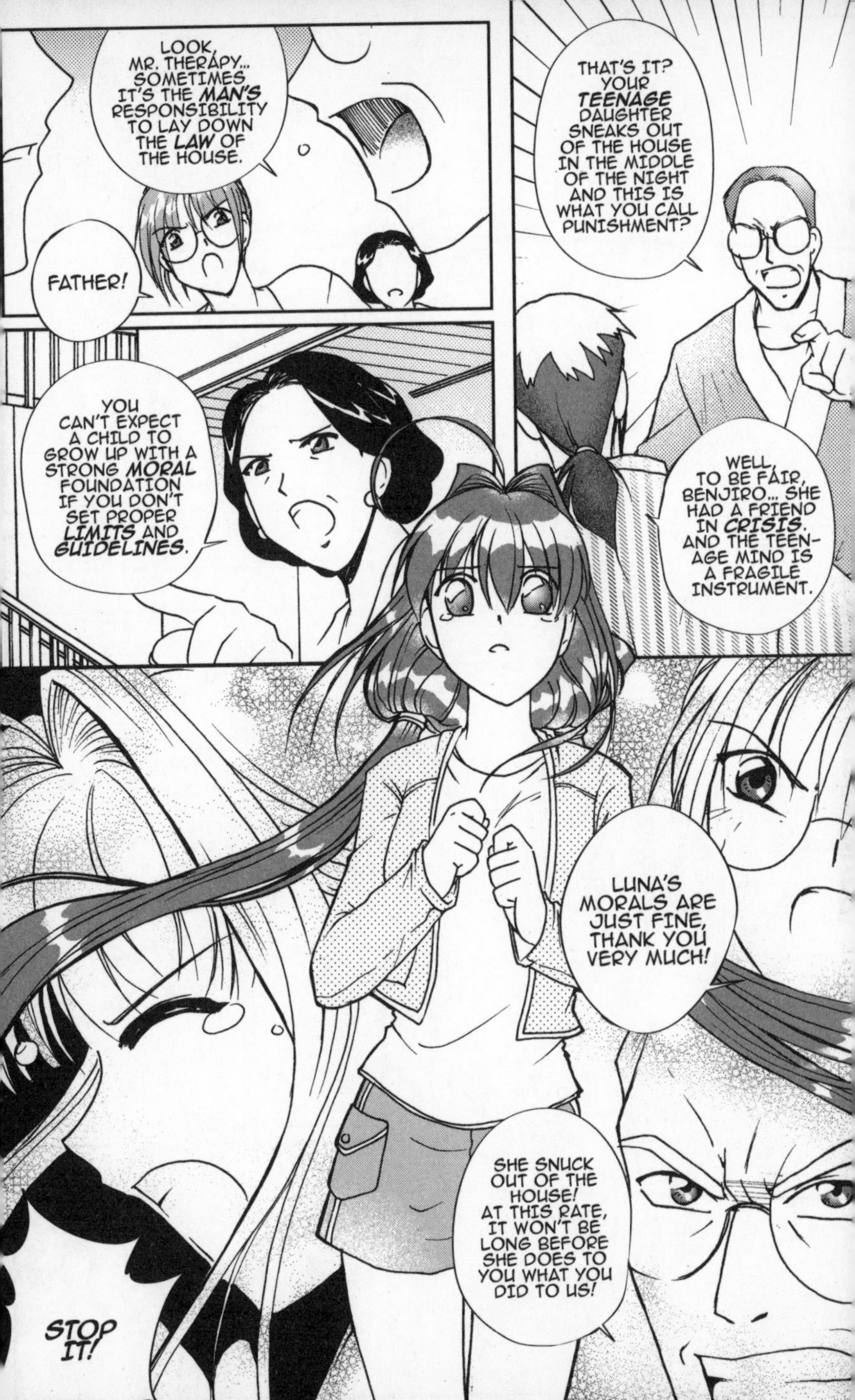
THAT'S IT? YOUR TEENAGE DAUGHTER SNEAKS OUT OF THE HOUSE IN THE MIDDLE OF THE NIGHT AND THIS IS WHAT YOU CALL PUNISHMENT?
WELL, TO BE FAIR, BENJIRO... SHE HAD A FRIEND IN CRISIS. AND THE TEENAGE MIND IS A FRAGILE INSTRUMENT.
LOOK, MR. THERAPY... SOMETIMES IT'S THE MAN'S RESPONSIBILITY TO LAY DOWN THE LAW OF THE HOUSE.
FATHER!
YOU CAN'T EXPECT A CHILD TO GROW UP WITH A STRONG MORAL FOUNDATION IF YOU DON'T SET PROPER LIMITS AND GUIDELINES.
LUNA'S MORALS ARE JUST FINE, THANK YOU VERY MUCH!
SHE SNUCK OUT OF THE HOUSE! AT THIS RATE, IT WON'T BE LONG BEFORE SHE DOES TO YOU WHAT YOU DID TO US!
STOP IT!

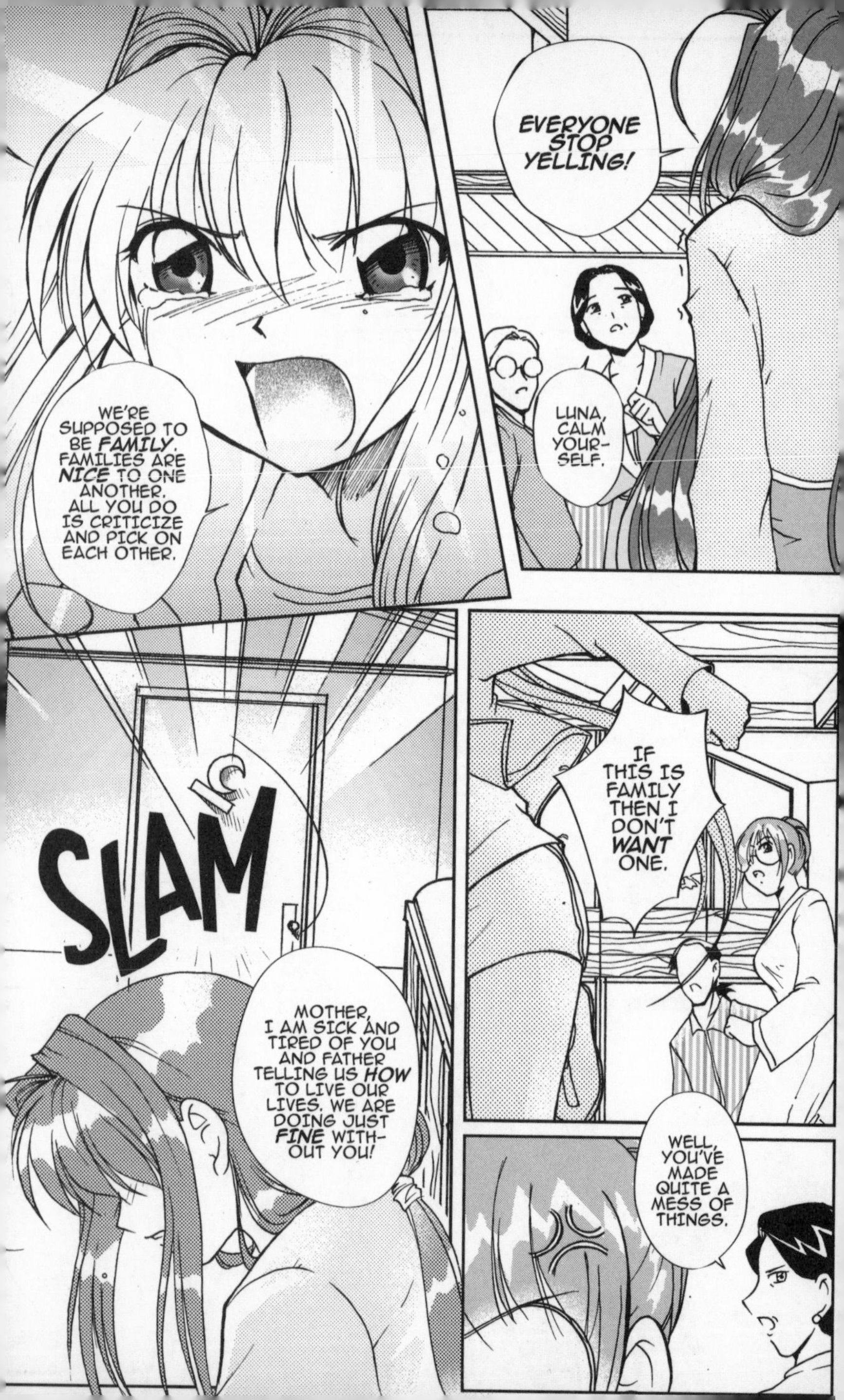
EVERYONE STOP YELLING!
LUNA, CALM YOUR-SELF.
WE'RE SUPPOSED TO BE *FAMILY*. FAMILIES ARE *NICE* TO ONE ANOTHER. ALL YOU DO IS CRITICIZE AND PICK ON EACH OTHER.
IF THIS IS FAMILY THEN I DON'T *WANT* ONE.
WELL, YOU'VE MADE QUITE A MESS OF THINGS.
SLAM
MOTHER, I AM SICK AND TIRED OF YOU AND FATHER TELLING US *HOW* TO LIVE OUR LIVES. WE ARE DOING JUST *FINE* WITH-OUT YOU!

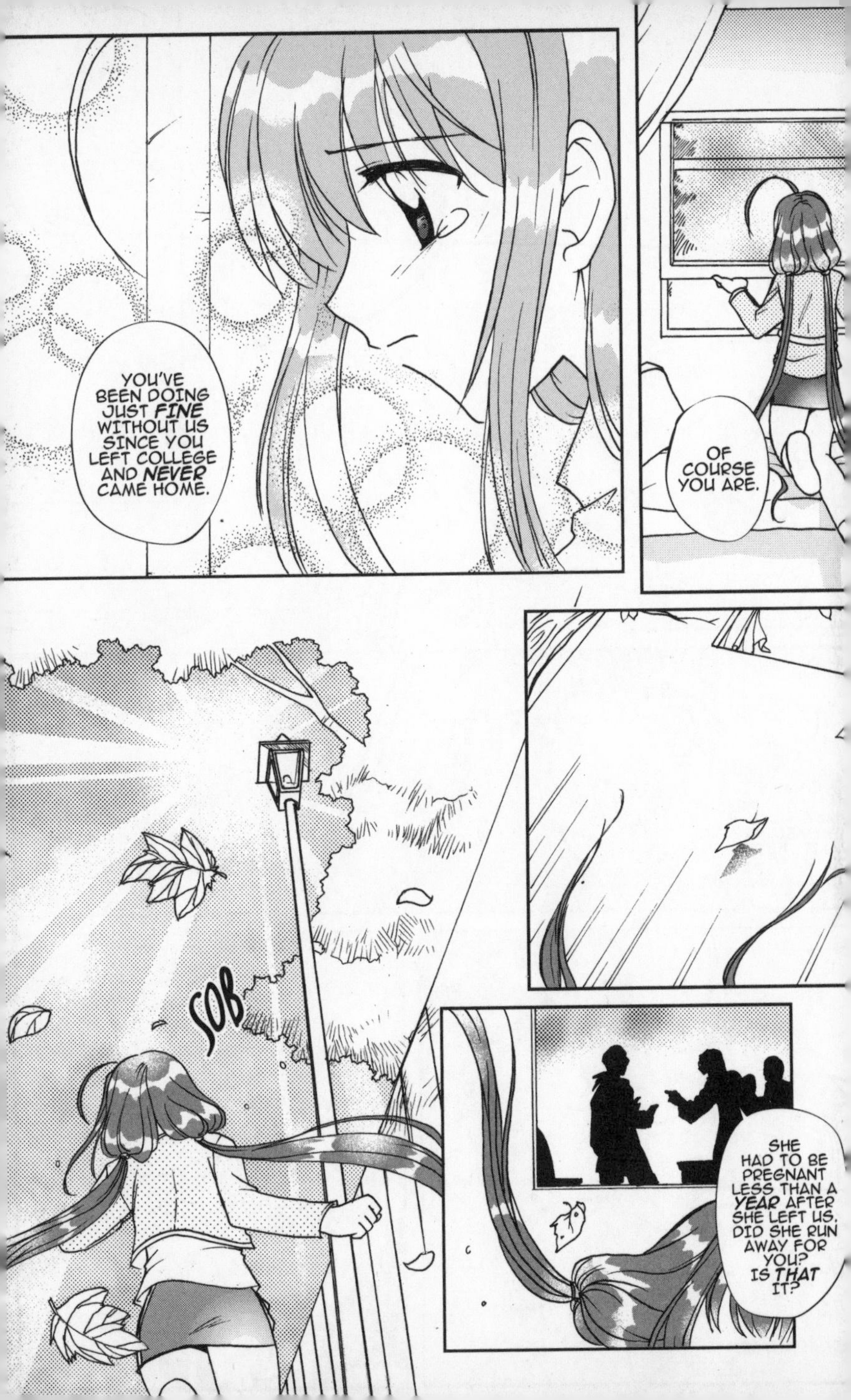
OF COURSE YOU ARE.
YOU'VE BEEN DOING JUST *FINE* WITHOUT US SINCE YOU LEFT COLLEGE AND *NEVER* CAME HOME.
SHE HAD TO BE PREGNANT LESS THAN A *YEAR* AFTER SHE LEFT US. DID SHE RUN AWAY FOR YOU? IS *THAT* IT?
SOB

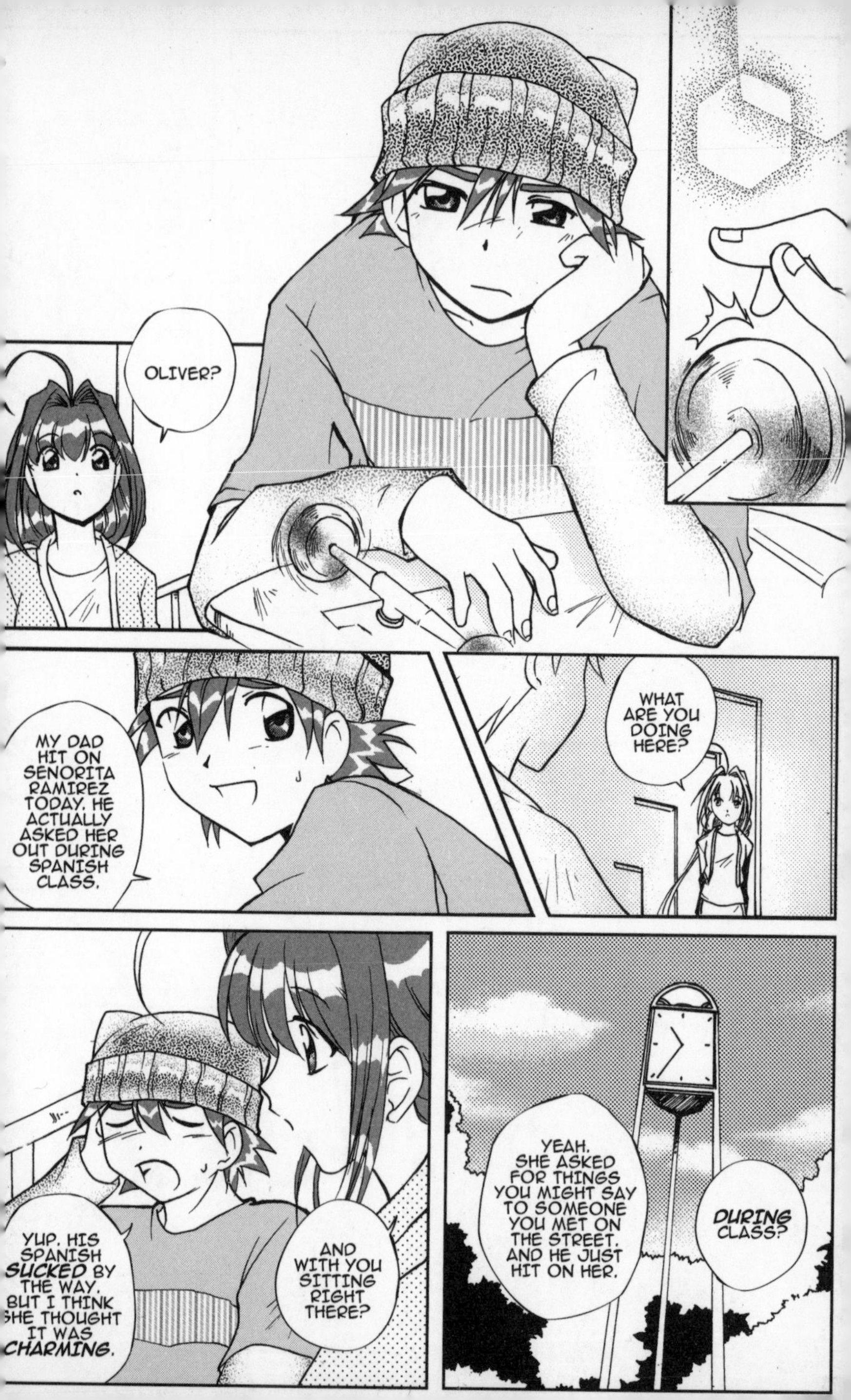
OLIVER?
WHAT ARE YOU DOING HERE?
MY DAD HIT ON SENORITA RAMIREZ TODAY. HE ACTUALLY ASKED HER OUT DURING SPANISH CLASS.
**DURING** CLASS?
YEAH. SHE ASKED FOR THINGS YOU MIGHT SAY TO SOMEONE YOU MET ON THE STREET. AND HE JUST HIT ON HER.
AND WITH YOU SITTING RIGHT THERE?
YUP. HIS SPANISH **SUCKED** BY THE WAY. BUT I THINK SHE THOUGHT IT WAS **CHARMING**.

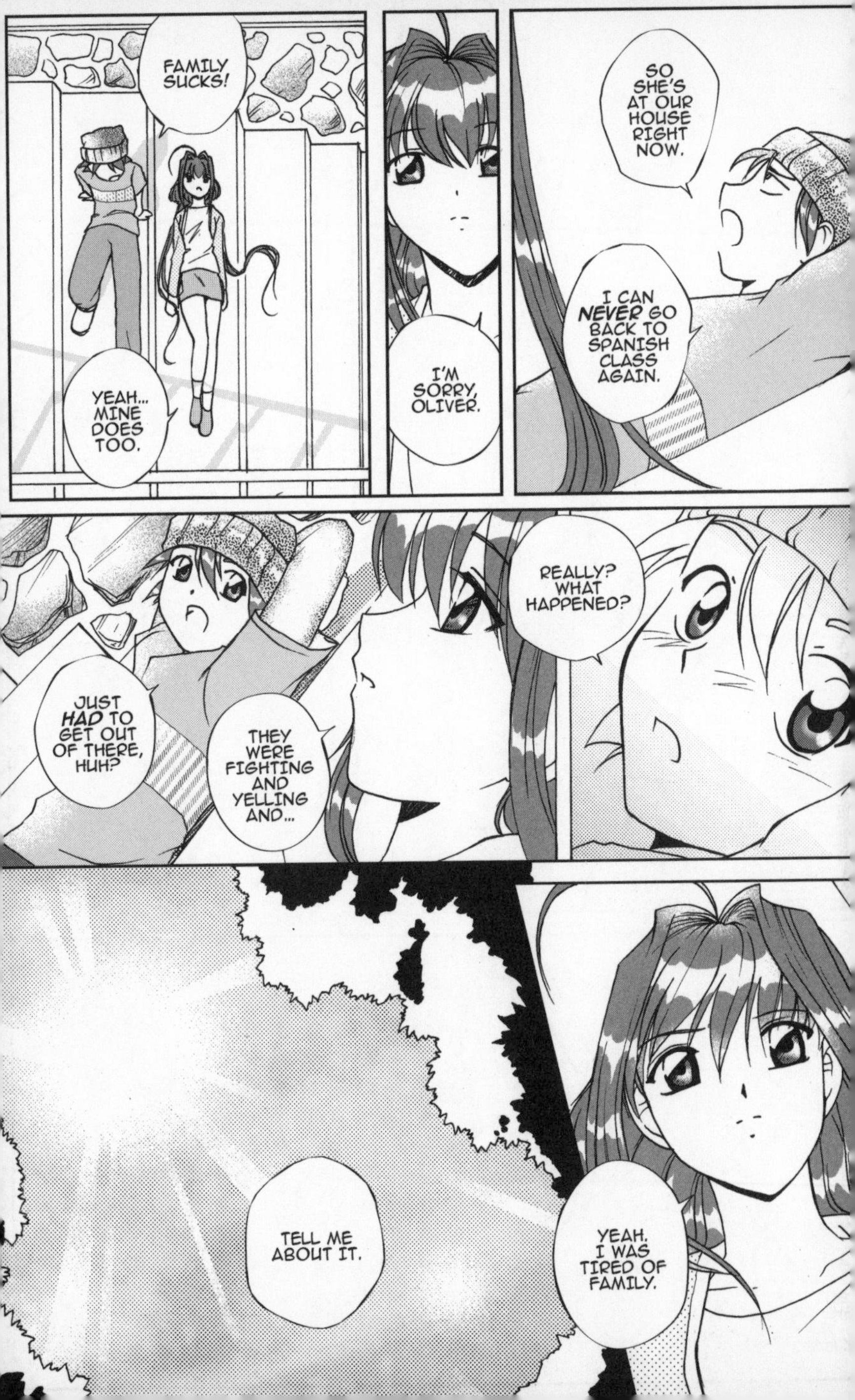
SO SHE'S AT OUR HOUSE RIGHT NOW.
I CAN *NEVER* GO BACK TO SPANISH CLASS AGAIN.
I'M SORRY, OLIVER.
FAMILY SUCKS!
YEAH... MINE DOES TOO.
REALLY? WHAT HAPPENED?
THEY WERE FIGHTING AND YELLING AND...
JUST *HAD* TO GET OUT OF THERE, HUH?
YEAH. I WAS TIRED OF FAMILY.
TELL ME ABOUT IT.

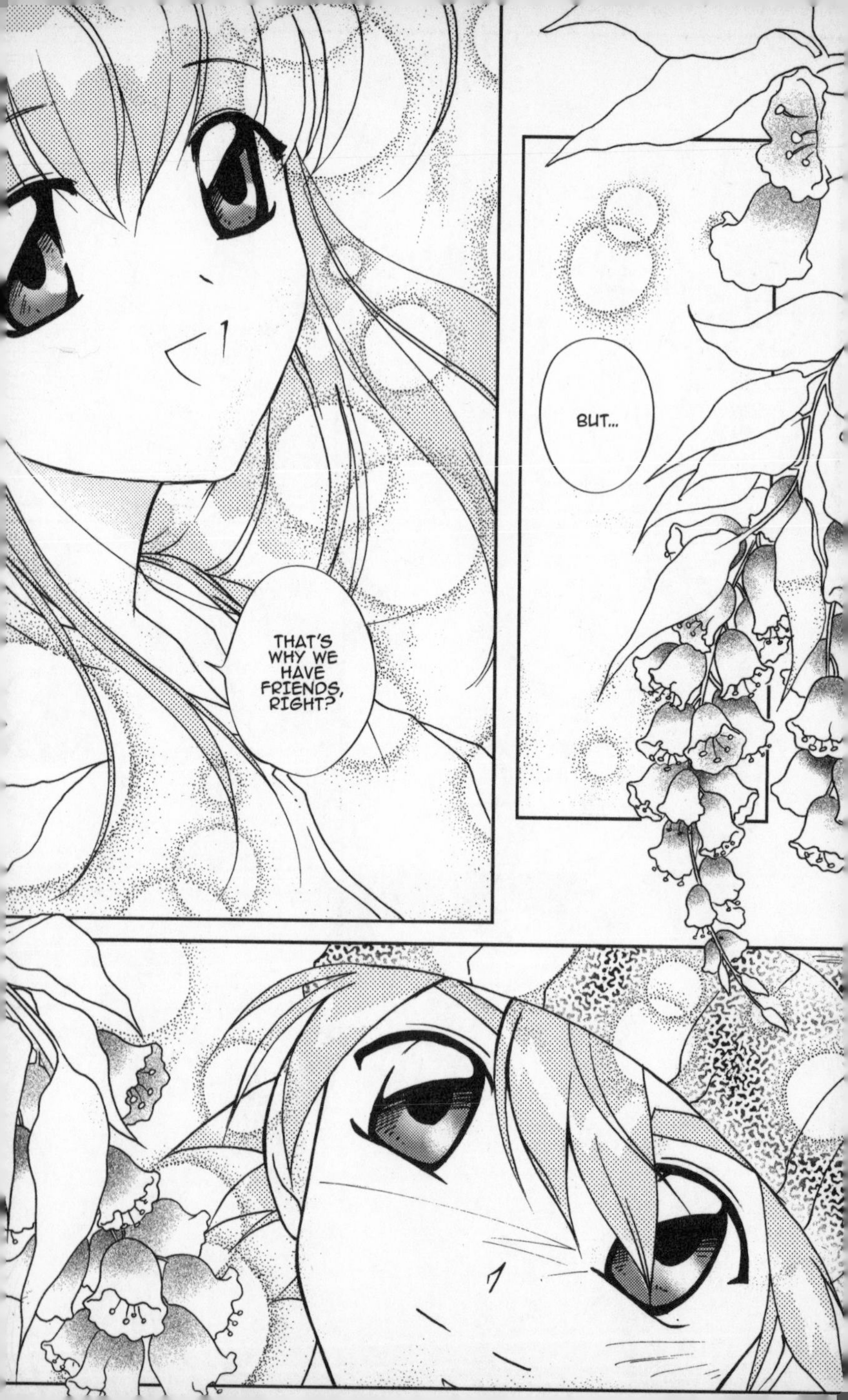
BUT...
THAT'S WHY WE HAVE FRIENDS, RIGHT?

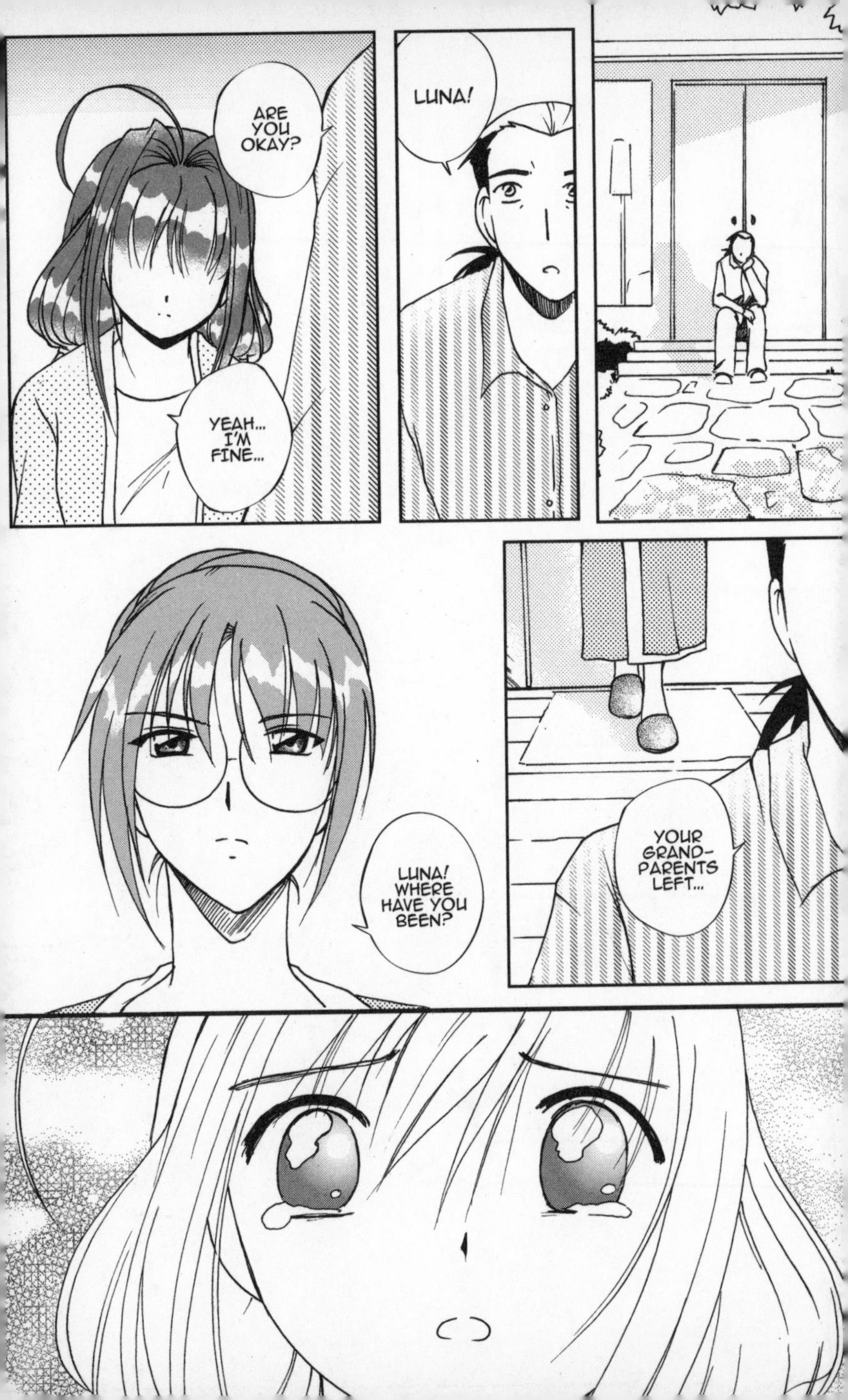
LUNA!
ARE YOU OKAY?
YEAH... I'M FINE...
YOUR GRAND-PARENTS LEFT...
LUNA! WHERE HAVE YOU BEEN?

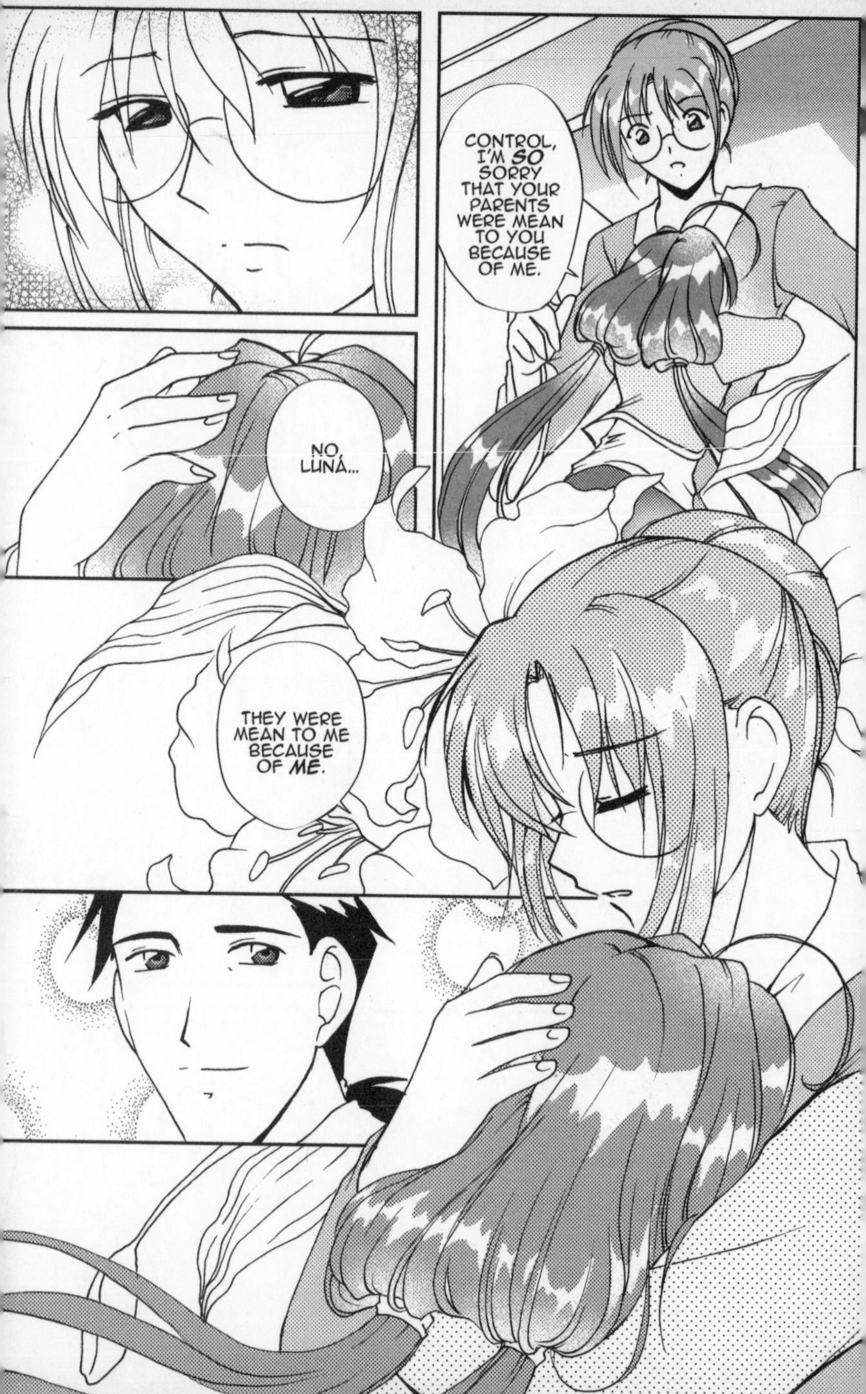
CONTROL, I'M SO SORRY THAT YOUR PARENTS WERE MEAN TO YOU BECAUSE OF ME.
NO, LUNA...
THEY WERE MEAN TO ME BECAUSE OF ME.

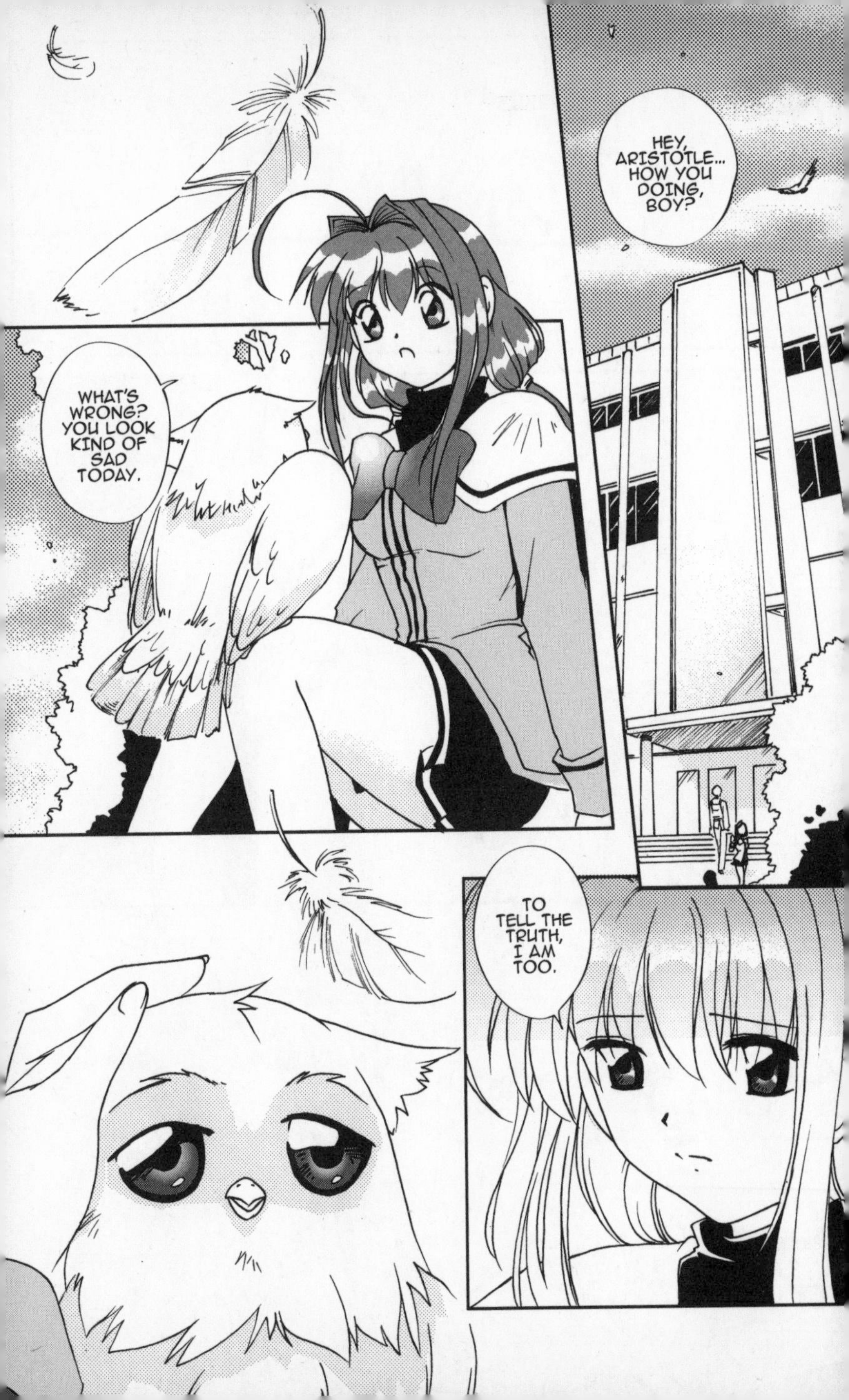
HEY, ARISTOTLE... HOW YOU DOING, BOY?
WHAT'S WRONG? YOU LOOK KIND OF SAD TODAY.
TO TELL THE TRUTH, I AM TOO.

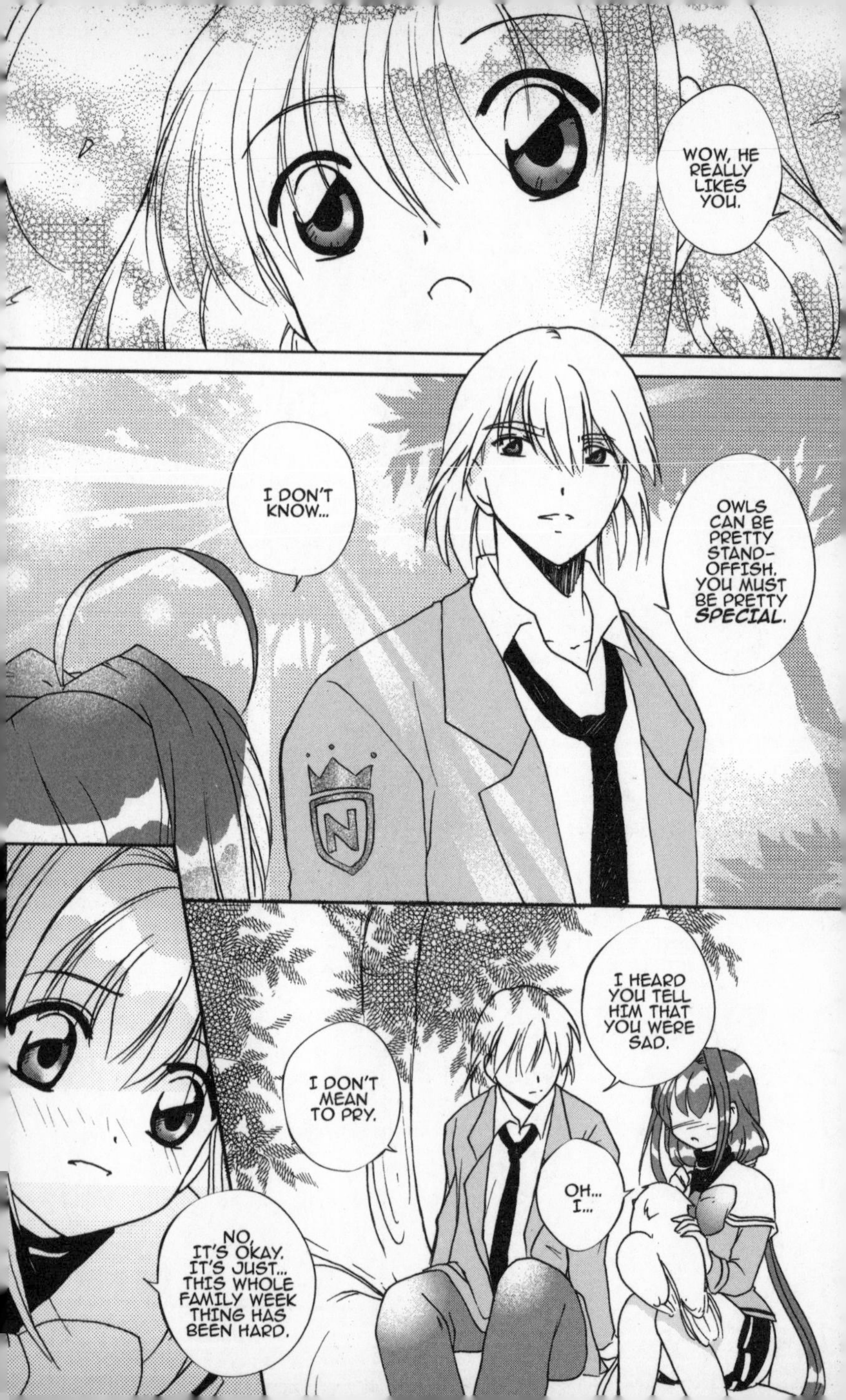
WOW, HE REALLY LIKES YOU.
OWLS CAN BE PRETTY STAND-OFFISH. YOU MUST BE PRETTY **SPECIAL**.
I DON'T KNOW...
I HEARD YOU TELL HIM THAT YOU WERE SAD.
OH... I...
I DON'T MEAN TO PRY.
NO, IT'S OKAY. IT'S JUST... THIS WHOLE FAMILY WEEK THING HAS BEEN HARD.

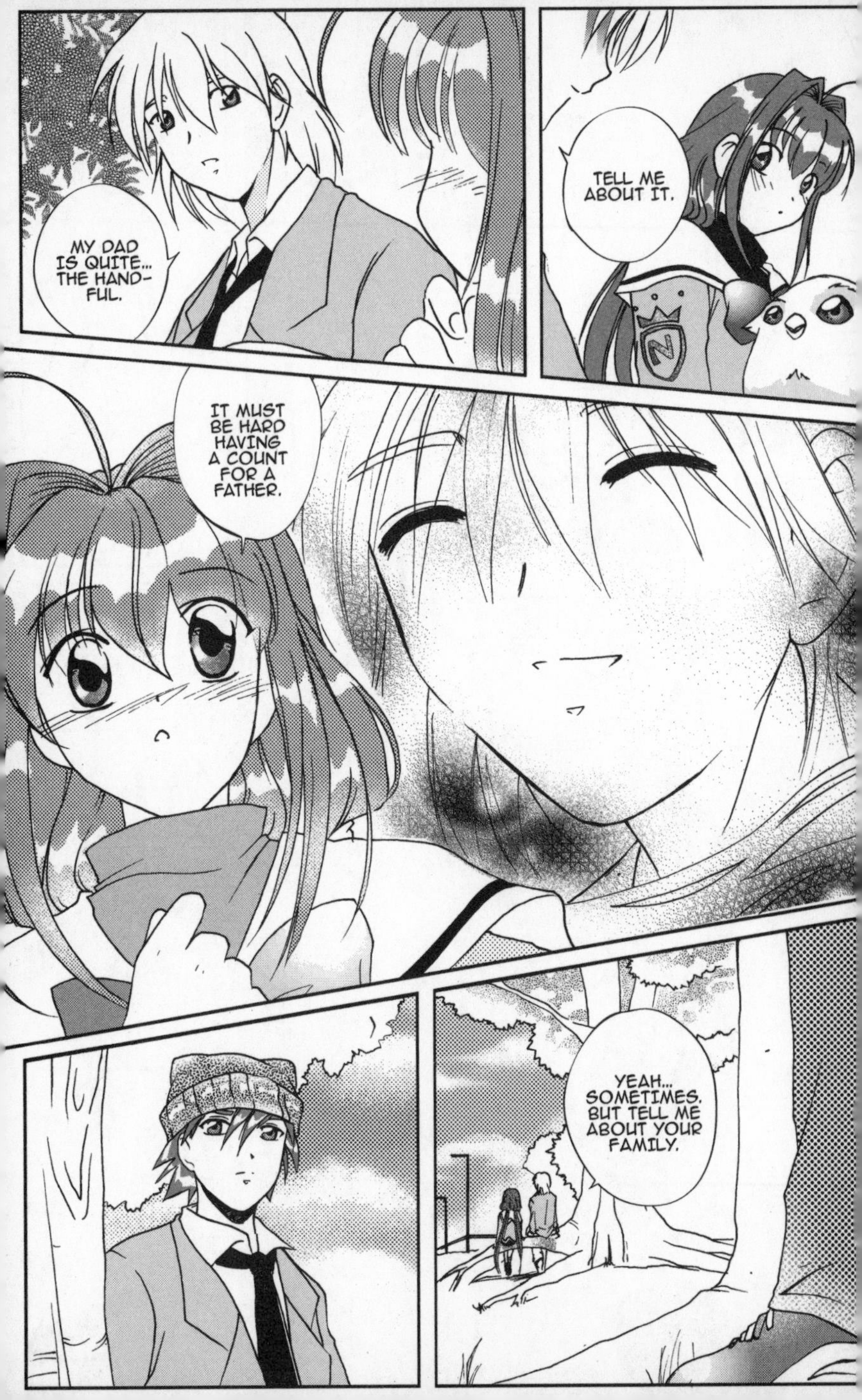
TELL ME ABOUT IT.
MY DAD IS QUITE... THE HAND-FUL.
IT MUST BE HARD HAVING A COUNT FOR A FATHER.
YEAH... SOMETIMES. BUT TELL ME ABOUT YOUR FAMILY.

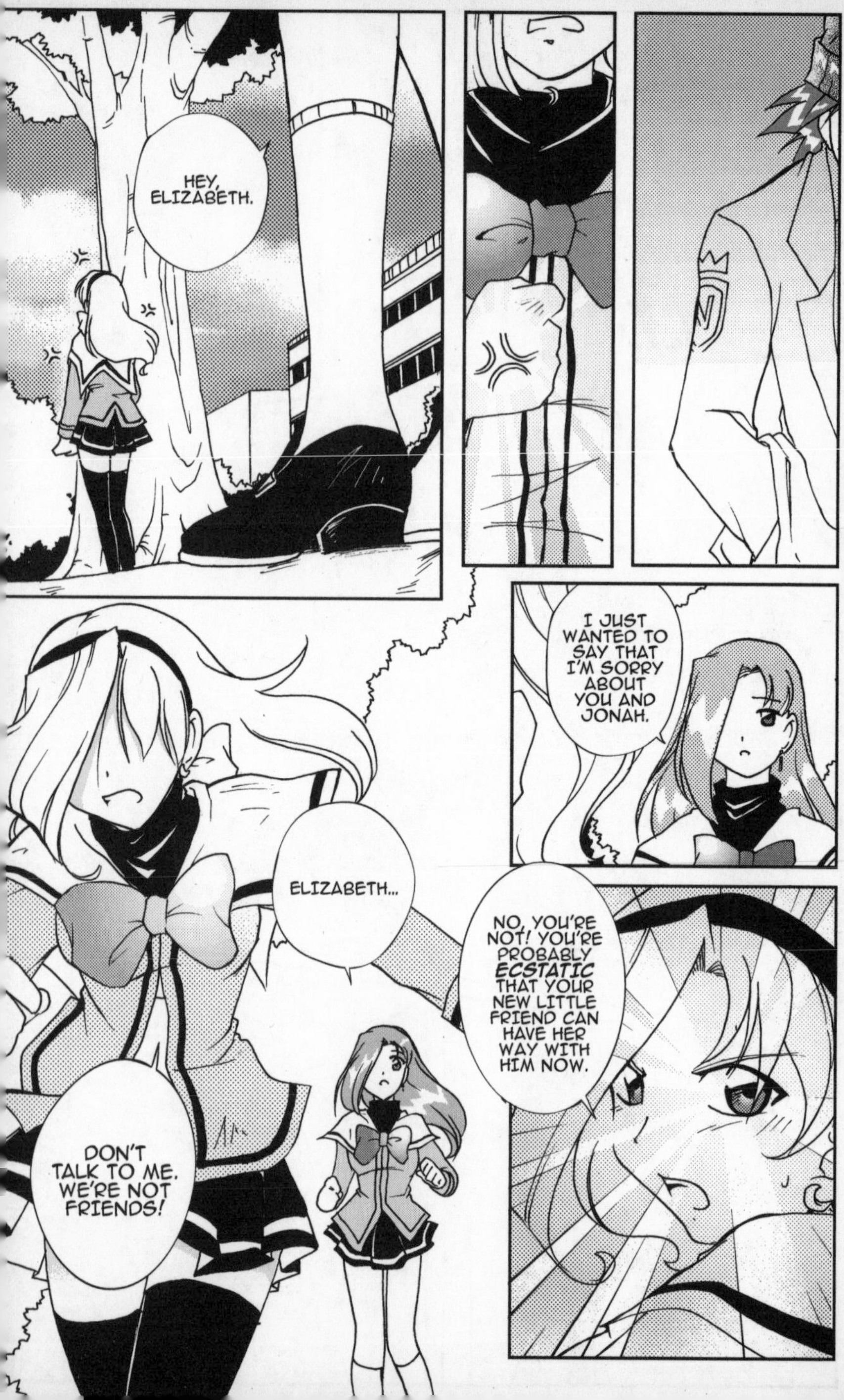
HEY, ELIZABETH.
I JUST WANTED TO SAY THAT I'M SORRY ABOUT YOU AND JONAH.
NO, YOU'RE NOT! YOU'RE PROBABLY *ECSTATIC* THAT YOUR NEW LITTLE FRIEND CAN HAVE HER WAY WITH HIM NOW.
ELIZABETH...
DON'T TALK TO ME. WE'RE NOT FRIENDS!

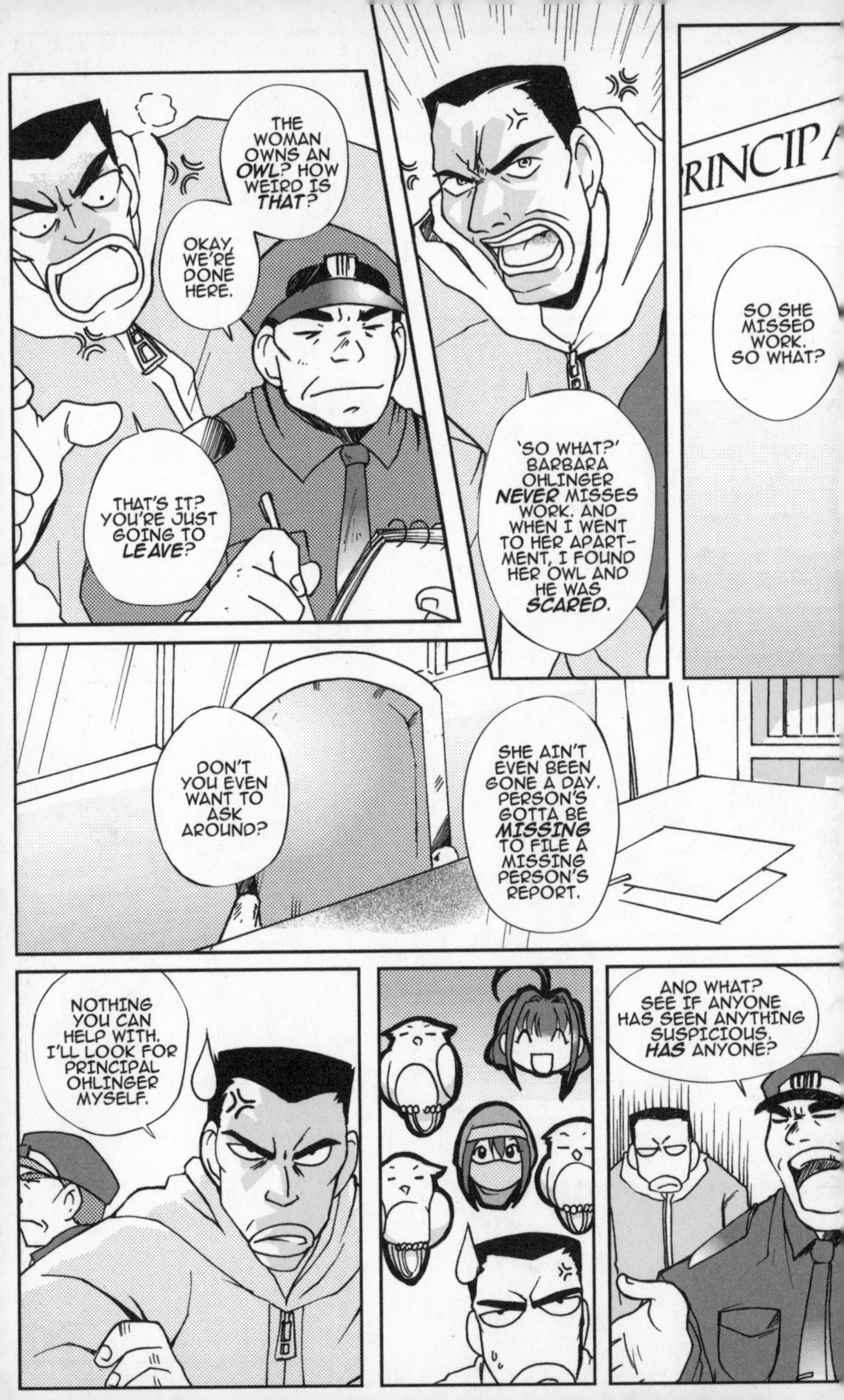
SO SHE MISSED WORK. SO WHAT?
'SO WHAT?' BARBARA OHLINGER NEVER MISSES WORK. AND WHEN I WENT TO HER APARTMENT, I FOUND HER OWL AND HE WAS SCARED.
THE WOMAN OWNS AN OWL? HOW WEIRD IS THAT?
OKAY, WE'RE DONE HERE.
THAT'S IT? YOU'RE JUST GOING TO LEAVE?
SHE AIN'T EVEN BEEN GONE A DAY. PERSON'S GOTTA BE MISSING TO FILE A MISSING PERSON'S REPORT.
DON'T YOU EVEN WANT TO ASK AROUND?
AND WHAT? SEE IF ANYONE HAS SEEN ANYTHING SUSPICIOUS. HAS ANYONE?
NOTHING YOU CAN HELP WITH. I'LL LOOK FOR PRINCIPAL OHLINGER MYSELF.

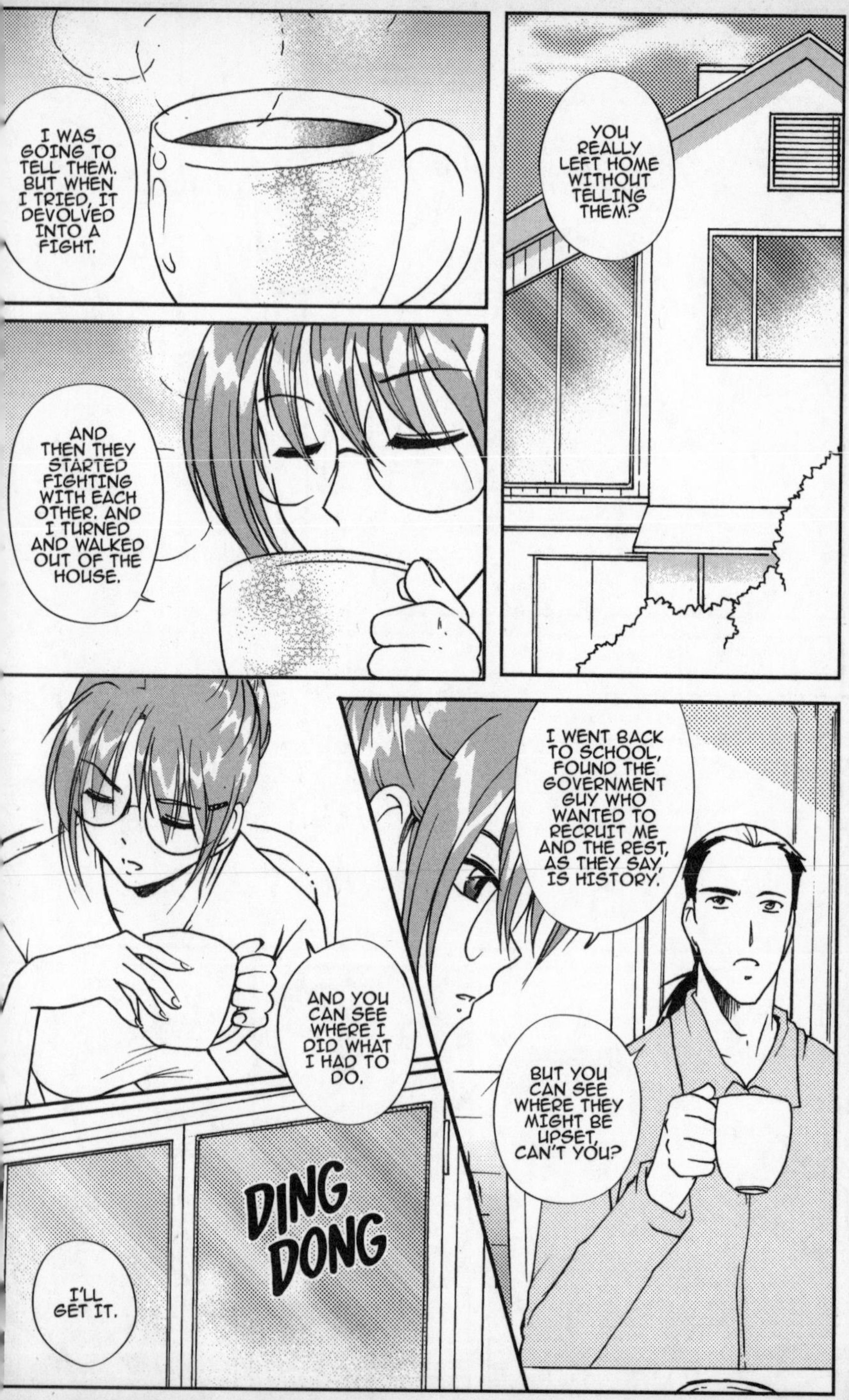
YOU REALLY LEFT HOME WITHOUT TELLING THEM?
I WAS GOING TO TELL THEM. BUT WHEN I TRIED, IT DEVOLVED INTO A FIGHT.
AND THEN THEY STARTED FIGHTING WITH EACH OTHER. AND I TURNED AND WALKED OUT OF THE HOUSE.
I WENT BACK TO SCHOOL, FOUND THE GOVERNMENT GUY WHO WANTED TO RECRUIT ME AND THE REST, AS THEY SAY, IS HISTORY.
BUT YOU CAN SEE WHERE THEY MIGHT BE UPSET, CAN'T YOU?
AND YOU CAN SEE WHERE I DID WHAT I HAD TO DO.
DING DONG
I'LL GET IT.

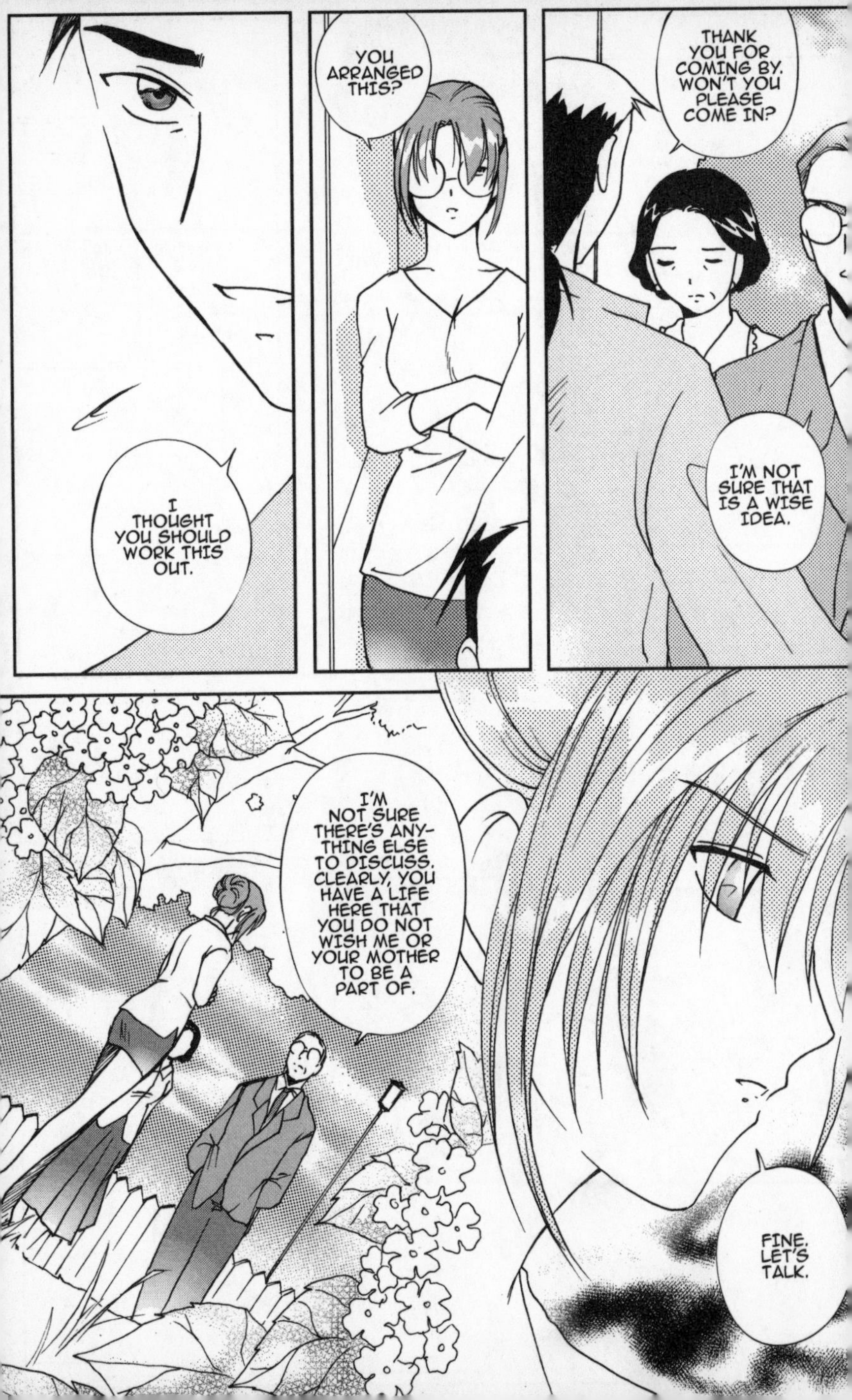
THANK YOU FOR COMING BY. WON'T YOU PLEASE COME IN?
I'M NOT SURE THAT IS A WISE IDEA.
YOU ARRANGED THIS?
I THOUGHT YOU SHOULD WORK THIS OUT.
I'M NOT SURE THERE'S ANY-THING ELSE TO DISCUSS. CLEARLY, YOU HAVE A LIFE HERE THAT YOU DO NOT WISH ME OR YOUR MOTHER TO BE A PART OF.
FINE. LET'S TALK.

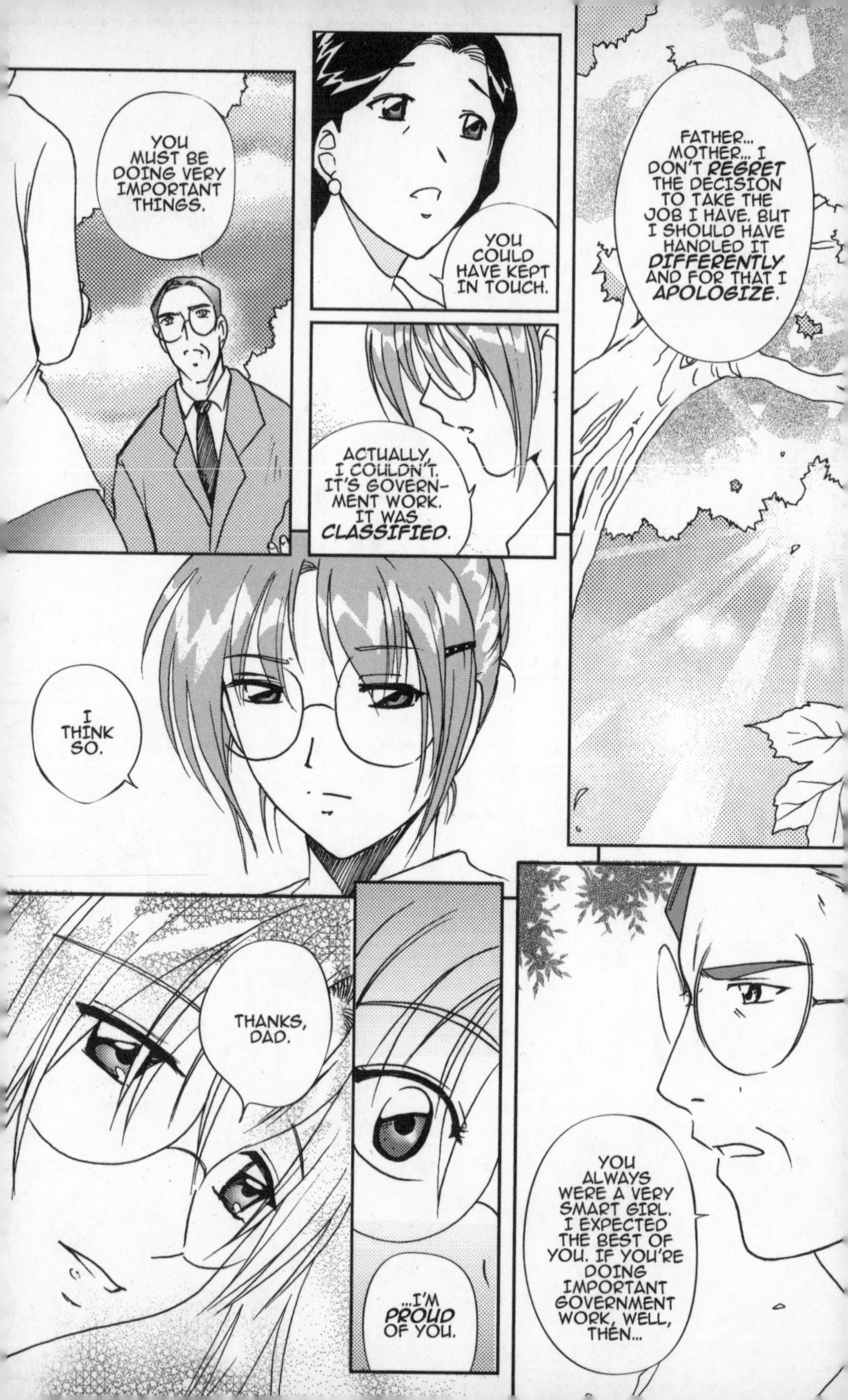
FATHER... MOTHER... I DON'T REGRET THE DECISION TO TAKE THE JOB I HAVE. BUT I SHOULD HAVE HANDLED IT DIFFERENTLY AND FOR THAT I APOLOGIZE.
YOU COULD HAVE KEPT IN TOUCH.
ACTUALLY, I COULDN'T. IT'S GOVERNMENT WORK. IT WAS CLASSIFIED.
YOU MUST BE DOING VERY IMPORTANT THINGS.
I THINK SO.
YOU ALWAYS WERE A VERY SMART GIRL. I EXPECTED THE BEST OF YOU. IF YOU'RE DOING IMPORTANT GOVERNMENT WORK, WELL, THEN...
...I'M PROUD OF YOU.
THANKS, DAD.

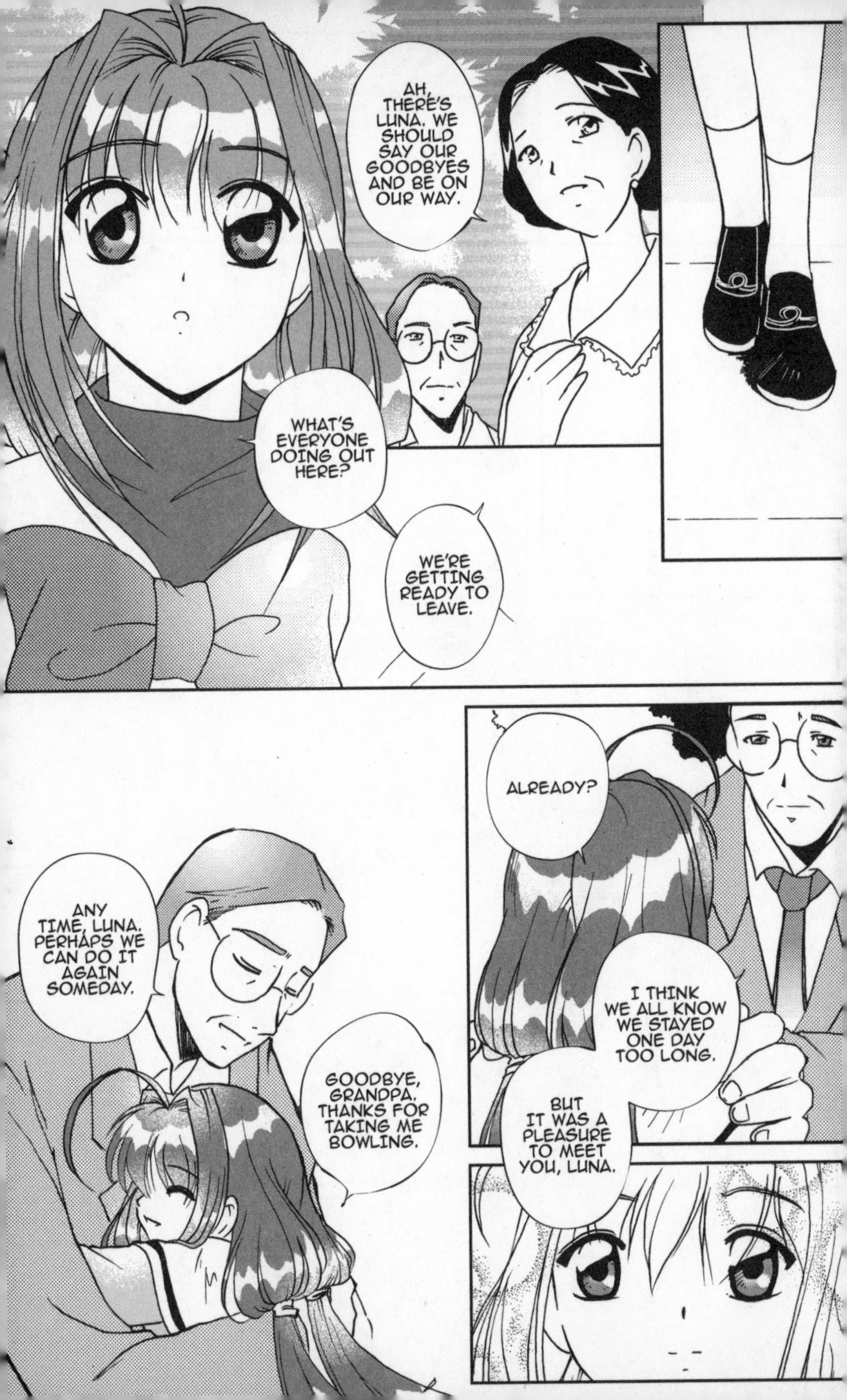
AH, THERE'S LUNA. WE SHOULD SAY OUR GOODBYES AND BE ON OUR WAY.
WHAT'S EVERYONE DOING OUT HERE?
WE'RE GETTING READY TO LEAVE.
ALREADY?
I THINK WE ALL KNOW WE STAYED ONE DAY TOO LONG.
BUT IT WAS A PLEASURE TO MEET YOU, LUNA.
GOODBYE, GRANDPA. THANKS FOR TAKING ME BOWLING.
ANY TIME, LUNA. PERHAPS WE CAN DO IT AGAIN SOMEDAY.

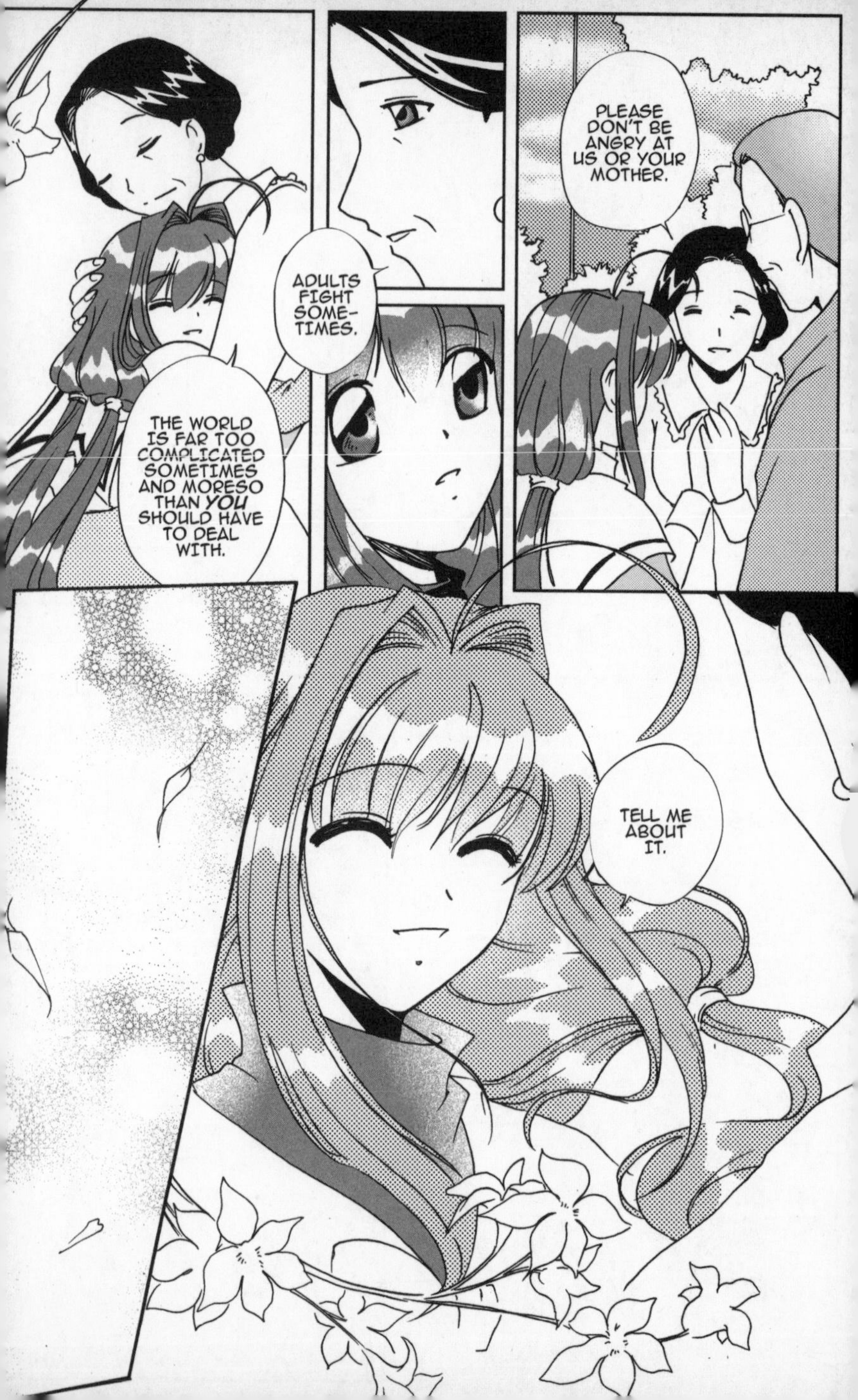
PLEASE DON'T BE ANGRY AT US OR YOUR MOTHER.
ADULTS FIGHT SOME-TIMES.
THE WORLD IS FAR TOO COMPLICATED SOMETIMES AND MORESO THAN *YOU* SHOULD HAVE TO DEAL WITH.
TELL ME ABOUT IT.

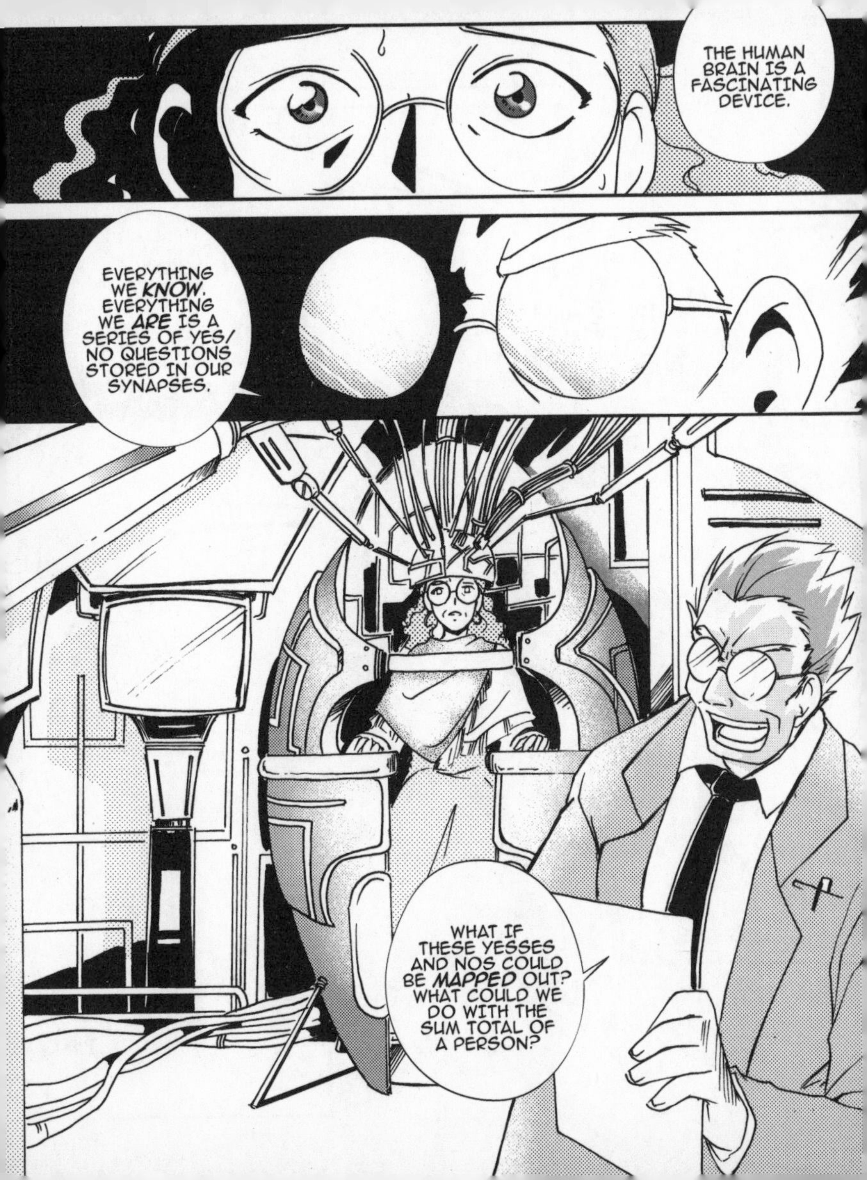
THE HUMAN BRAIN IS A FASCINATING DEVICE.
EVERYTHING WE KNOW. EVERYTHING WE ARE IS A SERIES OF YES/NO QUESTIONS STORED IN OUR SYNAPSES.
WHAT IF THESE YESSES AND NOS COULD BE MAPPED OUT? WHAT COULD WE DO WITH THE SUM TOTAL OF A PERSON?

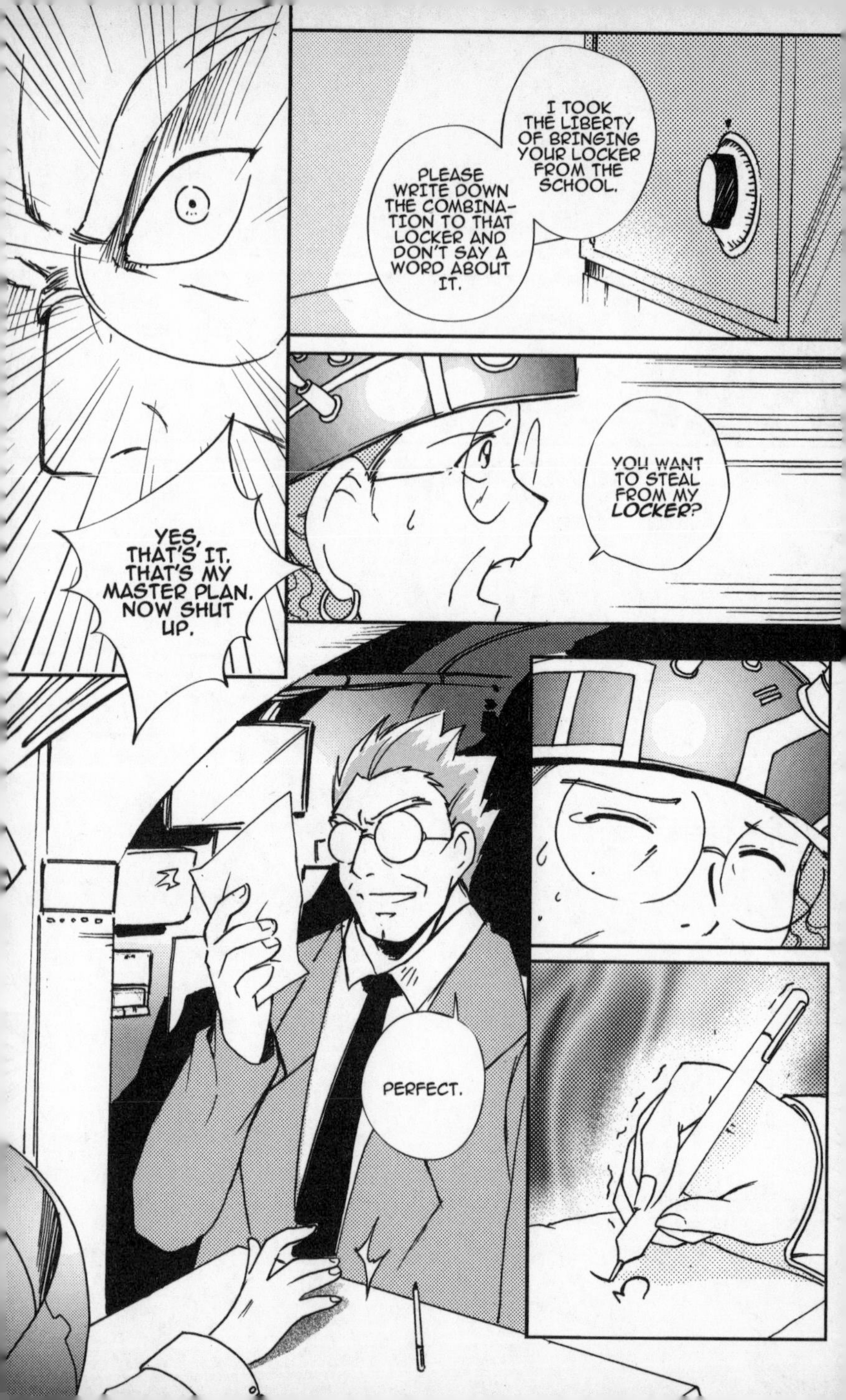

I TOOK THE LIBERTY OF BRINGING YOUR LOCKER FROM THE SCHOOL.
PLEASE WRITE DOWN THE COMBINATION TO THAT LOCKER AND DON'T SAY A WORD ABOUT IT.
YOU WANT TO STEAL FROM MY *LOCKER*?
YES, THAT'S IT. THAT'S MY MASTER PLAN. NOW SHUT UP.
PERFECT.

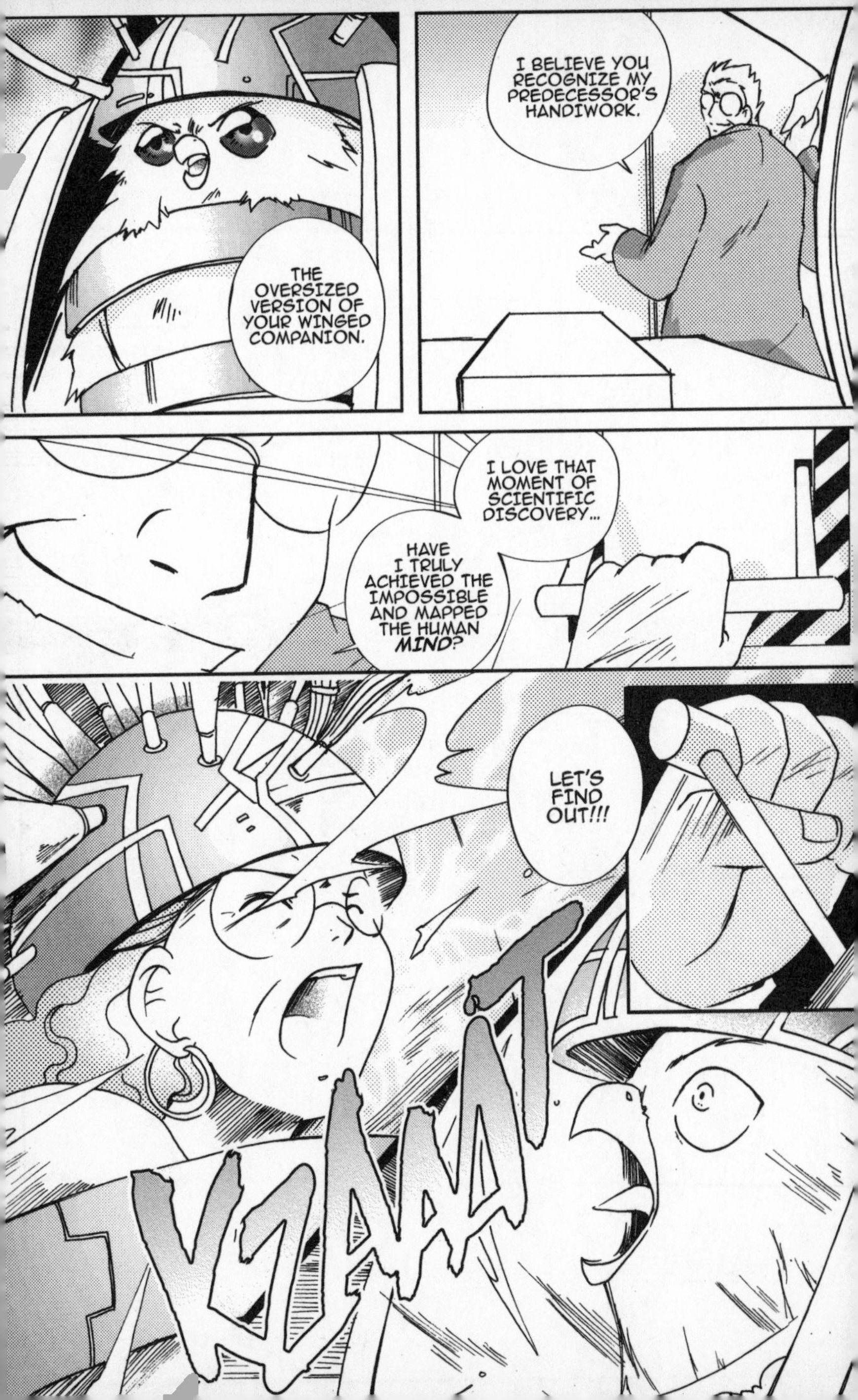
I BELIEVE YOU RECOGNIZE MY PREDECESSOR'S HANDIWORK.
THE OVERSIZED VERSION OF YOUR WINGED COMPANION.
I LOVE THAT MOMENT OF SCIENTIFIC DISCOVERY...
HAVE I TRULY ACHIEVED THE IMPOSSIBLE AND MAPPED THE HUMAN *MIND*?
LET'S FIND OUT!!!

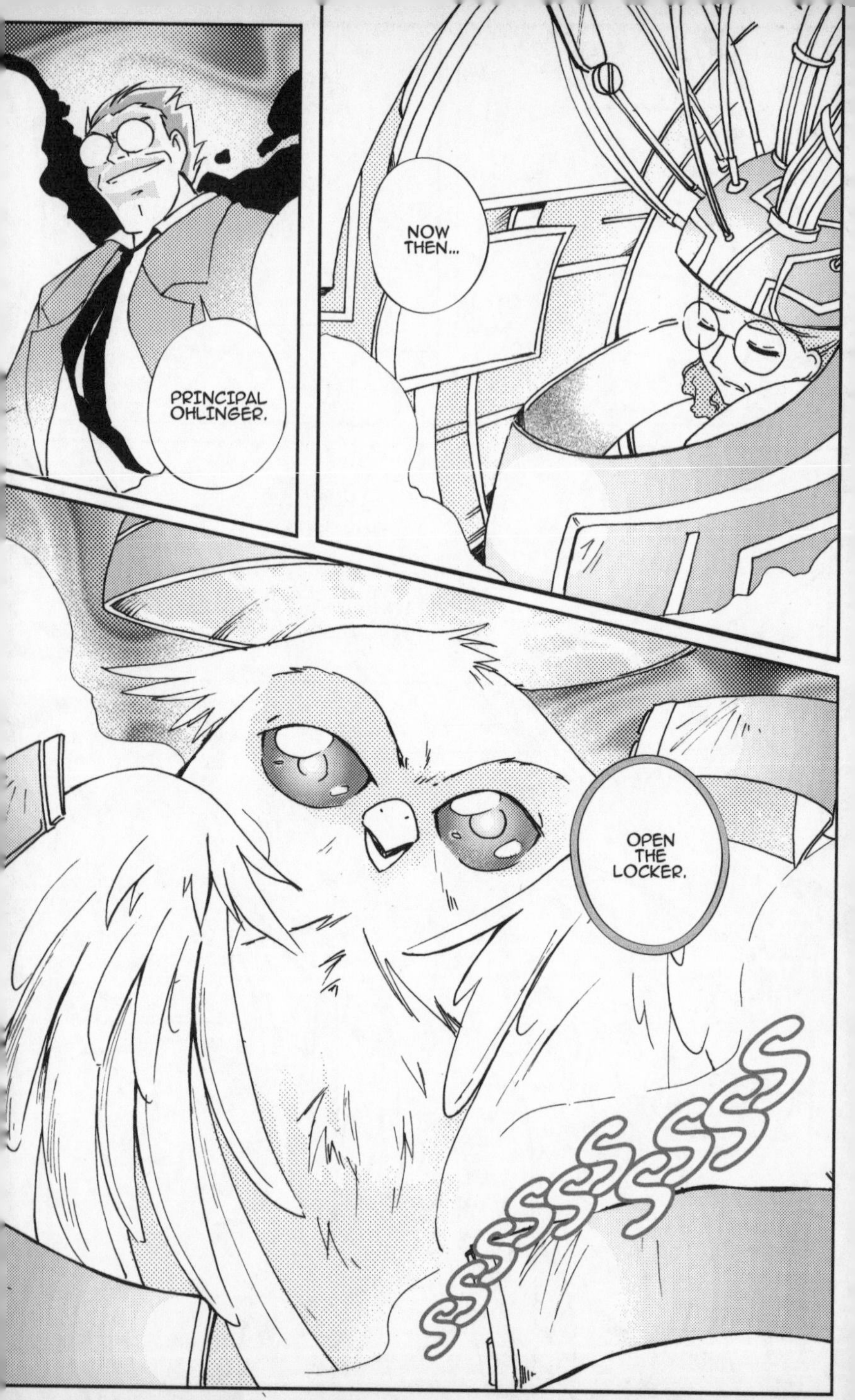
NOW THEN...
PRINCIPAL OHLINGER.
OPEN THE LOCKER.
SSSSSSSSS

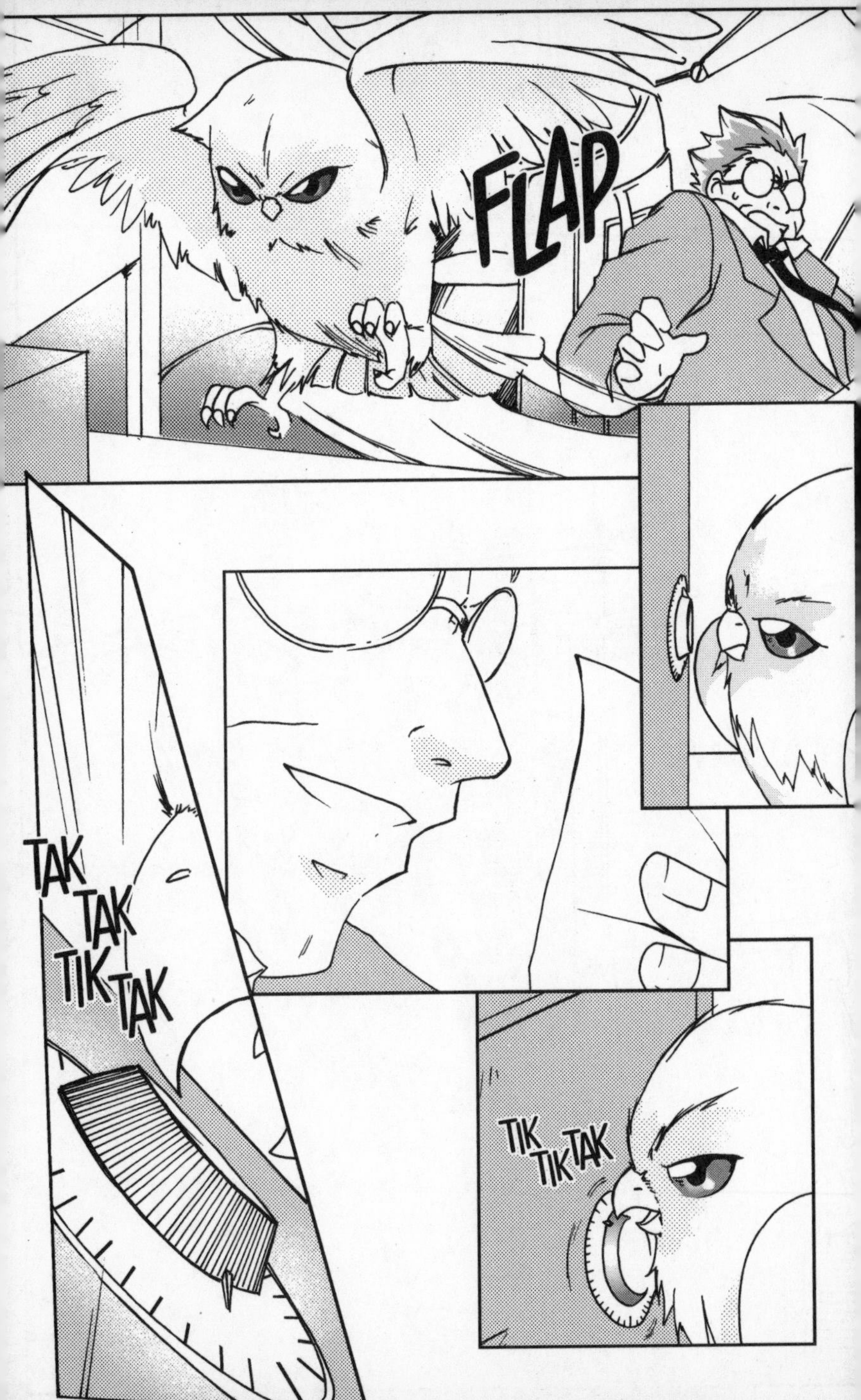
FLAP
TIK TIK TAK
TAK TAK TIK TAK

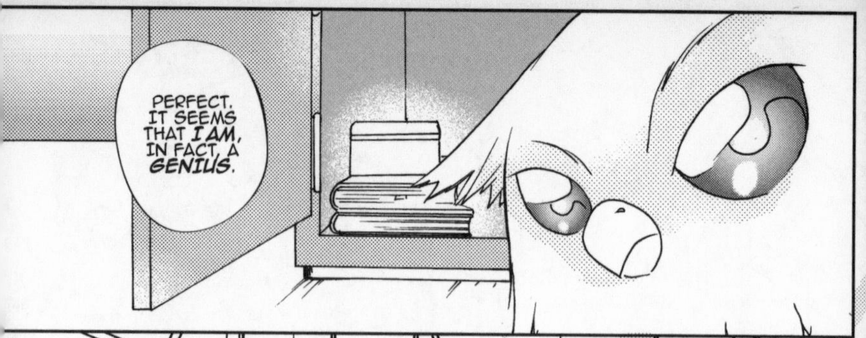
PERFECT. IT SEEMS THAT *I AM*, IN FACT, A *GENIUS*.

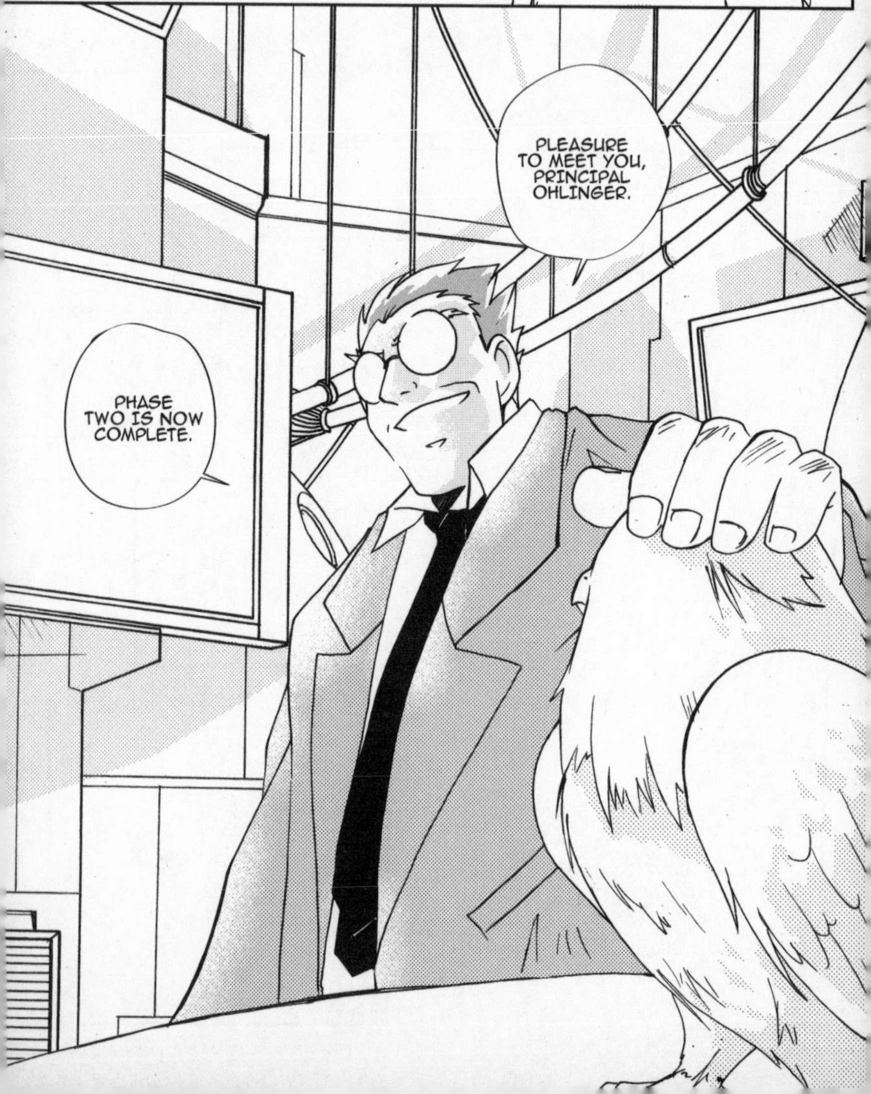
PLEASURE TO MEET YOU, PRINCIPAL OHLINGER.
PHASE TWO IS NOW COMPLETE.

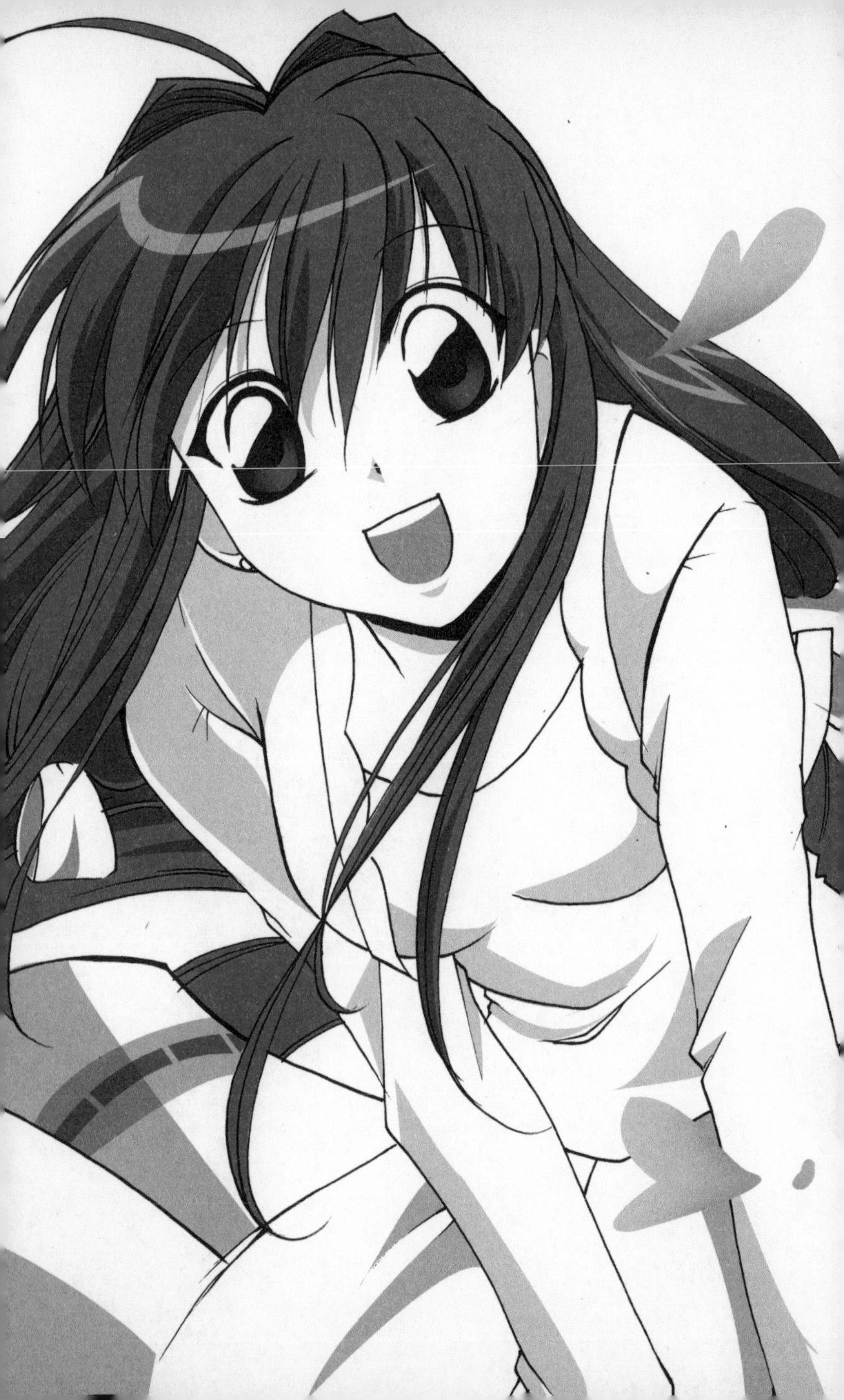

# File 11
# TEN YEARS AGO…

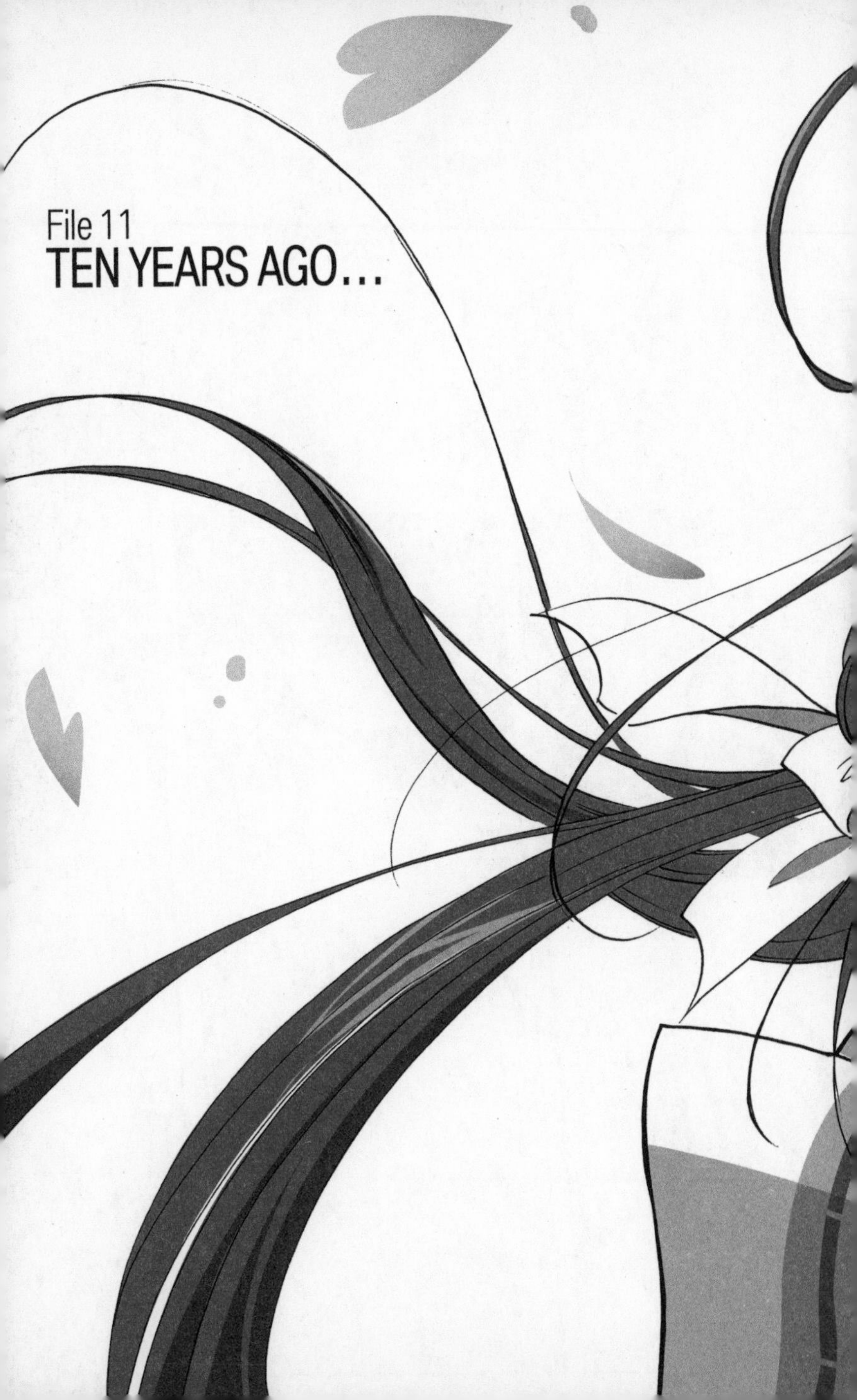

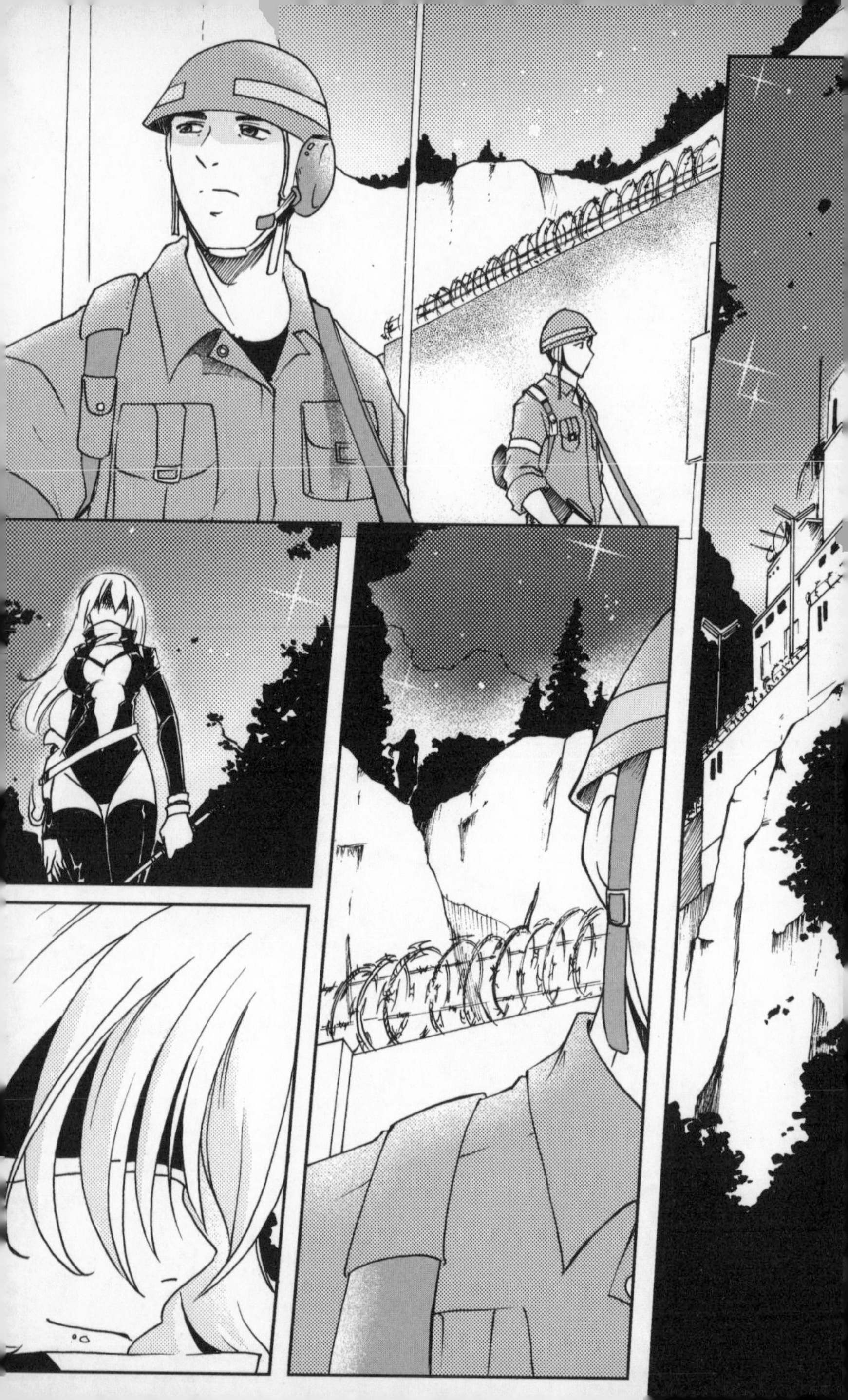

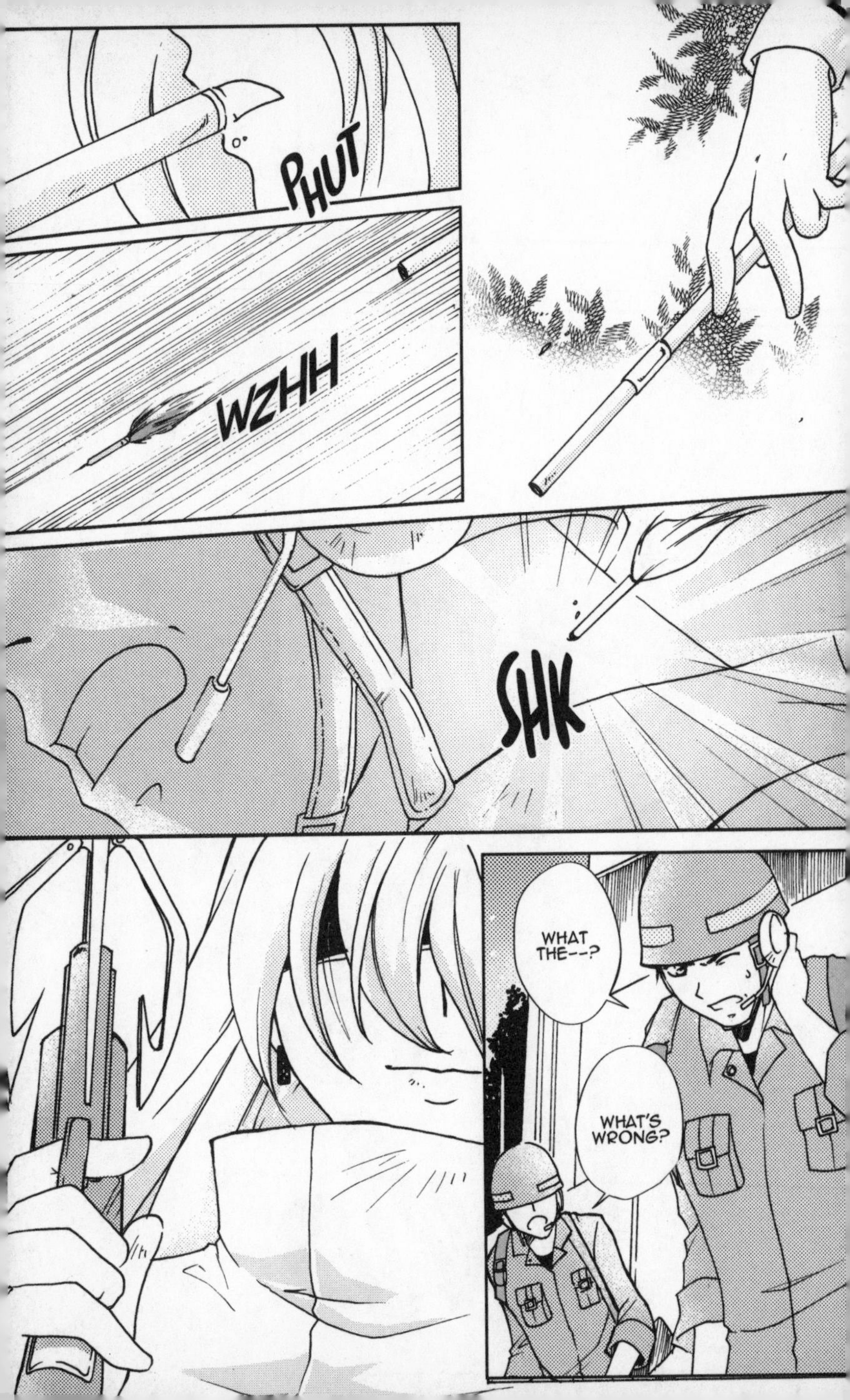
PHUT
WZHH
SHK
WHAT THE--?
WHAT'S WRONG?

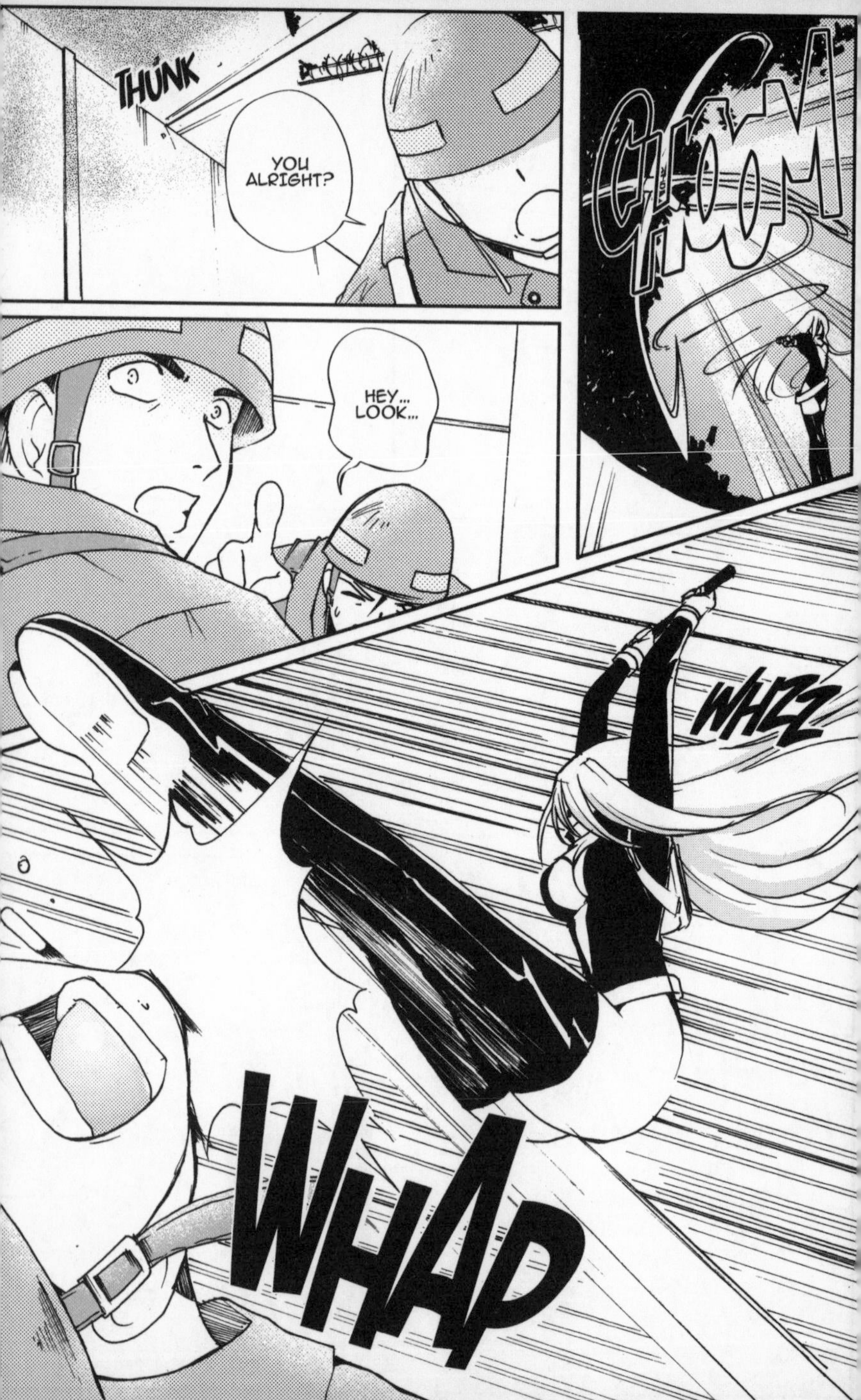
GROOM
THUNK
YOU ALRIGHT?
HEY... LOOK...
WHZZ
WHAP

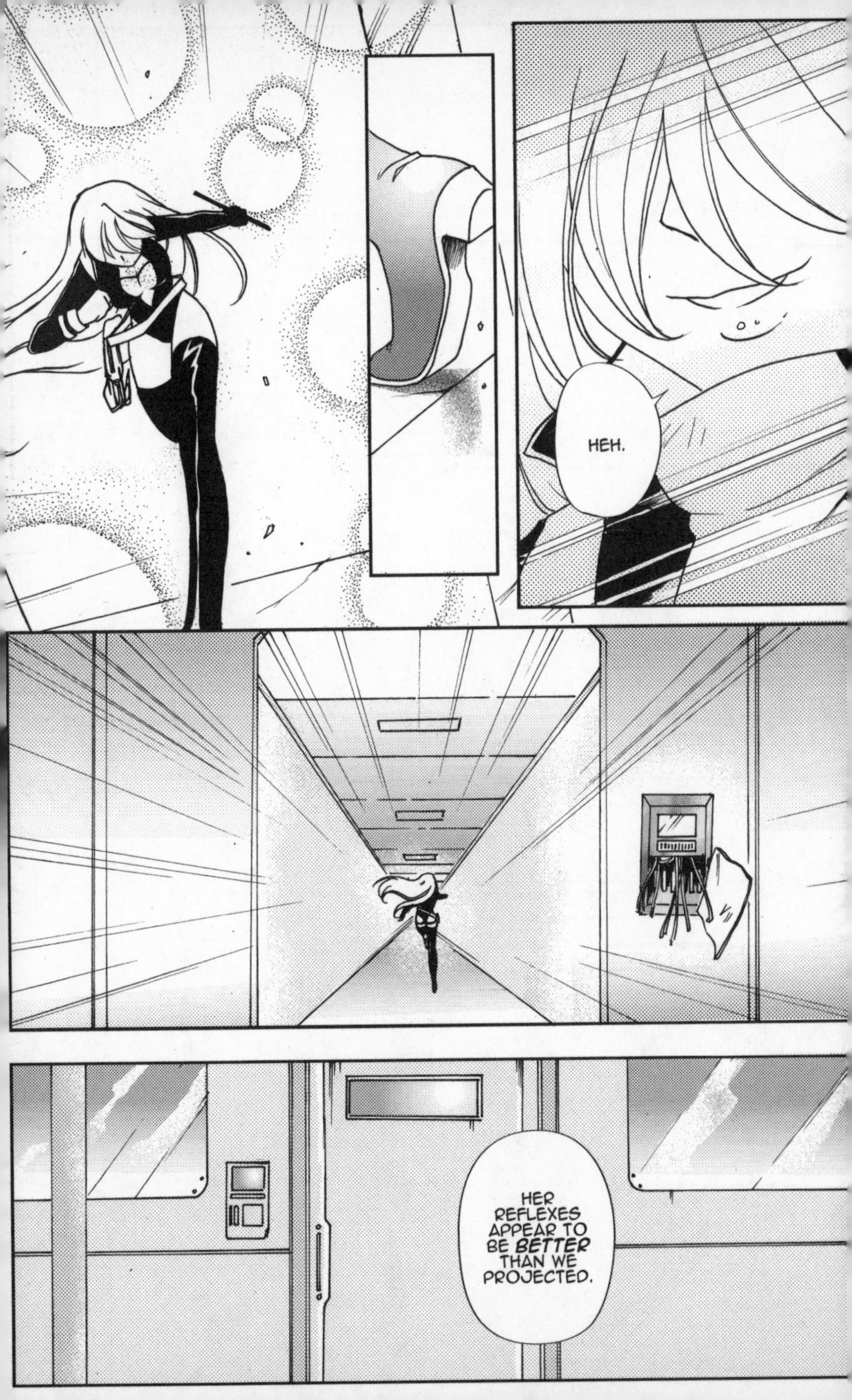
HEH.
HER REFLEXES APPEAR TO BE BETTER THAN WE PROJECTED.

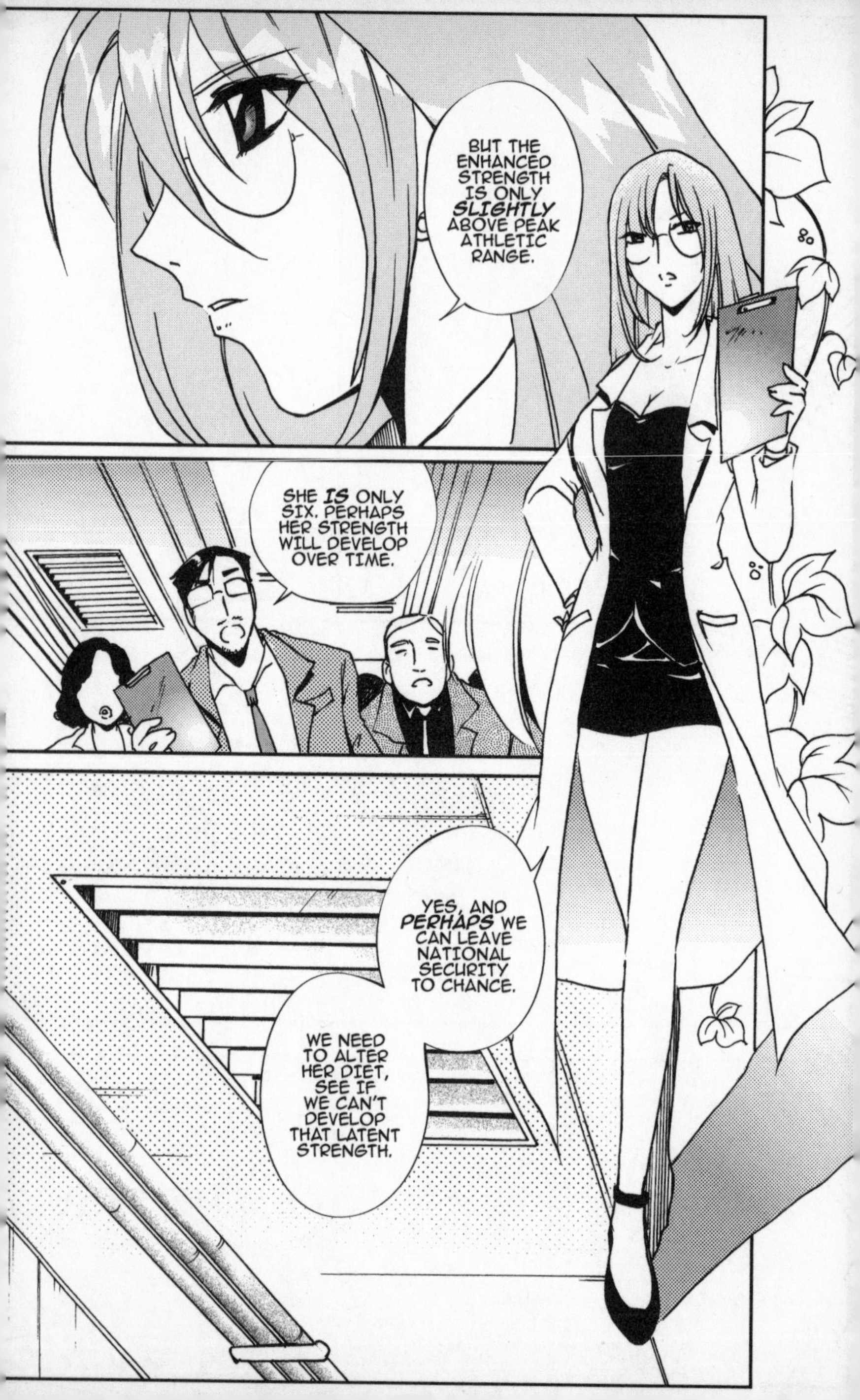
BUT THE ENHANCED STRENGTH IS ONLY *SLIGHTLY* ABOVE PEAK ATHLETIC RANGE.
SHE *IS* ONLY SIX. PERHAPS HER STRENGTH WILL DEVELOP OVER TIME.
YES, AND *PERHAPS* WE CAN LEAVE NATIONAL SECURITY TO CHANCE.
WE NEED TO ALTER HER DIET, SEE IF WE CAN'T DEVELOP THAT LATENT STRENGTH.

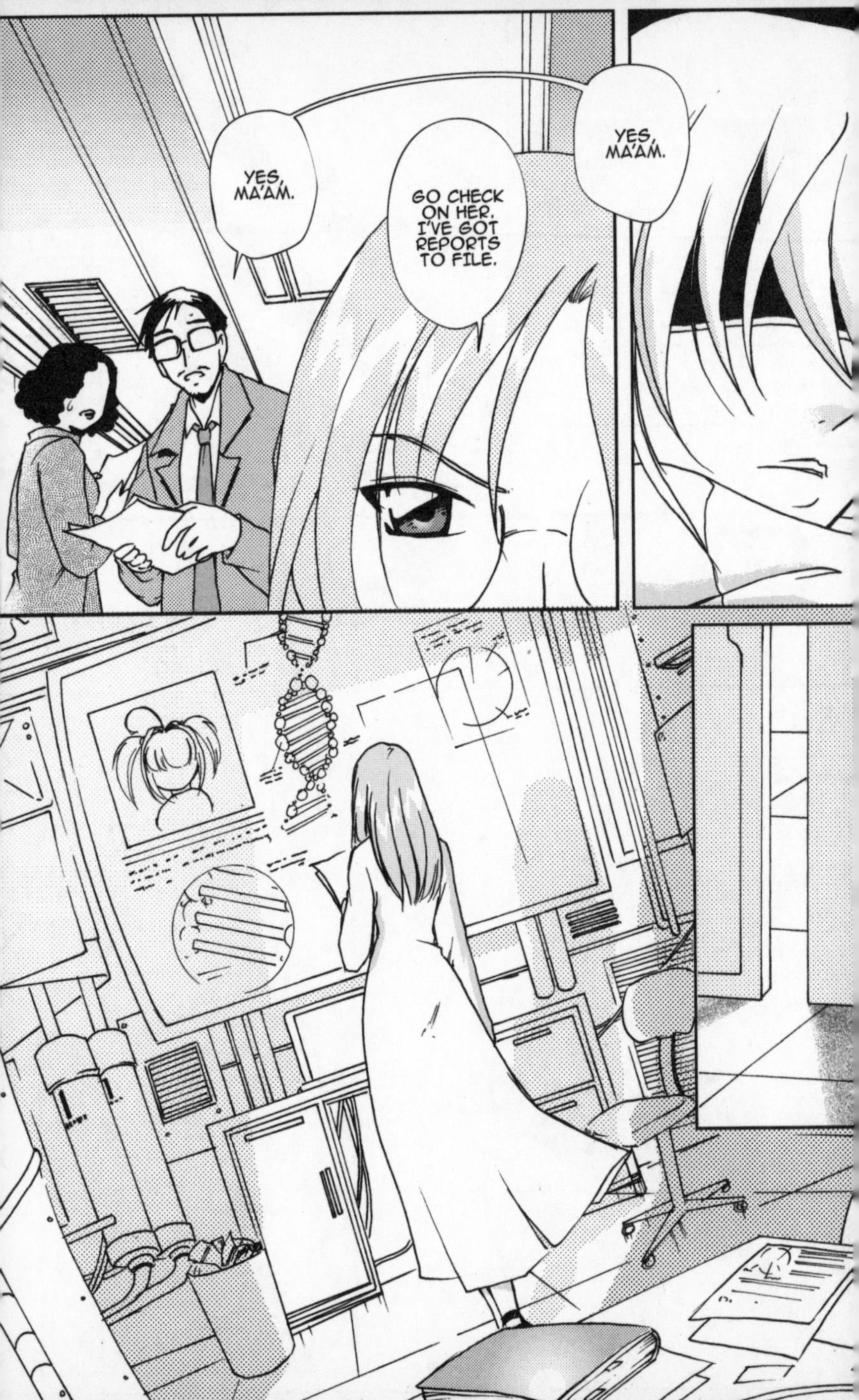
YES, MA'AM.
GO CHECK ON HER. I'VE GOT REPORTS TO FILE.
YES, MA'AM.

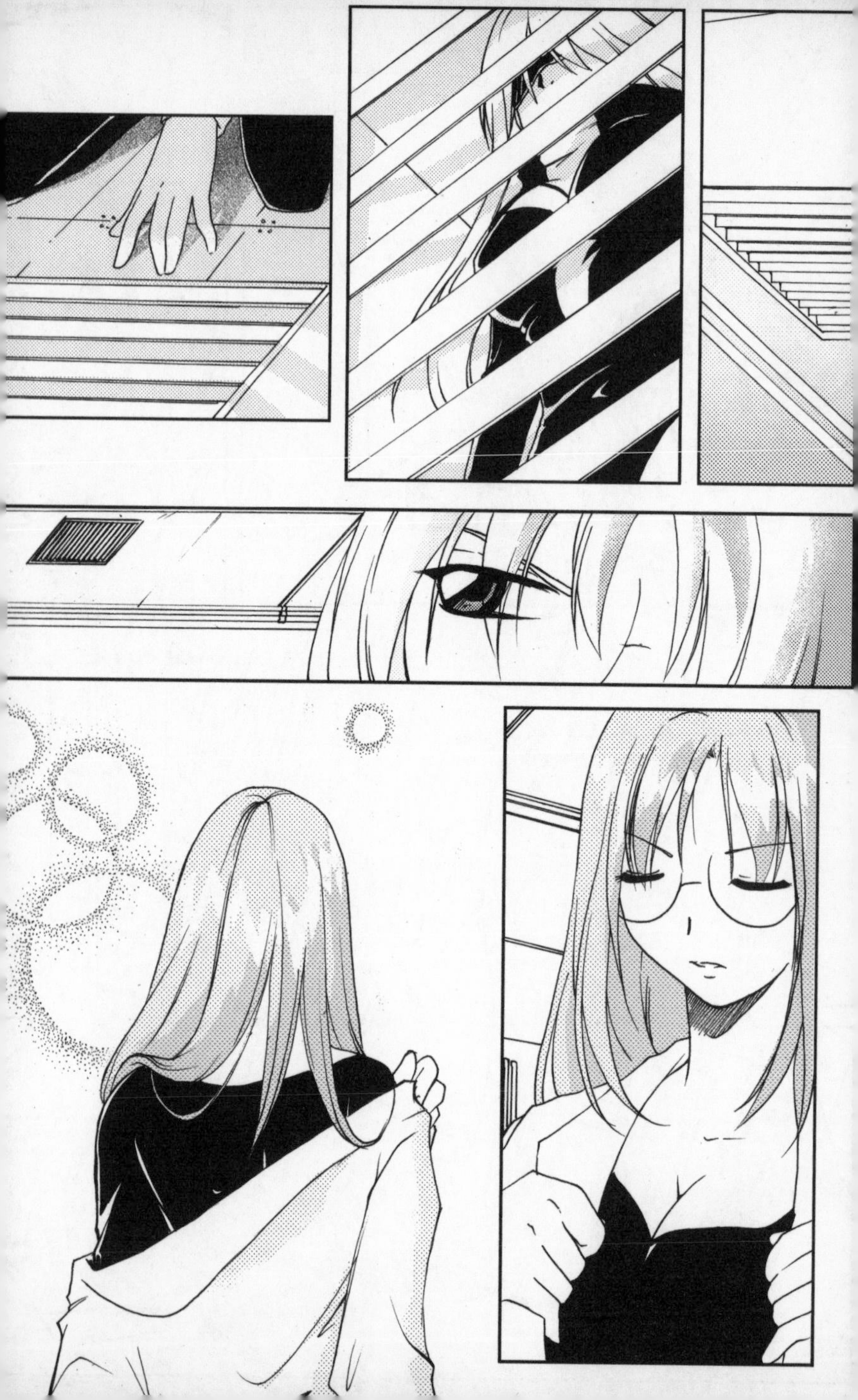

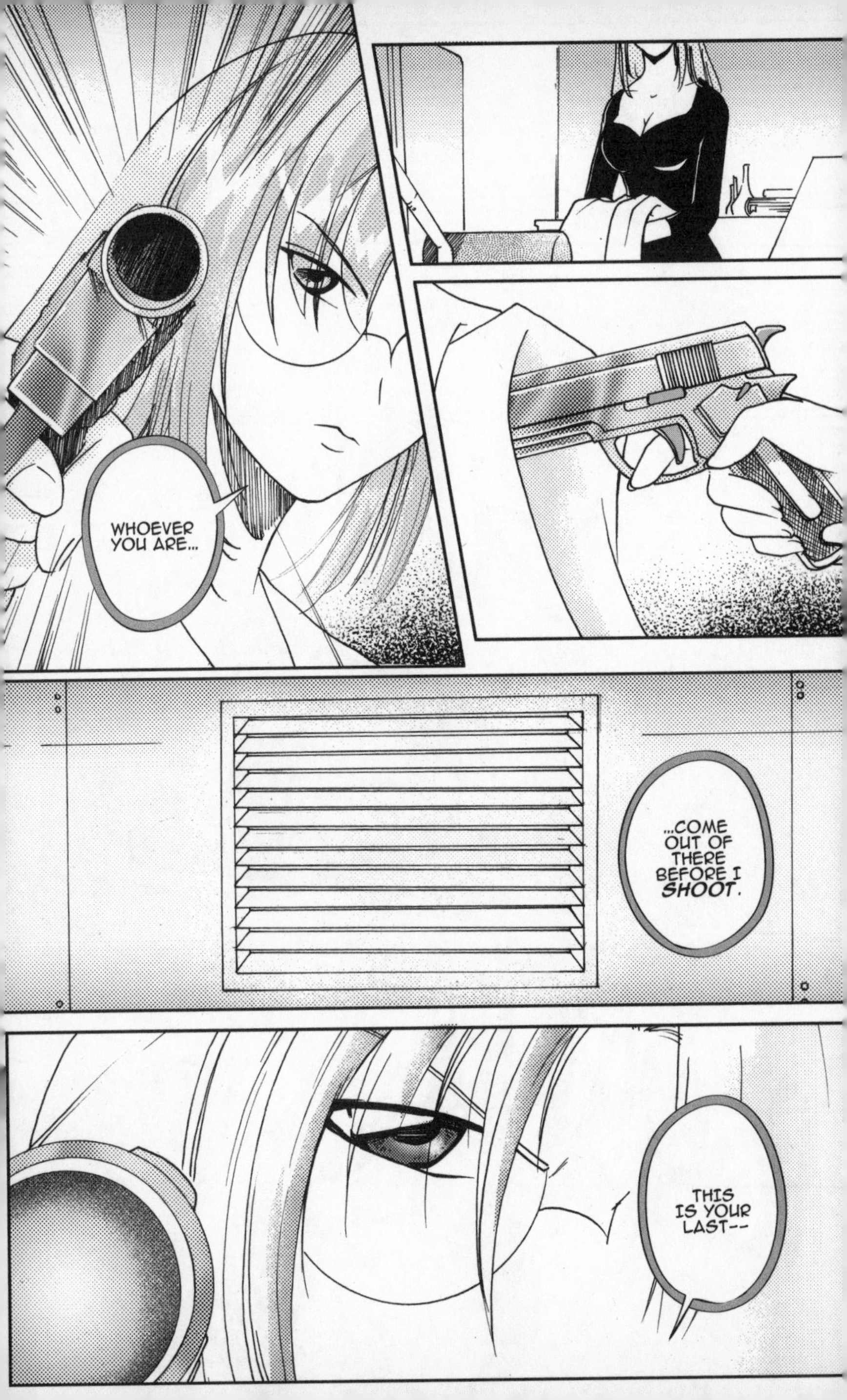
WHOEVER YOU ARE...
...COME OUT OF THERE BEFORE I *SHOOT*.
THIS IS YOUR LAST--

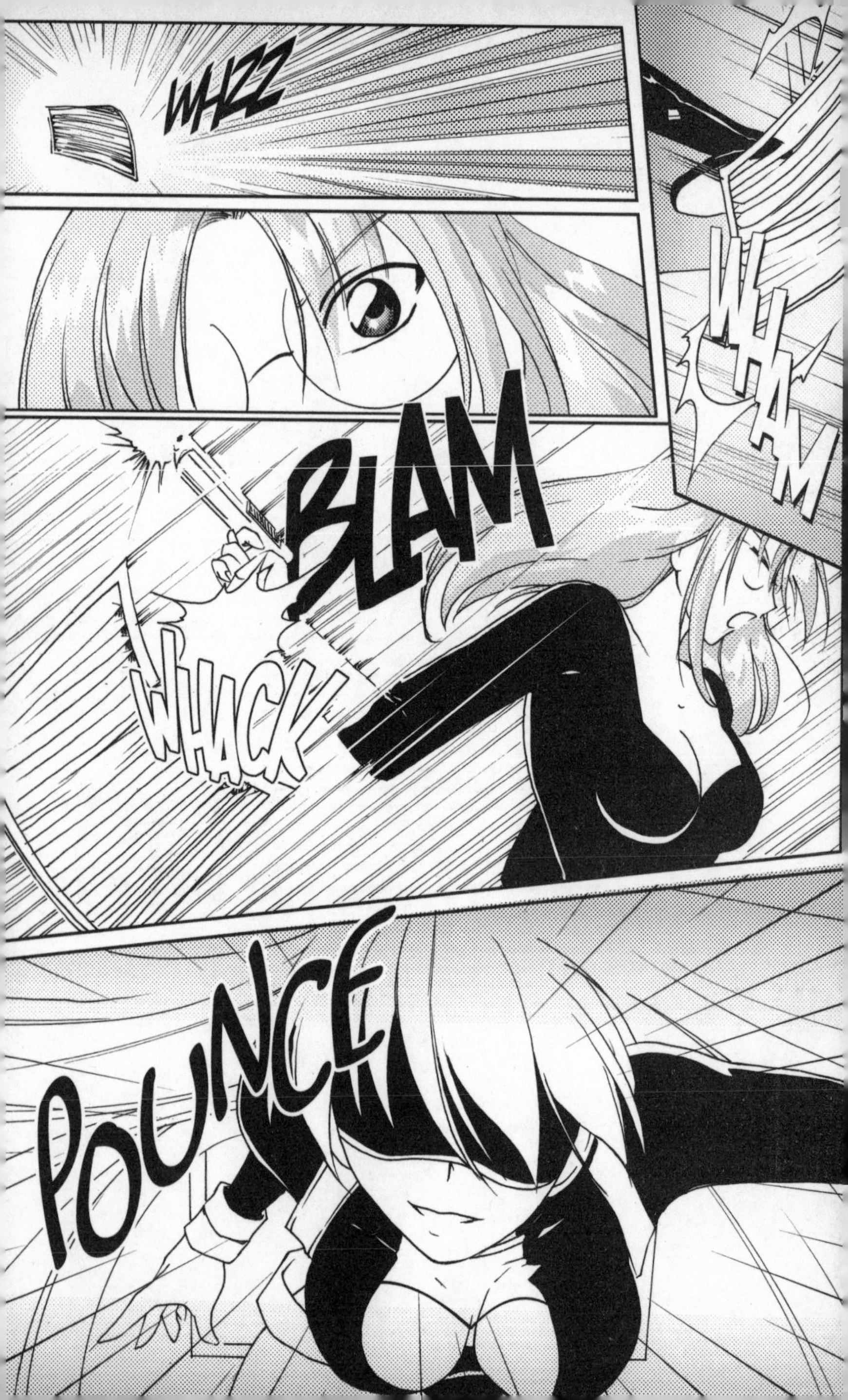
WHAM
WHIZZ
BLAM
WHACK
POUNCE

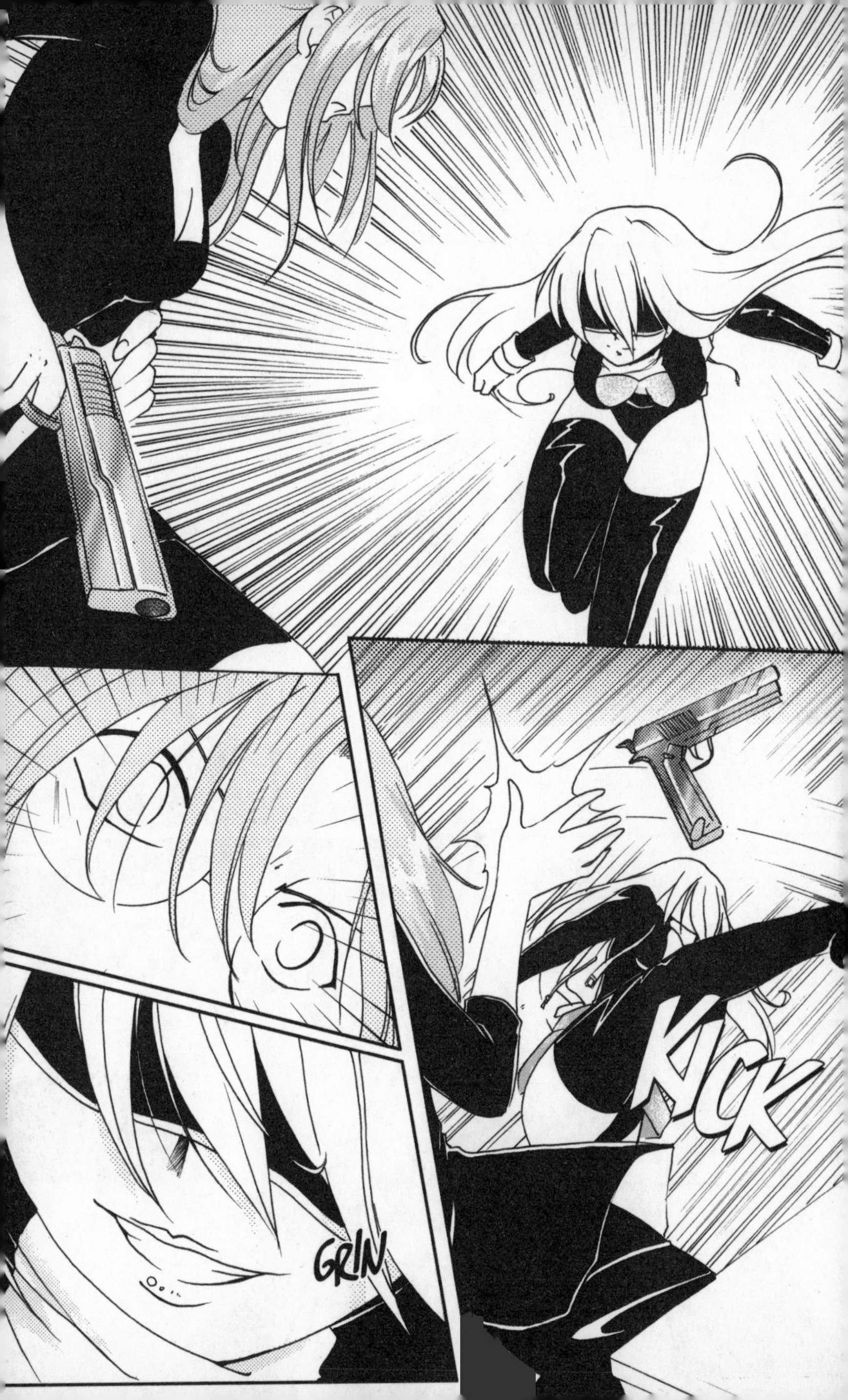
KICK
GRIN

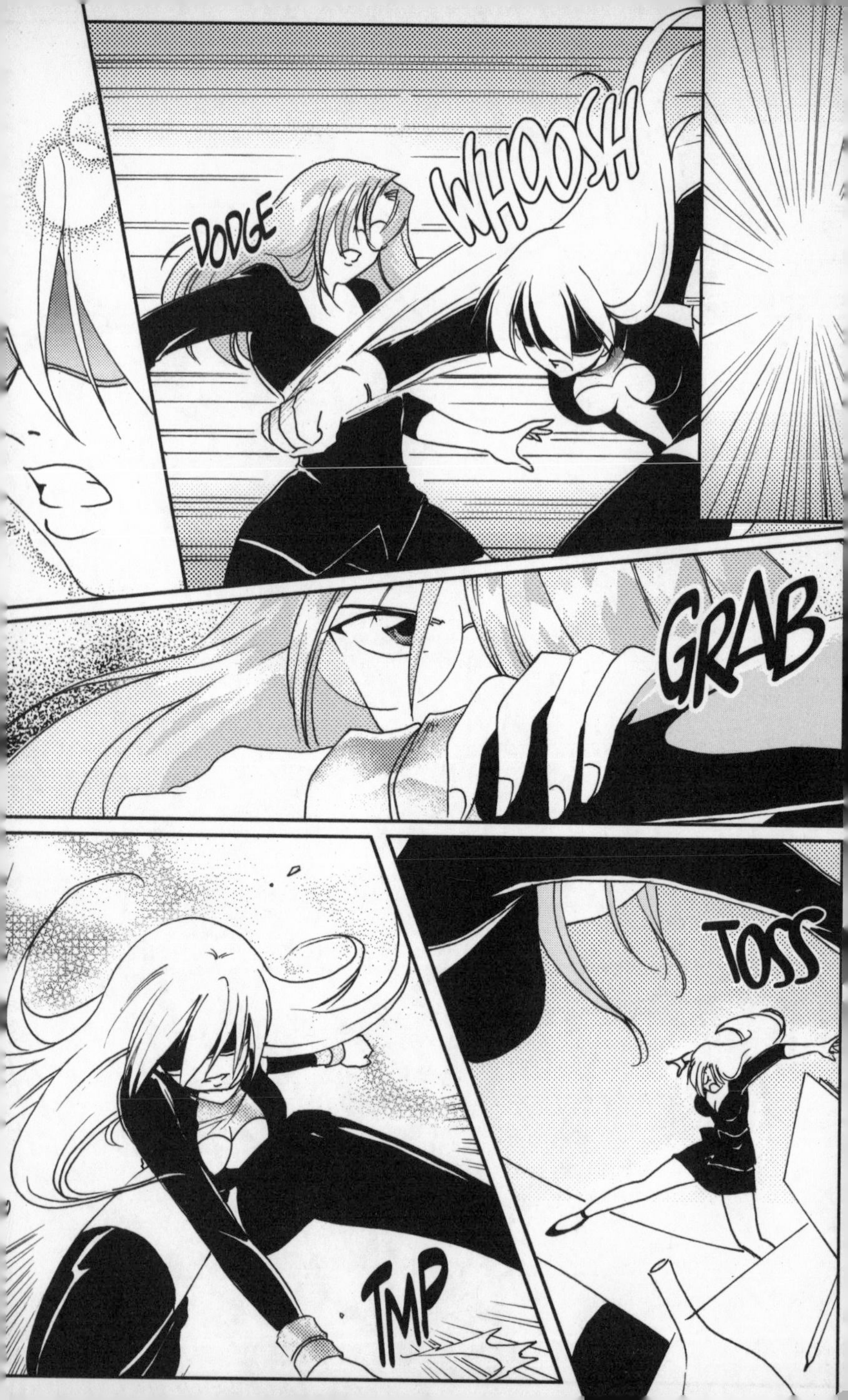
WHOOSH
DODGE
GRAB
TOSS
TMP

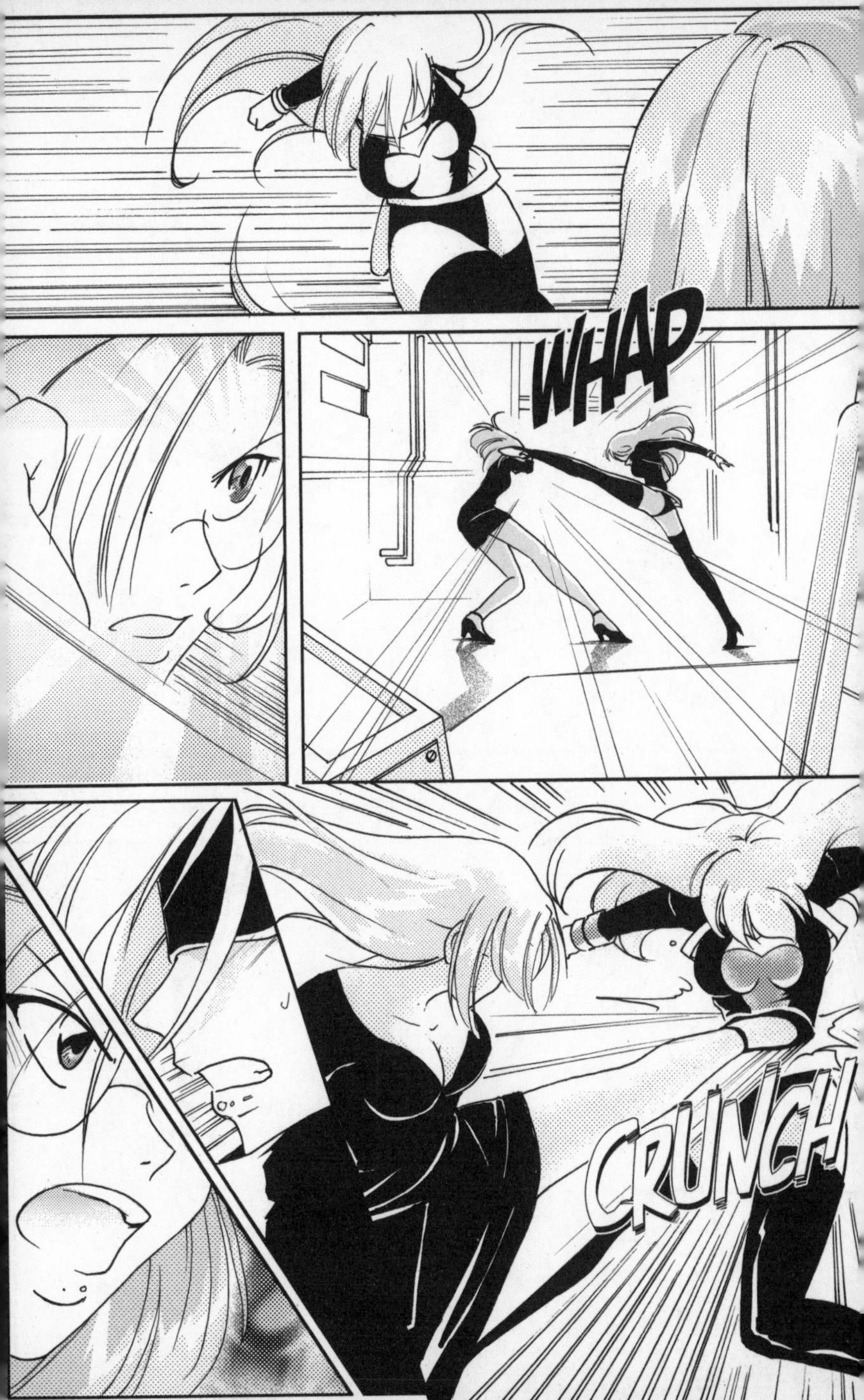
WHAP
CRUNCH

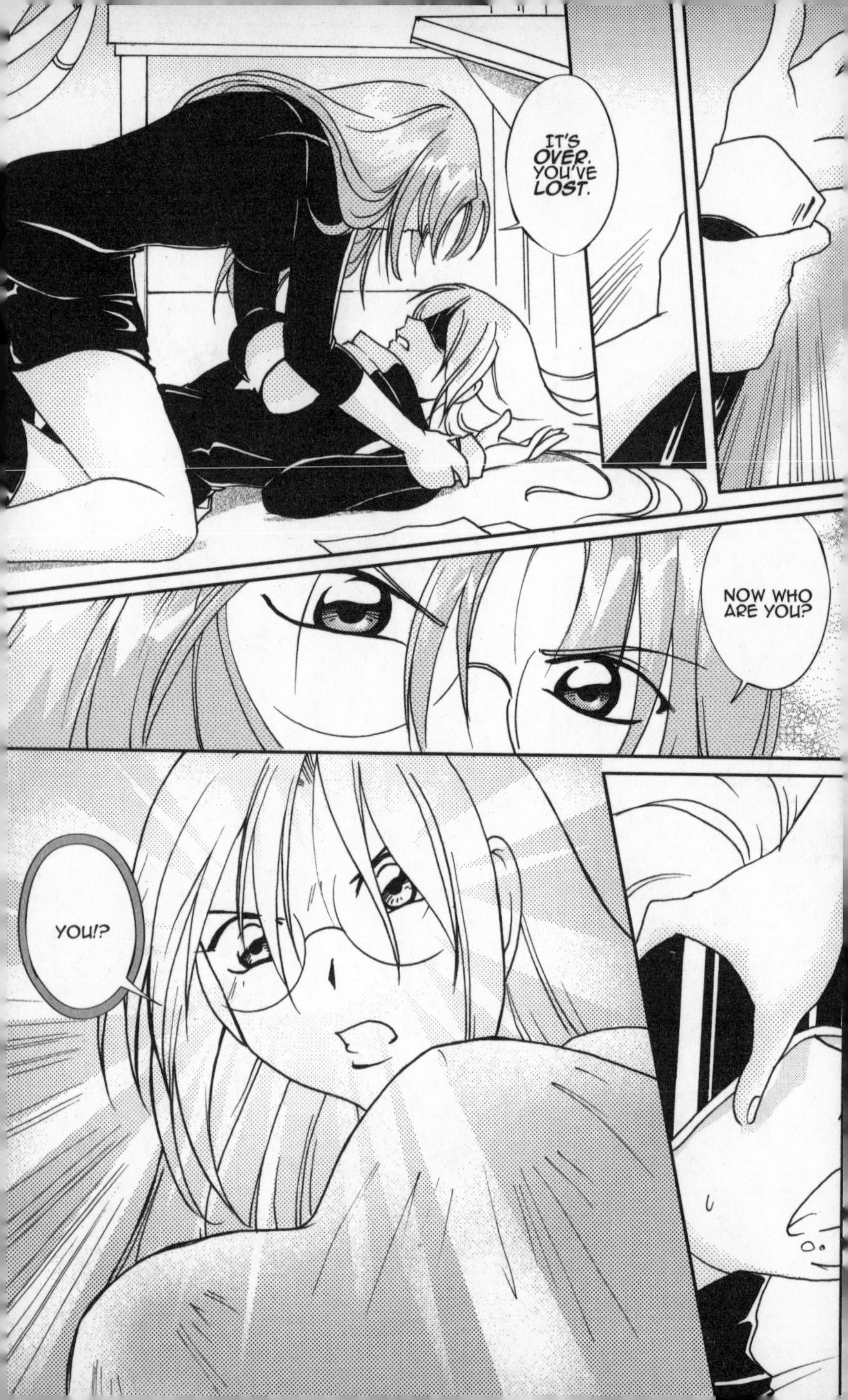
IT'S OVER. YOU'VE LOST.
NOW WHO ARE YOU?
YOU!?

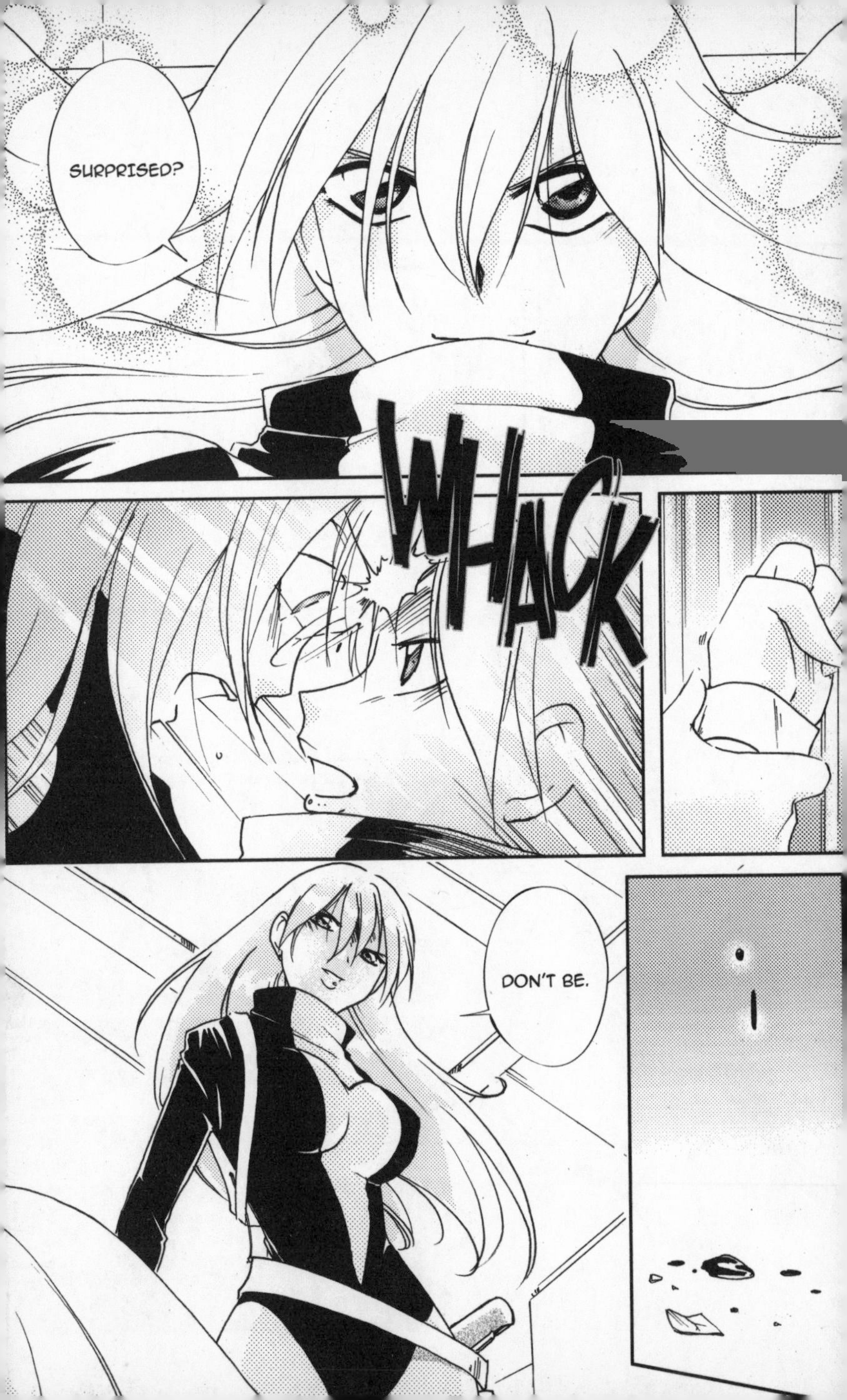
SURPRISED?
WHACK
DON'T BE.

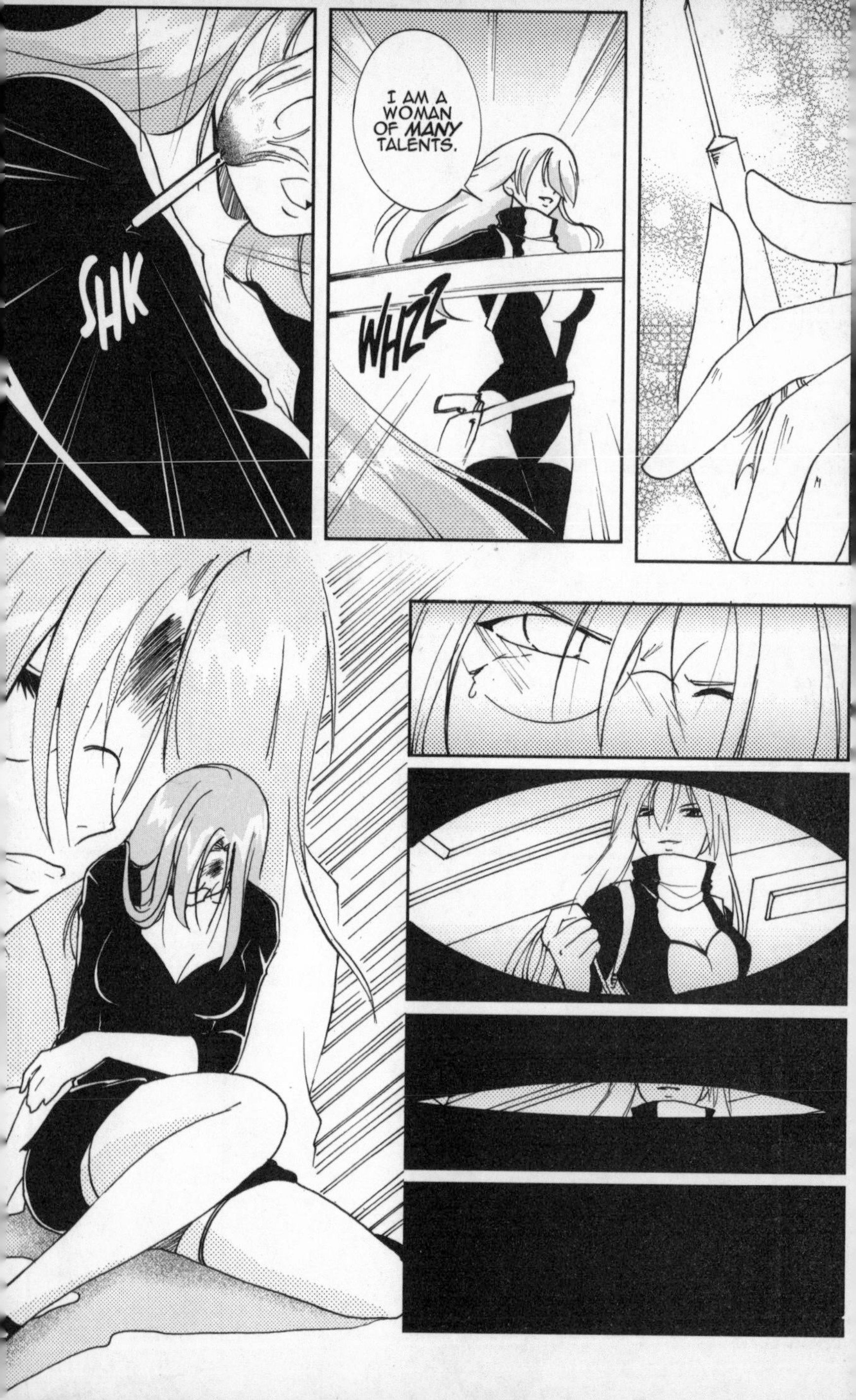
I AM A WOMAN OF MANY TALENTS.
WHZZ
SHK

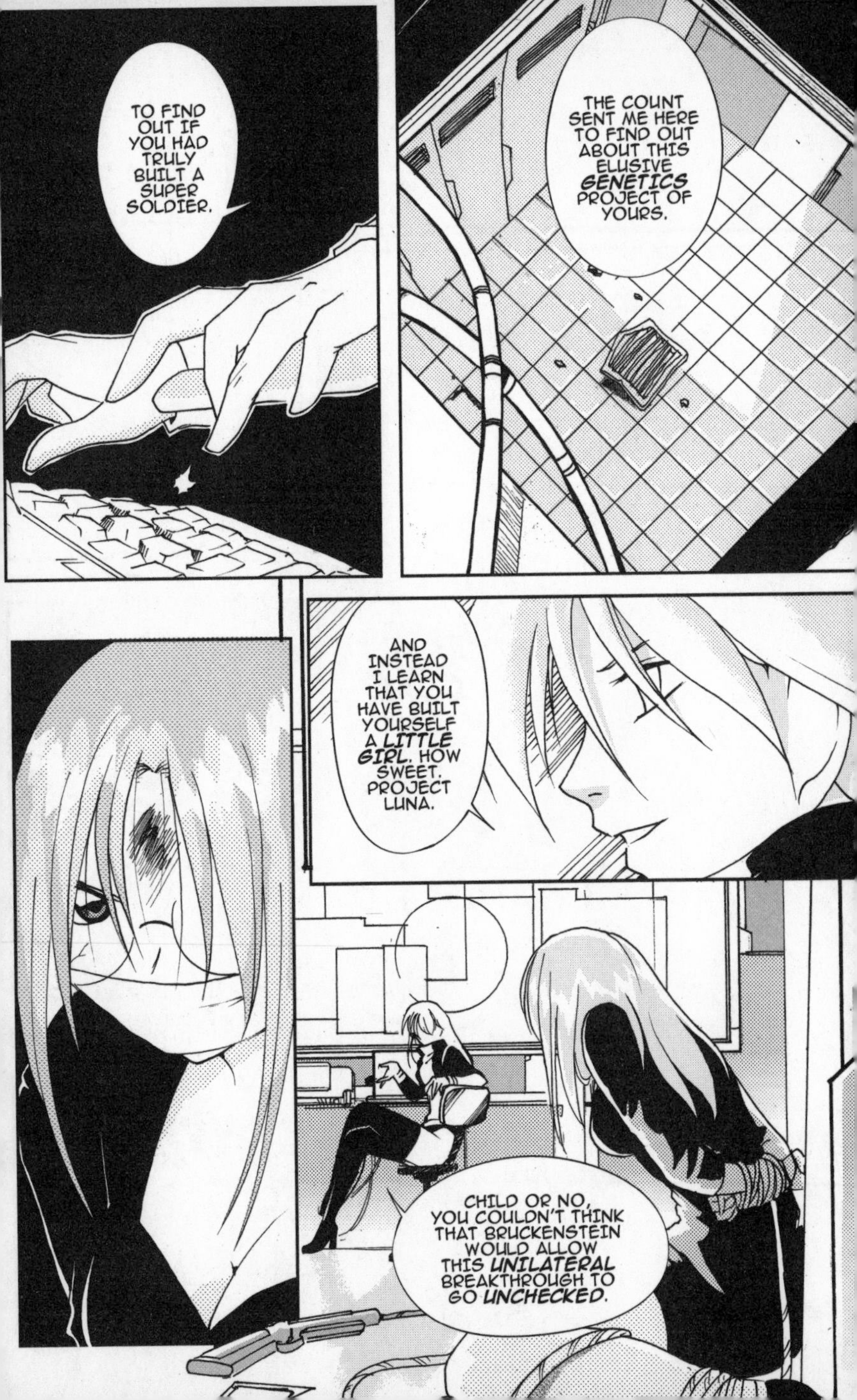
THE COUNT SENT ME HERE TO FIND OUT ABOUT THIS ELUSIVE **GENETICS** PROJECT OF YOURS.
TO FIND OUT IF YOU HAD TRULY BUILT A SUPER SOLDIER.
AND INSTEAD I LEARN THAT YOU HAVE BUILT YOURSELF A **LITTLE GIRL**. HOW SWEET. PROJECT LUNA.
CHILD OR NO, YOU COULDN'T THINK THAT BRUCKENSTEIN WOULD ALLOW THIS **UNILATERAL** BREAKTHROUGH TO GO **UNCHECKED**.

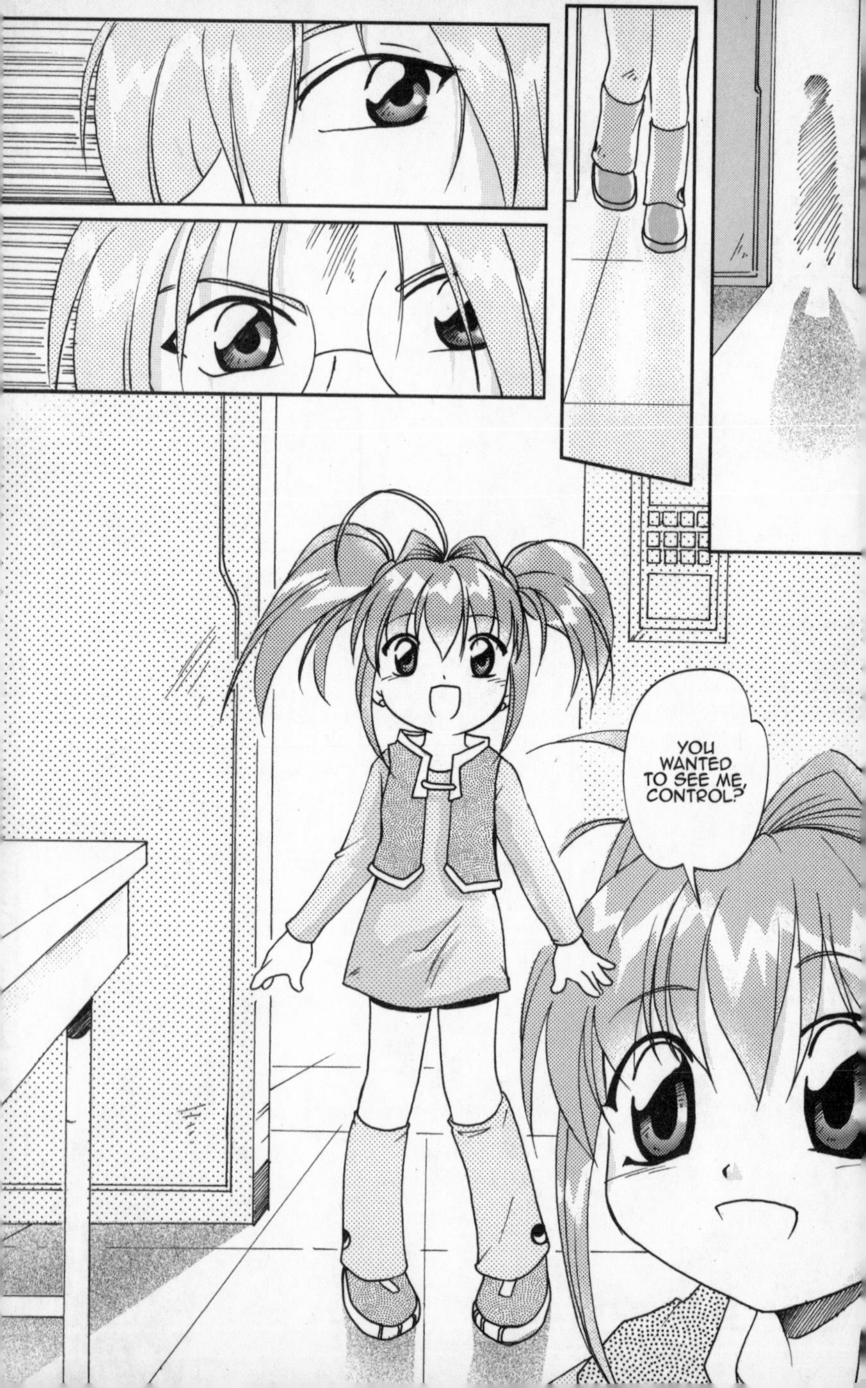
YOU WANTED TO SEE ME, CONTROL?

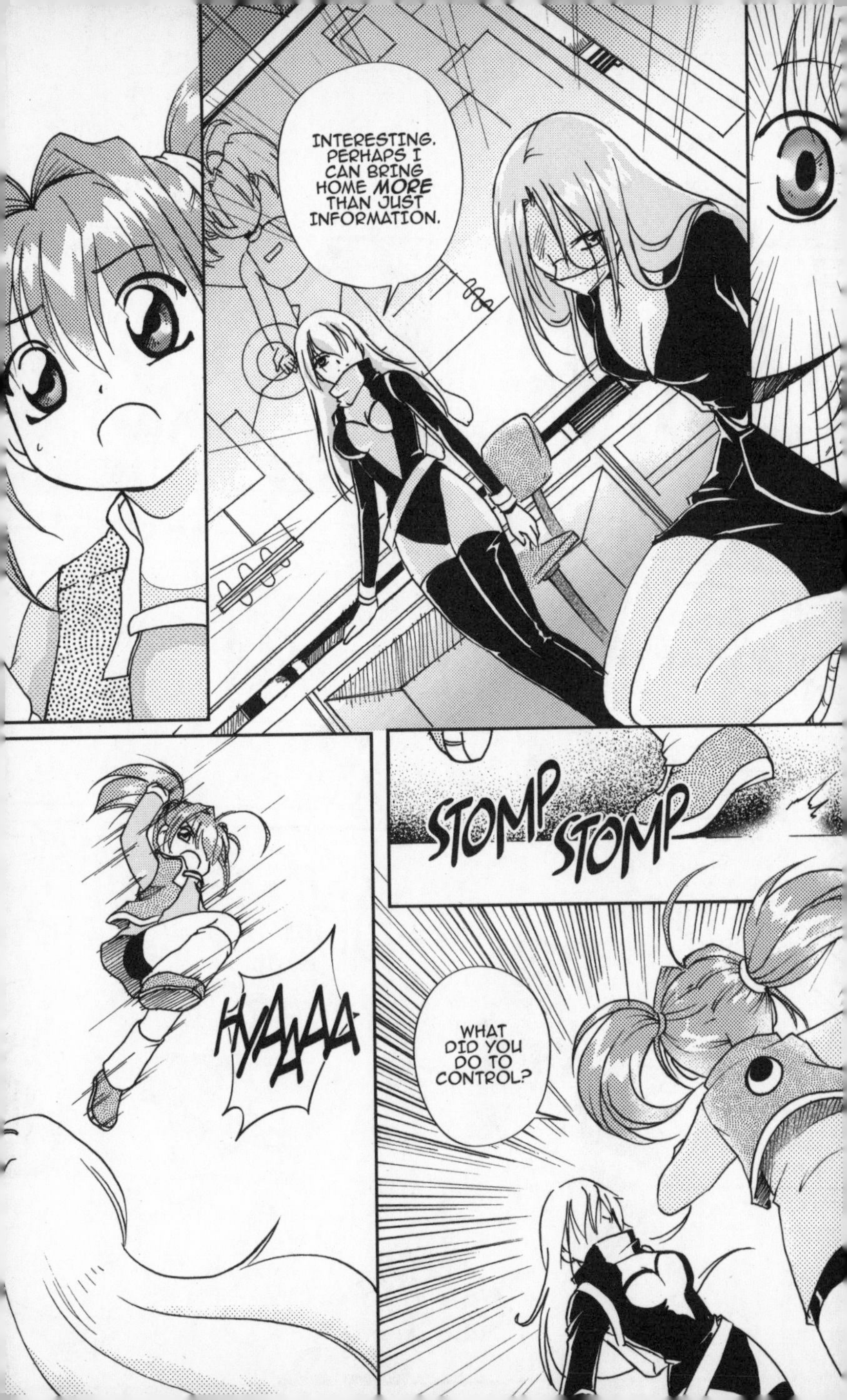
INTERESTING. PERHAPS I CAN BRING HOME *MORE* THAN JUST INFORMATION.
STOMP STOMP
WHAT DID YOU DO TO CONTROL?
KYAAAA

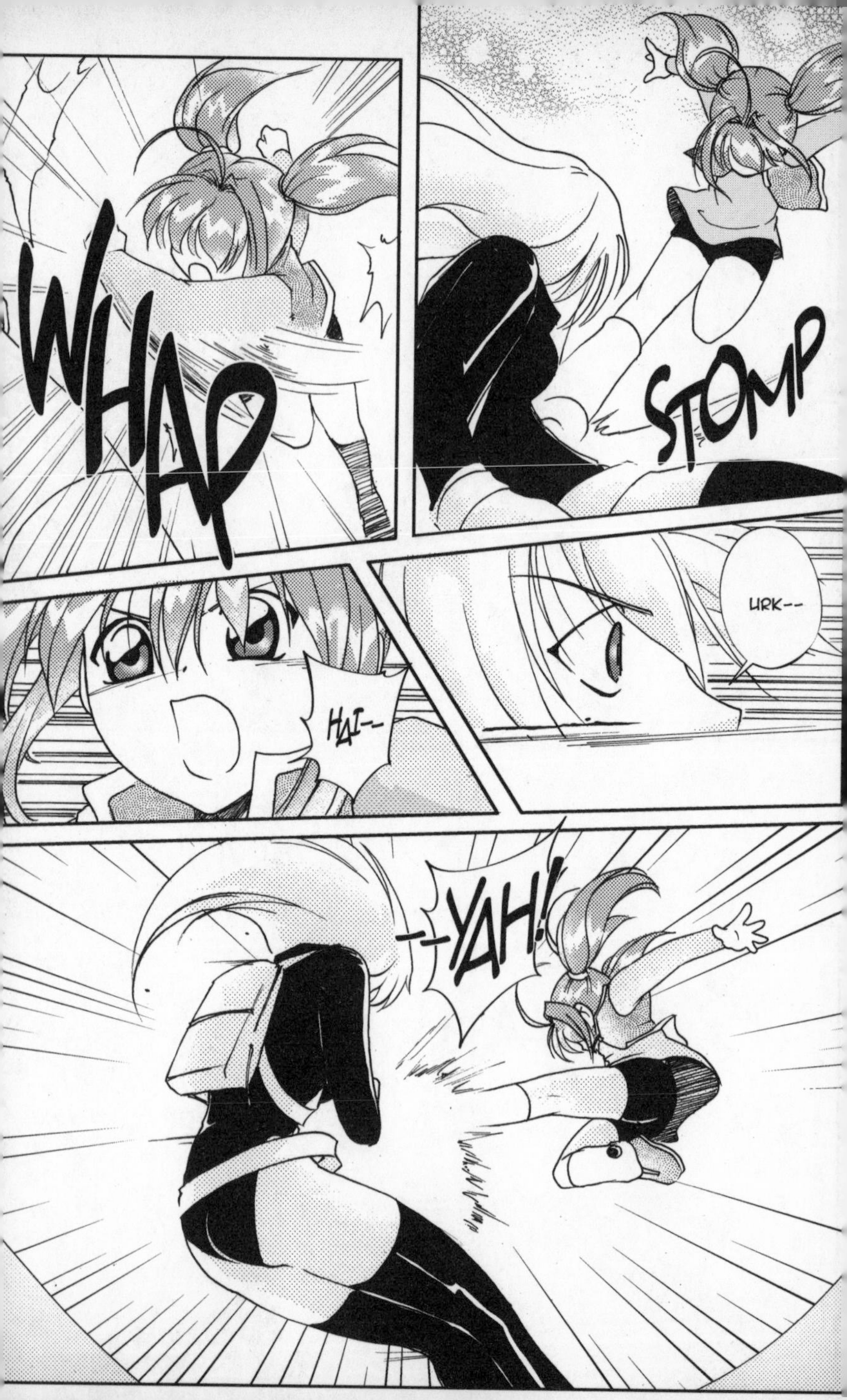
STOMP
WHAP
URK--
HAI--
--YAH!

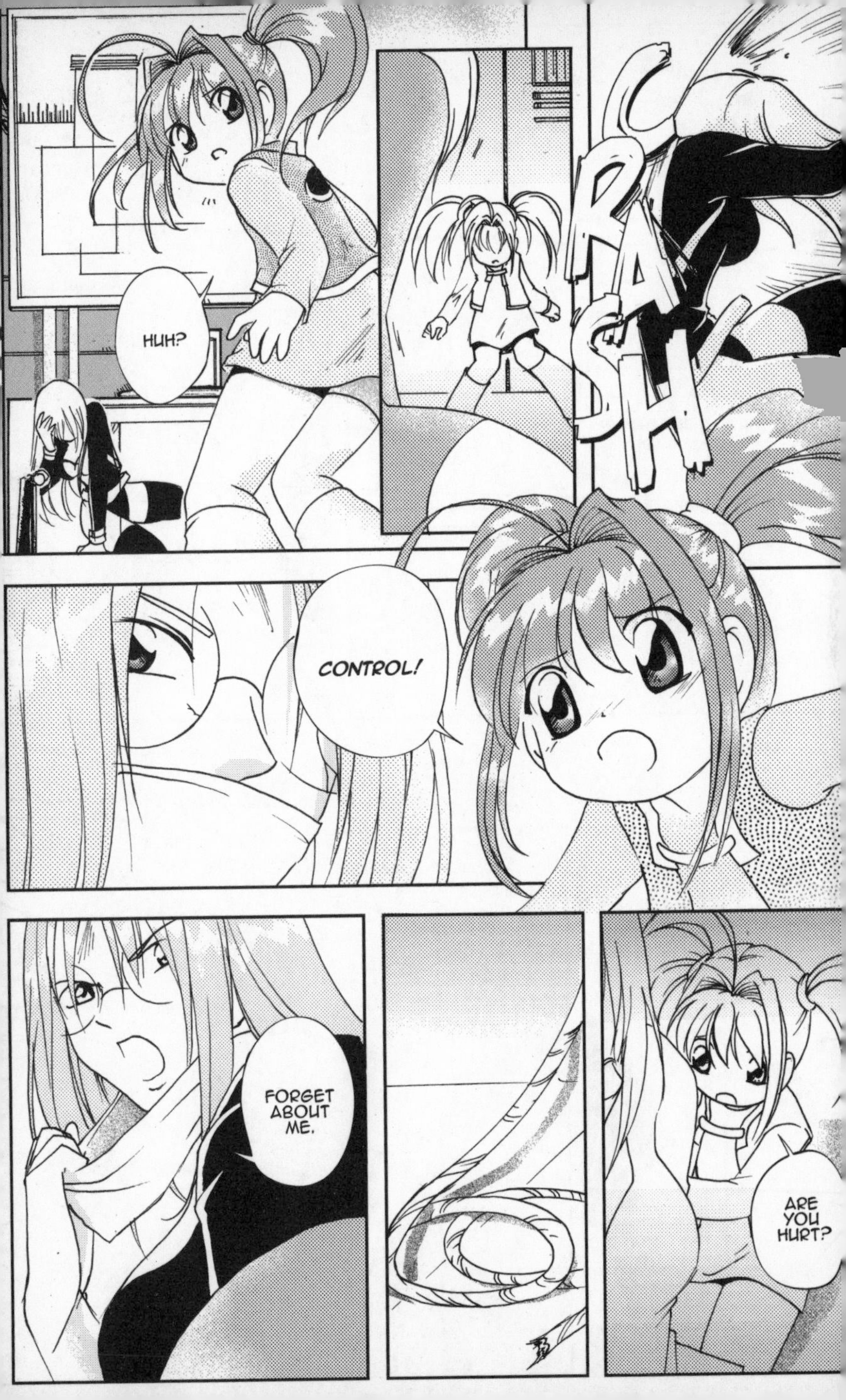
CRASH
HUH?
CONTROL!
ARE YOU HURT?
FORGET ABOUT ME.

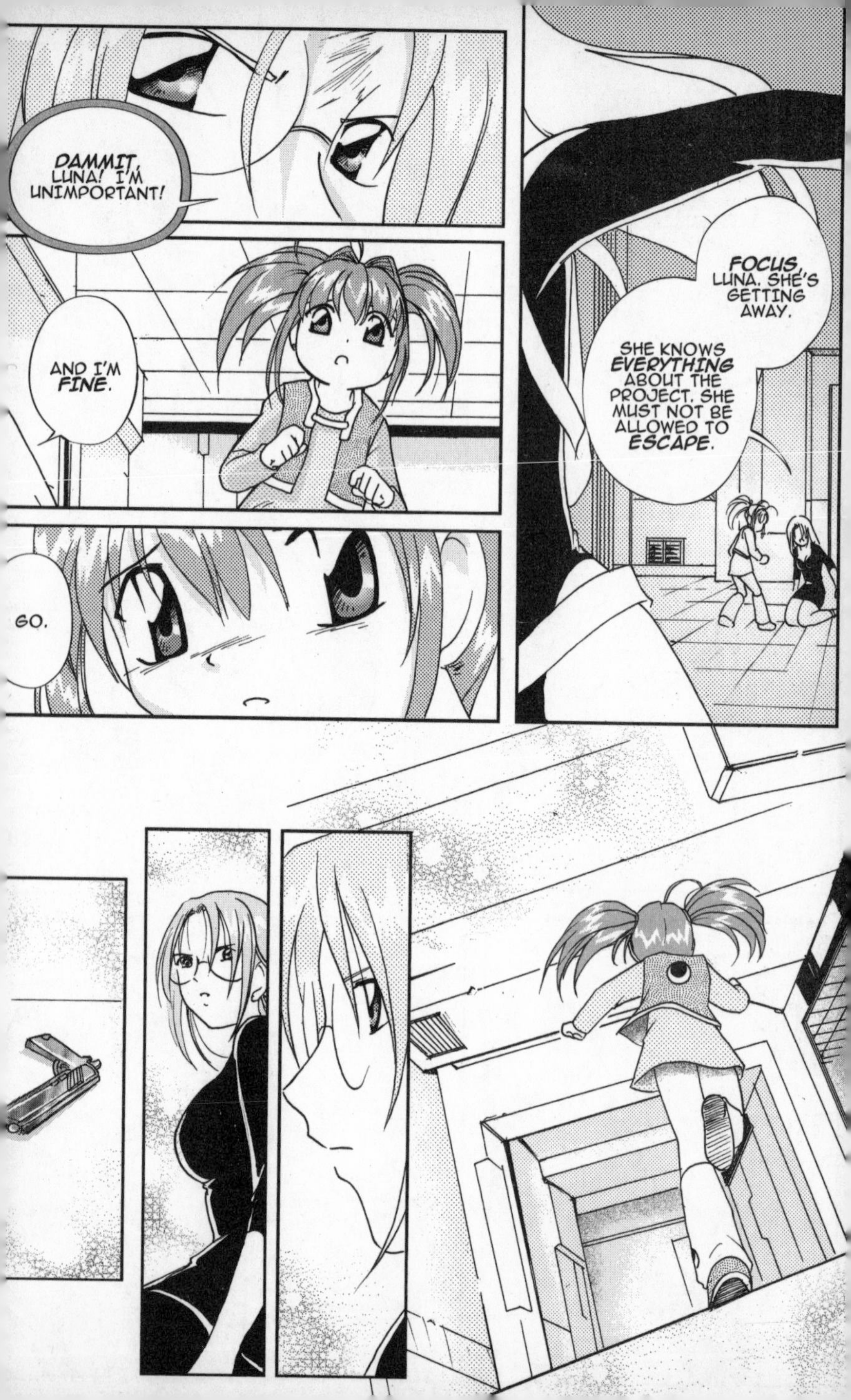
FOCUS, LUNA. SHE'S GETTING AWAY.
SHE KNOWS EVERYTHING ABOUT THE PROJECT. SHE MUST NOT BE ALLOWED TO ESCAPE.
DAMMIT, LUNA! I'M UNIMPORTANT!
AND I'M FINE.
GO.

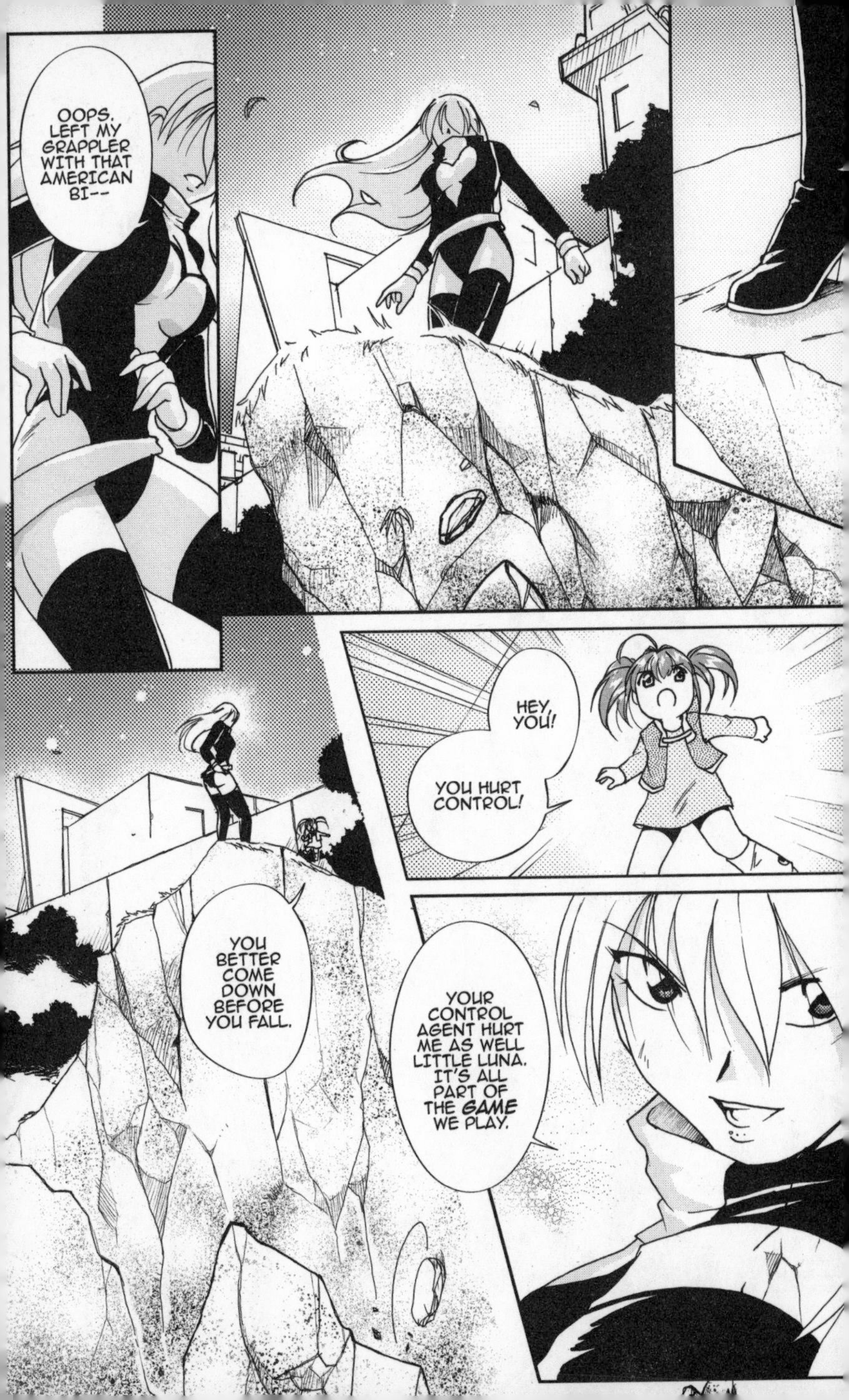
OOPS. LEFT MY GRAPPLER WITH THAT AMERICAN BI--
HEY, YOU!
YOU HURT CONTROL!
YOUR CONTROL AGENT HURT ME AS WELL LITTLE LUNA. IT'S ALL PART OF THE *GAME* WE PLAY.
YOU BETTER COME DOWN BEFORE YOU FALL.

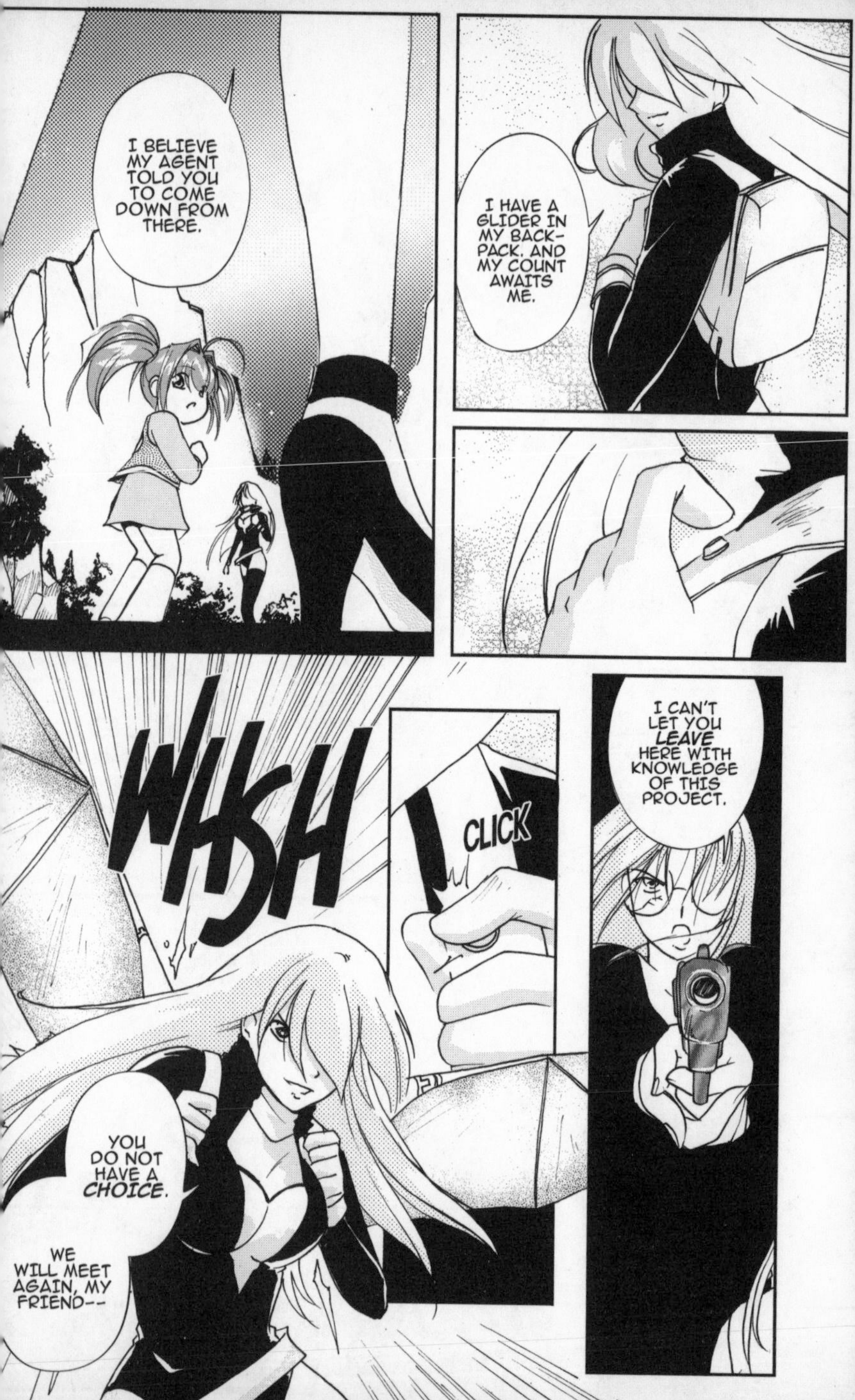
I HAVE A GLIDER IN MY BACK-PACK, AND MY COUNT AWAITS ME.
I BELIEVE MY AGENT TOLD YOU TO COME DOWN FROM THERE.
I CAN'T LET YOU *LEAVE* HERE WITH KNOWLEDGE OF THIS PROJECT.
CLICK
WHSH
YOU DO NOT HAVE A *CHOICE*.
WE WILL MEET AGAIN, MY FRIEND--

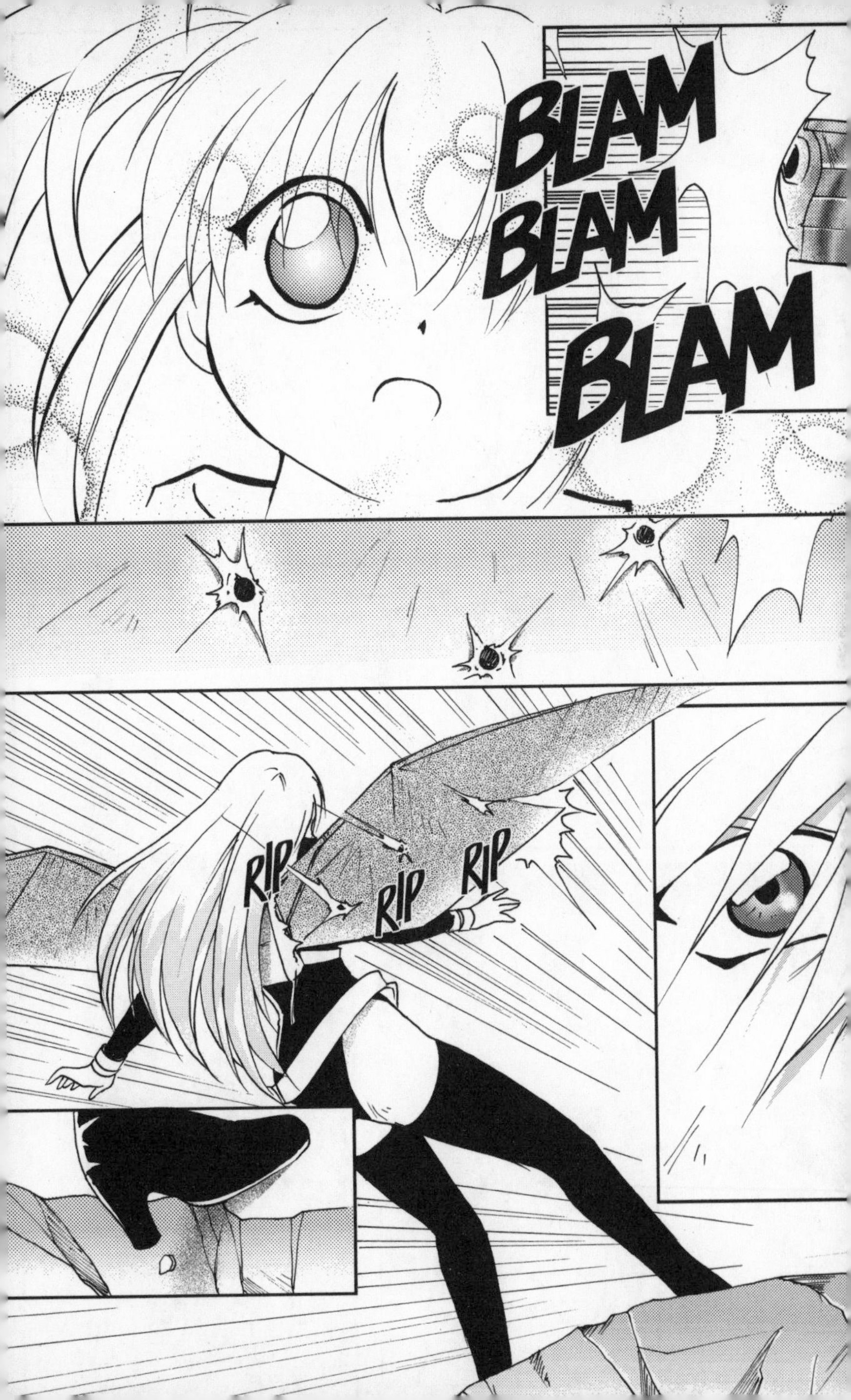
BLAM
BLAM
BLAM
RIP
RIP
RIP

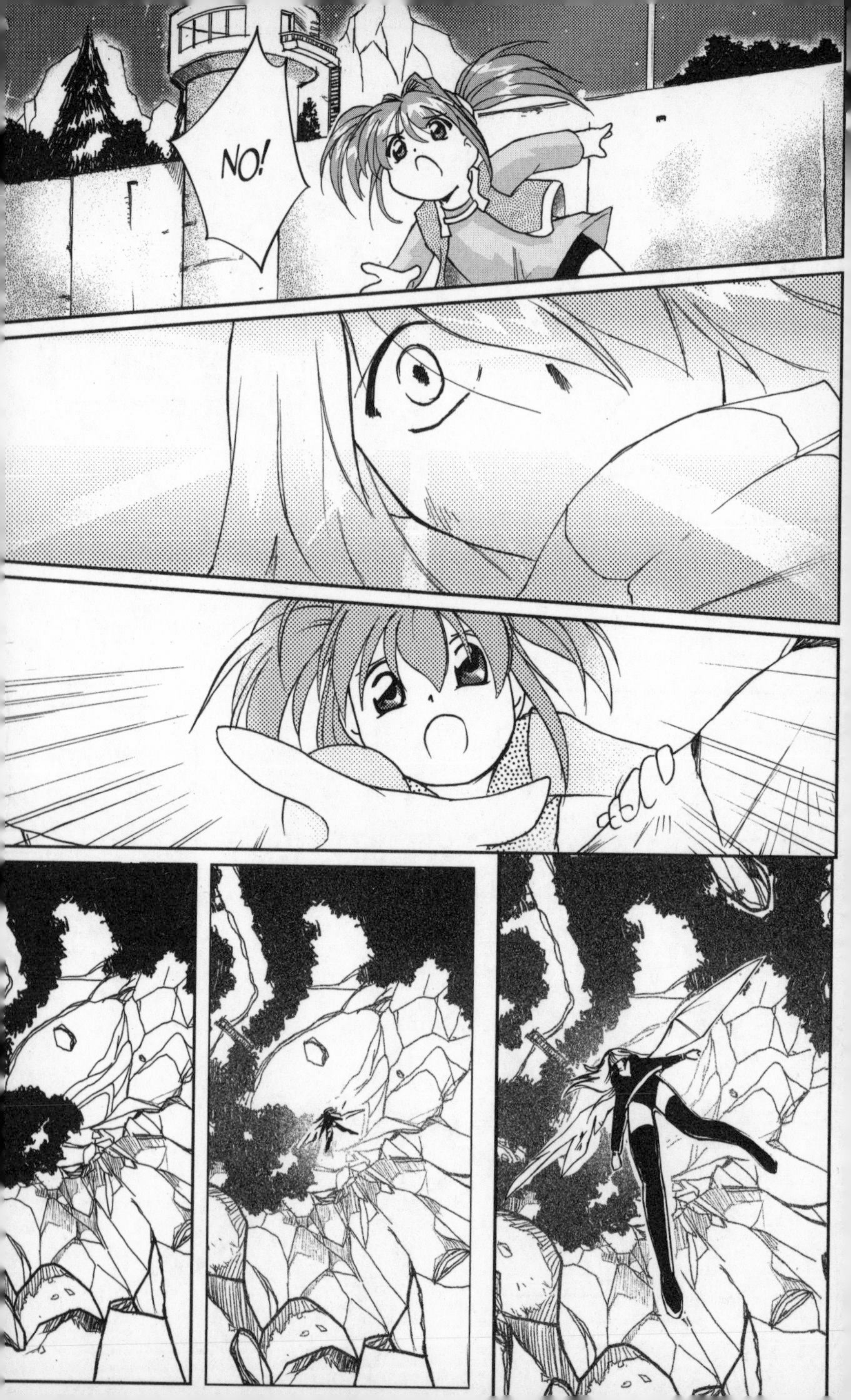
NO!

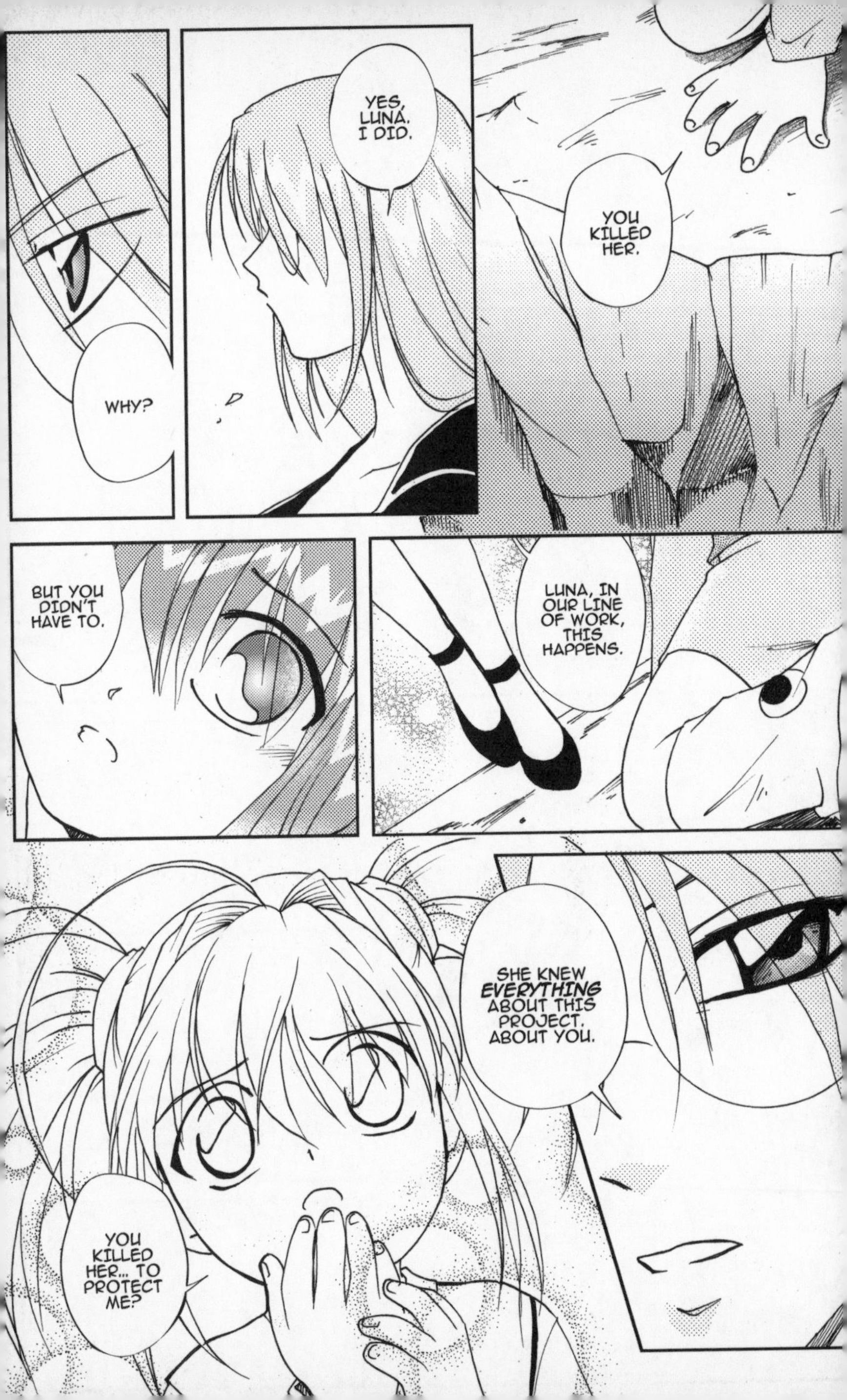
YOU KILLED HER.
YES, LUNA. I DID.
WHY?
LUNA, IN OUR LINE OF WORK, THIS HAPPENS.
BUT YOU DIDN'T HAVE TO.
SHE KNEW *EVERYTHING* ABOUT THIS PROJECT. ABOUT YOU.
YOU KILLED HER... TO PROTECT ME?

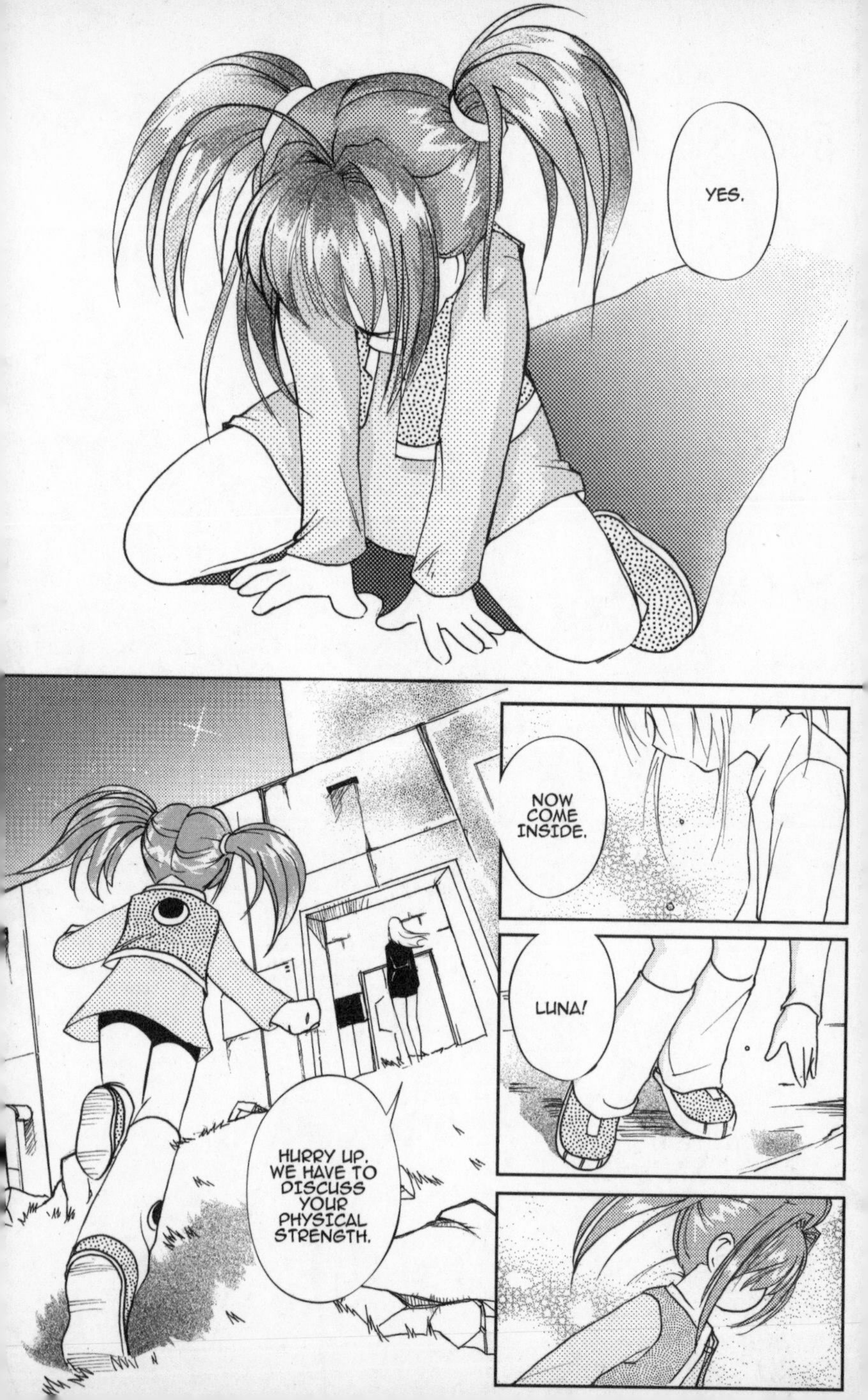
YES.
NOW COME INSIDE.
LUNA!
HURRY UP. WE HAVE TO DISCUSS YOUR PHYSICAL STRENGTH.

# File 12
# EVOLUTIONS

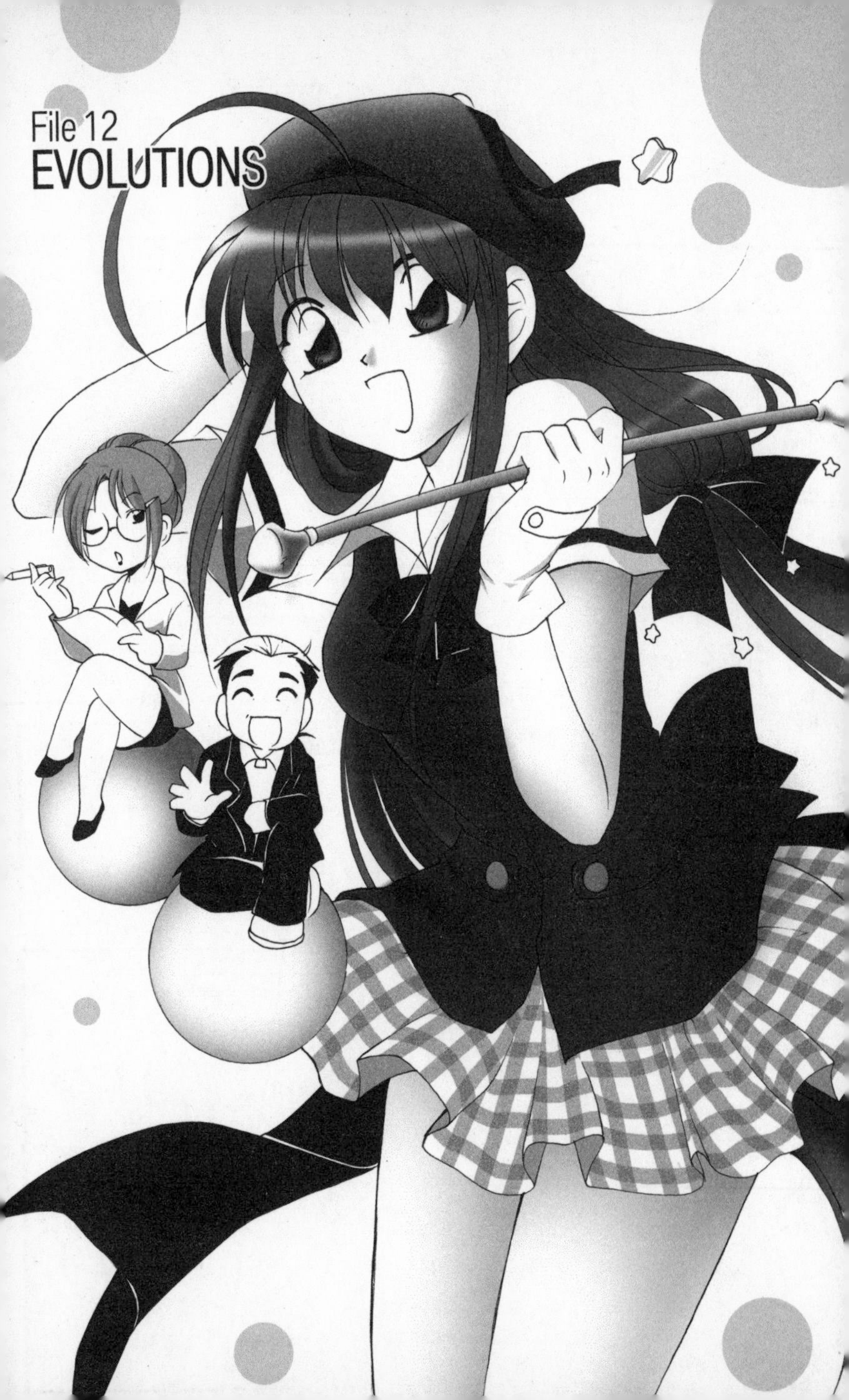

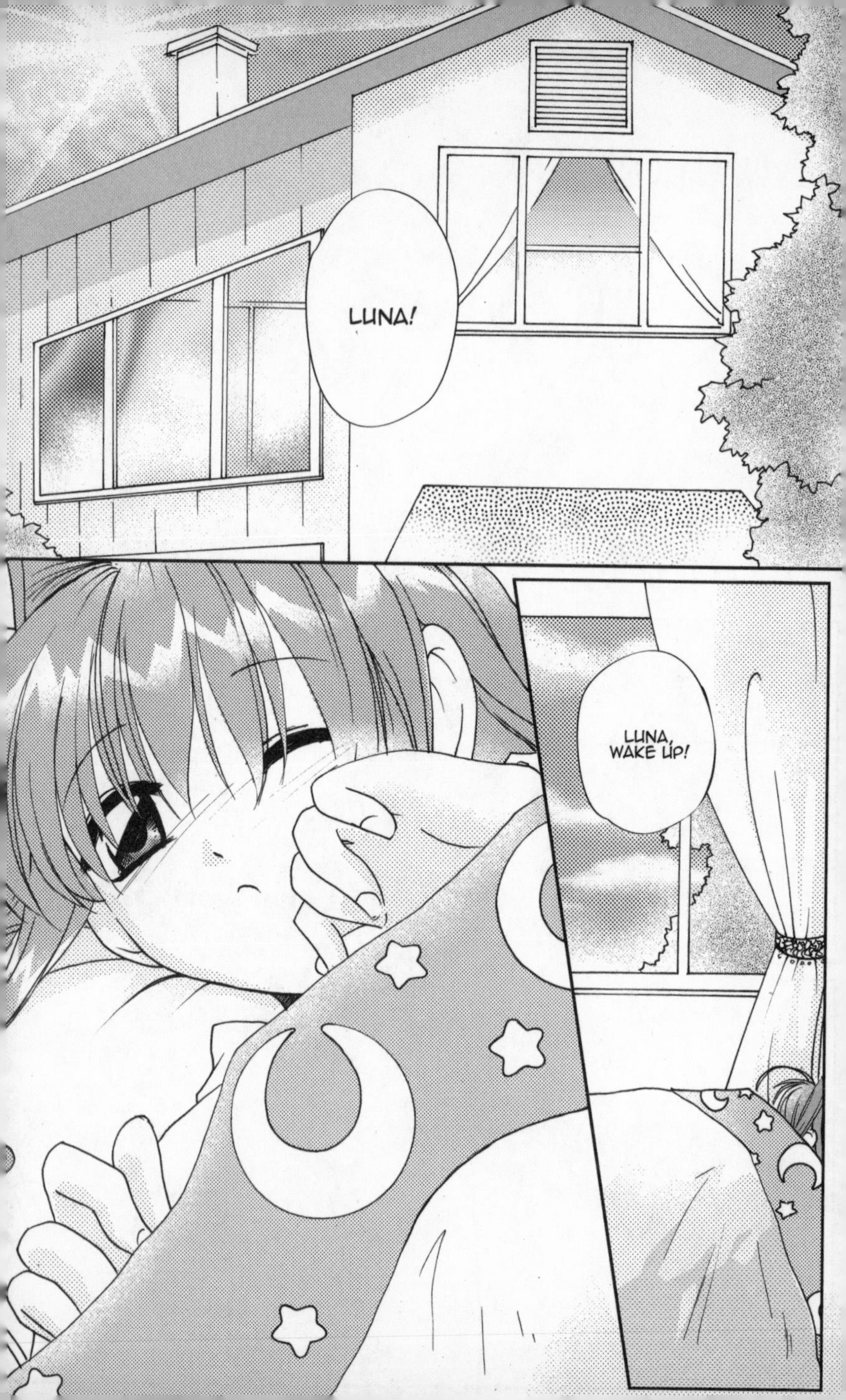
LUNA!
LUNA, WAKE UP!

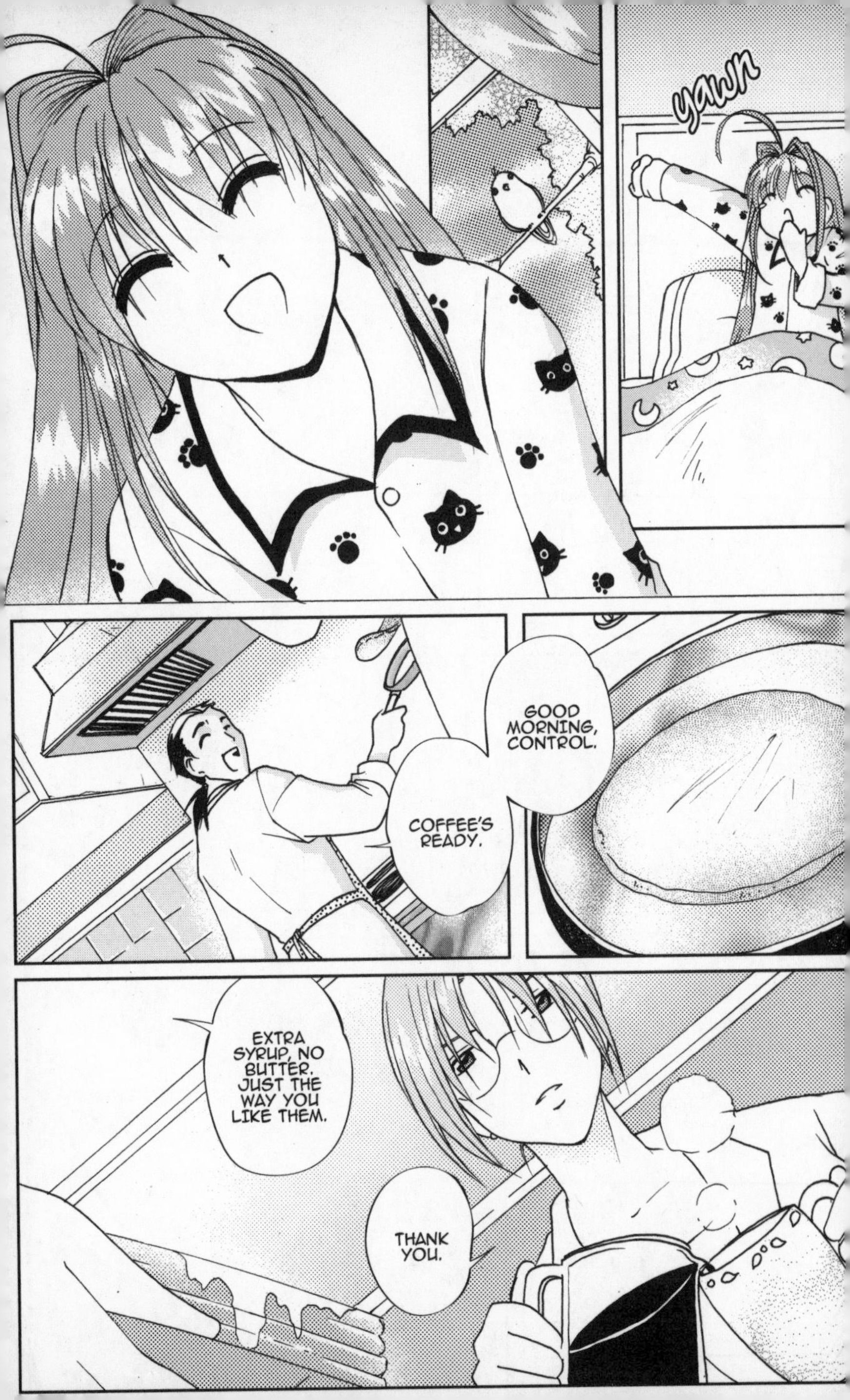
yawn
GOOD MORNING, CONTROL.
COFFEE'S READY.
EXTRA SYRUP, NO BUTTER. JUST THE WAY YOU LIKE THEM.
THANK YOU.

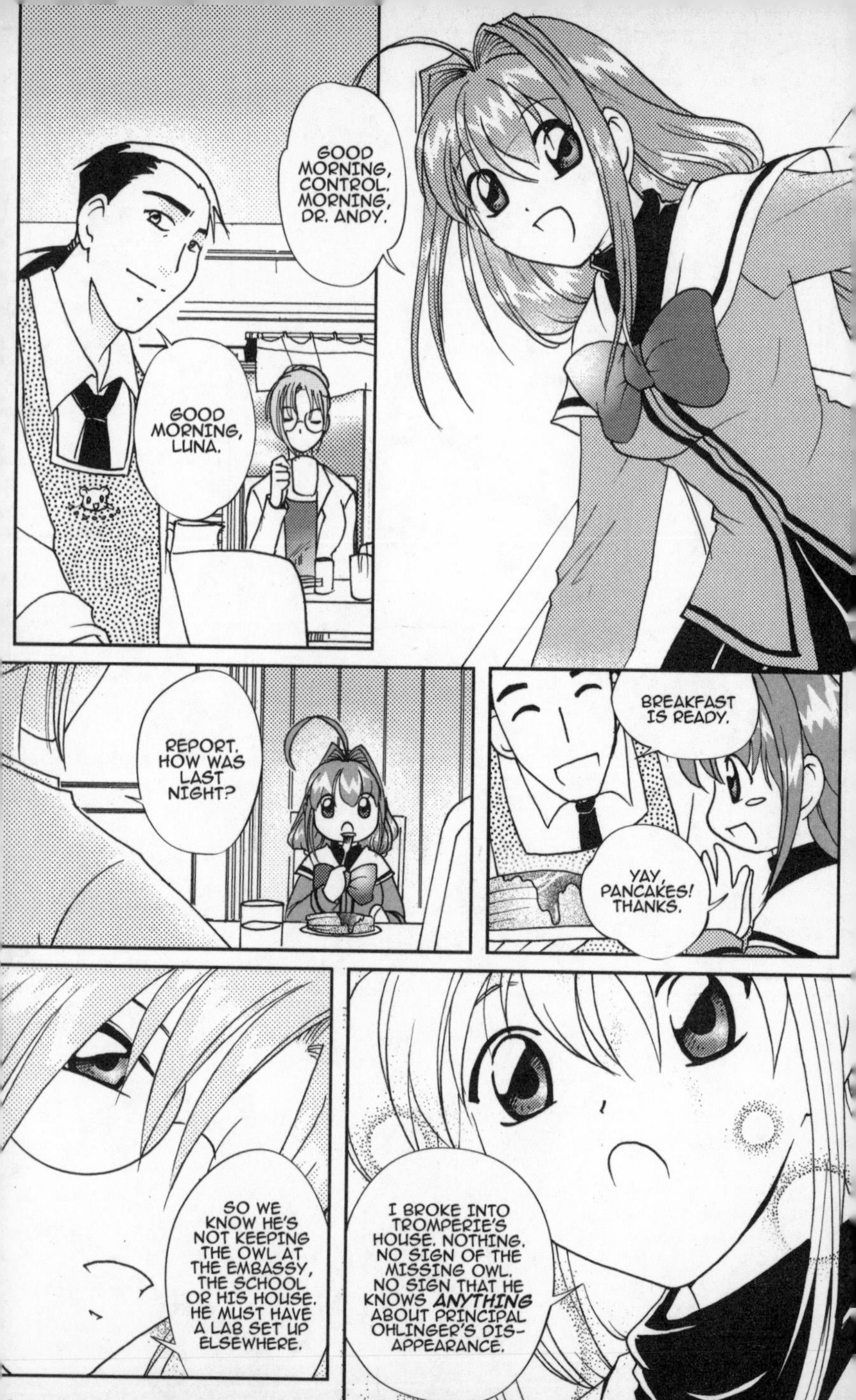
GOOD MORNING, CONTROL. MORNING, DR. ANDY.
GOOD MORNING, LUNA.
BREAKFAST IS READY.
YAY, PANCAKES! THANKS.
REPORT. HOW WAS LAST NIGHT?
I BROKE INTO TROMPERIE'S HOUSE. NOTHING. NO SIGN OF THE MISSING OWL. NO SIGN THAT HE KNOWS *ANYTHING* ABOUT PRINCIPAL OHLINGER'S DIS-APPEARANCE.
SO WE KNOW HE'S NOT KEEPING THE OWL AT THE EMBASSY, THE SCHOOL OR HIS HOUSE. HE MUST HAVE A LAB SET UP ELSEWHERE.

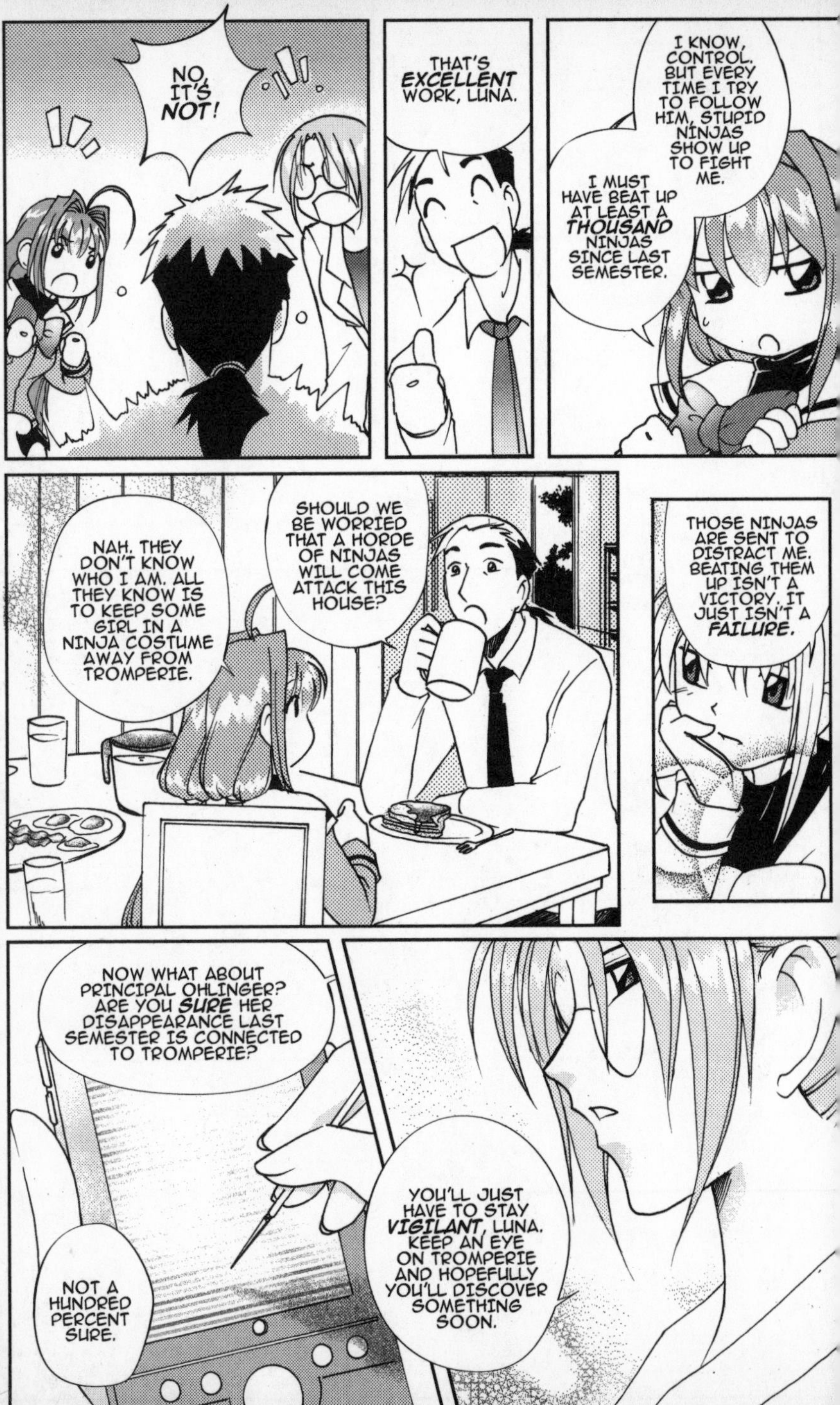
I KNOW, CONTROL. BUT EVERY TIME I TRY TO FOLLOW HIM, STUPID NINJAS SHOW UP TO FIGHT ME.
I MUST HAVE BEAT UP AT LEAST A *THOUSAND* NINJAS SINCE LAST SEMESTER.
THAT'S *EXCELLENT* WORK, LUNA.
NO, IT'S *NOT*!
THOSE NINJAS ARE SENT TO DISTRACT ME. BEATING THEM UP ISN'T A VICTORY. IT JUST ISN'T A *FAILURE.*
SHOULD WE BE WORRIED THAT A HORDE OF NINJAS WILL COME ATTACK THIS HOUSE?
NAH. THEY DON'T KNOW WHO I AM. ALL THEY KNOW IS TO KEEP SOME GIRL IN A NINJA COSTUME AWAY FROM TROMPERIE.
YOU'LL JUST HAVE TO STAY *VIGILANT*, LUNA. KEEP AN EYE ON TROMPERIE AND HOPEFULLY YOU'LL DISCOVER SOMETHING SOON.
NOW WHAT ABOUT PRINCIPAL OHLINGER? ARE YOU *SURE* HER DISAPPEARANCE LAST SEMESTER IS CONNECTED TO TROMPERIE?
NOT A HUNDRED PERCENT SURE.

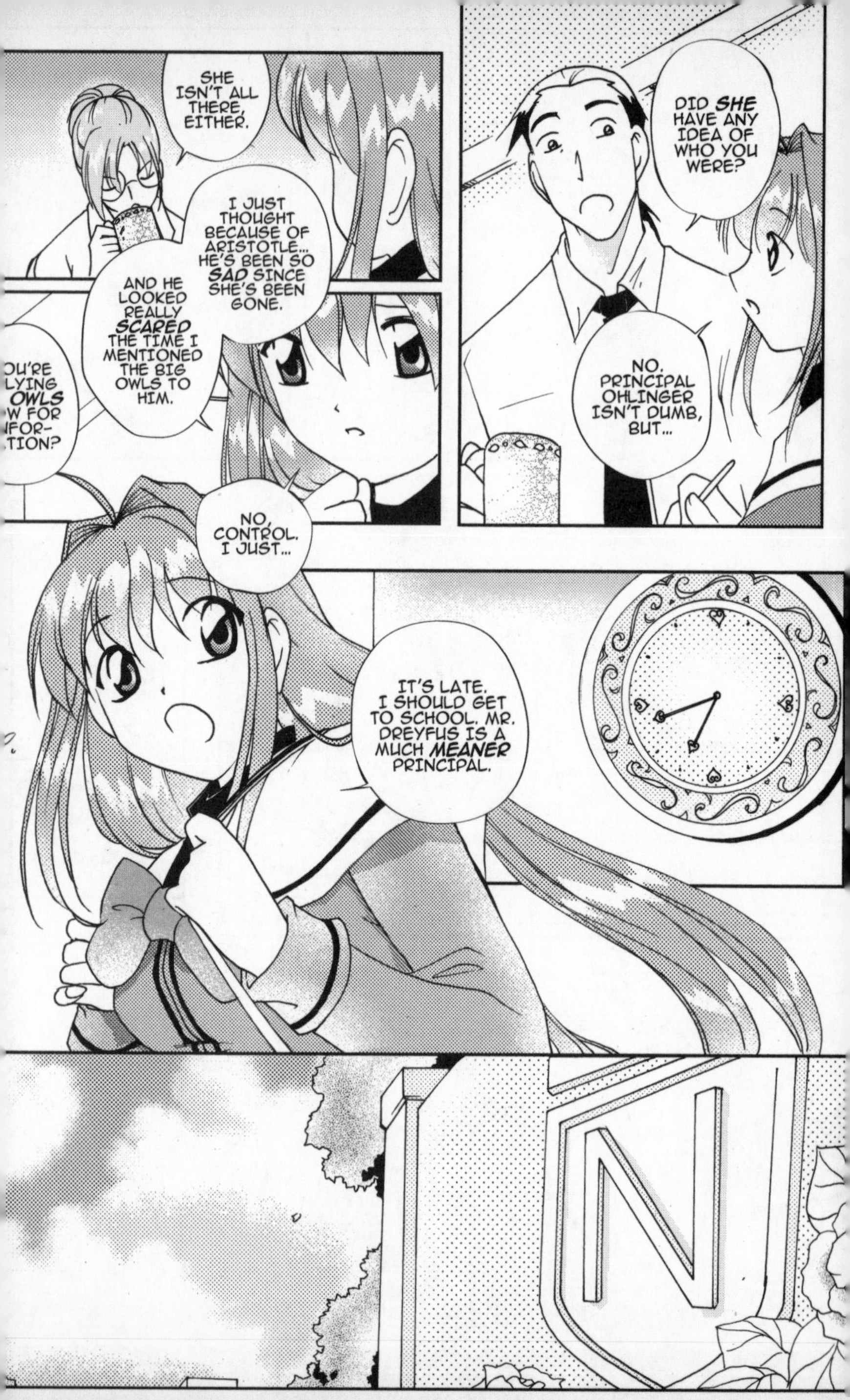
DID SHE HAVE ANY IDEA OF WHO YOU WERE?
NO. PRINCIPAL OHLINGER ISN'T DUMB, BUT...
SHE ISN'T ALL THERE, EITHER.
I JUST THOUGHT BECAUSE OF ARISTOTLE... HE'S BEEN SO SAD SINCE SHE'S BEEN GONE.
AND HE LOOKED REALLY SCARED THE TIME I MENTIONED THE BIG OWLS TO HIM.
NO, CONTROL. I JUST...
IT'S LATE. I SHOULD GET TO SCHOOL. MR. DREYFUS IS A MUCH MEANER PRINCIPAL.

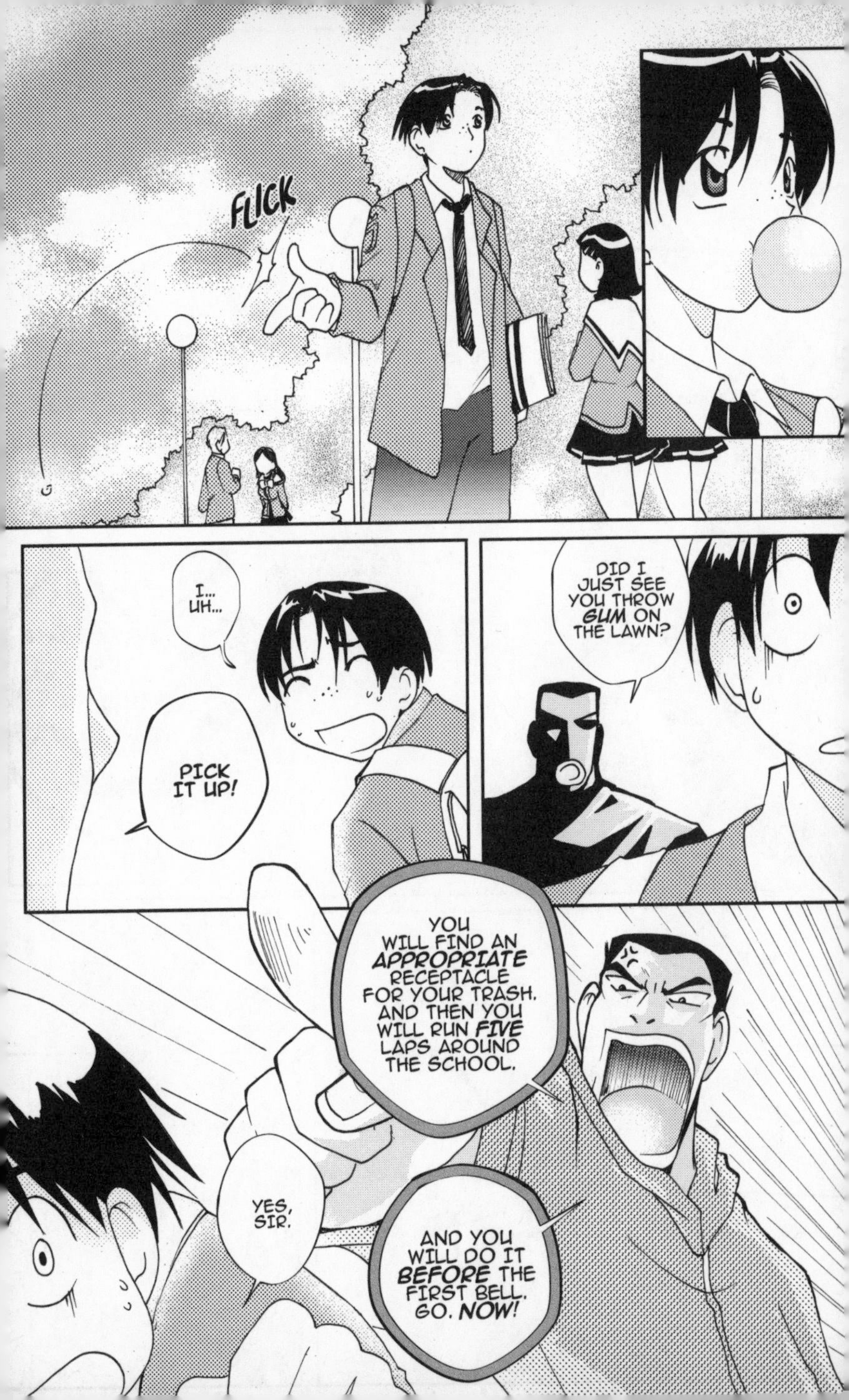
FLICK
DID I JUST SEE YOU THROW GUM ON THE LAWN?
I... UH...
PICK IT UP!
YOU WILL FIND AN APPROPRIATE RECEPTACLE FOR YOUR TRASH. AND THEN YOU WILL RUN FIVE LAPS AROUND THE SCHOOL.
AND YOU WILL DO IT BEFORE THE FIRST BELL. GO. NOW!
YES, SIR.

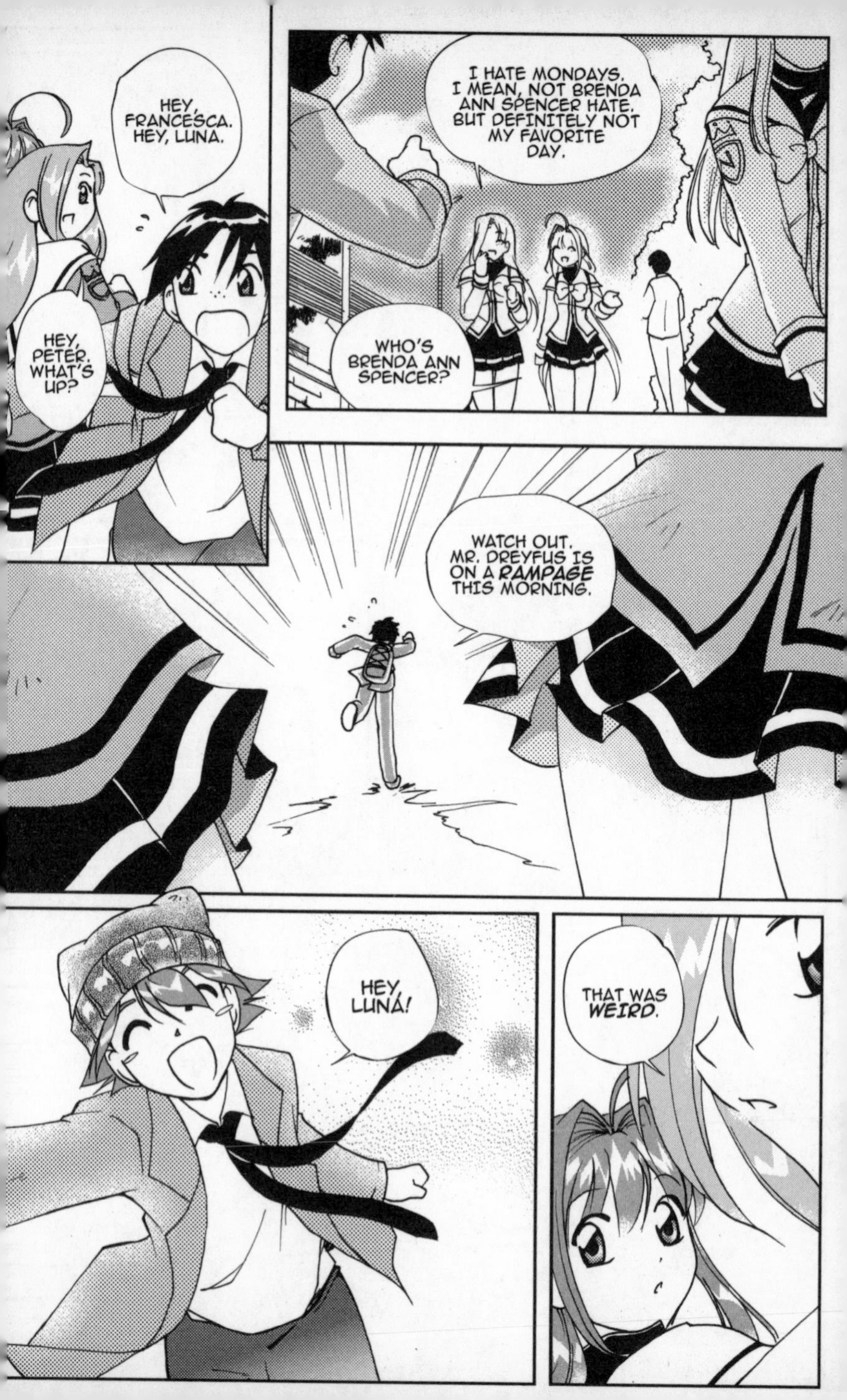
I HATE MONDAYS. I MEAN, NOT BRENDA ANN SPENCER HATE. BUT DEFINITELY NOT MY FAVORITE DAY.
WHO'S BRENDA ANN SPENCER?
HEY, FRANCESCA. HEY, LUNA.
HEY, PETER. WHAT'S UP?
WATCH OUT. MR. DREYFUS IS ON A *RAMPAGE* THIS MORNING.
THAT WAS *WEIRD*.
HEY, LUNA!

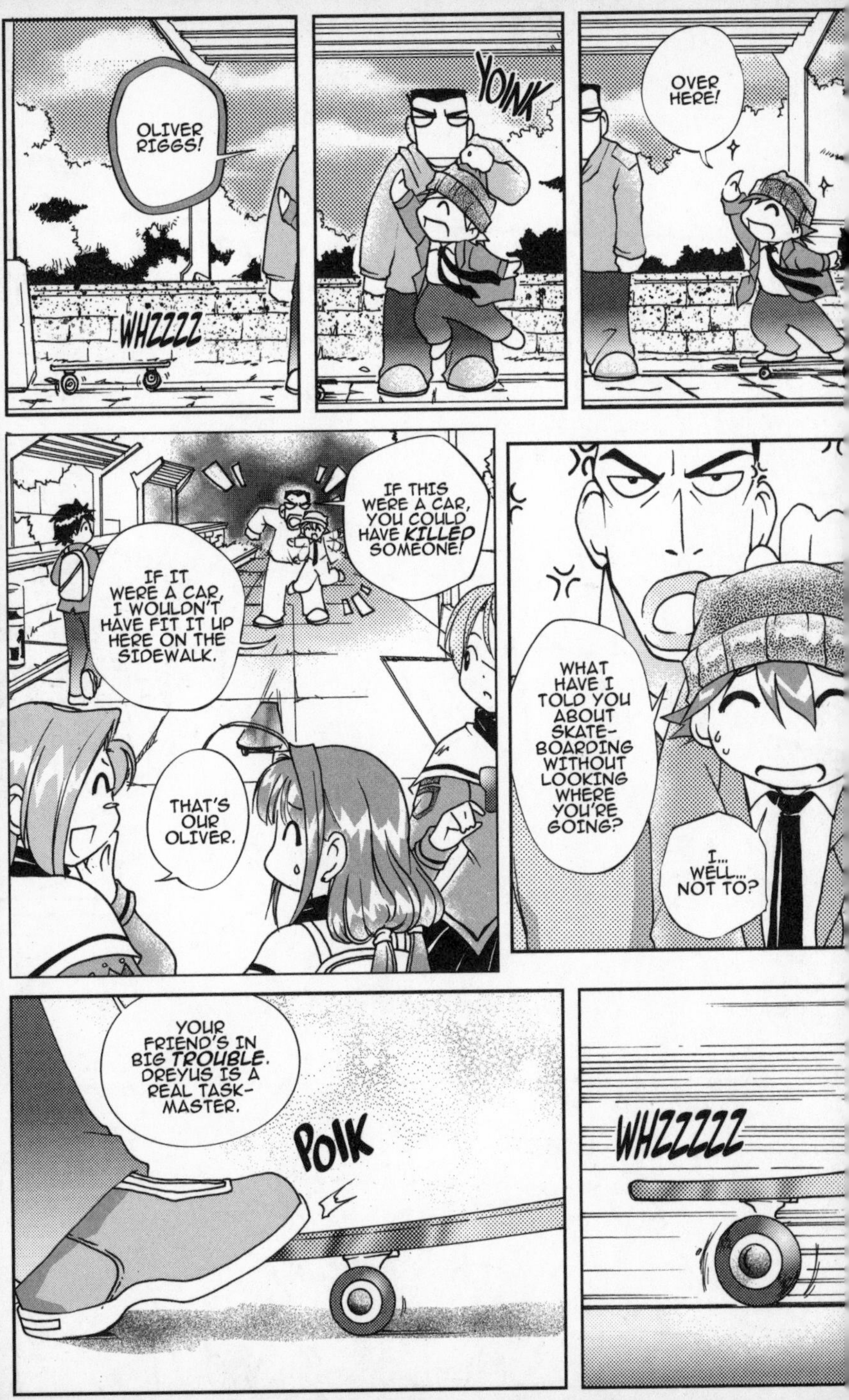
OVER HERE!
YOINK
OLIVER RIGGS!
WHZZZZ
WHAT HAVE I TOLD YOU ABOUT SKATE-BOARDING WITHOUT LOOKING WHERE YOU'RE GOING?
I... WELL... NOT TO?
IF THIS WERE A CAR, YOU COULD HAVE KILLED SOMEONE!
IF IT WERE A CAR, I WOULDN'T HAVE FIT IT UP HERE ON THE SIDEWALK.
THAT'S OUR OLIVER.
WHZZZZZ
YOUR FRIEND'S IN BIG TROUBLE. DREYUS IS A REAL TASK-MASTER.
POIK

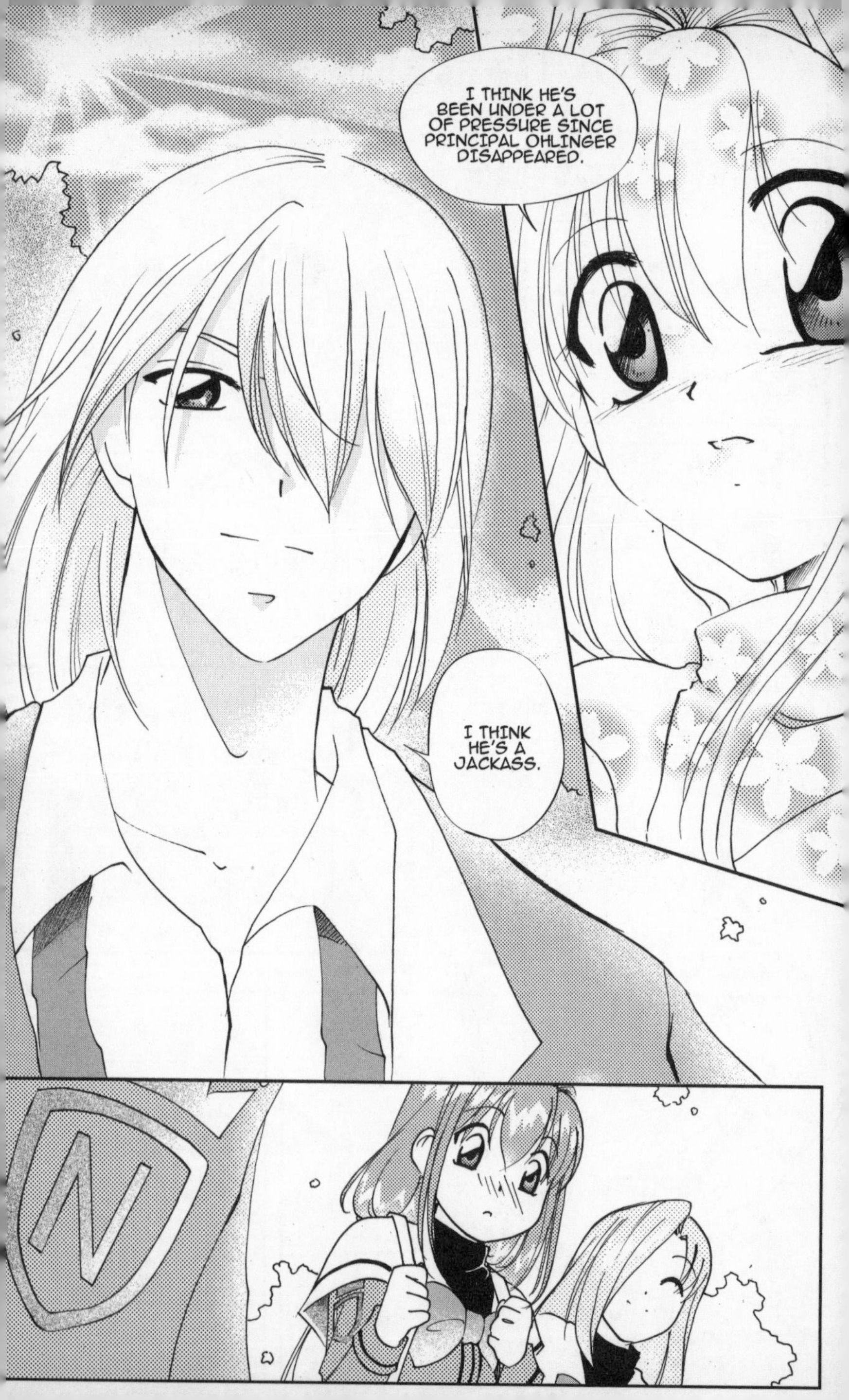
I THINK HE'S BEEN UNDER A LOT OF PRESSURE SINCE PRINCIPAL OHLINGER DISAPPEARED.
I THINK HE'S A JACKASS.
N

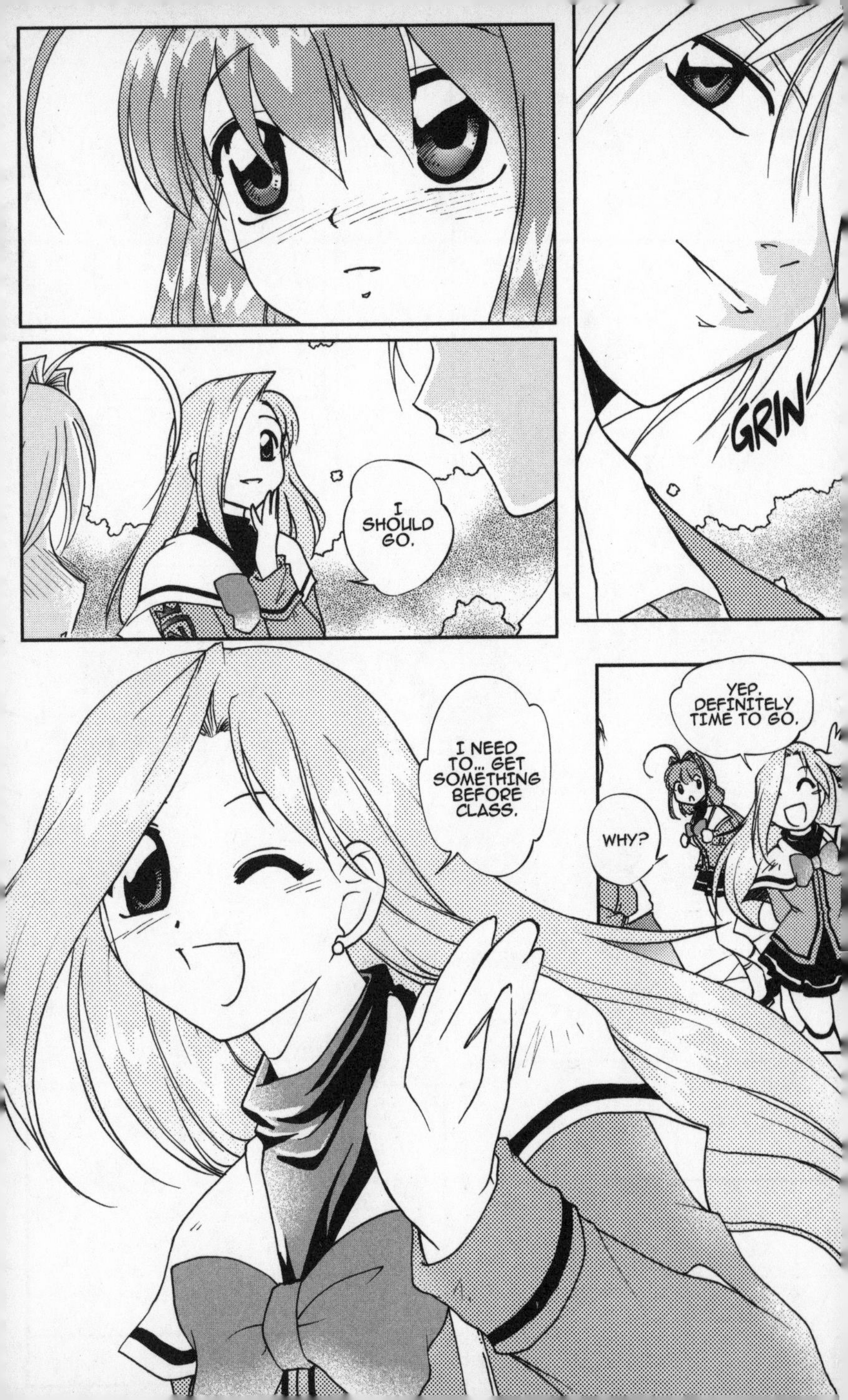
GRIN
I SHOULD GO.
YEP. DEFINITELY TIME TO GO.
WHY?
I NEED TO... GET SOMETHING BEFORE CLASS.

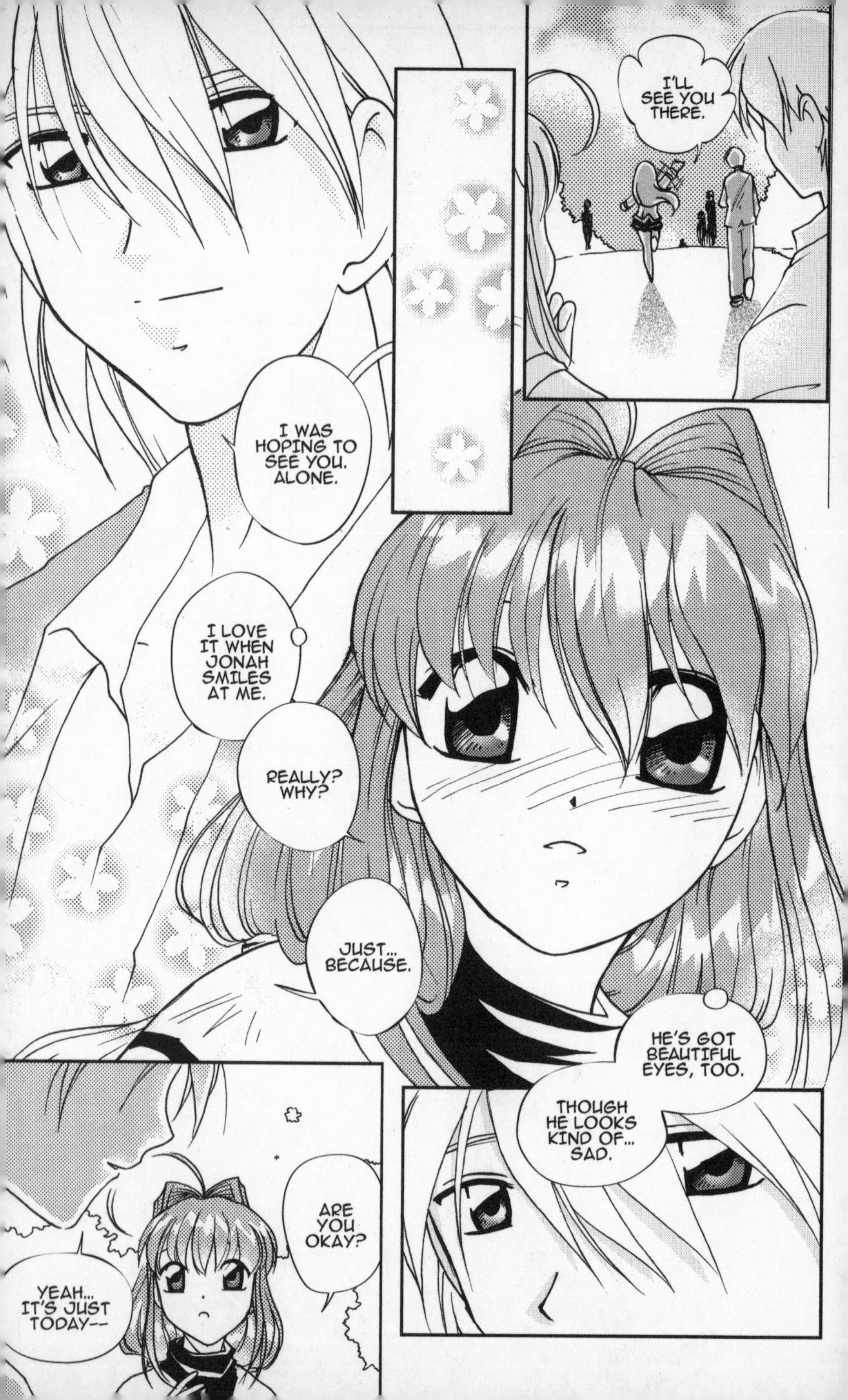
I'LL SEE YOU THERE.
I WAS HOPING TO SEE YOU. ALONE.
I LOVE IT WHEN JONAH SMILES AT ME.
REALLY? WHY?
JUST... BECAUSE.
HE'S GOT BEAUTIFUL EYES, TOO.
THOUGH HE LOOKS KIND OF... SAD.
ARE YOU OKAY?
YEAH... IT'S JUST TODAY--

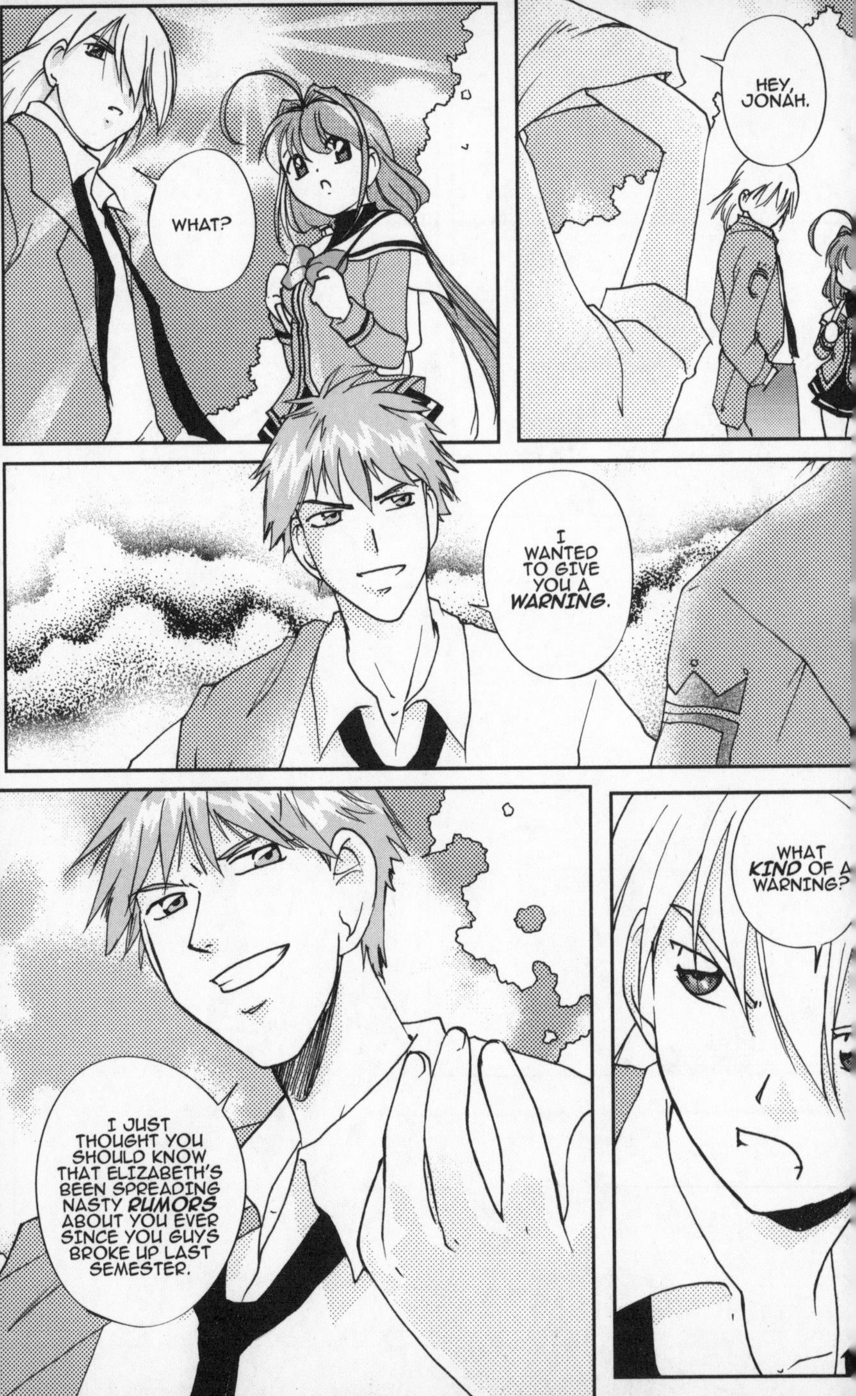
HEY, JONAH.
WHAT?
I WANTED TO GIVE YOU A WARNING.
WHAT KIND OF A WARNING?
I JUST THOUGHT YOU SHOULD KNOW THAT ELIZABETH'S BEEN SPREADING NASTY RUMORS ABOUT YOU EVER SINCE YOU GUYS BROKE UP LAST SEMESTER.

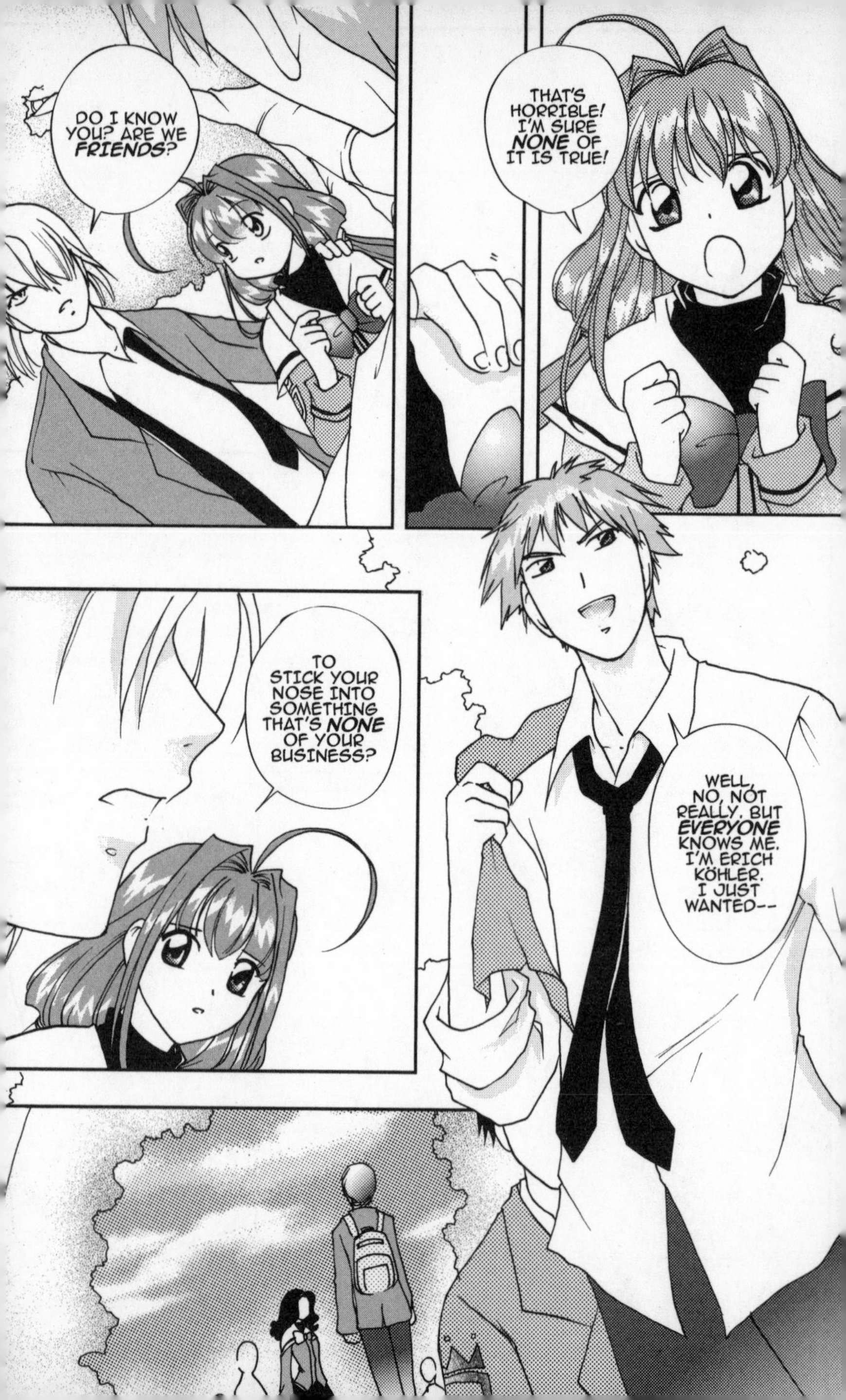
THAT'S HORRIBLE! I'M SURE NONE OF IT IS TRUE!
DO I KNOW YOU? ARE WE FRIENDS?
WELL, NO, NOT REALLY, BUT EVERYONE KNOWS ME. I'M ERICH KÖHLER. I JUST WANTED--
TO STICK YOUR NOSE INTO SOMETHING THAT'S NONE OF YOUR BUSINESS?

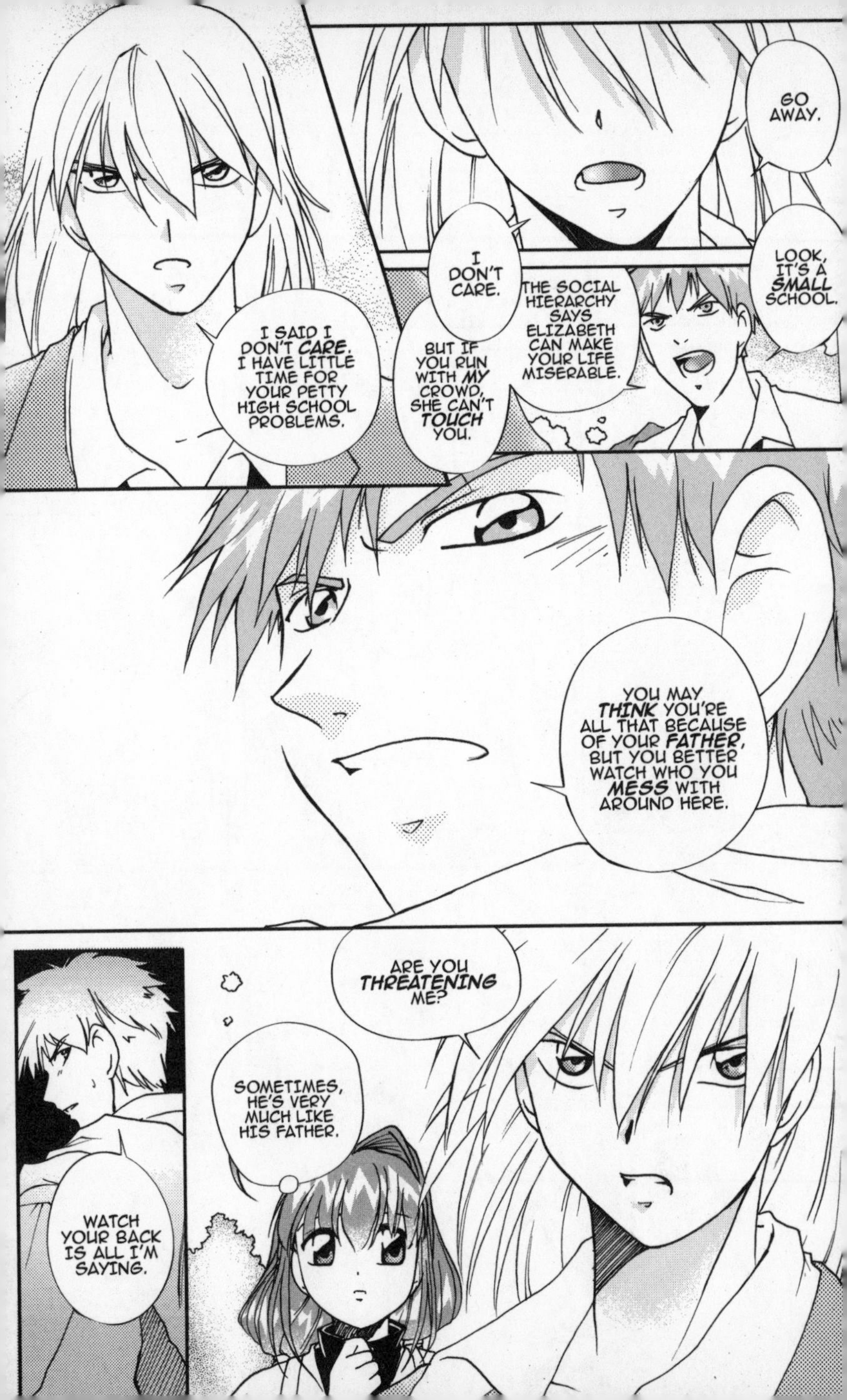

GO AWAY.
I DON'T CARE.
LOOK, IT'S A SMALL SCHOOL.
THE SOCIAL HIERARCHY SAYS ELIZABETH CAN MAKE YOUR LIFE MISERABLE.
BUT IF YOU RUN WITH MY CROWD, SHE CAN'T TOUCH YOU.
I SAID I DON'T CARE. I HAVE LITTLE TIME FOR YOUR PETTY HIGH SCHOOL PROBLEMS.
YOU MAY THINK YOU'RE ALL THAT BECAUSE OF YOUR FATHER, BUT YOU BETTER WATCH WHO YOU MESS WITH AROUND HERE.
ARE YOU THREATENING ME?
SOMETIMES, HE'S VERY MUCH LIKE HIS FATHER.
WATCH YOUR BACK IS ALL I'M SAYING.

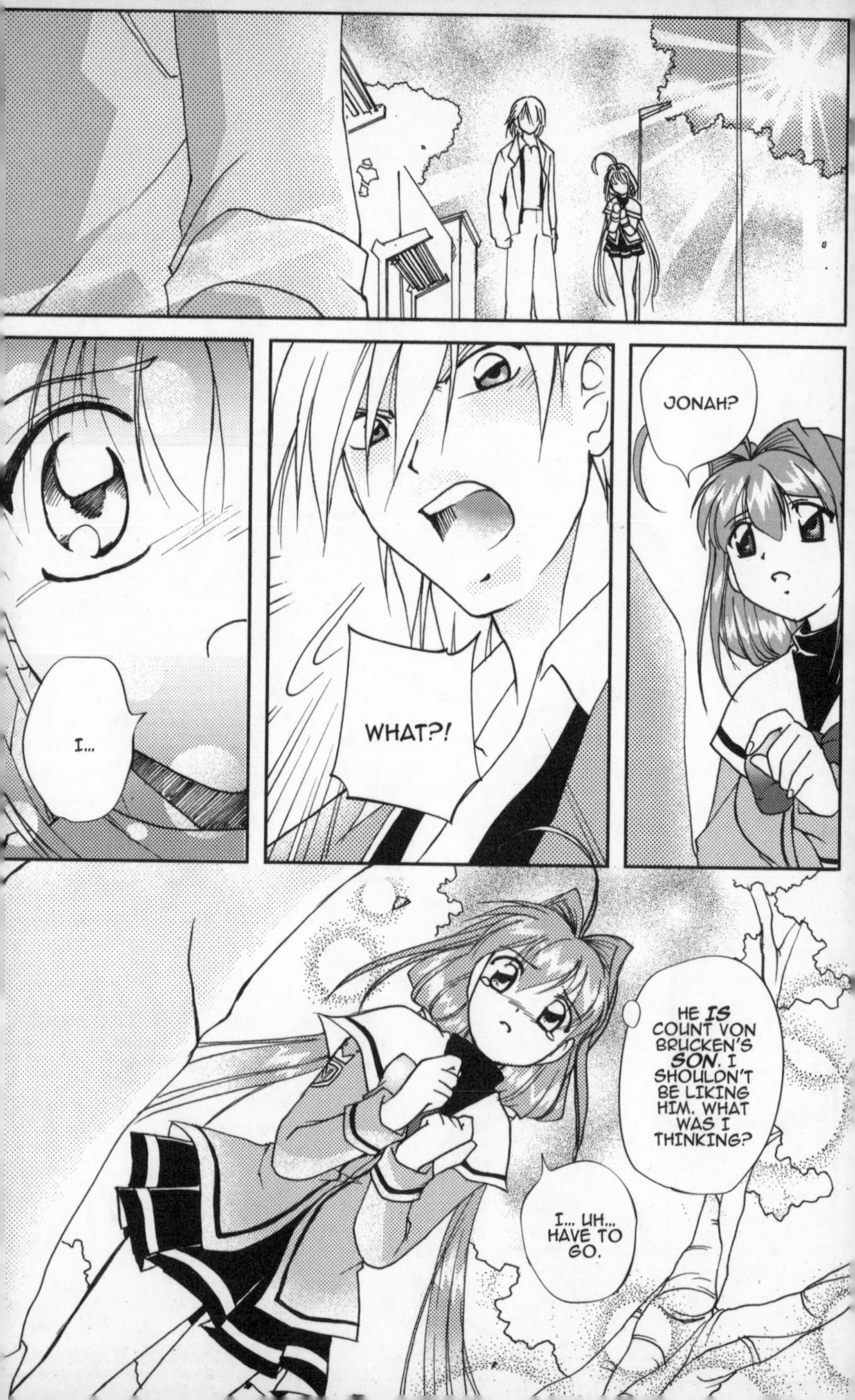
JONAH?
WHAT?!
I...
HE IS COUNT VON BRUCKEN'S SON. I SHOULDN'T BE LIKING HIM. WHAT WAS I THINKING?
I... UH... HAVE TO GO.

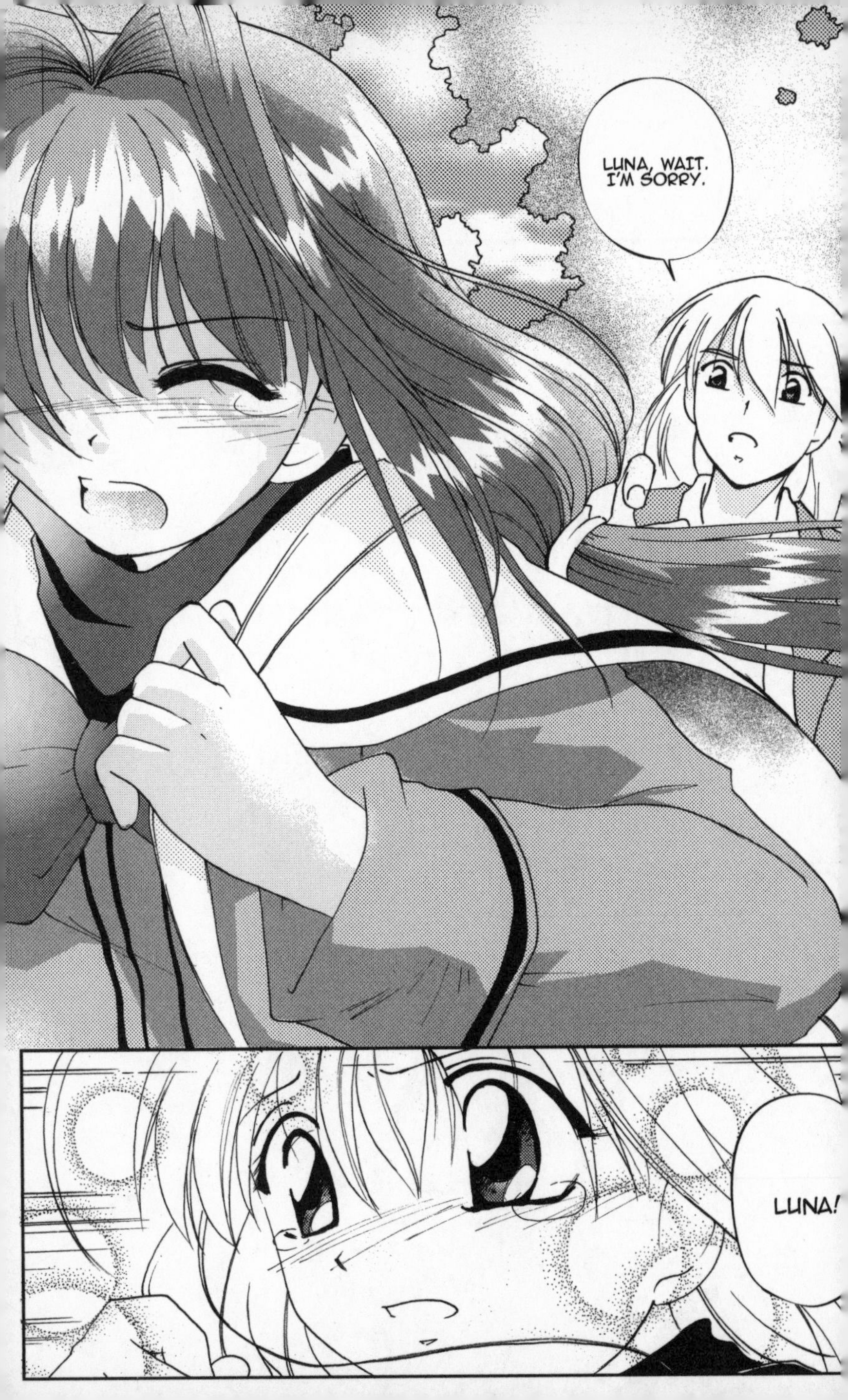
LUNA, WAIT. I'M SORRY.
LUNA!

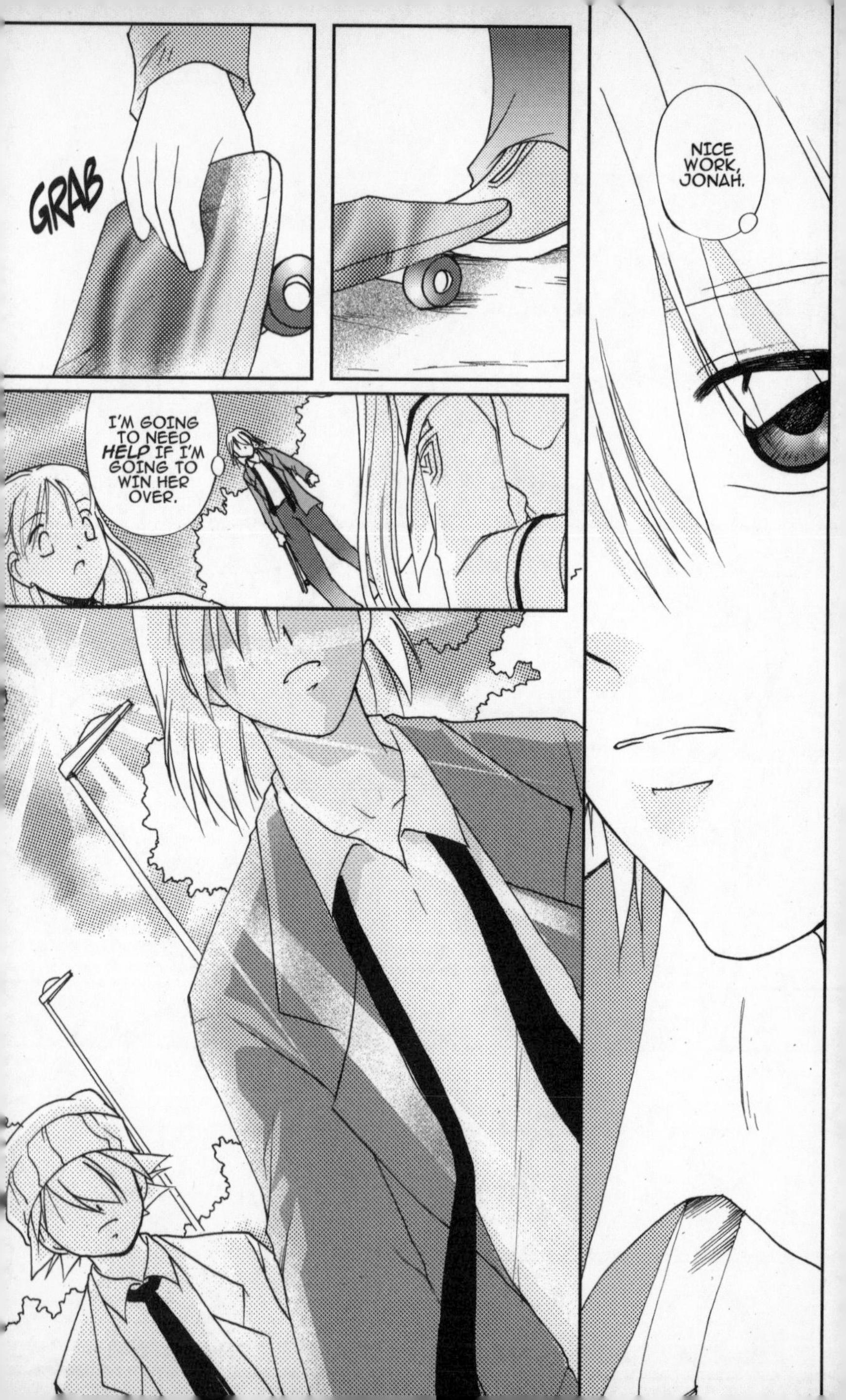
NICE WORK, JONAH.
GRAB
I'M GOING TO NEED HELP IF I'M GOING TO WIN HER OVER.

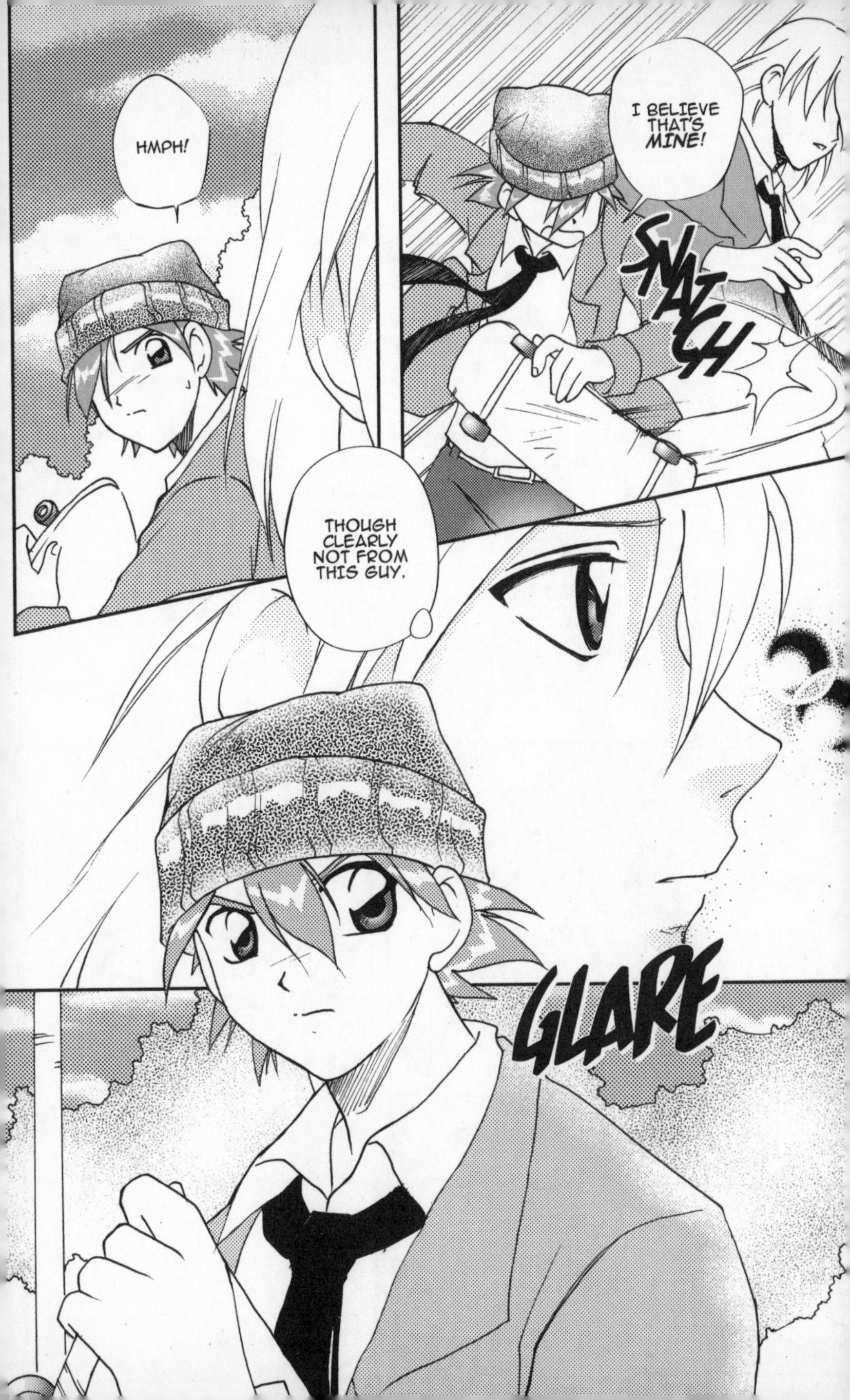
I BELIEVE THAT'S MINE!
SNATCH
HMPH!
THOUGH CLEARLY NOT FROM THIS GUY.
GLARE

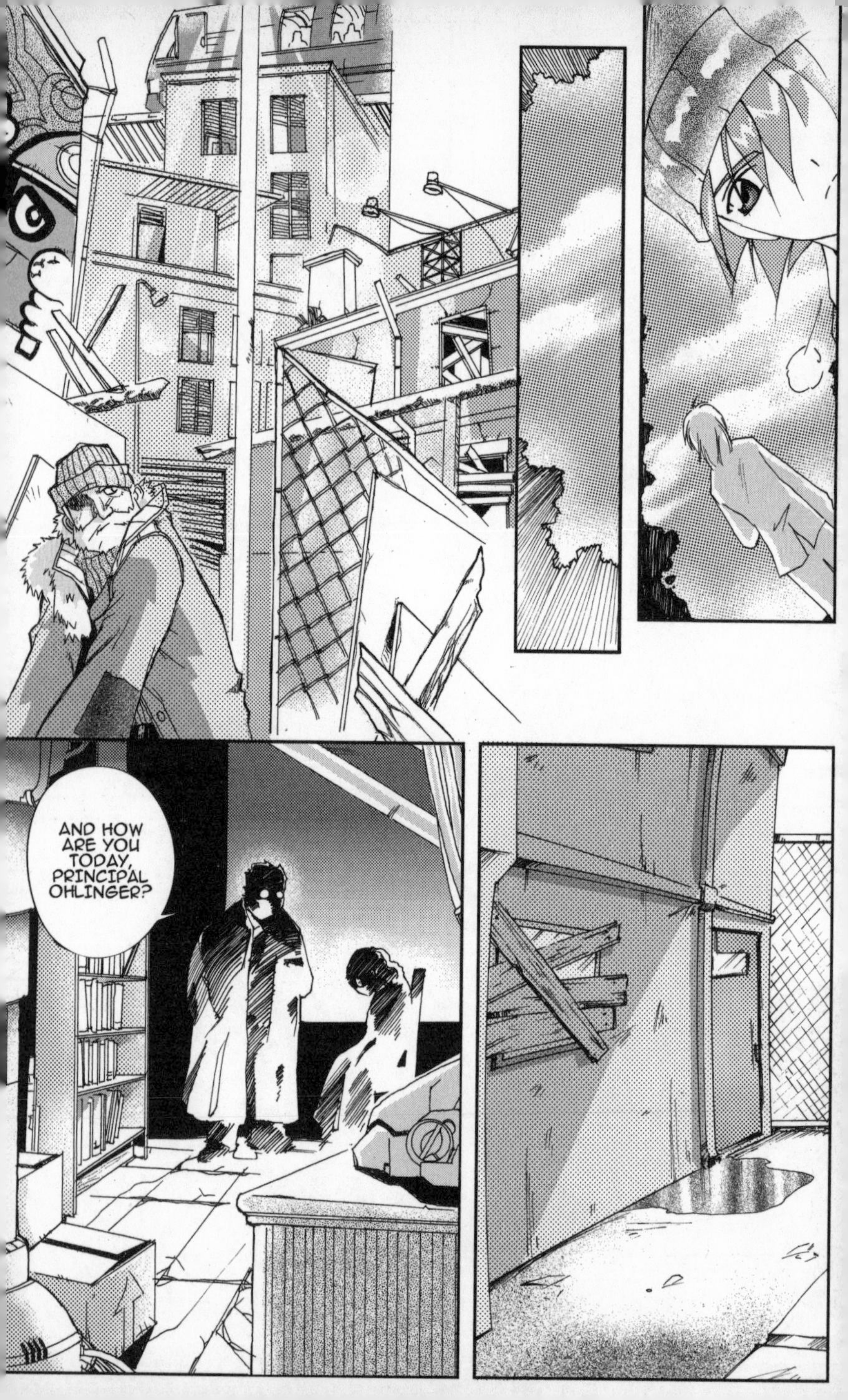
AND HOW ARE YOU TODAY, PRINCIPAL OHLINGER?

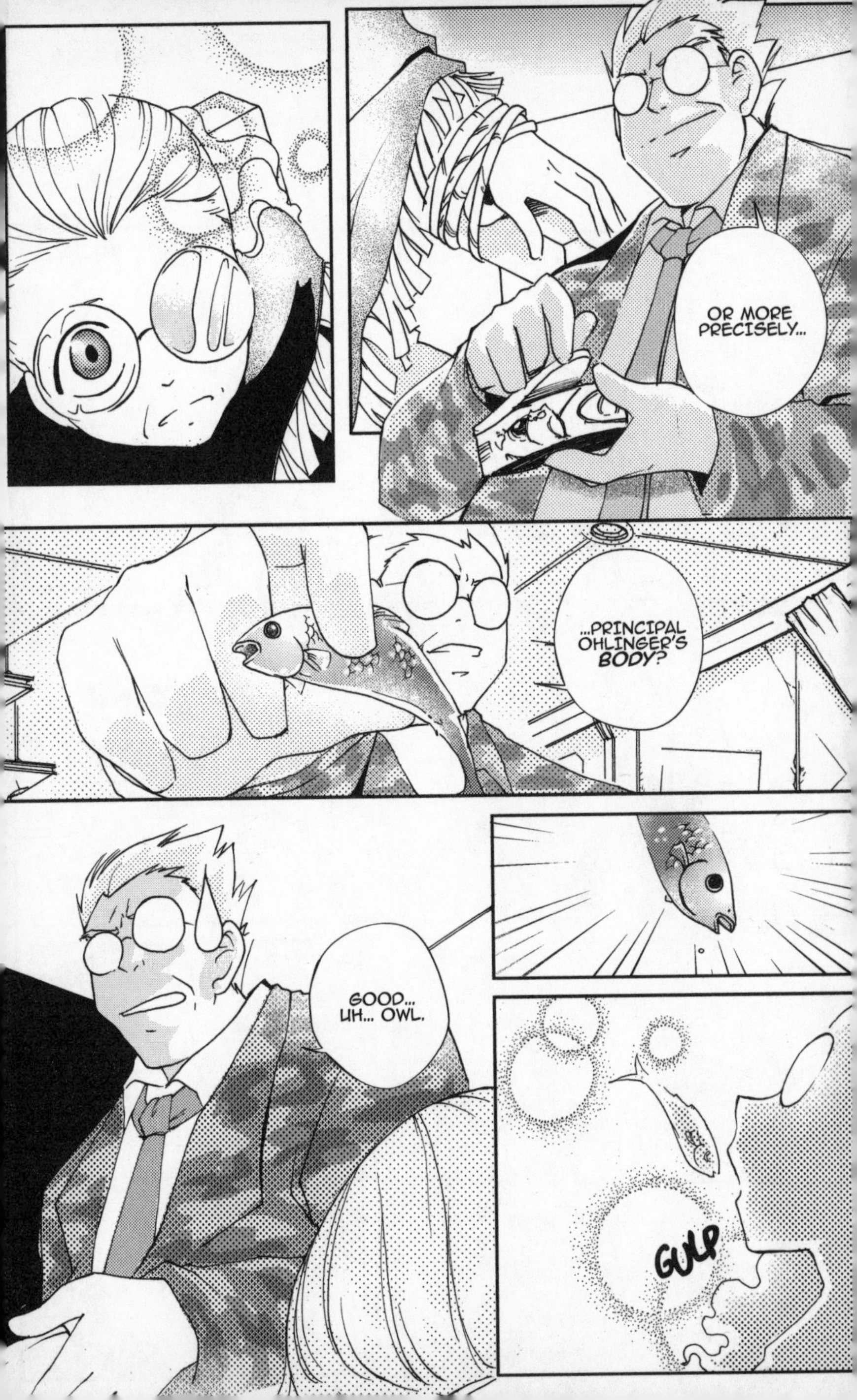
OR MORE PRECISELY...
...PRINCIPAL OHLINGER'S *BODY*?
GOOD... UH... OWL.
GULP

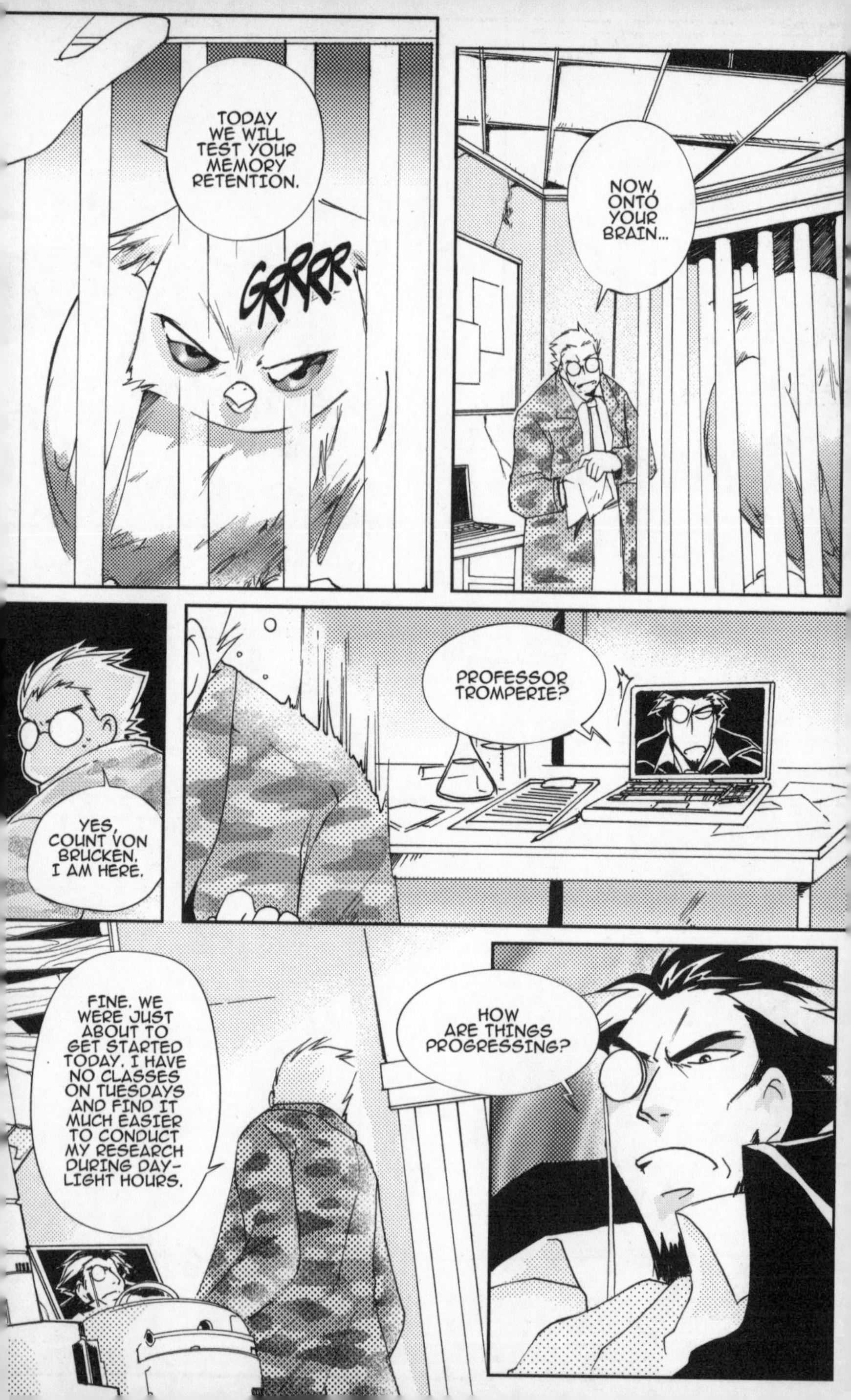
NOW, ONTO YOUR BRAIN...
TODAY WE WILL TEST YOUR MEMORY RETENTION.
GRRRR
PROFESSOR TROMPERIE?
YES, COUNT VON BRUCKEN. I AM HERE.
HOW ARE THINGS PROGRESSING?
FINE. WE WERE JUST ABOUT TO GET STARTED TODAY. I HAVE NO CLASSES ON TUESDAYS AND FIND IT MUCH EASIER TO CONDUCT MY RESEARCH DURING DAY-LIGHT HOURS.

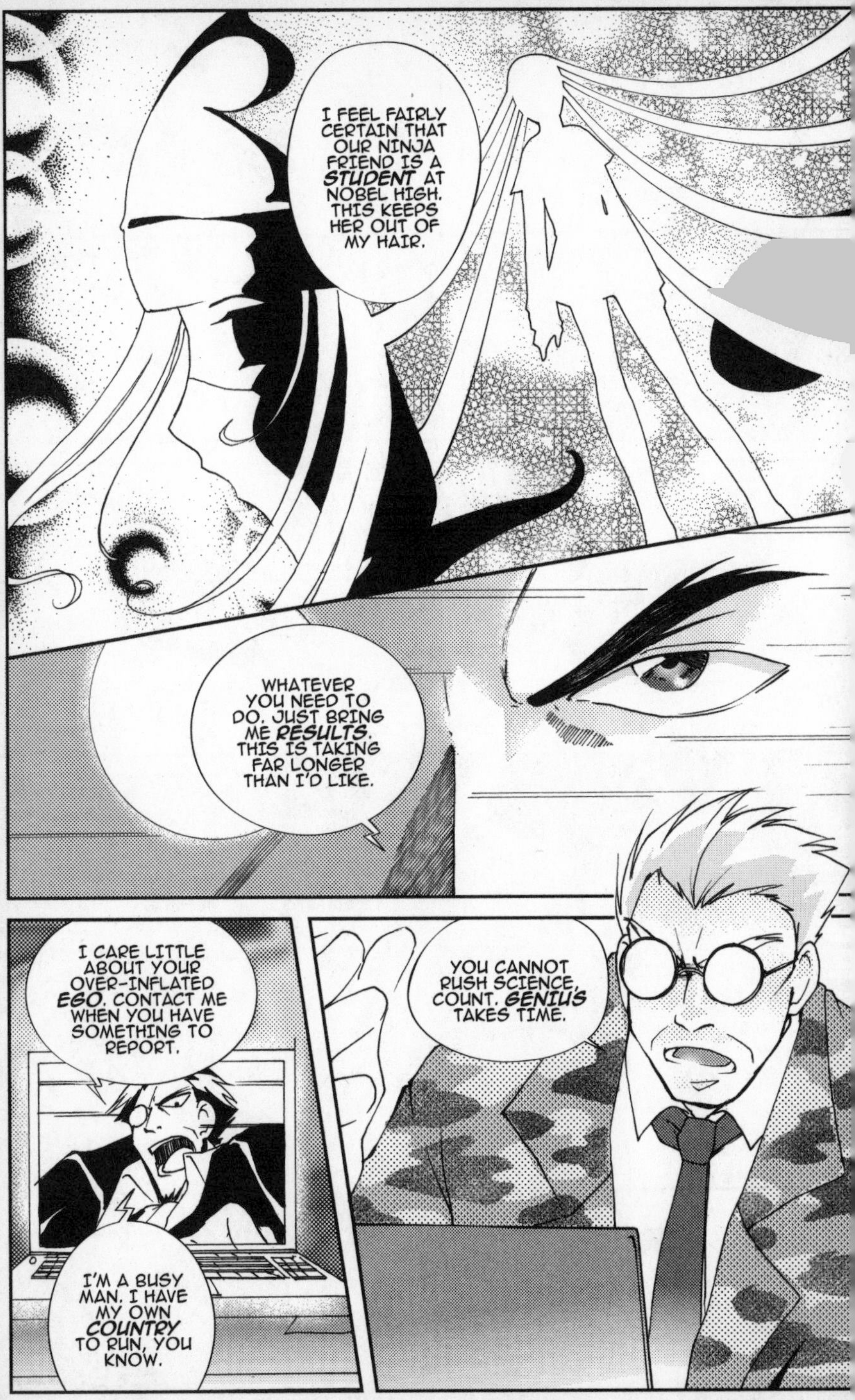
I FEEL FAIRLY CERTAIN THAT OUR NINJA FRIEND IS A STUDENT AT NOBEL HIGH. THIS KEEPS HER OUT OF MY HAIR.
WHATEVER YOU NEED TO DO. JUST BRING ME RESULTS. THIS IS TAKING FAR LONGER THAN I'D LIKE.
YOU CANNOT RUSH SCIENCE, COUNT. GENIUS TAKES TIME.
I CARE LITTLE ABOUT YOUR OVER-INFLATED EGO. CONTACT ME WHEN YOU HAVE SOMETHING TO REPORT.
I'M A BUSY MAN. I HAVE MY OWN COUNTRY TO RUN, YOU KNOW.

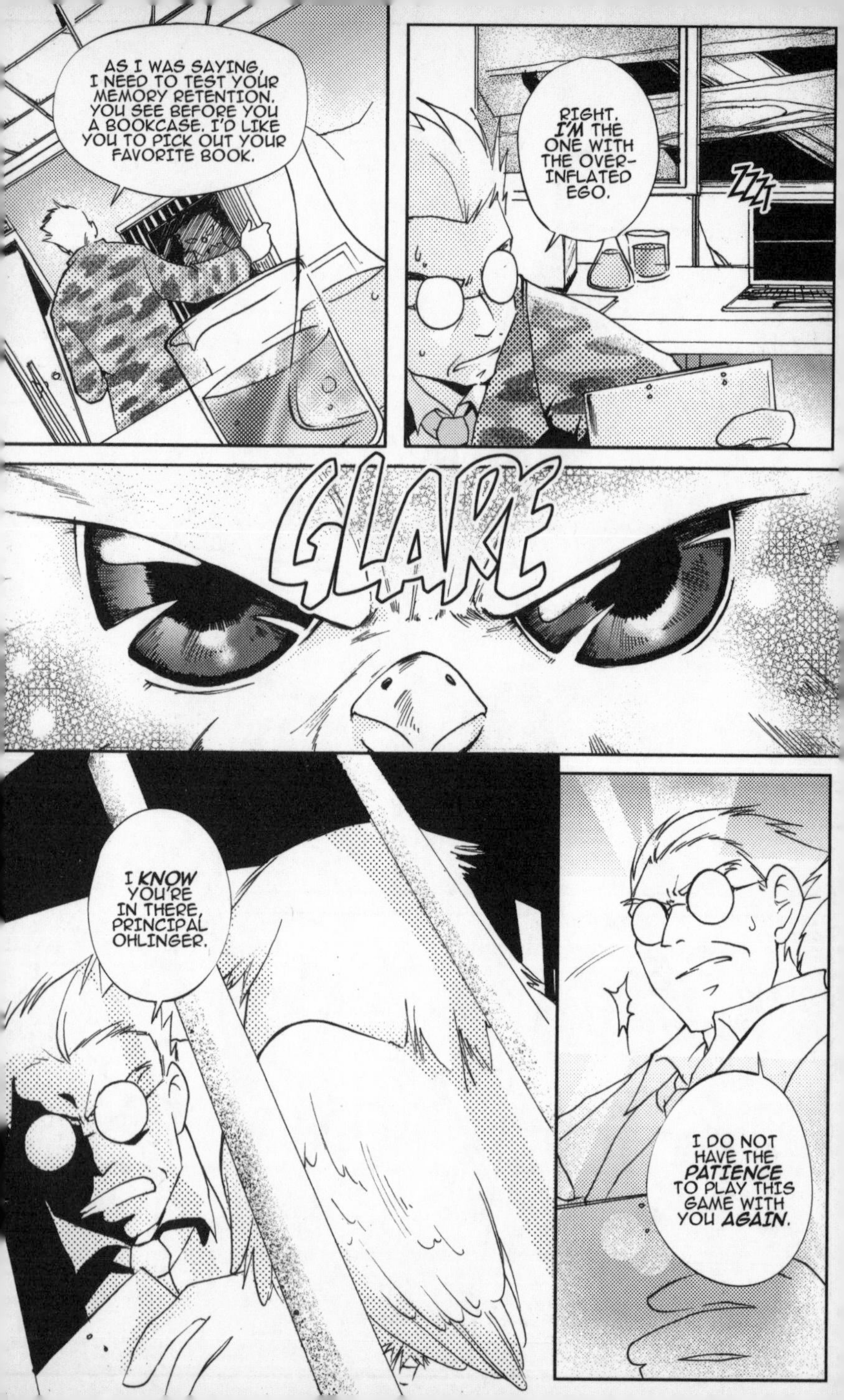
RIGHT. *I'M* THE ONE WITH THE OVER-INFLATED EGO.
ZZZT
AS I WAS SAYING, I NEED TO TEST YOUR MEMORY RETENTION. YOU SEE BEFORE YOU A BOOKCASE. I'D LIKE YOU TO PICK OUT YOUR FAVORITE BOOK.
GLARE
I DO NOT HAVE THE ***PATIENCE*** TO PLAY THIS GAME WITH YOU ***AGAIN***.
I ***KNOW*** YOU'RE IN THERE, PRINCIPAL OHLINGER.

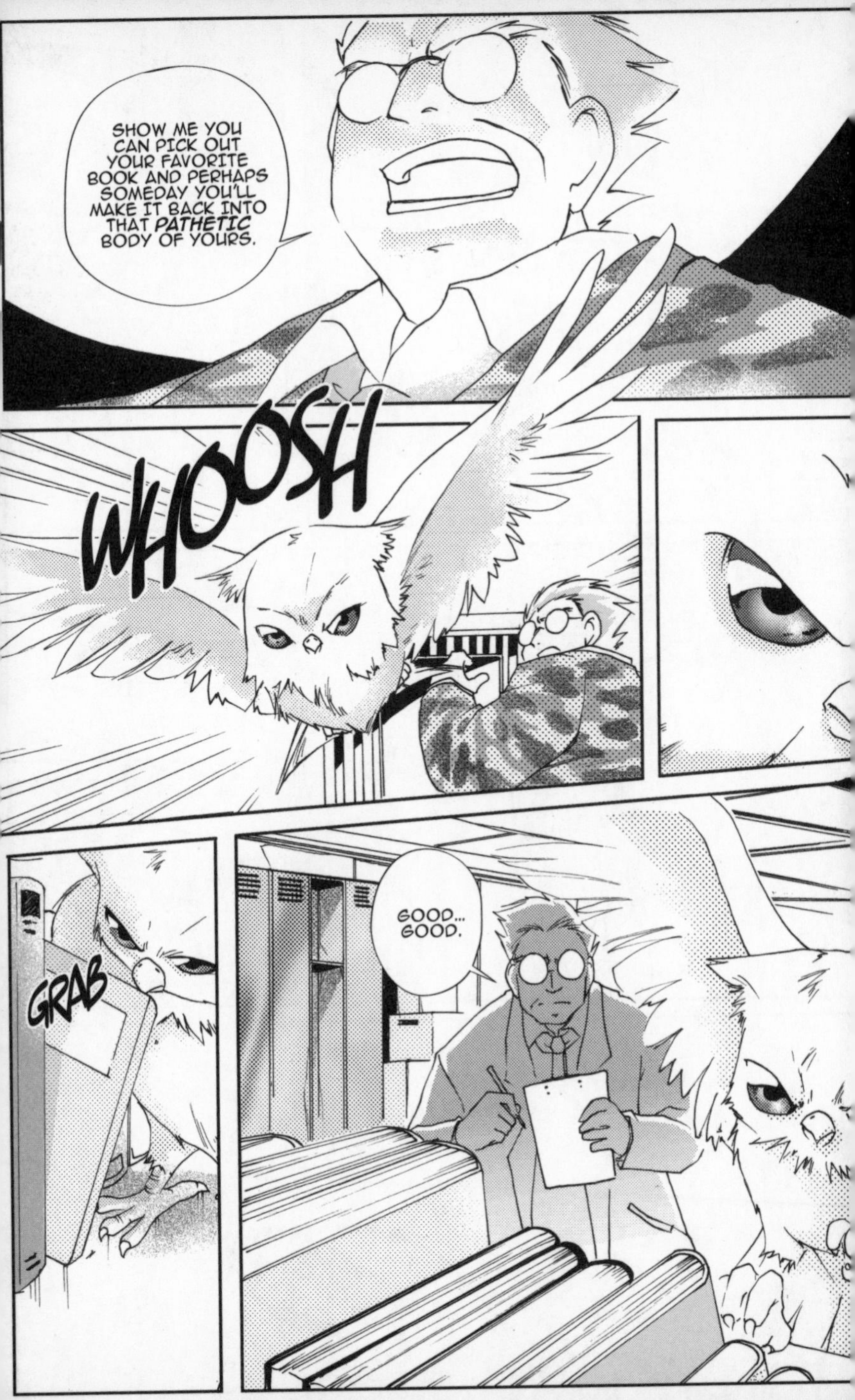
SHOW ME YOU CAN PICK OUT YOUR FAVORITE BOOK AND PERHAPS SOMEDAY YOU'LL MAKE IT BACK INTO THAT *PATHETIC* BODY OF YOURS.
WHOOSH
GOOD... GOOD.
GRAB

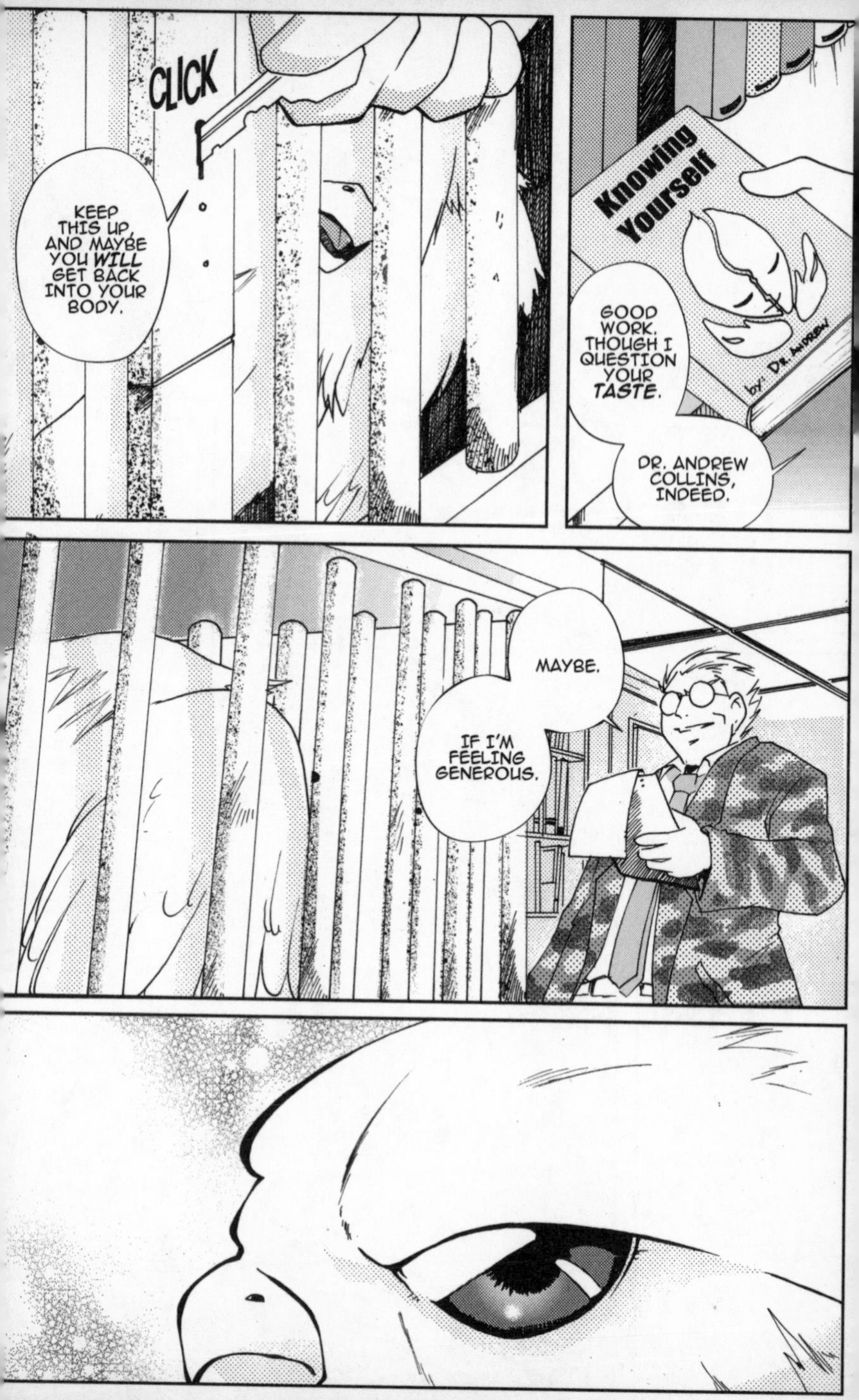
Knowing Yourself
by: Dr. Andrew
GOOD WORK. THOUGH I QUESTION YOUR TASTE.
DR. ANDREW COLLINS, INDEED.
CLICK
KEEP THIS UP, AND MAYBE YOU WILL GET BACK INTO YOUR BODY.
MAYBE.
IF I'M FEELING GENEROUS.

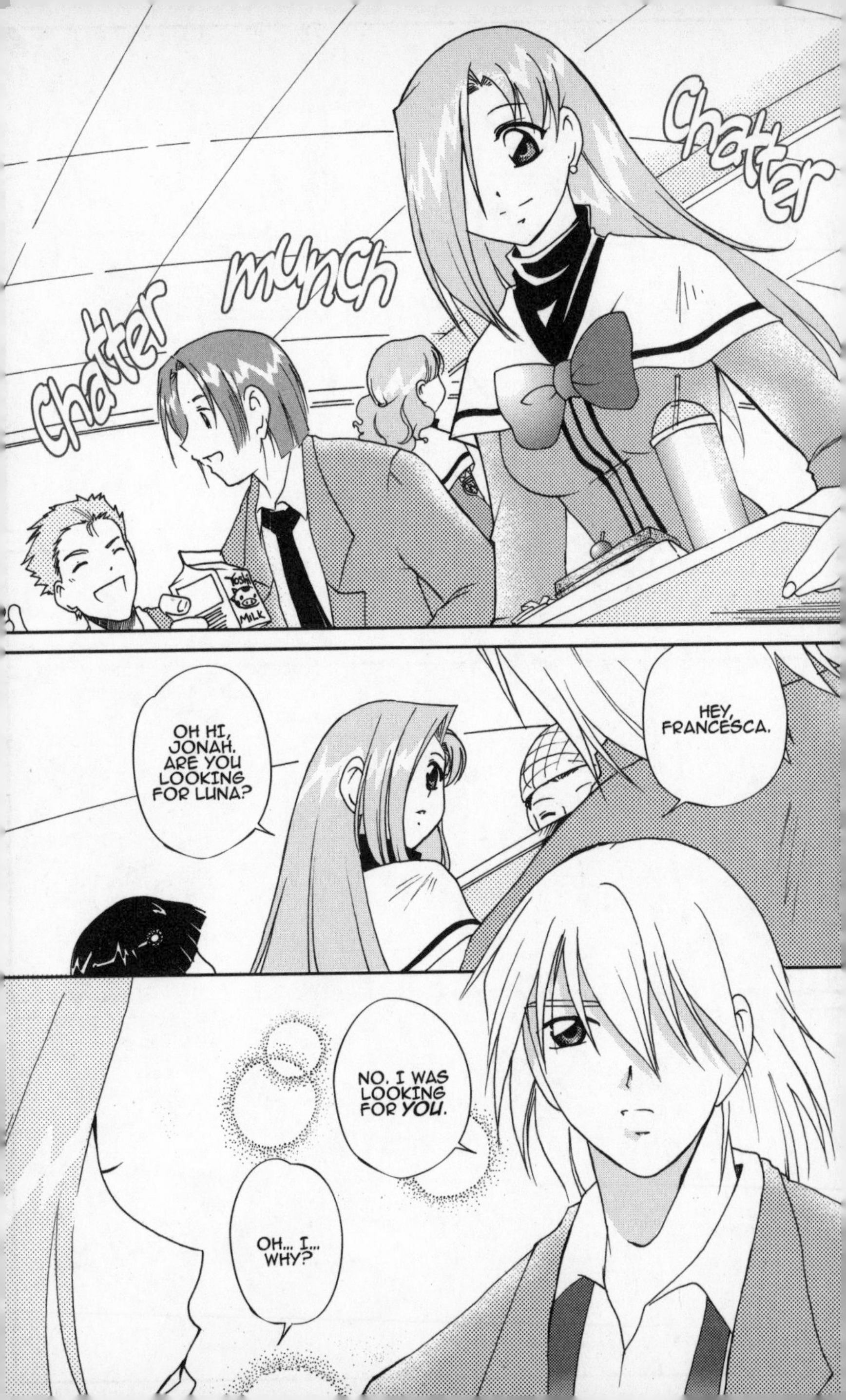
Chatter
munch
Chatter
Yoshi
MILK
HEY, FRANCESCA.
OH HI, JONAH. ARE YOU LOOKING FOR LUNA?
NO. I WAS LOOKING FOR *YOU*.
OH... I... WHY?

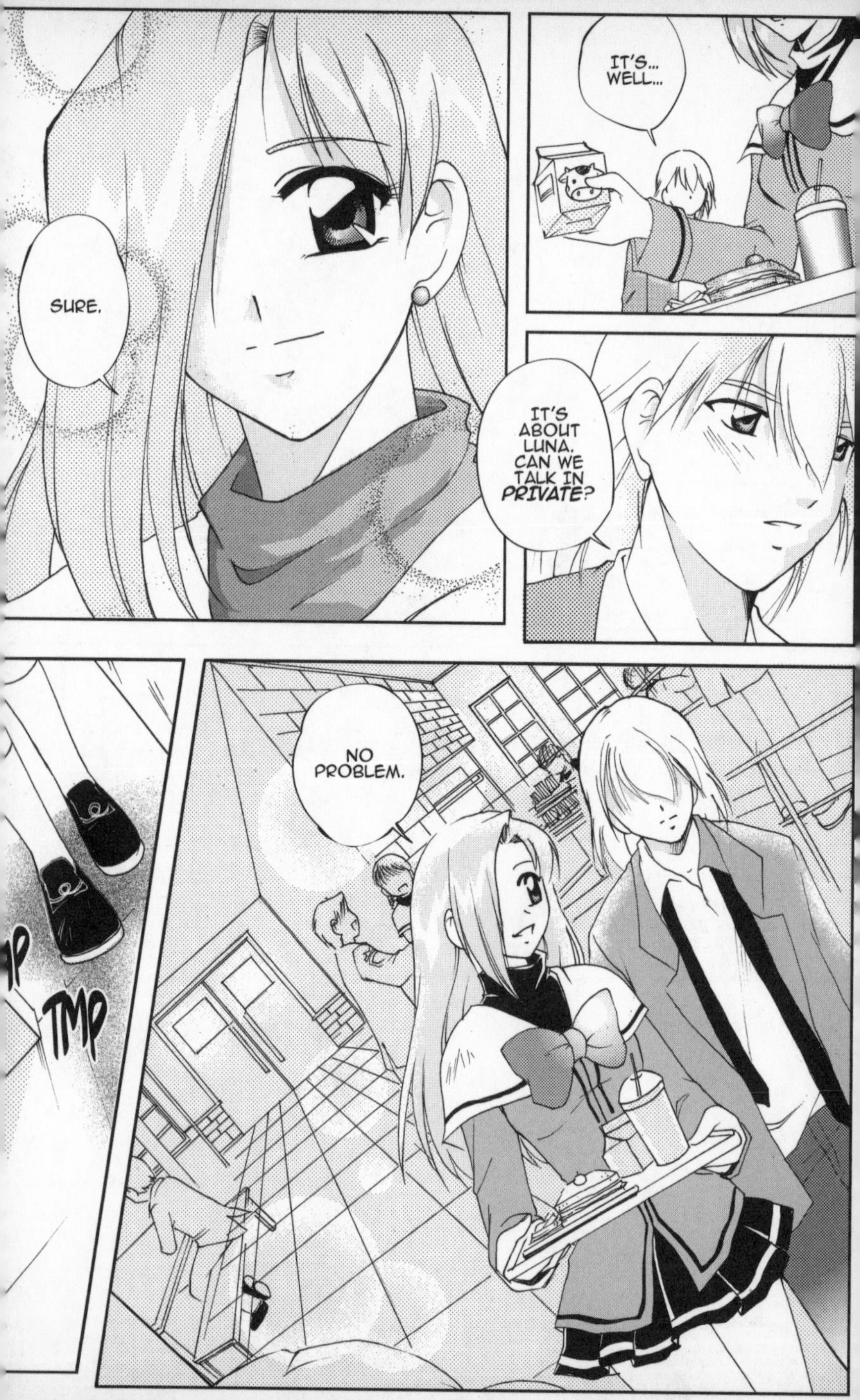
IT'S... WELL...
IT'S ABOUT LUNA. CAN WE TALK IN *PRIVATE*?
SURE.
NO PROBLEM.
TMP

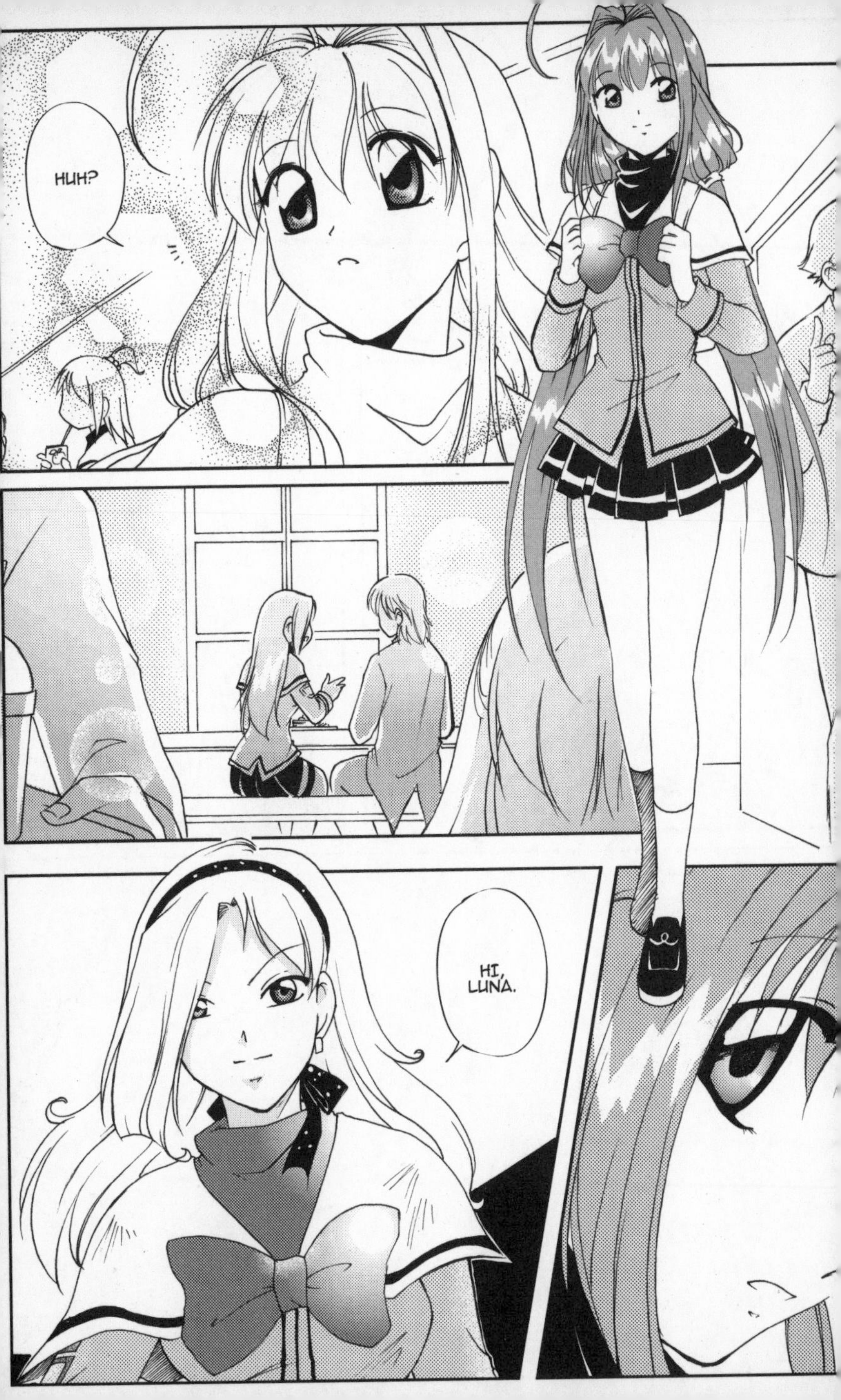
HUH?
HI, LUNA.

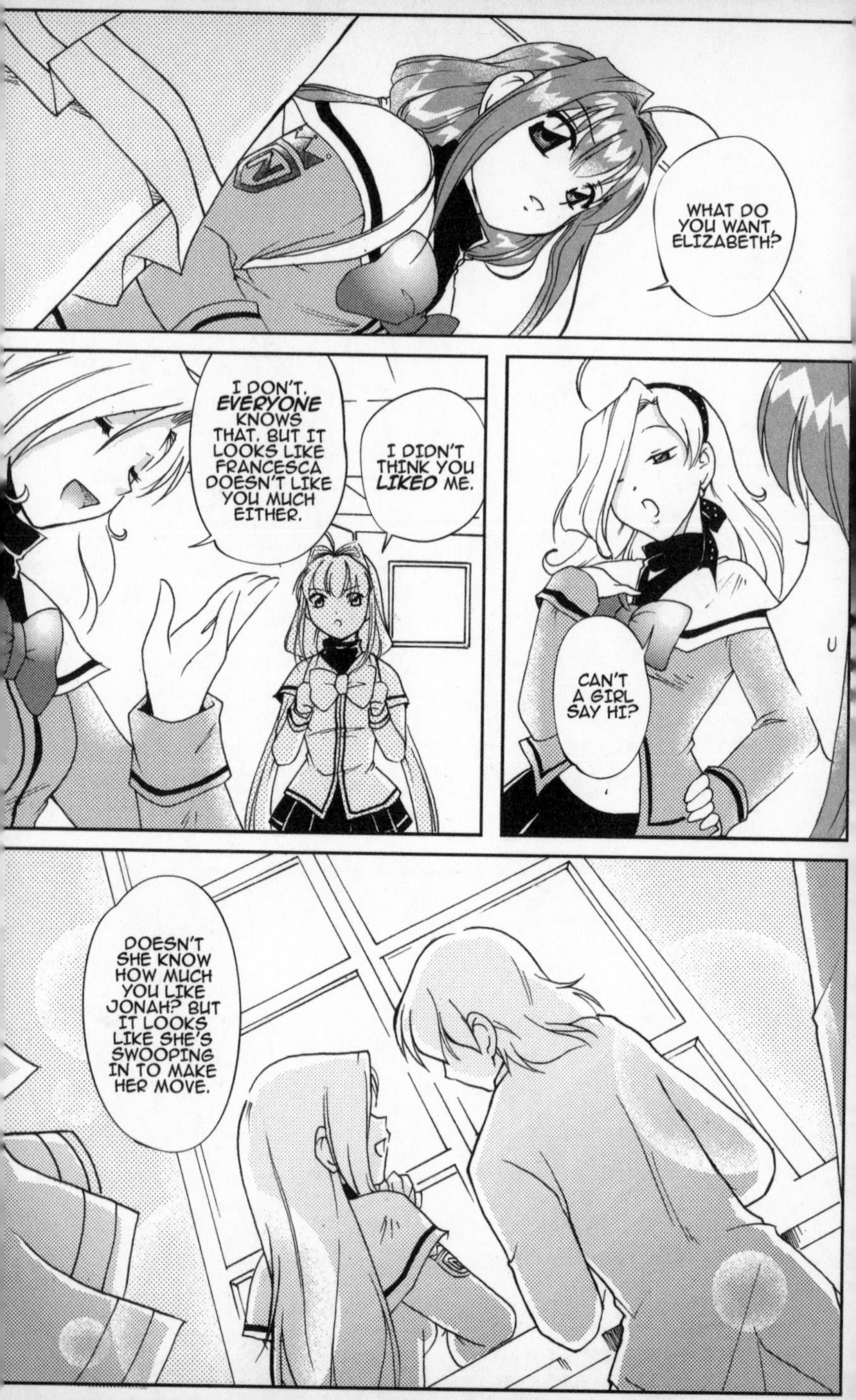
WHAT DO YOU WANT, ELIZABETH?
CAN'T A GIRL SAY HI?
I DIDN'T THINK YOU *LIKED* ME.
I DON'T. ***EVERYONE*** KNOWS THAT. BUT IT LOOKS LIKE FRANCESCA DOESN'T LIKE YOU MUCH EITHER.
DOESN'T SHE KNOW HOW MUCH YOU LIKE JONAH? BUT IT LOOKS LIKE SHE'S SWOOPING IN TO MAKE HER MOVE.

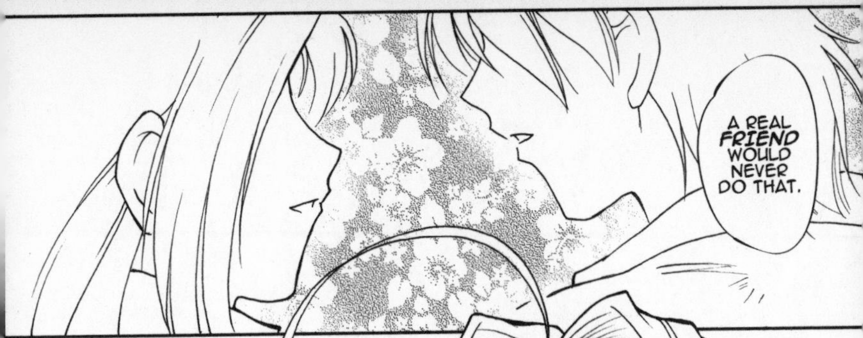
A REAL FRIEND WOULD NEVER DO THAT.
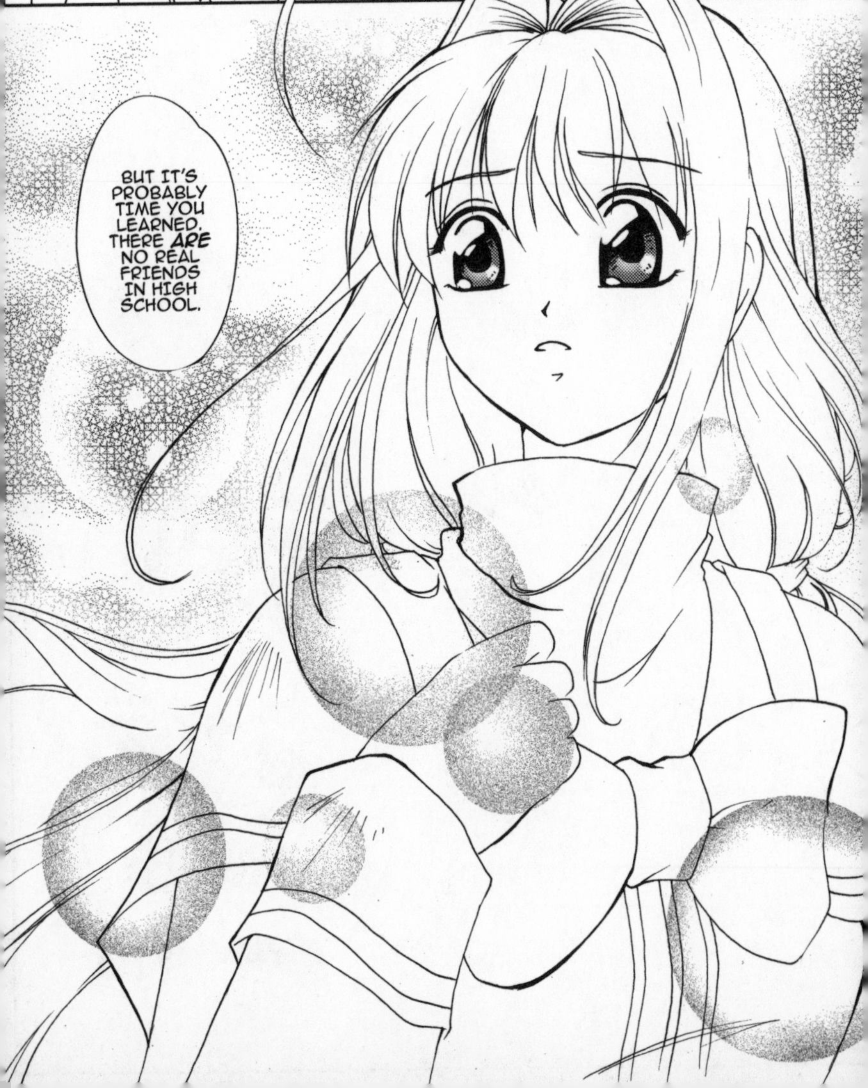
BUT IT'S PROBABLY TIME YOU LEARNED. THERE ARE NO REAL FRIENDS IN HIGH SCHOOL.

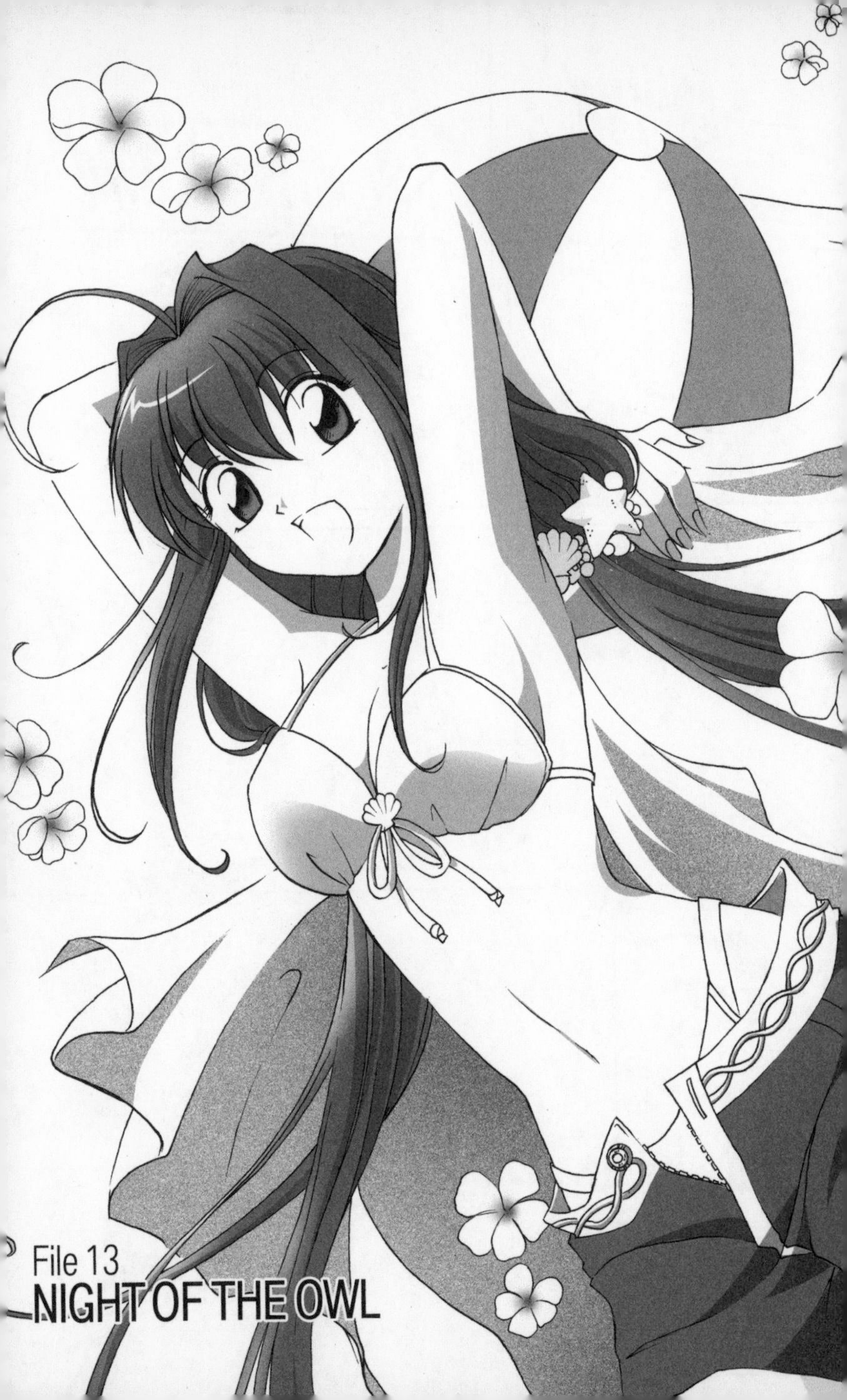
File 13
NIGHT OF THE OWL

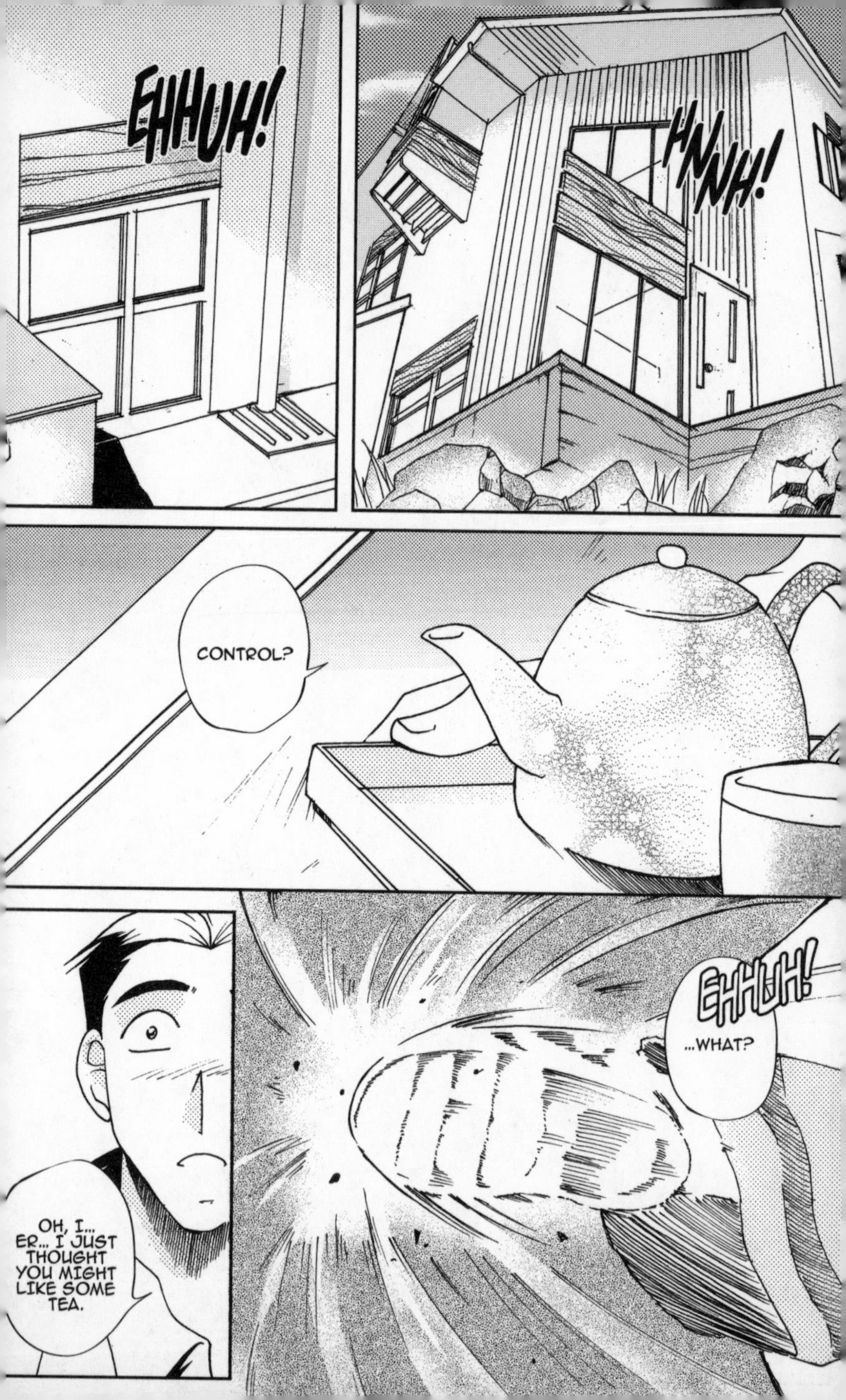
HNNH!
EHHUH!
CONTROL?
EHHUH!
...WHAT?
OH, I... ER... I JUST THOUGHT YOU MIGHT LIKE SOME TEA.

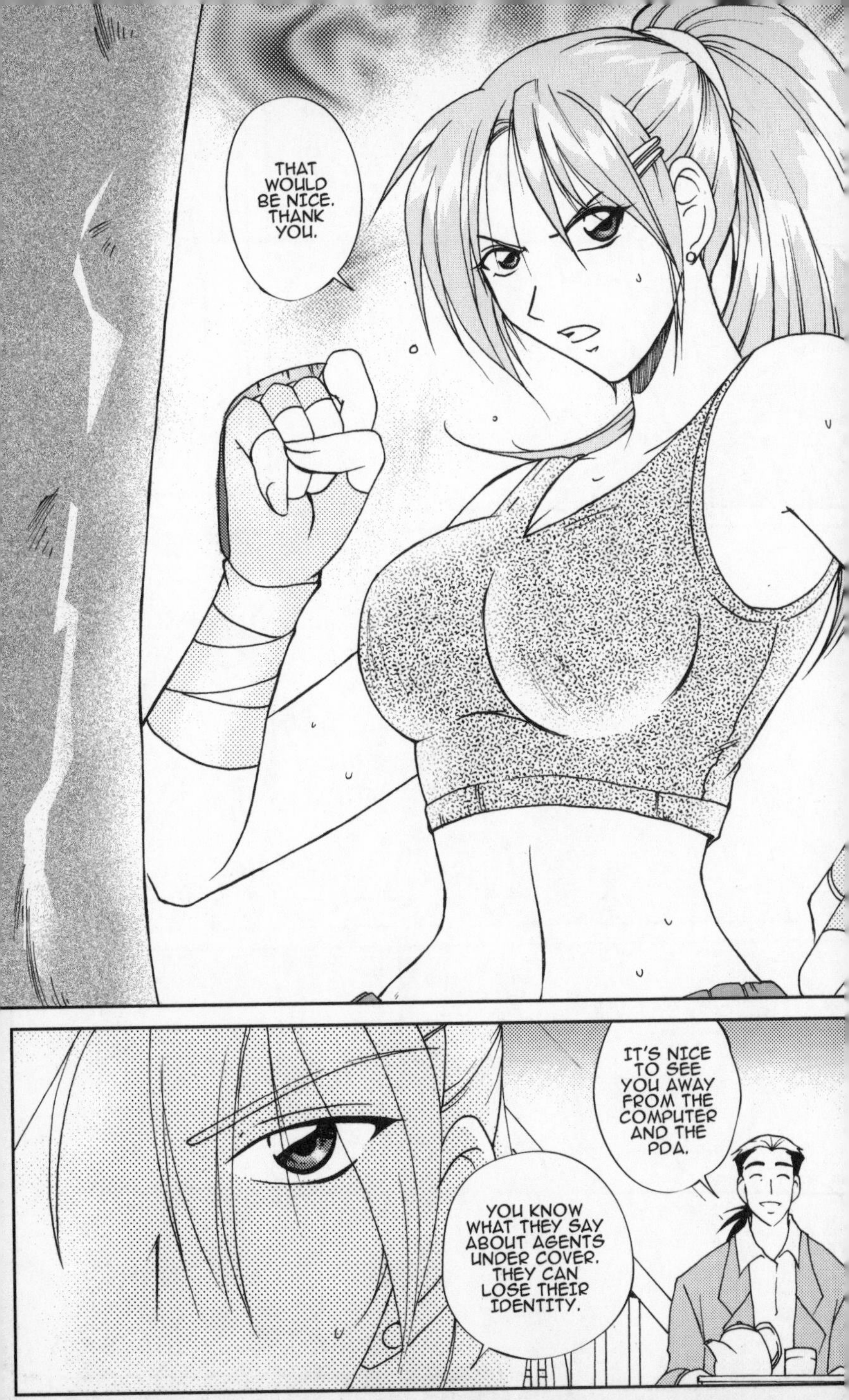
THAT WOULD BE NICE. THANK YOU.
IT'S NICE TO SEE YOU AWAY FROM THE COMPUTER AND THE PDA.
YOU KNOW WHAT THEY SAY ABOUT AGENTS UNDER COVER. THEY CAN LOSE THEIR IDENTITY.

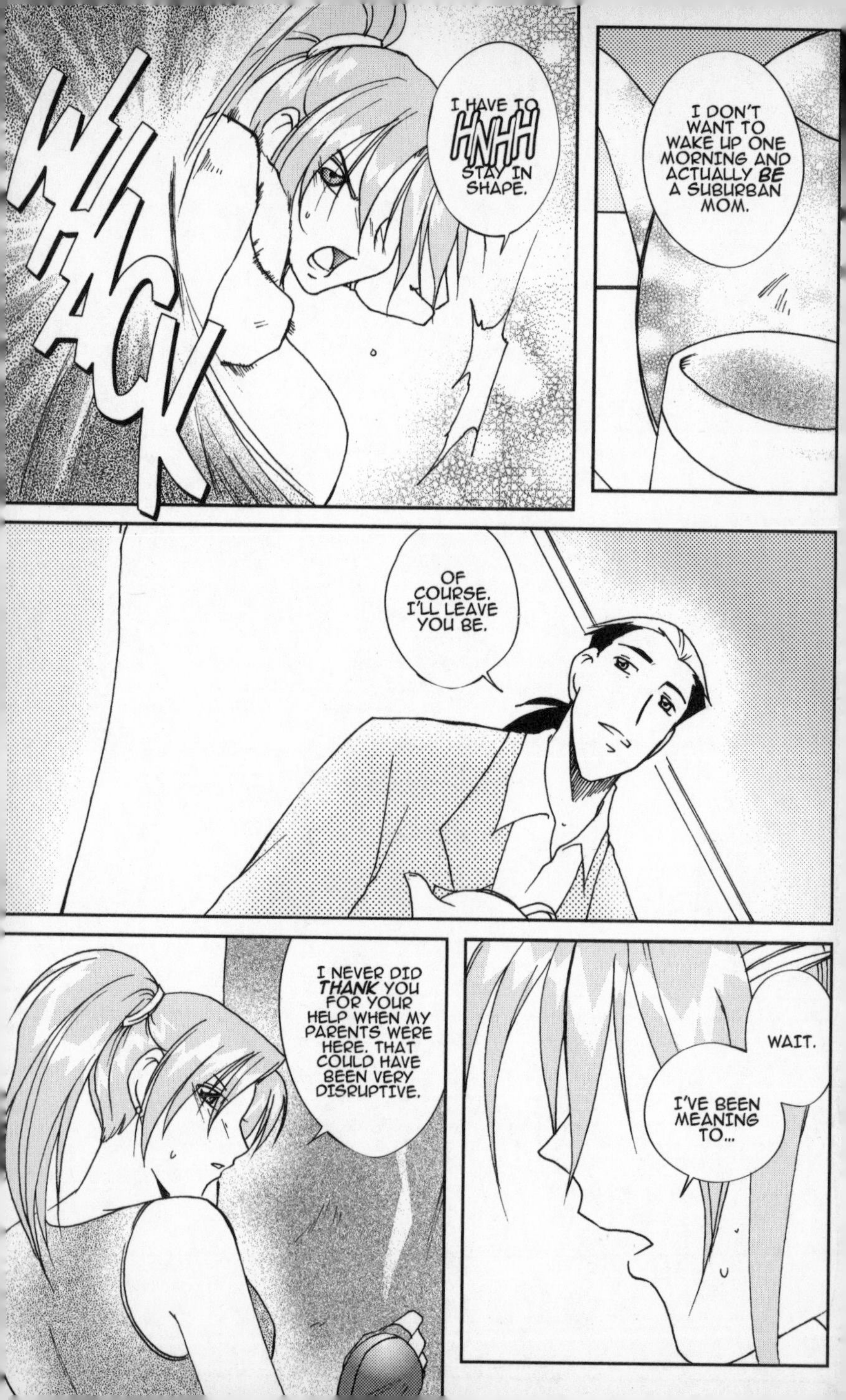
I DON'T WANT TO WAKE UP ONE MORNING AND ACTUALLY BE A SUBURBAN MOM.
I HAVE TO HNHH STAY IN SHAPE.
WHACK
OF COURSE. I'LL LEAVE YOU BE.
WAIT.
I'VE BEEN MEANING TO...
I NEVER DID THANK YOU FOR YOUR HELP WHEN MY PARENTS WERE HERE. THAT COULD HAVE BEEN VERY DISRUPTIVE.

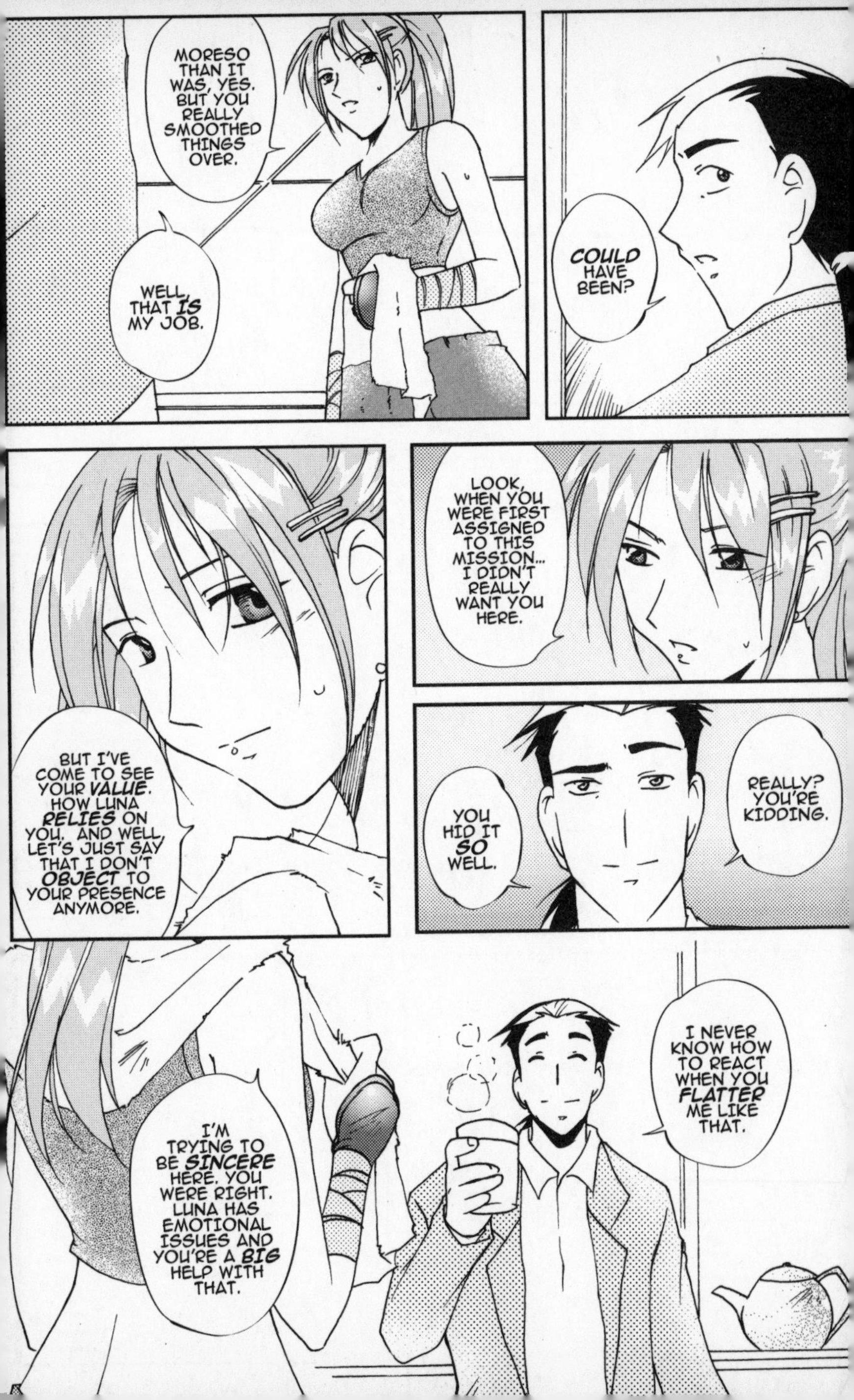

COULD HAVE BEEN?
MORESO THAN IT WAS, YES. BUT YOU REALLY SMOOTHED THINGS OVER.
WELL, THAT IS MY JOB.
LOOK, WHEN YOU WERE FIRST ASSIGNED TO THIS MISSION... I DIDN'T REALLY WANT YOU HERE.
REALLY? YOU'RE KIDDING.
YOU HID IT SO WELL.
BUT I'VE COME TO SEE YOUR VALUE. HOW LUNA RELIES ON YOU. AND WELL, LET'S JUST SAY THAT I DON'T OBJECT TO YOUR PRESENCE ANYMORE.
I NEVER KNOW HOW TO REACT WHEN YOU FLATTER ME LIKE THAT.
I'M TRYING TO BE SINCERE HERE. YOU WERE RIGHT. LUNA HAS EMOTIONAL ISSUES AND YOU'RE A BIG HELP WITH THAT.

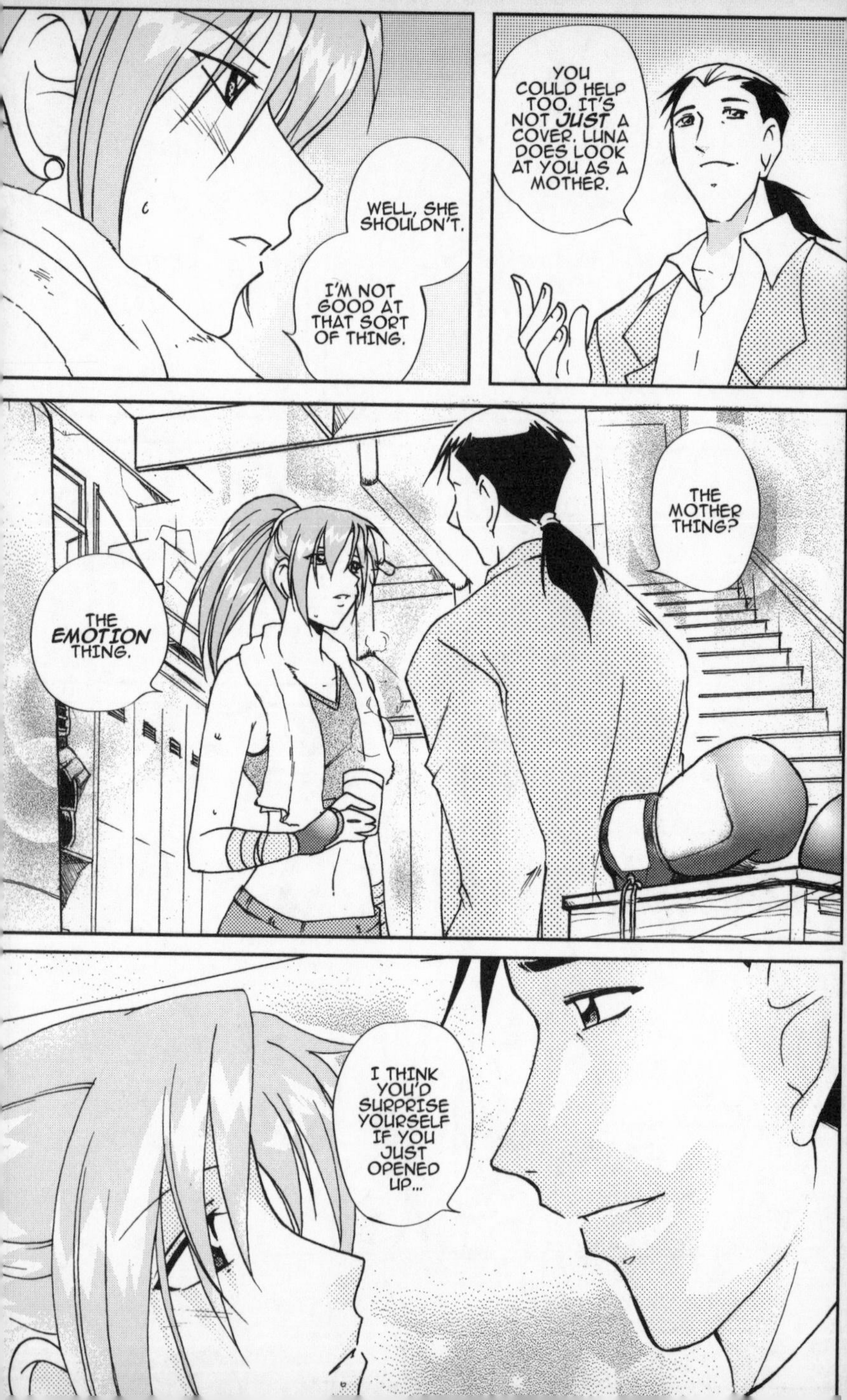
YOU COULD HELP TOO. IT'S NOT *JUST* A COVER. LUNA DOES LOOK AT YOU AS A MOTHER.
WELL, SHE SHOULDN'T.
I'M NOT GOOD AT THAT SORT OF THING.
THE MOTHER THING?
THE *EMOTION* THING.
I THINK YOU'D SURPRISE YOURSELF IF YOU JUST OPENED UP...

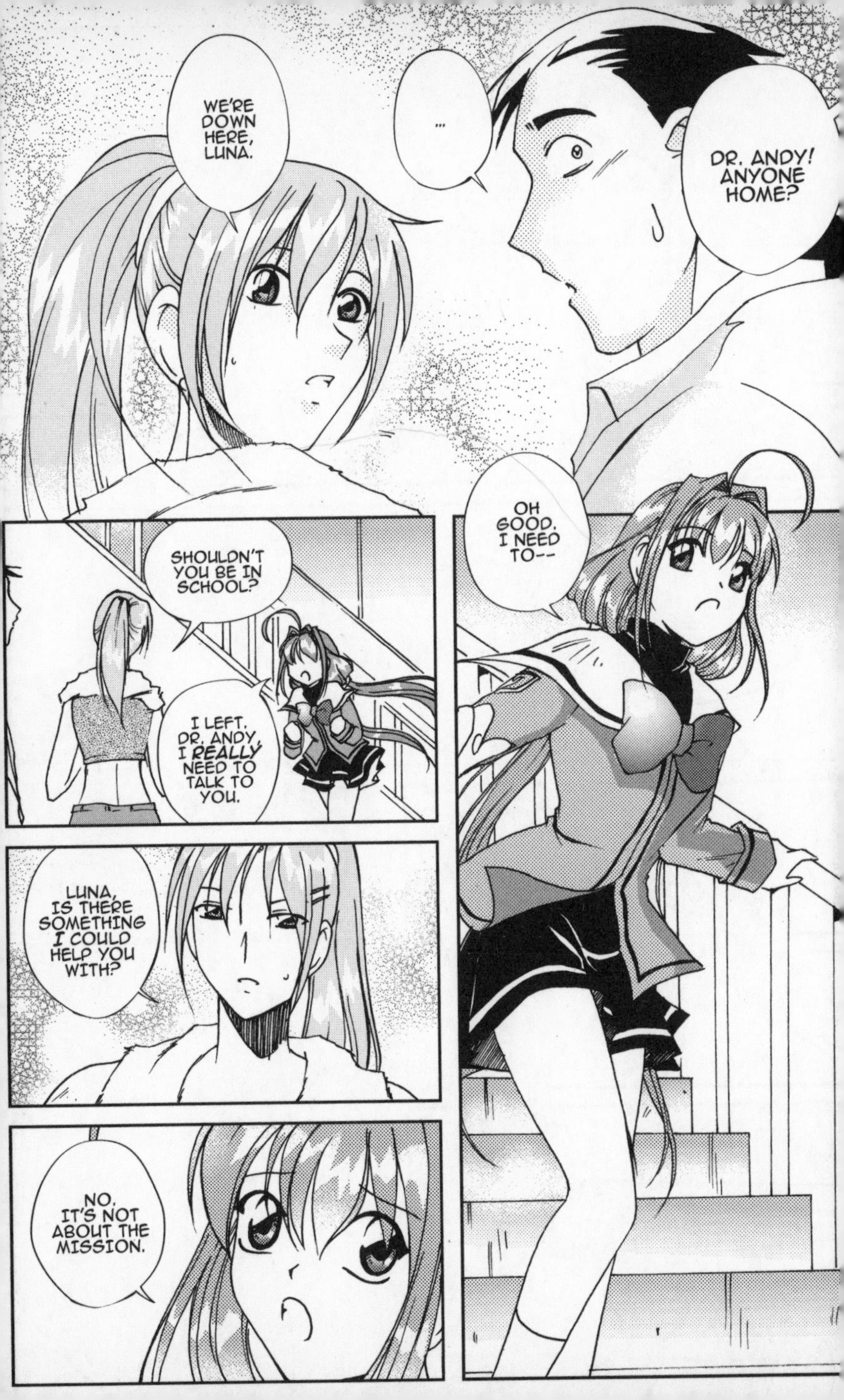
DR. ANDY! ANYONE HOME?
...
WE'RE DOWN HERE, LUNA.
OH GOOD. I NEED TO--
SHOULDN'T YOU BE IN SCHOOL?
I LEFT. DR. ANDY, I *REALLY* NEED TO TALK TO YOU.
LUNA, IS THERE SOMETHING *I* COULD HELP YOU WITH?
NO. IT'S NOT ABOUT THE MISSION.

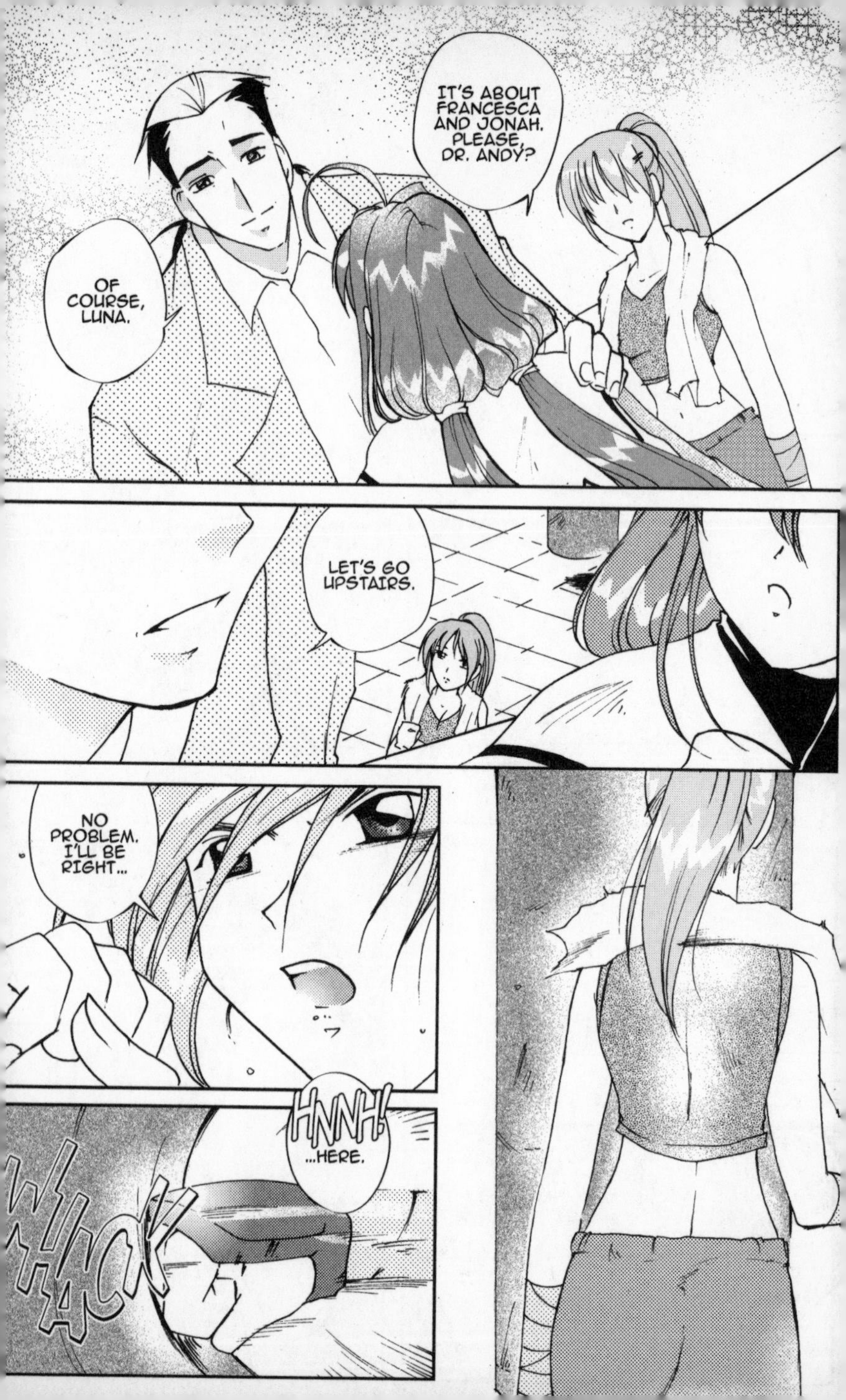
IT'S ABOUT FRANCESCA AND JONAH. PLEASE, DR. ANDY?
OF COURSE, LUNA.
LET'S GO UPSTAIRS.
NO PROBLEM. I'LL BE RIGHT...
HNNH!
...HERE.
WHACK

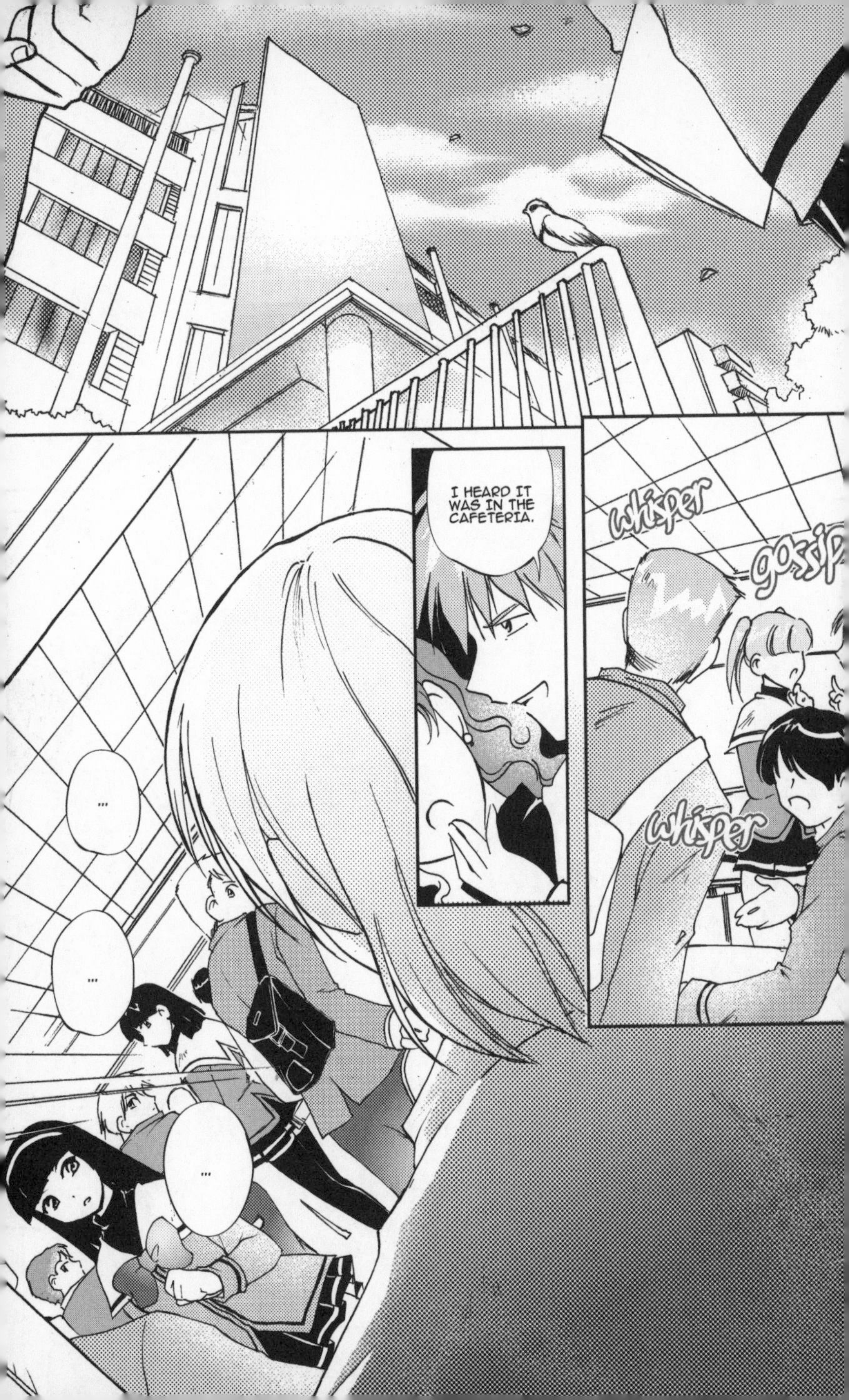
whisper
gossip
whisper
I HEARD IT WAS IN THE CAFETERIA.
...
...
...

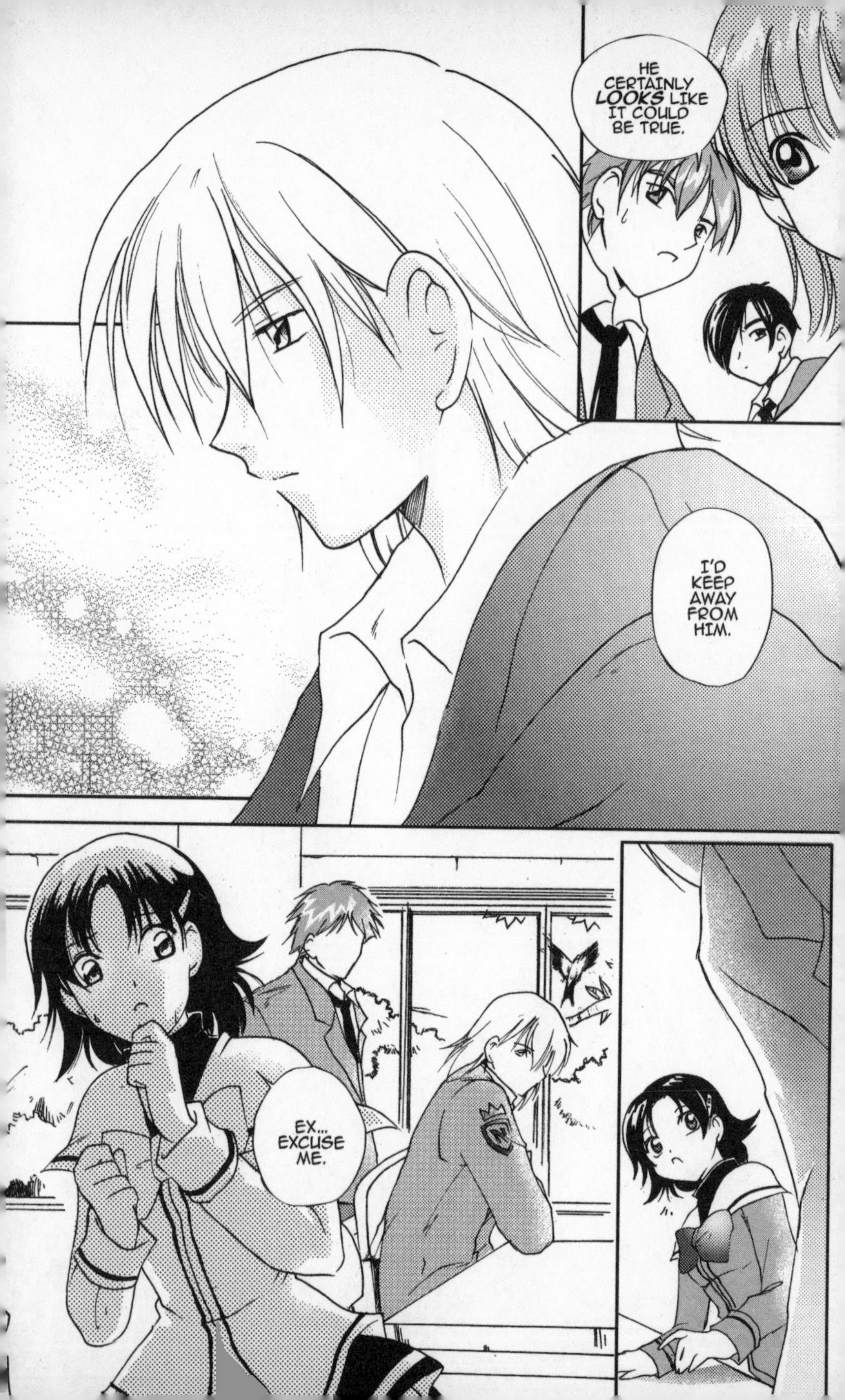
HE CERTAINLY LOOKS LIKE IT COULD BE TRUE.
I'D KEEP AWAY FROM HIM.
EX... EXCUSE ME.

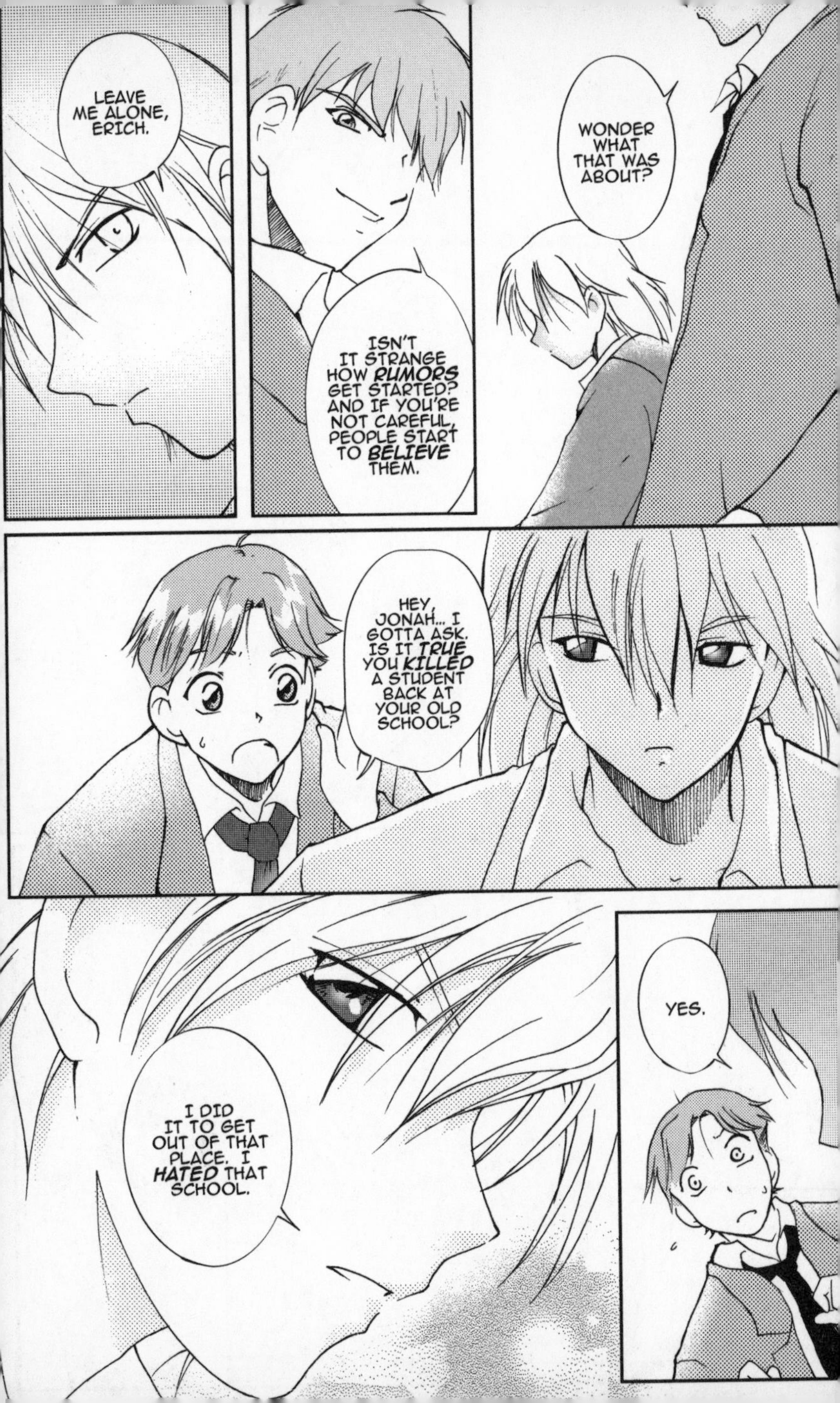
WONDER WHAT THAT WAS ABOUT?
ISN'T IT STRANGE HOW *RUMORS* GET STARTED? AND IF YOU'RE NOT CAREFUL, PEOPLE START TO *BELIEVE* THEM.
LEAVE ME ALONE, ERICH.
HEY, JONAH... I GOTTA ASK. IS IT *TRUE* YOU *KILLED* A STUDENT BACK AT YOUR OLD SCHOOL?
YES.
I DID IT TO GET OUT OF THAT PLACE. I *HATED* THAT SCHOOL.

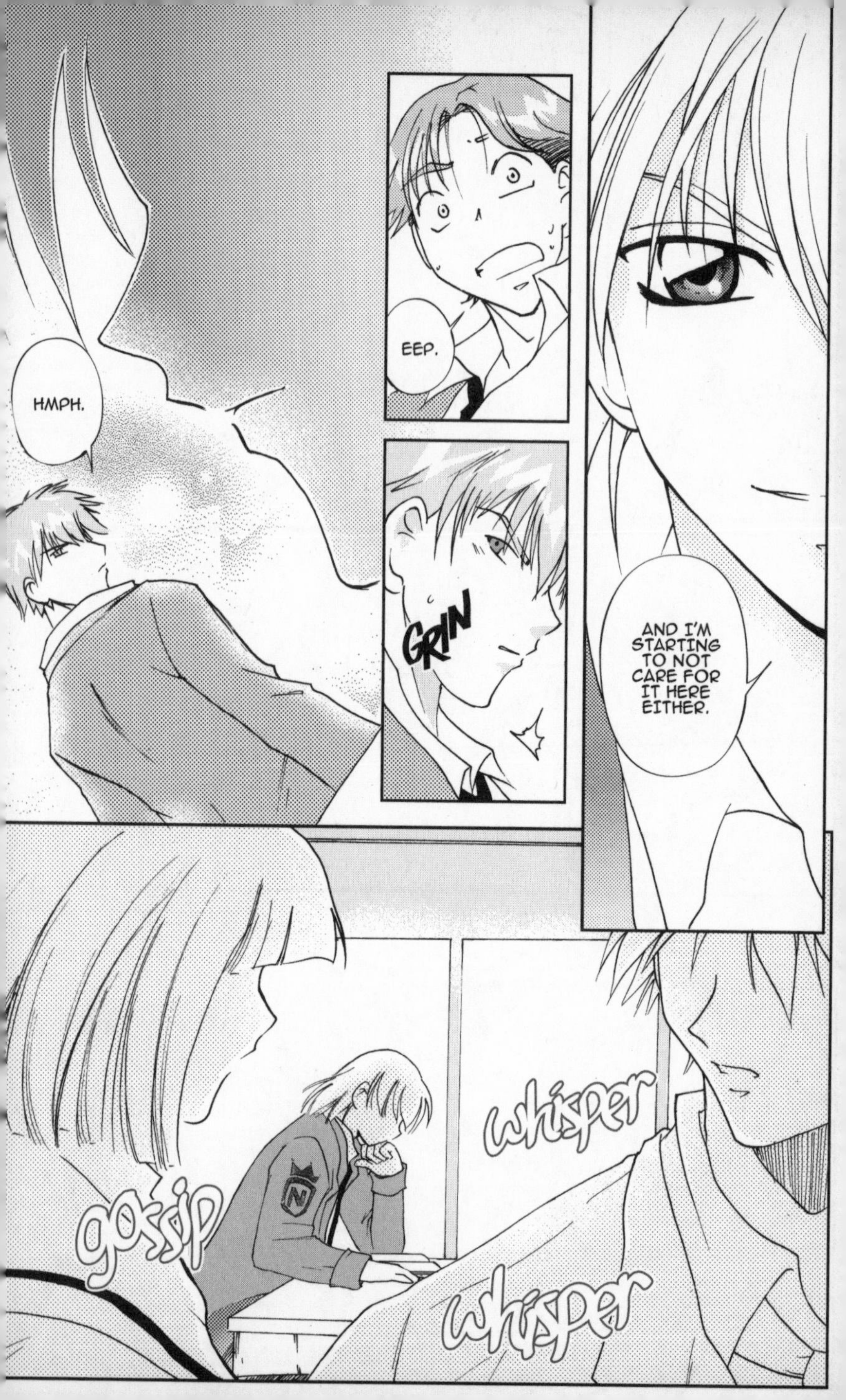
AND I'M STARTING TO NOT CARE FOR IT HERE EITHER.
EEP.
GRIN
HMPH.
whisper
gossip
whisper

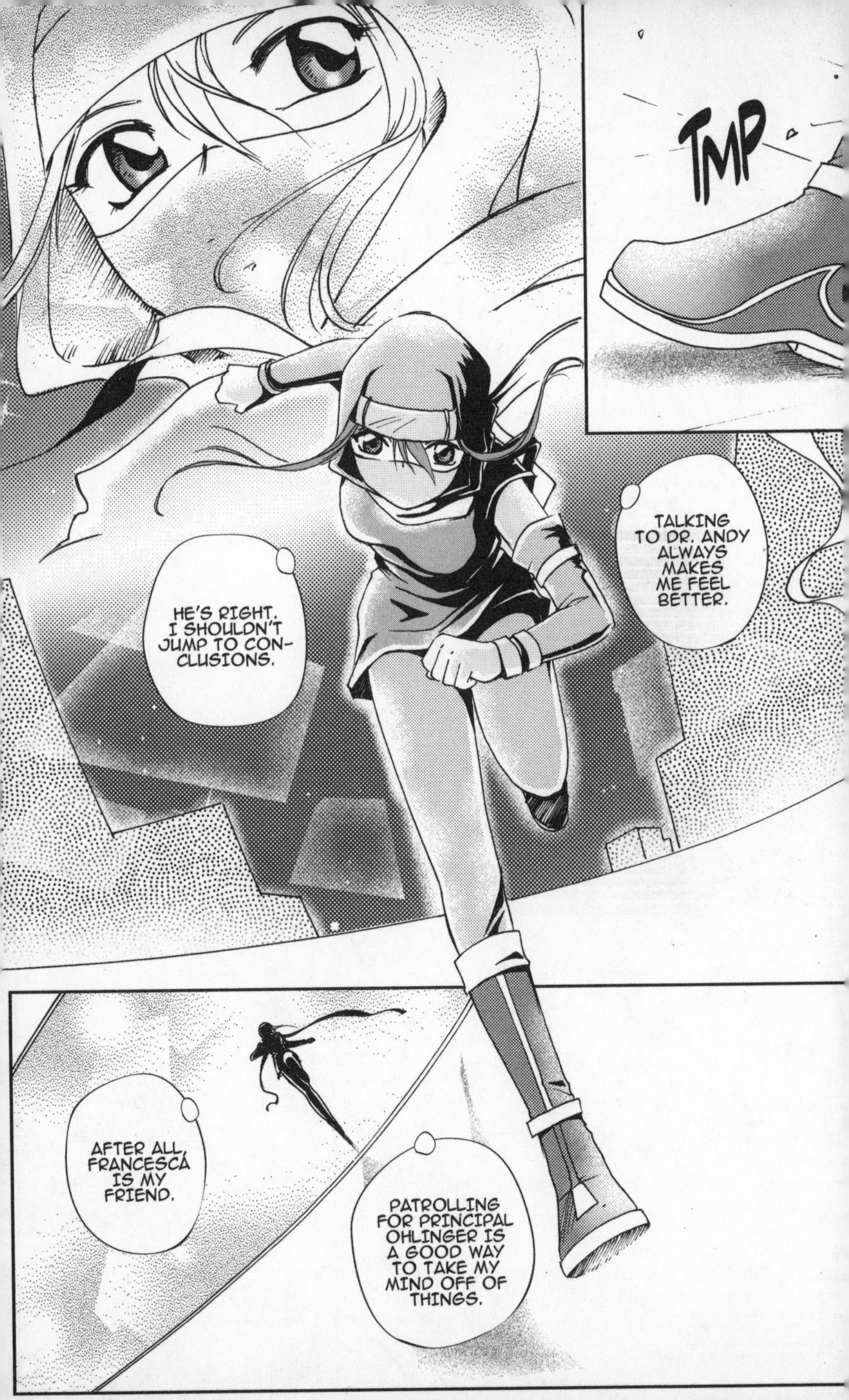
TMP
TALKING TO DR. ANDY ALWAYS MAKES ME FEEL BETTER.
HE'S RIGHT. I SHOULDN'T JUMP TO CON-CLUSIONS.
PATROLLING FOR PRINCIPAL OHLINGER IS A GOOD WAY TO TAKE MY MIND OFF OF THINGS.
AFTER ALL, FRANCESCA IS MY FRIEND.

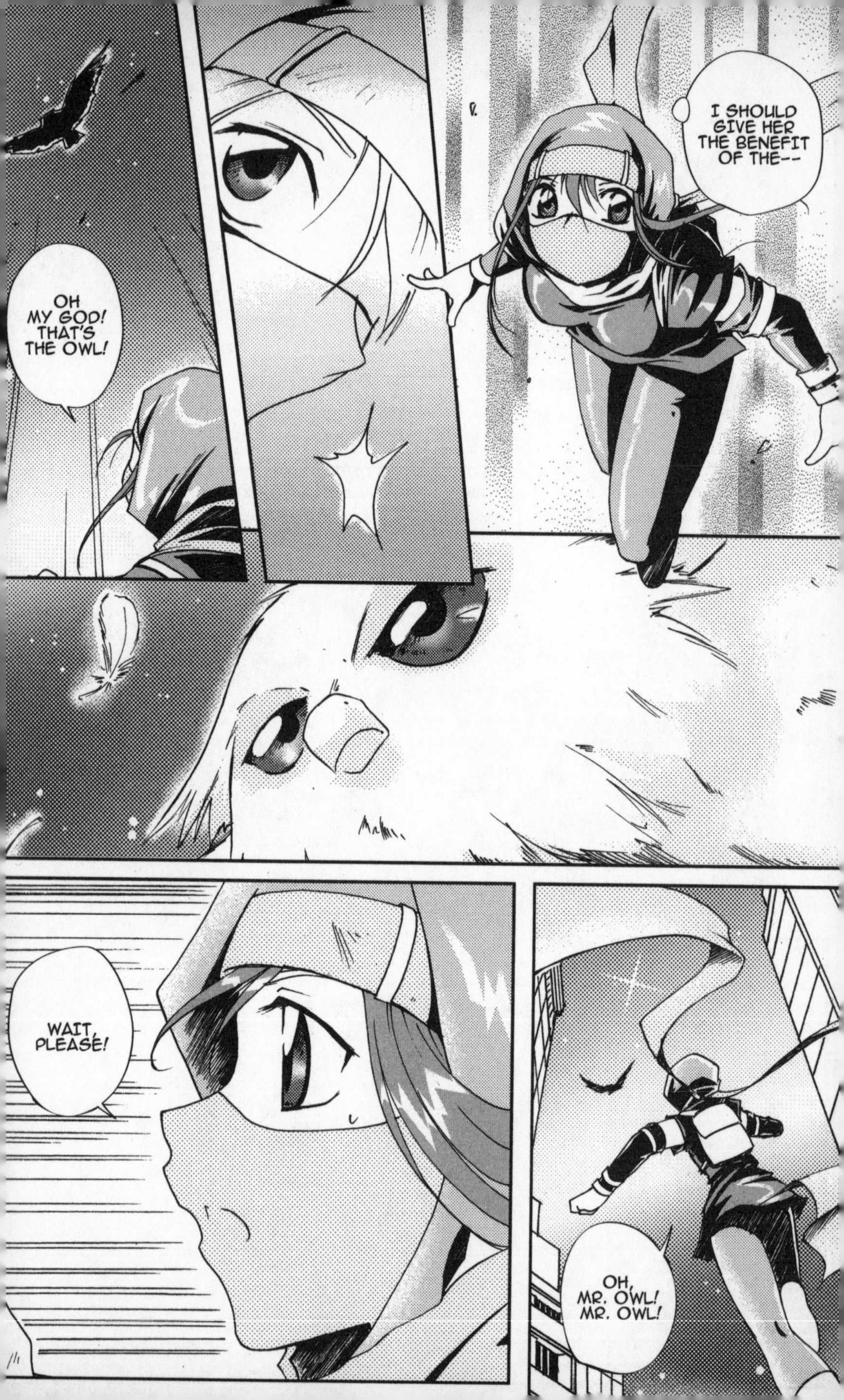
I SHOULD GIVE HER THE BENEFIT OF THE--
OH MY GOD! THAT'S THE OWL!
OH, MR. OWL! MR. OWL!
WAIT, PLEASE!

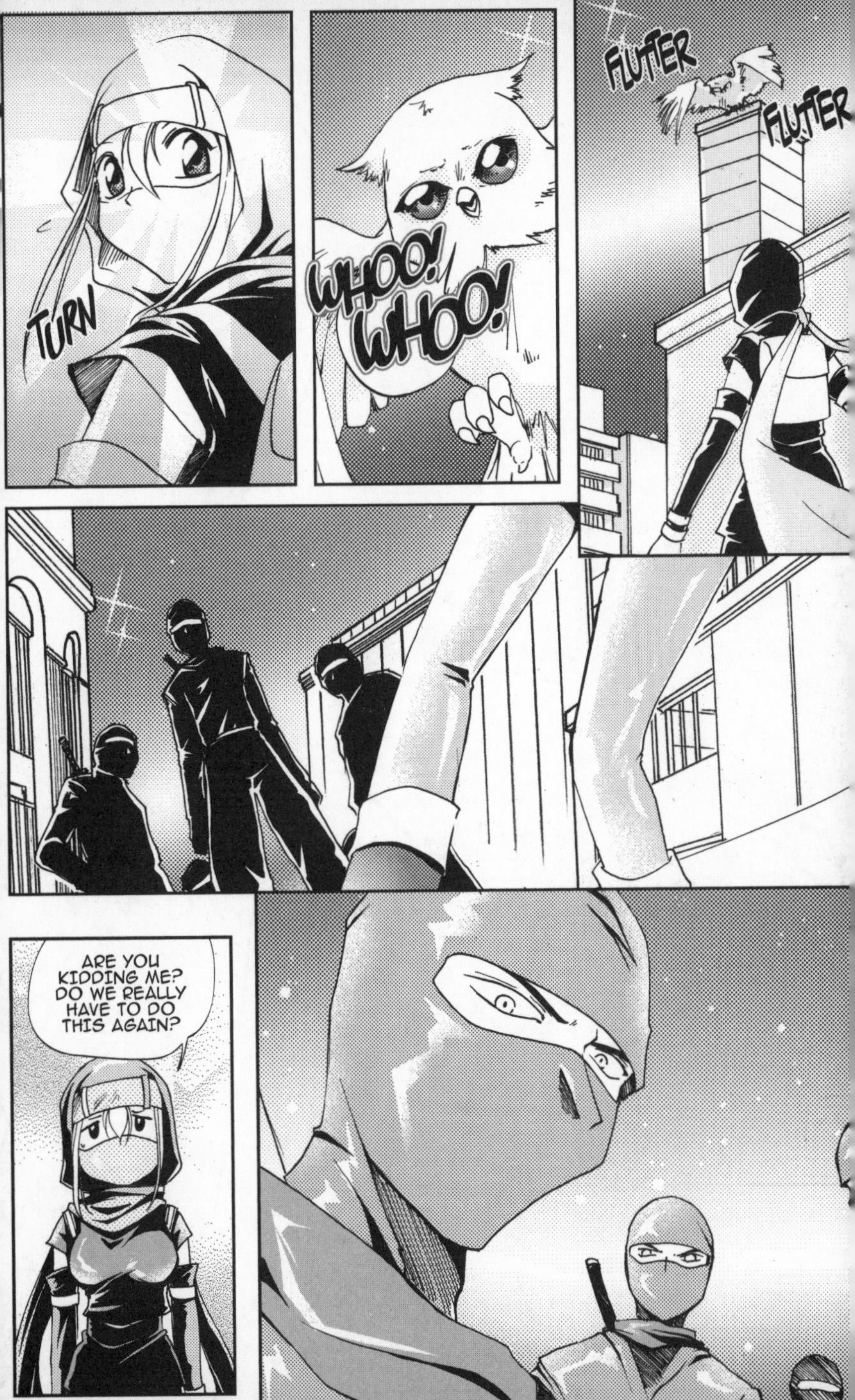
FLUTTER
FLUTTER
WHOO! WHOO!
TURN
ARE YOU KIDDING ME? DO WE REALLY HAVE TO DO THIS AGAIN?

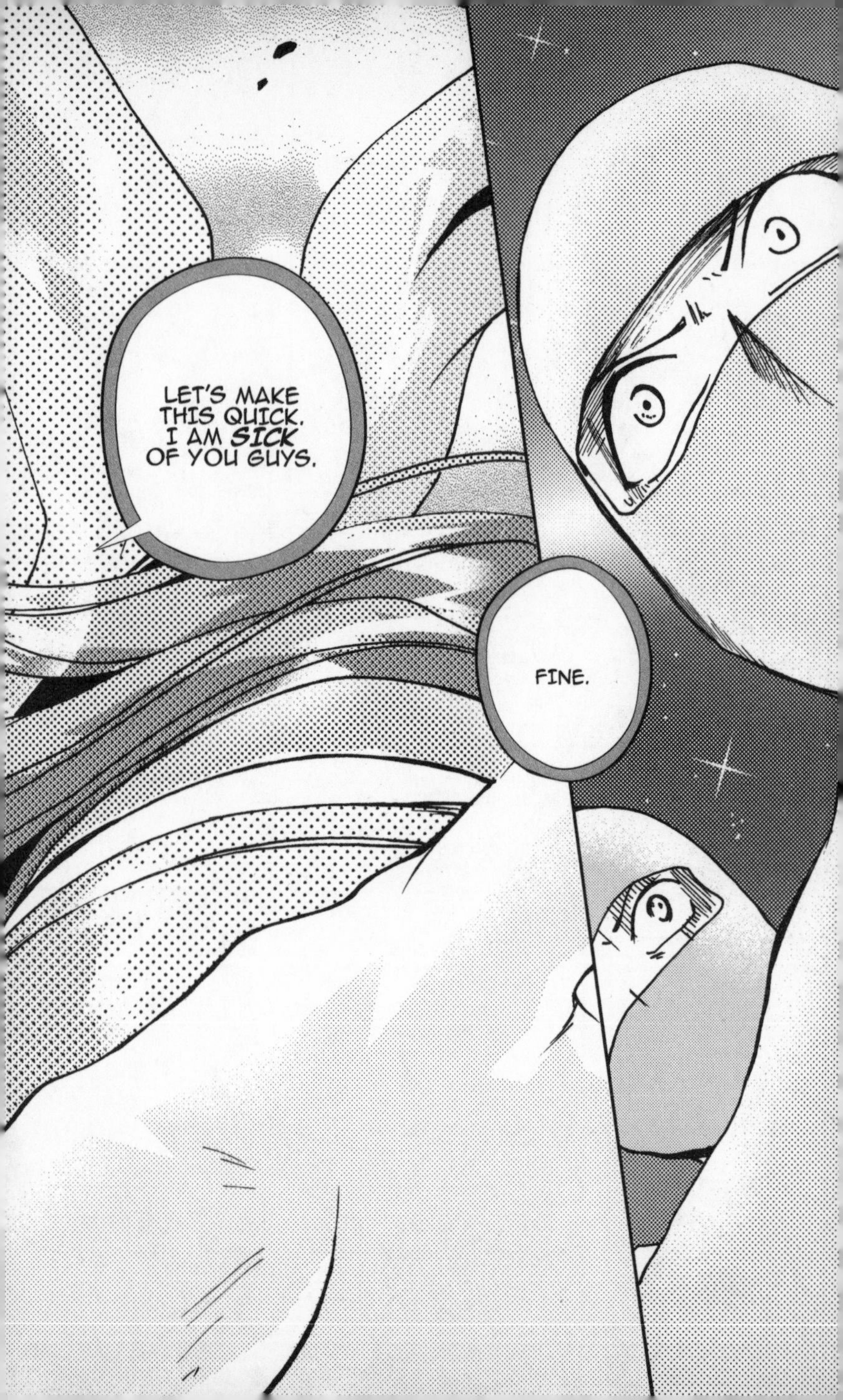
LET'S MAKE THIS QUICK. I AM SICK OF YOU GUYS.
FINE.

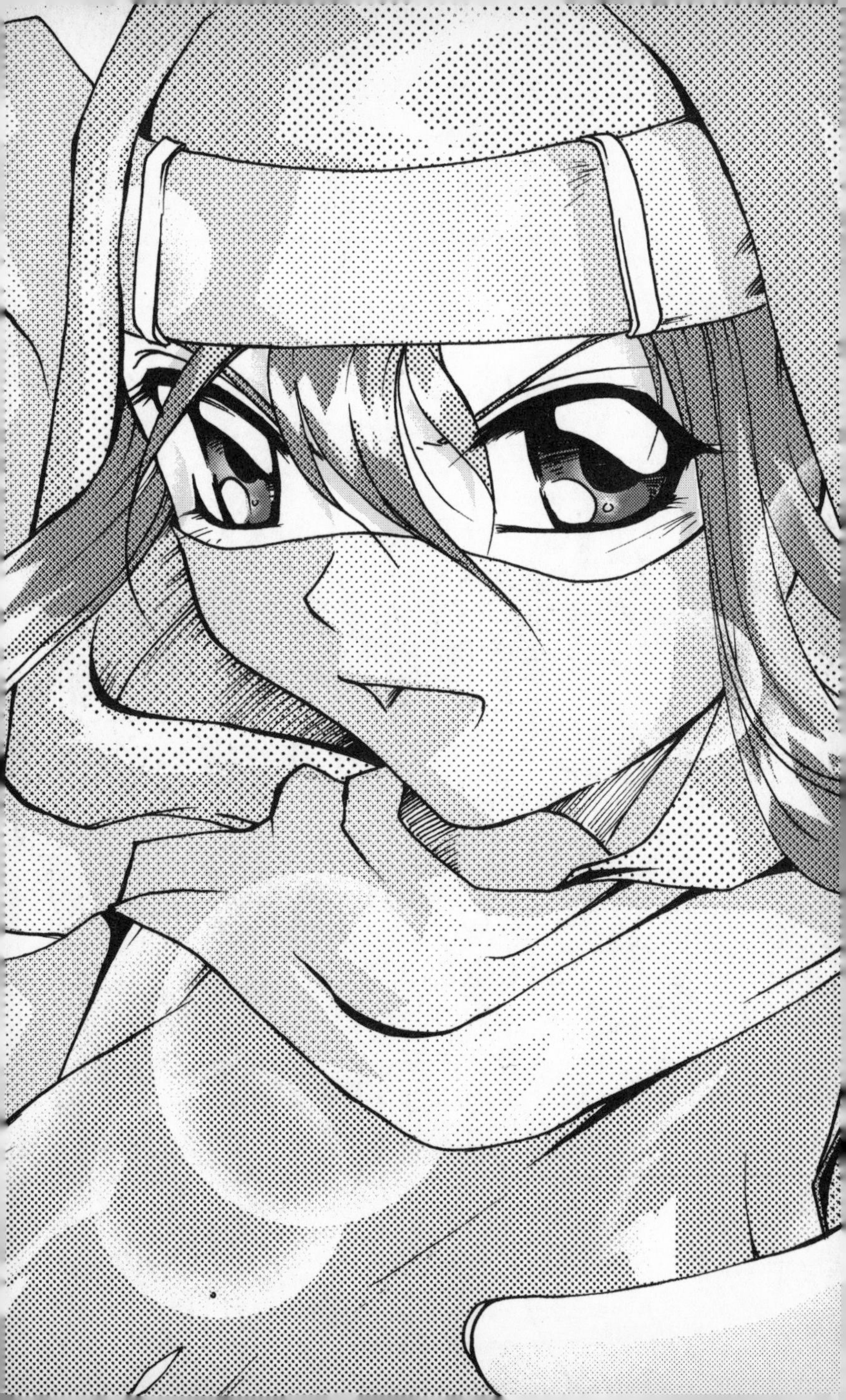

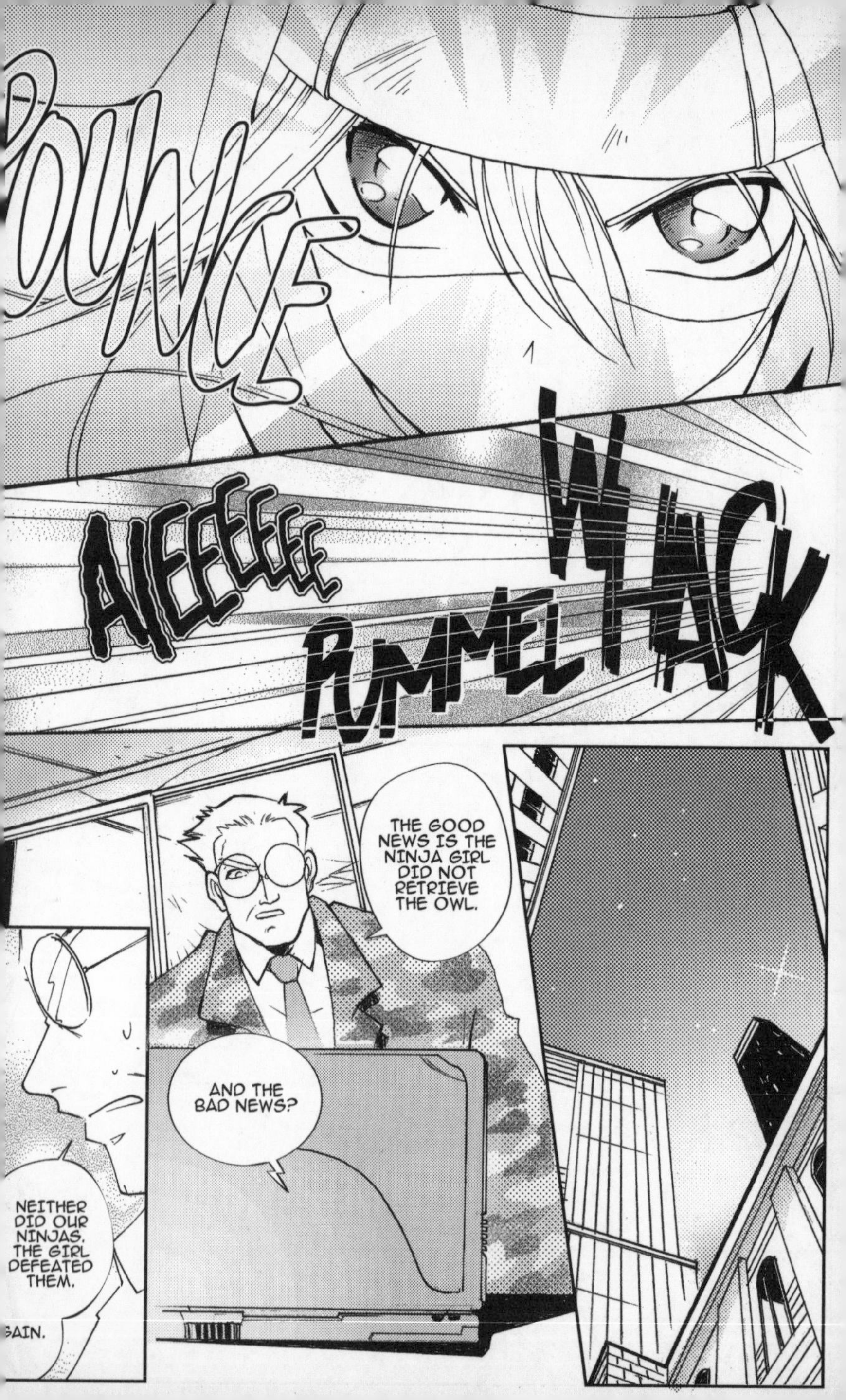
POUNCE
WHACK
HACK
PUMMEL
AIEEEEEE
THE GOOD NEWS IS THE NINJA GIRL DID NOT RETRIEVE THE OWL.
AND THE BAD NEWS?
NEITHER DID OUR NINJAS. THE GIRL DEFEATED THEM.
GAIN.

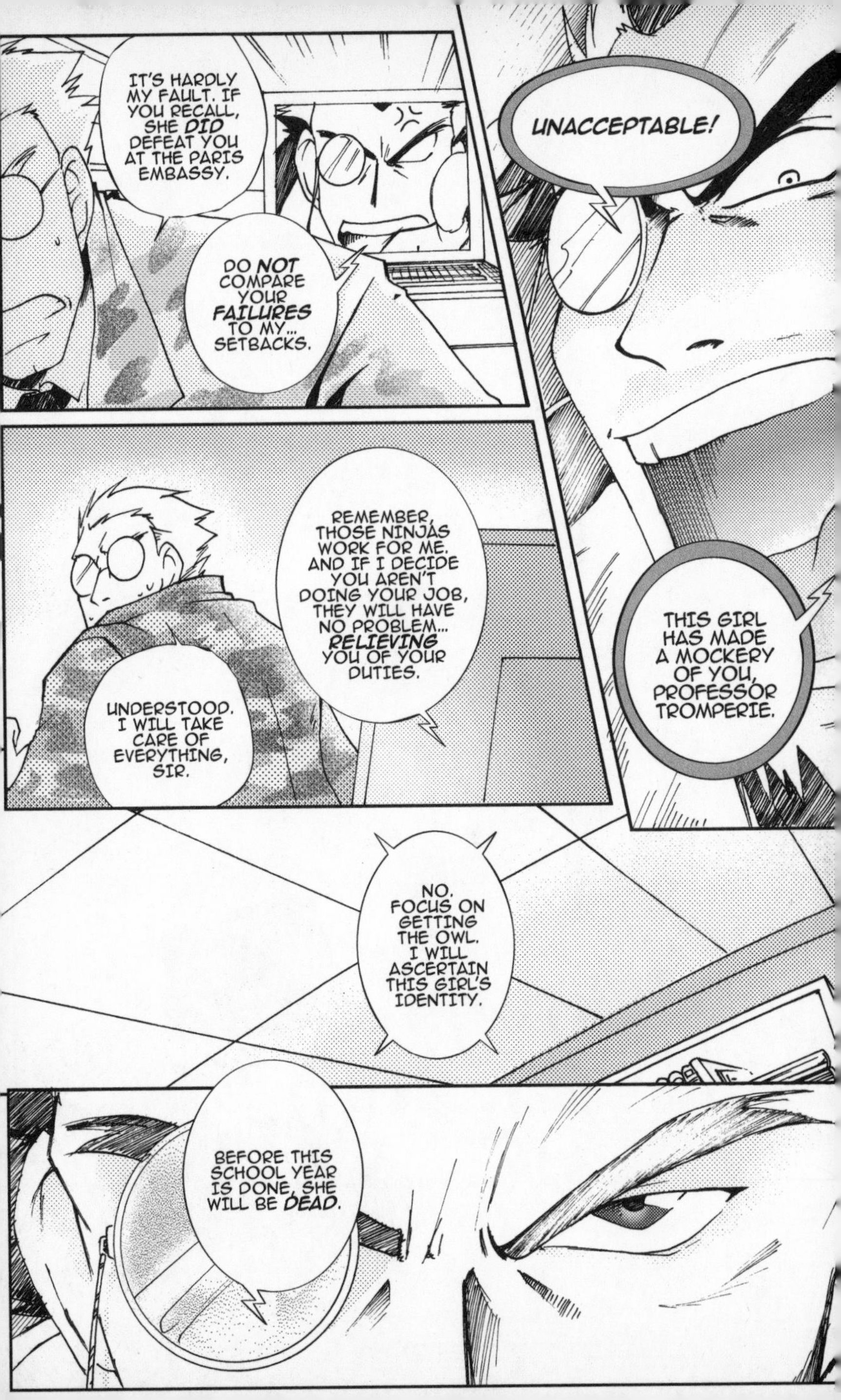
UNACCEPTABLE!
THIS GIRL HAS MADE A MOCKERY OF YOU, PROFESSOR TROMPERIE.
IT'S HARDLY MY FAULT. IF YOU RECALL, SHE DID DEFEAT YOU AT THE PARIS EMBASSY.
DO NOT COMPARE YOUR FAILURES TO MY... SETBACKS.
REMEMBER, THOSE NINJAS WORK FOR ME. AND IF I DECIDE YOU AREN'T DOING YOUR JOB, THEY WILL HAVE NO PROBLEM... RELIEVING YOU OF YOUR DUTIES.
UNDERSTOOD. I WILL TAKE CARE OF EVERYTHING, SIR.
NO. FOCUS ON GETTING THE OWL. I WILL ASCERTAIN THIS GIRL'S IDENTITY.
BEFORE THIS SCHOOL YEAR IS DONE, SHE WILL BE DEAD.

# File 14
# BEST FRIEND

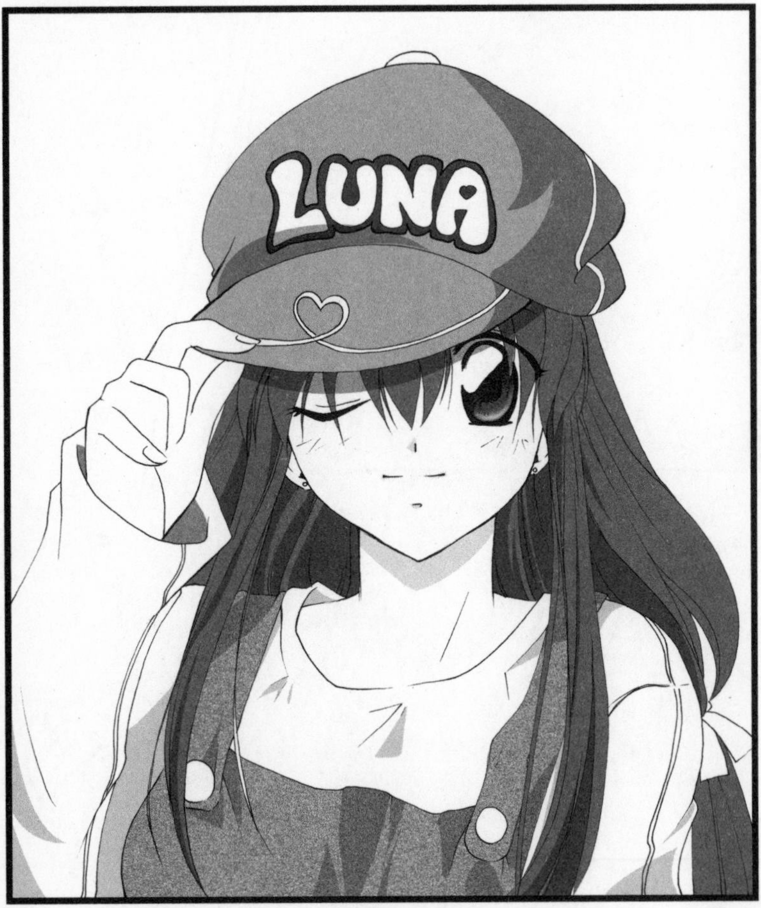
LUNA

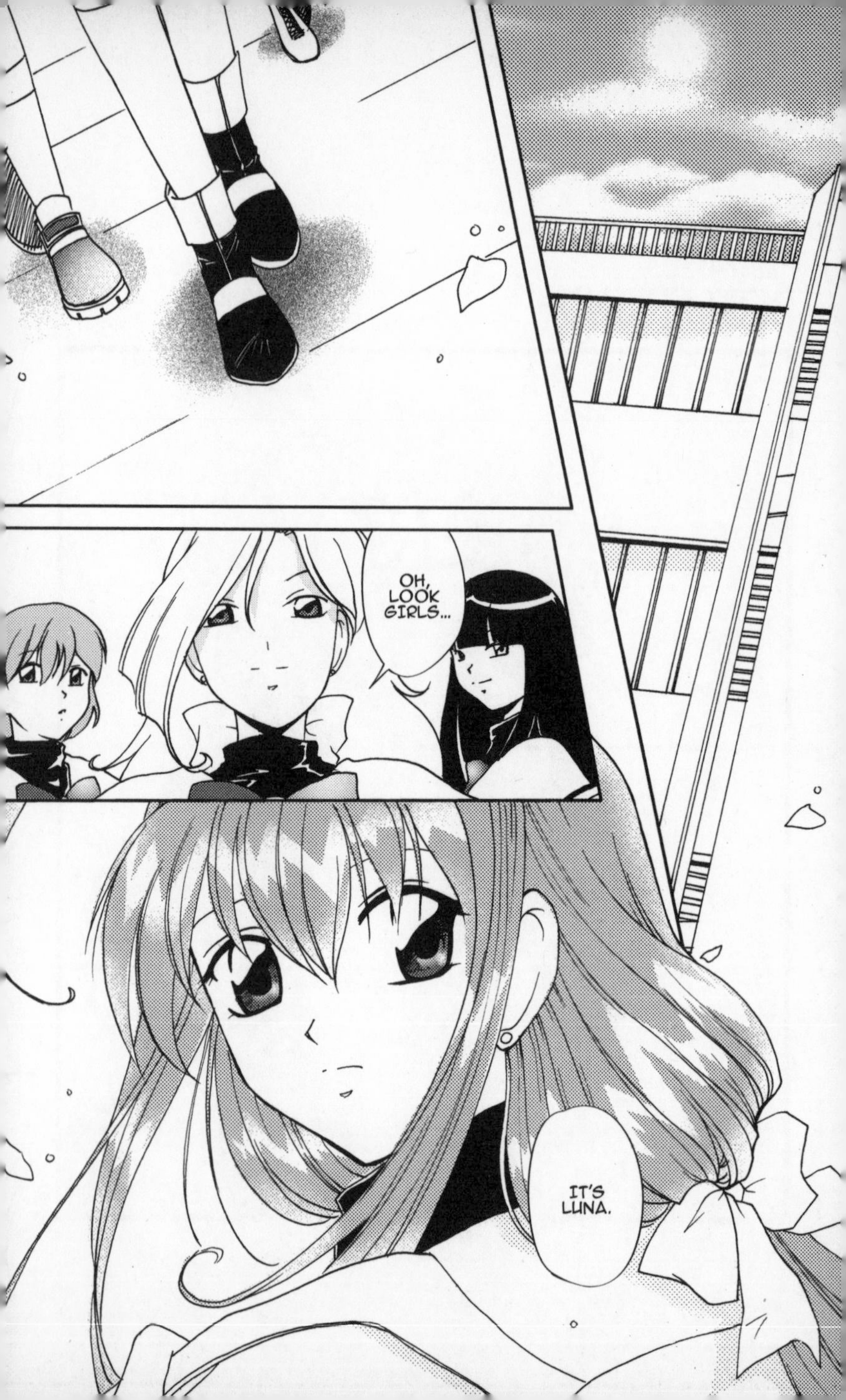
OH, LOOK GIRLS...
IT'S LUNA.

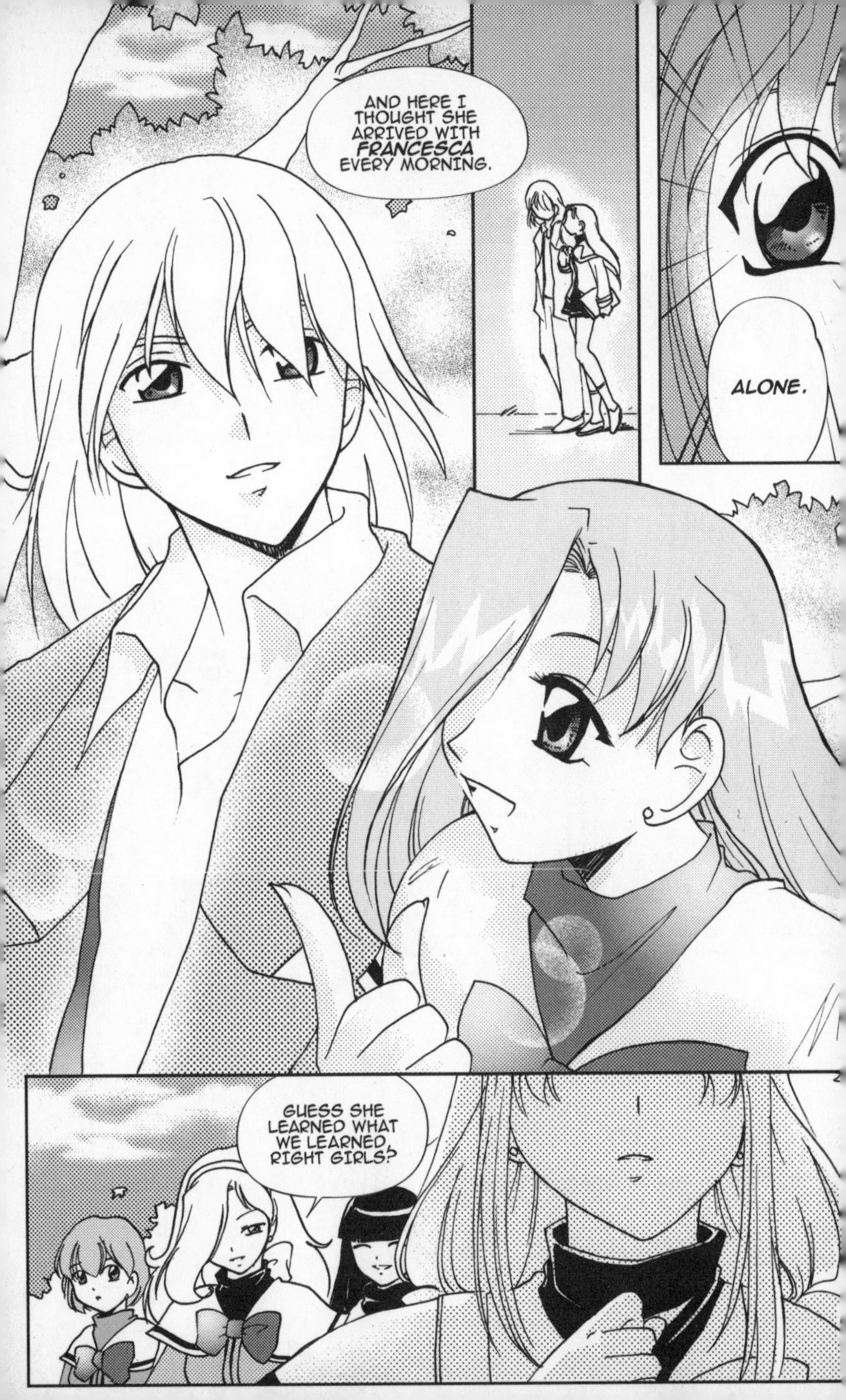
ALONE.
AND HERE I THOUGHT SHE ARRIVED WITH ***FRANCESCA*** EVERY MORNING.
GUESS SHE LEARNED WHAT WE LEARNED, RIGHT GIRLS?

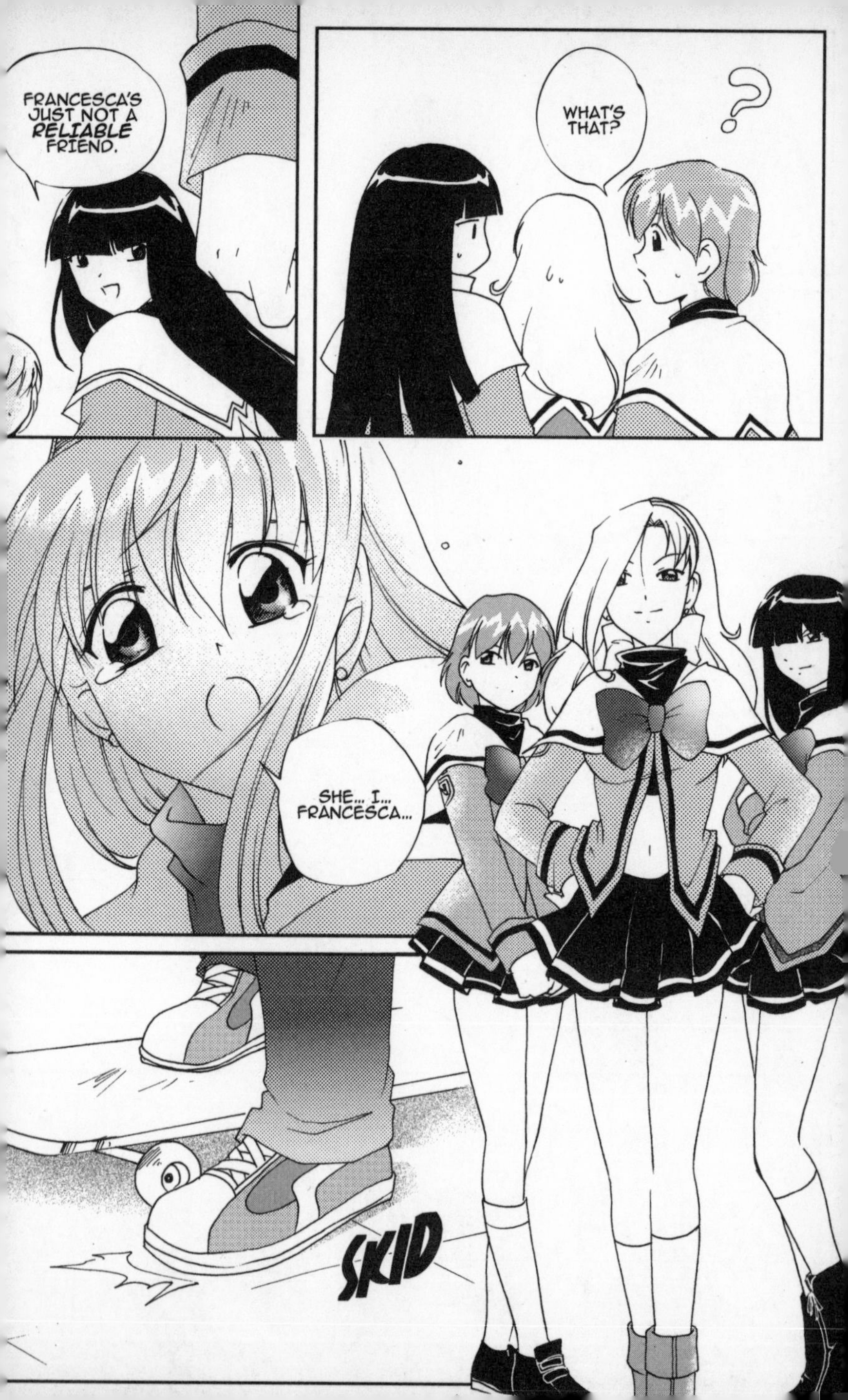
?
WHAT'S THAT?
FRANCESCA'S JUST NOT A RELIABLE FRIEND.
SHE... I... FRANCESCA...
SKID

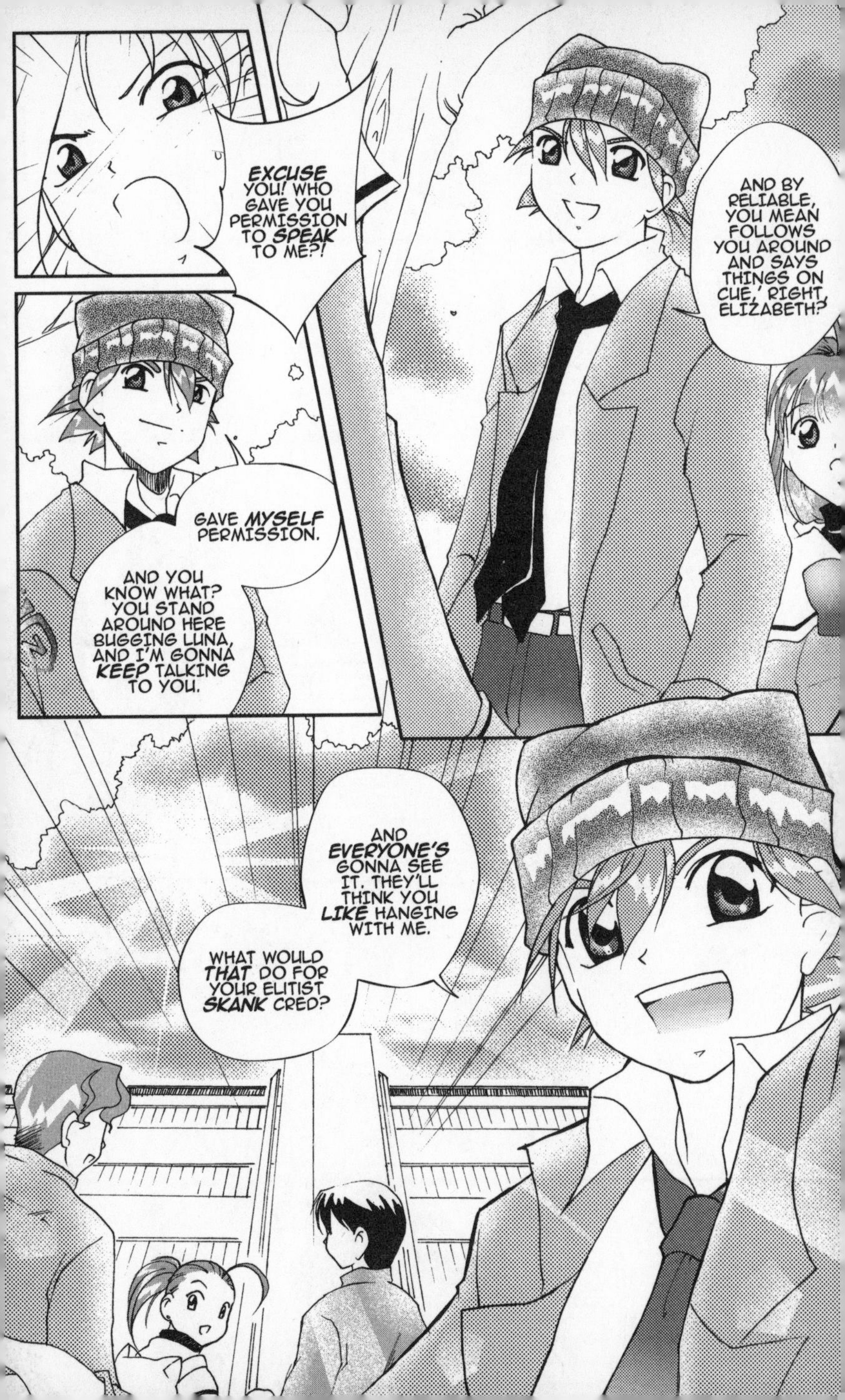
AND BY RELIABLE, YOU MEAN FOLLOWS YOU AROUND AND SAYS THINGS ON CUE,' RIGHT, ELIZABETH?
EXCUSE YOU! WHO GAVE YOU PERMISSION TO SPEAK TO ME?!
GAVE MYSELF PERMISSION.
AND YOU KNOW WHAT? YOU STAND AROUND HERE BUGGING LUNA, AND I'M GONNA KEEP TALKING TO YOU.
AND EVERYONE'S GONNA SEE IT. THEY'LL THINK YOU LIKE HANGING WITH ME.
WHAT WOULD THAT DO FOR YOUR ELITIST SKANK CRED?

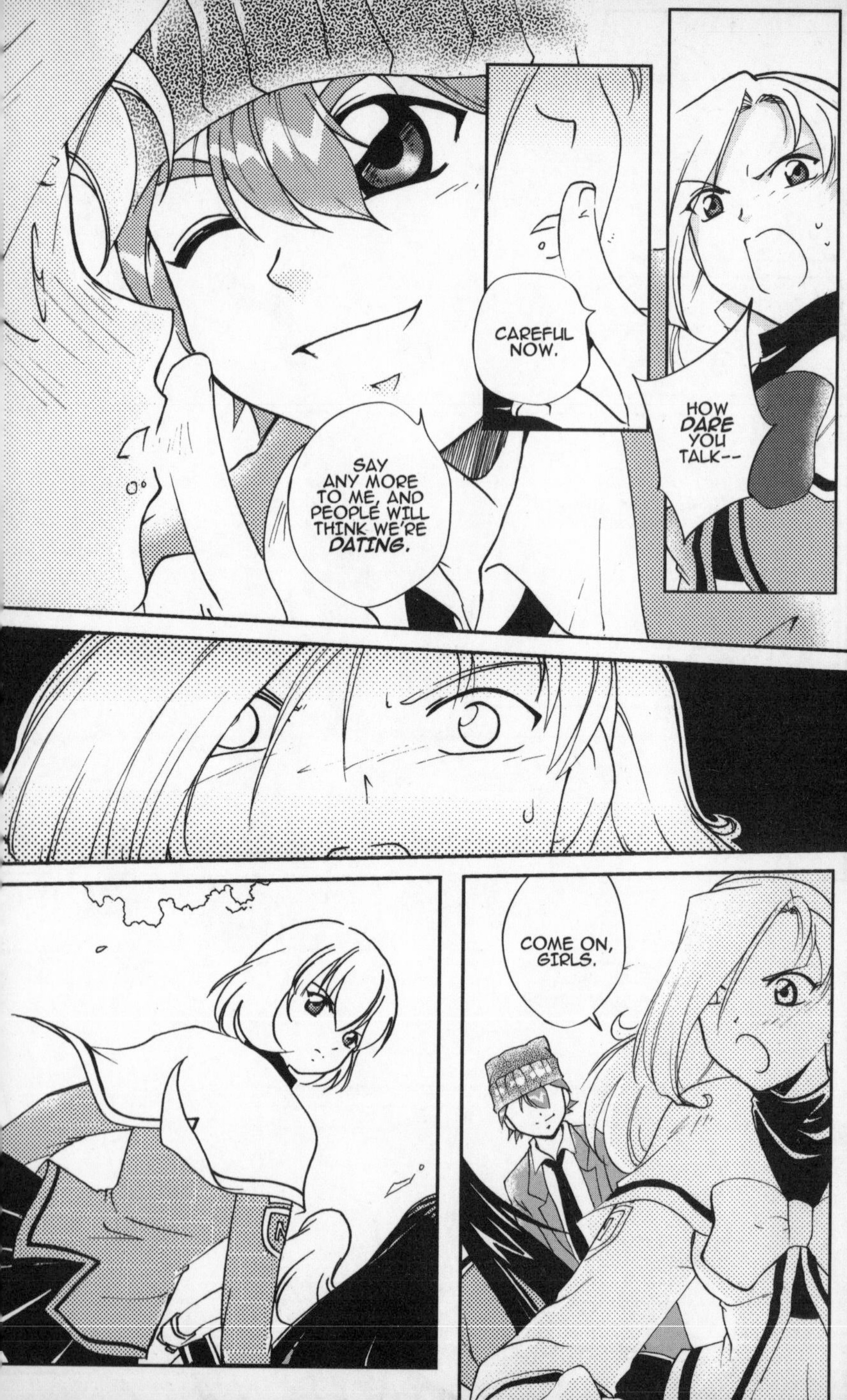
HOW DARE YOU TALK--
CAREFUL NOW.
SAY ANY MORE TO ME, AND PEOPLE WILL THINK WE'RE DATING.
COME ON, GIRLS.

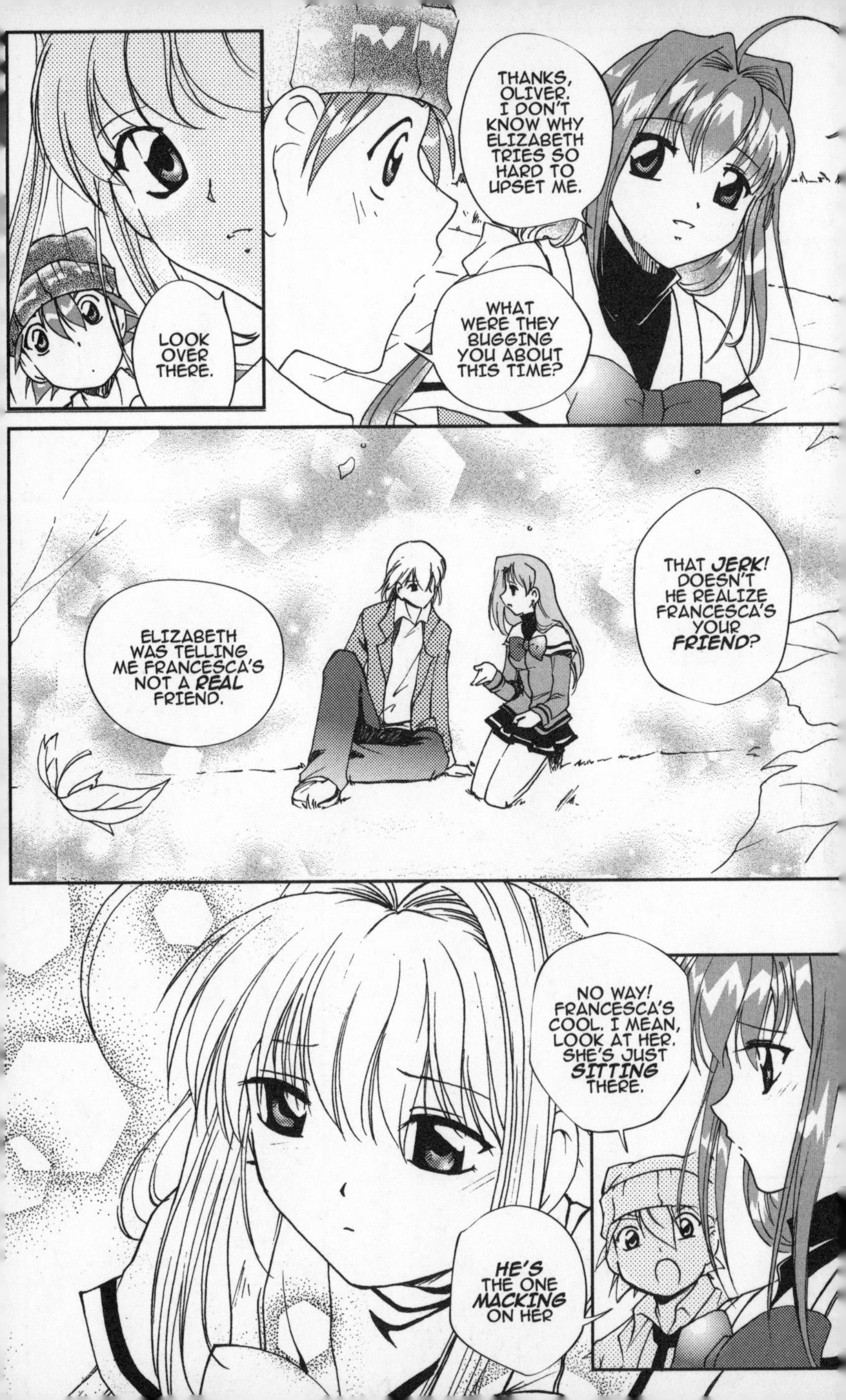
THANKS, OLIVER. I DON'T KNOW WHY ELIZABETH TRIES SO HARD TO UPSET ME.
WHAT WERE THEY BUGGING YOU ABOUT THIS TIME?
LOOK OVER THERE.
THAT JERK! DOESN'T HE REALIZE FRANCESCA'S YOUR FRIEND?
ELIZABETH WAS TELLING ME FRANCESCA'S NOT A REAL FRIEND.
NO WAY! FRANCESCA'S COOL. I MEAN, LOOK AT HER. SHE'S JUST SITTING THERE.
HE'S THE ONE MACKING ON HER

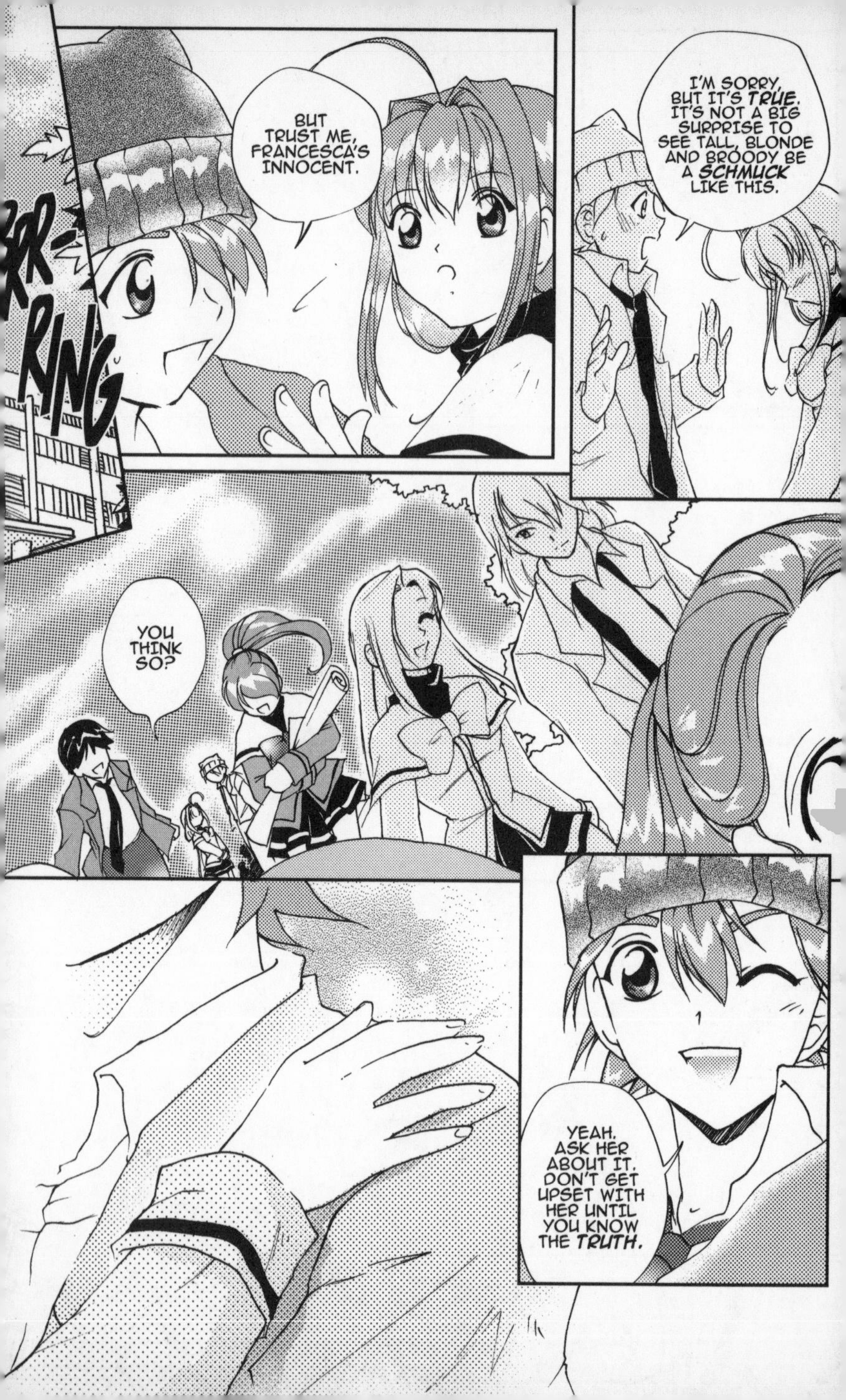
I'M SORRY, BUT IT'S TRUE. IT'S NOT A BIG SURPRISE TO SEE TALL, BLONDE AND BROODY BE A SCHMUCK LIKE THIS.
BUT TRUST ME, FRANCESCA'S INNOCENT.
RR-RING
YOU THINK SO?
YEAH. ASK HER ABOUT IT. DON'T GET UPSET WITH HER UNTIL YOU KNOW THE TRUTH.

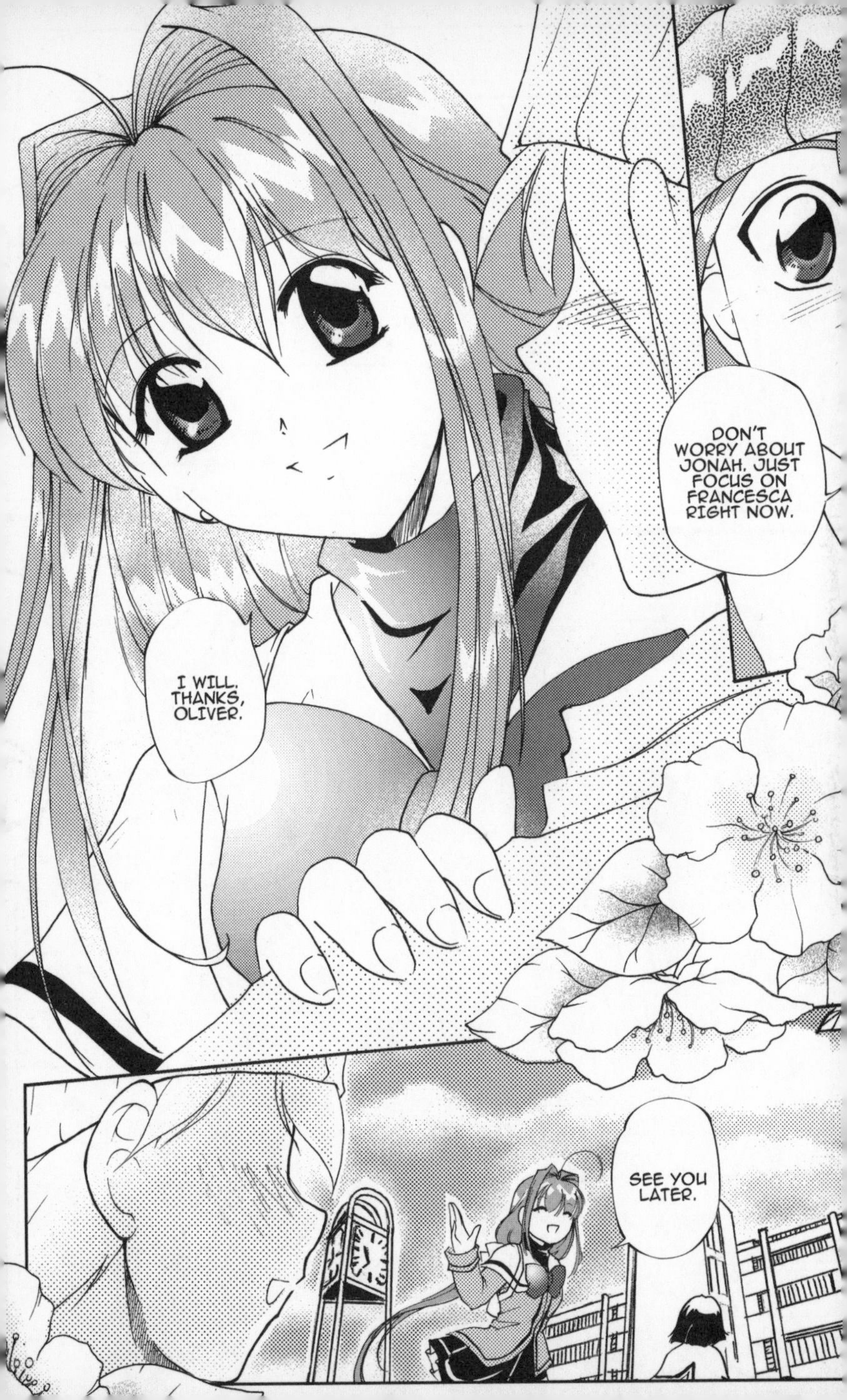
DON'T WORRY ABOUT JONAH. JUST FOCUS ON FRANCESCA RIGHT NOW.
I WILL. THANKS, OLIVER.
SEE YOU LATER.

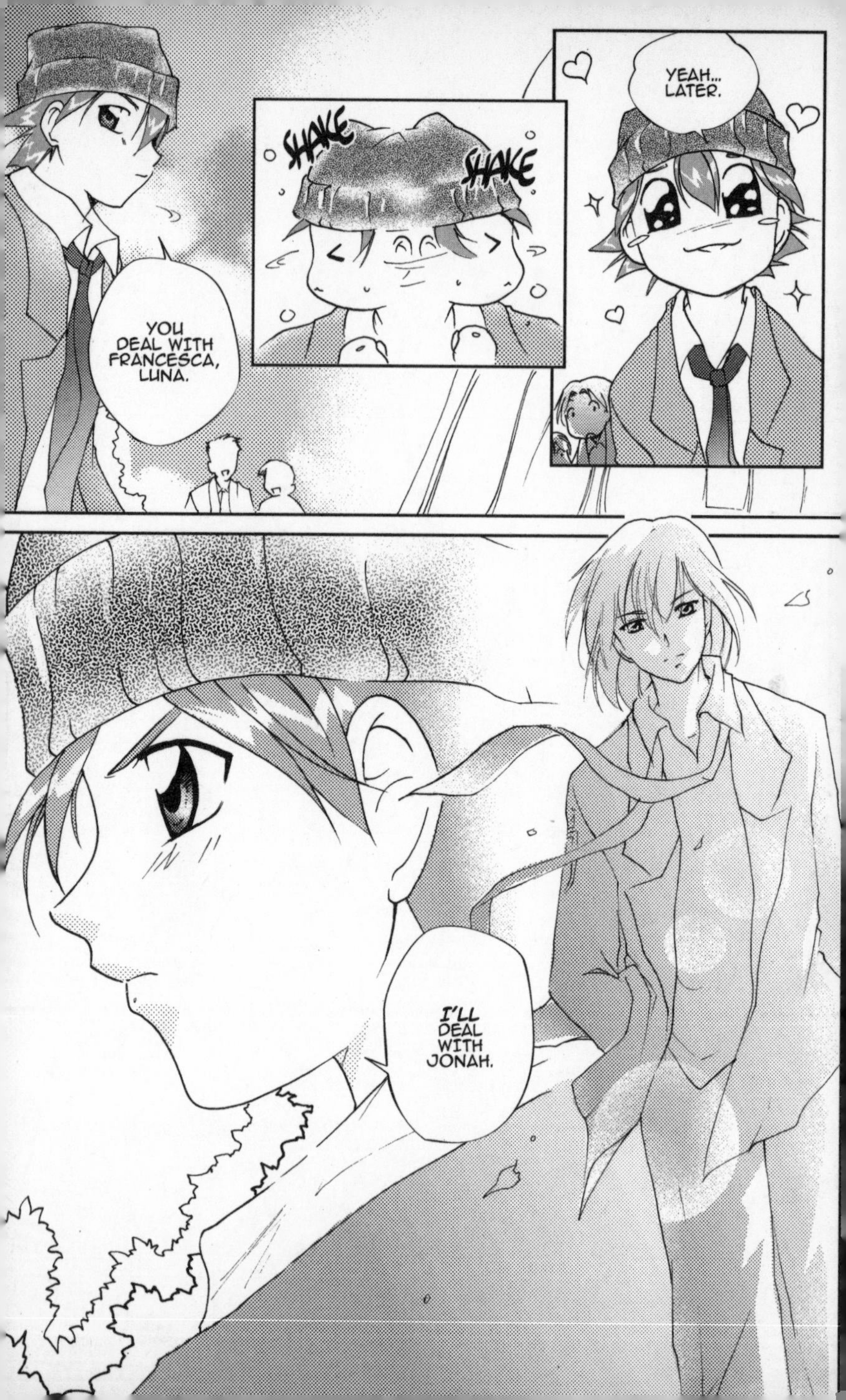
YEAH... LATER.
SHAKE
SHAKE
YOU DEAL WITH FRANCESCA, LUNA.
I'LL DEAL WITH JONAH.

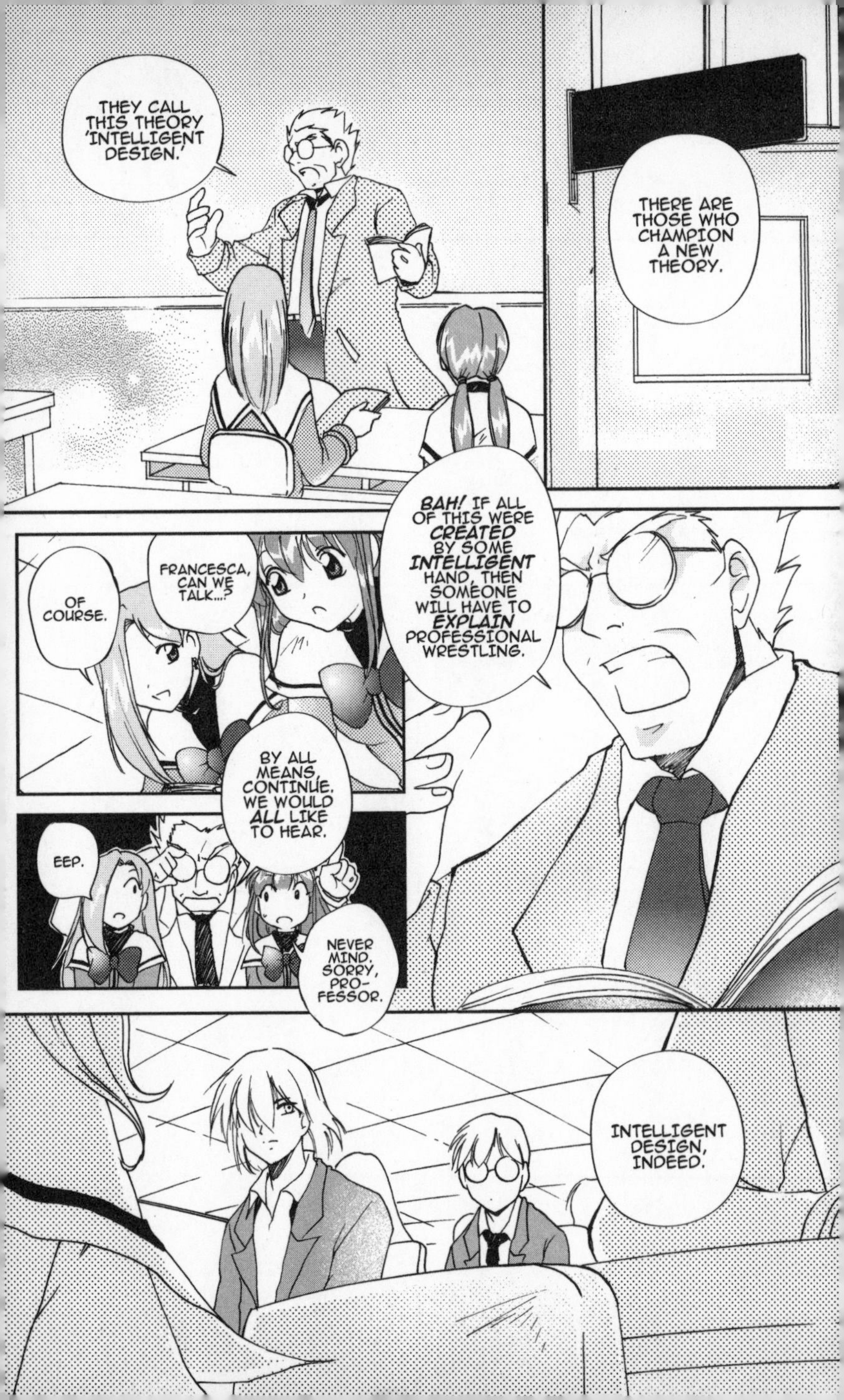
THERE ARE THOSE WHO CHAMPION A NEW THEORY.
THEY CALL THIS THEORY 'INTELLIGENT DESIGN.'
BAH! IF ALL OF THIS WERE CREATED BY SOME INTELLIGENT HAND, THEN SOMEONE WILL HAVE TO EXPLAIN PROFESSIONAL WRESTLING.
FRANCESCA, CAN WE TALK...?
OF COURSE.
BY ALL MEANS, CONTINUE. WE WOULD ALL LIKE TO HEAR.
EEP.
NEVER MIND. SORRY, PRO-FESSOR.
INTELLIGENT DESIGN, INDEED.

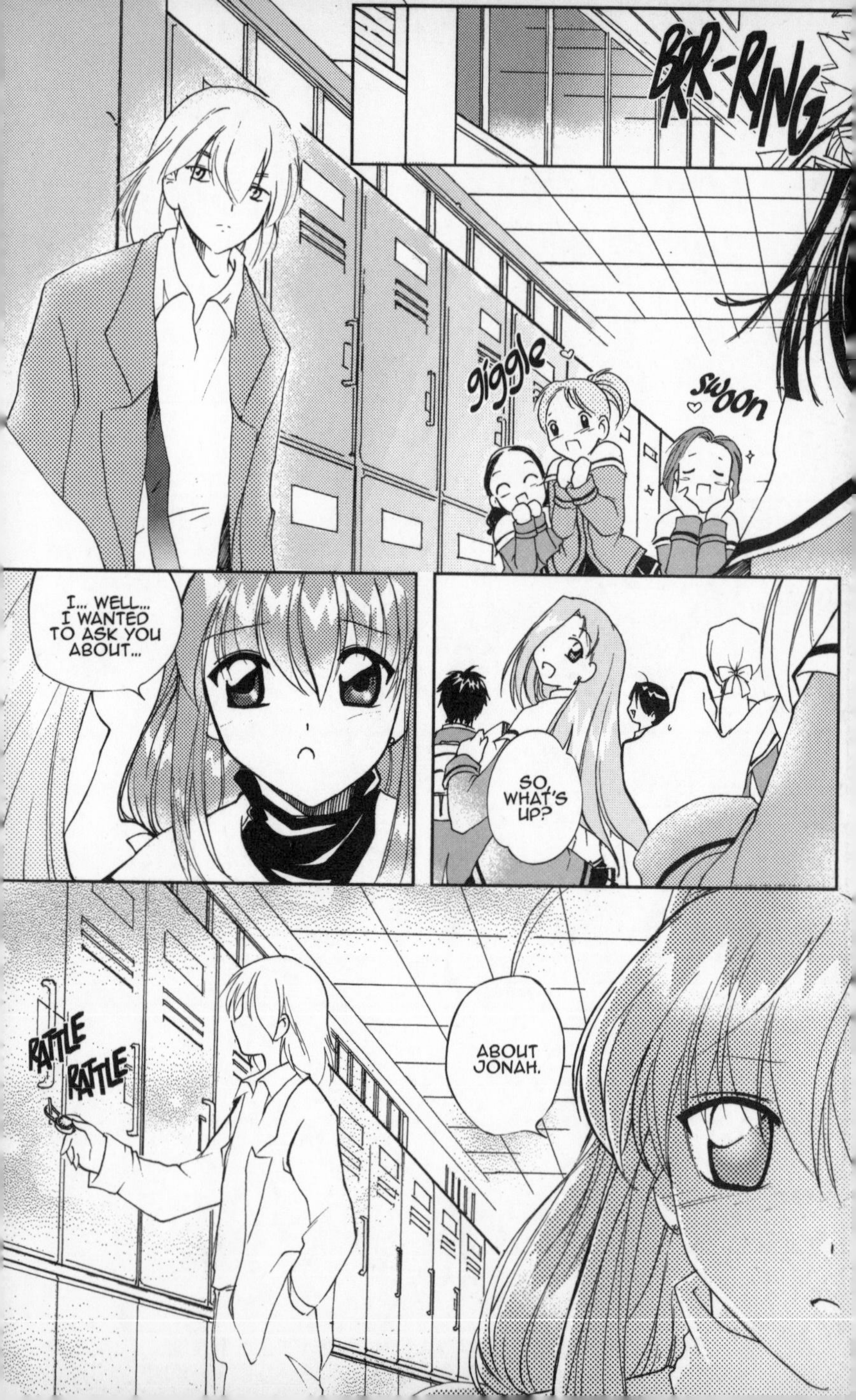
BRR-RING
swoon
giggle
SO, WHAT'S UP?
I... WELL... I WANTED TO ASK YOU ABOUT...
ABOUT JONAH.
RATTLE RATTLE

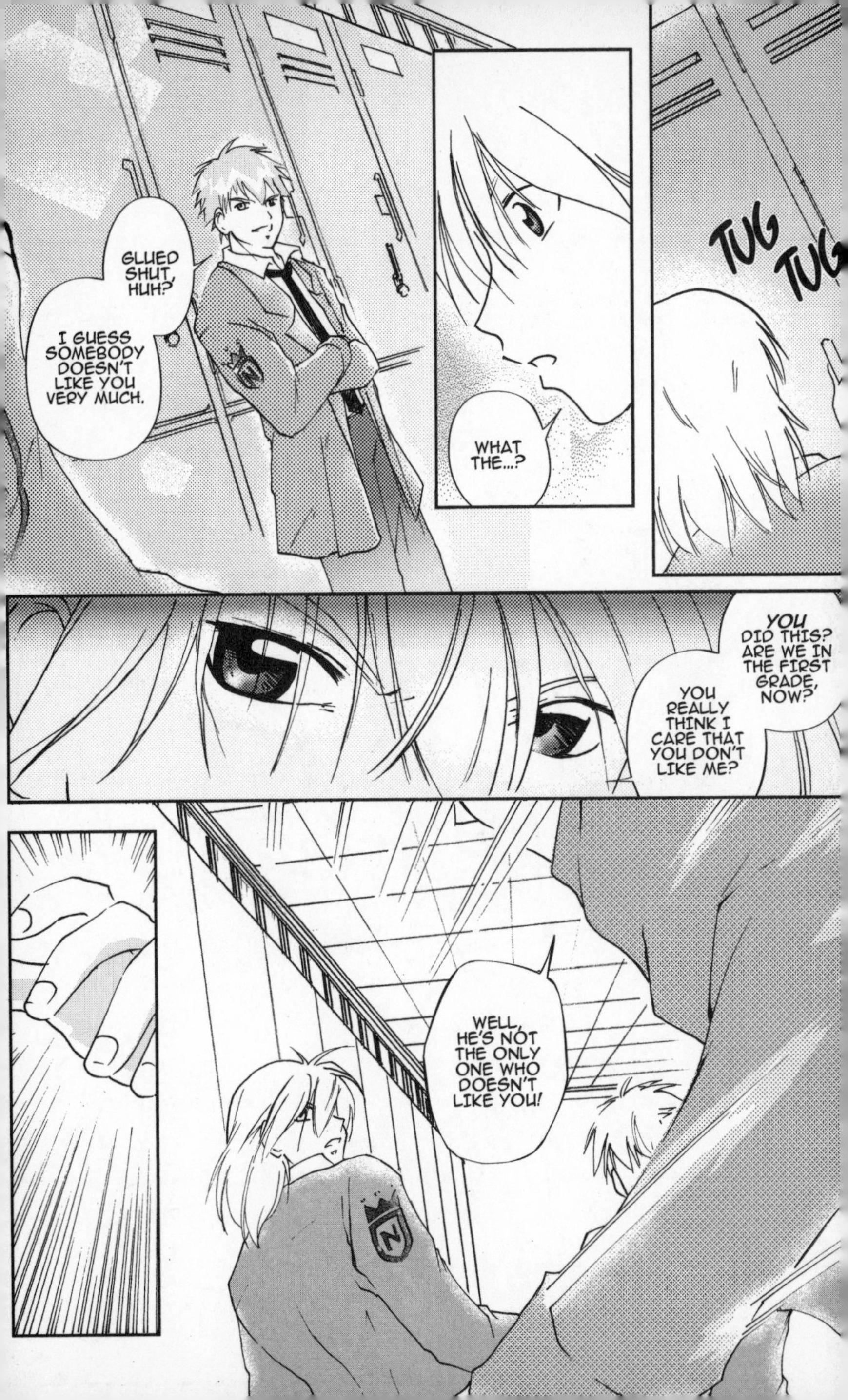
TUG TUG
WHAT THE...?
GLUED SHUT, HUH?
I GUESS SOMEBODY DOESN'T LIKE YOU VERY MUCH.
YOU DID THIS? ARE WE IN THE FIRST GRADE, NOW?
YOU REALLY THINK I CARE THAT YOU DON'T LIKE ME?
WELL, HE'S NOT THE ONLY ONE WHO DOESN'T LIKE YOU!

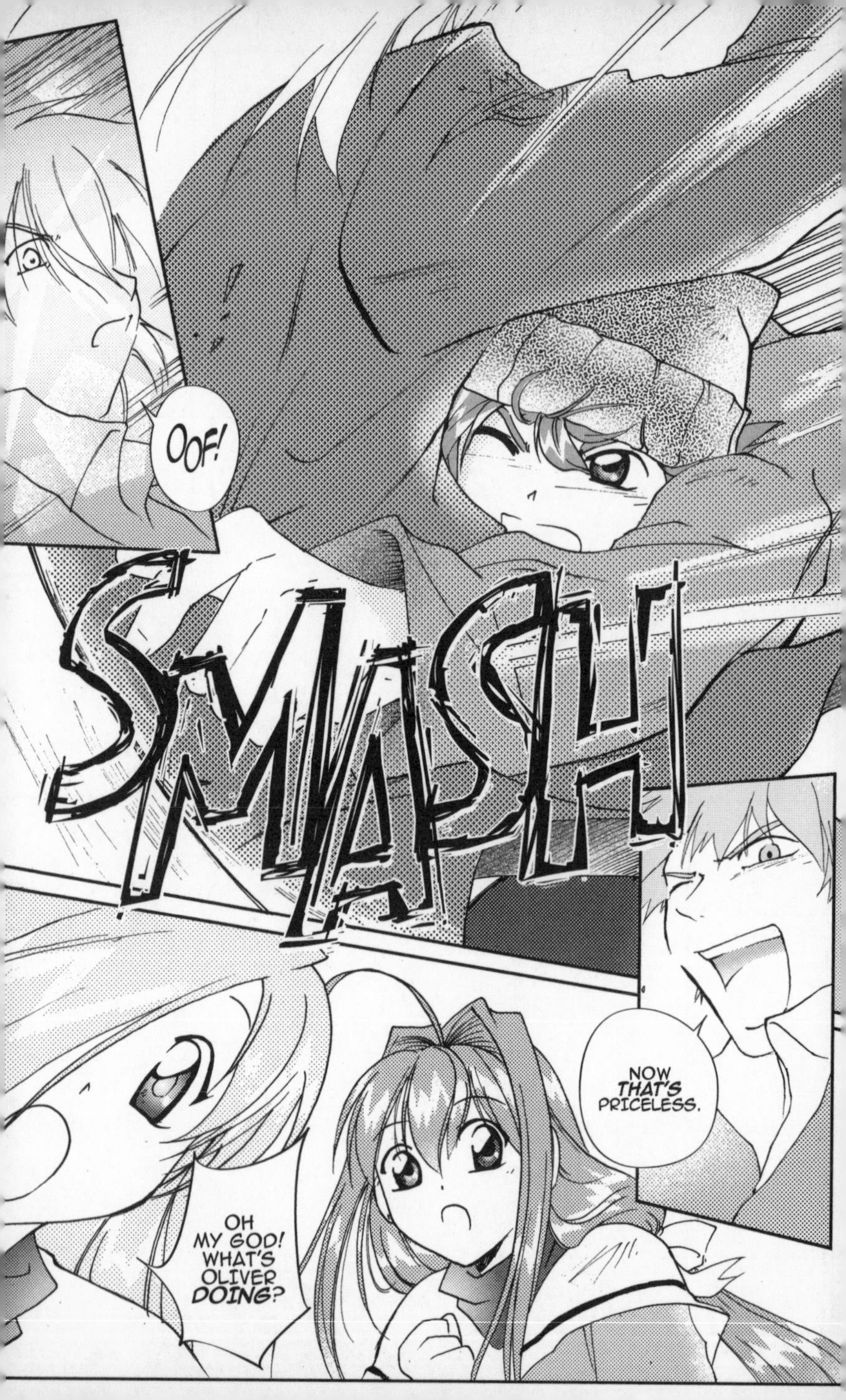

OOF!
SMASH
NOW THAT'S PRICELESS.
OH MY GOD! WHAT'S OLIVER DOING?

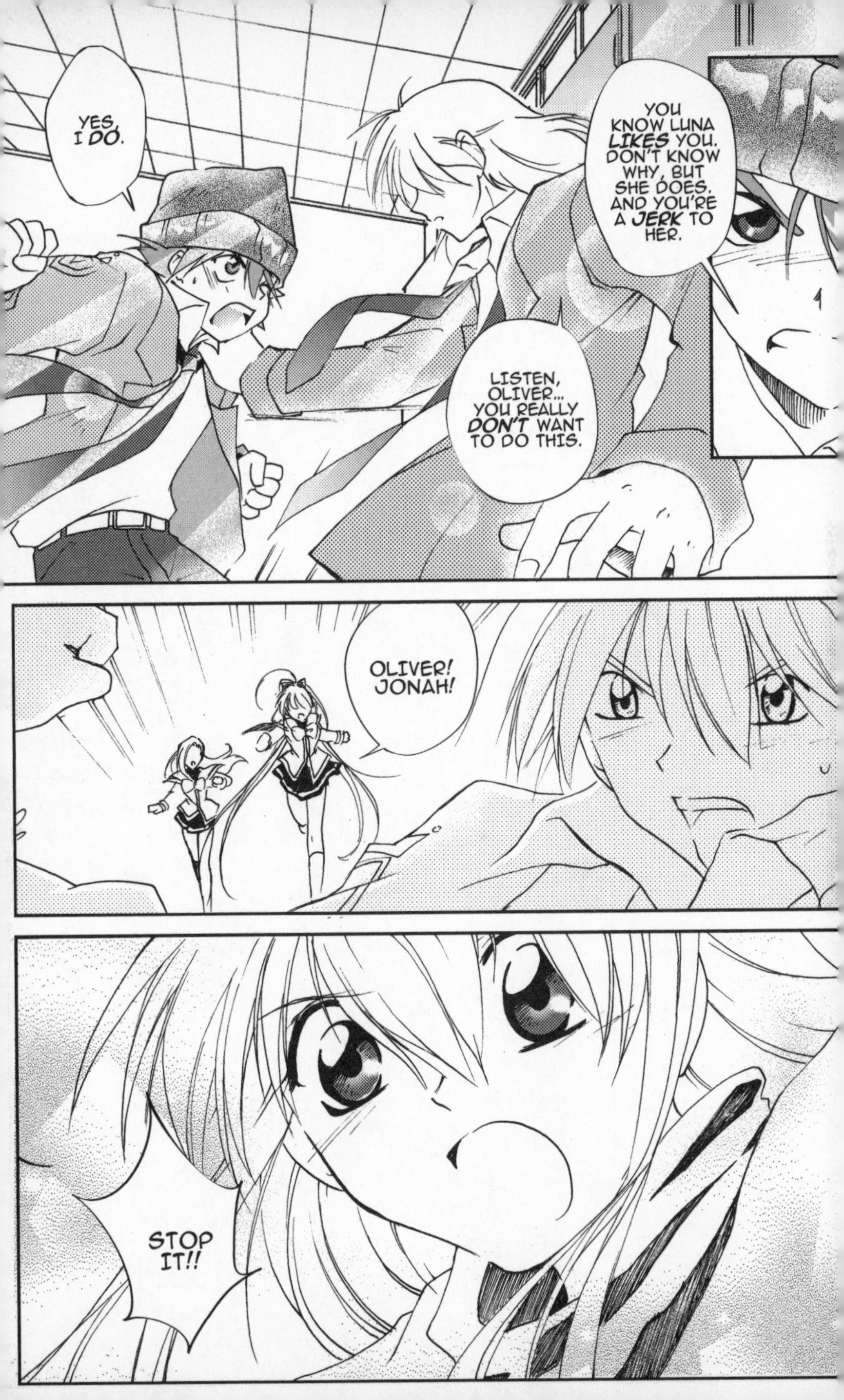
YOU KNOW LUNA LIKES YOU. DON'T KNOW WHY, BUT SHE DOES. AND YOU'RE A JERK TO HER.
LISTEN, OLIVER... YOU REALLY DON'T WANT TO DO THIS.
YES, I DO.
OLIVER! JONAH!
STOP IT!!

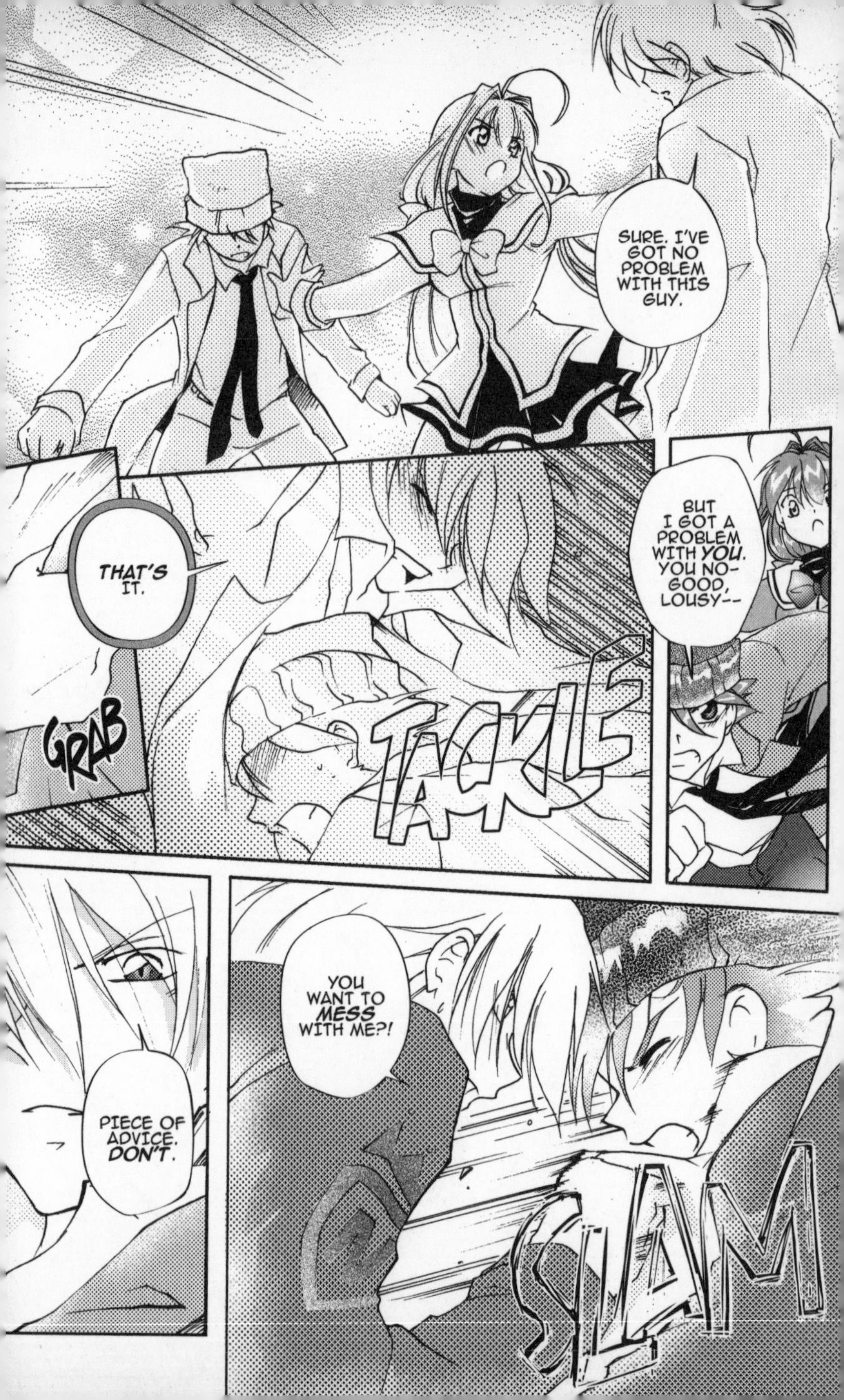
SURE. I'VE GOT NO PROBLEM WITH THIS GUY.
BUT I GOT A PROBLEM WITH *YOU*. YOU NO-GOOD, LOUSY--
*THAT'S* IT.
TACKLE
GRAB
YOU WANT TO *MESS* WITH ME?!
SLAM
PIECE OF ADVICE. *DON'T*.

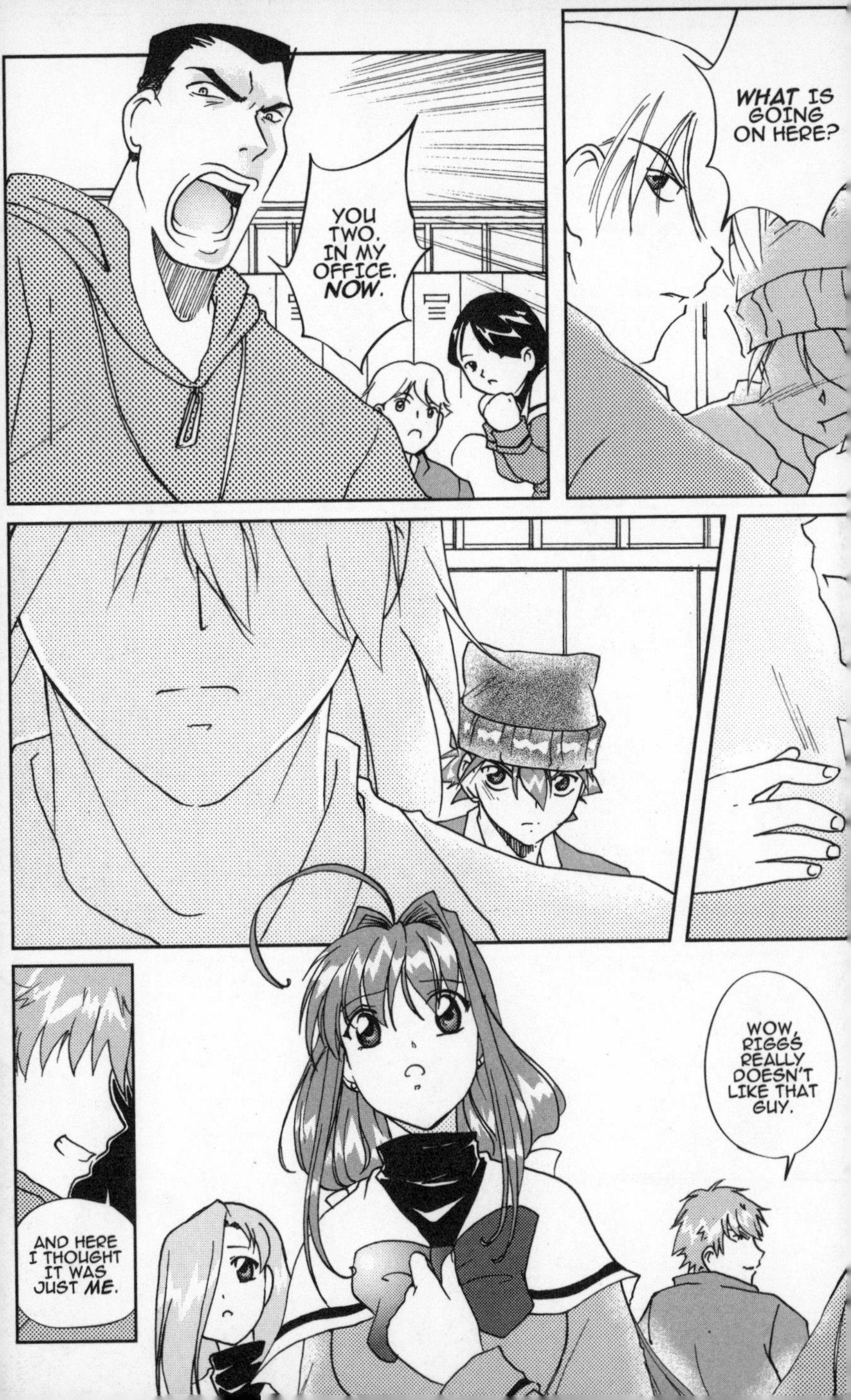
WHAT IS GOING ON HERE?
YOU TWO. IN MY OFFICE. NOW.
WOW, RIGGS REALLY DOESN'T LIKE THAT GUY.
AND HERE I THOUGHT IT WAS JUST ME.

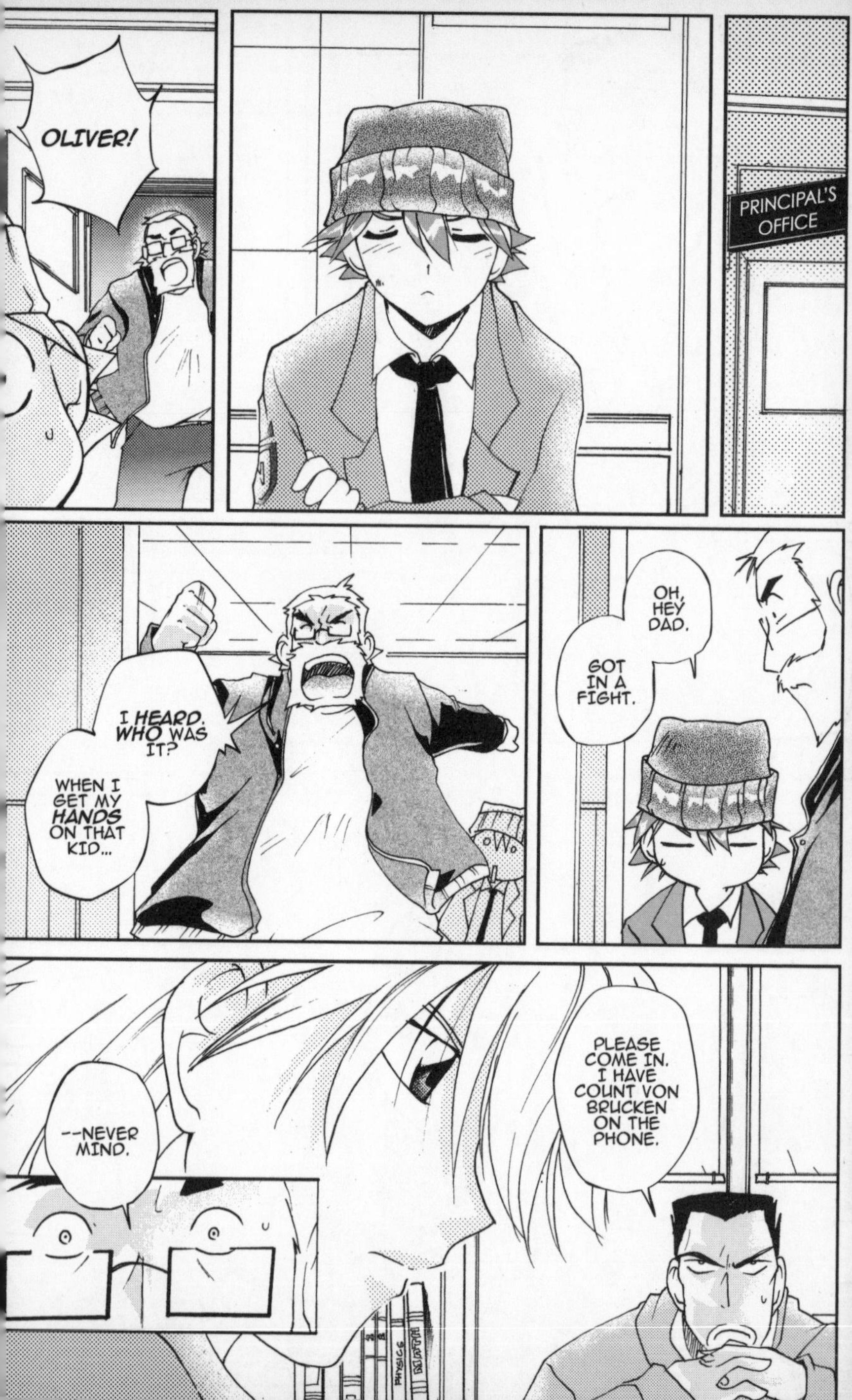
PRINCIPAL'S OFFICE
OLIVER!
OH, HEY DAD.
GOT IN A FIGHT.
I HEARD. WHO WAS IT?
WHEN I GET MY HANDS ON THAT KID...
PLEASE COME IN. I HAVE COUNT VON BRUCKEN ON THE PHONE.
--NEVER MIND.
PHYSICS

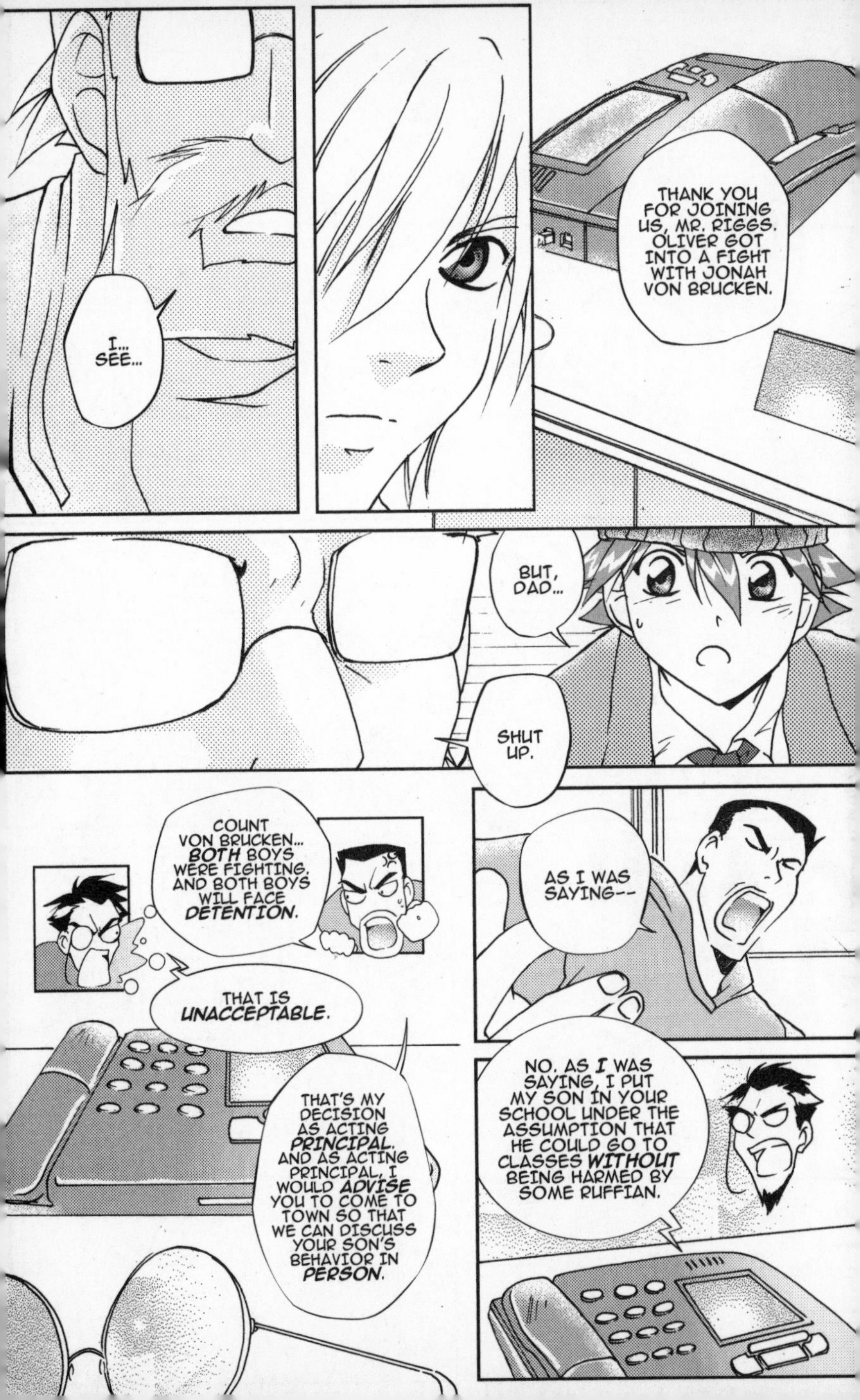
THANK YOU FOR JOINING US, MR. RIGGS. OLIVER GOT INTO A FIGHT WITH JONAH VON BRUCKEN.
I... SEE...
BUT, DAD...
SHUT UP.
AS I WAS SAYING--
COUNT VON BRUCKEN... BOTH BOYS WERE FIGHTING, AND BOTH BOYS WILL FACE DETENTION.
THAT IS UNACCEPTABLE.
NO. AS I WAS SAYING, I PUT MY SON IN YOUR SCHOOL UNDER THE ASSUMPTION THAT HE COULD GO TO CLASSES WITHOUT BEING HARMED BY SOME RUFFIAN.
THAT'S MY DECISION AS ACTING PRINCIPAL. AND AS ACTING PRINCIPAL, I WOULD ADVISE YOU TO COME TO TOWN SO THAT WE CAN DISCUSS YOUR SON'S BEHAVIOR IN PERSON.

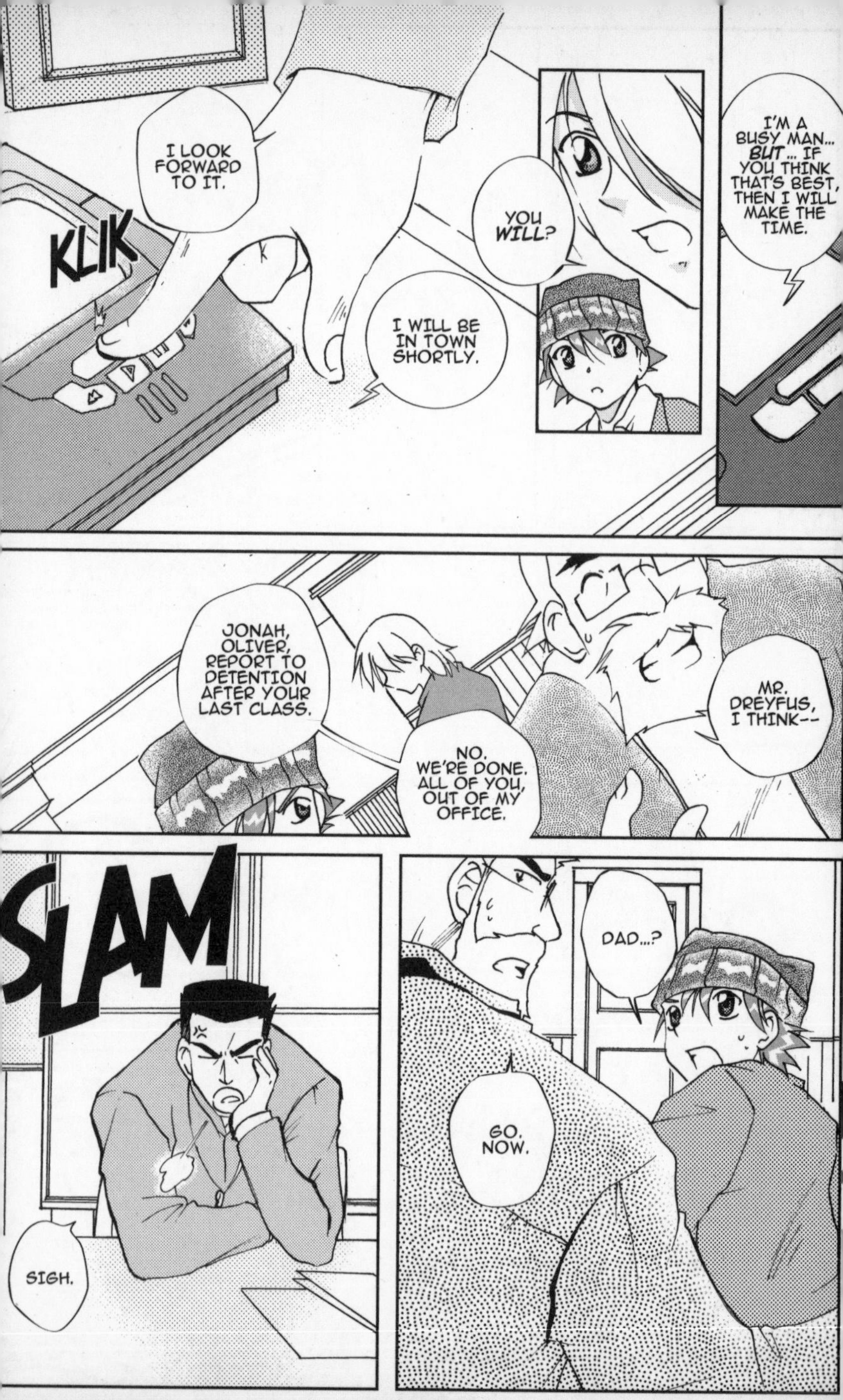
I'M A BUSY MAN... **BUT**... IF YOU THINK THAT'S BEST, THEN I WILL MAKE THE TIME.
YOU **WILL**?
I WILL BE IN TOWN SHORTLY.
I LOOK FORWARD TO IT.
KLIK
MR. DREYFUS, I THINK--
NO. WE'RE DONE. ALL OF YOU, OUT OF MY OFFICE.
JONAH, OLIVER, REPORT TO DETENTION AFTER YOUR LAST CLASS.
DAD...?
GO. NOW.
SLAM
SIGH.

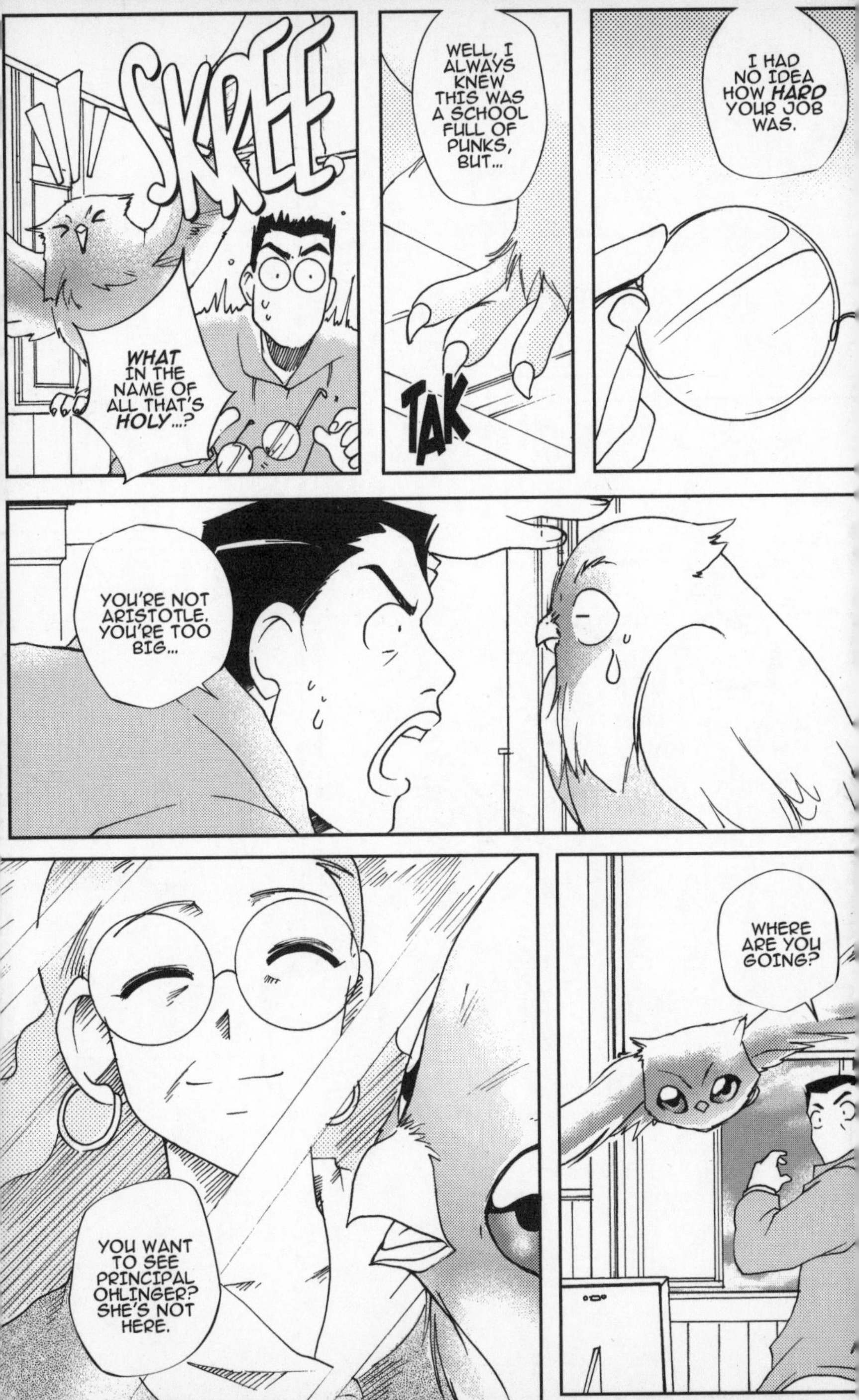
I HAD NO IDEA HOW HARD YOUR JOB WAS.
WELL, I ALWAYS KNEW THIS WAS A SCHOOL FULL OF PUNKS, BUT...
TAK
SKREE
WHAT IN THE NAME OF ALL THAT'S HOLY...?
YOU'RE NOT ARISTOTLE. YOU'RE TOO BIG...
WHERE ARE YOU GOING?
YOU WANT TO SEE PRINCIPAL OHLINGER? SHE'S NOT HERE.

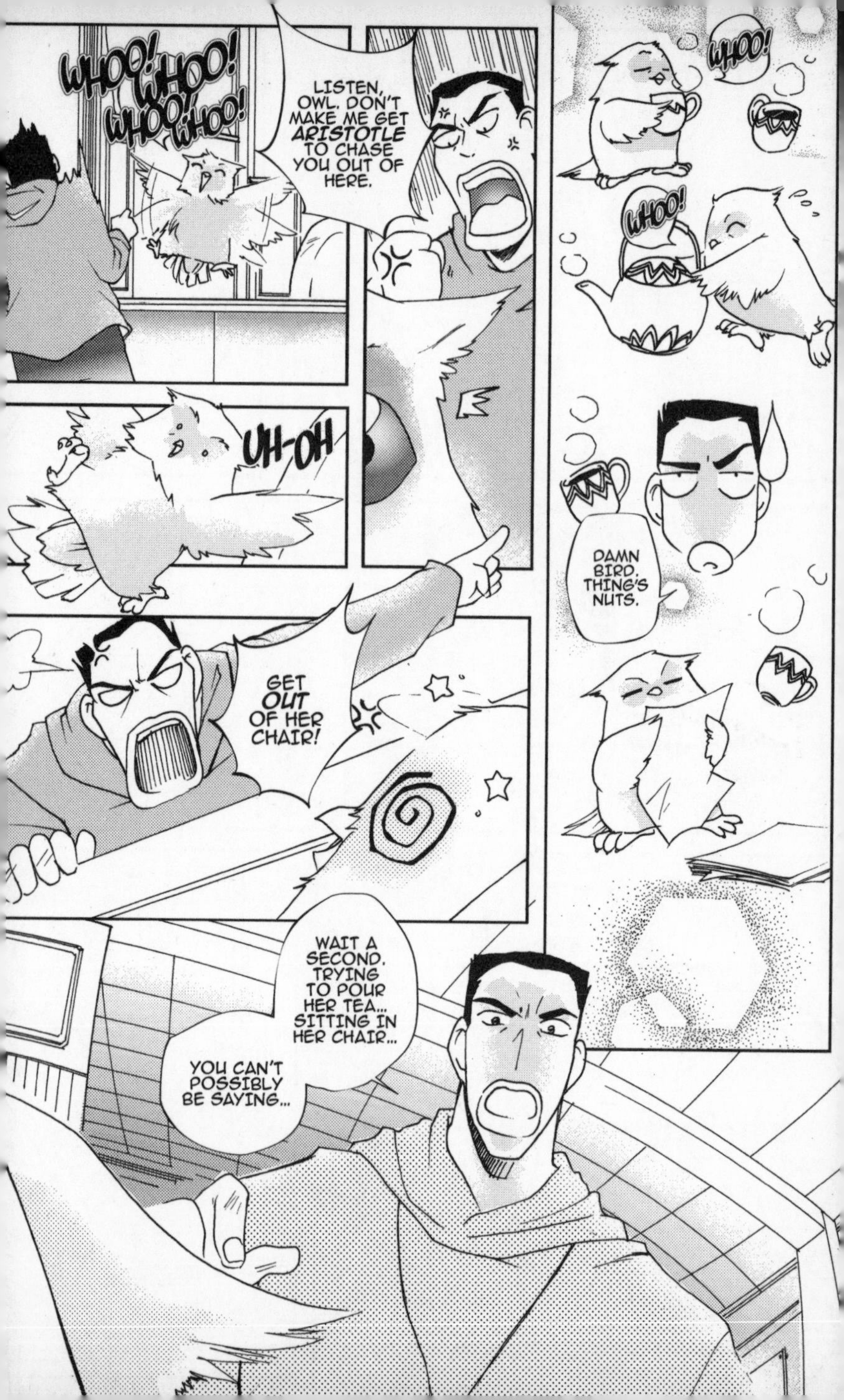
WHOO!
WHOO!
DAMN BIRD. THING'S NUTS.
LISTEN, OWL. DON'T MAKE ME GET ARISTOTLE TO CHASE YOU OUT OF HERE.
WHOO! WHOO! WHOO! WHOO!
UH-OH
GET OUT OF HER CHAIR!
WAIT A SECOND. TRYING TO POUR HER TEA... SITTING IN HER CHAIR...
YOU CAN'T POSSIBLY BE SAYING...

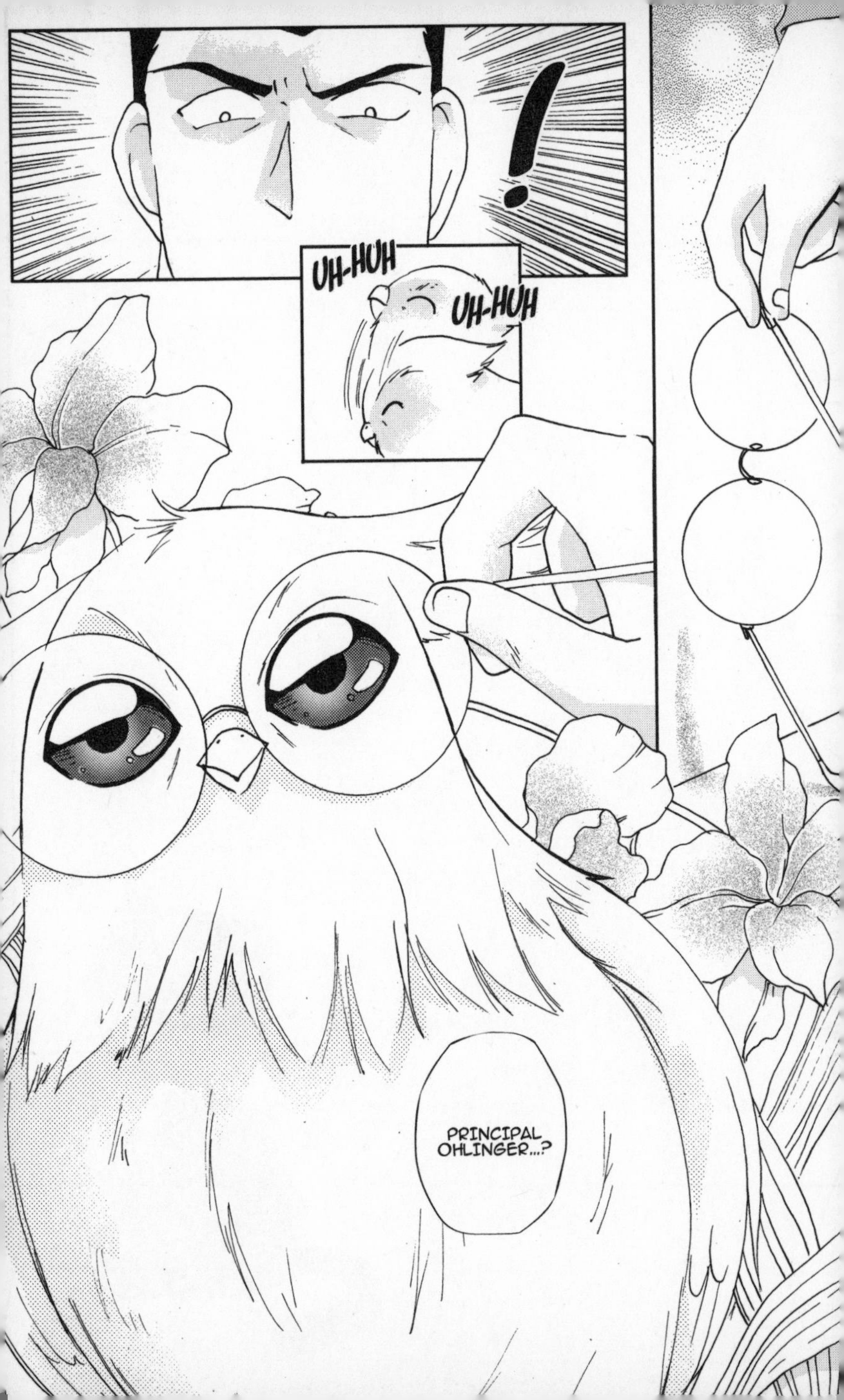
!
UH-HUH
UH-HUH
PRINCIPAL OHLINGER...?

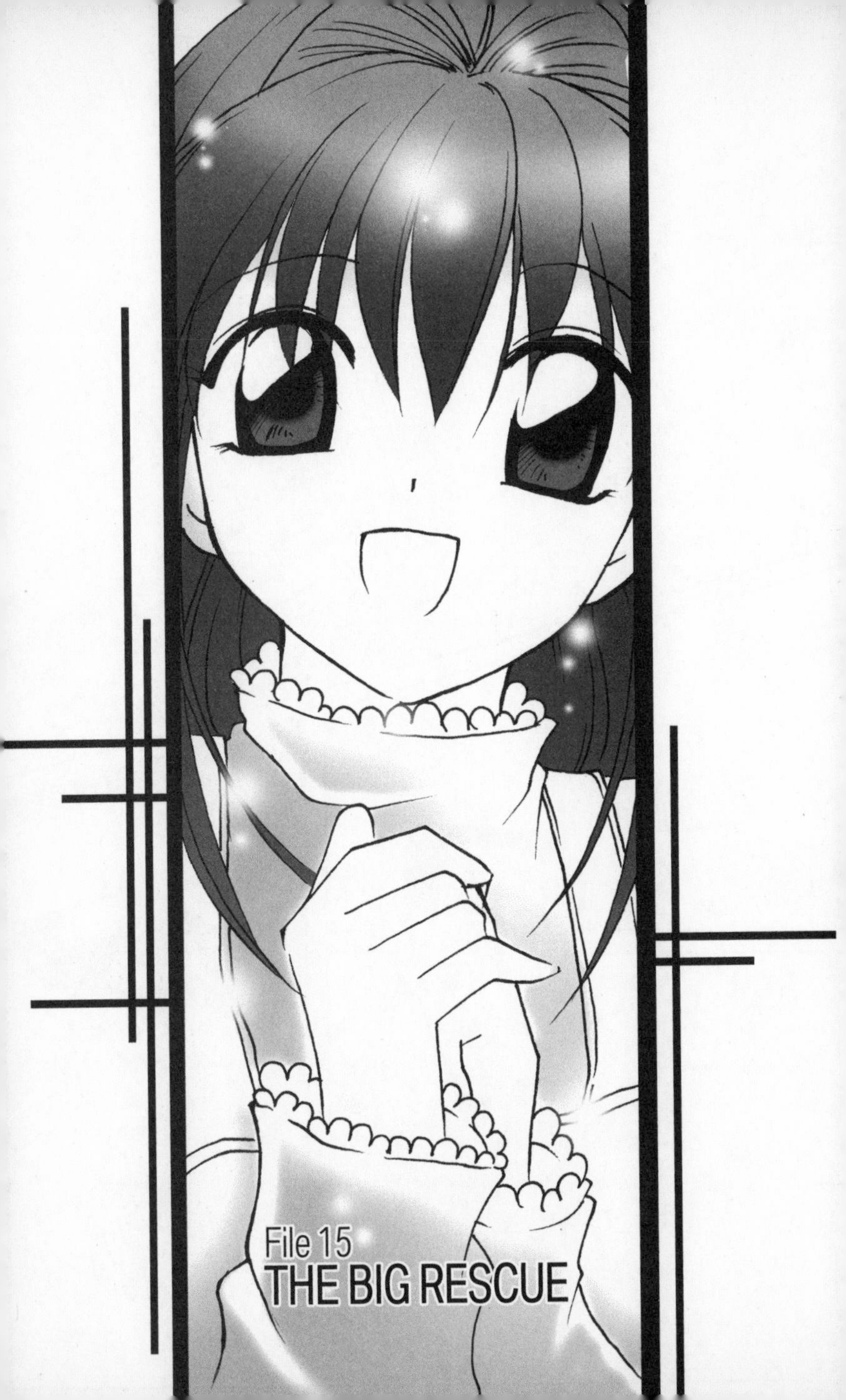
File 15
THE BIG RESCUE

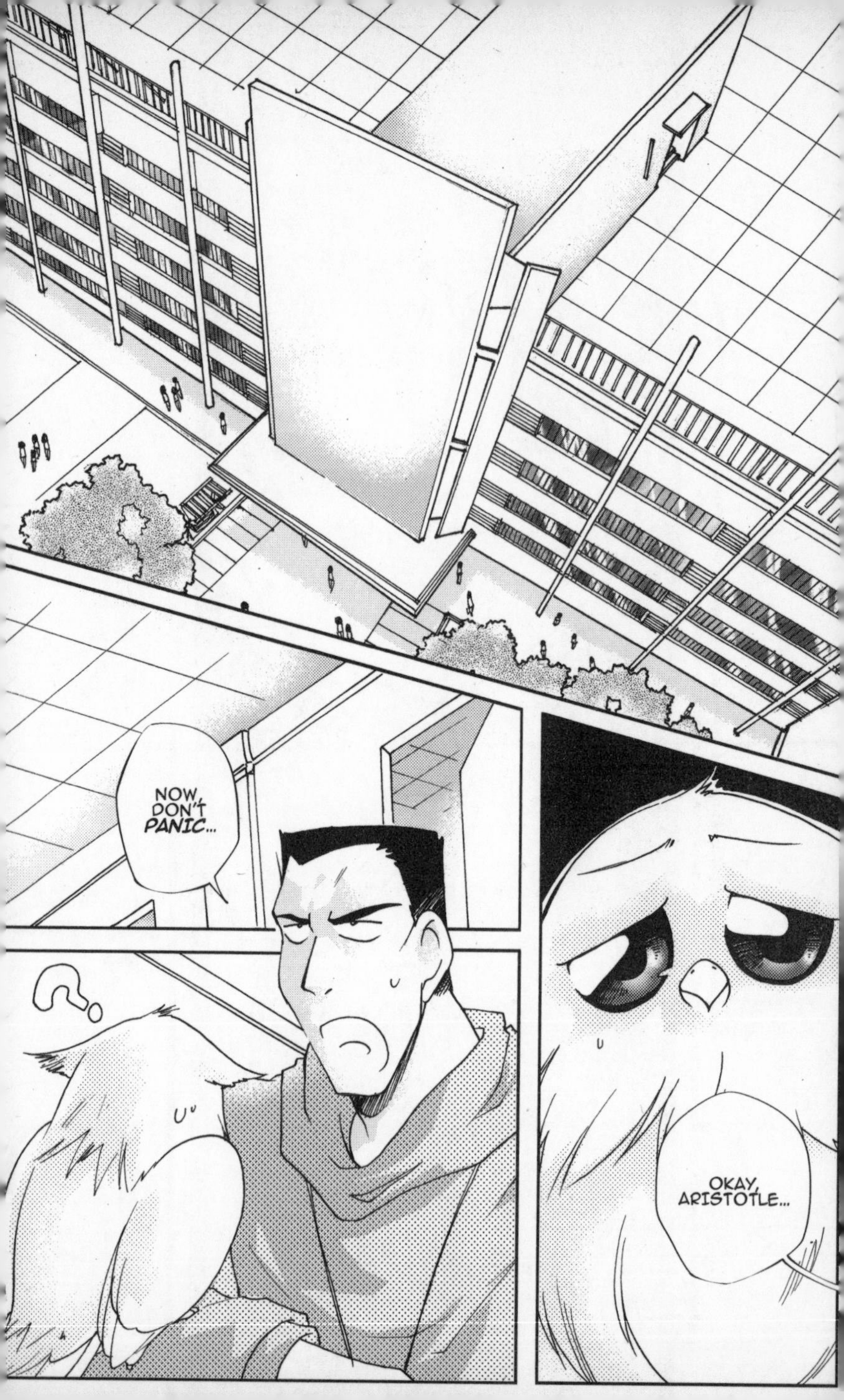
OKAY, ARISTOTLE...
NOW, DON'T PANIC...
?

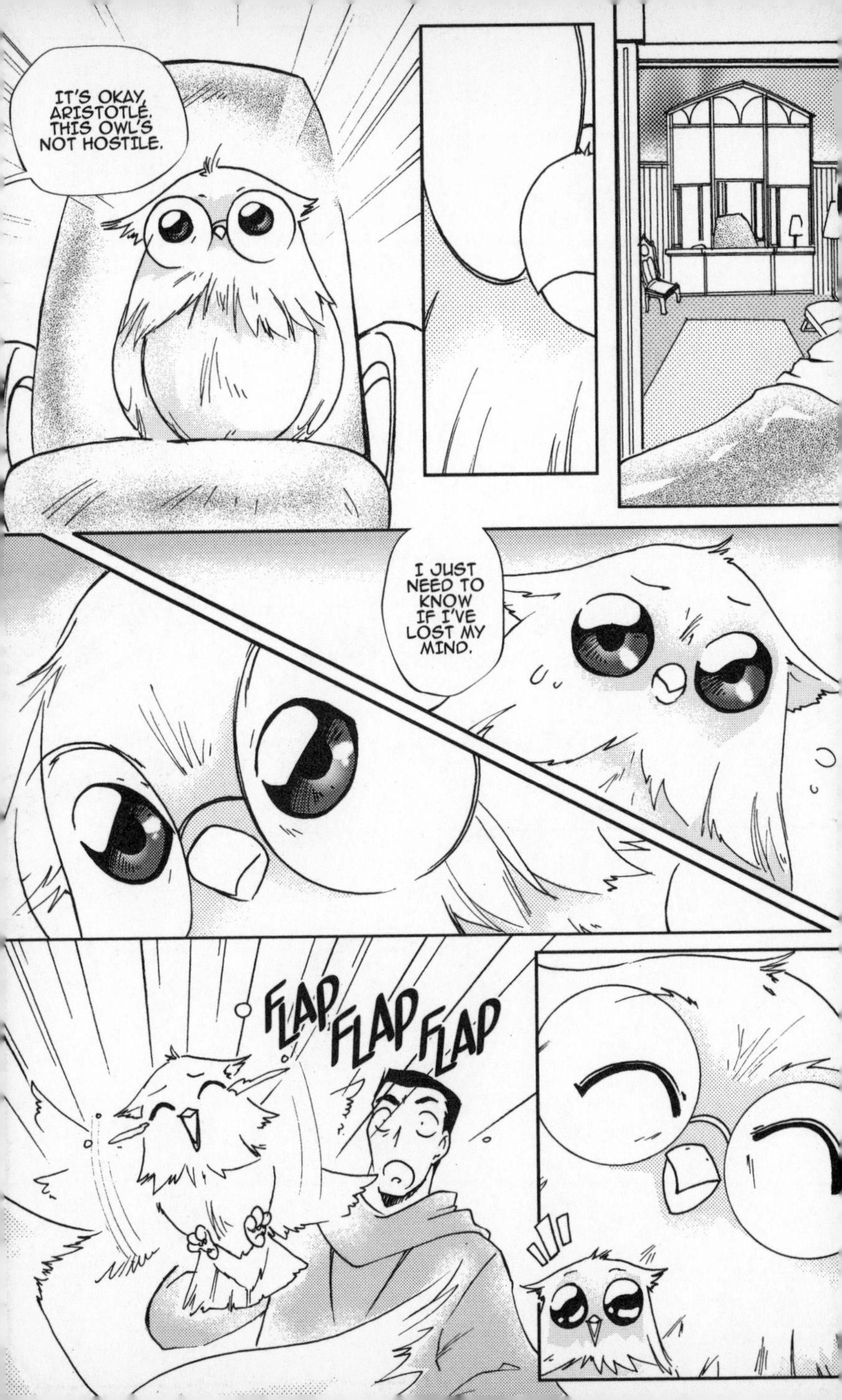
IT'S OKAY, ARISTOTLE. THIS OWL'S NOT HOSTILE.
I JUST NEED TO KNOW IF I'VE LOST MY MIND.
FLAP FLAP FLAP

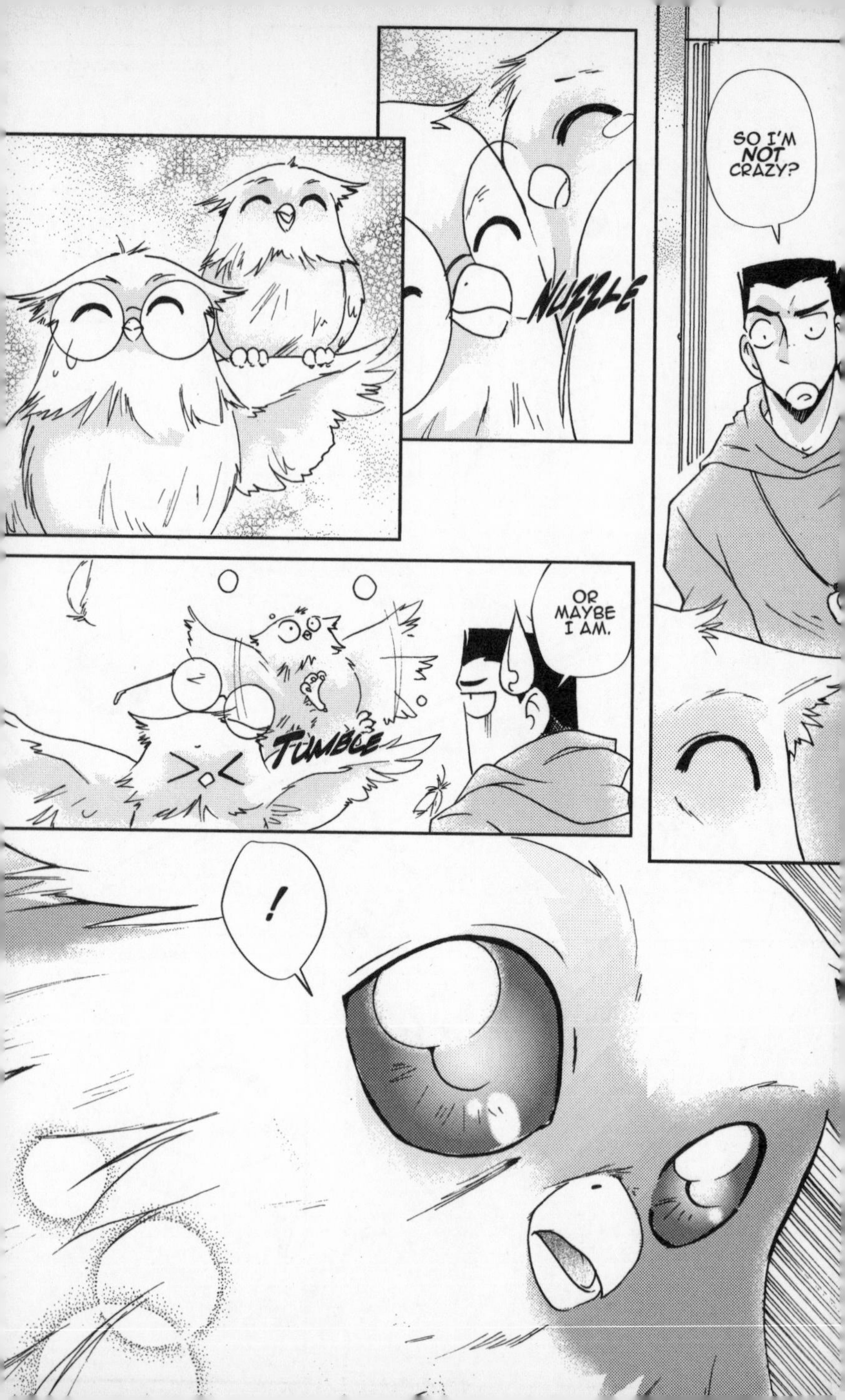
SO I'M NOT CRAZY?
NUZZLE
OR MAYBE I AM.
TUMBLE
!

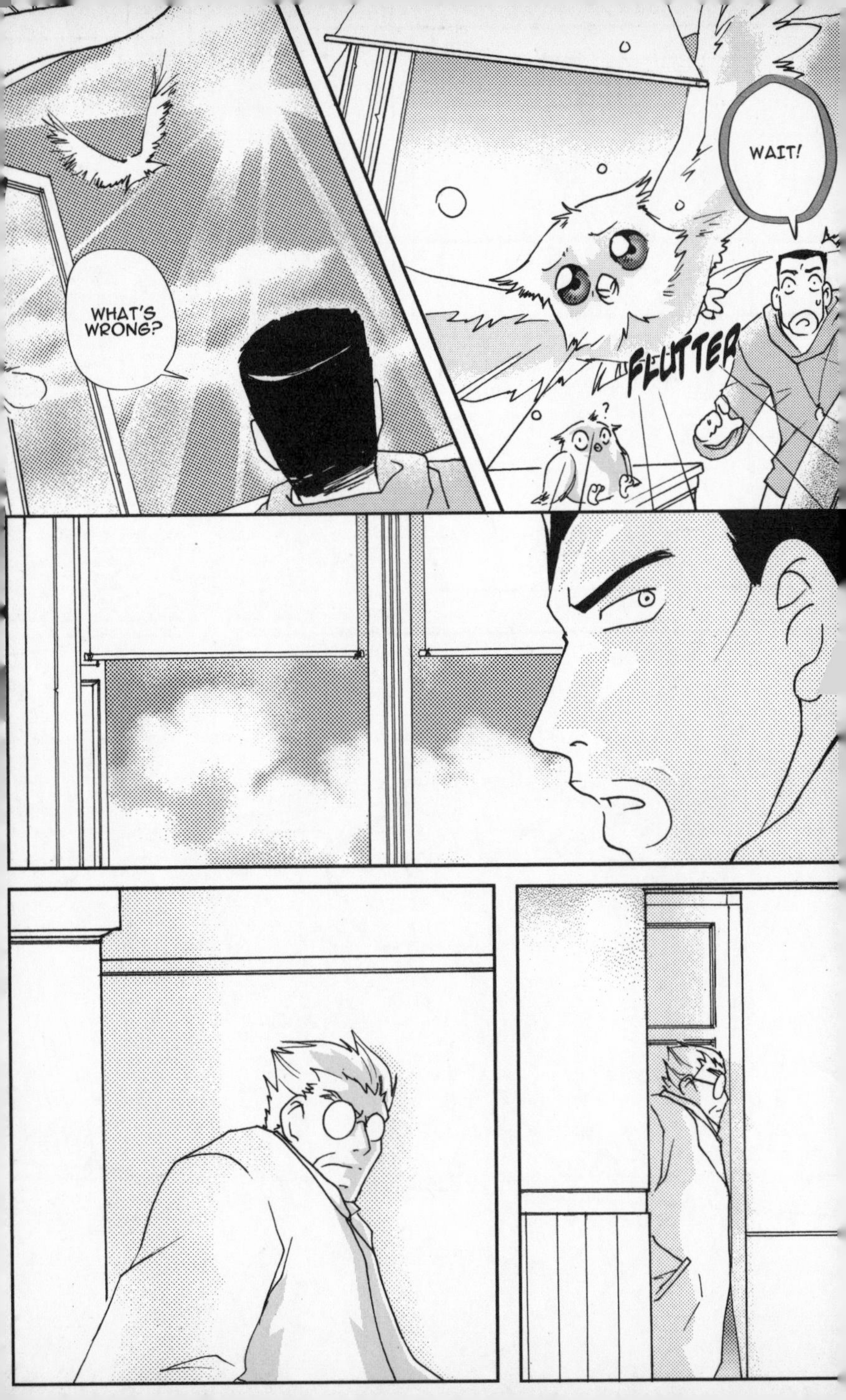
WAIT!
FLUTTER
WHAT'S WRONG?

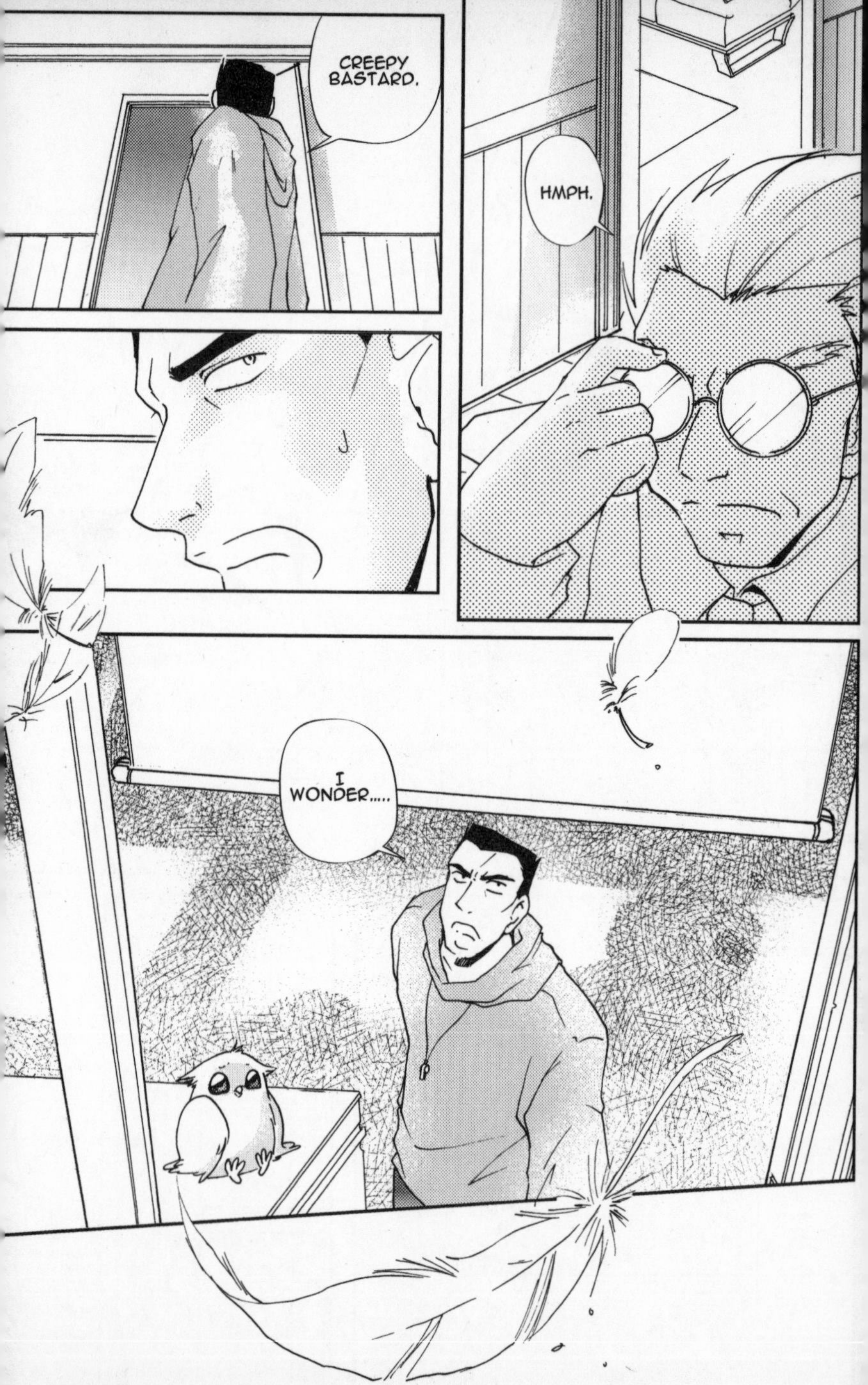
HMPH.
CREEPY BASTARD.
I WONDER.....

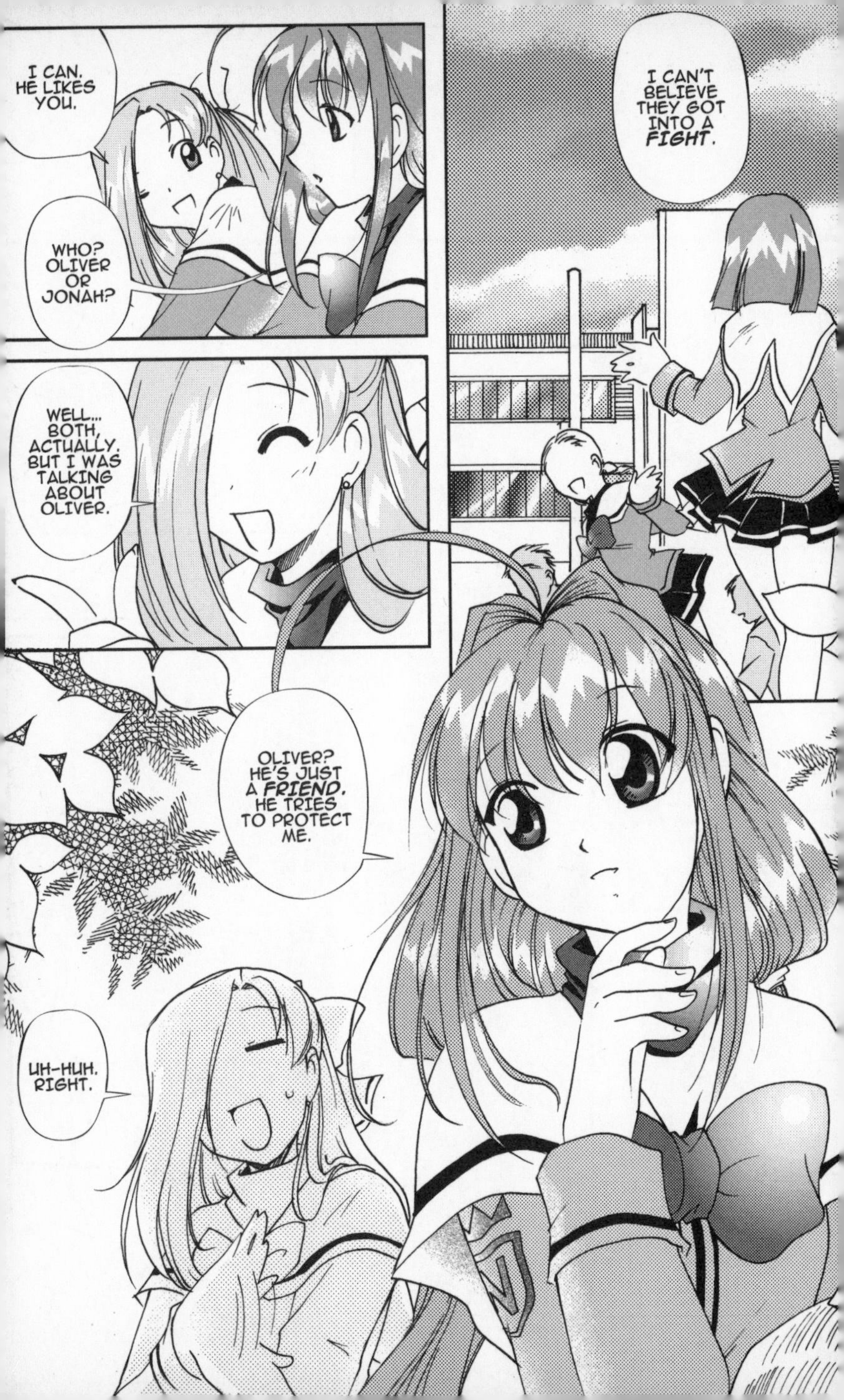
I CAN'T BELIEVE THEY GOT INTO A *FIGHT*.
I CAN. HE LIKES YOU.
WHO? OLIVER OR JONAH?
WELL... BOTH, ACTUALLY. BUT I WAS TALKING ABOUT OLIVER.
OLIVER? HE'S JUST A *FRIEND*. HE TRIES TO PROTECT ME.
UH-HUH. RIGHT.

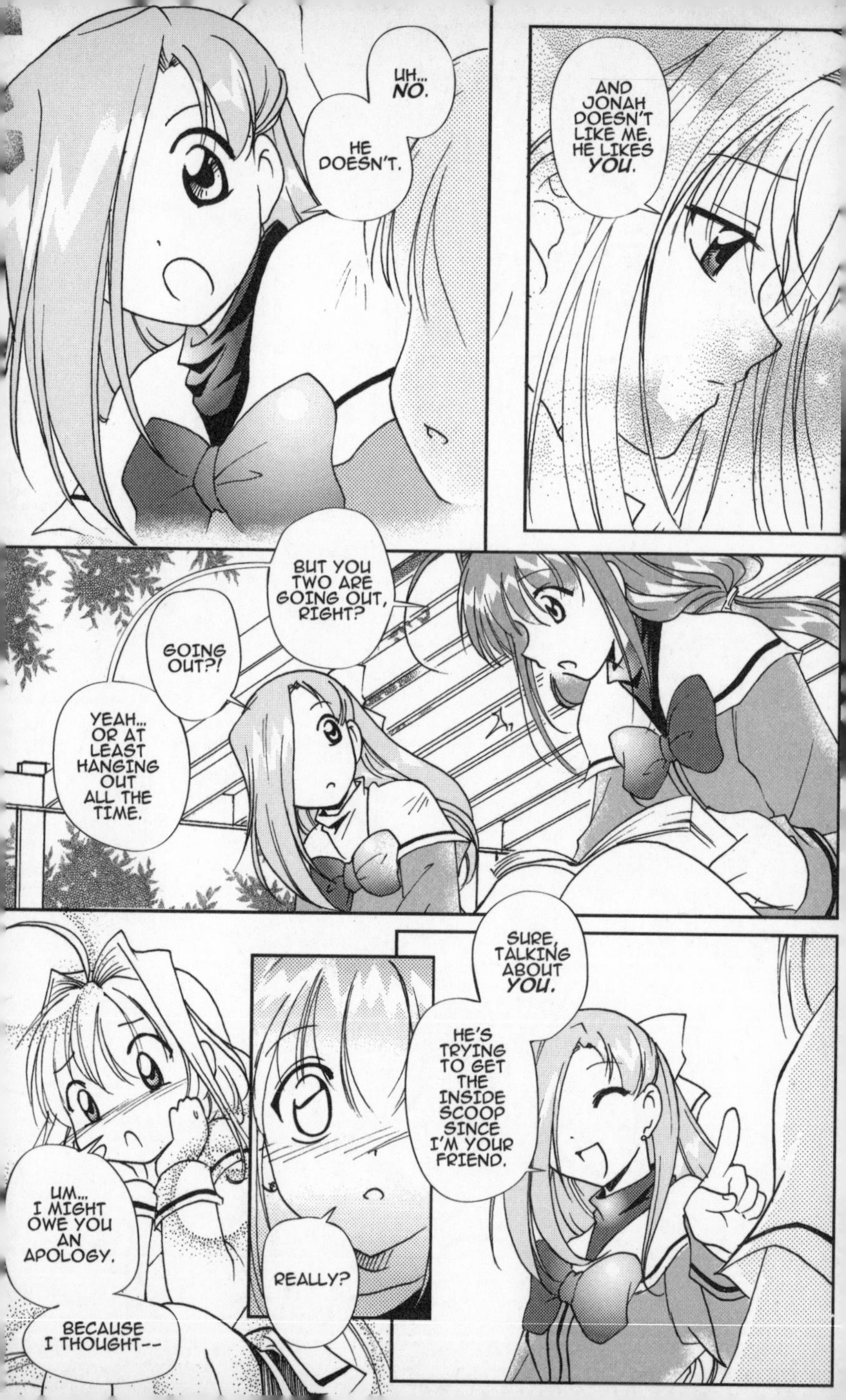
AND JONAH DOESN'T LIKE ME. HE LIKES *YOU*.
UH... *NO*.
HE DOESN'T.
BUT YOU TWO ARE GOING OUT, RIGHT?
GOING OUT?!
YEAH... OR AT LEAST HANGING OUT ALL THE TIME.
SURE, TALKING ABOUT *YOU*.
HE'S TRYING TO GET THE INSIDE SCOOP SINCE I'M YOUR FRIEND.
REALLY?
UM... I MIGHT OWE YOU AN APOLOGY.
BECAUSE I THOUGHT--

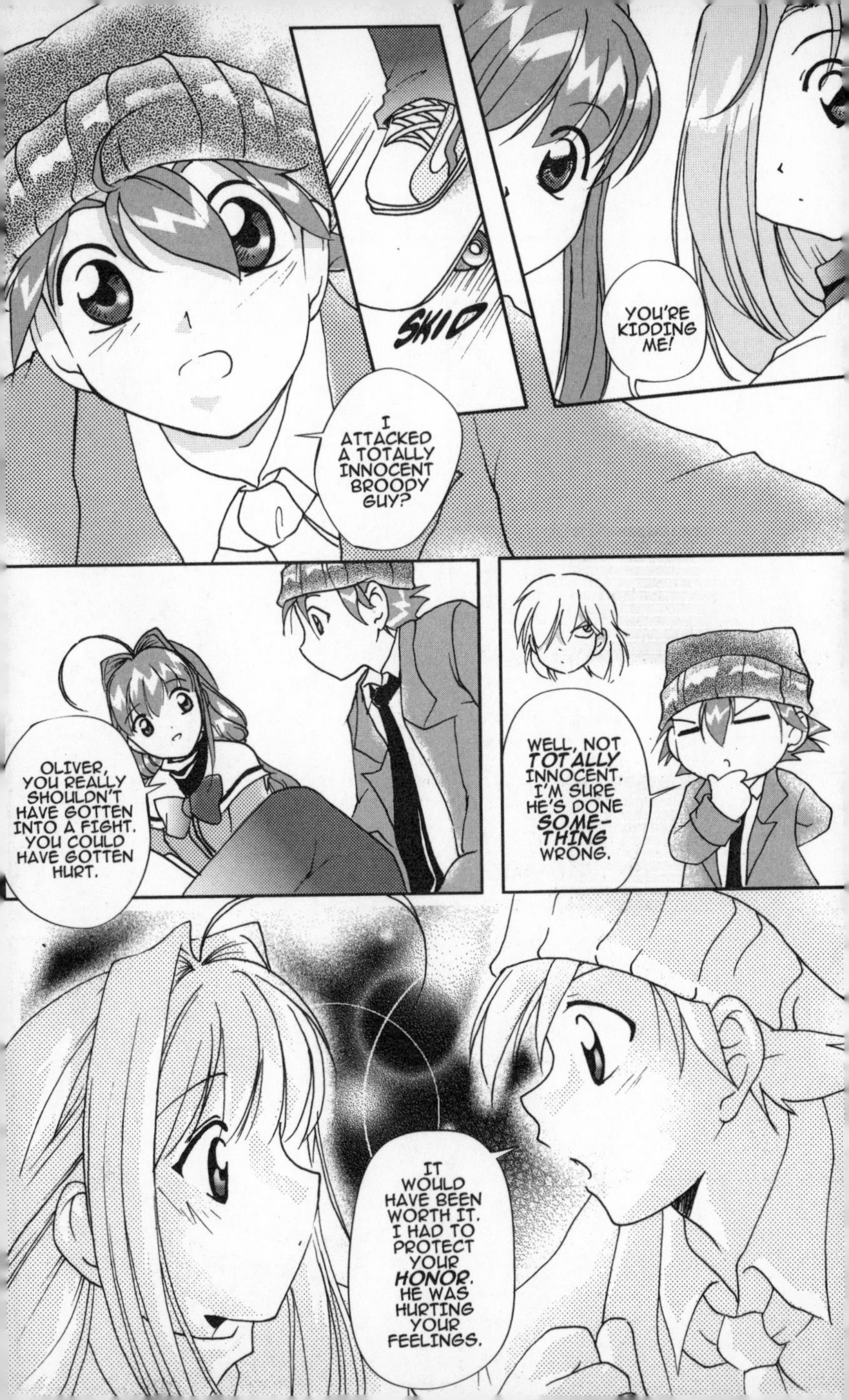

YOU'RE KIDDING ME!
SKID
I ATTACKED A TOTALLY INNOCENT BROODY GUY?
WELL, NOT *TOTALLY* INNOCENT. I'M SURE HE'S DONE ***SOME-THING*** WRONG.
OLIVER, YOU REALLY SHOULDN'T HAVE GOTTEN INTO A FIGHT. YOU COULD HAVE GOTTEN HURT.
IT WOULD HAVE BEEN WORTH IT. I HAD TO PROTECT YOUR ***HONOR***. HE WAS HURTING YOUR FEELINGS.

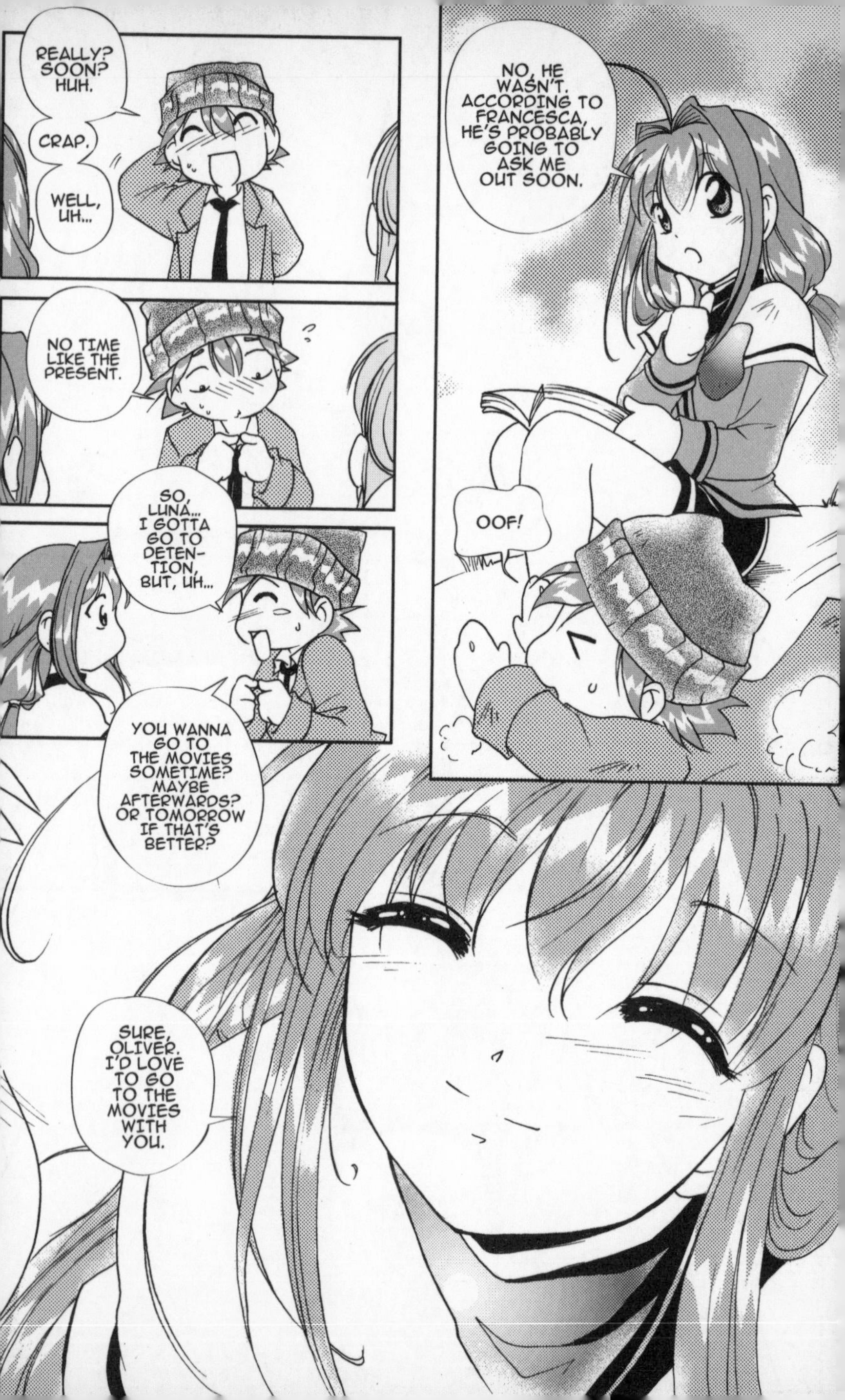
NO, HE WASN'T. ACCORDING TO FRANCESCA, HE'S PROBABLY GOING TO ASK ME OUT SOON.
OOF!
REALLY? SOON? HUH.
CRAP.
WELL, UH...
NO TIME LIKE THE PRESENT.
SO, LUNA... I GOTTA GO TO DETEN-TION, BUT, UH...
YOU WANNA GO TO THE MOVIES SOMETIME? MAYBE AFTERWARDS? OR TOMORROW IF THAT'S BETTER?
SURE, OLIVER. I'D LOVE TO GO TO THE MOVIES WITH YOU.

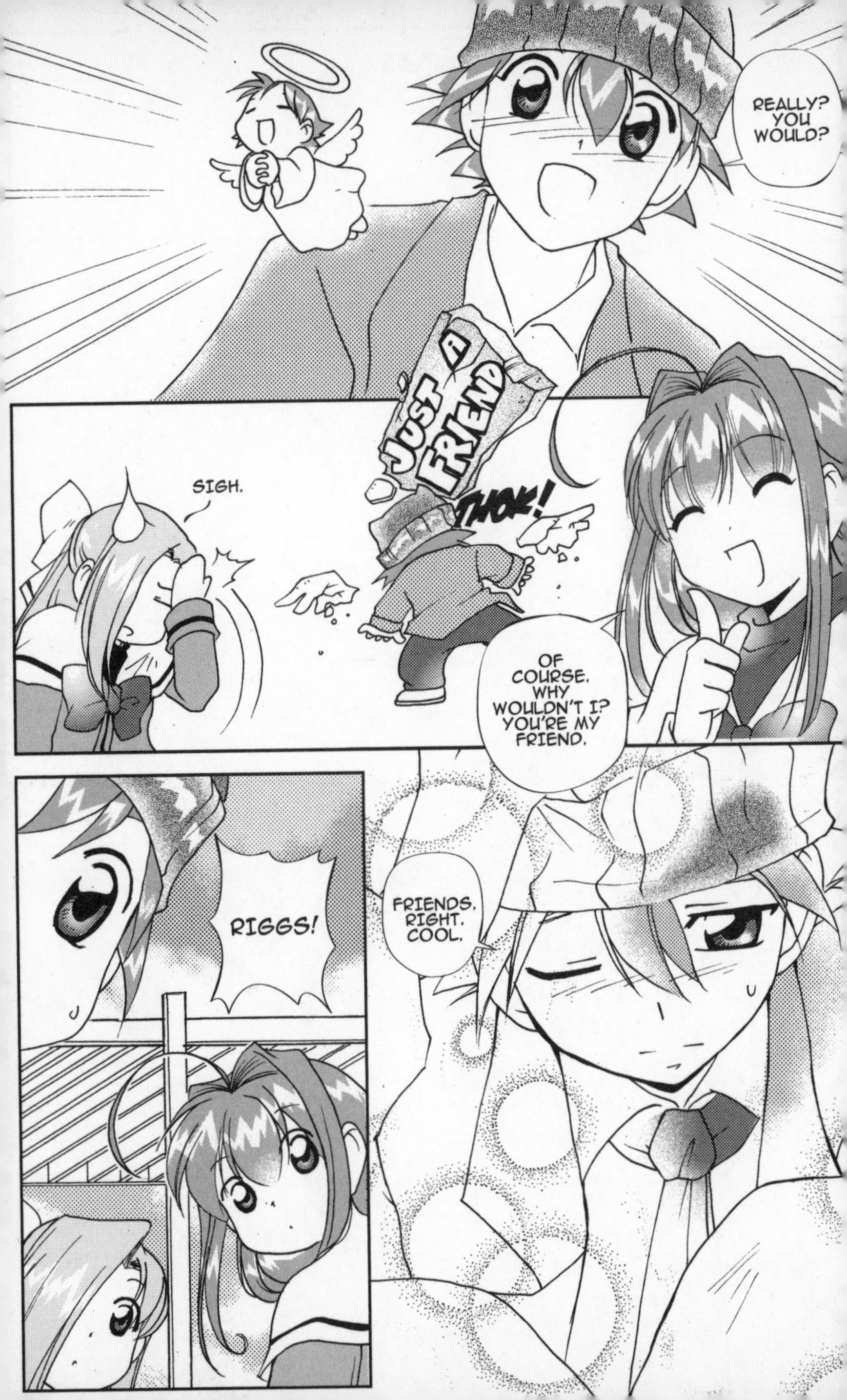
REALLY? YOU WOULD?
OF COURSE. WHY WOULDN'T I? YOU'RE MY FRIEND.
JUST A FRIEND
THOK!
SIGH.
FRIENDS. RIGHT. COOL.
RIGGS!

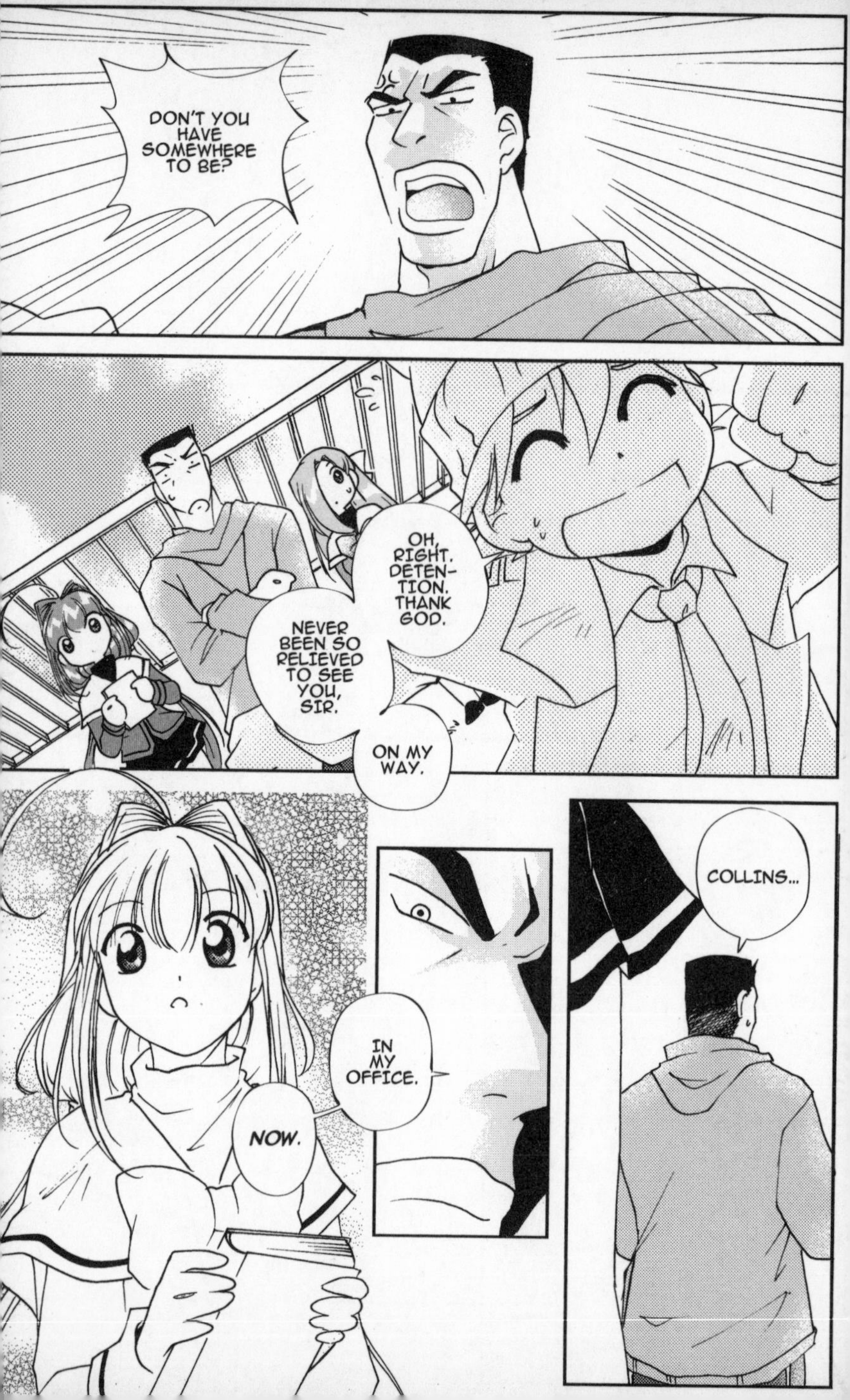
DON'T YOU HAVE SOMEWHERE TO BE?
OH, RIGHT. DETEN-TION. THANK GOD.
NEVER BEEN SO RELIEVED TO SEE YOU, SIR.
ON MY WAY.
COLLINS...
IN MY OFFICE.
NOW.

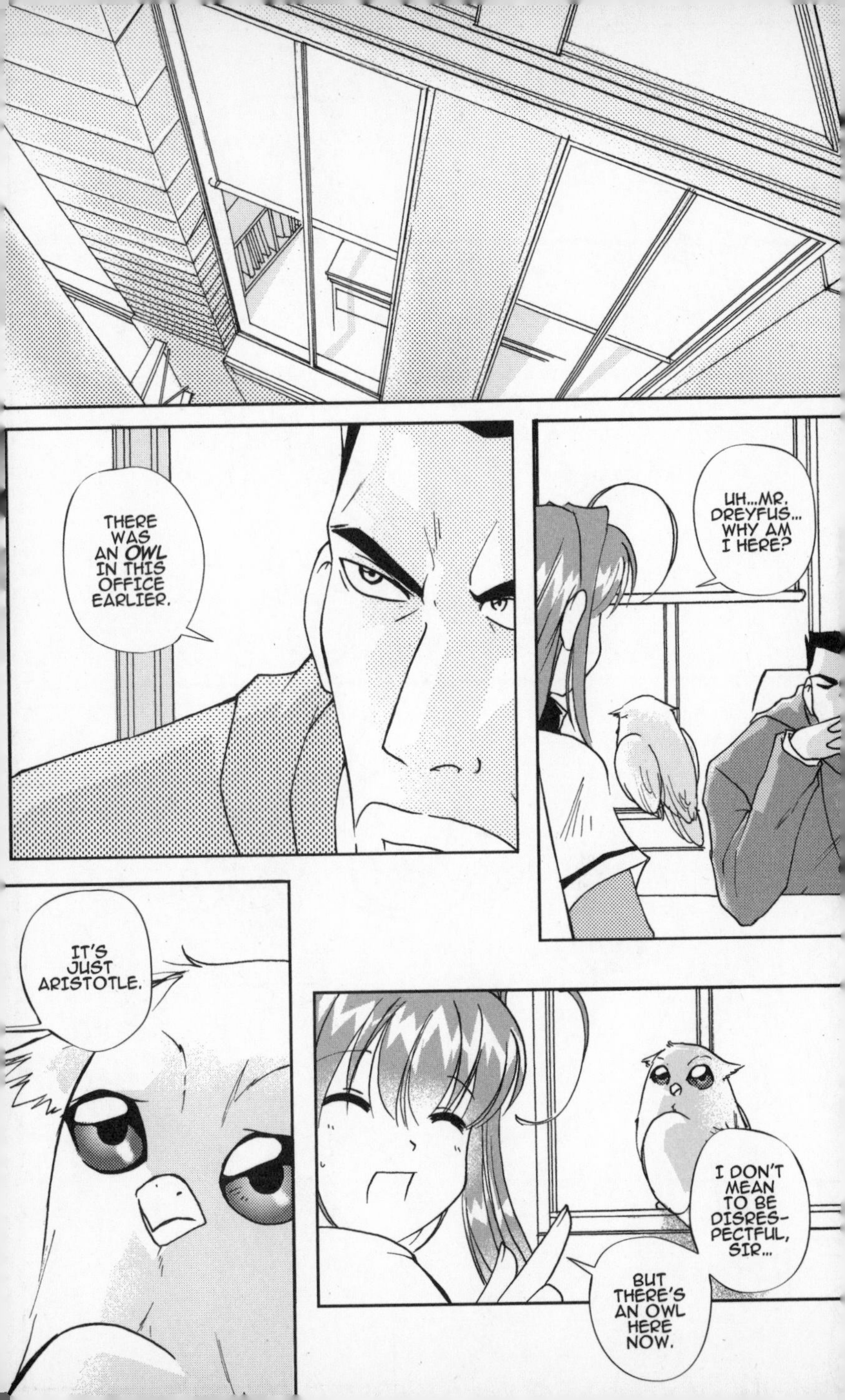
UH...MR. DREYFUS... WHY AM I HERE?
THERE WAS AN *OWL* IN THIS OFFICE EARLIER.
I DON'T MEAN TO BE DISRES-PECTFUL, SIR...
BUT THERE'S AN OWL HERE NOW.
IT'S JUST ARISTOTLE.

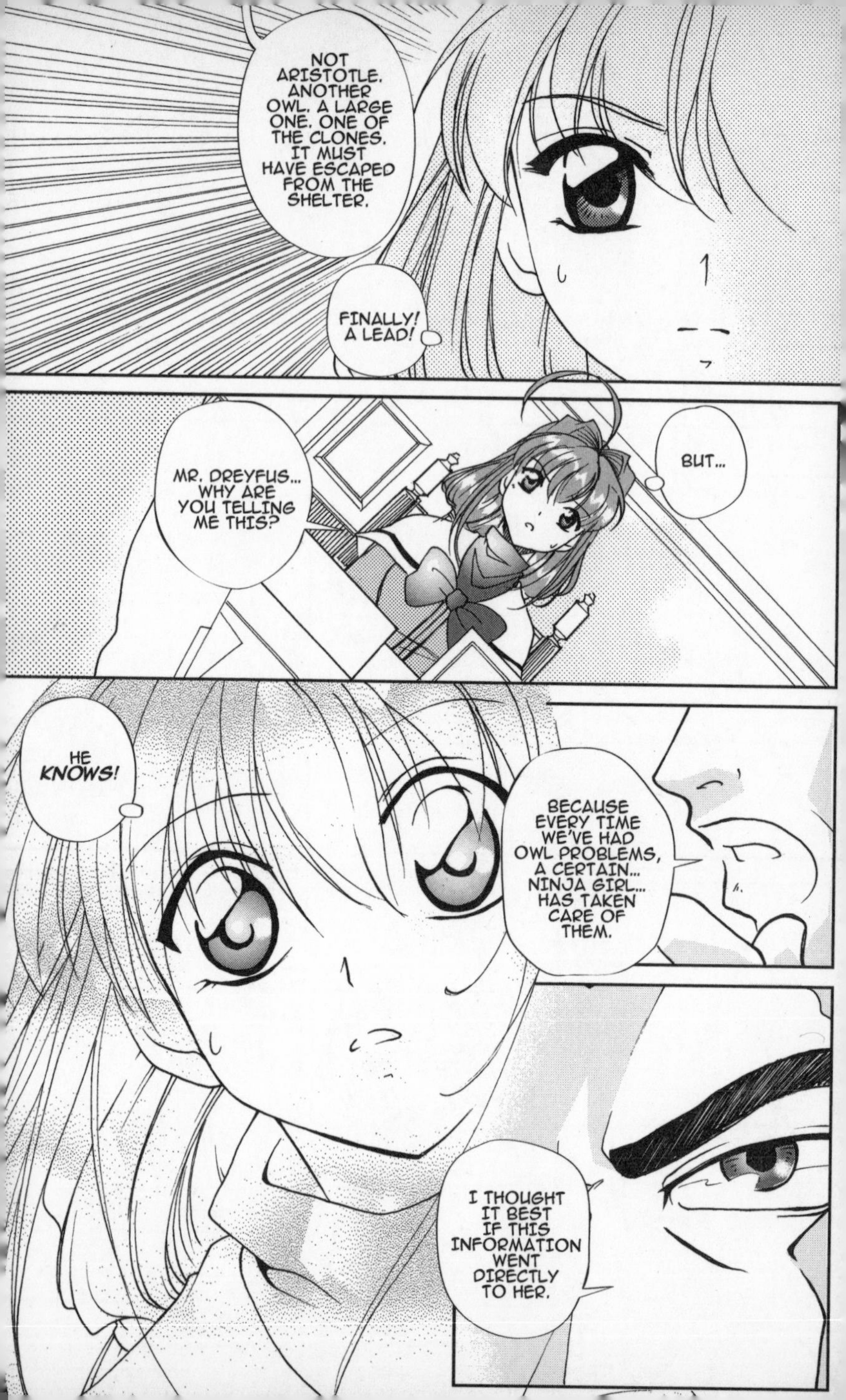
NOT ARISTOTLE. ANOTHER OWL. A LARGE ONE. ONE OF THE CLONES. IT MUST HAVE ESCAPED FROM THE SHELTER.
FINALLY! A LEAD!
BUT...
MR. DREYFUS... WHY ARE YOU TELLING ME THIS?
BECAUSE EVERY TIME WE'VE HAD OWL PROBLEMS, A CERTAIN... NINJA GIRL... HAS TAKEN CARE OF THEM.
I THOUGHT IT BEST IF THIS INFORMATION WENT DIRECTLY TO HER.
HE *KNOWS!*

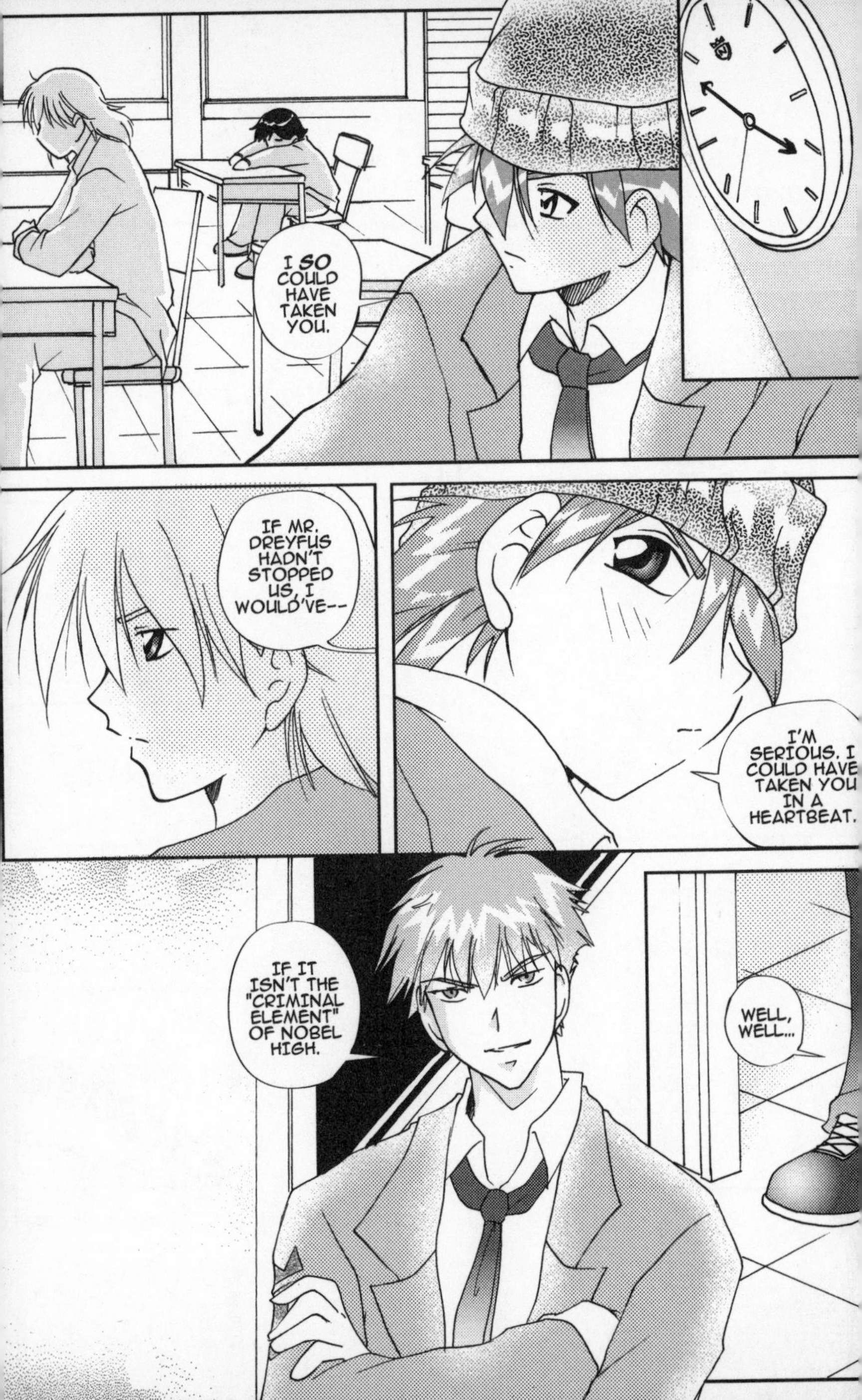
I SO COULD HAVE TAKEN YOU.
I'M SERIOUS. I COULD HAVE TAKEN YOU IN A HEARTBEAT.
IF MR. DREYFUS HADN'T STOPPED US, I WOULD'VE--
WELL, WELL...
IF IT ISN'T THE "CRIMINAL ELEMENT" OF NOBEL HIGH.

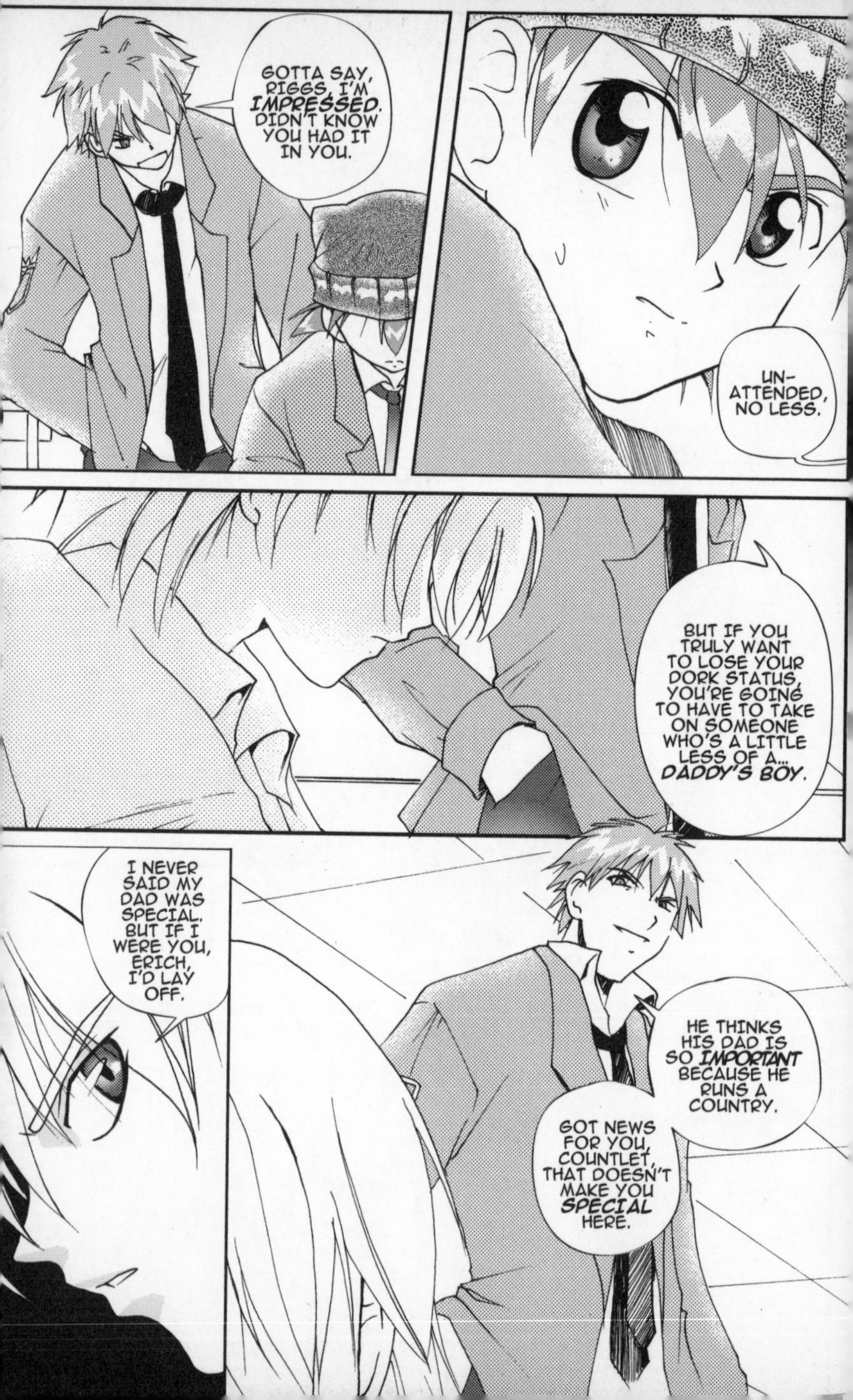
GOTTA SAY, RIGGS, I'M IMPRESSED. DIDN'T KNOW YOU HAD IT IN YOU.
UN-ATTENDED, NO LESS.
BUT IF YOU TRULY WANT TO LOSE YOUR DORK STATUS, YOU'RE GOING TO HAVE TO TAKE ON SOMEONE WHO'S A LITTLE LESS OF A... DADDY'S BOY.
HE THINKS HIS DAD IS SO IMPORTANT BECAUSE HE RUNS A COUNTRY.
GOT NEWS FOR YOU, COUNTLET, THAT DOESN'T MAKE YOU SPECIAL HERE.
I NEVER SAID MY DAD WAS SPECIAL. BUT IF I WERE YOU, ERICH, I'D LAY OFF.

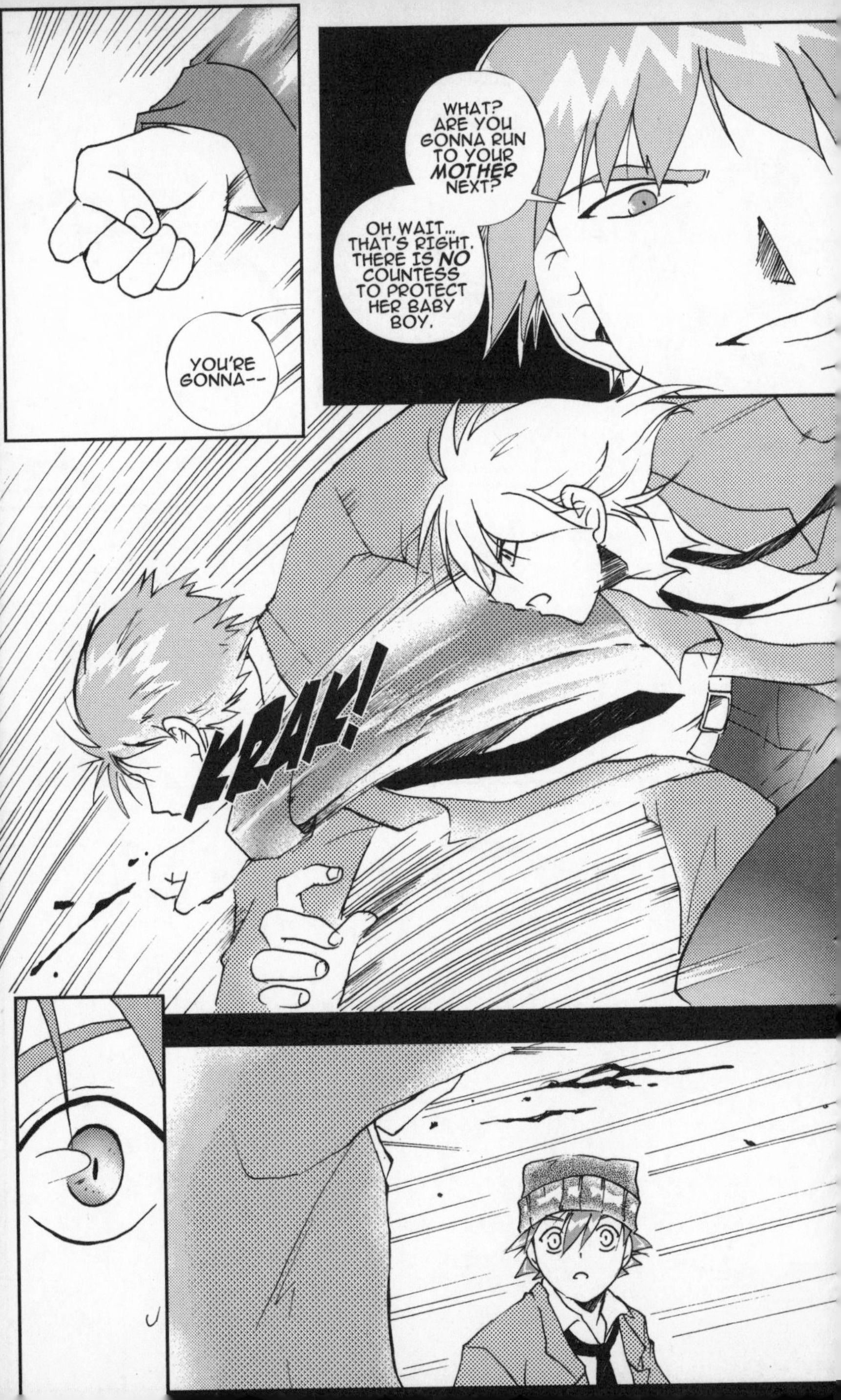
WHAT? ARE YOU GONNA RUN TO YOUR *MOTHER* NEXT?
OH WAIT... THAT'S RIGHT. THERE IS *NO* COUNTESS TO PROTECT HER BABY BOY.
YOU'RE GONNA--
KRAK!

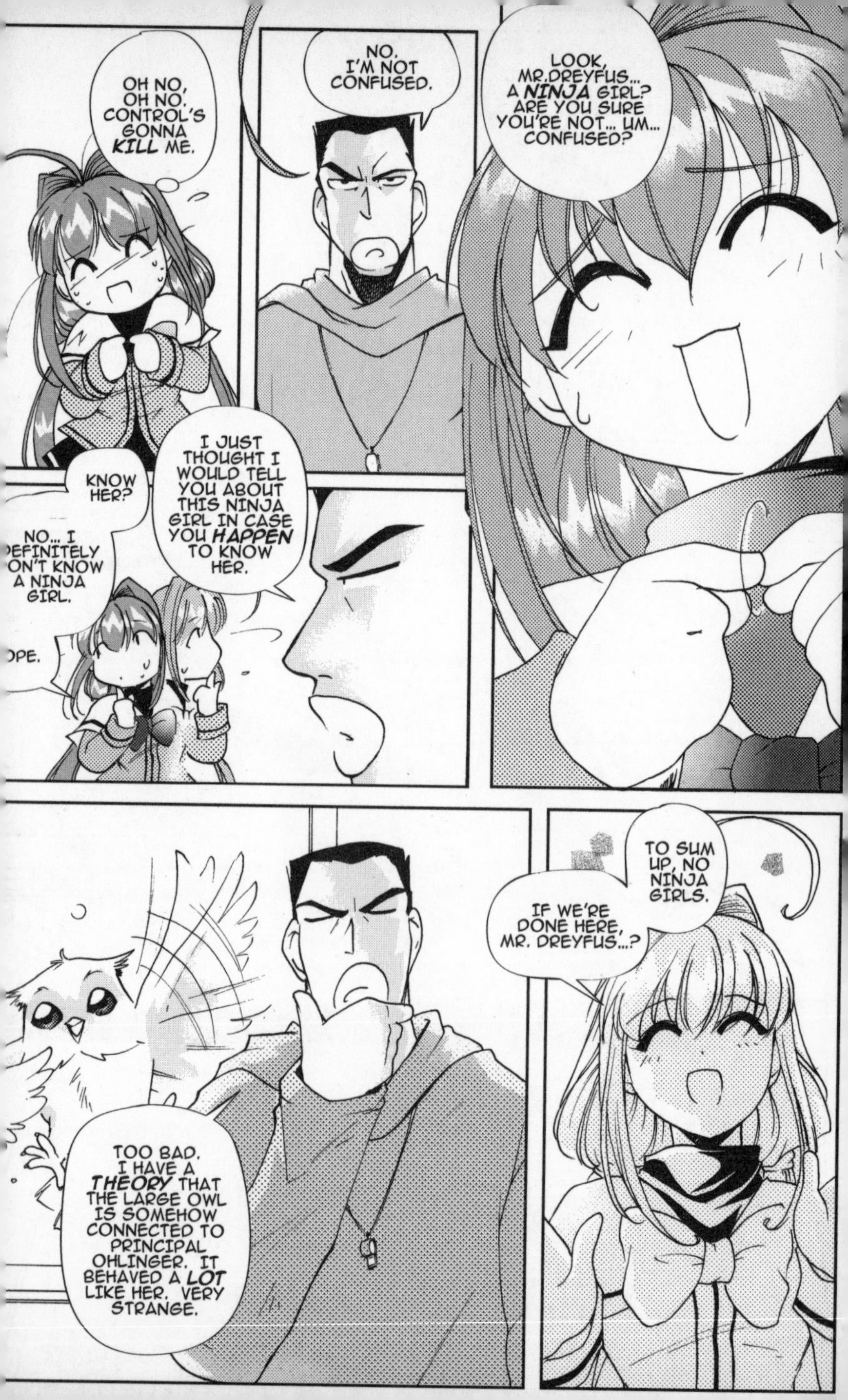
LOOK, MR.DREYFUS... A NINJA GIRL? ARE YOU SURE YOU'RE NOT... UM... CONFUSED?
NO. I'M NOT CONFUSED.
OH NO, OH NO. CONTROL'S GONNA KILL ME.
I JUST THOUGHT I WOULD TELL YOU ABOUT THIS NINJA GIRL IN CASE YOU HAPPEN TO KNOW HER.
KNOW HER?
NO... I DEFINITELY DON'T KNOW A NINJA GIRL.
OPE.
TO SUM UP, NO NINJA GIRLS.
IF WE'RE DONE HERE, MR. DREYFUS...?
TOO BAD. I HAVE A THEORY THAT THE LARGE OWL IS SOMEHOW CONNECTED TO PRINCIPAL OHLINGER. IT BEHAVED A LOT LIKE HER. VERY STRANGE.

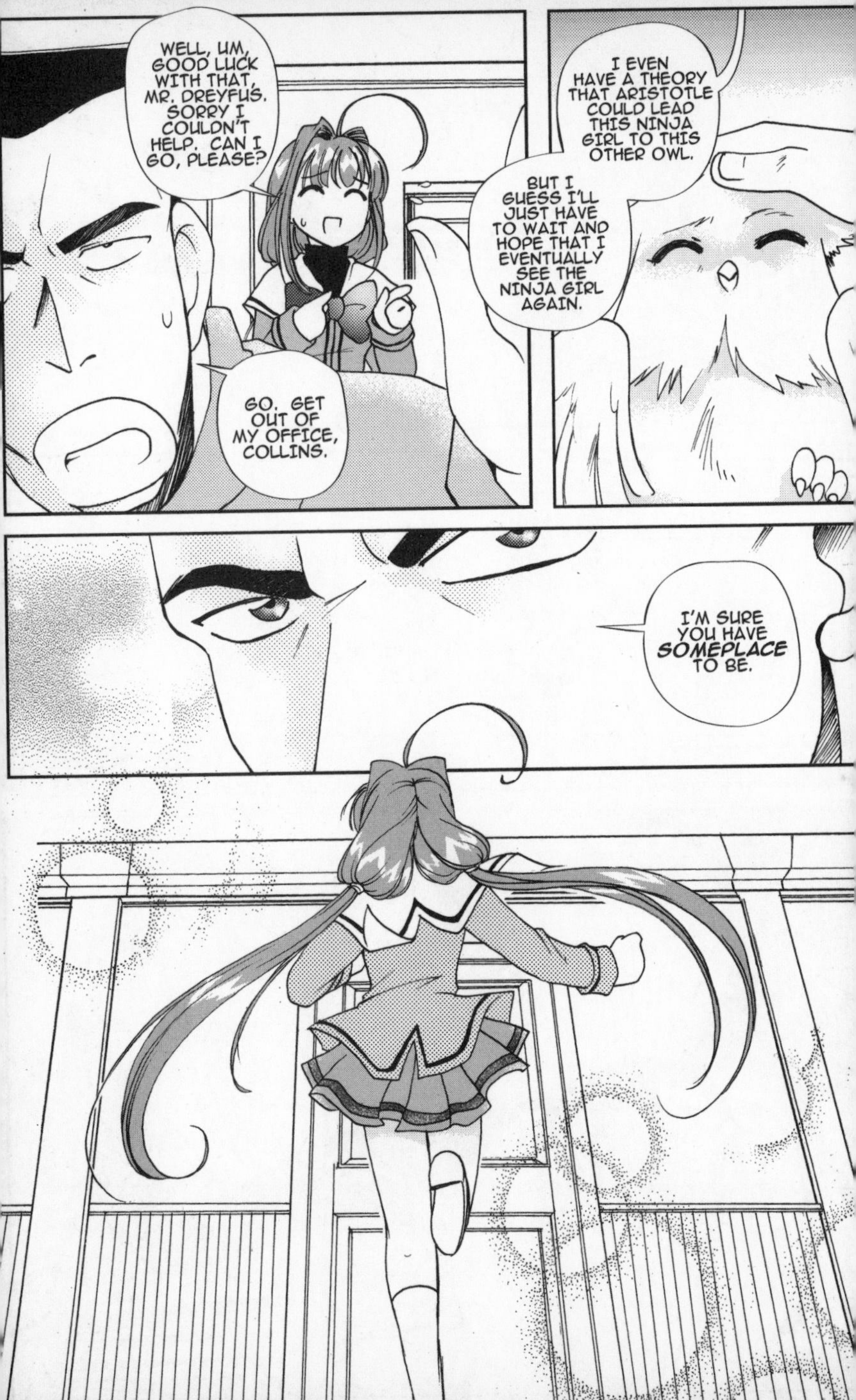
I EVEN HAVE A THEORY THAT ARISTOTLE COULD LEAD THIS NINJA GIRL TO THIS OTHER OWL.
BUT I GUESS I'LL JUST HAVE TO WAIT AND HOPE THAT I EVENTUALLY SEE THE NINJA GIRL AGAIN.
WELL, UM, GOOD LUCK WITH THAT, MR. DREYFUS. SORRY I COULDN'T HELP. CAN I GO, PLEASE?
GO. GET OUT OF MY OFFICE, COLLINS.
I'M SURE YOU HAVE ***SOMEPLACE*** TO BE.

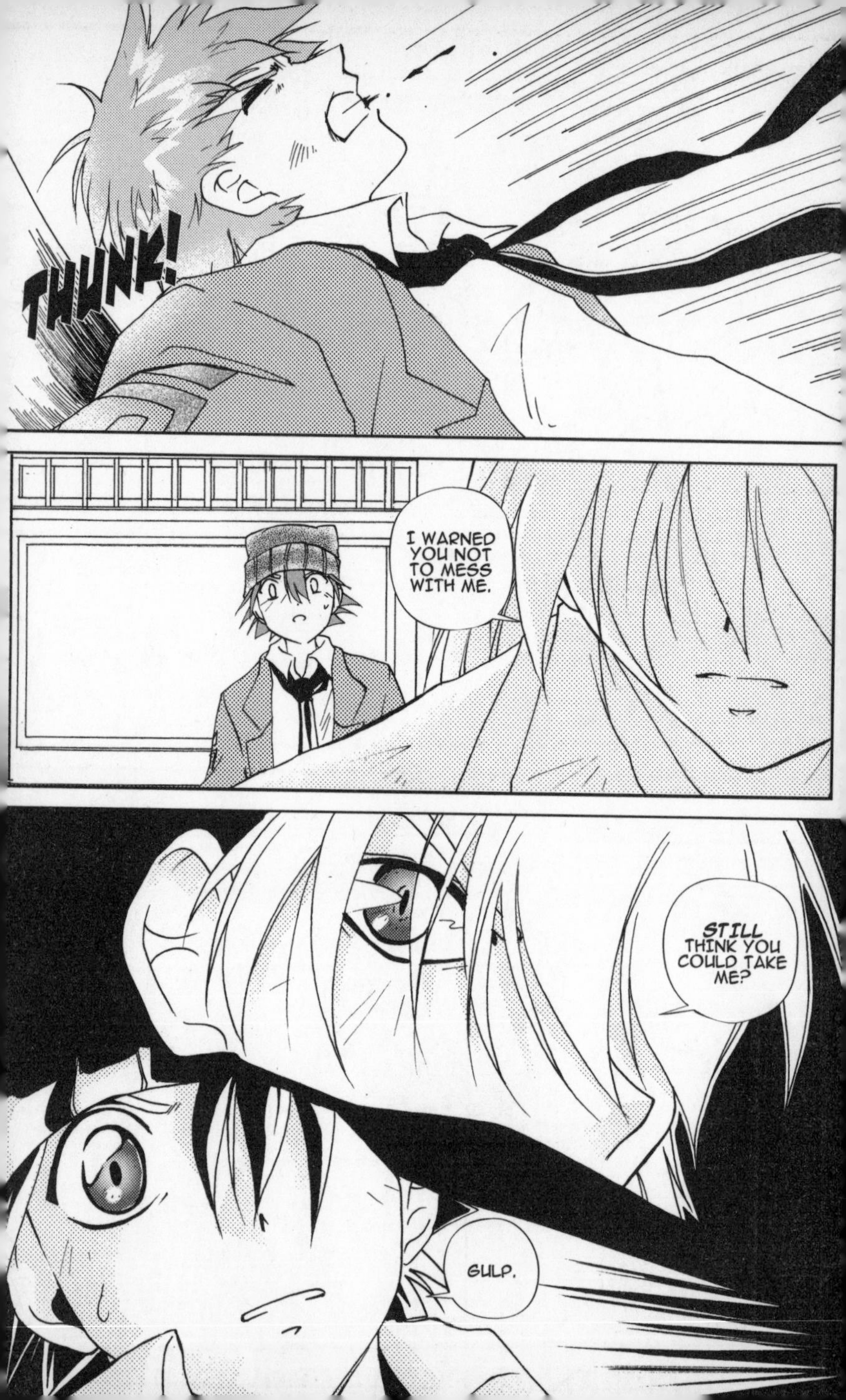

THUNK!
I WARNED YOU NOT TO MESS WITH ME.
STILL THINK YOU COULD TAKE ME?
GULP.

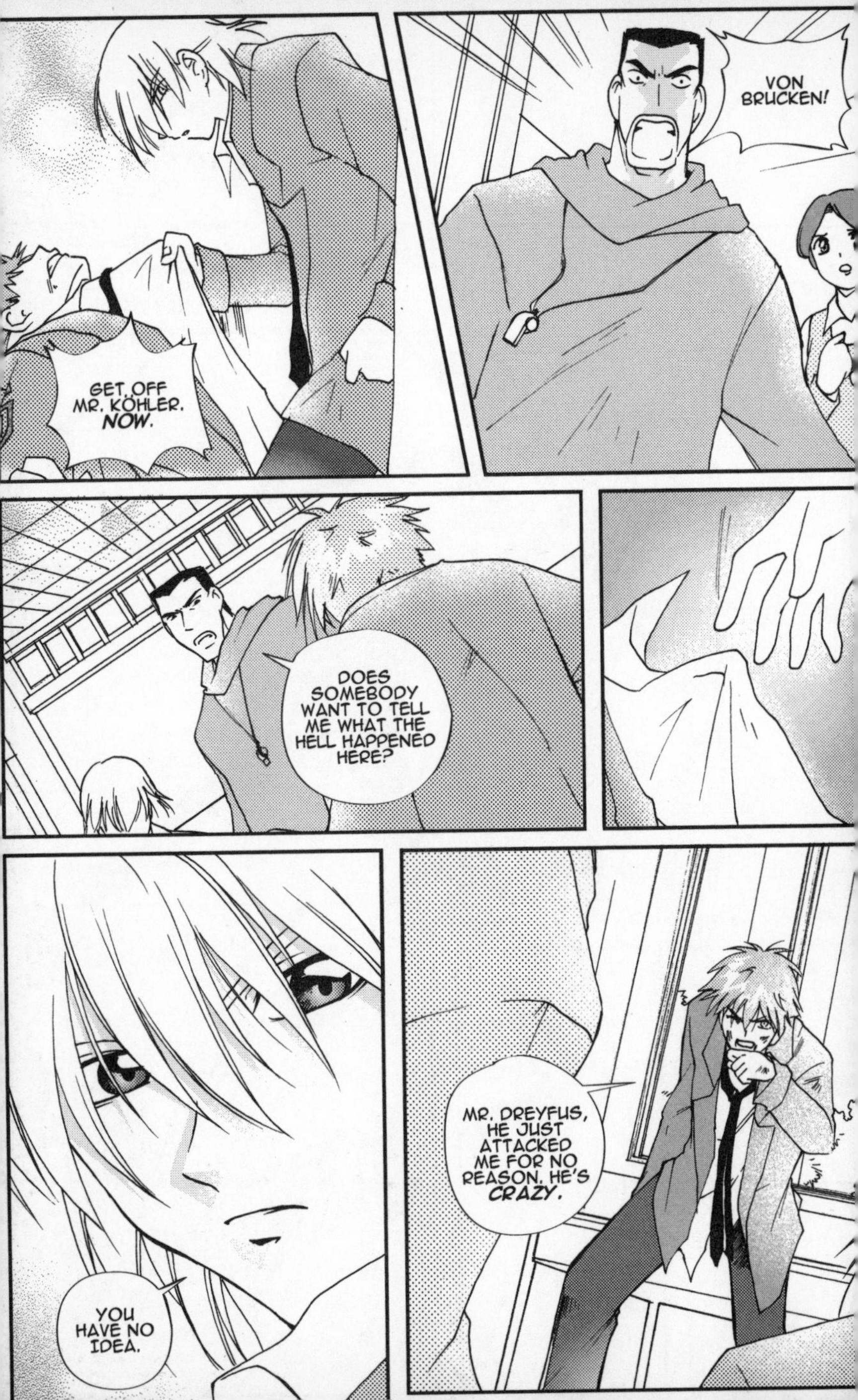
VON BRUCKEN!
GET OFF MR. KÖHLER. NOW.
DOES SOMEBODY WANT TO TELL ME WHAT THE HELL HAPPENED HERE?
MR. DREYFUS, HE JUST ATTACKED ME FOR NO REASON. HE'S CRAZY.
YOU HAVE NO IDEA.

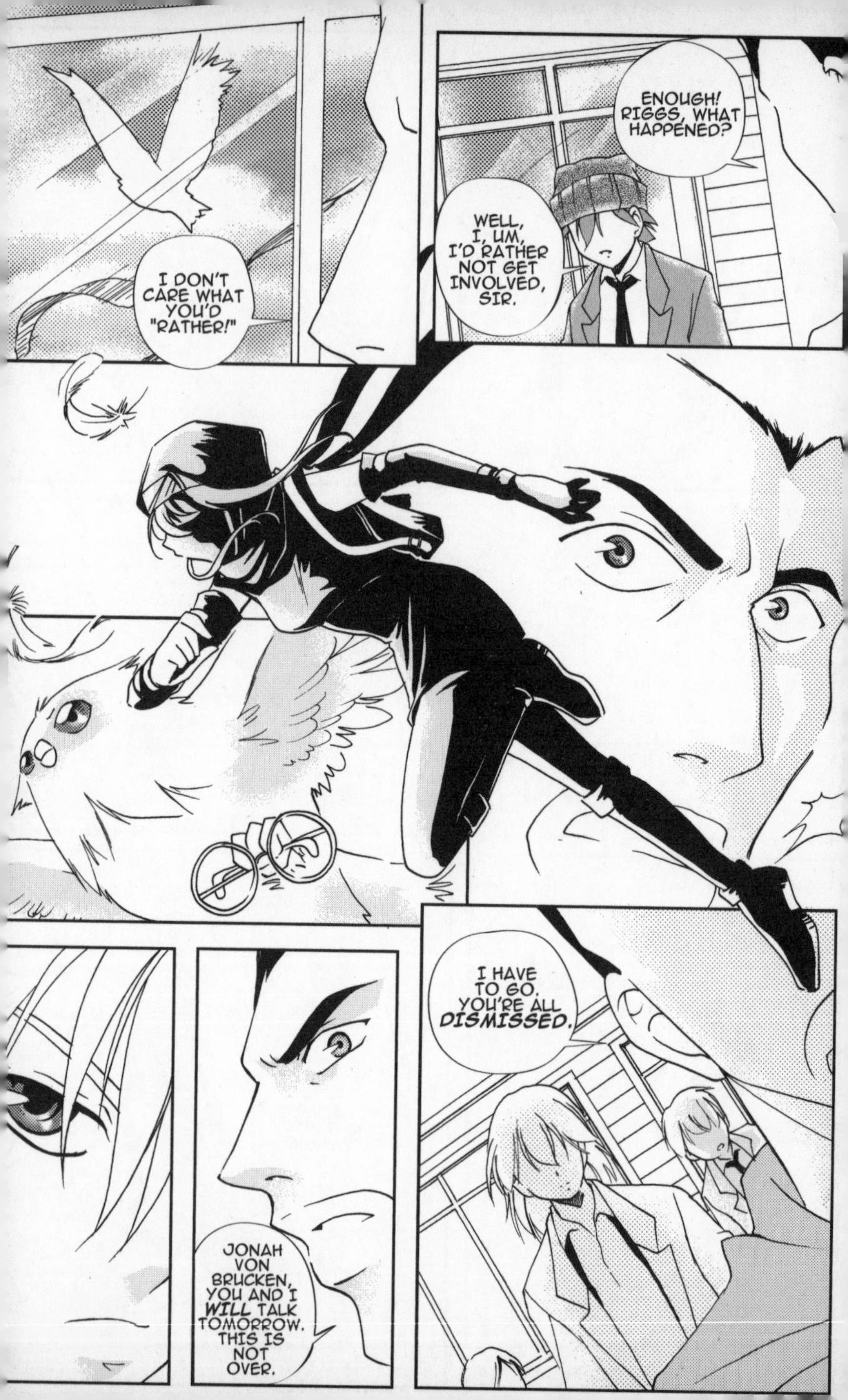
ENOUGH! RIGGS, WHAT HAPPENED?
WELL, I, UM, I'D RATHER NOT GET INVOLVED, SIR.
I DON'T CARE WHAT YOU'D "RATHER!"
I HAVE TO GO. YOU'RE ALL *DISMISSED*.
JONAH VON BRUCKEN, YOU AND I ***WILL*** TALK TOMORROW. THIS IS NOT OVER.

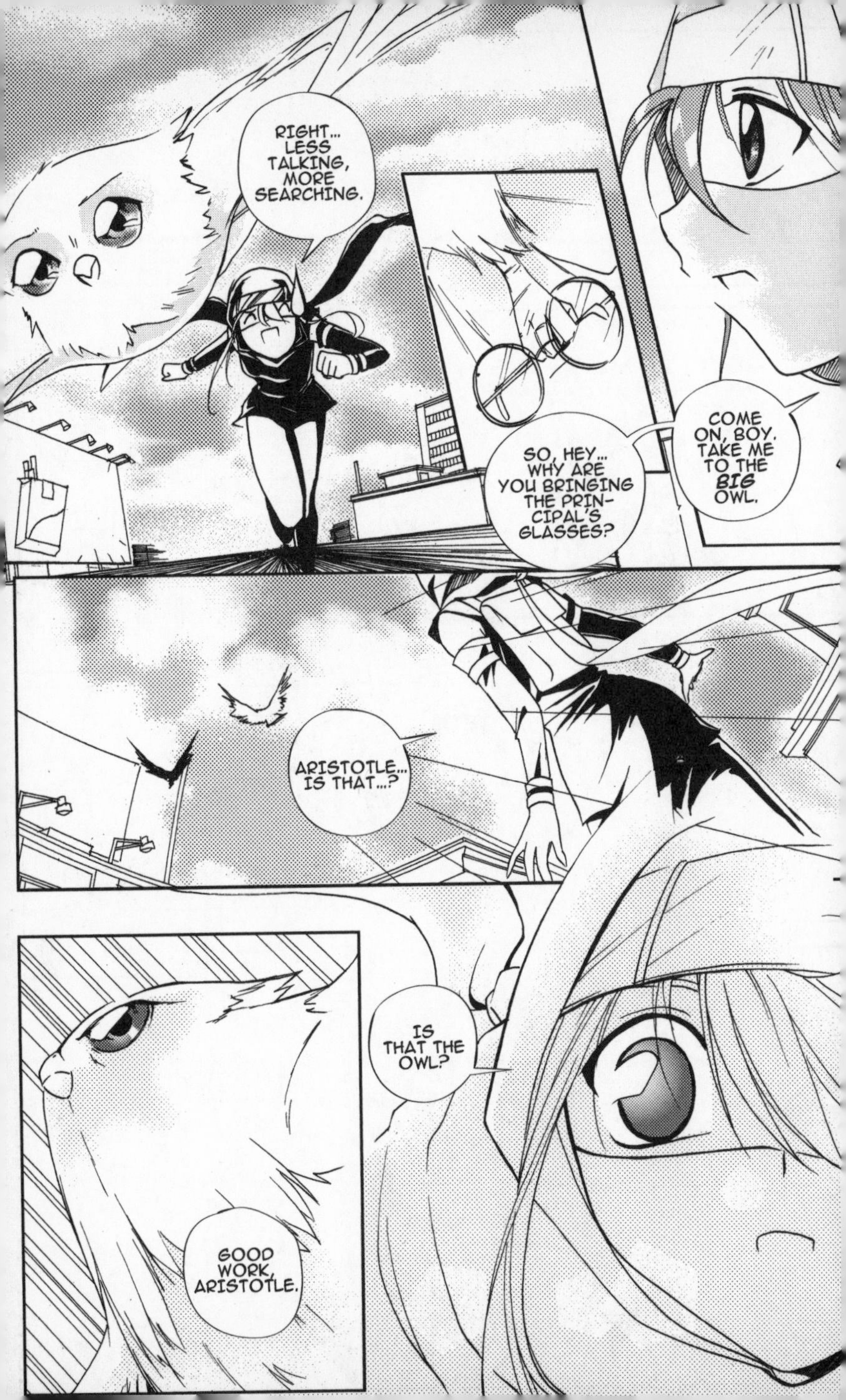
COME ON, BOY. TAKE ME TO THE *BIG* OWL.
SO, HEY... WHY ARE YOU BRINGING THE PRIN-CIPAL'S GLASSES?
RIGHT... LESS TALKING, MORE SEARCHING.
ARISTOTLE... IS THAT...?
IS THAT THE OWL?
GOOD WORK, ARISTOTLE.

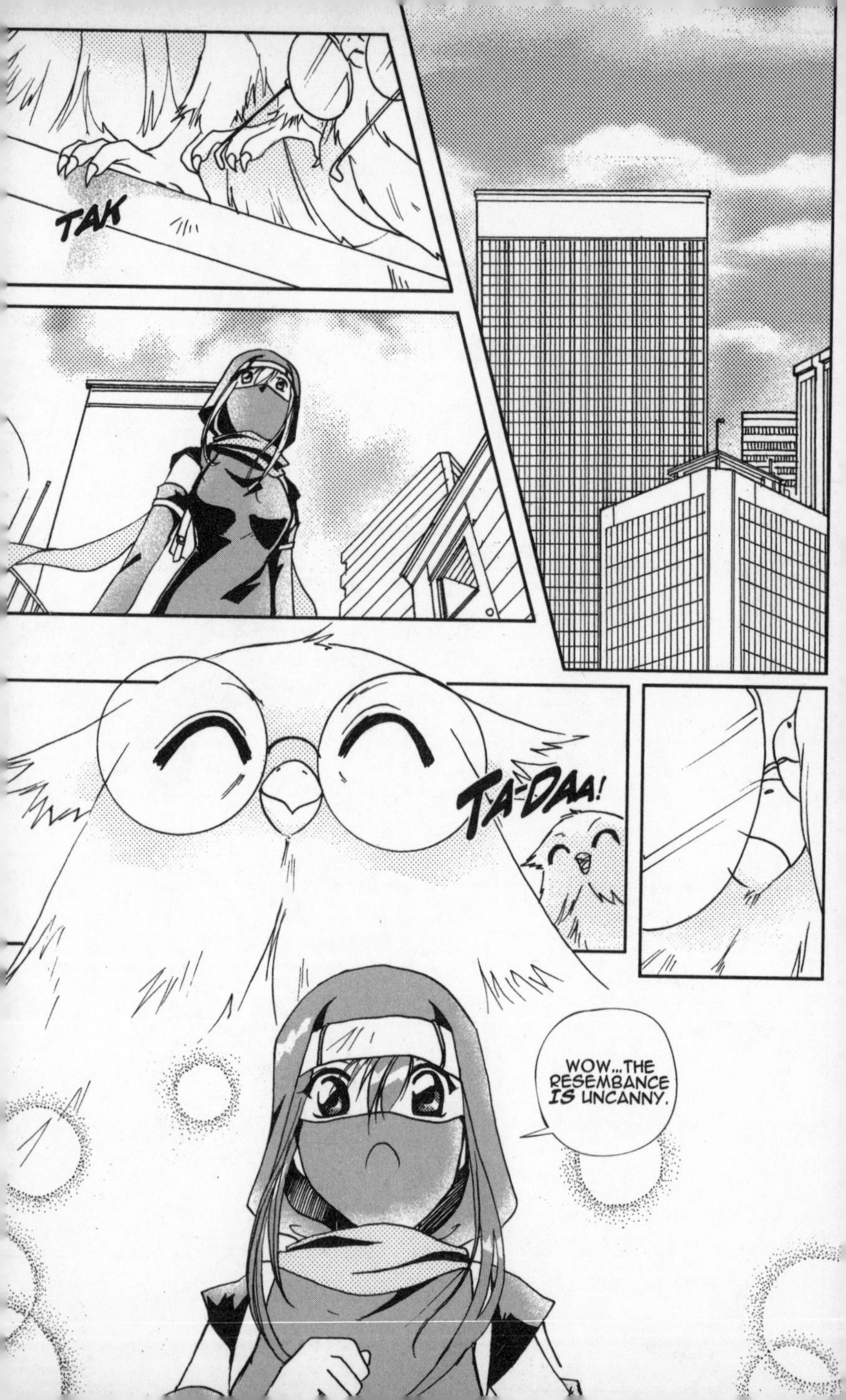
TAK
TA-DAA!
WOW...THE RESEMBANCE IS UNCANNY.

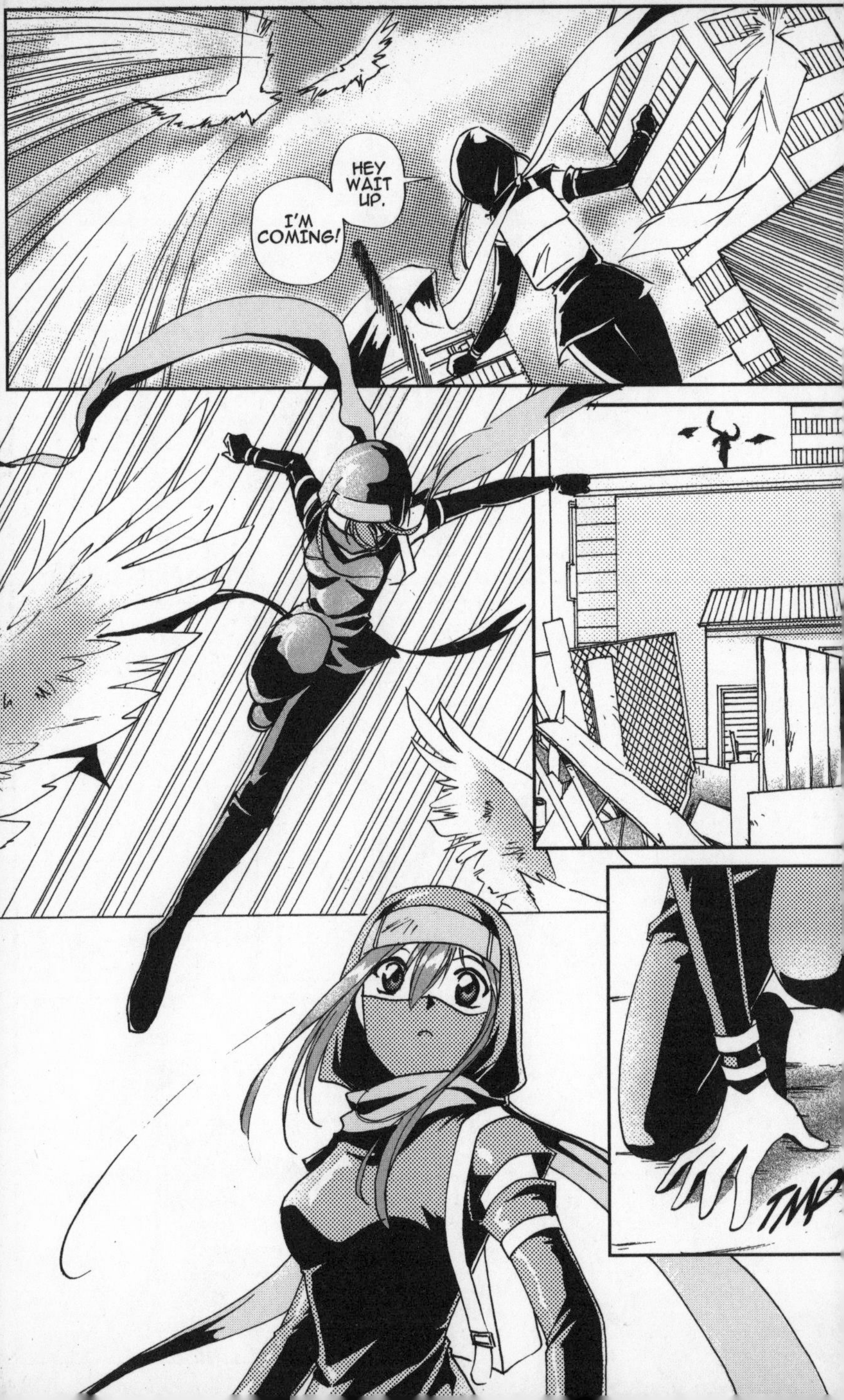
HEY WAIT UP.
I'M COMING!
TMP

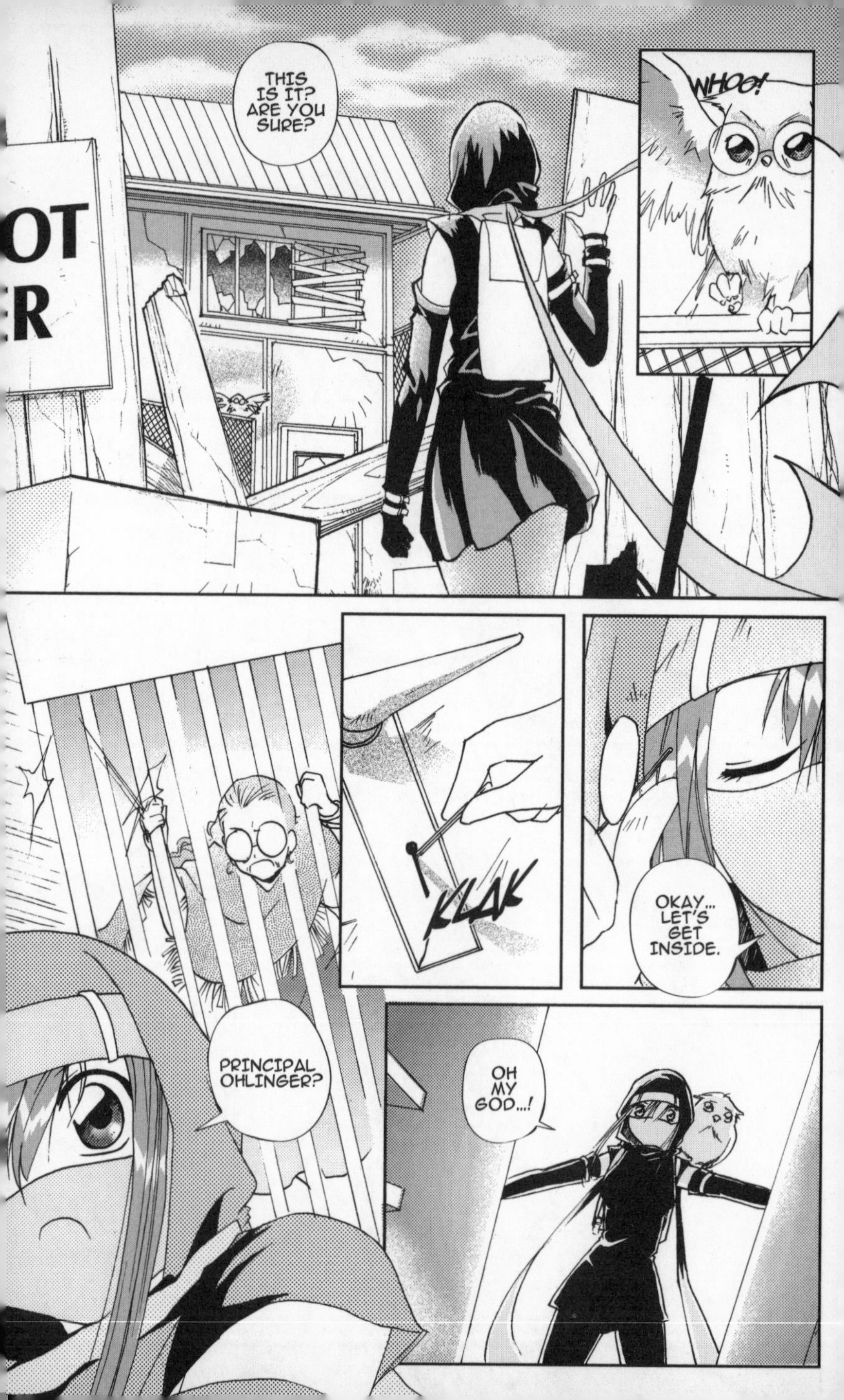
WHOO!
THIS IS IT? ARE YOU SURE?
OKAY... LET'S GET INSIDE.
KLAK
OH MY GOD...!
PRINCIPAL OHLINGER?

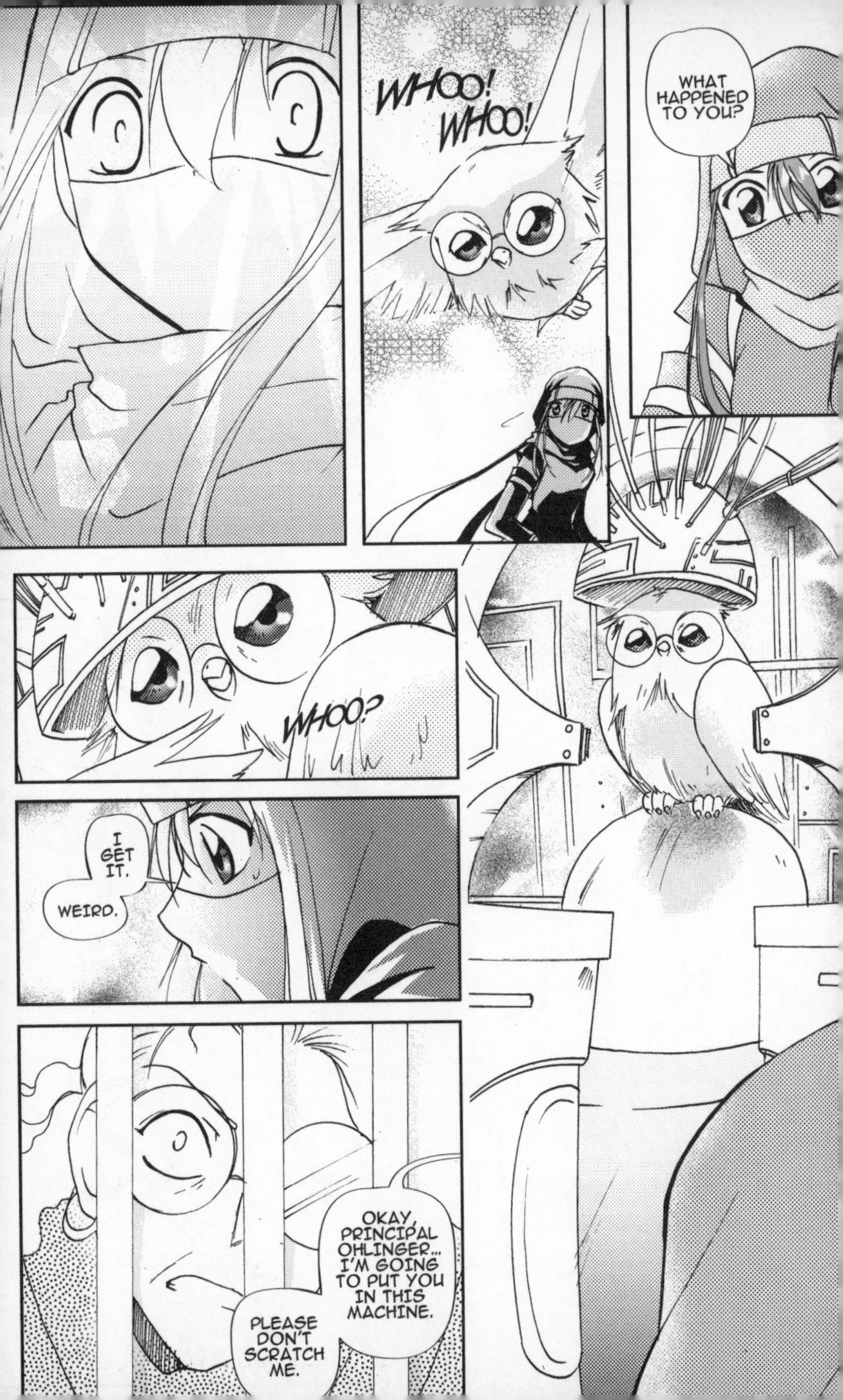
WHAT HAPPENED TO YOU?
WHOO! WHOO!
WHOO?
I GET IT.
WEIRD.
OKAY, PRINCIPAL OHLINGER... I'M GOING TO PUT YOU IN THIS MACHINE.
PLEASE DON'T SCRATCH ME.

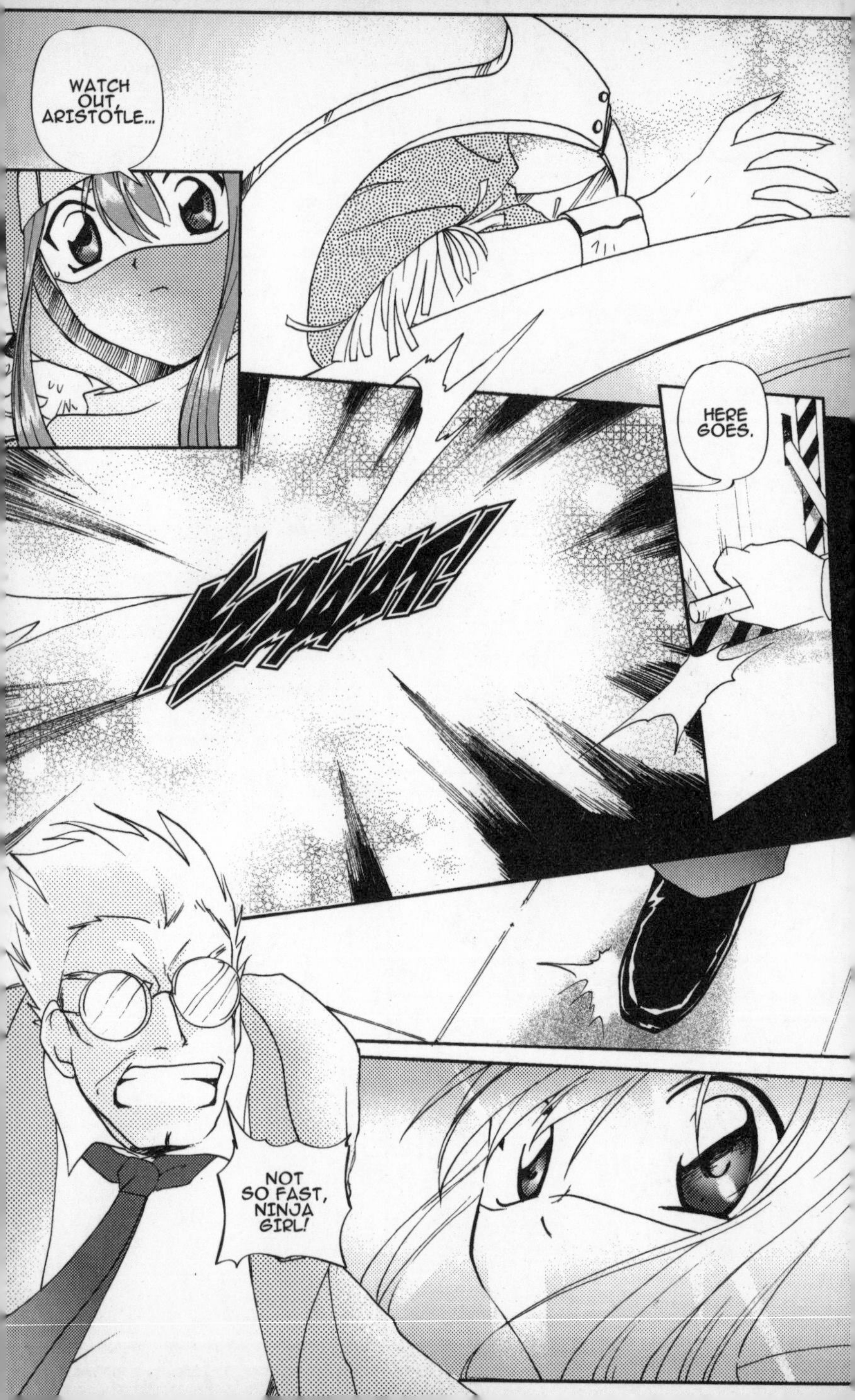
WATCH OUT, ARISTOTLE...
HERE GOES.
NOT SO FAST, NINJA GIRL!

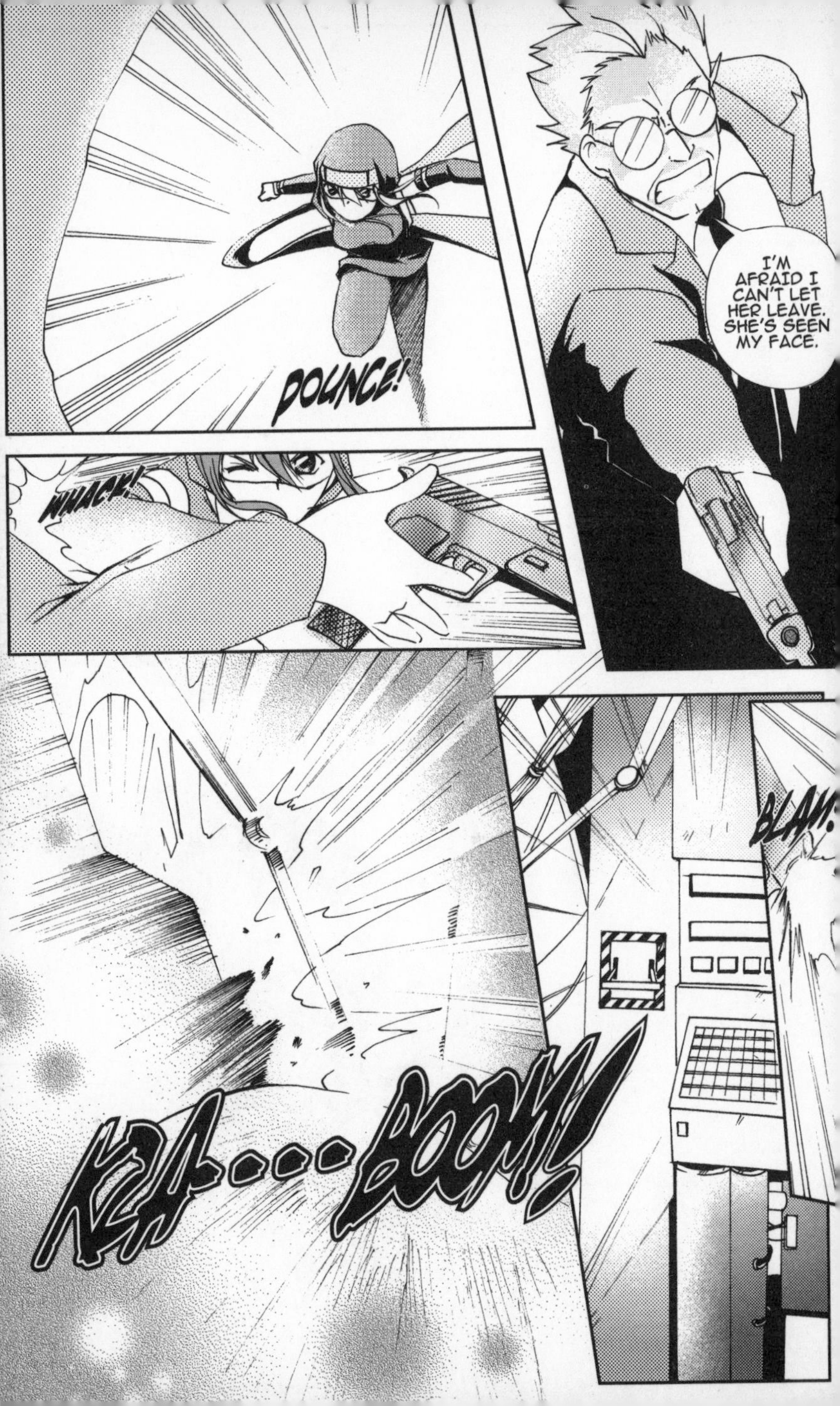
I'M AFRAID I CAN'T LET HER LEAVE. SHE'S SEEN MY FACE.
POUNCE!
WHACK!
BLAM!
KA...BOOM!

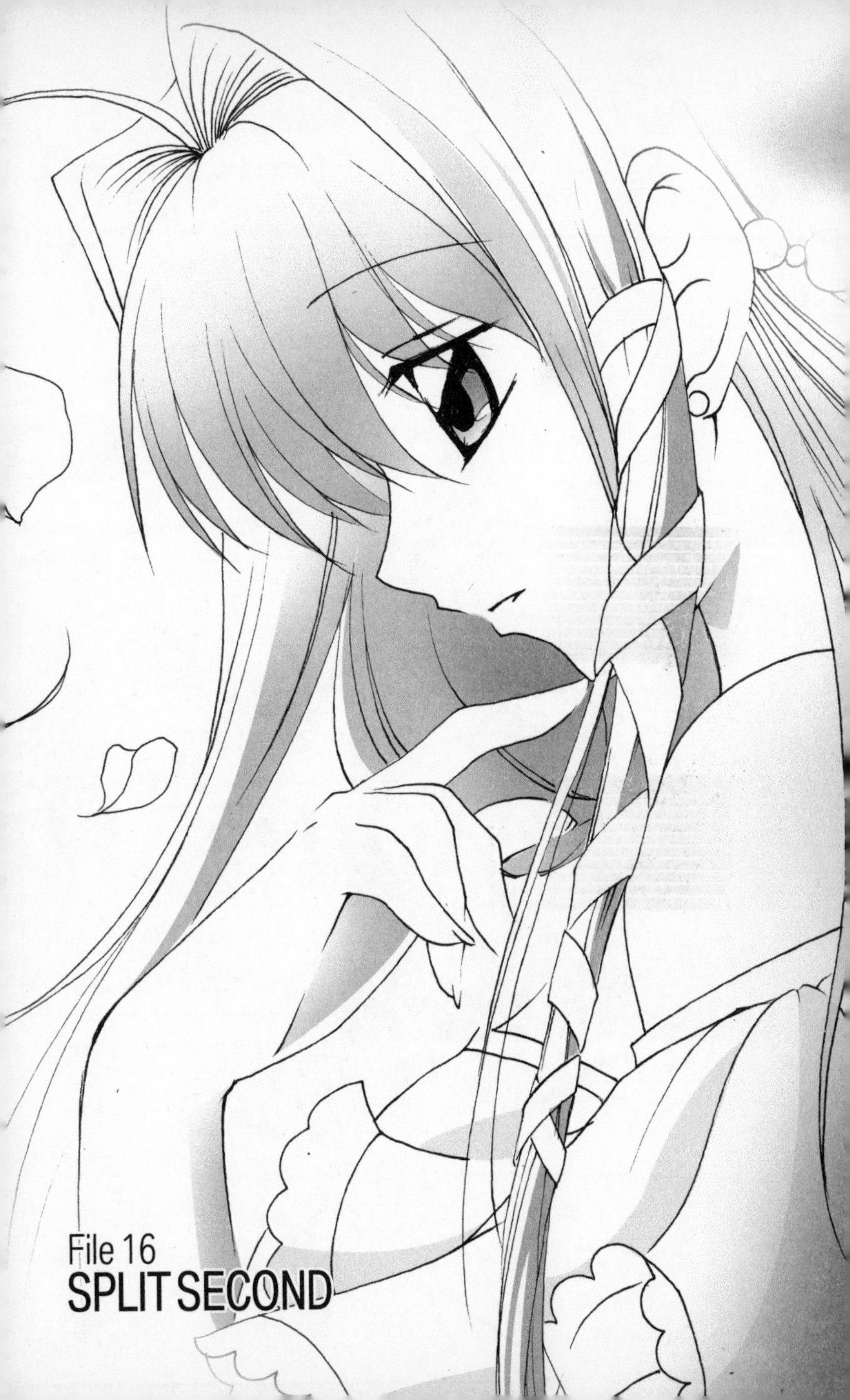

# File 16
# SPLIT SECOND

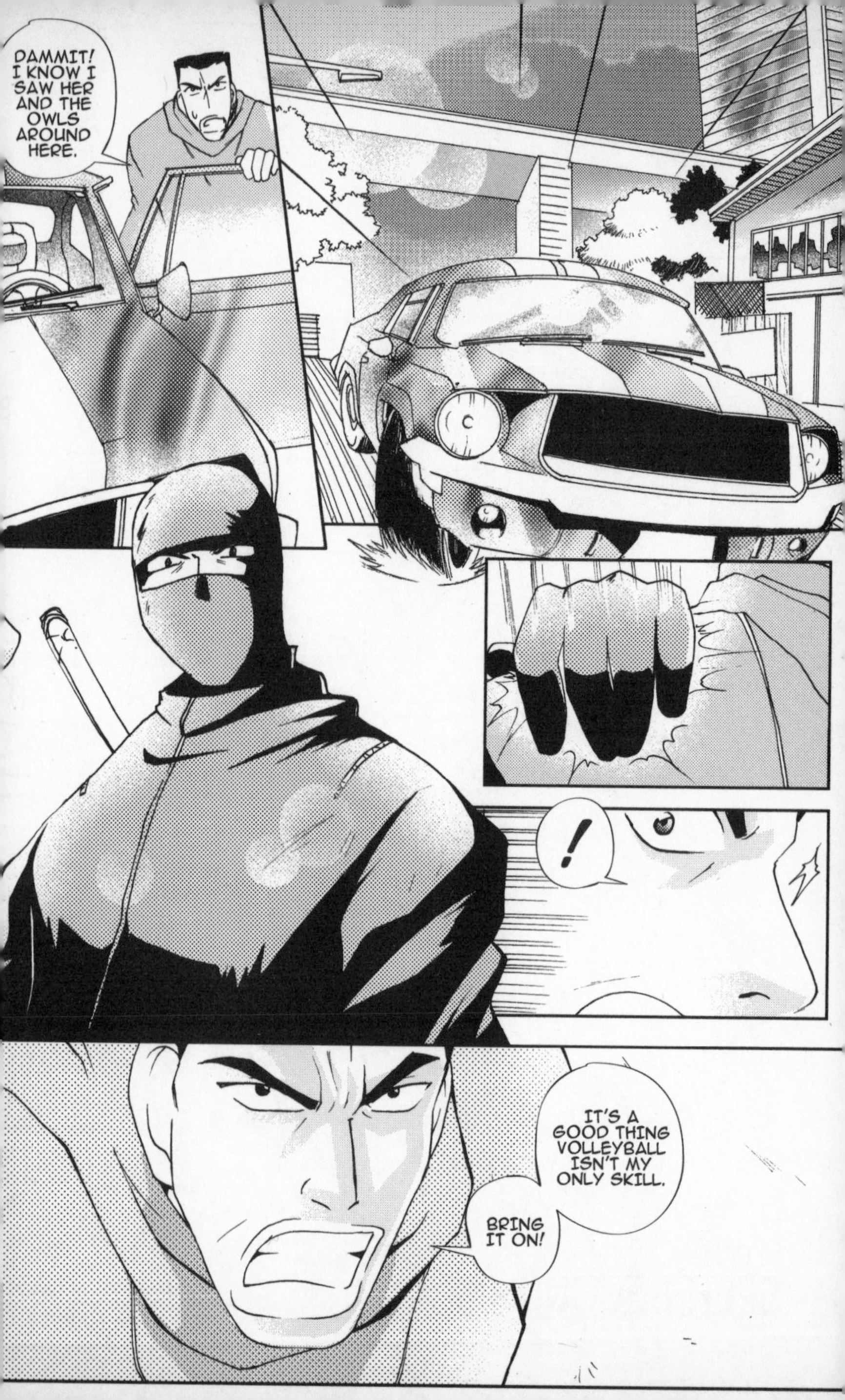
DAMMIT! I KNOW I SAW HER AND THE OWLS AROUND HERE.
!
IT'S A GOOD THING VOLLEYBALL ISN'T MY ONLY SKILL.
BRING IT ON!

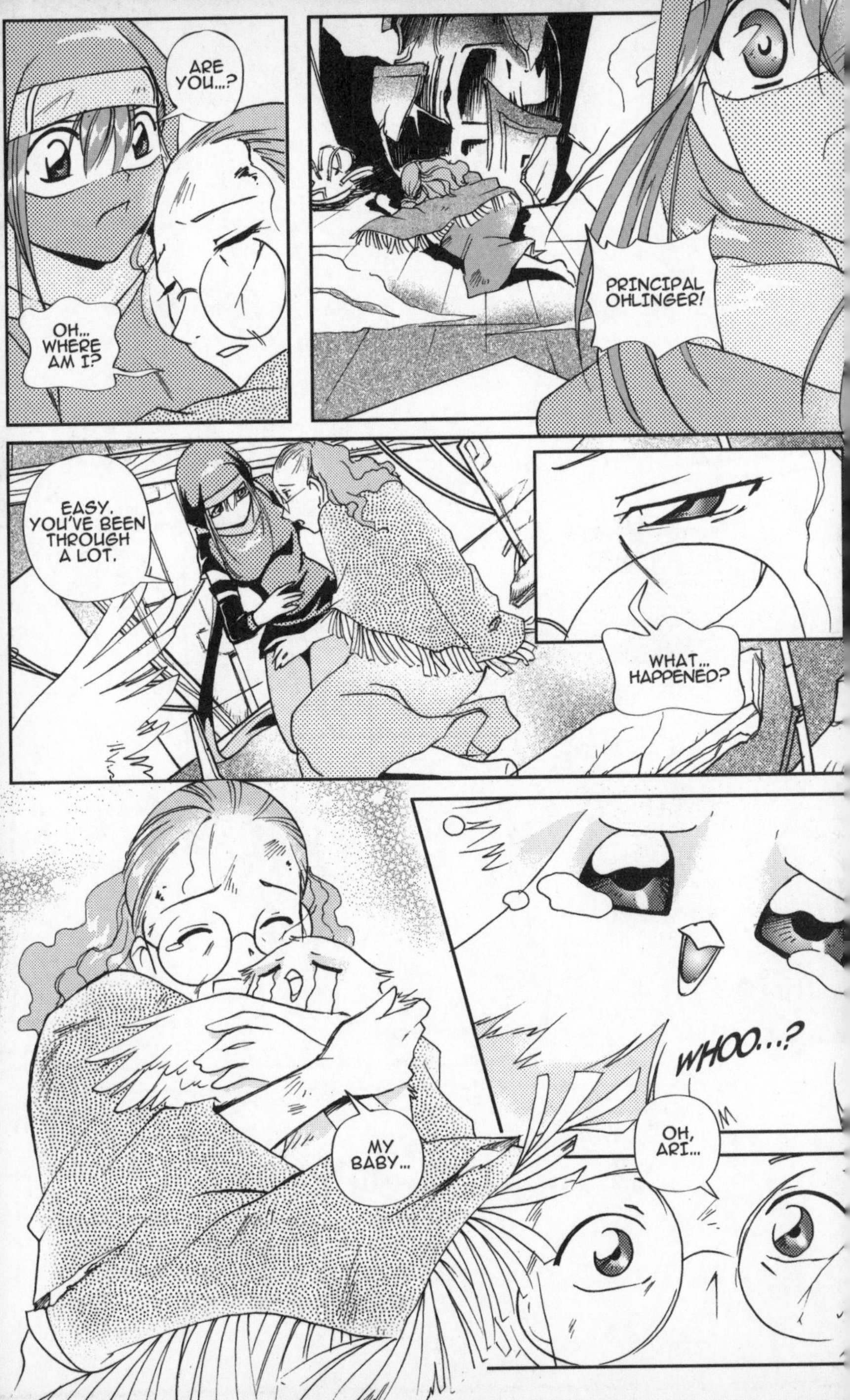
PRINCIPAL OHLINGER!
ARE YOU...?
OH... WHERE AM I?
WHAT... HAPPENED?
EASY. YOU'VE BEEN THROUGH A LOT.
WHOO...?
OH, ARI...
MY BABY...

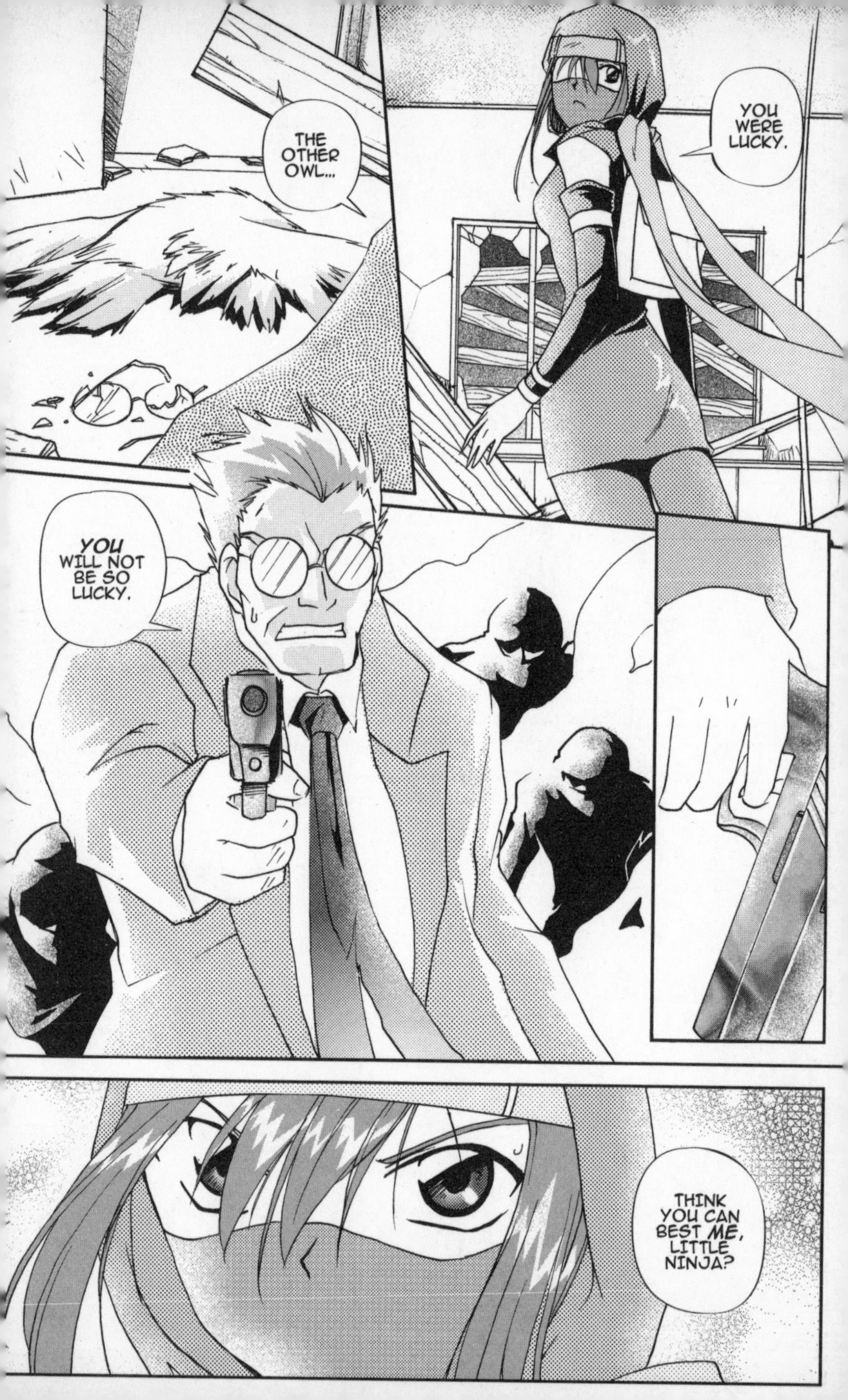
YOU WERE LUCKY.
THE OTHER OWL...
YOU WILL NOT BE SO LUCKY.
THINK YOU CAN BEST ME, LITTLE NINJA?

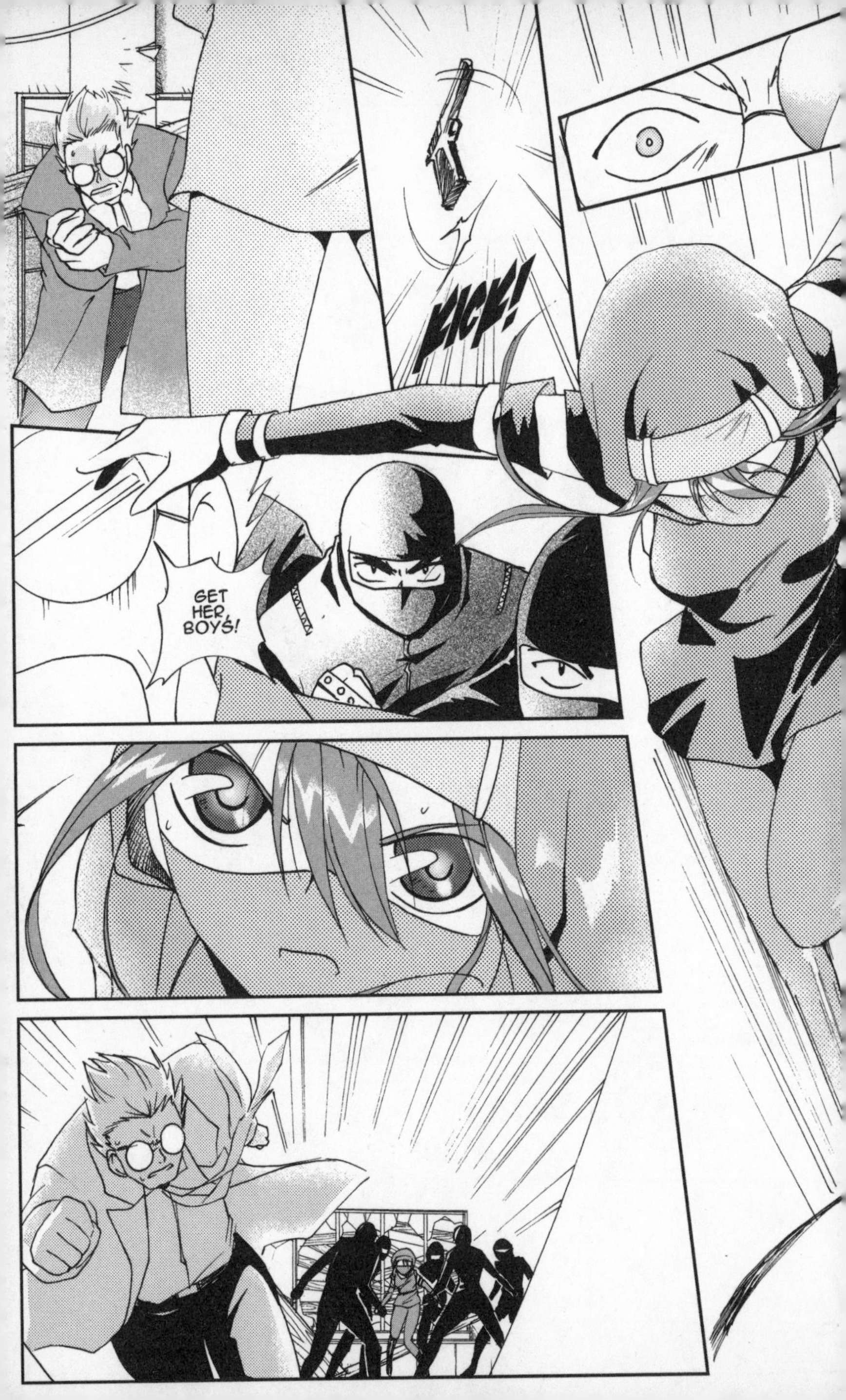
KICK!
GET HER, BOYS!

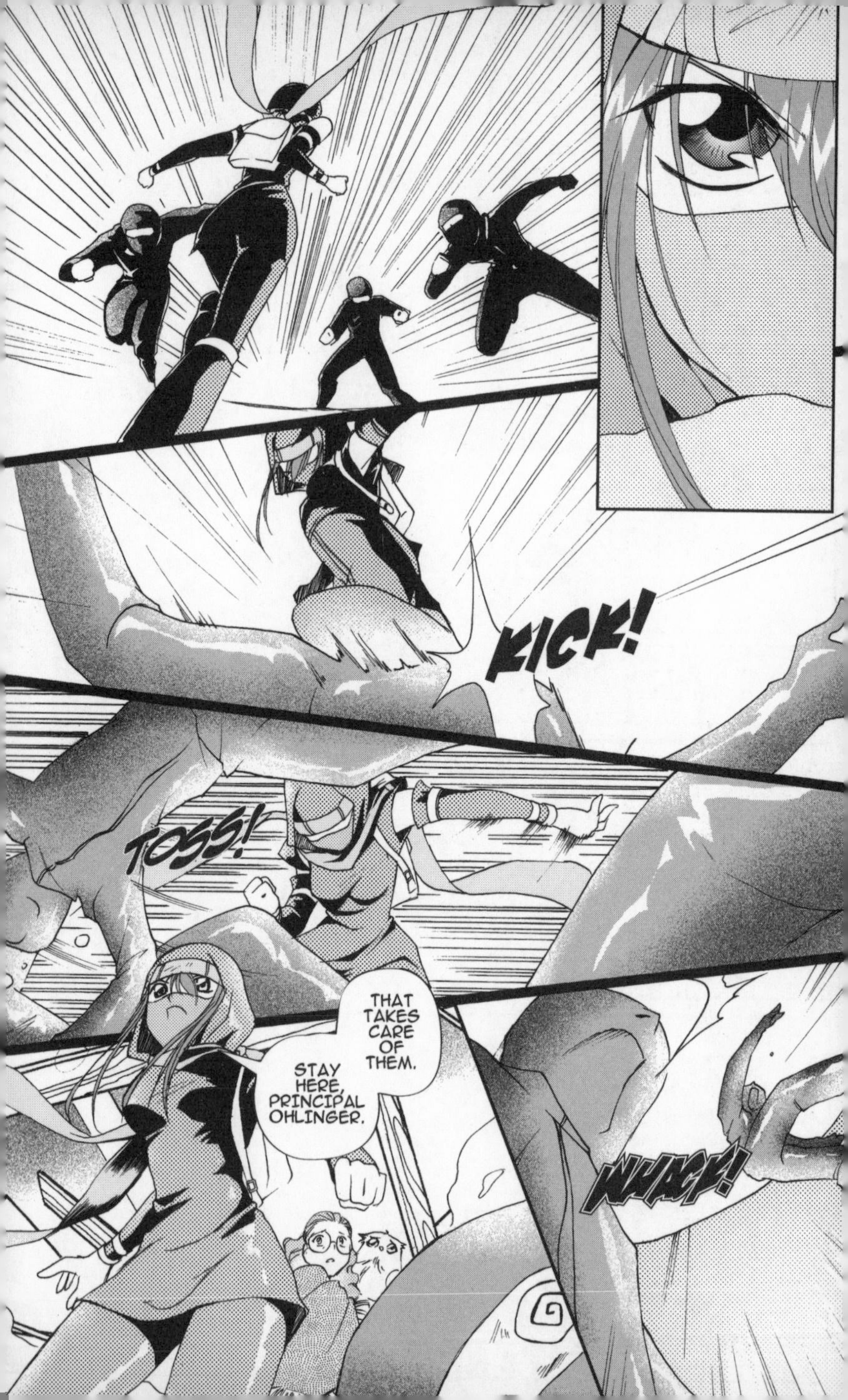
KICK!
TOSS!
WHACK!
THAT TAKES CARE OF THEM.
STAY HERE, PRINCIPAL OHLINGER.

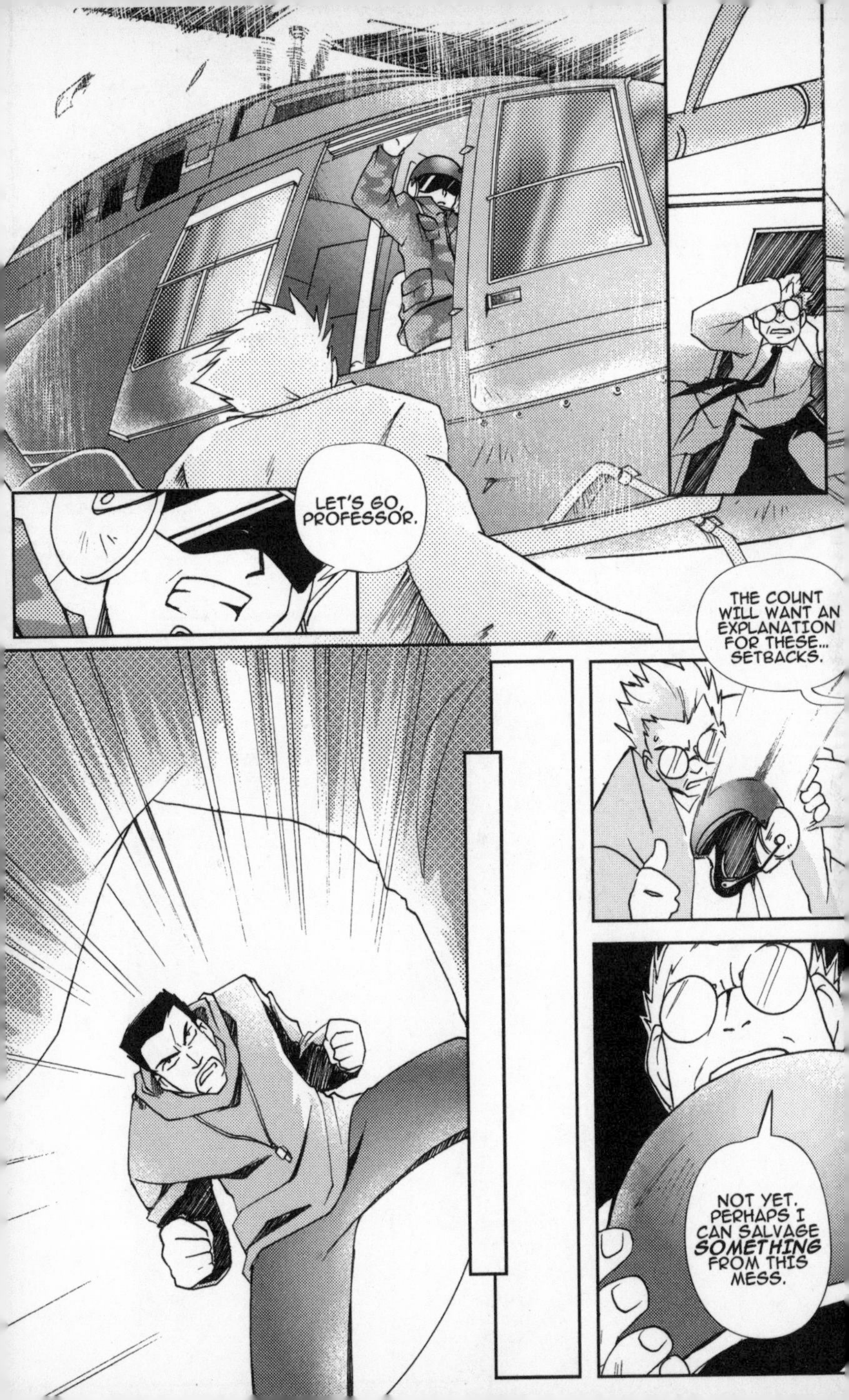
LET'S GO, PROFESSOR.
THE COUNT WILL WANT AN EXPLANATION FOR THESE... SETBACKS.
NOT YET. PERHAPS I CAN SALVAGE *SOMETHING* FROM THIS MESS.

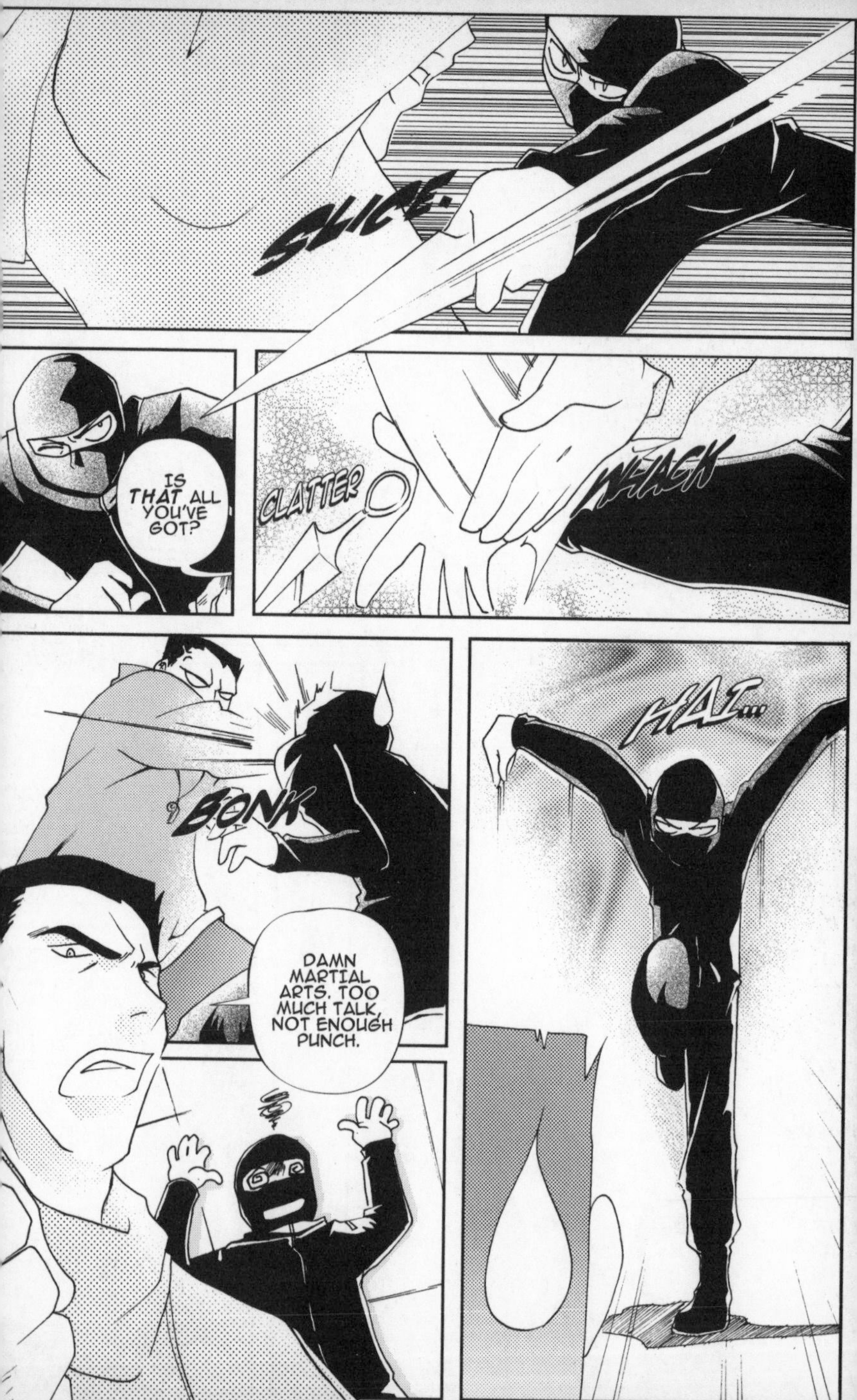
SLICE.
WHACK
CLATTER
IS THAT ALL YOU'VE GOT?
HAI...
BONK
DAMN MARTIAL ARTS. TOO MUCH TALK, NOT ENOUGH PUNCH.

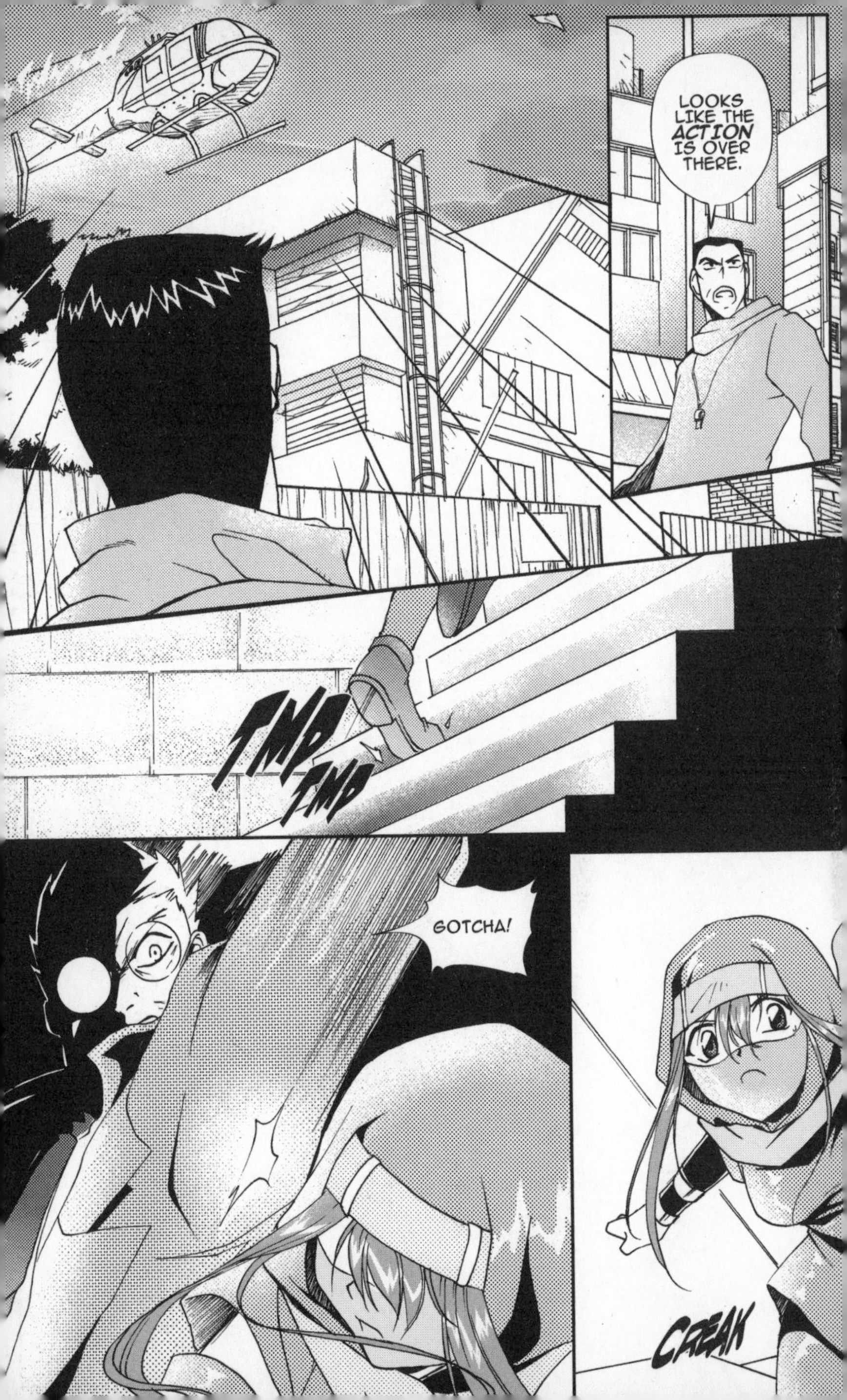
LOOKS LIKE THE ACTION IS OVER THERE.
TMP TMP
CREAK
GOTCHA!

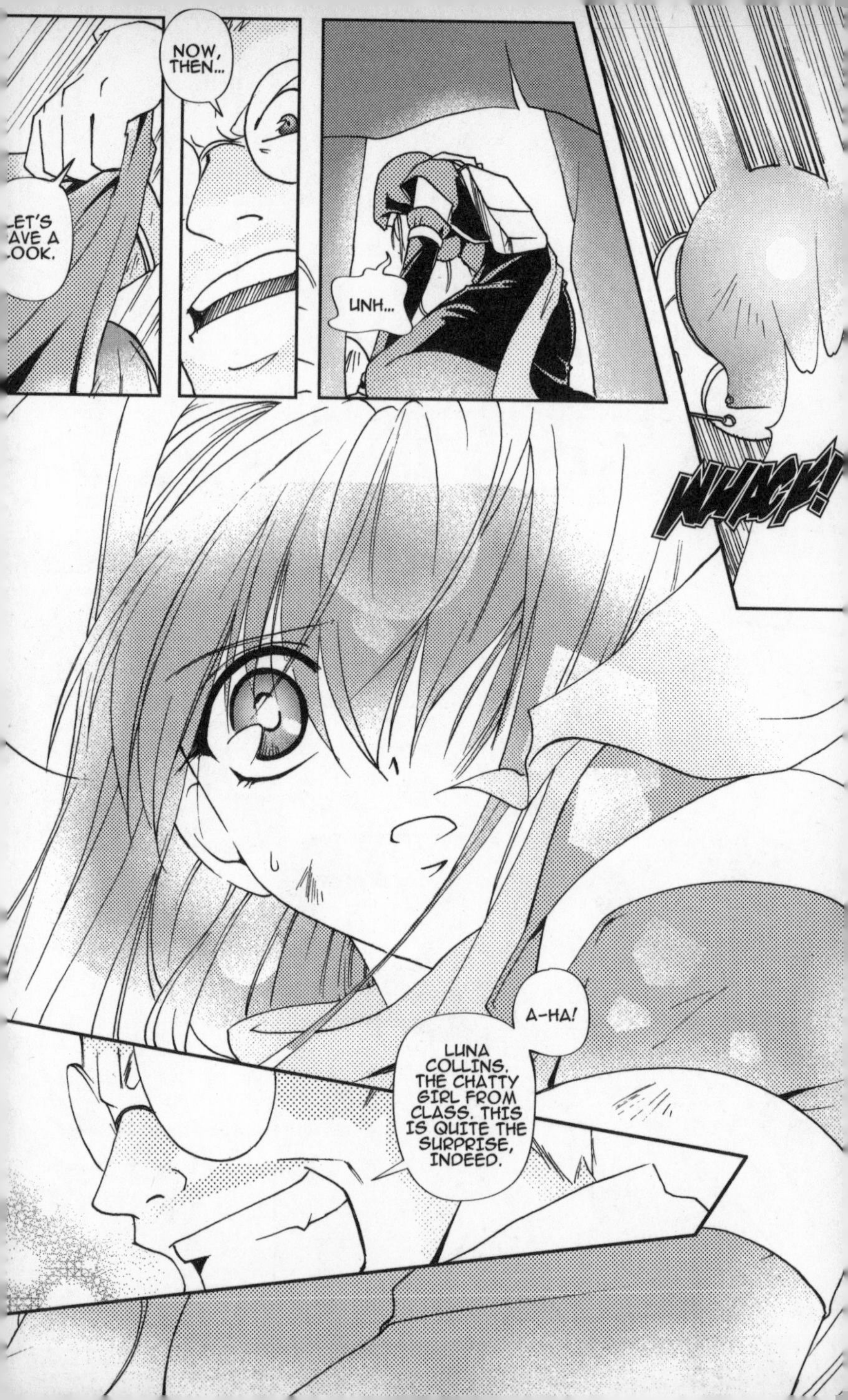
WHACK!
UNH...
NOW, THEN...
ET'S AVE A OOK.
A-HA!
LUNA COLLINS. THE CHATTY GIRL FROM CLASS. THIS IS QUITE THE SURPRISE, INDEED.

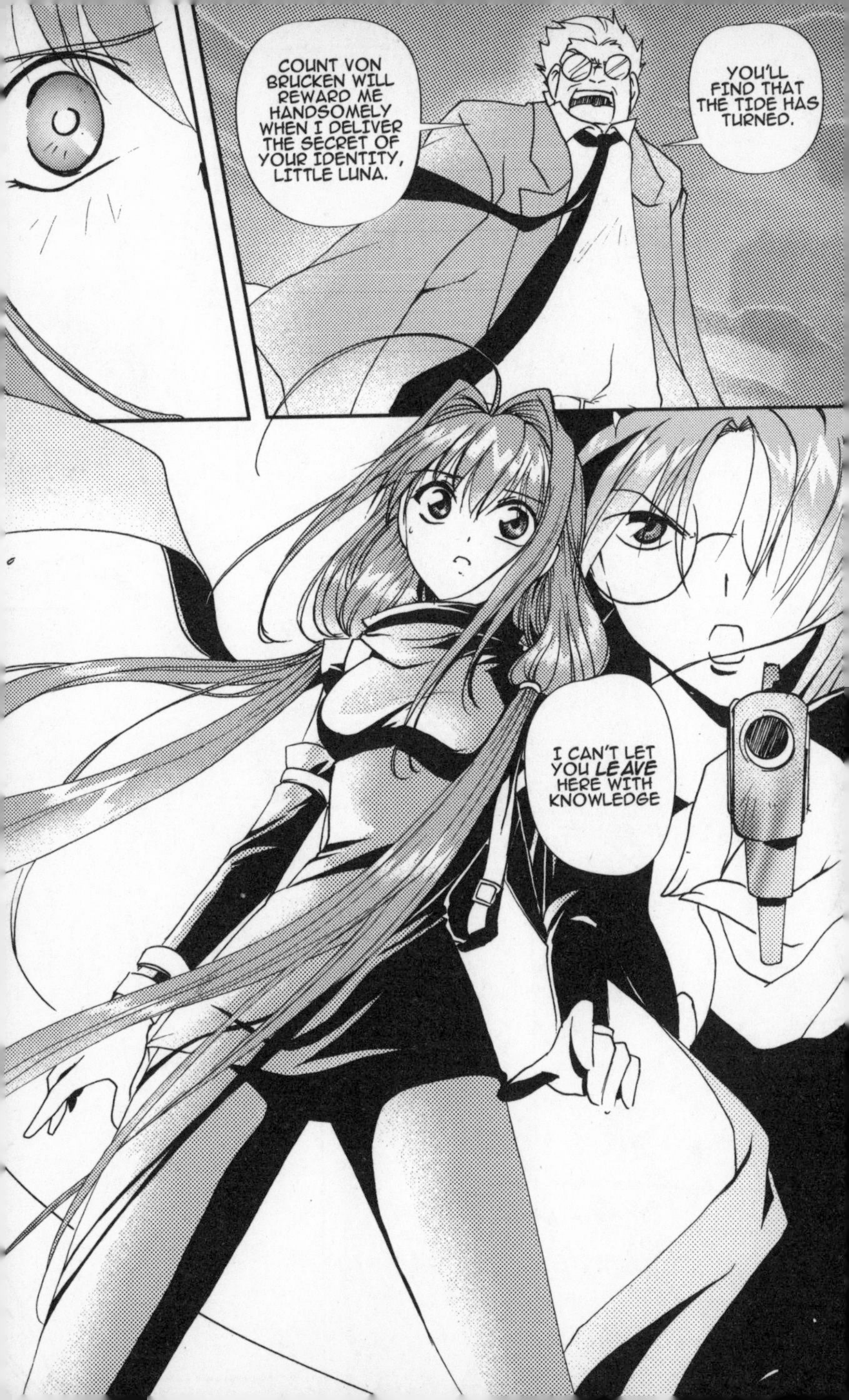
YOU'LL FIND THAT THE TIDE HAS TURNED.
COUNT VON BRUCKEN WILL REWARD ME HANDSOMELY WHEN I DELIVER THE SECRET OF YOUR IDENTITY, LITTLE LUNA.
I CAN'T LET YOU *LEAVE* HERE WITH KNOWLEDGE

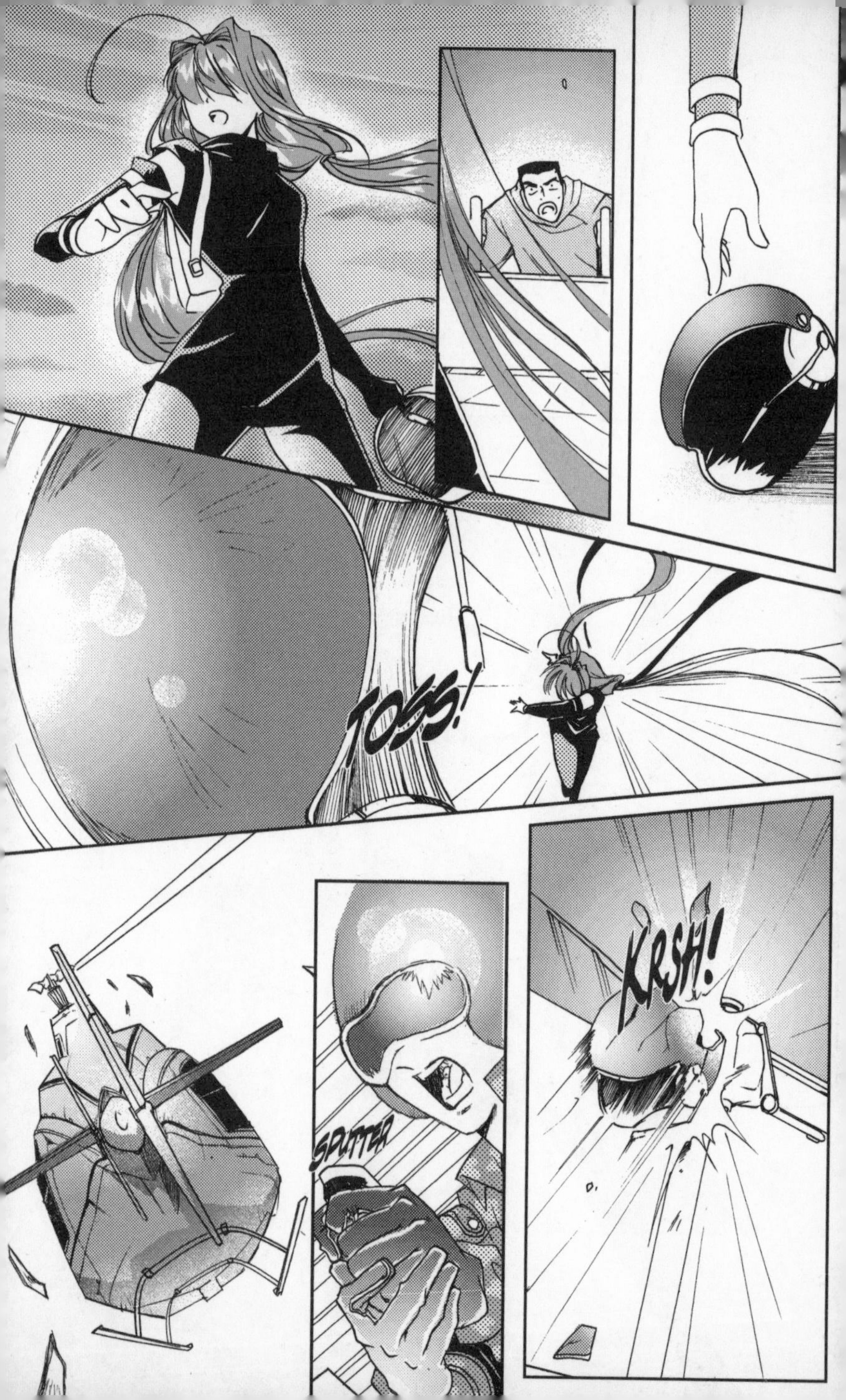
TOSS!
KRSH!
SPUTTER

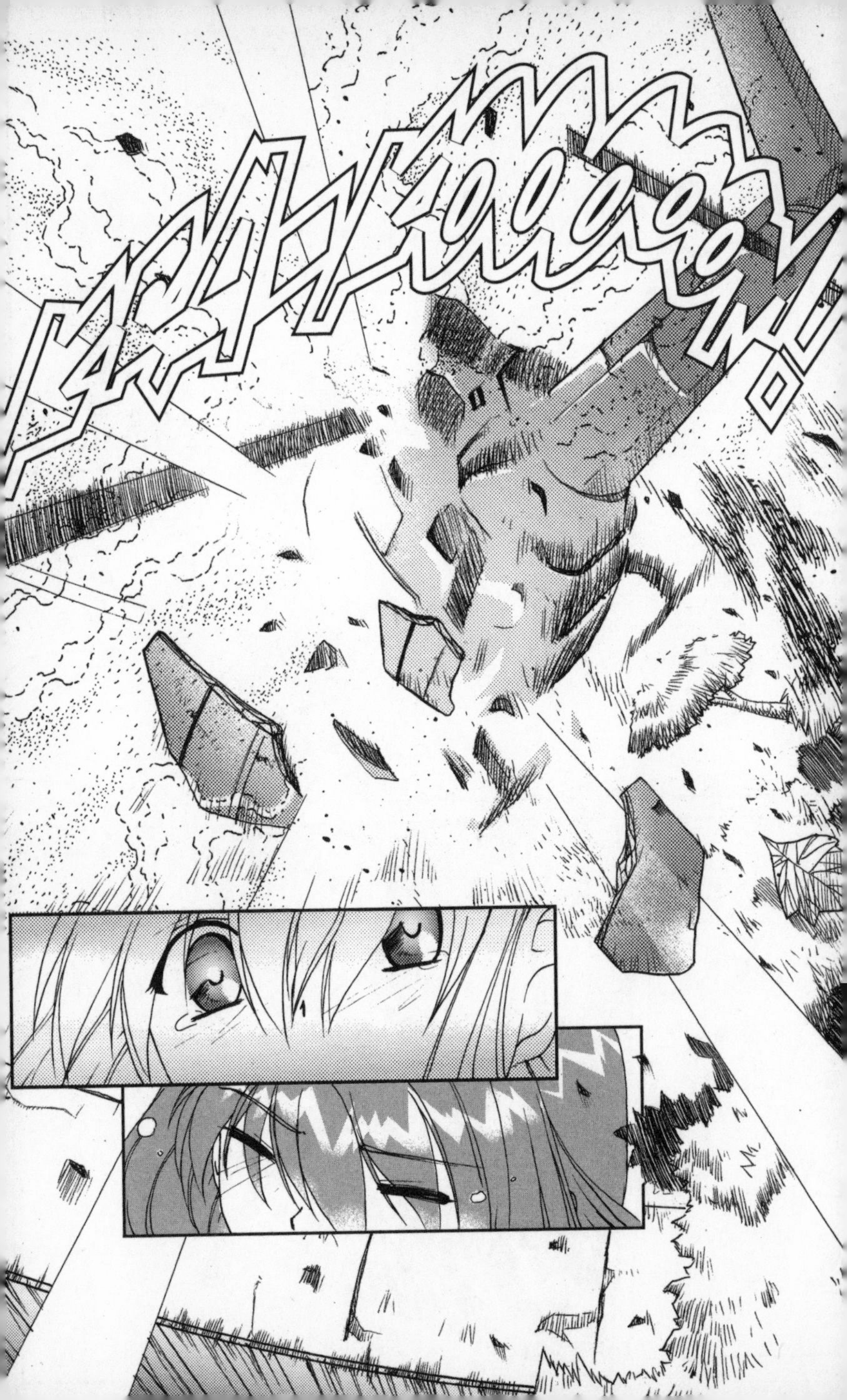

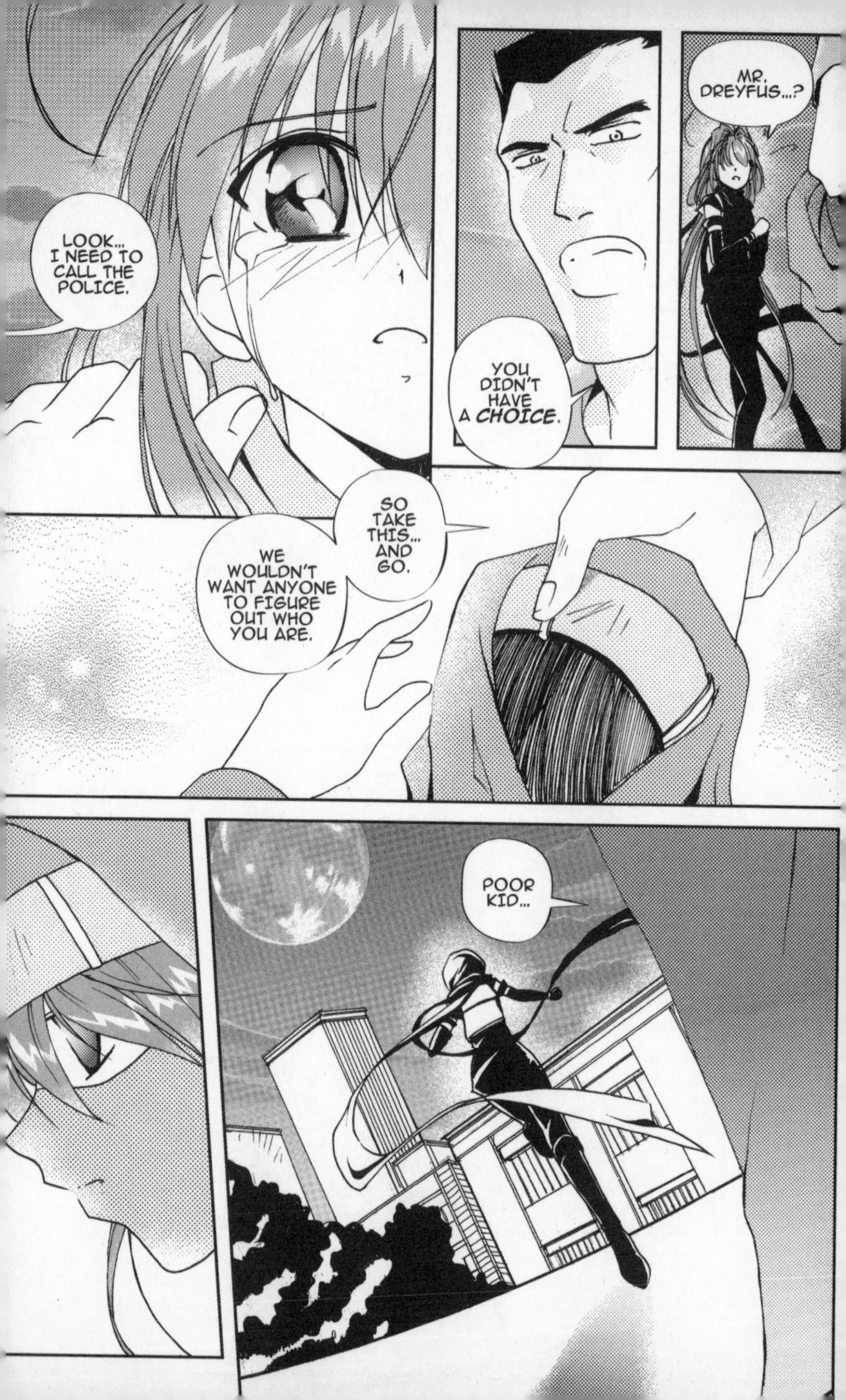
MR. DREYFUS...?
YOU DIDN'T HAVE A CHOICE.
LOOK... I NEED TO CALL THE POLICE.
SO TAKE THIS... AND GO.
WE WOULDN'T WANT ANYONE TO FIGURE OUT WHO YOU ARE.
POOR KID...

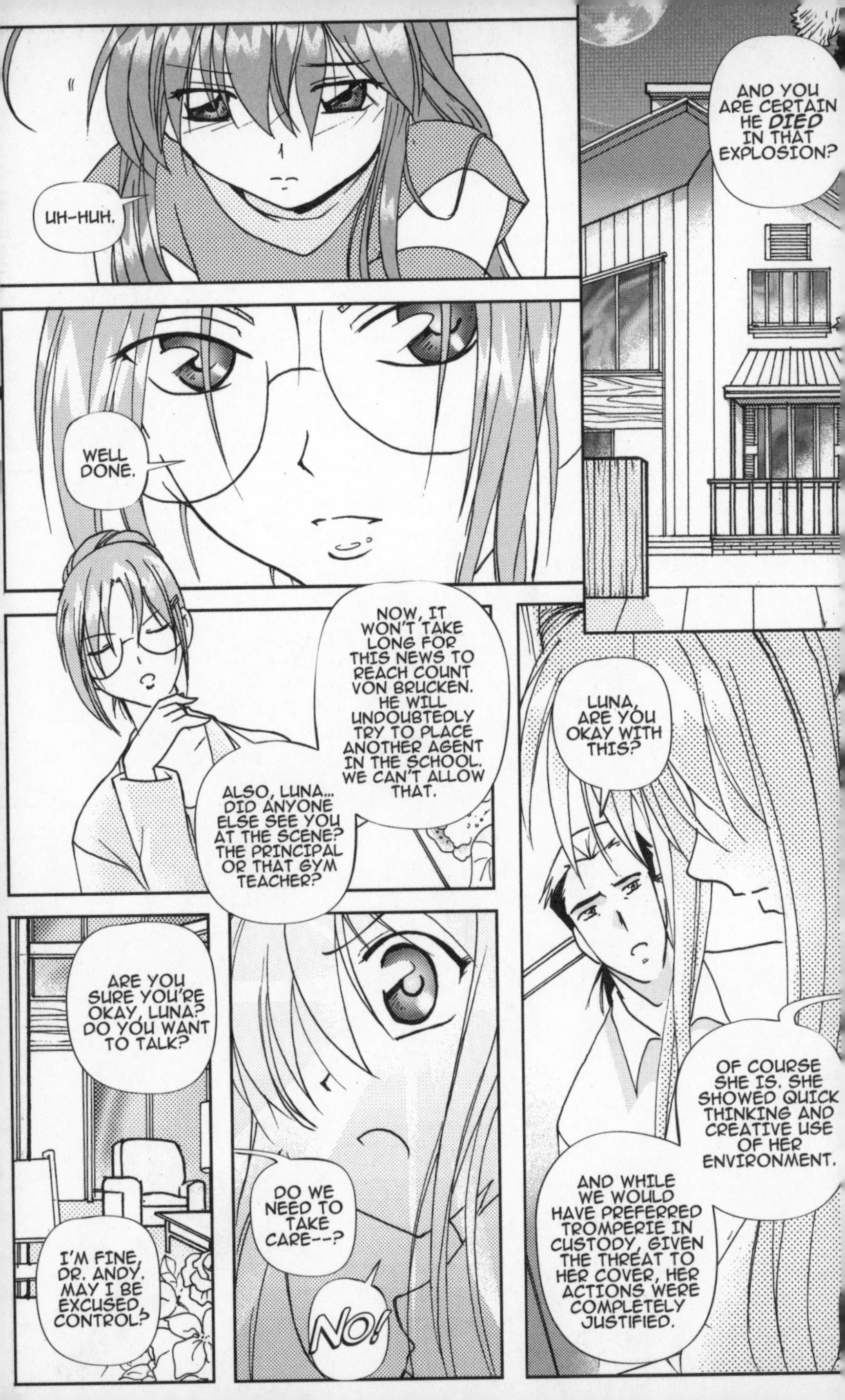
AND YOU ARE CERTAIN HE *DIED* IN THAT EXPLOSION?
UH-HUH.
WELL DONE.
LUNA, ARE YOU OKAY WITH THIS?
OF COURSE SHE IS. SHE SHOWED QUICK THINKING AND CREATIVE USE OF HER ENVIRONMENT.
AND WHILE WE WOULD HAVE PREFERRED TROMPERIE IN CUSTODY, GIVEN THE THREAT TO HER COVER, HER ACTIONS WERE COMPLETELY JUSTIFIED.
NOW, IT WON'T TAKE LONG FOR THIS NEWS TO REACH COUNT VON BRUCKEN. HE WILL UNDOUBTEDLY TRY TO PLACE ANOTHER AGENT IN THE SCHOOL. WE CAN'T ALLOW THAT.
ALSO, LUNA... DID ANYONE ELSE SEE YOU AT THE SCENE? THE PRINCIPAL OR THAT GYM TEACHER?
DO WE NEED TO TAKE CARE--?
NO!
ARE YOU SURE YOU'RE OKAY, LUNA? DO YOU WANT TO TALK?
I'M FINE, DR. ANDY. MAY I BE EXCUSED, CONTROL?

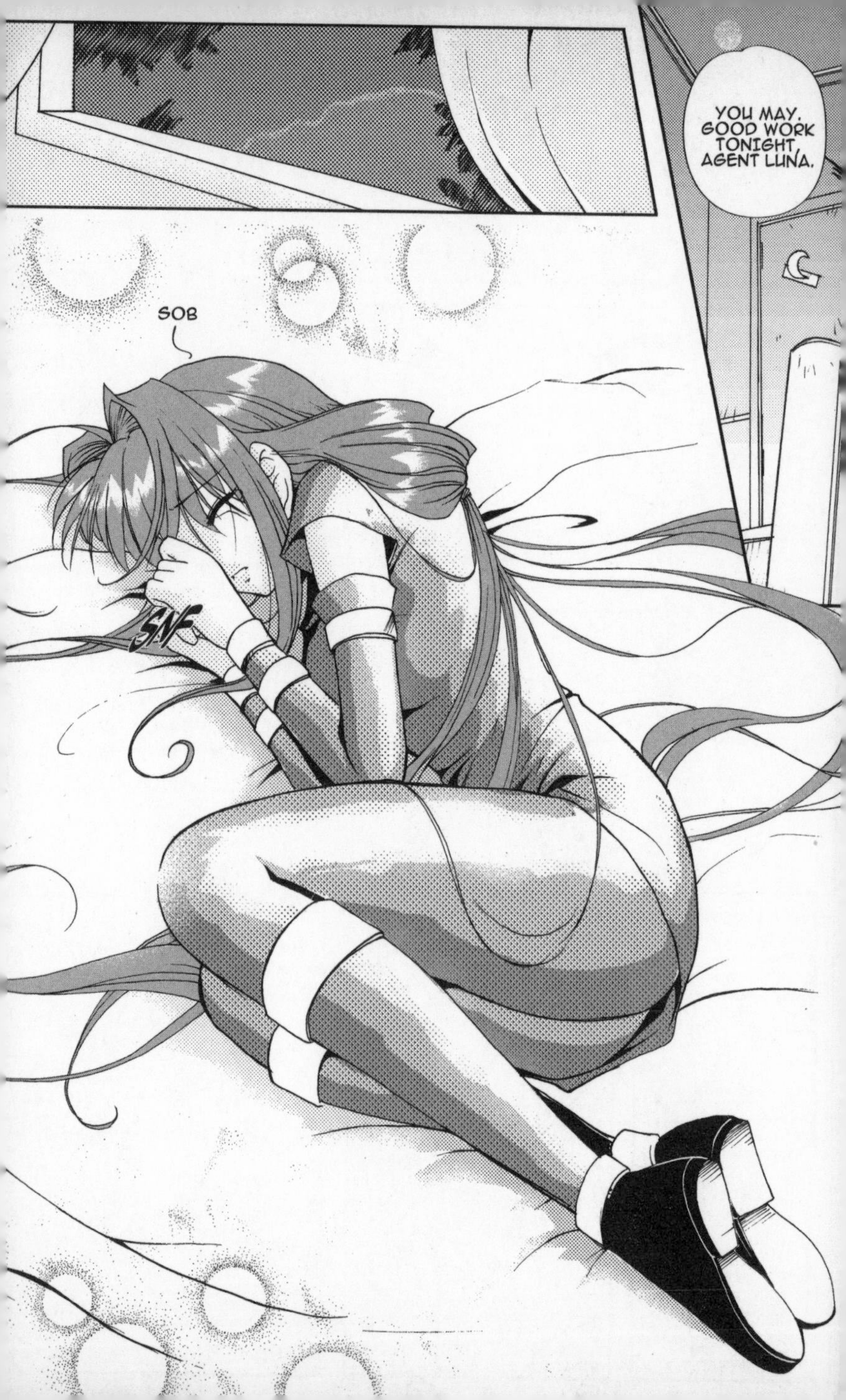
YOU MAY. GOOD WORK TONIGHT, AGENT LUNA.
SOB
SNF

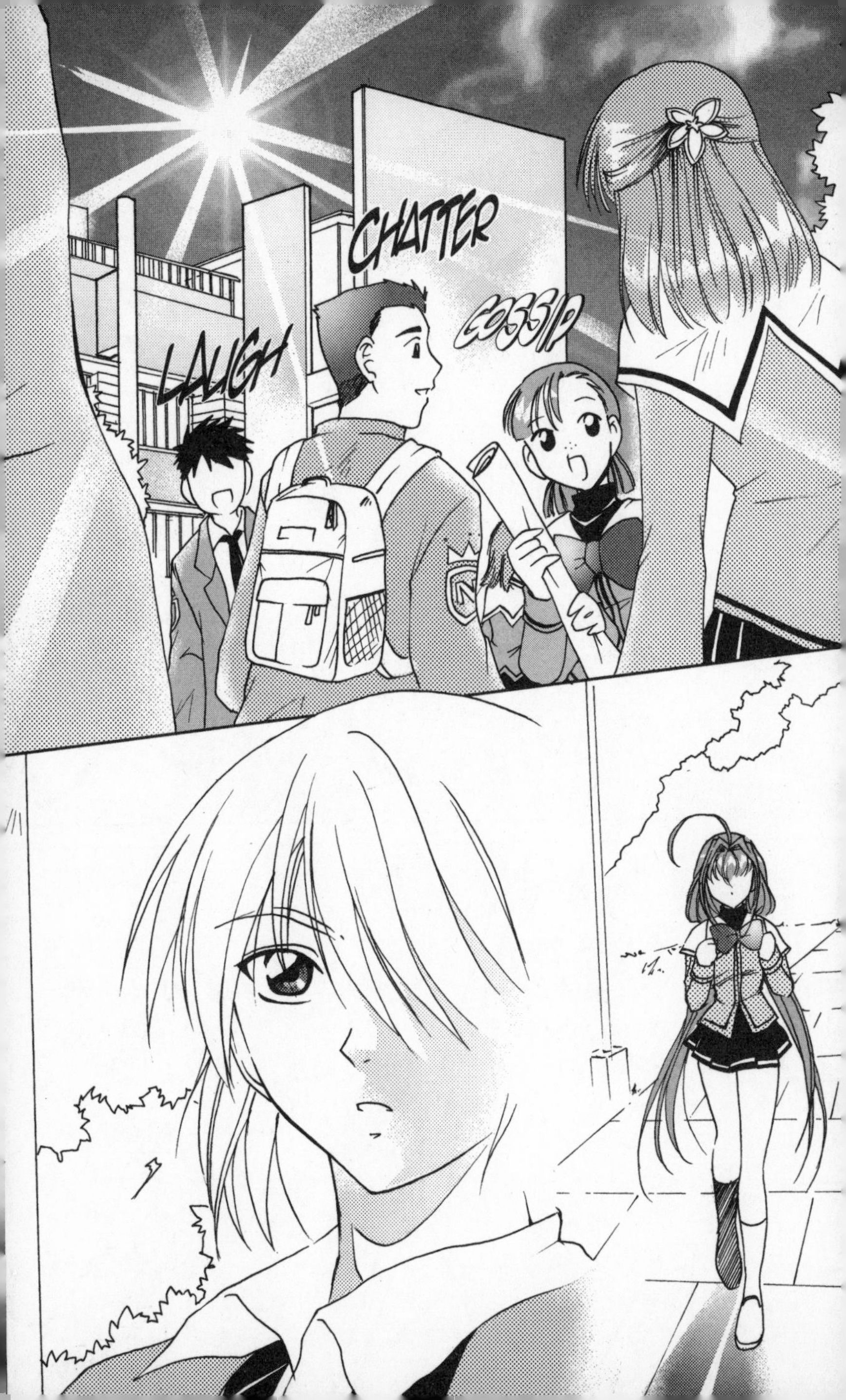

GOSSIP
CHATTER
LAUGH

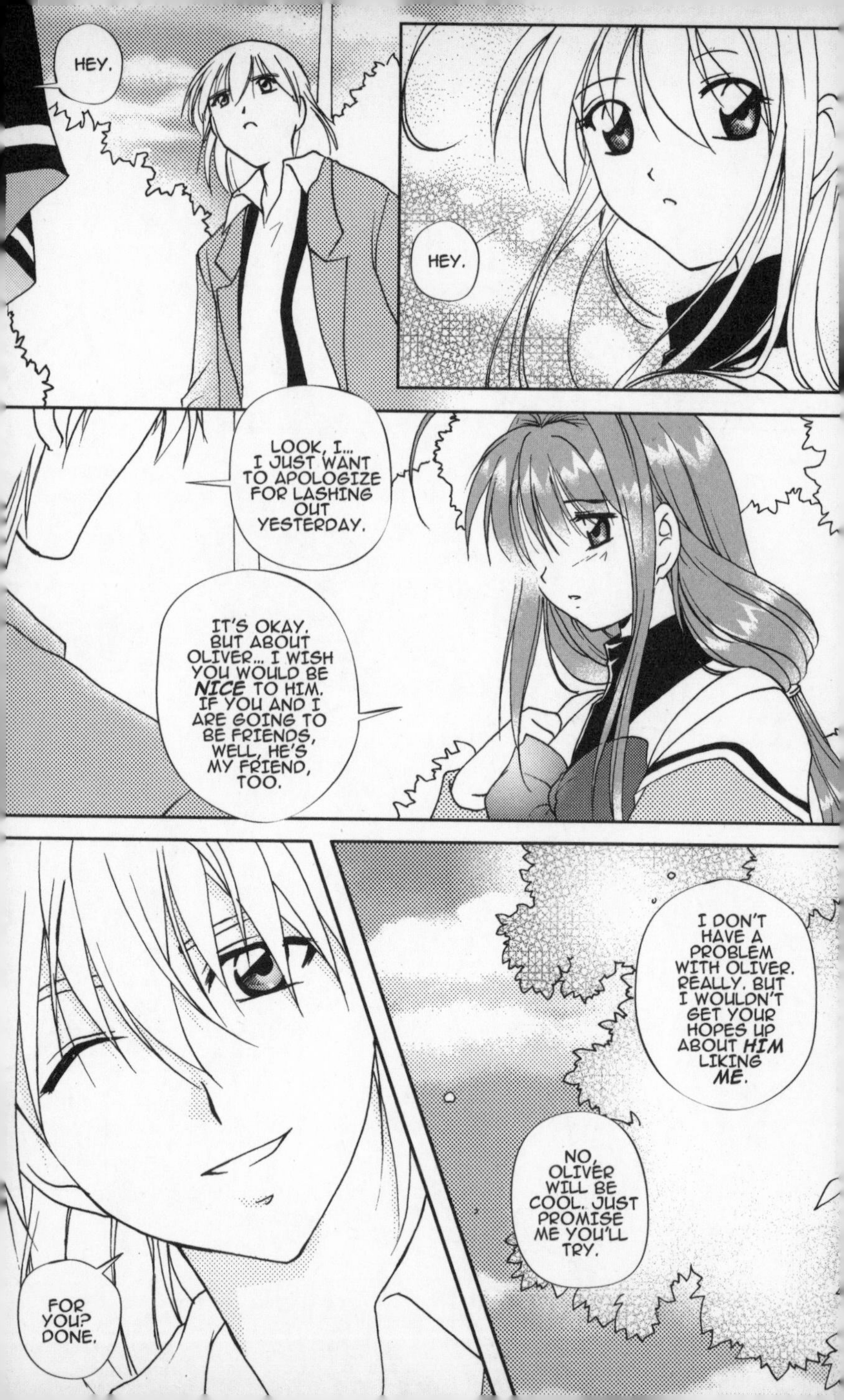
HEY.
HEY.
LOOK, I... I JUST WANT TO APOLOGIZE FOR LASHING OUT YESTERDAY.
IT'S OKAY. BUT ABOUT OLIVER... I WISH YOU WOULD BE NICE TO HIM. IF YOU AND I ARE GOING TO BE FRIENDS, WELL, HE'S MY FRIEND, TOO.
I DON'T HAVE A PROBLEM WITH OLIVER. REALLY. BUT I WOULDN'T GET YOUR HOPES UP ABOUT HIM LIKING ME.
NO, OLIVER WILL BE COOL. JUST PROMISE ME YOU'LL TRY.
FOR YOU? DONE.

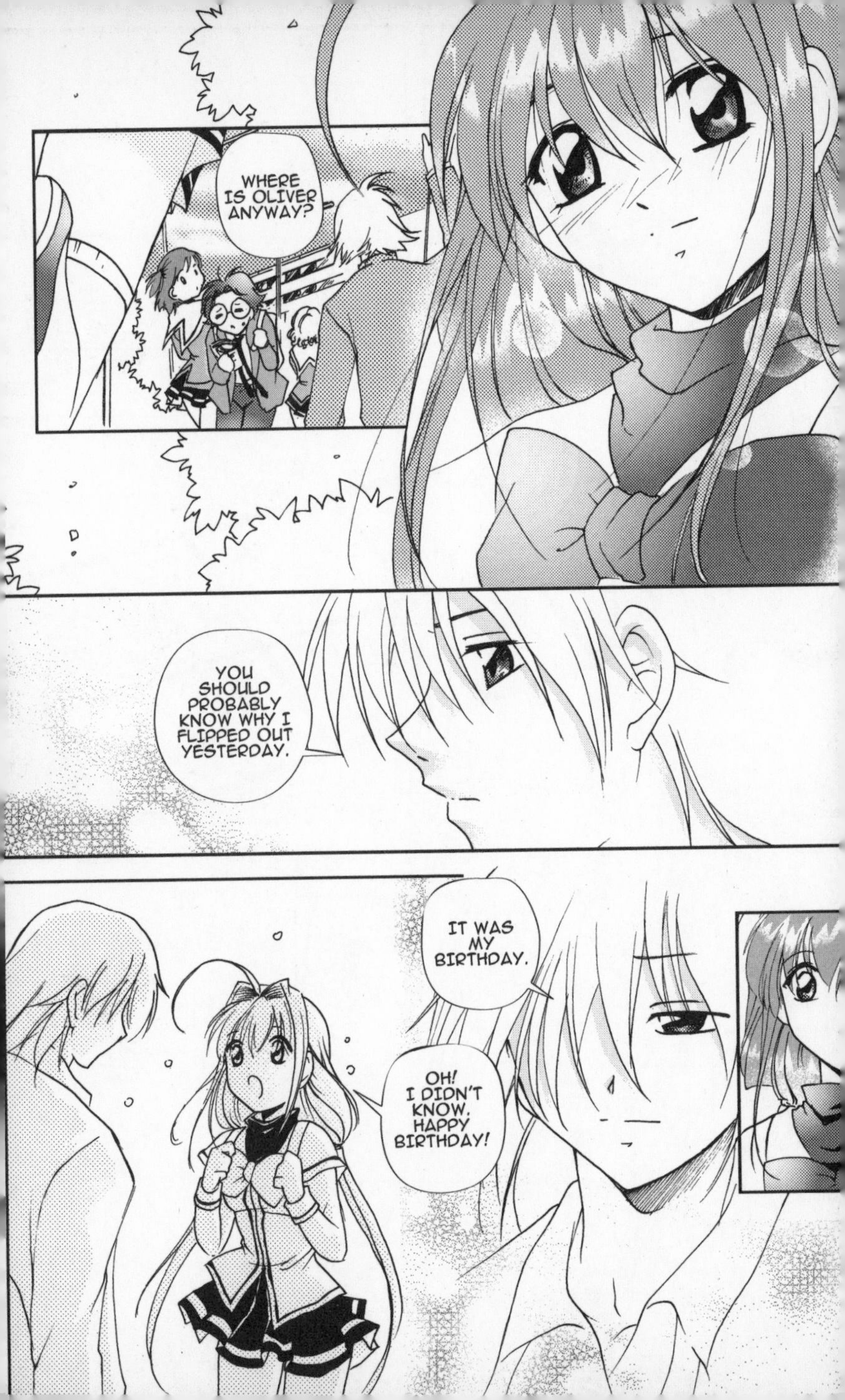
WHERE IS OLIVER ANYWAY?
YOU SHOULD PROBABLY KNOW WHY I FLIPPED OUT YESTERDAY.
IT WAS MY BIRTHDAY.
OH! I DIDN'T KNOW. HAPPY BIRTHDAY!

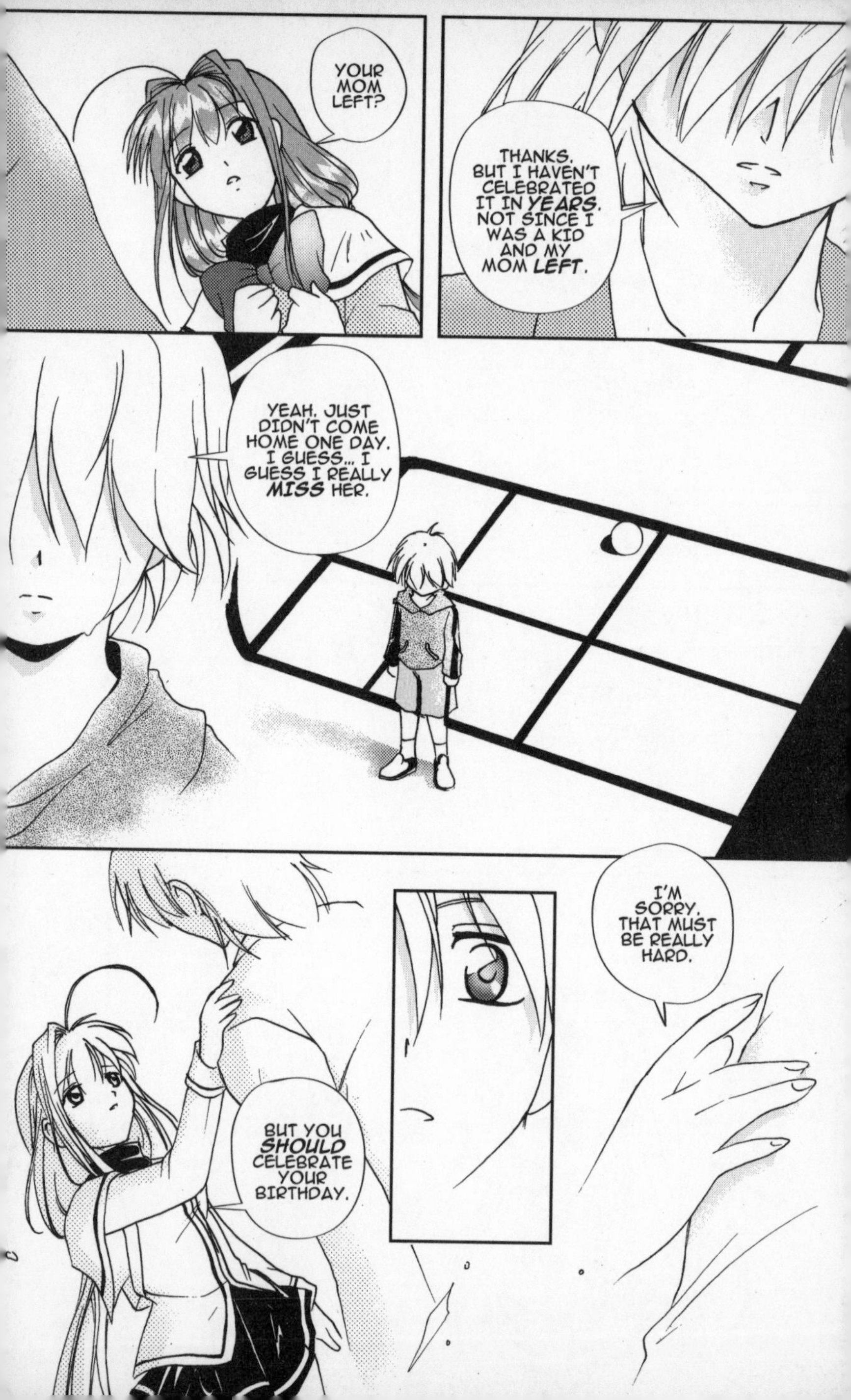
THANKS. BUT I HAVEN'T CELEBRATED IT IN *YEARS*. NOT SINCE I WAS A KID AND MY MOM *LEFT*.
YOUR MOM LEFT?
YEAH. JUST DIDN'T COME HOME ONE DAY. I GUESS... I GUESS I REALLY *MISS* HER.
I'M SORRY, THAT MUST BE REALLY HARD.
BUT YOU *SHOULD* CELEBRATE YOUR BIRTHDAY.

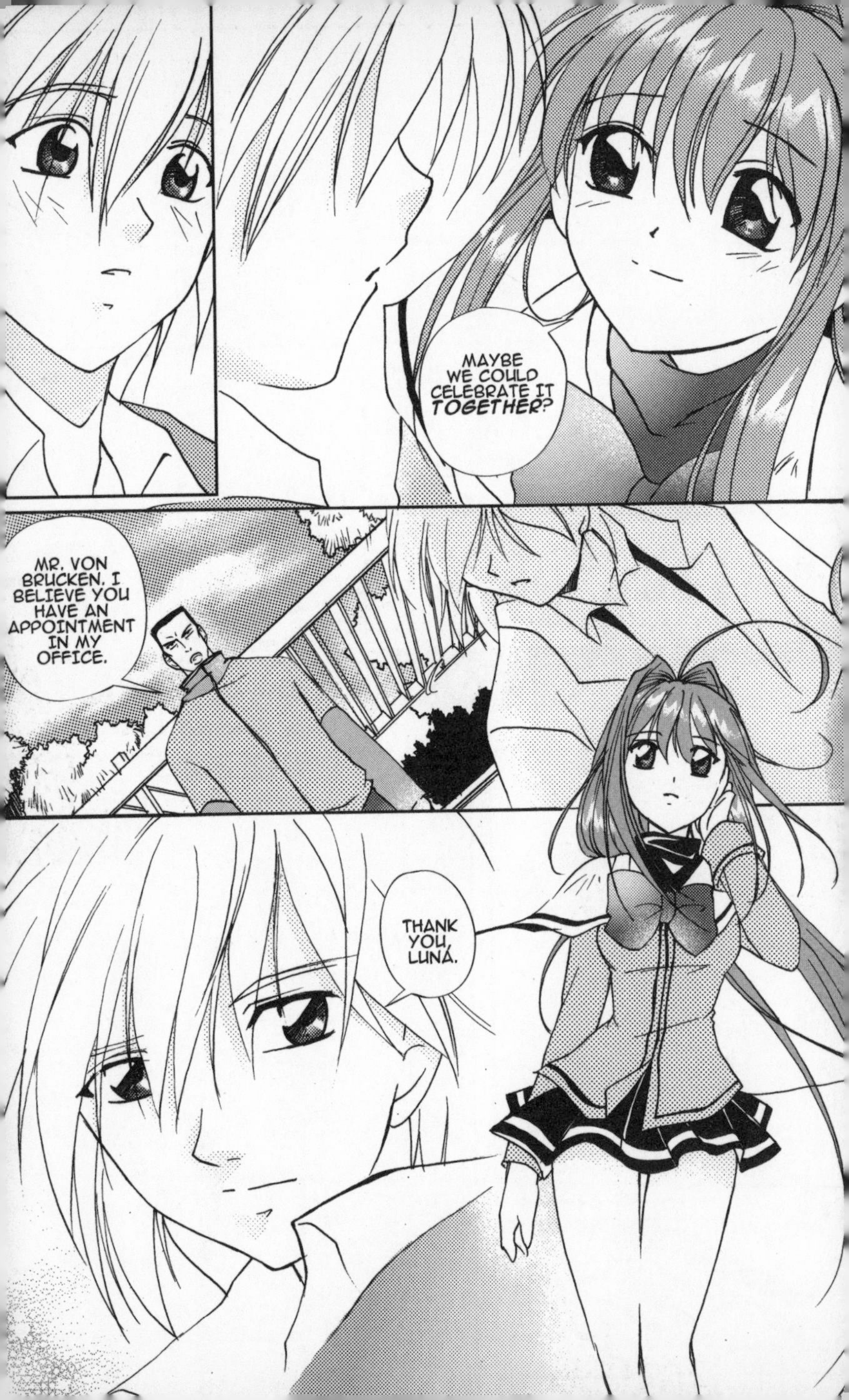
MAYBE WE COULD CELEBRATE IT TOGETHER?
MR. VON BRUCKEN. I BELIEVE YOU HAVE AN APPOINTMENT IN MY OFFICE.
THANK YOU, LUNA.

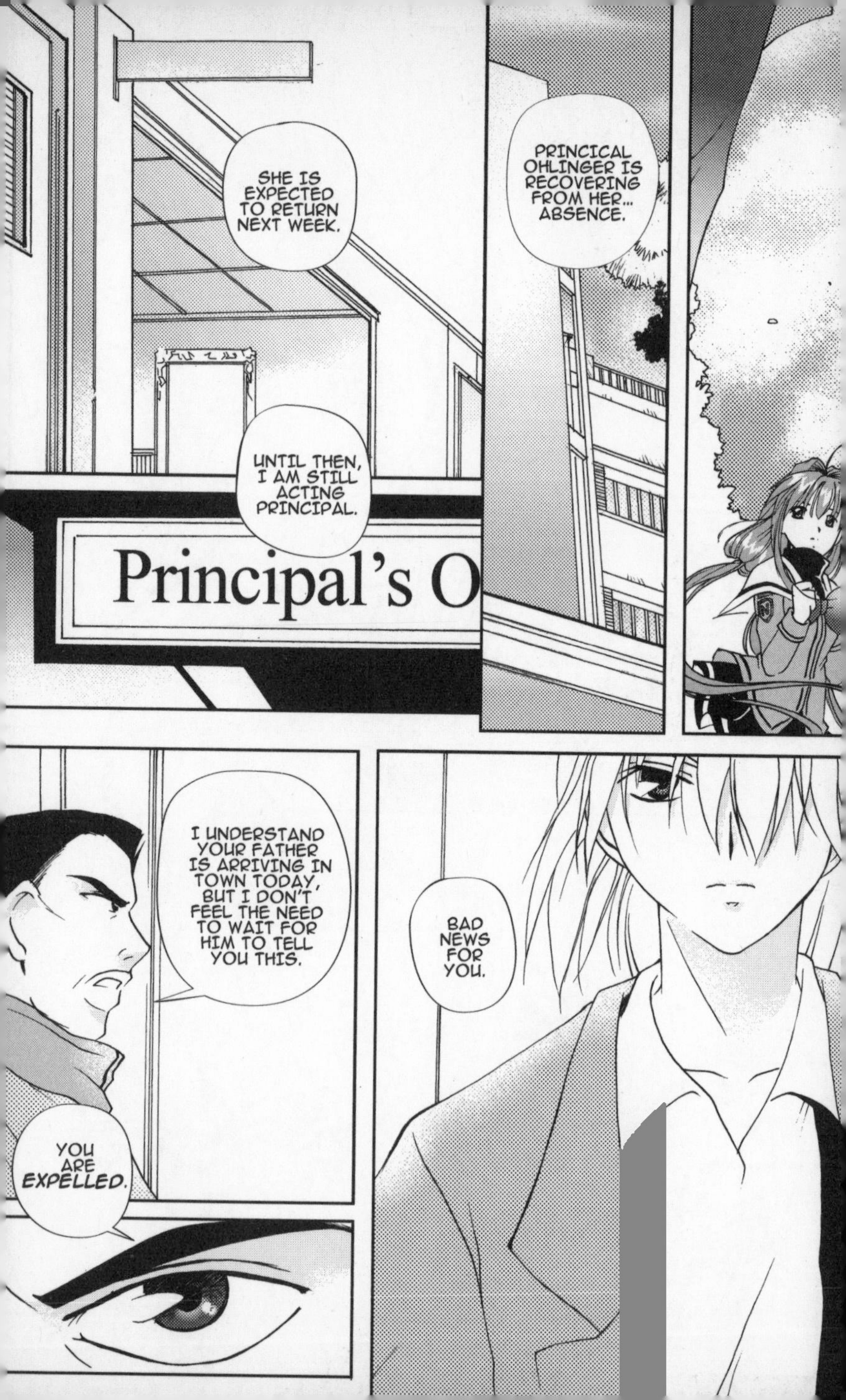
PRINCICAL OHLINGER IS RECOVERING FROM HER... ABSENCE.
SHE IS EXPECTED TO RETURN NEXT WEEK.
UNTIL THEN, I AM STILL ACTING PRINCIPAL.
Principal's O
BAD NEWS FOR YOU.
I UNDERSTAND YOUR FATHER IS ARRIVING IN TOWN TODAY, BUT I DON'T FEEL THE NEED TO WAIT FOR HIM TO TELL YOU THIS.
YOU ARE EXPELLED.

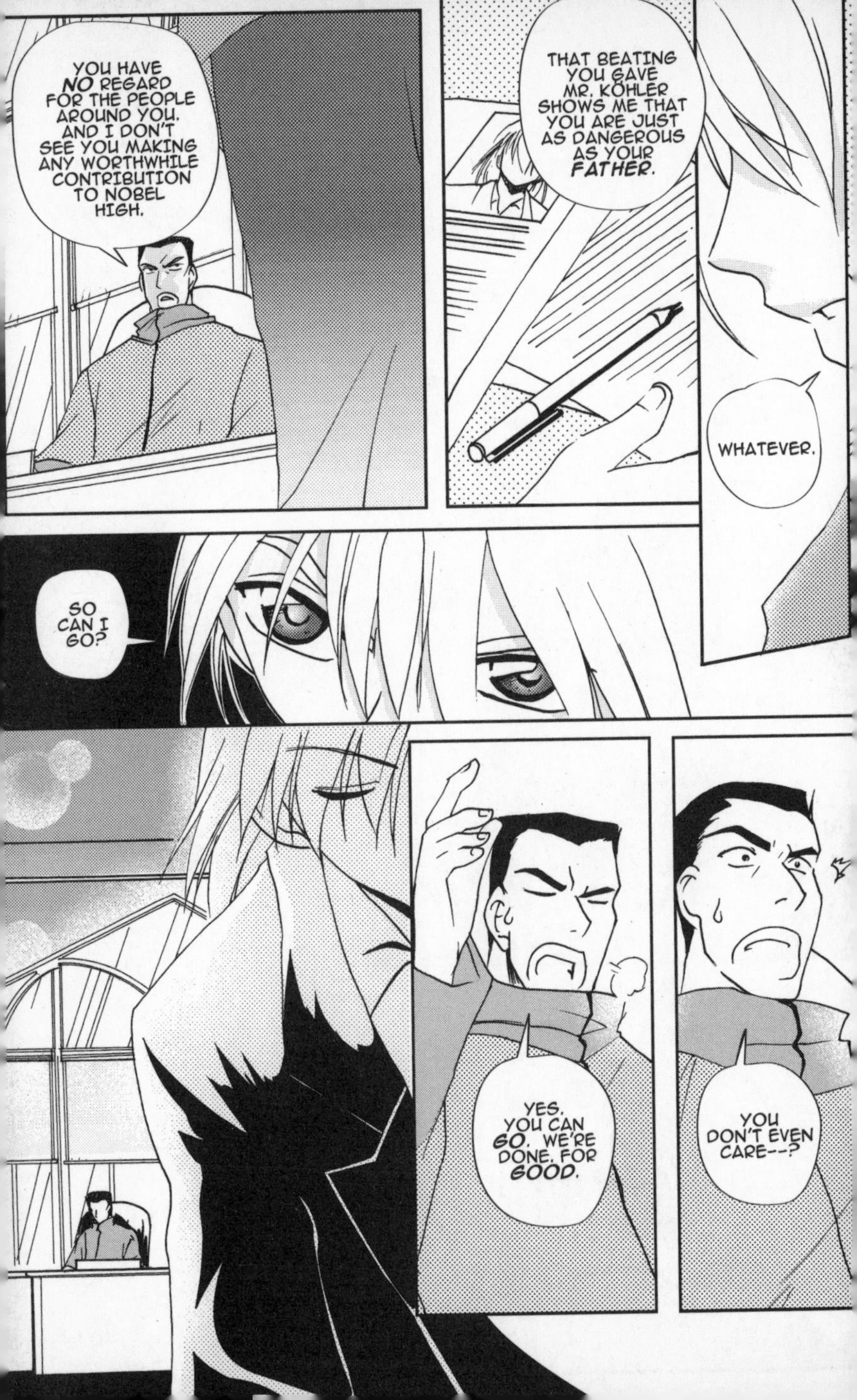
WHATEVER.
THAT BEATING YOU GAVE MR. KÖHLER SHOWS ME THAT YOU ARE JUST AS DANGEROUS AS YOUR **FATHER**.
YOU HAVE **NO** REGARD FOR THE PEOPLE AROUND YOU. AND I DON'T SEE YOU MAKING ANY WORTHWHILE CONTRIBUTION TO NOBEL HIGH.
SO CAN I GO?
YOU DON'T EVEN CARE--?
YES. YOU CAN **GO**. WE'RE DONE. FOR **GOOD**.

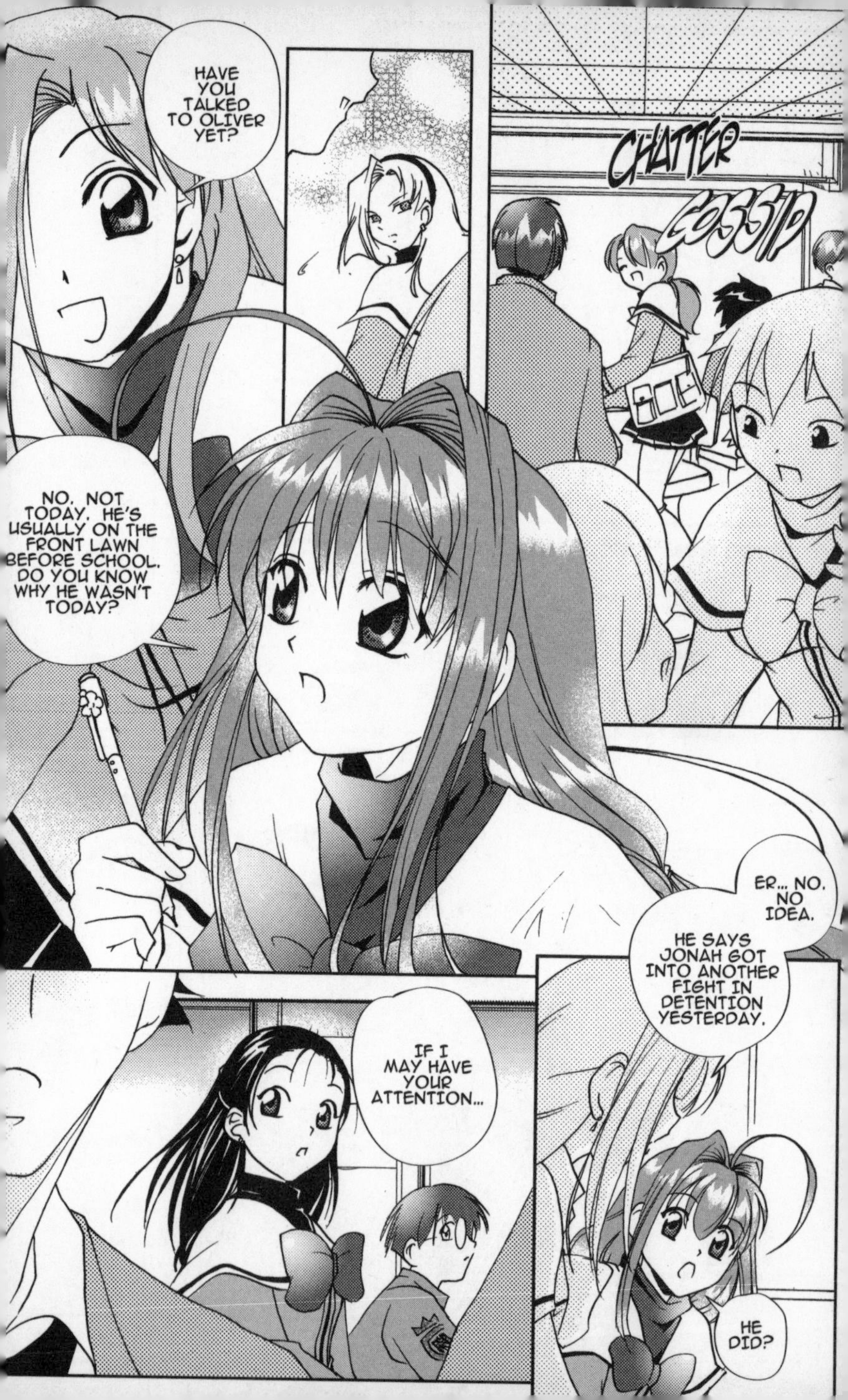
CHATTER
GOSSIP
HAVE YOU TALKED TO OLIVER YET?
NO. NOT TODAY. HE'S USUALLY ON THE FRONT LAWN BEFORE SCHOOL. DO YOU KNOW WHY HE WASN'T TODAY?
ER... NO. NO IDEA.
HE SAYS JONAH GOT INTO ANOTHER FIGHT IN DETENTION YESTERDAY.
HE DID?
IF I MAY HAVE YOUR ATTENTION...

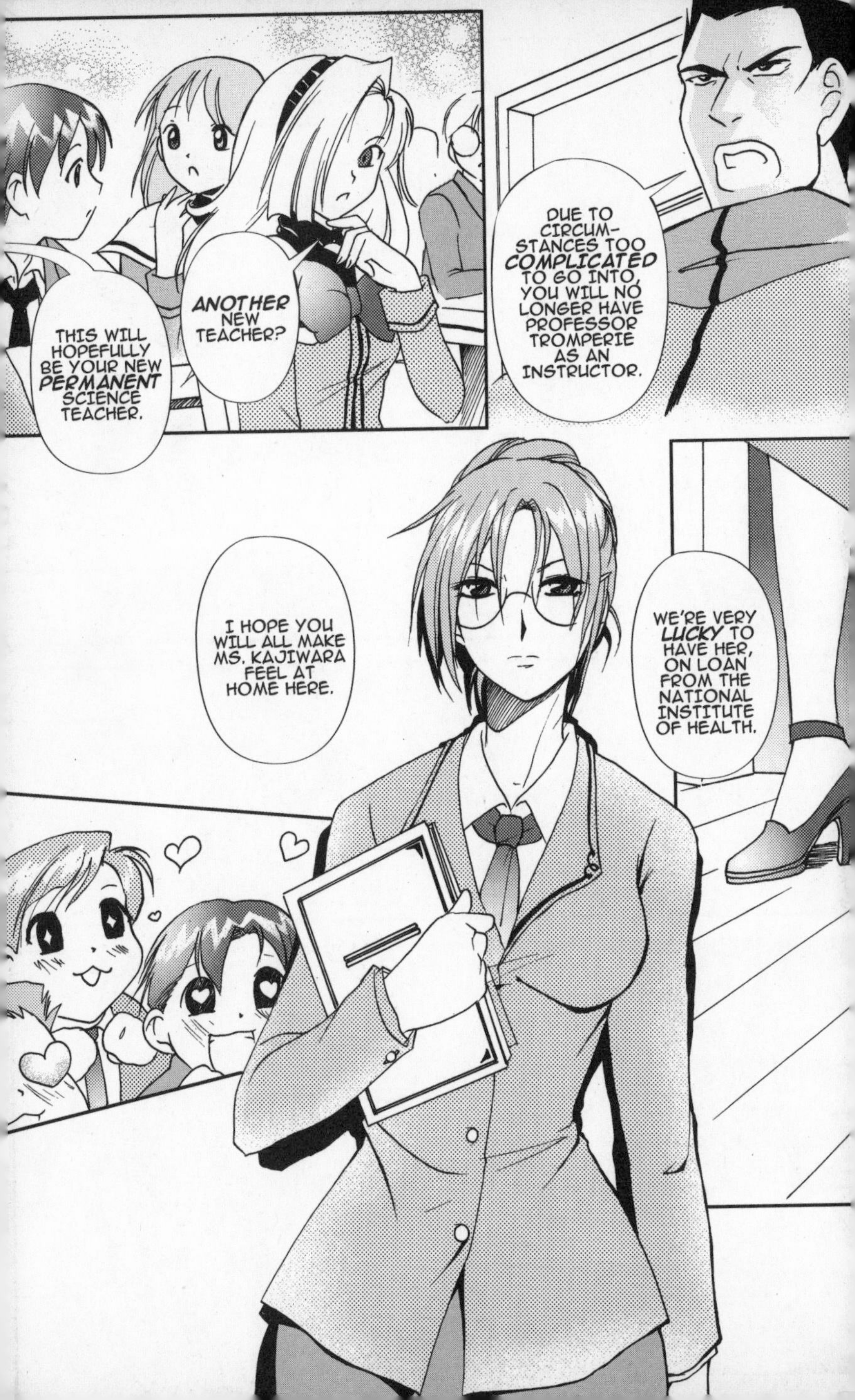

DUE TO CIRCUM-STANCES TOO *COMPLICATED* TO GO INTO, YOU WILL NO LONGER HAVE PROFESSOR TROMPERIE AS AN INSTRUCTOR.
*ANOTHER* NEW TEACHER?
THIS WILL HOPEFULLY BE YOUR NEW *PERMANENT* SCIENCE TEACHER.
WE'RE VERY *LUCKY* TO HAVE HER, ON LOAN FROM THE NATIONAL INSTITUTE OF HEALTH.
I HOPE YOU WILL ALL MAKE MS. KAJIWARA FEEL AT HOME HERE.

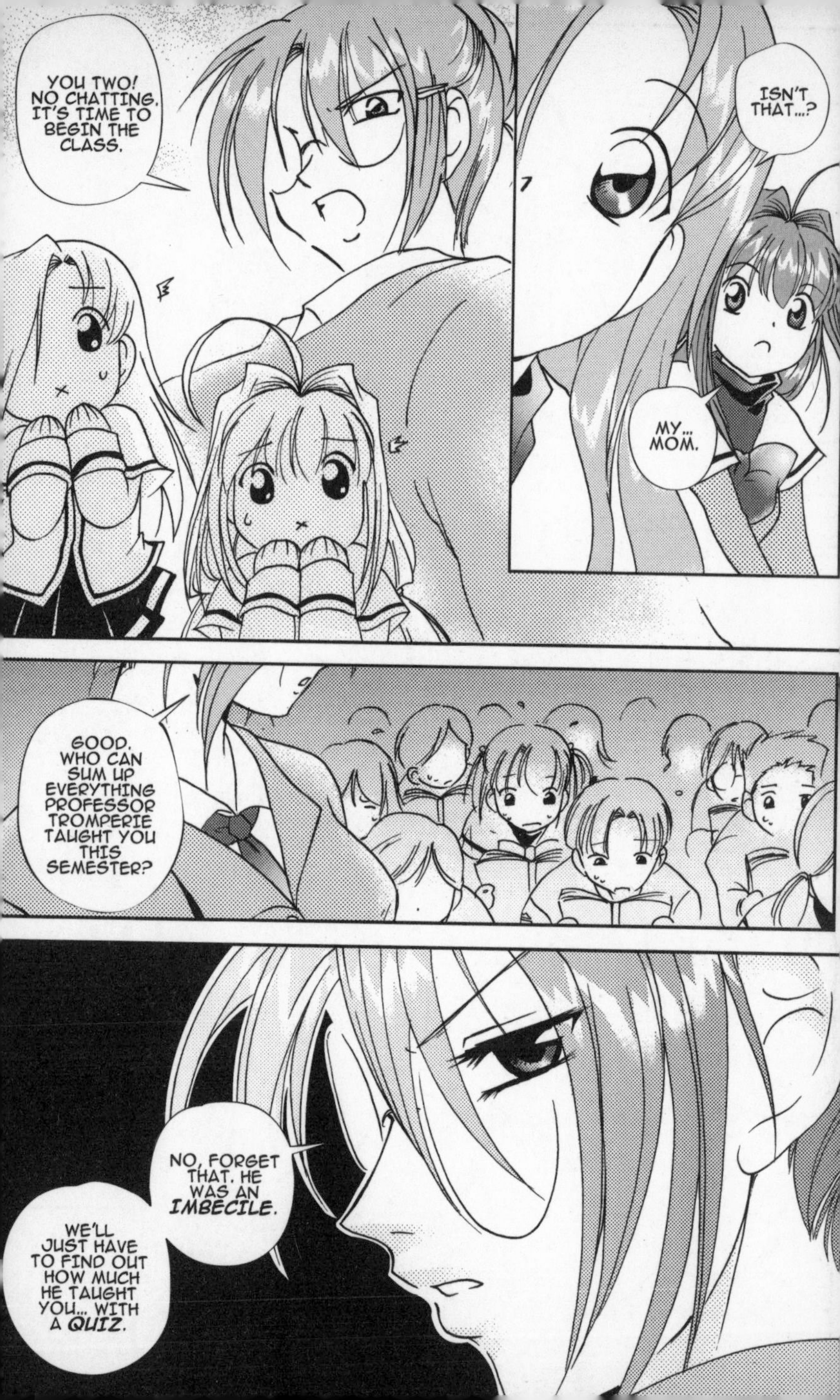
ISN'T THAT...?
MY... MOM.
YOU TWO! NO CHATTING. IT'S TIME TO BEGIN THE CLASS.
GOOD. WHO CAN SUM UP EVERYTHING PROFESSOR TROMPERIE TAUGHT YOU THIS SEMESTER?
NO, FORGET THAT. HE WAS AN IMBECILE.
WE'LL JUST HAVE TO FIND OUT HOW MUCH HE TAUGHT YOU... WITH A QUIZ.

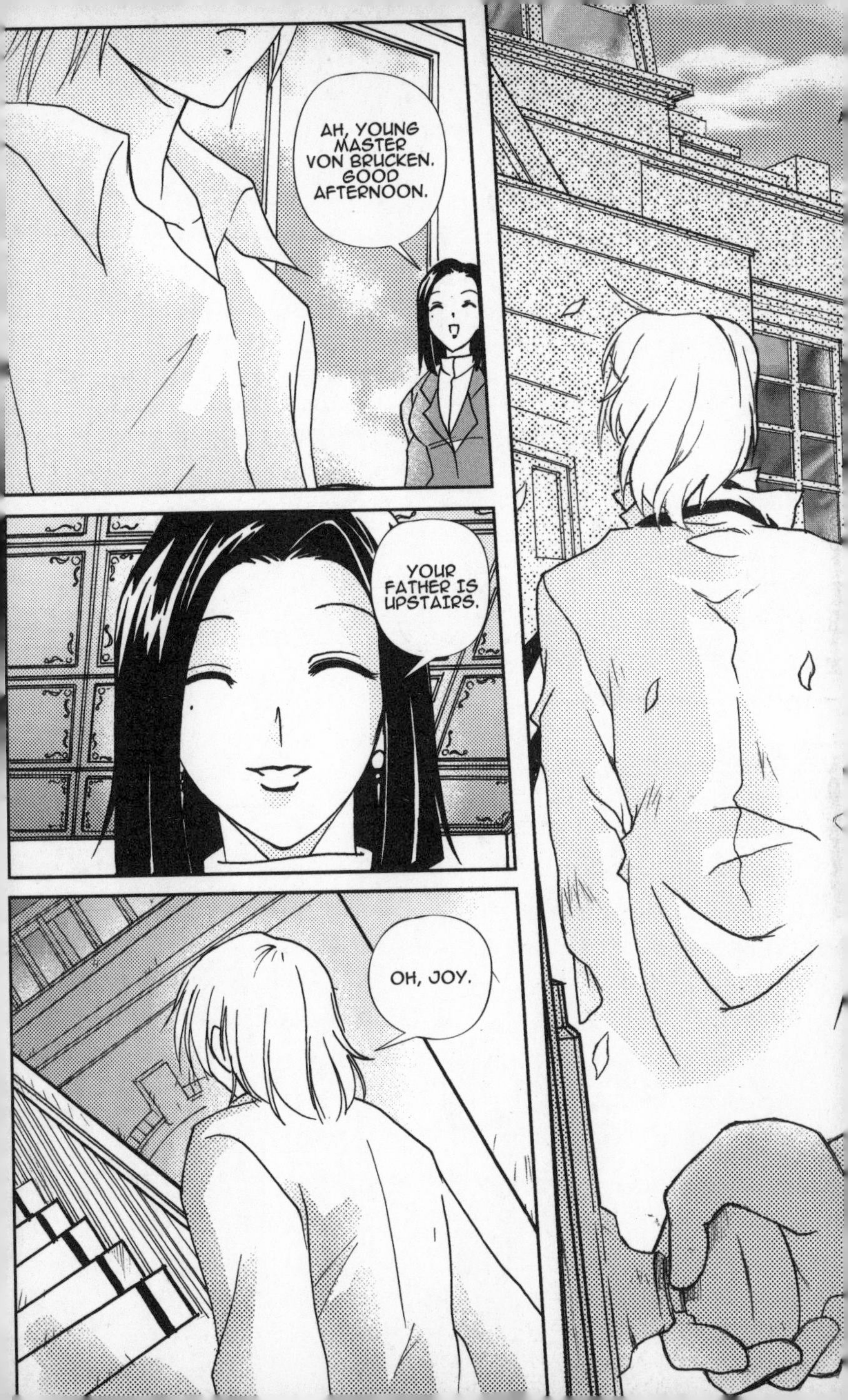
AH, YOUNG MASTER VON BRUCKEN. GOOD AFTERNOON.
YOUR FATHER IS UPSTAIRS.
OH, JOY.

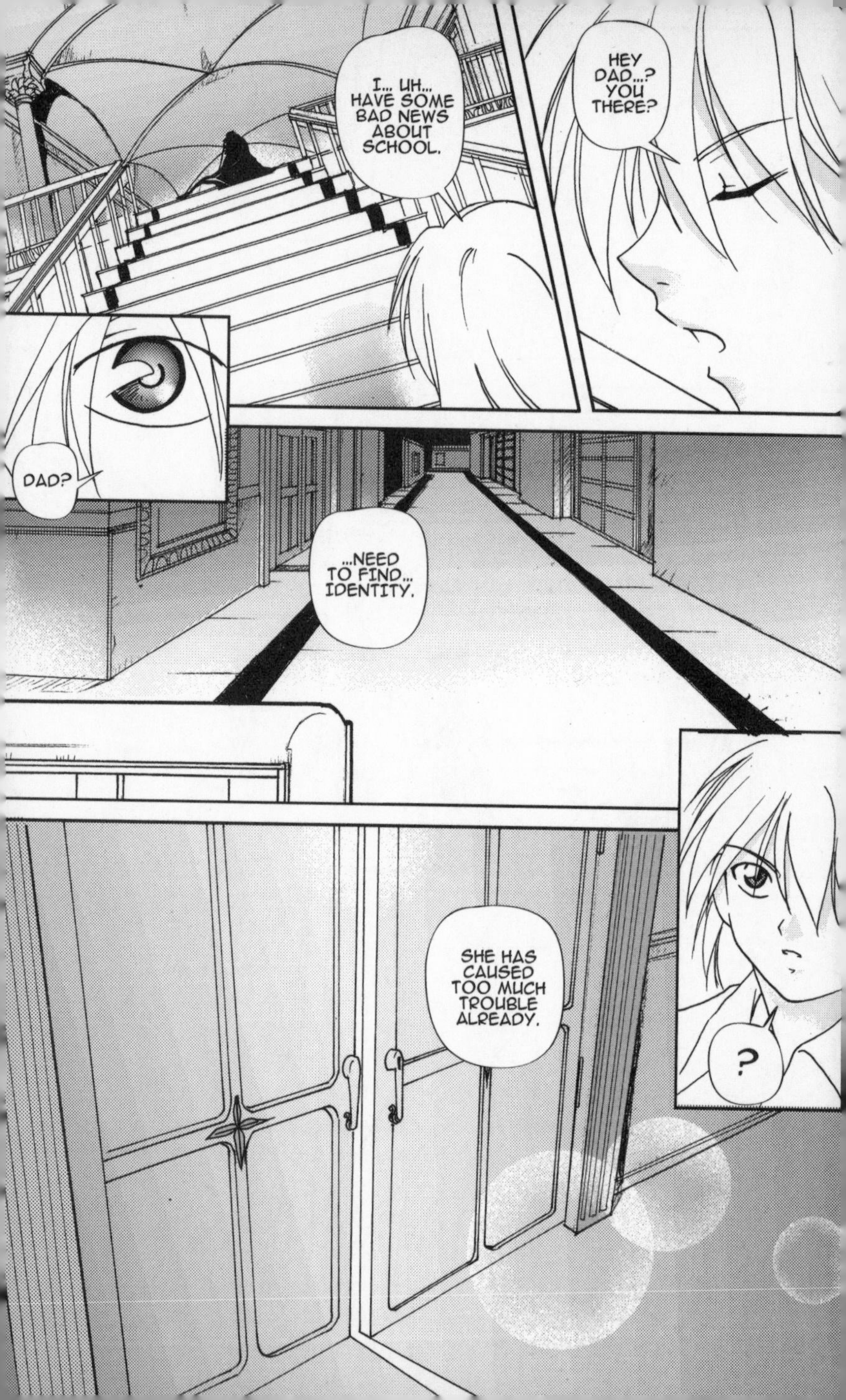
HEY DAD...? YOU THERE?
I... UH... HAVE SOME BAD NEWS ABOUT SCHOOL.
DAD?
...NEED TO FIND... IDENTITY.
?
SHE HAS CAUSED TOO MUCH TROUBLE ALREADY.

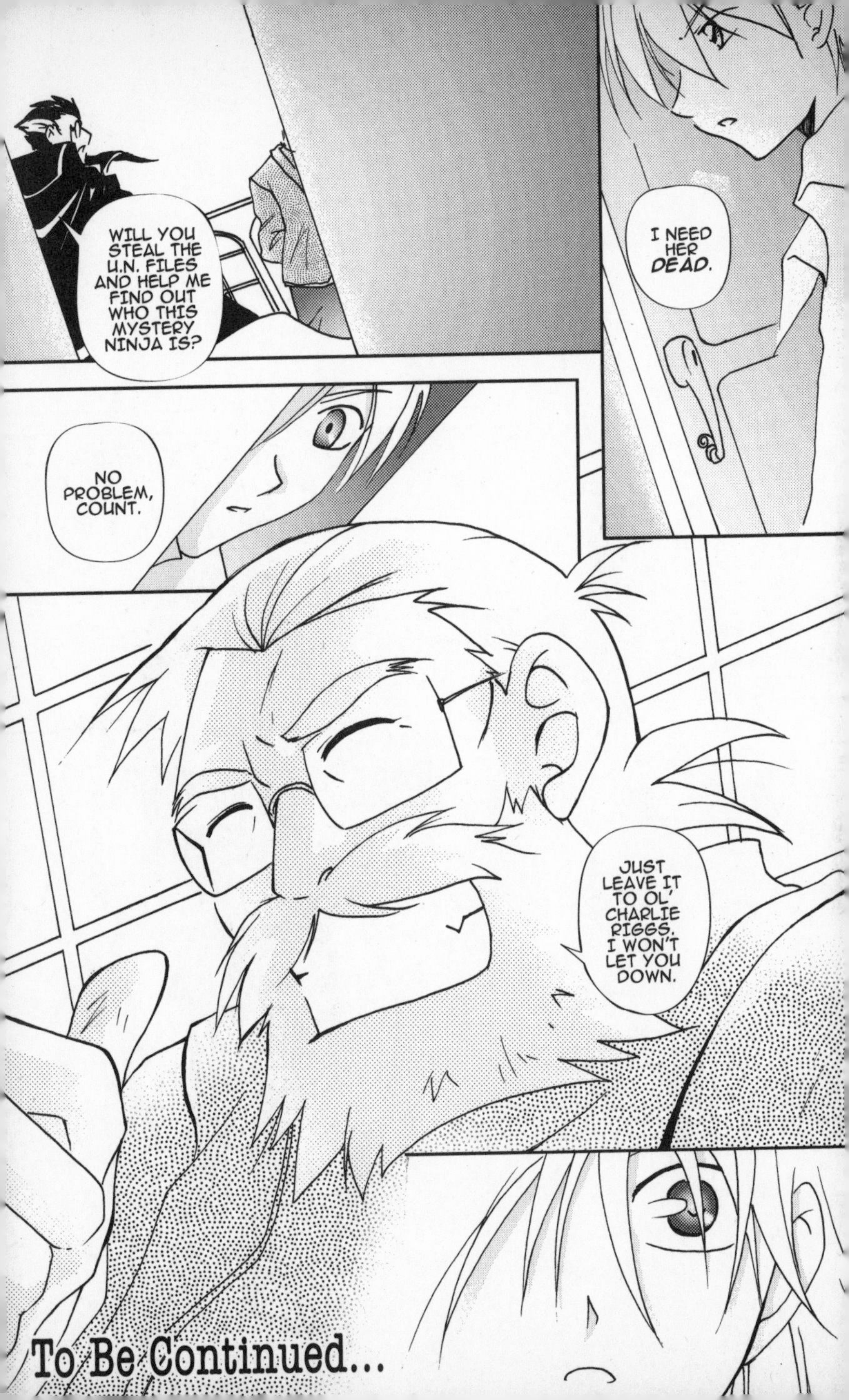
I NEED HER *DEAD*.
WILL YOU STEAL THE U.N. FILES AND HELP ME FIND OUT WHO THIS MYSTERY NINJA IS?
NO PROBLEM, COUNT.
JUST LEAVE IT TO OL' CHARLIE RIGGS. I WON'T LET YOU DOWN.
To Be Continued...

PROJECT LUNA DESIGN FILES

PROJECT LUNA DF 1504-00

**HERE'S A SNEAK PEEK AT NUNZIO AND CHRISTINA'S VERY FIRST PROPOSAL FOR AMAZING AGENT LUNA. NOTICE HOW DIFFERENT THE TITLE WAS BACK THEN.**

| SCOPE | TAB NO. |
|---|---|

SUBJECT ORIGINAL PROPOSAL

### OPERATION: HIGHSCHOOL
#### A proposal for an original manga series
#### By Nunzio DeFilippis & Christina Weir

Operation: Highschool (name subject to change in case it's in use) is the story of Luna, the perfect secret agent. A girl grown in a lab from the finest genetic material, she has been trained since her birth fifteen years ago to be the United States government's ultimate espionage weapon. But she will get an assignment that will test her to the utmost of her capacity – high school.

Luna has just defeated the evil Count Von Brucken, but his lab makes it clear something big and scary will be going down at Nobel High, the elite high school maintained by the U.N. for the children of diplomats, scientists and other international figures. This master plan is unspecified and will come down by graduation day for the class of 2007. Needing an agent who can work undercover at a high school, the government sends in Luna.

But the one thing Luna has not been trained to handle is her own feelings. They are powerful and out of control, your average teen, but without parents or real interaction to steer her. And worse, no one ever thought she'd need to figure them out. Putting her in high school is lighting the fuse on an emotional bomb of adolescent confusion. Especially when she starts to make friends, and have crushes, including a flirtation with Jonah, the son of Von Brucken.

**ON THE FOLLOWING PAGES YOU'LL FIND N & C'S EARLY NOTES ON THE CAST AND SHIEI'S CHARACTER DESIGNS. CAN YOU DETECT ALL THE CHANGES TO THE FINAL DESIGN AND STORYLINE?**

# Character sketches - LUNA

| RT PRODUCED AT | DATE PRODUCED | FILE PROCESSED BY | NATURE OF REPORT | FILE NO. |
|---|---|---|---|---|
| CHQ D-6 | | | [CLASSIFIED] | |

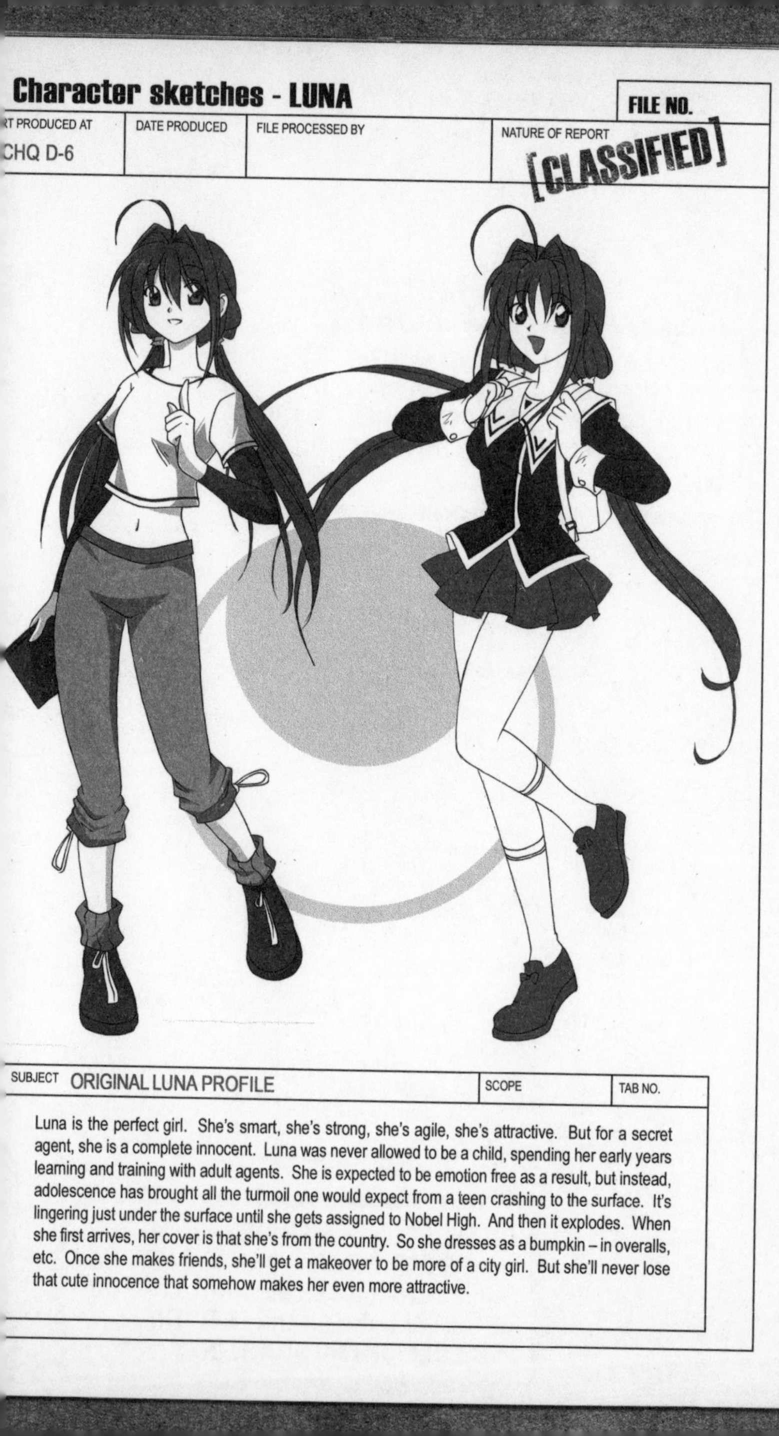

| SUBJECT ORIGINAL LUNA PROFILE | SCOPE | TAB NO. |
|---|---|---|

Luna is the perfect girl. She's smart, she's strong, she's agile, she's attractive. But for a secret agent, she is a complete innocent. Luna was never allowed to be a child, spending her early years learning and training with adult agents. She is expected to be emotion free as a result, but instead, adolescence has brought all the turmoil one would expect from a teen crashing to the surface. It's lingering just under the surface until she gets assigned to Nobel High. And then it explodes. When she first arrives, her cover is that she's from the country. So she dresses as a bumpkin – in overalls, etc. Once she makes friends, she'll get a makeover to be more of a city girl. But she'll never lose that cute innocence that somehow makes her even more attractive.

PROJECT LUNA DF 1304-00

# Character sketches - LUNA

| REPORT PRODUCED AT | DATE PRODUCED | FILE PROCESSED BY | NATURE OF REPORT | FILE NO. |
|---|---|---|---|---|
| CHQ D-6 | | | [CLASSIFIED] | |

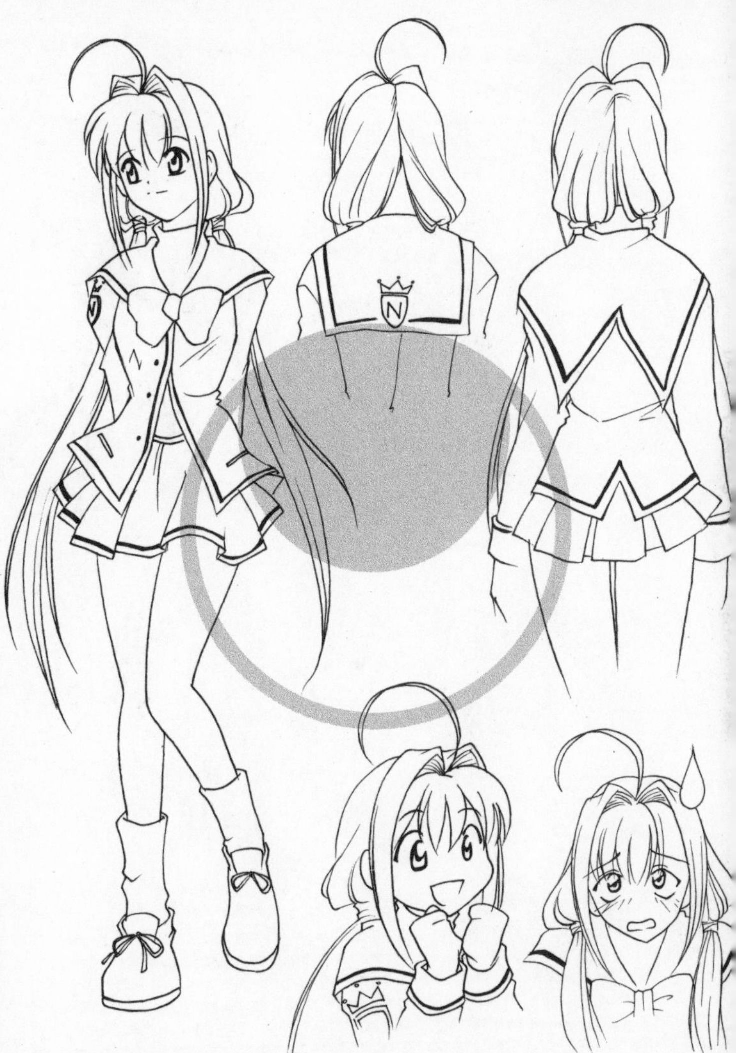

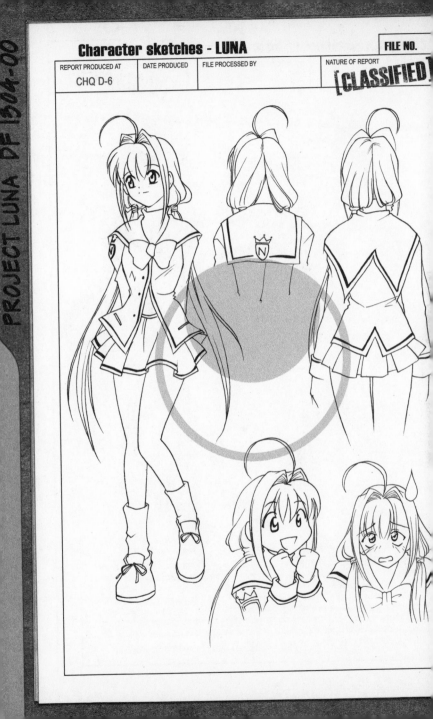

# Character sketches - COUNT HEINRICH VON BRUCKEN

| RT PRODUCED AT | DATE PRODUCED | FILE PROCESSED BY | NATURE OF REPORT | FILE NO. |
|---|---|---|---|---|
| CHQ D-6 | | | [CLASSIFIED] | |

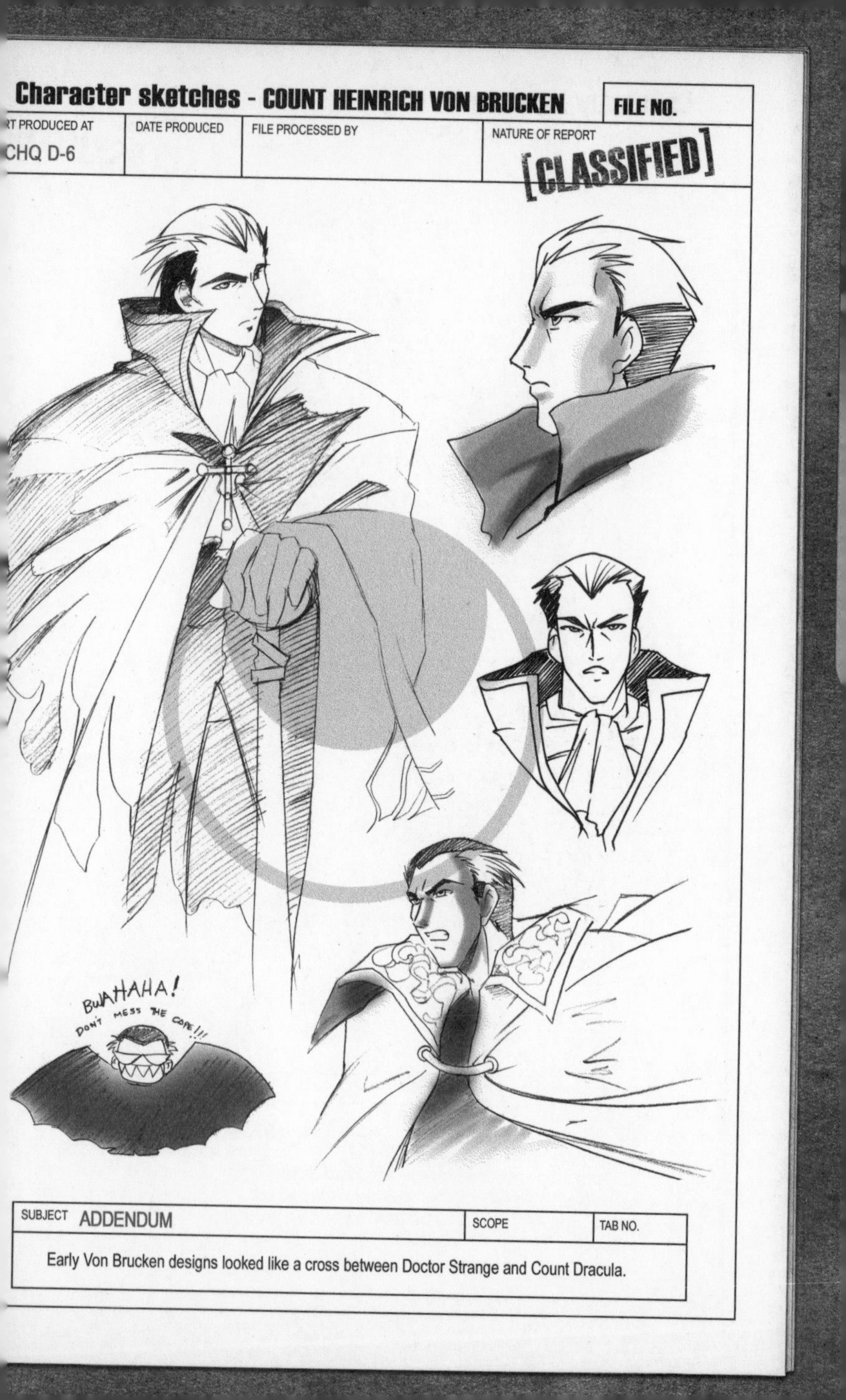
BWAHAHA!
DON'T MESS THE CAPE!!!

| SUBJECT ADDENDUM | SCOPE | TAB NO. |
|---|---|---|
| Early Von Brucken designs looked like a cross between Doctor Strange and Count Dracula. | | |

PROJECT LUNA DF 1304-00

## Character sketches - COUNT HEINRICH VON BRUCKEN

| REPORT PRODUCED AT | DATE PRODUCED | FILE PROCESSED BY | NATURE OF REPORT | FILE NO. |
|---|---|---|---|---|
| CHQ D-6 | | | [CLASSIFIED] | |

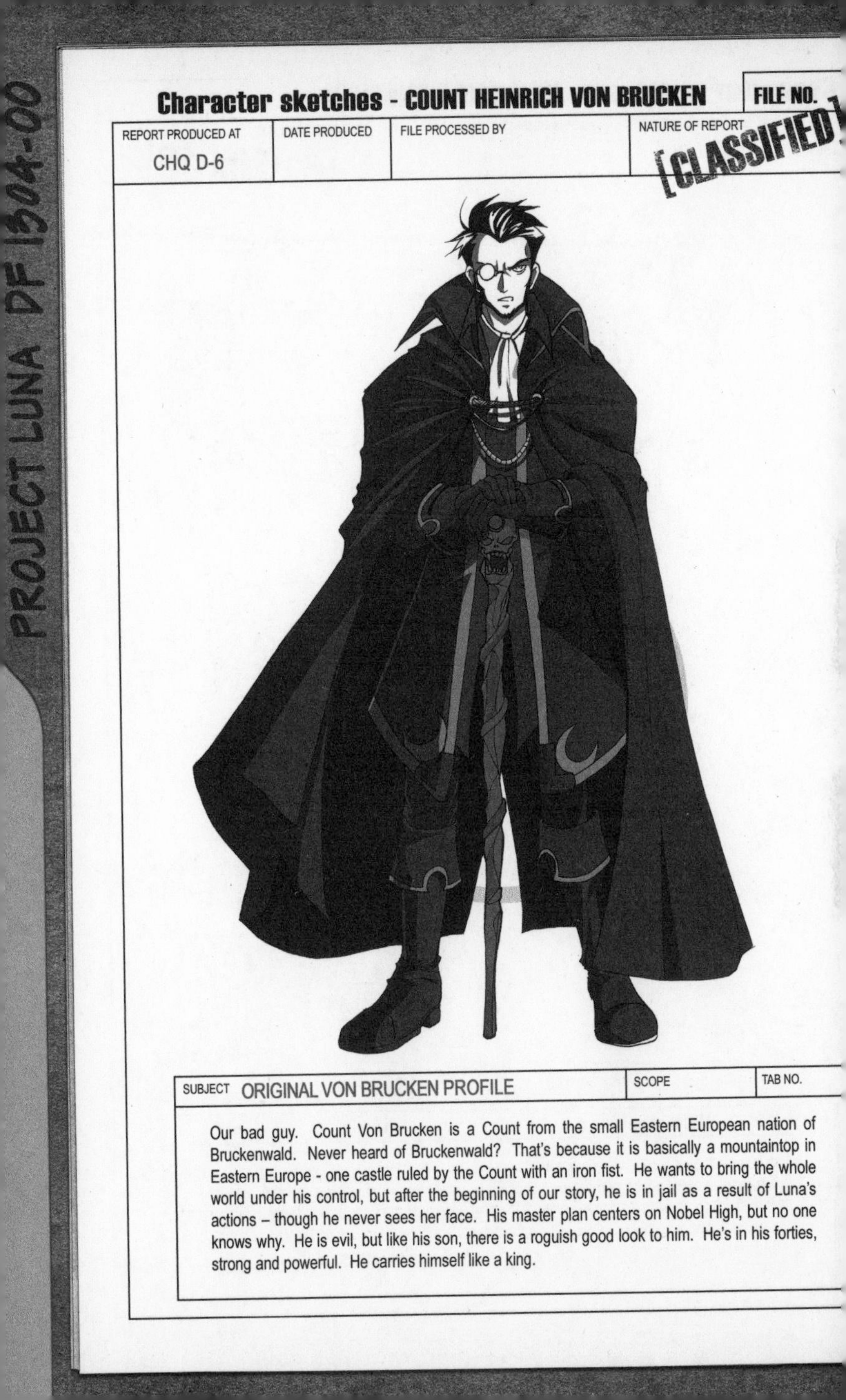

| SUBJECT ORIGINAL VON BRUCKEN PROFILE | SCOPE | TAB NO. |
|---|---|---|

Our bad guy. Count Von Brucken is a Count from the small Eastern European nation of Bruckenwald. Never heard of Bruckenwald? That's because it is basically a mountaintop in Eastern Europe - one castle ruled by the Count with an iron fist. He wants to bring the whole world under his control, but after the beginning of our story, he is in jail as a result of Luna's actions – though he never sees her face. His master plan centers on Nobel High, but no one knows why. He is evil, but like his son, there is a roguish good look to him. He's in his forties, strong and powerful. He carries himself like a king.

# Character sketches - JONAH VON BRUCKEN

| T PRODUCED AT | DATE PRODUCED | FILE PROCESSED BY | NATURE OF REPORT | FILE NO. |
|---|---|---|---|---|
| CHQ D-6 | | | [CLASSIFIED] | |

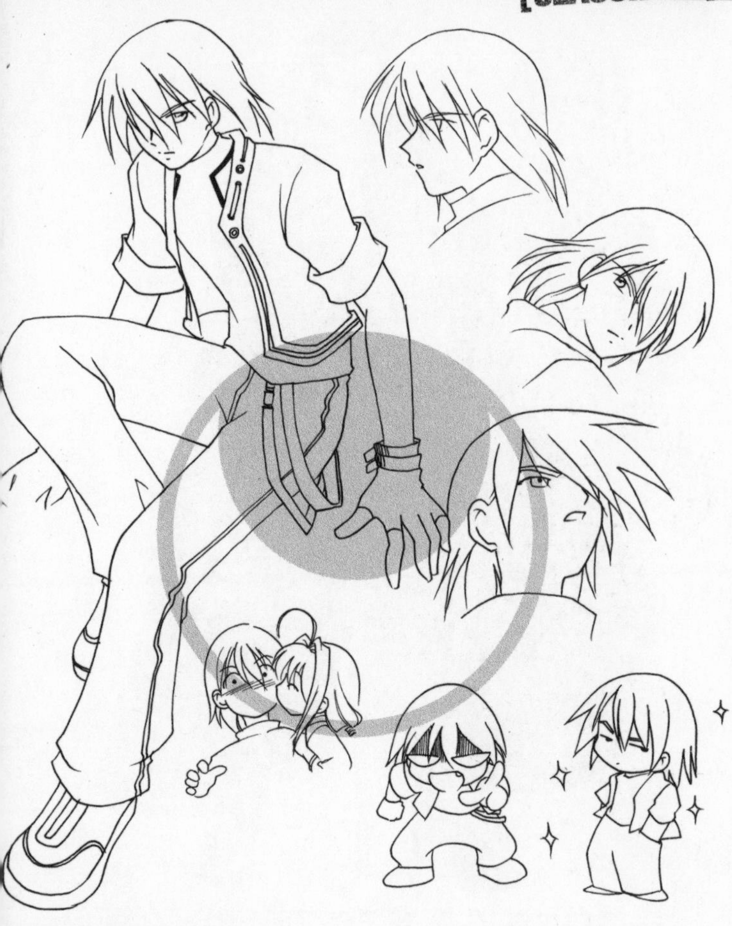

| SUBJECT ORIGINAL JONAH PROFILE | SCOPE | TAB NO. |
|---|---|---|

Jonah is the handsome, mysterious brooder, equally new to Nobel High. His connection to Count Von Brucken will make him number one suspect in whatever the Count's evil plans are. But Jonah's affiliation will remain a mystery up til the end. Jonah is the type to wear a long coat and stand alone in the moonlight. In short, he's the dangerous loner that high school girls shouldn't like, but always do. His arrival at Nobel High will have all the girls swooning.

PROJECT LUNA DF 1304-00

# Character sketches - OLIVER RIGGS

| REPORT PRODUCED AT | DATE PRODUCED | FILE PROCESSED BY | NATURE OF REPORT | FILE NO. |
|---|---|---|---|---|
| CHQ D-6 | | | [CLASSIFIED | |

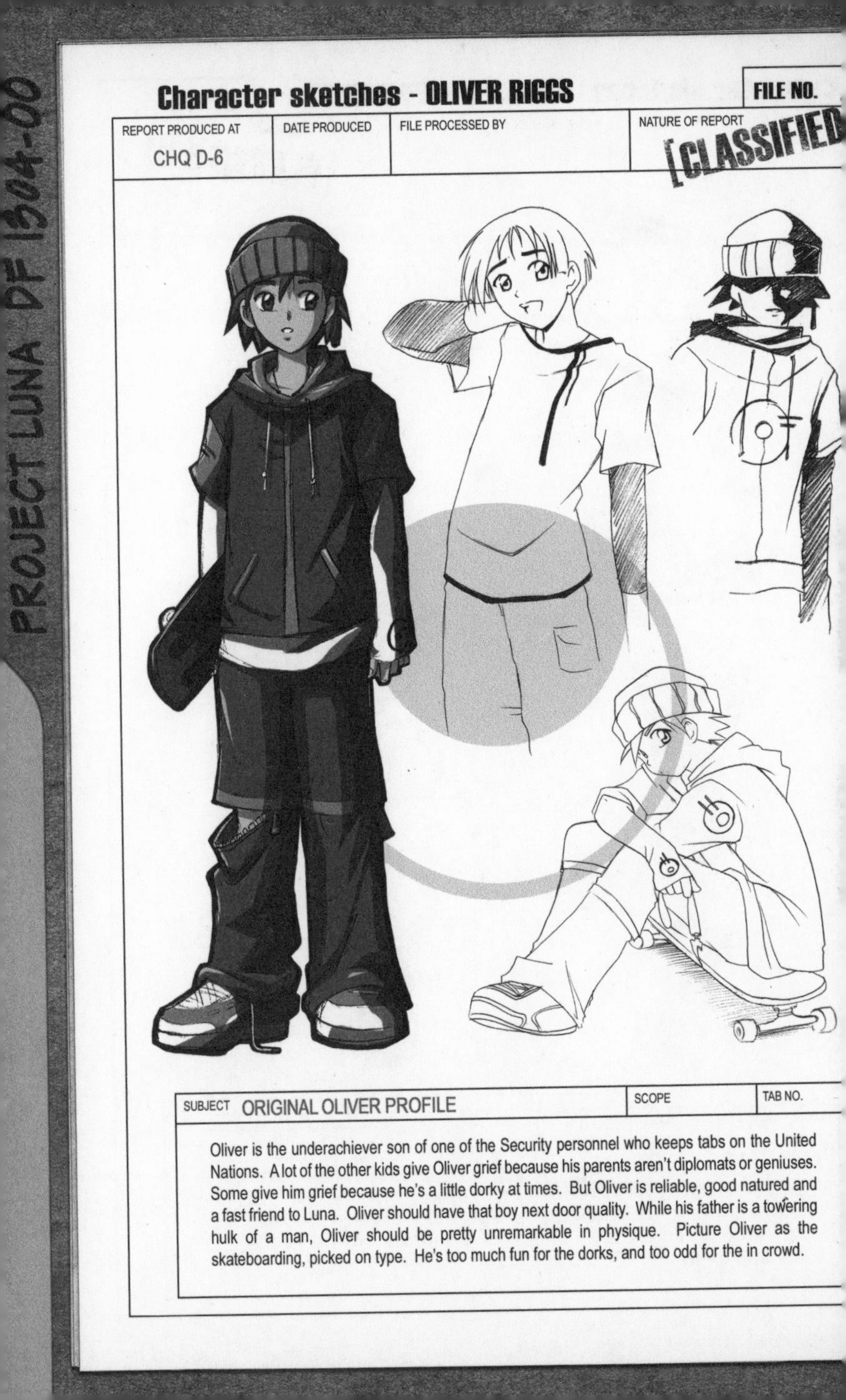

| SUBJECT ORIGINAL OLIVER PROFILE | SCOPE | TAB NO. |
|---|---|---|

Oliver is the underachiever son of one of the Security personnel who keeps tabs on the United Nations. A lot of the other kids give Oliver grief because his parents aren't diplomats or geniuses. Some give him grief because he's a little dorky at times. But Oliver is reliable, good natured and a fast friend to Luna. Oliver should have that boy next door quality. While his father is a towering hulk of a man, Oliver should be pretty unremarkable in physique. Picture Oliver as the skateboarding, picked on type. He's too much fun for the dorks, and too odd for the in crowd.

# Character sketches - ELIZABETH WESTBROOK

| FILE NO. | | | |
|---|---|---|---|
| T PRODUCED AT | DATE PRODUCED | FILE PROCESSED BY | NATURE OF REPORT |
| CHQ D-6 | | | [CLASSIFIED] |

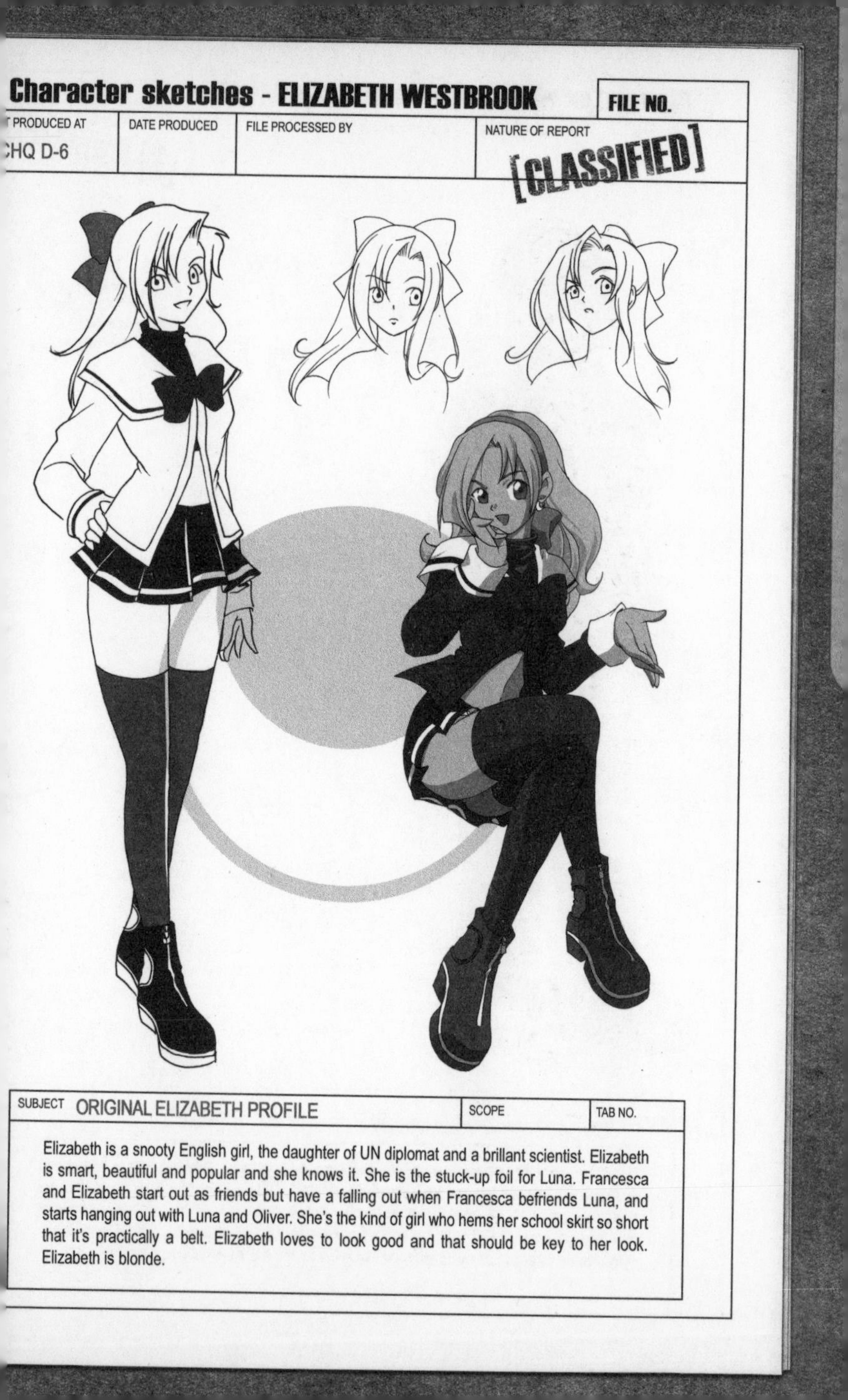

| SUBJECT ORIGINAL ELIZABETH PROFILE | SCOPE | TAB NO. |
|---|---|---|

Elizabeth is a snooty English girl, the daughter of UN diplomat and a brillant scientist. Elizabeth is smart, beautiful and popular and she knows it. She is the stuck-up foil for Luna. Francesca and Elizabeth start out as friends but have a falling out when Francesca befriends Luna, and starts hanging out with Luna and Oliver. She's the kind of girl who hems her school skirt so short that it's practically a belt. Elizabeth loves to look good and that should be key to her look. Elizabeth is blonde.

PROJECT LUNA DF 1304-00

# Character sketches - FRANCESCA ALDANA

FILE NO.

| REPORT PRODUCED AT | DATE PRODUCED | FILE PROCESSED BY | NATURE OF REPORT |
|---|---|---|---|
| CHQ D-6 | | | [CLASSIFIED] |

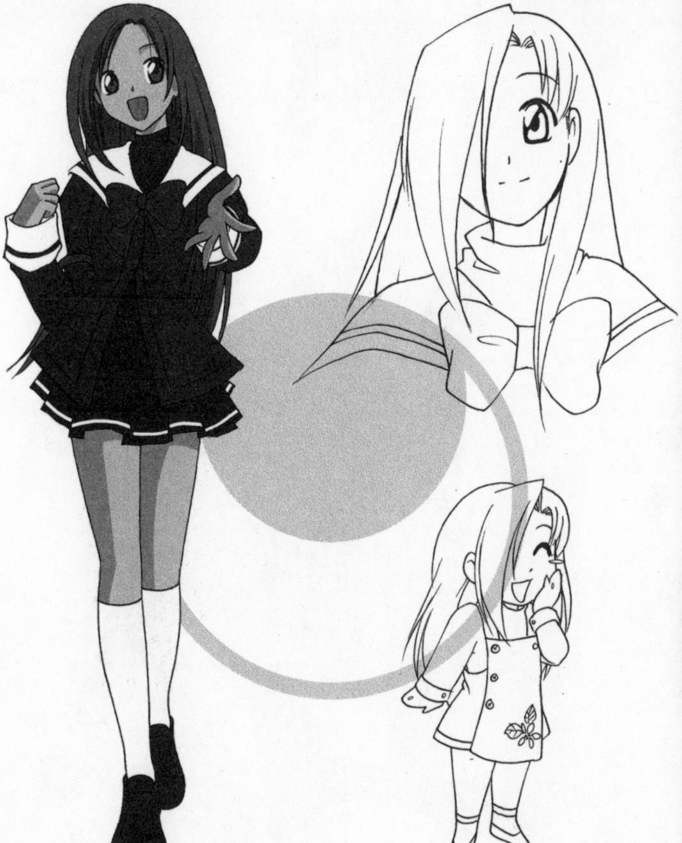

| SUBJECT ORIGINAL FRANCESCA PROFILE | SCOPE | TAB NO. |
|---|---|---|

Francesca is the fifteen year old daughter of Spanish diplomats. She is all grace and charm. She runs with the beautiful people crowd of high school, but isn't as stuck-up. She's the one who takes Luna on as a project for a makeover to try to get her in with the cool kids. When the cool kids continue to reject Luna, Francesca will have to make a choice. Francesca is hip, precociously sexy and always dressed in the latest fashion with long flowy hair.

# Character sketches - "CONTROL"/AGENT JENNIFER KAJIWARA | FILE NO.

| T PRODUCED AT | DATE PRODUCED | FILE PROCESSED BY | NATURE OF REPORT |
|---|---|---|---|
| CHQ D-6 | | | [CLASSIFIED] |

| SUBJECT | ORIGINAL CONTROL PROFILE | | SCOPE | TAB NO. |
|---|---|---|---|---|

Luna's by the book, hard as nails Control Agent. Jennifer is the daughter of a Japanese businessman and a American writer. Jennifer left home after college and never returned, disappearing into the mystery life of a secret agent. She gets a new assignment when Luna does. She'll remain a control agent, but with a new codename: Mom. Jennifer is in her mid-thirties, uptight, by the book and a little too sterile. She should be a variation on the sexy librarian. Glasses, very businesslike and probably quite the hottie if she ever let her hair down.

PROJECT LUNA DF 1304-00

## Character sketches - DR. ANDY COLLINS

FILE NO.

| REPORT PRODUCED AT | DATE PRODUCED | FILE PROCESSED BY | NATURE OF REPORT |
| --- | --- | --- | --- |
| CHQ D-6 | | | [CLASSIFIED |

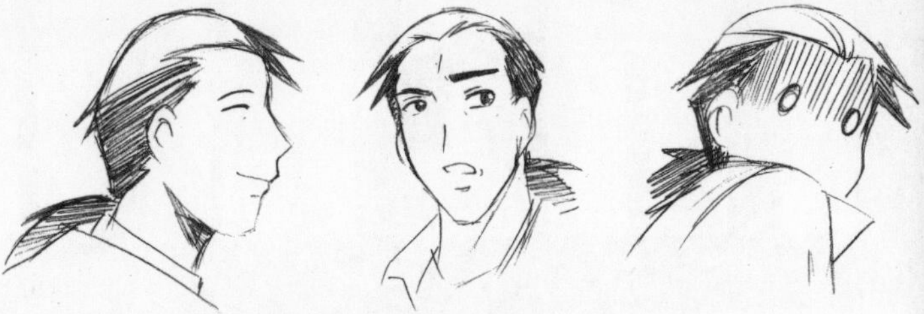

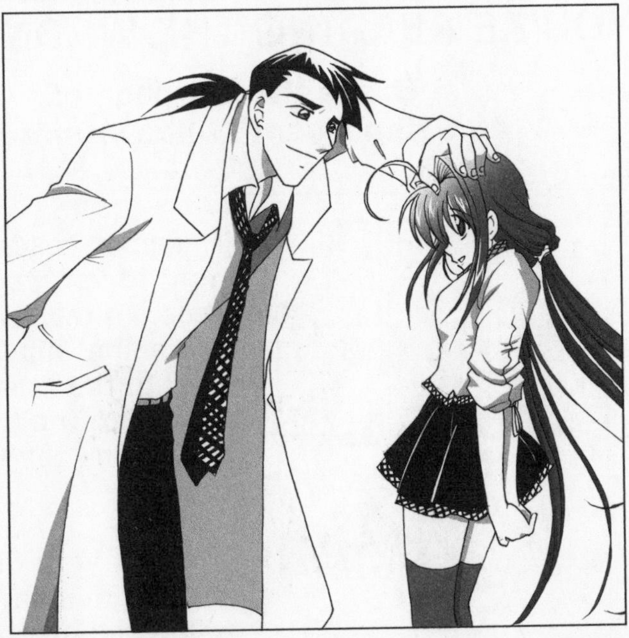

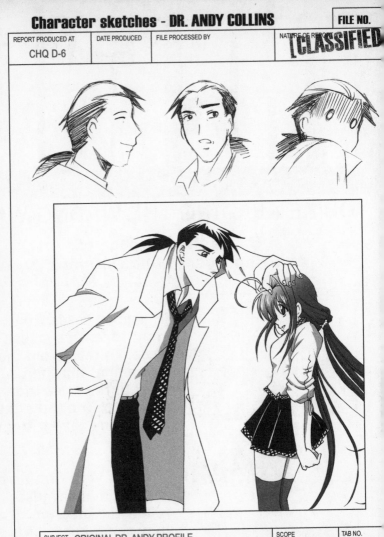

| SUBJECT ORIGINAL DR. ANDY PROFILE | SCOPE | TAB NO. |
| --- | --- | --- |

The government psychiatrist assigned to keep an eye on Luna when she hits her teen years. He's been saying all along that Luna needs training with her emotions, but Control never listened to him. Now that Luna's been assigned to High School, Dr. Andy will get re-assigned. He will play Luna's Dad, opposite Control, who he really can't stand. Dr. Andy is in his forties, laid back, good natured. A feel good kind of guy with a ponytail and an earring. He will love playing "Dad" to Luna because he thinks she really needs it.

# YOU'RE READING THE WRONG WAY

## This is the last page of
## *Amazing Agent Luna Omnibus I*

This book reads from right to left, Japanese style. To read from the beginning, flip the book over to the other side, start with the top right panel, and take it from there.

If this is your first time reading manga, just follow the diagram. It may seem backwards at first, but you'll get used to it! Have fun!